ANNUAL REVIEW OF PSYCHOLOGY

EDITORIAL COMMITTEE (1995)

ANNUAL REVIEW OF PSYCHOLOGY

VOLUME 46, 1995

JANET T. SPENCE, *Editor*
University of Texas, Austin

JOHN M. DARLEY, *Associate Editor*
Princeton University

DONALD J. FOSS, *Associate Editor*
University of Texas, Austin

ANNUAL REVIEWS INC.   4139 EL CAMINO WAY   P.O. BOX 10139   PALO ALTO, CALIFORNIA 94303-0139

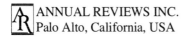
ANNUAL REVIEWS INC.
Palo Alto, California, USA

International Standard Serial Number: 0066-4308
International Standard Book Number: 0-8243-0246-X
Library of Congress Catalog Card Number: 50-13143

Annual Review and publication titles are registered trademarks of Annual Reviews Inc.

The paper used in this publication meets the minimum requirements of American National Standards for Information Sciences—Permanence of Paper for Printed Library
Materials, ANZI Z39.48-1984

Annual Reviews Inc. and the Editors of its publications assume no responsibility for
the statements expressed by the contributors to this *Review.*

Typesetting by Ruth McCue-Saavedra and the Annual Reviews Inc. Editorial Staff

PRINTED AND BOUND IN THE UNITED STATES OF AMERICA

PREFACE

For the past 26 years, Mark R. Rosenzweig has served as co-editor of the *Annual Review of Psychology* (*ARP*), first with Paul Mussen (1969–1973) and then, for over 20 years, with Lyman Porter (1974–1994). On behalf of the readers, we acknowledge the standards of intellectual leadership they established, and as their successors, we aspire to continue in the same tradition. We do not, however, aspire to rival their heroic length of service. With the agreement of the Annual Reviews Editorial Affairs Committee, our terms are for five years, a practice we suspect may continue in the future.

Psychologists continue to produce creative work and they do so at an increasing pace. The potential importance and usefulness of *ARP* in such an environment continues to grow. This would seem to be the appropriate occasion on which to review the procedures by which chapter topics and authors are chosen for each volume. Selection of topics is governed by a Master Plan, which specifies the major substantive and methodological areas of the field (currently about 20), ranging from Biological Psychology to Personnel and Organizational Psychology. These in turn are divided into a number of subareas, each of which is scheduled to be the subject of a review chapter at regular intervals ranging from two to eight or ten years, depending on the prominance of the topic in the research literature and the pace of accumulation of new knowledge. A prefatory chapter, written by a distinguished colleague on a topic of his or her own choosing, also appears in each volume. In the present volume, we are pleased that this chapter was prepared by R. Duncan Luce.

Nominations of potential authors are made by the editors and members of the *ARP* Editorial Committee. Our aim is to identify established investigators who are not only familiar with the relevant research data but who can also integrate and critically evaluate the literature. Often those who accept our invitation ask permission to include a colleague as a junior author, a request we are glad to accept.

The Master Plan that guides the selection of topics is reviewed each year at the annual meeting of the *ARP* Editiorial Committee to determine whether modifications are in order. In looking over the Master Plans of the past 25 years, we observed both stability and change. Only rarely were there major revisions or reorganizations of the Plan, usually occasioned as an aspect of the field underwent some kind of intellectual revolution. But changes over time in topics under the major headings—additions, deletions, revisions in both substance and timing—provide an interesting mirror on the progress of the field. We are impressed by the continued usefulness that the guidance of a Master Plan provides and with the continued dedication to the field on the part of the many psychologists who have been willing to take on the increasingly formidable task of reviewing the various and fast-moving fields of psychology.

We wish to acknowledge the contributions of the *ARP* Editorial Committee and to give special thanks to Donald Fowles, who has completed his five-year term. We welcome the new member of the Committee, William Greenough. Thanks are also due to Amy Marks, the Production Editor of *ARP,* for her patient guidance during our first year as editors.

Janet T. Spence, Editor
John M. Darley, Associate Editor
Donald J. Foss, Associate Editor

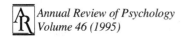
Annual Review of Psychology
Volume 46 (1995)

CONTENTS

INDEXES

SOME RELATED ARTICLES IN OTHER *ANNUAL REVIEWS*

From the *Annual Review of Neuroscience,* Volume 17 (1994)

Organization of Memory Traces in the Mammalian Brain, Richard F. Thompson and David J. Krupa

From the *Annual Review of Public Health,* Volume 15 (1994)

Child Abuse, Andrea M. Vandeven and Eli H. Newberger
Job Strain and Cardiovascular Disease, Peter L. Schnall, Paul A. Landsbergis, and Dean Baker
Methods for Quality-of-Life Studies, Marsha A. Testa and Johanna F. Nackley

From the *Annual Review of Sociology,* Volume 20 (1994)

Societal Taxonomies: Mapping the Social Universe, Gerhard Lenski
Sociobiology and Sociology, François Nielsen

Annu. Rev. Psychol. 1995. 46:1–26

FOUR TENSIONS CONCERNING MATHEMATICAL MODELING IN PSYCHOLOGY

R. Duncan Luce

Institute for Mathematical Behavioral Sciences, University of California, Irvine, California 92717

KEY WORDS: dynamic versus static models, error versus structure, mathematical modeling, normative versus descriptive models, phenomenological versus processing models

CONTENTS

0066-4308/95/0201-0001$05.00

WHY SHOULD MATHEMATICS PLAY A ROLE IN PSYCHOLOGY?

Structure, Pattern, and Process

Mathematics studies structures and patterns described by systems of propositions relating aspects of the entities in question. Deriving logically true statements from sets of assumed statements (often called axioms), uncovering symmetries and patterns, and evolving and understanding general structures are the concerns of mathematicians.

Mathematics becomes relevant to science whenever we uncover structure in what we are studying. One should not underestimate the difficulties in isolating such structure and the even more difficult task of finding good ways to describe it. After all, it took several millennia—albeit with some fairly inactive periods lasting centuries—to get to our current elaborate understanding of physical structures and processes.

As psychologists, we seek structure in aspects of human (and sometimes, animal) behavior. No one holds that all true statements we can make about a person's behavior are independent of each other. Some propositions surely follow as a consequence of others. Otherwise, any prediction of behavior would be impossible, and obviously we continually predict the behavior of others. People count on others to behave in certain ways depending on the situation or on various indicators about social roles, mood, etc. Without some predictable behavior, our social environments would seem random, which clearly they do not.

The existence of psychological structure cannot be in doubt. But what that structure is, is another matter. As we psychologists gradually disentangle its aspects, we also begin to describe it in more formal terms and, in some of the simpler cases, mathematics begins to play a significant role.

What Keeps Mathematical Psychology from Being an Oxymoron?

The existence of psychological structure means that mathematical theories are, at least in principle, a possibility in psychology. Nonetheless, such theories may not prove realizable in a deep sense; the attempt may really prove to be a contradiction in terms, an oxymoron. To avoid that danger, we must attempt to satisfy the following sensible but demanding criterion: Knowledge of an explicit, falsifiable psychological theory should not provide the (unaided) knower with the means to falsify it at will in every empirical context. Put another way, psychological theories should not turn out to be nonfulfilling prophecies any more than they should be self-fulfilling. In practice this means that the scientist should be confident that an experimental or field design exists that allows the theory to be tested despite the subject's knowledge of the theory. I call this the non-oxymoron criterion.

Such a principle holds for any science, but it is particularly significant for psychology. In other social sciences, which typically deal with situations aggregated over large numbers of individuals, widespread knowledge of a theory is less likely to lead to its rejection. This is partly because the impact of any single person on the behavior of large groups usually is minuscule.

Any psychologist who has reflected on the issue knows that this criterion is exceedingly difficult to satisfy and probably impossible to do so if subjects are permitted suitable external aids. For example, current mathematical models of the perception of aperture colors agree that the data can be represented in a three-dimensional (3-D) geometric space (Indow 1982; Krantz 1975a,b; Suppes et al 1989, pp. 131–153). Can a person with normal color vision systematically fool us into thinking his or her perception of nonreflected colors is either 4- or 2-D? I doubt that anyone without benefit of a physical spectrum analyzer and a computer model can simulate 4-D behavior. Faking 2-D behavior is, in principle, simpler because it only involves ignoring a distinction, such as that between red and green. But as a matter of fact it is quite difficult for an unaided person to do so successfully—witness the failures to simulate color blindness to avoid being drafted during our mid-century wars.

FOUR DISTINCTIONS

Four major contrasts are useful in discussing current mathematical modeling. Any particular model can be identified as falling somewhere on each of the distinctions. Some examples will be mentioned in illustrating these distinctions, and I will repeatedly raise the question of how we attempt to satisfy the non-oxymoron criterion for these specific models.

Phenomenological versus Process Models: Unopened and Opened Black Boxes

Phenomenological models treat a person as a "black box" that exhibits overall properties, but with no internal structure specified within the model. This approach is like that of classical physics, in which objects have properties— e.g. mass, charge, temperature—but no explicit molecular or atomic structure is attributed to them. Many psychological theories, including most mathematical modeling of judgment and decision making, are of this type; they attempt to characterize aspects and patterns of behavior without asking about the underlying, internal mechanisms that give rise to the behavior.

Another type of psychological modeling, commonly called information processing, attempts to analyze the black box in terms of internal mechanisms of information flow. The attempt is, in a functional sense, to open the black box. As will be noted later, various versions of information processing differ in the degree to which they take neurobiological observations seriously.

Descriptive versus Normative Models

Many psychological issues, especially those having to do with measurement, are related closely to well-articulated normative theories that describe how we should reason, draw inferences, and make decisions. Everyday reasoning is loosely coupled to formal logic; the ordinary inferences we draw have some relation to the formalized inferences of probability and statistics; and human decision making is sometimes replaced by formal theories of decisions. Nevertheless, in our ordinary lives we often fail to be fully logical in our deductions, to behave like skilled statisticians in drawing inferences from data, or to optimize a criterion when making decisions.

These normative sciences, in some sense, characterize our collective, and improving, understanding of ideal reasoning, inference, and decision making. To follow these collective dictates requires training, self consciousness, and auxiliary aids, such as a computer. Most of us revert to everyday modes of behavior unless we explicitly elect to act like a logician, statistician, or decision analyst for the occasion at hand.

Despite differences between the normative theories and everyday behavior, the fact is that these normative sciences have grown out of our natural, if imperfect, skills in dealing with such issues. So it is plausible to anticipate some degree of overlap in some of the basic principles, if not in the actual execution of reasoning and decisions. Moreover, humans are able to address issues of reasoning, induction, and decision making that our present formalized normative theories find exceedingly difficult to confront. For example, we are all masters at dealing with ambiguity, which is anathema to logic, mathematics, and computers. This is where we have the greatest difficulty in interfacing people with computers. A few scientists are attempting to model ambiguous reasoning, but no consensus yet exists.

Dynamic versus Static Modeling

We change and our environments change. Little is static except many of our theories. Why is this? Every time we introduce a new variable, the scientific problems become appreciably more complex, and so if we can omit time, so much the better. Moreover, statistical issues are much confounded when we deal with changing behavior: it is counterproductive to average over trials, because that is where the change is to be seen, or over subjects, because the changes they exhibit may be qualitatively different. Furthermore, the main devices used in the physical sciences for dealing with dynamics—differential, difference, and integral equations—have not, so far, proved well suited to most psychological problems. It is unclear whether this reflects a deep difference in the nature of the sciences or only our incomplete understanding of the mechanisms of change. But the fact is that only small portions of our theories purport to be dynamic in character. Most assume a static phenomenon. An important issue is how best to increase the dynamic character of our models.

Noise versus Models of Structure

Theories are about structure, and to be tentatively accepted as a "correct" theory, we confront it with data to determine whether the proposed structure agrees sufficiently well with the empirical data. In practice, this evaluation is confounded by various forms of error, systematic and nonsystematic. This is true of any science, but it is an especially severe problem for psychology. In the macro-physical sciences, refinements of procedure and equipment typically reduce the magnitude of nonsystematic errors toward zero. In psychology, as is also true for quantum theory at a scale many orders of magnitude finer, the object of study itself seems to be the irreducible source of that error. This apparent fact must not be used as an excuse for poor experimental design, incautious procedures, or the inclusion of experimental artifacts. Nonetheless, after many years of careful methodology, it is probably safe to conclude that an irreducible amount of nonsystematic error—perhaps randomness—is inherent in human behavior. In that case, our options are to tack statistics onto the algebraic models, to develop probabilistic models of structure, or to interpret the error as arising in some way from complex but systematic processes. Each approach is to some degree unsatisfactory, and a fully satisfactory solution has not yet evolved.

EXAMPLES OF PHENOMENOLOGICAL AND PROCESS MODELS

Phenomenological Models

TRADE-OFFS AND MEASUREMENT   All sciences study trade-offs, usually those among variables affecting an attribute (or dependent variable) of interest, in particular those combinations of independent variables that keep the attribute constant. Consider performance in signal detection (Green & Swets 1988, Macmillan & Creelman 1991). To improve detection, one must simultaneously increase hits and decrease false alarms. When an observer is operating below his or her performance limits, as shown in the hit versus false-alarm space of Figure 1, the observer can simultaneously improve both measures, in the region bounded by the horizontal and vertical lines from the point to the curve of

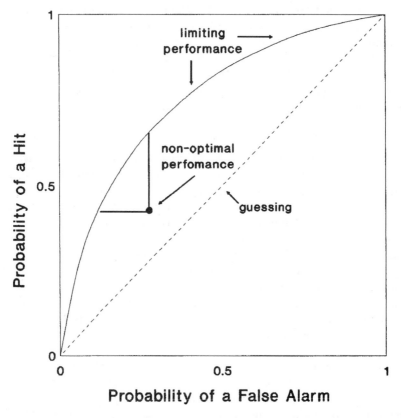

Figure 1   A plot of the probability of a hit (i.e. detecting a signal) versus the probability of a false alarm (i.e. saying a signal is present when it is not). The curve is the best performance possible for the signal in question. A point below the curve is always dominated by the points in the region under the curve bounded by the horizonal and vertical lines from the point to the curve.

limiting performance. But once the performance limit is reached, the only feasible movements while maintaining maximum detectability involve trading off an improvement in one dimension for a deterioration in the other. The limiting behavior is characterized by these being the only possible trade-offs that are not dominated by another feasible pattern of behavior. Such mathematical models of limits of behavior typically satisfy the non-oxymoron criterion because, without special aids, a person is incapable of overcoming these limits, even when fully familiar with the theory. This is one of several reasons why, when studying limiting performance, scientists often serve as their own subjects without the specter of experimenter bias being raised.

Another example where fairly sophisticated mathematical models have been developed is in studying speed-accuracy trade-offs in detection and discrimination contexts (see Luce 1986, Townsend & Ashby 1983). Once again, the focus is on the limits of performance, and so it is relatively immune to violations of the non-oxymoron principle.

REPRESENTATIONAL THEORIES OF MEASUREMENT   Equal-attribute or indifference curves represent a third example of trade-offs. In this case, stimuli have two or more factors that affect an attribute. The trade-off studied is that between the factors that keep the attribute constant (e.g. intensity and frequency pairs that maintain constant loudness, delays in receiving and amounts of food that maintain constant motivation, the combinations of several relevant features of a job that yield equal attractiveness). Here subjects are free to mislead us, although they probably have little motivation beyond laziness to do so. The cautious scientist typically collects redundant data. For example, we expect the judgments of equal attributes to be, within the limit of error, transitive: If tone s_1 is equally loud as s_2 and s_2 is equally loud as s_3, then if the subject is being consistent we expect s_1 to be equally loud as s_3. Such checks are commonly made.

Trade-offs become a source of measurement scales when we collect not only equal-attribute data but also when we order the indifference curves by the attribute. Key measurement questions are 1. What are the properties exhibited by the ordering? 2. Are they such that one can construct a numerical representation of the empirical information? A numerical representation involves two distinct constructions. The first consists of numerical measures associated with each of the independent factors. These describe how each factor affects the criterion attribute. In psychological examples these measures often are called psychological scales. The second construction is a rule for combining the scale values that yields a numerical measure of the criterion attribute. The rule must be such that the numerical order exactly reproduces the empirical order. Such rules are often referred to as "psychological laws."

The simplest representational problem posed by these examples was formulated and solved by the economist Debreu (1960) and, independently and somewhat more generally, by Luce & Tukey (1964). We provided a list of properties about the qualitative ordering of the attribute being studied over the two (or more) factors that, when satisfied, imply the existence of a multiplicative representation[1] of the ordering into the positive real numbers. This is the representation found in many common physical examples (e.g. kinetic energy, momentum, density). It goes under the generic name of *additive conjoint measurement*.

---

[1]
  Unlike physics, where measurement scales are into the positive real numbers and the combining rule is multiplication, social and psychological theorists often map into the entire real numbers and use an additive representation. The latter arises from the former by a logarithmic transformation.

It is a curiosity of the philosophy of science that the physicists, philosophers, and mathematicians who studied the bases of physical measurement at the end of the nineteenth century failed to come up with this result—or even to recognize that it was needed. Over half a century later, behavioral scientists saw its significance for measurement. The consequences have been considerable, not only for theory but also for widespread applications of the general idea of conjoint measurement in areas such as marketing (e.g. Green & Srinivasan 1990, Wittink & Cattin 1989).

Because the simple multiplicative rule is inadequate to describe many behavioral trade-offs, e.g. loudness, Narens and I generalized these results to far more complex rules (Narens & Luce 1976, Luce & Narens 1985; for a summary see Luce et al 1990). These representations continue to lead to numerical measures on the factors, but they combine in nonmultiplicative ways. Our models extend greatly the possibilities of measurement and are slowly finding applications in areas such as sensory psychology and decision making.

TESTING: PROPERTIES VERSUS REPRESENTATIONS   There are two ways to test the adequacy of an explicit measurement model.[2] One way is to study the individual phenomenological properties that give rise to the representation. Data collection is limited to carefully contrived sets of stimuli that are well suited for the study of the property in question. For example, transivity is the simplest property assumed to hold in all such theories. Let $\gtrsim$ denote the attribute ordering over the stimuli and suppose a, b, and c are any stimuli such that $a \gtrsim b$ and $b \gtrsim c$. Then transitivity is satisfied if $a \gtrsim c$ also holds. Other properties exhibit a somewhat similar form, stating that if certain inequalities hold, then certain others must also hold. For example, a key property of trade-off (or conjoint) measurement necessary for a multiplicative representation to exist is called double cancellation. Consider stimuli having two independently manipulable factors with a, b, and g (not necessarily numerical) values on the first and p, q, and x on the second. If $(a,x) \gtrsim (g,q)$ and $(g,p) \gtrsim (b,x)$, then $(a,p) \gtrsim (b,q)$. Note that the entity g of the first component and the entity x of the second component each appear on opposite sides of the first two inequalities and so can be "cancelled," leaving the resulting assertion. This necessary property of structures having a multiplicative representation is discussed thoroughly from a psychological perspective by Michell (1990), and it appears in every book on representation measurement published since 1970 (Krantz et al 1971, Narens 1985, Pfanzagl 1971, Roberts 1979).

2

   I use measurement model to mean the special types of models found in the axiomatic, representational theory of measurement. I do not mean the extensive statistical and geometric models that have been widely used in testing abilities and attitudes.

A naive test for the transitivity of behavior can easily fail the oxymoron criterion. If we present the three pairs of stimuli—$\{a,b\}$, $\{b,c\}$, and $\{a,c\}$—in immediate succession to a subject who, for whatever reason, wishes to defeat the postulate of transitivity, he or she will have no difficulty in doing so. Two tricks are used to bypass this problem. First, suppose the stimuli have an intrinsic value to the subject, who is informed at the outset that after the choices are completed a few of the pairs will be selected at random and from each such pair he or she will receive the choice made. It thus behooves subjects to reveal their true preferences. The second trick is to separate the several related pairs widely over hundreds of trials. Subjects find it impossible to hold in memory many of their past responses. Once again, a person provided with suitable aids to memory can readily violate the theory. Enforcement of the non-oxymoron criterion depends in this case on addressing the self interest of the subjects and on producing sufficient experimental complexity that, coupled with the familiar limitations of human memory, make intentional violations unlikely.

The other testing option is to collect data that sample relatively unselectively the whole space of stimuli and do not focus on any one property, and then attempt to fit the representation, which typically has several largely unspecified functions, to the entire body of data. Anderson (1981, 1982, 1991) and Tversky & Kahneman (1992) offer good examples of such an approach. Again subject honesty is sought in the same ways. A major problem with this approach is the considerable freedom of the model and, therefore, how best to establish stringent goodness-of-fit criteria. To my knowledge, no satisfactory general solution yet exists. Both of these testing approaches typically do not make room for error or noise in the data, although the data are invariably quite noisy. This issue remains sufficiently problematic in mathematical modeling that I devote a later section to it.

Process Models

OPENING THE BLACK BOX   Although a psychologist's interest lies primarily in behavior, process modeling attempts to explain some aspects of underlying mental and/or brain mechanisms and how they give rise to behavior. The attempt is to open the black box. The most extreme forms of opening it involve biological observations. Examples include readings of electrical spikes on individual neurons obtained from electrodes inserted into them, examination of the complex interactions taking place in a neural subnetwork, ablation techniques aimed at destroying a specific local region of a (nonhuman) brain to ascertain how behavior is affected differentially by the loss of that region, or the more-or-less passive EEG, CAT, and MRI scanning techniques that measure aspects of brain function under various tasks. Psychologists operate at these various levels.

In practice, most mathematical modelers, although sometimes inspired by neural data, postulate mechanisms far more abstract and functionally defined than are found at the neural level. Their strategy somewhat parallels the difference between understanding computer architecture and the actual detailed electronic connections among basic components. As with computer architecture, flow diagrams are a favorite device for communicating functional flows of information.

SOME FEATURES OF PROCESS MODELING   A few general remarks about information processing models are appropriate:

1. Process modeling is popular among mathematically oriented psychologists. Perhaps as many as three-quarters of the mathematical-theoretical papers in psychology adopt such an approach.
2. It relies heavily on computer modeling and simulation, which most psychologists find easier to learn than they do mathematics.
3. The approach is very flexible, which is both a virtue and a fault. It can be exceedingly difficult to be sure what about a particular processing model is correct. This is especially true when the processes are entirely hypothetical as was true, for example, in the early stimulus sampling models (Neimark & Estes 1967) and in the vast majority of response-time (Link 1992, Luce 1986, Townsend & Ashby 1983) and categorization (Ashby 1992) models.
4. All behavior obviously must arise from some internal activity. But it has been difficult to establish plausible connections between standard information processing ideas and some types of regular behavior (e.g. such as are described below in the section on individual decision making). Although Busemeyer & Townsend (1993) devised a processing model of decision making, they focused little on explaining the simple (often rational) behavioral properties that have been of concern to most decision theorists.
5. Sometimes exactly the opposite is true. There are cases where insights about behavior arise from information processing concepts and for which phenomenological approaches seem helpless. The following is one such example.

TRADE-OFFS AND PROCESSING   Direct recordings of electrical activity in the peripheral auditory (eighth) nerve, which departs the inner ear for the higher reaches of the brain, tell us that signal intensity is encoded, at least in part, by the rate at which electrical spikes occur. More intense signals yield higher rates. The observed values vary from about five spikes per second to hundreds per second. These observations are crudely analogous to heart rate, except for being much faster and varying over a far wider dynamic range.

If neural spikes are the information available to the brain about the signal— and current knowledge suggests that they may be—and if intensity (at least over a limited range) is encoded as spike rate, then a brain extracting intensity information has no option but to estimate the rate from brief samples of spikes. Assuming the brain includes the functional equivalent of a stopwatch and a simple counter—the evidence for which is entirely indirect—there are two extreme ways for the estimate to be made. One, called *timing,* is to see how long it takes to collect a prescribed number of spikes. The other, called *counting,* is to count how many spikes occur in a fixed time period. In both cases, the rate is estimated by dividing the count by the time.

When rates vary over a large range—a factor of about 100 in the neural case—the advantage of fixing the number of pulses is that the quality of decision, which varies with sample size, remains independent of signal level. The obvious disadvantage of that strategy is the time that it takes to achieve the sample depends significantly on signal strength. The organism can either maintain decision quality at the expense of slower responses to weak signals or maintain a fixed decision time at the expense of poorer quality performance. For weak signals, it cannot have high quality, fast responses. The problem either way—slow times or poor quality of information—is, of course, the reason why many predators employ a strategy of stealth coupled with a fast attack.

One empirical question is whether both options are actually available to human beings. Luce & Green (1972) showed mathematically that if both are available, then a dramatic difference should be evidenced in the resulting speed-accuracy trade-off. The two models result in differences in the slope of the hit versus false alarm (ROC) curve (see Figure 1) when replotted in z-score coordinates and in the resulting speed-accuracy trade-off. The slope of the ROC is considerably less than 1 for counting and considerably greater than 1 for timing.

To test this prediction, Green & Luce (1973) adopted a simple experimental procedure designed to induce the subjects to exhibit both modes of behavior, if they are available. Suppose in a detection situation we manipulate response times by imposing a fairly severe fine when a response deadline is missed. When the deadline applies to all trials, it is optimal to count the number of pulses in a fixed time, and when it applies only to signal trials, it is optimal to fix the count and measure the time. The latter is, of course, the payoff structure for potential prey relative to predators—it does not matter how long it takes to respond when the signal arises from nonpredator noise in the environment. The predictions were so clearly sustained by the data that no statistical test was needed. Wandell (1977) successfully replicated the study for visual intensity. In recent years, McGill & Teich (1991) have provided the main developments concerning such approaches.

MULTIPLE MODES OF BEHAVIOR   This above case is an unusually simple example of a pervasive dilemma for psychologists. People typically have several qualitatively different ways of coping with a situation. If we are unaware of these multiple possibilities or elect to ignore some of them, we are likely to become confused by the data, which when averaged over subjects is perforce some unknown mix of these possibilities. Even if we are sensitive to the issue, we may have considerable difficulty either in identifying the mode being used, especially if the subjects shift among them easily and frequently, or in controlling which is used. The case mentioned in the previous section involved experimental control of the mode, and other evidence suggests that subjects do not move readily between the two modes.

The so-called fast-guess model (Ollman 1966, Yellott 1971) offers a different example of alternate modes of behavior. This model suggests that if, in the speed-accuracy situation, one presses a subject to faster and faster behavior, there is a limit beyond which the subject can no longer pay attention to which of the two signals has been presented. Urged to go faster through the judicious use of money rewards, the subject can either refuse to do so or can give up on trying to achieve any accuracy at all and simply respond to the signal onset, but not its identity. This shift of mode occurs in humans and in such animals as pigeons (for a summary see Luce 1986, p. 224, 286–294). It is a strategy of frustration, which psychologists need to be alert about and take into account. This model initially postulated that the mode is selected at random, trial-by-trial. A careful sequential analysis by Swensson (1972) and Swensson & Edwards (1971) showed that, in fact, subjects stay in each mode for a number of trials before switching, which made possible a fairly accurate partition of the data into the fast guesses and the slower, more attentive responses.

These two examples are misleadingly simple and clear; rarely is it possible to see the modes so clearly. Caution and ingenuity are the only solutions I know of for dealing with the dilemma of multiple modes of behavior. A theory alleging only one mode of behavior may be easily rejected by a person having two or more available. To pass the non-oxymoron criterion—that knowing a theory should not be sufficient for the subject to falsify it—the theorist must work out the full range of modes and figure out ways either to induce a single one, as Green and I did using payoffs, or to partition an individual's data, as was necessary with the fast-guess model. To the degree we exhaust these options, the non-oxymoron criterion will be satisfied; but otherwise it will not be.

Invariance of Mechanisms Across Situations

One feature of the physical sciences is that as mechanisms and phenomena are uncovered and modeled, they become available for use, with whatever constants have been estimated, in wholly new situations. For example, the laws of thermodynamics and electromagnetism and their corresponding dimensional constants or, for another example, the existence of biological mechanisms such as genes, chromosomes, DNA, and RNA, once isolated, are assumed applicable whenever they are relevant. Little comparable invariance has evolved in psychology. It is moderately rare to find a psychologist who, when confronted by a new set of data, invokes already known mechanisms with parameters estimated from different situations. Newell (1990) claimed to do so in his computer-based, unified theory of cognition called SOAR, but I am not persuaded by the claim. When each model is unique to a particular experimental situation, all of the model's free parameters must be estimated from the data being explained. Frequently the resulting numbers of parameters outrun the degrees of freedom in the data. This reflects a failure of the science to be cumulative, an unfortunate feature of psychology and social science that is widely criticized by natural scientists. I view it as one of the greatest weaknesses of modeling (and other theory) in our science.

A DESCRIPTIVE/NORMATIVE EXAMPLE: DECISION MAKING

An area of current interest to me is how descriptive and normative decision theories relate. The problem, from my perspective, is to discover which underlying principles of normative behavior are descriptive and which must be modified to get a correct description of behavior. These theories seem to have more in common than one might expect, but there are significant deviations. To this end, it is convenient to class the phenomenological assumptions into three distinct groups followed by some consequences.

Normative Principles of Preference

Consider a situation of uncertainty in which some chance event partially determines the outcome. As an example, consider an entrepreneur contemplating an investment in a country on the fringe of the old Soviet empire. The expected profit from the investment depends, in part, on whether hostilities break out in that region during the time period of the investment and, if they do, their exact scope and nature. A widely accepted normative postulate about such gambles—which, of course, is what an investment is—asserts that if for a particular state of hostility the amount of profit is increased but otherwise the entire situation remains unchanged, then the modified alternative will be seen as better than the original one.

This apparently innocent truism, called consequence monotonicity, is in fact quite a strong property. Some empirical studies had led many to question its universal applicability, but recent work suggests that it is strongly descriptive as well as normative (von Winterfeldt et al 1994).

Normative Principles of Framing

People were initially misled about monotonicity because the original experimental designs also presupposed another normative postulate, which for some reason decision theorists failed to question (Luce 1992). According to this postulate, two alternate descriptions of the same situation should be treated as indifferent in preference by the decision maker. This normative postulate together with transitivity of choices and consequence monotonicity go a long way toward establishing the now classical rational representation called subjective expected utility (SEU), in which utilities of consequences are averaged using subjective probabilities over the events (Savage 1954; see also Fishburn 1982, 1988; Wakker 1989).

But as we know from the familiar example of whether to call a glass half full or half empty, descriptions of situations can matter. The impact of framing, as it is called, has been explored by Tversky & Kahneman (1986), has been formulated explicitly in a particular case by Luce (1990), and has led to some striking discoveries in, for example, the realm of medical decisions (McNeil et al 1982). Others have shown major impacts of the framing of questions in public opinion polls.

A Descriptive Principle

Closely related to these framing effects is the possibility that people replace a complex alternative by something simpler than but not exactly equivalent to the original gamble. For example, people often partition uncertain situations into two parts, each examined independently of the other: the chance of gains arising and, separately, the chance of losses arising. Each aspect is separately appraised and the two evaluations are summed in some fashion to get an overall evaluation of the original situation. Indeed, such a decomposition forms the basis of many risk-benefit analyses. Nonetheless, it is not fully rational to invoke such a decomposition because the separate, independent analyses are not fully equivalent, in general, to the original situation. Only three studies have examined this decomposition hypothesis, but all sustain it (Cho et al 1994, Payne & Braunstein 1971, Slovic & Lichtenstein 1968).

Rank- and Sign-dependent Utility Representation

This descriptive, but non-normative, principle coupled with the rational preference hypotheses of transitivity and consequence monotonicity, along with the simplest rational framing properties, yields a mathematical theory that is closely related to SEU, but appears to be more adequately descriptive. It is called rank- and sign-dependent utility (RSDU) by Luce (1991, Luce & Fishburn 1991) and cumulative prospect theory by Tversky & Kahneman

(1992, Kahneman & Tversky 1979, Wakker & Tversky 1993). In the RSDU representation the utility of a gamble is the weighted utility of its gains sub-gamble and its losses subgamble, but with weights that fail to sum to 1, as do the subjective probabilities of SEU. This representational oddity simply reflects the nonrational decomposition mentioned above. The utility of the gains subgamble is a weighted average representation like SEU except it is rank-dependent (RDU) in the sense that the weights attached to an event depend not only on the event but also on the rank-order position of the consequence arising with that event as compared with the other conse-quences from the subgamble. This rank dependence arises quite naturally from the process of rational reframing. Quiggin (1993) provides a general discussion of RDU models. Research on this topic is active, and experi-ence warns that, all too often, new data will surprise and perplex us. I fully expect the story to be somewhat different in a few years, but perhaps our empirical and theoretical knowledge will be cumulative rather than destructive in nature.

DYNAMIC AND SOMEWHAT DYNAMIC MODELS

Change is everywhere, and much of it is systematic. The major breakthrough in passing from Renaissance to modern physics was the creation of the calcu-lus as a way to capture physical change. So far, these classical mathematical methods have proved of limited help in dealing with psychological change, which appears to be of at least two distinct types, both of which are often referred to as learning, despite considerable qualitative differences. One type involves small, systematic adaptations; tennis and other skilled performances are (relatively complex) examples. The other type has to do with the acquisi-tion of concepts, their relation to previously existing concepts, and the repre-sentation of this knowledge in long-term memory. This is the sort of learning we associate with schools and textbooks, not tennis courts.

Models of Incremental Change

OPERATOR MODELS   Two approaches to changing behavior were pursued in the 1950s. A phenomenological approach assumed that each experimental trial was fully characterized by a probability vector over the possible responses, and that this vector was altered systematically depending on the choice actually made and the payoff received. The most fully developed of this class of incremental change models assumed linear changes (Bush & Mosteller 1955, Norman 1972). A class of nonlinear models was also studied but was rejected because of its inability to neglect experience from the distant past (Luce 1959, Sternberg 1963).

SEQUENTIAL EFFECTS   These simple operator models are ineffective in dealing with complex memory and learning processes (see below), but they have remained viable as descriptions of adjustment processes such as selecting the response criterion in signal detection. In particular, they seem somewhat useful for characterizing the sequential effects found in almost all psychophysical methods. The basic finding is that the response on trial n depends not only on the signal on trial n but on some of the past history of signals and responses. A central question is the actual depth of the dependency, which is not easy to decide because even if it only goes one step back, there will be an apparent dependency that goes back much further. These effects, which are seen in asymptotic behavior and can be quite large (on the order of 10–20% in response times), are mostly ignored by psychophysicists although they are found whenever they are sought. Attempts have been made to model them by incremental learning models (Luce 1986, pp. 292–298) and by linear regression (Ward 1979, Ward & Lockhead 1970); however, these models are inconsistent with the fact that the correlation between responses on successive trials has repeatedly been shown to depend on the signal separation, ranging from about 0.8 for repeated signals to 0 or even negative values for widely separated ones. Nothing adequate has yet been proposed.

NONLINEAR DYNAMICS   Until the advent of high speed computing, no science was able to work effectively at a theoretical level with profoundly nonlinear processes. Attempts were made to approximate these processes by linear models, and there was some understanding of asymptotic results in certain cases. Faster computers made it possible to simulate nonlinear processes in great detail, resulting in considerable surprises. One such finding was that small changes in parameter values do not always lead to small changes in the final result. Qualitatively very different modes of behavior sometimes result. Another finding was that some of these modes are very irregular (i.e. chaotic) and appear superficially to be totally random despite being entirely deterministic. This seems to be the nature of turbulence in fluid flows. These qualitative facts about many nonlinear systems strike a receptive chord in behavioral and social scientists because much of the behavior under their scrutiny seems to undergo radical transitions and often has to be described as chaotic.

Even something as prosaic as psychophysics may be modeled in this fashion. Perhaps the major proponent of this view is Gregson (1988). Unfortunately, many find his presentations obscure and, as a result, they have had less impact than might be expected. Nonetheless, this may well be an important development, provided that we can arrive at sensible dynamic models. Because of the partitioning of behavior into trials for the convenience of data collection, even at the cost of considerable unrealism, the types of equations that arise are difference rather than differential. A simple example, which has been used in studying population changes for a century and a half, is:

$$Y_{j+1} = -aY_j(1 - Y_j), 0<Y_j<1, j = 1,2,\ldots \qquad 1.$$

In this example the variable Y is, in principle, observable or at least estimable because it is, for example, the relative proportion of predators to prey. In the psychophysical case, Gregson proposed that some sort of underlying but unobservable state variable controls the observable responses. By what appears to have been a trial-and-error approach, various nonlinear recursions (considerably more complex than the one above) were explored until the desired system behavior was achieved. Because the testing of such models raises general issues, I devote a separate section to it.

ENVIRONMENTS DEPENDENT ON BEHAVIOR   Out of the operant animal literature has come an interesting development about choice behavior, one that appears equally applicable to human beings. Most modeling of choices in psychophysics and decision making assumes a totally static probabilistic environment. In the operant work on choice it is not static. The alternatives are designed to have features like those encountered by a foraging animal: the more uninterrupted time spent on one alternative, the lower the rate of reinforcements received, whereas the ignored alternatives become gradually richer.

Various schedules of this sort have been explored. One major finding is that subjects—ranging from rodents to humans—do not partition their time among alternatives to achieve a maximum total rate of reward, which requires equating all of the marginal rates of reward. Rather, they distribute their attention approximately so that each alternative yields the same average rate of reward (Herrnstein & Prelec 1991, Prelec 1982). At first, there was some doubt about this finding because, for most natural schedules, the difference between maximizing and averaging is comparatively small and, with data somewhat obscured by noise, it was difficult to be certain which was a more accurate description. Later studies, however, made the point unambiguously that it is averaging.

For example, consider the following two-choice design: Subjects received the same monetary reinforcement following every choice; however, it was only received after a delay that depended on which alternative was chosen, 1 or 2, and on the proportion of alternative 1 responses during the immediately preceding 10 trials. The functions used are shown in Figure 2. For each proportion, the delay for alternative 2 exceeds by 2 seconds that for alternative 1, and for each alternative separately, the delay increases linearly with the proportion of responses to alternative 1. The mean delay is shown by the dotted line in Figure 2. So, the optimal behavior is always to choose alternative 2, which yields the least mean delay. Yet, for any proportion of alternative 1

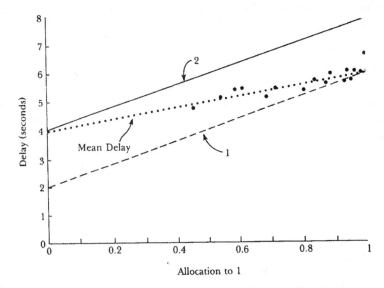

Figure 2   The delay for alternatives 1 and 2 as a function of the proportion of alternative 1 responses on the preceding 10 trials. The dotted line is the mean delay. The points are the behavior of 17 subjects in a 10 minute period after 100 practice trials. Reprinted from Figure 3 of Herrnstein & Prelec (1991).

responses, the delay is always 2 seconds less by choosing alternative 1. The dots show the behaviors of 17 subjects, and none is close to optimal.

An intuitively plausible mechanism, which Herrnstein & Vaughan (1980) called melioration, underlies this result. Suppose the subject decides (in some currently unknown fashion) that on average, alternative 1 is paying off at a higher rate than alternative 2. Then it is postulated that the time devoted to response 1 is increased at the expense of time to response 2. But once the pattern of relative returns is reversed (which generally happens, although it does not in the payoff structure of Figure 2), then the pressure is reversed to increase the time devoted to alternative 2. This continues, oscillating back and forth, until each alternative appears to be equally rewarding and the pressure evaporates. This is the same mechanism that underlies the fixed-point theorem proof of Nash's famed equilibrium theorem in game theory (Luce & Raiffa 1957, p. 391).

Concepts and Memory

After much experimentation and controversy, the early incremental models were for the most part abandoned. They were deemed not applicable to the learning of complex concepts, although they are still used to model the fine tuning found in some types of skill learning. A second approach, called stimulus sampling, which was pursued at about the same time, postulated a simple associative process that develops with experience (see Neimark & Estes 1967 for a collection of papers on stimulus sampling models). These processing models gradually evolved into a class of models concerned with memory and concept identification (for summaries see Ashby 1992, Healy et al 1992).

NEURAL NETWORKS AND ADAPTIVE PROCESSING   Some newer theoretical approaches to learning and memory stem from biological evidence that memories are not localized in single units but reside in larger neural networks. Minsky & Papert (1969) demonstrated the inability of the simplest type of network to acquire and retain concepts in the presence of competing ones. Computer simulation later showed that networks of greater complexity are able to acquire fairly complex concepts. (For more on this see Churchland & Sejnowski 1992, Grossberg 1982, McClelland et al 1986.)

3-D INFERENCES FROM SEQUENTIAL 2-D VIEWS   A major conceptual problem of visual perception is how the brain takes the two-dimensional (2-D) display on the retina (binocular vision is not required) and infers from it a (usually) unique 3-D world populated with objects, some partially obscured by others. It has long been known that from a single view, a continuum of 3-D worlds could have given rise to the 2-D display. So some degree of dynamic input is needed. It has been established empirically that very little additional information is sufficient, at least in sparse displays, to permit a unique 3-D inference. A second view adds so little information that the mathematical 3-D possibilities, although more constrained, are still not unique. Yet, human subjects typically report a unique percept. The conclusion, therefore, is that the brain must have built-in constraints on the inferences being made (Bennett et al 1989, Marr 1982, Ullman 1979). The major task, and it is a difficult one, is to characterize as fully as possible the nature of these built-in constraints. Solving such problems is not only of significance to psychology, but also promises to have a significant impact on the design of visually perceptive robots.

Comparable problems exist in hearing. It remains unknown how the brain partitions the temporal sound wave form, as transduced by the ear and peripheral nervous system, into streams of speech, music, or noise. Again, one suspects that an important contribution is to be made by mathematical formulations of the constraints and processes involved.

Problems of Testing Models of Change

A characteristic of many approaches to change, including neural networks and nonlinear dynamics, is the unobservable nature of the basic underlying mechanisms. The attempt is made to evaluate the models qualitatively in terms of the overall behavior. Little can be done to verify the underlying dynamics directly. This becomes a tricky issue for evaluation. It is not like complex processes in much of physics, which are built up from applications of basic fundamental laws that led to explicit equations such as the Navier-Stokes equations in fluid mechanics or Maxwell's equations in electromagnetism. We simply do not know the underlying nonlinear dynamics of psychological behavior; so, we attempt to infer it, using trial and error, from overall behavior of the system. This observation applies equally well to the attempts some have made to attribute complex social behavior to some unknown dynamic processes leading to complex patterns of behavior.

Even when explicit processes are postulated, such as the incremental models of the 1950s, it is extremely difficult to test their adequacy. Consider a situation for which there are choice probabilities, $P_j(i)$, for choosing alternative i on trial j. How does one estimate the probabilities to be able to study directly the dynamic recursion from $P_j(i)$ to $P_{j+1}(i)$? Surely, one cannot average responses over trials because, by the very nature of the topic, they are changing. Only in the strictly linear case is averaging over subjects justified, and even then considerable care is required not to confuse oneself. In nonlinear cases, averaging is completely unjustified unless one is working with actual clones, which may soon be possible with animals. The only solution that I know of to the estimation and testing problem is to work out the probability calculations for sequences of responses and to compare those with the patterns actually observed. Coupling our lack of knowledge about local dynamic mechanisms with these statistical difficulties, it is hard to be optimistic about our ability to test these nonlinear models effectively.

STRUCTURE AND NOISE

As scientists, our primary interest is in the structure imposed by the mental processes under study, witness the models mentioned earlier. However, we are always faced with variability in the data, which often makes it exceedingly difficult to judge the adequacy of a structural model. Three approaches for dealing with variable data are discussed below; none is yet fully satisfactory.

Statistical Modeling

The most conventional approach to noisy data is the statistician's. A structural model—often a simple additive one, as in regression and analysis of variance—is stated and a random variable is added to the result to describe the errors in observing the process. Psychologists are well acquainted with this style of modeling, and its methodology is de rigueur if one is to publish an empirical paper. Anderson (1981, 1982, 1991) and his group have used this approach extensively in studying the structure of a variety of psychological attributes.

Some of us are deeply skeptical about this approach. Perhaps the most thorough critique is Gigerenzer & Murray's (1987). One criticism is that only rarely can we expect that the particular linear (or log-linear) model in question describes simultaneously both the numerical measures obtained in our study and the assumed statistical model. Usually some a priori unknown transformation of the data should be made to put the observations into the simple structural form. But we do not have any reason to believe that the assumptions of the statistical model (often Gaussian distributions or equality of variances) hold for any but a very special, unknown transformation and not necessarily the one that leads to the structural model. There is no automatic compatibility between structure and statistics.

We attempt to brush these difficulties under the rug. We do computer simulations and attempt to establish some degree of robustness, and we try various ad hoc transformations of the data, but we do not really have a truly satisfactory way to arrive simultaneously at the underlying structure and statistics.

In this connection, evidence of interactions is usually a signal of trouble. It tells us that the statistical assumptions are grossly violated or that the structure is not what we had hoped it might be or both. Sometimes we are led to a transformation that successfully rids us of the interactions (Folk & Luce 1987), knowing full well that at least one of the statistical tests surely violated the assumptions of ANOVA. All too often, in my opinion, the interactions are treated as a finding and not as evidence of a lack of understanding of the combining rule for measures of the independent variables.

Probabilistic Models

A second tack is to suppose that the basic structure is not at all algebraic in character, but rather that the observables are response probabilities. The area of psychometric testing falls into this camp. In an area of interest to me, decision making, one postulates a probability $P(a,b)$ of choosing alternative a over alternative b rather than supposing they are simply ordered by preference, $a \succsim b$. We have already encountered examples of such modeling in signal detection.

This tack treats the probability as an inherent aspect of the model, rather than as a statistical add-on (Falmagne 1985, Doignon & Falmagne 1991). The difficulty with the approach appears once we go beyond the simplest case of just orderings and attempt to incorporate additional structure. We seem to encounter highly intractable conceptual problems. The only cases for which we have had any success involve, in one way or another, either an assumption analogous to Weber's law (Falmagne 1980, Falmagne & Iverson 1979, Narens

1994) or replacing the random variables by their medians (Falmagne 1976). For example, suppose we are modeling choices according to stimulus intensity and have as part of our structure the fact that intensities can be physically added. Let a and b be two intensities and let $a \circ b$ denote the joint presentation or concatenation of a and b. The problem is to understand how various choice probabilities relate. For example, how does $P(a \circ b, c \circ d)$ relate to $P(a,c)$, $P(a,d)$, $P(b,c)$, and $P(b,d)$? If Weber's law is true, we can say something; otherwise, we do not have the slightest idea how to proceed.

Lack of a Qualitative Theory of Structure and Noise

In my view, the problem of meshing structure and randomness is a very deep one, one for which we do not seem to have a good idea about how to proceed. It is a matter of putting into a single mathematical framework the axiomatic ideas of measurement that describe how to go from qualitative algebraic observations to their numerical representation and the numerical ideas of probability or statistics. The difficulty in doing so resides partly in the lack of a qualitative theory of randomness. We can discuss randomness only numerically, in terms of random variables. Thus, we do not have any natural way of putting together the qualitative ideas of measurement with the numerical ones of statistics.

Let me outline the kind of theory I believe we need in the simple case of concatenation. Let A denote a (dense) set of stimuli and $\circ$ a concatenation operation over them. In the usual algebraic theories of measurement there is, in addition, an ordering $\succsim$ over A. In the noisy case, we are unable to impose properties like transitivity and monotonicity because any observation we make may be spoiled by noise, so such regular patterns cannot be expected in our observations. But I don't know what to substitute for it. The idea would be to axiomatize whatever we have in such a fashion that the representation would be into a family of random variables $\{X_a : a \text{ in } A\}$. For example, in this case a suitable representation would be into a family of gamma-distributed random variables with the property that $E(X_{a \circ b}) = E(X_a) + E(X_b)$, where E denotes the expectation operator. In such a representation the expectations act like the classical algebraic theory for what are known as extensive structures (e.g. mass measurement).

Our failure to make any progress on this problem since it was recognized several decades ago is discouraging. Until we get some insight into its nature, I do not foresee a satisfactory solution for coping simultaneously with structure and error.

Chaos

Chaos theory—the newest kid on the block—is based on the premise that the process under study is fully deterministic, a nonlinear dynamic system. As mentioned earlier, simple nonlinear processes can generate exceedingly complex behavior. In particular, small changes in the parameters of such systems can lead to vastly different patterns, some of which are literally chaotic. This has become the primary approach taken with many physical systems (e.g. aerodynamic turbulence) for which previous theoretical treatments were not satisfactory.

The natural question is whether chaotic human or social behavior can and should be thought of as arising from deterministic dynamic systems, rather than being thought of statistically or probabilistically. Social phenomena sometimes exhibit marked discontinuities, and there certainly is a good deal of apparent randomness in behavior. The difficulty with this approach is the crudity with which the dynamic processes are known. Until they are pinned down in much more detail, one cannot view this approach as more than an interesting speculation.

CONCLUDING COMMENTS

Tensions are rarely resolved, but are adapted to and modified. Is that to be expected of these four?

PHENOMENOLOGICAL VERSUS PROCESS MODELING   In physics and applied physics they continue to co-exist, even when a detailed model at one level accounts, at least in principle, for the properties at a higher level. One does not predict the paths of space probes using particle physics. My guess is that any successful phenomenological model will always be seen as an explanatory challenge to process modelers, but that the latter will rarely supplant the former in all applications.

DESCRIPTIVE VERSUS NORMATIVE MODELING   Aside from metaphysical considerations, this is not a distinction made in the natural sciences. I do not see how psychology can avoid dealing with both types of models. Surely reasoning, inference, and decision making will be guided by normative principles—indeed, they are well established disciplines independent of psychology—and psychologists cannot but be intrigued by how these activities are actually conducted in daily practice. In particular, it is important to understand exactly when and how people depart from normative principles.

DYNAMIC VERSUS STATIC MODELING   If psychology is at all like the other sciences, it will tend increasingly toward dynamic descriptions. We are being held back from developing fully dynamic models not because we fail to recognize the importance of change. Rather, the data we deal with are inherently noisy, and the usual averaging procedures suitable in static situations are exceedingly difficult to use when subjects differ from one another either in the parameters of the process or by employing qualitatively different processes.

NOISE VERSUS STRUCTURE   We simply do not know how to model randomness at the same qualitative level at which we can model structure. Our attempts to bypass this discrepancy are, in my opinion, less than satisfactory. Moreover, the findings of the past 10 or 15 years about nonlinear dynamic systems call into question whether the actual source of the noise is randomness or ill-understood dynamics.

These last two, interrelated tensions strike me as the most significant. Here profound changes in mathematical modeling could take place, and until they do, modeling will remain limited and, to a degree, unsatisfactory.

ACKNOWLEDGMENTS

I thank Donald Hoffman and Geoffrey Iverson for useful comments on this manuscript, which is based, in part, on the University of California, Irvine 1994 Distinguished Lectureship Award for Research.

Literature Cited

Anderson NH. 1981. *Foundations of Information Integration Theory.* New York: Academic

Anderson NH. 1982. *Methods of Information Integration Theory.* New York: Academic

Anderson NH, ed. 1991. *Contributions to Information Integration Theory,* Vols. 1–3. Hillsdale, NJ: Erlbaum

Ashby FG, ed. 1992. *Multidimensional Models of Perception and Cognition.* Hillsdale, NJ: Erlbaum

Bennett B, Hoffman D, Prakash C. 1989. *Observer Mechanics: A Formal Theory of Perception.* New York: Academic

Busemeyer JR, Townsend JT. 1993. Decision field theory: a dynamic-cognitive approach to decision making in an uncertain environment. *Psychol. Rev.* 100:432–59

Bush RR, Mosteller F. 1955. *Stochastic Models for Learning.* New York: Wiley

Cho Y, Luce RD, von Winterfeldt D. 1994. Tests of assumptions about the joint receipt of gambles in rank- and sign-dependent utility theory. *J. Exp. Psychol.: Hum. Percept. Perf.* In press

Churchland PS, Sejnowski TJ. 1992. *The Computational Brain.* Cambridge, MA: MIT Press

Debreu G. 1960. Topological methods in cardinal utility theory. In *Mathematical Methods in the Social Sciences, 1959,* ed. KJ Arrow, S Karlin, P Suppes, pp. 16–26. Stanford, CA: Stanford Univ. Press

Doignon J-P, Falmagne J-C, eds. 1991. *Mathematical Psychology: Current Developments.* New York: Springer-Verlag

Falmagne J-C. 1976. Random conjoint measurement and loudness summation. *Psychol. Rev.* 83:65–79

Falmagne J-C. 1980. A probabilistic theory of extensive measurement. *Philos. Sci.* 47: 277–96

Falmagne J-C. 1985. *Elements of Psychophysical Theory.* New York: Oxford Univ. Press

Falmagne J-C, Iverson G. 1979. Conjoint Weber laws and additivity. *J. Math. Psychol.* 86:25–43

Fishburn PC. 1982. *The Foundations of Expected Utility.* Dordrecht: Reidel

Fishburn PC. 1988. *Nonlinear Preference and Utility Theory.* Baltimore, MD: Johns Hopkins Press

Folk MD, Luce RD. 1987. Effects of stimulus complexity on mental rotation rate of polygons. *J. Exp. Psychol.: Hum. Percept. Perf.* 13:395–404

Gigerenzer G, Murray DJ. 1987. *Cognition as Intuitive Statistics.* Hillsdale, NJ: Erlbaum

Green DM, Luce RD. 1973. Speed-accuracy trade off in auditory detection. In *Attention and Performance,* ed. S Kornblum, 4:547–69. New York: Academic

Green DM, Swets JA. 1988. *Signal Detection Theory and Psychophysics.* Palo Alto, CA: Peninsula

Green PE, Srinivasan V. 1990. Conjoint analysis in marketing: new developments with implications for research and practice. *J. Mark.* 54:3–19

Gregson RAM. 1988. *Nonlinear Psychophysical Dynamics.* Hillsdale, NJ: Erlbaum

Grossberg S. 1982. *Studies of Mind and Brain.* Dordrecht: Reidel

Healy AF, Kosslyn SM, Shiffrin RM, eds. 1992. *Essays in Honor of William K. Estes,* Vol. 1–2. Hillsdale, NJ: Erlbaum

Herrnstein RJ, Prelec D. 1991. Melioration: a theory of distributed choice. *J. Econ. Perspect.* 5:137–56

Herrnstein RJ, Vaughan W Jr. 1980. Melioration and behavioral allocation. In *Limits to Action: The Allocation of Individual Behavior,* ed. JER Staddon, pp. 143–76. New York: Academic

Indow T. 1982. An approach to geometry of visual space with no a priori mapping functions: multidimensional mapping according to Riemannian metrics. *J. Math. Psychol.* 26:204–36

Kahneman D, Tversky A. 1979. Prospect theory: an analysis of decision under risk. *Econometrica* 47:263–91

Krantz DH. 1975a. Color measurement and color theory. I. Representation theorem for Grassman structures. *J. Math. Psychol.* 12: 283–303

Krantz DH. 1975b. Color measurement and color theory. II. Opponent-colors theory. *J. Math. Psychol.* 304–27

Krantz DH, Luce RD, Suppes P, Tversky A. 1971. *Foundations of Measurement,* Vol. I. New York: Academic

Link SW. 1992. *The Wave Theory of Difference and Similarity.* Hillsdale, NJ: Erlbaum

Luce RD. 1959. *Individual Choice Behavior.* New York: Wiley

Luce RD. 1986. *Response Times: Their Role in Inferring Elementary Mental Organization.* New York: Oxford Univ. Press

Luce RD. 1990. Rational versus plausible accounting equivalences in preference judgments. *Psychol. Sci.* 1:225–34. Reprinted (with minor modifications) 1992. In *Utility Theories: Measurements and Applications,* ed. W Edwards, pp. 187–206. Boston: Kluwer

Luce RD. 1991. Rank- and sign-dependent linear utility models for binary gambles. *J. Econ. Theory* 53:75–100

Luce RD. 1992. Where does subjective-expected utility fail descriptively? *J. Risk Uncert.* 5:5–27

Luce RD, Fishburn PC. 1991. Rank- and sign-dependent linear utility models for finite first-order gambles. *J. Risk Uncert.* 4:29–59

Luce RD, Green DM. 1972. A neural timing theory for response times and the psychophysics of intensity. *Psychol. Rev.* 79:14–57

Luce RD, Krantz DH, Suppes P, Tversky A. 1990. *Foundations of Measurement,* Vol. 3. San Diego: Academic

Luce RD, Narens L. 1985. Classification of concatenation measurement structures according to scale type. *J. Math. Psychol.* 29: 1–72

Luce RD, Raiffa H. 1989. *Games and Decisions: Introduction and Critical Survey.* New York: Dover

Luce RD, Tukey JW. 1964. Simultaneous conjoint measurement: A new type of fundamental measurement. *J. Math. Psychol.* 1: 1–27

Luce RD, von Winterfeldt D. 1994. What common ground exists for descriptive, prescriptive and normative utility theories? *Manage. Sci.* 40:263–79

Macmillan NA, Creelman CD. 1991. *Detection Theory: A User's Guide.* New York: Cambridge Univ. Press

Marr D. 1982. *Vision.* San Francisco: Freeman

McClelland JL, Rumelhart DE, PDP Research Group. 1986. *Parallel Distributed Processing. Explorations in the Microstructure of Cognition,* Vols. 1–2. Cambridge, MA: MIT Press

McGill WJ, Teich M. 1991. Auditory signal detection and amplification in a neural transmission network. In *Signal Detection,* ed. M Commons, J Nevin, M Davison, pp. 1–37. Hillsdale, NJ: Erlbaum

McNeil BJ, Pauker SG, Sox HC Jr, Tversky A. 1982. On the elicitation of preference for alternative therapies. *N. Engl. J. Med.* 306: 1259–62

Michell J. 1990. *An Introduction to the Logic of Psychological Measurement.* Hillsdale, NJ: Erlbaum

Minsky M, Papert S. 1969. *Perceptrons.* Cambridge, MA: MIT Press

Narens L. 1985. *Abstract Measurement Theory.* Cambridge, MA: MIT Press

Narens L. 1994. The measurement theory of dense threshold structures. *J. Math. Psychol.* In press

Narens L, Luce RD. 1976. The algebra of

measurement. *J. Pure Appl. Math.* 8:197–233

Neimark ED, Estes WK, eds. 1967. *Stimulus Sampling Theory.* San Francisco: Holden-Day

Newell A. 1990. *Unified Theories of Cognition.* Cambridge, MA: Harvard Univ. Press

Norman MF. 1972. *Markov Processes and Learning Models.* New York: Academic

Ollman RT. 1966. Fast guesses in choice-reaction time. *Psychonomic Sci.* 6:155–56

Payne JW, Braunstein ML. 1971. Preferences among gambles with equal underlying distributions. *J. Exp. Psychol.* 87:13–18

Pfanzagl J. 1971. *Theory of Measurement.* Würzburg: Physica-Verlag. 2nd ed.

Prelec D. 1982. Matching, maximizing, and the hyperbolic reinforcement feedback function. *Psychol. Rev.* 89:189–230

Quiggin J. 1993. *Generalized Expected Utility Theory: The Rank-Dependent Model.* Boston: Kluwer

Roberts FS. 1979. *Measurement Theory.* Reading, MA: Addison-Wesley

Savage LJ. 1954. *The Foundations of Statistics.* New York: Wiley

Slovic P, Lichtenstein S. 1968. Importance of variance preferences in gambling decisions. *J. Exp. Psychol.* 78:646–54

Sternberg S. 1963. Stochastic learning theory. In *Handbook of Mathematical Psychology,* ed. RD Luce, RR Bush, E Galanter, 2:1–120. New York: Wiley

Suppes P, Krantz DH, Luce RD, Tversky A. 1989. *Foundations of Measurement,* Vol. 2. San Diego, CA: Academic

Swensson RG. 1972. The elusive trade-off: speed versus accuracy in visual discrimination tasks. *Percept. Psychophys.* 12:16–32

Swensson RG, Edwards W. 1971. Response strategies in a two-choice reaction task with a continuous cost for time. *J. Exp. Psychol.* 88:67–81

Townsend JT, Ashby FG. 1983. *Stochastic Modeling of Elementary Psychological Processes.* Cambridge: Cambridge Univ. Press

Tversky A, Kahneman D. 1986. Rational choice and the framing of decisions. *J. Bus.* 59:S251–78. Reprinted 1986 in *Rational Choice: The Contrast Between Economics and Psychology,* ed. RM Hogarth, MW Reder, pp. 67–94. Chicago: Univ. Chicago Press

Tversky A, Kahneman D. 1992. Advances in prospect theory: cumulative representation of uncertainty. *J. Risk Uncert.* 5:204–17

Ullman S. 1979. *The Interpretation of Visual Motion.* Cambridge, MA: MIT Press

von Winterfeldt D, Chung N-K, Luce RD, Cho Y. 1994. Tests of consequence monotonicity in decision making under uncertainty. *J. Exp. Psychol.: Learn. Mem. Cogn.* In press

Wakker PP. 1989. *Additive Representations of Preferences: A New Foundation of Decision Analysis.* Dordrecht: Kluwer

Wakker PP, Tversky A. 1993. An axiomatization of cumulative prospect theory. *J. Risk Uncert.* 7:147–76

Wandell BA. 1977. Speed-accuracy tradeoff in visual detection: applications of neural counting and timing. *Vis. Res.* 17:217–25

Ward LM. 1979. Stimulus information and sequential dependencies in magnitude estimation and cross-modality matching. *J. Exp. Psychol.: Hum. Peform. Percept.* 5:444–59

Ward LM, Lockhead GR. 1970. Sequential effects and memory in category judgments. *J. Exp. Psychol.* 84:27–34

Wittink DR, Cattin P. 1989. Commercial use of conjoint analysis: an update. *J. Mark.* 53:91–96

Yellott JI Jr. 1971. Correction for guessing and the speed-accuracy tradeoff in choice reaction time. *J. Math. Psychol.* 8:159–99

Annu. Rev. Psychol. 1995. 46:27–57

RESEARCH ASSESSING COUPLE AND FAMILY THERAPY

Jay L. Lebow

Chicago Center for Family Health, 445 E. Illinois, Chicago, Illinois 60611 and Department of Psychiatry, University of Chicago, Chicago, Illinois 60637

Alan S. Gurman

Department of Psychiatry, University of Wisconsin School of Medicine, Madison, Wisconsin 53792

KEY WORDS: couple and family therapy, process and outcome research, treatment efficacy

CONTENTS

0066-4308/95/0201-0027$05.00

INTRODUCTION

The field of couple and family therapy has come a long way since its early provocative beginnings. A diverse set of methods grounded in a number of well-articulated theories have developed, as have a number of distinct schools of practice. Couple and family therapy has received considerable attention, both in professional circles and in the popular culture, and is now among the most common forms of mental health treatment. Couple and family therapy is used to treat a variety of difficulties by therapists from all the mental health professions in all types of mental health settings. For issues such as marital difficulties and the possibility of impending divorce, couple and family therapy has become the treatment of choice, and is even an expectation in much of our culture.

The number of professionals who practice couple and family therapy has grown exponentially. The Family Psychology Division of the American Psychological Association and two multi-disciplinary organizations, the American Association for Marriage and Family Therapy and the American Family Therapy Academy, focus most of their attention on these therapies, as do several prominent journals: *Family Process, Journal of Marital and Family Therapy,* and *Journal of Family Psychology.* In the last twenty years, we have also seen the publication of a nearly endless series of titles dealing with the theory and practice of couple and family therapy, several of which have been auspicious in opening and developing areas of interest (e.g. normality in families in Walsh 1993; the family life-cycle in Carter & McGoldrick 1988; use of narrative methods in White & Epston 1990). In parallel with these developments in the field, society has also come to focus considerable attention on the importance of family life, and the risks to individuals within dysfunctional families.

This review focuses on research assessing couple and family therapy. We now have a number of well-articulated models of family-based intervention (Gurman & Kniskern 1981a, 1991), including the structural (Minuchin 1974), strategic (Watzlawick et al 1974), Milan systemic (Boscolo et al 1987), solution-focused (de Shazer 1985), object relations (Scharff & Scharff 1987), functional (Barton & Alexander 1981), contextual (Boszormenyi-Nagy & Ulrich 1981), intergenerational (Bowen 1978), behavioral (Jacobson & Margolin 1979, Patterson 1986), feminist (Goldner 1985), experiential (Whitaker & Keith 1981), and integrative (Gurman 1981, Pinsof 1983). Application of these models has extended across virtually all populations, especially to couples' difficulties (Jacobson & Gurman 1986), acting out in adolescence (Alexander & Parsons 1982, Patterson 1986), drug abuse in adolescents and adults (Liddle & Dakof 1994, Stanton & Todd 1982), disorders of childhood (Patterson 1986), depression (Jacobson et al 1991, O'Leary & Beach 1990), schizophrenia (Hogarty et al 1986), and across a variety of cultural groups and family forms (Boyd-Franklin 1989, Szapocznik et al 1990, Walsh 1993).

There has been a great deal of probing discussion of the theory underlying a family systems viewpoint, resulting in considerable elaboration and revision in recent years (Hoffman 1981). These developments in theory clearly have moved away from the earlier simplistic notion of the family as the exclusive etiologic agent in the development of difficulties, and as the sole preferred locus for intervention across all difficulties. An integrative viewpoint is emerging that includes concepts from various family methods of intervention, as well as interventions at the level of the individual (Lebow 1984, 1987a) and larger system (Breunlin et al 1992). Family therapy has also been examined from several pertinent and powerful vantage points including feminism (Goldner 1985, Hare-Mustin & Marecek 1988), culture (Boyd-Franklin 1989, McGoldrick et al 1988), and life-cycle development (Carter & McGoldrick 1988). The field has been boiling over with ideas and concepts, and ways of examining the family and how to have an impact on it. Treatments have emerged and been refined, theories have undergone considerable revision, and assumptions have been continually examined within the emerging perspectives about family within the broader society.

In reviewing the research base of couple and family therapy, one faces a basic dilemma. Traditional empirical research has not been the foundation for the development of these modes of practice, nor has it been part of the fabric of much of this work. At one time, most research on couple and family therapy was conducted with little connection to the outstanding clinical developments in the field. Alternative modes of investigation such as inductive reasoning, clinical observation, and deconstruction have dominated in the development of methods and treatment models. Some couple and family therapists have even been reluctant to acknowledge that empirical research has an important role. At one discouraging point, now fortunately past, there was considerable debate about whether traditional research had any relevant role in the development of family therapy (see critical comments in Tomm 1986, Keeney & Ray 1992, and rejoinders by Gurman 1983, Shields 1986).

Even with the assumption that research has value, the complexities of family therapy pose a formidable set of obstacles to investigation. Family interventions and therapy processes are rich and complex; the outcomes in family therapy include not only those of multiple individuals, but also of interactive variables that cross individuals. Further, as a developing set of methods, treatment is ever changing. Considered in the context of the formidable tasks involved, the research in couple and family therapy that has emerged is quite remarkable, particularly when one considers that much of the development of practice and theory has occurred away from the sites of traditional academia where resources and expertise in conducting research are greatest.

Much of this research also has been superior in methodology, an enormous change from the state of research a decade ago (Bednar et al 1988, Gurman et al 1986, Hazelrigg et al 1987). Most research on couple and family therapy has involved the study of behavioral techniques. This emphasis has come about as a result of the simpler questions asked in behavioral therapies, the more readily operationalized sets of interventions, and the prolific work of a few key researchers. Some of the work of behavioral couple and family researchers has been so idiomatic that it has had vast influence throughout the broader field of psychotherapy research (e.g. Jacobson & Revenstorf 1988). In contrast, all the other methods of couple and family therapy together have not produced as many research studies as have those of the behavioral methods. Three recent trends may be noted here: First, we are seeing more and better research on nonbehavioral methods. Second, behavioral studies now occur in the context of considerable prior work and, thus, ask more sophisticated questions about process and outcome than do studies of other approaches. Third, in the context of the integrative spirit in family therapy, we see much greater overlap in the practice of behavioral and nonbehavioral therapies. The closing of these gaps renders research on behavioral couple and family therapy much more relevant to the everyday practice of couple and family therapy than in the past.

DEFINING THE DOMAIN OF COUPLE AND FAMILY THERAPY

Delineating the domain of couple and family therapy is far from a trivial question. Is there a field of couple and family therapy? Does it make sense to review studies in so diverse a body of work together? Initially, marital and family therapies were grouped together simply because they shared the common ground of treating multiple members of the same family together. As conceptual sophistication grew, a relatively simple insight became apparent: Who was present was less important than whether the therapy was family based, i.e. focused on the family system and its relation to the change process. Treatments were developed that aimed at family-level intervention with sessions involving only a single person (Bowen 1978, Szapocznik et al 1983). Gurman et al (1986, p. 565) offered the following classic definition: "Family therapy may be defined as any psychotherapeutic endeavor that explicitly focuses on altering the interactions between or among family members and seeks to improve the functioning of the family as a unit, or its subsystems, and/or the functioning of individual members of the family."

In most family therapies, and in research on these therapies, more than one family member is seen. However, the presence of multiple members in conjoint sessions does not capture the essence of family therapy, which is about a viewpoint focused on the importance of altering ongoing interaction. This focus delineates the domain of couple and family therapy.

Recent arguments suggest that couple therapy and family therapy differ sufficiently to warrant two literatures and two sets of techniques (Alexander et al 1994). However, we believe the zeitgeist of the field over the last 40 years lies in the overarching importance of the system. With the tempering of some of the original radical systemic viewpoint into the kind of integrative multi-level family therapy that now is common, and the dissemination and transmutation of techniques across what were once absolutely separate theoretical frames, the logic for the preservation of a superordinate grouping of couple and family therapy is stronger than ever. This field should rightly include such diverse entities as couples therapy, sex therapy, behavioral parent training, and Milan systems family therapy, despite the obvious and enormous differences in their methods.

Family therapy is actually a number of different activities linked by these common understandings. Systemic concepts merely set a frame for possibilities; they do not limit the range of intervention. Both the mediating and ultimate goals of treatment may vary, as may the theoretical frame and the interventions (Gurman 1978). Therefore, it makes conceptual sense to sub-divide these therapies into ones that share common characteristics and operations. Family therapies can best be classified along two axes: the first defines who is seen in treatment (e.g. individual, couple, nuclear family, extended family), and the second defines the theoretical perspective (e.g. structural, strategic, object relations, or a type of integration). Both who is seen and the theory of the approach contribute to the differences between therapies at the level of operations. We must examine not only overall efficacy, but also the efficacy of the specific therapies that comprise couple and family therapy.

In examining this literature it is crucial to keep in focus the importance of treatment goals. In couple and family therapy, change in family process is always both a mediating and an ultimate goal. Most couple and family therapy has an additional goal, be it a change in the behavior of an individual or in a broader dimension of relational life (e.g. marital satisfaction). In examining research, one needs to consider the impact on both family process and these other entities.

It also should be mentioned that a fundamental change in nomenclature has occurred recently. "Marital and Family Therapy" has become "Couple and Family Therapy," out of respect for the diverse forms of family in our society (Walsh 1993). Consistent with this usage, we reserve use of the term "marital" to contexts in which we describe work specifically limited to married couples.

THE EFFICACY OF COUPLE AND FAMILY THERAPY

Reviews of the research literature conducted over the past 30 years conclude almost without exception that the outcomes achieved by treatment groups have exceeded those of control groups. This holds true for reviews considering the full range of couple and family therapy (Gurman & Kniskern 1978, Gurman et al 1986, Alexander et al 1994) and for reviews limited to couple therapy (Jacobson & Addis 1993, Baucom & Hoffman 1986). There have been dissenting views, especially about the documentation of the effectiveness of nonbehavioral treatments (Beach & O'Leary 1985, Bednar et al 1988), but with more and better recent research emerging in the last few years, the evidence for overall effectiveness has become unequivocal (e.g. Jacobson et al 1991, Snyder & Wills 1989). Although most studies have focused on behavioral treatments, there is now a considerable base of nonbehavioral treatment studies that point to treatment efficacy. Further, earlier concerns about possible confounds of treatment method that might mitigate this conclusion (Beach & O'Leary 1985, Gurman & Kniskern 1978, Bednar et al 1988, Lebow 1981) can now be put to rest; a range of excellent methodological studies confirms the general findings of efficacy found in less rigorous research.

In the last few years, meta-analytic techniques have been applied to the research data on couple and family therapy (Hazelrigg et al 1987 on family therapy, Hahlweg & Markman 1988 on behavioral couple therapy, and Shadish 1992 and Shadish et al 1993 on couple and family therapy). All have found impressive effect sizes. In the most methodologically sophisticated of these analyses, Shadish et al (1993) examined 63 studies conducted before 1988, all of which involved random assignment and a clinically distressed population with a mean treatment duration of 8 sessions. Shadish et al found a weighted least squares effect size of .51, suggesting that a therapy client at the mean was better off than 70% of control clients. Hazelrigg et al (1987) analyzed 15 studies of family therapy (i.e. involving at least a parent and child, excluding couple therapy) that included a control group. Random assignment was not required for inclusion in their analysis, although some effort to equate groups was needed. Hazelrigg et al reported a weighted mean effect size of .50 for behavior ratings, and .45 for family interaction. Hahlweg & Markman (1988) reported an effect size of .95 in their meta-analysis of studies of behavioral couple therapy. Shadish et al replicated both Hazelrigg et al's and Hahlweg & Markman's effect sizes in the relevant subset of studies in their meta-analysis. Couple and family therapies thus appear to produce statistically significant results and considerable effect sizes within traditional comparative designs; these effect sizes are not unlike those emerging for other successful psychosocial treatments.

In one of the most important recent developments in couple and family research and in psychotherapy research in general, Jacobson and his associates (Jacobson et al 1984, Jacobson & Addis 1993, Jacobson & Truax 1991) have drawn attention away from the statistical significance of differences between groups and have focused on the clinical significance of change. Specifically, they have examined how many couples in behavioral marital therapy reached the criterion of no longer being distressed. In these analyses, they found that even among these treatments, which are among the best documented for effectiveness, most achieved less than 50% success in helping individuals in distressed marriages to no longer be distressed. They also found further reductions in effectiveness rates with follow-up over time (Jacobson & Addis 1993, Jacobson et al 1987). Although Jacobson and his associates examined behavioral marital therapy, it would be inappropriate to suggest that issues of clinical significance and duration of change over time are unique to these therapies. Their work has raised the standard for demonstrating the clinical efficacy of therapy in general.

With regard to the ability of couple and family therapies to produce clinically significant change, the picture is not entirely negative. For example, in Shadish's meta-analysis, 41% of the treatment conditions in the behavioral couple treatments achieved the criterion of starting with distressed couples and moving them to nondistressed status, whereas none of the control conditions was able to do so.

Consensus is moving toward the use of both traditional statistical comparisons and the examination of clinical significance. Just as statistical criteria can set too trivial a standard, it is equally problematic to try to reach levels of efficacy out of keeping with the realities of clinical experience. Marital therapy is basically undertaken with distressed couples, many of whom are on the verge of divorce and for whom problems are so chronic and deeply rooted that positive change in marital satisfaction is highly unlikely. For many, marital therapy can help clients explore whether there is any hope in the relationship before they decide to divorce. For highly troubled samples, a 50% movement of couples into the genuinely nondistressed range may constitute effective treatment, and the changes that occur in the couples who do not meet the criterion for clinical significance may still make the difference between effective and ineffective patterns in such crucial areas as co-parenting. In some cases, divorce may be a positive alternative outcome. We require more data and discussion to set standards for clinical significance for treatments.

A few additional trends in effectiveness should be noted. Early investigations of treatments tend to show greater effects (Jacobson & Addis 1993) than do subsequent examinations. When investigators assess their own treatments, effects are also greater than when the assessment is conducted by others (Jacobson & Addis 1993, Shadish et al 1993). Published research also shows greater effects than do unpublished studies (Shadish et al 1993). The possible confounds implied by these trends should be considered in any evaluation of the outcome literature.

EFFICACY OF SPECIFIC TYPES OF COUPLE AND FAMILY THERAPY

Behavioral Couple and Family Therapy

The largest research literature focuses on behavioral couple therapy (BCT) and behavioral family therapy (BFT). Numerous reviews have documented findings demonstrating the efficacy of BCT in approximately 30 distinct studies (Alexander et al 1994, Baucom & Hoffman 1986, Gurman et al 1986, Hahlweg & Markman 1988, Jacobson & Addis 1993, Schmaling & Jacobson 1988, Shadish et al 1993). In meta-analyses of couple therapy, BCT produces the largest effect sizes (Shadish et al 1993). As noted above, Jacobson's commendable evaluation of these data for clinical significance point to some intrinsic limits: only about one-half the treated population reaches the point of no longer being distressed and effects tend to diminish on long-term follow-up.

Some studies have examined the components of change in BCT. Two basic ingredients have been identified: behavior exchange and communication/problem-solving treatment. There is some evidence that the combination of behavior exchange and communication/problem-solving treatment exceeds outcomes of therapies involving only one component (Jacobson 1984, Jacobson & Follette 1985), particularly in the maintenance of change (Jacobson et al 1987). Using meta-analysis, Shadish et al (1993) found an effect size of .85 for communication training, and .88 for behavior exchange, and .90 for the combination, suggesting all have similar levels of effectiveness.

There is also a large literature demonstrating the effectiveness of behavioral interventions with families, often in the context of parent training. This literature is discussed below in the context of specific problems.

Cognitive Therapy

Several studies have examined either the impact of a cognitive approach to couple therapy or the addition of a cognitive component to behavioral couple therapy. Although the relevant attribution literature suggests that cognitions in distressed and nondistressed relationships vary considerably (Bradbury & Fincham 1990), several studies on the efficacy of cognitive methods have found the treatments to effect the mediating goal of changing cognitions, but they produce mixed results in changing marital satisfaction and behavioral patterns (Emmelkamp et al 1988, Huber & Milstein 1985, Waring et al 1991). Similarly, the addition of cognitive interventions to behavioral ones provides additional impact on cognitions, but there is no apparent additional effect on marital satisfaction (Baucom & Lester 1986, Baucom et al 1990, Behrens et al 1990, Halford et al 1993).

Experiential Therapies

Emotionally focused couples therapy (EFT) (Greenberg & Johnson 1988), a treatment focused on the expression of emotion, has demonstrated effectiveness on short-term follow-up (Johnson & Greenberg 1985a,b; James 1991; Goldman & Greenberg 1992). The one study that has compared EFT to another treatment (Goldman & Greenberg 1992) found the effects of EFT comparable to an integrated systemic marital therapy (IST) with less maintenance of gains at follow-up than in IST.

Psychodynamic Therapies

Until recently, there was almost no research examining psychodynamic based couple and family therapies (Shadish et al 1993). Fortunately, Snyder and associates (Snyder & Wills 1989, Snyder et al 1991a, Wills et al 1987) have provided a model study of a manualized variant of psychodynamic marital therapy, termed Insight Oriented Marital Therapy (IOMT). This treatment emphasizes dealing with conflictual emotional processes that exist within one or both spouses separately, between spouses interactively, or within the broader family system. The research compared IOMT with a variant of BCT and a treatment on demand condition. Treatment averaged 19 sessions with follow-up at 6 months and 4 years. At termination and 6-month follow-up, both treatments were effective in reducing marital distress: 73% reached Jacobson's standard for clinical significance in IOMT and 62% in BCT, vs 15% in the control condition. At 4-year follow-up, the IOMT group had a much lower divorce rate (3% for IOMT vs 38% for BCT) and a higher level of marital satisfaction. Considerable debate has emerged about what these results mean (Gurman 1991; Jacobson 1991a,b,c; Snyder et al 1991b; Johnson & Greenberg 1991; Snyder & Wills 1991). Much of this debate surrounds the form of BCT treatment that was used. Supporters of BCT have argued that it was not a good example of BCT; however, the greatest importance of this study is its demonstration of the effectiveness of IOMT, which appears to have a powerful long-term effect on marital distress. This study gives some credibility to the long-standing claims of the effectiveness of psychodynamic methods. Clearly, replication and expansion of Snyder and associates' work are needed.

Structural and Systemic Therapies

Structural family therapy has a small, long-standing base of empirical support, almost exclusively in family therapy (Gurman et al 1986). Most recently, research on structural interventions is best represented in the integrative work of Szapocznik, Liddle, and associates (see below).

Strategic therapies have seldom been assessed and, therefore, have received limited support. Goldman & Greenberg (1992) found that a strategic Palo Alto–style model of couple therapy was as effective as short-term, emotionally focused therapy and had more lasting effects at follow-up. Green & Herget (1989, 1991) conducted a series of studies that have demonstrated the additional impact of a single Milan systemic team session within the context of a family therapy. Shadish et al's (1993) meta-analysis found the structural/strategic/systemic therapies to produce an effect size of .28.

Other Therapies

Little good research has examined other forms of couple and family therapy. As noted ten years ago (Gurman et al 1986), the evidence is especially weak for humanistic-experiential therapies. Shadish et al (1993) reported effect sizes for these treatments that did not differ significantly from 0. Few researchers have examined such influential forms of couple and family therapy as Bowen therapy (Bowen 1978), experiential therapy (Whitaker & Keith 1981), solution-focused therapy (de Shazer 1985), and narrative therapies (White & Epston 1990), or such recent heavily marketed approaches as "divorce busting" (which also make extraordinary claims of efficacy) (Weiner-Davis 1992).

It cannot be concluded that these treatments do not work. Snyder & Wills (1991) and Greenberg and his associates (Johnson & Greenberg 1985) show that treatments that have not been studied previously may be as effective as those that have been. However, the failure to conduct research on the efficacy of these methods stands as a major impediment to their credibility. Empirical evidence is needed, particularly in a field like couple and family therapy, where claims for effectiveness of a wide range of intervention are continually made within the popular media.

Integrative Therapies

Couple and family therapy has seen a movement toward the development of integrative methods that bring together aspects of many models (Lebow 1984, 1987a,b) and at times cross boundaries with individual therapy. Until recently, little research had been done on integrative methods of practice. The natural tendency to study pure forms of treatment first, coupled with the additional difficulties in research on more complex therapies, delayed study of couple and family therapy as it has come to be most frequently practiced. Recently, much more data have become available on integrative methods. Specific integrative programs have been designed, studied, and adapted to specific problems (e.g. see Liddle & Dakof 1994 on adolescent drug abuse). Further, school-based treatments currently being investigated are becoming more integrative. For example, Jacobson's (1992) behavioral couple therapy looks much like an integrative therapy. The breakdown of boundaries is most clearly expressed in the debate over Snyder & Wills' (1991) study that focused on how much the manual for insight-oriented therapy resembles the clinical practice of behavioral couple therapy (Jacobson 1991a).

Discussion

As noted earlier, there are a far greater number of studies of behavioral methods than of other approaches, and hence there is much better evidence for the effectiveness of these methods. Seldom have there been appropriate comparisons between behavioral methods and other modes of family therapy. Studies such as those of Snyder and associates and Greenberg and associates begin to suggest that the effectiveness of other approaches may be as strong or even stronger in nature.

The relationship between behavioral and other methods of couple and family therapy remains a complex one. Only a small percentage of couple and family therapists identify themselves as behavioral therapists, although most family therapists use a variety of behavioral methods (e.g. communication training, problem-solving, and creating consistency in parenting). An unanswered empirical question is how much data from the specific practice of behavioral methods can couple and family therapy claim as indicative of the effectiveness of typical methods of practice.

EFFICACY OF THERAPIES FOR SPECIFIC PROBLEMS

Research on couple and family therapy has moved to a greater focus on the ability of these therapies to have an effect on specific disorders and problems. These efforts follow research that has demonstrated powerful connections between family process and disorders such as depression (Coyne 1987), schizophrenia (Tarrier & Barrowclough 1990), and alcoholism (Steinglass et al 1987). Couple and family therapy have begun to emerge as effective in treating a wide array of specific problems.

ADOLESCENT DRUG ABUSE   Federal initiatives for research on the treatment of adolescent drug abuse have resulted in a considerable amount of investigation of the impact of family therapy. Liddle & Dakof's (1994) recent review suggested that all studies to date have found family treatments to exceed the impact of control conditions and/or alternative treatments. Retention in treatment has also been considerably better than in other treatments (Joanning et al 1992, Liddle & Dakof 1994). Szapocznik et al (1988) found 7% of the adolescents were drug-free at the beginning of their structurally oriented treatment, whereas 80% were at termination. Joanning et al (1992) found that a systemic therapy produced twice as many drug-free clients as did group therapy or a family drug education condition. Liddle et al found that 53% of their patients were using hard drugs at pretest vs 9% at posttest and 3% at one-year follow-up after integrative multidimensional family therapy. Further, 47% were drug-free and 34% were using marijuana or alcohol less than once per week after treatment. In these studies, family therapy was also found more effective than peer group meetings (Joanning et al 1992, Liddle & Dakof 1994), parent education (Joanning et al 1992, Lewis et al 1990), or multifamily group intervention (Liddle & Dakof 1994).

DEPRESSION   The literature examining depression has indicated that depression in women often is a problem in the couple relationship and always has implications for couples (Coyne 1987). Both Beach & O'Leary (1992) and Jacobson et al (1991) have examined BCT in relation to cognitive therapy, the most common psychological intervention for depression. O'Leary & Beach (1990) and Beach & O'Leary (1992) found that both BCT and cognitive therapy reduced depression in women in maritally discordant couples at termination and at one-year follow-up. Only the BCT resulted in improvement in marital satisfaction. Initial depression scores were not related to outcome, although initial levels of marital satisfaction were. In an interesting interaction, the more distressed women were in their pre-therapy relationship and the fewer cognitive errors they made pre-therapy, the more likely the BCT was to work better. Jacobson et al (1991, 1993) found cognitive-behavior therapy for depression, BCT, and a combined treatment all reduced depression in women. Couple therapy did not influence depression when the women were in nondistressed relationships, but it did when they were in distressed relationships. The combined treatment failed to produce more change in depression in either the maritally distressed or non–maritally distressed clients than the component treatments. Improvements in marital satisfaction occurred when the maritally distressed were treated with couple therapy or those who were not maritally distressed were treated with the combination therapy.

Given the high concordance rate between marital problems and depression in women, studies of marital therapy may include a significant percentage of depressed women. Sher et al (1990) found that a striking reduction in depression accompanied changes in the marital relationship with BCT. As a whole the literature offers strong evidence for behavioral couple treatment as a treatment for women who are depressed and in distressed marriages.

ALCOHOLISM   Several studies have used BCT in the treatment of alcoholism (for review, see Alexander et al 1994, Jacobson et al 1989). The research has found that BCT consistently adds to relationship satisfaction and frequently leads to a reduction in drinking (O'Farrell et al 1985, 1992; McCrady et al 1986, 1991).

DELINQUENCY   Tolan et al (1986), in reviewing this literature, found several studies demonstrating efficacy of family therapy in treating delinquency, but only a few of these studies were well designed. Considerable evidence is available for the impact of Functional Family Therapy on delinquency (Barton & Alexander 1981). More recently, Henggeler et al (1991, 1992) found that adolescents treated with Multi-systemic Therapy, a family therapy that includes attention to other systems, had fewer arrests and self-reported offenses and spent an average of 10 fewer weeks incarcerated.

PARENT TRAINING   The effects of parent training with aggressive and opposi- tional children and preadolescents have been summarized previously (e.g. Kazdin 1991, McMahon & Wells 1989, Miller & Prinz 1990, Patterson et al 1992), all finding high levels of efficacy. Parent training assumes that if one can alter the behavior of parents, the impact will pass on to their children. The efficacy of functional family therapy with acting-out adolescents and their families also is well documented (Alexander & Parsons 1973, Kazdin 1991). Parent training that reduces these problems also increases marital satisfaction (Sayger et al 1988, 1993). It should be noted, however, that Shadish et al's (1993) meta-analysis found family therapy less effective than individual therapy in the treatment of child and adolescent problems.

SCHIZOPHRENIA   Tarrier & Barrowclough (1990) and Hahlweg et al (1989) recently reviewed the literature on the efficacy of family therapies for schizo- phrenia. Family therapy that involves direct efforts to reduce expressed emotion dramatically reduces recidivism and symptomology in a schizophrenic popula- tion when combined with antipsychotic medication (Falloon et al 1985, Hogarty et al 1986). Falloon et al and Hogarty et al both developed psycho-educational programs that combined education, medication, interpersonal skill training, and family therapy. The Falloon study found a much lower relapse rate at 9 months (6% vs 44%) and 2 years (17% vs 83%) with the addition of family therapy. The Hogarty study found 41% relapse after 12 months in the control condition, 20% in a social skills condition, 19% with family management alone, and 0% with combined social skills and family management. As Tarrier & Barrowclough (1990) suggest, change in expressed emotion appears to be a strong predictor of outcome in schizophrenia. This finding suggests indirectly that the first-genera- tion family therapies for schizophrenia, which stimulate interaction and the sharing of powerful feelings and thus often increase expressed emotion, are unlikely to have a positive impact.

AGORAPHOBIA   Research examining the inclusion of spouses in treatment for agoraphobia (for review, see Alexander et al 1994, Jacobson et al 1989) has found evidence that spousal involvement adds to the effectiveness of behavioral exposure treatments (Arnow et al 1985, Barlow et al 1983, Cerny et al 1987).

OTHER PROBLEMS   The effects on other disorders and difficulties have yet to be demonstrated adequately. Despite considerable discussion of the use of a variety of couple and family therapies to help divorcing families, Lee et al (1994) were not able to locate any methodologically rigorous studies assessing the impact of family therapy in divorce. In their review, Lee et al found evidence that groups for adults encountering divorce do reduce distress, but groups for children have failed to show any consistent effect on their functioning. Some research has focused on hyperactivity (Barkley et al 1992), where family therapy has a clear but limited effect; on bi-polar disorder, where psycho-educational and other family interventions show promise (Miklowitz & Goldstein 1990, Retzer et al 1991), and on the family-based treatment of obesity (Epstein et al 1990). The efficacy of a variety of methods for intervention with couples in sexual dysfunction has been well documented (Emmelkamp 1994), but is beyond the realm of this review.

SUMMARY   A number of approaches to couple and family therapy have a positive effect on a range of important clinical problems and disorders. Research has begun to define subgroups of these populations for whom couple and family therapy may be the treatment of choice. However, there is a paucity of data examining the efficacy of couple and family therapy with some problems that are discussed frequently in the clinical literature (e.g. family violence, divorce, anorexia and other eating disorders, psychosomatic disorders, borderline and other personality disorders). Again, this data void does not necessarily suggest that commonly used treatments do not work, but it offers no evidence that they do.

EXAMINING THERAPY PROCESS

Although Pinsof (1981, 1988, 1989), Greenberg (1986, 1991), and others (Gurman et al 1986) have called for many years for the study of process in family therapy and its relation to both immediate and long-term outcomes, only in the last few years has a substantial body of work emerged. The task of analyzing process in complex interactions in which there are several partici- pants easily becomes daunting. Given the small literature studying many different specific treatments (which may highlight different processes), this research is best viewed as pointing to provocative possibilities and avenues for further exploration rather than to definitive conclusions.

Much of the pioneering work has occurred in the simpler research context of couples therapy, where Greenberg and associates have developed and refined several methods for studying process. A great deal of this work features a task analysis of key therapeutic events, with particular attention to the sequence marked by the emergence of a client problem, followed by therapist intervention, and ensuing client behavior. The work of Greenberg and associates has begun to produce a body of interesting findings.

By coding observed interactions, Johnson & Greenberg (1988) were able to compare the best sessions for couples attaining the best and worst outcomes. They found that those attaining successful outcomes had higher levels of experiencing, showed more affiliative actions, and had more experiences of softening of their feelings toward their partner. In a method centered on client views of the change process, Greenberg et al (1988) obtained retrospective accounts of critical change incidents four months after emotionally focused therapy and sorted these into categories of key events. Greenberg et al (1993) examined changes in process over time, finding more autonomous affiliative behaviors (e.g. support and understanding) later in therapy. Affiliative statements, depth of experiencing, and peak session events also were related. Further, spouses in emotionally focused therapy were more likely to respond affiliatively after the therapist facilitated intimate disclosure by their partner.

Interesting work has also emerged in behavioral approaches. Holtzworth-Munroe et al (1989) had clients and therapists report their session-by-session reactions to behavioral marital therapy. Both the clients' and therapists' reports of reactions were strongly related to outcome. Clients' collaborating in therapy and with homework assignments were related to ultimate marital satisfaction.

In a widely cited study, Patterson & Chamberlain (1992) attempted to track the process of resistance in behavioral parent training. They were able to identify how therapist behavior related to the genesis of resistance. This study is noteworthy for having documented a clinical phenomenon that was well known but uncharted in empirical investigation. Such analyses suggest potential pathways for improving treatment.

Other important developments have been in the study of the therapist-client relationship. Pinsof & Catherall (1986) have developed a promising methodology for studying the complexities of alliance in couple and family therapy that subdivides the alliance on one dimension into tasks, bonds, and goals; and along another dimension into individual, subsystem, and whole system alliance. This method allows for the study of the possibility of split alliance (i.e. different views across participants), which has emerged in this research

(Heatherington & Friedlander 1990). The relationships between alliance and outcome have only begun to be articulated. Bourgeois et al (1990) found alliance predicted outcome better for men in group couple therapy than for women, and, all told, only accounted for a small percentage of the variance in outcome. Green & Herget (1991) found a striking effect of therapist relationship skills in Milan-style team consultation, an approach in which these skills are typically viewed as unimportant.

Another window is opening through studies of the impact of gender on process, particularly within Functional Family Therapy. Newberry et al (1991) examined family members' responsiveness in relation to therapist behaviors such as structuring and supportiveness. Female therapists' supportive behaviors elicited higher probabilities of family supportive behaviors than did male therapists'. A different effect emerged in therapist structuring behaviors, where fathers responded more positively to structuring regardless of therapist sex. Mas et al (1985) found apparent differences such as less speaking by adolescents to female therapists and the use of different modes of expression by family members depending on therapist sex. A similar pattern emerged in Shields & McDaniel's (1992) study of structural/strategic family therapy. Although they found no sex difference in the retention of families, and found supportive statements to be equal across male and female therapists, families made more structuring or directive statements to male therapists while disagreeing with other family members more when the therapist was female. Male therapists also made more statements overall and more explanatory statements in response to family structuring or disagreement. Although the study of these relationships of gender to process and outcome has thus far been limited to the two approaches examined within these innovative investigations, these findings point to the likelihood of powerful effects of sex of therapist across all orientations.

PREDICTORS OF OUTCOME

Other efforts have looked at the relationship between independent variables and outcome, especially client characteristics. Several interesting relationships have been observed, particularly in the behavioral literature where there have been more opportunities to study these relationships. Alexander et al (1994) and Jacobson & Addis (1993) have reviewed predictors in BCT. According to this literature: 1. Couples who are more severely distressed are less likely to emerge without difficulties. 2. There is an inverse relationship between age and outcome. 3. Emotional disengagement is a bad prognostic sign. 4. Gender role preferences have an impact on outcome, but the direction has varied between studies. 5. Depression is a negative predictor of outcome. How well these findings extend to other couples therapy remains in question. Snyder et al (1993) found similar trends in their sample of couples treated with behavioral (BMT) and insight-oriented (IOMT) treatments. Couples who were most globally distressed and those who had poor problem-solving skills, low psychological resilience, and high levels of depression showed the poorest outcome. Snyder et al also found that those showing high levels of nonverbal negative affect while listening to their partners were more likely to divorce four years later and, paradoxically, that those who showed higher rates of problem-solving and information exchange at termination showed a poorer ultimate outcome.

Similar predictions have been attempted in behavioral parent training. Again, the findings have important practical implications. Dadds et al (1987a,b) found that families with marital problems were less likely to respond well to treatment, and Webster-Stratton & Hammond (1990) found that life stress affected outcome negatively. In addition, there have been clear trends toward worse outcomes in older children (Patterson et al 1992).

METHODOLOGICAL DEVELOPMENTS

The most striking developments in couple and family research lie in a vastly improved methodology. Couple and family research began with a number of flawed studies, followed by a sophisticated series of critiques and suggestions for improved methodology (Barton et al 1985, Beach & O'Leary 1985, Gurman & Kniskern 1978, Gurman et al 1986, Lebow 1981, Wynne 1988). Research has finally caught up with the recommendations of a decade ago, and although the quantity of work in most areas of investigation remains small, the quality of the work is now quite good (Shadish et al 1993). Several advances can be delineated:

1. Treatments are more clearly articulated. It is now typical to have manuals guiding the delivery of treatment in research (Jacobson et al 1991, Liddle & Dakof 1994, Snyder & Wills 1991), along with tests of the integrity of the treatment delivered (Waltz et al 1993, Wills et al 1987).
2. The use of multiple data sources has become common, providing a better understanding of outcome. Treatment outcomes almost invariably must examine change on both a relationship level and individual level. Client report, therapist report, and rater report often present quite different perspectives on change. Interaction on standard tasks in laboratory and inventories of behavior in natural settings add other sources of information.
3. Change is frequently assessed at multiple points in time. A few exemplary studies increased follow-up to as long as two (Jacobson et al 1987) or four years (Snyder et al 1993). These studies allow for a better understanding of the durability of change.

4. The impact of components of treatment are studied intensely. Particularly in behavioral studies, research has moved beyond the global assessment of treatments to assessments of what each intervention strategy adds to outcome and how each component can best be delivered.

5. The effects of treatment are compared to standardized treatments. In studies of depression treated with BCT, cognitive therapy, a well-researched therapy, has been used as a comparison. Similarly, Snyder & Wills (1991) have used BCT as a yardstick for assessing IOMT. Such comparisons help anchor the effectiveness of treatment in relation to a known entity.

6. Treatments under study have become more typical representations of practice. Research on family therapy began with studies of what were often atypical analogue treatments. Recent research (Snyder & Wills 1991, Green & Herget 1989, Goldman & Greenberg 1992) has operationalized treatments that are representative of the most widely disseminated models. More sophisticated versions of behavioral couple and family therapy also include many of the most prominent intervention strategies.

7. Good standardized measures for assessing process and outcome are more readily available (Grotevant 1989). In early research, it was typical for researchers to develop instruments while they studied specific questions, thereby limiting validity. Present research can draw on a number of well-validated instruments with documented histories of use. Examples include FACES (Olson 1986) and the Structural Family Systems Rating Scale (Szapocznik et al 1991) for assessing family structure, the Marital Satisfaction Inventory (Snyder 1981) and Dyadic Adjustment Scale (Spanier 1988) for assessing couple satisfaction, the Area of Change Questionnaire (Margolin et al 1983) for assessing areas of couple complaint, the Couple and Family Therapy Alliance Scales (Pinsof & Catherall 1986) for assessing the therapeutic alliance, the Couples Interaction Scoring System (Gottman 1979) and Marital Interaction Coding System (Weiss & Summers 1983) for coding couple interaction, and Family Goal Recording (Fleuridas et al 1990) for assessing family goal attainment. Critiques of extant instruments have also appeared that allow greater understanding of the data gathered through these instruments and suggest directions for the next generation of instruments (e.g. Kazak et al 1988, Heatherington & Friedlander 1990).

8. Greater efforts have been made to deal with threats to internal validity. Issues such as training of therapists and pre-therapy client status are now typically examined, thereby reducing such threats.

9. Results are more clearly reported and the limits of research are acknowledged. The most sophisticated critiques are often offered by researchers about their own work, including explication of the limits to external validity.

10. Clinical significance is emphasized. The work of Jacobson and his associates (Jacobson & Follette 1985, Jacobson & Revenstorf 1988) has led to widespread consideration of the clinical meaning of change. The standard for reporting now includes both effect size and measures of clinical significance.

11. Methods for studying treatment process examine both the proximal and distal effects of intervention. Greenberg and his associates have developed and described methods that allow for targeted process analysis of key events in treatment, thus removing many of the difficulties in conducting process research (Greenberg 1991, Rice & Greenberg 1984).

12. Innovative types of analysis are used, such as cost-effectiveness (Pike & Piercy 1990, Henggeler et al 1986) and qualitative analysis (Atkinson et al 1991, Moon et al 1990). The range of methods is broadening, with greater agreement about the advantages and limits of each method. Either/or dichotomies are being replaced by understanding of what can be gained from various methods of analysis.

13. Catalogs of generic therapist behaviors are being built (e.g. Figley & Nelson 1989). Such catalogs allow for more sophisticated study of therapy process.

14. Informed consent (Heatherington et al 1989), control groups, and other ethical dilemmas are better handled. Formal protocols for treatment on demand in control conditions and for gaining consent for treatment from multiple members in a family have replaced earlier more haphazard methods.

Not all research manifests these advances in method. However, a body of work is available that allows us to begin to delineate a well-validated base of specific findings and that provides a solid foundation for future efforts.

DIRECTIONS IN FAMILY THERAPY RESEARCH AND FAMILY THERAPY

1. There have been many important developments in the interface between researchers and clinicians. In a variety of settings, including two special conferences of the American Family Therapy Academy, the dialogue has moved from overtly hostile (Tomm 1986) to an examination of common ground and goals (Lebow 1988, Liddle 1991). Contentious thinking still remains on both sides (e.g. Keeney & Ray 1992), but the movement is clearly toward a rapprochement between research and practice. Researchers make more effort to translate their findings for clinicians, and clinicians increasingly consider the ramifications of research and suggest questions that are of interest.

Changes in the nature of treatment models and advances in research method have helped in this rapprochement. Most family therapies have moved away from radical systemic positions, which focused solely on interpersonal processes and viewed the etiology of disorder, treatment, and the assessment of change exclusively in terms of the properties of systems (e.g. circular causality and homeostasis). These radical systemic viewpoints showed little respect for any linear epistemology, including the methods of empirical research, and focused attention on a complex set of variables that were extremely difficult to measure. A shift has occurred in which interpersonal processes, feedback loops, and the system's role in problem generation and resolution are still emphasized; but attention has broadened to include individual functioning, the larger social system, and other levels of analysis. This shift has led to greater focus by clinicians on the kinds of questions about efficacy that are more amenable to research (e.g. With whom does a particular treatment approach work?), as well as to greater interest in the results of that research. In parallel, researchers have moved beyond the study of treatment analogues with little resemblance to actual practice to the study of more typical approaches to intervention. They have also gone beyond the more easily assessed aspects of process and outcome (e.g. individual functioning and marital satisfaction) to more complex assessments of the kinds of circular processes that have been central within the systemic viewpoint.

2. Family therapy models and methods are now better articulated and provide clearer guidelines for intervention and practice, making them more amenable to study. The early years of family therapy were marked by treatments that were very difficult to operationalize. More recent guidelines within the developing schools of family therapy have been clearer (Gurman & Kniskern 1981a, 1991), and there has been a far greater focus on orderly clinical decision-making (Pinsof 1983).

Treatments have become sufficiently articulated and orderly that manuals are readily created for their practice in research investigations. However, we must remain aware of what can be lost in the rigidity of a treatment manual. As Alexander et al (1994) note, manuals can limit exactly that kind of complex decision-making typical in the more complex variants of family therapy. In a pertinent study, Jacobson et al (1989) compared the manual-based version of BCT with a flexible version. Although the same outcomes were achieved at termination, the flexible treatment produced better results at follow-up. The best compromise appears to lie in manuals that allow some range of intervention strategy while clearly articulating decision trees. Research variants of couple and family treatments are always at some level analogues to treatment as represented in typical clinical practice. The treatment should be sufficiently replicable for research while also being as much like everyday treatment as possible. Recent research appears to be finding this best cross-over point.

3. With the convergence of findings of efficacy in studies using a variety of treatments and research methodologies, the question, Does couple and family therapy work? can be laid to rest. There is sufficient demonstration of effectiveness to serve as the cornerstone in any public policy discussion of couple and family therapy. Much more important for future investigations are questions at greater levels of specificity. For example, When and under what conditions are particular types of couple and family therapy effective?

4. The distribution of research across models of treatment is highly skewed. Differences in knowledge about models are even more pronounced than at the time of earlier reviews (Gurman et al 1986). We can also see the considerable influence a few good studies can have on the knowledge base within treatments (e.g. Snyder & Wills 1991, Greenberg & Johnson 1988), and the impact funding agencies can have in prioritizing work with certain populations (e.g. adolescent drug abuse). The gaping holes in our knowledge base need to be filled in.

5. We are seeing a trend toward more clinical trials research comparing treatments. Although some have cogently argued about the limits of these studies (Greenberg 1991), particularly in what they can suggest about how to improve practice, significant information has accrued from these efforts. The work becomes even more important when process analysis is added to the clinical trial.

6. Paradoxically, recent research also shows the impact that the intense study of process in a few cases can have, particularly when the cases are selected in relation to outcome and the methods for assessing process clearly focus on change events rather than engaging in a hunting expedition (Greenberg 1991). More work is emerging that links process to both short-term (e.g. behavior and feelings this week) and long-term (e.g. status at treatment completion) outcome. Both clinical trials and process and outcome analysis should be conducted, each supplementing the other.

7. The effectiveness of treatments appears to diminish over time. Research has begun to assess whether there are methods for increasing the durability of change. In particular, it is important to ask whether certain types of interventions increase the durability of change (Snyder et al 1993) or whether returning for booster sessions as a preventive strategy can do so (Jacobson 1991c). These research questions also point to challenges for clinical practice. In parallel, more clinicians are moving to open-ended views of treatment that may fit better with the realities of family life over the life-cycle than the notion of treatment as ending all difficulties forever (Lebow 1995).

8. Treatments utilized in research studies are converging, moving toward the delineation of a generic set of interventions, from which methods may be

constructed to meet the needs of specific populations. This trend parallels the movement in family therapy toward integrative treatments (Lebow 1984, 1987a). We require both studies within treatments that delineate the best means for conducting particular treatments and studies that look to the most effective combinations of ingredients across scholastic boundaries. We can begin to envision component analysis extending to important questions such as, How much do intergenerational, behavioral, and structural components add to problem resolution in specific kinds of cases?

9. Research remains at the level of methods testing within laboratories set up by those involved in the development of treatment methods, just as clinical methods in family therapy first tended to be developed and promoted in distinct locations. Meta-analytic studies have revealed considerable effect sizes in favor of whatever treatment was developed in the investigator's laboratory (Shadish et al 1993). We need to move to a broader base of research in which important couple and family therapies are examined across settings. The work done in laboratories in preparing manuals for various treatments is a step toward such efforts.

10. We are beginning to see research on treatments that transcend the labels of individual, couple, or family therapy, just as clinical methods are moving to transcend these boundaries (Lebow 1987a,b). Comparisons are needed of how different choices of participants and focus affect outcome. The substantial question remains: Under what conditions do family, couple, or individual sessions maximize impact? As yet, we have little data to suggest optimal choices of whom to include in what treatment, although some data suggest that couple and family intervention has particular relevance in certain kinds of disorder (e.g. depression in couples with low levels of marital satisfaction; schizophrenia in families high in expressed emotion). Research assessing when and how to blend family and child sessions in the treatment of child difficulties is especially needed (Fauber & Long 1992, Heincke 1990). To assess these types of questions concerning treatment integration, we must examine not only the research assessing couple and family therapy but also that examining other forms of treatment such as child therapy (Kazdin 1991).

11. Gender and culture have become major foci of attention in the family therapy literature. We are beginning to see some parallel efforts to address these issues in research. One method assesses special treatments for specific populations. For example, in a study involving Hispanic families, Szapocznik et al (1990) found considerable decrease in drop-out when culture-specific engagement procedures were used rather than typical techniques. Such efforts provide useful information about how to intervene best with specific groups.

At another level, data can be examined with an eye to these issues. For example, Jacobson and associates included analyses of the impact on outcome of the distribution of power in couples (Jacobson et al 1986, Whisman & Jacobson 1990). Even more importantly, we can probe for intrinsic biases. In their review of family therapy, Alexander et al (1994) called particular attention to assumptions about marriage and family that may be highly culture-based while becoming integral to methods of assessment (e.g. that "blissful enmeshment or codependency is the ultimate outcome goal" in some measures of marital satisfaction). Such self-critical examination helps provide the foundation for a meaningful research base.

12. An outstanding body of research is now available on family process and family development. This work suggests many clinical hypotheses that can serve as the base for treatment research. For example, Gottman and associates' breakthrough studies have added immeasurably to our knowledge of patterns and sequences of dysfunction in marriage (Buehlman et al 1992; Gottman 1991, 1992, 1993; Gottman & Krofkoff 1989). Certain patterns around conflict directly lead to decreasing levels of marital satisfaction and ultimately to divorce. Similarly, powerful bodies of research concerned with such issues as patterns in divorcing and remarried families (Bray & Hetherington 1993), family transitions around the birth of children (Cowan & Cowan 1992), and patterns in the alcoholic family (Steinglass et al 1987) suggest clear clinical implications. We are beginning to see research that builds on such work and there should be much more of it.

13. An increasing emphasis in family therapy has been on a life-cycle perspective (Carter & McGoldrick 1988). Except for the inclusion of age as a variable, there have been few efforts to look at treatment in relation to life-cycle changes and issues.

14. Research also has failed to attend sufficiently to issues of treatment acceptability and consumer satisfaction. Despite the central importance assigned the task of engagement in much of the clinical literature (Minuchin & Fishman 1981), acceptability of treatments, client satisfaction, and attrition are rarely reported. Provocative findings such as the disparate levels of client satisfaction in Milan treatment in two settings (Green & Herget 1991, Mashal et al 1989) require follow-up. There have been a few acceptability studies comparing aspects of behavioral couple or parenting interventions in nonclinical samples (Upton & Jensen 1991, Calvert & McMahon 1987) and some research has been concerned with treatment drop-out (e.g. Allgood & Crane 1991, Anderson et al 1985, Noel et al 1987), but this work has helped little in understanding under what conditions, to whom, and in what ways couple and family therapy is acceptable as a method of intervention.

15. If one issue has galvanized attention in the family therapy community, it is the meaning and methods for intervening in family violence (Avis 1992, Goldner et al 1990). Research has helped demonstrate the frequency of violence in the general population and in clinical samples (Babcock et al 1993, Burman et al 1993, Murphy & O'Leary 1989, O'Leary et al 1989), but has yet to examine the impact of any of the methods developed for intervention.

16. Biology is clearly emerging in the literature as an important variable in family life, in such disparate contexts as conflict in marriage (Gottman & Levenson 1992) and processes around schizophrenia in the family (Leff & Vaughn 1985). Family reactions to crises in health (Rolland 1994) and, more broadly, the field of family systems medicine occupy much attention. Treatment research must begin to attend more to these issues.

17. We still have few data about deterioration effects in couple and family therapy (Gurman & Kniskern 1978). When and under what conditions do clients worsen in the wake of these potent interventions? Are there contraindications for family therapy or alterations in method needed under particular circumstances to avoid such risks? Even the rates of deterioration in outcome studies are rarely reported.

18. Little effort has been made to consider family variables in the study of individual therapies. Systemic thinking suggests that the range of assessment should always extend beyond the individual to those who have intimate connections to the patient (Gurman & Kniskern 1981b). This theory is reinforced by findings in research comparing individual and couple or family treatments that use both types of measures and that show a variety of effects extending beyond the patient (e.g. Jacobson et al 1991).

19. Research on training of couple and family therapists (for review, see Avis & Sprenkle 1990), couple and family enrichment programs (for review, see Guerney & Maxson 1990, Bradbury & Fincham 1990, Giblin et al 1985), and efforts at family preservation in abuse and neglect has developed significantly over recent years.These studies suggest potential effective pathways for intervention, and these areas should continue to be examined in conjunction with research on family therapy.

20. Replication may represent the greatest single need in this body of work. Studies are difficult to execute, time-consuming, and costly. It is encouraging that despite these obstacles, we can now see the kind of replication and further inquiry that characterizes good science in a number of areas including behavioral couple therapy, parent training, and family therapy for adolescent substance abuse.

21. In conclusion, there appears to be a rapprochement between couple and family therapy research and the field of couple family therapy. Therapy research now examines treatments that look like typical therapies, re-

searchers and clinicians have dialogues, and an overarching set of concerns are evident in the work of both clinicians and researchers. This is not to overstate the level of agreement, because concerns and mistrust remain. However, the stage appears to be set for a fruitful and "clinically significant" next decade of research on couple and family therapy.

Literature Cited

Alexander JF, Holtzworth-Munroe A, Jameson P. 1994. The process and outcome of marital and family therapy: research review and evaluation. In *Handbook of Psychotherapy and Behavior Change,* ed. AE Bergin, SL Garfield, pp.595–630. New York: Wiley. 4th ed.

Alexander JF, Parsons B. 1973. Short-term behavioral intervention with delinquent families: impact on family process and recidivism. *J. Abnorm. Psychol.* 81:219–25

Alexander JF, Parsons B. 1982. *Functional Family Therapy: Principles and Procedures.* Carmel, CA: Brooks/Cole

Allgood SM, Crane DR. 1991. Predicting marital therapy dropouts. *J. Marital Fam. Ther.* 17:73–79

Anderson SW, Atilano RB, Bergen LP, Russell CS, Jurich AP. 1985. Dropping out of marriage and family therapy: intervention strategies and spouses' perceptions. *Am. J. Fam. Ther.* 13:39–54

Arnow BA, Taylor CB, Agras WS, Telch MJ. 1985. Enhancing agoraphobia treatment outcome by changing couple communication patterns. *Behav. Ther.* 16:452–67

Atkinson BJ, Heath AW, Chenail R. 1991. Qualitative research and the legitimization of knowledge. *J. Marital Fam. Ther.* 17: 161–66

Avis JM. 1992. Where are all the family therapists? Abuse and violence within families and family therapy's response. *J. Marital Fam. Ther.* 18:223–30

Avis JM, Sprenkle DH. 1990. Outcome research on family therapy training: a substantive and methodological review. *J. Marital Fam. Ther.* 16:241–64

Babcock JC, Waltz J, Jacobson NS, Gottman JM. 1993. Power and violence: the relation between communication patterns, power discrepancies, and domestic violence. *J. Consult. Clin. Psychol.* 61:40–50

Barkley RA, Guevremont DC, Anastopoulos AD, Fletcher KE. 1992. A comparison of three family therapy programs for treating family conflicts in adolescents with attention-deficit hyperactivity disorder. *J. Consult. Clin. Psychol.* 60:450–62

Barlow DH, O'Brien GT, Last CG, Holden AE. 1983. Couples treatment of agoraphobia: initial outcome. In *Advances in Clinical Behavior Therapy,* ed. KD Graig, RJ McMahon. New York: Brunner-Mazel

Barton C, Alexander JF. 1981. Functional family therapy. See Gurman & Kniskern 1981a, pp. 403–43

Barton C, Alexander JF, Sanders JD. 1985. Research and family therapy. In *The Handbook of Family Psychology and Therapy,* ed. L L'Abate, 1073–1107. Homewood IL: Dorsey

Barton C, Alexander JF, Waldron H, Turner CW, Warburton J. 1985. Generalizing treatment effects of functional family therapy: three replications. *Am. J. Fam. Ther.* 13:16–26

Baucom DH, Hoffman JA. 1986. The effectiveness of marital therapy: current status and application to the clinical setting. In *Clinical Handbook of Marital Therapy,* ed. N Jacobson, A Gurman, pp. 597–620. New York: Guilford

Baucom DH, Lester GW. 1986. The usefulness of cognitive restructuring as the adjunct to behavioral marital therapy. *Behav. Ther.* 17:385–403

Baucom DH, Sayers SL, Sher TG. 1990. Supplementing behavioral marital therapy with cognitive restructuring and emotional expressiveness training: an outcome investigation. *J. Consult. Clin. Psychol.* 58:636–45

Beach SRH, O'Leary KD. 1985. Current status of outcome research in marital therapy. In *The Handbook of Family Psychology and Therapy,* ed. L L'Abate, pp. 1035–72. Homewood, IL: Dorsey

Beach SRH, O'Leary KD. 1992. Treating depression in the context of marital discord: outcome and predictors of response of marital therapy versus cognitive therapy. *Behav. Ther.* 23:507–28

Bednar RL, Burlingame GM, Masters KS. 1988. Systems of family treatment: substance or semantics? *Annu. Rev. Psychol.* 39:401–34

Behrens BC, Sanders MR, Halford WK. 1990. Behavioral marital therapy: an evaluation of generalization of treatment effects across high and low risk settings. *Behav. Ther.* 21:423–33

Boscolo L, Cecchin G, Hoffman L, Penn P. 1987. *Milan Systemic Therapy.* New York: Basic Books

Boszormenyi-Nagy I, Ulrich DN. 1981. Contextual family therapy. See Gurman & Kniskern 1981a, pp. 159–86

Bourgeois L, Sabourin S, Wright J. 1990. Predictive validity of therapeutic alliance in group marital therapy. *J. Consult. Clin. Psychol.* 58:608–13

Bowen M. 1978. *Family Therapy in Clinical Practice.* Northvale, NY: Aronson

Boyd-Franklin N. 1989. *Black Families in Family Therapy: A Multi-systems Approach.* New York: Guilford

Bradbury TN, Fincham FD. 1990. Attributions in marriage: review and critique. *Psychol. Bull.* 107:3–33

Bray JH, Hetherington EM. 1993. Families in transition: introduction and overview. *J. Fam. Psychol.* 7:3–8

Breunlin D, Schwartz R, Karrer B. 1992. *Metaframeworks: Transcending the Models of Family Therapy.* San Francisco: Jossey-Bass

Buehlman KT, Gottman JM, Katz LF. 1992. How a couple views their past predicts their future: predicting divorce from an oral history interview. *J. Fam. Psychol.* 5:295–318

Burman B, Margolin G, John RS. 1993. America's angriest home videos: behavioral contingencies observed in home reenactments of marital conflict. *J. Consult. Clin. Psychol.* 61:28–39

Calvert SC, McMahon RJ. 1987. The treatment acceptability of a behavioral parent training program and its components. *Behav. Ther.* 2:165–79

Carter B, McGoldrick M. 1988. *The Changing Family Life Cycle: A Framework for Family Therapy.* Boston: Allyn, Bacon. 2nd ed.

Cerny JA, Barlow DH, Craske MG, Himadi WG. 1987. Couples treatment of agoraphobia: a two-year follow-up. *Behav. Ther.* 18:401–15

Cowan CP, Cowan PA. 1992. *When Partners Become Parents.* New York: Basic Books

Coyne JC. 1987. Depression, biology, marriage and marital therapy. *J. Marital Fam. Ther.* 13:393–407

Dadds MR, Sanders MR, James JE. 1987a. The generalization of treatment effects in parent training with multidistressed parents. *Behav. Psychother.* 15:289–313

Dadds MR, Schwartz S, Sanders MR. 1987b. Marital discord and treatment outcome in behavioral treatment of child behavior problems. *J. Consult. Clin. Psychol.* 55:396–403

de Shazer S. 1985. *Keys to Solution in Brief Therapy.* New York: Norton

Emmelkamp P. 1994. Behavior therapy with adults. In *Handbook of Psychotherapy and Behavior Change,* ed. A Bergin, S Garfield. New York: Wiley. 4th ed.

Emmelkamp P, van Linden G, van den Heuvell C, Ruphan M, Sanderman R, et al. 1988. Cognitive and behavioral interventions: a comparative evaluation with clinically distressed couples. *J. Fam. Psychol.* 1:365–77

Epstein LH, McCurley J, Wing RR, Valoski A. 1990. Five-year follow-up of family-based behavioral treatments for childhood obesity. *J. Consult. Clin. Psychol.* 58:661–64

Falloon IRH, Boyd JL, McGill CW, Williamson M, Razani J, et al. 1985. Family management in the prevention of morbidity of schizophrenia: clinical outcome of a two year longitudinal study. *Arch. Gen. Psychiatry* 42:887–96

Fauber RL, Long N. 1992. Children in context. The role of the family in child psychotherapy. *J. Clin. Consult. Ther.* 59:813–20

Figley C, Nelson TS. 1989. Basic family therapy skills. 1: Conceptualization and initial findings. *J. Marital Fam. Ther.* 15:349–65

Fleuridas C, Rosenthal DM, Leigh GF, Leigh TE. 1990. Family goal recording: an adaptation of goal attainment scaling for enhancing family therapy and assessment. *J. Marital Fam. Ther.* 16:389–406

Giblin P, Sprenkle DH, Sheehan R. 1985. Enrichment outcome research: a meta-analysis of premarital, marital, and family interventions. *J. Marital Fam. Ther.* 11:257–71

Goldman A, Greenberg L. 1992. Comparison of integrated systemic and emotionally focused approaches to couples therapy. *J. Consult. Clin. Psychol.* 60:1–8

Goldner V. 1985. Feminism in family therapy. *Fam. Process* 24:31–48

Goldner V, Penn P, Sheinberg M, Walter G. 1990. Love and violence: gender paradoxes in volatile attachments. *Fam. Process* 29:343–65

Gottman JM. 1979. *Marital Interaction: Experimental Investigations.* New York: Academic

Gottman JM. 1991. Predicting the longitudinal course of marriages. *J. Marital Fam. Ther.* 17:3–7

Gottman JM. 1992. The roles of conflict engagement, escalation, and avoidance in marital interaction: a longitudinal view of five types of couples. *J. Consult. Clin. Psychol.* 61:6–15

Gottman JM. 1993. A theory of marital dissolution and stability. *J. Fam. Psychol.* 7:57–75

Gottman JM, Krokoff L. 1989. Marital interaction and marital satisfaction: a longitudinal view. *J. Consult. Clin. Psychol.* 57:47–52

Gottman JM, Levenson RW. 1992. Marital processes predictive of later dissolution: behavior, physiology, and health. *J. Pers. Soc. Psychol.* 63:221–33

Green RJ, Herget M. 1989. Outcomes of systemic/strategic team consultation: I. overview and one-month results. *Fam. Process* 28:37–58

Green RJ, Herget M. 1991. Outcomes of systemic/strategic team consultation: III. the importance of therapist warmth and active structuring. *Fam. Process.* 30:321–36

Greenberg LS. 1986. Change process research. *J. Consult. Clin. Psychol.* 54:4–9

Greenberg LS. 1991. Research on the process of change. *Psychother. Res.* 1:3–16

Greenberg LS, Ford CL, Alden LS, Johnson SM. 1993. In-session change in emotionally focused therapy. *J. Consult. Clin. Psychol.* 61:78–84

Greenberg LS, James PS, Conry RF. 1988. Perceived change in couples therapy. *J. Fam. Psychol.* 2:5–23

Greenberg LS, Johnson SM. 1988. *Emotionally Focused Therapy for Couples.* New York: Guilford

Grotevant HD. 1989. Current issues in the assessment of marital and family systems. *J. Fam. Psychol.* 3:101–3

Guerney B Jr, Maxson P. 1990. Marital and family enrichment research: a decade review and look ahead. *J. Marriage Fam.* 52:1127–35

Gurman AS. 1978. Contemporary marital therapies. In *Marriage and Marital Therapy,* ed. T Paolino, B McCrady, pp. 445–566. New York: Brunner-Mazel

Gurman AS. 1981. Integrative marital therapy: toward the development of an interpersonal approach. In *Forms of Brief Therapy,* ed. S Budman, pp. 415–62. New York: Guilford

Gurman AS. 1983. Family therapy research and the "New Epistemology." *J. Marital Fam. Ther.* 9:227–34

Gurman AS. 1991. Back to the future, ahead to the past: Is marital therapy going in circles? *J. Fam. Psychol.* 4:402–6

Gurman AS, Kniskern DP. 1978. Research on marital and family therapy: progress, perspective, and prospect. In *Handbook of Psychotherapy and Behavior Change: An Empirical Analysis,* ed. SL Garfield, AE Bergin, pp. 817–901. New York: Wiley. 2nd ed.

Gurman AS, Kniskern DP, eds. 1981a. *Handbook of Family Therapy.* New York: Brunner-Mazel

Gurman AS, Kniskern DP. 1981b. Family therapy outcome research: knowns and unknowns. See Gurman & Kniskern 1981a, pp. 742–76

Gurman AS, Kniskern DP. 1991. *Handbook of Family Therapy,* Vol. II. New York: Brunner-Mazel

Gurman AS, Kniskern DP, Pinsof WM. 1986. Research on marital and family therapies. In *Handbook of Psychotherapy and Behavior Change,* ed. SL Garfield, AE Bergin, pp. 565–624. New York: Wiley. 3rd ed.

Hahlweg K, Feinstein E, Muller U, Dose M. 1989. Family therapies for schizophrenia. *Br. J. Psychiatry* 155(Suppl. 5):112–16

Hahlweg K, Markman HJ. 1988. The effectiveness of behavioral marital therapy: empirical status of behavioral techniques in preventing and alleviating marital distress. *J. Consult. Clin. Psychol.* 56:440–47

Hahlweg K, Schindler L, Revenstorf D, Brengelmann JC. 1984. The Munich marital therapy study. In *Marital Interaction: Analysis and Modification,* ed. K Hahlweg, NS Jacobson, pp. 3–26. New York: Guilford

Halford WK, Sanders MR, Behrens BC. 1993. A comparison of the generalization of behavioral marital therapy and enhanced behavioral marital therapy. *J. Consult. Clin. Psychol.* 61:51–60

Hare-Mustin RT, Marecek J. 1988. The meaning of difference: gender theory, postmodernism and psychology. *Am. Psychol.* 43:455–64

Hazelrigg MD, Cooper HM, Borduin CM. 1987. Evaluating the effectiveness of family therapies: an integrative review and analysis. *Psychol. Bull.* 101:428–42

Heatherington L, Friedlander ML. 1990. Couple and family therapy alliance scales: empirical considerations. *J. Marital Fam. Ther.* 16:299–306

Heatherington L, Friedlander ML, Johnson WF. 1989. Informed consent in family therapy research: ethical dilemmas and practical problems. *J. Fam. Psychol.* 2:373–85

Heincke CM. 1990. Toward generic principles of treating parents and children. *J. Clin. Consult. Ther.* 58:713–19

Henggeler SW, Borduin CM, Melton GFB, Mann BJ, Smith LA, et al. 1991. Effects of multisystemic therapy on drug use and abuse in serious juvenile offenders: a progress report from two outcome studies. *Fam. Dyn. Addict. Q.* 1:40–51

Henggeler SW, Melton GB, Smith LA. 1992. Family preservation using multisystemic therapy: an effective afternative to incarcerating serious juvenile offenders. *J. Consult. Clin. Psychol.* 60:953–61

Henggeler SW, Rodick JD, Borduin CM, Hanson CL, Watson SM, Urey JR. 1986. Multisystemic treatment of juvenile offenders: effects on adolescent behavior and family interaction. *Dev. Psychol.* 22:132–41

Hoffman L. 1981. *Foundations of Family Therapy.* New York: Basic Books

Hogarty G, Anderson CM, Reiss DJ, Kornblith SJ, Greenwald DP, et al. 1986. Family psychoeducation, social skills training and maintenance chemotherapy in the aftercare treatment of schizophrenia: I. One-year effects of a controlled study on relapse and expressed emotion. *Arch. Gen. Psychiatry* 43:633–42

Holtzworth-Munroe A., Jacobson NS, De-Klyen M, Whisman M. 1989. Relationship between behavioral marital therapy outcome and process variables. *J. Consult. Clin. Psychol.* 57:658–62

Huber CH, Milstein B. 1985. Cognitive restructuring and a collaborative set in couples' work. *Am. J. Fam. Ther.* 13:17–27

Jacobson NS. 1984. A component analysis of behavioral marital therapy: the relative effectiveness of behavior exchange and problem-solving training. *J. Consult. Clin. Psychol.* 52:295–305

Jacobson NS. 1991a. Behavioral versus insight-oriented marital therapy: Labels can be misleading. *J. Consult. Clin. Psychol.* 59:142–45

Jacobson NS. 1991b. To be or not to be behavioral when working with couples: What does it mean? *J. Fam. Psychol.* 4:436–45

Jacobson NS. 1991c. Toward enhancing the efficacy of marital therapy and marital therapy research. *J. Fam. Psychol.* 4:373–93

Jacobson NS. 1992. Behavioral couple therapy: a new beginning. *Behav. Ther.* 23:493–505

Jacobson NS, Addis ME. 1993. Research on couple therapy: What do we know? Where are we going? *J. Consult. Clin. Psychol.* 61:85–93

Jacobson NS, Dobson K, Fruzzetti A, Schmaling KB, Salusky S. 1991. Marital therapy as a treatment for depression. *J. Consult. Clin. Psychol.* 59:547–57

Jacobson NS, Follette WC. 1985. Clinical significance of improvement resulting from two behavioral marital therapy components. *Behav. Ther.* 16:249–62

Jacobson NS, Follette WC, Pagel M. 1986. Predicting who will benefit from behavioral marital therapy. *J. Consult. Clin. Psychol.* 54:518–22

Jacobson NS, Follette WC, Revenstorf D. 1984. Psychotherapy outcome research: methods for reporting variability and evaluating clinical significance. *Behav. Ther.* 15:336–52

Jacobson NS, Fruzzetti AE, Dobson K, Whisman M, Hops H. 1993. Couple therapy as a treatment for depression: II. The effects of relationship quality and therapy on depressive relapse. *J. Consult. Clin. Psychol.* 61:516–19

Jacobson NS, Gurman AS. 1986. *Clinical Handbook of Marital Therapy.* New York: Guilford

Jacobson NS, Holtzworth-Munroe A, Schmaling KB. 1989. Marital therapy and spouse involvement in the treatment of depression, agoraphobia, and alcoholism. *J. Consult. Clin. Psychol.* 57:5–10

Jacobson NS, Margolin G. 1979. *Marital Therapy: Strategies Based on Social Learning and Behavior Exchange Principles.* New York: Brunner-Mazel

Jacobson NS, Revenstorf D. 1988. Statistics for assessing the clinical significance of psychotherapy techniques: issues, problems, and new developments. *Behav. Assess.* 10:133–46

Jacobson NS, Schmaling KB, Holtzworth-Munroe A. 1987. Component analysis of behavioral marital therapy: two-year follow-up and prediction of relapse. *J. Marital Fam. Ther.* 13:187–95

Jacobson NS, Schmaling KB, Holtzworth-Munroe A, Katt JL, et al. 1989. Research-structured vs. clinically flexible versions of social learning-based marital therapy. *Behav. Res. Ther.* 27:173–80

Jacobson NS, Truax P. 1991. Clinical significance: a statistical approach to defining meaningful change in psychotherapy research. *J. Consult. Clin. Psychol.* 59:12–19

James PS. 1991. Effects of communication training component added to emotionally focused couples therapy. *J. Mar. Fam. Ther.* 17:263–75

Joanning H, Quinn W, Thomas F, Mullen R. 1992. Treating adolescent drug abuse: a comparison of family systems therapy, group therapy, and family drug education. *J. Marital Fam. Ther.* 18:345–56

Johnson SM, Greenberg LS. 1985a. Differential effects of experiential and problem-solving interventions in resolving marital conflict. *J. Consult. Clin. Psychol.* 53:175–84

Johnson SM, Greenberg LS. 1985b. Emotionally focused couples therapy: an outcome study. *J. Marital Fam. Ther.* 11:313–17

Johnson SM, Greenberg LS. 1988. Relating process to outcome in marital therapy. *J. Marital Fam. Ther.* 14:175–83

Johnson SM, Greenberg LS. 1991. There are more things in heaven and earth than dreamed of in BMT: a response to Jacobson. *J. Fam. Psychol.* 4:407–15

Kazak AE, Jarmas A, Snitzer L. 1988. The assessment of marital satisfaction: an evaluation of the Dyadic Adjustment Scale. *J. Fam. Psychol.* 2:82–91

Kazdin AE. 1991. Effectiveness of psychotherapy with children and adolescents. *J. Consult. Clin. Psychol.* 59:785–98

Keeney BP, Ray WA. 1992. Kicking research in the ass: provocations for reform. *AFTA Newsl.* 47(Spring):67–68

Lebow JL. 1981. Issues in the assessment of outcome in family therapy. *Fam. Process* 20:167–88

Lebow JL. 1984. On the value of integrating approaches to family therapy. *J. Marital Fam. Ther.* 10:127–38

Lebow JL. 1987a. Developing a personal integration in family therapy: principles for model construction and practice. *J. Marital Fam. Ther.* 13:1–14

Lebow JL. 1987b. Integrative family therapy: an overview of major issues. *Psychotherapy* 40:584–94

Lebow JL. 1988. From research into practice, from practice into research. *J. Fam. Psychol.* 2:337–51

Lebow JL. 1995. Open ended therapy. Termination in marital and family therapy. In *Family Psychology And Systems Therapy: A Handbook,* ed. RH Mikesell, D Lusterman, JS McDaniel. Washington, DC: Am. Psychol. Assoc.

Lee CM, Picard M, Blain MD. 1994. A methodological and substantive review of intervention outcome studies for families undergoing divorce. *J. Fam. Psychol.* 8:3–15

Leff J, Vaughn C. 1985. *Expressed Emotion in Families: Its Significance for Mental Illness.* New York: Guilford

Lewis RA, Piercy FP, Sprenkle DH, Trepper TS. 1990. Family-based interventions for helping drug-abusing adolescents. *J. Adol. Res.* 50:82–95

Liddle HA. 1991. Empirical values and the culture of family therapy. *J. Marital Fam. Ther.* 17:327–48

Liddle HA, Dakof GA. 1994. Family-based treatment for adolescent drug use: state of the science. In *Adolescent Drug Abuse: Assessment and Treatment,* ed. E Rahdert. Rockville, MD: Natl. Inst. Drug Abuse Res. Monogr. In press

Margolin G, Talovic S, Weinstein CD. 1983. Areas of change questionnaire: a practical approach to marital assessment. *J. Consult. Clin. Psychol.* 51:920–31

Mas CH, Alexander JF, Barton C. 1985. Modes of expression in family therapy: a process study of roles and gender. *J. Marital Fam. Ther.* 11:411–15

Mashal M, Feldman RB, Sigal JJ. 1989. The unraveling of a treatment paradigm: a followup study of the Milan approach to family therapy. *Fam. Process* 28:457–70

McCrady BS, Noel NE, Abrams DB, Stout RL, Nelson HF, Hay WM. 1986. Comparative effectiveness of three types of spouse involvement in outpatient behavioral alcoholism treatment. *J. Stud. Alcohol* 47:459–67

McCrady BS, Stout R, Noel N, Abrams D, Fisher-Nelson H. 1991. Effectiveness of three types of spouse-involved behavioral alcoholism treatment. *Br. J. Addict.* 86:1415–24

McGoldrick M, Pierce C, Giordano J. 1988. *Ethnicity and Family Therapy.* New York: Guilford

McMahon RJ, Wells KC. 1989. Conduct disorders. In *Treatment of Childhood Disorders,* ed. EJ Mash, RA Barkley, pp. 73–132. New York: Guilford

Miklowitz DJ, Goldstein MJ. 1990. Behavioral family treatment for patients with bipolar affective disorder. *Behav. Modif.* 14:457–89

Miller GE, Prinz RJ. 1990. Enhancement of social learning family interventions for childhood conduct disorder. *Psychol. Bull.* 108:291–307

Minuchin S. 1974. *Families and Family Therapy.* Cambridge, MA: Harvard Univ. Press

Minuchin S, Fishman HC. 1981. *Family Therapy Techniques.* Cambridge, MA: Harvard Univ. Press

Moon SM, Dillon DR, Sprenkle DH. 1990. Family therapy and qualitative research. *J. Marital Fam. Ther.* 16:357–73

Murphy CM, O'Leary KD. 1989. Psychological aggression predicts physical aggression in early marriage. *J. Consult. Clin. Psychol.* 57:579–82

Newberry AM, Alexander JF, Turner CW. 1991. Gender as a process variable in family therapy. *J. Fam. Psychol.* 5:158–75

Noel NE, McCrady BS, Stout RL, Fisher-Nelson F. 1987. Predictors of attrition from an outpatient alcoholism treatment program for couples. *J. Stud. Alcohol* 48:229–35

O'Farrell TJ, Cutter HS, Choquette K, Floyd F, Bayog R. 1992. Behavioral marital therapy for male alcoholics. *Behav. Ther.* 23:529–49

O'Farrell TJ, Cutter HSG, Floyd FJ. 1985. Evaluating behavioral marital therapy for male alcoholics: effects on marital adjustment and communication from before to after treatment. *Behav. Ther.* 16:147–67

O'Leary KD, Barling J, Arias I, Rosenbaum A, Malone J, Tyree A. 1989. Prevalence and stability of physical aggression between spouses: a longitudinal analysis. *J. Consult. Clin. Psychol.* 57:263–68

O'Leary KD, Beach SRH. 1990. Marital therapy: a viable treatment for depression and marital discord. *Am. J. Psychiatry* 147:183–86

Olson DH. 1986. Circumplex model VII: validation studies and FACES III. *Fam. Process* 25:337–51

Patterson GR. 1986. Performance models

for antisocial boys. *Am. Psychol.* 41:432–44

Patterson GR, Chamberlain P. 1992. A functional analysis of resistance (A neobehavioral perspective). In *Why Don't People Change? New Perspectives on Resistance and Noncompliance,* ed. H Arkowitz. New York: Guilford

Patterson GR, Dishion TJ, Chamberlain P. 1992. Outcomes and methodological issues relating to treatment of antisocial children. In *Effective Psychotherapy: A Handbook of Comparative Research,* ed. TR Giles. New York: Plenum

Pike CL, Piercy FP. 1990. Cost effectiveness research in family therapy. *J. Marital Fam. Ther.* 16:375–88

Pinsof WM. 1981. Family therapy process research. See Gurman & Kniskern 1981a, pp. 699–741

Pinsof WM. 1983. Integrative problem-centered therapy: toward the synthesis of family and individual psychotherapies. *J. Marital Fam. Ther.* 9:19–35

Pinsof WM. 1988. Strategies for the study of family therapy research. See Wynne 1988, pp. 159–74

Pinsof WM. 1989. A conceptual framework and methodological criteria for family therapy process resarch. *J. Consult. Clin. Psychol.* 57:53–59

Pinsof WM, Catherall DR. 1986. The integrative psychotherapy alliance: family, couple and individual therapy scales. *J. Marital Fam. Ther.* 12:137–51

Retzer A, Simon FB, Weber G, Stierlin H, Schmidt G. 1991. A followup study of manic-depressive and schizoaffective psychoses after systemic family therapy. *Fam. Process* 30:139–53

Rice L, Greenberg LS. 1984. *Patterns of Change: Intensive Analysis of Psychotherapy Process.* New York: Guilford

Rolland JS. 1994. *Families, Illness and Disability: An Integrative Treatment Model.* New York: Basic Books

Sayger TV, Horne AM, Glaser BA. 1993. Marital satisfaction and social learning family therapy for child conduct problems: generalization of treatment effects. *J. Marital Fam. Ther.* 19:393–402

Sayger TV, Horne AM, Walker JM, Passmore JL. 1988. Social learning family therapy with aggressive children: treatment outcome and maintenance. *J. Fam. Psychol.* 1:261–85

Scharff D, Scharff JS. 1987. *Object Relations Family Therapy.* New York: Aronson

Schmaling KB, Jacobson NS. 1988. Recent developments in family behavioral marital therapy. *Contemp. Fam. Ther.* 10:17–29

Shadish WR. 1992. Do family and marital psychotherapies change what people do? A meta-analysis of behavioral outcomes. In *Meta-analysis for Explanation: A Casebook,* ed. TD Cook, HM Cooper, DS Cordray, H Hortmann, LV Hedges, J Light, TA Louis, F Mosteller, pp. 129–208. New York: Russell Sage Found.

Shadish WR, Montgomery LM, Wilson P, Wilson MR, Bright I, Okwumabua T. 1993. Effects of family and marital psychotherapies: a meta-analysis. *J. Consult. Clin. Psychol.* 61:992–1002

Sher TG, Baucom DH, Larus JM. 1990. Communication patterns and response to treatment among depressed and nondepressed maritally distressed couples. *J. Fam. Psychol.* 4:63–79

Shields CG. 1986. Critiquing the new epistemologies: toward minimum requirements for a scientific theory of family therapy. *J. Marital Fam. Ther.* 12:359–72

Shields CG, McDaniel SH. 1992. Process differences between male and female therapists in a first family interview. *J. Marital Fam. Ther.* 18:143–51

Snyder DK. 1981. *Manual for the Marital Satisfaction Inventory.* Los Angeles: Western Psychol. Serv.

Snyder DK, Mangrum LF, Wills RM. 1993. Predicting couples' response to marital therapy: a comparison of short-and long-term predictors. *J. Consult. Clin. Psychol.* 61:61–69

Snyder DK, Wills RM. 1989. Behavioral versus insight-oriented marital therapy: effects on individual and interspousal functioning. *J. Consult. Clin. Psychol.* 57:39–46

Snyder DK, Wills RM. 1991. Facilitating change in marital therapy and research. *J. Fam. Psychol.* 4:426–35

Snyder DK, Wills RM, Grady-Fletcher A. 1991a. Long-term effectiveness of behavioral versus insight-oriented marital therapy. *J. Consult. Clin. Psychol.* 59:138–41

Snyder DK, Wills RM, Grady-Fletcher A. 1991b. Risks and challenges of long-term psychotherapy outcome research: Reply to Jacobson. *J. Consult. Clin. Psychol.* 59:146–49

Spanier GB. 1988. Assessing the strengths of the Dyadic Adjustment Scale. *J. Fam. Psychol.* 2:92–94

Stanton MD, Todd TC. 1982. *The Family Therapy of Drug Abuse and Addiction.* New York: Guilford

Steinglass P, Bennett L, Wolin S, Reiss D. 1987. *The Alcoholic Family.* New York: Basic Books

Szapocznik J, Kurtines W, Foote F, Perez-Vidal A, Hervis O. 1983. Conjoint versus one-person family therapy: some evidence for the effectiveness of conducting family therapy through one person. *J. Consult. Clin. Psychol.* 51:889–99

Szapocznik J, Kurtines W, Santisteban DA, Rio AT. 1990. Interplay of advances between theory, research, and applications in treatment interventions aimed at behavior problem children and adolescents. *J. Consult. Clin. Psychol.* 58:696–703

Szapocznik J, Perez-Vidal A, Brickman A, Foote FH, Santisteban D, et al. 1988. Engaging adolescent drug abusers and their families into treatment: a strategic structural systems approach. *J. Consult. Clin. Psychol.* 56:552–57

Szapocznik J, Rio AT, Hervis O, Mitrani VB, Kurtines W, Faraci AM. 1991. Assessing change in family functioning as a result of treatment: the structural family systems rating scale (SFSR). *J. Marital Fam. Ther.* 17:295–310

Tarrier N, Barrowclough C. 1990. Family interventions for schizophrenia. *Behav. Modif.* 14:408–40

Tarrier N, Barrowclough C, Baughn C, Bamrah JS, Porceddu K, Watts S, et al. 1988. The community management of schizophrenia: a controlled trial of a behavioural intervention with families to reduce relapse. *Br. J. Psychiatry* 153:532–42

Tolan PH, Cromwell RE, Brassell M. 1986. Family therapy with delinquents: a critical review of the literature. *Fam. Process* 26: 619–50

Tomm K. 1986. On incorporating the therapist in a scientific theory of family therapy. *J. Marital Fam. Ther.* 12:373–78

Upton LR, Jensen BJ. 1991. The acceptability of behavioral treatments for marital problems. *Behav. Modif.* 15:51–63

Walsh F, ed. 1993. *Normal Family Processes.* New York: Guilford. 2nd ed.

Waltz J, Addis ME, Koerner K, Jacobson NS. 1993. Testing the integrity of a psychotherapy protocol: assessment of adherence and competence. *J. Consult. Clin. Psychol.* 61: 620–30

Waring EM, Stalker CA, Carver CM, Gita MZ. 1991. Waiting list controlled trial of cognitive marital therapy in severe marital discord. *J. Marital Fam. Ther.* 17:243–56

Watzlawick P, Weakland J, Fisch R. 1974. *Change: Principles of Problem Formation and Problem Resolution.* New York: Norton

Webster-Stratton C, Hammond M. 1990. Predictors of treatment outcome in parent training for families with conduct problem children. *Behav. Ther.* 21:319–37

Weiner-Davis M. 1992. *Divorce Busting.* New York: Summit

Weiss RL, Summers KJ. 1983. Marital interaction coding system III. In *Marriage and Family Assessment: A Sourcebook for Family Therapy,* ed. EE Filsinger, pp. 85–115. Beverly Hills, CA: Sage

Whisman MA, Jacobson NS. 1990. Power, marital satisfaction, and response to marital therapy. *J. Fam. Psychol.* 4:202–12

Whitaker CA, Keith DV. 1981. Symbolic-experiential family therapy. See Gurman & Kniskern 1981a, pp. 187–225

White M, Epston D. 1990. *Narrative Means to Therapeutic Ends.* New York: Norton

Wills RM, Faitler SL, Snyder DK. 1987. Distinctiveness of behavioral versus insight-oriented marital therapy: an empirical analysis. *J. Consult. Clin. Psychol.* 55: 685–90

Wynne LC, ed. 1988. *The State of the Art in Family Therapy Research: Controversies and Recommendations.* New York: Family Process

Annu. Rev. Psychol. 1995. 46:59–90

ORGANIZATIONAL BEHAVIOR

B. Wilpert

Institut für Psychologie, Technische Universität Berlin, 10587 Berlin, Germany

KEY WORDS: micro OB, macro OB, organizational psychology, organization sciences

INTRODUCTION

Reexamining the eight review articles on organizational behavior (OB) that have appeared in the *Annual Review of Psychology* (*ARP*) since 1979 (Mitchell 1979, Cummings 1982, Staw 1984, Schneider 1985, House & Singh 1987, Ilgen & Klein 1988, O'Reilly 1991, Mowday & Sutton 1993) one cannot help but marvel about their achievement in conveying a remarkable degree of clarity and structure in discussing a generally ill-defined field.

This review focuses on systemic features of OB, that is, the more molar and pervasive aspects of organizational characteristics, antecedents and consequences of practices, as well as structures and processes in and of organizations. Presumably, such an approach places this review tendentially more into the macro than the micro camp of surmised OB traditions (i.e. examining the

0066-4308/95/0201-0059$05.00

behavior and characteristics of organizations vs the behavior and characteristics of individuals within organizations).

Finding an appropriate angle of review is further complicated, but in some ways eased, by the recent publication of the revised *Handbook of Industrial and Organizational Psychology* (Dunnette & Hough 1990, 1991, 1993; Dunnette et al 1994). The complication arises out of the comprehensiveness of the *Handbook,* which contains a rich review epilogue to its first three volumes that relates the emerging "meta trends" of the *Handbook*'s contributions to their historical forerunners (Katzell 1994). Such thoroughness leaves little room for additional review. However, the focus of the *Handbook*'s first three volumes on American industrial/organizational (I/O) psychology (similar to the previous *ARP* reviews, which also concentrated on United States sources) offers new options for the present reviewer: As the first European charged with this task, this reviewer has the opportunity to make a virtue out of a natural bias and to emphasize non-US work in an attempt to somewhat redress the past imbalance. Some recent reviews and meta-analyses (e.g. Austin & Villanova 1992, Erez & Earley 1993, Bass 1992, Bliesener 1992, Mitra et al 1992, Hom et al 1992) have covered topics not addressed in this review.

THEORETICAL DEVELOPMENTS

Organizations as Constructed Realities

Several publications view organizational phenomena as being socially constructed through the interaction of relevant actors. Such constructions may be myths, rituals, gossip, stories, symbols, negotiated structures and artifacts, or visionary goals—all of which provide the basis of and feed back into organizationally-specific sets of shared values and meanings.

ORGANIZATIONAL SYMBOLISM   Cummings (1982) predicted that symbolic aspects like myths and stories would become increasingly important in organization theory and Staw (1984) considered organizational culture as the hottest research topic at the time of his review. Their evaluations materialized Czarniawska-Joerges' (1992) stimulating book, which advocates the development of an anthropological approach to the analysis of complex organizations. In linking ethnomethodology and political anthropology to cover the practical (technological), symbolic, and political dimensions of large organizations, the book opens a multitude of vistas onto related concepts such as social representations (Moscovici 1984) or metaphors in organization theory (Morgan 1986) and provides a critique of the notion of organizational culture as well as of various methodologies.The book is concerned primarily with the problems of conceptualizing and analyzing the emergence and existence of intersubjectively shared meanings in organizations, on the one hand, and the felt need for a more comprehensive, holistic analysis of organizations, on the other hand. Lewin's concept of life space might have added another important and useful link to the former concern. The latter concern opens the important question, only treated in passing in the book, of where, in a complete analysis of an organization, one should draw organizational borders.

In a similar theoretical vein, one collection (Gagliardi 1992) examines artifacts (e.g. physical setting and space of organizations) as a source of sensory, emotional, and symbolic experience. The volume is the result of the Standing Conference on Organizational Symbolism (SCOS) of the European Group of Organization Studies and fills an apparent gap in organization theory (but see Pfeffer 1981). Fischer (1990) exemplifies the collective use, appropriation, and meaning of territory in work organizations. Other illustrations of the symbolic approach are found in the concept of symbolic domains in organizations (Schultz 1991) as different work locales endowed with collectively shared meanings and interpretations, or in storytelling and gossip in organizations as a means to provide understanding of processes and structures (Hansen & Kahnweiler 1993, Noon & Delbridge 1993).

Another SCOS volume (Turner 1990) pursues different aspects of organizational symbolism, including organizational style and aesthetics. The aesthetic understanding of organizational life is described as "an epistemological metaphor, a form of knowledge diverse from those based on analytical methods" (Strati 1992, p. 569). This approach epitomizes a variant of organizational inquiry that deliberately includes the ephemeral and ambiguous while stressing the criterion of plausibility in understanding the result of inquiry, which depends to a large extent on the researcher's and the reader's personal aesthetic experience.

Another perspective on the social construction of organizational reality is evoked by concepts such as collective ideation, group mind, organizational mind, social cognition, collective mind, and social representation, which all seem to be modern variations of Durkheim's notion of *conscience sociale* (1967). Although Weick & Roberts (1993) point out the danger of anthropomorphizing and reifying such terms, they also develop a concept of collective mind: Groups and organizations induce interrelationships of individual actions as if they had such a central collective control mechanism. In their case, the collective mind is enacted in the management of hazards on aircraft carriers. The authors point out that safe operations depend on "heedful" interrelations that "are constructed and reconstructed continually by individuals through the ongoing activities of contributing, representing, and subordinating" (pp. 365–366). In that sense, organizations are indeed a "network of intersubjectively shared meanings that are sustained through the development and use of a common language and everyday social interaction" (Walsh & Ungson 1991, p. 60).

In line with Cummings' prediction (1982), the symbolic approach has broadened the scope of legitimate topics in OB studies. It is thus on the way to establishing itself as a counterpoint to the traditional positivist agenda, a trend that finds its followers on both sides of the Atlantic.

ORGANIZATIONAL CLIMATE AND CULTURE   Despite more than 25 years of valiant attempts to introduce conceptually clear definitions of the constructs of organizational culture and climate, the field still lacks clarity (Moran & Volkwein 1992). Noting that sometimes the concepts of culture and climate are treated as synonyms, Moran & Volkwein argue emphatically for their separation, since these are "perhaps the two most potent constructs available for researchers for understanding the expressive, communicative, human dimensions of organizations" (p. 22). The authors examine and critique three approaches to the genesis of organizational climate—structural, perceptual, and interactive—and they propose a fourth—cultural. In structural traditions climate "is an objective manifestation of the organization's structure which individuals encounter and apprehend" (p. 25). The perceptual approach places the origin of climate mainly in the individual, but socially shared psychological representations of situations (Drory 1993). The interactive approach postulates that climate is the result of intersubjective processes of generating shared meanings about organizational "objective" conditions, thus avoiding the theoretical and methodological shortcomings of the purely structural and perceptual approaches (Schneider & Reichers 1983). Moran & Volkwein argue that the interactive approach neglects the implicit deeper level of social context that shapes interactions resulting in manifest climate characteristics. This deeper level is found in an organization's culture, the ideational system or abstract, usually "out-of-awareness" frame of reference that "contains the essential elements of values, negotiated understandings, and historically constituted meanings which imbue actions with purpose and consensual validation making possible organized efforts and, therefore, organizations" (Moran & Volkwein 1992, p. 33). Climate, although overlapping with these underlying deep-structures of culture inasmuch as it refers to more readily accessible aspects of it, must still be seen as distinct from it.

In an attempt to inductively identify dimensions of psychological climate (i.e. concentration on individual level measures instead of the organizational aggregate measures that reflect organizational climate) from previous publications, Koys & DeCotiis (1991) focus on some 80 descriptive perceptual measures, subsequently reduced to eight psychometrically acceptable scales. The authors hope that continuing their approach may ultimately lead to the identification of the universe of psychological climate perceptions.

A different type of induction is practiced in single firm studies. Sackmann (1992) used open interviews with an issue-focus followed by individual- and group-centered content analysis, validated through observation and document analysis, to reconstruct the "cognitive culture maps" existing in the firm. This study yielded evidence of the coexistence of an homogenous grouping with several subgroupings. Attempts to extract deeper meanings and myths from stories told in organizations fall into a similar category of inductive approaches (Boje 1991, Gabriel 1991).

In their study of a financial service firm, Schneider et al (1992) define organizational climate of the work setting as "employees' perceptions of events, practices, and procedures as well as their perceptions of behaviors that are rewarded, supported, and expected" (p. 705). In the study, semistructured group interviews were combined with a standardized questionnaire survey of about 350 employees on employee estimates of service perceived by the company's customers. Next to service-oriented practices, it was the firm's human resource practices (e.g. training, performance appraisal) that emerged as strongest correlates of service climate. In successfully combining qualitative and quantitative methods, Schneider et al show that rational and structural human resource practices can also generate meaning among employees. The finding suggests that higher order latent variables—concern for employees and concern for customers—seem to be important conceptual elements of service climate. The usefulness of including concern for outside stakeholders as part of a conceptualization of organizational climate is also corroborated by Burke et al (1992). Using confirmatory factor analysis, the authors were able to test their two-factor higher order model among more than 18,000 employees of a retail organization.

Harrison & Carroll (1991) use a strictly modeling approach in their thought-provoking computer simulation experiments on the stability and instability of organizational culture over time. They study the problem of cultural transmission as a consequence of intricate interactions among entry and exit rate of members, organizational growth rate, selectiveness of recruitment procedures, intensity of socialization process, and natural decay rate of socialization. The general problem of parameter setting in computer simulations is mitigated by placing the simulation runs into six ideal-typical organization forms as discussed in the extant literature (e.g. Japanese-style form, governmental-bureaucratic form, Z-type form). The findings are quite plausible and should stimulate further refined simulations.

The consequences of organizational culture are another dominant research topic. A series of studies by O'Reilly et al (1991) examine person-organizational environment fit and its correlates. In their attempt to ascertain the relationship between profiles of individual value preferences and value profiles characteristic of certain organizations, the authors developed the Organizational Culture Profile (OCP). The OCP was derived from 54 value statements that were used to generate individual as well as organizational Q-sort profiles. The organization-person fit can then be obtained by correlating the profile of values characteristic of the organization and the profile of individual preferences, interpretable as personality differences. Measures of organization-person fit were of predictive validity for individual commitment and satisfaction 12 months later as well as related to turnover 24 months later. Similar findings are reported by Sheridan (1992), who also used the OCP to study value profiles of different organizations and showed their association with an organization's capacity to retain new entrants. Companies with interpersonal relationship values were able to keep their employees longer than were companies stressing work task values. The person-organization fit paradigm also served as the framework for a longitudinal study of university graduates entering work life (von Rosenstiel 1989). Respondents were categorized according to a typology of work-related value preferences (e.g. career-oriented, leisure-oriented, alternatively oriented), terms of their job choices (e.g. industry, public administration, self employment), and socialization patterns based on work experience.

Calori & Sarnin (1991) examine the correlates of corporate culture (used synonymously with organizational culture) and economic performance. The authors developed their own instrument to assess organizational culture using items from other published sources presumed to be indicators of values and managerial practices (as manifestations of such values). The relationship was tested between correlated items of the Values and Managerial Practice Questionnaire and economic performance (based on return on investments, return on sales, growth rate) over a period of three years. Cultural company profile was clearly related to company growth, but considerably less so to profitability. Although the questionnaire lacks psychometric refinements, the study is laudable because it includes "hard" performance variables and acknowledges the need to include contingent factors not considered previously.

Research on organizational climate and culture continues to boom quantitatively in terms of the variety of theoretical and methodological approaches used. Significant attempts have been made to clarify the difficult theoretical delineations of the concepts involved, but many conceptualizations coexist. The subfield as a whole still seems to draw interest and attention from practitioners as well as researchers because of the broad gamut of notions that can be associated with climate and culture.

REMUNERATION SYSTEMS   In a conceptual review of the different meanings that pay and money have for employees, Thierry (1992) develops a model that should redirect future research on monetary remuneration into a focus on their motivational properties, performance feedback, social control potential, and purchasing power.

Most companies limit pay for performance principles to the extremes (low and upper end) of the performance distribution. Zenger's study (1992) of 984 engineering employees of two large companies investigates the determinants and consequences of such reward schemes, particularly in reference to turnover. The study demonstrates the dilemma of performance-based compensation schemes. Rewarding only extremely high performers and not rewarding extremely low performers may result in cost savings, because the 80-90% of nonextreme performers are neglected, but many employees in the middle ground may perceive pay injustice and leave the company. Cowherd & Levine (1992) investigate so-called interclass pay equity (i.e. the pay differential existing among lower and upper hierarchical strata in an organization) and its effects on organizational effectiveness. Combining equity theory (i.e. focusing on social comparisons of inputs) and relative deprivation theory (i.e. focusing on pay differentials) in a model to explain product quality of 102 business units, the authors show the positive effect of reward equity to unit performance. The study merits particular attention because it goes beyond the traditional path of studying the effect of reward equity on perceived justice and it effectively combines concepts of social justice with criteria of business economics.

Hatcher & Ross' (1991) longitudinal study examined the effects of switching from individual piecework remuneration to an organization-wide (systemic) gain sharing plan on grievances, product quality and quantity. Positive relationships were found between such systemic reward structures and performance criteria. Comparable findings were generated in Petty et al's (1992) study of an organizational incentive plan in an electrical utility company. These studies on systemic reward systems that favor positive interdependence of goals and expectancies of relevant actors point to an important, hitherto largely neglected relationship between goals and expectancies of relevant actors.

LEADERSHIP, CONTROL, AND POWER   Over the last 15 years a considerable body of theory development and empirical research has been collated that relates to transactional and tranformational leadership (Bass 1990). Although linked to House's (1977) conceptualization of charismatic leadership, Bass and collegues claim the two are not synonymous (Bass & Avolio 1993). Transformational leaders are those who respond positively to change and who actively induce change. The theory extends traditional transactional approaches to leadership as an exchange between leader and follower by adding the dimensions of charisma, inspirational motivation, intellectual stimulation, and individualized consideration, which are seen to "motivate followers to work for transcendental goals and for higher level self-actualizing needs instead of immediate self-interests" (Bass 1994). By adding these dimensions to transactional leadership factors (e.g. contingent reward and management-by-exception, which address follower needs in direct relation to the performance goals contracted with the leader), the explanatory power of measured leadership characteristics is increased (Bass 1985). Thus the theory covers a broader gamut of leadership behaviors from worst to best leaders.

An impressive example of the predictive power of the approach is provided by a recent longitudinal study of 186 randomly selected graduates from the United States Naval Academy and their later performance as US Navy officers (Yammarino et al 1993). The study used different instruments and different sources at multiple points in time. Performance appraisal of the officers at later stages in their career was significantly predicted by transactional leadership measures. Research with the Multifactor Leadership Questionnaire (MLQ) in various European and Asian countries supports the claim of the approach's universal application potential (Bass 1994). The single case account of an individual's tranformation of his visionary dream into reality may serve as an example of the transformational leadership concept although it is executed without references to the concepts above (Sooklal 1991).

Mowday & Sutton (1993) reported cautions that have been voiced by various authors in relation to tranformational leadership in terms of the possible dysfunctional consequences of immoral charismatic leaders and in terms of the social psychological contagion and attributional processes (e.g. romanticizing leaders) among followers. Transformational leadership theory still needs to solve the question of how much transformational input can be borne by an organization. The contention that if much transformational leadership is good, then more is better is clearly not tenable. After all, how much transformation can an organization afford? What is required again is the specification of criteria regarding the appropriate intensity of transformational energies.

A special SCOS issue of *Organization Studies* [1991, 12(4)] focuses on the role of leaders as creators of meaning. Pauchant (1991), searching for better insights into the underlying nature of charisma, suggests a depth psychological approach to leadership by focusing on the affective side of leader-follower dyads, which can be classified according to the given match of the self-developmental stages of leaders and followers linked to each other in respective transference patterns. Starting from a Jungian perspective, Czarniawska-Joerges & Wolff (1991) identify leaders, managers, and entrepreneurs as different archetypes of personalities and link their differential roles and emergence in organizations to varying sociopolitical and economic historical contexts as providers of meaning in organizational events.

To unravel the socially constructed and situationally embedded meanings of power, Fiol (1991) uses a semiotic approach to analyze the visible and invisible dimensions of power in terms of opposite leadership values (power to do and not to do vs powerlessness to do and not to do) as derived from autobiographies of business leaders such as Henry Ford and Lee Iacocca. In a deliberate attempt to stretch the limits of conventional logic, Calás & Smircich (1991) use a combination of Foucaultian genealogies, Derridian deconstructivism, and feminist poststructuralism to unveil the hidden interdependent meaning of leadership and (sexual) seduction, an attempt only topped by Mintzberg's (1991) postscript deconstructing this deconstructivist essay. Gemmill & Oakley's paper (1992) falls into the same epistemological tradition in which they attempt to unmask the leadership myth as creating the social pathology it purports to cure: learned helplessness of members of social systems. Wilson's (1992) linguistic analysis of gender-based power relations perpetuated by ideological metaphors of male dominance concurs with this orientation.

Leadership that offers opportunities for negotiated goal setting and encourages shared representations of organizational realities is using social constructionist thinking. A multiplicity of different approaches, some from mainstream leadership research such as transformational leadership, some from depth or psychoanalytic traditions, find their place here. Inasmuch as above reported treatments of leadership stress individual dispositions for (in)effective leadership they clearly fall into the recent meta-trend of the "revival of the personality" in OB research identified by Katzell (1994). If some of the stances taken transcend accepted logic and stringency of argument, that may have to be taken as a side effect of a thriving combative subfield.

Action Theory

Frese & Zapf (1994) provide the hitherto most comprehensive English language presentation of a large body of German theoretical and applied literature on action (control/regulation) theory. Action theory is a large umbrella (Lenk 1977–1984). The variant discussed here is a cognitive theory of goal-oriented work behavior (actions) that is considered to be regulated by feedback from different hierarchically organized action control levels (e.g. sensorimotor level, flexible action patterns, intellectual, and heuristic level). The approach has proven its fecundity in a variety of I/O research fields (e.g. human error, personality and competence development, work design, work and leisure).

The agent in this theoretical approach is traditionally the individual. This evokes the question concerning the social nature of any work, of division of labor and interrelated social action as discussed above. First attempts to complement the individual cognitive basis of the approach with the social dimension of action are, however, provided by von Cranach et al (1986). Another example for the need to link socially shared meanings and action control is given by Sandelands et al (1991), who demonstrate that supervisory feedback in its embeddedness in situational contexts and meaning goes far beyond a mechanistic performance control as suggested by the metaphoric use of technical feedback in the thermostat (Lord & Hanges 1987).

No systematic attempt seems to have been made to relate action (regulation) theory to Locke's goal setting and performance regulation theory (Latham & Locke 1991), which lies also "within the domain of purposefully directed action" (p. 213; Locke & Latham 1990). Early developments of Locke's theory date back to the 1960s; it relates volitional goal setting decisions to performance motivation, and its impressive research evidence illustrates the relevance of its basic premises for social and organizational contexts. This might be enhanced by conceptualizing the underlying dynamics of goal setting in terms of Lewin's (1926) *Vornahmehandlung* (i.e. the decision or intention to pursue a specific course of action that constitutes a quasi-need). This quasi-need in turn controls and sustains respective goal-oriented efforts. Studies in the tradition of Lewin's early experiments (1952) illustrate this effect in the pursuit of safety behavior with remarkable practical consequences (Misumi 1978, Brehmer et al 1991).

Starting from the notion of autopoeisis, which is defined as a permanent and structurally coupled adjustment of a living system to its given environment and its continuous systemic reproduction (Maturana et al 1980), Thereau (1992) develops another action theoretical approach under the guise of a "situated cognitive anthropology" in which the goal-oriented "course of action" constitutes the basic object of analysis with reference to individual and collective work (von Cranach et al 1982). The semiological nature of any analysis of a course of action is given by the postulate that a course of action is linked through triadic signs sensu Peirce (Houser & Kloesel 1992): the object (local situation with all its possibilities), *représentamen* (conscious representation of the situation), and *interprétant* (essentially unconscious *habitus*: the pursuit of a rule for requisite action). Together the signs imply the specific significance or meaning of the action, verbally communicable and communicated, thus creating the socially constructed reality. This explains the emphasis of the approach on linguistic data. On the whole, the approach is a valiant attempt to develop a general action theory, rich in its ramifications and applicable to the understanding of behavior in and of organizations, and beyond. Its precursors are the recently rediscovered American Peirce with his theory of meaning, the Russian Ochanine with his notion of operative image (1966), and the Belgian Faverge with his conceptualization of regulation of individual and social work (1966).

The notion of autopoeisis as a step beyond classical systems theory has received growing interest from various other organization theoreticians as well. Kickert (1993) discusses the original model developed in biology and its epigons in social sciences. After stripping the concept from its constrained usage in biology and mathematics, Kickert tests its applicability and usefulness as "the self-reproduction of the organization of the autopoeitic system" (p. 266) in the area of public administration and thus shows how the notion can fruitfully be applied to dynamic stability (continuous regeneration of the bureaucratic organization) as well as phenomena such as autonomy and self-governance of organizational actors in the public sphere. The parallelism to autogenesis of the organization process "through the self-organizing capacities of individuals interacting in a social field" (Drazin & Sandelands 1992) seems obvious, although the latter authors argue from the somewhat different theoretical bases of the work of Prigogine & Stengers (1984).

Starting from the unresolved contradictions of research concerned with the interaction of work life and life outside work, Baubion-Broye et al (1989a,b) develop a comprehensive interactive model (*système d'activités*), in which a person's activities in one life domain are viewed as potentially interacting with and influencing each other for three reasons: 1. Because an individual's activities use available limited resources, each activity constitutes constraints for other activities. 2. At the same time, activities in one life domain provide informational or material resources in other domains. 3. When the interaction of activities in different life domains is stressed, it becomes necessary to include in one's considerations the subjective salience of these activities, because activities in one domain will be partially controlled by their significance in other domains. The system of activities distinguishes three life domains as interdependent subsystems: family, work, and society, each with resources, constraints, and activities. Models of action (*modèle d'action*) as hierarchical representations of goals, action possibilities and of their intra- or inter-subsystemic relationships regulate activities in each subsystem. The ultimate control agent is a model of life (*modèle de vie*) wherein the subjective relative value of the three subsystems is represented. It inhibits or activates exchange processes among the subsystems. Research on unemployment has shown the basic validity of the theoretical model (Baubion-Broye et al 1989a,b).

TASK DESIGN   Job design chracteristics provide opportunities and constraints for work activity; hence, they are directly relevant to action theoretical approaches. As a recent review of rigorously designed case studies and experiments suggests (Kelly 1992), the job characteristics model (Hackman & Oldham 1976) still stimulates a considerable amount of research. Kelly's meta-analysis leads him to question the accepted proposition from job design theory that job redesign will affect both satisfaction and performance. Instead, he proposes a twin-track model in which satisfaction and performance are influenced by different determinants, the former by changing dimensions of job content, the latter by other organizational context variables not adequately taken into account by the job characteristics model. Thus, the twin-track model suggests an extension of the job characteristics model.

The frequently noted limitation to five job dimensions of the job characteristics model becomes particularly evident in the context of advanced manufacturing technology (Wall et al 1990, 1992). In addressing this aspect, Jackson et al (1993) develop measures for additional constructs reflecting work aspects such as control over timing and methods, monitoring and problem solving demand, and production responsibility. The complex curvilinear relationship of job scope and affective outcomes in relation to moderating impacts of work context satisfaction was investigated by Champoux (1992), resulting in suggestions for further elaborations of the basic job design theory. A study by Medcof (1991) on the use of computers as opportunities for growth by giving workers flexibility to do their jobs further illustrates the need to expand the original job characteristics model in terms of both independent and dependent variables.

Newton & Keenan (1991) pursue a different tack in their examination of the debate over whether dispositional or situational factors impact on job attitudes and affective reactions. The issue is of considerable theoretical and practical significance, because if temporally stable dispositions are primarily responsible for job attitudes, then job redesign would have limited impacts. Their results, however, are somewhat inconclusive in identifying relatively stable dispositional factors that seem, however, also to be influenced by situational factors.

Theoretical Controversies

An emotionally high-pitched controversy in OB erupted in the late 1970s to mid-1980s. The controversy, which pitted positivism against antipositivism, involved scholars from both sides of the Atlantic (Burrell & Morgan 1979, Clegg & Dunkerley 1980, Child 1988, Donaldson 1985, Hinings 1988) and has resumed in recent years (Astley & Zammuto 1992, Donaldson 1992, Marsden 1993). The debate addresses the epistemological basis required for OB as a science. Astley & Zammuto (1992) suggest that OB should be conceived of as a language game with myths, stories, culture, and symbols as meaning providing and legitimating concepts, with qualitative rather than quantitative methods. In response, Donaldson (1992) defends the positivist agenda and points out that the language game concept is no impediment to science-building and that a language game approach can easily be integrated into positivist practices. Marsden (1993) launches yet another broadside attack against positivism as expounded by Donaldson (1985, 1988) and proposes realism as a "rival concept of science" (Marsden, p. 93), based on the ontological writings of Bhaskar (1978) and Foucauldian conceptions of organization.

Adler & Borys (1993) present a second juxtaposition of contending theoretical positions, partially overlapping with the foregoing one—the longstanding debate concerning materialism and idealism in social science. They suggest potential strategies to overcome the conflict through a metatheoretical approach that promises to reconcile technical, economic, political, and symbolic features in OB theorizing.

METHODOLOGICAL APPROACHES

Cross-level Research

Cross-level research and theorizing (e.g. explaining the impact of influences across various system levels such as environment→organizational structure→individual behaviors) frequently have been demanded (O'Reilly 1991, Wilpert 1992), but little has been done. A few notable exceptions may be found in recent years. Earley & Brittain (1992) attempted to analyze cross-level effects on organizational performance by way of computer simulation on a population of 10,000 simulated firms using individual and organization-level runs iterated monthly over a period of ten years. Organizational environment (demographic processes), work environment (socialization), and individual processes (individual capability, effort, affect, and goal-directed behavior) are linked in mathematical functions and parameters estimated from evidence of previous research. Although the authors do not claim that their model represents everything that impacts on organizational performance, they purport to capture major factors integrating individual behavior and organizational action. Despite considerable plausibility of the results, the reader wonders how technology and organizational structure, so far left out of their model, would have affected the results.

Sorge (1991) develops what he calls a neo-contingency framework in which he summarizes the many studies of the "Aix group" (Rose 1985) in France, Germany, and Great Britain. Their findings convincingly portray the interactions of company specific profiles (e.g. innovation, business strategy, organization, human resources) and sectorally or nationally corresponding societal features. The Industrial Democracy in Europe (IDE) International Research Group has in a two-decade-spanning research program, hitherto the largest international comparative study of participation, shown the apparently causal relationship of formal rules for participation upon the level of intra-organizational participation. Similarly, the group demonstrated the impact of unemployment levels outside the organization upon participation, thus illustrating the possibility of systematically relating cross-level measurements (IDE 1981, 1992, 1993).

Spector & Jex (1991) examine the use of self-reported job characteristics and their relation to employee affect and behavior in order to test job characteristics theory. Their study showed significant relationships among rater judgments of jobs and job characteristics from the *U.S. Dictionary of Occupational Titles,* but failed to show similar relationships of such data to incumbent reports on job characteristics and employee outcomes. They advance two explanations for their results: job analysis data may provide poor indicators of the objective job situation or objective data may be poor predictors of subjective data; hence, job characteristics theory may be erroneous. Yammarino & Bass (1991) present a conceptual scheme that approaches leadership studies from a multi-level perspective covering person, situation, and person-situation from different points of view, thus demonstrating the need and possibility for multiple-level analyses of leadership.

The need for cross-level perspectives is not exclusive to the subdiscipline of OB as is illustrated by Hendrick's (1991) attempt to develop a macro-approach in ergonomics. Hendrick reviews the trend toward macroergonomics and suggests, from a "top-down" socio-technical systems approach, broadening the scope of ergonomics to include conceptions of technology, different aspects of the personnel subsystem (e.g. professionalism, psycho-social characteristics), and the relevant environment (e.g. environmental change and complexity) in organizational design and management considerations of ergonomics. Macroergonomics and the subdiscipline of OB thus appear to overlap or begin to merge to some extent.

Longitudinal Approaches

The need for longitudinal research strategies has often been articulated on two grounds: to document behavioral performance changes over time and to capture causal dynamics of change (Schaie & Hertzog 1982). Performance and change can be studied on the individual, group, and organizational level.

Focusing on autonomous work groups in two Australian mineral processing plants, Cordery et al (1991) measure perceived job characteristics, work role autonomy, satisfaction, organizational commitment, trust in management, absence, and turnover at two points in time (t_1 = 8 months and t_2 = 20 months later). The results confirm previous findings on positive relationships between autonomous working groups and member attitudes, but contrary to conventional wisdom, higher absentism and turnover are also found in such work groups. The need for a more systemic examination of work experience and its impact on psychological distress, perceived quality of life, and personality among different professional groups (e.g. teachers or police officers) is also demonstrated by the first publications of a comprehensive longitudinal Australian research program (Hart 1994, Hart et al 1994).

The IDE International Research Group conducted one of the few international comparative recapitulation studies in OB where participation in the same organizational units in ten different countries was studied with basically the same research design after an interval of ten years. The most important finding was that formal external and internal rules and regulations for participation (participative structure; PS) turned out in the replication (IDE 1992, 1993) to be less important predictors of participation than in the original research (IDE 1981). The longitudinal design facilitated the test of two explanatory models: a system inertia model, which assumes that employee groups with high participation levels at t_1 would persist even under unfavorable conditions while low participation groups would further lose ground over time. The second, a management strategy model, assumes that management would attempt to reduce participation of strongly participating groups and neglect low participation groups. The statistical analyses strongly support the management strategy model with unemployment levels functioning as moderators.

The Decisions in Organization study (Heller et al 1988) deepened the IDE approach by looking at 217 medium-term (tactical, control-oriented) and long-term (strategic, continuity- and growth-oriented) decision-making processes over a four-year period in seven British, Dutch, and Yugoslav companies (Koopman et al 1991, Drenth & Koopman 1992). The methods comprised interview schedules with key informants (tracing the history of a decision process through various decision phases), document analyses, participant observation, and the participation scales used in the IDE research. The total amount of participation in an organization was found to be strongly related to national context, and hierarchical level was identified as a large determinant of the level of participation.

Both results confirm findings from the IDE study. Furthermore, differential participation levels are found in different decision phases, however, this is moderated by national context as well. Status power, or normative rules and regulations for participation of a given group of employees (i.e. PS in IDE), significantly predicts skill utilization (if management is not involved) and other outcome variables (e.g. satisfaction, efficiency, and process).

Korunka et al (1993) relate the managerial implementation strategies in introducing new information and data processing technologies to strain reactions of employees in seven companies. Measures were taken 2 months prior to, during, and 12 months after the implementation process. Measurement of introductory strategy consisted of a specially developed instrument covering perception of project organization, employee involvement, and training. Various instruments for objective and subjective work analysis and stress measures (e.g. Zapf 1991), as well as measures of strain and satisfaction, complemented the instrument portfolio. The introduction and the use of new technologies both increased strain. Participatory introduction styles increased acceptance of new technologies and reduced strain reactions.

In a similar vein is Ledford & Mohrmann's (1993) study of a large-scale organizational change project in a 12-plant manufacturing division of a major company. High involvement management (devolution of information, power, and competence), drastic change in the organizations's character and performance, and self-design by organization members characterize this project as a participatory action research strategy (Whyte 1989). Ledford & Mohrmann provide insightful descriptions of the complexities involved in large-scale transformation projects, the variety of techniques and methods used (e.g. interviews, employee surveys at various points in time), the problems of appropriate choice of unit of analysis and of performance measures, the obstacles of establishing a learning network, and the ambiguities in the role of change agent in such projects.

Longitudinal studies of organizational behavior are gaining ground steadily. The more recent ones cover longer time horizons than did previous studies, and they display more refined in-depth observations of change processes. Both are important methodological developments because they offer opportunities to identify sustained changes.

CONTENT DOMAINS

New Technology

Tushman & Rosenkopf (1992), in a *tour de force* of organizational and interorganizational ideas and concepts, attempt to identify the major determinants of technological progress. Technological advance is seen to be intimately linked to a technology cycle of several phases: variation (innovations), era of ferment (competing technologies and diffusion), selection (dominant designs), and retention (era of incremental change). Social, political, and organizational influences upon technological evolution are presumed to be strongest under conditions of uncertainty (i.e. variation and era of ferment), while under conditions of relative certainty (i.e. incremental change), the process predominantly follows the logic of technology. More focused on organizational processes proper, Orlikowski (1992) draws on Giddens' (1979, 1984) theory of societal structuration and applies its basic principles of the continuous and reciprocal interaction of human action and structural organizational features in a case study of the use of technology over time. Orlikowski fruitfully combines cross-level and longitudinal approaches in his demonstration of how the structuration model of technology can be used. Clegg (1994) articulates the overall importance of new information technology for the discipline of psychology. He argues for a better integration of cognitive science and OB and follows closely the observations made above on the nature of organizations as socially constructed and shared realities among its interrelated members (Weick & Roberts 1993). The key notion is "cognition in action in organizations."

A slowly growing body of literature, again based mainly on case studies (e.g. Adler 1991), is concerned with computer-based advanced manufacturing technologies (AMT) such as flexible manufacturing systems or robotic installations. Clegg & Symon (1990) discuss the different approaches and philosophies that guide and impact on the utilization of AMT within organizations. Wall & Davids (1992) present a perceptive and measured review of the state of the art concerning the central social and organizational concomitants of AMT. Their review addresses the deskilling/enskilling debate, presumed work intensification and strain due to AMT, as well as theoretical approaches and empirical evidence on job design and AMT efficiency. Although the authors show convincingly that ideas and opinions about the implications of AMT are far ahead of empirical evidence, their main conclusions are quite plausible: AMT does not by itself result in simplified jobs; organizational decisions regarding division of labor seem to be the crucial factors in determining the nature of jobs; operator control opportunities, therefore, appear to provide the requisite conditions for operator learning and increased AMT efficiency; comparative, longitudinal, and experimental field studies are conspicuously amiss; theorizing and empirical research on AMT requires higher levels of integrating within I/O disciplinary boundaries as well as with other disciplines than presently is demonstrated.

Various studies investigate the differential consequences of alternative strategies for shop floor organization. On the one hand is the centralized/specialist systems control strategy ("knowledge based;" Rose 1992); on the other is the decentralized control strategy, where operator competence on the shop floor, including their implicit, experience based "tacit skills" (Leplat 1990), is used to optimize production processes and to compensate for technical component failures (Hirsch-Kreinsen et al 1990). Relevant "serendipitous" findings of increased machine use resulted from an unanticipated managerial decision in an engineering company to introduce an output-based bonus system that depended on machine usage (Wall et al 1992). This, in turn, induced shop floor operators to assume added responsibility for quick fault rectification. Unobtrusive measures of usage, stoppages, and downtime per stoppage in this longitudinal study suggest a dual process to have operated in increasing the efficiency of the system: a quick-response effect to fault rectification and an ensuing competence acquisition to anticipate and avoid potential breakdowns. For further evidence on the positive economic effects of decentralized, operator skill–based strategies, see Jackson & Wall (1991) and Snell & Dean (1992).

Studies of attitudes toward the introduction of new technologies form a further focus of NT studies (Hurley 1992). In a three wave questionnaire study of the introduction of a new office automation system, Parsons et al (1991) propose that system use and affective reactions to the new technology (NT) can be understood as an interaction between personal characteristics (e.g. attitudes, ability) and environmental facilitating or constraining factors (e.g. equipment convenience). In a multi-method action research type of study, Symon & Clegg (1991) report the problems encountered in introducing a computer aided design and manufacturing system in an engineering and manufacturing firm. Although the system was implemented, its technology-led implementation failed to meet the original objectives in the time expected because human and organizational factors were not considered. Rice & Aydin (1991) investigate the impact of social information on attitudes toward a new computerized health information system in a university's student health system. Their approach uses sophisticated network analysis techniques to specify various network-based proximity measures and to estimate their relative influence on attitudes toward the new technical system: relational proximity (extent and strength of direct and indirect interaction among individuals), positional proximity (positional equivalence and organizational proximity), and spatial proximity. In applying network analysis to organizational communication patterns, the authors demonstrate that the approach is also promising for the study of technology acceptance in organizations.

Various studies focus on training and learning in connection with new technologies, particularly with computers. Attitudinal components in learning regarding success, failure, and the process of trying are thematized in a study by Bagozzi et al (1992). A similar theme is also taken up in a comprehensive research program on self-organized learning (Greif 1992), which includes a series of controlled experiments to scrutinize the validity of the proposed procedures. The intriguing aspect of this training program is that it proceeds from the notion of minimal design (Carroll 1985) in software to favor increasing levels of complexity in order to accommodate growing learner expertise. Trainees are encouraged to choose learning tasks, help functions, and complexity levels themselves. "Exploratory error training" as a didactic device for diagnosing and coping with unavoidable errors is integrated systematically into the training. Frese et al (1991) also examine the positive role of errors in learning. The authors contrasted effects of specific error training and error avoidant training and found that the error trained groups performed better in solving difficult tasks in non-speed conditions and were less marked by frustration symptoms. Although these studies are based on small samples, they suggest important elaborations of accepted theories and approaches to training in technology contexts.

In studies of new technology, more so than in other areas, authors based in the United States and in Europe take little note of each others' theoretical underpinnings and rarely cross-reference each other. Particularly noticeable is the fact that various important conceptualizations of the introduction process of new technologies are not used as frameworks for empirical research (e.g. Blackler & Brown 1985, Mambrey & Oppermann 1983, Mumford & Weir 1979, Mumford 1983).

Participation

Some authors see direct employee involvement in decision-making (participative decision-making; PDM) as synonymous with participation (Locke & Schweiger 1979). Participation is usually defined as the behavior of individuals in terms of boss-subordinate cooperation, an understanding that is prominent in English-language publications (Cotton et al 1988). Shetzer (1993) develops a novel approach to direct participation in terms of an information processing model and schema theory. More systemic notions are evoked in the understanding of participation as statutorily induced employee involvement, in European sources usually referred to as industrial or organizational democracy. A recent encyclopedia (Széll 1992) and periodicals such as *Economic and Industrial Democracy* or the *International Yearbook/Handbook Series on Organizational Democracy and Participation* (Wiley/Oxford University Press) as well as reviews of conceptual and practical aspects (Cooke 1990, Lammers 1993, Martin 1994, Wilpert 1994) offer comprehensive summaries of participation research.

The links among PDM, perceived job autonomy, and control are investigated in a study of close to 600 teachers and computer firm employees (Evans & Fischer 1992). The study tests, by way of structural equation modeling, the hypothesis that a general second-order control dimension, such as the very second-order control dimension or factor, may explain the covariance among these three frequently and separately used variables. Results indicate considerable commonality among them as represented by a second-order control factor that the authors liken to the G-factor found in intelligence research. Future research may consider the measures as specific indicators of the latent control dimension.

More in line with traditional industrial relations research are single company studies on the effectiveness of joint committees (Peterson & Tracy 1992) or international comparative research programs in the European Community (EC), assessing the degree of participation in the introduction of new technologies in EC member countries (Gill & Krieger 1992). The latter study of the European Foundation for the Improvement of Living and Working Conditions surveys more than 7000 managers and employee representatives of some 2800 European companies with institutionalized worker participation (e.g. works councils). The empirical study uses a phase theoretical approach of introducing new technologies (i.e. planning, selection, implementation, evaluation phase). Its measure of participation is derived from the influence-power continuum (i.e. from no involvement to information to consultation to negotiation/ joint decision) already employed in the IDE studies (IDE 1981). Danish and German firms lead in the rank order of participativeness, and Italian, Luxembourg, and Portuguese firms fill the lowest ranks. Differences among countries are accounted for by a set of explanatory factors (e.g. dominant management style in the country, statutory rights and regulations, industrial relations system). Because these factors were not measured, nor were they controlled for, such *ex post facto* explanatory exercises are at best hypothesis generating.

A peculiar situation exists in some European countries where works council members are dependent employees on the one hand and equals to management in bargaining situations on the other. Kunst & Soeters (1991) examine the question of whether this role ambiguity influences career opportunities in a sample of Dutch works councillors. Although no objective career barriers were found, such constraints did exist in the perceptions of works councilors themselves. The authors suggest that personality variables may explain this apparent contradiction.

Autonomous work groups are often considered to offer the widest opportunities for employee involvement and self-management (Manz 1992). Pearson's (1992) well-designed longitudinal field experiment with pre-and post-test measurements addressed the question of subjective and objective consequences of working in autonomous versus traditional production teams. The results add further evidence to the frequently reported positive individual, social, and economic consequences of (semi)autonomous work groups in demonstrating "a substantial impact on perceived decision-making, job scope, role clarity, job satisfaction, productivity, attendance, and… a safer working climate" (p. 927). Another notable longitudinal field experiment under difficult conditions in the People's Republic of China (Jin 1993) similarly illustrates the positive consequences of self-selected work groups in terms of work motivation and quantitative as well as qualitative output.

Hazardous Work Systems

An increase in hazardousness is a likely concomitant of growing complexity and size of technical installations. Given that such growth can be observed in many societal domains (Roberts 1992), it is timely to refer to a still small but steadily emerging body of OB literature that centers on organizations characterized by large-scale potential hazards to people and environment. Labeled as high risk, high hazard, high reliability, or reliability enhancing organizations, they can be found in all contexts where high concentrations of energy or toxic substances must be contained (e.g. in high-speed earth-bound traffic, aviation, chemical process plants, nuclear energy production, nuclear powered submarines and aircraft carriers, off-shore oil drilling and oil transport). This line of research owes a lot to Perrow's stimulating analysis (Perrow 1984, Roberts

1990). Apostolakis (1991) provides a comprehensive overview of existing theoretical, methodological, and practical approaches to improving safety in complex hazardous systems.

Safety and reliability depend on failure avoidance and effective perform-ance control. The lesson learnt from many industrial disasters is that they occur not simply as a result of technical component failure or operator error, but also as a consequence of often intricate interactions of processes on all systems levels: technical, individual operator, work group, leadership and management, organization structures, and organizational environment (Wilpert & Klumb 1991). Critical contributing factors may often be far re-moved in space and time from actual triggering events (Brascamp et al 1993, Reason 1990). Hence, a systemic approach is called for in their analysis. A prime example of this approach is presented in the scrutiny of the Challenger disaster (Starbuck & Milliken 1988). The authors show the interplay of (*a*) decision-makers in fine-tuning the system, (*b*) group dynamics leading to erroneous decisions years before the accident but ultimately helping to bring it about, and (*c*) the influence of weather conditions on the launch day. The case study also highlights the difficulties and often misleading shortcomings of such *ex post facto* analyses.

The aftermath of the Chernobyl accident has popularized a new concept called safety culture (INSAG 1991). Clearly a derivative of organizational culture, the notion is perceived by many as a recipe for guaranteed failure-free operations of hazardous systems. Roberts et al (1993) describe the content of culture in two nuclear powered aircraft carriers in terms of the twelve dimen-sions composing the Organizational Culture Inventory (Cooke & Lafferty 1986). They enriched their database with interviews and intermittant partici-pant observations on language manifestations and rites over a period of two years. The authors were able to show the existence of both a dominant culture profile on the ships, oriented toward task security, power, opposition, and competition, as well as several group-specific subcultural variations.

Significant advances in analytic and practical terms may be expected by linking artificial intelligence approaches to situations of problem solving in high hazard situations. Roth et al (1992) developed a computer simulation technique (Cognitive Environment Simulation; CES) and showed how it can sucessfully be employed in studying the cognitive challenges imposed on operator teams in the dynamic sequences of simulated nuclear power plant incidents. The authors juxtaposed the results of the computer simulation with the results of experienced operator teams obtained in full-scale high-fidelity nuclear power plant simulators. They demonstrated the usefulness of CES for identifying the requisite competences of operators to handle the demands posed in the sequences of a given systems failure and to assess the environ-mental clues offered to problem solvers in dealing with the diagnostic tasks in highly complex systems dynamics. Such approaches seem to bring substantial progress to combining cognitive science and OB (Clegg 1994).

Organizational Learning

Dodgson (1993) offers an eclectic review of the literature on organizational learning and the characteristics of the learning organization. There are many reasons for the renewed interest in this field: demographic changes require readjustment of personnel policies; societal value changes alter industrial relations; the growth in worldwide competition imposes adaptation; rapid technological development requires new competences and behavioral repertoires; political events set new constraints and opportunities for organizations; and finally, the dynamic and integrative properties of the concept itself make learning an attractive concept in OB. Because organizational learning and organizational memory frequently are used in their metaphoric sense, they are liable to be used in questionable anthropomorphic generalizations. However, the literature is replete with examples where, for better or worse, organizations demonstrated their capacity to preserve knowledge of past experience (Walsh & Ungson 1991).

A special issue of *Organization Science* [1991, Vol. 2(1)] illustrates these points by assembling a set of important contributions "in honor of (and by) James G. March." The literature review therein by Huber (1991) focuses on four important conceptual notions related to organizational learning: knowledge acquisition, information distribution, information interpretation, and organizational memory. Huber asserts: "An entity learns if, through its processing of information, the range of potential behaviors is changed" (p. 89) and goes on to develop a classification of subconstructs and subprocesses, in particular those related to knowledge acquisition. The classification serves as a framework to discuss critically a wide range of literature. With reference to the voluminous literature on knowledge acquisition, Huber notes a lack of cumulative work and synthesis. In the work on information distribution he identifies a lack of research on how organizations may facilitate the retrieval of and access to existing knowledge in the organization. On the whole, "work on organizational learning has not led to research-based guidelines for increasing the effectiveness of organizational learning" (p. 108; for an enlightening exception, see Van der Schaaf et al 1991).

This last statement points to two unresolved fundamental issues raised in a stimulating paper by March et al (1991): 1. How do you make valid and reliable inferences from history (past experience), especially small histories and single cases? and 2. How do you organize and institutionalize organizational learning? The former issue poses an epistemological problem, the latter a practical problem of organizational design and development. Both mark the endpoints of the still widely open and largely untoiled core area of organizational learning. A valiant theoretical attempt to provide some answers to these problems is made by Reinhardt (1993) by integrating the (social-)systems theoretical positions of Maturana (1981), Maturana et al (1980), and Luhmann (1984, 1991). Self-reference and autonomy are in this context seen as central criteria for any attempt to facilitate organizational learning: "Organizations create their own learning capacity and reproduce themselves, if they take into account [self-reference and autonomy] in their communication and action" (Reinhardt 1993, p. 276).

On an empirical level, the structural impediments to organizational learning and adaptation are investigated in Amburgey et al's (1993) large-scale historical study of more than 1000 Finnish newspaper organizations. Based on Hannan & Freeman's (1984) structural inertia model and using archival data from 1771–1963, the authors tested a set of hypotheses regarding organizational change and mortality in their interaction with organization historical and environmental events. The results indicate that an organization's past experience with change and its location within the organization's life cycle are crucial in providing conditions for success or failure. Thus, the findings contribute to a better understanding of intra-organizational learning and environmental impacts.

Organization-Environment Relations

Many reviewers of OB have lamented the obvious neglect of contextual, environmental factors in research and theorizing (e.g. Cummings 1981, Near et al 1980, Cappelli & Sherer 1991, Wilpert 1992). This blind spot, despite the lip service given to conceptualizing organizations as open systems, gives rise to considerable concern from practical as well as theoretical points of view. Environmental impacts on OB make themselves undeniably felt at a time when technological and demographic changes in the work force induce novel ways of organizational adaptation, when border-transgressing activities of organizations abound, when the whole of middle and Eastern European economies find themselves in a veritable vortex. These are examples of the practical reasons to be concerned with organization-environment relations. But other reasons for favoring this focus go to the heart of the OB discipline itself. As Cappelli & Sherer (1991) emphasize, unless OB succeeds in bridging the micro-macro relationships, the field faces difficulties in establishing an independent identity. They find three factors responsible for the disregard for context in previous research: 1. the conservative role of the existing dominant paradigm, which impedes new approaches; 2. the consistency principle in science, which postulates that new theories ought to be consistent with accepted knowledge; and 3. the dominant focus on the individual as the unit of analysis combined with the present cognitivist bias. In consequence, "macro and micro organization theories are not reconcilable at least in part because they are not commensurate.... There is no way to relate macro theories, with their focus on the environment, to micro behavior, or vice versa" (Cappelli & Sherer 1991, p. 87).

Recent studies that address organization-environment links tend either to follow the traditional path of conceptualizing environments as perceived environments (McCabe & Dutton 1993) or to scrutinize, increasingly so, inter-organizational linkages by way of institutionalization theoretical approaches (Baum & Oliver 1991, Leblebici et al 1991), ecological perspectives (Boeker 1991, Staber 1992), or through employing network repertoires (Gerlach 1992, Galaskiewics & Burt 1991, Oliver 1991). Instead of opting either for the micro or the macro road, Cappelli & Sherer (1991) propose a mesoscopic-level approach to establish bridges between micro and macro on the assumption that "the environment shapes organizational characteristics and phenomena which in turn shape individual behavior and attitudes" (p. 89). The authors chose internal labor markets of organizations as an example of such bridging elements that buffer immediate environmental effects by providing organizational opportunities and constraints to behavior and attitudes (e.g. they offer job security, seniority, contractual arrangements, compensation).

The discussion of organization-environment relations is often bedeviled by a lack of clarity about what is meant by organizational context. As Cappelli & Sherer (1991) stress, for most OB research, context is the environment external to individuals (i.e. mainly characteristics of organizations). Quite different is the notion of organizational context as the environment external to organizations themselves, such as national or local labor market (IDE 1993), cultural traditions (Hofstede 1980), societal values (Inglehart 1989, MOW 1987), societal stratification (Maurice et al 1978), demographic changes in terms of female labor market participation [*Economic and Industrial Democracy,* 1994, Vol. 15(1)]. There is sufficient empirical evidence indicating that such environmental factors impact directly or in moderator roles upon intra-organizational processes and structures. "Yet these contextual explanations have in general not been incorporated into the paradigm of OB research" (Cappelli & Sherer 1991, p. 75). Furthermore, as a study by Miller (1992) demonstrates, striving for fit of internal contextual elements and striving for fit with external environments may be conceived of as disparate if not sometimes contradictory strategies that have to be pursued sequentially. Thus, Miller's study questions accepted theoretical notions of organization-environment fit as a critical condition for survival and efficiency.

CONCLUSIONS

The field of OB as a whole is on an expansive course. This review deliberately ventured into analyzing work not routinely referenced in English-language publications in order to alert the reader to currents in OB that otherwise receive little attention. A certain eclecticism is inevitable given constraints in time and space, but even so, this reviewer observes advances in the expanding scope of topics covered in OB, some important theoretical improvements or new developments, and a growing array of methodological refinements.

Undeniably, symbolic approaches are expanding their territory and are displaying remarkable vitality. This is directly apparent in areas of self-declared symbolic orientation in OB where almost no topic remains untouched. But it also emerges as a vital approach in studies of organizational culture and climate, leadership, new technologies and organization, hazardous work systems, and organizational adaptation.

Organizational symbolism and related theoretical strands are thorns in the flesh of accepted orientations and practices in OB. Offense and defense appear to be locked in a vicious circle. In consequence, doctrinaire zealotry often accompanies current conflicts. Without denying that basic epistemological foundations must principally be open to continuous critical analysis and eventual change ("anything-goes" is an anathema), the present conflictual discourse could certainly gain from a somewhat greater equanimity. The apparent swing of the pendulum in the direction of symbolism and social construction of organizational realities does not make extant traditions extinct. Nor will any new epistemological doctrine offer an all-encompassing mega-theory. The choice of a theoretical basis frequently is a function of the question to be answered. Although it seems perfectly legitimate to this reviewer to approach deeper lying value premises by way of myths and rituals with qualitative methods, he fails to understand why he should abrogate quantitative procedures if he happens to be interested in ascertaining the distribution of given myths and rituals. Paradigmatic studies have fruitfully combined both orientations. Time and proven usefulness in practical and theoretical terms will separate the wheat from the chaff. This is, however, easier said than done, given that theoretical controversies more often than not reflect fights over turf and territory.

As long as organizations are viewed as open socio-technical systems, their contextual embeddedness in surrounding environments is conceptually and implicitly given. Some important studies on (external) environment-organization relations have been published, but there is still a dearth of empirical studies of OB in vortical environments, such as Eastern Europe, in contexts of globalizing competition or changing societal value patterns. Moreover, content domains discussed above such as new technologies, hazardous organizations, and organizational learning all call for a systematic inclusion of environmental dimensions. These are, however, rarely realized in actual studies.

The study of environment-organization relationships requires cross-level conceptualizations and methodologies. The theoretical ground seems to be well prepared to tackle these issues on a broader front. Empirical studies have continued to demonstrate the feasibility of the strategy, thus confirming the trend identified by O'Reilly (1991). More ought to emerge in coming years, further advancing the integration of micro and macro OB.

Longitudinal studies are increasingly coming to the fore with lengthier time horizons and more sophisticated research designs. Length of time horizon depends greatly on the issue under study; however, if sustained organizational change is addressed, time horizons must be extended beyond the traditional perspective of a few months. This has practical as well as methodological implications (IDE 1993). The practical problems include maintaining funds, research teams and interest over long time periods, site accessibility, and the resultant output of fewer publications. Methodological difficulties may also arise (Schaie & Hertzog 1982), such as regression to the mean, mortality of units of analysis, changing sample composition, and reduced instrument validity. These are important reasons for why this type of longitudinal research is rarely conducted. Historical studies using archival data help to circumvent these problems. Multi-source studies also avoid some of the notorious problems of percept-percept research.

Previous authors of OB chapters in the *Annual Review of Psychology* touched upon the need to expand theoretical approaches by taking note of and by integrating various neighboring disciplines into OB research. It is not surprising that such appeals followed reflections upon research into organizational context and cross-level problems. The number of disciplines mentioned increased from sociology (Cummings 1982, Staw 1984); to sociology, economics, and psychology (O'Reilly 1991); and to sociology, history, economics, and political science (Mowday & Sutton 1993). OB internal dynamics, social and technological change suggest the desirability to expand that list even further. The burgeoning literature with a symbolic bias relies heavily on anthropological approaches (Czarniawska-Joerges 1994). The socioeconomic changes taking place in Eastern Europe imply a variety of issues such as changing property rights and legal prescriptions that cannot be left unnoticed by OB studies in such political contexts. The same is true in many western European countries where legal requirements guide employee participation and organizational control. Thus, jurisprudence is called for. Finally, technological change inundates industry and public administration all over the world. Task and job redesigns, which necessarily must follow these developments, cannot disregard the wide body of knowledge assembled by ergonomics. What is called for is an interdisciplinary openness that the pursuit of given problems demands.

ACKNOWLEDGMENTS

The writing of this review chapter was supported by a grant from the Deutsche Forschungsgemeinschaft and greatly facilitated through the stimulating environment of the *Maison des Sciences de l'Homme,* Paris. Further, I am grateful for the untiring critical support of Anne Theissen, assisted by Uta Boesch, in compiling reference materials used in this review. Helpful comments on earlier drafts were made by John M. Darley and Czarina Wilpert.

Literature Cited

Adler PS. 1991. Workers and flexible manufacturing systems: three installations compared. *J. Organ. Behav.* 12:447–60

Adler PS, Borys B. 1993. Materialism and idealism in organizational research. *Organ. Stud.* 14(5):657–79

Amburgey TL, Kelly D, Barnett WP. 1993. Resetting the clock: the dynamics of organizational change and failure. *Adm. Sci. Q.* 38:51–73

Apostolakis G, ed. 1991. *Probabilistic Safety Assessment and Management.* Amsterdam: Elsevier

Astley WG, Zammuto RF. 1992. Organization science, managers and language games. *Organ. Sci.* 3(4):443–60

Austin JT, Villanova P. 1992. The criterion problem: 1917–1992. *J. Appl. Psychol.* 77(6):836–74

Bagozzi RP, Davis FD, Warshaw PR. 1992. Development and test of a theory of technological learning and usage. *Hum. Relat.* 45(7):659–86

Bass BM. 1985. *Leadership and Performance Beyond Expectations.* New York: Free Press

Bass BM. 1990. *Bass' & Stogdill's Handbook of Leadership.* New York: Free Press

Bass BM. 1994. Is there universality in the full range model of leadership. *Int. J. Public Adm.* In press

Bass BM. 1992. Stress and leadership. In *Decision-Making and Leadership,* ed. F Heller, pp. 133–55. Cambridge: Cambridge Univ. Press

Bass BM, Avolio BJ. 1993. Transformational leadership: a response to critiques. In *Leadership Theory and Research: Perspectives and Directions,* ed. MM Chemers, RA Ayman, pp. 49–80. London: Academic

Baubion-Broye A, Curie J, Hajjar V. 1989a. Projets et transformations des activité des chômeurs. *Psychologie du travail. Nouveau Enjeux: Développement de l'homme au travail et développement des organisations,* pp. 362–70. Issy-les-Moulineaux: Editions EAP

Baubion-Broye A, Megemont JL, Sellinger M. 1989b. Evolution des sentiments de controle et de la réceptivité à l'information au cours du chomage. *Appl. Psychol.: Int. Rev.* 38(3):265–75

Baum JAC, Oliver C. 1991. Institutional linkages and organizational mortality. *Adm. Sci. Q.* 36:187–218

Bhaskar R. 1978. *A Realist Theory of Science.* Hemel Hempstead: Harvester Wheatsheaf

Blackler F, Brown C. 1985. Evaluation and the impact of information technologies on people in organizations. *Hum. Relat.* 38:213–31

Bliesener T. 1992. Ist die Validität biographischer Daten ein methodisches Artefakt? Ergebnisse einer meta-analytischen Studie. *Z. Arb. Organisationspsychol.* 36:12–21

Boeker W. 1991. Organizational strategy: an ecological perspective. *Acad. Manage. J.* 34(3):613–35

Boje DM. 1991. The storytelling organization: a study of story performance in an office-supply firm. *Adm. Sci. Q.* 36: 106–26

Brascamp MH, Koehorst LJB, van Steen JFJ. 1993. Management factors in safety. In *Safety and Reliability Assessment—An Integral Approach,* ed. P Kafke, J Wolf, pp. 35–48. Amsterdam: Elsevier

Brehmer B, Gregersen NP, Moren B. 1991. *Group methods in safety work.* Presented at Workshop New Technologies and Work, 10th, Bad Homburg, Germany

Burke MJ, Borucki CC, Hurley AE. 1992. Reconceptualizing psychological climate in a retail service environment: a multiple stakeholder perspective. *J. Appl. Psychol.* 77(5):717–29

Burrell G, Morgan G. 1979. *Sociological Paradigms and Organizational Analysis: Elements of the Sociology of Corporate Life.* London: Heinemann

Calás MB, Smircich L. 1991. Voicing seduction to silence leadership. *Organ. Stud.* 12(4):567–601

Calori R, Sarnin P. 1991. Corporate culture and economic performance: a French study. *Organ. Stud.* 12(1):49–73

Cappelli P, Sherer PD. 1991. The missing role of context in OB: the need for a meso-level approach. *Res. Organ. Behav.* 13:55–110

Carroll J. 1985. Minimals design for the active user. In *Human-computer Interaction IN-TER-ACT '84 ,* ed. B Shackle, pp. 39–44. Amsterdam: North-Holland

Champoux JE. 1992. A mulitivariate analysis of curvilinear relationships among job scope, work context satisfactions, and affective outcomes. *Hum. Relat.* 45(1):87-111

Child J. 1988. On organizations in their sectors. *Organ. Stud.* 9(1):13–19

Clegg C. 1994. Psychology and information technology: the study of cognitions in organizations. *Br. J. Psychol.* In press

Clegg C, Symon G. 1990. A review of human-centered manufacturing technology and a framework for its design and evaluation. *Int. Rev. Ergon.* 2:15–47

Clegg SR, Dunkerley D. 1980. *Organization, Class and Control.* London: Routledge/Kegan Paul

Cooke RA, Lafferty JC. 1986. *Level V: Organizational Culture Inventory.* Plymouth, MI: Human Synergistics

Cooke WN. 1990. *Labor-Management Cooperation: New Partnerships or Going in Circles?* Kalamazoo, MI: Upjohn Inst.

Cordery JL, Mueller WS, Smith LM. 1991. Attitudinal and behavioral effects of autonomous group working: a longitudinal field study. *Acad. Manage. J.* 34(2):464–76

Cotton JL, Vollrath DA, Frogatt KL, Lengnick-Hall ML, Jennings KR. 1988. Employee participation: diverse forms and different outcomes. *Acad. Manage. Rev.* 13:8–22

Cowherd DM, Levine DI. 1992. Product quality and pay equity between lower-level employees and top management: an investigation of distributive justice theory. *Adm. Sci. Q.* 37:302–20

Cummings LL. 1981. Organizational behavior in the 1980s. *Decis. Sci.* 12:365–77

Cummings LL. 1982. Organizational behavior. *Annu. Rev. Psychol.* 33:541–83

Czarniawska-Joerges B. 1992. *Exploring Complex Organizations. A Cultural Perspective.* London: Sage

Czarniawska-Joerges B. 1994. *The Three-Dimensional Organization: A Constructionist View.* Lund, Sweden: Chartwell Bratt

Czarniawska-Joerges B, Wolff R. 1991. Leaders, managers, entrepreneurs on and off the organizational stage. *Organ. Stud.* 12(4):529–46

Dodgson M. 1993. Organizational learning: a review of some literatures. *Organ. Stud.* 14(3):375–94

Donaldson L. 1985. *In Defence of Organization Theory: A Reply to Critics.* Cambridge: Cambridge Univ. Press

Donaldson L. 1988. In successful defence of organization theory: a routing of the critics. *Organ. Stud.* 9(1):28–32

Donaldson L. 1992. The Weick stuff: managing beyond games. *Organ. Sci.* 3(4):461–66

Drazin R, Sandelands L. 1992. Autogenesis: a perspective on the process of organizing. *Organ. Sci.* 3(2):230–49

Drenth PJD, Koopman PL. 1992. Duration and complexity in strategic decision-making. In *Decision Making and Leadership,* ed. FA Heller, pp. 58–70. Cambridge: Cambridge Univ. Press

Drory M. 1993. Perceived political climate and job attitudes. *Organ. Stud.* 14(1):59–71

Dunnette MD, Hough LM, eds. 1990. *Handbook of Industrial and Organizational Psychology,* Vol. 1. Palo Alto, CA: Consult. Psychol.

Dunnette MD, Hough LM, eds. 1991. *Handbook of Industrial and Organizational Psychology,* Vol. 2. Palo Alto, CA: Consult. Psychol.

Dunnette MD, Hough LM, Triandis H, eds. 1994. *Handbook of Industrial and Organizational Psychology,* Vol. 4. Palo Alto, CA: Consult. Psychol.

Durkheim M. 1967. *La Divison sociale du travail.* Paris: Presses Univ. France

Earley PC, Brittain J. 1992. Cross-level analysis of organizations: social resource management model. *Res. Organ. Behav.* 15:357–408

Erez M, Earley PC, eds. 1993. *Culture, Self-Identity and Work.* New York: Oxford Univ. Press

Evans BK, Fischer DG. 1992. A hierarchical model of participatory decision-making, job autonomy, and perceived control. *Hum. Relat.* 45(11):1169–89

Faverge JM. 1966. L'analyse de travail en terme de régulation. In *L'ergonomie des processus industriels,* ed. JM Faverge, M Olivier, F Delahaut, P Stephaneck, JC Falmagne, pp. 33–60. Bruxelles: Univ. Libre Bruxelles

Fiol CM. 1991. Seeing the empty spaces: towards a more complex understanding of the meaning of power in organizations. *Organ. Stud.* 12(4):547–66

Fischer GN. 1990. *Psychologie des Arbeitsraums.* Frankfurt: Campus

Frese M, Brodbeck F, Heinbokel T, Mooser C, Schleiffenbaum E, Thiemann P. 1991. Errors in training computer skills: on the positive function of errors. *Hum.-Comp. Interact.* 6: 77–93

Frese M, Zapf D. 1994. Action as the core of work psychology: a German approach. See Dunnette et al 1993, pp. 271–340

Gabriel Y. 1991. Turning facts into stories and stories into facts: a hermeneutic exploration of organizational folklore. *Hum. Relat.* 44(8):857–75

Gagliardi P, ed. 1992. *Symbols and Artifacts: Views on the Corporate Landscape.* New York: Aldine de Gruyter

Galaskiewicz J, Burt RS. 1991. Interorganization contagion in corporate philanthropy. *Adm. Sci. Q.* 36:88–105

Gemmill G, Oakley J. 1992. Leadership: an alienating social myth? *Hum. Relat.* 45(2): 113–29

Gerlach ML. 1992. The Japanese corporate network: a blockmodel analysis. *Adm. Sci. Q.* 37:105–39

Giddens A. 1979. *Central Problems in Social Theory: Action, Structure and Contradiction in Social Analysis.* Berkeley, CA: Univ. Calif. Press

Giddens A. 1984. *The Constitution of Society: Outline of the Theory of Structure.* Berkeley, CA: Univ. Calif. Press

Gill C, Krieger H. 1992. The diffusion of participation in new information technology in Europe: survey results. *Econ. Ind. Dem.* 13:331–58

Greif S. 1992. *Software-Design und selbstorganisiertes Lernen aus Fehlern.* Bericht zum Projekt "Multifunktionale Büro-Software und Qualifizierung (MBO)." Fachbereich Arbeits- und Organisationspsychologie: Univ. Osnabrück

Hackman JR, Oldham GR. 1976. Motivation through the design of work: test of a theory. *Organ. Behav. Hum. Perform.* 16: 250–79

Hannan MT, Freeman J. 1984. Structural inertia and organizational change. *Am. Soc. Rev.* 49:149–64

Hansen CD, Kahnweiler WM. 1993. Storytelling: an instrument for understanding the dynamics of corporate relationships. *Hum. Relat.* 46(12):1391–409

Harrison JR, Carroll GR. 1991. Keeping the faith: a model of cultural transmission in formal organizations. *Adm. Sci. Q.* 36:552–82

Hart PM. 1994. Teacher quality of worklife: integrating work experiences, psychological distress and morale. *J. Occup. Organ. Psychol.* In press

Hart PM, Waering AJ, Headey B. 1994. Assessing police work experiences: development of the police daily hassles, uplifts scales. *J. Crim. Justice.* In press

Hatcher L, Ross TL. 1991. From individual incentives to an organization-wide gainsharing plan: effects on teamwork and product quality. *J. Organ. Behav.* 12:169–83

Heller FA, Drenth PJD, Koopman PL, Rus V. 1988. *Decisions in Organizations: A Three-Country Comparative Study.* London: Sage

Hendrick HW. 1991. Ergonomics in organizational design and management. *Ergonomics* 34(6):743–56

Hinings CR. 1988. Defending organization theory: a British view from North America. *Organ. Stud.* 9(1):2–7

Hirsch-Kreinsen H, Schultz-Wild R, Köhler C, Behr M. 1990. *Einstieg in die rechnerintegrierte Produktion. Alternative Entwicklungspfade der Industriearbeit im Maschinenbau.* Frankfurt: Campus

Hofstede G. 1980. *Culture's Consequences.* London: Sage

Hom PW, Caranikas-Walker F, Prussia GE. 1992. A meta analytical structural equations analysis of a model of employee turnover. *J. Appl. Psychol.* 77(6):890–909

House RJ. 1977. A 1976 theory of charismatic leadership. In *Leadership: The Cutting Edge,* ed. JG Hunt, LL Larson, pp. 189–207. Cardondale: S. Ill. Univ. Press

House RJ, Singh JV. 1987. Organizational behavior: some new directions for I/O psychology. *Annu. Rev. Psychol.* 38:669–718

Houser N, Kloesel C, eds. 1992. *The Essential Peirce: Selected Philosophical Writings,* Vol. 2. Bloomington: Indiana Univ. Press

Huber GP. 1991. Organizational learning: the contributing processes and the literatures. *Organ. Sci.* 2(1):88–115

Hurley JJP. 1992. Towards an organizational psychology model for the acceptance and utilisation of new technology in organisations. *Irish J. Psychol.* 13(1):17–31

IDE (International Research Group). 1981. *Industrial Democracy in Europe.* London: Oxford Univ. Press

IDE (International Research Group). 1992. *Industrial Democracy in Europe Revisited:* summary and conclusions. *Soc. Sci. Inform.* 4:773–85

IDE (International Research Group). 1993. *Industrial Democracy in Europe Revisited.* London: Oxford Univ. Press

Ilgen DR, Klein HJ. 1988. Organizational behavior. *Annu. Rev. Psychol.* 40:327–51

Inglehart R. 1989. *Cultural Change.* Princeton, NJ: Princeton Univ. Press

INSAG. 1991. *Safety Culture.* Vienna: Int. Atomic Energy Agency

Jackson PR, Wall TD. 1991. How does operator control enhance performance of advanced manufacturing technology? *Ergonomics* 34(10):1301–11

Jackson PR, Wall TD, Martin R, Davids K. 1993. New measures of job control, cognitive demand and production responsibility. *J. Appl. Psychol.* 78(5):753–62

Jin P. 1993. Work motivation and productivity in voluntarily formed work teams: a field study in China. *Organ. Behav. Hum. Decis. Mak. Proc.* 54:133–55

Katzell RA. 1994. Contemporary meta-trends in industrial and organizational psychology. See Dunnette et al 1993, pp. 1–93

Kelly J. 1992. Does job re-design theory explain job re-design outcomes? *Hum. Relat.* 45(8):753–75

Kickert WJM. 1993. Autopoiesis and the science of (public) administration: essence, sense and nonsense. *Organ. Stud.* 14(2): 261–78

Koopman P, Drenth P, Heller F, Rus V. 1991. Strategic and tactical decisions: a comparative analysis of 217 decisions in three countries. In *Contemporary Issues in Cross-Cultural Psychology,* ed. N Bleichroth, PJD Drenth, pp. 137–51. Amsterdam: Zeitlinger

Korunka C, Weiss A, Karetta B. 1993. Die Bedeutung des Umstellungsprozesses bei der Einführung neuer Technologien. Eine interdisziplinäre Längsschnittstudie. *Z. Arb. Organisationspsychol.* 37:10–18

Koys DJ, DeCotiis TA. 1991. Inductive measures of psychological climate. *Hum. Relat.* 44(3):265–85

Kunst P, Soeters J. 1991. Works council membership and career opportunities. *Organ. Stud.* 12(1):75–93

Lammers CJ. 1993. International democracy. In *Interdisciplinary Perspectives on Organization Studies,* ed. S Lindenberg, H Schreuder, pp. 323–37. Oxford: Pergamon

Latham GP, Locke E. 1991. Self-regulation through goal setting. *Organ. Behav. Hum. Decis. Mak. Proc.* 50:212–47

Leblebici H, Salancik GR, Copay A, King T. 1991. Institutional change and the transformation of interorganizational fields: an organizational history of the US broadcasting industry. *Adm. Sci. Q.* 36:333–63

Ledford GE Jr, Albers Mohrman S. 1993. Self-design in high involvement: a large scale organizational change. *Hum. Relat.* 46(1): 143–73

Lenk H, ed. 1977–1984. *Handlungstheorien interdisziplinär,* Vols. 1–4 München: Fink

Leplat J. 1990. Skills and tacit skills: a psychological perspective. *Appl. Psychol.* 39(2): 143–54

Lewin K. 1926. Vorsatz, Wille und Bedürfnis. *Psychol. Forsch.* 7: 294–385

Lewin K. 1952. Group decision and social change. In *Outside Readings in Social Psychology,* ed. GE Swanson, TM Newcomb, EL Hartley, pp. 459–73. New York: Holt

Locke EA, Latham G. 1990. *A Theory of Goals and Performance.* Englewood Cliffs, NJ: Prentice Hall

Locke EA, Schweiger DM. 1979. Participation in decision making: one more look. In *Research in Organizational Behavior,* ed. B. Staw, LL Cummings, 1:265–369. Greenwich, CT: JAI

Lord RG, Hanges PJ. 1987. A control system model of organizational motivation: theoretical development and applied implications. *Behav. Sci.* 32:161–78

Luhmann N. 1984. *Soziale Systeme. Grundriß einer allgemeinen Theorie.* Frankfurt: Suhrkamp

Luhmann N. 1991. *Die Wissenschaft der Gesellschaft.* Frankfurt: Suhrkamp

Mambrey P, Oppermann R, eds. 1983. *Beteiligung von Betroffenen bei der Entwicklung von Informationssystemen.* Frankfurt: Campus

Manz CC. 1992. Self-leading work teams: moving beyond self-management myths. *Hum. Relat.* 45(11):1119–41

March JG, Sproull LS, Tamuz M. 1991. Learning from samples of one or fewer. *Organ. Sci.* 2(1):1–13

Marsden R. 1993. The politics of organizational analysis. *Organ. Stud.* 14(1):93–124

Martin D. 1994. *Démocratie industrielle: la participation directe dans les entreprises.* Paris: Presses Univ. France

Maturana HR, Varela FJ, Cohen RS. 1980. *Autopoiesis and Cognition: The Realisation of Living.* Boston: Reidel

Maurice H, Sorge A, Warner M. 1978. Societal differences in organizing manufacturing units: a comparison of France, West-Germany and Great Britain. *Organ. Stud.* 1(1): 59–86

McCabe DL, Dutton JE. 1993. Making sense of the environment: the role of perceived effectiveness. *Hum. Relat.* 46(5):623–43

Medcof JW. 1991. A test of a revision of the job characteristics model. *Appl. Psychol.* 40(4):381–93

Miller D. 1992. Environmental fit versus internal fit. *Organ. Sci.* 3(2):159–78

Mintzberg H. 1991. A letter to Marta Calás and Linda Smircich. *Organ. Stud.* 12(4):602–3

Misumi J. 1978. *The effects of organizational climate variables, particularly leadership variables and group decision, on accident prevention.* Presented at Int. Congr. Appl. Psychol., 19th, Munich

Mitchell TR. 1979. Organizational behavior. *Annu. Rev. Psychol.* 30:243–81

Mitra A, Jenkins GD Jr, Gupta N. 1992. A meta-analytic review of the relationship between absence and turnover. *J. Appl. Psychol.* 77(6):879–89

Moran ET, Volkwein JF. 1992. The cultural

approach to the formation of organizational climate. *Hum. Relat.* 45(1):19–47

Morgan G. 1986. *Images of Organizations.* Beverly Hills, CA: Sage

Moscovici S. 1984. The phenomenon of social representations. In *Social Representations,* ed. R Farr, S. Moscovici, pp. 3–69. Cambridge: Cambridge Univ. Press

MOW (Meaning of Working) International Research Team. 1989. *The Meaning of Working.* London: Academic

Mowday RT, Sutton RI. 1993. Organizational behavior: linking individuals and groups to organizational contexts. *Annu. Rev. Psychol.* 44:195–229

Mumford E. 1983. Participative systems design: practice and theory. *J. Occup. Behav.* 4:47–57

Mumford E, Weir M. 1979. *Computer Systems in Work Design: The Ethics Method.* London: Assoc. Bus.

Near JP, Rice RW, Hunt RG. 1980. The relationship between work and nonwork domains: a review of empirical research. *Acad. Manage. Rev.* 5:415–29

Newton T, Keenan T. 1991. Further analyses of the dispositional argument in organizational behavior. *J. Appl. Psychol.* 76(6): 781–87

Noon M, Delbridge R. 1993. News from behind my hand: gossip in organizations. *Organ. Stud.* 14(1):23–36

Ochanine D. 1966. *The operative image of controlled object in "man-automatic-machine" systems.* Presented at Int. Congr. Psychol., 17th, Moscow

Oliver C. 1991. Network relations and loss of organizational autonomy. *Hum. Relat.* 44(9):943–61

O'Reilly CA. 1991. Organizational behavior: where we've been, where we're going. *Annu. Rev. Psychol.* 42:427–58

O'Reilly CA, Chatman JA, Caldwell D. 1991. People and organizational culture: a Q-sort approach to assessing person-organization fit. *Acad. Manage. J.* 34:487–516

Orlikowski WJ. 1992. The duality of technology: rethinking the concept of technology in organizations. *Organ. Sci.* 3(3):398–447

Parsons CK, Liden RC, O'Connor EJ, Nagao DH. 1991. Employee responses to technologically-driven change: the implementation of office automation in a service organization. *Hum. Relat.* 44(12):1331–55

Pauchant TC. 1991. Transferential leadership. Towards a more complex understanding of charisma in organizations. *Organ. Stud.* 12(4):507–28

Pearson CAI. 1992. Autonomous workgroups: an evaluation at an industrial site. *Hum. Relat.* 45(9):905–36

Perrow C. 1984. *Normal Accidents: Living with High-risk Technologies.* New York: Basic

Peterson RB, Tracy L. 1992. Assessing effectiveness of joint committees in a labor-management cooperation program. *Hum. Relat.* 45:467–88

Petty MM, Singleton B, Conell DW. 1992. An experimental evaluation of an organizational incentive plan in the electric utility industry. *J. Appl. Psychol.* 77(4):427–36

Pfeffer J. 1981. Organizational theory and structural perspectives on management. *J. Manage.* 17:789–803

Prigogine I, Stengers I. 1984. *Order Out of Chaos.* Toronto: Bantam

Reason J. 1990. *Human Error.* Cambridge: Cambridge Univ. Press

Reinhardt R. 1993. *Das Modell organisationaler Lernfähigkeit und die Gestaltung lernfähiger Organisationen.* Frankfurt: Lang

Rice RE, Aydin C. 1991. Attitudes toward new organizational technology: network proximity as a mechanism for social information processing. *Adm. Sci. Q.* 36:219–44

Roberts KH. 1990. Some characteristics of one type of high reliability in organization. *Organ. Sci.* 1(2):160–76

Roberts KH. 1992. Structuring to facilitate migrating decisions in reliability enhancing organizations. In *Top Management and Executive Leadership in High Technology. Advances in Global High-Technology Management,* ed. L Gomez-Mehia, MW Lawless, pp. 171–91. Greenwich, CT: JAI

Roberts KH, Rousseau DM, La Porte TR. 1993. The culture of high reliability: quantitative and qualitative assessment aboard nuclear-powered aircraft carriers. *J. High Technol. Manage.* In press

Rose H. 1992. Erfahrungsgeleitete Arbeit als Fokus für Arbeitsgestaltung und Technikentwicklung. *Z. Arb. Organisationspsychol.* 36:22–29

Rose M. 1985. Universalism, culturalism and the Aix Group. *Eur. Soc. Rev.* 1:145–48

Roth EM, Woods DD, Pople HE Jr. 1992. Cognitive simulation as a tool for cognitive task analysis. *Ergonomics* 35(10):1163–98

Sackmann SA. 1992. Culture and subcultures: an analysis of organizational knowledge. *Adm. Sci. Q.* 37:140–61

Sandelands L, Glynn MA, Larson JR Jr. 1991. Control theory and social behavior in the workplace. *Hum. Relat.* 44(10):1107–30

Schaie WK, Herzog C. 1982. Longitudinal methods. In *Handbook of Developmental Psychology,* ed. BB Waldman, pp. 91–115. New York: Prentice Hall

Schneider B. 1985. Organizational behavior. *Annu. Rev. Psychol.* 36: 573–611

Schneider B, Reichers AE. 1983. On the etiology of climates. *Pers. Psychol.* 36:19–40

Schneider B, Wheeler JK, Cox JF. 1992. A passion for service: using content analysis to explicate service climate themes. *J. Appl. Psychol.* 77(5):705–16

Schultz M. 1991. Transitions between symbolic domains in organizations. *Organ. Stud.* 12(4):489–506

Sheridan JE. 1992. Organizational culture and employee retention. *Acad. Manage. J.* 35(5):1036–56

Shetzer L. 1993. A social information processing model of employee participation. *Organ. Sci.* 4(2):252–68

Snell SA, Dean JW Jr. 1992. Integrated manufacturing and human resource management: a human capital perspective. *Acad. Manage. J.* 33(3):467–504

Sooklal L. 1991. The leader as a broker of dreams. *Hum. Relat.* 44(8):833–57

Sorge A. 1991. Strategic fit and social effect: interpreting cross-national comparisons of technology, organization and human resources. *Organ. Stud.* 12(2):161–90

Spector PE, Jex SM. 1991. Relations of job characteristics from multiple data sources with employee affect, absence, turnover intentions and health. *J. Appl. Psychol.* 76(1):46–53

Staber U. 1992. Organizational interdependence and organizational mortality in the cooperative sector: a community ecology perspective. *Hum. Relat.* 45:1191–1212

Starbuck WH, Milliken FJ. 1988. Challenger: fine-tuning the odds until something breaks. *J. Manage. Stud.* 25(4):320–40

Staw BM. 1984. Organizational behavior: a review and reformulation of the field's outcome variables. *Annu. Rev. Psychol.* 35: 627–66

Strati A. 1992. Aesthetic understanding of organizational life. *Acad. Manage. Rev.* 17(3):568–81

Symon G, Clegg CW. 1991. Technology-led change: a study of the implementation of CADCAM *J. Occup. Psychol.* 64:273–90

Széll G, ed. 1992. *Concise Encyclopedia of Participation and Cooperative Management.* Berlin: de Gruyter

Thereau J. 1992. *Le cours dáction: analyse semio-logique.* Bern: Lang

Thierry H. 1992. Which meanings are rewarding? *Am. Behav. Sci.* 35(6):694–707

Turner BA, ed. 1990. *Organizational Symbolism.* Berlin: de Gruyter

Tushman ML, Rosenkopf L. 1992. Organizational determinants of technological change: toward a sociology of technological evolution. *Res. Organ. Behav.* 14:311–47

Van der Schaaf TW, Lucas DA, Hale AR, eds. 1991. *Near Miss Reporting as a Safety Tool.* Oxford: Butterman-Heinemann

von Cranach M, Kalbermatten U, Indermühle K, Gugler B. 1982. *Goal-directed Action.* London: Academic

von Cranach M, Ochsenbein G, Valach L. 1986. The group as a self-active system (outline of a theory of group action). *Eur. J. Soc. Psychol.* 16:193–229

von Rosenstiel L. 1989. Selektions- und Sozialisationseffekte beim Übergang vom Bildungs- ins Beschäftigungssystem. *Z. Arb. Organisationspsychol.* 33(1):21–32

Wall TD, Corbett JM, Clegg CW, Jackson PR, Martin R. 1990. Advanced manufacturing technology and work design: towards a theoretical framework. *J. Organ. Behav.* 11:201–19

Wall TD, Davids K. 1992. Shopfloor work organization and advanced manufacturing technology. *Int. Rev. Ind. Organ. Psychol.* 7:364–98

Wall TD, Jackson PR, Davids K. 1992. Operator work design and robotics system performance: a serendipitous field study. *J. Appl. Psychol.* 77(3):353–62

Walsh JP, Ungson GR. 1991. Organizational memory. *Acad. Manage. Rev.* 16(1):57–91

Weick KE, Roberts KH. 1993. Collective mind in organizations: headful interrelating on flight decks. *Adm. Sci. Q.* 38(3): 357–81

Whyte WF. 1989. Action research for the twenty-first century: participation, reflection, and practice. *Am. Behav. Sci.* 32(5): 513–551

Wilpert B. 1992. Organization-environment relations. In *Organizational and Work Psychology,* ed. J Misumi, B Wilpert, H Motoaki, pp. 66–88. Hove, UK: Erlbaum

Wilpert B. 1994. Konzept der Partizipation in der Arbeits- und Organisationspsychologie. In *Arbeits- und Organisationspsychologie im Spannungsfeld zwischen grundlagenwissenschaftlicher Orientierung und Angewandter Forschung,* ed. W Bungard, T Herrmann, pp. 357–68. Bern: Huber

Wilpert B, Klumb P. 1991. Störfall Biblis A. *Z. Arb.* 45(1):51–54

Wilson F. 1992. Language, technology, gender, and power. *Hum. Relat.* 45(9).883–97

Yammarino FJ, Bass BM. 1991. Person and situation views of leadership: a multiple levels of analysis approach. *Leadership Q.* 2(2):121–39

Yammarino FJ, Spangler WD, Bass BM. 1993. Transformational leadership and performance: a longitudinal investigation. *Leadership Q.* 4:81–102

Zapf D. 1991. Streßbezogene Arbeitsanalyse bei der Arbeit mit unterschiedlichen Bürosoftwaresystemen. *Z. Arb. Organisationspsychol.* 35:2–14

Zenger TR. 1992. Why do employers only reward extreme perfomance? Examining the relationship between performance, pay and turnover. *Adm. Sci. Q.* 37:198–219

Annu. Rev. Psychol. 1995. 46:91–120

LANGUAGE COMPREHENSION:
Sentence and Discourse Processing

Patricia A. Carpenter, Akira Miyake, and Marcel Adam Just

Department of Psychology, Carnegie Mellon University, Pittsburgh, Pennsylvania 15213-3890

KEY WORDS: natural language processing, computational models of language, modularity and interactivity, cognitive architecture, individual and population differences

CONTENTS

INTRODUCTION

Language has been the venue in which several key questions about cognition have been asked. Language was one area in which Lashley examined the problem of serial order in behavior, arguing that the timing and organization of speech could not be explained by pairwise associations. Language was also one of the main battlefields in which the cognitivist perspective, as represented by Chomsky, gained ascendancy over the behaviorist view, represented by Skinner. Whorf, reflecting on the relation of thought to language from a

0066-4308/95/0201-0091$05.00

cross-linguistic perspective, proposed a relation in which some aspects of cognition are subordinated to linguistic organization. Fodor made many of his arguments concerning the modularity of mind in the context of various components of language processing. Language has been considered a prototype of a complex, well-learned, multi-tiered intellectual activity that reflects the fundamental architecture of cognition. As a result, language comprehension research is no longer just an esoteric specialty field, but one among several paths to scientific insight, and perhaps an especially fruitful path at that. In this spirit, this review considers how recent findings on language comprehension have illuminated our understanding of the organization of cognition.

Although the key questions about cognition continue to echo in language research, methodological and theoretical advances provide new answers to old questions, in many cases causing the questions to be recast. More extensive use of on-line methodologies, such as self-paced reading, eye-fixation monitoring, priming, and event-related potentials, provide detailed information about the real-time properties of comprehension, which is, after all, a real-time process. At the same time, theoretical advances, particularly in the computational modeling of comprehension, have enabled the framing of precise and integrated questions about comprehension, many of which are answerable with the new methodologies. Concomitant with these advances, the field has broadened to include language processing in other populations, such as aging adults, aphasics, and deaf signers.

Marr's Analysis

A theoretical framework that is broad and neutral enough to encompass many of the findings we will report is Marr's (1982) analysis of complex information processing devices. Marr proposed that there are three levels at which a complex information processing system (like the human brain) can be understood. We briefly describe these levels here because many of the comprehension phenomena to be discussed later can be illuminated by reference to some of these levels.

The most abstract level, which Marr called computational theory, characterizes the performance of an information-processing device in terms of a goal-oriented mapping between one kind of information and another. For example, this level of understanding of a device that adds natural numbers would map from (3,4) to (7), would follow associative and commutative laws, and would include negative numbers and zero and their special properties. Note that this level would be the same regardless of whether the device was a 5-year-old, an adult, or an electronic calculator. Although Marr formulated his framework to analyze visual cognition, he was well aware of its potential application to language, citing Chomsky's (1965) theory of syntactic competence as a prime example of understanding at the abstract computational level.

At the second level, a task can be analyzed into the representations and algorithms needed to perform the computations specified by the first level. In the domain of language, an example of an algorithm is the procedure that deals with a temporary ambiguity. Consider two apparently contradictory algorithms that have been proposed. One algorithm requires that the comprehender retain both interpretations of the ambiguity until it is later resolved, whereas the other requires that only the more likely interpretation (selected by an embedded algorithm) be retained. Most research in language comprehension (and perhaps in cognitive psychology) addresses this level of understanding, often asking which of several possible algorithms people actually use. At this same level, there are also questions about representation: Some researchers ask how a given linguistic structure is typically represented. It should be noted that algorithms and representations come in pairs, such that a given algorithm is not meaningful unless accompanied by an appropriate representation, and vice versa.

The third level is what Marr called the implementation level—the particular way in which the algorithms and representations are physically realized within some given computational architecture, such as the human mind. Until recently, this level was neglected in language research, perhaps because in Chomsky's bipartite distinction between *competence* and *performance,* the term *performance* fails to distinguish Marr's second and third levels. Many recent findings and emerging principles can be explained best in terms of the implementation level. Although Marr's implementational concerns were related to neurophysiology, the implementational determinants addressed in this review are limitations in the human working memory for language. Such limitations constrain the resources available for both storage and computation.

Computational Architectures for Language

Language research has increasingly been related to computational frameworks that are primarily at Marr's second level (i.e. concerned with algorithms and processes). One type of computational framework has assumed a symbolic architecture, like a production system, in which productions (condition-action rules) are units of procedural knowledge that operate on a working memory, without any central executive. Linguistic rules, such as syntactic parsing rules, can be represented directly in a symbolic system, enabling it to perform the fundamental computations of language, namely to assign an interpretation to a set of familiar representational elements that are in a particular configuration (Fodor & Pylyshyn 1988, Fodor & McLaughlin 1990). In a symbolic system it is straightforward to assign different interpretations to the sentences "John told

Mary" and "Mary told John," or to interpret a recursive structure such as, "John told Mary that he had told her."

A second approach involves the use of connectionist models, which postulate that cognition occurs through a network of linked nodes. The nodes integrate activation through their excitatory and inhibitory links, and they also propagate activation that reflects what they have integrated. This type of model has proven useful in accounting for processing at the level of individual words and inter-word relations and also has been applied to sentence comprehension. There is considerable attractiveness in the concepts of graded representations (nodes at various levels of activation), parallel processing, and the general idea that processing takes place gradually, over time, using mechanisms like activation and suppression. Such concepts help to account for the fine grain of the time course of many component processes of comprehension.

The relative merits of the two computational approaches to language modeling have been debated (Fodor & Pylyshyn 1988, Pinker & Prince 1988; see also Reilly & Sharkey 1992). Symbolic and connectionist approaches contain mechanisms that apparently are relevant to sentence and text comprehension, so it is interesting to consider how the strengths of the two approaches can be combined.

HYBRID MODELS   Symbolic-connectionist hybrid models attempt to meld the combinatorial power of a symbol system with the attributes of the parallel, activation-based, processing system. One hybrid model explores mechanisms for binding together distributed connectionist representations of properties and relations, so that the result is effectively a symbol (Dyer et al 1992). Another type of hybrid uses symbolic rules in conjunction with connectionist-like graded symbols and parallel processing (Just & Carpenter 1992, Kintsch 1988). As important as the choice of model (symbolic, connectionist, or hybrid) is the consideration of constraints imposed by limitations of the human mind (Marr's third level), and how these constraints are accommodated within each type of model. The review of recent findings below on sentence and discourse-level processes indicates which facets of the various models are particulary illuminating.

SENTENCE COMPREHENSION

Because language comprehension is a multi-level process (containing component processes like lexical processing, syntactic analysis, and thematic analysis), it raises the question of how processing at the various levels is coordinated, temporally and functionally. At one extreme, a particular component process or subsystem of comprehension (e.g. syntactic analysis) could operate autonomously of the other processes. This position, called modularity, was clarified by Fodor's (1983) proposal that the mind might contain a set of cognitive modules, each of which is an autonomous subsystem, and in addition, an extremely complex central cognitive system. The research emphasis has been on the modules. Within a module, once a set of initiating conditions starts it on a minimal quantum of processing, it is uninfluenced by certain classes of information that may develop elsewhere in the system. This lack of influence is called informational encapsulation, and it has been proposed as a particularly important distinguishing property of a cognitive module (Garfield 1989). One of Fodor's examples is the encapsulation of motion perception from kinesthetic information. A viewer perceives the world to be moving, even when the perception is caused by the viewer pushing his own eye with his finger; the information about the finger movement apparently is not available to, nor is it used by, the processes that interpret input from the retina, even though some part of the cognitive system knows that the motion is not real. The functional rationale that Fodor offers for encapsulation is that modular systems have to operate rapidly (without allocating time to consider all possible relevant information) and veridically, somewhat like a reflex.

At the other extreme, all subsystems may be completely interactive, continuously taking into account any new relevant information as it is made available by other subsystems, and also making their own outputs available to other subsystems as soon as they are developed. Although these two positions represent extremes of cognitive architecture, they do not define a useful set of research strategies by themselves. Instead, the two extremes help generate a set of second-order research questions about the nature of encapsulation or interaction in various aspects of language processing. One such question concerns the time course over which syntactic, semantic, and pragmatic information interact in contributing to comprehension. Two subsystems whose degree of modularity/interaction have been examined are lexical access and syntactic analysis.

Lexical Ambiguity

Lexical ambiguity research has examined how word-level information interacts with contextual information (see Simpson 1994 for a recent review). The initial data, obtained in cross-modal priming studies, were consistent with the hypothesis that the lexicon constitutes a cognitive module, indicating that immediately after a homograph was read, the response times to both the contextually appropriate and inappropriate meanings were facilitated compared to a neutral control (Swinney 1979). However, lexical access may not be as impervious to contextual influences as was once thought. More recent cross-modal priming studies have demonstrated immediate effects of context, showing that strong biasing contexts can lead to the facilitation of only the contextually appropriate meaning, even immediately after the occurrence of the homograph (Simpson & Krueger 1991, Tabossi & Zardon 1993). An event-related potential study also suggests that, even though both meanings are activated, prior contexts can slow down the activation of contextually inappropriate meanings (Van Petten & Kutas 1987). Rather than treating the modularity or interactivity of lexical access as dichotomous possibilities, current research suggests that the time course of ambiguity resolution is influenced by the strength or type of a prior biasing context (Tabossi 1988) and the relative frequencies of a homograph's multiple meanings (Gorfein & Bubka 1989). Whether or not prior contexts lead to a selective activation of the contextually appropriate meaning depends, at least in part, on the values on these two dimensions.

The conjoint effects of context and relative frequency on the resolution of lexical ambiguity were demonstrated in an eye tracking study with college-age readers (Duffy et al 1988). Neutral contexts or contexts biased toward the subordinate meaning preceded two types of homographs, those with equally frequent interpretations (balanced) and those with one much more frequent interpretation (polarized). In the absence of prior biasing context, readers integrated only the dominant meaning for polarized homographs, but both meanings for balanced homographs, suggesting that the accessing of rare meanings (i.e. the subordinate meaning of a polarized homograph) may not occur quickly enough to permit successful integration. When the context favored the subordinate meaning, however, the opposite pattern of data was obtained, indicating the integration of both meanings for polarized homographs and only the dominant meaning for balanced homographs. These results suggest that the prior contexts had a strong impact such that the meanings of polarized homographs became more or less balanced, whereas those of balanced homographs became polarized. Such data, along with other compatible findings (Dopkins et al 1992, Miyake et al 1994b), specify the conditions under which there appears to be selective access of a single meaning or access of multiple meanings.

Several recent activation-based computational models can naturally capture such findings and provide an important first step toward a coherent and comprehensive account of ambiguity resolution processes (Kawamoto 1993; LC Twilley & P Dixon, submitted). These models characterize ambiguity resolution as a constraint satisfaction process, in which multiple possible interpretations of an ambiguity compete with one another, based on inputs from multiple sources of information, such as context and frequency. When context and frequency provide converging support for a single interpretation of a homograph, usually only that interpretation is highly activated, showing the pattern consistent with selective access. In contrast, when the two factors favor different interpretations, then both interpretations are usually activated in proportion to the amount of support that each interpretation receives. This latter pattern of activation trajectories, consistent with the prevalent view of exhaustive access, has traditionally been considered to reflect the informational encapsulation of the lexical access module in the lexical ambiguity literature. However, the fact that such activation trajectories can also be demonstrated by interactive, constraint satisfaction models provides a challenge for the strictly modular account of lexical access and ambiguity resolution.

Syntactic Processing

The modularity hypothesis applied to the syntactic domain has also provided a rationale for research on the structural aspects of sentence comprehension (Garfield 1989). The hypothesis was that syntactic processing constitutes a module that initially is encapsulated from nonsyntactic information, such as the pragmatic context or real world knowledge, although the pragmatic or semantic information is ultimately brought to bear on the final interpretation. Thus, the primary focus has been on the time course of processing syntactic information.

A second facet of this research area has examined various heuristic-based parsers that are used for mapping from the surface structure of a sentence onto its underlying relations, and have the potential for explaining why similar syntactic structures might differ in difficulty, or why comprehenders may prefer one interpretation of a structurally ambiguous sentence to another. Some of these parsers make specific reference to working memory limitations in the proposed parsing principles (Abney & Johnson 1991, Gibson 1990). One influential model proposed that preferences arise from a limit on the number of structural elements that can be maintained during parsing or from a preference for a simpler geometry in the developing parsing tree (Frazier 1978). A heuristic that has been the topic of considerable research is called minimal attachment, which proposes a preference to introduce the fewest possible new nodes in a parsing representation when attaching a new phrase. For example, consider the incomplete sentence, "The city council argued the mayor's position...." According to this preference, the phrase "the mayor's position" would be interpreted as a simple direct object, rather than the subject of a sentential complement, as in "The city council argued the mayor's position was entirely unsupported," because the former interpretation is structurally simpler. Such specific heuristics, along with the more general hypothesis that syntactic analysis has temporal priority, have been the basis of several studies (see below).

The various proposals for how parsing is implemented can be distinguished along several dimensions. A major dimension is whether or not syntactic processing is assumed to have temporal priority by virtue of its nature (the modularity hypothesis). Thus, are some processes inherently serial or do some circumstances allow for parallel computations of both syntactic and semantic information? Another dimension is the extent to which extra resources are presumed to be required to construct and maintain multiple interpretations (Just & Carpenter 1992, Mitchell 1994). A final dimension that differentiates proposals is the unit of text that is subject to syntactic and semantic analysis before the two levels are presumed to interact. Because comprehension shows strong evidence of immediacy in reading (Just & Carpenter 1980) and listening (Marslen-Wilson & Tyler 1980), the unit may be the individual word for some types of computations. However, some parsing models assume a larger unit of analysis (e.g. three words) (Marcus 1980).

One serial model proposed that only structural information dictated the initial output proposed by the syntactic parser, and that this step was followed by a thematic processor that evaluated the acceptability of the output in light of semantic and pragmatic information (Rayner et al 1983). If the decision of the thematic processor was negative, the syntactic parser presumably went through another iteration and proposed some alternative structure without being influenced by semantics. According to a recent version of this model, a decision to reject an analysis may be delayed until sufficient information is available from the text-based thematic processor (Perfetti 1990). By contrast, a "weak" interactive parallel model hypothesized that the syntactic parser autonomously proposed multiple analyses, while semantic and pragmatic information adjudicated among the alternatives, causing some analyses to be abandoned and others to be pursued (Altmann & Steedman 1988). Other parallel models propose that multiple alternatives may be computed, with no preference necessarily given to the syntactic processes, and that interaction among various sources determines the extent to which a particular interpretation is supported (McClelland et al 1989).

Results of early eye-tracking studies indicated that contextual information did not override the initial preference of the syntactic parsing module (Rayner et al 1983). These studies showed longer initial reading times associated with parts of the sentence that were disambiguated in an unpreferred direction. Consider, for example, one of the most studied syntactic ambiguities, involving the past tense or past participle interpretations, as in the sentence "The defendant *examined* by the lawyer shocked the jury." The verb *examined* is temporarily ambiguous, because it could either be the main verb or, as it turns out, a past participle. One study favoring the modular account of syntactic processing (Ferreira & Clifton 1986) compared such temporarily ambiguous sentences with analogous yet semantically constrained sentences, such as "The evidence *examined* by the lawyer shocked the jury," in which the inanimate status of the head noun (i.e. *evidence*) ruled out the possibility of the main verb interpretation on semantic/pragmatic grounds. Surprisingly, the eye-fixation data suggested that readers showed garden path effects on the first-pass reading of the disambiguating *by*-phrase for both types of sentences, in spite of the potential availability of semantic/pragmatic cues to guide the interpretation in the case of the *evidence* sentence. The lack of immediate influence on the syntactic processing was considered consistent with the informational encapsulation of the syntactic module. Other studies also failed to find an immediate effect on processing time of either pragmatic information (Rayner et al 1992) or biasing contextual information (Mitchell et al 1992).

The data from recent studies present a more complex picture than the modular view of syntactic processing, one that is analogous to the picture for lexical ambiguity. First, individuals differ systematically in whether they show an immediate effect of context on their first-pass reading times on the *by*-phrase following a main verb/past participle ambiguity, depending on their working memory capacity (Just & Carpenter 1992). Second, the properties of the sentences can also have large effects. For example, one self-paced reading time study demonstrated that, depending on the context, the comprehenders' parsing preferences could either be consistent or inconsistent with the minimal attachment heuristic (Taraban & McClelland 1988).

Current research suggests that the frequency information associated with each verb's argument or thematic role structure is another important factor constraining the process of syntactic ambiguity resolution (Boland & Tanenhaus 1991, MacDonald 1994). For example, the verbs *remember* and *claim* can be followed by either a noun phrase complement (e.g. "John remembered my birthday") or a sentence complement (e.g. "John remembered my birthday is coming"). However, *remember* is followed more frequently by a noun phrase complement and *claim* by a sentence complement. A series of studies on syntactic ambiguity resolution found that readers can use such frequency information rapidly, in time to influence their processing of the next word of the sentence (Trueswell et al 1993). Even in the absence of structural ambiguity, the speed of verb processing can be influenced by which argument structure associated with the verb is most frequent or most preferred by the reader (Shapiro et al 1993). A meta-analysis (MacDonald et al 1994) of ten syntactic ambiguity studies suggests that such differences in the strength of the bias associated with the specific verbs may help explain why some studies found an immediate influence of context with the main verb/past participle ambiguity and others did not. The verbs used in the studies that failed to show the immediate effect of context (e.g. Ferreira & Clifton 1986) had significantly lower past participle frequencies (49.7% on average) than did those used in the studies that showed such effects (64.5% on average). These results suggest that the presence of semantic/pragmatic context is more likely to influence the final interpretation when the alternative structural assignments are more evenly matched in frequency.

Some researchers explain away such discrepancies in the data by pointing out that there are methodological differences between the studies that demonstrated the immediate effect of context and those that did not (Clifton & Ferreira 1989). The main claim is that eye-fixation studies provide more sensitive measures of the temporal characteristics of processing than do studies of self-paced word-by-word reading (Rayner et al 1992), and that those studies that used the eye-fixation technique tended to find no immediate effect of context on ambiguity resolution. This methodological point entails an important theoretical one. The answers to many questions about the organization of processes, such as whether two processes are informationally encapsulated from each other, or whether a representation is constructed gradually versus discretely, are relative to the grain size of the measurement and analysis. The grain size of the measurement must be fine enough to resolve the phenomenon of interest.

A more subtle theoretical implication to this methodological point is that the characterization of comprehension needs to take the increasing fineness of grain into account. The formulation of syntactic encapsulation 20 years ago sometimes treated an entire clause as the unit of processing, and the duration of such processing can easily take two seconds or more. However, recent investigations treat the processing of a single word or just the first pass fixations on a word as the unit of analysis. If the temporal resolution is fine enough, the precise answer about encapsulation becomes moot. If syntactic processing turns out to be encapsulated, but only for a few milliseconds, before being influenced by pragmatic information, then it would still be, relative to the time scale of comprehension, a very interactive process. The implicit result from many studies is that comprehension is much more interactive and continuous than was initially suspected or measurable.

It appears likely that in processing a sentence, various alternative representational structures are partially activated, and that the speed of activation depends partly on the relative frequencies of the associated interpretations. The structural alternatives may then be pursued in parallel, at least for some period of time, depending on their support from the prior and subsequent context. Other evidence for parallelism comes from a task involving rapid grammaticality judgments, which requires the subject to read a string of words, and after some brief but variable interval, determine if it is grammatically acceptable (McElree 1993). The critical measure is the accuracy of the judgments as a function of interval length. Specifically, the rate and asymptote of the accuracy function reflects the rate at which evidence accumulates for an interpretation. If the parsing were serial, and if the more frequent interpretation of an ambiguous verb were always tried before the less frequent one, then the rates of the accuracy functions should differ for the two interpretations. The results showed that the functions for the more frequent and less frequent interpretations were similar, which is consistent with the hypothesis that both of the activated interpretations are pursued in parallel.

The suggestion that parsing alternatives are pursued in parallel, at least over some time period, is also consistent with a reading time study that involved the ambiguity between a main verb/reduced relative interpretation (MacDonald et al 1992). Readers with a large working memory capacity for language showed interference from the ambiguity, in the form of longer reading times after an ambiguity and at its point of resolution, when compared to the reading time on an unambiguous sentence. Such results, and others described below, are consistent with the idea that multiple interpretations may be partially activated, that the speed of activation might reflect the relative frequency of the interpretation, as well as the local context, and that the multiple interpretations may be pursued in parallel.

As is the case for lexical ambiguity, the emerging models shift the emphasis of the research from the modular vs nonmodular dichotomy to a more continuous view of how context may influence syntactic analysis. More specifically, these new models emphasize how the processing of an ambiguous word or phrase depends on the simultaneous influence from multiple sources of information, such as the type or strength of the context, and the relative frequencies of the multiple interpretations. Hence, the models suggest that these factors conjointly influence the rapidity with which context can affect the interpretation of an ambiguity. Moreover, several studies suggest that there may be implementational constraints, often manifested in systematic individual differences, on the time course over which context and frequency manifest their influence.

Working Memory and Sentence Processing

Because it is widely acknowledged that resource limitations in working memory affect comprehension, it is particularly important to characterize these limitations within some theoretical model of the system. One recent proposal embeds the resource constraints within an activation-based production system, 3CAPS, in which both processing and information maintenance are fueled by activation (Just & Carpenter 1992). Storage in working memory is fueled by activation because the representational strength of an element (representing a word, phrase, proposition, etc) is determined by its activation level. Activation also underlies the computations, which are performed within a production system architecture. The productions manipulate representational elements by modifying their activation levels or by constructing new elements. The resource constraint is imposed by limiting the total amount of activation available to the system. Any activation shortage can be borne by the storage function, resulting in a functional loss or forgetting of information; by the computational function, resulting in a slow-down in processing; or by both functions. This type of conjoint limitation on processing and storage has been extremely useful in accounting for individual differences and task differences in various language processes such as ambiguity processing and the interaction/encapsulation of syntax and pragmatics (Carpenter et al 1994).

An individual's capacity to simultaneously process and store verbal information, as assessed with a reading-span task (Daneman & Carpenter 1980), correlates with how fast and accurately the individual can process the demanding regions of syntactically complex sentences (King & Just 1991). Working memory capacity also limits how many interpretations of lexical and syntactic ambiguities can be pursued simultaneously (MacDonald et al 1992, Miyake et al 1994b). It may also modulate the individual's ability to rapidly integrate multiple sources of information. In a replication of Ferreira & Clifton's (1986) study, low-capacity readers showed the garden path effects with reduced relative clause sentences (such as "The evidence examined by the lawyer...."). However, high-capacity readers were influenced by the inanimacy of the head noun in interpreting the syntactic ambiguity (Just & Carpenter 1992). Such data suggest that the failure of the pragmatic cue to influence the syntactic processing in some readers could be the result of a capacity constraint, rather than a structural encapsulation. In sum, a variety of studies suggest that resource limitations, that is, an implementational factor, influence processes that were previously thought to reflect structural factors (representations and algorithms).

In contrast to the emphasis on resource limitations, some researchers have pursued a more traditional, structural view of short-term memory. For example, echoing Miller's (1956) classic analysis of short-term memory, some computational models of parsing and discourse comprehension regard working memory as a buffer of fixed size that can passively store, at any given time, a fixed number of items, such as words or propositions (Berwick & Weinberg 1984, Kintsch & van Dijk 1978). In more recent network models of language comprehension, this type of structural constraint has been implemented as the number of nodes that can be active simultaneously (Kintsch 1988). Similarly, a proposal for a variable binding mechanism has also suggested a constraint on the number of variables that can be activated simultaneously (Shastri & Ajjanagadde 1993).

Another working memory approach addresses the short-term phonological memory buffer and rehearsal process that Baddeley (1986) called the articulatory-phonological loop. It is a slave system to the central executive in Baddeley's multi-component model of working memory and is dedicated to the maintenance of articulatory and phonological information. The role of the loop, however, seems to be only secondary in higher-level comprehension processes. Various studies have documented the lack of correlation between language comprehension performance and measures of the capacity of the articulatory loop system, such as digit or word span (Gathercole & Baddeley 1993). An important finding is that severe impairments in this system due to brain damage (resulting in the inability to verbally reproduce more than two or three words or digits) does not necessarily entail severe impairments in sentence comprehension (Martin 1993). One proposal attributes to the articulatory loop a role as a back-up resource that the language system can use when the first-pass analysis of the sentence fails and a second-pass analysis is necessary (Caplan & Waters 1990). In contrast to its role in comprehension, this loop system plays a critical role in learning to read and acquiring vocabulary among children (Gathercole & Baddeley 1993). Although the loop may not be needed to access the meaning of familiar words, phonological codes seem to be activated automatically and temporarily stored in the system, whether the orthography is alphabetic (Daneman & Reingold 1993) or logographic (Zhang & Perfetti 1993, Wydell et al 1993).

Individual and Population Differences

Studies of individual and population differences are not only of practical interest; they are of theoretical importance as well. Systematic variations in performance could indicate which facets of language comprehension performance are consequences of the way in which the human language processing system is implemented, and which are a function of more general architectural factors. Nevertheless, such studies tend to be correlational in nature and, thus, are inherently open to alternative causal interpretations.

INDIVIDUAL DIFFERENCES AMONG COLLEGE-AGE ADULTS   As described above, individual differences among adults have been an important source of constraint on models of sentence processing. One measure of individual differences is performance on the reading span task (Daneman & Carpenter 1980), which assesses the individual's ability to simultaneously process and store verbal information. The measure correlates with the comprehender's reading as well as spoken language comprehension ability among college-age adults (Rankin 1993) and children (Engle et al 1991, Swanson 1992), suggesting that, for most comprehenders, the limiting factors in comprehension are general, rather than being specific to reading.

Another source of individual differences is the efficiency with which one can suppress irrelevant or inappropriate information. For example, less skilled college-age comprehenders are slower in suppressing the contextually inappropriate interpretations of lexical ambiguities (Gernsbacher et al 1990). Such individual differences in the efficiency of inhibitory processes seem to be domain-general and also apply to the processing of nonlinguistic pictorial information (Gernsbacher & Faust 1991), supporting the view that language comprehension shares common mechanisms with other domains of cognition.

EFFECTS OF AGING   Although language functions are commonly believed to be relatively robust to the effects of aging, recent studies have found specific age-correlated deficits (Kemper 1992). The age-related decline is not across-the-board, because older adults often rival younger adults on tasks that mainly require simple retrieval of previously acquired knowledge (e.g. vocabulary tests). The decline seems most apparent in tasks that impose a heavy demand on working memory. For example, age-related differences in auditory comprehension accuracy are almost absent for simple sentences, but are large for more complex sentences, such as relative clause sentences (Kemper & Anagnopoulos 1993, Obler et al 1991). Similarly, an increased rate of speech input is particularly detrimental to elderly adults' comprehension and memory for text when compared to that for young adults (Riggs et al 1993).

Such effects of processing demands on elderly adults suggest that the circumscribed decline in language processing may be attributable, in part, to reductions in working memory capacity (Carpenter et al 1994, Cohen 1988). These reductions may further be mediated by other more micro-level changes, such as reductions in speed of processing (Salthouse 1994), subtle impairments in perceptual processes (MK Pichora-Fuller, BA Schneider & M Daneman, submitted), and the weakening of inhibitory processes (Hasher & Zacks 1988). The suggestion that decrements occur in spite of the accumulation of knowledge and expertise often associated with older age (Morrow et al 1992) indicates that some effects of knowledge and expertise may be separable from implementational constraints, such as working memory constraints, even though these two factors are often correlated and difficult to tease apart.

SYNTACTIC COMPREHENSION DISORDERS IN APHASIA   A recent surge of interest in cognitive neuropsychology has yielded an important body of evidence that illustrates the neurological underpinnings of the human cognitive architecture (Shallice 1988) and, more specifically, the language system (Caplan 1992, Sarno 1991). In explaining language processing deficits in aphasics, particularly with respect to syntactic comprehension disorders (McNeil et al 1991), the research illuminates how language comprehension may be implemented in the brain. Auditory syntactic comprehension is often difficult for aphasic patients, particularly when there are no semantic or pragmatic cues to guide interpretation, as in semantically reversible sentences, like "The boy that the girl is hitting is tall" (Caplan & Hildebrandt 1988). Previous accounts of the deficits have tended to postulate a loss of language-specific knowledge (i.e. competence) that is needed to perform complete syntactic analysis (Berndt & Caramazza 1980). For example, the inability to co-index "traces" (as they are defined within Chomsky's Government and Binding Framework) has been proposed as the source of one particular syntactic comprehension deficit (Grodzinsky 1986).

This trace-deletion hypothesis has been refined in two independent linguistically-sophisticated proposals (Hickok et al 1993, Mauner et al 1993).

In contrast, a new trend is to view aphasic patients' comprehension problems as implementational deficits that originate from severe limitations in their processing capacity or efficiency, rather than from a loss of competence (Frazier & Friederici 1991, Haarmann & Kolk 1991, Miyake et al 1994a). In fact, some patients with relatively intact competence (as indicated by their ability to make reasonably accurate judgments of the grammaticality of sentences) (Linebarger et al 1983, Berndt et al 1988) still demonstrate agrammatic comprehension. Consistent with the hypothesis of an implementational deficit, some aphasic patients show improvements in their syntactic comprehension performance when the speech rate is slowed (Blumstein et al 1985). Furthermore, when the sentence presentation rate is accelerated, even normal adults exhibit some of the key characteristics of aphasic comprehension breakdown, suggesting that reductions in available capacity or available time can similarly degrade comprehension (Miyake et al 1994a). This view has led to an expanded use of on-line studies of language comprehension (Hagoort 1993, Shankweiler et al 1989, Tyler 1992). For example, the results from a word monitoring study indicate that, possibly because of a pathological limitation in cognitive resources used in parsing, patients with Broca's aphasia suffer from abnormally fast "forgetting" of partial products of syntactic analysis (Haarmann & Kolk 1994). This suggests that some aphasic patients' problems may reside mainly in the time course of language comprehension processes. These findings support the view that an account of syntactic comprehension breakdown needs to be based on deficits in the processes by which the preserved structural knowledge base is accessed and deployed in real time.

Recent studies of individuals who use American Sign Language (ASL) and have suffered a left-hemisphere stroke indicate that the subsequent language impairments are analogous to those observed in speech-based languages (Bellugi et al 1993). The initial results suggest that the language-specific functions of ASL, despite their spatial and gestural modality, tend to be lateralized in the left hemisphere, as they are for a majority of aphasics who use spoken language. Current studies of impaired signers support the hypothesis of an implementation-based impairment, consistent with the hypothesis as applied to aphasics who use spoken language. For example, a case study of the deficits of a native signer suffering from Parkinson's disease indicated that although the patient had spared linguistic knowledge, some implementational limitation (in this case, associated with production) severely restricted his ability to access or use this knowledge (Brentari & Poizner 1994).

SENTENCE PROCESSING PROBLEMS AMONG CHILDREN   Another domain that reflects a similar trend toward performance constraints concerns comprehension difficulty among children with reading disabilities. Their problems are not always specific to word decoding, and some children have difficulty comprehending complex spoken sentences as well. Previously, the auditory comprehension problem was thought to arise from a delay in the acquisition of complex syntactic structures (Stein et al 1984). However, reducing the processing demands by introducing presentation changes can elicit better comprehension performance from poor readers on the same problematic sentence types (Smith et al 1989). With appropriate pragmatic settings, poor readers can also be induced to produce, as successfully as good readers, the exact syntactic structures they have difficulty comprehending (Bar-Shalom et al 1993). These findings suggest that poor readers already have knowledge of complex sentence structures, but some implementational factors restrict their ability to use this knowledge.

Cross-linguistic Studies

Cross-linguistic studies provide important information that distinguishes those aspects of comprehension that are specific to one language, typically English, from those that reflect more general principles of language processing. Cuetos & Mitchell (1988) examined whether the principle of late closure, a parsing heuristic proposed for English, also exists for Spanish. The late closure principle posits that, in sentences such as "Andrew had dinner yesterday with the niece of the teacher who belonged to the Communist party," comprehenders tend to attach the relative clause, "who belonged to the Communist party," to the teacher, the latter of the two candidate noun phrases, rather than to the niece, yielding the interpretation that the teacher is a Communist, not the niece. Reading-time data from native speakers of English support the existence of such a preference. Interestingly, however, native speakers of Spanish reading equivalent Spanish sentences tended to attach the relative clause to the earlier noun phrase (i.e. the niece). The predominance of the early closure for this sentence type in Spanish indicates that the late closure is not a universal principle that applies to all languages and all sentence constructions.

MacWhinney & Bates (1989) examined how different types of cues are weighed in the interpretation of sentences in a wide range of languages. According to their model, one facet of sentence interpretation is viewed as the competition and convergence of multiple cues that are processed concurrently, including cues that are semantic (such as animacy), grammatical (such as word order), and morphological (such as number agreement). When different cues provide conflicting information regarding the interpretation of a sentence, the relative strengths of the cues determine the final interpretation, according to a constraint-satisfaction algorithm. Language acquisition entails the adjustment of weights associated with various types of cues, weights that differ from language to language. When subjects are asked to indicate which noun phrase is the agent of a pseudo-sentence, like "The pencils the cow are kicking," in which the different cues are pitted against each other, the dominance order among cues varies across languages. For example, English listeners are highly influenced by word order, but Hungarian listeners rely heavily on inflectional markers. A comparable study of Chinese, which has little inflectional morphology, indicates that, rather than relying on one dominant cue, Chinese listeners use a variety of cues in complex configurations. For example, cues in Chinese are ordered from strongest to weakest as follows: passive marker (*bei*) > animate noun > word order > object marker (*ba*) > indefinite marker (*yi*) (Li et al 1993). The fact that the ordering interweaves several types of cues, morphosyntactic, syntactic, and semantic, is also consistent with the claim that such cues interact to determine interpretation.

This paradigm has been applied to a variety of language-related processes, including sentence production (Sridhar 1989) and second language acquisition (Heilenman & McDonald 1993, Sasaki 1994). Also, a series of studies of language breakdown among aphasics has been conducted within this framework (see Bates et al 1991 for an overview). This aphasia work has demonstrated that the difference among patient groups (e.g. Broca's vs Wernicke's aphasics) has less impact on performance than does the difference among languages. Aphasics tend to preserve the relative weights associated with different cues in their native language.

Conceptual Combination and Integration

Beyond activating information, comprehension centrally involves what is sometimes called conceptual combination or integration. The computational issue is highlighted by considering the comprehension of novel phrases or metaphors, or a familiar word used in a different way. The proposals bring to the forefront the crucial role of world knowledge in language interpretation.

Recent hypotheses concerning the mechanisms underlying combination assume that a word's representation has considerable internal structure, using the notion of a schema with slots and fillers. The internal structure of a noun concept, for example, could include features (such as color, function) and possible values (such as red, food), and in some models (Smith et al 1988), information about the value's salience or frequency and the feature's diagnosticity in distinguishing the concept from related concepts. One model of noun-noun combination also makes considerable reference to world knowledge in a two-stage process (Murphy 1990). To interpret a novel phrase, such as *elephant tie,* one of the features of the head noun is given a value specified by the modifying term. But what feature of *tie* is to be modified? In the example of *elephant tie,* is it the owner, the function, or the size? The choice of feature to modify may depend on a feature's typicality or on context or general knowledge. World knowledge is also invoked in a postulated elaboration stage that involves subsequently refining the representation of the combination. The slot filling mechanism may be too limited to accommodate all of the novel noun-noun interpretation processes. Wisniewski & Gentner (1991) invoke reasoning mechanisms that are used in analogical reasoning, including the mapping between relational structures. For example, to interpret a *pony chair* as a "small chair," the subjects are apparently mapping the size feature of ponies relative to their superordinate (horses) and attributing that property to chairs.

The combinatorial issue is also central to the comprehension of figurative language, such as metaphors. Several taxonomic theories have been proposed for clarifying the relation among various types of figurative language, such as metaphors, similes, and comparisons (Ortony 1979, Tourangeau & Rips 1991). For example, one recent proposal is that metaphors, such as "My job is a jail," are class-inclusion statements, in which the vehicle term (e.g. *jail*) functions as a stand-in name for a category (Glucksberg & Keysar 1990). The taxonomic relations among various types of figurative expressions are still unclear. However, one informative and repeatedly examined issue in this domain is the overall time course of comprehending figurative language. Several studies using a variety of figurative constructions have found that the comprehension of figurative statements does not take longer than does the comprehension of their literal counterparts (Pollio et al 1990). Such results suggest strongly that figurative comprehension does not entail constructing a complete literal interpretation before consulting world knowledge. Perhaps several interpretations are computed in parallel, and at some point during the on-line comprehension process, the world knowledge is sufficiently salient to override the literal interpretation.

Pragmatics also provides a compatible perspective on concept combinatorics and on the importance of world knowledge (Green 1989). Even the comprehension of everyday, relatively simple constructions can entail inferences that override the literal interpretation (Clark 1993). For example, a cafe waitress might say to the cook, "The ham sandwich wants an order of fries," which would be perfectly comprehensible, in spite of the novel mapping between the phrase *ham sandwich* and its customer referent. From this perspective, the comprehension process is shaped fundamentally by the listener's knowledge of the situation, including the inferred goals of the speaker. World knowledge must be rapidly available and sufficiently salient to dominate other knowledge sources. This perspective brings the process of language comprehension into the domain of general thinking.

DISCOURSE COMPREHENSION

Discourse comprehension requires that mental connections be made between various parts of a text in order to understand it. A pair of easily comprehensible sentences, "John had a severe headache. He went to check the medicine cabinet," illustrates this point. The major research issues concern the mechanisms and algorithms with which such connections are made. There are two important and related points about the connections that readers have to make to generate the coherence among the sentences of a text. First, the knowledge basis on which these types of connections are made is often knowledge of the world, rather than knowledge of language per se. Second, an indefinitely large number of connections could be inferred, and the challenge is to specify which subset of connections are made, and what modulates the size and nature of the subset.

Establishing Coherence

Research on discourse processing has traditionally asked what types of inferences are drawn during reading and under what circumstances they are drawn. The empirical research has focused on the types of inferences (e.g. instrumental, causal) highly likely to be drawn (see Graesser & Bower 1990, Singer 1990). For example, a sentence that describes someone sweeping a floor invites the inference that a broom was the instrument used. Should a subsequent sentence mention the word *broom,* having made the inference would facilitate a connection between the two instances of *broom,* one of which was only implicit. Clearly, many such inferences could be drawn, but do readers draw them all when they are reading normally? Although there have been attempts to characterize the types of inferences that are typically drawn, the research discussed below suggests that the evolving theory must also take into account the information's salience (McKoon & Ratcliff 1992a). Inferences, like other types of linguistic information, should be viewed as having graded activation (Murray et al 1993) over a time course.

In answer to the question of what inferences are drawn, a minimalist position, outlined by McKoon & Ratcliff (1992a), claims that in normal reading, the only inferences made automatically are those required to establish local (typically, sentence-to-sentence) coherence and those lexical-level inferences that are based on well-known general knowledge (such as the relation between "the dog" and "the collie") (Fletcher & Bloom 1988). According to this view, a reader may make other elaborative inferences and establish global coherence only under special circumstances, for example, as a result of specific goal-directed strategies. McKoon & Ratcliff (1992a) contrast this minimalist position with a constructivist position, in which more elaborate inferences, including global coherence, are routinely constructed to instantiate a detailed representation of the situation or logic of the narrative or to link disparate parts of the text.

Although several studies reported in McKoon & Ratcliff (1992a) found no evidence for automatic encoding of constructivist inferences, the contrast between the minimalist and constructivist positions is complicated by the fact that theories in the latter category vary in what type of knowledge they posit to be necessary for establishing global coherence. In one approach, particular types of information are assumed to be needed for global coherence by virtue of the roles they have in an abstract relational structure, such as a schema, text grammar, script, or memory organization packets (MOP). Causal relations have been deemed particulary important for global coherence in several models of text comprehension, supported in part by the behavioral data showing that readers are relatively fast to verify and likely to recall causal propositions and their inferential links (Singer et al 1992, Trabasso & Suh 1993, van den Broek 1990).

In a second approach, the representational organization is provided by a mental model, which is a higher-level representation of a situation described in a text, in which the dynamics of a physical or functional interaction are symbolized (Johnson-Laird 1983). This mental model, based on text information and knowledge of the world, is constructed in parallel with a meaning representation of the text itself that may preserve the text's linguistic properties. Consider the following passage: "John was preparing for a marathon in August. After doing a few warm-up exercises, he *put on/took off* his sweatshirt and went jogging. He jogged halfway around the lake without too much difficulty...." According to the mental model framework, the concept of *sweatshirt* should be differentially available in the two versions of the text, because only in the *put on* version would the sweatshirt remain in the activated portion of the mental model. A probe recognition study found that the verification times to a probe such as *sweatshirt* at the end of the text were indeed faster when the protagonist and the target object were in physical proximity (e.g. when John put on his sweatshirt before jogging) than when they were spatially segregated (e.g. when he took it off) (Glenberg et al 1987). This result supports the conclusion that comprehenders may construct a mental model that includes detailed spatial information (Morrow et al 1989, Taylor & Tversky 1992).

Although much of the work on mental models has been in the spatial domain, other researchers argue that the underlying processes are much more general. Several types of nonspatial information may also be part of the representation of a situation or mental model: for example, procedures (Glenberg & Langston 1992), the main character's emotional states (Gernsbacher & Robertson 1992), and goal information (Huitema et al 1993). Similar processes may evoke the generation of a mental empathetic commentary in reaction to a protagonist's likely successes or failures (Allbritton & Gerrig 1991).

Related pictures may aid the construction of a mental model by facilitating the accessibility of certain information in working memory (Glenberg & Langston 1992). Some aspects of mental model construction can be inferred from the way pictures and texts are inspected during reading. In a study of readers' eye fixations as they read descriptions of various pulley systems and scanned a diagram of the described system (Hegarty & Just 1993), diagram inspection patterns were interwoven with the text reading. One type of inspection, confined to a small number of pulley components, seemed to be used to obtain details about a particular component, to establish coreference between text phrases and parts of the diagram, and to help in converting the text-based representation to a mental model of the components. Another type of pattern encompassed more pulley system components, with repeated gazes on components, and longer times on each, and may reflect the integration of the component representations into a more complete mental model.

Constructing a mental model sometimes helps comprehenders maintain coherence at both a local and global level. In one study, for example, subjects read a passage in which the information contained in an initial sentence (e.g. that the protagonist is inside a building) was contradicted by a critical sentence that occurred several sentences later (O'Brien & Albrecht 1992). The readers experienced difficulty comprehending the critical sentence, even though it was perfectly consistent with immediately preceding sentences. Thus, comprehenders can and do establish some aspect of global coherence, even when local coherence is maintained, particularly if the global information is salient. On the other hand, there are boundary conditions on when minor aspects of the situation are likely to be represented and actively updated. Obviously, readers do not always keep track of the spatial location of objects that have been mentioned in a narrative. Readers are only likely to construct and update a representation of spatial relations among objects if the task explicitly requires them to keep track of a protagonist's location within a situation (Wilson et al 1992).

The apparent conflict between the minimalist and constructivist positions may be resolved by considering other determinants of inference-making (besides inference type), such as the salience of the information relevant to the to-be-made inference in a particular context (McKoon & Ratcliff 1992a), the time course of the inferential process (Murray et al 1993), and its dependence on working memory capacity (Whitney et al 1991).

When connecting inferences are activated, the information need not remain activated throughout the processing of the remainder of the text. The constructed information may be activated only for a short time, while it is potentially relevant to the focus of the passage (Millis & Just 1994, Murray et al 1993, Whitney et al 1992). In contrast to earlier studies indicating that predictive inferences were not generated by readers (Potts et al 1988), several newer studies have emphasized that such information appears to be relatively accessible but only for a brief time. For example, a study that used a word-naming task to probe for predictive inferences found facilitation for probes that occurred immediately after the relevant information, but no facilitation for probes that were delayed until after a 7-s interference task (Keefe & McDaniel 1993). Hence, predictive inferences are not "made" or "not made," so much as they are temporarily and provisionally accessible. Whether or not the information becomes part of the final representation may depend on how the text unfolds, on the task, and on other factors that influence whether or not the information is maintained in working memory so that it can be integrated with other information.

Working memory capacity emerges as a central construct in explaining the conditions under which comprehenders can maintain both local and global coherence. Capacity was evoked as an explanation for the differential ways of coping with a demanding passage by high-capacity and low-capacity college readers (Whitney et al 1991). In this study, the stimulus passages were filled with vaguely specified referents and actions (e.g. *things* and *do*) so that neither the overall topic nor the specific events and references could be inferred easily. The think-aloud protocols describing the developing interpretations indicated that low-capacity readers faced a trade-off between constructing a globally coherent interpretation of the passage and maintaining local sentence-to-sentence coherence. Some low-capacity readers committed themselves to a particular global interpretation early in the text and forced the remaining text to fit into it, whereas other low-capacity readers opted for local coherence and frequently changed their global interpretations as they read, without being able to figure out what the entire passage was about. In contrast, high-capacity readers produced protocols indicating that they considered more cues and delayed their commitment to a final interpretation until later in the passage. Such differences suggest that resource constraints are partial determinants of whether the reader establishes global coherence during reading. Several studies conducted with children also conclude that limitations in working memory capacity may account for some young readers' problems in text comprehension, particularly their problems in establishing global coherence and detecting inconsistencies in the text (Yuill et al 1989).

In sum, a sharply drawn contrast between a minimalist and constructivist position does not capture the complexity of discourse comprehension. The extent to which readers maintain global coherence may depend on the ease of accessing the representational structure that permits such an organization, as well as the reader's goals, knowledge, and working memory capacity. Finally, research from both minimalist and constructivist perspectives indicates that such inferences are best construed as graded in their accessibility over the time course of comprehension.

Algorithms in Text Comprehension

Computational modelers have also been interested in how a language comprehension system can make the right type and right number of connections to process a discourse. The connections to be made are among parts of the text representation, but these connections typically are mediated by a representation of some relevant world knowledge. What types of mechanisms allow such connections to be made? The mechanism that cognitive psychologists often invoke in theories of discourse comprehension is spreading activation, which is an instance of a more general mechanism called marker passing, both of which entail the passing of a marker from one representational element in a data-structure to another element (Hendler 1986). In the *headache–medicine cabinet* example above, the relation between the two expressions would presumably be mediated by knowledge that headaches are undesirable pains and that medicine cabinets are a location for getting appropriate pain relievers. The mediation would occur when activation spreads between the representations of the two initial expressions and somehow intersects or defines an interconnecting path. Although spreading activation makes sense at the abstract level of the computational theory, the underlying algorithms, let alone their implementation, are far from obvious. Marker passing in a large network is hard to keep track of because of a potential combinatorial explosion between source and destination elements of the markers (Fahlman 1979). Just as *headache* and *medicine cabinet* could be related through other paths (e.g. hitting one's head on the medicine cabinet), there could be many sources and destinations for markers in the representation of a longer text.

Several algorithms have been proposed to cope with this marker-passing explosion problem. One model draws on an analogy to neural firing rates to suggest that rate be used as an indexical marker. Specifically, feature patterns that all refer to the same concept could be temporarily bound together and, consequently, act as a unit by virtue of having a synchronous firing rate (Shastri & Ajjanagadde 1993). Shastri & Ajjanagadde argue that such variable binding enables their model to account for what they call reflexive reasoning, making easily available linguistic inferences. For example, consider the sentence "John gave the book to Mary." A unit (or set of units) representing *John* will fire in synchrony, and at a phase that distinguishes it from *Mary.* Moreover, prior relations appropriately link the construct of *giving* to the concept of *recipient,* instantiating the knowledge that if someone is given something, then they possess it. The assumptions that Shastri & Ajjanagadde make about the specific properties of the temporal binding window and the speed of neural firing turn out to limit the number of variables that can be distinguished to approximately five. This property is consistent with the classical short-term memory limitations.

Another model, the construction-integration model, proposes a specific algorithm for using marker passing in text comprehension (Kintsch 1988). The model has two main phases of processing. In the construction phase, possible connections between the input propositions are generated fairly indiscriminately based on argument overlap, propositional embedding, and highly likely implications, such as a consequence of some event. The integration phase uses a connectionist-like settling algorithm to prune away the irrelevant activations and to converge on a set of connections that define the final inter-propositional connectivity. The final set of activations then can predict some performance measures, such as the probability of recall of a given proposition.

The central assumption concerning resource constraints in Kintsch's (1988) model is that only propositions that reside in working memory simultaneously can be connected. The mechanism that permits connection between different sentences is a limited buffer (typically having a capacity of two propositions) in which propositions emanating from an earlier portion of a text can be carried forward. Thus, whether or not a proposition is carried forward has a crucial effect on whether it can be integrated. A variant of Kintsch's model, implemented on the capacity-constrained architecture called 3CAPS (Just & Carpenter 1992), replaces the fixed, two-slot buffer with an overall constraint on available resources, which in turn determines which and how many propositions are carried over to the next cycle (Goldman & Varma 1994).

The computational work indicates that it is unlikely that marker passing is indiscriminate and unconstrained, thereby posing questions about the nature of the constraint and the nature of the algorithm (Hendler 1986). For example, does marker passing indicate only connectedness between two nodes? Or does it also provide information about the connecting path? If so, what is this information? Are all the intermediate nodes along the path also activated (McKoon & Ratcliff 1992b; McNamara 1992)? Although the nature of the implementation is different in humans and computers, computational modeling helps define an interesting set of questions for discourse research concerning the algorithm for relating concepts in a text.

Another contribution to discourse processing from the perspective of computational models is that connecting inferences, like other propositions, can be graded in their level of activation, reflecting their degree of support (St. John 1992, Kintsch 1988). Such gradedness allows the process and product to be conditional on the degree of textual support and availability of resources, providing a mechanism for integrating connecting inferences from different domains and for gracefully altering expectations if new contradictory information is encountered.

Recent research suggests that discourse comprehension issues might be reformulated in three ways. First, connective inferences, like other types of information, may vary in the strength with which they are represented, rather than being either present or absent. Second, like other types of information, the activation of a connective inference has a time course. Consequently, whether or not it is accessible depends on when it is probed or what other information is processed subsequently. Third, readers' goals and their working memory capacity may influence the amount and perhaps the type of inferences that are temporarily activated.

CONCLUSIONS

Many of the accounts of sentence and text comprehension are converging on a common set of principles that underlie general cognitive mechanisms. One converging principle is that the representation of information is graded, such that it can be in intermediate states other than present or absent. Furthermore, a representation's construction and decay may be gradual rather than discrete. A second, related principle concerns the mechanisms of spreading activation (or in its more general form, marker passing) and suppression, which operate in language, as they have been shown to operate in various motor and sensory modalities, such as visual perception. These mechanisms provide a gradedness of processing to accompany the gradedness of representation. Gradedness is inherent in connectionist models, but it is also entirely compatible with symbolic models. A third principle concerns resource constraint. Limitations on cognitive resources can account for many types of individual differences and processing strategies in language comprehension, but language is surely not the only domain in which such limitations exist. These central principles in the psychology of language comprehension are likely the hallmarks of all of cognition.

ACKNOWLEDGMENTS

The writing of this article was supported by the National Institute of Mental Health grant MH29617 and Research Scientist Awards MH00661 and MH00662 to Patricia A. Carpenter and Marcel Adam Just.

Literature Cited

Abney SP, Johnson M. 1991. Memory requirements and local ambiguities of parsing strategies. *J. Psycholinguist. Res.* 20:233–50

Allbritton DW, Gerrig RJ. 1991. Participatory responses in text understanding. *J. Mem. Lang.* 30:603–26

Altmann G, Steedman M. 1988. Interaction with context during human sentence processing. *Cognition* 30:191–238

Baddeley AD. 1986. *Working Memory.* New York: Oxford Univ. Press

Bar-Shalom EG, Crain S, Shankweiler D. 1993. A comparison of comprehension and production abilities of good and poor readers. *Appl. Psycholinguist.* 14:197–227

Bates E, Wulfeck B, MacWhinney B. 1991. Cross-linguistic research in aphasia: an overview. *Brain Lang.* 41:123–48

Bellugi U, Poizner H, Klima ES. 1993. Language, modality and the brain. In *Brain Development and Cognition,* ed. M Johnson, pp. 403–23. London: Blackwell

Berndt RS, Caramazza A. 1980. A redefinition of the syndrome of Broca's aphasia: implications for a neuropsychological model of language. *Appl. Psycholinguist.* 1:225–78

Berndt RS, Salasoo A, Mitchum CC, Blumstein SE. 1988. The role of intonation cues in aphasic patients' performance of the grammaticality judgment task. *Brain Lang.* 34:65–97

Berwick RC, Weinberg AS. 1984. *The Grammatical Basis of Linguistic Performance.* Cambridge, MA: MIT Press

Blumstein SE, Katz B, Goodglass H, Shrier R, Dworetsky B. 1985. The effects of slowed speech on auditory comprehension in aphasia. *Brain Lang.* 24:246–65

Boland J, Tanenhaus MK. 1991. The role of lexical representations in sentence processing. In *Understanding Word and Sentence,* ed. GB Simpson, pp. 331–66. Amsterdam: North-Holland

Brentari D, Poizner H. 1994. A phonological analysis of a Parkinsonian signer. *Lang. Cogn. Process.* 9:69–99

Caplan D. 1992. *Language: Structure, Processing, and Disorders.* Cambridge, MA: MIT Press

Caplan D, Hildebrandt N. 1988. *Disorders of Syntactic Comprehension.* Cambridge, MA: MIT Press

Caplan D, Waters GS. 1990. Short-term memory and language comprehension: a critical review of the neuropsychological literature. In *Neuropsychological Impairments of Short-term Memory,* ed. G Vallar, T Shallice, pp. 337–89. New York: Cambridge Univ. Press

Carpenter PA, Miyake A, Just MA. 1994. Working memory constraints in comprehension: evidence from individual differences, aphasia, and aging. In *Handbook of Psycholinguistics,* ed. M Gernsbacher, pp. 1075–1122. San Diego, CA: Academic

Chomsky N. 1965. *Aspects of the Theory of Syntax.* Cambridge, MA: MIT Press

Clark HH. 1993. *Arenas of Language Use.* Chicago: Univ. Chicago Press

Clifton C Jr, Ferreira F. 1989. Ambiguity in context. *Lang. Cogn. Process.* 4:77–103

Cohen G. 1988. Age differences in memory for texts: production deficiency or processing limitations? In *Language, Memory, and Aging,* ed. LL Light, DM Burke, pp. 171–90. New York: Cambridge Univ. Press

Cuetos F, Mitchell DC. 1988. Cross-linguistic differences in parsing: restrictions on the use of Late Closure strategy in Spanish. *Cognition* 30:73–105

Daneman M, Carpenter PA. 1980. Individual differences in working memory and reading. *J. Verb. Learn. Verb. Behav.* 19:450–66

Daneman M, Reingold E. 1993. What eye fixations tell us about phonological recoding during reading. *Can. J. Exp. Psychol.* 47:153–78

Dopkins S, Morris RK, Rayner K. 1992. Lexical ambiguity and eye fixations in reading: a test of competing models of lexical ambiguity resolution. *J. Mem. Lang.* 31:461–76

Duffy SA, Morris RK, Rayner K. 1988. Lexical ambiguity and fixation times in reading. *J. Mem. Lang.* 27:429–46

Dyer MG, Flowers M, Wang YA. 1992. Distributed symbol discovery through symbol recirculation: toward natural language processing in distributed connectionist networks. In *Connectionist Approaches to Natural Language Processing,* ed. RG Reilly, NE Sharkey, pp. 21–48. Hillsdale, NJ: Erlbaum

Engle RW, Carullo JJ, Collins KW. 1991. Individual differences in working memory for comprehension and following directions. *J. Educ. Res.* 84:253–62

Fahlman SE. 1979. *NETL: A System for Representing and Using Real World Knowledge.* Cambridge, MA: MIT Press

Ferreira F, Clifton C Jr. 1986. The independence of syntactic processing. *J. Mem. Lang.* 25:348–68

Fletcher CR, Bloom CP. 1988. Causal reasoning in the comprehension of simple narrative texts. *J. Mem. Lang.* 27:235–44

Fodor JA. 1983. *The Modularity of Mind.* Cambridge, MA: MIT Press

Fodor JA, McLaughlin BP. 1990. Connectionism and the problem of systematicity: why Smolensky's solution doesn't work. *Cognition* 35:183–204

Fodor JA, Pylyshyn ZW. 1988. Connectionism and cognitive architecture: a critical analysis. *Cognition* 28:3–71

Frazier L. 1978. *On comprehending sentences: syntactic parsing strategies.* PhD thesis. Univ. Conn., Distr. by Ind. Univ. Linguist. Club

Frazier L, Friederici A. 1991. On deriving the properties of agrammatic comprehension. *Brain Lang.* 40:51–66

Garfield JL, ed. 1989. *Modularity in Knowledge Representation and Natural-Language Understanding.* Cambridge, MA: MIT Press

Gathercole SE, Baddeley AD. 1993. *Working Memory and Language.* Hillsdale, NJ: Erlbaum

Gernsbacher MA, Faust ME. 1991. The mechanism of suppression: a component of general comprehension skill. *J. Exp. Psychol.: Learn. Mem. Cogn.* 17:245–62

Gernsbacher MA, Robertson RRW. 1992. Knowledge activation versus sentence mapping when representing fictional characters' emotional states. *Lang. Cogn. Process.* 7:353–71

Gernsbacher MA, Varner KR, Faust M. 1990. Investigating differences in general comprehension skill. *J. Exp. Psychol.: Learn. Mem. Cogn.* 16:430–45

Gibson E. 1990. Recency preferences and garden-path effects. In *The Proceedings of the Twelfth Annual Conference of the Cognitive Science Society,* pp. 372–79. Hillsdale, NJ: Erlbaum

Glenberg AM, Langston WE. 1992. Comprehension of illustrated text: pictures help to build mental models. *J. Mem. Lang.* 31:129–51

Glenberg AM, Meyer M, Lindem K. 1987. Mental models contribute to foregrounding during text comprehension. *J. Mem. Lang.* 26:69–83

Glucksberg S, Keysar B. 1990. Understanding metaphorical comparisons: beyond similarity. *Psychol. Rev.* 97:3–18

Goldman SR, Varma S. 1994. CAPing the construction-integration model of discourse comprehension. In *Discourse Comprehension: Models of Processing Revisited,* ed. C Weaver, S Mannes, C Fletcher. Hillsdale, NJ: Erlbaum. In press

Gorfein DS, Bubka A. 1989. A context-sensitive frequency-based theory of meaning achievement. In *Resolving Semantic Ambiguity,* ed. DS Gorfein, pp. 84-106. New York: Springer-Verlag

Graesser AC, Bower GH, eds. 1990. *The Psychology of Learning and Motivation: Inferences and Text Comprehension.* San Diego, CA: Academic

Green GM. 1989. *Pragmatics and Natural Language Understanding.* Hillsdale, NJ: Erlbaum

Grodzinsky Y. 1986. Language deficits and the theory of syntax. *Brain Lang.* 27:135–59

Haarmann HJ, Kolk HHJ. 1991. A computer model of the temporal course of agrammatic sentence understanding: the effects of variation in severity and sentence complexity. *Cogn. Sci.* 15:49–87

Haarmann HJ, Kolk HHJ. 1994. On-line sensitivity to subject-verb agreement violations in Broca's aphasics: the role of syntactic complexity and time. *Brain Lang.* 46:493–516

Hagoort P. 1993. Impairments of lexical-semantic processing in aphasia: evidence from the processing of lexical ambiguities. *Brain Lang.* 45:189–232

Hasher L, Zacks R. 1988. Working memory, comprehension, and aging: a review and a new view. In *The Psychology of Learning and Motivation,* ed. GH Bower, 22:193–225. New York: Academic

Hegarty M, Just MA. 1993. Constructing mental models of machines from text and diagrams. *J. Mem. Lang.* 32:717–42

Heilenman LK, McDonald JL. 1993. Processing strategies in L2 learners of French: the role of transfer. *Lang. Learn.* 43:507–57

Hendler J. 1986. *Issues in the design of marker-passing systems.* Tech. Rep. TR-1636. College Park: Dept. Comput. Sci., Univ. Maryland

Hickok G, Zurif E, Canseco-Gonzales E. 1993. Structural description of agrammatic comprehension. *Brain Lang.* 45:371–95

Huitema JS, Dopkins S, Klin CM, Myers JL. 1993. Connecting goals and actions during reading. *J. Exp. Psychol.: Learn. Mem. Cogn.* 19:1053–60

Johnson-Laird PN. 1983. *Mental Models.* Cambridge, MA: Harvard Univ. Press

Just MA, Carpenter PA. 1980. A theory of reading: from eye fixations to comprehension. *Psychol. Rev.* 87:329–54

Just MA, Carpenter PA. 1992. A capacity theory of comprehension: individual differences in working memory. *Psychol. Rev.* 99:122–49

Kawamoto AH. 1993. Nonlinear dynamics in the resolution of lexical ambiguity: a parallel distributed processing account. *J. Mem. Lang.* 32:474–516

Keefe D, McDaniel MA. 1993. The time course and durability of predictive inferences. *J. Mem. Lang.* 32:446–63

Kemper S. 1992. Language and aging. In *The Handbook of Aging and Cognition,* ed. FIM Craik, TA Salthouse, pp. 213-70. Hillsdale, NJ: Erlbaum

Kemper S, Anagnopoulos C. 1993. Adult use of discourse constraints on syntactic processing. In *Adult Information Processing: Limits on Loss,* ed. J Cerella, J Rybash, W Hoyer, ML Commons, pp. 489–507. San Diego, CA: Academic

King J, Just MA. 1991. Individual differences in syntactic processing: the role of working memory. *J. Mem. Lang.* 30:580–602

Kintsch W. 1988. The role of knowledge in discourse comprehension: a construction-integration model. *Psychol. Rev.* 95:163–82

Kintsch W, van Dijk TA. 1978. Toward a model of text comprehension and production. *Psychol. Rev.* 85:363–94

Li P, Bates E, MacWhinney B. 1993. Processing a language without inflections: a reaction time study of sentence interpretation in Chinese. *J. Mem. Lang.* 32:169–92

Linebarger MC, Schwartz MF, Saffran EM. 1983. Sensitivity to grammatical structure in so-called agrammatic aphasics. *Cognition* 13:361–92

MacDonald MC. 1994. Probabilistic constraints and syntactic ambiguity resolution. *Lang. Cogn. Process.* 9:157–201

MacDonald MC, Just MA, Carpenter PA. 1992. Working memory constraints on the processing of syntactic ambiguity. *Cogn. Psychol.* 24:56–98

MacDonald MC, Pearlmutter NJ, Seidenberg MS. 1994. Syntactic ambiguity resolution as lexical ambiguity resolution. In *Perspectives on Sentence Processing,* ed. C Clifton, L Frazier, K Rayner, pp. 123-53. Hillsdale, NJ: Erlbaum

MacWhinney B, Bates E. 1989. *The Cross-Linguistic Study of Sentence Processing.* New York: Cambridge Univ. Press

Marcus MP. 1980. *A Theory of Syntactic Recognition for Natural Language.* Cambridge, MA: MIT Press

Marr D. 1982. *Vision.* San Francisco, CA: Freeman

Marslen-Wilson W, Tyler LK. 1980. The temporal structure of spoken language understanding. *Cognition* 8:1–71

Martin RC. 1993. Short-term memory and sentence processing: evidence from neuropsychology. *Mem. Cogn.* 21:176–83

Mauner G, Fromkin VA, Cornell TL. 1993. Comprehension and acceptability judgments in agrammatism: descriptions in the syntax of referential dependency. *Brain Lang.* 45:340–70

McClelland JL, St. John MF, Taraban R. 1989. Sentence comprehension: a parallel distributed processing approach. *Lang. Cogn. Process.* 4:287–335

McElree B. 1993. The locus of lexical preference effects in sentence comprehension: a time-course analysis. *J. Mem. Lang.* 32: 536–71

McKoon G, Ratcliff R. 1992a. Inference during reading. *Psychol. Rev.* 99:440–66

McKoon G, Ratcliff R. 1992b. Spreading activation versus compound cue accounts of priming: mediated priming revisited. *J. Exp. Psychol.: Learn. Mem. Cogn.* 18: 1155–72

McNamara TP. 1992. Theories of priming: I. Associative distance and lag. *J. Exp. Psychol.: Learn. Mem. Cogn.* 18:1173–90

McNeil MR, Odell K, Tseng C-H. 1991. Toward the integration of resource allocation into a general theory of aphasia. *Clin. Aphas.* 20:21–39

Miller GA. 1956. The magical number seven, plus or minus two: some limits on our capacity for processing information. *Psychol. Rev.* 63:81–97

Millis KK, Just MA. 1994. The influence of connectives on sentence comprehension. *J. Mem. Lang.* 33:128–47

Mitchell DC. 1994. Sentence parsing. In *Handbook of Psycholinguistics,* ed. M Gernsbacher, pp. 375–409. San Diego, CA: Academic

Mitchell DC, Corley MMB, Garnham A. 1992. Effects of context in human sentence parsing: evidence against a discourse-based proposal mechanism. *J. Exp. Psychol.: Learn. Mem. Cogn.* 18:69–88

Miyake A, Carpenter PA, Just MA. 1994a. A capacity approach to syntactic comprehension disorders: making normal adults perform like aphasic patients. *Cogn. Neuropsychol.* In press

Miyake A, Just MA, Carpenter PA. 1994b. Working memory constraints on the resolution of lexical ambiguity: maintaining multiple interpretations in neutral contexts. *J. Mem. Lang.* 33:175–202

Morrow DG, Bower GH, Greenspan SE. 1989. Updating situation models during narrative comprehension. *J. Mem. Lang.* 28:292–312

Morrow DG, Leirer V, Altieri P. 1992. Aging, expertise, and narrative processing. *Psychol. Aging* 7:376–88

Murphy GL. 1990. Noun phrase interpretation and conceptual combination. *J. Mem. Lang.* 29:259–88

Murray JD, Klin CM, Myers J. 1993. Forward inferences in narrative text. *J. Mem. Lang.* 32:464–73

Obler LK, Fein D, Nicholas M, Albert ML. 1991. Auditory comprehension and aging: decline in syntactic processing. *Appl. Psycholinguist.* 12:433–52

O'Brien EJ, Albrecht JE. 1992. Comprehension strategies in the development of a mental model. *J. Exp. Psychol.: Learn. Mem. Cogn.* 18:777–84

Ortony A. 1979. Beyond literal similarity. *Psychol. Rev.* 86:161–80

Perfetti CA. 1990. The cooperative language processors: Semantic influences in an autonomous syntax. In *Comprehension Processes in Reading,* ed. DA Balota, GB Flores d'Arcais, K Rayner, pp. 205–30. Hillsdale, NJ: Erlbaum

Pinker S, Prince A. 1988. On language and connectionism: analysis of a parallel distributed processing model of language acquisition. *Cognition* 28:73–193

Pollio HR, Smith MK, Pollio M. 1990. Figurative language and cognitive psychology. *Lang. Cogn. Process.* 5:141–67

Potts GR, Keenan JM, Golding JM. 1988. Assessing the occurrence of elaborative inferences: lexical decision versus naming. *J. Mem. Lang.* 27:399-415

Rankin JL. 1993. Information-processing differences of college-age readers differing in reading comprehension and speed. *J. Read. Behav.* 25:261–78

Rayner K, Carlson M, Frazier L. 1983. The interaction of syntax and semantics during sentence processing: eye movements in the analysis of semantically biased sentences. *J. Verb. Learn. Verb. Behav.* 22:358–74

Rayner K, Garrod S, Perfetti CA. 1992. Discourse influences during parsing are delayed. *Cognition* 45:109–39

Reilly RG, Sharkey NE, eds. 1992. *Connectionist Approaches to Natural Language Processing*. Hillsdale, NJ: Erlbaum

Riggs KM, Wingfield A, Tun PA. 1993. Passage difficulty, speech rate, and age differences in memory for spoken text: speech recall and the complexity hypothesis. *Exp. Aging Res.* 19:111–28

Salthouse TA. 1994. The nature of the influence of speed on adult age differences in cognition. *Dev. Psychol.* 30:240–59

Sarno MT, ed. 1991. *Acquired Aphasia*. San Diego, CA: Academic. 2nd ed.

Sasaki Y. 1994. Paths of processing strategy transfers in learning Japanese and English as foreign languages. *Stud. Second Lang. Acquisit.* 16:43–72

Shallice T. 1988. *From Neuropsychology to Mental Structure*. Cambridge: Cambridge Univ. Press

Shankweiler D, Crain S, Gorrell P, Tuller B. 1989. Reception of language in Broca's aphasia. *Lang. Cogn. Process.* 4:1–33

Shapiro LP, Nagel HN, Levine BA. 1993. Preferences for a verb's complements and their use in sentence processing. *J. Mem. Lang.* 32:96–114

Shastri L, Ajjanagadde V. 1993. From simple associations to systematic reasoning: a connectionist representation of rules, variables, and dynamic bindings using temporal synchrony. *Behav. Brain Sci.* 16:417–94

Simpson GB. 1994. Context and the processing of ambiguous words. In *Handbook of Psycholinguistics,* ed. MA Gernsbacher, pp. 359–74. San Diego, CA: Academic

Simpson GB, Krueger MA. 1991. Selective access of homograph meanings in sentence context *J. Mem. Lang.* 30:627–43

Singer M. 1990. *Psychology of Language: An Introduction to Sentence and Discourse Processes*. Hillsdale, NJ: Erlbaum

Singer M, Halldorson M, Lear JC, Andrusiak P. 1992. Validation of causal bridging inferences in discourse understanding. *J. Mem. Lang.* 31:507–24

Smith EE, Osherson DN, Rips LJ, Keane M. 1988. Combining prototypes: a modification model. *Cogn. Sci.* 12:485–528

Smith S, Macaruso P, Shankweiler D, Crain S. 1989. Syntactic comprehension in young poor readers. *Appl. Psycholinguist.* 10: 429–54

Sridhar SN. 1989. Cognitive structures in language production: a crosslinguistic study. In *The Cross Linguistic Study of Sentence Processing,* ed. B MacWhinney, E Bates, pp. 209–24. New York: Cambridge Univ. Press

St. John M. 1992. The story gestalt: a model of knowledge-intensive processes in text comprehension. *Cogn. Sci.* 16:271–306

Stein CL, Cairns HS, Zurif EB. 1984. Sentence comprehension limitations related to syntactic deficits in reading-disabled children. *Appl. Psycholinguist.* 5:305–22

Swanson LH. 1992. Generality and modifiability of working memory among skilled and less skilled readers. *J. Educ. Psychol.* 84: 473–88

Swinney DA. 1979. Lexical access during sentence comprehension: reconsideration of context effects. *J. Verb. Learn. Verb. Behav.* 18:645–59

Tabossi P. 1988. Accessing lexical ambiguity in different types of sentential contexts. *J. Mem. Lang.* 27:324–40

Tabossi P, Zardon F. 1993. Processing ambiguous words in context. *J. Mem. Lang.* 32:359–72

Taraban R, McClelland JL. 1988. Constituent attachment and thematic role assignment in sentence processing: influences of content-based expectations. *J. Mem. Lang.* 27:597–632

Taylor HA, Tversky B. 1992. Spatial mental models derived from survey and route descriptions. *J. Mem. Lang.* 31:261–92

Tourangeau R, Rips L. 1991. Interpreting and evaluating metaphors. *J. Mem. Lang.* 30: 452–72

Trabasso T, Suh S. 1993. Understanding text: achieving explanatory coherence through on-line inferences and mental operations in working memory. *Discourse Process.* 16: 3–34

Trueswell JC, Tanenhaus MK, Kello C. 1993. Verb-specific constraints in sentence processing: separating effects of lexical preference from garden-paths. *J. Exp. Psychol.: Learn. Mem. Cogn.* 19:528–53

Tyler LK. 1992. *Spoken Language Comprehension: An Experimental Approach to Disordered and Normal Processing*. Cambridge, MA: MIT Press

van den Broek P. 1990. Causal inferences and the comprehension of narrative texts. In *The Psychology of Learning and Motivation: Inferences and Text Comprehension,* ed. AC Graesser, GH Bower, 25:175–94. San Diego, CA: Academic

Van Petten C, Kutas M. 1987. Ambiguous words in context: an event-related potential analysis of the time course of meaning activation. *J. Mem. Lang.* 26:188–208

Whitney P, Ritchie BG, Clark MB. 1991. Working-memory capacity and the use of elaborative inferences in text comprehension. *Discourse Process.* 14:133–45

Whitney P, Ritchie BG, Crane RS. 1992. The effect of foregrounding on reader's use of predictive inferences. *Mem. Cogn.* 20:424–32

Wilson SG, Rinck M, McNamara TP, Bower GH, Morrow D. 1992. Mental models and narrative comprehension: some qualifications. *J. Mem. Lang.* 32:141–54

Wisniewski EJ, Gentner D. 1991. On the combinatorial semantics of noun pairs: minor and major adjustments to meaning. In *Understanding Word and Sentence,* ed. GB Simpson, pp. 241–84. Amsterdam: North-Holland

Wydell TN, Patterson KE, Humphreys GW. 1993. Phonological mediated access to meaning for Kanji: Is a rows still a rose in Japanese Kanji? *J. Exp. Psychol.: Learn.* *Mem. Cogn.* 19:491–514

Yuill N, Oakhill J, Parkin A. 1989. Working memory, comprehension ability and the resolution of text anomaly. *Br. J. Psychol.* 80:351–61

Zhang S, Perfetti CA. 1993. The tongue-twister effect in reading Chinese. *J. Exp. Psychol.: Learn. Mem. Cogn.* 19:1082–93

Annu. Rev. Psychol. 1995. 46:121–53

DIAGNOSIS AND CLASSIFICATION OF PSYCHOPATHOLOGY: Challenges to the Current System and Future Directions

L. A. Clark, D. Watson, and S. Reynolds

Department of Psychology, The University of Iowa, Iowa City, Iowa 52242-1407

KEY WORDS: diagnosis, classification, *DSM-IV*, psychopathology

CONTENTS

0066-4308/95/0201-0121$05.00

INTRODUCTION

In an effort to improve and substantiate the empirical basis of the Fourth Edition of the *Diagnostic and Statistical Manual of Mental Disorders* [*DSM-IV*; American Psychiatric Association (APA) 1994], the *DSM-IV* Task Force commissioned the review of literatures pertaining to a vast array of psychological disorders from a variety of perspectives. One hundred and fifty of these reviews are published as three of the five-volume *DSM-IV Source Book* (Widiger et al 1994). Together with papers published since those reviews were completed, the sheer bulk of relevant scholarly material is prodigious and has made reviewing the literature on the diagnosis and classification of psychopathology a formidable challenge.

Although the empirical data base regarding the diagnosis of psychopathology has increased greatly as a result of this activity, regrettably little attention was paid to the science of classification itself, in part because the Task Force accepted the obligation to conform the *DSM-IV* to the organization of the *International Classification of Diseases.* Accordingly, our review focuses on difficulties, problems, and limitations in the *DSM*'s categorical approach to diagnostic classification and considers directions that need to be taken for the development of a truly scientific taxonomy of psychopathology.

PURPOSES OF A DIAGNOSTIC TAXONOMY

Over the years, many people have tackled the various thorny issues involved in delineating the elements and goals of classification, both medical and psychiatric (see Millon 1991). This section highlights a few issues that have been the subject of recent writings and debates regarding psychiatric classification.

Clinical Utility

As reflected in the now somewhat outmoded title, the *DSM*s evolved from an earlier need to collect uniform statistics in psychiatric hospitals in the early 1900s. It was not until after World War II that a more detailed and comprehensive diagnostic nomenclature based on a system developed by the Armed Forces and modified by a survey of American Psychiatric Association members was developed for general use (for discussions of historical developments, see APA 1994, Widiger et al 1991, Wilson 1993). Research findings first played a major role in the process with *DSM-III* and have been emphasized in the development of the *DSM-IV*. Nevertheless, the stated rationale of the *DSM-IV* remains true to its applied origins: to facilitate clinical practice and communication (Frances et al 1991; see Widiger & Trull 1993, for elaboration of how this has been operationalized).

Given the degree to which science has been highlighted in the most recent revision process (Widiger et al 1991), the reaffirmation that clinical utility is accorded the highest priority may come as a surprise to some. The important question is whether the goal of clinical utility directed the process in nonscientific ways. The *DSM-IV* Task Force states that the various uses of the *DSM* are usually compatible (APA 1994, p. xv), but it is not clear whether this assertion has ever been evaluated empirically. Although several *DSM-III-R* diagnoses will be simplified in *DSM-IV* because they have proved cumbersome in everyday practice (Frances et al 1990), at least some data suggest that this will not impact validity adversely (e.g. TA Widiger, R Cadoret, R Hare, L Robins, M Rutherford, et al, submitted for publication). Treatment and patient management considerations also affect diagnostic formulations, as the cutoff point for determining a case is debated (e.g. Davidson & Foa 1991). To their credit, the framers of the *DSM-IV* have recognized the tension between these potentially conflicting goals (Frances et al 1990) and have been clear about their priorities.

Research Facilitation

There is no question that research has been stimulated and facilitated by having a standard set of diagnostic criteria. However, the existence of an official taxonomy also has become an unintended straitjacket, as most researchers have limited themselves to the *DSM* criteria rather than investigating diverse sets of criteria (Frances et al 1990). Davidson & Foa (1991) lamented that the frequent changes (i.e. from *DSM-III* to *III-R* to *IV*) hampered thorough assessment of the criterion sets: "Once a criterion set becomes obsolete, there is little interest in spending significant time on its evaluation" (Davidson & Foa 1991, p. 351). This widespread attitude is unfortunate, because it means that the *DSM* is driving science as well as vice versa. Perhaps researchers across disciplines—as well as editors, reviewers, and granting agencies—have endorsed each successive set of *DSM* criteria too readily. In this regard, it is noteworthy that the *DSM-IV* Task Force made explicit that the specific criteria "are meant to serve as guidelines to be informed by clinical judgment and are not meant to be used in a cookbook fashion" (APA 1994, p. xxiii). Why, then, have researchers overwhelmingly confined themselves to the officially defined domain?

Scientific Understanding

There are conflicting views regarding the feasibility of developing a scientific taxonomy of psychopathology. Kendler (1990) asserts that some nosological questions involve "value judgments" (p. 971) that are fundamentally nonempirical. In contrast, Widiger & Trull (1993) assert that what Kendler calls value judgments are actually choices between competing theoretical formulations, that is, scientific decisions based on the degree of empirical support for each theoretical position. The issue of value versus science is also central to Wakefield's (1992) proposal that disorders—including mental disorders—are harmful dysfunctions, a definition that has both value (harmful) and scientific (dysfunction) components.

Many writers (e.g. Blashfield & Livesley 1991, Carson 1991, Livesley & Jackson 1991, Morey 1991) have asserted the general relevance of construct validity in the development of a scientific classification of psychopathology. These writers emphasize that the discovery of the broad structure and internal organization of natural entities is best pursued through an iterative process involving both theory and data. In addition to direct empirical tests of a proposed taxonomy, criteria such as testability and parsimony would be used to compare competing systems. These writers uniformly reject recent *DSM* attempts to be atheoretical with regard to the fundamental etiology and developmental nature of psychological disorder, asserting that shared phenomenology is only one of many possible ways to organize psychopathology. Etiology, course, treatment response, biological precursors and concomitants, and family and genetic relations all are potentially useful as well (cf Robins & Guze 1970). In a remarkably frank disclosure, the *DSM* leadership acknowledge that "the descriptive system is only a temporary way station to be replaced...with more incisive pathogenetic and etiologic models of classification" (Frances et al 1991, p. 411). Carson (1991) suggests that the latter models might also have superior clinical utility.

DEVELOPMENT OF *DSM-IV*

Descriptive Approach and the Structure of DSM-IV

It has been stated repeatedly that the *DSM* approach is descriptive (e.g. Widiger & Trull 1993), emphasizing observed or reported clinical features rather than underlying causal mechanisms. It is also well known that the *DSM* adheres to a categorical approach in which patients either meet or do not meet criteria for a diagnosis. However, most of the *DSM* diagnoses are defined polythetically, meaning that diagnosis is based on meeting a certain number of equally weighted criteria. Because it is not necessary that a case meet all criteria but only that it pass a required threshold, patients with the same diagnosis "are likely to be heterogeneous even in regard to the defining features of the diagnosis" (APA 1994, p. xxii). Dimensional models of classification have been proposed as alternatives to address this problem (e.g. Blashfield 1989, Widiger 1992a), but these were rejected by the Task Force for a variety of reasons, especially lack of consensus, issues of clinical utility, and insufficient empirical support (APA 1994). Nevertheless, there are problems inherent in using discrete entities to describe "the objectively seamless blendings of disordered behavior" (Carson 1991, p. 302; Frances et al 1991; Frances et al 1990). Much of this review is devoted to an examination of the scope and severity of these inherent problems, which we believe have been understated in the literature.

The rationale for the manual's overall organization is less well known than is its use of a descriptive, categorical approach. Eleven of the sixteen major diagnostic classes are based on shared phenomenological features (e.g. mood disorders, sleep disorders). Also, as part of the *DSM-IV* reorganization, each of the individual disorders comprising the sections "Mental Disorders Due to a General Medical Condition" and "Substance-Related Disorders" is placed within the particular diagnostic class with which it shares phenomenology (e.g. "Mood Disorder Due to a General Medical Condition" is placed in the Mood Disorders section). By contrast, the class "Disorders Usually First Diagnosed in Infancy, Childhood, or Adolescence" includes disorders with a wide range of phenomenological features grouped solely on the basis of common age at first presentation. Similarly, "Delirium, Dementia, Amnestic and Other Cognitive Disorders" are placed together "because of their priority in differential diagnosis" (APA 1994, p. 10); the very title of this section suggests the somewhat tenuous connection among them. Finally, the Adjustment Disorders are grouped based on their common etiology ("maladaptive reaction to a stressor"; APA 1994, p. 10). Thus, from the outset it is apparent that this is not a unified scientific taxonomy; the organization is eclectically pragmatic and serves more as a heuristic system for filing diagnoses than as an integrated scientific classification of psychological disorders. The question of whether data should inform this overall organization apparently was not considered. Rather, the primary concern was to facilitate differential diagnosis (APA 1994).

Considerations of the relative weighting of empirical evidence versus clinical utility thus were applied almost exclusively to the lower level of organization—the subdivision into specific disorders. The *DSM-IV* work groups directed significant efforts at deciding whether to add, eliminate, combine, subtype, or split diagnoses. Both clinical utility and empirical criteria such as clarity, complexity, comprehensiveness, and coverage were brought to bear in making these decisions. Additional work groups considered Axes III through V of the *DSM*'s multiaxial system as well as potential additional axes for defense mechanisms, culturally related syndromes, and so forth.

Process

The three-pronged process—involving at least 150 literature reviews, 50 data reanalyses, and 12 field trials—through which empirical data influenced the *DSM-IV* has been widely publicized (e.g. First 1994, Widiger et al 1991) and the enormity of this effort must be recognized. However, the limitations of this process have not been acknowledged sufficiently. Most importantly, the literature reviews were based on research that was conducted largely within the *DSM* framework. These reviews examined specific *DSM* diagnoses but generally did not consider alternative approaches or conceptualizations (Spitzer 1991). A major exception is the work on the Axis II personality disorders from a dimensional perspective (Clark 1993, Costa & Widiger 1994, Livesley 1991, Widiger 1992a). Although the field trials had an opportunity to break this mold, they also tended not to be designed to examine the comparative validity of alternative conceptualizations of disorders (Spitzer 1991). Thus, although empirical considerations played a major role in the revision process, they invariably began "with the implicit assumption that what is already in place in the way of major differentiations correctly demarcates the main outlines of the domain and that fine tuning of the system is all that is required" (Carson 1991, p. 303).

DATA THAT CHALLENGE CATEGORICAL MODELS OF PSYCHOPATHOLOGY

Certain types of data challenge categorical models of psychopathology in general and the current *DSM-IV* system in particular. Following are discussions of problems of comorbidity, heterogeneity both within and across diagnostic boundaries, and the overall organization of *DSM-IV*.

Comorbidity

BACKGROUND INFORMATION

Historical overview   In the past few years, comorbidity—that is, the co-occurrence of two or more disorders in the same individual—has come to be viewed as a major problem. In fact, Kendall & Clarkin (1992) described it as the "premier challenge facing mental health professionals in the 1990s" (p. 833). This contemporary focus on comorbidity can be traced to the publication of the *DSM-III* (APA 1980), which included hierarchical exclusionary rules affecting some 60% of all disorders (Boyd et al 1984). In this system, diagnoses were excluded from consideration if they were judged to occur only during the course of a coexisting disorder that was deemed to occupy a higher position in the diagnostic pecking order (Boyd et al 1984, Brown & Barlow 1992).

These exclusion criteria proved highly controversial. One major problem was that the architects of *DSM-III* offered virtually no theoretical rationale or empirical evidence to justify the exclusionary rules. In addition, the "not due to" criteria were vague and difficult to apply. Finally, the use of these criteria made it extremely difficult to study disorders occupying a less privileged position in the diagnostic hierarchy. Accordingly, researchers soon began to explore the implications of ignoring these criteria (Boyd et al 1984). In doing so, they discovered not only that there were widespread comorbidities among disorders, but also that these comorbidities had important diagnostic and treatment implications. On the basis of this rapidly accumulating evidence, most of these exclusion criteria were dropped in *DSM-III-R* (APA 1987).

Factors affecting comorbidity   Freed of these exclusionary rules, research on comorbidity has exploded in the last five years. This literature is already so vast that it can only be sampled here. Before reviewing relevant data, it must be emphasized that comorbidity estimates necessarily reflect a number of methodological factors, so that specific numbers must be interpreted with some caution. For instance, comorbidity rates are influenced by time frame (e.g. concurrent or lifetime diagnostic co-occurrence), severity criteria (e.g. whether subsyndromal manifestations are included), and the range of disorders considered (e.g. only Axis I, Axis II, or both) (Brown & Barlow 1992).

The diagnostic method used also can influence both prevalence and comorbidity estimates. Self-reports almost invariably yield higher prevalence rates than do interview methods (e.g. Zimmerman et al 1991). Significantly different prevalence rates also have been obtained using two different structured interviews (e.g. Oldham et al 1992). Moreover, the level and pattern of comorbidity also varied by interview, which Oldham et al attributed to different interview formats. Furthermore, over the course of a structured interview, respondents may recognize that an affirmative response leads to more detailed questions; therefore, unless precautions are taken, respondents may underreport disorders examined later in the interview, thereby affecting both prevalence and comorbidity rates (Kessler et al 1994).

Help-seeking is perhaps the most important factor that influences comorbidity rates. Comorbidity estimates tend to be higher for clinical than nonselected community samples, partly because individuals with comorbid conditions are more likely to seek treatment than are those with a single disorder (Galbaud du Fort et al 1993, Schneier et al 1992, Simpson et al 1992, Kessler et al 1994).

THE EXTENT OF THE PROBLEM

General comorbidities: community samples   Two large national epidemiological surveys have indicated that more than half of all individuals with a *DSM* disorder also have at least one additional comorbid disorder. Sixty percent of the respondents in the Epidemiological Catchment Area (ECA) study with at least one lifetime *DSM* disorder also had at least one comorbid disorder (Robins et al 1991).[1] Similarly, 56% of the respondents in the National Comorbidity Survey (NCS) with at least one lifetime disorder had two or more disorders (Kessler et al 1994). Furthermore, in the NCS data, individuals with comorbid conditions accounted for 79% of all lifetime disorders and 82% of all 12-month diagnoses. Even more striking was the fact that a relatively small group (14% of the total sample) of individuals with three or more lifetime disorders accounted for nearly 90% of all severe disorders.

Community samples have also yielded very high comorbidity rates for specific *DSM* disorders. For example, analyses of the ECA data using lifetime diagnoses indicated that 91% of individuals diagnosed with panic disorder, 91% of schizophrenics, 75% of depressives, 69% of those with social phobia, and 52% of those with alcohol abuse or dependence had at least one comorbid condition (Robins et al 1991, Schneier et al 1992). Similarly, studies of other community samples have found at least one comorbid disorder in 83% of individuals with generalized anxiety disorder (GAD; Breslau et al 1991) and 77% of bulimics (Kendler et al 1991). In an analysis of a Canadian epidemiological sample, Galbaud du Fort et al (1993) reported moderate to very high comorbidity rates for a variety of disorders, including alcohol abuse or dependence (46%), major depression (48%), phobia (48%), obsessive-compulsive disorder (OCD) (74%), drug abuse or dependence (77%), panic disorder (91%), and antisocial personality disorder (PD) (93%). Similarly, in a community sample of Australian twins, Andrews et al (1990) obtained comorbidity rates ranging from 40% (for GAD) to greater than 80% (for major depression and dysthymia). Finally, in a sample of high school students, Lewinsohn et al (1993) reported moderate to high lifetime comorbidity rates for adjustment disorders (29%), major depression (43%), anxiety disorders (61%), and substance use disorders (66%). Thus, for many disorders, pure and uncomplicated symptom pictures are somewhat atypical.

General comorbidities: clinical samples   Using clinical samples, high concurrent and/or lifetime comorbidity rates have been demonstrated for virtually all of the Axis I *DSM* disorders. In many clinical settings it may be difficult to find pure diagnostic cases that do not also suffer from other types of psychopathology. For example, two studies of patients with multiple personality disorder (MPD) identified an average of 2.7 (Ross et al 1989) and 3.6 (Putnam et al 1986) comorbid diagnoses per subject. Sanderson and colleagues (1990) found that 65% of dysthymics and 59% of patients with major depression had at least one

---

[1]
    It may be argued that using lifetime diagnoses exaggerates the comorbidity problem (cf the lifetime comorbidity for strep throat and stomach flu, which probably is quite high but meaningless). However, the use of lifetime diagnoses reflects the common practice of diagnosing, for example, "major depression, in remission," but not "strep throat, in remission."

concurrent Axis I disorder. Halmi et al (1991) obtained current and lifetime comorbidity rates of 77% and 93%, respectively, in a sample of anorexics; corresponding rates reported for patients with OCD were 96% and 100%, respectively (Leonard et al 1993). Those for a sample of drug addicts were 80% and 83%, respectively (Hendriks 1990). In addition, lifetime comorbidity rates ranging from 68% to 100% have been reported for patients with GAD (Brawman-Mintzer et al 1993), panic or agoraphobia (Andrews et al 1990), hypochondriasis (Barsky et al 1992), body dysmorphic disorder (BDD; Phillips et al 1993), substance abuse (Nace et al 1991), cocaine abuse (Rounsaville et al 1991), alcoholism (Roy et al 1990), attention deficit disorder (Steingard et al 1992), kleptomania (McElroy et al 1991), and trichotillomania (Christenson et al 1991).

Studies of high-risk groups also have yielded very high comorbidity rates. For instance, Pribor & Dinwiddie (1992) reported an average of 7.1 lifetime diagnoses per subject in a sample of incest victims, and Mellman et al (1992) found an average of 3.1 disorders in a sample of combat veterans. Rudd et al (1993) reported an average of 4.0 current disorders per subject in a high-risk sample of suicidal patients.

Although these Axis I data are striking, comorbidity rates for the Axis II personality disorders tend to be even higher. Available data indicate that relatively few patients meet criteria for a given personality disorder without also meeting criteria for one or more other *DSM* diagnoses (for reviews see Gunderson et al 1991a, b; Hirschfeld et al 1991; Pfohl 1991; Widiger & Rogers 1989). In a sample of more than 2000 patients assigned an Axis II diagnosis, Fabrega et al (1992) found that 79% also suffered from at least one Axis I disorder. Oldham et al (1992) reported that more than 80% of patients with a personality disorder had at least one comorbid Axis II disorder; moreover, the average number of personality disorder diagnoses per subject was 3.4. In terms of specific disorders, Widiger & Rogers (1989) found that across four studies 96% of patients with borderline PD also met criteria for at least one other Axis II diagnosis. Similar results have been reported for histrionic, narcissistic, avoidant, and other personality disorders (e.g. Gunderson et al 1991a, Hirschfeld et al 1991, Pfohl 1991).

Comorbidities with specific disorders   Recent data also indicate that comorbidity, while rampant, is not random. Most disorders show systematic comorbidities with specific diagnoses or diagnostic classes. For instance, various anxiety disorders have been found to be strongly comorbid with other anxiety disorders, depression and dysthymia, alcoholism, and personality disorders (e.g. Brown & Barlow 1992, Kushner et al 1990, Sutker et al 1991, Tynes et al 1990). Similarly, hypochondriasis, somatization, and other somatoform disorders are strongly linked with depression, anxiety, substance abuse, and personality disorders (e.g. Katon et al 1991, Kirmayer et al 1994). Depression and dysthymia show strong comorbidities with the anxiety disorders, personality disorders, and substance abuse (e.g. Brown & Barlow 1992, Farmer & Nelson-Gray 1990, Shea et al 1992). Comparable statements could be offered for many other conditions.

To illustrate the breadth and magnitude of these diagnostic affinities, we offer a few specific examples. Shea et al (1990) reported that 74% of their depressed outpatients also suffered from at least one personality disorder, and Sanderson et al (1990) found that 43% of their depressed or dysthymic patients had a concurrent anxiety disorder. In a sample of combat veterans with post-traumatic stress disorder (PTSD), Davidson and colleagues (1990) obtained lifetime comorbidity rates of 64% with GAD, 59% with major depression, and 59% with alcoholism. Barsky et al (1992) found that 71% of their hypochon-driacal patients had a lifetime diagnosis of GAD, and 86% had some type of anxiety disorder; in addition, 55% of the patients met lifetime criteria for either major depression or dysthymia. In a large sample of MPD patients, Ross et al (1990) observed concurrent comorbidity rates of 91% with major depression, 64% with borderline PD, and 61% with somatization disorder. Halmi et al (1991) found that 84% of anorexics met lifetime criteria for a mood disorder and 65% had a comorbid anxiety disorder. In a large sample of individuals with antisocial PD, Dinwiddie & Reich (1993) reported that lifetime comor-bidity rates were 76% with alcoholism, 63% with drug dependence, and 34% with depression. In a sample of cocaine abusers, Rounsaville et al (1991) found that 61% met lifetime criteria for some type of mood disorder; more-over, 35% had attention deficit disorder and 21% had some type of anxiety disorder. Finally, in an analysis of the ECA data, Mueser and colleagues (1992) reported that 47% of schizophrenics met lifetime criteria for a sub-stance use disorder.

Data demonstrating co-occurrences between specific disorders are subject to various interpretations (see Biederman et al 1992, Brown & Barlow 1992, Widiger & Shea 1991). In some instances, the comorbidity appears artifactual, reflecting the fact that the *DSM* allows two separate diagnoses to be assigned to what may be expressions of a single disorder. For example, the extremely high comorbidity between avoidant PD and social phobia largely reflects the fact that these disorders share several symptom criteria (Widiger 1992b, Widi-ger & Shea 1991), Similar observations have been made regarding the rela-tions between antisocial PD and substance abuse, mood disorder and border-line PD, and schizotypal PD and schizophrenia (Widiger & Shea 1991).

In other instances, one disorder may develop as a secondary complication of another. For example, recent evidence indicates that comorbid conditions such as depression and substance abuse typically develop after the onset of social phobia (Schneier et al 1992). Still another possibility is that two quasi-distinct disorders share a common diathesis or vulnerability factor. For example, liability to major depression and GAD may be influenced by the same genetic factors (Kendler et al 1992), and a shared genetic vulnerability also appears to be at least partly responsible for the observed comorbidity between depression and alcoholism (Kendler et al 1993). One interesting research possibility would be a systematic examination of comorbidity patterns to elucidate the broad, higher-order structure of phenotypic psychopathology, which in turn might guide the search for putative genetic structures.

RELATIONS WITH COURSE, OUTCOME, AND SEVERITY   The foregoing data suggest that pure, unmixed cases are not likely to be representative of the overall population of individuals with a disorder. Moreover, individuals with comorbid conditions differ in important ways from pure cases. Most notably, individuals with comorbid conditions generally have a more chronic and complicated course, poorer prognosis, and lessened response to treatment. Much of the relevant research has examined the complicating influence of an Axis II disorder on an Axis I condition. Comorbid personality disorders have been found to be negative prognostic signs in patients with major depression (Diguer et al 1993, Farmer & Nelson-Gray 1990, Shea et al 1990, Shea et al 1992), OCD (Baer et al 1992), eating disorders (Sansone & Fine 1992), and substance abuse (Nathan 1991, Nurnberg et al 1993). However, similar effects have been observed for comorbid Axis I disorders. For example, studies have demonstrated the complicating effects of comorbid anxiety on depression (Coryell et al 1992), major depression on panic disorder (Laberge et al 1993), ADD on cocaine abuse (Carroll & Rounsaville 1993), and cocaine abuse on schizophrenia (Brady et al 1990).

The complicating influence of comorbidity can be seen clearly in relation to suicide attempts and suicidal ideation. In an analysis of the ECA data, Johnson et al (1990) reported that the rate of suicide attempts among individuals with uncomplicated panic disorder was only 7.0% but rose to 26% in those who also had at least one comorbid condition. Similarly, Schneier et al (1992) found suicide attempt rates of 1.1% among individuals with no psychiatric disorder, 0.9% for those with uncomplicated social phobia, and 15.7% among social phobics with a comorbid diagnosis. One might argue that this marked rise in suicide rates occurs simply because the comorbid diagnoses (e.g. depression) are associated with a higher suicide rate than are panic disorder or social phobia. However, similar data have been reported for depression: Johnson et al (1990) reported a suicide rate of 8% for pure cases of major depression, but 20% for depressives with comorbid disorders.

To a considerable extent, the complicating effects of diagnostic comorbidity may be attributed to its strong association with the severity of disorder, which also is a negative prognostic indicator (Keller et al 1992). Furthermore, comorbidity rates tend to be substantially higher in individuals with more severe conditions (Clarkin & Kendall 1992, Diguer et al 1993, Katon et al 1991, Kendall et al 1992, Kessler et al 1994). Putting these considerations together, the data suggest that the severity of disorder—as indicated both by the magnitude and the breadth of the observed dysfunction—is a crucial factor in course, treatment, and outcome. In many contexts, assessing the severity of dysfunction may be as or more important than specifying the precise nature of the disorder. (For a general discussion of the importance of severity and of various approaches to assessing it, see Mezzich & Sullivan 1995.)

Heterogeneity

Two highly prevalent types of heterogeneity further challenge the validity and utility of the *DSM*'s polythetic categorical approach to psychopathology: 1. within-category heterogeneity of defining features and 2. mixed symptom presentations that fall between diagnostic boundaries [i.e. Not Otherwise Specified (NOS) diagnoses]. To the extent that diagnosis is used to inform treatment or to predict course, its purpose is defeated by either type of hetero-geneity. From a scientific viewpoint, both phenomena suggest an inadequate taxonomy: Excessive within-category heterogeneity challenges the basis for classification, while an overabundance of unclassifiable boundary cases indi-cates poor coverage.

WITHIN-CATEGORY HETEROGENEITY   A polythetic format was adopted more broadly in *DSM-III-R,* both to enhance reliability and to increase coverage, because many *DSM-III* diagnoses that were defined monothetically (i.e. all features required for diagnosis) had very low base rates (e.g. Morey 1988). However, because the *DSM* diagnostic criteria typically reflect multiple symp-tom dimensions, this format necessarily promotes within-category heterogene-ity (see Tellegen 1993). For example, the nine criteria for borderline PD reflect a wide range of personality trait dimensions, from uncontrollable anger to identity disturbance. Two patients who both meet criteria for the diagnosis may share all nine criterion traits or they may share only a single one and exhibit rather different personality pathologies.

Of course, heterogeneity is not simply an artifact of the *DSM* diagnostic format. Heterogeneity exists in patient populations, and any categorical system must either ignore it (as in *DSM-III,* which sacrificed coverage by creating rigidly and unrealistically homogeneous categories) or accept and incorporate it (as in *DSM-III-R* and *DSM-IV*). However, owing to the multidimensional nature of most *DSM* diagnoses, the resulting within-category heterogeneity is quite troublesome. Consequently, many schemes for subtyping diagnoses have been proposed to try to create more homogeneous groupings. In this section, we illustrate and discuss problems of within-category heterogeneity using selected diagnostic categories.

Schizophrenia is a category that is well known for its within-group variability and may represent a set of etiologically distinct disorders rather than a single diagnosis (Tsuang et al 1990). Many efforts have been made to define subtypes, and the scheme used in *DSM-III-R* remains problematic (Keefe et al 1991). For example, patients often display symptoms of more than one type and may change subtypes in later episodes (Andreasen & Carpenter 1993). However, some researchers argue for the viability of at least one of the classic groups—the paranoid subtype. Nicholson & Neufeld (1993) offer a model that comprises two independent dimensions: severity of disorder (which refers to the type of symptom—paranoid vs nonparanoid) and severity of symptoms (which refers to the frequency and prominence of the symptoms). Importantly, this perspective represents a departure from qualitative (i.e. categorical) distinctions and instead asserts that the symptoms of schizophrenia should be described dimensionally.

McGlashan & Fenton (1992) note that many of the attempts to subtype schizophrenia seem to correspond to the positive-negative symptom distinction [e.g. acute (positive) vs chronic (negative); reactive (positive) vs process (negative)]. Recent evidence, however, suggests that two dimensions may be insufficient to categorize schizophrenic symptoms. One factor-analytic study (Arndt et al 1991) indicated that three dimensions were needed: a negative or deficit dimension plus two dimensions of positive symptomatology—hallucinations or delusions and disorganization (bizarre behavior plus formal thought disorder). This subtyping scheme appears in a *DSM-IV* appendix. Lenzenweger et al (1991) also found evidence for three factors underlying the disorder; however, positive symptoms and negative symptoms each formed a single dimension, with premorbid social functioning as the third. Thus, no broad consensus on subtyping schizophrenia has emerged and its heterogeneity remains a vexing problem (Andreasen & Carpenter 1993).

Affective psychosis presents a related and equally long-standing problem. Listed as a subtype of schizophrenia in *DSM-II*, schizoaffective disorder was recognized as an independent category in *DSM-III*, and recent research on treatment response has suggested that there may be two variants of schizoaffective disorder, one more schizophrenic and one more affective (Aubert & Rush 1994). Considering that the *DSM* also provides for the subtyping of major depressive disorder with or without psychotic features that may be mood-congruent or incongruent, it is not surprising that some writers have questioned the adequacy of the traditional categorical approach in this domain and speculated about the existence of a continuum ranging from schizophrenia to nonpsychotic mood disorders (e.g. Maier et al 1992, Taylor et al 1993).

The eating disorder category also encompasses widely diverse patients. Analyses of symptomatology in bulimia nervosa patients (Gleaves et al 1993, Tobin et al 1991) have identified multifactorial structures underlying the disorder that reflect a sufficiently wide range of concomitant clinical features to question the unity of the diagnosis. Various subtyping schemes—with or without a history of anorexia nervosa, with or without a history of obesity, obese vs normal weight, and purging vs nonpurging—have been proposed to deal with the observed heterogeneity (Mitchell 1992). Only the last subtyping option had sufficient empirical support to convince the *DSM-IV* work group of its utility: Nonpurging bulimics show distinctive and less-severe associated psychopathology than do those who purge (Mitchell 1992).

Anorexia nervosa also will be subdivided in *DSM-IV*—into restrictor (i.e. reducing through diet and exercise alone) and bulimic subtypes. Restricting anorexics tend toward constraint and compulsivity, whereas bulimic anorexics are more likely to show impulsivity and emotional lability and are generally prone to more severe and diffuse psychopathology (Vitousek & Manke 1994). Thus, although these subtypes are based on clinical features of eating pathology, personality dimensions actually may constitute the underlying causal factors. Similarly, in a second-order factor analysis of the symptomatology in bulimia nervosa patients mentioned earlier, the factors that best defined the general factor were not specifically related to eating (Tobin et al 1991). Rather, factors such as personality disturbance, depression, and ineffectiveness accounted for most of the higher-order variance. Thus, personality factors may link subgroups of disordered eaters with patients whose primary clinical presentation is on Axis II (cf Johnson 1993).

Personality variables also appear to characterize subtypes of patients within the closely linked categories of substance abuse and antisocial PD. Sher & Trull (1994) note that these disorders each represent broad, heterogeneous constructs, although they share a common core of disinhibition. Sher & Trull suggest that both alcoholism and antisocial PD can be divided into at least two subtypes of patients with different personality characteristics—one group has more purely psychopathic attributes, whereas the other is characterized by emotional reactivity (neuroticism) (see also Gerstley et al 1990, Stein et al 1993). Similarly, Nathan (1993) proposes that the current categories of alcohol abuse and dependence might be supplemented by dimensional coding based on the prominent five-factor model of personality. He argues that defining alcoholism subtypes based on associated personality traits could provide more accurate description and identify important differences among patients who currently are lumped together. Finally, Hare and colleagues (1990) have identified two correlated but distinct factors of psychopathy—an affective interpersonal component (e.g. callousness) and social deviance (e.g. criminality)—that may be related differentially to comorbidity patterns. For example, Smith &

Newman (1990) found that only the social deviance factor was associated with lifetime alcohol use disorders in a sample of prison inmates.

Heterogeneity also exists within anxiety disorders, and these disorders illustrate the range of variables that have been suggested as bases for subtyping. For example, the wide variety of symptomatology that PTSD encompasses may reflect, at least in part, the nature of the precipitating stressor. Patients experiencing a single-impact traumatic event are more likely to reexperience the trauma, whereas multiple or chronic stressors are more strongly associated with dissociative symptoms (McNally 1991). Moreover, stressors of human origin are associated with greater severity (APA 1994). It is interesting to note, however, that in the *DSM-IV*, PTSD will be subdivided simply into acute, chronic, and delayed onset subtypes based on the onset and duration of symptoms (Liebowitz 1992), despite the lack of empirical data supporting the validity of these distinctions (Rothbaum & Foa 1993).

Various subclassifications of social phobia also have been considered, including two-group models focusing on single or few vs multiple fears and on performance vs interactional fears, as well as a three-group model based on performance vs limited interactional vs widespread interactional fears. However, the social phobia work group concluded that there were insufficient data to warrant a change from the current subtype formulation of generalized versus nongeneralized social phobia (Schneier et al 1994). At the same time, there is little evidence to suggest that the current dichotomous model actually reflects a qualitative difference (Schneier et al 1994). Turner et al (1992) found that patients with generalized social phobia showed greater severity and pervasiveness of distress, leading the authors to question the advantage of subtyping over simple, continuous ratings of severity.

It is increasingly clear that OCD patients also vary on a number of dimensions (e.g. degree of insight, overvalued ideation, psychotic thought processes, anxiety or depressive features, presence of both obsessions and compulsions or only one type of symptom; see Tynes et al 1990). Arts et al (1993) differentiated patients with obsessions alone from those with both features of the disorder on the basis of demographic characteristics, age of onset, severity of disorder, and degree of depressive symptomatology. It is not clear whether this heterogeneity represents systematic variation along a continuous severity dimension or reflects the existence of fundamentally different types of psychopathology.

Finally, the mood disorders represent a particularly complex case. Even limiting the example to major depression—which has a venerable history of subtyping schemes—we find that this disorder is subtyped in *DSM-IV* using a number of cross-sectional features that may or may not show cross-episode stability (e.g. melancholic, atypical, or catatonic features; with or without mood-congruent or incongruent features; postpartum onset) and course specifiers (with or without full interepisode recovery and seasonal pattern). The symptom presentations (and, consequently, the treatment implications) are so diverse that the validity of considering them all to reflect a single diagnosis must be questioned. We have used these examples to illustrate particular points; however, within-category heterogeneity is characteristic of most, if not all, of the *DSM* diagnoses, so similar considerations apply broadly across the taxonomy. Clearly, within-group heterogeneity remains a theoretical and empirical challenge.

FREQUENCY OF NOS DIAGNOSES   The second type of problematic heterogeneity is the large proportion of atypical or subthreshold cases who receive boundary diagnoses (e.g. schizoaffective disorder) or who fall under the rubric of "not otherwise specified" (NOS). High rates of NOS diagnoses are found within the mood disorders, for example. In epidemiological data from the Zurich Study—based on a community sample deemed at high risk for depression—52% had diagnoses consistent with depressive disorder NOS (Angst 1992b). Two large-scale surveys of psychiatric populations (Mezzich et al 1989, Saxena & Prasad 1989) also indicated that the clear majority of dissociative patients received an atypical dissociative diagnosis. Similarly, Spiegel & Cardeña (1991) concluded that dissociative disorder NOS is the most common condition within this diagnostic class. The diagnosis of personality disorder NOS also is relatively common. In a national sample of patients with personality disorder, Morey (1992) found that 22.3% were best described as PDNOS on the basis of a symptom checklist completed by their therapists. Notably, however, this diagnosis was assigned by these same therapists only 10.3% of the time, leading Morey to conclude that clinicians underuse this category in favor of standard diagnoses.

One strategy for reducing the high number of NOS diagnoses has been to elevate groups within a NOS category to distinct diagnoses. For example, bipolar II, a form of bipolar disorder characterized by depression and hypomanic symptoms rather than full-blown mania, was classified as bipolar disorder NOS in *DSM-III-R*. Cases of bipolar II appear with relatively high frequency, and 5–15% of bipolar II patients eventually will be reclassified as having bipolar I disorder, suggesting a common underlying diathesis (Blacker & Tsuang 1992, Dunner 1993). In a study that examined first-degree relatives of bipolar I or bipolar II probands, the rate of bipolar II (40%) far exceeded that of bipolar I (22%), the established form of bipolar disorder (Simpson et al 1992). These authors consequently proposed that bipolar II is the prototypic phenotype of the genetic form of bipolar disorder. Bipolar II will appear as a distinct category in *DSM-IV*. This obviously (and it would seem appropriately) will reduce the number of bipolar disorder NOS patients considerably; however, it is unclear whether creating a new diagnosis optimally represents the bipolar domain.

In other cases, new diagnostic categories proposed to increase coverage and reduce the number of NOS cases were rejected by the relevant *DSM-IV* work group, but a compromise was effected in which the proposed criteria were included as an example of a specific NOS symptom picture. For instance, to encompass the large number of patients who present with significant distress and impairment but who do not meet criteria for an established anxiety or mood disorder (Katon & Roy-Byrne 1991, Zinbarg et al 1994), proposals were made to include mixed anxiety-depression in *DSM-IV* (Clark & Watson 1991, Zinbarg & Barlow 1991). Similarly, Angst (1992a,b) documented the prevalence of two mood syndromes—recurrent brief depression and minor depression—in a longitudinal community-based high-risk study. Each of these three proposed diagnoses are listed, complete with criteria, as subtypes of either mood or anxiety disorder NOS. As a result, the number of NOS patients in these diagnostic classes may be expected to increase dramatically and to rival, or perhaps exceed, those with standard diagnoses.

The foregoing data document that the so-called atypical case often is more properly characterized as the typical diagnosis. Furthermore, additional data document the relative rarity of true prototypical cases. For example, Blashfield et al (1992), who established that a prototypic personality disorder (PD) was defined conceptually by clinicians as a patient meeting eight or more of a criterial set, found that 15% of a sample of 151 psychiatric patients could be characterized as prototypic PDs. Not surprisingly, however, in light of previously presented comorbidity data, most of these prototypic PD patients also met criteria for several other PDs. When only those prototypic PD patients who met criteria for a single PD were considered, the number of pure prototypic cases was reduced to only 1%. Analysis of a second sample of 320 nationally drawn patients showed similar rates of prototypic PDs—14% and 3%, respectively.

Much of the data related to NOS diagnoses are drawn from community samples, high-risk family studies, or primary care settings rather than inpatient or outpatient psychiatric settings. Indeed, prototypicality, severity, and comorbidity may interact such that comorbidity of full diagnoses is the norm at the severe end of the psychopathological spectrum, whereas mixed, subsyndromal symptom pictures are more common at the mild end. In either case, single, prototypic diagnoses appear to be the exception rather than the rule.

Finally, it is worth noting that comorbidity and heterogeneity are related issues. Problematic comorbidity exists, in part, because patients differ widely (i.e. they show within-group heterogeneity) in diagnostic features that are shared across diagnoses. That is, if patients sharing a diagnosis were relatively homogeneous with regard to the diagnosis' defining features and if the defining features were both structurally coherent and distinct from each other, then neither a comorbidity nor a heterogeneity problem would exist.[2]

Organizational Problems in DSM-IV

The viability of the *DSM-IV* taxonomy also has been questioned with regard to (*a*) the validity of the distinction between clinical syndromes and personality disorders and (*b*) problems in its phenomenological organization (i.e. concerns about the placement of specific disorders and the need for new diagnostic classes).

AXIS I VERSUS AXIS II   A primary innovation of *DSM-III* was the introduction of a multiaxial system for diagnosis, in which one important change was that clinical syndromes (coded on Axis I) are now separated from personality disorders (coded on Axis II).[3] There were several reasons for the creation of a separate Axis II, one of which was to increase the attention paid to personality disorders. Unquestionably, this purpose has been accomplished. Research in personality disorders has increased many-fold over the past decade, societies and journals devoted to their study have arisen, and personality disorders are now commonly diagnosed in clinical settings. More recently, however, the validity of the distinction has been questioned on both empirical (Widiger & Shea 1991) and conceptual grounds (Livesley et al 1994).

The separation of schizotypal PD from schizophrenia is perhaps the most inconsistent with current theory and data. A sizable body of evidence regarding family history, symptomatology, treatment response, and biological markers indicates that schizotypal PD is closely related to schizophrenia and perhaps shares one or more vulnerability dimensions (Grove et al 1991, Lenzenweger & Korfine 1992, Widiger & Shea 1991). Siever & Davis (1991) propose a new class of schizophrenic spectrum disorders that would include schizophrenia and the Axis II schizoid and schizotypal PDs.

Another particularly problematic boundary area is the distinction between avoidant PD and social phobia, generalized type (Herbert et al 1992, Holt et al 1992, Schneier et al 1991, Turner et al 1992). These diagnoses obviously share overlapping symptomatology: Avoidant PD involves pervasive social discomfort, whereas generalized social phobia (GSP) involves a persistent, irrational fear of social situations. Moreover, GSP typically has an early onset so that the disorders cannot be distinguished on the basis of course. Empiri-

---

[2]   We are grateful to Roger Blashfield and Auke Tellegen for pointing out this connection, although we are responsible if we have misrepresented their arguments.

[3]   Specific developmental disorders also were coded on Axis II originally, but we limit our attention to the personality disorders.

cally, the diagnostic distinction is characterized primarily by degree of severity without a clear or substantial boundary: GSP occurs without avoidant PD, but avoidant PD in the absence of GSP is rare. On the basis of these data, Widiger (1992b) argued against the assignment of dual diagnoses to what is essentially a single form of psychopathology and suggested alternative modes of classification, such as listing the disorder on both axes or using dimensional ratings of social avoidance. In a review of relations between anxiety and personality disorders, Stein et al (1993) presented evidence that panic disorder also is related to avoidant PD, as well as more generally to the Cluster B personality disorders. They suggested that the common component is broader than social avoidance and speculated about possible psychobiological mechanisms.

The relation between borderline PD and the mood disorders has been a matter of some debate (Blacker & Tsuang 1993, Widiger & Shea 1991). Reversing an earlier stance that the two were linked through nonspecific etiologic variables (Gunderson & Elliott 1985), Gunderson & Phillips (1991) concluded that these disorders coexist but are essentially unrelated. This position has been challenged, however, with the heterogeneity of depression arising as a key issue (Heritch 1992). If borderline pathology is related to some forms of depression but not to others, then dimensional analyses of the common and distinctive features may be helpful in resolving the controversy. Furthermore, Stein et al (1993) have suggested that borderline PD and certain mood and anxiety disorders may all share a nonspecific neurobiological substrate.

The relation between antisocial PD and substance use disorders also has received considerable attention. It must be noted that definitional and design issues confound the study of these disorders (Sher & Trull 1994). For example, the criteria for antisocial PD are highly influenced by substance use behaviors and some of the criteria are conceptually equivalent (Widiger & Shea 1991). Sher & Trull (1994) thoroughly analyzed several models of the relation between alcoholism and antisocial PD and found that the heterogeneity of both disorders precludes any simple or clear conclusions. As mentioned earlier, they argue for at least two subtypes of each disorder, linked by common personality traits or underlying vulnerabilities.

PROBLEMS IN PHENOMENOLOGICAL ORGANIZATION

Placement of disorders in particular diagnostic classes   Many researchers have argued that some disorders currently are placed in the wrong diagnostic class. For instance, Kihlstrom (1992) and Nemiah (1991) have suggested that conversion disorder shares essential phenomenological features with the dissociative disorders and so should be placed there, rather than within the somatoform disorders (for a rebuttal, see Martin 1992). Others have suggested that PTSD—which is associated with depersonalization, detachment, and elevated levels of dissociative symptomatology—is better viewed as a dissociative than as an anxiety disorder (Davidson & Foa 1991, Spiegel & Cardeña 1991). Ironically, the newly defined acute stress disorder, which is classified as an anxiety disorder along with PTSD, originated as a proposal for a brief reactive dissociative disorder, owing to its predominant dissociative symptomatology. Côté et al (1994) have argued that at least one form of hypochondriasis—that defined primarily by the fear that one has a disease—may be characterized more accurately as an anxiety disorder, perhaps as a variant of specific phobia. Similarly, because of its strong link with OCD, it may be preferable to categorize BDD as an anxiety disorder (Hollander et al 1992, Phillips 1991).

These diverse proposals all highlight a taxonomic problem for which no satisfactory solution has been found. That is, although the major phemonologically based diagnostic classes may seem intuitively compelling and relatively straightforward, several specific disorders do not fit comfortably into any one of them. Many disorders are phenomenological hybrids that encompass dysfunction characteristic of two or more diagnostic classes. For example, to some extent, conversion disorder is both a somatoform and a dissociative disorder, hypochondriasis is both a somatoform and an anxiety disorder, PTSD is both an anxiety and a dissociative disorder, and generalized social phobia and avoidant PD are both anxiety and personality disorders. Widely discussed in the work group meetings, this issue of phenomenologic complexity is largely ignored in the official document, although *DSM-IV* explicitly acknowledges evidence linking conversion disorder (which remains categorized as a somatoform disorder) to the dissociative disorders (see Martin 1992).

New phenomenological classes   Others have argued for the creation of entirely new phenomenological classes. For instance, some authors have emphasized the phenomenologic similarities among the substance disorders, paraphilias, bulimia, and the impulse control disorders (e.g. trichotillomania, kleptomania) and have argued that such disorders should be included in a new class of impulse control disorders (for a review, see McElroy et al 1992). Similarly, Tynes et al (1990) have highlighted the centrality of obsessive-compulsive symptomatology in a variety of disorders (e.g. the impulse control disorders, hypochondriasis, BDD, anorexia, and bulimia), and they have proposed a nosological revision in which these disorders are recognized as variants of OCD (see also Hollander 1993, Hollander et al 1992, McElroy et al 1992, Phillips 1991).

IMPLICATIONS FOR CHANGE IN THE TAXONOMY

Implications of Comorbidity

INHERENT LIMITATIONS OF CATEGORICAL SYSTEMS   As the magnitude of the comorbidity problem has become apparent, psychopathologists increasingly have argued that these data demonstrate serious problems in the *DSM* taxonomy. Admittedly, some of the co-occurrence is related in a superficial way to the sheer proliferation of diagnostic categories, which ironically occurred, in part, to increase coverage. Over time, the number of officially recognized diagnostic categories has increased from 106 diagnostic categories in *DSM-I* to 182 in *DSM-II*, 265 in *DSM-III*, and 292 in *DSM-III-R*. Owing to the Task Force's conservative approach to the addition of new diagnoses, the count in *DSM-IV* has remained steady at 297 (not including those in appendices).

More fundamentally, however, a growing number of investigators are concluding that the comorbidity problem stems from an inherent incompatibility between the nature of psychopathology and categorical taxonomies. That is, perhaps no categorical system can classify psychopathology adequately (e.g. Clarkin & Kendall 1992, Widiger & Shea 1991). Reviewing data on the somatoform disorders, Kirmayer and colleagues (1994) concluded: "The fact that patients commonly have multiple diagnoses in a system made up of disjunctive categories reflects not so much the terrible irony of lightning striking twice in the same place as it does the limited ability of these categories to capture the natural covariation of forms of distress" (p. 131).

Because the bulk of research examining comorbidity was begun after the publication of *DSM-III-R*, these data did not have a major impact on *DSM-IV*. Brown & Barlow (1992), however, predict that "With the 12- to 15-year lag anticipated before the appearance of *DSM-V*, data on comorbidity, and the conceptual advances that will emanate from these data, should profoundly affect the clinical science" (p. 842).

THE NECESSITY OF COMPREHENSIVE ASSESSMENT   The data on comorbidity also challenge the meaningfulness of a classic psychopathology research paradigm in which investigators identify a group of individuals who share a common diagnosis and then examine them on variables hypothesized to be relevant to the etiology, course, or treatment of the disorder. The problem with this paradigm is that the selected diagnostic group can be expected to show a very diffuse pattern of psychopathology. For example, most bulimics do not suffer simply from bulimia; they also show high rates of depression, anxiety, and personality disorders (Kendler et al 1991, Sunday et al 1993). Accordingly, it is impossible to say whether any observed correlates of bulimia have a specific affinity with eating disorder; rather, they may reflect the confounding influence of some other psychopathology. (For a discussion of this issue, see Johnson et al 1990.)

One possible solution is to study only the pure, non-comorbid manifestations of the disorder, but there are two basic problems with this approach. First, these pure, uncomplicated cases may be difficult to find. Second and more importantly, even if a sample of non-comorbid cases can be identified, they are likely to be atypical and unrepresentative of the overall population of individuals with the disorder. A better approach to this interpretative problem is to assess psychopathology comprehensively in order to analyze the influence of comorbid conditions directly. Clearly, new research designs are needed that reflect the complexity of psychopathological conditions.

Implications of Heterogeneity

As with comorbidity, researchers are only gradually realizing the scope and magnitude of this problem. Because most psychopathology research is focused on a limited range of disorders, researchers typically are aware of within-group heterogeneity and boundary problems in their own area, but are less cognizant that similar issues plague the field as a whole. Moreover, the *DSM* may be a victim of its own success. The development and use of structured assessment methods in connection with the recent *DSM*s has helped to reveal the extent of comorbidity, while increased awareness of psychopathology in primary care settings has highlighted the inability of the taxonomy to categorize patients with mixed symptom pictures at the milder end of the pathological spectrum.

As mentioned, problems of heterogeneity have been addressed in the recent *DSM*s through subtyping and the addition of new categories. Although these strategies increase coverage for previously undiagnosable patients, they also create an increasingly cumbersome taxonomy with many categories that rarely are used in clinical practice (Blashfield et al 1990). Regrettably, new categories become reified, even when there is little evidence of their validity, so that it has proved far more difficult to remove diagnoses from the *DSM*s than to add them (First 1994). More importantly, adding categories to improve coverage ultimately may be futile. Frances et al (1991) note that it is not possible to encompass the wide range of symptom presentations in patient populations and that atypical cases are an inevitable by-product of categorical classification. Indeed, division of diagnoses into separate disorders will simply replace old areas of diagnostic confusion with new boundary or residual cases.

Implications of Problems in Organization

AXIS I VERSUS AXIS II   Frances et al (1991) have pointed out that there is no compelling conceptual or definitional justification for separating personality disorders from Axis I syndromes. Accordingly, the placement of some disorders seems arbitrary and inconsistent. For example, one could argue with consider-able justification that certain chronic Axis I disorders (e.g. cyclothymia, dys-thymia, GAD, GSP) have personality-disorder-like features that merit their being switched to Axis II or, conversely, that schizotypal PD, because of its relation to schizophrenia, should be coded on Axis I. In fact, some investigators have charged that the division exists primarily for pragmatic rather than scien-tific reasons (Livesley et al 1994). Hirschfeld (1993) has proposed five distinc-tive features of personality disorder: early onset, stability and persistence, pervasiveness, interpersonal focus, and impairment; but the validity of these features has not been tested.

Livesley et al (1994) discuss three conceptual rationales that have been put forward for the separation of mental states (Axis I syndromes) and personality disorders: etiology, formal structure of psychopathology, and temporal stabil-ity. They conclude that there is little conceptual or empirical support for the distinction from any of these viewpoints; "nor does there appear to be any reliable and valid criterion for making the distinction" (p. 14). Interestingly, they call for the inclusion of personality disorder on Axis I, with the separate coding of personality traits on Axis II, arguing that manifestations of both clinical syndromes and personality disorders may stem from underlying traits. In light of increased evidence for the role of personality in relation to both Axis I and Axis II pathology (e.g. Cloninger 1994, Watson & Clark 1994), this position is perhaps not as radical as it may seem at first glance.

PHENOMENOLOGICAL ORGANIZATION   The proposed phenomenologically based revisions (e.g. placing conversion disorder within the dissociative disor-ders) demonstrate, first, that accepting a descriptive taxonomic scheme does not necessarily imply endorsement of all of the current groupings. More fundamen-tally, these proposals highlight the fact that the phenomenology of the current system is poorly articulated and that remarkably little attention has been given to the nature and composition of the various diagnostic classes. In many instances it is even difficult to understand the rationale for placing a disorder into a particular higher-order class.

As an illustration, consider the class of somatoform disorders. The *DSM-IV* states that "The common feature of the Somatoform Disorders is the presence of physical symptoms that suggest a general medical condition...and are not fully explained by a general medical condition" (p. 445). Initially, this organiz-ing principle seems straightforward. An examination of the disorders sub-sumed within this category, however, reveals that some are not concerned with prominent physical symptomatology at all. For instance, a diagnosis of hypo-chondriasis does not require significant physical symptoms unless a symptom is taken to mean any bodily sensation (e.g. Côté et al 1994, Kihlstrom 1992). Even more clearly, patients with BDD have no "physical symptoms that suggest a general medical condition"; rather, they are preoccupied with "an *imagined* defect in appearance" (APA 1994, p. 468; emphasis added). With the current definition, there is no compelling justification for placing these disorders within the class of somatoform disorders. An alternative formulation that incorporates patient (mis)perceptions of physical sensations and characteristics might encompass the currently defined set of diagnoses more adequately, but the point remains that the organizing principle seems to reflect semantics rather than natural groupings.

Recognizing this point raises an even more fundamental issue. The various proposals for organizational revision of the *DSM* all reflect the implicit assumption that diagnostic class membership is important. That is, there is little point in debating whether conversion disorder is a dissociative or somatoform disorder unless its placement has important diagnostic implications. Therefore, it is surprising to find that placement may *not* have important diagnostic implications. For instance, in discussing the organizing role of diagnostic classes, Spitzer (1991) states that they "are easy to remember given that they correspond to the way that clinicians and researchers think about these disorders" (pp. 295–296), which suggests that their primary function is to facilitate the location of disorders in the manual. Moreover, there is nothing in the manual to indicate that any particular significance should be attached to diagnostic class membership.

In contrast, the recent proliferation of debates on this issue indicates that those in the field do attach significance to class membership. Furthermore, the existence of class-based clinics (e.g. specializing in sleep, anxiety, or mood disorders) and journals (e.g. *Journal of Personality Disorders, International Journal of Eating Disorders*) attests to the continuing power of these diagnostic categories to shape both treatment and research.

RECONSIDERATION OF THE CLASSIFICATION SYSTEM

Alternatives to a Phenomenological, Descriptive Approach

As described earlier, the *DSM* disorders are not grouped, for the most part, on etiological or other theoretical grounds; rather, disorders are placed into the major classes on the basis of shared symptomatology. Many critiques of the existing taxonomy directly challenge phenomenology as the primary organizing principle (e.g. Andreasen & Carpenter 1993, Perry 1990), while others emphasize the lack of theoretical justification for current groupings (e.g. Carson 1991). Few dispute the desirability of an increased role for theory on conceptual grounds, but views differ markedly on the urgency and viability of developing a theory-based classification system (Frances et al 1991, Millon 1991, Morey 1991, Perry 1990).

ETIOLOGY   Some proposals emphasize the desirability of etiologically based classification. For example, Andreasen & Carpenter (1993) discuss limitations of both the traditional symptom-based approach to the diagnosis and classification of schizophrenia and the use of external validators as proposed by Robins & Guze (1970). Andreasen & Carpenter emphasize the need to identify etiologic mechanisms as the defining features of a disorder in order to understand the core of the disorder and to explain the observed heterogeneity. Others assert that etiological explanations are needed to account for the observed comorbidities between, for example, anxiety and eating disorders (Schwalberg et al 1992), antisocial PD and substance abuse (Sher & Trull 1994), anxiety and depressive disorders (Clark & Watson 1991), and the newly proposed group of impulse control disorders (Hollander et al 1992, Tynes et al 1990).

Hudson & Pope (1990) discuss the merits of a variant of etiologically based classification. They note that several disorders (e.g. major depression, bulimia, panic disorder, OCD, ADD) respond favorably to antidepressant drugs. Accordingly, they propose that these disorders reflect a common pathophysiologic mechanism and should be grouped together under the label of affective spectrum disorder.

Others have proposed new etiologically based classes. For example, several investigators have asserted that PTSD and the adjustment disorders should be grouped together in a category of stress disorders or trauma disorders that recognizes the necessary etiological role of stressful life events in the development of these conditions (Brett 1993, Davidson & Foa 1991). One problem with this notion is that, when compared to identified etiological agents such as germs, toxins, and tumors, the exact etiological role of trauma is much less precise, especially since many individuals exposed to trauma do not develop a disorder (Breslau et al 1991, Davidson & Foa 1991). Furthermore, stress, trauma, and abuse have been linked to many other conditions, including conversion disorder, somatization disorder, borderline PD, and various dissociative disorders (Gunderson & Sabo 1993; Martin 1992; Pribor et al 1993; Ross et al 1989, 1990; Spiegel & Cardeña 1991); hence, it is unclear how broad and inclusive this proposed new category should be.

DIMENSIONAL APPROACHES   Psychopathologists increasingly are advocating a partial or complete abandonment of the current categorical system; in its place, many favor the expanded use of a dimensional system in which symptomatology is assessed on a linear continuum of graded severity. Advocacy of a dimensional system has been particularly strong among researchers of personality disorder, who are closest to a consensus that the domain is characterized better by a relatively small set of personality trait dimensions than by a set of categorical diagnoses (e.g. Clark 1993, 1994; Harkness 1992; Livesley et al 1994; Costa & Widiger 1994; Widiger & Shea 1991). However, the issue also has been raised for schizophrenia (Andreasen & Carpenter 1993), depersonalization disorder (Simeon & Hollander 1993), and the somatoform (Katon et al 1991, Kirmayer et al 1994), anxiety (Brown & Barlow 1992), bipolar (Blacker & Tsuang 1992), substance abuse (Helzer 1994, Tarter et al 1992), eating (Gleaves et al 1993, Tobin et al 1991), and obsessive-compulsive spectrum or impulse control (Hollander 1993) disorders.

Moving to a dimensional system offers at least two major advantages. First, it would replace the current set of approximately 300 diagnostic categories with a much smaller set of basic dimensions. Second, it affords a greater role to the critical factor of severity of disorder. The framers of *DSM-IV* acknowledge the lack of fit between the system and reality (e.g. Frances et al 1991 noted that "nature seems to abhor clear boundaries," p. 408), but, not unreasonably, they rejected the adoption of a dimensional system in the *DSM-IV* as premature. Their objections ranged from the pragmatic (e.g. the unfamiliarity of clinicians with dimensional systems) to the irrelevant (e.g. the vividness of categorical names) to the perfectly valid assertion that "there is as yet no agreement on the choice of the optimal dimensions to be used for classification purposes" (APA 1994, p. xxii).

Even the term "dimensional" is not used consistently among researchers (Clark 1994). For example, dimensions may refer to (*a*) degrees of severity for defined sets of symptoms; (*b*) individual phenotypic symptom or personality trait dimensions, which in varied combinations produce the wide array of observed psychopathology; (*c*) underlying single or multifactorial genetic vulnerabilities; or (*d*) specific biological parameters. Thus, although the value of dimensional approaches for specific disorders or classes of disorders is easily and widely recognized, the issues involved in developing a dimension-based taxonomy will be at least as complex as those facing the *DSM-IV* Task Force. For example, future research must explore such difficult problems as whether a single unified set of dimensions is adequate to describe the entire domain of psychopathology and, even if so, which types of dimensions (even more problematic, which specific dimensions) are most valid for classification purposes. Moreover, multifactorial dimensional systems typically have a hierarchical structure (Watson et al 1994), with higher- versus lower-order levels of analysis yielding different types of information, whose relevance for classification would need explication. Finally, it should be made clear that opposing dimensional versus categorical approaches is a false dichotomy (Tellegen 1993). It is an empirical question whether a particular set of dimensional indicators will support or refute the existence of a given categorical entity.

On the one hand, dimensional approaches hold promise and deserve serious exploration while, on the other hand, a tremendous amount of work needs to be done before psychopathologists can even begin to contemplate replacing the current system with a dimension-based taxonomy. It would not be much of an improvement—and would probably be more cumbersome and less useful—to replace the current set of categorical diagnoses with an unintegrated hodge-podge of dimensions. Thus, it is time to halt the general call for dimensional systems and to begin the hard work of developing specific dimensional proposals in targeted domains, such as personality disorder, where the current categorical system has proved to be most problematic.

CONCLUDING REMARKS

The *DSM-IV* reflects a compromise of interests (Frances et al 1991). Its primary goal was clinical utility; the interests of lawyers, insurers, parole officers, disability claims personnel, statisticians, educators, and so forth also played a role, however minor. Although empirical considerations were weighted especially strongly in the latest revision, many decisions were made on the basis of expert consensus in the absence of data. Perhaps the *DSM-IV* is best viewed as a document with mixed origins and purposes, based in part on scientific principles but also reflecting other influences. In this regard, it is noteworthy that there will be two versions of the *International Classification of Diseases*: one for clinicians and one for researchers. In the long run, of course, the most clinically useful system will be one that has maximal predictive power regarding course and treatment because it is based on a scientific understanding of the relevant parameters.

Second, the *DSM-IV* describes a collection of disorders, not an integrated system of psychopathology. The science of psychopathology is still primitive and thus is best applied in lower-order, local systems, which is well reflected in the highly decentralized nature of the current research enterprise and the *DSM-IV* revision process. However, this focus on local problems—which provides the richness of phenotypic description that is one of the *DSM*'s strengths—also inhibits discovering the interconnections across domains.

Finally, another strength of the operational approach of the recent *DSM*s is that it permits explicit empirical testing. Our review has documented some limitations of the current classification of psychopathology thus revealed, and we predict that problems in the current system will only become more apparent with further research. We are hopeful, however, that a more logical, coherent, and valid taxonomy will emerge from the interplay of compelling, integrative theories of psychopathology with empirical data across domains from behavior to neurophysiology.

ACKNOWLEDGMENTS

We wish to thank Roger Blashfield, David Freides, Allen Frances, Robert Spitzer, Auke Tellegen, Tom Widiger, and Mark Zimmerman for their insightful comments on a previous draft of this paper.

Literature Cited

Am. Psychiatr. Assoc. 1980. *Diagnostic and Statistical Manual of Mental Disorders.* Washington, DC: Am. Psychiatr. Assoc. 3rd ed.

Am. Psychiatr. Assoc. 1987. *Diagnostic and Statistical Manual of Mental Disorders.* Washington, DC: Am. Psychiatr. Assoc. 3rd ed. rev.

Am. Psychiatr. Assoc. 1994. *Diagnostic and Statistical Manual of Mental Disorders.* Washington, DC: Am. Psychiatr. Assoc. 4th ed.

Andreasen NC, Carpenter WT. 1993. Diagnosis and classification of schizophrenia. *Schizophr. Bull.* 19:199–214

Andrews G, Stewart G, Morris-Yates A, Holt P, Henderson S. 1990. Evidence for a general neurotic syndrome. *Br. J. Psychiatr.* 157:6–12

Angst J. 1992a. Minor depression and recurrent brief depression. In *Chronic Depressions and Their Treatment,* ed. HS Akiskal, GB Cassano. New York: Guilford

Angst J. 1992b. Recurrent brief psychiatric syndromes of depression, hypomania, neurasthenia, and anxiety from an epidemiological point of view. *Neurol. Psychiatr. Brain Res.* 1:5–12

Arndt S, Alliger RJ, Andreasen NC. 1991. The distinction of positive and negative symptoms: the failure of a two-dimensional model. *Br. J. Psychiatr.* 158:317–22

Arts W, Hoogduin K, Schaap C, De Haan E. 1993. Do patients suffering from obsessions alone differ from other obsessive-compulsives? *Behav. Res. Ther.* 31:119–23

Aubert JL, Rush JA. 1994. Schizoaffective disorder: a review for DSM-IV. See Widiger et al 1994, Vol. 2:In press

Baer L, Jenike MA, Black DW, Treece C, Rosenfeld MS, Greist J. 1992. Effect of Axis II diagnoses on treatment outcome with clomipramine in 55 patients with obsessive-compulsive disorder. *Arch. Gen. Psychiatr.* 49:862–66

Barsky AJ, Wyshak G, Klerman GL. 1992. Psychiatric comorbidity in *DSM-III-R* hypochondriasis. *Arch. Gen. Psychiatr.* 49: 101–8

Biederman J, Faraone SV, Lapey K. 1992. Comorbidity of diagnosis in attention-deficit hyperactivity disorder. *Child Adol. Psychiatr. Clin. N. Am.* 1:335–60

Blacker D, Tsuang MT. 1992. Contested boundaries of bipolar disorder and the limits of categorical diagnosis in psychiatry. *Am. J. Psychiatr.* 149:1473–83

Blashfield RK. 1989. Alternative taxonomic models of psychiatric classification. In *The Validity of Psychiatric Diagnosis,* ed. LN Robins, JE Barrett, pp. 77–97. New York: Raven

Blashfield RK, Livesley WJ. 1991. Metaphorical analysis of psychiatric classification as a psychological test. *J. Abnorm. Psychol.* 100:262–70

Blashfield RK, McElroy RA, Pfohl B, Blum N. 1992. *Are there any prototypic personality disorder patients?* Presented at Annu. Conv. Am. Psychol. Assoc., 100th, Washington, DC

Blashfield RK, Sprock J, Fuller AK. 1990. Suggested guidelines for including or excluding categories in the *DSM-IV. Compr. Psychiatr.* 31:15–19

Boyd JH, Burke JD Jr, Gruenberg E, Holzer CE III, Rae DS, et al. 1984. Exclusion criteria of *DSM-III* : a study of hierarchy-free syndromes. *Arch. Gen. Psychiatr.* 41:983–89

Brady K, Anton R, Ballenger JC, Lydiard RB, Adinoff B, Selander J. 1990. Cocaine abuse in schizophrenic patients. *Am. J. Psychiatr.* 147:1164–67

Brawman-Mintzer O, Lydiard RB, Emmanuel N, Payeur R, Johnson M, et al. 1993. Psychiatric comorbidity in patients with generalized anxiety disorder. *Am. J. Psychiatr.* 150:1216–18

Breslau N, Davis GC, Andreski P, Peterson E. 1991. Traumatic events and posttraumatic stress disorder in an urban population of young adults. *Arch. Gen. Psychiatr.* 48: 216–22

Brett E. 1993. Classifications of posttraumatic stress disorder in *DSM-IV*: anxiety disorder, dissociative disorder, or stress disorder? In *Posttraumatic Stress Disorder,* ed. JRT Davidson, EB Foa, pp. 191–204. Washington, DC: Am. Psychiatr. Press

Brown TA, Barlow DH. 1992. Comorbidity among anxiety disorders: implications for treatment and *DSM-IV. J. Consult. Clin. Psychol.* 60:835–44

Carroll KM, Rounsaville BJ. 1993. History and significance of childhood attention deficit disorder in treatment-seeking cocaine abusers. *Compr. Psychiatr.* 34:75–82

Carson RC. 1991. Dilemmas in the pathway of the *DSM-IV. J. Abnorm. Psychol.* 100:302–7

Christenson GA, Mackenzie TB, Mitchell JE. 1991. Characteristics of 60 adult chronic hair pullers. *Am. J. Psychiatr.* 148:365–70

Clark LA. 1993. *Manual for the Schedule for Nonadaptive and Adaptive Personality.* Minneapolis: Univ. Minn. Press

Clark LA. 1994. Dimensional approaches to personality disorder assessment and diagnosis. See Cloninger 1994. In press

Clark LA, Watson D. 1991. Tripartite model of anxiety and depression: psychometric evidence and taxonomic implications. *J. Abnorm. Psychol.* 100:316–36

Clarkin JF, Kendall PC. 1992. Comorbidity and treament planning: summary and future directions. *J. Consult. Clin. Psychol.* 60:904–8

Cloninger CR, ed. 1994. *Personality and Psychopathology.* Washington, DC: Am. Psychiatr. Press. In press

Coryell W, Endicott J, Winokur G. 1992. Anxiety syndromes as epiphenomena of primary major depression: outcome and familial psychopathology. *Am. J. Psychiatr.* 149:100–7

Costa PT Jr, Widiger TA, eds. 1994. *Personality Disorders and the Five-factor Model of Personality.* Washington, DC: Am. Psychol. Assoc.

Côté G, O'Leary T, Barlow DH, Strain J. 1994. Hypochondriasis: integrative review. See Widiger et al 1994, Vol. 2:In press

Davidson JRT, Foa EB. 1991. Diagnostic issues in posttraumatic stress disorder: considerations for the *DSM-IV. J. Abnorm. Psychol.* 100:346–55

Davidson JRT, Kudler HS, Saunders WB, Smith RD. 1990. Symptom and comorbidity patterns in World War II and Vietnam veterans with posttraumatic stress disorder. *Compr. Psychiatr.* 31:162–70

Diguer L, Barber JP, Luborsky L. 1993. Three concomitants: personality disorders, psychiatric severity, and outcome of dynamic psychotherapy of major depression. *Am. J. Psychiatr.* 150:1246–48

Dinwiddie SH, Reich T. 1993. Attribution of antisocial symptoms in coexistent antisocial personality disorder and substance abuse. *Compr. Psychiatr.* 34:235–42

Dunner DL. 1993. A review of the diagnostic status of 'bipolar II' for the DSM-IV work group on mood disorders. *Depression* 1:2–10

Fabrega H Jr, Ulrich R, Pilkonis P, Mezzich JE. 1992. Pure personality disorders in an intake psychiatric setting. *J. Pers. Disord.* 6:153–61

Farmer R, Nelson-Gray RO. 1990. Personality

disorders and depression: hypothetical relations, empirical findings, and methodological considerations. *Clin. Psychol. Rev.* 10:453–76

First MB. 1994. *Preparing for DSM-IV.* Presented at the Clin. Assess. Conf. Kona, Hawaii

Frances AJ, First MB, Widiger TA, Miele GM, Tilly SM, et al. 1991. An A to Z guide to *DSM-IV* conundrums. *J. Abnorm. Psychol.* 100:407–12

Frances AJ, Pincus HA, Widiger TA, Davis WW, First MB. 1990. *DSM-IV*: work in progress. *Am. J. Psychiatr.* 147:1439–48

Galbaud du Fort G, Newman SC, Bland RC. 1993. Psychiatric comorbidity and treatment seeking: sources of selection bias in the study of clinical populations. *J. Nerv. Ment. Dis.* 181:467–74

Gerstley LJ, Alterman AI, McLellan AT, Woody GE. 1990. Antisocial personality disorder in patients with substance abuse disorders: a problematic diagnosis? *Am. J. Psychiatr.* 147:173–78

Gleaves DH, Williamson DA, Barker SE. 1993. Confirmatory factor analysis of a multidimensional model of bulimia nervosa. *J. Abnorm. Psychol.* 102:173–76

Grove WM, Lebow BS, Clementz BA, Cerri A, Medus C, Iacono WG. 1991. Familial prevalence and coaggregation of schizotypy indicators: a multitrait family study. *J. Abnorm. Psychol.* 100:115–21

Gunderson JG, Elliott GR. 1985. The interface between borderline personality and affective disorder. *Am. J. Psychiatr.* 142:277–88

Gunderson JG, Phillips KA. 1991. A current view of the interface between borderline personality disorder and depression. *Am. J. Psychiatr.* 148:967–75

Gunderson JG, Ronningstam E, Smith LE. 1991a. Narcissistic personality disorder: A review of data on *DSM-III-R* descriptions. *J. Pers. Disord.* 5:167–77

Gunderson JG, Sabo AN. 1993. The phenomenological and conceptual interface between borderline personality disorder and PTSD. *Am. J. Psychiatr.* 150:19–27

Gunderson JG, Zanarini MC, Kisiel CL. 1991b. Borderline personality disorder: a review of data on *DSM-III-R* descriptions. *J. Pers. Disord.* 5:340–52

Halmi KA, Eckert E, Marchi P, Sampugnaro V, Apple R, Cohen J. 1991. Comorbidity of psychiatric diagnoses in anorexia nervosa. *Arch. Gen. Psychiatr.* 48:712–18

Hare RD, Harpur TJ, Hakstian AR, Forth AE, Hart SD, Newman JP. 1990. The revised psychopathy checklist: reliability and factor structure. *Psychol. Assess.* 2:338–41

Harkness AR. 1992. Fundamental topics in the personality disorders: candidate trait dimensions from lower regions of the hierarchy. *Psychol. Assess.* 4:251–59

Helzer JE. 1994. Psychoactive substance abuse and its relation to dependence. See Widiger et al 1994, 1:33–44

Hendriks VM. 1990. Psychiatric disorders in a Dutch addict population: rates and correlates of *DSM-III* diagnosis. *J. Consult. Clin. Psychol.* 58:158–65

Herbert JD, Hope DA, Bellack AS. 1992. Validity of the distinction between generalized social phobia and avoidant personality disorder. *J. Abnorm. Psychol.* 101:332–39

Heritch AJ. 1992. Borderline personality disorder and depressive disorder. *Am. J. Psychiatr.* 149:852

Hirschfeld RMA. 1993. Personality disorders: definition and diagnosis. *J. Pers. Disord.* 7:9–17 (Suppl.)

Hirschfeld RMA, Shea MT, Weise R. 1991. Dependent personality disorder: perspectives for *DSM-IV*. *J. Pers. Disord.* 5:135–49

Hollander E. 1993. Obsessive-compulsive spectrum disorders: an overview. *Psychiatr. Ann.* 23:355–58

Hollander E, Neville D, Frenkel M, Josephson S, Liebowitz MR. 1992. Body dysmorphic disorder: diagnostic issues and related disorders. *Psychosomatics* 33:156–65

Holt CS, Heimberg RG, Hope DA. 1992. Avoidant personality disorder and the generalized subtype of social phobia. *J. Abnorm. Psychol.* 101:318–25

Hudson JI, Pope HG Jr. 1990. Affective spectrum disorder: Does antidepressant response identify a family of disorders with a common pathophysiology? *Am. J. Psychiatr.* 147:552–64

Johnson J, Weissman MM, Klerman GL. 1990. Panic disorder, comorbidity, and suicide attempts. *Arch. Gen. Psychiatr.* 47:805–8

Johnson TM. 1993. Vomiting as a manifestation of borderline personality disorder in primary care. *J. Am. Board Fam. Pract.* 6:385–94

Katon W, Lin E, Von Korff M, Russo J, Lipscomb P, Bush T. 1991. Somatization: a spectrum of severity. *Am. J. Psychiatr.* 148:34–40

Katon W, Roy-Byrne PP. 1991. Mixed anxiety and depression. *J. Abnorm. Psychol.* 100: 337–45

Keefe RSE, Lobel DS, Mohs RC, Silverman JM, Harvey PD, et al. 1991. Diagnostic issues in chronic schizophrenia: Kraepelinian schizophrenia, undifferentiated schizophrenia, and state-independent negative symptoms. *Schizophr. Res.* 4:71–79

Keller MB, Lavori PW, Mueller TI, Endicott J, Coryell W, et al. 1992. Time to recovery, chronicity, and levels of psychopathology in major depression: a 5-year prospective follow-up of 431 subjects. *Arch. Gen. Psychiatr.* 49:809–16

Kendall PC, Clarkin JF. 1992. Introduction to Special Section: comorbidity and treatment implications. *J. Consult. Clin. Psychol.* 60: 833–34

Kendall PC, Kortlander E, Chansky TE, Brady EU. 1992. Comorbidity of anxiety and depression in youth: treatment implications. *J. Consult. Clin. Psychol.* 60:869–80

Kendler KS. 1990. Towards a scientific psychiatric nosology: strengths and limitations. *Arch. Gen. Psychiatr.* 47:969–73

Kendler KS, Heath AC, Neale MC, Kessler RC, Eaves LJ. 1993. Alcoholism and major depression in women: a twin study of the causes of comorbidity. *Arch. Gen. Psychiatr.* 50:690–98

Kendler KS, MacLean C, Neale M, Kessler RC. 1991. The genetic epidemiology of bulimia nervosa. *Am. J. Psychiatr.* 148:1627–37

Kendler KS, Neale MC, Kessler RC, Heath AC, Eaves LJ. 1992. Major depression and generalized anxiety disorder: same genes, partly different environments? *Arch. Gen. Psychiatr.* 49:716–22

Kessler RC, McGonagle KA, Zhao S, Nelson CB, Hughes M, et al. 1994. Lifetime and 12-month prevalence of *DSM-III-R* psychiatric disorders in the United States: results from the National Comorbidity Study. *Arch. Gen. Psychiatr.* 51:8–19

Kihlstrom JF. 1992. Dissociative and conversion disorders. In *Cognitive Science and Clinical Disorders*, ed. DJ Stein, J Young, pp. 247–70. San Diego: Academic

Kirmayer LJ, Robbins JM, Paris J. 1994. Somatoform disorders: personality and the social matrix of somatic distress. *J. Abnorm. Psychol.* 103:125–36

Kushner MG, Sher KJ, Beitman BD. 1990. The relation between alcohol problems and the anxiety disorders. *Am. J. Psychiatr.* 147:685–95

Laberge B, Gauthier JG, Côté G, Plamondon J, Cormier HJ. 1993. Cognitive-behavioral therapy of panic disorder with secondary major depression: a preliminary investigation. *J. Consult. Clin. Psychol.* 61:1028–37

Lenzenweger MF, Dworkin RH, Wethington E. 1991. Examining the underlying structure of schizophrenic phenomenology: evidence for a three-process model. *Schizophr. Bull.* 17:515–24

Lenzenweger MF, Korfine L. 1992. Confirming the latent structure and base rate of schizotypy: a taxometric analysis. *J. Abnorm. Psychol.* 101:567–71

Leonard HL, Swedo SE, Lenane MC, Rettew DC, Hamburger SD, et al. 1993. A 2- to 7-year follow-up study of 54 obsessive-compulsive children and adolescents. *Arch. Gen. Psychiatr.* 50:429–39

Lewinsohn PM, Hops H, Roberts RE, Seeley JR, Andrews JA. 1993. Adolescent psychopathology: I. Prevalence and incidence of depression and other *DSM-III-R* disorders in high school students. *J. Abnorm. Psychol.* 102:133–44

Liebowitz MR. 1992. Diagnostic issues in anxiety disorders. In *Review of Psychiatry,* ed. A Tasman, MB Riba, 11:247–59. Washington, DC: Am. Psychiatr. Press

Livesley WJ. 1991. Classifying personality disorders: ideal types, prototypes, or dimensions? *J. Pers. Disord.* 5:52–59

Livesley WJ, Jackson DN. 1991. Construct validity and the classification of personality disorders. In *DSM-III-R Axis II: Perspectives in Validity,* ed. J Oldham, pp. 1–22. Washington, DC: Am. Psychiatr. Press

Livesley WJ, Schroeder ML, Jackson DN, Jang KL. 1994. Categorical distinctions in the study of personality disorder: implications for classification. *J. Abnorm. Psychol.* 103:6–17

Maier W, Lichtermann D, Klingler T, Heun R, Hallmayer J. 1992. Prevalences of personality disorders (DSM-III-R) in the community. *J. Pers. Disord.* 6:187–96

Martin RL. 1992. Diagnostic issues for conversion disorder. *Hosp. Commun. Psychiatr.* 43:771–73

McElroy SL, Hudson JI, Pope HG Jr, Keck PE Jr, Aizley HG. 1992. The *DSM-III-R* impulse control disorders not elsewhere classified: clinical characteristics and relationship to other psychiatric disorders. *Am. J. Psychiatr.* 149:318–27

McElroy SL, Pope HG Jr, Hudson JI, Keck PE Jr, White KL. 1991. Kleptomania: a report of 20 cases. *Am. J. Psychiatr.* 158:652–57

McGlashan TH, Fenton WS. 1992. The positive-negative distinction in schizophrenia. *Arch. Gen. Psychiatr.* 49:63–72

McNally RJ. 1991. Assessment of posttraumatic stress disorder in children. *Psychol. Assess.* 3:531–37

Mellman TA, Randolph CA, Brawman-Mintzer O, Flores LP, Milanes FJ. 1992. Phenomenology and course of psychiatric disorders associated with combat-related posttraumatic stress disorder. *Am. J. Psychiatr.* 149:1568–74

Mezzich JE, Fabrega H, Coffman GA, Haley R. 1989. DSM-III disorders in a large sample of psychiatric patients: frequency and specificity of diagnoses. *Am. J. Psychiatr.* 146:212–19

Mezzich JE, Sullivan PF. 1995. *On measuring syndromic severity: a review paper for DSM–IV.* See Widiger et al 1994, Vol. 3:In press

Millon T. 1991. Classification in psychopathology: rationale, alternatives, and standards. *J. Abnorm. Psychol.* 100:245–61

Mitchell JE. 1992. Subtyping of bulimia nervosa. *Int. J. Eating Disord.* 11:327–32

Morey LC. 1988. Personality disorders in *DSM-III* and *DSM-III-R*: convergence, coverage, and internal consistency. *Am. J. Psychiatr.* 145:573–77

Morey LC. 1991. Classification of mental disorder as a collection of hypothetical constructs. *J. Abnorm. Psychol.* 100:289–93

Morey LC. 1992. *Personality disorder NOS: specifying patterns of the otherwise unspecified.* Presented at Annu. Conv. Am. Psychol. Assoc., 100th, Washington, DC

Mueser KT, Bellack AS, Blanchard JJ. 1992. Comorbidity of schizophrenia and substance use: implications for treatment. *J. Consult. Clin. Psychol.* 60:845–56

Nace EP, Davis CW, Gaspari JP. 1991. Axis II comorbidity in substance abusers. *Am. J. Psychiatr.* 148:118–20

Nathan PE. 1991. Substance use disorders in the *DSM-IV. J. Abnorm. Psychol.* 100:356–61

Nathan PE. 1993. Can alcohol abuse and dependence be dimensionalized—and should they be? *Psychol. Inq.* 4:113–15

Nemiah JC. 1991. Dissociation, conversion, and somatization. In *Review of Psychiatry,* ed. A Tasman, SM Goldfinger, 10:248–60. Washington, DC: Am. Psychiatr. Press

Nicholson IR, Neufeld RWJ. 1993. Classification of the schizophrenias according to symptomatology: a two-factor model. *J. Abnorm. Psychol.* 102:259–70

Nurnberg HG, Rifkin A, Doddi S. 1993. A systematic assessment of the comorbidity of *DSM-III-R* personality disorders in alcoholic outpatients. *Compr. Psychiatr.* 34:447–54

Oldham JM, Skodol AE, Kellman HD, Hyler SE, Rosnick L, Davies M. 1992. Diagnosis of *DSM-III-R* personality disorders by two structured interviews: patterns of comorbidity. *Am. J. Psychiatr.* 149:213–20

Perry JC. 1990. Challenges in validating personality disorders: beyond description. *J. Pers. Disord.* 4:273–89

Pfohl B. 1991. Histrionic personality disorder: a review of available data and recommendations for *DSM-IV. J. Pers. Disord.* 5:150–66

Phillips KA. 1991. Body dysmorphic disorder: the distress of imagined ugliness. *Am. J. Psychiatr.* 148:1138–49

Phillips KA, McElroy SL, Keck PE, Pope, HG, Hudson JI. 1993. Body dysmorphic disorder: 30 cases of imagined ugliness. *Am. J. Psychiatr.* 150:302–8

Pribor EF, Dinwiddie SH. 1992. Psychiatric correlates of incest in childhood. *Am. J. Psychiatr.* 149:52–56

Pribor EF, Yutzy SH, Dean JT, Wetzel RD. 1993. Briquet's Syndrome, dissociation, and abuse. *Am. J. Psychiatr.* 150:1507–11

Putnam FW, Guroff JJ, Silberman EK, Barban L. 1986. The clinical phenomenology of multiple personality disorder: review of

100 recent cases. *J. Clin. Psychiatr.* 47: 285–93

Robins E, Guze SB. 1970. Establishment of diagnostic validity in psychiatric illness: its application to schizophrenia. *Am. J. Psychiatr.* 145:983–87

Robins LN, Locke BZ, Regier DA. 1991. An overview of psychiatric disorders in America. In *Psychiatric Disorders in America,* ed. LN Robins, BZ Locke, pp. 328–66. New York: Free

Ross CA, Miller SD, Reagor P, Bjornson L, Fraser GA, Anderson G. 1990. Structured interview data on 102 cases of multiple personality disorder from four centers. *Am. J. Psychiatr.* 147:596–601

Ross CA, Norton GR, Wozney K. 1989. Multiple personality disorder: an analysis of 236 cases. *Can. J. Psychiatr.* 34:413–18

Rothbaum BO, Foa EB. 1993. Subtypes of posttraumatic stress disorder and duration of symptoms. In *Posttraumatic Stress Disorder: DSM-IV and Beyond,* ed. JRT Davidson, EB Foa, pp. 23–36. Washington, DC: Am. Psychiatr. Press

Rounsaville BJ, Anton SF, Carroll K, Budde D, Prusoff BA, Gawin F. 1991. Psychiatric diagnoses of treatment-seeking cocaine abusers. *Arch. Gen. Psychiatr.* 48:43–51

Roy A, Lamparski D, DeJong J, Moore V, Linnoila M. 1990. Characteristics of alcoholics who attempt suicide. *Am. J. Psychiatr.* 147: 761–65

Rudd MD, Dahm PF, Rajab MH. 1993. Diagnostic comorbidity in persons with suicidal ideation and behavior. *Am. J. Psychiatr.* 150:928–34

Sanderson WC, Beck AT, Beck J. 1990. Syndrome comorbidity in patients with major depression or dysthymia: prevalence and temporal relationships. *Am. J. Psychiatr.* 147:1025–28

Sansone RA, Fine MA. 1992. Borderline personality as a predictor of outcome in women with eating disorders. *J. Pers. Disord.* 6:176–86

Saxena S, Prasad K. 1989. *DSM-III* subclassifications of dissociative disorders applied to psychiatric outpatients in India. *Am. J. Psychiatr.* 146:261–62

Schneier FR, Johnson J, Hornig CD, Liebowitz MR, Weissman MM. 1992. Social phobia: comorbidity and morbidity in an epidemiologic sample. *Arch. Gen. Psychiatr.* 49:282–88

Schneier FR, Liebowitz MR, Beidel DC, Fyer AJ, George MS, et al. 1994. Social phobia. See Widiger et al 1994, Vol. 2:In press

Schneier FR, Spitzer RL, Gibbon M, Fyer AJ, Liebowitz MR. 1991. The relationship of social phobia subtypes and avoidant personality disorder. *Compr. Psychiatr.* 32: 496–502

Schwalberg MD, Barlow DH, Alger SA,

Howard LJ. 1992. Comparison of bulimics, obese binge eaters, social phobics, and individuals with panic disorder on comorbidity across *DSM-III-R* anxiety disorders. *J. Abnorm. Psychol.* 101:675–81

Shea MT, Pilkonis PA, Beckham E, Collins JF, Elkin I, et al. 1990. Personality disorders and treatment outcome in the NIMH Treatment of Depression Collaborative Research Program. *Am. J. Psychiatr.* 147: 711–18

Shea MT, Widiger TA, Klein MH. 1992. Comorbidity of personality disorders and depression: implications for treatment. *J. Consult. Clin. Psychol.* 60:857–68

Sher KJ, Trull, TJ. 1994. Personality and disinhibitory psychopathology: alcoholism and antisocial personality disorder. *J. Abnorm. Psychol.* 103:92–102

Siever LJ, Davis KL. 1991. A psychobiological perspective on the personality disorders. *Am. J. Psychiatr.* 148:1647–58

Simeon D, Hollander E. 1993. Depersonalization disorder. *Psychiatr. Ann.* 23:382–88

Simpson SG, Al-Mufti R, Andersen AE, DePaulo JR. 1992. Bipolar II affective disorder in eating disorder inpatients. *J. Nerv. Ment. Dis.* 180:719–22

Smith SS, Newman JP. 1990. Alcohol and drug abuse-dependence disorders in psychopathic and nonpsychopathic criminal offenders. *J. Abnorm. Psychol.* 99:430–39

Spiegel D, Cardeña E. 1991. Disintegrated experience: the dissociative disorders revisited. *J. Abnorm. Psychol.* 100:366–78

Spitzer RL. 1991. An outsider-insider's views about revising the *DSM*s. *J. Abnorm. Psychol.* 100:294–96

Stein DJ, Hollander E, Skodol AE. 1993. Anxiety disorders and personality disorders: a review. *J. Pers. Disord.* 7:87–104

Steingard R, Biederman J, Doyle A, Sprich-Buckminster S. 1992. Psychiatric comorbidity in attention deficit disorder: impact on the interpretation of Child Behavior Checklist results. *J. Am. Acad. Child Adolesc. Psychiatr.* 31:449–54

Sunday SR, Levey CM, Halmi KA. 1993. Effects of depression and borderline personality traits on psychological state and eating disorder symptomatology. *Compr. Psychiatr.* 34:70–74

Sutker PB, Uddo-Crane M, Allain AN Jr. 1991. Clinical and research assessment of posttraumatic stress disorder: a conceptual overview. *Psychol. Assess.* 3:520–30

Tarter RE, Moss HB, Arria A, Mezzich AC, Vanyukov MM. 1992. The psychiatric diagnosis of alcoholism: critique and proposed reformulation. *Alcohol. Clin. Exp. Res.* 16:106–16

Taylor MA, Berenbaum SA, Jampala VC, Cloninger CR. 1993. Are schizophrenia and affective disorder related? Preliminary data from a family study. *Am. J. Psychiatr.* 150:278–85

Tellegen A. 1993. Folk concepts and psychological concepts of personality and personality disorder. *Psychol. Inq.* 4:122–30

Tobin DL, Johnson C, Steinberg S, Staats M, Dennis AB. 1991. Multifactorial assessment of bulimia nervosa. *J. Abnorm. Psychol.* 100:14–21

Tsuang MT, Lyons MJ, Faraone SV. 1990. Heterogeneity of schizophrenia: conceptual models and analytic strategies. *Br. J. Psychiatr.* 156:17–26

Turner SM, Beidel DC, Townsley RM. 1992. Social phobia: a comparison of specific and generalized subtypes and avoidant personality disorder. *J. Abnorm. Psychol.* 101: 326–31

Tynes LI, White K, Steketee GS. 1990. Toward a new nosology of obsessive compulsive disorder. *Compr. Psychiatr.* 31:465–80

Vitousek K, Manke F. 1994. Personality variables and disorders in anorexia nervosa and bulimia nervosa. *J. Abnorm. Psychol.* 103: 137–47

Wakefield JC. 1992. The concept of mental disorder: on the boundary between biological facts and social values. *Am. Psychol.* 47:373–88

Watson D, Clark LA, eds. 1994. Special Issue on Personality and Psychopathology. *J. Abnorm. Psychol.* 101:3–158

Watson D, Clark LA, Harkness AR. 1994. Structures of personality and their relevance to psychopathology. *J. Abnorm. Psychol.* 103:18–31

Widiger TA. 1992a. Categorical versus dimensional classification. *J. Pers. Disord.* 6: 287–300

Widiger TA. 1992b. Generalized social phobia versus avoidant personality disorder: a commentary on three studies. *J. Abnorm. Psychol.* 101:340–43

Widiger TA, Frances AJ, Pincus H, Davis W, First M. 1991. Towards an empirical classification for the *DSM-IV. J. Abnorm. Psychol.* 100:280–88

Widiger TA, Frances AJ, Pincus H, First M, Ross R, eds. 1994. *DSM-IV Sourcebook,* Vols. 1–3. Washington, DC: Am. Psychiatr. Press

Widiger TA, Rogers JH. 1989. Prevalence and comorbidity of personality disorders. *Psychiatr. Ann.* 19:132–36

Widiger TA, Shea T. 1991. Differentiation of Axis I and Axis II disorders. *J. Abnorm. Psychol.* 100:399–406

Widiger TA, Trull TJ. 1993. The scholarly development of DSM-IV. In *International Review of Psychiatry,* ed. JA Costa, E Silva, CC Nadelson, 1:59-78. Washington, DC: Am. Psychiatr. Press

Wilson M. 1993. DSM-III and the transformation of American psychiatry: a history. *Am. J. Psychiatr.* 150:399–410

Zimmerman M, Pfohl B, Coryell WH, Corenthal C, Stangl D. 1991. Major depression and personality disorder. *J. Affect. Disord.* 22:199–210

Zinbarg RE, Barlow DH. 1991. Mixed anxiety-depression: a new diagnostic category? In *Chronic Anxiety: Generalized Anxiety Disorder and Mixed Anxiety-Depression,* ed. RM Rapee, DH Barlow, pp. 136–52. New York: Guilford

Zinbarg RE, Barlow DH, Liebowitz M, Street L, Broadhead E, et al. 1994. The *DSM-IV* field trial for mixed anxiety-depression. *Am. J. Psychiatr.* 151:1153–56

Annu. Rev. Psychol. 1995. 46:155–81

ACQUIRING INTELLECTUAL SKILLS

J. F. Voss and J. Wiley

Learning Research and Development Center, University of Pittsburgh, Pittsburgh, Pennsylvania 15260

M. Carretero

Universidad Autonoma de Madrid, Madrid, Spain

KEY WORDS: learning, reasoning, domain-related skills, general skills, social context

CONTENTS

INTRODUCTION

This review is concerned with how intellectual skills are acquired, and covers the literature from 1988 to 1993. As we use the terms, *intellectual* refers to skills important to human mental activity and *acquisition* refers to how such skills are learned. Although the review follows most closely from Glaser & Bassok's (1989) review of instructional psychology, the present chapter's title acknowledges that intellectual skill acquisition takes place in non-classroom as well as classroom situations. This review addresses four topics: domain-related intellectual skill acquisition, general intellectual skills, social contexts, and some significant issues.

DOMAIN-RELATED INTELLECTUAL SKILL ACQUISITION

Three domains are considered here: mathematics and physics, in which most of the research has occurred, and history, which has received increasing attention. The research generally has been concerned with how a priori conceptual knowledge influences learning and reasoning.

Mathematics

In recent years there has been a relatively large amount of research on mathematics learning concerned with 1. students' prior knowledge, including preschool intuitions and out-of-school learning, 2. the interaction of language and symbolic mathematical expressions, 3. metacognitive skills; and 4. socially interactive processes.

INTUITIVE MATHEMATICS   What constitutes intuitive knowledge of preschool children and how such knowledge impacts mathematics learning have been questions of interest. Resnick (1989) noted that young children's knowledge of size differences, of concepts such as big and little, of increases or decreases in amount, and of part-whole relationships are reasonably well established before school years, as sometimes are counting skill and calculation strategies. Resnick (1989) therefore suggests that formal instruction, generally emphasizing mathematical routines, may be more beneficial if built upon intuitions, as exemplified by Resnick & Singer's (1993) study of ratio reasoning. Similarly, Levine et al (1992) reported results consistent with the idea that young children's ideas of adding and subtracting emerge from combining and separating objects in the real world.

MATHEMATICS LEARNING   Studying the acquisition of addition, subtraction, and multiplication skills and working within a competition-of-response model, Siegler has examined strategy learning in subtraction (Siegler & Jenkins 1989), strategy choice as related to domain-specific and domain-general knowledge (Siegler 1989), and intraindividual variability in strategy selection (Siegler & Jenkins 1989), the latter also studied by Ohlsson & Bee (1991).

The study of solving algebra word problems has indicated that a deficit in language processing is more critical to problem solving than is a deficit in the use of mathematical algorithms (Cummins et al 1988). In addition, better learners more accurately map the understanding of the problem statement to the needed equations (Nathan et al 1992), and poorer students show poor understanding of the mathematical symbol system and the described situation (Greeno 1989, Hall et al 1989). Understanding of word problems is also related to the discrimination of relevant and irrelevant problem information (Littlefield & Rieser 1993) and to the ability to indicate the necessary and sufficient conditions required to solve a problem (Low & Over 1989).

Sweller (1988) has argued that students can solve problems without improving in their problem solving skill. Strategy-based operations, such as means-ends analysis, take up working memory capacity, thereby providing little opportunity for schema acquisition, that is, learning to categorize problems and to apply particular rules (e.g. Ayres & Sweller 1990, Zhu & Simon 1987).

STREET MATHEMATICS AND CULTURE   Cross-cultural research, comparing American, Japanese, and Taiwanese first and fifth graders, has indicated that students in the United States spend less time in school and less time on academic tasks than do students in Japan or Taiwan (Stevenson et al 1987). Fernandez et al (1992) also demonstrated that Japanese students enter class with better mathematical representations than do American students. In home life, Asian families take education more seriously than do American families, with Japanese and Taiwanese students spending more time doing homework and academic-related activities (Stevenson & Stigler 1992).

Reviewing a series of Brazilian studies, Nunes et al (1993) concluded that mathematics learning has two components: 1. the social component of how mathematics is practiced in the real world, and 2. the logical or symbolic component of how mathematics is acquired in school. Coconut vendors aged 9–15 correctly performed price computations in the market place but did not perform as well when the problems were stated formally. Saxe (1988, 1991) also found that vendor and nonvendor groups matched for age and schooling represented numerical quantities in similar ways but vendors developed better computational strategies. Schliemann & Acioly (1989) found that bookies aged 23–65, varying in schooling from 0 to 11 years, were accurate when selling mathematically complex lotteries, but more schooling yielded better justification of the calculations and better performance on unusual problems. Nunes et al (1993) also reported that uneducated fishermen, based on their work demands, developed a general schema for calculating quantity and price in proportionality problems. Nunes et al suggest that "realistic mathematical problems" (i.e. those that capitalize on the real world experience of students) should be used in school.

TEACHING OF MATHEMATICS   The Cognition and Technology Group at Vanderbilt (CTGV) has combined a theoretical position with technology in its research on mathematics instruction. The CTGV program involves presenting a video-based narrative adventure of a fictitious character, after which a realistic and relatively complex problem is asked that is based on the video contents. Students, usually working as a class or in small groups, subsequently generate a detailed solution plan. The instructional program assumes that student learning is anchored in complex, realistic situational events in which students can engage (CTGV 1990). The program has yielded results superior to typical instruction in specific calculations and general problem orientation (CTGV 1993). In addition, assessment measures have yielded positive outcomes (CTGV 1992).

Schoenfeld (1987, 1988, 1991) has stressed that children need to use mathematics as a tool for recognizing and solving problems, instead of trying to find the answer as quickly as possible. Schoenfeld (1988) has noted that traditional instruction does not accomplish this goal even when students learn the course contents. Schoenfeld has also discussed the importance of metacognition and social factors to mathematics instruction, that is, how knowledge of one's own thought processes and the use of self-monitoring procedures as well as participation in small groups facilitate performance (Schoenfeld 1987).

Lampert (1990) has emphasized collaborative argumentation in a classroom as a means of developing mathematical proofs. Lampert suggests that students need to see mathematics as both a deductive and an inductive process. To do this, students must engage in mathematical arguments in which they develop and defend strategies, state hypotheses, and question and defend assumptions. Movement toward this goal was demonstrated in a fifth grade class that emphasized these procedures. Fennema et al (1993) have demonstrated that when a first grade teacher used their cognitive approach, termed Cognitively Guided Instruction, the students performed above a national standard level.

Physics

Recent research in physics has largely been a continuation and refinement of work of the 1980s, which emphasized physical concepts as they are held by naive subjects, especially in relation to misconceptions (e.g. McCloskey 1983, McCloskey & Kargon 1987). Current research generally constitutes an extension of this work.

PERSISTENCE OF NAIVE PERCEPTIONS   Studies continue to indicate that although studying physics improves performance on physics problems, naive conceptions of physics are maintained with complex problems (Pozo & Carretero 1992, Villani & Pacca 1990), with more familiar problems (Kaiser et al 1986), and as a function of problem type (Donley & Ashcraft 1992). However, by providing appropriate experiences, Levin et al (1990) were able to produce conceptual change that reduced the maintenance of naive conceptions.

PIECEMEAL KNOWLEDGE AND COHERENT KNOWLEDGE   A controversial issue has been whether naive performance reflects an incorrect but coherent theory of physical causation versus the use of bits of knowledge that are applied to particular situations (see Ranney 1994). diSessa (1993) has argued that naive individuals do not have a coherent theory but have basic phenomenological primitives, pieces of knowledge related to physical activity. The primitives are activated by stimuli and provide a "sense of mechanism" regarding the physical world. Learning then takes place as the primitives, serving as part of a developing structure, increasingly serve as cues and heuristics to access acquired principles. Supporting the position with student protocols, diSessa (1993) noted that traditional physics instruction emphasizes concepts and problem solving and neglects the more naive piecemeal knowledge structures upon which principles are built. McCloskey & Kargon (1987), on the other hand, argue that misconceptions stem from systematic beliefs or intuitive theories.

UNDERSTANDING PHYSICS CONCEPTS   Better learners not only have a more developed understanding of the specific physics concepts under study but they also have more usable knowledge that supports understanding of the meaning and application of the concepts. Reif & Allen (1992) supported this conclusion with respect to the concept of acceleration and Robertson (1990) did so for Newton's second law. Also, Dufresne et al (1992) found that requiring novices to perform a qualitative analysis of the concepts of physics problems before solving them improved novice understanding. Difficulties in understanding the concept of matter have been studied in students aged 13–16, with matter viewed at one extreme as a homogeneous substance and at the other as a particle system (Renstrom et al 1990).

ACQUIRING PHYSICS CONCEPTS: SELF-EXPLANATIONS   Chi et al (1989) found that compared to poor learners, good learners in solving physics problems explain each step to themselves; refine, elaborate, and evaluate conditions needed to take a step in the solution process; consider sequences of actions; explain the meaning of quantitative expressions; monitor their understanding; and refer back to examples with a specific goal in mind rather than trying to find the solution. Also, good solvers are likely to construct inference rules relating concepts and quantitative expressions (Chi & VanLehn 1991). Using text describing the human circulatory system and prompting subjects for self-explanation, Chi et al (1994) also found that high explainers learned more and had better mental models when prompted to explain than did low explainers.

History

Researchers studying the acquisition of historical concepts are faced not only with the question of what skills need to be acquired in history, but also with controversial issues concerning the goals of historical inquiry and instruction. Seixas (1993a), for example, notes that the teaching of history often is used to embrace student identity, but in the United States there are politically volatile arguments about what identity to embrace. In American history, the traditional approach emphasizes the Revolutionary War, Lincoln and the Civil War, etc, while more recent social history emphasizes the historical origins of different ethnic cultures, thereby facilitating student identity with appropriate minority groups. Despite these problematic issues, research on learning in history has focused on concept acquisition, causal reasoning, and learning from text.

ACQUIRING HISTORICAL-POLITICAL CONCEPTS   Although limited in number, studies involving the acquisition of historical-political concepts have shown that the ability to acquire such concepts is a function of age. Working within a Piagetian framework, Berti (1994) studied how children develop political concepts (e.g. state or government). She found that such concepts were incomplete for third graders, had emerged by fifth grade, and became more developed by eighth grade. Delval (1994) found a similar pattern of concept learning across cultures. von Borries (1994) showed that student understanding of historical concepts is not based solely on cognitive considerations. For example, students sometimes respond to questions about the Crusades in moral as well as emotional ways, and students' moral standards can play a role in such reasoning. Carretero et al (1991a) showed that students are relatively poor estimators of the sequence of historical events. Seixas (1993c) found that students of a particular cultural background regard events of that culture as historically significant, based in part on knowledge they have acquired from their families.

CAUSATION AND EXPLANATION   Consider the quote attributed to Pascal, "If Cleopatra's nose would have been one-quarter inch longer (thereby making her less attractive), would the course of Western civilization have been different?" Scientific reasoning tends to focus on isolating single causes and their possible interactions, but history must deal with the issue of multiple causation, and with causation over time. There is also the question of the extent to which causes are based on particular theoretical explanations of history (Leinhardt et al 1994b).

Furthermore, causal agents in history can refer to individuals, groups, institutions, or to a set of particular conditions (e.g. economic and class issues in Marxist theory). From a learning perspective, however, research has not been concerned with the meta-issues of causation and explanation per se, but rather with how individuals perceive historical causation.

Students regard the actions of individuals as more important than the influence of societal and institutional structures, which are often emphasized by historians (Halldén 1986, Shemilt 1987). Halldén (1986) concluded that the failure of students to understand the nature of history as a subject matter is the primary problem of history learning. Halldén (1993) also showed that although in the classroom Swedish secondary students learned institutional explanations for Sweden's industrial revolution and establishment of democracy, they nevertheless had an alternative framework, attributing these changes to the suffering of and demands made by the people. Similarly, Carretero et al (1994) found that in rating six causes of why Columbus sailed, sixth and eighth graders rated personal motives as the most important while tenth graders, psychology students, and history students rated economic conditions first. Personal motives were rated second by the tenth graders and psychology students, and fifth by the history students. Voss et al (1994), however, found that students considered both structural and personal factors when writing essays about why the Soviet Union collapsed (e.g. structural factors produced the need for personal action). Students also rated immediate causes as more important than those remote in time. In another study, Hindu students of India tended to emphasize the context as more important than the specific agents (Miller 1986), thereby suggesting that what historical factors are emphasized as causal may be related to culture.

DOCUMENTS   Examining written documents and pictorial representations of the 1775 Battle of Lexington, Wineburg (1991a,b) found that expert ratings of document reliability were inversely related to novice ratings. Historians also used three heuristics more frequently than did novices: 1. corroboration—comparing sources for consistency, 2. sourcing—looking at the origin of a source before examining it, and 3. contextualization—determining when and where the event in the document took place. Wineburg (1991a) also noted that historians, but not novices, construct a subtext (i.e. they provide historical meaning to documents, considering especially when and why a text was likely written, who wrote it, and the writer's possible motives). Perfetti et al (1994) have found that the use of documents as an instructional tool facilitates student learning.

THE TEACHING OF HISTORY   A question considered in the field of history as well as other domains is the extent to which students in the domain should be taught the skills of the domain professional, as opposed to being taught the products of the domain-related research. Seixas (1993b) has noted four characteristics that differentiate the scholarly community from the classroom community: the role of authority, exclusiveness (who is accepted in the community as a member), education, and training. However, Seixas also suggested that both communities need to emphasize inquiry. Holt (1990) has suggested that inquiry may be facilitated by having students generate historical reports using historiographic methods, and Hahn (1994) has recommended the use of historical conflict to facilitate hypothesis testing and development of skills involving evaluation of evidence.

Beck et al (1989) found that the contents of history texts assumed knowledge of concepts that students did not have, that the contents lacked coherence, and that the text goals were not clearly stated. Correcting these deficits, Beck et al (1991) produced texts that yielded improvement in student learning. At a more general level, much text processing research has used the narrative genre, and such research may be applicable to learning from narrative historical accounts. The question of the extent to which history should be regarded as narrative is debatable. Mink (1987), for example, regards narrative as a cognitive instrument, while other writers consider historical writing as narrative as well as expository (cf Topolski 1990).

Leinhardt et al (1994a) studied the role of teacher explanation in history instruction and found that quality teaching in history varies. In one case, instruction involved the reinstatement of basic historical concepts in different historical contexts, whereas in another case teaching involved the study of historical concepts over time. Leinhardt (1994) also has provided an overview of issues of history instruction.

GENERAL INTELLECTUAL SKILLS

Scientific Reasoning Skills

In recent years a substantial amount of research has been conducted on scientific reasoning. The primary focus has been on the interaction between hypotheses and evidence, and the related issue of how evidence produces conceptual change.

REASONING BY SCIENTISTS   Dunbar (1994) studied the reasoning of scientists in four biological laboratories. He found that cognitive restructuring occurred when data inconsistent with a hypothesis were obtained, and that project laboratory meetings were especially important when members of a laboratory challenged a presenter's hypotheses and data interpretation (see also Amigues 1988). Conceptual change also occurred via the use of "local" analogies, but such changes decreased with the distance of analogy from the basic issue. Moreover, "far" analogies, such as those crossing disciplines, did not occur.

Scientists' notebooks have been used to examine the reasoning of scientists. After studying Michael Faraday's notebooks,Tweney (e.g. 1985, 1991) was able to show how Faraday tested hypotheses and integrated different principles and observations in making his discovery of electromagnetic induction. More recently, Ippolito & Tweney (1994) considered Faraday's work on visual deceptions, pointing out how Faraday, as other scientists, started from the senses of the real world and constructed a symbolic reality that was in a sense more real than the "real" world of the senses.

The discovery process of scientific thinking has also been modeled from the contents of diaries, recollections, and other sources. Kulkarni & Simon (1988), in modeling Krebs's synthesis of urea, concluded that the heuristics generally used by scientists were important, as were domain knowledge and idiosyncratic factors such as the learning of new techniques. Similarly, Qin & Simon (1990) demonstrated that Kepler's third law could be "discovered" by college students if they used many of the same heuristics as Kepler.

SCIENTIFIC THINKING BY CHILDREN AND OTHER NAIVE SUBJECTS   Research on scientific reasoning in naive subjects has focused on the extent to which naive subjects think like scientists (Nisbett & Ross 1980), and on whether cognitive restructuring is found in response to contrary evidence. In addition, analogy has been studied as a vehicle to facilitate scientific thinking.

Kuhn (1989) has argued that the core relation in scientific thinking is differentiating theory and evidence and correctly evaluating evidence in relation to theory. She has found that children have considerable difficulty in separating theory and evidence when performing covariation tasks (Kuhn 1989, Kuhn et al 1988). However, Richardson (1992), Sodian et al (1991), and Ruffman et al (1993) have found that children as young as 6 or 7 are able to show an appropriate hypothesis-evidence relationship, given an appropriate context. Karmiloff-Smith (1988) has argued that children are theorists, demonstrating that children aged 4 and 5 provide some theoretical ideas and that children aged 8 and 9 develop more extensive theoretical representations of the problem.

In other work on the hypothesis-evidence relation, Klahr & Dunbar (1988) asked subjects about an unknown control function of a robot tank and found that adult subjects used two problem spaces, a hypothesis space and an experimental space. Individuals tended to fall into two categories: the theorists, who searched for hypotheses, and the experimentalists, who attempted to draw conclusions from prior experimental results. Theorists solved the problem in less time and tested hypotheses more specifically, running about one-half the number of experiments as experimentalists. Klahr & Dunbar also found that confirmed hypotheses were retained about 75% of the time while disconfirmed hypotheses were changed about 45% of the time. Confirmed hypotheses may not have been maintained more frequently because confirmation is often ambiguous (Klayman & Ha 1987). Disconfirmed hypotheses may not have been changed more often because of bias or because subjects could not think of other hypotheses (Klahr & Dunbar 1988).

The question of whether children restructure their concepts in relation to experience has been addressed by Vosniadou & Brewer (1992), who asked first, third, and fifth grade children about the shape of the earth. Although responses were not accurate, 82% of the inconsistencies were explained by five student mental models of the earth; namely, a rectangle, a disc, a dual earth, a hollow sphere, and a flattened sphere. The authors argued that the concepts were based on experiential preconceptions, and that children eventually accept earth as a sphere as a result of changes in their presuppositions that occur via cultural exposure. Brewer & Samarapungavan (1991) have argued further that children, in constructing their models, use thought processes similar to those of scientists, with performance differences attributable to the scientists' greater amount of institutionalized knowledge. In addition, Samarapungavan (1992) has shown that children are able to choose among competing scientific theories if the theories are described in a simple way.

Chinn & Brewer (1993) delineated seven types of responses to anomalous data, one of which was changing the theory. The authors found that the likelihood of theory change is influenced by factors such as the type of anomalous data and the characteristics of an alternative theory, while resistance to theory change is the result of factors such as entrenched beliefs, epistemological considerations, and lack of background knowledge. However, such factors were found to facilitate change on occasion. In an instructional context, Burbules & Linn (1988) presented data contradictory to that previously given and found that the new data produced conceptual change. In sum, the likelihood of cognitive restructuring in relation to specific evidential input apparently varies as a function of a number of factors, including certainty of beliefs and possibility of alternative hypotheses, and, noting Dunbar's results with scientific training, exposure to critical analysis.

Analogy has been regarded as an important aspect of scientific reasoning, and research on the topic has focused on how an individual maps from a base domain to a target domain. Gentner (1988) has proposed a structure mapping model in which the mapping of the base domain to the target domain involves not the predicate per se but the system of relations (Clement & Gentner 1991). Brown & Clement (1989) have described the difficulties in using analogy to overcome misconceptions. In analyzing analogy usage of children, Goswami

(1991) has concluded that analogical skill competence is followed by meta-cognitive skill development.

LEARNING SCIENTIFIC THINKING SKILLS   Schauble et al (1991) have demonstrated that good and poor learners engage in different strategies in solving electrical circuit problems. Good learners were superior in the planning and the control of variables. They also generated more hypotheses, of which a greater proportion was correct, and they were better at data management. Studying transfer in causal reasoning, Kuhn et al (1992) pretested subjects in each of two domains, and subsequently provided experience in one domain, measured performance in that domain, and at intervals measured performance in the second domain. They found that learning occurred in both domains, and attributed the findings to the use of appropriate strategies and to the growth of metacognitive awareness.

Other intervention studies have also demonstrated facilitation in scientific thinking. Linn & Songer (1993) measured student ideas of scientific explanations, parsimony, and relevance of science to everyday problems, and found that a preliminary course emphasizing the integration of science concepts with everyday thinking improved learning. Similarly, Shayer & Adey (1993) obtained facilitation, even three years after the intervention, when they provided conceptual experience with the use of variables, cognitive conflict, metacognition, and knowledge of strategies. Schauble et al (1994) found that teachers who had been trained in scientific reasoning, and later gave sixth graders a three-week course on experimentation, produced significant improvement in student understanding of experimentation. The authors concluded that without curriculum change, there is substantial opportunity for teachers to provide instruction about experimentation. Carey (1986) and Carey et al (1989) found students' views of science as a passive and accurate copy of the world changed toward a more constructivist view when students were provided with appropriate instruction.

Another intervention study (Rosebery et al 1992), conducted in a minority classroom with students generally naive to science, used a collaborative procedure in which science was viewed as one type of literacy and as part of an interdisciplinary instructional effort. After studying hypotheses involving water taste and purity, students demonstrated significant improvement with respect to scientific thinking. Lock (1990) showed that low-ability students could profit from training in planning and interpretation. In a relatively rare longitudinal study, first and second grade children were instructed in physics and biology concepts and interviewed periodically from first through twelfth grade (Novak & Musonda 1991). Subjects who received training provided more valid conceptions and fewer misconceptions than did controls, with the difference persisting through twelfth grade.

Informal Reasoning Skills

Informal reasoning is a loose term referring generally to the probabilistic reasoning taking place in everyday situations. Such reasoning is characteristically goal-related and has the argument as its core structure. Goals include justifying one's own position and/or attacking another person's, making a decision, persuading others, or resolving a conflict. The argument usually takes the form of an enthymeme, that is, a claim (conclusion) supported by a reason (premise). One premise of the argument is thus not made explicit, the missing premise in Toulmin's (1958) terms being the warrant of the argument (cf Voss et al 1991 for a more extensive discussion of informal reasoning). Research in this area has focused on skills in the use of argumentation, which are relatively poor in the general population.

JUSTIFYING ONE'S POSITION   In studies of informal reasoning, individuals are often asked to generate an answer to a question, to justify the answer, and to state counterarguments (Kuhn 1991, Means & Voss 1994). Or, individuals may be given arguments to evaluate. Results of such studies indicate that 1. individuals have relatively poor argumentation skills (Kuhn 1991, Means & Voss 1994); 2. informal reasoning skills are related to intellectual ability level (Perkins 1985) and to educational level, which may be interpreted as ability level (Baron et al 1993, Kuhn 1991, Voss et al 1986); 3. informal reasoning skill sometimes improves with age although the results may often be attributed to knowledge differences (Kuhn 1991, Means & Voss 1994); 4. individuals, while sometimes providing good evidence, also provide pseudoevidence, essentially a narrative of how, for example, a given person may have failed in school, rather than stating a causal analysis (Kuhn 1991), and 5. students apparently do not develop informal reasoning skill in school (Perkins 1985). Voss & Means 1991 have suggested ways to provide such instruction and practice in schools.

DECISION PROCESSES   A common normative assumption is that rationality includes examining both sides of a claim (Baron 1988). However, individuals usually provide more justification for their own side than for the other (Baron et al 1993, Perkins 1985). This deficiency is possibly the result of an inadequate search (Baron 1988). Perkins et al (1983) suggest that individuals often only search to the point of providing an answer that makes sense, rather than providing a critical epistemology, which involves more search and evaluation, what Baron (1988) terms fairness. Further, Roussey & Gombert (1994) found that children had difficulty constructing a two-sided argument unless the children were good writers and were placed in a dyad situation.

PERSUASION   From a developmental perspective, preschool children use persuasive arguments when trying to convince mother or when buying or sharing a toy. They use sanctions, requests, and assertions as persuasive mechanisms. Older children use more positive sanctions to persuade while younger children rely more on assertions per se (Weiss & Sachs 1991).

CONFLICT RESOLUTION   Stein & Miller (1991) found that children as young as five understand the nature of conflict, with such disputes arising typically over the possession of objects or through social behavior. Stein & Miller (1993a,b) also concluded that children as young as second graders are able to provide support for their arguments and can provide counterarguments. Slomkowski & Killen (1992) have shown that children as young as four provide different justifications in relation to context: Children provide personal justifications if asked about transgressions involving friends, but they use moral or social-conventional justifications for transgressions involving non-friends. Hofer & Pikowsky (1993) studied mother-daughter conflict and found that the goals and arguments of the conflict differed. Mothers desired to control the argument and daughters desired independence, trying to weaken their mothers' position. Stein et al (1994) studied argumentation skill of adolescents in a negotiating situation in which compromise was sought. They found that initial knowledge had little to do with outcome; social factors occurring during the negotiation played a critical role.

LANGUAGE AND ARGUMENTATION   In general, older children are better at writing argumentative text than are younger children (Coirier & Golder 1993, Golder 1992). In a study of children aged 7–16, the youngest children did not express a position, slightly older children took a position without justifying it, still older children developed minimal arguments, later providing elaborated arguments, and counterargument occurred typically at about age 14 (Coirier & Golder 1993). Golder (1993) also found that personal involvement with the topic is related to better argument generation. Zammuner (1987) had subjects write about their position on abortion and found that the construction of argumentative text was more elaborated for individuals favoring abortion. The result was attributed to the anti-abortion sociocultural atmosphere of Italy, where the study took place.

TEACHING CRITICAL THINKING SKILLS   Common to a number of critical thinking programs are the skills of defining problems, evaluating information, and generating and evaluating alternatives (Adams 1989, Idol et al 1991). Some researchers suggest that students need a critical-thinking disposition (Halpern 1989, Norris 1989), that is, the willingness to engage in activities such as planning, learning from mistakes, persistence, and open-mindedness. Simply having a student serve as task designer, strategist, monitor, or challenger in group problem solving on everyday problems has yielded positive effects, with retention found up to 8 weeks after training (Riesenmy et al 1991). Costa (1991) provides a summary of programs used successfully for the teaching of higher mental skills.

Verbal Skills

LEARNING FROM TEXT   Kintsch (1986) distinguished between remembering text contents and learning from text, that is, recalling text contents vs using the contents for inference generation and problem solving. Although Kintsch (1994) reported that more coherent texts produce better recall than do less coherent texts, the latter may produce better learning because individuals need to generate inferences to understand the text, thereby producing integration of a priori knowledge and information in the text. Similarly, Voss & Silfies (1994) showed that when using an expanded history text in which causal statements were "unpacked," recall performance was correlated significantly with reading comprehension scores but not with history knowledge; however, for an unexpanded text, recall performance was related to prior history knowledge but not to reading comprehension. The authors concluded that in the unpacked text individuals use their prior knowledge to fill in gaps, whereas the expanded text reduces the role of knowledge and makes reading comprehension more important. In another study, a mismatch between a text outline and the text organization itself resulted in better performance on inference tasks than when the text and outline agreed (Mannes & Kintsch 1987). Roller (1990) concluded that text structure is of greatest importance when the subject matter is somewhat unfamiliar.

Work on learning from text has indicated that generating explanations to questions about a text facilitates learning (Pressley et al 1992). Other research has examined the role of prior knowledge (cf Alexander & Judy 1988) and the role of interest (e.g. Garner et al 1991, Hidi & Baird 1988, Wade 1992). Texts other than narratives have also been used, including expository text (e.g. Varnhagen 1991) as well as editorials and literature (cf Britton & Graesser 1994). Causal narrative structure has been found to be significantly related to learning (Trabasso et al 1989, Trabasso & Nickels 1992).

WRITING   Bereiter & Scardamalia (1987) have suggested that less-advanced writers view writing as a knowledge-telling exercise, while more-advanced writers see writing as knowledge transforming. The latter also revise at a more global level than do the former (cf Hayes 1990). Methods to improve the skill of less-advanced writers include providing students with a clear understanding of the task (Nelson & Hayes 1988), although this procedure can only be effective when the younger students have other requisite skills. Thus, Wright & Rosenberg (1993) found that fourth graders could not recognize or produce coherent text, while students were able to by eighth grade. Experienced writers are better at recognizing potential obstacles for a reader and at taking a reader's perspective (Schriver 1990). Also, use of a word processor may increase productivity, but writing via a computer tends to produce more grammatical errors (D'Odorico & Zammuner 1993), engenders less planning before and during writing, and tends to inhibit a spatial sense of text organization (Haas & Hayes 1986).

QUESTIONING   McKeown et al (1993) found that a procedure they termed "Questioning the author," which involves students asking questions of the text, facilitated student learning. Singer (1990) discussed the various cognitive components involved in question answering, especially in relation to inference generation, and Graesser & Person (1994) found that individuals asked more questions in a tutoring context than in the classroom.

SOCIAL CONTEXTS OF INTELLECTUAL SKILL ACQUISITION

One of the most profound movements in the study of intellectual skill acquisition has been the study of how social and cultural factors are related to skill acquisition. Two related lines of such work are described below: One involves collaborative learning and the other is concerned with situated learning and apprenticeship.

Collaborative Learning

Brown & Palincsar (1989) reviewed the literature on collaborative learning and its relation to acquisition. A point emphasized is that collaborative learning success is related to the generation of explanation and elaboration, processes that trigger the need to reflect and the need to deal with conflict. They also note that change "is not the result of social qua social, motivational qua motivational, or even conflict qua conflict, it is the result of certain social settings that force the elaboration and justification of various positions" (p. 408). Another analysis of cooperative learning (Slavin 1987) integrated motivational and social-developmental interpretations. Slavin suggested that a social context can set a motivational context so that individuals will provide more explanations and elaborations.

At the empirical level, Brown et al (1993) observed conceptual change in both teachers and students in a classroom situation under conditions of distributed expertise (in which different students researched particular subtopics of a domain and reported their findings). Four factors related to classroom learning were noted: the presence of guided discovery; the student serving as teacher, researcher, and monitor of progress; active student inquiry; and thinking as basic literacy. These components, Brown et al argued, established a community of learners.

Orsolini & Pontecorvo (1992) found that with children aged 5 and 6, classroom discussion about a story facilitates argumentation, with children challenging not the facts of the story but the claims of other students. The disputes produced positive outcomes, such as learning to justify and stating explanations and counterarguments. Pontecorvo & Girardet (1994) also found that 9-year-old children in a non-teacher guided discussion sometimes arrived at a higher level of cognitive activity than they did when teachers were present. Gilly (1991), citing a study by Are, indicated that children aged 7 and 8 rarely questioned how to solve a problem with no possible solution when in the classroom, but while working with an adult or a peer, students produced more questioning and rejection of the problem.

In a review of peer interaction effects in the context of small groups, Webb (1989) concluded that group activity yielded high levels of elaboration and explanation as well as better achievement. The relative homogeneity or heterogeneity of the group was also important, as was personality, with extroverts obtaining more attention than did introverts.

Blaye et al (1991) found that pairs of 11-year-olds working on a computer-based problem solving task performed better than did individuals working alone, both with respect to original learning and when working alone on a transfer task (cf Azmitia 1988). Clements & Gullo (1984) also found positive dyad effects in the development of planning strategies, while Perlmutter et al (1989) reported that with children aged 4–11, the older children benefitted from peer interaction more than did younger children, especially for complex tasks. Juel (1991) found that in a cross-age tutoring procedure, young at-risk children improved in reading skill when tutored by college athletes, who also benefitted from the program.

Situated Learning and Apprenticeship

The concept of situated learning has emphasized the cultural context in which intellectual skill acquisition takes place. The concept generally holds that skill acquisition and the sociocultural context cannot be separated (Brown et al 1989, Lave 1989, Lave & Wenger 1991). Activity in turn is cued by the situation, a view that leads to a distinct view of transfer (Säljö 1991, Säljö & Wyndhamn 1990). Lave (1989) argued that although transfer traditionally focuses on learning of a skill in one context and applying it to another context, such transfer is difficult to obtain. The situated learning model considers transfer to have occurred when a new situation cues or triggers a response. Although the situated learning concept contains a sociocultural component, the strong version of the position is akin to behaviorism in that it assumes that environmental stimuli produce behavior. The situated learning model was in part derived from findings suggesting that theories built upon mental structures (e.g. Piaget's) had difficulty in dealing with performance variability (Guberman & Greenfield 1991). Guberman & Greenfield further noted that the situational view needed to be integrated with views about what was going on in the heads of individuals. This integrative process has been the subject of recent research. Cole (1989), for example, pointed out the importance of culture in the development of literacy. Guberman & Greenfield (1991) also argued that goal-setting is a function of a person's interaction with the social context, and an individual's mental representation then constitutes the mental structure of the goal in the social context. These authors cited Cheng & Holyoak's (1985) work on pragmatic schema as an example of such integration of situational and representational components. A similar line of research showed that knowledge of procedure acquired in a particular context leads to a mental representation consisting of an abstraction of the procedure in that context (Hatano 1988).

Apprenticeship has been defined as the teaching of crafts by means of practical activity in one-to-one relationship with an expert of the field (Gardner 1991, Hamilton 1990), and as such constitutes learning in a particular situated context. The apprenticeship process consists of observation, coaching, and practice (Lave & Wenger 1991), with the learner building a conceptual model of the task. The model becomes more developed during the guidance and practice phases as the learner integrates feedback from the master. Apprenticeship thus takes place in the context of particular learning environments. Rogoff (1990) stressed the importance of social interaction in apprenticeship learning, but Radziszewska & Rogoff (1988, 1991) found that only particular forms of peer interaction yield instructional benefits. Not only must one partner be more skilled than the other, but the more-skilled partner must also supply explanations for particular strategies, and also allow the less-skilled partner to participate in decisions. Thus, without both guidance and participation, the less-skilled partner does not benefit from the interaction. Further, the studies suggest that the benefit of apprenticeship might be limited by age. Even when given guidance and the chance to participate, the youngest students that were studied, aged 4–5, seemed unable to benefit from interaction with a skilled partner.

Establishing appropriate learning environments has also been addressed by developing computer-based contexts to facilitate learning. Examples of such work include the development of tutoring systems in economics (Achtenhagen 1991, Shute & Glaser 1991), medical diagnosis (Clancey 1987), and computer programming (Harel & Papert 1990). De Corte (1990) has developed a learning environment for mathematics designed to foster the development of successful problem solving.

SOME SIGNIFICANT ISSUES

Individual Differences

With the exception of the study of prior knowledge, little research has been carried out on individual differences in intellectual skill acquisition. However, research on individual differences will likely increase, as suggested by recent work on prior knowledge, motivation, interest, and ability level.

Studies have generally indicated that greater knowledge of a given subject matter domain facilitates the acquisition of new domain-related information. However, research (e.g. Reif & Allen 1992) has indicated that a person's general world knowledge and his or her beliefs, attitudes, and values are also important. Tishman et al (1993) have suggested that individuals in given situations have predisposing tendencies to act in particular ways, which in turn can influence intellectual skill acquisition. What constitutes a disposition, however, is not clear. What might be expected in the future is that the relation of acquisition and prior knowledge will be studied with a more precise measurement of prior knowledge as well as a broadening definition of what constitutes relevant prior knowledge and tendencies to use it in particular ways.

Research on the roles of motivation and emotion in acquiring intellectual skills has increased. Dweck & Leggett (1988), for example, have shown that a student's goal orientation (in terms of whether to please via performance or to learn competence), the student's own perceived ability, and the student's view of intelligence (as fixed or malleable) are related to intellectual skill acquisition. Also, Boekaerts (1993) has shown that how anger is controlled, rather than anger per se, is related to school performance. The related issue of how interest facilitates acquisition of intellectual skill has also been studied (see Renninger et al 1992). Ability level is one of the most important individual differences that requires study (Perkins 1985, Means & Voss 1994). Although much has been written about intelligence, two key questions remain unanswered: 1. What is the basis of ability-level differences? and perhaps even more importantly, 2. To what extent can intellectual skill acquisition for low ability-level individuals really be facilitated?

General versus Specific Skills

Research indicates that both general and specific skills exist, as found, for example, in the use of general heuristics and metacognitive skills on the one hand and specific domain-related skills on the other. The potential controversy emerges, however, in relation to how these skills are acquired and especially the extent to which they transfer. Detterman (1993) holds an extreme position, arguing that transfer effects are primarily found only when subjects are told how and what to transfer (cf Ceci & Ruiz 1993). Perkins & Salomon (1989), however, in reviewing the history of the controversy, noted that there was an early adherence to the general skills position, followed by adherence to the specific skills position, but that currently there is a return to a more general skills position, with transfer occurring in relation to the use of general heuristics and metacognitive strategies, such as those used by Brown & Palincsar (1989).

Studies have demonstrated transfer of relatively specific skills. Brown & Kane (1988), for example, using learning-to-learn and example-based learning paradigms, found that children aged 3–5 could transfer in both paradigms: The children responded not to surface but to underlying features. Brown & Kane also found that reflection about the problem facilitated transfer and that children who explained their learning transferred more than when information was provided by the experimenter. Lehman et al (1988) demonstrated that training in psychology, medicine, and law yielded positive transfer with respect to conditional reasoning while chemistry training did not. Psychology and medical students also showed significant gains in statistical-methodological reasoning while law and chemistry students did not. Fong et al (1986) showed that training in statistics led to a significant improvement in everyday thinking. Studies in computer science have also demonstrated positive transfer effects (Black et al 1988, Klahr & Carver 1988, Reed & Palumbo 1992). In some cases, however, transfer has been difficult to obtain. For example, Bassok & Holyoak (1993) found a lack of transfer across isomorphic word problems in physics and algebra, while Leshowitz (1989) observed difficulty in transferring what is learned in social science courses.

The most reasonable position seems to be that transfer of specific skills is difficult to obtain, but it can be facilitated by training that includes elaboration and explanation as well as self-monitoring metacognitive processes. The use of general heuristics, however they are acquired, seems to occur to the extent that individuals had training in their use and that a particular situation arose that activated the heuristics. This topic, however, has been a long-standing matter of controversy, and the future will likely produce more evidence indicating that transfer "depends on...." We also agree with Sternberg (1989), who has argued that the general-specific distinction is overstated and that the research requires consideration of factors such as context and personality.

The Sociocultural Revolution and Active Processing

THE SOCIOCULTURAL REVOLUTION   Although psychology has been experiencing a cognitive revolution since the 1950s, the most recent decade has produced what may be termed a sociocultural revolution. Although intellectual skill acquisition has traditionally been and still is regarded as primarily the responsibility of formal education, research in the last decade has aptly demonstrated that considerable skill in intellectual functioning can be and often is acquired outside of the classroom. Furthermore, such acquisition takes place because the sociocultural context creates the need for individuals to acquire such skills (e.g. Lave 1989, Nunes et al 1993). This relation of sociocultural context and an individual's intellectual development suggests, moreover, that such development is based on socially derived goals involving motivation and emotion. Indeed, Bruner (1990) has emphasized such factors in his plea for the study of "folk psychology." Along with greater study of out-of-school learning there has been increasing concern regarding the relation of such learning to the classroom. Thus, one question is that of two-directional transfer: To what extent can in-school knowledge be used to facilitate out-of-school learning, and to what extent should out-of-school learning be built upon in the classroom?

Another aspect of the sociocultural revolution is the general finding of positive results in the acquisition of intellectual skills through social interaction. Such results tend to change the view of learning from the strong emphasis placed on individual learning to a more collective form of systemic learning.

ACTIVE PROCESSING   While in recent years the importance of the sociocultural influence upon learning has been increasingly recognized, strong evidence has also underscored the individual as an active learner. Some time ago the idea that the individual is an active and not a passive learner became a cliché. Nevertheless, recent evidence indicates that intellectual skill acquisition is facilitated when individuals generate their own solutions to problems, explain and elaborate upon their solutions, and employ metacognitive skills. The sociocultural influence can act to produce more processing, in terms of elaboration and justification, than may otherwise occur (e.g. Brown & Palincsar 1989). This outcome has been demonstrated in many domains, and future research will likely produce a better understanding of how such learning occurs. In sum, recent studies of the acquisition of intellectual skills have generated research and theory about the nature of learning these skills and how they may be used (cf Bruer 1993). At the same time, the work has produced the need for theory development, and has reinforced Jenkins's (1979) point that because learning seems to depend on the context, the nature of materials, the task, and the ability, knowledge, motivation, and interest of individuals, the idea of arriving at invariance seems quite remote.

ACKNOWLEDGMENTS

The preparation of this chapter was supported by the Office of Educational Research and Improvement of the United States Department of Education via an award of the Center for the Study of Learning to the Learning Research and Development Center, and by the Mellon Foundation. The contribution of the third author has been supported by a grant (PB91-0028-C03-03) from DGCYT, Spain. The contents of the chapter do not necessarily reflect the position of any of these organizations. The authors also thank Laurie Ney Silfies, Joyce Holl, and Marguerita Limon for their assistance in preparing this manuscript.

Literature Cited

Achtenhagen F. 1991. Development of problem solving skills in natural settings. See Carretero et al 1991, pp. 49–66

Adams MJ. 1989. Thinking skills curricula: their promise and progress. *Educ. Psychol.* 24(1):25–77

Alexander PA, Judy JE. 1988. The interaction of domain-specific and strategic knowledge in academic performance. *Rev. Educ. Res.* 58(4):375–404

Amigues R. 1988. Peer interaction in solving physics problems: sociocognitive confrontation and metacognitive aspects. *J. Exp. Child Psychol.* 45(1):141–58

Ayres P, Sweller J. 1990. Locus of difficulty in multistage mathematics problems. *Am. J. Psychol.* 103(2):167–93

Azmitia M. 1988. Peer interaction and problem solving: When are two heads better than one? *Child Dev.* 59(1):87–96

Baron J. 1988. *Thinking and Deciding.* New York: Cambridge Univ. Press

Baron J, Granato L, Spranca M, Teubal E. 1993. Decision-making biases in children and early adolescents: exploratory studies. *Merrill-Palmer Q.* 39(1):22–46

Bassok M, Holyoak KJ. 1993. Pragmatic knowledge and conceptual structure: determinants of transfer between quantitative domains. See Detterman & Sternberg 1993, pp. 68–98

Beck IL, McKeown MG, Gromoll EW. 1989. Learning from social studies texts. *Cogn. Instr.* 6(2):99–158

Beck IL, McKeown MG, Sinatra GM, Loxterman JA. 1991. Revising social studies text from a text-processing perspective: evidence of improved comprehensibility. *Read. Res. Q.* 26(3):251–76

Bereiter C, Scardamalia M. 1987. *The Psychology of Written Composition.* Hillsdale, NJ: Erlbaum

Berti AE. 1994. Children's understanding of the concept of the state. See Carretero & Voss 1994, pp. 49–75

Black JB, Swan K, Schwartz DL. 1988. Developing thinking skills with computers. *Teach. Coll. Rec.* 89(3):384–407

Blaye A, Light P, Joiner R, Sheldon S. 1991. Collaboration as a facilitator of planning and problem solving on a computer-based task. *Br. J. Dev. Psychol.* 9(4):471–83

Boekaerts M. 1993. Anger in relation to school learning. *Learn. Instr.* 3(4):269–80

Brewer WF, Samarapungavan A. 1991. Children's theories vs. scientific theories: differences in reasoning or differences in knowledge? In *Cognition and the Symbolic Processes: Applied and Ecological Perspectives*, ed. RR Hoffman, DS Palermo, pp. 209–32. Hillsdale, NJ: Erlbaum

Britton BF, Graesser AC, ed. 1994. *Models of Understanding.* Hillsdale, NJ: Erlbaum. In press

Brown AL, Ash D, Rutherford M, Nakagawa K, Gordon A, Campione JC. 1993. Distributed expertise in the classroom. In *Distributed Cognitions*, ed. G Salomon, pp. 188–228. New York: Cambridge Univ. Press

Brown AL, Kane MJ. 1988. Preschool children can learn to transfer: learning to learn and learning from example. *Cogn. Psychol.* 20(4):493–523

Brown AL, Palincsar AS. 1989. Guided, cooperative learning and individual knowledge acquisition. In *Knowing, Learning, and Instruction. Essays in Honor of Robert Glaser*, ed. LB Resnick, pp. 393–451. Hillsdale, NJ: Erlbaum

Brown DE, Clement J. 1989. Overcoming misconceptions via analogical reasoning: abstract transfer versus explanatory model construction. *Instr. Sci.* 18(4):237–61

Brown JS, Collins A, Duguid P. 1989. Situated cognition and the culture of learning. *Educ. Res.* 18(1):32–42

Bruer JT. 1993. *Schools For Thought. A Science of Learning in the Classroom.* Cambridge, MA: MIT Press

Bruner J. 1990. *Acts of Meaning.* Cambridge, MA: Harvard Univ. Press

Burbules NC, Linn MC. 1988. Response to contradiction: scientific reasoning during adolescence. *J. Educ. Psychol.* 80(1):67–75

Carey S. 1986. Cognitive science and science education. *Am. Psychol.* 41(10): 1123–30

Carey S, Evans R, Honda M, Woods JE, Unger C. 1989. 'An experiment is when you try it and see if it works': a study of grade 7 students' understanding of the construction of scientific knowledge. *Int. J. Sci. Educ.* 11:514–29

Carretero M, Asensio M, Pozo JI. 1991. Cognitive development, historical time representation and causal explanations in adolescence. See Carretero et al 1991, pp. 27–48

Carretero M, Jacótt L, Limón M, Lopez-Manjón A, León JA. 1994. Historical knowledge: cognitive and instructional implications. See Carretero & Voss 1994, pp. 357–76

Carretero M, Pope M, Simons R-J, Pozo JI, eds. 1991. *Learning and Instruction: European Research in an International Context,* Vol. 3. Oxford: Pergamon

Carretero M, Voss JF, eds. 1994. *Cognitive and Instructional Processes in History and the Social Sciences.* Hillsdale, NJ: Erlbaum. In press

Ceci SJ, Ruiz A. 1993. Transfer, abstractness, and intelligence. See Detterman & Sternberg 1993, pp. 168–91

Cheng PW, Holyoak KJ. 1985. Pragmatic reasoning schemas. *Cogn. Psychol.* 17(4): 391–416

Chi MTH, Bassok M, Lewis MW, Reimann P, Glaser R. 1989. Self-explanations: how students study and use examples in learning to solve problems. *Cogn. Sci.* 13(2): 145–82

Chi MTH, deLeeuw N, Chiu M, LaVancher C. 1994. Eliciting self-explanations improves understanding. *Cogn. Sci.* In press

Chi MTH, VanLehn KA. 1991. The content of physics self-explanations. *J. Learn. Sci.* 1(1):69–105

Chinn CA, Brewer WF. 1993. The role of anomalous data in knowledge acquisition: a theoretical framework and implications for science instruction. *Rev. Educ. Res.* 63(1):1–49

Clancey WJ. 1987. *Knowledge-Based Tutoring: The Guidon Program.* Cambridge, MA: MIT Press

Clement CA, Gentner D. 1991. Systematicity as a selection constraint in analogical mapping. *Cogn. Sci.* 15(1):89–132

Clements DH, Gullo DF. 1984. Effects of computer programming on young children's cognition. *J. Educ. Psychol.* 76(6):1051–58

Cognition and Technology Group at Vanderbilt. 1990. Anchored instruction and its relationship to situated cognition. *Educ. Res.* 19(5):2–10

Cognition and Technology Group at Vanderbilt. 1992. The Jasper series as an example of anchored instruction: theory, program description, and assessment data. *Educ. Psychol.* 27(3):291–315

Cognition and Technology Group at Vanderbilt. 1993. The Jasper series: theoretical foundations and data on problem solving and transfer. In *The Challenge in Mathematics and Science Education: Psychology's Response,* ed. LA Penner, GM Batsche, HM Knoff, DL Nelson, pp. 113–52. Washington, DC: Am. Psychol. Assoc.

Coirier P, Golder C. 1993. Writing argumentative text: a developmental study of the acquisition of supporting structures. *Eur. J. Psychol. Educ.* 8(2):169–81

Cole M. 1989. Cultural psychology: a once and future discipline. In *Nebraska Symposium on Motivation: Cross-cultural Perspectives,* ed. J Berman, 37:279–335. Lincoln: Univ. Nebr. Press

Costa AL. 1991. *Developing Minds.* Alexandria, VA: Assoc. Superv. Curric. Dev.

Cummins DD, Kintsch W, Reusser K, Weimer R. 1988. The role of understanding in solving word problems. *Cogn. Psychol.* 20(4): 405–38

De Corte E. 1990. Towards powerful learning environments for the acquisition of problem-solving skills. *Eur. J. Psychol. Educ.* 5(1):5–19

Delval J. 1994. Stages in the child's construction of social knowledge. See Carretero & Voss 1994, pp. 77–102

Detterman DK. 1993. The case for the prosecution: transfer as an epiphenomenon. See Detterman & Sternberg 1993, pp. 1–24

Detterman DK, Sternberg RJ, eds. 1993. *Transfer on Trial: Intelligence, Cognition, and Instruction.* Norwood, NJ: Ablex

diSessa AA. 1993. Toward an epistemology of physics. *Cogn. Instr.* 10(2&3):101–4

D'Odorico L, Zammuner V. 1993. The influence of using a word processor on children's story writing. *Eur. J. Psychol. Educ.* 8(1):51–64

Donley RD, Ashcraft MH. 1992. The methodology of testing naive beliefs in the physics classroom. *Mem. Cogn.* 20(4):381–91

Dufresne RJ, Gerace WJ, Hardiman PT, Mestre JP. 1992. Constraining novices to perform expertlike problem analyses: effects on schema acquisition. *J. Learn. Sci.* 2(3): 307–31

Dunbar K. 1994. How scientists really reason: scientific reasoning in real-world laboratories. See Sternberg & Davidson 1994. In press

Dweck CS, Leggett EL. 1988. A social-cognitive approach to motivation and personality. *Psychol. Rev.* 95(2):256–73

Fennema E, Franke ML, Carpenter TP, Carey DA. 1993. Using children's mathematical knowledge in instruction. *Am. Educ. Res. J.* 30(3):555–83

Fernandez C, Yoshida M, Stigler JW. 1992. Learning mathematics from classroom instruction: on relating lessons to pupils' interpretations. *J. Learn. Sci.* 2(4): 333–65

Fong GT, Krantz DH, Nisbett RE. 1986. The effects of statistical training on thinking about everyday problems. *Cogn. Psychol.* 18(3):253–92

Gardner H. 1991. *The Unschooled Mind: How Children Think and How Schools Should Teach.* New York: Basic

Garner R, Alexander PA, Gillingham MG, Kulikowich JM, Brown R. 1991. Interest and learning from text. *Am. Educ. Res. J.* 28(3):643–59

Gentner D. 1988. Metaphor as structure mapping: the relational shift. *Child Dev.* 59(1): 47–59

Gilly M. 1991. Social psychology of cognitive constructions: European perspectives. See Carretero et al 1991, pp. 99–123

Glaser R, Bassok M. 1989. Learning theory and the study of instruction. *Annu. Rev. Psychol.* 40:631–66

Golder C. 1992. Production of elaborated argumentative discourse: the role of cooperativeness. *Eur. J. Psychol. Educ.* 7(1): 49–57

Golder C. 1993. Framed writing of argumentative monologues by sixteen- and seventeen-year-old students. *Argumentation* 7(3):343–58

Goswami U. 1991. Analogical reasoning: What develops? A review of research and theory. *Child Dev.* 62(1):1–22

Graesser AC, Person NK. 1994. Question asking during tutoring. *Am. Educ. Res. J.* 31(1):104–37

Greeno JG. 1989. Situation models, mental models, and generative knowledge. In *Complex Information Processing: The Impact of Herbert A. Simon*, ed. D Klahr, K

Kotovsky, pp. 285–318. Hillsdale, NJ: Erlbaum

Guberman SR, Greenfield PM. 1991. Learning and transfer in everyday cognition. *Cogn. Dev.* 6(3):233–60

Haas C, Hayes JR. 1986. What did I just say? Reading problems in writing with the machine. *Res. Teach. Engl.* 20(1):20–35

Hahn CL. 1994. Controversial issues in history instruction. See Carretero & Voss 1994, pp. 201–19

Hall R, Kibler D, Wenger E, Truxaw C. 1989. Exploring the episodic structure of algebra story problem solving. *Cogn. Instr.* 6(3): 223–83

Halldén O. 1986. Learning history. *Oxford R. Educ.* 12(1):53–66

Halldén O. 1993. Learners' conceptions of the subject matter being taught. A case from learning history. In *Learning Discourse: Qualitative Research in Education*, ed. R Säljö. *Int. J. Educ. Res.* 19:317–25

Halpern DF. 1989. *Thought and Knowledge: An Introduction to Critical Thinking.* Hillsdale, NJ: Erlbaum

Hamilton SF. 1990. *Apprenticeship for Adulthood: Preparing Youth for the Future.* New York: Free

Harel I, Papert S. 1990. Software design as a learning environment. *Interact. Learn. Environ.* 1(1):1–32

Hatano G. 1988. Social and motivational bases for mathematical understanding. In *Children's Mathematics: New Directions for Child Development*, ed. GB Saxe, M Gearhart, 41:55–70. San Francisco: Jossey-Bass

Hayes JR. 1990. Individuals and environments in writing instruction. In *Dimensions of Thinking and Cognitive Instruction*, ed. BF Jones, L Idol, pp. 241–63. Hillsdale, NJ: Erlbaum

Hidi S, Baird W. 1988. Strategies for increasing text-based interest and students' recall of expository text. *Read. Res. Q.* 23(4): 465–83

Hofer M, Pikowsky B. 1993. Validation of a category system for arguments in conflict discourse. *Argumentation* 7(2):135–48

Holt T. 1990. *Thinking Historically: Narrative, Imagination, and Understanding.* New York: College Entrance Examination Board

Idol L, Jones BF, Mayer RE. 1991. Classroom instruction: the teaching of thinking. In *Educational Values and Cognitive Instruction: Implications for Reform*, ed. L Idol, BF Jones, pp. 65–119. Hillsdale, NJ: Erlbaum

Ippolito MF, Tweney RD. 1994. The inception of insight. See Sternberg & Davidson 1994. In press

Jenkins JJ. 1979. Four points to remember: a tetrahedral model of memory experiments.

In *Levels of Processing in Human Memory*, ed. LS Cermak, FIM Craik, pp. 429–46. Hillsdale, NJ: Erlbaum

Juel C. 1991. Cross-age tutoring between student athletes and at-risk children. *Read. Teach.* 45(3):178–86

Kaiser MK, Jonides J, Alexander J. 1986. Intuitive reasoning about abstract and familiar physics problems. *Mem. Cogn.* 14(4):308–12

Karmiloff-Smith A. 1988. The child is a theoretician, not an inductivist. *Mind Lang.* 3(3):183–95

Kintsch W. 1986. Learning from text. *Cogn. Instr.* 3(2):87–108

Kintsch W. 1994. Text comprehension, memory, and learning. *Am. Psychol.* 49(4):294–303

Klahr D, Carver SM. 1988. Cognitive objectives in a LOGO debugging curriculum: instruction, learning, and transfer. *Cogn. Psychol.* 20(3):362–404

Klahr D, Dunbar K. 1988. Dual space search during scientific reasoning. *Cogn. Sci.* 12(1):1–48

Klayman J, Ha Y. 1987. Confirmation, disconfirmation, and information in hypothesis testing. *Psychol. Rev.* 94(2):211–28

Kuhn D. 1989. Children and adults as intuitive scientists. *Psychol. Rev.* 96(4):674–89

Kuhn D. 1991. *The Skills of Argument.* New York: Cambridge Univ. Press

Kuhn D, Amsel E, O'Loughlin M. 1988. *The Development of Scientific Thinking Skills.* San Diego: Academic

Kuhn D, Schauble L, Garcia-Mila M. 1992. Cross-domain development of scientific reasoning. *Cogn. Instr.* 9(4):285–327

Kulkarni D, Simon HA. 1988. The processes of scientific discovery: the strategy of experimentation. *Cogn. Sci.* 12(2):139–75

Lampert M. 1990. When the problem is not the question and the solution is not the answer: mathematical knowing and teaching. *Am. Educ. Res. J.* 27(1):29–63

Lave J. 1989. *Cognition in Practice: Mind, Mathematics, and Culture in Everyday Life.* New York: Cambridge Univ. Press

Lave J, Wenger E. 1991. *Situated Learning: Legitimate Peripheral Participation.* New York: Cambridge Univ. Press

Lehman DR, Lempert RO, Nisbett RE. 1988. The effects of graduate training on reasoning: formal discipline and thinking about everyday-life events. *Am. Psychol.* 43(6):431–42

Leinhardt G. 1994. History: a time to be mindful. In *Teaching and Learning in History*, ed. G Leinhardt, IL Beck, C Stainton, pp. 209–55. Hillsdale, NJ: Erlbaum

Leinhardt G, Stainton C, Virji SM. 1994a. A sense of history. *Educ. Psychol.* 29(2):In press

Leinhardt G, Stainton C, Virji SM, Odoroff E.

1994b. Learning to reason in history: mindlessness to mindfulness. See Carretero & Voss 1994, pp. 131–58

Leshowitz B. 1989. It is time we did something about scientific illiteracy. *Am. Psychol.* 44(8):1159–60

Levin I, Siegler RS, Druyan S, Gardosh R. 1990. Everyday and curriculum-based physics concepts: When does short-term training bring change where years of schooling have failed to do so? *Br. J. Dev. Psychol.* 8(3):269–79

Levine SC, Jordan NC, Huttenlocher J. 1992. Development of calculation abilities in young children. *J. Exp. Child Psychol.* 53(1):72–103

Linn MC, Songer NB. 1993. How do students make sense of science? *Merrill-Palmer Q.* 39(1):47–73

Littlefield J, Rieser JJ. 1993. Semantic features of similarity and children's strategies for identifying relevant information in mathematical story problems. *Cogn. Instr.* 11(2):133–88

Lock R. 1990. Pupil ability and practical skill performance in science. *Educ. Rev.* 42(1):65–76

Low R, Over R. 1989. Detection of missing and irrelevant information within algebraic story problems. *Br. J. Educ. Psychol.* 59(3):296–305

Mannes SM, Kintsch W. 1987. Knowledge organization and text organization. *Cogn. Instr.* 4(2):91–115

McCloskey M. 1983. Naive theories of motion. In *Mental Models*, ed. D Gentner, AL Stevens, pp. 299–324. Hillsdale, NJ: Erlbaum

McCloskey M, Kargon R. 1987. The meaning and use of historical models in the study of intuitive physics. In *Ontogeny, Phylogeny and Historical Development*, ed. S Strauss, 2:49–67. Norwood, NJ: Ablex

McKeown MG, Beck IL, Worthy MJ. 1993. Grappling with text ideas: questioning the author. *Read. Teach.* 46(7):560–66

Means ML, Voss JF. 1994. Who reasons well? Two studies of informal reasoning among children of different grade, ability, and knowledge levels. *Cogn. Instr.* In press

Miller JG. 1986. Early cross-cultural commonalities in social explanation. *Dev. Psychol.* 22(4):514–20

Mink LO. 1987. Narrative form as a cognitive instrument. In *Historical Understanding*, pp. 182–203. Ithaca, NY: Cornell Univ. Press

Nathan MJ, Kintsch W, Young E. 1992. A theory of algebra-word-problem comprehension and its implications for the design of learning environments. *Cogn. Instr.* 9(4):329–89

Nelson J, Hayes JR. 1988. *How the writing context shapes college students' strategies for writing from sources.* Tech. Rep. No. 16 (ERIC Doc. 297 374). Cent. Stud. Writ., Carnegie Mellon Univ./Univ. Calif., Berkeley

Nisbett RE, Ross L. 1980. *Human Inference: Strategies and Shortcomings of Social Judgment.* Englewood Cliffs, NJ: Prentice-Hall. 334 pp.

Norris SP. 1989. Can we test validly for critical thinking? *Educ. Res.* 18(9):21–26

Novak JD, Musonda D. 1991. A twelve-year longitudinal study of science concept learning. *Am. Educ. Res. J.* 28(1):117–53

Nunes T, Carraher DW, Schliemann AD. 1993. *Street Mathematics and School Mathematics.* New York: Cambridge Univ. Press

Ohlsson S, Bee N. 1991. Intra-individual differences in fractions arithmetic. *Proc. 15th Psychol. Math. Educ. Conf.,* Assissi, Italy, pp. 121–28

Orsolini M, Pontecorvo C. 1992. Children's talk in classroom discussions. *Cogn. Instr.* 9(2):113–36

Perfetti CA, Britt MA, Rouet J, Georgi MC, Mason RA. 1994. How students use text to learn about historical uncertainty. See Carretero & Voss 1994, pp. 257–83

Perkins DN. 1985. Postprimary education has little impact on informal reasoning. *J. Educ. Psychol.* 77(5):562–71

Perkins DN, Allen R, Hafner J. 1983. Difficulties in everyday reasoning. In *Thinking: The Expanding Frontier,* ed. W Maxwell, pp. 177–89. Philadelphia: Franklin Inst.

Perkins DN, Salomon G. 1989. Are cognitive skills context-bound? *Educ. Res.* 18(1):16–25

Perlmutter M, Behrend SD, Kuo F, Muller A. 1989. Social influences on children's problem solving. *Dev. Psychol.* 25(5):744–54

Pontecorvo C, Girardet H. 1994. Arguing and reasoning in understanding historical topics. *Cogn. Instr.* In press

Pozo JI, Carretero M. 1992. Causal theories, reasoning strategies, and conflict resolution by experts and novices in Newtonian mechanics. In *Neo-Piagetian Theories of Cognitive Development. Implication and Applications for Education,* ed. A Demetriou, A Efklides, M Shayer, pp. 231–55. London: Routledge

Pressley M, Wood E, Woloshyn VE, Martin V, King A, Menke D. 1992. Encouraging mindful use of prior knowledge: attempting to construct explanatory answers facilitates learning. *Educ. Psychol.* 27(1):91–109

Qin Y, Simon HA. 1990. Laboratory replication of scientific discovery processes. *Cogn. Sci.* 14(2):281–312

Radziszewska B, Rogoff B. 1988. Influence of adult and peer collaborators on children's planning skills. *Dev. Psychol.* 24(6):840–48

Radziszewska B, Rogoff B. 1991. Children's guided participation in planning imaginary errands with skilled adult or peer partners. *Dev. Psychol.* 27(3):381–89

Ranney M. 1994. Relative consistency and subjects' "theories" in domains such as naive physics: common research difficulties illustrated by Cooke and Breedin. *Mem. Cogn.* In press

Reed WM, Palumbo DB. 1992. The effect of BASIC instruction on problem solving skills over an extended period of time. *J. Educ. Comp. Res.* 8(3):311–25

Reif F, Allen S. 1992. Cognition for interpreting scientific concepts: a study of acceleration. *Cogn. Instr.* 9(1):1–44

Renninger KA, Hidi S, Krapp A, eds. 1992. *The Role of Interest in Learning and Development.* Hillsdale, NJ: Erlbaum

Renstrom L, Andersson B, Marton F. 1990. Students' conceptions of matter. *J. Educ. Psychol.* 82(3):555–69

Resnick LB. 1989. Developing mathematical knowledge. *Am. Psychol.* 44(2):162–69

Resnick LB, Singer JA. 1993. Protoquantitative origins of ratio reasoning. In *Rational Numbers: An Integration of Research,* ed. TP Carpenter, E Fennema, TA Romberg, pp. 107–30. Hillsdale, NJ: Erlbaum

Richardson K. 1992. Covariation analysis of knowledge representation: some developmental studies. *J. Exp. Child Psychol.* 53(2):129–50

Riesenmy MR, Ebel D, Mitchell S, Hudgins B. 1991. Retention and transfer of children's self-directed critical thinking skills. *J. Educ. Res.* 85(1):14–25

Robertson WC. 1990. Detection of cognitive structure with protocol data: predicting performance on physics transfer problems. *Cogn. Sci.* 14(2):253–80

Rogoff B. 1990. *Apprenticeship in Thinking: Cognitive Development in Social Context.* New York: Oxford Univ. Press

Roller CM. 1990. The interaction between knowledge and structure variables in the processing of expository prose. *Read. Res. Q.* 25(2):79–89

Rosebery AS, Warren B, Conant FR. 1992. Appropriating scientific discourse: findings from language minority classrooms. *J. Learn. Sci.* 2(1):61–94

Roussey J, Gombert A. 1994. Improving argumentative writing skills: effect of two types of aids. *Argumentation.* In press

Ruffman T, Perner J, Olson DR, Doherty M. 1993. Reflecting on scientific thinking: children's understanding of the hypothesis-evidence relation. *Child Dev.* 64(6):1617–36

Säljö R. 1991. Learning and mediation: fitting reality into a table. *Learn. Instr.* 1(3):261–72

Säljö R, Wyndhamn J. 1990. Problem solving,

academic performance, and situated reasoning: a study of joint cognitive activity in the formal setting. *Br. J. Educ. Psychol.* 60(3):245–54

Samarapungavan A. 1992. Children's judgments in theory choice tasks: scientific rationality in childhood. *Cognition* 45(1):1–32

Saxe GB. 1988. The mathematics of child street vendors. *Child Dev.* 59(5):1415–25

Saxe GB. 1991. *Culture and Cognitive Development: Studies in Mathematical Understanding.* Hillsdale, NJ: Erlbaum

Schauble L, Glaser R, Duschl RA, Schulze S, John J. 1994. Students' understanding of the objectives and procedures of experimentation in the science classroom. *J. Learn. Sci.* In press

Schauble L, Glaser R, Raghavan K, Reiner M. 1991. Causal models and experimentation strategies in scientific reasoning. *J. Learn. Sci.* 1(2):201–38

Schliemann AD, Acioly NM. 1989. Mathematical knowledge developed at work: the contribution of practice versus the contribution of schooling. *Cogn. Instr.* 6(3): 185–221

Schoenfeld AH. 1987. What's all the fuss about metacognition? In *Cognitive Science and Mathematics Education*, ed. AH Schoenfeld, pp. 189–215. Hillsdale, NJ: Erlbaum

Schoenfeld AH. 1988. When good teaching leads to bad results: the disasters of "well taught" mathematics classes. *Educ. Psychol.* 23(2):145–66

Schoenfeld AH. 1991. On mathematics as sense-making: an informal attack on the unfortunate divorce of formal and informal mathematics. See Voss et al 1991, pp. 311–43

Schriver KA. 1990. *Evaluating text quality: The continuum from text-focused to reader-focused methods.* Tech. Rep. No. 41 (ERIC Doc. 318 009). Cent. Stud. Writ., Carnegie Mellon Univ./Univ. Calif., Berkeley

Seixas P. 1993a. Parallel crises: history and the social studies curriculum in the USA. *J. Curric. Stud.* 25(3):235–50

Seixas P. 1993b. The community of inquiry as a basis for knowledge and learning: the case of history. *Am. Educ. Res. J.* 30(2): 305–24

Seixas P. 1993c. Historical understanding among adolescents in a multicultural setting. *Curric. Inq.* 23(3):301–27

Shayer M, Adey PS. 1993. Accelerating the development of formal thinking in middle and high school students: IV. Three years after a two-year intervention. *J. Res. Sci. Teach.* 30(4):351–66

Shemilt D. 1987. Adolescent ideas about evidence and methodology in history. In *The History Curriculum for Teachers*, ed. C Portal, pp. 39–61. Philadelphia: Falmer

Shute VJ, Glaser R. 1991. An intelligent tutoring system for exploring principles of economics. In *Improving Inquiry in Social Science: A Volume in Honor of Lee J Cronbach*, ed. RE Snow, D Wiley, pp. 333–66. Hillsdale, NJ: Erlbaum

Siegler RS. 1989. How domain-general and domain-specific knowledge interact to produce strategy choices. *Merrill-Palmer Q.* 35(1):1–26

Siegler RS, Jenkins E. 1989. *How Children Discover New Strategies.* Hillsdale, NJ: Erlbaum

Singer M. 1990. Answering questions about discourse. *Disc. Process.* 13(3):261–77

Slavin RE. 1987. Developmental and motivational perspectives on cooperative learning: a reconciliation. *Child Dev.* 58(5): 1161–67

Slomkowski CL, Killen M. 1992. Young children's conceptions of transgressions with friends and nonfriends. *Int. J. Behav. Dev.* 15(2):247–58

Sodian B, Zaitchik D, Carey S. 1991. Young children's differentiation of hypothetical beliefs from evidence. *Child Dev.* 62(4): 753–66

Stein NL, Bernas RS, Calicchia DJ, Wright A. 1994. A model of argument understanding: the dynamics of negotiation. In *Models of Understanding*, ed. B Britton, A Graesser, Hillsdale, NJ: Erlbaum. In press

Stein NL, Miller CA. 1991. I win—you lose: the development of argumentative thinking. See Voss et al 1991, pp. 265–90

Stein NL, Miller CA. 1993a. Argumentative understanding: relationships among position preference, judgments of goodness, memory and reasoning. *Argumentation* 7(2):183–204

Stein NL, Miller CA. 1993b. The development of memory and reasoning skill in argumentative contexts: evaluating, explaining, and generating evidence. In *Advances in Instructional Psychology*, ed. R Glaser, 4: 285–335. Hillsdale, NJ: Erlbaum

Sternberg RJ. 1989. Domain-generality versus domain-specificity: the life and impending death of a false dichotomy. *Merrill-Palmer Q.* 35(1):115–30

Sternberg RJ, Davidson J, eds. 1994. *The Nature of Insight.* Cambridge, MA: MIT Press

Stevenson HW, Stigler JW. 1992. *The Learning Gap: Why Our Schools are Failing and What We Can Learn from Japanese and Chinese Education.* New York: Summit

Stevenson HW, Stigler JW, Lucker GW, Lee S, Hsu CC, Kitamura S. 1987. Classroom behavior and achievement of Japanese, Chinese, and American children. In *Advances in Instructional Psychology*, ed. R Glaser, 3:153–204. Hillsdale, NJ: Erlbaum

Sweller J. 1988. Cognitive load during problem solving: effects on learning. *Cogn. Sci.* 12(2):257–85

Tishman S, Jay E, Perkins DN. 1993. Teaching thinking dispositions: from transmission to enculturation. *Theory Prac.* 32:147–53

Topolski J. 1990. Towards an integrated model of historical explanation. *Hist. Theor.* 30(3):324–38

Toulmin SE. 1958. *The Uses of Argument.* Cambridge, MA: Cambridge Univ. Press

Trabasso T, Nickels M. 1992. The development of goal plans of action in the narration of a picture story. *Disc. Process.* 15(3):249–75

Trabasso T, van den Broek P, Suh S. 1989. Logical necessity and transitivity of causal relations in stories. *Disc. Process.* 12(1):1–25

Tweney RD. 1985. Faraday's discovery of induction: a cognitive approach. In *Faraday Rediscovered: Essays on the Life and Work of Michael Faraday, 1791-1867*, ed. D Gooding, FAJL James, pp. 189–210. New York: Macmillan

Tweney RD. 1991. Reasoning in science. See Voss et al 1991, pp. 3–16

Varnhagen CK. 1991. Text relations and recall for expository prose. *Disc. Process.* 14(4):399–422

Villani A, Pacca JLA. 1990. Spontaneous reasoning of graduate students. *Int. J. Sci. Educ.* 12(5):589–600

von Borries B. 1994. (Re-)constructing history and moral judgment. On relationships between interpretations of the past and perceptions of the present. See Carretero & Voss 1994, pp. 339-55

Vosniadou S, Brewer WF. 1992. Mental models of the earth: a study of conceptual change in childhood. *Cogn. Psychol.* 24(4):535–85

Voss JF, Blais J, Means ML, Greene TR, Ahwesh E. 1986. Informal reasoning and subject matter knowledge in the solving of economics problems by naive and novice individuals. *Cogn. Instr.* 3(4):269–302

Voss JF, Carretero M, Kennet J, Silfies LN. 1994. The collapse of the Soviet Union: a case study in causal reasoning. See Carretero & Voss 1994, pp. 403–29

Voss JF, Means ML. 1991. Learning to reason via instruction in argumentation. *Learn. Instr.* 1(4):337–50

Voss JF, Perkins DN, Segal JW, eds. 1991. *Informal Reasoning and Education.* Hillsdale, NJ: Erlbaum

Voss JF, Silfies LN. 1994. Learning from history text: the interaction of knowledge and comprehension skill with text structure. *Cogn. Instr.* In press

Wade SE. 1992. How interest affects learning from text. In *The Role of Interest in Learning and Development*, ed. KA Renninger, S Hidi, A Krapp, pp. 255–77. Hillsdale, NJ: Erlbaum

Webb NM. 1989. Peer interaction and learning in small groups. *Int. J. Educ. Res.* 13(1):21–39

Weiss DM, Sachs J. 1991. Persuasive strategies used by preschool children. *Disc. Process.* 14(1):55–72

Wineburg SS. 1991a. Historical problem solving: a study of the cognitive processes used in the evaluation of documentary and pictorial evidence. *J. Educ. Psychol.* 83(1):73–87

Wineburg SS. 1991b. On the reading of historical texts: notes on the breach between school and academy. *Am. Educ. Res. J.* 28(3):495–519

Wright RE, Rosenberg S. 1993. Knowledge of text coherence and expository writing: a developmental study. *J. Educ. Psychol.* 85(1):152–58

Zammuner VL. 1987. For or against: the expression of attitudes in discourse. *Text* 7(4):411–34

Zhu X, Simon HA. 1987. Learning mathematics from examples and by doing. *Cogn. Instr.* 4(3):137–66

Annu. Rev. Psychol. 1995. 46:183–207
Copyright © 1995 by Annual Reviews Inc. All rights reserved

INTERPERSONAL RELATIONS:
Mixed-Motive Interaction

Samuel S. Komorita

Department of Psychology, University of Illinois, Champaign, Illinois 61820

Craig D. Parks

Department of Psychology, Washington State University, Pullman, Washington 99164

KEY WORDS: bargaining, coalition formation, social dilemma, commons dilemma, public goods dilemma, cooperation

CONTENTS

0066-4308/95/0201-0183$05.00

183

INTRODUCTION

The concept of mixed-motive conflict was first introduced by economist Thomas Schelling (1960) to refer to a situation in which two or more parties are faced with a conflict between the motives to cooperate and to compete with each other. Two-person bargaining is a classic example of a mixed-motive relationship in which the bargainers must make concessions to reach a compromise agreement, but at the same time, they must compete to achieve a good bargain. Although mixed-motive interactions are involved in several research areas, this review covers only bargaining and social dilemmas [i.e. situations in which payoffs to the participants (rewards and costs) are specified, and it is assumed that all parties are motivated to maximize their payoffs]. Excluded are studies of social loafing, which has been interpreted as a special case of a social dilemma (Kerr & Bruun 1983), as well as group decision making and various forms of bargaining involving nontangible rewards and motives (e.g. face-saving, ideological issues, fear, guilt) involved in marital conflict or political-international conflict.

What remains are two basic types of mixed-motive situations: bargaining and social dilemmas. These two classes of situations (in game theory) are special cases of cooperative and noncooperative games, respectively. In a cooperative game, side-payments are possible and are enforced by an external agent, whereas in a noncooperative game, side-payments are not possible, and payoffs are based on the joint choices of two or more players. These two types of situations may be further subdivided into two-person vs N-person (N > 2) cases, resulting in a 2 × 2 classification scheme. In the two-person case we have dyadic bargaining and the classic prisoner's dilemma and their variants (e.g. the game of Chicken). In the N-person case we have research on coalition formation and N-person social dilemmas (e.g. public goods and resource dilemmas).

Many social scientists are interested in mixed-motive interaction, and an enormous number of experiments have been conducted by investigators in other disciplines. Thus, a review of all of these studies would be an impossible task. Fortunately, there are several excellent reviews of the literature in other disciplines. Because Carnevale & Pruitt (1992) have recently reviewed psychological research on bargaining, our discussion of bargaining focuses on coalition research as well as the nonpsychological literature, the latter to inform the reader of approaches and variables other than those typically of interest to social psychologists. However, because it has been more than ten years since the last extensive review of psychological social dilemma research (Messick & Brewer 1983), our discussion of social dilemmas focuses almost entirely on psychological work.

BARGAINING

As might be expected, bargaining is of fundamental concern to economists and political scientists. What is surprising is their emphasis on experimental studies of bargaining, especially in the last 15 to 20 years. The emphasis on laboratory studies of economic behavior was stimulated by several prominent researchers (Plott 1979, 1982; Roth 1988; Smith 1980, 1982). A similar movement was led in Germany by Sauermann & Selten (1960). Smith (1993) has presented an interesting history of this movement.

Kagel & Roth (1994) provide the most recent review of the literature in experimental economics. In political science, Palfrey (1991) classifies experimental research into three major areas: 1. laboratory elections, 2. committee decision making, and 3. coordination and cooperation. The first two areas are not reviewed here, but the third is touched upon in our later discussion of social dilemmas.

The Economic Approach to Bargaining

One of the striking differences between studies conducted by economists and those by social psychologists is that economists attempt to test some theoretical principle, such as the core (von Neumann & Morgenstern 1947), the Nash equilibrium (1950), or more recently, the perfect equilibria criteria (Selten 1975). In general, their theoretical principles are based on axiomatic (rational choice) models, and as might be expected, the results of some studies support the models and the results of others do not. The problem then is to determine under what conditions a given model is valid. Such inconsistencies have led to stimulating controversies regarding the relevance of rational choice models (cf Hogarth & Reder 1987, Smith 1991).

A notable exception to this approach is Selten's (1972) research on bounded (limited) rationality, as first proposed by Simon (1957). Selten's work (in addition to Sauermann's) has led to an interdisciplinary approach to mixed-motive research in general (cf Tietz et al 1986). A more recent development is a rapprochement between the axiomatic (i.e. prescriptive) and behavioral (i.e. descriptive) approaches to research in negotiations, called the behavioral decision approach to negotiation (Neale & Bazerman 1991, Neale & Bazerman 1992). It is an important development because it encourages cross-fertilization between the economic and psychological approaches to bargaining.

Ultimatum Bargaining

Studies on ultimatum bargaining (Guth 1988) illustrate the difference between studies conducted by social psychologists and by economists. In ultimatum bargaining, two bargainers must negotiate the division of a given amount of money, denoted c. One of the players (randomly selected) demands how much of c she wishes; then the other player accepts or rejects player 1's demand. If player 2 accepts player 1's demand, player 1 receives the demand and player 2 receives the remainder of c. If player 2 rejects player 1's demand, each receives 0. The optimal strategy for player 1, according to game theory, is to demand $c - \varepsilon$, where ε is some small quantity. For example, if $c = \$100$, player 1 should demand \$99. Player 2 is then left with a choice between \$1 (accept) vs \$0 (reject), and according to game theory, player 2 should accept.

Several variations of this game have been used, including (*a*) allowing more than one round of bargaining (if player 2 rejects player 1's demand, player 2 is allowed to demand a share of c and player 1 is faced with an ultimatum to accept or reject player 2's demand); (*b*) using multiple rounds of bargaining with a "shrinking cake" (the value of c becomes smaller with each successive round of demands); and (*c*) auctioning of player position (the highest bidder becomes player 1). Guth & Tietz's (1990) review of several studies presents a striking conclusion: the game theoretic prediction is clearly not supported. Because player 1 frequently demands a 50–50 (equal) split, Guth (1988) concludes that norms of fairness (distributive justice) clearly affect subjects' behavior—both in the demands of player 1, as well as player 2's decision to accept or reject player 1's demand. In this context, Roth raises an interesting question about the role of incentives in bargaining experiments. Suppose the value of c is \$100 million (instead of \$100 in our example). How many of us (as Player 2) would reject 1 million dollars if Player 1 demanded 99 million?

The results of ultimatum bargaining experiments have important implications for theories of justice and reward allocation, widely studied by social psychologists (cf Bierhoff et al 1986). The results also have implications for some social dilemma games, e.g. sequential "best-shot" public good games (Harrison & Hirshleifer 1989). Roth (1994) provides an excellent discussion of the role of cultural-social-psychological factors on the validity of game-theoretic models.

Disagreements

Another unique aspect of the economic literature on bargaining is the concern with variables that lead to disagreements. One obvious factor is the cost of disagreement: The greater the penalties for a stalemate in negotiations, the greater the incentive to avoid disagreement. But Roth (1994) argues that disagreements and costly delays occur frequently even when it is advantageous to reach agreement. He cites Kennan & Wilson's (1990) claim that "most strikes are eventually settled on terms that could have been reached earlier, without incurring the costs that the strike imposes on all parties" (p. 42).

Attempts to isolate the factors underlying disagreements are complicated by the fact that face-to-face bargaining evokes much lower rates of disagreement than does anonymous bargaining via written notes. Because face-to-face interaction provides more information about the bargainer's preferences than does anonymous bargaining, another explanation for disagreements is that bargainers have incomplete information and are uncertain about the important aspects of each other's situation. Roth concludes that bargaining models of incomplete information do not provide an adequate explanation of the frequency of disagreements.

A review of a large number of experiments suggests that disagreements are based on differences in the expectations of the bargainers about what is a fair or reasonable division of the payoffs. The intriguing question is how such differences in expectations are resolved to reach an agreement. Carnevale & Pruitt's (1992) coverage of the bargaining process, especially the cognitive processes involved in bargaining, is pertinent here. We do not review this literature here, but the reader is referred to reviews by Messick & Mackie (1989) and Thompson & Hastie (1990). In addition, Bazerman et al (1991) have reviewed the bargaining literature from a variety of perspectives: economic, political science, and in particular, organizational behavior.

COALITION FORMATION

From one perspective, research on two-person bargaining can be interpreted as a special case of coalition formation, where each bargainer has more than one person with whom he/she can reach an agreement. Consider a three-person game in which players A, B, and C can form two-person coalitions AB, AC, or BC. Each possible coalition, including one-person coalitions, is given a value, denoted $v(C_j)$, and members of coalition C_j must negotiate and reach agreement on the division of $v(C_j)$. For example, suppose $v(AB) = 100$; $v(AC) = 80$; $v(BC) = 60$; and $v(A) = v(B) = v(C) = 0$. The problem for theories of coalition formation is to predict which coalition is likely to form and to predict the payoff shares negotiated by the coalition members. This type of game is called a multivalued game (Komorita & Kravitz 1983). One of the more accurate theories for multivalued games is the equal excess model (Komorita 1979), which predicts that the AB coalition is most likely to form for a 55–45 split of $v(AB)$ for players A and B respectively. Similar payoff predictions are made by the alpha-power model (Rapoport & Kahan 1982) and by the equal division Kernel (Crott & Albers 1981).

When the value of the three-person coalition, $v(N)$, is very large, e.g. $v(ABC) = 150$, the game is called superadditive. For such games, Michener (1992) has developed a behavioral theory, called the Central-Union Theory, that yields probability predictions of coalition formation, as well as payoff shares of the coalition members. Although this is a remarkable achievement, the theory requires estimates of three parameters to derive predictions. As a result, evaluation of the theory will be difficult, and thus far, no attempt has been made to competitively evaluate its predictions against the predictions of other theories.

Simple Games

In a *simple game,* all coalitions have one of two values: one value for all winning coalitions and a second value for all losing coalitions (e.g. 100 and 0, respectively). For example, consider a four-person game with winning coalitions AB, AC, AD, and BCD, and losing coalitions BC, BD, CD (as well as all one-person coalitions). Player A has an advantage (greater bargaining strength) because A needs only one other player to form a winning coalition (AB, AC, or AD), whereas players B, C, and D each need both of the other two weak players to form the weak-union (BCD). For a review of research on simple games and other coalition games, see Komorita (1984).

Levine & Moreland (1990) have concluded that research on simple games provides the greatest support for the weighted probability model (Komorita 1974), bargaining theory (Komorita & Chertkoff 1973), and equal excess theory (Komorita 1979). For multivalued games, Levine & Moreland claim that the data "provide a murky theoretical picture," and "although equal excess theory seemed ascendant a few years ago (Komorita 1984), the situation today is less clear" (p. 610). Their conclusions are based on the results of studies showing that situational factors affect the validity of various theories (Komorita & Ellis 1988); some theories are more accurate in one situation but less accurate in others. To complicate matters, some theories may be more accurate in predicting which coalitions are likely to form, but less accurate in predicting the payoff shares of the coalition members. Thus, one of the basic problems for future research is to determine the boundary conditions of various theories.

Types of Coalition Theories

A surprisingly large number of coalition theories have been proposed, and they can be classified according to their assumptions about the motives for forming a coalition (Komorita 1984). Various theories assume that the parties are motivated either to maximize control over other members, maximize status in the group, maximize similarity of attitudes and values, or minimize conflict among its members. However, the majority of theories assume that the parties are motivated to maximize some external reward, such as money or points.

Among theories that are based on reward maximization, many are axiomatic (prescriptive) theories. These theories predict the payoff shares of various possible coalitions, but they do not yield predictions about the likelihood of these coalitions. Most social scientists are interested in both of these response measures (see below); thus, we restrict our review to theories that predict both coalition formation and the payoff shares. For a review of axiomatic theories, see Kahan & Rapoport (1984) and Selten (1987); for a review of other types of theories, see Cook & Gilmore (1984), Ordeshook (1986), Schofield (1985), and Wilke (1985).

Critique of Coalition Research

As in many areas of psychological research, there is disagreement on the extent to which theories should be broad and general, or specific enough to allow rigorous tests of the theory. Almost all the theories discussed in this review are quite narrow in scope, but sufficiently specific so that they are vulnerable to rejection. However, in recent years, there have been several critiques of and pleas to broaden the scope of coalition research (Cook & Gilmore 1984, Murnighan 1986, Pearce et al 1986).

One way to extend the generality of theories is to enlarge the number of motives of the parties to form coalitions (e.g. all members are motivated to maximize reward, status, common goals) but with different weights for each factor. Stryker (1972) suggested this approach when he recommended that we extend coalition theories to situations in which "rewards are internal to the triadic relationship, rather than emanating from outside" (p. 373).

Stryker's suggestion is quite compelling because in many real-life situations, the rewards are indeed internal to the relationships within the group. However, Komorita (1984) argued that "such an approach would involve multiple (unspecified) motives among the participants and would be highly intractable. Some members may be motivated to maximize rewards or achieve the goals of the group, some may be motivated to maximize control or status, while others may be motivated by similarity of attitudes and values" (p. 187). Such an approach would be a formidable task without specifying the strength of each motive of each participant and would represent an attempt to develop a general theory of groups.

A less formidable approach is to restrict the theory to the two-person case . This approach was first proposed by Thibaut & Kelley (1959) and includes many variants of two-person bargaining (e.g. Lawler & Yoon 1993). Another approach is to retain the reward maximization paradigm but embed the task in a larger, more realistic social context (Cook & Gilmore 1984, Mannix & White 1992, Miller & Komorita 1986, Molm 1987, Murnighan 1986, Murnighan & Brass 1990, Stolte 1990). For example, Cook & Gilmore (1984) asked subjects to maximize points worth 2 or 3 cents each, but unlike the typical coalition experiment, subjects bargained with incomplete information: All players knew the value of the coalitions that included them but were uninformed about the values of other coalitions.

In contrasting the work of economists and social psychologists, we indicated that economists emphasize formal (axiomatic) theory, whereas psychologists tend to emphasize cognitive-motivational approaches. We also cited the work of Selten and his associates (Tietz et al 1986), who emphasize a bounded rationality approach to mixed-motive interaction. Their work demonstrates the influence of psychological research, but with some notable exceptions (e.g. Dawes, Rapoport and their associates), social psychologists do not seem to have been influenced by research in economics. This lack of cross-fertilization between economists and social psychologists is unfortunate, but seems to be changing—witness the *Journal of Economic Psychology* and the International Association for Research in Economic Psychology (IAREP).

Research on coalition formation has declined markedly. During the past five years, fewer than a half-dozen studies were published in psychology journals. This decline is partly because the vast majority of coalition studies lack social relevance (ecological validity). Although we described several ways to extend the generality of coalition research, we should point out that these approaches do not attempt to evaluate theories of coalition formation, but focus on social psychological variables that affect coalition behavior. This is the major weakness of this approach. If we increase the complexity of the situation (in the interest of ecological validity), it is difficult to develop theories that yield clear predictions. Predictions cannot be derived logically, and the increased realism is attained at the cost of theoretical precision.

This dilemma suggests another direction for future research—the development of process theories of bargaining and coalition formation. Komorita & Ellis (1988), for example, note that there is considerable variability in payoff shares in various coalition games. The most plausible explanation for this variability is that differences in the sequence and process of sending and rejecting offers affect the final outcome. Several investigators have emphasized the development of a process theory (e.g. Kahan & Rapoport 1984, Komorita 1984), and several attempts have been made to examine coalition processes (e.g. Kahan & Rapoport 1984, Komorita et al 1983). Thus far, these attempts have been discouraging. Perhaps more innovative methods such as protocol analysis (Ericsson & Simon 1980) may yield more promising results.

SOCIAL DILEMMAS

A social dilemma can be defined as a situation in which a group of persons must decide between maximizing selfish interests or maximizing collective interests. It is generally more profitable to maximize selfish interests, but if all do so, all are worse off than if everyone had maximized collective interests. Since Messick & Brewer's (1983) review, there has been increasing interest in social dilemmas in a variety of disciplines. Scientists have used social dilemma analyses to explain topics such as evolution (e.g. Alexander 1987, Boyd 1988), international security (e.g. Lichbach 1990), and funding of governmental programs (e.g. Kotlikoff 1987). Psychologists have used its logic to explain the suboptimal performance of decision-making (e.g. Kameda et al 1992) and task-performing laboratory groups (Shepperd 1993), as well as real work groups (Rutte 1990, Tomer 1987). Research has centered upon three paradigms: the prisoner's dilemma, public goods, and resource dilemmas.

Prisoner's Dilemma

Although the popularity of the prisoner's dilemma (PDG) as a research tool has clearly declined, this paradigm is still used in some work. Much of this work involves the use of reciprocity as a gaming strategy. The simplest of these strategies, tit-for-tat (TFT), involves cooperation on the first trial, followed by imitation of the opponent's move on each succeeding trial. In a now-classic computer simulation, Axelrod (1984; see also Axelrod & Dion 1988) demonstrated the effectiveness of tit-for-tat in comparison against a variety of other strategies. Many researchers have since conducted computer tournaments to test the effectiveness of various strategies under different constraints. These results provide a baseline for cooperation rates and an evaluation of the effectiveness and limitations of various types of strategies.

COMPUTER SIMULATIONS   Researchers have altered the PDG to assess the robustness of TFT. Reciprocity seems to be effective in asymmetric games (Swistak 1989), and a more lenient version (in which retaliation for defection is not as severe) works well with an expanded (5 × 5) choice matrix (To 1988). In noisy environments (i.e. when the likelihood of an action being misperceived is nonzero), TFT is suboptimal, although it is not clear whether the best strategy should involve some unconditional cooperation (Bendor et al 1991, Molander 1985) or be harsh and unforgiving (Mueller 1987). Also, strategies that are effective in two-person games are not necessarily effective in N-person games (Molander 1992).

Investigators have also devised and tested new strategies that were not included in Axelrod's simulation. Messick & Liebrand (1993) tested a "win-cooperate, lose-defect" strategy, which involves cooperation if the payoff is at least as large as the average of the other players, and defection otherwise. This strategy always converges upon cooperation in a homogeneous environment. Marinoff (1992) found that utility-maximization (MEU) strategies consistently outperform reciprocal strategies in a standard game (except, interestingly, when playing another MEU). Boyd & Richerson (1992) proposed a "moralistic" strategy, which is selective in nature: Retaliation is invoked only against noncooperators and those who allow defection to go unpunished. Moralistic strategies are similar to Yamagishi's (1986a,b) notion of a sanctioning system (see below).

Finally, a recent simulation has compared social dilemmas to physical thermodynamics. This simulation indicates that an initially homogeneous group of strategies tends to remain homogeneous, even if noise is introduced into the system (Glance & Huberman 1993).

LABORATORY STUDIES OF TFT   Reciprocity has also been tested in the laboratory. Komorita et al (1991) studied immediate versus delayed reciprocation and found it much more important to immediately reciprocate cooperation than defection. They also showed that TFT's "niceness" (initial cooperative choice) inhibits cooperation over time. Tit-for-tat's effectiveness declines as group size increases (Komorita et al 1992) and is minimal when there is little incentive to cooperate (Komorita et al 1993). Data also suggest that TFT's effectiveness lies partially in the perceived control it instills in its target; a reciprocated individual completely determines TFT's choices and outcomes, conditions that tend to foster cooperation (Friedland 1990). In asymmetric games, mutual cooperation appears to be suboptimal, probably because the temptation to defect differs for each player. A strategy of complex alternation seems to maximize total payoff (King & Murnighan 1987, Murnighan 1991, Murnighan & King 1992, Murnighan et al 1990).

Other factors encourage cooperation in PDG-type games. One important factor is group identity, or caring about one's fellow group members (Orbell et al 1988). Instigation of group identity has been found to enhance cooperation in standard PDG games (Wit & Wilke 1992). Group identity has been researched much more heavily in public goods games (see below).

It has long been suspected that the way in which the dilemma is framed will affect behavior. Most recent work on this question has been spurred by Brewer & Kramer's (1986) finding that cooperation is more frequent when the dilemma is framed as gains rather than losses. Subsequent studies, however, have not totally supported this finding. Some researchers have replicated the positive effects of gain frame (Komorita 1987), but others have not (Aquino et al 1992, Komorita & Carnevale 1992, Rutte et al 1987b). Still others have found interactions with how the opponent's payoff is framed (de Dreu et al 1992) and with the opponent's behavior (Fleishman 1988).

Public Goods

The social dilemma that has received the greatest attention in the last decade is the public goods paradigm. A public good is a commodity (or service) that can be provided only if group members contribute something (e.g. money, effort) toward its provision. However, all persons—contributors and noncontributors—may use it. If one does not have to give to use the good, the individually rational action is to not contribute (behavior known as free riding). Of course, if everyone reasons this way, then there will be no contributions, the good is not provided, and all are worse off. A special case of a public good is the Volunteer's Dilemma (Diekmann 1985, 1986; Weesie 1993; see also An Rapoport 1988a), in which only one contributor is necessary for the good to be provided.

Two types of public good paradigms are frequently used. The most common is the linear model, in which the value of the public good varies directly with the total amount contributed by the group members. In the second paradigm, called the step-level paradigm, there is a provision point such that the public good is provided (all-or-none) if the total amount contributed exceeds the provision point. Thus, in the step-level paradigm, the value of the public good is fixed, and there is an optimal level of contribution: Once the provision point is attained, it is not optimal for additional persons to contribute. In contrast, in the linear model, each additional person increases the value of the public good, and it is optimal for all members to contribute.

FACTORS IN CONTRIBUTION BEHAVIOR   An important problem in public goods research is the question of when people will sacrifice self-interest to help the group. One important factor is self-efficacy. Group members are more likely to cooperate if they feel that their contribution is critical. In large groups, members tend to believe that their efforts will be insignificant (Kerr 1989, Rapoport 1985), and this belief persists even when in reality it is inaccurate (Kerr 1989). Conversely, group members who perceive their contribution as critical are exceedingly likely to cooperate (Rapoport et al 1989, van de Kragt et al 1986).

Related to self-efficacy are expectations about the actions of fellow group members. We would be foolish to contribute if we believed no one else was going to do so. Complementary lines of research have shown that people seem to make heterogeneous assumptions about others, i.e. they believe that some people are more likely to contribute than are others (Rapoport 1985, 1987, 1988; Rapoport & Bornstein 1987). Also, expectations are often based on our own behavior, i.e. we expect most others to act as we do (Dawes & Orbell 1994, Orbell & Dawes 1991).

Endowment size, or the amount of a person's contributable resource, also affects expectations, either inversely (i.e. resource-poor individuals are expected to give more than the wealthy, because the poor have less to lose if the good is not provided), or directly (i.e. the wealthy are expected to give more than the poor because they can more easily afford it). Research tends to support the latter perspective. Most studies show that subjects are more likely to contribute as their wealth increases (Kerr 1992, Rapoport 1988, van Dijk & Grodzka 1992, van Dijk & Wilke 1991, Wit et al 1989a). However, the inverse relationship occurs when the gap between rich and poor is quite large (Aquino et al 1992). Moreover, groups with unequal endowments across members are less successful at public goods provision than are groups with equal endowments (Rapoport & Suleiman 1993).

Most real-life social dilemmas involve very large groups, and group size also affects contribution behavior. The sheer size of the group increases the opportunity for one's free riding to go unnoticed. Removing the element of anonymity by providing explicit feedback about each member's actions produces significant increases in cooperation (Sell & Wilson 1991, Sniezek et al 1990). Large group size may also instill feelings of low self-efficacy (see Weick 1984), although the empirical evidence for this relation is mixed at best (Kaufman & Kerr 1993).

As we might expect, fear and greed (Coombs 1973) seem to moderate contribution behavior—fear that one's contribution will be wasted, and the greedy desire to both maintain wealth and enjoy the public good. Many studies have found greed to play an important role in the contribution decision (Bruins et al 1989, Dawes et al 1986, Liebrand et al 1986b, Poppe & Utens 1986, Rapoport & Eshed-Levy 1989). The effects of fear are not as clear. Some studies have found fear to contribute significantly to competition (Bruins et al 1989, Liebrand et al 1986b, Rapoport & Eshed-Levy 1989), but others have not (Dawes et al 1986, Poppe & Utens 1986). Yamagishi & Sato (1986) have argued that the effects of fear and greed depend on whether provision of the good is conjunctive (i.e. determined by the worst member, which produces fear) or disjunctive (i.e. determined by the best, which produces greed).

Vested interest represents one's utility for the good (Kemp 1991), and recent research shows that vested interest affects contribution behavior. Wit et al (1989a) have shown that individuals who stand to receive a larger payoff than others have higher contribution rates. However, this seems to hold true only in equity-type situations, where the strong-interest individuals have been selected at random rather than on an effort basis (van Dijk & Wilke 1993; see also Sniezek & May 1990).

ENHANCING COOPERATION   Whereas some researchers are interested in why people contribute, others are more concerned with how we can improve contribution rates. One approach is to allow group members to discuss the dilemma before making a contribution choice. The benefits of group discussion in social dilemmas are well established, and recent research has demonstrated its effectiveness with public goods (Bornstein & Rapoport 1988, Braver & Wilson 1986, Orbell et al 1988, van de Kragt et al 1986). Several explanations have been suggested for why discussion is so effective. For example, group members use discussion to make explicit, unanimous promises of cooperative behavior (Orbell et al 1988, 1990, 1991); discussion enhances group identity (Orbell et al 1988); it allows groups to plan and coordinate their contributions (Bornstein &

Rapoport 1988); and it triggers a general "norm of cooperation" (Kerr 1994, Kondo 1990; but see Orbell et al 1988).

Arguing for the coordination explanation, Ledyard (1994) hypothesizes that face-to-face communication should have a greater effect on contribution rates in the step-level paradigm than in the linear paradigm, because the problem for step-level groups is to coordinate behaviors and designate which members should contribute. However, Orbell et al's (1988) work on group identity, which has been replicated consistently (see Dawes et al 1988), suggests that the function of communication is not to facilitate coordination but to alter motivational-normative processes. This problem is analogous to the problem of coordination vs motivational factors in Steiner's (1974) process losses, and we currently have little (if any) data on the validity of Ledyard's hypothesis.

Yamagishi (1986a,b) has argued for the use of a sanctioning system to enhance cooperation in public goods. Under this system, group members would cooperate both in the provision of the good and in the provision of some means of punishing noncooperators. The punishment could be tangible (e.g. restricted access to the good) or intangible (e.g. embarrassment). Research on sanctioning suggests that such a system is particularly effective when dealing with distrustful group members (Yamagishi 1986a, 1988b) and when the temptation to defect is high (Yamagishi 1988a).

Finally, cooperation may be inhibited by the constraints of the experimental paradigm. In many laboratory experiments, contribution behavior is discrete (i.e. subjects give all of their endowment or none of it) and simultaneous (i.e. all subjects act at the same time). However, cooperation rates increase when choice is continuous (Suleiman & Rapoport 1992) or sequential (Budescu et al 1992, Erev & Rapoport 1990, Rapoport et al 1993; see also Bolle & Ockenfels 1990), situations that seem to more closely simulate real-world processes.

Resource Dilemmas

The other major type of social dilemma (in terms of research attention) is a resource dilemma, in which group members may harvest from a common resource pool that is replenished periodically. The dilemma is that if all take as much of the resource as they want, it will run out quickly. As with public goods, researchers interested in resource dilemmas attempt to isolate factors underlying harvesting behavior, although some have begun to apply laboratory findings in attempts to solve real-life dilemmas (Samuelson 1990, Thompson & Stoutemyer 1991; see also Huppes & Midden 1991, Vlek & Keren 1992). In fact, Ostrom (1990) has compiled an insightful book dedicated to analyses of real-life resource dilemmas, as well as an evaluation of the role of game-theoretic models in real dilemmas.

CHOICE MOTIVATION   There seem to be three motives behind harvest choices: 1. individual rationality, or acting in one's self interest; 2. responsibility, or the desire to counteract abuses by others; and 3. conformity. The latter two motives are well established (e.g. Fleishman 1988; Rutte et al 1987a; Samuelson & Messick 1986a,b; Wilke et al 1986). Individuals may actively seek conformity because they do not want their choices to be deviant from others (Liebrand et al 1986a,b, Wilke & Braspenning 1989). Abusers seem more likely to conform to underuse behavior than are underusers to abusive behavior (Chapman 1991).

Other aspects of resource dilemma behavior have also been addressed. Individuals in negative moods have difficulty managing a resource (Knapp & Clark 1991), seemingly because the negative mood makes the self-interest motive predominant. Individual harvests increase as uncertainty about the exact size of the pool increases (Budescu et al 1990, Rapoport et al 1992).

SOLUTIONS TO RESOURCE DILEMMAS   Solving a resource dilemma means finding ways to make optimal harvests, where an optimal harvest is defined as an amount that maintains the pool. Implementation of a solution may be difficult, because subjects tend to view their (and others') choices as being cooperative, even when in reality they are not (O'Connor & Tindall 1990). Group members may thus be hesitant to adopt a new system if they believe behavior to be optimal under the current one.

Some studies emphasize *structural solutions,* in which the basic choice procedure is altered in some way. The alteration most often studied involves elimination of free choice of harvest size. Such a solution is effective but unpopular, particularly if members view it as a violation of rights or unfair punishment of nonabusers (Baron & Jurney 1993). A useful alternative is a leader-based system, under which one group member decides for all (Samuelson 1991, Samuelson & Messick 1986a), although it is very unpopular with noncooperators (Samuelson 1993). Support for the leader is affected by the amount of success the group experiences (Wit & Wilke 1988) and by the consistency of resource replenishment (Wit et al 1989b).

An equality norm, under which all members receive the same harvest, has more support (Allison & Messick 1990, Rutte et al 1987a, Samuelson & Messick 1986b), but the resource must be easily divisible (Allison et al 1992, Allison & Messick 1990) and relatively small (Allison & Messick 1990). Equality will be violated if a subject believes he or she has a valid reason for doing so (Samuelson & Allison 1994).

Another class of solutions, called *individual solutions,* involves introducing manipulations aimed at changing the behavior of group members. Many such manipulations have been investigated. As with public goods, group discussion substantially improves harvesting behavior (Messick et al 1988, Ostrom & Walker 1991, Ostrom et al 1992). Other interventions that have positive effects on harvest behavior are individualized training in resource management (Allison & Messick 1985), enhancement of social identity (Brewer & Kramer 1986, Dawes et al 1988), punishment for overconsumption (Bell et al 1989, Martichuski & Bell 1991), detailed description of the dilemmatic properties of a commons (Mio et al 1993, An. Rapoport 1988b), and verbal reinforcement of conservation (Birjulin et al 1993). Interestingly, neither concern for the environment nor prior commons experience (Moore et al 1987) seems to affect conservation (Smith & Bell 1992).

Samuelson & Messick (1994) have synthesized this research into a decision model of resource dilemmas. They assume that preference for change is a function of dissatisfaction with current outcomes and that it varies with the attribution as to the cause of the problem. Individual solutions are preferred over structural solutions because they are easier to implement and can be undertaken without consent of the entire group. The model also assumes that several factors affect the choice of a specific structural solution (e.g. fairness, efficiency).

DILEMMAS WITH INCOMPLETE INFORMATION   Our review thus far assumes the availability of considerable information about resource size and the behavior of others. But in the real world, it is often difficult to acquire this information. When there is uncertainty about the resource (environmental uncertainty) and/or actions of others (social uncertainty) communication is effective at reducing both (Messick et al 1988). For situations in which interaction is not possible, Suleiman & Rapoport have developed expected utility (1988) and game-theoretic (Rapoport & Suleiman 1992) models of the individual decision process, but both need systematic testing.

ORGANIZATIONAL DILEMMAS   An organization can be thought of as a pool of resources (e.g. labor, information) from which workers can draw (Kramer 1991a,b). If the organization uses a reward-for-performance system, then a limited resource pool presents a social dilemma. Workers or work teams may overuse resources, a strategy that benefits the team, but hurts the company as a whole. In a series of studies, Mannix (1991, 1993; Mannix & White 1992) has observed that workers in competition for resources often form coalitions, and that these coalitions are poor at managing a resource, giving too much to coalition members and not leaving enough for others.

Other Factors in Cooperation

PERSONALITY   Research on social values has established that one's personality plays an important role in mixed-motive behavior. Many social values have been identified, but three have received the greatest support: competition (i.e. maximize the difference between payoffs), cooperation (i.e. maximize joint payoff), and individualism (i.e. maximize own payoff). Some researchers continue to study the values themselves. For example, the competitive orientation can be primed, producing even lower levels of cooperation in such people (Neuberg 1988). Values are predictive of the amount of help offered in helping situations (McClintock & Allison 1989) and of response latencies on interpersonal decision tasks (Liebrand & McClintock 1988). Whether or not a social value predicts cooperative behavior seems to be based on the payoff structure of the dilemma (Parks 1994).

Most studies have focused on how persons with different value orientations view cooperation. Cooperators seem to believe that cooperative behavior reflects intelligence and is the correct way to behave, while noncooperators see cooperation as a sign of weakness and defection as a sign of strength (Liebrand et al 1986a, McClintock & Liebrand 1988, van Lange & Liebrand 1991a, van Lange et al 1990; see also Samuelson 1993). This is referred to as the "might versus morality" hypothesis. That cooperators view cooperation in moral terms is well supported, but some studies have failed to show that noncooperators think in power terms (Beggan et al 1988, Sattler & Kerr 1991). In addition, individuals perceived as truly moral (e.g. priests) are expected to be highly cooperative (Orbell et al 1992) and are not expected to be exploited by noncooperators (van Lange & Liebrand 1989, 1991b).

Intergroup Relations

How groups interact with other groups in mixed-motive settings has received considerable attention in recent years. In social dilemmas, Rapoport, Bornstein, and colleagues have studied group competition for a public good. They have devised a simple paradigm, called an intergroup public goods (IPG) game, in which groups of individuals compete for a good that only the winners may use (Rapoport & Bornstein 1987). Several studies show that a larger group will not necessarily prevail over a smaller group (Rapoport & Bornstein 1989, Rapoport et al 1989). Preplay discussion within each group (though not between groups) substantially increases contribution rates (Bornstein & Rapoport 1988, Bornstein et al 1989, Rapoport & Bornstein 1989), although this result may be true only for step-level goods (Bornstein 1992).

Insko and colleagues have shown that interaction between groups is more contentious and less cooperative compared with individuals interacting with other individuals. The phenomenon is known as individual-group discontinuity and is very robust. Insko & Schopler (1987) offer two explanations for discontinuity. The "social support for shared self interest" hypothesis argues that self-interested behaviors (i.e. competition) receive support within a group that isolated individuals cannot obtain. According to the "schema-based distrust" hypothesis, group members maintain beliefs that intergroup interactions are by nature contentious and, thus, act accordingly. Support for schema-based distrust is equivocal. Intergroup interactions are expected to be competitive and hostile (Hoyle et al 1989), but groups rarely choose to withdraw from such interactions (Insko et al 1993). The fact that greed is a significant motivator in intergroup choice (Insko et al 1990, Schopler et al 1993) makes the social support explanation seem more plausible.

CRITIQUE OF MIXED-MOTIVE RESEARCH

Mixed-motive interaction continues to be a popular research topic, and we doubtless will learn considerably more about such interaction in the near future. However, there are some definite weaknesses that we feel researchers have not adequately addressed.

We have already touched upon what we see as a weakness in coalition research: the lack of any process-oriented theories. Many theories are able to predict which coalitions will form, but these theories are superficial and do not address the psychological factors involved in the coalescing process. Many theorists have emphasized the need for process theories, but with the exception of Friend et al (1977), none have appeared. Unfortunately, Friend and colleagues' theory is restricted to a "game of status," which is a special type of coalition game and is not applicable to the more general coalition situation. However, their work may serve as a guide for theorists who wish to develop a process theory of coalition formation.

By contrast, social dilemma researchers have made some theoretical progress. As we have seen, several psychological variables have been researched in-depth regarding their role in facilitating cooperation. Group identity, self-efficacy, uncertainty, and expectations, for example, have been shown to affect cooperation across a broad range of dilemmas. What is missing is a general model of cooperative behavior that postulates how these factors are interrelated. We are not alone in calling for such a theory. Liebrand (1992) identified 14 factors that conclusively affect dilemma behavior, yet he noted that almost nothing is known about how these factors interact.

Accordingly, mixed-motive researchers should become more process-oriented. In particular, coalition researchers need to shift their focus away from prediction of coalitions and concentrate on psychological variables that will facilitate the development of a process theory. By contrast, social dilemma researchers have done an excellent job of documenting the psychological factors that drive cooperation. It is time to integrate these factors to obtain a more complete picture of how cooperation evolves in a group.

SOME CONCLUDING COMMENTS

Psychologists are not alone in pondering mixed-motive problems. Economists in particular are also interested in bargaining, coalition formation, and social dilemmas (see Ledyard 1994), as are sociologists (see Yamagishi 1994) and political scientists (see Palfrey 1991). But to date, many social psychologists have largely ignored economic principles and concepts. At least in the social dilemma area, many economists seem to be similarly unaffected by psychological research (see Ledyard 1994). However, some economic theories of bargaining draw freely from basic psychological work.

This lack of sharing between the two disciplines is unfortunate. Given that the research goals of psychologists and economists are often complementary, the potential exists for fruitful collaboration. Happily, there are many indicators that this state of affairs may be changing. For example, economic psychology continues to grow as a viable subdiscipline; important interdisciplinary publications have appeared recently (see Hogarth & Reder 1987, Lopes 1994; see also the *Journal of Behavioral Decision Making*); and psychological articles have been published in nonpsychology journals. Perhaps these developments will encourage the kinds of cooperation and collaboration we are calling for.

A Final Comment

Experimental research on mixed-motive interaction was once dominated by social psychologists. During the last decade this dominance has been called into question. In 1986 Steiner warned us that "if social psychologists do not research the group, someone else surely will" (p. 238). In response to Steiner, Levine & Moreland (1990) concluded that "Steiner's warning comes too late. Despite all the excellent research on small groups within social psychology, that discipline has already lost its dominance in this field" (p. 620). They also stated that "the torch has been passed to colleagues in other disciplines, particularly organizational psychology." Although psychologists involved in mixed-motive research have not yet "passed the torch," that point may be approaching rapidly. Bargaining and coalition research is now dominated by economists and organizational behaviorists, and a sizable amount of social dilemma research is also conducted by investigators outside of social psychology. Mixed-motive research may not regain the prominence it had when prisoner's dilemma research was at its peak, but neither is it ready to be abandoned. There are simply too many interesting psychological variables yet to be explored.

Literature Cited

Alexander RD. 1987. *The Biology of Moral Systems*. Hawthorne, NY: Aldine de Gruyter

Allison ST, McQueen LR, Schaerfl LM. 1992. Social decision making processes and the equal partitionment of shared resources. *J. Exp. Soc. Psychol.* 28:23–42

Allison ST, Messick DM. 1985. Effects of experience on performance in a replenishable resource trap. *J. Pers. Soc. Psychol.* 49:943–48

Allison ST, Messick DM. 1990. Social decision heuristics in the use of shared resources. *J. Behav. Decis. Mak.* 3:195–204

Aquino K, Steisel V, Kay A. 1992. The effects of resource distribution, voice, and decision framing on the provision of public goods. *J. Confl. Resolut.* 36:665–87

Axelrod R. 1984. *The Evolution of Cooperation*. New York: Basic Books

Axelrod R, Dion D. 1988. The further evolution of cooperation. *Science* 242:1385–90

Baron J, Jurney J. 1993. Norms against voting for coerced reform. *J. Pers. Soc. Psychol.* 64:347–55

Bazerman MH, Lewicki RJ, Sheppard BH. 1991. *Research on Negotiation in Organizations*, Vol. 3. Greenwich, CT: JAI

Beggan JK, Messick DM, Allison ST. 1988. Social values and egocentric bias: two tests of the might over morality hypothesis. *J. Pers. Soc. Psychol.* 55:606–11

Bell PA, Petersen TR, Hautaluoma JE. 1989. The effect of punishment probability on overconsumption and stealing in a simulated commons. *J. Appl. Soc. Psychol.* 19:1483–95

Bendor J, Kramer RM, Stout S. 1991. When in doubt...: cooperation in a noisy prisoner's dilemma. *J. Confl. Resolut.* 35:691–719

Bierhoff HW, Cohen RL, Greenberg J. 1986. *Justice in Social Relations*. New York: Plenum

Birjulin AA, Smith JM, Bell PA. 1993. Monetary reward, verbal reinforcement, and harvest strategy of others in the commons dilemma. *J. Soc. Psychol.* 133:207–14

Bolle F, Ockenfels P. 1990. Prisoners' dilemma as a game with incomplete information. *J. Econ. Psychol.* 11:69–84

Bornstein G. 1992. The free-rider problem in intergroup conflicts over step-level and continuous public goods. *J. Pers. Soc. Psychol.* 62:597–606

Bornstein G, Rapoport Am. 1988. Intergroup competition for the provision of step-level public goods: effects of preplay communication. *Eur. J. Soc. Psychol.* 18:125–44

Bornstein G, Rapoport Am, Kerpel L, Katz T. 1989. Within- and between-group communication in intergroup competition for public goods. *J. Exp. Soc. Psychol.* 25:422–31

Boyd R. 1988. The evolution of reciprocity in sizeable groups. *J. Theor. Biol.* 132:337–56

Boyd R, Richerson PJ. 1992. Punishment allows the evolution of cooperation (or anything else) in sizable groups. *Ethol. Sociobiol.* 13:171–95

Braver SR, Wilson LA. 1986. Choices in social dilemmas: effects of communication within subgroups. *J. Confl. Resolut.* 30:51–62

Brewer MB, Kramer RM. 1986. Choice behavior in social dilemmas: effects of social identity, group size, and decision framing. *J. Pers. Soc. Psychol.* 50:543–49

Bruins JJ, Liebrand WBG, Wilke HAM. 1989. About the saliency of fear and greed in social dilemmas. *Eur. J. Soc. Psychol.* 19:155–61

Budescu DV, Rapoport Am, Suleiman R. 1990. Resource dilemmas with environmental uncertainty and asymmetric players. *Eur. J. Soc. Psychol.* 20:475–87

Budescu DV, Rapoport Am, Suleiman R. 1992. Simultaneous vs. sequential requests in resource dilemmas with incomplete information. *Acta Psychol.* 80:297–310

Carnevale PJ, Pruitt DG. 1992. Negotiation and mediation. *Annu. Rev. Psychol.* 43:531–82

Chapman JG. 1991. The impact of socially projected group composition on behavior in a commons dilemma: a self-attention perspective. *Curr. Psychol. Res. Rev.* 10:183–98

Cook KS, Gilmore MR. 1984. Power, dependence, and coalitions. *Adv. Group Process.* 1:27–58

Coombs CH. 1973. A reparameterization of the prisoner's dilemma game. *Behav. Sci.* 18:424–28

Crott NW, Albers W. 1981. The equal division kernel: an equity approach to coalition formation and payoff distribution in N-person games. *Eur. J. Soc. Psychol.* 11:285–306

Dawes RM, Orbell JM. 1994. The benefit of optional play in anonymous one-shot prisoner's dilemma games. In *Barriers to Conflict Resolution*, ed. K Arrow, R Mnookin, L Ross, A Tversky, R Wilson. New York: Norton. In press

Dawes RM, Orbell JM, Simmons RT, van de Kragt AJC. 1986. Organizing groups for collective action. *Am. Polit. Sci. Rev.* 80:1171–85

Dawes RM, van de Kragt AJC, Orbell JM. 1988. Not me or thee but we: the importance of group identity in eliciting cooperation in dilemma situations. *Acta Psychol.* 68:83–97

de Dreu CKW, Emans BJM, Van de Vliert E.

1992. Frames of reference and cooperative social decision-making. *Eur. J. Soc. Psychol.* 22:297–302

Diekmann A. 1985. Volunteer's dilemma. *J. Confl. Resolut.* 29:605–10

Diekmann A. 1986. Volunteer's dilemma: a social trap without a dominant strategy and some empirical results. In *Paradoxical Effects of Social Behavior,* ed. A Diekmann, P Mitter, pp. 187–97. Heidelberg: Physica Verlag

Erev I, Rapoport Am. 1990. Provision of step-level public goods: the sequential contribution mechanism. *J. Confl. Resolut.* 34:401–25

Ericsson KA, Simon HA. 1980. Verbal reports as data. *Psychol. Rev.* 87:215–51

Fleishman JA. 1988. The effects of decision framing and others behavior on cooperation in a social dilemma. *J. Confl. Resolut.* 32:162–80

Friedland N. 1990. Attribution of control as a determinant of cooperation in exchange situations. *J. Appl. Soc. Psychol.* 20:303–20

Friend KE, Laing JD, Morrison RJ. 1977. Game-theoretic analysis of coalition behavior. *Theory Decis.* 8:127–57

Glance NS, Huberman BA. 1993. The outbreak of cooperation. *J. Math. Sociol.* 17:281–302

Guth W. 1988. On the behavioral approach to distributive justice: a theory and experimental investigation. In *Applied Behavioural Economics,* ed. S Maital, 2:703–17. New York: New York Univ. Press

Guth W, Tietz R. 1990. Ultimatum bargaining behavior: A survey and comparison of experimental results. *J. Econ. Psychol.* 11:417–49

Harrison GW, Hirshleifer J. 1989. An experimental evaluation of weakest-link/best-shot models of public goods. *J. Polit. Econ.* 97:201–25

Hogarth RM, Reder MW. 1987. *Rational Choice.* Chicago: Univ. Chicago Press

Hoyle RH, Pinkley RL, Insko CA. 1989. Perceptions of social behavior: evidence of differing expectations for interpersonal and intergroup interaction. *Pers. Soc. Psychol. Bull.* 15:365–76

Huppes G, Midden CJH. 1991. Regulations and incentives as solutions to the social dilemma in wetland management. *Land. Urban Plan.* 20:197–204

Insko CA, Schopler J. 1987. Categorization, competition, and collectivity. *Rev. Pers. Soc. Psychol.* 8:213–51

Insko CA, Schopler J, Drigotas SM, Graetz KA, Kennedy JF, et al. 1993. The role of communication in interindividual-intergroup discontinuity. *J. Confl. Resolut.* 37:108–38

Insko CA, Schopler J, Hoyle RH, Dardis GJ,

Graetz KA. 1990. Individual-group discontinuity as a function of fear and greed. *J. Pers. Soc. Psychol.* 58:68–79

Kagel J, Roth AE. 1994. *Handbook of Experimental Economics.* Princeton, NJ: Princeton Univ. Press

Kahan JP, Rapoport Am. 1984. *Theories of Coalition Formation.* Hillsdale, NJ: Erlbaum

Kameda T, Stasson MF, Davis JH, Parks CD, Zimmerman SK. 1992. Social dilemmas, subgroups, and motivation loss in task-oriented groups: in search of an "optimal" team size in work division. *Soc. Psychol. Q.* 55:47–56

Kaufman CM, Kerr NL. 1993. Small wins: perceptual focus, efficacy, and cooperation in a stage-conjunctive social dilemma. *J. Appl. Soc. Psychol.* 23:3–20

Kemp S. 1991. Magnitude estimation of the utility of public goods. *J. Appl. Psychol.* 76:533–40

Kennan J, Wilson R. 1990. Theories of bargaining delays. *Science* 249:1124–28

Kerr NL. 1989. Illusions of efficacy: the effects of group size on perceived efficacy in social dilemmas. *J. Exp. Soc. Psychol.* 25:287–313

Kerr NL. 1992. Efficacy as a causal and moderating variable in social dilemmas. See Liebrand et al 1992, pp. 59–80

Kerr NL. 1994. Norms in social dilemmas. In *Social Dilemmas,* ed. D. Schroeder. New York: Praeger. In press

Kerr NL, Bruun SE. 1983. Dispensability of member effort and group motivation losses: free-rider effects. *J. Pers. Soc. Psychol.* 44:78–94

King TR, Murnighan JK. 1986. Stability and outcome tradeoffs in asymmetric dilemmas: conditions promoting the discovery of alternating solutions. See Tietz et al, pp. 85–94

Knapp A, Clark MS. 1991. Some detrimental effects of negative mood on individuals' ability to solve resource dilemmas. *Pers. Soc. Psychol. Bull.* 17:678–88

Komorita SS. 1974. A weighted probability model of coalition formation. *Psychol. Rev.* 81:242–56

Komorita SS. 1979. An equal excess model of coalition formation. *Behav. Sci.* 24:369–81

Komorita SS. 1984. Coalition bargaining. *Adv. Exp. Soc. Psychol.* 18:184–247

Komorita SS. 1987. Cooperative choice in decomposed social dilemmas. *Pers. Soc. Psychol. Bull.* 13:53–63

Komorita SS, Carnevale PJ. 1992. Motivational arousal vs. decision framing in social dilemmas. See Liebrand et al 1992, pp. 209–24

Komorita SS, Chan DKS, Parks CD. 1993. The effects of reward structure and reciprocity in social dilemmas. *J. Exp. Soc. Psychol.* 29:252–67

Komorita SS, Chertkoff JM. 1973. A bargaining theory of coalition formation. *Psychol. Rev.* 80:149–62

Komorita SS, Ellis AL. 1988. Level of aspiration in coalition bargaining. *J. Pers. Soc. Psychol.* 54:421–31

Komorita SS, Hilty JA, Parks CD. 1991. Reciprocity and cooperation in social dilemmas. *J. Confl. Resolut.* 35:494–518

Komorita SS, Kravitz DA. 1983. Coalition formation: A social psychological approach. In *Basic Group Processes,* ed. PB Paulus, pp. 145–51. Hillsdale, NJ: Erlbaum

Komorita SS, Parks CD, Hulbert LG. 1992. Reciprocity and the induction of cooperation in social dilemmas. *J. Pers. Soc. Psychol.* 62:607–17

Kondo T. 1990. Some notes on rational behavior, normative behavior, moral behavior, and cooperation. *J. Confl. Resolut.* 34:495–530

Kotlikoff LJ. 1987. Justifying public provision of Social Security. *J. Policy Anal. Manage.* 6:674–89

Kramer RM. 1991a. The more the merrier? Social psychological aspects of negotiations in organizations. See Bazerman et al 1991, pp. 307–32

Kramer RM. 1991b. Intergroup relations and organizational dilemmas: the role of categorization processes. *Res. Organ. Behav.* 13:191–228

Lawler EJ, Yoon J. 1993. Power and emergence of commitment behavior in negotiated exchange. *Am. Sociol. Rev.* 58:465–88

Ledyard JO. 1994. Is there a problem with public good provision? See Kagel & Ross 1994

Lewicki RJ, Sheppard BN, Bazerman MN. 1986. *Research on Negotiation in Organizations,* Vol. 1. Greenwich, CT: JAI

Levine JM, Moreland RL. 1990. Progress in small group research. *Annu. Rev. Psychol.* 41:585–634

Lichbach MI. 1990. When is an arms rivalry a prisoner's dilemma? Richardson's models and 2 × 2 games. *J. Confl. Resolut.* 34:29–56

Liebrand WBG. 1992. How to improve our understanding of group decision making with the help of artificial intelligence. *Acta Psychol.* 80:279–95

Liebrand WBG, Jansen RWTL, Rijken VM, Suhre CJM. 1986a. Might over morality: social values and the perception of other players in experimental games. *J. Exp. Soc. Psychol.* 22:203–15

Liebrand WBG, McClintock CM. 1988. The ring measure of social values: a computerized procedure for assessing individual differences in information processing and social value orientation. *Eur. J. Pers.* 2:217–30

Liebrand WBG, Messick DM, Wilke HAM. 1992. *Social Dilemmas.* Tarrytown, NY: Pergamon

Liebrand WBG, Wilke HAM, Vogel R, Wolters FJM. 1986b. Value orientation and conformity. *J. Confl. Resolut.* 30:77–97

Lopes LL. 1994. Psychology and economics: perspectives on risk, cooperation, and the marketplace. *Annu. Rev. Psychol.* 45:197–227

Mannix EA. 1991. Resource dilemmas and discount rates in decision making groups. *J. Exp. Soc. Psychol.* 27:379–91

Mannix EA. 1993. Organizations as resource dilemmas: the effects of power balance on coalition formation in small groups. *Organ. Behav. Hum. Decis. Process.* 55:1–22

Mannix EA, White SB. 1992. The impact of distributive uncertainty on coalition formation in organizations. *Organ. Behav. Hum. Decis. Process.* 51:198–219

Marinoff L. 1992. Maximizing expected utilities in the prisoner's dilemma. *J. Confl. Resolut.* 36:183–216

Martichuski DK, Bell PA. 1991. Reward, punishment, privatization, and moral suasion in a commons dilemma. *J. Appl. Soc. Psychol.* 21:1356–69

McClintock CG, Allison ST. 1989. Social value orientation and helping behavior. *J. Appl. Soc. Psychol.* 19:353–62

McClintock CG, Liebrand WBG. 1988. Role of interdependence structure, individual value orientation, and another's strategy in social decision making: a transformational analysis. *J. Pers. Soc. Psychol.* 55:396–409

Messick DM, Allison ST, Samuelson CD. 1988. Framing and communication effects on groups members' responses to environmental and social uncertainty. In *Applied Behavioural Economics,* ed. S Maital, 2:677-700. New York: New York Univ. Press

Messick DM, Brewer MB. 1983. Solving social dilemmas: a review. *Rev. Pers. Soc. Psychol.* 4:11–44

Messick DM, Liebrand WBG. 1993. Computer simulations of the relationship between individual heuristics and global cooperation in prisoner's dilemmas. *Soc. Sci. Comput. Rev.* 11:301–12

Messick DM, Mackie DM. 1989. Interpersonal relations. *Annu. Rev. Psychol.* 40:45–81

Michener HA. 1992. Coalition anomalies in light of the central-union theory. *Adv. Group Process.* 9:65–88

Miller CE, Komorita SS. 1986. Coalition formation in organizations: What laboratory studies do and do not tell us. See Lewicki et al 1986, pp. 117–38

Mio JS, Thompson SC, Givens GH. 1993. The commons dilemma as metaphor: memory, influence, and implications for environmental conservation. *Metaph. Symbol. Activ.* 8:23–42

Molander P. 1985. The optimal level of generosity in a selfish, uncertain environment. *J. Confl. Resolut.* 29:611–18

Molander P. 1992. The prevalence of free riding. *J. Confl. Resolut.* 36:756–71

Molm LD. 1987. Power-dependence theory: Power processes and negative outcomes. *Adv. Group Process.* 4:171–98

Moore SF, Shaffer LS, Pollak EL, Taylor-Lemke P. 1987. The effects of interpersonal trust and prior commons problem experience on commons management. *J. Soc. Psychol.* 127:19–29

Mueller U. 1987. Optimal retaliation for optimal cooperation. *J. Confl. Resolut.* 31:692–724

Murnighan JK. 1986. The structure of mediation and intravention: Comments on Carnevale's strategic choice model. *Negot. J.* 2:351–6

Murnighan JK. 1991. Cooperating when you know your outcomes will differ. *Simul. Games* 22:463–75

Murnighan JK, Brass DJ. 1990. Intraorganizational coalitions. See Bazerman et al 1991, pp. 283–306

Murnighan JK, King TR. 1992. The effects of leverage and payoffs on cooperative behavior in asymmetric dilemmas. See Liebrand et al 1992, pp. 163–80

Murnighan JK, King TR, Schoumaker F. 1990. The dynamics of cooperation in asymmetric dilemmas. *Adv. Group Process.* 7:251–82

Nash JF. 1950. The bargaining problem. *Econometrics* 18:155–62

Neale MA, Bazerman MH. 1991. *Cognition and Rationality in Negotiation.* New York: Free Press

Neale MA, Bazerman MH. 1992. Negotiator cognition and rationality: a behavioral decision theory perspective. *Organ. Behav. Hum. Decis. Process.* 51:157–75

Neuberg SL. 1988. Behavioral implications of information presentation outside of conscious awareness: the effect of subliminal presentation of trait information on behavior in the prisoner's dilemma game. *Soc. Cogn.* 6:207–30

O'Connor BP, Tindall DB. 1990. Attributions and behavior in a commons dilemma. *J. Psychol.* 124:485–94

Orbell JM, Dawes RM. 1991. A "cognitive miser" theory of cooperators' advantage. *Am. Polit. Sci.* Rev. 85:515–28

Orbell JM, Dawes RM, van de Kragt AJC. 1990. The limits of multilateral promising. *Ethics* 100:616–27

Orbell JM, Goldman M, Mulford M, Dawes RM. 1992. Religion, context, and constraint toward strangers. *Ration. Soc.* 4:291–307

Orbell JM, van de Kragt AJC, Dawes RM. 1988. Explaining discussion-induced cooperation. *J. Pers. Soc. Psychol.* 54:811–19

Orbell JM, van de Kragt AJC, Dawes RM. 1991. Covenants without the sword: the role of promises in social dilemma circumstances. In *Social Norms And Economic Institutions,* ed. KJ Koford, JB Miller, 3: 117-33. Ann Arbor, MI: Univ. Mich. Press

Ordeshook PC. 1986. *Game Theory and Political Theory.* New York: Cambridge Univ. Press

Ostrom E. 1990. *Governing the Commons.* New York: Cambridge Univ. Press

Ostrom E, Walker JM. 1991. Communication in a commons: cooperation without external enforcement. See Palfrey 1991, pp. 287–322

Ostrom E, Walker JM, Gardner R. 1992. Covenants with and without a sword: self-governance is possible. *Am. Polit. Sci. Rev.* 86: 404–17

Palfrey TR. 1991. *Laboratory Research in Political Economy.* Ann Arbor, MI: Univ. Mich. Press

Parks CD. 1994. The predictive ability of social values in resource dilemmas and public good games. *Pers. Soc. Psychol. Bull.* In press

Pearce JL, Stevenson WB, Porter LW. 1986. Coalitions in the organizational context. See Lewicki 1986 et al, pp. 97–116

Plott CR. 1979. The application of laboratory experimental methods to public choice. In *Collective Decision Making,* ed. CS Russell, pp. 137–60. Baltimore: Johns Hopkins Univ. Press

Plott CR. 1982. Industrial organization theory and experimental economics. *J. Econ. Lit.* 20:1485–527

Poppe M, Utens L. 1986. Effects of greed and fear of being gypped in a social dilemma situation with changing pool size. *J. Econ. Psychol.* 7:61–73

Rapoport Am. 1985. Provision of public goods and the MCS experimental paradigm. *Am. Polit. Sci. Rev.* 79:148–55

Rapoport Am. 1987. Research paradigms and expected utility models for the provision of step-level public goods. *Psychol. Rev.* 94: 74–83

Rapoport Am. 1988. Provision of step-level public goods: effects of inequality in resources. *J. Pers. Soc. Psychol.* 54:432–40

Rapoport Am, Bornstein G. 1987. Intergroup competition for the provision of binary public goods. *Psychol. Rev.* 94:291–99

Rapoport Am, Bornstein G. 1989. Solving public good problems in competition between equal and unequal size groups. *J. Confl. Resolut.* 33:460–79

Rapoport Am, Bornstein G, Erev I. 1989. Intergroup competition for public goods: effects of unequal resources and relative group size. *J. Pers. Soc. Psychol.* 56:748–56

Rapoport Am, Budescu DV, Suleiman R. 1993. Sequential requests from randomly distributed shared resources. *J. Math. Psychol.* 37:241–65

Rapoport Am, Budescu DV, Suleiman R, Weg E. 1992. Social dilemmas with uniformly distributed resources. See Liebrand et al 1992, pp. 43-58

Rapoport Am, Eshed-Levy D. 1989. Provision of step-level public goods: effects of greed and fear of being gypped. *Organ. Behav. Hum. Decis. Process.* 44:325–44

Rapoport Am, Kahan JP. 1982. The power of a coalition and payoff disbursement in three-person negotiable conflicts. *J. Math. Sociol.* 8:193-225.

Rapoport Am, Suleiman R. 1992. Equilibrium solutions for resource dilemmas. *Group Decis. Negot.* 1:269–94

Rapoport Am, Suleiman R. 1993. Incremental contribution in step-level public goods with asymmetric players. *Organ. Behav. Hum. Decis. Process.* 55:171–94

Rapoport An. 1988a. Experiments with n-person social traps. I: Prisoner's dilemma, weak prisoner's dilemma, volunteer's dilemma, and largest number. *J. Confl. Resolut.* 32:457–72

Rapoport An. 1988b. Experiments with n-person social traps. II: Tragedy of the commons. *J. Confl. Resolut.* 32:473–88

Roth AE. 1988. Laboratory experimentation in economics: a methodological overview. *Econ. J.* 98:974–1031

Roth AE. 1994. Bargaining. See Kagel & Roth 1994

Rutte CG. 1990. Solving organizational social dilemmas. *Soc. Behav.* 5:285–94

Rutte CG, Wilke HAM, Messick DM. 1987a. Scarcity or abundance caused by people or the environment as determinants of behavior in the resource dilemma. *J. Exp. Soc. Psychol.* 23:208–16

Rutte CG, Wilke HAM, Messick DM. 1987b. The effects of framing social dilemmas as give-some or take-some games. *Br. J. Soc. Psychol.* 26:103-8

Samuelson CD. 1990. Energy conservation: a social dilemma approach. *Soc. Behav.* 5:207–30

Samuelson CD. 1991. Perceived task difficulty, causal attributions, and preferences for structural change in resource dilemmas. *Pers. Soc. Psychol. Bull.* 17:181-87

Samuelson CD. 1993. A multiattribute evaluation approach to structural change in resource dilemmas. *Organ. Behav. Human Decis. Process.* 55:298–324

Samuelson CD, Allison ST. 1994. Cognitive factors affecting the use of social decision heuristics in resource sharing tasks.

Organ. Behav. Human Decis. Process. 58:1–27

Samuelson CD, Messick DM. 1986a. Alternative structural solutions to resource dilemmas. *Organ. Behav. Human Decis. Process.* 37:139–55

Samuelson CD, Messick DM. 1986b. Inequities in access to and use of shared resources in social dilemmas. *J. Pers. Soc. Psychol.* 51:960–67

Samuelson CD, Messick DM. 1994. When do people want to change the rules for allocating shared resources? In *Social Dilemmas,* ed. D Schroeder. New York: Praeger

Sattler DN, Kerr NL. 1991. Might versus morality explored: motivational and cognitive bases for social motives. *J. Pers. Soc. Psychol.* 61:756–65

Sauermann H, Selten R. 1960. An experiment in oligopoly. In *General Systems Yearbook,* ed. L von Bertalanffy, An. Rapoport, 5:85-114. Ann Arbor, MI: Soc. Gen. Syst. Res.

Schelling TC. 1960. *The Strategy of Conflict.* Cambridge, MA: Harvard Univ. Press

Schofield N. 1985. Equilibria in simple dynamic games. In *Social Choice and Welfare,* ed. PK Pattanaik, M Salles, pp. 269–84. New York: North-Holland

Schopler J, Insko CA, Graetz KA, Drigotas SM, Smith VA, et al. 1993. Individual-group discontinuity: further evidence for mediation by fear and greed. *Pers. Soc. Psychol. Bull.* 19:419–31

Sell J, Wilson RK. 1991. Levels of information and contributions to public goods. *Soc. Forces* 70:107–24

Selten R. 1972. Equal share analysis of characteristic function experiments. In *Contributions to Experimental Economics,* ed. H. Sauermann, 3:130-65. Tubingen: Mohr

Selten R. 1975. Re-examination of the perfectness concept for equilibrium points in extensive games. *Int. J. Game Theor.* 4:25–55

Selten R. 1987. Equity and coalition bargaining in experimental 3-person games. In *Laboratory Experimentation in Economics,* ed. AE Roth, pp. 42–98. New York: Cambridge Univ. Press

Shepperd JA. 1993. Productivity loss in performance groups: a motivation analysis. *Psychol. Bull.* 113:67–81

Simon HA. 1957. *Administrative Behavior.* New York: Macmillan

Smith JM, Bell PA. 1992. Environmental concern and cooperative-competitive behavior in a simulated commons dilemma. *J. Soc. Psychol.* 132:461–68

Smith VL. 1980. Relevance of laboratory experiments to testing resource allocation theory. In *Evaluation of Econometric Models,* ed. J Kmenta, JB Ramsey, pp. 345–77. New York: Harcourt Brace Jovanovich

Smith VL. 1982. Microeconomic systems as an

experimental science. *Am. Econ. Rev.* 72: 923–55

Smith VL. 1991. Rational choice: the contrast between economics and psychology. *J. Polit. Econ.* 99:877–97

Smith VL. 1993. Game theory and experimental economics: beginnings and early influences. *Hist. Polit. Econ.* 24 (Suppl.)

Sniezek JA, May DR. 1990. Conflict of interests and commitment in groups. *J. Appl. Soc. Psychol.* 20:1150–65

Sniezek JA, May DR, Sawyer JE. 1990. Social uncertainty and interdependence: a study of resource allocation decisions in groups. *Organ. Behav. Human Decis. Process.* 46: 155–80

Steiner ID. 1974. Whatever happened to the group in social psychology? *J. Exp. Soc. Psychol.* 10:94–108

Steiner ID. 1986. Paradigms and groups. *Adv. Exp. Soc. Psychol.* 19:251–89

Stolte JF. 1990. Power processes in structures of dependence and exchange. *Adv. Group Process.* 7:129–50

Stryker S. 1972. Coalition behavior. In *Experimental Social Psychology,* ed. CG McClintock, pp. 338-80. New York: Holt, Reinhart, & Winston

Suleiman R, Rapoport Am. 1988. Environmental and social uncertainty in single-trial resource dilemmas. *Acta Psychol.* 68:99–112

Suleiman R, Rapoport Am. 1992. Provision of step-level public goods with continuous contribution. *J. Behav. Decis. Mak.* 5:133–54

Swistak P. 1989. How to resist invasion in the repeated prisoner's dilemma game. *Behav. Sci.* 34:151–53

Thibaut JW, Kelley HH. 1959. *The Social Psychology of Groups.* New York: Wiley

Thompson L, Hastie R. 1990. Judgment tasks and biases in negotiation. *Res. Negot. Organ.* 2:31–54

Thompson SC, Stoutemyer K. 1991. Water use as a commons dilemma: the effects of education that focuses on long-term consequences and individual action. *Environ. Behav.* 23:314–33

Tietz R, Albers W, Selten R. 1986. *Bounded Rational Behavior in Experimental Games and Markets.* Berlin: Springer-Verlag

To T. 1988. More realism in the prisoner's dilemma. *J. Confl. Resolut.* 32:402–8

Tomer JF. 1987. Productivity through intrafirm cooperation: a behavioral economic analysis. *J. Behav. Econ.* 16:83–95

van de Kragt AJC, Dawes RM, Orbell JM, Braver SR, Wilson LA. 1986. Doing well and doing good as ways of resolving social dilemmas. In *Experimental Social Dilemmas,* ed. HAM Wilke, DM Messick, CG Rutte, pp. 177–204. Frankfurt: Verlag Peter Lang

van Dijk E, Grodzka M. 1992. The influence of endowments asymmetry and information level on the contribution to a public step good. *J. Econ. Psychol.* 13:329–42

van Dijk E, Wilke HAM. 1991. De invloed van legitimiteit van middelen-asymmetrie op de contributie aan een lineair publiek goed. *Fund. soc. psychol.* 5:222–42 (In Dutch)

van Dijk E, Wilke HAM. 1993. Differential interests, equity, and public good provision. *J. Exp. Soc. Psychol.* 29:1–16

van Lange PAM, Liebrand WBG. 1989. On perceiving morality and potency: social values and the effects of person perception in a give-some dilemma. *Eur. J. Pers.* 3: 209–25

van Lange PAM, Liebrand WBG. 1991a. Social value orientation and intelligence: a test of the Goal Prescribes Rationality Principle. *Eur. J. Soc. Psychol.* 21:273–92

van Lange, PAM, Liebrand WBG. 1991b. The influence of other's morality and own social value orientation on cooperation in the Netherlands and in the USA. *Int. J. Psychol.* 26:429–49

van Lange PAM, Liebrand WBG, Kuhlman DM. 1990. Causal attributions of choice behavior in three n-person prisoner's dilemmas. *J. Exp. Soc. Psychol.* 26:34–48

Vlek C, Keren G. 1992. Behavioral decision theory and environmental risk management: assessment and resolution of four survival dilemmas. *Acta Psychol.* 80:249–78

von Neumann J, Morgenstern O. 1947. *Theory of Games and Economic Behavior.* New York: Wiley

Weesie J. 1993. Asymmetry and timing in the volunteer's dilemma. *J. Confl. Resolut.* 37: 569–90

Weick KE. 1984. Small wins: redefining the scale of social problems. *Am. Psychol.* 39: 40–49

Wilke HAM. 1985. *Coalition Formation.* New York: Elsevier

Wilke HAM. 1991. Greed, efficiency and fairness in resource management situations. *Eur. Rev. Soc. Psychol.* 2:165–87

Wilke HAM, Braspenning J. 1989. Reciprocity: choice shift in a social trap. *Eur. J. Soc. Psychol.* 19:317–26

Wilke HAM, de Boer KL, Liebrand WBG. 1986. Standards of justice and quality of power in a social dilemma situation. *Br. J. Soc. Psychol.* 25:57–65

Wit AP, Wilke HAM. 1988. Subordinates' endorsement of an allocating leader in a commons dilemma: an equity theoretical approach. *J. Econ. Psychol.* 9:151–68

Wit AP, Wilke HAM. 1992. The effects of social categorization on cooperation in three types of social dilemmas. *J. Econ. Psychol.* 13:135–51

Wit AP, Wilke HAM, Oppewal H. 1989a.

Asymmetrische sociale dilemmas: Het effect van verschillen in middelen en profijt tussen groepsleden op hun bijdrage aan een gemeenschapplijk belang. *Fund. soc. psychol.* 3:93–110 (In Dutch)

Wit AP, Wilke HAM, van Dijk E. 1989b. Attribution of leadership in a resource management situation. *Eur. J. Soc. Psychol.* 19: 327–38

Yamagishi T. 1986a. The provision of a sanctioning system as a public good. *J. Pers. Soc. Psychol.* 51:110–16

Yamagishi T. 1986b. The structural goal/expectation theory of cooperation in social dilemmas. *Adv. Group Process.* 3:51–87

Yamagishi T. 1988a. Seriousness of social dilemmas and the provision of a sanctioning system. *Soc. Psychol. Q.* 51:32–42

Yamagishi T. 1988b. The provision of a sanctioning system in the United States and Japan. *Soc. Psychol. Q.* 51:265–71

Yamagishi T. 1994. Social dilemmas. In *Sociological Perspectives on Social Psychology,* ed. KS Cook, GA Fine, J House. In press

Yamagishi T, Sato K. 1986. Motivational bases of the public goods problem. *J. Pers. Soc. Psychol.* 50:67–73

Annu. Rev. Psychol. 1995. 46:209–35

EMOTION: Clues from the Brain

Joseph E. LeDoux

Center for Neural Science, Department of Psychology, New York University, New York, New York 10003

KEY WORDS: cognition, fear, amygdala, memory, learning

CONTENTS

INTRODUCTION

Despite the obvious importance of emotion to human existence, scientists concerned with human nature have not been able to reach a consensus about what emotion is and what place emotion should have in a theory of mind and behavior. Controversy abounds over the definition of emotion, the number of emotions that exist, whether some emotions are more basic than others, the commonality of certain emotional response patterns across cultures and across species, whether different emotions have different physiological signatures, the extent to which emotional responses contribute to emotional experiences, the role of nature and nurture in emotion, the influence of emotion on cognitive processes, the dependence of emotion on cognition, the importance of conscious versus unconscious processes in emotion, and on and on (see Ekman & Davidson 1994).

Although there has been no shortage of psychological research on these topics, the findings have not resolved many of the issues in a compelling manner. But psychological research is not the only source of information about the nature of emotion. Information about the representation of emotion in the brain may shed light on the nature of emotional processes. First, information about how emotion is represented in the brain can provide constraints that could help us choose between alternative hypotheses about the nature of some emotional process. Second, findings about the neural basis of emotion might also suggest new insights into the functional organization of emotion that were not apparent from psychological findings alone. The brain, in other words, can constrain and inform our ideas about the nature of emotion.

This review examines the neural basis of emotion and considers how research on brain mechanisms can potentially help us to understand emotion as a psychological process.

NEURAL BASIS OF EMOTION

Studies of the neural basis of emotion have a long history within neuroscience (see LeDoux 1987, 1991). This research culminated around mid-century in the limbic system theory of emotion (MacLean 1949, 1952), which claimed to have identified the limbic system as the mediator of emotion. However, in recent years both the limbic system concept (Brodal 1982, Swanson 1983, Kotter & Meyer 1992) and the limbic system theory of emotion (LeDoux 1991) have been questioned. Despite problems with the conceptualization of the brain system that mediates emotion in general, there has been a great deal of systematic and productive research on the neural basis of specific emotions. It is not known whether there is a general purpose system of emotion in the brain, but if there is it will be identified readily by synthesizing across studies of specific emotions. This review focuses on the neural basis of fear, an emotion that has been studied extensively at the neural level.

Neural Basis of Fear

Fear is an especially good emotion to use as a model. It is a common part of life, almost from the beginning. The expression of fear is conserved to a large extent across human cultures and at least to some extent across human and nonhuman mammalian species, and possibly across other vertebrates as well. There are well-defined experimental procedures for eliciting and measuring fear, and many of these can be used in more or less identical ways in humans and experimental animals. Further, disorders of fear regulation are at the heart of many psychopathologic conditions, including anxiety, panic, phobic, and posttraumatic stress disorders. It would be an important achievement if, by focusing on fear, we were able to generate an adequate theory of fear, even if it applied to no other emotion.

The following survey of the neural basis of fear concentrates on studies of fear conditioning. This approach has been particularly successful in identifying the neural system that mediates learned fear and in uncovering some of the cellular mechanisms that might be involved.

Fear conditioning is a form of Pavlovian (classical) conditioning. Pavlov is best remembered for his studies of alimentary conditioning, in which he elicited salivation in dogs by presenting stimuli that had been associated with the delivery of food (Pavlov 1927). He also determined that animals will exhibit conditioned reflexes that allow them to protect themselves against harmful stimuli by responding to warning signals. Pavlov referred to the latter as defense conditioning. Today, Pavlovian defense conditioning is usually referred to as fear conditioning (Brown et al 1951, Kamin 1965, McAllister & McAllister 1971, Millenson & de Villiers 1972, Bouton & Bolles 1980, Davis 1992, Kapp et at 1992, Fanselow 1980, LeDoux 1993a).

In a typical fear conditioning experiment, the subject is exposed to a tone or light (the conditioned stimulus, CS) that is followed by a brief shock (the unconditioned stimulus, US; see Figure 1). Conditioning occurs after only a few pairings (one pairing is enough if the US is sufficiently intense) (Fanselow & Bolles 1979). The effects of conditioning can be assessed directly by measuring defense responses elicited by the CS, including freezing responses (Blanchard & Blanchard 1972, Bouton & Bolles 1980, Fanselow 1980, LeDoux et al 1984) or changes in autonomic (Smith et al 1980, Cohen & Randall 1984, LeDoux et al 1984) and endocrine (Mason 1968, van de Kar et al 1991) activity. These are hard-wired or innate reactions to threat that come to be coupled to the CS through the conditioning process. The effects of fear conditioning can also be assessed indirectly by measuring the potentiation of reflexes, such as the eyeblink or startle reflex (e.g. Brown et al 1951, Davis et al 1987, Weisz et al 1992), in the presence of the CS, by measuring the inhibition of pain by the CS (e.g. Watkins & Mayer 1982, Fanselow & Helmstetter 1988), or by measuring the degree to which the animal's ongoing behavior is interfered with or suppressed by the CS (e.g. Estes & Skinner 1941, Hunt & Brady 1955, Bouton & Bolles 1980, Leaf & Muller 1965).

Neural Pathways Mediating Fear Conditioning

The logic underlying the search for the neural pathways in fear conditioning is straightforward. Conditioning is believed to involve the intersection in the brain of pathways transmitting information about the CS and the US (Pavlov 1927, Konorski 1967, Hebb 1949). Because the US must intersect a variety of CS pathways originating in different sensory systems, it seems that the crucial changes that underlie conditioning should involve modifications in the network that is involved in the processing of the specific CS used. Thus, if one were able to follow the processing of the CS through its sensory system and beyond to the motor system controlling the conditioned responses (CRs), the circuitry within which conditioning occurs would presumably be known.

How, then, should one attempt to follow the processing of the CS? The strategy that has worked best uses the classical lesion method in conjunction with modern neuroanatomical tracing techniques. For example, if the CS is an acoustic stimulus, then the CS pathway must begin in the auditory system and should continue as an efferent projection out of the auditory system. Since the auditory system is a linearly organized system involving relays from lower to higher centers, it is possible to determine, with the lesion method, whether the auditory CS has to rise through the entire pathway for conditioning to occur. By using neuroanatomical tracing techniques it is then possible to examine the connections of the highest auditory station required and, thereby, define the

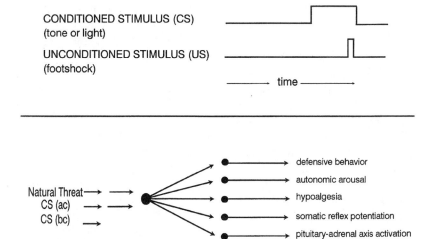

Figure 1   Fear conditioning involves the temporal association of an innocuous conditioned stimulus (CS), such as a light or tone, with a noxious unconditioned stimulus (US), such as footshock. After conditioning (ac), but not before conditioning (bc), the CS acquires the capacity to activate a variety of brain systems involved in the control of defensive responses. These same responses are elicited by natural or unlearned threatening stimuli. Fear conditioning is stimulus learning, not response learning, and it allows new stimuli to gain control over hard-wired, evolutionarily perfected, defensive response control networks.

next possible links in the pathway, which can each in turn be lesioned to determine which one constitutes the key link.

Research in the early 1980s showed that lesions of the midbrain and thalamic stations of the auditory pathway prevented conditioning but that lesions of the auditory cortex had no effect (LeDoux et al 1984). This suggested that the CS must exit the auditory system at the level of the thalamus. Anatomical tracing techniques were then used to show that the auditory thalamus projects not only to the auditory cortex but also to the amygdala (LeDoux et al 1985). Additional studies showed that interruption of the connections between the auditory thalamus and the amygdala interferes with conditioning (LeDoux et al 1986, Iwata et al 1986) and that the lateral nucleus of the amygdala is the crucial region for the reception of the auditory stimulus (LeDoux et al 1990a,b; Clugnet et al 1990).

Although the auditory cortex is not necessary for conditioning, projections from the auditory thalamus through the auditory cortex and to the amygdala (Romanski & LeDoux 1993a,b) are sufficient to mediate simple acoustic fear conditioning (conditioning with a single auditory CS paired with the US) (Romanski & LeDoux 1992). This suggests that the thalamo-amygdala and thalamo-cortico-amygdala pathways are equipotential in mediating simple conditioning (Romanski & LeDoux 1992). However, auditory cortical areas, and presumably cortico-amygdala connections, are required for differential conditioning (in which two auditory stimuli are presented, one paired with the US and the other not) (Jarrell et al 1987).

The direct thalamic pathway to the amygdala is shorter and thus faster, but its capacity to represent the auditory stimulus is more limited (Bordi & LeDoux 1994a,b). The thalamo-cortico-amygdala pathway, which involves several cortico-cortical links before reaching the amygdala (Romanski & LeDoux 1993a,b), is longer and slower, but its capacity to represent the auditory stimulus is considerably greater. The thalamic pathway is sufficient for the rapid triggering of emotion by simple stimulus features (as in simple conditioning), whereas the cortical pathway appears to be needed for emotional reactions coupled to perceptually complex stimulus objects (as in differential conditioning). Within the amygdala, the quick-and-dirty thalamic inputs and the slower but more accurate cortical inputs converge in the lateral nucleus (LeDoux et al 1991). The lateral nucleus is the sensory interface of the amygdala and possibly a crucial site of integration of information from parallel auditory projections during fear conditioning (LeDoux et al 1990b, LeDoux 1992).

Whenever a CS is paired with a US, some conditioning accrues to the background or to contextual stimuli that are also present in the environment (e.g. Rescorla & Wagner 1972). Recent studies have shown that contextual conditioning, like conditioning to a CS, is dependent on the amygdala, but unlike CS conditioning, it is also dependent upon the hippocampus (Phillips & LeDoux 1992b, Kim & Fanselow 1992, Selden et al 1991). Although the exact direction of information flow between these structures is not known, the hippocampus (by way of the subiculum) projects to the lateral nucleus (and several other amygdala nuclei) (Ottersen 1982, Phillips & LeDoux 1992a). As a result, the hippocampus, long believed to be involved in complex information processing functions, including spatial, contextual, and relational processing (O'Keefe & Nadel 1978, Eichenbaum 1992, McNaughton & Barnes 1990, Nadel & Willner 1980, Rudy & Sutherland 1992), may be a kind of higher-order sensory structure in fear conditioning. That is, the hippocampus may relay environmental inputs pertaining to the conditioning context to the amygdala, where emotional meaning is added to context just as it is added to thalamic or cortical sensory information. Once learned, this kind of contextual fear conditioning might allow the organism to distinguish between those situations in which it is appropriate to defend oneself against a stimulus vs situations in which it is not necessary (e.g. a bear in the woods vs in the zoo).

Just as the lateral nucleus is the input system of the amygdala, the central nucleus is the output system (LeDoux 1993a, Davis 1992, Kapp et al 1984, 1990). Lesions of the central nucleus interfere with the expression of conditioned responses expressed through a variety of motor modalities, including freezing behavior, sympathetic and parasympathetic autonomic responses, neuroendocrine responses, the potentiation of startle and eyeblink reflexes, and the suppression of pain. Most interestingly, lesions of areas to which the central nucleus projects interfere separately with individual responses. For example, projections to the central gray are involved in freezing responses (Iwata et al 1987, LeDoux et al 1988, Wilson & Kapp 1994); projections to the lateral hypothalamus are involved in sympathetic autonomic responses (Smith et al 1980, Iwata et al 1987, LeDoux et al 1988); projections to the bed nucleus of the stria terminalis are involved in neuroendocrine responses (van de Kar et al 1991); and projections to the nucleus reticularis caudalis pontis are involved in the potentiation of startle responses (Rosen et al 1991).

The amygdala is involved in both the acquisition and the expression of fear conditioning (e.g. LeDoux 1987, 1990, 1992; Davis et al 1987; Davis 1992; Kapp et al 1984, 1990, 1992; Gentile et al 1986). Even with extensive overtraining, posttraining lesions of the amygdala interfere with fear conditioning (Kim & Davis 1993).

Although much of the work on fear conditioning has used auditory CSs, some studies have used visual stimuli (e.g. Davis et al 1987; Davis 1992; LeDoux et al 1989). In general, the circuitry involved appears to be quite similar. However, because the visual connections with the amygdala in the rat are poorly understood, the input circuitry is not as clear as it is for auditory conditioning.

In summary, the neural pathways through which defense responses are conditioned and expressed to auditory stimuli have been well defined (see Figure 2). The amygdala appears to play a central role in this circuitry. It is located between the sensory system that processes the CS and the motor systems that control the conditioned responses. Although some learning may occur in the sensory and motor systems (see below), important aspects of fear conditioning probably occur in the amygdala because it is the only part of the

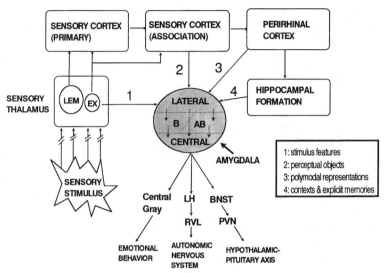

Figure 2   Neural circuits of fear conditioning. The neural pathways by which a sensory CS elicits emotional responses involve the relay of sensory inputs to the thalamus. While the lemniscal nuclei (LEM) transmit only to the primary sensory cortex, the extralemniscal areas (EX) transmit to primary sensory and association regions of the cortex, as well as to the lateral nucleus of the amygdala. This region of the amygdala also receives inputs from sensory association areas of the neocortex, as well as from polymodal areas such as the perirhinal cortex and the hippocampal formation. The thalamo-amygdala sensory projection (1) has been implicated in simple fear conditioning [one conditioned stimulus (CS) paired with an unconditioned stimulus (US)]; the cortico-amygdala sensory projection (2) in differential fear conditioning (one CS paired with US, another not paired); and the hippocampo-amygdala projection (4) in contextual conditioning (conditioning to situational cues other than the CS). The hippocampal projection may also be involved in conditioning of fear to explicit or declarative memories that occur in the presence of an US, but this has not been studied. The role of the perirhinal projection to amygdala (3) is not known, but it may have something to do with the elicitation of fear by complex polymodal stimulus representations. The central nucleus of the amygdala is the interface with motor systems, as it connects with various brainstem areas involved in the regulation of specific defense response networks. Projections to the central gray control freezing and other defensive behaviors; projections to the lateral hypothalamus (LH) and from there to the rostral ventral lateral medulla (RVL) control sympathetic autonomic nervous system responses; and projections to the bed nucleus of the stria terminalis (BNST) and paraventricular hypothalamus control stress reactions involving the pituitary-adrenal axis. The amygdala nuclei are the sensory- and motor-independent parts of the circuitry and are likely to play important integrative roles in fear conditioning.

circuitry that is involved independent of the CS and CR modalities. Studies of cellular mechanisms have thus focused on the amygdala.

Cellular Mechanisms Involved in Fear Conditioning

A main reason for wanting to understand the neural circuit underlying conditioning is that such information isolates from the vast numbers of neurons and their connections the particular neurons and connections that must be modified during learning and within which the changes might be stored either temporarily or permanently. The neural systems level of analysis thus guides the cellular level analysis, and findings at the cellular level reveal mechanisms about how the brain actually works. Although the search for the cellular basis of fear conditioning is in its infancy, important discoveries have begun to shed light on the underlying mechanisms.

CS-US CONVERGENCE   The neural basis of classical conditioning involves convergence of the CS and US pathways in the brain (Pavlov 1927, Hebb 1949, Konorski 1967). If, as the systems level of analysis suggests, the amygdala is a crucial site of conditioning, then cells in the amygdala should respond to both the CS and the US. Recent studies have mapped the responses of amygdala neurons to auditory stimuli similar to those used in conditioning experiments (Bordi et al 1992, 1993; Romanski et al 1993). This work has shown that neurons in the lateral nucleus of the amygdala are particularly responsive to auditory CS-like stimulation. Responses in other areas tend to be weaker and to have longer latencies. This reinforces the conclusion that the lateral nucleus is the sensory interface of the amygdala. Romanski et al (1993) found that essentially every cell that responded to auditory stimuli also responded to noxious somatosensory stimulation similar to that used as a US. The lateral nucleus of the amygdala is thus a site of CS-US convergence and may be a crucial site of the cellular changes that underlie learning. However, one of the key missing pieces of information about the neural basis of fear conditioning is the origin of the US inputs to the amygdala.

PHYSIOLOGICAL PLASTICITY INDUCED BY CS-US PAIRING   Neurons in a number of brain regions undergo physiological changes during aversive classical conditioning (see Thompson et al 1983). This fact discourages the use of unit recording techniques to find the critical locus of learning. An alternative strategy is to first identify the essential neural circuit underlying a particular learned response through lesion studies and then examine the plastic properties of the neurons in the circuit. These are the neurons that are most likely to undergo changes in physiological responsivity that are essential to the learning task.

With key aspects of the fear learning circuitry now identified (see above), it is useful to consider the extent of physiological plasticity that has been observed in these areas. Studies of the physiology of learning have suggested that many brain regions exhibit physiological changes during learning. Thus, it is perhaps not surprising that plasticity has been found throughout the fear conditioning circuitry: in the auditory thalamic areas that project to the amygdala (Gabriel et al 1976, Ryugo & Weinberger 1978, Edeline & Weinberger 1992); in the auditory cortex (Weinberger & Diamond 1987, Edeline & Weinberger 1993); in the lateral, basolateral, and central nuclei of the amygdala (LeGal LaSalle & Ben-Ari 1981, Muramoto et al 1993, Pascoe & Kapp 1985); and in the lateral hypothalamus (Ono et al 1988). This ubiquitous plasticity in the conditioning circuitry would be trivial if plasticity in all levels of the pathway reflects learning by some early station (such as the auditory thalamus). On the other hand, it would be significant if it means that each link in the pathway is plastic and that plasticity in different locations serves different functions. Plasticity in the sensory structures could make stimulus processing more efficient; plasticity in motor systems could make the execution of the responses more efficient; and plasticity in the amygdala could represent the integrative (stimulus- and response-independent) aspects of learning.

LTP AND THE AMYGDALA   Learning at the cellular level is generally believed to involve changes in synaptic transmission (Hebb 1949, Kandel & Spencer 1968, Squire 1987). A great deal of work has thus sought to identify the mechanisms by which experience modifies the efficiency of synaptic transmission. Most of this work has involved long-term potentiation (LTP). In an LTP experiment, a pathway is stimulated at a high frequency, and as a result, the response to a low-frequency test stimulus is amplified. LTP has been studied most extensively in the hippocampus (Lynch 1986, Cotman et al 1988, Brown et al 1988, Malenka & Nicoll 1993, Madison et al 1991, Bliss & Collingridge 1993) but has also been demonstrated in other brain regions, including the lateral and basal nuclei of the amygdala (Clugnet & LeDoux 1990, Chapman et al 1990).

Several properties of LTP make it attractive as a memory mechanism (Lynch 1986, Brown et al 1988). LTP is experience dependent and synapse specific: Cells receive many inputs, but the response is only amplified for those inputs that were stimulated. LTP exhibits cooperativity: The induction of LTP depends on the simultaneous activation of many afferents. LTP exhibits associativity: It can be produced by simultaneous stimulation of two pathways using stimuli that are not effective individually. LTP is stable and long lasting. Although the relationship between LTP and behavioral learning and memory is still unclear and controversial (Teyler & DiScenna 1987, Morris 1992, McNaughton & Barnes 1990, O'Keefe 1993), an LTP-like phenomenon might underlie some aspects of learning, including fear conditioning mediated by the amygdala.

PHARMACOLOGICAL SIMILARITY OF LTP AND FEAR CONDITIONING   One way to link LTP to learning and memory is to determine whether similar pharmacological manipulations are involved (Lynch et al 1991, Staubli 1994). The pharmacology of the classic form of LTP has been well characterized (e.g. Lynch et al 1991, Madison et al 1991, Malenka & Nicoll 1993). It involves the binding of the excitatory amino acid transmitter, L-glutamate, to two classes of postsynaptic excitatory amino acid receptors, NMDA and non-NMDA receptors. The NMDA receptor channel is normally opened only when the cell membrane is depolarized by the prior binding of Glu to non-NMDA receptors. The opening of the NMDA channel is a crucial step in LTP. LTP does not occur if the channel is blocked by an antagonist. In contrast, the expression of established LTP is not affected by NMDA blockade.

In 1949 Hebb postulated that learning at the cellular level involved the simultaneous activity of pre- and postsynaptic neurons. That is, if the postsynaptic neuron is depolarized when the presynaptic input arrives, the connection will be strengthened. The NMDA receptor appears to be a neural instantiation of the Hebb rule. It requires that presynaptically released Glu bind to postsynaptic NMDA receptors while the postsyanptic cell is active or depolarized.

If the classic form of LTP is a mediator of fear conditioning, then blockade of NMDA receptors in the amygdala should have two consequences: 1. The establishment but not the expression of LTP in the amygdala should be disrupted, and 2. the acquisition but not the expression of fear conditioning should be disrupted. Existing data are, for the most part, consistent with this line of reasoning. Recent studies have shown that LTP induced in the amygdala by stimulation of the endopyriform nucleus is dependent on NMDA receptors (Gean et al 1993). However, induction of LTP in the same regions by stimulation of the external capsule does not exhibit the same dependence (Chapman & Bellavance 1992). Regardless, these studies have focused on the basal nucleus, which is not necessarily the only or even the main site of plasticity in fear conditioning (recall that the cells receiving CS-US convergent inputs are in the lateral nucleus). Further, these studies have not stimulated known CS or US pathways in their LTP paradigms. Although LTP has been demonstrated in a CS pathway to the lateral amygdala, the thalamo-amygdala auditory pathway (Clugnet & LeDoux 1990), the pharmacology of LTP in this pathway has yet to be determined. Blockade of NMDA receptors in the lateral/basal amygdala interferes with the acquisition but not the expression of Pavlovian fear conditioning to a CS (e.g. Miserendino et al 1990) or to contextual stimuli (Fanselow & Kim 1994). Because of the small size of these brain areas it is not possible to conclude whether the site of action is in the lateral or basal nucleus. Nevertheless, NMDA receptors in this region seem to be involved.

SUMMARY   Important steps have been taken toward understanding the cellular basis of fear conditioning. While much work remains, this is a young research area and it holds great promise for elucidating mechanisms through which an important aspect of emotional learning occurs. Findings to date are consistent with the view that an NMDA-dependent, LTP-like phenomenon in the amygdala might mediate fear conditioning, but this remains unproved.

Extinction of Conditioned Fear

Extinction is the process through which the strength of a conditioned response is weakened by repeated exposure to the CS in the absence of the US. Considerable evidence suggests that extinction of conditioned fear does not occur passively (i.e. the memory persists in the absence of explicit extinction training), and when extinction occurs it is not passive forgetting but instead is an active process, quite possibly involving new learning (Bouton & Swartzentruber 1991). Further, conditioned fear reactions are notoriously difficult to extinguish and once extinguished they can recur spontaneously or can be reinstated by stressful experiences (e.g. Rescorla & Heth 1975, Jacobs & Nadel 1985, Campbell & Jaynes 1966). Because fear conditioning processes may contribute to such disorders as phobia, excessive fear, anxiety, posttraumatic stress, and panic, understanding how the effects of fear conditioning are modulated by extinction is of great clinical interest.

The neural basis of extinction has been studied much less extensively than has the neural basis of acquisition, but some key discoveries have been made. Although cortical areas are not required for the acquisition of conditioned defense (see above), cortical lesions can interfere with extinction. For example, lesions of auditory (Teich et al 1989) or visual (LeDoux et al 1989) cortex have no effect on simple conditioning involving an auditory or visual CS. However, with such lesions extinction is greatly prolonged if not prevented. This suggests that the subcortical sensory projections to the amygdala mediate learning in this situation (since the relevant cortical areas have been removed) and that subcortical learning of this type is relatively indelible (LeDoux et al 1989). The cortical lesions, in other words, may have unmasked the existence of relatively permanent memories. Extinction, by this account, might be a process by which the cortex regulates the expression of these indelible memories. A recent study failed to replicate these effects (Falls et al 1992), but a number of procedural differences between the studies might be responsible for the failure to replicate.

Additional studies have shown that extinction is prolonged by damage to the medial prefrontal cortex (Morgan et al 1993), which may be the link between sensory cortex and the amygdala in behavioral extinction. That is, the medial prefrontal cortex may modulate the expression of defense responses at the level of the amygdala. A related conclusion was reached on the basis of studies recording unit activity in the prefrontal cortex and the amygdala during appetitive conditioning (e.g. Thorpe et al 1983, Rolls 1992).

Blockade of NMDA receptors in the amygdala interferes with the extinction of conditioned fear (Falls et al 1992). This reinforces the view that extinction is not passive forgetting but an active form of learning and suggests that NMDA-dependent synaptic plasticity may be involved. The synapses between the frontal cortex and the amygdala might be the plastic synapses in this case. Although extinction plasticity may involve modifications in the strength of the existing associations, extinction plasticity may also involve changes in the propensity with which existing memories are expressed.

Conditioned Fear and Instrumental Action (Coping)

A stimulus that warns of impending danger elicits defense responses, such as those discussed above, but it also has other consequences. Once the organism is acted on by the CS, it then prepares to act back on the environment, figuring out how to escape and/or avoid danger and the stimuli that are associated with danger. These instrumental emotional responses, which might be thought of as coping responses (Lazarus 1966, 1991), have been studied experimentally using avoidance conditioning procedures. Fear conditioning is generally assumed to be the first step in the learning of avoidance (e.g. Mowrer 1960, Mackintosh 1983). That is, the state of conditioned fear is assumed to be unpleasant or undesirable, and in the effort to reduce fear, the organism learns to escape from and ultimately avoid situations or stimuli that lead to the arousal of fear. It might therefore be expected that damage to the amygdala, which will prevent fear conditioning, would interfere with avoidance conditioning.

The literature on the effects of brain lesions on avoidance conditioning is large and fairly confusing, and is not reviewed in detail here. Several features of this literature are highlighted below.

First, many studies of active and passive avoidance demonstrate that lesions of the amygdala interfere with the acquisition of avoidance responses (Panksepp et al 1991, Sarter & Markowitsch 1985). It is not clear why some studies fail to find this effect, but an analysis of the underlying task demands might be revealing. Even for those tasks in which the amygdala is involved, the input and output connections and intra-amygdala circuitry are not very well understood, possibly because of the variability in the eliciting stimulus conditions and in the emitted instrumental responses. At the same time, the simplicity of the eliciting stimuli and elicited responses in fear conditioning probably contribute to the greater success achieved in uncovering brain mechanisms with this procedure.

Second, most studies of passive avoidance find that the septo-hippocampal system is important. This observation provides part of the conceptual foundation for Gray's septo-hippocampal theory of fear and anxiety (Gray 1982, 1987). Although the theory is based on an impressive survey of the literature, it is unclear to what extent the septo-hippocampal system is involved in the fear part or in the stimulus processing (e.g. contextual processing) aspect of many passive avoidance tasks. As noted above, the hippocampus is involved in fear conditioning if the CS is the context in which the US occurs rather than a discrete signal. The same may be true of passive avoidance, in which diffuse contextual cues usually serve as the Pavlovian CS. Other aspects of the septo-hippocampal model of anxiety have been discussed elsewhere (see commentaries in Gray 1982, LeDoux 1992, Panksepp 1990).

Third, although the amygdala is often required for the acquisition of avoidance, it is less important and probably unnecessary for the long-term maintenance of well-trained avoidance responses. Thus, after learning is established, the defense system involving the amygdala is no longer a necessary part of the avoidance circuitry. It is thus important to keep the phase of training in mind when asking questions about brain involvement in avoidance.

Fourth, the instrumental aspects of avoidance, unlike the Pavlovian elicited responses, may require connections between the amygdala and the ventral striatum for their acquisition and/or expression (Everitt & Robbins 1992). In particular, the nucleus accumbens of the ventral striatum may be a crucial area for the initiation and control of instrumental responses motivated by either appetitive or aversive processes, possibly resulting from its innervation by dopaminergic pathways.

In summary, although the literature on avoidance is somewhat confusing, studies of avoidance conditioning, like studies of fear conditioning, point to the amygdala as probably playing some role. This should not be surprising since avoidance conditioning is believed to involve Pavlovian fear conditioning (which requires the amygdala) followed by the learning of the instrumental avoidance response. The amygdala almost certainly contributes to the Pavlovian part of avoidance learning but its role in the instrumental part is less clear.

Fear Conditioning: Conclusions

Studies of fear conditioning have successfully identified the neural system that underlies this important form of learning and memory process. Part of the reason that researchers have been so successful is that in fear conditioning, simple, well-defined stimuli can be used to elicit stereotyped or at least repeatable responses that require little training. It is always much easier to trace neural pathways when the stimulus and the response can both be precisely identified and quantified. This probably accounts for the greater success of studies of fear conditioning than of studies of avoidance conditioning in mapping the pathways of fear. At the same time, we have to be aware that the brain mechanisms of fear conditioning may not generalize to all aspects of fear. Whether fear of failure or fear of authority or fear of being afraid are mediated by the same basic system, with some cognitive baggage added on, remains to be determined.

Relation of the Neural Basis of Fear to Other Emotions

As noted above, the neural basis of fear conditioning has been studied so extensively and successfully because there are good techniques available for eliciting and quantifying conditioned fear responses. For the same reason, there has been a relative paucity of research on the neural basis of most other emotions, especially positive emotions.

Some studies have examined the neural basis of positive affective reactions and approach behavior. Unlike studies of defensive behavior, which are relevant to the emotion of fear, these studies are less specifically related to a well-defined emotion, except possibly pleasure. Most of this work has involved three paradigms: brain stimulation reward (Rolls 1975, Olds 1977, Gallistel et al 1981), stimulus-reward association learning procedures (see Aggleton & Mishkin 1986, Gaffan 1992, Everitt & Robbins 1992, Rolls 1992, Ono & Nishijo 1992), and appetitive classical conditioning (Gallagher & Holland 1992). The neural network underlying these tasks overlaps somewhat with the fear system in that the amygdala is involved to some extent in each of these tasks [but see Cahill & McGaugh (1990) for a comparison of the relative contribution of the amygdala to appetitive and aversive learning]. Unfortunately, the neural system is poorly understood for these positive emotional phenomena and much more work is needed. The creation of new models of positive affect is also important.

Given that the amygdala is involved to some extent in both positive and negative emotional reactions, one might be tempted to conclude that the amygdala is the centerpiece of an emotional system of the brain. However, this would be a mistake. We know far too little about the neural system–mediating emotions other than fear and far too little about variants of fear other than simple forms of conditioned fear. The amygdala is a sufficiently complex brain region that it could be involved in fear and reward processes in completely different ways and for different reasons. Other attempts at identifying emotion with a single system of the brain (e.g. the limbic system) have fared poorly (see LeDoux 1991), and we should be cautious not to overinterpret the role of the amygdala.

IMPLICATIONS OF THE NEURAL BASIS OF FEAR FOR UNDERSTANDING EMOTION

Examining emotion from the point of view of the nervous system allows us to see questions about this complex process from a unique angle. Several issues have been raised about the nature of emotion in light of the neural systems analysis of emotion just presented.

Cognitive-Emotional Interactions

The nature of cognitive-emotional interactions is one of the most debated topics in the psychology of emotion (e.g. Zajonc 1980, 1984; Lazarus 1982, 1984, 1991; Mandler 1984; Leventhal & Scherer 1987; Frijda 1986; LeDoux 1987, 1993b; Parrott & Schulkin 1993a,b; Izard 1992; Oatley & Johnson-Laird 1987; Ortony et al 1988; Ekman 1992). Knowledge of the neural system underlying emotion can help constrain our thinking on this topic. As we have seen, the system that mediates the emotion fear is well characterized. We can thus examine how cognitive processes participate in and interact with the neural system of fear.

DEPENDENCE OF EMOTIONAL PROCESSING (APPRAISAL) ON COGNITION   By most accounts, the amygdala plays a crucial role in deciding whether a stimulus is dangerous or not. Functions mediated by the amygdala are likely to be the neural instantiation of the emotional process know as appraisal (Arnold 1960, Lazarus 1966, 1991; Ekman 1977, 1992; Leventhal & Scherer 1987, Ellsworth 1991, Scherer 1991), at least for the appraisal of danger. The anatomical inputs to the amygdala from systems involved in stimulus processing define the kinds of events that can be appraised by the amygdala and the kinds of cognitive factors that might be important in this evaluation.

For example, the amygdala receives inputs from sensory processing areas in the thalamus and cortex (summarized in Figure 1; see LeDoux 1992 for review). The former provide course representations, but reach the amygdala quickly, while the latter provide detailed stimulus information, but reach the amygdala more slowly because of the additional processing stations involved at the cortical level. The thalamic inputs thus may be useful for producing rapid responses on the basis of limited stimulus information, whereas cortical inputs are required to distinguish between stimuli. Rapid response to danger has obvious survival value (Ohman 1986, 1992; Ekman 1992; LeDoux 1986, 1990), suggesting the possible significance of a quick-and-dirty subcortical pathway. The amygdala also receives inputs from the hippocampal formation (Ottersen 1982, Amaral et al 1992). These set the context in which an emotional stimulus is to be evaluated (Phillips & LeDoux 1992b, Kim & Fanselow 1992, Selden et al 1991, Penick & Solomon 1991, Good & Honey 1991), possibly allowing the amygdala to respond to a stimulus as threatening in one situation and not in another. In addition, given the role of the hippocampus in declarative or explicit memory (Squire 1992, Eichenbaum 1992), the hippocampal inputs may also allow fear responses to be activated by explicit or conscious memories of past experiences. When the functions of the other cortical areas that project to the amygdala have been elucidated we will be able to make additional predictions about the kinds of inputs that the amygdala appraises.

The anatomical organization of the fear system thus tells us that emotional responses can be elicited by processing in a wide range of systems. The issue of whether emotional processing is dependent on prior cognitive processing is reduced to a question of how we define cognition. If cognition is defined broadly to include sensory information processing, such as that occurring in the sensory thalamus and/or sensory cortex, as well as the processing that occurs in complex association areas of cortex in the frontal lobes or hippocampus, then emotional processing by the amygdala is highly dependent on cognitive processing. If cognitive processing is defined narrowly to include only the higher mental functions most likely mediated by complex association cortex, then emotion is not necessarily dependent on prior cognitive processing.

Emotional responses also might occur in the absence of inputs from cognitive systems. On the one hand, the amygdala receives inputs about the state of various internal organs of the body (e.g. Cechetto & Calaresu 1984) and these subcortical sensory inputs, like other exteroceptive sensory inputs, might be capable of triggering emotional responses. It is known that internal signals can precipitate emotional reactions, as in panic attacks (Klein 1993), but it is not known whether the coding of the signal by the amygdala is involved. On the other hand, in some situations spontaneous discharges of the amygdala might generate emotional responses, but little evidence supports this possibility.

In the past, cognitive-emotional interactions have often been discussed without much consideration of what the terms cognition and emotion mean. I have limited this discussion to the emotion of fear and have examined how specific cognitive processes (such as sensory processing in the thalamus, perceptual processing in the neocortex, spatial and contextual processing in the hippocampus, or mnemonic processing in the hippocampus) can influence the amygdala and thereby elicit fear responses. This perspective forces us to abandon discussions of cognitive-emotional interactions in terms of vague monolithic cognitive processes and instead consider exactly which cognitive processes are involved in fear reactions. This is a more practical and tractable problem than the problem of how cognition and emotion, in the broader sense of the terms, interact. All we have to do is to determine how a particular cognitive process is organized in the brain and then determine how that brain region interacts with the amygdala. We can then hypothesize the nature of that particular cognitive-emotional interaction, at least within the fear domain.

EMOTIONAL INFLUENCES ON COGNITION   A similar situation holds for the other side of the cognitive-emotional dyad. That is, we can examine projections from the amygdala to areas involved in cognitive processing and make predictions about how the appraisal of danger by the amygdala might affect these processes (see Figure 3). The role of these projections in information processing has not been studied empirically, but the anatomical observations are suggestive of the functions served. For example, the amygdala projects back to the cortical sensory processing systems that send projections to the amygdala (Price et al 1987, Amaral et al 1992). Although the amygdala receives inputs from only the later stages of sensory processing, its back projections innervate the earlier stages as well. These projections from the amygdala to sensory processing areas may allow the amygdala's appraisals of danger to influence ongoing perceptions of the environment (Rolls 1992, LeDoux 1992). The amygdala does not project back to the thalamus, but the cortical areas that receive amygdala inputs do,

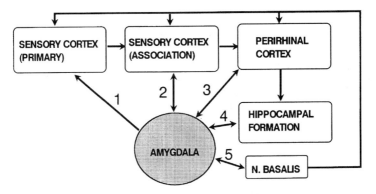

Figure 3 Amygdala influences on cortical cognitive processing. Once an emotional stimulus activates the amygdala, the amygdala can in turn impact cognitive processes organized in the neocortex. The amygdala receives inputs from sensory association areas but not primary sensory cortex (see Figure 2). However, it appears to project back to primary sensory cortex (1) and to association areas (2). These projections allow the amygdala and its coding of emotional significance to control the ongoing flow of sensory information and may represent channels by which emotional processing can influence perception. The amygdala receives inputs from and projects to the perirhinal cortex and hippocampal formation (3, 4). These structures have been implicated in explicit or declarative memory processing and the interconnections may account for emotional influences on memory processing. The hippocampus is also important in adding context to emotional situations, and the interconnections between the amygdala and the hippocampus may play a role in making context an emotional stimulus. The nucleus basalis (N. Basalis) is the source of cholinergic inputs to widespread areas of the cortex (5) and plays an important role in cortical arousal and attention. Projections from the amygdala to this region may be important in attention and arousal processes.

allowing for an indirect modulation of thalamic processing. Additionally, the amygdala projects to the nucleus basalis (Price et al 1987, deOlmos et al 1985), which provides widespread cholinergic modulation of cortical arousal. These projections may allow the amygdala to participate in selective attention (Weinberger 1993, Kapp et al 1992, Gallagher & Holland 1992). The amygdala also projects to the hippocampus (Amaral et al 1992, Price et al 1987), allowing the appraisal of danger to modulate hippocampal functions, including spatial behavior (O'Keefe & Nadel 1978, O'Keefe 1993, McNaughton & Barnes 1990, Muller et al 1991), contextual processing (Phillips & LeDoux 1992b, Kim & Fanselow 1992, Selden et al 1991, Nadel & Willner 1980, Good & Honey 1991, Penick & Solomon 1991), and explicit or declarative memory storage or retrieval (Squire 1992, Eichenbaum 1992). Many other examples could be given, but these illustrate the usefulness of a neuroanatomical perspective in suggesting predictions about the nature of cognitive-emotional interactions.

IS EMOTIONAL PROCESSING COGNITIVE PROCESSING?   It has been argued that appraisal involves information processing; therefore, emotion is cognition (Lazarus 1982, 1984). However, as Zajonc (1984) and Izard (1992) have noted, cognitive processing is but one example of information processing. Noncognitive biological information processing systems include the immune system and the genome. Just because emotion involves information processing does not mean that emotion is cognition.

The issue, again, depends on how cognition is defined. It can be defined to include emotion, motivation, and similar processes, but this would seem to defeat the purpose of having a designation of cognition as opposed to the more general term mind. Hilgard (1980) has reminded psychology that cognition historically has been thought of as part of a trilogy of mind that also includes emotion and will (motivation) rather than as an all-encompassing description of mind. Certainly, early pioneers of cognitive science did not view emotion as a cognitive process. According to Neisser (1967), emotion was one of the many aspects of psychology not included in the cognitive approach.

Studies of the processing rules and transformations in areas of the brain that are involved in cognition and areas involved in emotion might be able to address the question of whether emotional and cognitive processing are fundamentally different. Studies of the brain mechanisms of emotion have pointed to the amygdala as an important part of an aversive emotional memory system, and to the hippocampus as part of the system involved in cognitive or declarative form of memory (for a discussion of emotional and cognitive memory systems, see LeDoux 1993a). This does not prove that the systems operate by different information processing rules, but it certainly leaves open the possibility. For example, given that cells in the amygdala and hippocampus both "learn" during conditioning, one might ask whether comparable representations are encoded. Although a lot has been learned about the nature of hippocampal information processing from studies of the physiology of hippocampal neurons (for review, see O'Keefe 1993), we know very little about how amygdala neurons process information. If and when physiological studies of the amygdala catch up with studies of the hippocampus, it may be possible to determine whether these systems use different processing rules or whether they simply do different things on the basis of similar processing functions.

Conscious versus Unconscious Processes in Emotion

The issue of what is conscious or unconscious in emotion was around even before James (1884) popularized it with his famous question about whether we run from a bear out of fear (conscious or subjective emotion) or whether fear comes from running away. However, all animals, invertebrates as well as vertebrates, must have a way of defending themselves from danger. When a fruitfly is conditioned to avoid shock by flying out of the chamber where the shock occurred (Tully 1991), it is unlikely that a conscious state of fear intervenes between the reception of the stimulus and the production of the response. Comparative psychologists long ago learned the importance of parsimony in explaining findings across species. If we do not need subjective fear to explain defensive responses in lower species, then we should not explain defensive responses in higher species in this way either. At least amongst vertebrates, the neural system involved in detecting danger and producing defense responses is similarly organized in all species studied. This suggests that evolution long ago figured out how to organize the defense system and has continued to use this organizational blueprint. Subjective fear, in this view, is what occurs when the evolutionary old defense system is activated, but only in a species that also has the capacity for subjective conscious states.

This view highlights the value of studies of experimental animals in understanding emotional systems. Because the system that generates emotional responses is strongly conserved in evolution (the amygdala and its connections are involved in all vertebrates studied), we can learn about human defense or fear reactions by studying other creatures. And if fear responses and conscious emotional states of fear are the result of activation of an evolutionarily conserved system that detects danger, then studying how the neural system produces fear responses in animals will also shed light on mechanisms that contribute to conscious states of fear in humans.

Volitional Control of Emotion

Whether emotional responses are under voluntary control is an important issue with a great deal of practical application to legal issues. What seems clear from the neural systems perspective is that there are both involuntary and voluntary responses, each mediated by different neural networks emanating out of the amygdala.

Many defense responses are respondents rather than operants. That is, the responses are controlled by their antecedents rather than by their consequences (Bouton & Bolles 1980). Borrowing a term from ethology, these responses are released by the presence of stimuli that have their releasing capacity either as a result of genetic programming or associative learning processes. These responses are, in the language of cognitive psychology, effortless and automatic, and probably are controlled by unconscious appraisal processes. These involuntary emotional responses include behavioral (e.g. freezing and flight reactions, facial expressions) as well as visceral (e.g. autonomic and endocrine) responses.

Emotional respondents are only part of the story of emotional responsivity. Once emotional respondents are expressed, emotional operants begin to occur. These are instrumental responses. A rat exposed to a cat will automatically freeze in order to minimize the possibility of an attack. During the freezing episode, the rat begins planning strategies that might lead to successful escape, using information stored from past experience and expectations about possible outcomes. These kinds of processes are related to what has been called risk-assessment behavior (Blanchard et al 1993). This may be the point at which Gray's (1982, 1987) septo-hippocampal system (which may be involved in the instrumental and cognitive phase of fear and anxiety) meets the amygdala-based system (which is probably more involved in the automatic, elicited aspects of fear and anxiety).

Respondents are not learned. They are hard-wired into the nervous system, and are subject to Pavlovian conditioning. But conditioning does not modify the responses; it allows new stimuli to activate the responses. In contrast, emotional operants are learned through instrumental (operant) conditioning procedures. Although the respondents are controlled by outputs of the amygdala to brainstem motor systems, the instrumental actions (such as escape and avoidance) appear to be mediated by projections from the amygdala to a forebrain region know as the ventral striatum (Everitt & Robbins 1992), an important link to the extrapyramidal motor system. The emotional respondent system has been examined in detail, but less is known about emotional operants, which are much more difficult to study because they are considerably more complex. However, this is an important area for future research because it may help shed light on emotional coping responses (Lazarus 1991).

Psychopathological Issues

Disorders of fear regulation make up an important set of psychopathologic conditions. To the extent that we understand the anatomy of these systems, we will be in a better position to develop more selective drug therapies that are targeted for the specific brain networks involved in fear regulation. In addition, knowledge of the anatomy of fear may help us understand some other aspects of pathological fear, and perhaps other emotions, as well.

The anatomy of the fear processing system tells us that fear can be triggered by many different kinds of information processing functions that lead to the amygdala. If, for genetic or experiential reasons, the lower-order pathways are more efficient at triggering the amygdala than are the higher-order pathways in some individuals, we would expect those individuals to have rather limited insight into the nature of their emotional reactions. People have different degrees of insight into their emotions and the anatomical findings suggest a possible explanation.

Another point to consider is that emotional memories mediated by the amygdala system are indelible. That is, the memories persist even after emotional behavior is extinguished. This has been demonstrated in behavioral studies (e.g. Bouton & Swartzentruber 1991), but is also illustrated dramatically by studies showing that with cortical lesions, extinction can be prolonged or eliminated (Teich et al 1989, LeDoux et al 1989, Morgan et al 1993). Extinction thus appears to involve cortical inhibition of indelible, amygdala-mediated memories. It is not a process of emotional memory erasure. The role of therapy may be to allow the cortex to establish more effective and efficient synaptic links with the amygdala.

Finally, consider the issues of infantile amnesia and the inaccessibility of memory for early trauma. Jacobs & Nadel (1985) made the intriguing suggestion that our inability to remember early experiences may be because the hippocampus is not sufficiently mature to allow us to form declarative or conscious memories until around the second or third year of life. They suggest that early trauma might not be accessible consciously because the system that encodes conscious memories is not fully functional. At the same time, we know that early trauma can have long lasting influences on behavioral and mental states, which suggests that the system that encodes these unconscious traumatic memories is present and functional. We know that the amygdala is crucial for at least some forms of aversive or traumatic learning and memory, but little definitive work has been done on the maturational time course of the amygdala that would allow us to clearly state whether it develops before the hippocampus. However, a recent study showed that rats can be conditioned to an auditory CS at an earlier age than they can to contextual stimuli (Rudy 1993). This finding implies strongly that the amygdala matures earlier than does the hippocampus.

There are several implications of these observations. First, early memories may be emotional memories (and not explicit, declarative conscious memories) because the emotional memory system (and not the declarative system) is functional at the time. Second, early emotional memories, including traumatic as well as nontraumatic memories, may be inaccessible to consciousness not because of active repression but because of the time course of brain maturation. Third, the extent to which one can gain conscious access to these early memories, which were encoded in the absence of the conscious or declarative memory system, may be limited.

CONCLUSIONS

Progress in understanding the neural basis of fear has been rapid in the last decade. We now understand the anatomy of this system in great detail. This information can help us see emotions in a different light and suggests some insights and constraints concerning important issues about the nature of emotion. Although much remains to be done, especially in terms of determining the generality of the findings, we are well on the way to understanding how one important aspect of emotional life is represented in the brain.

Any *Annual Review* chapter, as well as any article cited in an *Annual Review* chapter, may be purchased from the Annual Reviews Preprints and Reprints service.
1-800-347-8007; 415-259-5017; email: arpr@class.org

Literature Cited

Aggleton JP. 1992. *The Amygdala: Neurobiological Aspects of Emotion, Memory, and Mental Dysfunction.* New York: Wiley-Liss

Aggleton JP, Mishkin M. 1986. The amygdala: sensory gateway to the emotions. In *Emotion: Theory, Research and Experience,* ed. R Plutchik, H Kellerman, 3:281–99. Orlando: Academic

Amaral DG, Price JL, Pitkänen A, Carmichael ST. 1992. Anatomical organization of the primate amygdaloid complex. See Aggleton 1992, pp. 1–66

Arnold MB. 1960. *Emotion and Personality.* New York: Columbia Univ. Press

Blanchard DC, Blanchard RJ. 1972. Innate and conditioned reactions to threat in rats with amygdaloid lesions. *J. Comp. Physiol. Psychol.* 81(2):281–90

Blanchard RJ, Yudko EB, Rodgers RJ, Blanchard DC. 1993. Defense system psychopharmacology: an ethological approach to the pharmacology of fear and anxiety. *Behav. Brain Res.* 58:155–66

Bliss TVP, Collingridge GL. 1993. A synaptic model of memory: long-term potentiation in the hippocampus. *Nature* 361: 31–39

Bordi F, LeDoux J. 1992. Sensory tuning beyond the sensory system: an initial analysis of auditory properties of neurons in the lateral amygdaloid nucleus and overlying areas of the striatum. *J. Neurosci.* 12(7): 2493–2503

Bordi F, LeDoux JE. 1994a. Response properties of single units in areas of rat auditory thalamus that project to the amygdala. I: Acoustic discharge patterns and frequency receptive fields. *Exp. Brain Res.* 98:261–74

Bordi F, LeDoux JE. 1994b. Response properties of single units in areas of rat auditory thalamus that project to the amygdala. II: Cells receiving convergent auditory and somatosensory inputs and cells antidromically activated by amygdala stimulation. *Exp. Brain Res.* 98:275–86

Bordi F, LeDoux JE, Clugnet MC, Pavlides C. 1993. Single unit activity in the lateral nucleus of the amygdala and overlying areas of the striatum in freely-behaving rats: rates, discharge patterns, and responses to acoustic stimuli. *Behav. Neurosci.* 107: 757–69

Bouton ME, Bolles RC. 1980. Conditioned fear assessed by freezing and by the suppression of three different baselines. *Anim. Learn. Behav.* 8:429–34

Bouton ME, Swartzentruber D. 1991. Sources of relapse after extinction in Pavlovian and instrumental learning. *Clin. Psychol. Rev.* 11:123–40

Brodal A. 1982. *Neurological Anatomy.* New York: Oxford Univ. Press

Brown JS, Kalish HI, Farber IE. 1951. Conditioned fear as revealed by magnitude of startle response to an auditory stimulus. *J. Exp. Psychol.* 41:317–28

Brown TH, Chapman PF, Kairiss EW, Keenan CL. 1988. Long-term synaptic potentiation. *Science* 242:724–28

Cahill L, McGaugh JL. 1990. Amygdaloid complex lesions differentially affect retention of tasks using appetitive and aversive reinforcement. *Behav. Neurosci.* 104:532–43

Campbell BA, Jaynes J. 1966. Reinstatement. *Psychol. Rev.* 73:478–80

Cechetto DF, Calaresu FR. 1984. Units in the amygdala responding to activation of carotid baro- and chemoreceptors. *Am. J. Physiol.* 246:R832–36

Chapman PF, Bellavance LL. 1992. NMDA receptor-independent LTP in the amygdala. *Synapse.*

Chapman PF, Kairiss EW, Keenan CL, Brown TH. 1990. Long-term synaptic potentiation in the amygdala. *Synapse* 6:271–78

Clugnet MC, LeDoux JE. 1990. Synaptic plasticity in fear conditioning circuits: induction of LTP in the lateral nucleus of the amygdala by stimulation of the medial geniculate body. *J. Neurosci.* 10:2818–24

Clugnet MC, LeDoux JE, Morrison SF. 1990. Unit responses evoked in the amygdala and striatum by electrical stimulation of the medial geniculate body. *J. Neurosci.* 10:1055–61

Cohen DH, Randall DC. 1984. Classical conditioning of cardiovascular responses. *Annu. Rev. Physiol.* 46:187–97

Cotman CW, Monaghan DT, Ganong AH. 1988. Excitatory amino acid neurotransmission: NMDA receptors and Hebb-type synaptic plasticity. *Annu. Rev. Neurosci.* 11:61–80

Davis M. 1992. The role of the amygdala in conditioned fear. See Aggleton 1992, pp. 255–306

Davis M, Hitchcock JM, Rosen JB. 1987. Anxiety and the amygdala: pharmacological and anatomical analysis of the fear-potentiated startle paradigm. In *The Psychology of Learning and Motivation,* ed. GH Bower, 21:263–305. San Diego: Academic

deOlmos J, Alheid G, Beltramino C. 1985. Amygdala. In *The Rat Nervous System,* ed. G Paxinos, pp. 223–334. Orlando: Academic

Edeline J-M, Weinberger NM. 1992. Associative retuning in the thalamic source of input to the amygdala and auditory cortex: receptive field plasticity in the medial division of the medial geniculate body. *Behav. Neurosci.* 106:81–105

Edeline J-M, Weinberger NM. 1993. Receptive field plasticity in the auditory cortex during frequency discrimination training: selective retuning independent of task difficulty. *Behav. Neurosci.* 107:82–103

Eichenbaum H. 1992. The hippocampal system and delclarative memory in animals. *J. Cogn. Neurosci.* 4(3):217–31

Ekman P. 1977. Biological and cultural contributions to body and facial movement. In *Anthropology of the Body,* ed. J Blacking, pp. 39–84. London: Academic

Ekman P. 1992. An argument for basic emotions. *Cogn. Emot.* 6:169–200

Ekman P, Davidson R. 1994. *The Nature of Emotion: Fundamental Questions.* New York: Oxford Univ. Press

Ellsworth P. 1991. Some implications of cognitive appraisal theories of emotion. In *International Review of Studies on Emotion,* ed. KT Strongman, pp. 143–61. Chichester, UK: Wiley

Estes WK, Skinner BF. 1941. Some quantitative properties of anxiety. *J. Exp. Psychol.* 29:390–400

Everitt BJ, Robbins TW. 1992. Amygdala-ventral striatal interactions and reward-related processes. See Aggleton 1992, pp. 401–29

Falls WA, Miserendino MJD, Davis M. 1992. Extinction of fear-potentiated startle: blockade by infusion of an NMDA antagonist into the amygdala. *J. Neurosci.* 12(3): 854–63

Fanselow MS. 1980. Conditional and unconditional components of postshock freezing. *Pavlovian J. Biol. Sci.* 15:177–82

Fanselow MS, Bolles RC. 1979. Naloxone and shock-elicited freezing in the rat. *J. Comp. Physiol. Psychol.* 93(4):736–44

Fanselow MS, Helmstetter FJ. 1988. Conditional analgesia, defensive freezing, and benzodiazepines. *Behav. Neurosci.* 102(2): 233–43

Fanselow MS, Kim JJ. 1994. Acquisition of contextual Pavlovian fear conditioning is blocked by application of an NMDA receptor antagonist D,L-2-amino-5-phosphonovaleric acid to the basolateral amygdala. *Behav. Neurosci.* 108:210–12

Frijda N. 1986. *The Emotions.* Cambridge: Cambridge Univ. Press

Gabriel M, Slatwick SE, Miller JD. 1976. Multiple unit activity of the rabbit medial geniculate nucleus in conditioning, extinction, and reversal. *Physiol. Psychol.* 4:124–34

Gaffan D. 1992. Amygdala and the memory of reward. See Aggleton 1992, pp. 471–483

Gallagher M, Holland PC. 1992. Understanding the function of the central nucleus: Is simple conditioning enough? See Aggleton 1992, pp. 307–21

Gallistel CR, Shizgal P, Yeomans JS. 1981. A portrait of the substrate for self-stimulation. *Psychol. Rev.* 88:228–73

Gean P-W, Chang F-C, Huang C-C, Lin J-H, Way L-J. 1993. Long-term enhancement of EPSP and NMDA receptor-mediated synaptic transmission in the amygdala. *Brain Res. Bull.* 31:7–11

Gentile CG, Jarrell TW, Teich A, McCabe PM, Schneiderman N. 1986. The role of amygdaloid central nucleus in the retention of differential Pavlovian conditioning of bradycardia in rabbits. *Behav. Brain Res.* 20: 263–73

Good M, Honey RC. 1991. Conditioning and contextual retrieval in hippocampal rats. *Behav. Neurosci.* 105:499–509

Gray JA. 1982. *The Neuropsychology of Anxiety.* New York: Oxford Univ. Press

Gray JA. 1987. *The Psychology of Fear and Stress.* New York: Cambridge Univ. Press

Hebb DO. 1949. *The Organization of Behavior.* New York: Wiley

Hilgard ER. 1980. The trilogy of mind: cognition, affection, and conation. *J. Hist. Behav. Sci.* 16:107–17

Hunt HF, Brady JV. 1955. Some effects of punishment and intercurrent "anxiety" on a simple operant. *J. Comp. Physiol. Psychol.* 48:305–10

Iwata J, Chida K, LeDoux JE. 1987. Cardiovascular responses elicited by stimulation of neurons in the central amygdaloid nucleus in awake but not anesthetized rats resemble conditioned emotional responses. *Brain Res.* 418:183–88

Iwata J, LeDoux JE, Meeley MP, Arneric S, Reis DJ. 1986. Intrinsic neurons in the amygdaloid field projected to by the medial geniculate body mediate emotional responses conditioned to acoustic stimuli. *Brain Res.* 383:195–214

Izard CE. 1992. Four systems for emotion activation: cognitive and noncognitive. *Psychol. Rev.* 99:561–65

Jacobs WJ, Nadel L. 1985. Stress-induced recovery of fears and phobias. *Psychol. Rev.* 92:512–31

James W. 1884. What is emotion? *Mind* 9: 188–205

Jarrell TW, Gentile CG, Romanski LM, McCabe PM, Schneiderman N. 1987. Involvement of cortical and thalamic auditory regions in retention of differential bradycardia conditioning to acoustic conditioned stimuli in rabbits. *Brain Res.* 412: 285–94

Kamin LJ. 1965. Temporal and intensity characteristics of the conditioned stimulus. In *Classical Conditioning,* ed. WF Prokasy,

pp. 118–47. New York: Appleton-Century-Crofts

Kandel ER, Spencer WA. 1968. Cellular neurophysiological approaches to the study of learning. *Physiol. Rev.* 48:65–134

Kapp BS, Pascoe JP, Bixler MA. 1984. The amygdala: a neuroanatomical systems approach to its contributions to aversive conditioning. In *Neuropsychology of Memory,* ed. N Buttlers, LR Squire, pp. 473–88. New York: Guilford

Kapp BS, Whalen PJ, Supple WF, Pascoe JP. 1992. Amygdaloid contributions to conditioned arousal and sensory information processing. See Aggleton 1992, pp. 229–54

Kapp BS, Wilson A, Pascoe J, Supple W, Whalen PJ. 1990. A neuroanatomical systems analysis of conditioned bradycardia in the rabbbit. In *Learning and Computational Neuroscience: Foundations of Adaptive Networks,* ed. M Gabriel, J Moore, pp. 53–90. Cambridge, MA: MIT Press

Kim JJ, Fanselow MS. 1992. Modality-specific retrograde amnesia of fear. *Science* 256: 675–77

Kim M, Davis M. 1993. Lack of a temporal gradient of retrograde amnesia in rats with amygdala lesions assessed with the fear-potentiated startle paradigm. *Behav. Neurosci.* 107:1088–92

Klein DF. 1993. False suffocation alarms and spontaneous panics: subsuming the CO_2 hypersensitivity theory. *Arch. Gen. Psychiatry* 50:306–17

Konorski J. 1967. Transient (or dynamic) memory. In *Integrative Activity of the Brain,* ed. Anonymous, pp. 490–505. Chicago: Univ. Chicago Press

Kotter R, Meyer N. 1992. The limbic system: a review of its empirical foundation. *Behav. Brain Res.* 52:105–27

Lazarus RS. 1966. *Psychological Stress and the Coping Process.* New York: McGraw Hill

Lazarus RS. 1982. Thoughts on the relations between emotion and cognition. *Am. Psychol.* 37:1019–24

Lazarus RS. 1984. On the primacy of cognition. *Am. Psychol.* 39:124–29

Lazarus RS. 1991. Cognition and motivation in emotion. *Am. Psychol.* 46(4):352–67

Leaf RC, Muller SA. 1965. Simple method for CER conditioning and measurement. *Psychol. Rep.* 17:211–15

LeDoux JE. 1986. Sensory systems and emotion. *Integr. Psychiatry* 4:237–48

LeDoux JE. 1987. Emotion. In *Handbook of Physiology. 1: The Nervous System,* ed. F Plum, 5:419–60. Bethesda, MD: Am. Physiol. Soc.

LeDoux JE. 1990. Information flow from sensation to emotion: plasticity in the neural computation of stimulus value. See Kapp et al 1990, pp. 3–52

LeDoux JE. 1991. Emotion and the limbic system concept. *Concepts Neurosci.* 2:169–99

LeDoux JE. 1992. Brain mechanisms of emotion and emotional learning. *Curr. Opin. Neurobiol.* 2:191–98

LeDoux JE. 1993a. Emotional memory systems in the brain. Behav. *Brain Res.* 58:69–79

LeDoux JE. 1993b. Cognition versus emotion, again—this time in the brain: a response to Parrott and Schulkin. *Cogn. Emot.* 7:61–64

LeDoux JE, Cicchetti P, Xagoraris A, Romanski LM. 1990a. The lateral amygdaloid nucleus: sensory interface of the amygdala in fear conditioning. *J. Neurosci.* 10:1062–69

LeDoux JE, Farb C, Ruggiero DA. 1990b. Topographic organization of neurons in the acoustic thalamus that project to the amygdala. *J. Neurosci.* 10:1043–54

LeDoux JE, Farb CR, Romanski L. 1991. Overlapping projections to the amygdala and striatum from auditory processing areas of the thalamus and cortex. *Neurosci. Lett.* 134:139–44

LeDoux JE, Iwata J, Cicchetti P, Reis DJ. 1988. Different projections of the central amygdaloid nucleus mediate autonomic and behavioral correlates of conditioned fear. *J. Neurosci.* 8:2517–29

LeDoux JE, Romanski LM, Xagoraris AE. 1989. Indelibility of subcortical emotional memories. *J. Cogn. Neurosci.* 1:238–43

LeDoux JE, Ruggiero DA, Reis DJ. 1985. Projections to the subcortical forebrain from anatomically defined regions of the medial geniculate body in the rat. *J. Comp. Neurol.* 242:182–213

LeDoux JE, Sakaguchi A, Iwata J, Reis DJ. 1986. Interruption of projections from the medial geniculate body to an archi-neostriatal field disrupts the classical conditioning of emotional responses to acoustic stimuli in the rat. *Neuroscience* 17:615–27

LeDoux JE, Sakaguchi A, Reis DJ. 1984. Subcortical efferent projections of the medial geniculate nucleus mediate emotional responses conditioned by acoustic stimuli. *J. Neurosci.* 4(3):683–98

LeGal La Salle G, Ben-Ari Y. 1981. Unit activity in the amygdaloid complex: a review. In *The Amygdaloid Complex,* ed. Y Ben-Ari, pp. 227–237. New York: Elsevier/North-Holland Biomed. Press

Leventhal H, Scherer K. 1987. The relationship of emotion to cognition: a functional approach to a semantic controversy. *Cogn. Emot.* 1:3–28

Lynch G. 1986. *Synapses, Circuits, and the Beginnings of Memory.* Cambridge, MA: MIT Press

Lynch G, Larson J, Staubli U, Granger R. 1991. Variants of synaptic potentiation and different types of memory operations in hippocampus and related structures. In *Memory: Organization and Locus of Change,* ed. LR Squire, NM Weinberger, G Lynch, JL McGaugh, pp. 330–63. New York: Oxford Univ. Press

Mackintosh NJ. 1983. *Conditioning and Associative Learning.* New York: Oxford Univ. Press

MacLean PD. 1949. Psychosomatic disease and the "visceral brain": recent developments bearing on the Papez theory of emotion. *Psychosom. Med.* 11:338–53

MacLean PD. 1952. Some psychiatric implications of physiological studies on frontotemporal portion of limbic system (visceral brain). *Electroencephalogr. Clin. Neurophysiol.* 4:407–18

Madison DV, Malenka RC, Nicoll RA. 1991. Mechanisms underlying long-term potentiation of synaptic transmission. *Annu. Rev. Neurosci.* 14:379–97

Malenka RC, Nicoll RA. 1993. NMDA-receptor-dependent synaptic plasticity: multiple forms and mechanisms. *Trends Neurosci.* 16:521–27

Mandler G. 1984. *Mind and Body: The Psychology of Emotion and Stress.* New York: Norton

Mason JW. 1968. A review of psychoendocrine research on the sympathetic-adrenal medullary system. *Psychosom. Med.* 30:631–53

McAllister WR, McAllister DE. 1971. Behavioral measurement of conditioned fear. In *Aversive Conditioning and Learning,* ed. FR Brush, pp. 105–79. New York: Academic

McNaughton BL, Barnes CA. 1990. From cooperative synaptic enhancement to associative memory: bridging the abyss. *Sem. Neurosci.* 2:403–16

Millenson JR, de Villiers PA. 1972. Motivational properties of conditioned anxiety. In *Reinforcement: Behavioral Analyses,* ed. RM Gilbert, JR Millenson, pp. 98–128. New York: Academic

Miserendino MJD, Sananes CB, Melia KR, Davis M. 1990. Blocking of acquisition but not expression of conditioned fear-potentiated startle by NMDA antagonists in the amygdala. *Nature* 345:716–18

Morgan MA, Romanski LM, LeDoux JE. 1993. Extinction of emotional learning: contribution of medial prefrontal cortex. *Neurosci. Lett.* 163:109–13

Morris RGM 1992. Is there overlap between the characteristics of learning and the physiological properties of LTP? In *Encyclopedia of Learning and Memory,* ed. LR Squire, pp. 369–72. New York: Macmillan

Mowrer OH. 1960. *Learning Theory and Behavior.* New York: Wiley

Muller RU, Kubie JL, Saypoff R. 1991. The hippocampus as a cognitive graph (abridged version). *Hippocampus* 1(3): 243–46

Muramoto K, Ono T, Nishijo H, Fukuda M. 1993. Rat amygdaloid neuron responses during auditory discrimination. *Neuroscience* 52:621–36

Nadel L, Willner J. 1980. Context and conditioning: a place for space. *Physiol. Psychol.* 8:218–28

Neisser U. 1967. *Cognitive Psychology.* New York: Appleton-Century-Crofts

Oatley K, Johnson-Laird P. 1987. Towards a cognitive theory of emotion. *Cogn. Emot.* 1:29–50

Ohman A. 1986. Face the beast and fear the face: animal and social fears as prototypes for evolutionary analyses of emotion. *Psychophysiology* 23:123–45

Ohman A. 1992. Fear and anxiety as emotional phenomena: clinical, phenomenological, evolutionary perspectives, and information-processing mechanisms. In *Handbook of the Emotions,* ed. M Lewis, JM Haviland, pp. 511–36. New York: Guilford

O'Keefe J. 1993. Hippocampus, theta, and spatial memory. *Curr. Opin. Neurobiol.* 3: 917–24

O'Keefe J, Nadel L. 1978. *The Hippocampus as a Cognitive Map.* Oxford: Clarendon

Olds J. 1977. *Drives and Reinforcement.* New York: Raven

Ono T, Nakamura K, Nishijo H, Tamura R, Tabuchi E. 1988. Lateral hypothalamus and amygdala involvement in rat learning behavior. *Adv. Biosci.* 70:123–26

Ono T, Nishijo H. 1992. Neurophysiological basis of the Kluver-Bucy Syndrome: responses of monkey amygdaloid neurons to biologically significant objects. See Aggleton 1992, pp. 167–90

Ortony A, Clore GL, Collins A. 1988. *The Cognitive Structure of Emotions.* Cambridge: Cambridge Univ. Press

Ottersen OP. 1982. Connections of the amygdala of the rat. IV: Corticoamygdaloid and intraamygdaloid connections as studied with axonal transport of horseradish peroxidase. *J. Comp. Neurol.* 205:30–48

Panksepp J. 1990. Gray zones at the emotion/cognition interface: a commentary. *Cogn. Emot.* 4:289–302

Panksepp J, Sacks DS, Crepau LJ, Abbot BB. 1991. The psycho- and neurobiology of fear systems in the brain. In *Fear, Avoidance, and Phobias,* ed. MR Denny, pp. 7–59. Hillsdale, NJ: Erlbaum

Parrott WG, Schulkin J. 1993a. What sort of system could an affective system be? A reply to LeDoux. *Cogn. Emot.* 7:65–69

Parrott WG, Schulkin J. 1993b. Neuropsychol-ogy and the cognitive nature of the emotions. *Cogn. Emot.* 7:43–59

Pascoe JP, Kapp BS. 1985. Electrophysiological characteristics of amygdaloid central nucleus neurons during Pavlovian fear conditioning in the rabbit. *Behav. Brain Res.* 16:117–33

Pavlov IP. 1927. *Conditioned Reflexes.* New York: Dover

Penick S, Solomon PR. 1991. Hippocampus, context, and conditioning. *Behav. Neurosci.* 105:611–17

Phillips RG, LeDoux JE. 1992a. Overlapping and divergent projections of CA1 and the ventral subiculum to the amygdala. *Soc. Neurosci. Abstr.* 18:518

Phillips RG, LeDoux JE. 1992b. Differential contribution of amygdala and hippocampus to cued and contextual fear conditioning. *Behav. Neurosci.* 106:274–85

Price JL, Russchen FT, Amaral DG. 1987. The limbic region. II: The amygdaloid complex. In *Handbook of Chemical Neuroanatomy.* Vol. 5: *Integrated Systems of the CNS,* ed. A Bjorklund, T Hokfelt, LW Swanson, pp. 279–388. Amsterdam: Elsevier

Rescorla RA, Heth CD. 1975. Reinstatement of fear to an extinguished conditioned stimulus. *J. Exp. Psychol. Anim. Behav.* 104:88–96

Rescorla RA, Wagner AR. 1972. A theory of Pavlovian conditioning: variations in the effectiveness of reinforcement and nonreinforcement. In *Classical Conditioning II: Current Research and Theory,* ed. AA Black, WF Prokasy, pp. 64–99. New York: Appleton-Century-Crofts

Rolls ET. 1975. *The Brain and Reward.* Oxford: Pergamon

Rolls ET. 1992. Neurophysiology and functions of the primate amygdala. See Aggleton 1992, pp. 143–65

Romanski LM, Clugnet MC, Bordi F, LeDoux JE. 1993. Somatosensory and auditory convergence in the lateral nucleus of the amygdala. *Behav. Neurosci.* 107:444–50

Romanski LM, LeDoux JE. 1992. Equipotentiality of thalamo-amygdala and thalamo-cortico-amygdala projections as auditory conditioned sitmulus pathways. *J. Neurosci.* 12:4501–9

Romanski LM, LeDoux JE. 1993a. Information cascade from primary auditory cortex to the amygdala: corticocortical and corticoamygdaloid projections of temporal cortex in the rat. *Cerebr. Cortex* 3:515–32

Romanski LM, LeDoux JE. 1993b. Organization of rodent auditory cortex: anterograde transport of PHA-L from MGv to temporal neocortex. *Cerebr. Cortex* 3:499–514

Rosen JB, Hitchcock JM, Sananes CB, Miserendino MJD, Davis M. 1991. A direct projection from the central nucleus of the amygdala to the acoustic startle pathway: anterograde and retrograde tracing studies. *Behav. Neurosci.* 105:817–25

Rudy JW. 1993. Contextual conditioning and auditory cue conditioning dissociate during development. *Behav. Neurosci.* 107:887–91

Rudy JW, Sutherland RJ. 1992. Configural and elemental associations and the memory coherence problem. *J. Cogn. Neurosci.* 4(3): 208–16

Ryugo DK, Weinberger NM. 1978. Differential plasticity of morphologically distinct neuron populations in the medial geniculate body of the cat during classical conditioning. *Behav. Biol.* 22:275–301

Sarter M, Markowitsch HJ. 1985. Involvement of the amygdala in learning and memory: a critical review, with emphasis on anatomical relations. *Behav. Neurosci.* 99:342–80

Scherer KR. 1991. Criteria for emotion-antecedent appraisal: a review. In *Cognitive Perspectives on Motivation and Emotion,* ed. V Hamilton, GH Bower, NH Fridja, pp. 89–126. Dordrecht: Kluwer

Selden NRW, Everitt BJ, Jarrard LE, Robbins TW. 1991. Complementary roles for the amygdala and hippocampus in aversive conditioning to explicit and contextual cues. *Neuroscience* 42(2):335–50

Smith OA, Astley CA, Devito JL, Stein JM, Walsh RE. 1980. Functional analysis of hypothalamic control of the cardiovascular responses accompanying emotional behavior. *Fed. Proc.* 39(8):2487–94

Squire LR. 1987. Memory: neural organization and behavior. In *Handbook of Physiology.* 1: *The Nervous System,* ed. F Plum, 5:295–371. Bethesda, MD: Am. Physiol. Soc.

Squire LR. 1992. Memory and the hippocampus: a synthesis from findings with rats, monkeys, and humans. *Psychol. Rev.* 99: 195–231

Staubli U. 1994. Parallel properties of LTP and memory. In *Brain and Memory: Modulation and Mediation of Neuroplasticity,* ed. JL McGaugh. New York: Oxford Univ. Press. In press

Swanson LW. 1983. The hippocampus and the concept of the limbic system. In *Neurobiology of the Hippocampus,* ed W Seifert, pp. 3–19. London: Academic

Teich AH, McCabe PM, Gentile CC,

Schneiderman LS, Winters RW, et al. 1989. Auditory cortex lesions prevent the extinction of Pavlovian differential heart rate conditioning to tonal stimuli in rabbits. *Brain Res.* 480:210–18

Teyler TJ, DiScenna P. 1987. Long-term potentiation. *Annu. Rev. Neurosci.* 10:131–61

Thompson RF, Berger TW, Madden J IV. 1983. Cellular processes of learning and memory in the mammalian CNS. *Annu. Rev. Neurosci.* 6:447–91

Thorpe SJ, Rolls ET, Maddison S. 1983. The orbitofrontal cortex: neuronal activity in the behaving monkey. *Exp. Brain Res.* 49: 93–115

Tully T. 1991. Genetic dissection of learning and memory in *Drosophila melanogaster.* In *Neurobiology of Learning, Emotion and Affect,* ed. JI Madden, pp. 29–66. New York: Raven

van de Kar LD, Piechowski RA, Rittenhouse PA, Gray TS. 1991. Amygdaloid lesions: differential effect on conditioned stress and immobilization-induced increases in corticosterone and renin secretion. *Neuroendocrinology* 54:89–95

Watkins LR, Mayer DJ. 1982. Organization of endogenous opiate and nonopiate pain control systems. *Science* 216:1185–92

Weinberger NM. 1993. Learning-induced changes of auditory receptive fields. *Curr. Opin. Neurobiol.* 3:570–77

Weinberger NM, Diamond DM. 1987. Physiological plasticity in auditory cortex: rapid induction by learning. *Prog. Neurobiol.* 29: 1–55

Weisz DJ, Harden DG, Xiang Z. 1992. Effects of amygdala lesions on reflex facilitation and conditioned response acquisition during nictitating membrane response conditioning in rabbit. *Behav. Neurosci.* 106: 262–73

Wilson A, Kapp BS. 1994. The effect of lesions of the ventrolateral periequiductal gray on the Pavlovian conditioned heart response in the rabbit. *Behav. Neural Biol.* In press

Zajonc R. 1980. Feeling and thinking: preferences need no inferences. *Am. Psychol.* 35: 151–75

Zajonc RB. 1984. On the primacy of affect. *Am. Psychol.* 39:117–23

Annu. Rev. Psychol. 1995. 46:237–64

UNDERSTANDING HUMAN RESOURCE MANAGEMENT IN THE CONTEXT OF ORGANIZATIONS AND THEIR ENVIRONMENTS

Susan E. Jackson

Department of Psychology, New York University, 6 Washington Place, New York, NY 10003

Randall S. Schuler

Department of Management, New York University, 40 W. 4th Street, New York, NY 10012

KEY WORDS: international, personnel, strategic, industrial/organizational

CONTENTS

0066-4308/95/0201-0237$05.00

INTRODUCTION

The Need for Understanding Human Resource Management (HRM) in Context

Applied psychologists have developed sophisticated tools and techniques intended to improve the effectiveness of organizations, and substantial evidence attesting to the value of these has accrued (e.g. Denison 1990; Hansen & Wernerfelt 1989; Kaufman 1992; MacDuffie & Krafcik 1992; Macy & Izumi 1993; Terpstra & Rozell 1993; United States Department of Labor 1993; MA Huselid, unpublished; ER Schnell, Olian JD, KG Smith, HP Sims Jr, JA Scully, KA Smith, unpublished). Nevertheless, US employers have been slow to adopt the "best" practices, i.e. those widely discussed in organizations as being the most effective (Bretz et al 1992, Rynes & Boudreau 1986, Saari et al 1988). Commentators have suggested that the acontextual nature of the scientific evidence is part of the problem (e.g. Johns 1993, Murray & Dimick 1978); consequently, calls for new human resource management (HRM) research that takes context more seriously have become more frequent (e.g. Begin 1991, Dobbins et al 1991, James et al 1992, Latham 1988). At the same time, a growing body of empirical evidence is beginning to shed light on the relationship between contextual conditions and HRM. Our objective for this review is to increase the momentum associated with this emerging field.

We use HRM as an umbrella term that encompasses (*a*) specific human resource practices such as recruitment, selection, and appraisal; (*b*) formal human resource policies, which direct and partially constrain the development of specific practices; and (*c*) overarching human resource philosophies, which specify the values that inform an organization's policies and practices. Ideally, these comprise a system that attracts, develops, motivates, and retains employees who ensure the effective functioning and survival of the organization and its members. To understand HRM in context we must consider how these three components of HRM are affected by the internal and external environments of organizations. The internal contextual factors we discuss are technology, structure, size, organizational life cycle stage, and business strategy. We treat organizational culture as inextricably bound to HRM and therefore not meaningful if separated from it. The external contextual factors are legal, social, and political environments; unionization; labor market conditions; industry characteristics; and national cultures.

Theoretical Perspectives Relevant to Understanding HRM in Context

Theoretical perspectives based in sociology, economics, management, and psychology focus on different aspects of the domain of HRM in Context (Wright & McMahan 1992). We begin by offering brief summaries of the perspectives that have guided most of the empirical studies reviewed in this chapter and that we feel are most likely to drive future research.

GENERAL SYSTEMS THEORY   In general systems theory, the unit of analysis is understood as a complex of interdependent parts (von Bertalanffy 1950). An open (vs closed) system is dependent on the environment for inputs, which are transformed during throughput to produce outputs that are exchanged in the environment. Open systems models seldom address organizations or large units within organizations. Katz & Kahn's (1978) *The Social Psychology of Organizations* is an exception in that it treats HRM as a subsystem embedded in a larger organizational system. The open systems view of HRM has been developed further by Wright & Snell (1991), who used it to describe a competence management model of organizations. Skills and abilities are treated as inputs from the environment; employee behaviors are treated as throughput; and employee satisfaction and performance are treated as outputs. In this model, the HRM subsystem functions to acquire, utilize, retain, and displace competencies. Similarly, Snell's (1992) description of HRM as a control system is based in open systems theory. In a more narrow discussion, Kozlowski & Salas (1994) presented a multilevel organizational systems approach for understanding training implementation and transfer. Many of the more specific theories used to understand HRM in Context assume that organizations function like open systems (see below).

ROLE BEHAVIOR PERSPECTIVE   Katz & Kahn (1978) focused on roles as the interdependent components that make up an organization system. Instead of using specific behaviors and job performances as the fundamental components, this perspective shifts the focus from individuals to social systems characterized by multiple roles, multiple role senders, and multiple role evaluators. Katz & Kahn defined role behaviors as "the recurring actions of an individual, appropriately interrelated with the repetitive activities of others so as to yield a predictable outcome." HRM is the organization's primary means for sending role information through the organization, supporting desired behaviors, and evaluating role performances; it is effective, therefore, when it communicates internally consistent expectations and evaluates performances in ways that are congruent with the system's behavioral requirements (e.g. see Frederickson 1986). System requirements are, in turn, presumed to depend on contextual factors such as business strategies and the nature of the industry. Role theory recognizes that the behavioral expectations of all role partners can influence the behavior of organizational members. By implication, effective HRM helps employees meet the expectations of role partners within the organization (i.e. supervisors, peers, subordinates), at organizational boundaries (i.e. customers and clients), and beyond (i.e. family and society). Thus the expectations of these role partners must be incorporated into an understanding of HRM in Context.

INSTITUTIONAL THEORY   A role theory perspective assumes individuals respond to normative pressures as they seek approval for their performance in socially defined roles. Similarly, institutional theory views organizations as social entities that seek approval for their performances in socially constructed environments. Organizations conform to gain legitimacy and acceptance, which facilitate survival (Meyer & Rowan 1977, Zucker 1977). Because multiple constituencies control needed resources, legitimacy and acceptance are sought from many stakeholders.

Research on institutionalization (Scott 1987, Zucker 1987) focuses on pressures emanating from the internal and external environments. Internally, institutionalization arises out of formalized structures and processes, as well as informal or emergent group and organization processes. Forces in the external environment include those related to the state (e.g. laws and regulations), the professions (e.g. licensure and certification), and other organizations—especially those within the same industrial sector. Regardless of the source of institutional pressures, two central assertions of this perspective are (*a*) institutionalized activities are resistant to change and (*b*) organizations in institutionalized environments are pressured to become similar (Meyer & Rowan 1977, DiMaggio & Powell 1983). Thus, in this theoretical perspective, context is the major explanation for both resistance to change and the adoption of new HRM approaches. The first assertion suggests that HRM activities have deep historical roots in the organization, so they cannot be understood completely without analyzing the organization's past. From the second assertion it follows that HRM activities may be adopted by an organization simply because other organizations have done so. Thus, "managerial fads and fashions" ebb and flow in part because a few legitimate organizations become fashion leaders that are imitated by other organizations that view imitation as a low-risk way to gain acceptance (Abrahamson 1991). Tolbert & Zucker (1983) showed, for example, that institutionalization resulting from imitation partially explained the rate at which reforms in civil service selection procedures spread throughout the country at the turn of the century.

RESOURCE DEPENDENCE THEORY   Like institutional theory, resource dependence theory focuses on the relationship between an organization and its constituencies. However, resource dependence theory emphasizes resource exchanges as the central feature of these relationships, rather than concerns about social acceptability and legitimacy (Pfeffer & Cohen 1984). According to this perspective, groups and organizations gain power over each other by controlling valued resources. Furthermore, HRM activities and processes are assumed to reflect the distribution of power within a system. For example, personnel departments acquire power over other departments to the extent they make others dependent upon them by controlling the flow of human resources into and through the organization (Osterman 1984, 1992; Pfeffer & Cohen 1984). Thus this theoretical perspective is somewhat similar to an interactionist perspective within psychology in that the actor (an organization or unit) and the environment work in conjunction as explanations for the behavior of the actor.

Institutional theory and resource dependence theory were developed in the context of understanding large public bureaucracies, where efficiency may not be among the most important goals (see Ostroff & Schmitt 1993). In contrast, the theories we discuss next—human capital theory, transaction costs theory, agency theory, and resource-based theory—were developed in the context of understanding business enterprises, for which issues of efficiency are presumed to be central.

HUMAN CAPITAL THEORY   In the economics literature, human capital refers to the productive capabilities of people (Becker 1964). Skills, experience, and knowledge have economic value to organizations because they enable it to be productive and adaptable; thus, people constitute the organization's human capital. Like other assets, human capital has value in the market place, but unlike other assets, the potential value of human capital can be fully realized only with the cooperation of the person. Therefore, all costs related to eliciting productive behaviors from employees—including those related to motivating, monitoring, and retaining them—constitute human capital investments made in anticipation of future returns (Flamholtz & Lacey 1981).

Organizations can use HRM in a variety of ways to increase their human capital (Cascio 1991, Flamholtz & Lacey 1981). For example, they can "buy" human capital in the market (e.g. by offering desirable compensation packages) or "make" it internally (e.g. by offering extensive training and development opportunities). Investments of either type have associated costs, which are justifiable only to the extent the organization is able to productively utilize the accumulated capital (Tsang et al 1991). In human capital theory, contextual factors such as market conditions, unions, business strategies, and technology are important because they can affect the costs associated with alternative approaches to using HRM to increase the value of the organization's human capital and the value of the anticipated returns, such as productivity gains (e.g. see Boudreau & Berger 1985, Russell et al 1993).

TRANSACTION COSTS THEORY   Transaction cost economics assumes that business enterprises choose governance structures that economize transaction costs associated with establishing, monitoring, evaluating, and enforcing agreed upon exchanges (Williamson 1979, 1981). Predictions about the nature of the governance structure an enterprise will use incorporate two behavioral assumptions: bounded rationality and opportunism (i.e. the seeking of self-interest with guile). These assumptions mean that the central problem to be solved by organizations is how to design governance structures that take advantage of bounded rationality while safeguarding against opportunism. To solve this problem, implicit and explicit contracts are established, monitored, enforced, and revised. The theory has direct implications for understanding how HRM practices are used to achieve a governance structure for managing the myriad implicit and explicit contracts between employers and employees (Wright & McMahan 1992). For example, organizations that require firm-specific knowledge and skills are predicted to create internal labor markets that bind self-interested and boundedly rational employees to the organization, while organizations that do not require these skills can gain efficiencies by competing for self-interested and boundedly rational talent in an external labor market (Williamson 1981, 1991). Contextual factors, in turn, partly determine whether the types and amounts of skills and knowledge a firm needs are likely to be available in the external labor market, the costs of acquiring them from the external market, the organization's capability for developing them internally, and the costs of doing so.

AGENCY THEORY   Agency theory focuses attention on the contracts between a party (i.e. the principal) who delegates work to another (i.e. the agent) (Jensen & Meckling 1976). Agency relations are problematic to the degree that (*a*) the principal and agent have conflicting goals and (*b*) it is difficult or expensive for the principal to monitor the agent's performance (Eisenhardt 1989). Contracts are used to govern such relations. Efficient contracts align the goals of principals and agents at the lowest possible cost. Costs can arise from providing incentives and obtaining information (e.g. about the agent's behavior and/or the agent's performance outcomes). Agency theory appears to be particularly useful for understanding executive and managerial compensation practices, which are viewed as a means for aligning the interests of the owners of a firm (i.e. principals) with the managers in whom they vest control (i.e. agents). For example, agency theory suggests several conditions under which contracts are more likely to monitor behavior (e.g. salary-plus-merit pay systems) and/or outcomes (e.g. commissions) (see Conlon & Parks 1990; Eisenhardt 1988, 1989; Milkovich et al 1991; Tosi & Gomez-Mejia 1989). Agency theory also has been used to predict occupation-based differences in job pricing methods (i.e. job evaluation vs market pricing) and in pay variability (Newman & Huselid 1992).

Agency and transaction costs theories share many similar assumptions about human behavior (Eisenhardt 1989) and may be most useful when combined. For example, using these two theories, Jones & Wright (1992) offer an insightful interpretation of the HRM literature focusing on implications of the economic perspective for HRM utility estimates. Their discussion suggests various reasons for predicting that the utility of HRM activities will vary with conditions in both the internal and external environments of organizations. Such conditions include the other human resource practices that are used by the organization, government regulations and their enforcement, technologies, union activities, and labor market conditions. These contextual factors can affect both the costs and potential gains associated with a particular human resource practice (e.g. a recruitment program, a selection test, or a training program).

RESOURCE-BASED THEORY   The resource-based theory of the firm blends concepts from organizational economics and strategic management (Barney 1991, Conner 1991). A fundamental assumption of this view is that organizations can be successful if they gain and maintain competitive advantage (see Porter 1985). Competitive advantage is gained by implementing a value-creating strategy that competitors cannot easily copy and sustain (Barney 1991) and for which there are no ready substitutes. For competitive advantage to be gained, two conditions are needed: First, the resources available to competing firms must be variable among competitors, and second, these resources must be immobile (i.e. not easily obtained). Three types of resources associated with organizations are (a) physical (plant; technology and equipment; geographic location), (b) human (employees' experience and knowledge), and (c) organizational (structure; systems for planning, monitoring, and controlling activities; social relations within the organization and between the organization and external constituencies). HRM greatly influences an organization's human and organizational resources and so can be used to gain competitive advantage (Schuler & MacMillan 1984). Presumably, the extent to which HRM can be used to gain competitive advantage, and the means of doing so, are partly determined by the environments in which organizations operate (Wright et al 1994). For example, in some industries, technologies can substitute for human resources, whereas in others the human element is fundamental to the business. To illustrate, contrast labor-intensive and knowledge-intensive industries. The latter context may be more conducive to the use of HRM as a means to gain competitive advantage.

CONCLUSION   This brief and selective overview of theoretical perspectives is intended to facilitate the reader's understanding and interpretation of some of the empirical research we review below. In addition, we believe these perspectives can inform new research on HRM in Context. Although many of the internal and external factors considered below are likely to be related, few studies control for all possible interdependencies; similarly, we treat the contextual factors as if they are independent while recognizing that this approach is overtly simplistic.

REVIEW OF EMPIRICAL RESEARCH

HRM and the Internal Contexts of Organizations

TECHNOLOGY   Technology refers to a system's processes for transforming inputs into usable outputs. These processes can vary along many dimensions, including the degree of continuity in the production system (e.g. Woodward 1965), the types and levels of knowledge required by the system (Hulin & Roznowski 1985), the degree to which tasks are routinized and predictable (Perrow 1967), and the linkages and interdependencies among tasks and people (Thompson 1967). The impact of technology on the social dynamics within organizations has long been recognized, but only recently have US researchers begun to address systematically the implications of technology for HRM (Katzell 1994).

Following human capital theory and a systems theory view of the relationship between human and technical subsystems, Snell & Dean (1992) hypothesized that HRM would be directly influenced by the presence of advanced manufacturing technology (AMT), total quality management (TQM), and just-in-time inventory control (JIT). Using data from 512 manufacturing firms, they found that firms using traditional technologies were less likely than firms using AMT to engage in selective hiring, comprehensive training, developmental appraisal, and externally equitable compensation (see Clark 1993 for a similar conclusion). Jackson et al (1989) used the role behavior perspective to predict and explain why, compared to firms engaged in mass production, firms using technologies for flexible specialization were more likely to use performance appraisals in determining pay and training needs. Kozlowski & Hults (1987) did not directly invoke roles as explanatory constructs in their study of engineers, but the association they found between an organization's technical complexity and HRM indicative of a "climate for technical updating" also are consistent with the role behavior perspective. It appears that research informed by both role theory and human capital theory could improve our understanding of how technology shapes HRM, as well as the role of HRM in implementing new technology (e.g. see Zammuto & O'Connor 1992).

STRUCTURE   Organization structure describes the allocation of tasks and responsibilities among individuals and departments; it designates the nature and means of formal reporting relationships as well as the groupings of individuals within the organization (Child 1977). The structural forms generally recognized for domestic firms include functional departmentalization, product-based divisionalization, geographical divisionalization, and matrix organization (with dual reporting relationships). Different forms are presumed to result from and be associated with a variety of internal and external forces, including technological demands, organizational growth, environmental turbulence, and business strategy (e.g. see Randolph & Dess 1984). Furthermore, each structural form probably faces some unique challenges that have implications for HRM. For example, Jackson et al (1989) argued that divisionalized firms should be more likely than those structured around functional departments to emphasize results over process, reflecting greater integration across units and a more externally oriented focus. Consistent with this expectation, they found that divisionalized firms relied relatively more on stock ownership and bonuses for company-wide performance as components of their HRM systems.

Van Sluijs et al (1991) argued that HRM has been shaped by its evolution within the context of functionally departmentalized organizations. Congruent with functional departmentalization, the traditional approach to managing people focuses on selection, training, performance appraisal, and compensation for individuals in specific jobs versus, for example, team players employed as members of an organization (cf Bowen et al 1991). It also presumes hierarchies of control rather than horizontal work-flow sequences (cf Whyte 1991). A realization is emerging, however, that when organizations are (re)structured around teamwork (in place of individual performers), there are major consequences for HRM. For example, Klimoski & Jones (1994) suggest that organizations with team-based designs may need to use new methods of job analysis, assessment, recruitment, and socialization activities. Jackson et al (1994) argued that greater reliance on teams has been an important factor in generating more concern about the HRM implications of workforce diversity.

The impact of structure on HRM is particularly evident in discussions of multinational firms and international joint ventures. Structures for organizations that span across national borders include multinational, global, international, or transnational forms (Phatak 1992, Ghoshal & Bartlett 1990). These forms represent alternative solutions to the problems of differentiation, integration, uncertainty, and risk management in an international environment (SJ Kobrin, unpublished), and each form has unique implications for HRM (Dowling et al 1994, Kochan et al 1992). The fundamental challenge is how to use HRM to link globally dispersed units while also adapting to the societal requirements of host societies (Laurent 1986). Similar problems must be solved when firms from different countries collaborate in a joint venture (e.g. Schuler et al 1991, 1992; Schuler & van Sluijs 1992; Slocum & Lei 1993).

SIZE   Institutional theory suggests that larger organizations should adopt more sophisticated and socially responsive HRM activities because these more visible organizations are under more pressure to gain legitimacy. Economic theories suggest that, because of the costs associated with many aspects of HRM, acceptable economies of scale must be reached before sophisticated HRM systems can be implemented. Consistent with both perspectives, considerable evidence shows that HRM varies systematically with organization size.[1] Specifically, compared to smaller organizations, larger ones are more likely to (a) adopt due process procedures (Dobbin et al 1988); (b) adopt employee involvement practices (Lawler et al 1992); (c) rely less on temporary staff (Davis-Blake & Uzzi 1993); (d) use more sophisticated staffing (Terpstra & Rozell 1993) and training and development (Saari et al 1988) procedures, and have more highly developed internal labor markets (Baron et al 1986a, see also Ferris et al 1992); (e) pay their employees more (Mellow 1982), but also put more pay at risk through the use of bonuses and long-term incentives (Gerhart & Milkovich 1990); and (f) engage in drug testing (Guthrie & Olian 1991a).

LIFE CYCLE STAGES   The literature on organization life cycle stages directs attention to the changing managerial priorities that characterize organizations in various developmental stages such as start-up, growth, maturity, and perhaps decline and revival (Baird & Meshoulam 1988, Smith et al 1985). These changing priorities, in turn, have implications for HRM. For example, a description of how managerial roles change across phases of the organizational life cycle was used by Gerstein & Reisman (1983) to argue that selection criteria and assessment methods for top-level executives need to be matched to life cycle stages. Similarly, Datta & Guthrie (1994) suggested that the role requirements of CEOs in rapidly growing firms help explain why outsider CEOs are more likely to be hired during this phase. Ferris et al (1984) also used a role perspective to develop propositions regarding the staffing needs and their implications under conditions of decline. Research and theory relating life cycle stages to changes in managerial requirements presumes that managerial roles change across life cycle stages, but the validity of this assumption has not been established empirically, for example, through the use of systematic job analyses (Szilagyi & Schweiger 1984).

In the studies just described, the research questions address the types of employees who best match the needs of organizations in various life cycle stages. Other studies have addressed the issue of how much attention is directed toward staffing issues, and here economic arguments seem more relevant. For example, Buller & Napier (1993) found that CEOs and human resource executives in rapidly growing firms viewed recruitment and selec-

---

[1]   In HRM research, number of employees is the most commonly used size indicator, but financial indicators such as the dollar value of capital assets and/or the dollar value of sales also are reported sometimes.

tion as by far the most important aspect of HRM, whereas in mature firms there was more concern for a broad array of activities, such as those related to maintaining an internal labor market (see also Kotter & Sathe 1978). Economic explanations also have been used to predict and explain associations between life cycle stages and pay levels (see Gerhart & Milkovich 1992).

To date, empirical research on HRM and organizational life cycles has adopted a deterministic view, predicting that life cycle stage constrains and shapes HRM. But more complex contingency models also have been proposed. In these models, the assumption is that HRM reflects choices made by organizational decision makers; wise choices lead to a good fit between life cycle stage and HRM, which results, in turn, in organizational effectiveness (e.g. Cook & Ferris 1986, Lengnick-Hall & Lengnick-Hall 1988, Milliman et al 1991, Kozlowski et al 1993). The validity of such models has not been assessed empirically, however.

BUSINESS STRATEGY Typologies for characterizing the business strategies used by firms abound, but the two most frequently cited in discussions of HRM were proposed by Miles & Snow (1978) and Porter (1980, 1985). Miles & Snow classified organizations as prospectors, analyzers, or defenders (later, reactors were added). Prospectors actively seek new products and markets and, therefore, seek to grow; analyzers also seek to grow, but in a more stable and predictable way through the internal development of new products rather than creation of new markets; defenders seek to maintain the same limited product line with emphasis on high volume and low cost (Miles & Snow 1984). These postures toward the environment should have implications for the quantity and pace of human resource flows. Defenders, for instance, are less concerned about recruiting new applicants externally and more concerned about developing current employees. Therefore, performance appraisal is used more for developmental purposes than for evaluation (Snow & Snell 1993). In contrast, prospectors are growing and so are more concerned about recruiting and using performance appraisal results for evaluation rather than for longer-term development (Olian & Rynes 1984, see also Slocum et al 1985).

Porter's (1985) competitive strategies distinguish among firms that compete on the basis of cost leadership, product differentiation, and market focus. In a study of airlines, Johnson et al (1989) showed that, in a deregulated environment, wage rates were related significantly to which of these strategies airlines pursued. In an adaptation of Porter's typology, Schuler & Jackson (1987a) used the role behavior perspective to describe the possible HRM implications of cost-reduction, innovation, and quality enhancement strategies. Jackson et al (1989) supported Schuler & Jackson's argument that, because an innovation strategy requires risk-taking and tolerance of inevitable failures,

HRM in firms pursuing this strategy should be used to give employees a sense of security and encourage a long-term orientation. Peck (1994) and Milkovich et al (1991) also support a relationship between an innovation strategy and the use of HRM to support a longer-term orientation. Consistent with predictions regarding behaviors needed for a quality strategy is Cowherd & Levine's (1992) finding that egalitarian pay structures are associated with greater product quality.

This brief review of the strategic HRM literature is by no means exhaustive (e.g. see Lengnick-Hall & Lengnick-Hall 1988) and does not fully consider the possible complexity of and alternative models for describing the relationship between strategy and HRM (e.g. see Kerr 1985, Snow & Snell 1993), but the studies clearly support the assertion that strategy is a contextual factor with important implications for HRM. Thus, we are especially optimistic about recent efforts to establish linkages between strategic considerations and psychologically oriented HRM research on selection and utility (see Russell et al 1993).

HRM and the External Contexts of Organizations

LEGAL, SOCIAL, AND POLITICAL ENVIRONMENTS   Within the United States, almost all aspects of HRM are affected by the legal and regulatory environment. In the process of attending to the legal environment, the field also responds to the social and political environments that give rise to and shape the promulgation, interpretation, and enforcement of acts of Congress, executive orders, tax codes, and even funding for HRM innovations (see Cascio 1992, Landy et al 1994, Mahoney 1987, Miller & O'Leary 1989, Noe & Ford 1992, Sharf 1994, Wigdor & Sackett 1993). As US corporations expand their operations abroad, however, they face additional legal concerns. For example, in European countries, organizations are obliged to set aside specific sums of money for formal training and development (Brewster et al 1993). And for corporations that employ expatriates abroad, immigration and taxation treaties can influence staffing decisions (Dowling et al 1994). Global corporations also encounter additional social and political realities. For example, in some countries, civil laws and religious laws coexist and jointly define a legal context for HRM (Florkowski & Nath 1993). Looking ahead, institutional theory and resource dependence theory appear to be particularly useful guides for research on how the legal, social, and political environments impact HRM (see Konrad & Linnehan 1992). Potential topics for investigation include the conditions and processes that facilitate or inhibit the adoption and transfer of HRM innovations (e.g. see Johns 1993) and the feedback processes through which the HRM activities of organizations create changes in their social, legal, and political environments.

UNIONIZATION   In the United States, unionized employees have received wages estimated to be up to 33% greater than those of nonunion employees, and unions are often credited with improving working conditions and safety (Lawler & Mohrman 1987). Unions give voice to their members; establish policies and procedures for handling wage and working condition grievances; provide for job security; and secure health and retirement benefits (Baron et al 1986b, Freeman & Medoff 1984, Jackson et al 1989, Kochan et al 1992, Youngblood et al 1992). In addition to helping their own members, unions have probably motivated nonunion employers to provide many of these same benefits (Foulkes 1980). Nevertheless, recent years have witnessed a decline in unionization due to the environmental forces of deregulation, international competition, and the shift to a service economy. Consequently, some unions have moved out of their traditional collective bargaining roles and adversarial relationships with management and are beginning to work cooperatively on issues such as plant designs and locations (Adler 1993, Lewandowski & MacKinnon 1992, Noble 1993, Woodruff 1993); work team design (Lawler & Mohrman 1987); team-oriented pay plans such as gainsharing and employee ownership (Miller & Schuster 1987, Rosen et al 1986); recruitment and selection procedures including selecting members for representation on the board of directors (Collins et al 1993); retraining and relocation (Hoerr 1991, Marshall 1992); and quality improvement (Bognanno & Kleiner 1992, Brett et al 1990, Lawler et al 1992, Reid 1992). Changing union-management relations mean that researchers can no longer simply compare union to nonunion firms. Now they must also take into consideration whether union-management relations with each firm are adversarial or cooperative (e.g. see Cutcher-Gershenfeld 1991).

As the process of globalizing unfolds, both unions and multinational enterprises (MNEs) are recognizing that they need to understand how the institutions of union-management relations and collective bargaining differ around the world (Dowling et al 1994). Prahalad & Doz (1987) found that lack of such understanding often results in conflicts between MNE managers and local communities. To facilitate adaptation to local conditions, it helps US MNEs to know, for example, that in Europe the collective bargaining process and class struggle are more intertwined than they are in the United States (Bournois & Chauchat 1990; Marginson 1992; Poole 1986a,b), and labor institutions are often much stronger (Ofori-Dankwa 1994, Western 1993). MNEs must consider these histories and institutions when developing company-wide human resource philosophies, policies, and practices (Hamill 1983). HRM researchers on almost every topic also must recognize, understand, and incorporate these realities into their work (Kochan et al 1992) if it is to be useful for organizations operating in a global context.

LABOR MARKET CONDITIONS   Labor market conditions can be characterized along several dimensions including unemployment levels, labor diversity, and labor market structure. Unemployment levels and labor market structures have long been recognized as important macroeconomic variables, whereas the importance of labor diversity has been recognized more recently.

Unemployment levels reflect the demand for labor relative to the supply. Macroeconomic research conducted at the national level indicates that in the capitalist United States, excess demand typically results in low unemployment while excess supply typically results in high unemployment. Furthermore, as unemployment drops, wages and costs increase and profits and investments decline; these conditions, in turn, reduce demand for labor (Levine & Tyson 1990). Conversely, as unemployment rises, absenteeism and turnover rates tend to decrease (Kerr 1954, Markham 1985) and the link between employee dissatisfaction and turnover is weakened (Carsten & Spector 1987).

Perhaps because recruitment activities regulate organizational inputs, recruitment researchers have been more sensitive than others to the potential importance of unemployment levels (Rynes 1991, Rynes & Barber 1990). Consistent with transaction costs theory, recruitment strategies appear to vary with unemployment levels. When the labor supply is tight, organizations use more expensive and intensive recruiting methods (Hanssens & Levien 1983), increase the geographic scope of their recruitment activities (Malm 1955), and appear to forego preemployment drug screening (Bennett et al 1994). Other responses to a tight labor supply include improving wages, benefits, and working conditions in order to attract and retain employees (Lakhani 1988) and reducing hiring standards as a means to fill vacant positions (Thurow 1975). Such responses to the labor pool may have significant implications for other human resource practices (e.g. lower selection standards may mean that more training is needed). Thus, the consequences of the external environment may ultimately include fundamental changes in the nature of the employment relationship (e.g. see Levine & Tyson 1990).

The US labor market is evolving toward greater diversity in terms of gender, age, and ethnicity (Johnston & Packer 1987, see also Triandis et al 1994b), although demographic diversity varies markedly among occupations and across status levels. The implications of increasing diversity have been mostly ignored by HRM researchers, as have the implications of differing degrees of homogeneity across segments of the labor market (cf Katzell 1994, Triandis et al 1994b). This is somewhat surprising, given the field's long history of research on bias and discrimination and substantial evidence showing that feelings, cognitions, and behaviors are all influenced by conditions of group homogeneity vs diversity (see Cox 1993, Jackson et al 1994). These effects undoubtedly have consequences for recruitment, selection, and attrition (see Jackson et al 1991, Pfeffer 1983, Schneider 1987); socialization (Jackson et al 1993); training, development, and mentoring (Morrison 1992, Ohlott et al 1994, Powell & Butterfield 1994, Thomas 1993); and perhaps assessment and reward systems (Pfeffer & Langton 1988). To date, however, the HRM implications of increasing diversity have received relatively more attention from large businesses than from academic researchers. Large businesses are experimenting with a variety of HRM interventions in order to adjust systems that evolved in the context of relative homogeneity to fit the new conditions of relative diversity (e.g. see Jackson & Associates 1992, Morrison & Crabtree 1992, Morrison et al 1993, Zedeck 1992).

The above discussion regarding how unemployment levels can impact HRM implicitly assumes a labor market structure that is undifferentiated. But stratification of the external labor market as well as the internal labor market along the somewhat related dimensions of price and status is acknowledged widely; methods of recruitment, forms of compensation, severance arrangements, employee autonomy, and numerous other aspects of HRM are known to differ as one moves up through price and status levels (e.g. Guthrie & Olian 1991a, Osterman 1984, Rynes 1991, Schuler & Jackson 1987b). Substantial evidence suggests that HRM systems differ across occupational groups, reflecting occupational subcultures that vary in their orientations toward work, control, and authority structures, self-identification, and career expectations (Althauser 1989, Bridges & Villemez 1991, Sonnenstuhl & Trice 1991, Van Maanen & Barley 1984). Thus, even if firms have a single HRM philosophy and a single set of HRM policies, these are likely to manifest themselves in different practices across subgroups of employees. By extension, the "same" HRM intervention should be expected to be differentially interpreted and received across these subgroups.

INDUSTRY CHARACTERISTICS   The term "industry" refers to a distinct group of productive or profit-making enterprises. A full discussion of how HRM is affected by industry-level factors would consider HRM in the public vs private sectors (Rosen et al 1986, Molnar & Rogers 1976), in regulated vs unregulated industries (Guthrie & Olian 1991b, Guthrie et al 1991, Johnson et al 1989), and in industries characterized by high vs low stability or change (Ghoshal & Bartlett 1990, Evans 1992), among other topics. Due to space limitations, only the simple classification of manufacturing vs service industries is discussed below.

Bowen & Schneider (1988) described three characteristics that distinguish the activities of services from manufacturing organizations: First, a service is generally intangible; second, in services the customer and employee usually collaborate in the service production-and-delivery process; third, in services, production and consumption are usually simultaneous. Because customers play a central role in services, they can be thought of as partial employees who are subject to human resource management (Bowen 1986, Mills & Morris 1986). Consistent with this notion, Jackson & Schuler (1992) found that employers in the service sector were more likely to include customers as sources of input for performance appraisal. Differences in the nature of manufacturing and service also appear to have implications for other aspects of HRM systems, including recruitment and selection, training, compensation, stress management, use of temporary workers, and the development and maintenance of appropriate organizational climates and cultures (see Davis-Blake & Uzzi 1993, Delaney et al 1989, Guthrie & Olian 1991a, Jackson & Schuler 1992, Jackson 1984, Schneider et al 1992, Terpstra & Rozell 1993).

In summary, although not yet widely incorporated into research paradigms, industry characteristics may have far-reaching implications for HRM. Industries, like national cultures, are the contexts within which meanings are construed, effectiveness is defined, and behaviors are evaluated (e.g. see Hofstede 1991).

NATIONAL CULTURE   The globalization of national economies and the evolution of multinational enterprises have resulted in increased awareness and documentation of the differences in how human resources are managed among countries (Brewster & Hegewisch 1994, Towers Perrin 1992). Because countries often have unique cultures (i.e. values, norms, and customs) it is widely presumed that multinational enterprises must understand the culture(s) of the region(s) in which they operate in order to effectively manage their human resources.

The most widely known framework for comparing national cultures is that developed by Hofstede (1980), who identified four dimensions of culture: individualism, masculinity, uncertainty avoidance, and power distance. A fifth dimension, time orientation, has been added more recently, but most available research considers only the four original dimensions (Hofstede 1993). Other authors have identified additional dimensions of culture, including informality, materialism, and change orientation (Adler 1991, Phatak 1992, Ronen 1994).

There has been considerable speculation about the possible implications for HRM of cultural variations along these dimensions (Erez & Earley 1993, Mendoca & Kanungo 1994, Slocum & Lei 1993), but empirical studies seldom include direct measures of both culture and HRM. Instead, researchers generally have compared HRM across countries and then argued that cultural values and orientations are determinants of the differences found (see Arvey et al 1991, Bhagat et al 1990, Brewster & Tyson 1991, Begin 1992, Carroll 1988, Eberwien & Tholen 1993, Erez 1994, Hickson 1993, Maruyama 1992, Yu &

Murphy 1993). It must be recognized, however, that culture may not explain all HRM differences found across countries (Lincoln 1993). Country differences may also be the result of differences in economic and political systems (e.g. Carroll et al 1988), laws and regulations (e.g. Florkowski & Nath 1993), industrial relations systems (Strauss 1982), and labor market conditions (e.g. Lévy-Leboyer 1994). Recently, Hofstede (1991) even suggested that organizational and industry characteristics may be more important than national cultures as determinants of managerial practices and employee behaviors. This argument is consistent with evidence that some types of HRM systems can be used effectively across countries that are culturally quite dissimilar (MacDuffie & Krafcik 1992, Wickens 1987). Our understanding of the role of national culture in HRM could benefit from investigations that focus on the question of how globally expanding companies develop HRM systems that are simultaneously consistent with multiple and distinct local cultures and yet internally consistent in the context of a single organization (cf Heenan & Perlmutter 1979, Phatak 1992, Schwartz 1992, Tung 1993).

AN INTEGRATIVE PERSPECTIVE FOR RESEARCH ON HRM IN CONTEXT

Figure 1 represents a summary view of the many relationships between context and HRM described in this review. The relationships we described are depicted as part of a larger model, which includes several important components that are beyond the focus of our discussion. The component labeled "Sense-making and Decision-making" has been the subject of a growing body of research that investigates how and why organization leaders, acting individually and in concert, characterize and interpret their environments, and the implications of these processes for eventual action (e.g. Hambrick 1994, Jackson 1992, Jackson & Dutton 1988). In our integrative model of HRM, these processes are assumed to be intimately bound with the implicit and explicit prioritizing of objectives. These, in turn, are translated into HRM philosophies, programs, and practices (Schuler 1992). In other words, our model presumes that the phenomena represented in the left-most box in Figure 1 are key mediators that help explain vertical linkages between context and HRM.

Individual-, organizational-, and societal-level outcomes (right-most boxes in Figure 1) are also major components of an integrative model. A list of specific outcomes could be readily derived by readers familiar with the scientific and practice-oriented HRM literature. We wish to encourage interested researchers to expand their conceptualizations of outcomes to go beyond individual-level behavior in work settings. In addition, outcomes that describe small and large groups (e.g. groups, organizations, society) should be consid-

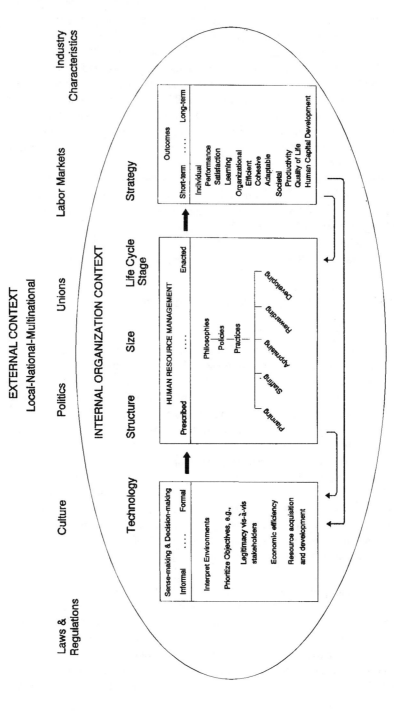

Figure 1 Integrative framework for understanding HRM in Context. Copyright by SE Jackson & RS Schuler. Used with permission.

ered and the phenomena studied should reflect the reality that HRM activities may affect outcomes beyond the traditional boundaries of the target organization (e.g. families, schools, communities).

Understanding and advancing HRM in Context requires an integrative perspective that recognizes and incorporates all of the relationships depicted in Figure 1. Within the discipline of psychology, however, linkages involving the macro-level internal and external environments have been largely ignored. Fortunately, a realization is now emerging that this state of affairs should not continue. Much research is needed to understand how internal and external environments shape (a) the nature of human resource philosophies, policies, and practices; (b) the employee behaviors and attitudes that should be valued, and which are likely to be exhibited; (c) the criteria that define employee effectiveness and achieved levels of employee effectiveness; and (d) the criteria that define organizational effectiveness and achieved levels of organizational effectiveness. In addition, future research needs to recognize that contexts may moderate the observed relationships between HRM and various outcomes.

Our review of the literature has revealed to us how seldom research addresses the horizontal linkages among HRM activities, although such linkages are implied by most of the theories we reviewed and, we would argue, by most psychological theories about employee attitudes and behaviors. Employees do not respond to specific human resource policies and practices in isolation. They attend to and interpret the entire array of information available and from this they discern cultural values and behavioral norms. Unfortunately, we know surprisingly little about how various combinations of human resource policies and practices are interpreted by employees, nor do we know how complex HRM systems influence the attitudes and behaviors of current and potential organizational members. Our understanding of vertical linkages between HRM and contexts cannot proceed without attending to the horizontal interdependencies that exist among human resource policies and practices.

Theory-Driven Research

The theories we have identified represent possible explanations for some of the empirical relationships between environmental conditions and HRM, but the available theories are admittedly inadequate. Each deals with pieces of the larger phenomenon and none addresses the whole domain of HRM in Context. Thus, in the near future, the best work will be informed by multiple theoretical perspectives. Furthermore, because the theories we have discussed were generally not formulated specifically for the purpose of understanding HRM in Context, some translation and adaptation of these theories may be required. This translation process is likely to proceed in iterative steps, with consensus emerging slowly. Nevertheless, research driven by incomplete theories is more likely to accumulate to form a meaningful body of knowledge, compared to research driven by no theory at all.

Methodological Issues

Although imperfect, potentially useful theories are relatively plentiful. Much less plentiful are psychometrically sound, agreed-upon approaches for measuring relevant constructs and testing key theoretical propositions. Through methodological contributions, industrial-organizational psychology is in an excellent position to contribute to the advance of knowledge about HRM in Context. Contributions will not come through "research as usual," however. Several shifts in approach will be required: from treating organizational settings as sources of error variance to attending as closely to them as we have traditionally attended to individual characteristics; from focusing on individuals to treating social systems as the target for study; from focusing on single practices or policies to adopting a holistic approach to conceptualizing HRM systems; from research conducted in single organizations at one point in time to research comparing multiple organizations and/or studying dynamic changes in organizations across times and places; and from a search for the "one best way" to a search for the fundamental features that characterize the many possible ways to design and maintain effective systems.

These shifts in perspective are fundamental in many respects. In other respects, however, they require little more than a change from defining the essential features of situations as jobs (as industrial-organizational psychology often does) to a recognition that jobs are merely the first level of context in a many-level complex system of contexts. By extension, we would argue that future HRM research should elevate organization analysis (and perhaps extra-organization analysis) to a status equal to that currently enjoyed by job analysis. We already understand and act on the principle that effective selection systems, performance appraisal methods, compensation plans, and training programs cannot be developed without a scientifically valid diagnosis of the job-as-situation. Similarly, the design of effective HRM systems cannot be developed without a valid diagnosis of the organization-as-situation.[2] Current methods for conducting job analysis are not adequate for conducting organizational analysis. However, if motivated to do so, thoughtful researchers undoubtedly could apply the principles of sound job analysis for the purpose of developing sophisticated methods for measuring organizational contexts.

2

   This principle is, of course, widely accepted in the training literature—but it is also widely ignored.

Also needed are measurement tools that capture the essential features of HRM philosophies, policies, and practices, while yielding information that facilitates meaningful comparisons among organizations and across environmental contexts. Research that simply identifies and describes the most common configurations of prescribed HRM systems and the most common forms of received HRM should serve as the foundation for future investigations of HRM in Context. Ideally, such research will reflect the reality of rapid globalization and the international context of most large organizations. Indeed, globalization may be the most potent catalyst for an explosion of research on HRM in Context: for those operating in a global environment, the importance of context is undeniable—it cannot be ignored. Multinational organizations strive for consistency in their ways of managing people on a worldwide basis while also adapting their ways to the specific cultural requirements of different societies (Laurent 1986). To meet this challenge, those responsible for the design of globally effective HRM must shift their focus away from the almost overwhelming variety of specific practices and policies found around the world and look instead at the more abstract, fundamental dimensions of contexts, HRM systems, and dimensions of employees' reactions (e.g. see Fulkerson & Schuler 1992). If they succeed in identifying these dimensions and the relationships between them, they may be able to more easily design HRM systems that can be used effectively in multiple country locations (e.g. see MacDuffie & Krafcik 1992).

Literature Cited

Abrahamson E. 1991. Managerial fads and fashions: the diffusion and rejection of innovations. *Acad. Manage. Rev.* 16:586–612

Adler NJ. 1991. *International Dimensions of Organizational Behavior.* Boston: PWS-Kent

Adler PS. 1993. Time-and-motion regained. *Harvard Bus. Rev.* 73:97

Althauser RP. 1989. Internal labor markets. *Annu. Rev. Sociol.* 15:143–61

Arvey RD, Bhagat RS, Salas E. 1991. Cross-cultural and cross-national issues in personnel and human resources management: Where do we go from here? *Res. Pers. Hum. Res. Manage.* 9:367–407

Baird L, Meshoulam I. 1988. Managing the two fits of strategic human resource management. *Acad. Manage. Rev.* 13:116–28

Barney J. 1991. Firm resources and sustained competitive advantage. *J. Manage.* 17:99–120

Baron JN, Davis-Blake A, Bielby W. 1986a. The structure of opportunity: how promotion ladders vary within and among organizations. *Admin. Sci. Q.* 31:248–73

Baron JN, Dobbin FR, Jennings PD. 1986b. War and peace: the evolution of modern personnel administration in US industry. *Am. J. Sociol.* 92:350–83

Becker GS. 1964. *Human Capital.* New York: Natl. Bur. Econ. Res.

Begin JP. 1991. *Strategic Employment Policy.* Englewood Cliffs, NJ: Prentice-Hall

Begin JP. 1992. Comparative human resource management (HRM): a systems perspective. *Int. J. Hum. Res. Manage.* 3:379–408

Bennett N, Blum TC, Roman PM. 1994. Presence of drug screening and employee assistance programs: exclusive and inclusive human resource management practices. *J. Organ. Behav.* 15: In press

Bhagat RS, Kedia BL, Crawford SE, Kaplan MR. 1990. Cross-cultural issues in organizational psychology: emergent trends and directions for research in the 1990's. *Int. Rev. Ind. Organ. Psychol.* 5:196–231

Bognanno M, Kleiner M. 1992. Introduction: labor market institutions and the future role of unions. *Ind. Relat.* 31:1–12

Boudreau JW, Berger CJ. 1985. Decision-theoretic utility analysis applied to employee separations and acquisitions. *J. Appl. Psychol.* 70:581–612

Bournois F, Chauchat J-H. 1990. Managing managers. *Eur. Manage. J.* 8:56–71

Bowen DE. 1986. Managing customers as human resources in service organizations. *Hum. Res. Manage.* 25:371–83

Bowen DE, Ledford GE Jr, Nathan BR. 1991. Hiring for the organization, not the job. *Acad. Manage. Exec.* 5(4):35–51

Bowen DE, Schneider B. 1988. Services marketing and management: implications for organizational behavior. *Res. Organ. Behav.* 10:43–80

Brett JM, Goldberg SB, Ury WL. 1990. Designing systems for resolving disputes in organizations. *Am. Psychol.* 45:162–70

Bretz R Jr, Milkovich G, Read W. 1992. The current state of performance appraisal research and practice: concerns, directions, and implications. *J. Manage.* 18:111–37

Brewster C, Hegewisch A, Lockhart T, Holden L, eds. 1993. *The European Human Resource Management Guide.* New York: Academic

Brewster C, Hegewisch A, eds. 1994. *Policy and Practice in European Human Resource Management.* London: Routledge

Brewster C, Tyson S, eds. 1991. *International Comparisons in Human Resource Management.* London: Pitman

Bridges WP, Villemez WJ. 1991. Employment relations and the labor market: integrating institutional and market perspectives. *Am. Sociol. Rev.* 56:748–64

Buller PF, Napier NK. 1993. Strategy and human resource management integration in fast growth versus other mid-sized firms. *Br. J. Manage.* 4:273–91

Carroll GR, Delacroix J, Goodstein J. 1988. The political environments of organizations: an ecological view. *Res. Organ. Behav.* 10:359–92

Carroll SJ. 1988. Asian HRM philosophies and systems: Can they meet our changing HRM needs? In *Personnel and Human Resource Management,* ed. RS Schuler, SA Youngblood, VL Huber, pp. 442–55. St. Paul, MN: West

Carsten JM, Spector PE. 1987. Unemploy-

ment, job satisfaction, and employee turnover: a meta-analytic test of the Muchinsky Model. *J. Appl. Psychol.* 72:374–81

Cascio WF. 1991. *Costing Human Resource: The Financial Impact of Behavior in Organizations.* Boston: PWS-Kent

Cascio WF. 1992. Reconciling economic and social objectives in personnel selection: impact of alternative decision rules. *New Approaches Empl. Manage.: Fairness Empl. Sel.* 1:61–86

Child J. 1977. *Organization.* New York: Harper & Row

Clark J. 1993. Managing people in a time of technical change: conclusions and implications. In *Human Resource Management and Technical Change,* ed. J Clark, pp. 212–22. Newbury Park, CA: Sage

Collins D, Hatcher L, Ross TL. 1993. The decision to implement gainsharing: the role of work climate, expected outcomes, and union status. *Pers. Psychol.* 46:77–104

Conlon E, Parks J. 1990. The effects of monitoring and tradition on compensation arrangements: an experiment on principal/agent dyads. *Acad. Manage. J.* 3: 603–22

Conner KR. 1991. A historical perspective of resource-based theory and five schools of thought within industrial organization economics: Do we need a new theory of the firm? *J. Manage.* 17:121–54

Cook DS, Ferris GR. 1986. Strategic human resource management and firm effectiveness in industries experiencing decline. *Hum. Res. Manage.* 25:441–58

Cowherd DM, Levine DI. 1992. Product quality and pay equity between lower-level employees and top management: an investigation of distributive justice theory. *Admin. Sci. Q.* 37:302–20

Cox T Jr. 1993. *Cultural Diversity in Organizations: Theory, Research and Practice.* San Francisco: Berrett-Koehler

Cutcher-Gershenfeld J. 1991. The impact on economic performance of a transformation in workplace relations. *Ind. Labor Relat. Rev.* 44:241–60

Datta DK, Guthrie JP. 1994. Executive succession: organizational antecedents of CEO characteristics. *Strat. Manage. J.* In press

Davis-Blake A, Uzzi B. 1993. Determinants of employment externalization: a study of temporary workers and independent contractors. *Admin. Sci. Q.* 38:195–223

Delaney JT, Lewin D, Ichniowski C. 1989. *Human Resource Policies and Practices in American Firms.* Washington, DC: US Dept. Labor, US Govt. Print. Off.

Denison D. 1990. *Corporate Culture and Organizational Effectiveness.* New York: Wiley

DiMaggio PJ, Powell WW. 1983. The iron cage revisited: institutional isomorphism and collective rationality in organizational fields. *Am. Sociol. Rev.* 35:147–60

Dobbin FR, Edelman L, Meyer JW, Scott WR, Swidler A. 1988. The expansion of due process in organizations. In *Institutional Patterns and Organizations: Culture and Environment,* ed. LG Zucker, pp. 71–98. Cambridge, MA: Ballinger

Dobbins GH, Cardy RL, Carson KP. 1991. Examining fundamental assumptions: a contrast of person and system approaches to human resource management. *Res. Pers. Hum. Res. Manage.* 9:1–38

Dowling PJ, Schuler RS, Welch DE. 1994. *International Dimensions of Human Resource Management.* Belmont, CA: Wadsworth

Eberwein W, Tholen J. 1993. Euro-manager or splendid isolation? *Int. Manage.—An Anglo-German Comparison* 9:266

Eisenhardt KM. 1988. Agency and institutional explanations of compensation in retail sales. *Acad. Manage. J.* 31:488–511

Eisenhardt KM. 1989. Agency theory: an assessment and review. *Acad. Manage. Rev.* 14:57–74

Erez M. 1994. Towards a model of cross-cultural I/O psychology. See Triandis et al 1994a, pp. 559–608

Erez M, Earley PC. 1993. *Culture, Self-Identity, and Work.* New York: Oxford Univ. Press

Evans P. 1992. Management development as glue technology. *Hum. Res. Plan.* 15:85–106

Ferris GR, Buckley MR, Allen GM. 1992. Promotion systems in organizations. *Hum. Res. Plan.* 15:47–68

Ferris GR, Schellenberg DA, Zammuto RF. 1984. Human resource management strategies in declining industries. *Hum. Res. Manage.* 23: 381–94

Flamholtz EG, Lacey JM. 1981. *Personnel Management, Human Capital Theory, and Human Resource Accounting.* Los Angeles: Inst. Ind. Relat., Univ. Calif.

Florkowski GW, Nath R. 1993. MNC responses to the legal environment of international human resource management. *Int. J. Hum. Res. Manage.* 4:305–24

Foulkes FK. 1980. *Personnel Policies in Large Nonunion Companies.* Englewood Cliffs, NJ: Prentice-Hall

Frederiksen N. 1986. Toward a broader conception of human intelligence. *Am. Psychol.* 41:445–52

Freeman RB, Medoff JL. 1984. *What Do Unions Do?* New York: Basic

Fulkerson JR, Schuler RS. 1992. Managing worldwide diversity at Pepsi-Cola International. In *Diversity in the Workplace: Human Resources Initiatives,* ed. SE Jackson, pp. 248–76. New York: Guilford

Gerhart B, Milkovich GT. 1990. Organiza-

tional differences in managerial compensation and financial performance. *Acad. Manage. J.* 33:663–91

Gerhart B, Milkovich GT. 1992. Employee compensation: research and practice. In *Handbook of Industrial and Organizational Psychology,* ed. HC Triandis, MD Dunnette, LM Hough, 3:481–569. Palo Alto, CA: Consult. Psychol.

Gerstein M, Reisman H. 1983. Strategic selection: matching executives to business conditions. *Sloan Manage. Rev.* 24:33–49

Ghoshal S, Bartlett CA. 1990. The multinational corporation as an interorganizational network. *Acad. Manage. Rev.* 15:603–25

Guthrie JP, Grimm CM, Smith KG. 1991. Environmental change and management staffing: an empirical study. *J. Manage.* 17:735–48

Guthrie JP, Olian JD. 1991a. Drug and alcohol testing programs: Do firms consider their operating environment? *Hum. Res. Plan.* 14:221–32

Guthrie JP, Olian JD. 1991b. Does context affect staffing decisions? The case of general managers. *Pers. Psychol.* 44:283–96

Hambrick DC. 1994. Top management groups: a conceptual integration and reconsideration of the "team" label. *Res. Org. Behav.* 16:171–214

Hamill J. 1983. The labor relations practices of foreign-owned and indigenous firms. *Empl. Relat.* 5:14–16

Hansen GS, Wernerfelt B. 1989. Determinants of firm performance: relative importance of economic and organizational factors. *Strat. J. Manage.* 10:399–411

Hanssens DM, Levien HA. 1983. An econometric study of recruitment marketing in the US Navy. *Manage. Sci.* 29:1167–84

Heenan DA, Perlmutter HV. 1979. *Multinational Organization Development.* Reading, MA: Addison-Wesley

Hickson DJ. 1993. Management in Western Europe. *Soc. Cult. Org. Twelve Nations* 14:290

Hoerr J. 1991. What should unions do? *Harvard Bus. Rev.* May-June:30–45

Hofstede G. 1980. *Cultures Consequences.* Beverly Hills, CA: Sage

Hofstede G. 1991. *Cultures and Organizations.* London: McGraw-Hill

Hofstede G. 1993. Cultural constraints in management theories. *Acad. Manage. Exec.* 7: 81–94

Hulin CL, Roznowski M. 1985. Organizational technologies: effects on organizations' characteristics and individuals' responses. *Res. Organ. Behav.* 7:39–85

Jackson SE. 1984. Organizational practices for preventing burnout. In *Handbook of Organizational Stress Coping Strategies,* ed. AS Sethi, RS Schuler, pp. 89–111. Cambridge, MA: Ballinger

Jackson SE. 1992. Consequences of group composition for the interpersonal dynamics of strategic issue processing. *Adv. Strat. Manage.* 8:345–82

Jackson SE, Associates, eds. 1992. *Diversity in the Workplace: Human Resources Initiatives.* New York: Guilford

Jackson SE, Brett JF, Sessa VI, Cooper DM, Julin JA, Peyronnin K. 1991. Some differences make a difference: individual dissimilarity and group heterogeneity as correlates of recruitment, promotions and turnover. *J. Appl. Psychol.* 76:675–89

Jackson SE, Dutton JE. 1988. Discerning threats and opportunities. *Admin. Sci. Q.* 33:370–87

Jackson SE, May KE, Whitney K. 1994. Understanding the dynamics of diversity in decision making teams. In *Team Decision Making Effectiveness in Organizations,* ed. RA Guzzo, E Salas. San Francisco, CA: Jossey-Bass. In press

Jackson SE, Schuler RS. 1992. HRM practices in service-based organizations: a role theory perspective. *Adv. Serv. Mark. Manage.* 1:123–57

Jackson SE, Schuler RS, Rivero JC. 1989. Organizational characteristics as predictors of personnel practices. *Pers. Psychol.* 42:727–86

Jackson SE, Stone VK, Alvarez EB. 1993. Socialization amidst diversity: the impact of demographics on work team oldtimers and newcomers. *Res. Organ. Behav.* 15:45–109

James LR, Demaree RG, Mulaik SA, Ladd RT. 1992. Validity generalization in the context of situational models. *J. Appl. Psychol.* 77:3–14

Jensen M, Meckling W. 1976. Theory of the firm: managerial behavior, agency costs, and ownership structure. *J. Financ. Econ.* 3:305–60

Johns G. 1993. Constraints on the adoption of psychology-based personnel practices: lessons from organizational innovation. *Pers. Psychol.* 46:569–91

Johnson NB, Sambharya RB, Bobko P. 1989. Deregulation, business strategy, and wages in the airline industry. *Ind. Relat.* 28:419–30

Johnston WB, Packer AE. 1987. *Workforce 2000: Work and Workers for the 21st Century.* Washington, DC: US Dept. Labor

Jones GR, Wright PM. 1992. An economic approach to conceptualizing the utility of human resource management practices. *Res. Pers. Hum. Res. Manage.* 10:271–99

Katz D, Kahn RL. 1978. *The Social Psychology of Organizations.* New York: Wiley

Katzell RA. 1994. Contemporary meta-trends in industrial and organizational psychology. See Triandis et al 1994a, pp. 1–89

Kaufman R. 1992. The effects of IM-

PROSHARE on productivity. *Ind. Labor Relat. Rev.* 45:311–22

Kerr C. 1954. The Balkanization of labor markets. In *Labor Mobility and Economic Opportunity,* ed. EW Bakke, PM Hauser, GL Palmer, CA Myers, D Yoder, C Kerr, pp. 93–109. New York: Wiley

Kerr JL. 1985. Diversification strategies and managerial rewards: an empirical study. *Acad. Manage. J.* 28:155–79

Klimoski RJ, Jones RG. 1994. Suppose we took staffing for effective group decision making seriously? In *Team Decision Making Effectiveness in Organizations,* ed. RA Guzzo, E Salas. San Francisco, CA: Jossey-Bass. In press

Kochan TA, Batt R, Dyer L. 1992. International human resource studies: a framework for future research in research frontiers. In *Industrial Relations and Human Resources,* ed. D Lewin, OS Mitchell, PD Sherer, pp. 147–67. Madison, WI: Ind. Relat. Res. Assoc.

Konrad AM, Linnehan F. 1992. The implementation and effectiveness of equal opportunity employment. In *Best Papers Proceedings,* ed. F Hoy. pp. 380–84. Anaheim, CA: Acad. Manage.

Kotter J, Sathe V. 1978. Problems of human resource management in rapidly growing companies. *Calif. Manage. Rev.* Winter: 29–36

Kozlowski SWJ, Chao GT, Smith EM, Hedlund J. 1993. Organizational downsizing: strategies, interventions, and research implications. *Int. Rev. Ind. Org. Psychol.* 8: 263–332

Kozlowski SWJ, Hults BM. 1987. An exploration of climates for technical updating and performance. *Pers. Psychol.* 40:539–63

Kozlowski SWJ, Salas E. 1994. A multilevel organizational systems approach for the implementation and transfer of training. In *Improving Training Effectiveness in Work Organizations,* ed. JK Ford & Associates. Hillsdale, NJ: Erlbaum

Lakhani H. 1988. The effect of pay and retention bonuses on quit rates in the US Army. *Ind. Labor Relat. Rev.* 41:430–38

Landy FJ, Shankster LJ, Kohler SS. 1994. Personnel selection and placement. *Annu. Rev. Psychol.* 45:261–96

Latham GP. 1988. Human resource training and development. *Annu. Rev. Psychol.* 39: 545–82

Laurent A. 1986. The cross-cultural puzzle of international human resource management. *Hum. Res. Manage.* 25:91–102

Lawler EE III, Mohrman SA. 1987. Unions and the new management. *Acad. Manage. Exec.* 1:293–300

Lawler EE III, Mohrman SA, Ledford GE. 1992. *Employee Involvement and Total Quality Management: Practices and Re-*

sults in *Fortune 1000 Companies.* San Francisco, CA: Jossey-Bass

Lengnick-Hall CA, Lengnick-Hall ML. 1988. Strategic human resources management: a review of the literature and a proposed topology. *Acad. Manage. Rev.* 13:454–70

Levine DI, Tyson LD. 1990. Participation, productivity, and the firm's environment. In *Paying for Productivity,* ed. A Blinder, pp. 183–235. Washington, DC: Brookings Inst.

Lévy-Leboyer C. 1994. Selection and assessment in Europe. See Triandis et al 1994a, pp. 173–90

Lewandowski JL, MacKinnon WP. 1992. What we learned at Saturn. *Pers. J.* 37:31–32

Lincoln JR. 1993. Work organization in Japan and the United States. In *Country Competitiveness: Technology and the Organizing of Work,* ed. B Kogut, pp. 93–124. Oxford: Oxford Univ. Press

MacDuffie JP, Krafcik J. 1992. Integrating technology and human resources for high-performance manufacturing. In *Transforming Organizations,* ed. T Kochan, M Useem, pp. 210–26. New York: Oxford Univ. Press

Macy B, Izumi H. 1993. Organizational change, design, and work innovation: a meta-analysis of 131 North American field studies—1961–1991. In *Research in Organizational Change and Development,* ed. R Woodman, W Pasmore, 7:147–70. Greenwich, CT: JAI

Mahoney TA. 1987. Understanding comparable worth: a societal and political perspective. *Res. Organ. Behav.* 9:209–45

Malm FT. 1955. Hiring procedures and selection standards in the San Francisco Bay area. *Ind. Labor Relat. Rev.* 8:231–52

Marginson P. 1992. European integration and transnational management-union relations in the enterprise. *Br. J. Ind. Relat.* 30:529–45

Markham SE. 1985. An investigation of the relationship between unemployment and absenteeism: a multi-level approach. *Acad. Manage. J.* 28:228–34

Marshall R. 1992. The future role of government in industrial relations. *Ind. Relat.* 31:31–49

Maruyama M. 1992. Changing dimensions in international business. *Acad. Manage. E.* 6:88–96

Mellow W. 1982. Employer size and wages. *Rev. Econ. Stat.* 64:495–501

Mendoca M, Kanungo RN. 1994. Managing human resources: the issue of cultural fit. *J. Manage. Inq.* In press

Meyer JW, Rowan B. 1977. Institutionalized organizations: formal structure as myth and ceremony. *Am. J. Sociol.* 83:340–63

Miles RE, Snow CC. 1978. *Organizational Strategy, Structure, and Process.* New York: McGraw-Hill

Miles RE, Snow CC. 1984. Designing strategic human resources systems. *Org. Dyn.* 16:36–52

Milkovich GT, Gerhart B, Hannon J. 1991. The effects of research and development intensity on managerial compensation in large organizations. *J. High Technol. Manage. Res.* 2:133–50

Miller CS, Schuster MH. 1987. Gainsharing plans: a comparative analysis. *Org. Dyn.* Summer:44–67

Miller P, O'Leary T. 1989. Hierarchies and American ideals, 1900–1940. *Acad. Manage. Rev.* 14:250–65

Milliman J, von Glinow MA, Nathan M. 1991. Organizational life cycles and strategic international human resource management in multinational companies: implications for congruence theory. *Acad. Manage. Rev.* 16:318–39

Mills PK, Morris JH. 1986. Clients as "partial" employees of service organizations: role development in client participation. *Acad. Manage. Rev.* 11:726–35

Molnar JJ, Rogers DL. 1976. Organizational effectiveness: an empirical comparison of the goal and system resource approaches. *Sociol. Q.* 17:401–13

Morrison AM. 1992. *The New Leaders: Guidelines on Leadership Diversity in America.* San Francisco, CA: Jossey-Bass

Morrison AM, Crabtree KM. 1992. *Developing Diversity in Organizations: A Digest of Selected Literature.* Greensboro, NC: Cent. Creative Leadersh.

Morrison AM, Ruderman MN, Hughes-James M. 1993. *Making Diversity Happen.* Greensboro, NC: Cent. Creative Leadersh.

Murray VV, Dimick DE. 1978. Contextual influences on personnel policies and programs: an explanatory model. *Acad. Manage. Rev.* 12:750–61

Newman JM, Huselid MA. 1992. The nature of behavioral controls in boundary occupations: agency theory at the edge. *Adv. Global High-Technol. Manage.* 2:193–212

Noble BP. 1993. More than labor amity at AT&T. *New York Times* March 14:F25

Noe RA, Ford JK. 1992. Emerging issues and new directions for training research. *Res. Pers. Hum. Res. Manage.* 10:345–84

Ofori-Dankwa J. 1994. Murray and Reshef revisited: towards a typology and theory of paradigms of national trade union movements. *Acad. Manage. Rev.* 18:269–92

Ohlott PJ, Ruderman MN, McCauley CD. 1994. Gender differences in managers' developmental job experiences. *Acad. Manage. J.* 37:46–67

Olian JD, Rynes SL. 1984. Organizational staffing: integrating practice with strategy. *Ind. Relat.* 23:170–83

Osterman PO. 1984. *Internal Labor Markets.* Cambridge, MA: London

Osterman PO. 1992. Internal labor markets in a changing environment: models and evidence. In *Research Frontiers in Industrial Relations and Human Resources*, ed D Lewin, OS Mitchell, PD Sherer, pp. 273–308. Madison, WI: Ind. Relat. Res. Assoc.

Ostroff C, Schmitt N. 1993. Configurations of organizational effectiveness and efficiency. *Acad. Manage. J.* 36:1345–61

Peck SR. 1994. Exploring the link between organizational strategy and the employment relationship: the role of human resources policies. *J. Manage. Stud.* 31: In press

Perrow C. 1967. A framework for the comparative analysis of organizations. *Am. Sociol. Rev.* 32:194–208

Pfeffer J. 1983. Organizational demography. *Res. Organ. Behav.* 5:299–357

Pfeffer J, Cohen Y. 1984. Determinants of internal labor markets in organizations. *Admin. Sci. Q.* 29:550–72

Pfeffer J, Langton N. 1988. Wage inequality and the organization of work: the case of academic departments. *Admin. Sci. Q.* 33: 588–606

Phatak AV. 1992. *International Dimensions of Management.* Boston: PWS-Kent

Poole M. 1986a. Managerial strategies and styles in industrial relations: a comparative analysis. *J. Gen. Manage.* 12:40–53

Poole M. 1986b. *Industrial Relations: Origins and Patterns of National Diversity.* London: Routledge

Porter ME. 1980. *Competitive Strategy: Techniques for Analyzing Industries and Competitors.* New York: Free Press

Porter ME. 1985. *Competitive Advantage: Creating and Sustaining Superior Performance.* New York: Free Press

Powell GN, Butterfield DA. 1994. Investigating the "Glass Ceiling" phenomenon: an empirical study of actual promotions to top management. *Acad. Manage. J.* 37:68–86

Prahalad CK, Doz YL. 1987. *The Multinational Mission: Balancing Local Demands and Global Vision.* New York: Free Press

Randolph WA, Dess GG. 1984. The congruence perspective of organization design: a conceptual model and multivariate research approach. *Acad. Manage. Rev.* 9: 114–27

Reid J Jr. 1992. Future unions. *Ind. Relat.* 31: 122–36

Ronen S. 1994. An underlying structure of motivational need taxonomies: a cross-cultural confirmation. See Triandis et al 1994a, pp. 241–70

Rosen CM, Klein KJ, Young KM. 1986. *Employee Ownership in America.* Lexington, MA: Lexington

Russell CJ, Colella A, Bobko P. 1993. Expanding the context of utility: the strategic impact of personnel selection. *Pers. Psychol.* 46:781–801

Rynes SL. 1991. Recruitment, job choice, and post-hire consequences: a call for new research directions. In *Handbook of Industrial and Organizational Psychology,* ed. MD Dunnette, LM Hough, 2:399–444. Palo Alto, CA: Consult. Psychol.

Rynes SL, Barber AE. 1990. Applicant attraction strategies: an organizational perspective. *Acad. Manage. Rev.* 15:286–310

Rynes SL, Boudreau JW. 1986. College recruiting in large organizations: practice, evaluation, and research implications. *Pers. Psychol.* 39:729–57

Saari LM, Johnson TR, McLaughlin SD, Zimmerle DM. 1988. A survey of management training and education practices in US companies. *Pers. Psychol.* 41:731–43

Schneider B. 1987. The people make the place. *Pers. Psychol.* 40:437–53

Schneider B, Wheeler JK, Cox JF. 1992. A passion for service: using content analysis to explicate service climate themes. *J. Appl. Psychol.* 77:705–16

Schuler RS. 1992. Strategic human resource management: linking people with the needs of the business. *Organ. Dyn.* 21:19–32

Schuler RS, Dowling PJ, DeCieri H. 1992. The formation of an international joint venture: Marley Automotive Components. *Eur. Manage. J.* 10:304–9

Schuler RS, Jackson SE. 1987a. Linking competitive strategy and human resource management practices. *Acad. Manage. Exec.* 3: 207–19

Schuler RS, Jackson SE. 1987b. Organizational strategy and organization level as determinants of human resource management practices. *Hum. Res. Plan.* 10(3):125–41

Schuler RS, Jackson SE, Dowling PJ, DeCieri H. 1991. Formation of an international joint venture: Davidson Instrument Panel. *Hum. Res. Plan.* 14:51–59

Schuler RS, MacMillan IC. 1984. Gaining competitive advantage through HR management practices. *Hum. Res. Manage.* 23: 241–55

Schuler RS, van Sluijs E. 1992. Davidson-Marley BV: establishing and operating an international joint venture. *Eur. Manage. J.* 10:428–37

Schwartz SH. 1992. Universals in the content and structure of values: theoretical advances and empirical tests in 20 countries. *Adv. Exp. Soc. Psychol.* 25:1–66

Scott WR. 1987. The adolescence of institutional theory. *Admin. Sci. Q.* 32:493–511

Sharf J. 1994. Legal and EEO issues impacting on personal history inquiries. In *Biodata Handbook: Theory, Research, & Application,* ed. GS Stokes, MD Mumford, WA

Owens. Palo Alto, CA: Consult. Psychol. In press

Slocum JW, Lei D. 1993. Designing global strategic alliances: integrating cultural and economic factors. In *Organizational Change and Redesign: Ideas and Insights for Improving Performance,* ed. GP Huber, WH Glick, pp. 295–322. New York: Oxford Univ. Press

Slocum JW Jr, Cron WL, Hansen RW, Rawlings S. 1985. Business strategy and the management of plateaued employees. *Acad. Manage. J.* 28:133–54

Smith KG, Mitchell TR, Summer CE. 1985. Top level management priorities in different stages of the organizational life cycle. *Acad. Manage. J.* 28:799–820

Snell SA. 1992. Control theory in strategic human resource management: the mediating effect of administrative information. *Acad. Manage. Rev.* 35:292–327

Snell SA, Dean JW Jr. 1992. Integrated manufacturing and human resource management: a human capital perspective. *Acad. Manage. J.* 35:467–504

Snow CC, Snell SA. 1993. Staffing as strategy. In *Personnel Selection in Organizations,* ed. N Schmitt, WC Borman, & Associates, pp. 448–78. San Francisco, CA: Jossey-Bass

Sonnenstuhl WJ, Trice HM. 1991. Linking organizational and occupational theory through the concept of culture. *Res. Sociol. Organ.* 9:295–318

Strauss G. 1982. Workers participation in management: an international perspective. *Res. Organ. Behav.* 4:173–265

Szilagyi AD Jr, Schweiger DM. 1984. Matching managers to strategies: a review and suggested framework. *Acad. Manage. Rev.* 9:626–37

Terpstra DE, Rozell EJ. 1993. The relationship of staffing practices to organizational level measures of performance. *Pers. Psychol.* 46:27–48

Thomas DA. 1993. Racial dynamics in cross-race developmental relationships. *Admin. Sci. Q.* 38:169–94

Thompson JD. 1967. *Organizations in Action.* New York: McGraw-Hill

Thurow L. 1975. *Generating Inequality.* New York: Basic

Tolbert PS, Zucker LG. 1983. Institutional sources of change in the formal structure of organizations: the diffusion of Civil Service Reform, 1880–1935. *Admin. Sci. Q.* 28: 22–39

Tosi HL Jr, Gomez-Mejia LR. 1989. The decoupling of CEO pay and performance: an agency theory perspective. *Admin. Sci. Q.* 34:169–89

Towers Perrin. 1992. *Priorities for Competitive Advantage.* New York: Towers Perrin

Triandis HC, Dunnette MD, Hough LM, eds. 1994a. *Handbook of Industrial and Organizational Psychology,* Vol. 4. Palo Alto, CA: Consult. Psychol. 2nd ed.

Triandis HC, Kurowski LL, Gelfand MJ. 1994b. Workplace diversity. See Triandis et al 1994a, pp. 769–827

Tsang MC, Rumberger RW, Levin HM. 1991. The impact of surplus schooling on worker productivity. *Ind. Relat.* 30:209–28

Tung RL. 1993. Managing cross-national and intra-national diversity. *Hum. Res. Manage.* 32:461–77

United States Department of Labor. 1993. *High Performance Work Practices and Firm Performance.* Washington, DC: US Dept. Labor

Van Maanen J, Barley SR. 1984. Occupational communities: culture and control in organizations. *Res. Organ. Behav.* 6:287–365

van Sluijs E, van Assen A, den Hertog JF. 1991. Personnel management and organizational change: a sociotechnical perspective. *Eur. Work Org. Psychol.* 1:27–51

von Bertalanffy L. 1950. The theory of open systems in physics and biology. *Science* 111:23–29

Western B. 1993. Postwar unionization in eighteen advanced capitalist countries. *Am. Sociol. Rev.* 58:266–82

Whyte WF, ed. 1991. *Social Theory for Action: How Individuals and Organizations Learn to Change.* Newbury Park, CA: Sage

Wickens P. 1987. *The Road to Nissan.* London: MacMillan

Wigdor AK, Sackett PR. 1993. Employment testing and public policy: the case of the general aptitude test battery. In *Personnel Selection and Assessment: Individual and Organizational Perspectives,* ed. H Schuler, JL Farr, M Smith, pp. 183–204. Hillsdale, NJ: Erlbaum

Williamson OE. 1979. Transaction-cost economics: the governance of contractual relations. *J. Law Econ.* 22(2):233–61

Williamson OE. 1981. The modern corporation: origins, evolution, attributes. *J. Econ. Lit.* 19:1537–68

Williamson OE. 1991. Comparative economic organization: the analysis of discrete structural alternatives. *Admin. Sci. Q.* 36:269–96

Woodruff D. 1993. Saturn: labor's love lost? *Bus. Week* Feb. 8:122–23

Woodward J. 1965. *Industrial Organization: Theory and Practice.* London: Oxford Univ. Press

Wright PM, McMahan GC. 1992. Theoretical perspectives for strategic human resource management. *J. Manage.* 18:295–320

Wright PM, McMahan GC, McWilliams A. 1994. Human resources and sustained competitive advantage: a resource-based perspective. *Int. J. Hum. Res. Manage.* 5(2): 299–324

Wright PM, Snell SA. 1991. Toward an integrative view of strategic human resource management. *Hum. Res. Manage. Rev.* 1: 203–25

Youngblood SA, Tevino LK, Favia M. 1992. Reactions to unjust dismissal and third-party dispute resolution: a justice framework. *Empl. Responsib. Rights J.* 5(4): 283–307

Yu J, Murphy KR. 1993. Modesty bias in self-ratings of performance: a test of the cultural relativity hypothesis. *Pers. Psychol.* 46:357–66

Zammuto RF, O'Connor EJ. 1992. Gaining advanced manufacturing technologies' benefits: the roles of organization design and culture. *Acad. Manage. Rev.* 17:701–28

Zedeck S. 1992. *Work, Families, and Organizations.* San Francisco, CA: Jossey-Bass

Zucker LG. 1977. The role of institutionalization in cultural persistence. *Am. Sociol. Rev.* 42:726–43

Zucker LG. 1987. Institutional theories of organization. *Annu. Rev. Sociol.* 13:443–64

Annu. Rev. Psychol. 1995. 46:265–93

ADOLESCENT DEVELOPMENT: Pathways and Processes of Risk and Resilience

Bruce E. Compas, Beth R. Hinden, and Cynthia A. Gerhardt

Department of Psychology, University of Vermont, Burlington, Vermont 05405

KEY WORDS: adolescence, developmental psychology, aggression, depression

CONTENTS

INTRODUCTION

The close of the twentieth century represents both the best of times and the worst of times for adolescents. The lay public and health professionals have gradually changed their views of adolescence from a time of inherent stress and storm to one of opportunities for growth and positive development (e.g. Feldman & Elliott 1990, Millstein et al 1993, Petersen 1988). Youth in many countries throughout the world, especially Eastern Europe, have the opportunity to grow up in and contribute to democratic societies that were unimagin-

0066-4308/95/0201-0265$05.00

able less than a decade ago. In stark contrast, the lives of large segments of today's adolescents in the United States and worldwide are threatened by violence, disease, poverty, and limited opportunities for the future. This is the challenging context for the psychology of adolescence—one of opportunity and of enormous responsibility.

A similar contrast can be found in the juxtaposition of research on adolescence and the status of adolescents themselves. The recent history of research and theory on adolescent development has been characterized by rapid growth. Evidence of the vitality of a psychology of adolescence is reflected in a variety of indicators, including the continued growth of a strong interdisciplinary scientific society (the Society for Research on Adolescence), the presence of several scientific journals devoted specifically to the topic (e.g. *The Journal of Research on Adolescence, The Journal of Youth and Adolescence, The Journal of Adolescent Research*), increased interest in this area from other scientific and professional groups (e.g. the Adolescent Medicine branch of the American Medical Association), the allocation of resources from several major foundations (e.g. the Carnegie Corporation of New York, the Johan Jacobs Foundation, the MacArthur Foundation, the William T. Grant Foundation), and concern for the well-being of adolescents expressed at the level of national policy (e.g. Dougherty 1993, United States Congress/Office of Technology Assessment 1991).

Paradoxically, the robust growth of a psychology of adolescence has been accompanied by a decline in the overall well-being and health status of adolescents. Although morbidity rates for most other age groups have declined in recent decades, adolescent morbidity has increased (Hamburg 1992). The challenges faced by today's youth are reflected in a host of problems, including adolescent suicide (Garland & Zigler 1993), depression (Petersen et al 1993), violence and death due to violence (Earls et al 1993, Hammond & Yung 1993), unplanned pregnancy (Brooks-Gunn & Paikoff 1993), substance abuse (Leventhal & Keeshan 1993), and sexually transmitted diseases (Brooks-Gunn & Paikoff 1993). Further evidence that problems of adolescence are on the rise comes from longitudinal research indicating that rates of emotional and behavioral problems of adolescents (and children) have increased over the past ten years (Achenbach & Howell 1993).

This review highlights recent developments in theory and research methods and summarizes exemplary research findings that contribute to our understanding of psychological development during the second decade of life. We begin by identifying three important themes in research and theory on adolescence: (*a*) the emergence of broad integrative models of adolescent development that include psychological, biological, social, and contextual factors; (*b*) the identification of developmental pathways or trajectories during adolescence that are linked to prior growth during childhood and subsequent adult development; and (c) the investigation of risk and protective processes that distinguish adaptive and maladaptive developmental paths in the face of adversity. We then offer a critical analysis of these themes by examining their contributions to the understanding of two important problems during adolescence—depression and aggression or antisocial behavior. Finally, we identify directions for future research that will both enhance our understanding of the nature of adolescent development and contribute to improving the quality of the lives and development of adolescents now and in the future.

EMERGENT THEMES IN THEORY AND RESEARCH ON ADOLESCENCE

As any area of scientific inquiry moves toward maturity, there is an inevitable convergence of separate lines of thinking and research. Investigators and theorists who are engaged in particular lines of study discover cross-cutting themes in their work, yielding increasingly more integrative and comprehensive models and methods than those that existed separately. There are a number of indicators that such a convergence has occurred in research on adolescent development (Zaslow & Takanishi 1993).

Models of Adolescent Development: Transactional, Interdisciplinary, and Contextual Approaches

Early attempts to conceptualize the psychology of adolescence took the form of rather straightforward main effects models. These approaches attempted to understand the significant characteristics of adolescent development as a direct function of either intrapsychic (e.g. Freud 1958), biological (e.g. Hall 1904, Kestenbaum 1968), or environmental factors. Recent attempts to conceptualize psychological development during adolescence have reflected a fundamental shift to more interdisciplinary and transactional models. We have selected three recent examples of emerging models of adolescent development that illustrate this broad perspective.

BIOPSYCHOSOCIAL MODELS   Human development and behavior unfold simultaneously on multiple levels. Physical and biological maturation, including the development of the brain and the central nervous system, continue well into the adolescent decade (Brooks-Gunn & Reiter 1990). Thinking processes, such as social cognition, problem-solving skills, language capacity, and visio-spatial skills, also develop during adolescence (Harter 1990, Keating 1990). These developmental changes are accompanied by changes in the nature of the social environments in which adolescents function, as well as in their socially defined roles in these contexts (Brown 1990, Furstenberg 1990, Entwisle 1990). Recognition of the interrelatedness of these aspects of development characterizes recent biopsychosocial models of adolescent development (e.g. Brooks-Gunn 1987, Buchanan et al 1992, Crockett & Petersen 1993, Lerner & Mulkeen 1990).

One the foremost examples of biopsychosocial models can be found in recent conceptualizations of the relationship of pubertal development to behavior, cognition, emotion, and social relationships (e.g. Brooks-Gunn & Reiter 1990, Buchanan et al 1992, Paikoff & Brooks-Gunn 1991). The hormonal changes that define puberty influence growth and functioning of the brain, the central nervous system, and neurotransmitter processes within the central nervous system, and contribute to observable changes in body shape and morphology, including breast development, gonadal development, and growth of facial and pubic hair (Paikoff & Brooks-Gunn 1991).

Much of the early research on pubertal development was quite naturally concerned with charting the basic biological changes that occur in adolescents (Brooks-Gunn & Reiter 1990). More recent research has pursued a broad biopsychosocial focus in trying to define the relationship between hormonal development and changes in mood and behavior (Buchanan et al 1992), as well as the impact of pubertal development on parent-child relationships (Paikoff & Brooks-Gunn 1991), the interaction of pubertal development with social factors in contributing to adolescent sexual behavior (Rogers & Rowe 1993), and the association between hormonal changes and specific problems such as depression (e.g. Brooks-Gunn et al 1994) and aggression (e.g. Susman et al 1987). Furthermore, these recent efforts have investigated the reciprocal and interactive relationships of hormonal changes with other aspects of cognitive, emotional, behavioral, and interpersonal development (e.g. Belsky et al 1991, Steinberg 1988, Trickett & Putnam 1993).

The association of pubertal development with mood and behavior has represented one of the most active areas of integrative research. The evidence suggests that hormonal changes are linked to mood and behavior, although these relations are complex and the data often inconsistent (Buchanan et al 1992, Crockett & Petersen 1993, Richards & Larson 1993). The links between hormones and mood or behavior appear to differ for boys and girls, with age, for different types of hormones and their interaction with one another, and as a function of pubertal status (e.g. Nottelmann et al 1987, Susman et al 1991, Susman et al 1987).

Another integrative approach involves research concerned with pubertal onset not just as a biological event but as an event that has social and interpersonal ramifications. This research has examined the timing of puberty relative to one's peer group rather than the onset of puberty per se. This research has recognized that the developmental impact of hormonal changes on behavior and emotion are in part mediated by the responses that pubertal changes elicit from others in the social environment. Specifically, it appears that the onset of puberty early or late relative to the timing of this event for one's peers is an important predictor of behavioral and emotional adjustment (Nottelmann et al 1987, Petersen et al 1991).

Research has also examined the impact of puberty and pubertal timing on the nature of parent-child relationships, especially on parent-child conflict (Paikoff & Brooks-Gunn 1991). Puberty appears to have a predictable but small effect on family relationships, although this association is moderated by a variety of factors including child gender, age at puberty, and family structure (e.g. Hill 1988, Holmbeck & Hill 1991, Papini et al 1988, Steinberg 1987). Researchers have now begun to investigate the processes underlying the observed associations, including responses to biological change, changes in social cognitive processes, self-definitional or identity-related changes, individual or familial characteristics, ethnicity, other social relationship changes, and multiple life-event changes (Paikoff & Brooks-Gunn 1991).

DEVELOPMENTAL BEHAVIORAL SCIENCE   Models of adolescent development that consider multiple levels of functioning and analyses have led to a call for interdisciplinary research that draws on the collective knowledge base of several disciplines concerned with human behavior. The most formal proposal for an interdisciplinary approach to the study of adolescent development is reflected in Jessor's call for a "developmental behavioral science" (Jessor 1991, 1992, 1993; Jessor et al 1991). A central element of developmental behavioral science is the abandonment of traditional, parochial models within psychology, as well as an abandonment of a strictly positivist epistemology (Jessor 1993). Research traditions and methods that have developed in sociology, anthropology, child psychiatry, pediatrics, criminology, life course development, demography, and education can all inform a psychology of adolescence. In addition to the integration of traditionally distinct scientific disciplines, developmental behavioral science also includes an integration of the often distinct arenas of basic and applied research. In particular, the high-risk social environments of minority youth are believed to be contexts in which the integration of basic and applied research will be most beneficial.

Developmental behavioral science also holds the concept of interrelatedness as central. For example, research has recognized that the impact of various social contexts (e.g. family, peer, school, and work environments) are each dependent in part on the effects of the other (e.g. Durbin et al 1993, Mortimer et al 1992). Further, developmental behavioral science recognizes the interrelatedness of both healthy and maladaptive developmental outcomes. This has been observed in the interrelatedness of a set of problem behaviors (e.g. substance abuse, delinquency, and drunk driving) that reflect a health-compromising lifestyle (Elliott 1993, Windle et al 1992) and the covariation of syndromes of psychological problems or the comorbidity of psychiatric disorders (Angold & Costello 1993, Compas & Hammen 1994).

MODELS OF PERSON-CONTEXT MATCH   A third perspective on broad integrative models of adolescent development can be found in conceptualizations of adolescent development as a function of the match or fit between the characteristics of the individual and the social environment (e.g. Eccles & Midgley 1989, Eccles et al 1993, Lerner 1985, Lerner & Tubman 1989, Windle & Lerner 1986). Such models construe adolescent development as a dynamic interaction of individual and environmental characteristics. Adolescents evoke differential reactions from the environment as a result of their physical and behavioral characteristics, and environments contribute to individual development through the feedback that they provide to adolescents. The quality of this feedback is dependent on the degree of fit or match between the characteristics of the individual and the expectations, values, and preferences of the social environment. Problematic development is viewed as a function of a "mismatch between the needs of developing adolescents and the opportunities afforded them by their social environments" (Eccles et al 1993, p. 90). The person-environment match model expands in complexity with the recognition that there may be variability in the degree of fit between an individual adolescent and multiple contexts (e.g. school, peer group, family) at the same time (Eccles et al 1993). Moreover, the expectations and demands of these contexts may or may not be in synch with one another.

A mismatch may occur in the form of expectations or demands from the environment that exceed the developmental capacities of the individual. Some demands that challenge current adaptive capacities may provide a stimulus and opportunity for the development of new competencies, whereas other demands may overwhelm the current capacities of the adolescent and may result in high levels of distress and disorder. For example, Elder and colleagues found that in families subjected to economic hardship during the 1930s, many adolescents were given increased responsibilities within the family that challenged their current resources (Elder & Caspi 1988, Elder et al 1984). The long-term outcomes for these individuals, however, appear to have been positive, suggesting that the increased responsibilities presented an opportunity to develop new coping capacities and skills. In contrast, Compas et al (1994) found that adolescents who were faced with the stress of the diagnosis and treatment of cancer in one of their parents showed poorer adjustment than did preadolescent children in their families. The highest levels of anxiety and depression in these families were experienced by girls whose mothers were ill. The increased distress in these girls was accounted for by the increased levels of family responsibilities and duties they were given while their mothers were incapacitated (KE Grant & BE Compas, unpublished manuscript). These contrasting examples suggest that environmental demands may vary in the degree to which they represent an appropriate or inappropriate fit with adolescents' adaptive capacities. Furthermore, mismatches between the demands of the environment and the adaptive capacities of the individual may show different short- and long-term effects.

Pathways and Trajectories of Development

Current perspectives on adolescent development have evolved significantly since early conceptualizations of adolescence as a period of stress and turmoil for most or all adolescents (Hall 1904). The search for universal descriptions for all adolescents has been replaced by recognition of the wide variability that characterizes psychological development during the second decade of life. Further, individual differences in the associations between childhood functioning and adolescent development, and between adolescent and adult functioning are also recognized. These observations have contributed to interest in individual differences in the paths and trajectories of personal development from childhood through adolescence to adulthood (e.g. Block 1971, Moffitt 1993, Petersen 1993, Powers et al 1989, Rutter 1989, Rutter & Rutter 1993). Identification of developmental paths requires longitudinal data on the same individuals over time, or accelerated longitudinal designs (e.g. Stanger et al 1994, Stanger & Verhulst 1994).

Research on normative and problematic adolescent development has identified five developmental trajectories (see Figure 1). These can be characterized as stable adaptive functioning (Path 1), stable maladaptive functioning (Path 2), adolescent turnaround or recovery (Path 3), adolescent decline (Path 4), and temporary deviation or maladaptation during adolescence (Path 5). Empirical evidence for each of these paths has come from a variety of research endeavors. Stable adaptive functioning is best reflected in youth who traverse adolescence in relatively low-risk environments (Path 1). For example, the development of many adolescents is marked by the absence of involvement in delinquent, antisocial activities or serious emotional problems (e.g. Achenbach 1991). Similarly, the majority of adolescents maintain a positive sense of self throughout adolescence (e.g. Harter 1990). Stable maladaptive functioning is found in the trajectories of individuals who enter adolescence with a personal history of problems or disorder, and who are exposed to chronic stress and adversity in the absence of resources to mitigate against these risks (Path 2). For example, youth with a prior history of aggressive, antisocial behavior during childhood have a high probability of maintaining this pattern throughout adolescence.

Pathways that involve significant change during adolescence are relatively more rare than are stable trajectories, but they are also potentially more informative regarding the personal and contextual factors that account for developmental patterns. One subgroup of adolescents is characterized by a temporary pattern of deviance that is limited to the adolescent years. For example, Moffitt (1993) describes a subgroup of youth who engage in aggressive or delinquent

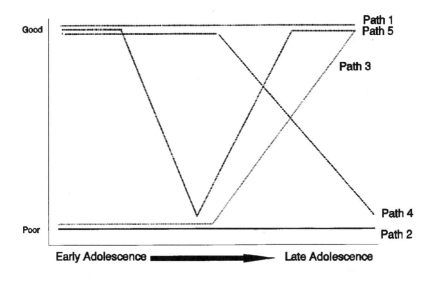

Figure 1 Divergent pathways of development during adolescence. Path 1: stable adaptive functioning; Path 2: stable maladaptive functioning; Path 3: adolescent turnaround; Path 4: adolescent decline; Path 5: temporary deviation or maladaptation during adolescence.

behavior that is limited to adolescence—it is not preceded by such problems in childhood and is not followed by antisocial problems in adulthood (Path 5). Some patterns of temporary deviance during adolescence may represent experimentation with risk-taking behaviors during adolescence but do not reflect the development of a broader deviant lifestyle. A second subgroup can be identified by a pattern of decline in functioning during adolescence following a relatively successful period of development during childhood (Path 4). This pattern is exemplified by exposure to dramatic changes in environmental circumstances during adolescence. For example, changes in family structure such as divorce or remarriage during adolescence can contribute to negative outcomes for some youth. Changes in development can also be the result of biologically-based shifts that do not emerge until adolescence, as some genetic effects do not "turn on" until adolescence or even later in development (Rutter & Rutter 1993). A third pathway involves a turnaround or recovery in which a previously negative developmental pattern is reversed during adolescence (Path 3). Rutter & Rutter (1993) have outlined how important life events and opportunities during adolescence can contribute to an upturn in a developmental trajectory. One example can be found in the apparent opportunities in the military that are afforded to some individuals whose prior developmental course was headed in a negative direction (Elder 1986).

These different developmental paths have been examined in four ways: 1. paths of development during adolescence (e.g. Alsaker & Olweus 1992, Petersen et al 1991), 2. pathways from childhood to adolescence (e.g. Sameroff et al 1993), 3. pathways from adolescence to adulthood (e.g. Aseltine & Gore 1993, Brooks-Gunn et al 1993, Hammen et al 1994), and 4. lifespan research in which individuals have been followed from early childhood through adolescence into adulthood (e.g. Block et al 1991).

Processes of Risk and Resilience

Recognition of individual differences in pathways of adolescent development is closely linked to interest in those factors that place individuals at risk for a negative trajectory and factors that protect others from these negative paths in spite of exposure to known sources of risk (Anthony & Cohler 1987, Garmezy 1985, Haggerty et al 1994, Rutter & Rutter 1993). Risk factors are those characteristics of the person or the environment that are associated with an increased probability of maladaptive developmental outcomes. Protective factors are hypothesized to interact with sources of risk such that they reduce the probability of negative outcomes under conditions of high risk but do not show an association with developmental outcomes under low risk.

Early research in this area was concerned with the identification of rather static factors or markers that served as predictors of negative outcomes. For example, gender and socioeconomic status are static markers of increased risk for certain negative health and mental health outcomes during adolescence (e.g. Leadbeater et al 1994, Nolen-Hoeksema & Girgus 1994). Some risk markers have been conceptualized in terms of characteristics of individuals, such as genetic predispositions toward specific disorders or a difficult temperament. Similarly, environmental factors, such as exposure to stressful or traumatic life events or chronic poverty and adversity, can be markers of risk.

Although risk factors or markers serve an important function in the identification of individuals with a high probability of subsequent problems, they do not help to explain how or why problems develop. For this reason, research in this area has turned to the search for the processes or mechanisms that account for negative outcomes during adolescence.

One way to conceptualize risk processes is to examine the chain or sequence of events that can unfold as a result of exposure to certain risk factors (e.g. Quinton & Rutter 1988). The impact of stressful major life events on adolescent adjustment also appears to be mediated by more proximal processes in the social environment. Specifically, major life events are related to emotional and behavioral difficulties primarily as a function of the ongoing, chronic stresses and strains to which they give rise (e.g. Compas et al 1989a; KE Grant & BE Compas, unpublished manuscript; Wagner et al 1988). Stressful events such as parental divorce, personal illness, illness of a parent, or a family move contribute to short-term emotional distress. However, the long-term impact of these events is more the result of chronic disruptions, demands, and strains that they create in the adolescent's social environment (Compas 1994).

The effects of exposure to chronic adversity also appear to be mediated by characteristics of the family environment and chronic stress processes. Conger and colleagues have reported on the relationship of family economic hardship and symptoms of psychological distress among adolescents. For example, Ge et al (1992) reported that economic stress had a direct impact on the quality of the parents' marital relationship, which, in turn, disrupted parent-child relationships, leading to increased adolescent distress. Finally, controlled preventive intervention trials can provide evidence that strengthening certain protective factors or processes can reduce the likelihood of negative developmental outcomes among adolescents who are at risk (e.g. Coie et al 1993).

EXEMPLARY RESEARCH ON PROBLEMS OF ADOLESCENCE

Developments in theory and research on the emergence and course of conduct problems (including aggression and delinquency) and depression during adolescence provide important examples of integrative models, identification of developmental paths, and the search for sources of risk and protective mechanisms.

Aggression and Antisocial Behavior

Although most adolescents become well-adjusted adults, a substantial proportion of adolescent males will have some experience with delinquent behavior.[1] A recent analysis of a large New Zealand sample revealed that 93% of males acknowledged some delinquent activity prior to age 18 (Moffitt 1993). These results echo similar findings showing that one third of US males report police contact by adulthood for serious crimes, and four fifths report contact for more minor offenses (Moffitt 1993). These data suggest that adolescent delinquency is common and prevalent for boys and may even be described as normative. Moffitt (1993) suggests that for many boys, delinquency is not only normative

---

[1]
Aggression and antisocial behavior have been studied far more extensively in males than in females, as the prevalence of these behaviors is markedly higher in males. Recent work (Caspi & Moffitt 1991, Caspi et al 1993) with female samples, however, suggests that there may be similarities between antisocial boys and girls.

but is also "adjustive" in that it serves a developmental function by expressing autonomy. The frequency and apparent normality of these behaviors should not, however, obscure their seriousness. Adolescent offenses are often serious and result in negative consequences for the adolescent and for society as a whole.

How do we understand and explain aggression as both a phenomenon of individual development and as a defining feature of a particular developmental period? Recent research in this area has been creative and fruitful, generating hypotheses that promise to help illuminate the nature, etiology, and processes of risk and resilience associated with aggression and delinquency.

BIOPSYCHOSOCIAL MODELS OF AGGRESSION DURING ADOLESCENCE   Integrative models of adolescent aggression can be divided into two types. The first type looks to early and chronic biological, psychological, and social factors that influence the development of an aggressive, antisocial personality or behavioral style that manifests itself in adolescence as delinquency. The second type looks to more proximal factors to explain these behaviors during adolescence. It now seems likely that these divergent models describe qualitatively different processes leading to similar negative outcomes.

Investigators of antisocial behavior have noted that aggression is a profoundly persistent, chronic, and intractable characteristic of certain individuals (e.g. Caspi et al 1990, Farrington et al 1990, Robins 1985). Caspi et al (1990) proposed that antisocial behavior reflects an "ill-tempered" interactional style that is developed initially in childhood and persists through adulthood. This interactional style is believed to develop from an insidious transactional process between subtle, congenital neuropsychological deficits and criminologic environments that inadvertently reward aggressive behavior (Moffitt 1993). This style is also thought to be most salient when unfamiliar environments need to be negotiated or during periods of uncertainty such as developmental transitions (Caspi et al 1990). Once developed, individuals who display this interactional style continue to select environments that favor and sustain them, thus creating a lifelong disposition to antisocial behavior (Caspi et al 1990). Longitudinal research (e.g. Farrington et al 1990) has shown that these characteristics are stable and are related to the environmental risks outlined by Caspi et al (1990). In addition, recent findings have supported this model by explaining adolescent aggression in girls. In a sample of 348 girls from New Zealand, Caspi & Moffitt (1991) found that girls predisposed to behavior problems in childhood were more likely to exhibit increases in aggressive and delinquent behavior during adolescence as a result of early maturation.

A second integrative model that examines multidimensional, early and chronic factors to explain adolescent aggression and antisocial behavior is Jessor's "problem behavior" or "risk behavior" theory. Jessor (1993) proposes that risk behavior is a lifestyle created by the interaction of the individual's biological-genetic characteristics, social environment, perceived environment, personality, and behavior. This model is supported by empirical studies showing that each of these factors, when considered independently or in combination with others, predicts aggressive or antisocial outcomes (e.g. Cohen et al 1990, Farrington et al 1990).

Other investigators have approached adolescent behavior problems as a more developmentally specific issue involving more proximal causal factors, such as school and contemporaneous family environments. For example, Eccles et al (1993) have suggested that poor person-environment fit for the adolescent, at home or in school, may account for the increase in behavior problems observed in community school samples of adolescents. Their research reveals that with increasing age and educational level, adolescents desire more participation in classroom and family decision-making but have decreasing opportunity to do so. They hypothesize, therefore, that adolescent "acting out" stems from the failure of schools or families to accommodate and reflect adolescents' increasing needs for autonomy and control.

Moffitt (1993) offers an integrative model for adolescent antisocial behavior that complements and extends person-environment fit models. She hypothesizes that the bulk of adolescent delinquency results from a historical phenomenon—a maturity gap—created by the incongruity of achieving biological maturity at adolescence without simultaneously being awarded adult status. Under these circumstances, delinquency becomes an avenue for self-definition and expression of autonomy, a maturity substitute. It is an adaptive attempt by the adolescent to bridge the gap between changing self perceptions and circumscribed social roles.

The potential role of physiological changes in the manifestation of adolescent aggressive and/or antisocial behavior has also been recognized in recent research. Animal studies and studies of adult criminality and violent behavior have largely supported the view that hormonal processes influence the expression of aggression (e.g. Inoff-Germain et al 1988). Recent work on the relation of hormones to aggressive behavior in adolescents suggests that the levels of circulating hormones related to sexual development may be related to measures of aggressive behavior for boys and girls (Susman et al 1987, Inoff-Germain et al 1988). In addition to hormonal influences on aggression, Robins & McEvoy (1990) have suggested that biological factors may play an important role in both conduct problems and substance abuse. Their findings show that conduct problems in childhood and adolescence are related to early drug use, which is strongly and independently related to serious, long-term substance abuse problems. They suggest that the powerful, independent relationship of early drug use to long-term problems may result from the use of drugs during a biologically critical period prior to completion of puberty, when effects of drugs may be more salient.

DEVELOPMENTAL PATHWAYS OF AGGRESSION   Developmental data on aggression and antisocial, delinquent behavior present an intriguing puzzle—these problems are persistent yet they increase dramatically in frequency during adolescence. A stable portion of males appear to develop aggressive and conduct problems early in life and sustain these behaviors into adulthood (Farrington et al 1990, Robins 1985). Virtually all men diagnosed with adult antisocial personality disorder carried a diagnosis of conduct disorder in childhood (Robins 1985). Thus, there is ample empirical support for an identified chronic antisocial, delinquent, criminal pathway. In contrast to the observed chronicity of this antisocial pathway, however, delinquency is also distinctly a problem of adolescence, with numbers of crimes and variety of crimes increasing dramatically during this period (Moffitt 1993, LeBlanc 1990). This increase appears to be the result of an increase both in the numbers of crimes and in the number of individuals involved in criminal activity, such that individuals not previously committing delinquent acts begin to do so during adolescence. This increase during adolescence declines in early adulthood to rates similar to those reported prior to adolescence (LeBlanc 1990, Moffitt 1993).

The apparent contradictory observations that aggression and delinquency are both transient and stable is resolved by recognition of two distinct subgroups of males who display these problems and follow two distinct developmental pathways. The first involves a trajectory of chronic poor adjustment— early conduct problems that escalate and manifest as juvenile delinquency in adolescence. The second is represented by an adolescent deviance trajectory in which great numbers of previously well-adjusted adolescent males experiment with delinquent behavior and join their more chronic, delinquent peers (Moffitt 1993; see also Figure 1 above).

The two different pathways of antisocial behavior have been hypothesized to have different causal factors and processes. Moffitt (1993) suggests that a small group of adolescent males represents a chronic, persistent course of delinquency, evolving from the interaction of early biological and environmental factors. During adolescence, these antisocial boys seem relatively independent and mature, and thus become temporary role models to other more well-adjusted boys who are seeking self-definition and mature status. This model is supported by numerous findings of changing prevalence of antisocial behavior across the life course, and identified risk and resilience factors for early conduct versus later conduct problems (e.g. Farrington et al 1990, LeBlanc 1990). Moffitt's model reconciles the apparent contradictory realities of persistent versus transient offending and the latter's distinct relation to adolescence.

A third trajectory of adolescent decline (see Figure 1), although less discussed and explored in the literature, may be extrapolated from Moffitt's model. As she suggests, previously well-adjusted adolescents may experiment with particular delinquent behaviors that have long-term effects, such as alcohol and substance abuse and/or irresponsible sexual activity. Through such behaviors and their consequences (e.g. drug dependence, pregnancy, HIV infection), these adolescents may enter a course of steady decline. This group may consist of relatively more adolescent girls, whose antisocial activities are less documented and perhaps less understood. Early-maturing adolescent girls in particular have been identified as a risk group for adjustment problems in general. They are certainly more vulnerable for the long-term consequences of teenage pregnancy and may be more at risk for serious substance abuse problems (Robins & McEvoy 1990), making them likely candidates for a trajectory of adolescent decline.

Lastly, a trajectory of adolescent turnaround (see Figure 1) may be hypothesized from the literature on aggressive children. Farrington et al (1990) have identified a group of boys with hyperactivity-impulsivity-attentional problems who do not present with serious conduct problems. These boys, though troublesome and difficult as children and at risk for juvenile convictions, are unlikely to develop criminal careers in adulthood. For example, Farrington et al (1990) found that fewer boys in the hyperactivity-impulsivity, nonconduct problem group had adult convictions than did boys in the well-adjusted childhood group (8% vs 14.3%). Thus, these boys may represent a group whose earlier problematic functioning improves as they pass through adolescence into adulthood.

RISK AND RESILIENCE   Identification of risk and resilience factors and processes is of necessity closely linked to correct identification of developmental pathways. Investigators of adolescent aggression and delinquency have focused on both distal and proximal processes. Moffitt's (1993) model of two distinct pathways to antisocial behavior in adolescence hypothesizes that early-life risk factors may be associated with the more chronic life-course-persistent trajectory and that more contemporary risk factors such as puberty and changing social definition are associated with adolescence-limited antisocial behavior.

Demographic variables (e.g. gender, low SES, and large family size), environmental characteristics (e.g. neighborhood crime and poor housing), parenting behaviors (e.g. poor paternal interactions, poor supervision, low level of control, and power-assertive punishment), and parent characteristics (e.g. low maternal competence, paternal alcoholism, and/or criminality) have been associated with aggressive, adolescent antisocial behaviors and juvenile delinquency (Farrington et al 1990, McCord 1990, Cohen et al 1990, Moffitt 1993). Many of these variables have been associated with long-term, chronic criminal offending and alcoholism as well, and as such may be more defining of Moffitt's "life-course persistent" group and not as relevant to the adolescent-limited group.

In addition to these demographic and psychosocial variables, childhood behavior problems such as oppositional behavior and childhood hyperactivity predict juvenile delinquency. Comorbidity of these problem areas appears to be additive in effect, increasing risk for juvenile delinquency (Farrington et al 1990). Early onset of conduct problems, prior to age 9, is a risk factor for stable and frequent offending (LeBlanc 1990). Conduct problems in childhood also predict earlier adolescent substance use and long-term substance abuse problems.

Moffitt (1993) suggests that adolescent-limited delinquency is a risk of industrialized cultures where children attain biological maturity before they attain adult status. This gap is a key risk factor and provides the motivation and contingencies for temporary acting out. The experience of this gap appears to be more prevalent for boys, and for early maturing girls who are at increased risk for delinquency (Moffitt 1993, Caspi & Moffitt 1991), and seems to be mediated for girls by exposure to boys who would be delinquent peers. Thus, boys who are increasing their delinquent behavior appear to be a risk factor for girls both in that they provide delinquent models and in that relationships with boys may provide a sense of maturity for girls.

Depression During Adolescence

Depression remains one of the most significant mental health problems throughout the lifespan as reflected in its high prevalence among adults (Weissman et al 1991), the debilitating effects of moderate to severe expressions on overall functioning (Gotlib & Hammen 1992), and its association with other negative outcomes including substance abuse (Weissman et al 1991). Recent research has pointed to adolescence as an important developmental period for understanding depression, because many significant changes in depressive problems occur during adolescence (Petersen et al 1993).

DEFINING DEPRESSION DURING ADOLESCENCE   Recent integrative perspectives have recognized the significance of three levels of operationalizing depression during adolescence (e.g. Angold 1988, Compas et al 1993a). Depressed mood (Kandel & Davies 1982), an anxious-depressed syndrome (Achenbach 1991), and depressive disorders (American Psychiatric Association 1994) all have important implications and unique contributions for understanding significant psychological problems during adolescence and all contain unique features during adolescence. Compas et al (1993a) have proposed a sequential and hierarchical model for the associations among these multiple levels of depression: A large portion (30–40%) of adolescents experience significant depressed mood at any one point in development, with a smaller group (5–6%) experiencing significant levels of a depressive syndrome, and a still smaller segment (2–3%) of the population experiencing depressive disorders. These groups are viewed as embedded within one another, with each group in the hierarchy representing a subgroup of the others. Further, these levels of depression are hypothesized to develop sequentially over time. Initial empirical investigations have provided partial support for such a model (e.g. Edelbrock & Costello 1988).

BIOPSYCHOSOCIAL MODELS OF DEPRESSION DURING ADOLESCENCE   Current models of depression recognize the significance of biological, psychological, and social factors (e.g. Gotlib & Hammen 1992, Shelton et al 1991, Petersen et al 1993). Biological factors that are implicated in the emergence and course of depression during adolescence include neuroendocrine processes, dysregulation of neurotransmitters, dysregulation of biological rhythms such as sleep patterns, and a family history of depression that is suggestive of a genetic risk for the disorder (e.g. Brooks-Gunn et al 1994; Dahl et al 1991, 1992). Cognitive or psychological factors that are associated with depression during adolescence include a dysfunctional style of attributing the causes of success and failure (Kaslow 1994), negative perceptions about the self (Garber et al 1993), hopelessness about the future (Kazdin et al 1986), and a maladaptive style of coping with stress (Compas et al 1993b). Social factors associated with adolescent depression entail family dysfunction (including parental depression), psychosocial stress, and poor peer relationships (Cole 1991, Compas et al 1994a, Hammen 1991).

When these various perspectives on depression during adolescence are considered together it is apparent that dozens of factors may interact in their relationship with depressive problems among adolescents. For example, Brooks-Gunn & Warren (1989) found that pubertal stage was not related to symptoms of depression or social withdrawal in a sample of adolescent girls. However, negative life events were more likely to be associated with these symptoms in pre- than in postmenarcheal girls. Early maturing girls (Petersen et al 1991) and late maturing boys (Nottelmann et al 1987) report more depressed affect, again indicating that the social ramifications of puberty are important. In a novel study that integrated biological and psychological factors related to depression, Ewart & Kolodner (1994) found that negative affect, including depressed mood and anger, was related to prevailing blood pressure levels in adolescents. Further, this association was found to be moderated by gender, a nonverbal expressive style, and social setting (e.g. in a classroom vs with friends). Drawing on a general diathesis-stress framework, Robinson and colleagues (NS Robinson, J Garber, R Hilsman, unpublished manuscript) found that a negative attributional style interacted with recent stressors to predict depressive symptoms but not externalizing behavior problems. The need for integrative research is further reflected in the recognition of the high degree of co-occurrence of depressive symptoms and the comorbidity of depressive disorders with other symptoms and disorders during adolescence (e.g. Angold & Costello 1993, Compas & Hammen 1994, Nottelmann & Jensen 1994).

The challenges for researchers in this area are clear—to distinguish correlates from causes, to identify how these factors interact to contribute to the cause versus maintenance of depression, to delineate the processes that account for depression in some adolescents and not others, and to distinguish risk factors associated with depressed mood versus syndrome versus disorders. These goals will not be achieved by continued pursuit of these factors in isolation; integrative models and research are necessary.

DEVELOPMENTAL PATHWAYS OF DEPRESSION   Some of the most provocative empirical evidence on depression during adolescence has come from longitudinal studies of developmental paths that entail depressive problems. Early to middle adolescence marks a point of increased depressed mood, depressive syndromes, and depressive disorders (e.g. Rutter 1986). Increased rates of depressive problems, as well as the substantially higher rates of these problems for females as compared to males, emerge during adolescence and remain relatively stable into adulthood (Petersen et al 1993). Thus, longitudinal data suggest that there is something special about adolescence in understanding developmental processes in depression. An important next step in this research involves documenting the paths of depressive problems during adolescence.

Data from one of the largest investigations of the course of depression and other disorders during adolescence revealed high rates of relapse (Lewinsohn et al 1991, 1993; Rohde et al 1991), which suggests that depression is recurrent among adolescents who have experienced an initial episode. Data on the recurrent nature of depressive disorders indicates that the course of clinical depression is characterized by both change and continuity. That is, depression is episodic rather than stable and unremitting over long periods of time. On the other hand, depression shows continuity—once an individual has experienced a significant depressive episode, she or he is at substantially increased risk for a recurrence in the future (Lewinsohn et al 1991). Therefore, the stable maladaptive pathway described above characterizes a subgroup of adolescents who experience depression, with the qualification that even the group that shows the most persistent pattern of depression will experience sustained periods in which they do not meet diagnostic criteria for a depressive disorder (Lewinsohn et al 1991).

The probability that significant depression will be first observed during adolescence is much greater than an initial onset during childhood, suggesting the group characterized by an adolescent decline in adaptation is larger than a group whose depressive problems have continued since childhood. The available evidence also suggests that individuals who experience significant levels of depression during adolescence are unlikely to experience a complete turnaround, because they are at high risk to experience a reoccurrence during adulthood (Harrington et al 1990). Furthermore, those individuals who have experienced conditions that are comorbid with depression during adolescence appear to be at even greater risk for continued depression or recurrences (Hammen et al 1994).

As noted above, depressed mood, depressive syndromes, and depressive disorders all co-occur with other problems at a high rate (Compas & Hammen 1994). Studies of co-occurrence and comorbidity indicate that depressive problems typically follow rather than precede other problems (e.g. Kovacs et al 1984, 1988).

Longitudinal studies also show that the course of depressive problems differs for males and females. In a longitudinal study of 335 adolescents randomly selected from two school districts, Petersen et al (1991) found no significant sex differences in measures of depressed affect or number of depressive episodes in early adolescence (grades 6–8), but there were significant gender differences in the twelfth grade follow-up assessment. Girls began to show an increase in depressed affect in the eighth grade, with boys remaining at a relatively stable level. In the twelfth grade, girls scored significantly worse on measures of depressed affect and emotional tone and had a significantly higher number of depressive episodes than did boys. Block et al (1991) investigated the role of behavior and personality antecedents in the manifestation of depressive symptoms at 18 years of age. For males and females displaying depressive tendencies at age 18, the authors note several significant correlates at ages 3/4, 7, and 11 years, which correspond to proposed internalizing and externalizing personality profiles. These correlates are less exhaustive but similar to those found at age 14. In addition, males who were subsequently depressed at age 18 were more likely to acknowledge the use of marijuana at age 14, whereas the dysthymic females were more likely to acknowledge the use of harder drugs. The authors suggest that this unexpected finding for females "may represent a desperate, convoluted attempt to escape a personal situation, already viewed as hopeless, by changing the inner world" (Block et al 1991). These findings suggest that personality characteristics may serve to explain the sex differences in the expression of depression during adolescence.

RISK AND PROTECTIVE MECHANISMS   Consistent with a biopsychosocial perspective on depression during adolescence, there is evidence for sources of risk in the biological, psychological, and social domains. Clearly the four most significant markers of risk for depression during adolescence are age, gender, a family history of depression, and exposure to stressful events and life circumstances. Early to mid-adolescence marks a time of significant increase in the risk for depression as compared with childhood (Petersen et al 1993). Gender is an equally strong marker; adolescent girls are at least twice as likely as boys to develop depression (e.g. Nolen-Hoeksema & Girgus 1994), a pattern that is not evident in childhood. Parental depression places children and adolescents at increased risk for depressive problems as well as a host of other emotional and behavioral difficulties (Cummings & Davies 1994, Downey & Coyne 1990, Hammen 1991, Lee & Gotlib 1991). Finally, stressful life events and chronic stress or adversity also are associated with increased risk for depressive symptoms and disorders (Compas et al 1994b).

In the biological realm, there is some evidence that the sleep onset mechanism is impaired in some depressed adolescents, as evidenced by decreased growth hormone secretion, increased cortisol, and increased time until sleep in a subgroup of depressed adolescents who expressed suicidal intent (Dahl et al 1992). Genetic loading may be higher for depression that has an initial onset during childhood or adolescence (Puig-Antich 1987, Strober et al 1988).

Research examining mechanisms of risk that may explain how and why risk markers lead to depression has been relatively rare. One active area of research on risk mechanisms has focused on parent-child interactions in families with a depressed parent, most typically a depressed mother. Hammen and her colleagues have found that the interactions between depressed mothers and their children (including adolescents) are characterized by irritability and negativity, and that levels of mother and child stress and strain closely coincide (e.g. Adrian & Hammen 1993, Hammen et al 1991). A second area of risk-mechanism research has focused on stress processes. The accumulation of negative life events also serves as a marker of subsequent increases in depressed mood and symptoms of depressive syndromes and disorders (e.g. Compas et al 1989a; Dubois et al 1994; NS Robinson, J Garber & R Hilsman, unpublished manuscript; KE Grant & BE Compas, unpublished manuscript). Discrete stressful life events appear to contribute to depressive outcomes at least partly through chronic or minor stress in the proximal environment.

In an effort to explain the sex difference in adolescent depression, Petersen et al (1991) proposed and tested a model for the development of mental health in adolescence. This model incorporated prior mental health difficulties, timing and nature of life events (stressful or normative), and the buffering effects of family and peer support and coping responses. They found that gender differences in depressed affect were related to the synchronicity of pubertal and school change, and sex differences in the number of depressive episodes were related to early pubertal timing in girls. The authors note that since only girls showed long-term negative effects of early puberty and since they are more likely to experience pubertal change simultaneously with school change, this may further explain the increase in depression in girls during adolescence. Petersen et al (1991) suggested that these stressful events may actually improve boys' confidence and coping skills, thus providing a buffering effect. Lastly, although an adolescent's relationship with a best friend was not associated significantly with depressed affect, closeness with parents, especially fathers appeared to moderate the effects of early adolescent changes. Specifically, closeness with mothers buffered negative effects of family changes, while closeness with fathers buffered both family change and synchronous school and pubertal change.

In a longitudinal study of cognitive and ego development, Block and colleagues investigated gender differences in depressive symptoms along with their familial and personality antecedents. Relative to nondysphoric males and females and dysphoric females, male adolescents with depressive tendencies were observed as relatively antagonistic, unrestrained, unhappy with self, and unconventional in thought and behavior, and described themselves as alienated and relatively aggressive, having a tendency to worry, feeling vulnerability, and a lack of a sense of psychological well-being (Gjerde et al 1988). In a similar comparison, dysphoric females were not observed as socially impaired or aggressive, but they described themselves as relatively aggressive, unrestrained, alienated from others, and having low self-esteem (Gjerde et al 1988).

To elaborate on the involvement of personality characteristics in the manifestation of depression at age 18, Block & Gjerde (1990) analyzed data obtained during childhood. Females with high depressive symptom scores at age 18 performed significantly higher on the performance IQ subscale and the full IQ scale as assessed at age 4. At age 14, girls displayed personality traits, termed collectively as ego brittleness, including feelings of vulnerability, anxiety, somatization, concern with adequacy, rumination, and feelings of little personal meaning in their lives. Additionally, low self-esteem assessed at age 14 was significantly related to depressive symptoms in 18-year-old females. Although 14-year-old boys also exhibited ego brittleness similar to their female counterparts, antisocial and hostile characteristics became even more prominent for these males. Further, females who exhibited dysphoric tendencies at age 18 tended to display concern with morality and loss in play at age 11. Females who scored relatively low or high on the depression scale also displayed more anger, themes of loss, and were more overcontrolling of impulse as compared to those in the middle range. Males who scored relatively high or low on the depressive symptoms measure exhibited more anger and concern with loss than did males in the middle range. Contrary to results found for females, these males also tended to be less controlling of impulse.

EMERGENT THEMES ON ADOLESCENT DEVELOPMENT

Contributions

The gradual emergence of integrative models that consider pathways of development as a function of risk and protective processes has had a number of benefits for the psychology of adolescence. First, these approaches have facilitated interdisciplinary research, breaking down the often artificial boundaries that contribute to fragmentation of theory and research and unproductive battles over intellectual turf. Collaborative efforts that draw on skilled researchers from psychology, medicine, education, sociology, and other disciplines have been developed to tackle significant problems pertaining to adolescent development. These efforts should yield more comprehensive perspectives on both normal and atypical development during adolescence.

Second, these research themes underscore the importance of adhering to a developmental perspective that captures both the continuities and discontinuities of individual development. Most adolescents traverse this developmental period without major psychological or behavioral problems. A growing segment of the adolescent population, however, is represented by other developmental trajectories that include in some cases brief and in other cases enduring problems. Longitudinal research efforts have been undertaken to chart these individual differences in pathways through adolescence. Attention to individual differences in the course of adolescent development will help resolve the apparently contradictory results that are found when only aggregated data are examined (Moffitt 1993).

Third, these themes capture the transactional nature of development and behavior, in which both person and context as well their mutual influences on one another are examined. Simple main effects models in which aspects of the person or the environment are given precedence over the other are insufficient to explain the complexity of different developmental paths through adolescence. The findings described above are clear in their implications for understanding problems of aggression and depression, as well as other aspects of adolescent development.

A fourth benefit of these themes has been their contribution to research on a number of important aspects of normative development during adolescence (e.g. parent-adolescent relationships, identity development, effects of schooling) as well as atypical development (e.g. alcohol, tobacco, and substance abuse; teen pregnancy; suicide; delinquency). Continued integration of research on normative and deviant development during adolescence will be useful to the field, as research on normative and clinical populations can inform each other.

Limitations

Despite the significance of these themes for the development of a psychology of adolescence, they have some limitations. First, overly broad conceptual models violate the fundamental scientific principle of parsimony. That is, broad integrative models that include multiple levels of analysis run the risk of describing much but explaining little. A challenge for proponents of biopsychosocial models is to determine which elements are necessary and sufficient to explain the important features of adolescent development. For example, although broad contextual factors are important correlates of significant problems during adolescence, they may carry no additional weight in explaining individual differences in developmental paths after accounting for more proximal characteristics of the environment. Similarly, family history of a specific problem may be interpreted as consistent with a genetic process when it may be fully accounted for by a history of dysfunctional interactions and relationships within the family. The identification of correlates of adolescent functioning at multiple levels of analysis does not insure that these correlates all play important causal roles in adolescent development.

Second, basic psychological models (e.g. learning theory) have been misrepresented and used as straw targets for arguments that enhance the appearance of integrative models at the expense of increasingly complex models that already are available. Learning- or conditioning-based explanations of development have frequently been criticized for being mechanistic and reductionistic (e.g. Jessor 1993). More recent conceptualizations of fundamental processes of learning and conditioning are far from mechanistic in nature, drawing instead on the rich tradition of associationist models (e.g. Rescorla 1988). As the field continues to develop broad interdisciplinary models, there is an increased risk of losing what is unique in the perspective of psychology as a discipline.

Third, recent approaches to research on adolescent development value macro-level longitudinal research to the extent that micro-level studies, including laboratory experimental methods, may be overlooked. For example, research on the nature and development of coping processes during adolescence has been influenced strongly by a paradigm of coping research that relies exclusively on self reports of coping in natural contexts (Compas 1987). Some of the complex cognitive processes that are involved in coping with stress cannot be understood adequately without additional information that can only be obtained in controlled laboratory contexts (e.g. Nolen-Hoeksema 1991). Further, microanalytic studies of the subtle changes of mood and behavior that characterize the daily lives of adolescents make important contributions that complement broader longitudinal studies (e.g. Richards & Larson 1993).

Fourth, the broad themes that are guiding adolescent research may not be useful in the search for specificity in some developmental processes or some problems or forms of psychopathology. Although many of the problems of adolescence are interrelated, they may be the result of separate risk mechanisms. For example, depression and aggression may co-occur but as a result of separate risk processes (e.g. Downey & Coyne 1990). Marital conflict and discord is associated with child and adolescent aggression, and parental depression is a risk factor for child and adolescent depression. Marital discord and parental depression are highly intercorrelated, however, and may function as distinct but correlated risk factors for separate but correlated outcomes. Attention to specific risk mechanisms will be important for understanding the etiology of distinct but related problems during adolescence (Garber & Hollon 1991).

Fifth, more cross-cultural research and research with ethnic minority adolescents is needed to place adolescent development in its social context. The adolescent population in the United States continues to become a more ethnically diverse group, partly as a result of immigration. Understanding the experiences of these populations has become an increasing focus of adolescent research. For example, Feldman et al (1991) have examined conduct problems and family environments in Hong Kong, Australia, and the United States; Chiu et al (1992) examined the influence of immigration on parental behavior and adolescent distress in Chinese families residing in the United States and Australia; Linares et al (1991) identified subgroups among African-American and Hispanic-American adolescent mothers; and Rosenthal & Feldman (1991) have examined the influence of perceived family and personal factors on school performance of Chinese and Western high school students.

CONCLUSION

These recent trends in research and theory concerned with adolescent development offer a solid foundation for continued understanding of both normative and atypical developmental processes and paths during the second decade of life. The field will benefit from renewed debate about the usefulness of fundamental psychological models for understanding adolescent development. Recognition of the significance of biological, psychological, and social processes provides a broad framework for understanding adolescent development. More specific models are needed, however, to add greater precision to theory and research on delineated aspects of adolescent functioning. Continued consideration of models from learning theory, cognitive science, and social psychology will be useful in pursuing research on adolescent development. Furthermore, integration of longitudinal and laboratory experimental research, including the integration of research with animal and human populations, will provide a more complete and rich understanding of adolescent development.

Finally, increased attention to the implications of research for interventions is needed to improve the quality of life for adolescents and to guide the development of sound public policy (Dougherty 1993, Zaslow & Takanishi 1993). In spite of the significance of psychosocial problems of adolescence, well-designed and evaluated interventions for the prevention and treatment of these problems have been rare. The strong knowledge base on biopsychosocial processes in adolescent development provides a foundation for the continued development of interventions to address the problems of adolescence.

Literature Cited

Achenbach TM. 1991. *Integrative Guide for the 1991 CBCL/4-18, YSR, and TRF Profiles.* Burlington, VT: Univ. Vermont, Dept. Psychiatr.

Achenbach TM, Howell CT. 1993. Are American children's problems getting worse? A 13-year comparison. *J. Am. Acad. Child Adol. Psychiatr.* 32:1145–54

Adrian C, Hammen C. 1993. Stress exposure and stress generation in children of depressed mothers. *J. Consult. Clin. Psychol.* 61:354–59

Alsaker FD, Olweus D. 1992. Stability of global self-evaluations in early adolescence: a cohort longitudinal study. *J. Res. Adol.* 2:123–45

American Psychiatric Association. 1994. *Diagnostic and Statistical Manual for Mental Disorders.* Washington, DC: Am. Psychiatr. Press. 4th ed.

Angold A. 1988. Childhood and adolescent depression. I: Epidemiological and aetiological aspects. *Br. J. Psychiatr.* 152:601–17

Angold A, Costello EJ. 1993. Depressive comorbidity in children and adolescents: empirical, theoretical, and methodological issues. *Am. J. Psychiatr.* 150:1779–91

Anthony EJ, Cohler BJ. 1987. *The Vulnerable Child.* New York: Guilford

Aseltine RH, Gore S. 1993. Mental health and social adaptation following the transition from high school. *J. Res. Adol.* 3:247–70

Belsky J, Steinberg L, Draper P. 1991. Childhood experience, interpersonal development and reproductive strategy: an evolutionary theory of socialization. *Child Dev.* 62:647–70

Block J. 1971. *Lives Through Time.* Berkeley, CA: Bankroft

Block J, Gjerde PF. 1990. Depressive symptoms in late adolescence: a longitudinal perspective on personality antecedents. In *Risk and Protective Factors in the Development of Psychopathology,* ed. JE Rolf, A Masten, D Cicchetti, KH Nuechterlein, S Weintraub, pp. 334–59. New York: Cambridge Univ. Press

Block J, Gjerde PF, Block JH. 1991. Personality antecedents of depressive tendencies in 18-year-olds: a prospective study. *J. Pers. Soc. Psychol.* 60:726–38

Brooks-Gunn J. 1987. Pubertal processes and girls' psychological adaptation. In *Biological-psychosocial Interactions in Early Adolescence: A Lifespan Perspective,* ed. RM Lerner, TT Foch, pp. 123–53. Hillsdale, NJ: Earlbaum

Brooks-Gunn J, Guo G, Furstenberg F. 1993. Who drops out of and who continues beyond high school? A 20-year follow-up of black urban youth. *J. Res. Adol.* 3:271–94

Brooks-Gunn J, Paikoff RL. 1993. "Sex is a gamble, kissing is a game": adolescent sexuality and health promotion. See Millstein et al 1993, pp. 180–208

Brooks-Gunn J, Petersen AC, Compas BE. 1994. What role does biology play in childhood and adolescent depression? In *Mood Disorders in Childhood and Adolescence,* ed. IM Goodyer. New York: Cambridge Univ. Press. In press

Brooks-Gunn J, Reiter EO. 1990. The role of pubertal processes. See Feldman & Elliott 1990, pp. 16–53

Brooks-Gunn J, Rock D, Warren MP. 1989. Comparability of constructs across the adolescent years. *Dev. Psychol.* 25:51–60

Brooks-Gunn J, Warren MP. 1989. Biological and social contributions to negative affect in young adolescent girls. *Child Dev.* 60: 40–55

Brown BB. 1990. Peer groups and peer cultures. See Feldman & Elliott 1990, pp. 171–96

Buchanan CM, Eccles JS, Becker JB. 1992. Are adolescents the victims of raging hormones: evidence for the activational effects of hormones on moods and behavior at adolescence. *Psychol. Bull.* 111:62–107

Caspi A, Elder GH, Herbener ES. 1990. Childhood personality and the prediction of life-course patterns. See Robins & Rutter 1990, pp. 13–35

Caspi A, Lyman D, Moffitt TE, Silva PA. 1993. Unraveling girls' delinquency: biological, dispositional, and contextual contributions to adolescent misbehavior. *Dev. Psychol.* 29:19–30

Caspi A, Moffitt TE. 1991. Individual differences are accentuated during periods of social change: the sample case of girls at puberty. *J. Pers. Soc. Psychol.* 61:157–68

Chiu ML, Feldman SS, Rosenthal DA. 1992. The influence of immigration on parental behavior and adolescent distress in Chinese families residing in two western nations. *J. Res. Adol.* 2:205–39

Cohen P, Brood JS, Cohen J, Velez CN, Garcia M. 1990. Common and uncommon pathways to adolescent psychopathology and problem behavior. See Robins & Rutter 1990, pp. 242–58

Coie JD, Watt NF, West SG, Hawkins JD, Asarnow JR, et al. 1993. The science of prevention: a conceptual framework and some directions for a national research program. *Am. Psychol.* 48:1013–22

Cole D. 1991. Preliminary support for a competency-based model of depression in children. *J. Abnorm. Psychol.* 100:181–90

Compas BE. 1987. Coping with stress during childhood and adolescence. *Psychol. Bull.* 101:393–403

Compas BE. 1994. Promoting successful coping during adolescence. In *Psychosocial Disturbances in Young People: Challenges for Prevention*, ed. M Rutter. Cambridge: Cambridge Univ. Press. In press

Compas BE, Ey S, Grant KE. 1993a. Taxonomy, assessment, and diagnosis of depression during adolescence. *Psychol. Bull.* 114:323–44

Compas BE, Grant KE, Ey S. 1994a. Psychosocial stress and child/adolescent depression: Can we be more specific? In *Handbook of Depression in Children and Adolescents*, ed. WM Reynolds, H Johnston. New York: Plenum. In press

Compas BE, Hammen CL. 1994. Child and adolescent depression: covariation and comorbidity in development. See Haggerty et al 1994, pp. 225–67

Compas BE, Howell DC, Phares V, Williams RA, Giunta C. 1989a. Risk factors for emotional/behavioral problems in young adolescents: a prospective analysis of adolescent and parental stress and symptoms. *J. Consult. Clin. Psychol.* 57:732–40

Compas BE, Howell DC, Phares V, Williams RA, Ledoux N. 1989b. Parent and child stress and symptoms: an integrative analysis. *Dev. Psychol.* 25:550–59

Compas BE, Orosan PG, Grant KE. 1993b. Adolescent stress and coping: implications for psychopathology during adolescence. *J. Adol.* 16:331–49

Compas BE, Worsham N, Epping JE, Howell DC, Grant KE, et al. 1994b. When mom or dad has cancer: markers of psychological distress in patients, spouses, and children. *Health Psychol.* In press

Crockett LJ, Petersen AC. 1993. Adolescent development: health risks and opportunities for health promotion. See Millstein et al 1993, pp. 13–37

Cummings EM, Davies PT. 1994. Maternal depression and child development. *J. Child Psychol. Psychiatr.* 35:73–112

Dahl RE, Ryan ND, Puig-Antich J, Nguyen NA, al-Shabbout M, et al. 1991. 24-hour cortisol measures in adolescents with major depression: a controlled study. *Biol. Psychiatr.* 30:25–36

Dahl RE, Ryan ND, Williamson DE, Ambrosini PJ, Rabinovich H, et al. 1992. Regulation of sleep and growth hormone in adolescent depression. *J. Am. Acad. Child Adol. Psychiatr.* 31:615–21

Dougherty DM. 1993. Adolescent health: reflections on a report to the U.S. Congress. *Am. Psychol.* 48:193–201

Downey G, Coyne JC. 1990. Children of depressed parents: an integrative review. *Psychol. Bull.* 108:50–76

Dubois DL, Felner RD, Meares H, Krier M. 1994. A prospective investigation of the effects of socioeconomic disadvantage, life stress, and social support on early adolescent adjustment. *J. Abnorm. Psychol.* In press

Durbin DL, Darling N, Steinberg L, Brown BB. 1993. Parenting style and peer group membership among European-American adolescents. *J. Res. Adol.* 3:87–100

Earls F, Cairns RB, Mercy JA. 1993. The control of violence and the promotion of nonviolence in adolescents. See Millstein et al 1993, pp. 159–79

Eccles JS, Midgley C. 1989. Stage/environment fit: developmentally appropriate classrooms for early adolescents. In *Research on Motivation in Education*, ed. RE

Ames, C Ames, 3:139–86. San Diego, CA: Academic

Eccles JS, Midgley C, Wigfield A, Buchanan CM, Reuman D, et al. 1993. Development during adolescence: the impact of stage-environment fit on adolescents' experiences in schools and families. *Am. Psychol.* 48: 90–101

Edelbrock C, Costello AJ. 1988. Convergence between statistically derived behavior problem syndromes and child psychiatric diagnoses. *J. Abnorm. Child Psychol.* 16: 219–31

Elder GH. 1986. Military times and turning points in men's lives. *Dev. Psychol.* 22: 233–45

Elder GH, Caspi A. 1988. Human development and social change: an emerging perspective on the life course. In *Persons in Context: Developmental Processes,* ed. N Bolger, A Caspi, G Downey, M Moorehouse, pp. 77–113. Cambridge: Cambridge Univ. Press

Elder GH, Liker J, Cross C. 1984. Parent-child behavior in the Great Depression: life course and inter-generational influences. In *Life-span Development and Behavior,* ed. PB Baltes, OG Brim, 6:109–58. New York: Academic

Elliott DS. 1993. Health-enhancing and health-compromising lifestyles. See Millstein et al 1993, pp. 119–45

Entwisle DR. 1990. Schools and the adolescent. See Feldman & Elliott 1990, pp. 197–224

Ewart CK, Kolodner KB. 1994. Negative affect, gender, and expressive style predict elevated ambulatory blood pressure in adolescents. *J. Pers. Soc. Psychol.* 66:596–605

Farrington D, Loeber R, Van Kammen WB. 1990. Long-term criminal outcomes of hyperactivity-impulsivity-attention deficit and conduct problems in childhood. See Robins & Rutter 1990, pp. 62–81

Feldman SS, Elliott GR, eds. 1990. *At the Threshold: The Developing Adolescent.* Cambridge, MA: Harvard Univ. Press

Feldman SS, Rosenthal DA, Mont-Reymond R, Leung K, Lau S. 1991. Ain't misbehavin': adolescent values and family environments as correlates of misconduct in Australia, Hong Kong, and the United States. *J. Res. Adol.* 1:109–34

Freud A. 1958. Adolescence. *Psychoanal. Stud. Child.* 13:255–78

Furstenberg FF. 1990. Coming of age in a changing family system. See Feldman & Elliott 1990, pp. 147–70

Garber J, Hollon SD. 1991. What can specificity designs say about causality in psychopathology research? *Psychol. Bull.* 110: 129–36

Garber J, Weiss B, Shanley N. 1993. Cognitions, depressive symptoms, and development in adolescents. *J. Abnorm. Psychol.* 102:47–57

Garland AF, Zigler E. 1993. Adolescent suicide prevention: current research and social policy implications. *Am. Psychol.* 48:169–82

Garmezy N. 1985. Stress-resistant children: the search for protective factors. In *Recent Research in Developmental Psychopathology. J. Child Psychol. Psychiatr. Book Suppl.* 4:213–33, ed. JE Stevenson. Oxford: Pergamon

Ge X, Conger RD, Lorenz FO, Elder GH, Montague RB, Simons RL. 1992. Linking family economic hardship to adolescent distress. *J. Res. Adol.* 2:351–78

Gjerde PF, Block J, Block JH. 1988. Depressive symptoms and personality during late adolescence: gender differences in the externalization-internalization of symptom expression. *J. Abnorm. Psychol.* 97: 475–86

Gotlib IH, Hammen C. 1992. *Psychological Aspects of Depression: Toward a Cognitive-interpersonal Integration.* New York: Wiley

Haggerty RJ, Garmezy N, Rutter M, Sherrod L, eds. 1994. *Risk and Resilience in Children: Developmental Approaches.* New York: Cambridge Univ. Press

Hall GS. 1904. *Adolescence: Its Psychology and its Relation to Psychology, Anthropology, Sociology, Sex, Crime, Religion, and Education.* Englewood Cliffs, NJ: Prentice-Hall

Hamburg DA. 1992. *Today's Children: Creating a Future for a Generation in Crisis.* New York: New York Times Books

Hammen C. 1991. *Depression Runs in Families.* New York: Springer-Verlag

Hammen C, Burge D, Adrian C. 1991. Timing of mother and child depression in a longitudinal study of children at risk. *J. Consult. Clin. Psychol.* 59:341–45

Hammen C, Daley S, Rudolph K, Burge D. 1994. *Depression comorbidity in late adolescent women.* Presented at Biannu. Meet. Soc. Res. Adol., San Diego, Feb.

Hammond WR, Yung B. 1993. Psychology's role in the public health response to assaultive violence among young African-American men. *Am. Psychol.* 48:142–54

Harrington R, Fudge H, Rutter M, Pickles A, Hill J. 1990. Adult outcome of childhood and adolescent depression. *Arch. Gen. Psychiatr.* 47:465–73

Harter S. 1990. Self and identity development. See Feldman & Elliott 1990, pp. 352–87

Hill JP. 1988. Adapting to menarche: familial control and conflict. In *Minnesota Symposium on Child Development,* ed. M Gunnar, WA Collins, 21:43–77. Hillsdale, NJ: Earlbaum

Holmbeck GN, Hill JP. 1991. Conflictive engagement, positive affect, and menarche in families with seventh grade girls. *Child Dev.* 62:1030–48

Inoff-Germain G, Arnold GS, Nottelmann ED, Susman EJ, Cutler GB, Chousos GP. 1988. Relations between hormone levels and observational measures of aggressive behavior of young adolescents in family interactions. *Dev. Psychol.* 24:129–39

Jessor R. 1991. Behavioral science: an emerging paradigm for social inquiry? In *Perspectives on Behavioral Science: The Colorado Lectures,* ed. R Jessor, pp. 309–16. Boulder, CO: Westview

Jessor R. 1992. Risk behavior in adolescence: a psychosocial framework for understanding and action. *Dev. Rev.* 12:374–90

Jessor R. 1993. Successful adolescent development among youth in high-risk settings. *Am. Psychol.* 48:117–26

Jessor R, Donovan JD, Costa F. 1991. *Beyond Adolescence: Problem Behavior and Young Adult Development.* New York: Cambridge Univ. Press

Kandel DB, Davies M. 1982. Epidemiology of depressive mood in adolescents. *Arch. Gen. Psychiatr.* 39:1205–12

Kaslow N. 1994. Contemporary psychological theories. In *Handbook of Depression in Children and Adolescents,* ed. WM Reynolds, H Johnston. New York: Plenum

Kazdin AE, Rodgers A, Colbus D. 1986. The Hopelessness Scale for Children: psychometric characteristics and concurrent validity. *J. Consult. Clin. Psychol.* 54:241–45

Keating D. 1990. Adolescent thinking. See Feldman & Elliott 1990, pp. 54–89

Kestenbaum JS. 1968. Phases of adolescence with suggestions for a correlation of psychic and hormonal organizations: Part 3. Puberty growth, differentiation, and consolidation. *J. Am. Acad. Child Psychiatr.* 7:108–51

Kovacs M, Feinberg TL, Crouse-Novak MA, Paulauskas SL, Finkelstein R. 1984. Depressive disorders in childhood: I. A longitudinal prospective study of characteristics and recovery. *Arch. Gen. Psychiatr.* 41:219–39

Kovacs M, Paulauskas S, Gatsonis C, Richards C. 1988. Depressive disorders in childhood: III. A longitudinal study of comorbidity with and risk for conduct disorders. *J. Affect. Disord.* 15:205–17

Leadbeater BJ, Blatt SJ, Quinlan DM. 1994. Gender-linked vulnerabilities to depressive symptoms, stress, and problem behaviors in adolescence. *J. Res. Adol.* In press

LeBlanc M. 1990. Two processes of the development of persistent offending: activation and escalation. See Robins & Rutter 1990, 82–100

Lee CM, Gotlib IH. 1991. Family disruption, parental availability, and child adjustment: an integrative review. In *Advances in the Behavioral Assessment of Children and Families,* ed. RJ Prinz, 5:166–99. Greenwich, CT: JAI

Lerner RM. 1985. Adolescent maturational changes and psychosocial development: a dynamic interactional perspective. *J. Youth Adol.* 14:355–72

Lerner RM, Mulkeen P. 1990. Commentary. *Dev. Rev.* 33:179–84

Lerner RM, Tubman JG. 1989. Conceptual issues in studying continuity and discontinuity in personality development across life. *J. Pers.* 57:343–73

Leventhal H, Keeshan P. 1993. Promoting healthy alternatives to substance abuse. See Millstein et al 1993, pp. 260–84

Lewinsohn PM, Hops H, Roberts RE, Seeley JR, Andrews JA. 1993. Adolescent psychopathology: I. Prevalence and incidence of depression and other DSM-III-R disorders in high school students. *J. Abnorm. Psychol.* 102:133–44

Lewinsohn PM, Rohde P, Seeley JR, Hops H. 1991. The comorbidity of unipolar depression: I. Major depression with dysthymia. *J. Abnorm. Psychol.* 100:205–13

Linares LO, Leadbeater BJ, Kato PM, Jaffe L. 1991. Predicting subgroup outcomes for minority groups adolescent mothers: Can subgroups be identified? *J. Res. Adol.* 1:379–400

McCord J. 1990. Long-term perspectives on parental absence. See Robins & Rutter 1990, pp. 116–34

Millstein SG, Petersen AC, Nightingale EO, eds. 1993. *Promoting the Health of Adolescents: New Directions for the Twenty-first Century.* New York: Oxford Univ. Press

Moffitt TE. 1993. Adolescence-limited and life-course-persistent antisocial behavior: a developmental taxonomy. *Psychol. Rev.* 100:674–701

Mortimer JT, Finch M, Shanahan M, Ryu S. 1992. Adolescent work history and behavioral adjustment. *J. Res. Adol.* 2:59–80

Nolen-Hoeksema S. 1991. Responses to depression and their effects on the duration of depressive episodes. *J. Abnorm. Psychol.* 100:569–82

Nolen-Hoeksema S, Girgus JS. 1994. The emergence of gender differences in depression during adolescence. *Psychol. Bull.* 115:424–43

Nottelmann ED, Jensen PS. 1994. Comorbidity of disorders in children and adolescents: developmental perspectives. In *Advances in Clinical Child Psychology,* ed. T Ollendick, R Prinz, Vol. 17. New York: Plenum. In press

Nottelmann ED, Susman E, Inoff-Germain G, Cutler G, Loriaux D, Chrousos G. 1987. Developmental processes in early adolescence: relationships between adolescent adjustment problems and chronological age, pubertal status, and puberty-related serum hormone levels. *J. Pediatr.* 110:473–80

Paikoff RL, Brooks-Gunn J. 1991. Do parent-child relationships change during puberty? *Psychol. Bull.* 110:47–66

Papini DR, Datan N, McCluskey-Fawcett KA. 1988. An observational study of affective and assertive family interactions during adolescence. *J. Youth Adol.* 17:477–92

Petersen AC. 1988. Adolescent development. *Annu. Rev. Psychol.* 39:583–607

Petersen AC. 1993. Presidential address: Creating adolescents: the role of context and process in developmental trajectories. *J. Res. Adol.* 3:1–18

Petersen AC, Compas BE, Brooks-Gunn J, Stemmler M, Ey S, Grant KE. 1993. Depression during adolescence. *Am. Psychol.* 48:155–68

Petersen AC, Sarigiani PA, Kennedy RE. 1991. Adolescent depression: Why more girls? *J. Youth Adol.* 20:247–71

Powers SI, Hauser ST, Kilner LA. 1989. Adolescent mental health. *Am. Psychol.* 44:200–8

Puig-Antich J. 1987. Sleep and neuroendocrine correlates of affective illness in childhood and adolescence. *J. Adol. Health Care* 8:505–29

Quinton D, Rutter M. 1988. *Parenting Breakdown: The Making and Breaking of Intergenerational Links.* Aldershot, England: Avebury

Rescorla RA. 1988. Pavlovian conditioning: It's not what you think. *Am. Psychol.* 43:151–59

Richards MH, Larson R. 1993. Pubertal development and the daily subjective states of young adolescents. *J. Res. Adol.* 3:145–69

Robins LN. 1985. The epidemiology of antisocial personality. In *Psychiatry,* ed. JO Cavenar, 3:1–14. Philadelphia: Lippincott

Robins LN, McEvoy L. 1990. Conduct problems as predictors of substance abuse. See Robins & Rutter 1990, pp. 182–204

Robins LN, Rutter M, eds. 1990. *Straight and Devious Pathways from Childhood to Adulthood.* New York: Oxford Univ. Press

Rogers JL, Rowe DC. 1993. Social contagion and adolescent sexual behavior: a developmental EMOSA model. *Psychol. Rev.* 100:479–510

Rohde P, Lewinsohn PM, Seeley JR. 1991. Comorbidity of unipolar depression: II. Comorbidity with other mental disorders in adolescents and adults. *J. Abnorm. Psychol.* 100:214–22

Rosenthal DA, Feldman SS. 1991. The influence of perceived family and personal factors on self-reported school performance of

Chinese and western high school students. *J. Res. Adol.* 1:135–54

Rutter M. 1986. The developmental psychopathology of depression: issues and perspectives. In *Depression in Young People: Developmental and Clinical Perspectives,* ed. M Rutter, CE Izard, PB Read, pp. 3–30. New York: Guilford

Rutter M. 1989. Pathways from childhood to adult life. *J. Child Psychol. Psychiatr.* 30:23–51

Rutter M, Rutter M. 1993. *Developing Minds: Challenge and Continuity Across the Life Span.* New York: Basic Books

Sameroff AJ, Seifer R, Baldwin AL, Baldwin CA. 1993. Stability of intelligence from preschool to adolescence: the influence of social and family risk factors. *Child Dev.* 64:80–97

Shelton RC, Hollon SD, Purdon SE, Loosen PT. 1991. Biological and psychological aspects of depression. *Behav. Ther.* 22:201–28

Stanger C, Achenbach TM, Verhulst FC. 1994. Accelerating longitudinal research in child psychopathology: a practical example. *Psychol. Assess.* 6:102–7

Stanger C, Verhulst FC. 1994. Accelerated longitudinal designs. In *The Epidemiology of Child and Adolescent Psychopathology,* ed. FC Verhulst, H Koot. London: Oxford Univ. Press. In press

Steinberg L. 1987. Impact of puberty on family relations: effects of pubertal status and pubertal timing. *Dev. Psychol.* 23:451–60

Steinberg L. 1988. Reciprocal relation between parent-child distance and pubertal maturation. *Dev. Psychol.* 24:122–28

Strober M, Morrell W, Burroughs J, Lampert C, Danforth H, Freeman R. 1988. A family study of Bipolar I disorder in adolescence: early onset of symptoms linked to increased familial loading and lithium resistance. *J. Affect. Disord.* 15:255–68

Susman E, Dorn LD, Chrousos GP. 1991. Negative affect and hormone levels in young adolescents: concurrent and predictive waves. *J. Youth Adol.* 20:167–90

Susman EJ, Inoff-Germain G, Nottelmann ED, Loriaux DL, Cutler GB, Chrousos GP. 1987. Hormones, emotional dispositions, and aggressive attributes in young adolescents. *Child Dev.* 58:1114–34

Trickett PK, Putnam FW. 1993. Impact of child sexual abuse on females: toward a developmental psychological integration. *Psychol. Sci.* 4:81–87

United States Congress/Office of Technology Assessment. 1991. *Adolescent Health.* Vol. 1: *Summary and Policy Options* (OTA-H-464). Washington, DC: US Gov. Print. Off.

Wagner BM, Compas BE, Howell DC. 1988. Daily hassles and major life events: a test of an integrative model of psychosocial stress. *Am. J. Commun. Psychol.* 16:189–205

Weissman MM, Bruce ML, Leaf PJ, Florio LP, Holzer C. 1991. Affective disorders. In *Psychiatric Disorders in America,* ed. LN Robins, DA Regier, pp. 53–80. New York: Free

Windle M, Lerner RM. 1986. The "goodness of fit" model of temperament-context rela-tions: interaction or correlation? *New Dir. Child Dev.* 31:109–20

Windle M, Miller-Tutzauer C, Domenico D. 1992. Alcohol use, suicidal behavior, and risky activities among adolescents. *J. Res. Adol.* 2:317–30

Zaslow J, Takanishi R. 1993. Priorities for re-search on adolescent development. *Am. Psychol.* 48:185–92

Annu. Rev. Psychol. 1995. 46:295–328

PERSONALITY PROCESSES

William Revelle

Department of Psychology, Northwestern University, Evanston, Illinois 60208

KEY WORDS: personality traits, evolution, behavior genetics, biological bases, affect

CONTENTS

INTRODUCTION

The development of psychological theory tends to oscillate between optimistic advances and self-critical analyses and retrenchment. Personality theory is no different. In the past 40 years personality research has seen at least one full cycle of uncritical enthusiasm turn into bleak pessimism and again to enthusiasm. Recent events suggest that the field is again becoming a focal area of psychological study. Exciting discoveries are being made in behavior genetics, there is a growing consensus about the relationship between personality traits and emotional states, biological theorists of adult personality are exchanging ideas with theorists of childhood temperament, and long-term studies of personality development across the life span are delivering on the promises made many years ago. Upon reading the most recent *Handbook of Personality* (Pervin 1990a) one cannot help being excited by the progress that has been made since the previous edition (Borgatta & Lambert 1968). Many of the tentative findings of the early 1950s (Eysenck 1952, MacKinnon 1951, Sears 1950) have led to substantial contributions that continue to influence our thinking. This claim of a renaissance in personality theory has, however, been made before (Allport & Vernon 1930, Bronfenbrenner 1953, Pervin 1990b). Unfortunately, many promising approaches have led nowhere.

Personality theories attempt to account for individual behavior. The scope of such theories is vast. They describe how genetic predispositions and biological mechanisms combine with experience as children develop into young adults who will show behavioral consistencies over their life spans. Personality researchers report heritability coefficients, relate MRI scans and EEG activity to intellectual performance and emotional reactions, and predict job outcomes and lifetime satisfaction. They examine the dimensions of self-description and the many ways feelings, knowledge, and beliefs combine in behavior. Personality research ranges from tests of evolutionary theories of jealousy to analyses of the structure and content of one's life story.

After 20 years there is a resurgence of interest in the fundamental questions of personality, including 1. What are the relevant dimensions of individual differences in personality? 2. How do genetic mechanisms lead to individual differences? 3. Does personality have a biological basis? 4. How does personality develop? 5. How does personality change? 6. What are the social determinants of personality?

Personality constructs are again being seen in the literature of behavior genetics, cognitive psychology, developmental psychology, evolutionary psychology, physiological psychology, psychopathology, and social psychology. This review focuses on these related areas partly to clarify their links to personality theory and also to guide those who might be interested in recent advances in personality theory. In addition, it is meant to guide personality researchers to developments reported outside the usual personality journals. Because personality is the study of the whole person, this review focuses on the interrelationships of personality theory with other areas of psychology. Just as other areas of psychology have become more aware of advances in personality, theoreticians within the field must be aware of recent advances in related disciplines.

The earliest reviews of personality were able to address the entire field. Starting with Atkinson (1960), issues of personality dynamics were separated from those of structure and development because it was no longer possible to give adequate coverage in less than book form (if at all). Similarly, this review focuses more on the how and why of personality processes than on the what of personality taxonomy and structure (Digman 1990, Wiggins & Pincus 1992). I consider the metatheoretic question of what is personality and what are the appropriate ways to study it.

A METATHEORETIC TAXONOMY OF PERSONALITY THEORIES AND PROCESSES: THREE DIMENSIONS OF PERSONALITY THEORY

The questions that scientists ask about the world are driven by their scientific metaphors. The chasm between the two disciplines of psychological inquiry so well described by Atkinson (1960), Cronbach (1957, 1975), Eysenck (1966), and Vale & Vale (1969) was a split between two world views, two scientific metaphors, and two data-analytic strategies. The experimentalists emphasized control, manipulation, and the t-test. The individual differences psychologists emphasized adaptation, variation, and the correlation coefficient.

Unfortunately, theoretical and research emphases have splintered beyond even two disciplines. Even within the field of personality there are many different, seemingly unrelated approaches. Current research in personality can be organized along three dimensions: level of generality between people, levels of analysis, and degree of adaptability of the behavior. The first dimension ranges from generalizing to all people to focusing on single individuals and was captured by Kluckhohn & Murray (1948) as emphasizing how all people are the same, some people are the same, and no people are the same. These ways of knowing (McAdams 1994a) can be crossed with a second dimension of analysis, ranging from analyses of the genetic code, through biological mechanisms, learning and developmental processes, and temporary cognitive and emotional structures and processes, to the study of overall life meaning and satisfaction. Phenomena at one level of analysis are only loosely coupled with those at different levels (Figure 1). The third dimension, not shown in the figure, is one of adaptability and functioning. Personality theories need to account for normal adaptive processes as well as extreme psychopathologies. Although broad theories consider issues across these three dimensions, most theorists focus on phenomena that range across levels of analysis at one level of generality, or across levels of generality at one level of explanation.

A conceptual organization of personality theory and research

Levels of analysis	Species typical		adjustment - well being / life satisfaction	proprium / self concept / possible selves	Individual (narrative structure)
Life meaning/identity	identity / ego ideal		adjustment - well being / life satisfaction	proprium / self concept / possible selves	narrative structure
Cognitive-affective structures	ego/superego secondary process; id primary process	knowledge / social skills; attributional styles	intelligence / interpersonal skills / motivational direction; dimensions of affect / motivational intensity	self schemas / personal constructs / conscious awareness	narrative content; affective reactions
Learning and experience	gratification fixations	schedules of reinforcement	differential sensitivities / temperament	childhood experiences	
Biological substrates and constraints	reproductive fitness and sexual drive		c.n.s. and CNS / BIS/BAS/FFS / 5HT/DA/GABA		
Genetic predisposition/evolutionary selection	evolution of species typical behaviors	behavior genetics of shared environmental effects	behavior genetics of individual differences		

Levels of generality: from the species to the individual

Figure 1. A conceptual organization of the multiple approaches to personality. Theories differ in level of analysis as well as in level of generality. The third dimension, levels of functioning, has not been shown. Cell entries are representative of phenomena studied. Specific theorists are discussed in the text. Broader theories account for phenomena across more cells than do narrower theories. Theorists tend to emphasize either multiple levels of analysis at the same level of generality or multiple levels of generality at the same level of analysis. Solid lines indicate larger differences of level than do dashed lines.

Levels of Generality—From the Species to the Individual

Just as psychology is the study of behavior, personality is the study of individual behavior. Although to many the study of individual behavior has meant the study of individual differences in behavior, an adequate theory of personality process and structure must also account for similarities in behavior. A complete personality theory needs to focus on the three levels of personality identified by Kluckhohn & Murray (1948).

The classical test theory metaphor used by applied and personnel psychologists, and the analysis of variance metaphor used by the interactionists, although compelling, both emphasize sources of variation rather than sources of consistency. Although it is important to consider the interaction of persons and situations as well as the effects of individual and situational differences, by using either a correlational or an analysis of variance metaphor we are unable to ask questions other than how some people are the same and some are different.

A generalization of the analysis of variance metaphor is to consider the other components of the general linear model. Estimates of any particular behavior are expressed in terms of the central tendency across all people, the responsivity to particular situational and person variables, the interaction between the situational and person variables, as well as the reliable within-person variance and that associated with unknown sources of variance.

Theories differ in their central focus as well as in their range of generalizability. Evolutionary personality theory, psychoanalytic theory, behavior theory, and sociology emphasize the commonalities of individual behaviors. Every member of every species needs to meet the challenges of survival and of reproduction. How these challenges are met within a species reflects species-typical solutions. By understanding how these problems are answered by humans as a species we can understand the fundamentals of human nature. Trait theorists focus on systematic individual differences and similarities among people. Although some emphasize how general laws lead to behavioral differences (Eysenck 1990), at the extreme, this approach consciously shuns universal theories (Hofstee 1991). Social constructionists, phenomenologists, and biographers focus on the unique patterns of a life story after species-typical and broad individual differences and trait influences have been removed (Allport 1962; but see Holt 1962).

Levels of Explanation—From the Gene to the Society

Current research in personality and individual differences ranges from attempts to identify particular genetic sequences associated with behavior to studies of how one's life meaning can be affected by societal changes such as the Depression or a world war. Species-typical behaviors that are the result of genetic selection are proposed by evolutionary psychologists who ask about the origins and reasons for human nature. Behavior geneticists examine the genetic architecture of specific traits as well as the covariances of traits with each other and with different parts of the environment. Behavior genetic analyses also demonstrate within-family and between-family environmental effects. Genes affect particular dimensions of individual differences by modifying biological structures and regulating ongoing processes. Rather than the evolutionary question of *why,* explanations at the biological level ask *how.* Although ultimately rooted in biology, cognition, affect, and behavior may be studied independently of biological mechanisms. These are studies of *what* is human nature. Examining individual differences in behavior in terms of cognitive structures and affective reactions is perhaps the most common personality research. Broad questions of meaning tend to be associated with philosophically and clinically oriented theorists who emphasize how people organize their lives in terms of recurrent themes and problems. Research on the effect of the self-concept, self-esteem, career choice, personality disorders, satisfaction, and development throughout the life span also emphasizes this highest level of analysis.

Levels of Functioning

Personality theories are not just theories of normal functioning. They also address dysfunctional as well as high-level behavior. Although many limit their studies to unselected groups of adolescents and adults, others examine selected groups such as prisoners, patients, and professionals.

RECENT TRENDS IN PERSONALITY AND RELATED FIELDS

Recent *Annual Review of Psychology* chapters on personality theory and research reflect the breadth and scope of the field. Buss (1991) proposed that evolutionary theory provides the necessary framework for the study of personality. Evolutionary personality theory addresses the goals and mechanisms to achieve them that are typical of our species. It also focuses on individual strategies that are used to meet species-typical challenges. Magnusson & Törestad (1993) evoked biological models and systems theory to emphasize the need to consider dynamic processes of cognitive construals as active, purposeful agents interact with their world. Digman (1990) reviewed the consistent findings in personality taxonomic work and reported strong agreement across different research groups on the number and identification of the basic dimensions of personality. Wiggins & Pincus (1992) elaborated on structural questions of the assessment of basic dimensions and concluded that there is strong agreement on personality structure from those examining enduring dispositions, dyadic-interactions, social competencies, or natural language. Ozer & Reise (1994) shared that view and emphasized methodological rather than substantive issues in personality assessment.

Even with the diversity of perspectives seen in the above chapters, personality theory is too broad to be included in a single review. A complete review of personality processes needs to include recent social psychology advances in self-theory and social cognition, cross-cultural sources of variation, biological theories of memory structure, and techniques of brain imaging. Theoretical advances in the biological nature of schizophrenia and the affective disorders shed light on both normal and psychopathological functioning. Techniques of treatment of the anxiety disorders are relevant to theories of normal personality. These topics and more have appeared in recent issues of the *Annual Review of Psychology.*

In addition, there has been a proliferation of "handbooks" devoted to various aspects of personality. For an overview of the field, the *Handbook of Personality Theory* (Pervin 1990a) is essential reading. Gale & Eysenck (1992) review advances in biological approaches. Smith & Jones (1992) review individual differences in trait and states as they affect human performance. Conferences and edited volumes sponsored by the American Psychological Association have emphasized longitudinal research (Funder et al 1993, Heatherton & Weinberger 1994), temperament (Bates & Wachs 1994), and the application of personality assessment to psychopathology (Costa & Widiger 1994). Special issues of the *Journal of Personality* have been devoted to long-term stability and change in personality (West & Graziano 1989), the biological foundations of personality (Buss 1990), personality and daily experience (Tennen et al 1991), the five-factor model (McCrae 1992), and personality judgment (Funder & West 1993). Special issues of *Cognition and Emotion* particularly relevant to personality processes have addressed the psychobiological aspects of relationships between emotion and cognition (Gray 1990, Watts 1993), the question of whether there are basic emotions (Stein & Oatley 1992), and the role that cognitive appraisals play in emotion (Frijda 1993).

ALL PEOPLE ARE THE SAME: THE STUDY OF SPECIES-TYPICAL BEHAVIOR

It is easy to forget, when considering human behavior, how similar we all are to each other. Demonstrations of this similarity include the compelling "Barnum effect" observed when judging the accuracy of self-descriptions based on human universals. That one experiences some anxiety when meeting an attractive stranger, or sometimes thinks about things that other people might find peculiar, is not a sign of uniqueness but rather something one shares with everyone. Rather than dismissing these similarities, evolutionary theorists, psychodynamicists, sociologists, and others hope to find an understanding of the universalities and general laws of human nature.

Evolutionary Personality Psychology

Evolutionary personality theory focuses on the *why* of behavior, rather than the *how* of biological models, or the *what* of descriptive taxonomies. It is "best regarded as a theory about the origins, rather than the content of human nature" (Buss 1991, p. 463). It has been described as providing a grand framework that "links the field with what is known about the processes that govern all forms of life [and identifies] the central human goals and the psychological and behavioral strategic means deployed to obtain these goals" (p. 486). "Evolutionary psychology is simply psychology that is informed by the additional knowledge that evolutionary biology has to offer, in the expectation that understanding the process that designed the human mind will advance the discovery of its architecture" (Cosmides et al 1992, p. 3).

Evolutionary Causes for Individual Differences

Although focusing on general laws, evolutionary theory tries to explain individual differences. The problem of reconciling genetic diversity within species with principles of evolutionary adaptation is complex: "Both the psychological universals that constitute human nature and the genetic differences that contribute to individual variation are the product of the evolutionary process.... [Personality is from an] evolutionary perspective, analyzable as either (a) an adaptation, (b) an incidental by-product of an adaptation, (c) the product of noise in the system, or (d) some combination of these" (Tooby & Cosmides 1990, p. 19).

Evolutionary theorists ask why there are genetically based individual differences. Individual differences might result from frequency-dependent selection pressures that can lead to complex polymorphisms and maintain a stable mix of genotypes. In an environment with many potential niches, individuals, by being different, can select the niches that maximize their own fitness, and thus the population is a mix of multiple genotypes each searching for and creating optimal environments (D Wilson 1994, D Wilson et al 1993, D Wilson et al 1994).

Another intriguing hypothesis for the adaptive significance of individual differences, for sexual reproduction, as well as for much greater genetic diversity within rather than between racial groups, is that variation and recombination is a response to parasites. "Large, complex, long-lived organisms constitute ecological environments for immense numbers of short-lived, rapidly evolving parasites—disease causing microorganisms. ...Parasites and hosts are locked in an antagonistic coevolutionary race" (Tooby & Cosmides 1990, p. 32). Sexual reproduction, although genetically costly (without assortative mating, sexual reproduction assesses a 50% "inheritance tax" at each generation), produces offspring with a genetic makeup that one's parasites have never before encountered. The function of individual differences and sexual rather than asexual reproduction might be to survive this constant onslaught of parasitic infestation. In humans, the importance of physical appearance (a sign of pathogen resistance) in mate selection may be associated with pathogen prevalence (Gangestad & Buss 1993).

Sexual Strategies

Survival and reproduction are the two fundamental challenges of evolution. This general principle leads to individual differences between the sexes in terms of reproductive strategies. Males and females differ in the costs associated with reproduction and use different strategies to maximize their fitness. Although males are potentially almost unlimited in their number of offspring, females are not. Females can be certain about motherhood, but males can never be certain of paternity. From these biological realities, several interesting predictions have been tested. Male swallows, dunnocks, and humans "take a proprietary view of women's sexuality and reproductive capacity" (M Wilson & Daly 1992, p. 289). Males, thought to be concerned with paternity certainty, are more upset by sexual infidelity of their partners, while females, thought to be concerned with the long-term emotional investment of their partners, are more concerned about emotional infidelity (Buss et al 1992). In general (but see Gangsted & Simpson 1990), females are more choosy about sexual partners than are males, even though males and females do not differ in their preferences for long-term relationships (Kenrick et al 1990). In a powerful example of the theoretical possibilities, Buss & Schmitt (1993) formalized the predictions of evolutionary personality theory with nine hypotheses about human mating patterns.

Sociology of Generational Effects

Sociological approaches to personality are strikingly different from evolutionary personality theory in terms of level of analysis, but they are similar with respect to the level of generality. For example, it is easy for personality theorists to forget that different generations have experienced significantly different challenges and opportunities throughout their life spans. The experience of war, national economic collapse, or the threat of nuclear extinction have had profound effects on those who have experienced them. Although these are universal experiences for all alive at the time, only generational cohorts share both the experience as well as the timing at the same stage in their lives. Detection of potential generational effects requires many waves of longitudinal data for people of different age cohorts. A single longitudinal study that focuses on the experiences of a particular cohort will show impressive consistencies and coherencies over large parts of the life span but will fail to detect the effect on personality of the timing of major life events. Data from several of the classic longitudinal studies have been used to address such generational effects on personality through the life span (Elder 1994).

Archival data from the 12 waves (1922 through 1986) of the Terman (1925) study show cohort effects on later career achievement, transitions, and trajectories (Elder & Pavalko 1993). The age of experiencing the Great Depression and the disruption of career upon entry into the military during World War II had reliable effects on lifetime accomplishment for this group.

Psychodynamic Theory

Psychoanalytic approaches "take as axiomatic the importance of conflicting mental processes; unconscious processes; compromises among competing psychological tendencies that may be negotiated unconsciously; defense and self-deception; the influence of the past on current functioning; the enduring effects of interpersonal patterns laid down in childhood; and the role of sexual and aggressive wishes in consciously and unconsciously influencing thought, feeling, and behavior" (Westen 1990, p. 21). With such an inclusive definition, it is not surprising that discussions of psychodynamic approaches integrate findings from more experimental areas of psychology about self (Markus & Cross 1990), unconscious awareness (Kihlstrom 1987, 1990), and even biological distinctions in memory systems.

Psychodynamic theories with an emphasis on cognitive representations rather than biological drives (i.e. object relations theory) are more compatible with the research paradigms of social cognition (Westen 1991). Obstacles to integration of these two approaches, however, include strong differences in the data used for theory building (clinical insights versus systematic laboratory-based data) and in the level of generality that the theory addresses (Westen 1990). Some psychiatric theories propose useful links of psychodynamic with psychobiological approaches to personality and the personality disorders (Siever & Davis 1991).

SOME PEOPLE ARE THE SAME: THE STUDY OF INDIVIDUAL DIFFERENCES AND SIMILARITIES

That people who share a similar upbringing are more similar than those who do not is obvious. Similarities based on linguistic and cultural background have never been denied. The utility of using individual differences in one situation to predict individual differences in another situation, however, has been hotly contested. Debates about the relative importance of situational versus individual causes of consistencies and differences dominated a disproportionate amount of the literature of the 1970s and 1980s but became less virulent as both sides developed more tolerance, became exhausted, or developed a richer understanding of the underlying issues. By changing their emphases, both sides have made theoretical advances by better understanding their limits.

Trait-Based Differences and Similarities

In a tradition strongly associated with prediction and selection (Kanfer et al 1994), the study of individual differences in personality represents the greatest amount of personality research. Indeed, so much work has been done that to some the field of personality *is* the study of individual differences (Buss 1989). Just as personality theories can be organized in terms of their level of explanation and level of generality, so can studies of individual differences be further organized along two dimensions: cognitive versus affective-temperamental and descriptive versus causal-explanation.

COGNITIVE ABILITIES VERSUS AFFECTIVE-TEMPERAMENTAL TRAITS   The first dimension distinguishes analyses of intellectual abilities from those of noncognitive variables associated with affective reactions and behavior. The cognitive-noncognitive distinction runs throughout the field and some personality theorists specifically rule out cognitive ability as an area of study. Others include both cognitive abilities and temperamental traits as part of personality structure, whereas still others discuss personality and intelligence as separate domains but routinely study both. The distinction between cognitive and affective components of personality is both clarified and muddied by the labels given to measures in these two domains: tests of intellectual ability and tests of personality.

Ackerman and Kanfer and their colleagues have attempted to integrate individual differences in cognitive and noncognitive function in applied settings. Not only do cognitive and noncognitive measures differ in content, but they also differ in typicality. Intelligence tests are meant to be maximal performance measures, whereas most noncognitive scales are measures of typical behavior. Furthermore, cognitive tasks are direct behavioral measures, whereas noncognitive measures are typically based on self-reports of average behaviors or of intentions (Brody 1994). The predictive relationship with performance outcome of cognitive and noncognitive measures changes as people become more experienced with the task at hand. Noncognitive measures and typical intellectual engagement become more important predictors over trials and maximal cognitive performance becomes less important (Ackerman 1994). Further clarifying the relationship between maximal and typical performance, Goff & Ackerman (1992) report that typical intellectual engagement, although independent of fluid intelligence, is correlated positively with crystallized intelligence. Typical intellectual engagement is highly related to the "Big 5" dimension of openness (Rocklin 1994) but differs somewhat at lower-order components of both openness and typical intellectual engagement (Ackerman & Goff 1994).

An innovative use of cognitive and noncognitive variables in the study of creativity is proposed by Eysenck (1993). Eysenck reviews the J-shaped distribution of creative output and suggests that it results from the interactive product of cognitive ability, societal constraints and opportunities, and noncognitive variables including confidence, nonconformity, and originality. He places particular emphasis on the role that the psychoticism dimension plays in creative productions.

Experimental analyses have shown systematic although complex relationships between noncognitive personality variables and cognitive performance. These relationships are moderated by a variety of situational manipulations that affect motivational states (Anderson 1994; Anderson & Revelle 1994; Matthews et al 1989, 1990; Revelle 1989). These are theoretically driven tests of the arousal model of extraversion (Eysenck 1967, 1990) and its modification and extension to impulsivity (Humphreys & Revelle 1984). Helpful reviews of the effects on performance of extraversion (Matthews 1992a) and anxiety (Mueller 1992) summarize many theoretical approaches to the combination of cognitive and noncognitive individual differences.

In applied settings, cognitive measures have been used since at least the Army Alpha Test in World War I. Noncognitive variables have a long and checkered past but "the emergence of an acceptable taxonomy of personality during the 1980s has provided applied psychologists with a sorely needed organizational framework for investigation of personality-work linkages" (Kanfer et al 1994, p. 30). Conscientiousness, experience, and ability combine to predict job performance (Schmidt & Hunter 1992).

DESCRIPTIVE TAXONOMIES VERSUS CAUSAL THEORY   After many years of bitterly fought debate about the appropriate number and identification of the fundamental dimensions of personality, the past several years have seen a remarkable consensus among most but not all descriptive taxonomists around five robust factors (the "Big 5" or B5): extraversion, emotional (in)stability or neuroticism, agreeableness, conscientiousness, and openness or culture (see Digman 1990; Goldberg 1992, 1993a,b; John 1990; Ozer & Reise 1994; Widiger & Costa 1994; Wiggins & Pincus 1992). Critics have suggested that this consensus is premature and overstated (Pervin 1994). Although much of the work on the B5 addresses the number and identification of personality dimensions, there are some particular instantiations such as the Five Factor Model (FFM) that are more concerned with underlying mechanisms (John & Robins 1993, McCrae & Costa 1990, 1994).

Descriptive taxonomies of individual differences have been a tradition in personality theories since Plato and Galen. Most taxonomic systems of cognitive and noncognitive attributes are hierarchical: clustering similar behaviors into narrow traits, then clustering these into higher-order traits, and eventually into a limited number of dimensional types (Eysenck 1991a). At any level of this hierarchy, behaviors and traits can be found that represent blends of separate dimensions, resisting any appearance of factorial simple structure and requiring a horizontal as well as a vertical structure (Goldberg 1993a,b). The problem for taxonomists thus becomes determining the optimal number of factors to describe these structures. Optimality means different things to different investigators, but includes being parsimonious, replicable, and useful. It is not surprising that there is not perfect agreement among all taxonomists given the many assumptions implicit to factor or principal components analysis.

There is strong agreement that the dimensions of extraversion-introversion and neuroticism–emotional stability are fundamental parts of any personality taxonomy. But proponents of what can be called "The Even Bigger 3" (EB3) suggest that openness is more of a cognitive than noncognitive construct, and that agreeableness and conscientiousness are both parts of a higher-order factor of psychoticism (Eysenck 1990, 1991b), or psychoticism-impulsivity–sensation seeking (Zuckerman 1991, 1994).

The dimensions of the B5 and the EB3 can be used to classify and provide order to the multiplicity of psychiatric diagnoses found useful by therapists and clinical researchers. The numerous personality disorders listed in the *Diagnostic and Statistical Manual of Mental Disorders (DSM-IIIR)* (American Psychiatric Association 1987) may be organized parsimoniously in terms of the FFM (Widiger & Costa 1994). Neuroticism is a risk factor for depression and anxiety, and introversion in combination with neuroticism increases risk of depression (Clark et al 1994, Costa & McCrae 1993). The hypothesized biological basis of the EB3 has been used to organize both the Axis I and Axis II dimensions of the *DSM-IIIR* (Siever & Davis 1991). A reconceptualization of the EB3 has been used to categorize the personality disorders (Cloninger 1987). It is uncertain whether personality traits are the causal sources of psychopathology, co-occurring signs, or the resulting psychological scars left by experiencing these disorders. Taxonomic work on interpersonal problems suggests a general factor of distress and a two-dimensional–circumplex structure that has been described in terms of love and trust or the B5 dimensions of emotional stability, extraversion, and agreeableness (Gurtman 1992, 1994).

Taxonomic studies of individual differences in mood have extended the earlier work of Tellegen (1985), Russell (1979), Thayer (1989), and Watson & Tellegen (1985) on identifying two independent dimensions of mood and emotion that are associated with positive and negative affect or energetic and tense arousal. These two dimensions of mood are, in turn, related to the EB3 and the B5. Extraversion is associated with measures of positive affect, and neuroticism is associated with measures of negative affect (Meyer & Shack 1989, Saucier 1992, Watson et al 1994).

CAUSAL MODELS OF INDIVIDUAL DIFFERENCES   The descriptive taxonomies associated with the proponents of the B5 are in contrast to those theories concerned with developing causal models of individual differences. Much of the recent consensus around the B5 has been on the number of dimensions useful in the description of individual differences rather than on any causal basis for these purported structures. Descriptive taxonomists suggest that before it is possible to develop causal explanations it is necessary to agree on the fundamental dimensions to be explained. Causal theorists, on the other hand, have focused on biological explanations of the EB3 and have emphasized the relationships of biological mechanisms of emotional reactivity with dimensions of stable individual differences. These theorists have suggested that problems of taxonomy can best be solved in terms of underlying mechanisms.

Until recently, this work has followed two related paths: demonstrations of the genetic basis of particular traits and explorations of particular biological mechanisms thought to be associated with individual differences in the major affective and cognitive traits (see Buss 1990). Among the mechanisms proposed are differences in relative activation of specific brain structures as well as differences in the relative amounts of specific neurotransmitters. More recently, some causal explanations for individual differences of some of the B5 have been proposed in terms of evolutionary theory (MacDonald 1992).

Genetics of individual differences in behavior   Recent evidence suggests that practically any trait of interest has a substantial genetic component. Excellent monograph-length reviews summarize studies of the heritabilities of the B5 (Loehlin 1992), review how behavior genetic studies help clarify the "nature of nurture" (Plomin 1994), or integrate many different approaches (Plomin & McClearn 1993). Behavioral patterns as complex as sexual orientation for males (Bailey & Pillard 1991) and females (Bailey et al 1993), political attitudes (Tessor 1993), or various personality disorders (Nigg & Goldsmith 1994) show strong evidence for heritability. Direct comparisons of results from cognitive and noncognitive studies suggest higher heritabilities of cognitive measures than of B5 or EB3 noncognitive dimensions (Brody 1993, 1994), although this may be the result of differences in scale reliability.

Kimble (1993) points out that the sudden resurgence of debates about nature versus nurture is surprising for those who remember learning that asking which is more important is like asking which contributes more to the area of a rectangle, the width or the length. That almost all of the major personality dimensions seem to have a substantial (50% +/– 20%) heritability is no longer a point of contention. What is more interesting is the genetic nature of the covariances between traits, the way in which one's environment contributes the remaining 30–70% of the variance (Brody 1993, Plomin 1994), and thus, the way that genotypes lead to phenotypes.

Heritability is a population value reflecting the amount of between-individual variability associated with additive (narrow heritabilty) or total (broad heritability) genetic variation. Heritability does not imply immutability; a lack of heritability does not imply a lack of a biological mechanism; nor does a high heritability imply a simple biological mechanism. Thus, that 90% of the variance in height is under additive genetic control does not preclude a several centimeter increase in height due to improved nutrition. That there is no additive genetic component to the sex of one's offspring does not imply that sex chromosomes don't matter. And finally, that 52% of the variability in the likelihood of divorce is under genetic control (McGue & Lykken 1992) does not imply that there is a divorce gene, nor does it imply that there is a divorce nucleus somewhere in the limbic system, nor is it inconsistent with large temporal variation in divorce rates. Complex behaviors reflect the sum and interaction of many separate predispositions. Although the similarity of monozygotic twins reared apart allows for estimates of broad heritability (Bouchard et al 1990, Bouchard & McGue 1990), these estimates may be inflated estimates of narrow (additive) genetic influences due to the effects of scaling, dominance, and gene-gene interactions (epistasis, also called emergenesis by Lykken et al 1992).

Creative research designs take advantage of the power of structural modeling procedures to estimate genetic and environmental parameters from adopted and biological siblings living together, biological siblings living apart, parent-child correlations for adopted and biological children, and many of the other living arrangements modern society provides (Eaves et al 1989, Loehlin 1992, Plomin et al 1990). Each unique family constellation can be fitted with alternative genetic models and the resulting path diagrams allow one to choose the most parsimonious.

One consequence of systematic modeling is that much more is known about environmental influences on personality development than was known before behavior genetic modeling was done. Just as classic behavior genetics analysis allows for a decomposition of genetic variance into additive and nonadditive within- and between-family genetic effects, so can estimates be derived for shared and unshared family environment effects. A striking conclusion is that in general, the shared family environment contributes little if anything to the similarity of children growing up in the same home. That is, within a similar culture, biologically related children growing up together tend to be as similar on most personality traits as they would be growing up apart, and unrelated children growing up together tend to be no more similar than unrelated children in general. In fact, it is likely that some similarities of child rearing practices that are experienced by children are largely the result of the genetic similarity of the children. Environment means more than one's family, for it includes cultural as well as prenatal environments.

Behavior genetic techniques can be applied to the covariances between traits as well as to the variances of traits. These techniques, although long available, have become more useful as larger samples and more powerful algorithms have become available. A useful example of such modeling is the examination of the genetic covariance of neuroticism, anxiety, and depression to analyze the direction of causation between them (Carey & DiLalla 1994).

The consistency of the behavior genetic evidence can be interpreted in two ways. Rather than showing whether or not environments are important determinants of personality, genetic modeling has shown how dynamic is the process of personality development. Gene-environment covariation suggests that people are selecting and shaping the environments in which they live, rather than being passively acted on by the environment. Children shape the action of their parents just as parents try to modify the behavior of their children (Rowe & Waldman 1993, Scarr 1992).

Biological substrates   Genes do not act directly on behavior. Genes code for proteins that in turn affect structures and regulate processes. Most biologically based theorists have asked what particular structure, neural pathway, transmitter, or hormone is associated with a particular individual difference in affect, cognition, or behavior. Much of this theorizing has been at the level of the conceptual nervous system (cns) rather than actually describing the Central Nervous System (CNS). That is, broad-brush behavioral systems have been described and linked, sometimes closely, sometimes loosely, to known physiological structures and transmitters. To the biologically oriented radical trait theorists, taxonomies should be developed in terms of cns or CNS biological systems rather than phenotypic behaviors. Individual differences in the functioning of these systems are believed to cause differential sensitivities to environmental cues, leading to differential affective and cognitive states. Traits refer to the probabilities of being in a particular state, or to the latency to achieve a state following a specific environmental elicitor. Although it is not necessary to know the specifics of a neural system to test the implications of a conceptual system, by limiting theorizing to known neural architectures, personality theories become more constrained.

That the proposed biological mechanisms for these conceptual systems differ from investigator to investigator should not be taken as a sign of theoretical weakness but rather as a sign of the complexity of the purported systems. No single structure, transmitter, or gene controls the entire system, but rather each plays a supporting and limiting role. Consider by analogy the case of oxygen flow to the brain. Experimental demonstrations of the importance of the heart to oxygen levels in the cortex or low correlations across subjects between measures of heart and lung functioning do not imply that the lungs, veins, arteries, and vagal nerve are not also involved in oxygen transport and regulation, for they are all in fact part of the same circulatory system.

Further complicating any simple review is the multiplicity of analytic techniques. Data are reported in terms of structures, transmitters, and electrophysiology. Generalizations are drawn from rodents, primates, and humans. Dominant EEG frequencies for children are labeled in terms of higher frequencies found in adults. Correlations are made with structures identified by MRI and PET, or with functioning observed by evoked potentials or hormone levels.

Most experimental and theoretical statements concerning the biological substrates of personality are directly or indirectly related to the theories of Hans Eysenck, whose theory of the biological basis of introversion-extraversion, neuroticism-stability, and socialization-psychoticism (Eysenck 1990) has evolved from taxonomic work (Eysenck 1947) to a proposed biological model (Eysenck 1967) that has been the basis of a variety of suggested modifications (Cloninger 1987; Gray 1972, 1981, 1991, 1994). In broad strokes, Eysenck's theory and subsequent modifications (1990, 1991a) are theories of approach and reward, inhibition and punishment, and aggression and flight. All three constructs have been, of course, fundamental concerns for many years and have been the basis for descriptive as well as nonbiological theories of motivation and learning (Atkinson 1960, Dollard & Miller 1950). Approach and withdrawal are behavioral characteristics of amoebae, insects, and human infants (Schneirla 1959). Unifying recent biological work is an emphasis on these three interrelated biological and behavioral systems as sources of individual differences in affective reactions and interpersonal behavior. Although differing in the particular mechanisms proposed at the level of the CNS, these models show striking agreement at the behavioral and conceptual (cns) level.

Central constructs of Eysenck's biological theory of introversion-extraversion (I-E) and stability-neuroticism were cortical arousal and limbic activation (Eysenck 1967). Arousal was originally postulated as reflecting activation of the Ascending Reticular Activating System (ARAS) and the associated cortical-reticular loop. Activation reflected limbic activity of the hippocampus, amygdala, singulum, septum, and hypothalamus. Introverts were thought to have higher levels of resting arousal than did extraverts. With the assumption that some intermediate level of arousal was preferred, the stimulus-seeking behavior of extraverts was explained as a compensation for a lower resting level. With the recognition that ARAS arousal was too broad a concept, Eysenck subsequently modified his theory to include a limbic arousal system, the monoamine oxidase system, and the pituitary-adrenocortical system (1990). He suggested that the apparent diversity of multiple arousal mechanisms "may not prevent the systems from operating in a relatively unified fashion" (p. 249). He associates subjective arousal with Thayer's (1989) measures of energetic arousal (feelings of energy, vigor, and pep). Extraversion and feelings of energetic arousal are both associated with approach behavior and with positive affect following reward or cues for reward.

Stelmack (1990) summarized 20 years of psychophysiological research on Eysenck's hypothesis that introverts have higher arousal levels than extraverts and concluded that there "is a good deal of evidence that introverts are characterized by greater physiological reactivity to sensory stimulation than extraverts...[but] there is little compelling evidence that introverts and extraverts differ in tonic or basal levels" (p. 307). Indirect tests of the arousal hypothesis have examined the relationship between extraversion and cognitive performance under various experimentally induced arousers. These studies do not support the hypothesis of a stable I-E difference in tonic arousal levels, but they do show that I-E, or the impulsivity component of I-E, moderates the relationship between induced arousal and performance (Anderson 1994; Anderson & Revelle 1994; Matthews 1992a; Matthews et al 1989, 1990; Revelle 1993).

The Behavioral Approach System (BAS) (Gray 1994), also known as the Behavioral Activation System (Fowles 1988), or Behavioral Facilitation System (Depue & Iacono 1989), activates approach behaviors in response to cues for reward or nonpunishment. It may be associated neurophysiologically with the motor programming system. "The key components are the basal ganglia (the dorsal and ventral striatum, and dorsal and ventral pallidum); the dopaminergic fibers that ascend from the mesencephalon (substantia nigra and nucleus A 10 in the ventral tegmental area) to innervate the basal ganglia; thalamic nuclei closely linked to the basal ganglia; and similarly, neocortical areas (motor, sensorimotor, and prefrontal cortex) closely linked to the basal ganglia." (Gray 1994, p 41). Dopamine is said to play an essential moderating role in the functioning of the BAS (Depue & Iacono 1989, Depue et al 1994), but the full relationship of dopaminergic activation and reward is less than clear (Wise and Rompre 1989).

The cluster of approach traits of extraversion (Eysenck 1990), impulsivity (Barratt 1994, Gray 1994, Zinbarg & Revelle 1989), novelty seeking (Cloninger 1987), and positive affectivity (Depue & Iacono 1989, Depue et al 1994, Tellegen 1985) as well as the states resulting from approach or reward, energetic arousal (Thayer 1989), and positive affect (Watson et al 1994) have all been discussed in terms of the BAS.

If the BAS is the engine of behavior, the Behavioral Inhibition System (BIS) is the braking system. Signals of punishment, nonreward, novel stimuli, and innate fear stimuli lead to behavioral inhibition, an increment in tense arousal, and increased attention. The BIS may be considered as both a cognitive and a physiological system (Fowles 1988, Gray 1982). Cognitively, the role of the BIS is to compare the current state of the world with expectations, and to inhibit and modify behavior that leads to deviations from expectation. Physiologically, the comparator function of the BIS is associated with the septohippocampal system. Input to this system comes from the prefrontal cortex, and output flows through the noradrenergic fibers of the locus coeruleus and the serotonergic fibers from the median raphe (Gray 1994). More detailed reviews of the neurophysiology of the BIS emphasize the role of seretonin (Clonginger 1987, Depue & Iacono 1989, Spoont 1992) and the amygdala (Kagan et al 1993).

Just as approach traits are associated with the BAS, so are avoidant and inhibitory traits associated with the BIS. Anxiety and neuroticism are believed to reflect chronically high levels of BIS function (Gray 1994). Negative affect and state anxiety are both state markers of BIS activation. Depression has been proposed to reflect high BIS and low BAS activity (Clark & Watson 1991).

Aggression and hostility have been associated with the third dimension of the EB3, psychoticism. In terms of the B5, psychoticism is a combination of (dis)agreeableness and (un)conscientiousness. Neurologically, the Fight Flight System has been associated with the amygdala, the medial hypothalamus, and the central gray of the midbrain (Gray 1994). Neurochemically, serotonin, gamma-aminobutyric acid, the endorphins, and testosterone have been implicated in aggression and hostility (Dabbs & Morris 1990).

In partial agreement with the dichotomization of affect into positive and negative systems are studies of the lateralization of emotionality that suggest an association between left-frontal activation and approach-related positive affect and right-frontal activation and inhibitory or withdrawal-related behavior and negative affect (Davidson 1992, 1993a, 1994). Unfortunately, identification of particular biological systems with particular personality traits or psychopathological disorders tends to ignore the complexity of neural architecture. The brain has evolved to solve many different problems and primitive systems are controlled by later, more complex systems (Derryberry & Tucker 1992, MacLean 1990).

Amelang & Ullwer (1991) and Fahrenburg (1991) discuss data that are quite critical of the uniform acceptance of simple relationships between self-report dimensions and biological systems. Their criticism is twofold: The complex specification of parameters necessary to find the purported results make theories overly complicated, and based on their empirical investigations, there is little evidence for the proposed mechanisms.

The need to optimally specify parameters to detect presumed relationships has long plagued the field of personality research (Eysenck & Levey 1972). It is useful to consider this issue in some detail, for appropriate parameter values are a consistent difficulty in personality research. At the most naive level, individual differences in a trait would be expected to produce consistent individual differences in an associated construct independent of other parameters. This assumption is typical of classical test theory, which assumes that equal true score differences are equally discernible (i.e. will lead to equal observed score differences) at all levels of true score. More recent approaches (e.g. item response theory), however, make it clear that this is not the case. Observed scores are a monotonic but nonlinear function of individual differences on some underlying attribute. They also reflect differential response probabilities (difficulty) associated with the situation (item) being measured. That is, even large differences on a latent trait are not easily detectable if the situational parameters are inappropriately specified. Such scaling artifacts include ceiling or floor effects. These scaling problems can lead to inappropriate inferences about group differences as well as about interactions of multiple variables (Revelle & Anderson 1992).

Another problem arises when consistent individual differences reverse direction depending on the value of a specific parameter. This is not a problem of mere scaling but can be a much more serious theoretical challenge. Some reversals are predictable consequences of nonmonotonic relationships (Anderson 1990, 1994; Humphreys & Revelle 1984; Yerkes & Dodson 1908). But other reversals cannot be explained in terms of theory-related parameters. For example, the supposed greater rate of decay in performance over time for high impulsives than for low impulsives reverses when studies are conducted in the morning versus the evening (Anderson & Revelle 1994).

Temperament and development   In parallel with the development of the biological models of personality developed from rodents and adult humans is the work on children. As all parents know, children are different from each other. Some are shy, some are bold, some are slow to warm up, some are unafraid of new challenges. Child developmental research concerned with seemingly biological traits has emphasized the temperamental aspects of personality development. This work on temperament has, until recently, been somewhat independent of the adult research literature in personality, although "a complete understanding of personality and psychopathology must be a developmental one" (Rothbart & Ahadi 1994, p. 55). Theories of adult personality and childhood temperament, besides being isolated from each other, have tended to be parochial, with a lack of communication between American and Eastern European researchers. Attempts have been made to reverse both of these trends. Recent conferences and edited volumes reporting work on both adults and children have included contributions by both Eastern and Western researchers (Bates & Wachs 1994, Strelau & Angleitner 1991).

Temperament may be seen "as constitutionally based individual differences in reactivity and self-regulation, influenced over time by heredity, maturation, and experience" (Rothbart & Ahadi 1994, p. 55). Aspects of reactivity include activation of physiological and behavioral systems. Regulatory processes that modulate reactivity include selective attention and processing of cues to reward and punishment, as well as approach and inhibition to novel stimuli (Rothbart et al 1994). Discussions of reactivity and regulatory processes bear a striking resemblance to those of approach and avoidance traits in adults (Strelau 1987, 1994).

Temperamental differences in reactivity to novelty and to strangers (Kagan et al 1992) show striking correlates with hemispheric differences in activation (Davidson 1993b). Shy or inhibited children identified at 31 months showed more right hemispheric activation than did uninhibited children when they were tested at 38 months. This effect seems to be due to a deficit in the left-frontal approach system for the inhibited children rather than to a hyperactivation of the right-frontal withdrawal system (Calkins & Fox 1994, Davidson 1993a). Gray's model of approach and avoidance is discussed in the context of infants and the neural structure of temperament (Nelson 1994, Strelau 1994). In a discussion of the relationship between temperament and attachment, Goldsmith & Harman (1994) point out that physiological measures do not explain temperament and suffer the same difficulties in interpretation as do behavioral measures.

Longitudinal studies of temperamental differences suggest long-term consistencies in behavior (Caspi & Bem 1990). In a continuing study of the antecedents and correlates of delinquency, B5 measures were found by Robins et al (1994) to be related to dynamic conceptions of ego-control and ego-resiliency. In a 15-year-long study of impulsivity and disinhibitory behavior, children diagnosed as hyperactive or attention-deficit disordered continue to show impulsive behavior in early adulthood and to be at greater risk for alcoholism and committing violence (af Klinteberg et al 1994).

Affective and cognitive processes—how traits relate to states Traits are not behavior. They are summary statements describing likelihood of and rates of change in behavior in response to particular situational cues. In addition to their relationship to the probability and latency of response, stable predispositions may be conceptualized in terms of differential sensitivities to situations and differential response biases. Intervening between traits, situations, and responses are momentary affective and cognitive states.

Taxonomic analyses of mood and emotion disagree about categorical versus dimensional representations. Do the many separate emotional terms in the natural language describe many different emotions, or are there a limited number of affective states that differ in intensity and duration? Two affective dimensions that relate to stable personality traits are positive and negative affect (Meyer & Shack 1989, Watson et al 1994) or the related constructs of energetic and tense arousal (Thayer 1989). Extraversion tends to be related to positive affect, neuroticism with negative affect. These relationships, however, are not strong and interact predictably with the situation. In positive, rewarding situations, extraversion is associated with positive affect, but this relationship vanishes in threatening situations. Similarly, neuroticism is related to negative affect under threat but not under reward conditions (Larsen & Ketallar 1989). Although these relationships are consistent with theories of traits and states, they are small enough to require assessing traits and states separately in order to study relationships with performance (Matthews 1992b).

Further complicating the trait-state relationship is its dynamic nature. When free to choose situations, individuals sensitive to negative affect (neurotics) will try to avoid threatening situations. It is the emotionally stable individual who is more likely to participate voluntarily in activities that are likely to induce negative affect. Thus, it is necessary to distinguish between externally imposed and freely selected situations as well as within- and between-subject differences in the use of affective scales.

Traits as well as emotional states affect the detection, encoding, storage, retrieval, and integration of information (Christianson 1993). Trait and state effects may be seen at each of these conceptual stages (Revelle 1993). Impulsivity interacts with time of day to affect energetic arousal, which in turn is related to the detection and storage of information (Anderson & Revelle 1994, Revelle & Loftus 1993). Anxiety shifts attention to threat-related cues whereas depression biases memory toward depression-related material (Mathews 1993, Mueller 1992). Relations between anxiety and memory vary as a function of trait and state anxiety as well as implicit and explicit memory conditions (Eysenck & Mogg 1993).

Life satisfaction, identity, and death   Personality characteristics of young adults predict lifelong risks for neuroticism, emotional health, and even death (McCrae 1994). The effect of neuroticism and extraversion on psychological distress over a ten-year period has been estimated to be four times greater than the effects of psychological interventions to reduce distress (Brody 1994).

Conley (1985) examined the multitrait-multimethod-multitime structure of self-reports and peer ratings of neuroticism, social extraversion, and impulse control from the Kelly longitudinal study measures taken in 1935–1938, 1954–1955, and 1980–1981. Neuroticism at times 1 and 2 reliably predicted neuroticism and emotional health at time 3. Similarly, social extraversion measures at times 1 and 2 predicted social extraversion and social activity at time 3.

Measures of conscientiousness taken in 1922 as part of the Terman (1925) study predicted mortality risk through 1986 through age 76 with a relative hazard of death of roughly .75. Stated differently, for someone at the 25th percentile of conscientiousness at age 12, there is a 35% greater risk of dying before age 70 than for someone at the 75th percentile (Friedman et al 1993).

Situation-Based Differences and Similarities

Social learning theory explains consistent individual differences in behavior in terms of stabilities in the supporting environment rather than in terms of an individual's characteristics. Consistency across situations reflects similarity of situations rather than stable individual traits. Behavior can be modified by changing the environmental cues. Total reliance on prior learning experiences rather than on individual readiness is as much a straw man for social learning theory as total cross-situational consistency is for trait theory. Adherents of social learning theory now emphasize the need to understand how individual cognitive representations of the environment lead to behavior (Cantor 1990, Cantor & Zirkel 1990).

Some of the clearest evidence for the effect of the formative and sustaining environment on determining individual differences comes from behavioral genetic analyses. That identical twins are not perfectly concordant for extraversion, neuroticism, schizophrenia, or homosexuality demonstrates environmental effects. More importantly, that identical twins growing up together seem to be no more similar than those growing up apart (Eaves et al 1989, Tellegen et al 1988) implies that the formative environment is not the set of experiences shared within a family, but is either unique to each individual or common to their culture.

Part of the unique family environment is birth order. Although genetically related, siblings differ in age, experience, and in reproductive value to their parents. Differences between siblings growing up together can be magnified by contrast effects. Sulloway (1995) applies an evolutionary perspective on sibling rivalry in a meta-analysis of birth order effects on the traits of the B5 and reports that first-borns are more extraverted and conscientious but less emotionally stable, agreeable, or open than are later-borns. Later-borns are more likely to adopt radical innovations in science than are first-borns.

Trait-by-Situation Interactions

Although interactionism was claimed to be the new and improved way to study personality (Magnusson & Endler 1976), most personality research has gone beyond the simple assertion that consistencies exist in the interactions of traits and situations. Theoretically driven trait theorists have long recognized that stable individual differences produce predictably different patterns of results in different situations. Failure to change one's actions across situations is a sign of pathology, not adaptive behavior. The utility of demonstrations of trait-by-situation interactions lies in the exclusion of many competing hypotheses, as well as in the setting of boundary conditions for individual and situational effects, for theories are best tested at their limits.

Consider delinquency as an example of the setting of boundary conditions. Delinquency may be conceived as the outcome of the interaction of lack of social constraints with a biological propensity. When social constraints are diminished, the relationship between testosterone and delinquency and antisocial behavior increases (Dabbs et al 1990, Dabbs & Morris 1990). Among lower-SES military veterans there is a positive relationship between testosterone and antisocial behavior, but this relationship vanishes among higher-SES subjects. These results might be due to a lack of social control or, alternatively, to the existence of more legal ways to seek stimulation among higher-SES groups than among lower-SES groups.

Interactions also allow for tests of theories. Consider the relationship between impulsivity and cognitive performance, which changes as a function of caffeine (Anderson 1994) or time of day (Anderson & Revelle 1994) and differs as a function of the particular task used (Revelle et al 1987). These interactive results allow for precise tests of the competing theories relating to the arousal interpretations of impulsivity (Revelle & Anderson 1992).

In a thoughtful review of the many meanings of person-by-situation interactions, Higgins (1990) emphasizes the interplay between situational standards and individual beliefs. Differences in cognitive representations and activation prime reactions to specific situational cues. This social psychological emphasis on contextual priming of memories relates to the personality concern with individual differences in cognitive structures.

NO PERSON IS THE SAME: THE STUDY OF UNIQUE PATTERNS OF BEHAVIOR

Individual differences research is not the same as theories of personality of the individual (Rorer 1990). A person is not just the simple combination of universals of human nature and specific values on two, three, five, or even ten independent trait dimensions. A person is also a dynamic information processor whose unique memories and perceptual structures lead to a unique cognitive, affective, and behavioral signature. Structural studies of individual differences emphasize between-subject correlational patterns of variables. But these structures are not the same as studying the coherent patterns of an individual over a lifetime, or even across different situations (York & John 1992). Those theorists emphasizing uniqueness have tended to be more cognitively oriented than are the biologically oriented trait theorists, or the pragmatic psychometricians concerned with cross-situational prediction.

Social-cognitive theorists emphasize the dynamic and flexible use of multiple cognitive structures as one solves the problems of day-to-day interaction.

Although recognizing the importance of dispositional structures (i.e. traits), the focus is on the adaptive use of schemas, tasks, and strategies (Cantor 1990). Schema-driven processing describes the assimilation of new information into existing cognitive structures and recognizes that physically identical inputs will lead to dramatically different outputs depending on prior knowledge and beliefs. Although this cognitive orientation at first seems different from the dispositional approach, in fact, biological theorists also suggest that information is processed differently according to existing structures (e.g. Gray's description of anxiety and impulsivity as sensitivities to cues for punishment and reward). The difference is thus one of emphasis on the particular schemas, tasks, and strategies that one uses rather than on the determination of the causes for differences.

Although it is logically possible to study the effects of unique organizations of biological structures (anatomical texts emphasize the similarities of structure, but anatomists quickly realize the variation and unique patterning that exist), the primary emphasis on individuality is expressed by those studying cognitive structures and processes. By emphasizing the uniqueness of individual construals, cognitive theorists attempt to move beyond the "psychology of the stranger" (McAdams 1994b) characteristic of trait theory and instead study the personalities of individuals.

Personal Construals

The study of cognitive aspects of personality is not new (Kelly 1955) but has become a focal point of social-cognitive theorists as they apply cognitive theory to the study of individuality. People are seen as active processors of information, forming, testing, and acting on hypotheses about their selves and others. This active social construal process can be seen as the basis of the lexical hypothesis that individuals will code important phenomena linguistically. What is important to people in the aggregate becomes coded into the language.

SELF-SCHEMAS   The multiple hypotheses one has about one's self guide one's perceptions, thoughts, and actions. Self is the insider's view of personality (Markus & Cross 1990). As a fundamentally social construal (Banaji & Prentice 1994), the "working self-concept is influential in the shaping and controlling of intrapersonal behavior (self-relevant information processing, affect regulation, and motivational processes) and interpersonal processes, which include social perception, social comparison, and social interaction" (Markus & Cross 1990, p. 578). One's theory of intelligence guides one's responses to success and failure and resulting school achievement (Dweck 1991), and a negative self-concept leads to seeking self-verification through failure (Swann 1992).

REVERSAL THEORY—DYNAMIC CONCEPTUALIZATIONS OF SITUATION   Changes in interpreting motivational phenomena such as arousal in terms of metamotivational states (e.g. the telic state that emphasizes goal driven behaviors versus the paratelic state that emphasizes the behaviors themselves) can lead to dramatic reversals of thought and action (Apter 1989). When in a telic state of trying to achieve an important goal, high arousal is associated with anxiety and low arousal with relaxation. In contrast, when in a paratelic state of playfulness, high arousal is exciting and low arousal is boring. Phenomenological interpretation of a situation affects physiological responses in that situation (Apter & Svebak 1992).

The dynamic pattern of reversals over time that occur in a constant situation are reminiscent of those modeled by the dynamics of action (Atkinson & Birch 1970, Revelle 1986). Although the emphasis in reversal theory is on the metamotivational state within an individual and the reversals in behavior resulting from changes in state, most research studies use between-individual analyses of dominant or typical state.

Life Histories and the Study of Lives

An attempt at understanding the coherencies within individuals rather than within variables has been a theme of the longitudinal studies done at Berkeley (Block 1971, Block & Robins 1993, Helson 1993, Helson & Roberts 1992, York & John 1992). These were ambitious studies when initiated, and have shown the costs, difficulties, and benefits of "studying personality the long way" (Block 1993). These longitudinal studies emphasize person-centered as well as variable-centered analyses and represent a powerful blend of psychometric and theoretical sophistication. For example, Block & Robins (1993) report that mean self-esteem, indexed as the correlation between self and ideal-self ratings, increases slightly for males and decreases slightly for females from ages 14 to 23. Individual differences in self-esteem are more consistent across this period for females than for males and show different correlates of change across the two genders. Personality correlates of later drug use, political attitudes, or even subsequent parental divorce show strong and meaningful patterns that are not detectable in cross-sectional analyses (Block 1993).

Life Stories

Whereas the Berkeley group focuses on the coherencies over time of individual life histories, others emphasize the autobiographical story of the self that makes up one's identity (McAdams 1990, 1993, Runyan 1990). McAdams suggests that the narrative tone of a life story is set by the quality of early experience and the forming of attachment. As children mature they are exposed to many different legends and myths as they develop their own life story and their conception of their self. Story scripts change with age and tend to be concerned with future generations. Studying the origins, characters, settings, and scripts of a life story is said to provide "a framework for conceptualizing the development of the whole person, from birth to death" (McAdams 1990, p. 192).

FUTURE DIRECTIONS: CHALLENGES AND PROMISES

Based on the mixed success of previous reviewers and prognosticators, it is risky to make any strong predictions about the future. There are several themes, however, that have emerged in the past several years that offer both promises and challenges to the field of personality research.

Challenges

As the rise of neuroscience and cognitive science threatens to split the discipline of psychology, so does the emphasis on biological mechanisms of individual differences and cognitive mechanisms of uniqueness threaten personality theory. There is an unfortunate tendency for the more biologically oriented to dismiss cognitive approaches as focusing on epiphenomena, and for cognitive theorists to ignore the advances in biological bases as irrelevant for understanding a person. There are far too few researchers emphasizing how cognitive interpretations can affect physiological state and in turn, how physiological structures and processes constrain and affect cognitive and affective reactions.

Promises

The past few years have seen a resurgence of interest in personality. Research spanning the range from genes to the life span, from the individual to the species, and from the normal to the pathological is being carried out in the name of personality theory. Once again, researchers and theorists from all parts of psychology are working on the fundamental questions of personality. What is integrating much of this work is an emphasis not just on description, but on the functions that personality serves. Evolutionary, biological, sociological, developmental, cognitive, and clinical approaches all provide unique perspectives to the field. What the next decade promises is an integration of these many separate foci.

ACKNOWLEDGMENTS

Preparation of this chapter was supported in part by contract MDA903-93-K-0008 from the US Army Research Institute to William Revelle and Kristen Anderson. The views, opinions, and findings contained in this chapter are those of the author and should not be construed as an official Department of the Army position, policy, or decision, unless so designated by other official documentation. I would like to thank KJ Anderson, D Billings, E Gilboa, G Rogers, S Sutton, and the members of the Northwestern Personality Group for their helpful comments on parts of this manuscript.

Literature Cited

Ackerman PL. 1994. Intelligence, attention, and learning: maximal and typical performance. In *Current Topics in Human Intelligence. Vol. 4: Theories of Intelligence,* ed. DK Detterman. Norwood, NJ: Ablex. In press

Ackerman PL, Goff M. 1994. Typical intellectual engagement and personality: reply to Rocklin 1994. *J. Educ. Psychol.* 86:150–53

Allport G. 1962. The general and the unique in psychological science. *J. Pers.* 30:405–21

Allport GW, Vernon PE. 1930. The field of personality. *Psychol. Bull.* 27:677–730

Amelang M, Ullwer U. 1991. Correlations between psychometric measures and psychophysiological as well as experimental variables in studies of extraversion and neuroticism. See Strelau & Angleitner 1991, pp. 297–315

American Psychiatric Association. 1987. *Diagnostic and Statistical Manual of Mental Disorders.* Washington, DC: Am. Psychiatr. Assoc. 3rd ed. rev.

Anderson KJ. 1990. Arousal and the inverted-u hypothesis—a critique of Neiss's reconceptualizing arousal. *Psychol. Bull.* 107: 96–100

Anderson KJ. 1994. Impulsivity, caffeine, and task difficulty: a within-subjects test of the Yerkes-Dodson law. *Pers. Indiv. Diff.* 16: 813–30

Anderson KJ, Revelle W. 1994. Impulsivity and time of day: Is rate of change in arousal a function of impulsivity? *J. Pers. Soc. Psychol.* 67:334–44

Apter MJ. 1989. *Reversal Theory: Motivation, Emotion and Personality.* London: Routledge

Apter MJ, Svebak S. 1992. Reversal theory as a biological approach to individual differences. See Gale & Eysenck 1992, pp. 324–53

Atkinson JW. 1960. Personality dynamics. *Annu. Rev. Psychol.* 11:255–90

Atkinson JW. 1974. Strength of motivation and efficiency of performance. In *Motivation and Achievement,* ed. JW Atkinson, JO Raynor, pp. 117–42. New York: Winston (Halsted/Wiley)

Atkinson JW, Birch D. 1970. *The Dynamics of Action.* New York: Wiley

Bailey JM, Pillard RC. 1991. A genetic study of male sexual orientation. *Arch. Gen. Psychiatry* 48:1089–96

Bailey JM, Pillard RC, Neale MC, Agyei Y. 1993. Heritable factors influence sexual orientation in women. *Arch. Gen. Psychiatry* 50:217–23

Banaji MR, Prentice DA. 1994. The self in social contexts. *Annu. Rev. Psychol.* 45: 297–332

Barratt ES. 1994. Impulsivity: integrating cognitive, behavioral, biological, and environmental data. In *The Impulsive Client: Theory, Research, and Treatment,* ed. W McCown, M Shure. Washington, DC: Am. Psychol. Assoc. In press

Bates JE, Wachs TD, eds. 1994. *Temperament: Individual Differences at the Interface of Biology and Behavior.* Washington, DC: Am. Psychol. Assoc.

Block J. 1971. *Lives Through Time.* Berkeley, CA: Bancroft

Block J. 1993. Studying personality the long way. In *Studying Lives Through Time,* ed. D Funder, RD Parke, C Tomlinson-Keasey, K Widaman, pp. 9–44. Washington, DC: Am. Psychol. Assoc.

Block J, Robins RW. 1993. A longitudinal study of consistency and change in self-esteem from early adolescence to early adulthood. *Child. Dev.* 64:909–23

Borgatta EF, Lambert WW, eds. 1968. *Handbook of Personality: Theory and Research.* Chicago: Rand McNally

Bouchard TJ Jr, Lykken DT, McGue M, Segal NL, Tellegen A. 1990. Sources of human psychological differences: the Minnesota study of twins reared apart. *Science* 250: 223–28

Bouchard TJ Jr, McGue M. 1990. Genetic and rearing environmental influences on adult personality: an analysis of adopted twins reared apart. *J. Pers.* 58:263–92

Brody N. 1993. Intelligence and the behavioral genetics of personality. See Plomin & McClearn 1993, pp. 161–78

Brody N. 1994. .5+ or –.5: continuity and

change in personal dispositions. See Heatherton & Weinberger 1994, pp. 59–81

Bronfenbrenner U. 1953. Personality. *Annu. Rev. Psychol.* 4:157–82

Buss AH. 1989. Personality as traits. *Am. Psychol.* 44:1378–88

Buss DM, ed. 1990. Biological foundations of personality: evolution, behavioral genetics, and psychophysiology. *J. Pers.* 58 (Special Issue)

Buss DM. 1991. Evolutionary personality psychology. *Annu. Rev. Psychol.* 42:459–91

Buss DM. 1995. Evolutionary psychology: a new paradigm for psychological science. *Psychol. Inq.* 6: In press

Buss DM, Larsen RJ, Westen D, Semmelroth J. 1992. Sex differences in jealousy: evolution, physiology, and psychology. *Psychol. Sci.* 3:251–55

Buss DM, Schmitt DP. 1993. Sexual strategies theory: an evolutionary perspective on human mating. *Psychol. Rev.* 100:204–32

Calkins SD, Fox NA. 1994. Individual differences in the biological aspects of temperament. See Bates & Wachs 1994, pp. 199–217

Cantor N. 1990. From thought to behavior: "having" and "doing" in the study of personality and cognition. *Am. Psychol.* 45:735–50

Cantor N, Zirkel S. 1990. Personality, cognition, and purposive behavior. See Pervin 1990a, pp. 135–64

Carey G, DiLalla DL. 1994. Personality and psychopathology: genetic perspectives. *J. Abnorm. Psychol.* 103:32–43

Caspi A, Bem DJ. 1990. Personality continuity and change across the life course. See Pervin 1990a, pp. 549–75

Christianson SA, ed. 1993. *The Handbook of Emotion and Memory: Research and Theory.* Hillsdale, NJ: Erlbaum

Clark LA, Watson D. 1991. Tripartite model of anxiety and depression: psychometric evidence and taxonomic implications. *J. Abnorm. Psychol.* 100:316–36

Clark LA, Watson D, Mineka S. 1994. Temperament, personality, and the mood and anxiety disorders. *J. Abnorm. Psychol.* 103:103–16

Cloninger CR. 1987. A systematic method for clinical description and classification of personality variants—a proposal. *Arch. Gen. Psychiatry* 44:573–88

Conley JJ. 1985. Longitudinal stability of personality traits: a multitrait-multimethod-multioccasion analysis. *J. Pers. Soc. Psychol.* 49:1266–82

Cosmides L, Tooby J, Barkow JH. 1992. Introduction: evolutionary psychology and conceptual integration. In *The Adapted Mind: Evolutionary Psychology and the Generation of Culture,* ed. JH Barkow, L Cos-

mides, J Tooby, pp. 3–15. New York: Oxford Univ. Press

Costa PT Jr, McCrae RR. 1993. Depression as an enduring disposition. In *Diagnosis and Treatment of Depression in Late Life: Results of the NIH Consensus Development Conference,* ed. LS Schneider, CF Reynolds III, BD Lebowitz, AJ Friedhoff, pp. 173–87. Washington, DC: Am. Psychiatr. Press

Costa PT Jr, Widiger TA, ed. 1994. *Personality Disorders and the Five-factor Model of Personality.* Washington, DC: Am. Psychol. Assoc.

Cronbach LJ. 1957. The two disciplines of scientific psychology. *Am. Psychol.* 12:671–84

Cronbach LJ. 1975. Beyond the two disciplines of scientific psychology. *Am. Psychol.* 30:116–27

Dabbs JM, Hopper CH, Jurkovic GJ. 1990. Testosterone and personality among college-students and military veterans. *Pers. Indiv. Diff.* 11:1263–69

Dabbs JM, Morris R. 1990. Testosterone, social-class, and antisocial-behavior in a sample of 4,462 men. *Psychol. Sci.* 1:209–11

Davidson RJ. 1992. Emotion and affective style: hemispheric substrates. *Psychol. Sci.* 3:39–43

Davidson RJ. 1993a. Cerebral asymmetry and emotion: conceptual and methodological conundrums. *Cognit. Emot.* 7:115–38

Davidson RJ. 1993b. Childhood temperament and cerebral asymmetry: a neurobiological substrate of behavioral inhibition. In *Social Withdrawal, Inhibition and Shyness in Childhood,* ed. K Rubin, J Asendorpf, pp. 31–48. Hillsdale, NJ: Erlbaum

Davidson RJ. 1994. Temperament, affective style and frontal lobe asymmetry. In *Human Behavior and the Developing Brain,* ed. G Dawson, K Fisher, pp. 518–36. New York: Guilford

Depue RA, Iacono WG. 1989. Neuro-behavioral aspects of affective-disorders. *Annu. Rev. Psychol.* 40:457–92

Depue RA, Luciana M, Arbisi P, Collins P, Leon A. 1994. Dopamine and the structure of personality: relation of agonist-induced dopamine activity to positive emotionality. *J. Pers. Soc. Psychol.* 67:485–98

Derryberry D, Tucker DM. 1992. Neural mechanisms of emotion. *J. Consult. Clin. Psychol.* 60:329–38

Digman JM. 1990. Personality structure—emergence of the 5-factor model. *Annu. Rev. Psychol.* 41:417–40

Dollard J, Miller N. 1950. *Personality and Psychotherapy: An Analysis in Terms of Learning, Thinking and Culture.* New York: McGraw-Hill

Dweck CS. 1991. Self-theories and goals: their

role in motivation, personality, and development. In *Perspectives on Motivation: Nebraska Symposium on Motivation,* ed. RA Dienstbier, 38:129–235. Lincoln: Univ. Nebr. Press

Eaves L, Eysenck HJ, Martin NG. 1989. *Genes, Culture, and Personality.* New York: Academic

Elder GH Jr. 1994. The life course paradigm and social change: historical and developmental perspectives. In *Perspectives on the Ecology of Human Development,* ed. P Moen, GH Elder Jr, K Luscher. Washington, DC: Am. Psychol. Assoc. In press

Elder GH Jr, Pavalko EK. 1993. Work careers in men's later years: transitions, trajectories, and historical change. *J. Gerontol.: Soc. Sci.* 48(4):S180–91

Endler NS, Magnusson D, eds. 1976. *Interactional Psychology and Personality.* New York: Halstead (Wiley)

Eysenck HJ. 1947. *Dimensions of Personality.* New York: Praeger

Eysenck HJ. 1952. Personality. *Annu. Rev. Psychol.* 3:151–74

Eysenck HJ. 1966. Personality and experimental psychology. *Bull. Br. Psychol. Soc.* 19: 1–28

Eysenck HJ. 1967. *The Biological Basis of Personality.* Springfield, IL: Thomas

Eysenck HJ. 1990. Biological dimensions of personality. See Pervin 1990, pp. 244–76

Eysenck HJ. 1991a. Dimensions of personality: 16: 5 or 3? criteria for a taxonomic paradigm. *Pers. Indiv. Diff.* 12:773–90

Eysenck HJ. 1991b. Dimensions of personality: the biosocial approach to personality. See Strelau & Angleitner 1991, pp. 87–103

Eysenck HJ. 1993. Creativity and personality: suggestions for a theory. *Psychol. Inq.* 4: 147–78

Eysenck HJ, Levey A. 1972. Conditioning, introversion-extraversion and the strength of the nervous system. In *Biological Bases of Individual Behavior,* ed. VD Nebylitsyn, JA Gray, pp. 206–20. New York: Academic

Eysenck MW, Mogg K. 1993. Clinical anxiety, trait anxiety, and memory bias. See Christianson 1993, pp. 429–50

Fahrenberg J. 1991. Differential psychophysiology and the diagnosis of temperament. See Strelau & Angleitner 1991, pp. 317–33

Friedman HS, Tucker JS, Tomlinson-Keasey C, Schwartz JE, Wingard DL, Criqui MH. 1993. Does childhood personality predict longevity? *J. Pers. Soc. Psychol.* 65:176–85

Frijda NH. 1993. Appraisal and beyond: the issue of cognitive determinants of emotion. *Cognit. Emot.* 7 (Special Issue)

Fowles DC. 1988. Psychophysiology and psychopathology: a motivational approach. *Psychophysiology* 25:373–91

Funder D, Parke RD, Tomlinson-Keasey C, Widaman K, eds. 1993. *Studying Lives Through Time.* Washington, DC: Am. Psychol. Assoc.

Funder DC, West SG. 1993. Viewpoints on personality: consensus, self-other agreement, and accuracy in personality judgement. *J. Pers.* 61 (Special Issue)

Gale A, Eysenck MW, eds. 1992. *Handbook of Individual Differences: Biological Perspectives.* Chichester, UK: Wiley

Gangestad SW, Buss DM. 1993. Pathogen prevelance and human mate selection. *Ethol. Sociobiol.* 14:89–96

Gangestad SW, Simpson JA. 1990. Toward an evolutionary history of female sociosexual variation. *J. Pers.* 58:69–96

Goff M, Ackerman PJ. 1992. Personality-intelligence relations: assessment of typical intellectual engagement. *J. Educ. Psychol.* 84:537–52

Goldberg LR. 1992. The development of markers for the big-five factor structure. *Psychol. Assess.* 4:26–42

Goldberg LR. 1993a. The structure of phenotypic personality traits. *Am. Psychol.* 48: 26–34

Goldberg LR. 1993b. The structure of personality traits: vertical and horizontal aspects. See Funder et al 1993, pp. 169–88

Goldsmith HH, Harman C. 1994. Temperament and attachment: individuals and relationships. *Curr. Dir. Psychol. Sci.* 3:53–57

Gray JA. 1972. The psychophysiological basis of introversion-extraversion: a modification of Eysenck's theory. In *The Biological Basis of Individual Behavior,* ed. VD Nebylitsyn, JA Gray, pp. 182–205. New York: Academic

Gray JA. 1981. A critique of Eysenck's theory of personality. In *A Model for Personality,* ed. HJ Eysenck, pp. 246–76. Berlin: Springer-Verlag

Gray JA. 1982. *Neuropsychological Theory of Anxiety: An Investigation of the Septal-hippocampal System.* Cambridge: Cambridge Univ. Press

Gray JA. 1990. Psychobiological aspects of relationships between emotions and cognition. *Cognit. Emot.* 4 (Special Issue)

Gray JA. 1991. The neuropsychology of temperament. See Strelau & Angleitner 1991, pp. 105–28

Gray JA. 1994. Framework for a taxonomy of psychiatric disorder. In *Emotions: Essays on Emotion Theory,* ed. SHM van Goozen, NE van de Poll, J Sergeant, pp. 29–59. Hillsdale NJ: Erlbaum

Gurtman MB. 1992. Trust, distrust, and interpersonal problems: a circumplex analysis. *J. Pers. Soc. Psychol.* 62:989–1002

Gurtman MB. 1994. A methodological primer for using the circumplex to differentiate normal and abnormal personality. In *Dif-*

ferentiating Normal and Abnormal Personality, ed. S Strack, M Lorr. New York: Springer-Verlag. In press

Heatherton T, Weinberger J, eds. 1994. *Can Personality Change?* Washington, DC: Am. Psychol. Assoc.

Helson R. 1993. Comparing longitudinal studies of adult development: toward a paradigm of tension between stability and change. See Funder et al 1993, pp. 93–119

Helson R, Roberts B. 1992. The personality of young adult couples and wives' work patterns. *J. Pers.* 60:575–97

Higgins TE. 1990. Personality, social psychology, and person-situation relations: standards and knowledge activation as a common language. See Pervin 1990, pp. 301–38

Hofstee WKB. 1991. The concepts of personality and temperament. See Strelau & Angleitner 1991, pp. 177–88

Holt RR. 1962. Individuality and generalization in the psychology of personality: an evaluation. *J. Pers.* 30:377–402

Humphreys MS, Revelle W. 1984. Personality, motivation, and performance—a theory of the relationship between individual-differences and information-processing. *Psychol. Rev.* 91:153–84

John OP. 1990. The "Big Five" factor taxonomy: dimensions of personality in the natural language and in questionnaires. See Pervin 1990, pp. 66–100

John OP, Robins RW. 1993. Gordon Allport: Father and critic of the five-factor model. In *Fifty Years of Personality Psychology,* ed. KH Craik, R Hogan, R Wolfe, pp. 215–36. New York: Plenum

Kagan J, Arcus D, Snidman N. 1993. The idea of temperament: Where do we go from here? See Plomin & McClearn 1993, pp. 197–212

Kagan J, Snidman N, Arcus DM. 1992. Initial reactions to unfamiliarity. *Curr. Dir. Psychol. Sci.* 1:171–74

Kanfer R, Ackerman PL, Murtha T, Goff M. 1994. Personality and intelligence in industrial and organizational psychology. In *International Handbook of Personality and Intelligence,* ed. DH Saklofske, M Zeidner. New York: Plenum. In press

Kelly GA. 1955. *The Psychology of Personal Constructs.* New York: Norton

Kenrick DT, Sasalla EK, Groth G, Trost M. 1990. Evolution, traits, and the stages of human courtship: qualifying the parental investment model. *J. Pers.* 58:97–116

Kihlstrom JF. 1987. The cognitive unconscious. *Science* 237:1445–52

Kihlstrom JF. 1990. The psychological unconscious. See Pervin 1990, pp. 445–64

Kimble GA. 1993. Evolution of the nature-nurture issue in the history of psychology. See Plomin & McClearn 1993, pp. 3–26

af Klinteberg B, Andersson T, Magnusson D, Stattin H. 1994. Hyperactive behavior in childhood as related to subsequent alcohol problems and violent offending: a longitudinal study of male subjects. *Pers. Indiv. Diff.* In press

Kluckhohn C, Murray HA. 1948. Personality formation: the determinants. In *Personality: In Nature, Society and Culture,* ed. C Kluckhohn, HA Murray, pp. 35–48. New York: Knopf

Larsen RL, Ketellar T. 1989. Extraversion, neuroticism and susceptibility to positive and negative mood induction procedures. *Pers. Indiv. Diff.* 10:1221–28

Locke EA, Latham GP. 1990. *A Theory of Goal Setting and Task Performance.* Englewood Cliffs, NJ: Prentice Hall

Loehlin JC. 1992. *Genes and Environment in Personality Development.* Newbury Park, CA: Sage

Lykken DT, McGue M, Tellegen A, Bouchard TJ Jr. 1992. Emergenesis: genetic traits that may not run in families. *Am. Psychol.* 47:1565–77

MacDonald K. 1992. Warmth as a developmental construct: an evolutionary analysis. *Child Dev.* 63:752–73

MacKinnon DW. 1951. Personality. *Annu. Rev. Psychol.* 2:113–36

MacLean PD. 1990. *The Triune Brain in Evolution: Role in Paleocerebral Functions.* New York: Oxford Univ. Press

Magnusson D, Endler NS. 1976. *Personality at the Crossroads: Current Issues in Interactional Psychology.* Hillsdale, NJ: Erlbaum

Magnusson D, Törestad B. 1993. A holistic view of personality: a model revisited. *Annu. Rev. Psychol.* 44:427–52

Markus H, Cross S. 1990. The interpersonal self. See Pervin 1990, pp. 576–608

Mathews A. 1993. Anxiety and the processing of emotional information. In *Progress in Experimental Personality and Psychopathology Research: Models and Methods of Psychopathology,* ed. LJ Chapman, JP Chapman, D Fowles, pp. 254–90. New York: Springer-Verlag

Matthews G. 1992a. Extraversion. See Smith & Jones 1992, pp. 95–126

Matthews G. 1992b. Mood. See Smith & Jones 1992, 3:161–93

Matthews G, Davies DR, Lees JL. 1990. Arousal, extroversion, and individual-differences in resource availability. *J. Pers. Soc. Psychol.* 59:150–68

Matthews G, Jones DM, Chamberlain AG. 1989. Interactive effects of extraversion and arousal on attentional task-performance—multiple resources or encoding processes. *J. Pers. Soc. Psychol.* 56:629–39

McAdams DP. 1990. Unity and purpose in human lives: the emergence of identity as a life story. In *Studying Persons and Lives,* ed. AI Rabin, RA Zucker, RA Emmons, S Frank, pp. 148–200. New York: Springer-Verlag

McAdams DP. 1993. *The Stories We Live By: Personal Myths and the Making of the Self.* New York: Morrow

McAdams DP. 1994a. *The Person: An Introduction to Personality Psychology.* Fort Worth, TX: Harcourt Brace

McAdams DP. 1994b. A psychology of the stranger. *Psychol. Inq.* 5:145–48

McCrae RR, ed. 1992. The five-factor model: issues and applications. *J. Pers.* 60 (Special Issue)

McCrae RR. 1994. New goals for trait psychology. *Psychol. Inq.* 5:148–53

McCrae RR, Costa PT Jr. 1990. *Personality in Adulthood.* New York: Guilford

McCrae RR, Costa PT Jr. 1994. Toward a new generation of personality theories: theoretical contexts for the five factor model. In *The Five-factor Model of Personality,* ed. JS Wiggins. New York: Guilford. In press

McGue M, Lykken DT. 1992. Genetic influence on risk of divorce. *Psychol. Sci.* 3: 368–73

Meyer GJ, Shack JR. 1989. Structural convergence of mood and personality: evidence for old and new directions. *J. Pers. Soc. Psychol.* 57:691–706

Mueller JH. 1992. Anxiety and performance. See Smith & Jones 1992, 3:127–60

Nelson CA. 1994. The neural bases of infant temperament. See Bates & Wachs 1994, pp. 47–82

Nigg JT, Goldsmith HH. 1994. Genetics of personality disorders: perspectives from personality and psychopathology research. *Psychol. Bull.* 115:346–80

Ozer DJ, Reise SP. 1994. Personality assessment. *Annu. Rev. Psychol.* 45:357–88

Pervin LA, ed. 1990a. *Handbook of Personality: Theory and Research.* New York: Guilford

Pervin LA. 1990b. See Pervin 1990a, pp. 3–18

Pervin LA. 1994. A critical analysis of current trait theory. *Psychol. Inq.* 5:103–13

Plomin R. 1994. *Genetics and Experience: The Interplay Between Nature and Nuture.* Thousand Oaks, CA: Sage

Plomin R, Chipuer HM, Loehlin JC. 1990. Behavioral genetics and personality. See Pervin 1990a, pp. 225–43

Plomin R, McClearn GE, eds. 1993. *Nature, Nurture, and Psychology.* Washington, DC: Am. Psychol. Assoc.

Revelle W. 1986. Motivation and efficiency of cognitive performance. In *Frontiers of Motivational Psychology: Essays in Honor of John W. Atkinson,* ed. DR Brown, J Veroff, pp. 107–31. Berlin: Springer

Revelle W. 1989. Personality, motivation, and cognitive performance. In *Learning and Individual Differences: Abilities, Motivation, and Methodology,* ed. P Ackerman, R Kanfer, R Cudeck, pp. 297–341. Hillsdale, NJ: Erlbaum

Revelle W. 1993. Individual differences in personality and motivation: 'non-cognitive' determinants of cognitive performance. In *Attention: Selection, Awareness and Control: A Tribute to Donald Broadbent,* ed. A Baddeley, L Weiskrantz, pp. 346–73. Oxford: Oxford Univ. Press

Revelle W, Anderson KJ. 1992. Models for the testing of theory. See Gale & Eysenck 1992, pp. 81–113

Revelle W, Anderson KJ, Humphreys MS. 1987. Empirical tests and theoretical extensions of arousal based theories of personality. In *Personality Dimensions and Arousal,* ed. J Strelau, HJ Eysenck, pp. 17–36. London: Plenum

Revelle W, Loftus D. 1993. The implications of arousal effects for the study of affect and memory. See Christianson 1993, pp. 113–49

Robins RW, John OP, Caspi A. 1994. Major dimensions of personality in early adolescence: the big five and beyond. In *The Developing Structure of Temperament and Personality from Infancy to Adulthood,* ed. CF Halverson, GA Kohnstamm, RP Martin, pp. 267–91. Hillsdale, NJ: Erlbaum

Rocklin T. 1994. Relation between typical intellectual engagement and openness: comment of Goff and Ackerman 1992. *J. Educ. Psychol.* 86:145–49

Rorer LG. 1990. Personality assessment: a conceptual survey. See Pervin 1990a, pp. 693–720

Rothbart MK, Ahadi SA. 1994. Temperament and the development of personality. *J. Abnorm. Psychol.* 103:55–66

Rothbart MK, Derryberry D, Posner MI. 1994. A psychobiological approach to the development of temperament. See Bates & Wachs 1994, pp. 83–116

Rowe DC, Waldman ID. 1993. The question "how" reconsidered. See Plomin & McClearn 1993, pp. 355–73

Runyan WM. 1990. Individual lives and the structure of personality psychology. In *Studying Persons and Lives,* ed. AI Rabin, RA Zucker, RA Emmons, S Frank, pp. 10–40. New York: Springer

Russell JA. 1979. Affective space is bipolar. *J. Pers. Soc. Psychol.* 37:345–56

Saucier G. 1992. Benchmarks: integrating affective and interpersonal circles with the big-five personality factors. *J. Pers. Soc. Psychol.* 62:1025–35

Scarr S. 1992. Developmental theories for the 1990s: development and individual differences. *Child Dev.* 63:1–19

Schmidt FL, Hunter JE. 1992. Development of a causal model of processes determining job performance. *Curr. Dir. Psychol. Sci.* 1:89–92

Schneirla T. 1959. An evolutionary and developmental theory of biphasic processes underlying approach and withdrawal. In *Nebraska Symposium on Motivation,* ed. M Jones, pp. 27–58. Lincoln: Univ. Nebr. Press

Sears RR. 1950. Personality. *Annu. Rev. Psychol.* 1:105–18

Siever LJ, Davis KL. 1991. A psychobiological perspective on the personality disorders. *Am. J. Psychiatry* 148:1647–58

Smith AP, Jones DM, eds. 1992. *Handbook of Human Performance.* London: Academic

Spoont MR. 1992. Modulatory role of serotonin in neural information-processing—implications for human psychopathology. *Psychol. Bull.* 112:330–50

Stein NL, Oatley K. 1992. Basic emotions. *Cognit. Emot.* 6 (Special Issue)

Stelmack RM. 1990. Biological bases of extraversion—psychophysiological evidence. *J. Pers.* 58:293–311

Strelau J. 1987. Emotion as a key concept in temperament research. *J. Res. Pers.* 21: 510–28

Strelau J. 1994. The concepts of arousal and arousability as used in temperament studies. See Bates & Wachs 1994, pp. 117–41

Strelau J, Angleitner A. 1991. *Explorations in Temperament: International Perspectives on Theory and Measurement.* London: Plenum

Sulloway FJ. 1995. Birth order and evolutionary psychology: a meta-analytic overview. *Psychol. Inq.* 6(1):In press

Swann WB Jr. 1992. Seeking "truth," finding despair: some unhappy consequences of a negative self-concept. *Curr. Dir. Psychol. Sci.* 1:15–18

Tellegen A. 1985. Structures of mood and personality and their relevance to assessing anxiety, with an emphasis on self-report. In *Anxiety and the Anxiety Disorders,* ed. AH Tuma, J Maser, pp. 681–706. Hillsdale, NJ: Erlbaum

Tellegen A, Lykken DT, Bouchard TJ Jr, Wilcox KJ, Rich S, Segal NL. 1988. Personality similarity in twins reared apart and together. *J. Pers. Soc. Psychol.* 54:1031–39

Tennen H, Suls J, Affleck G, eds. 1991. Personality and daily experience. *J. Pers.* 59 (Special Issue)

Terman LM. 1925. *Genetic Studies of Genius: I. Mental and Physical Traits of a Thousand Gifted Children.* Stanford, CA: Stanford Univ. Press

Tessor A. 1993. The importance of heritability in psychological research: the case of attitudes. *Psychol. Rev.* 100:129–42

Thayer RE. 1989. *The Biopsychology of Mood and Arousal.* New York: Oxford Univ. Press

Tooby J, Cosmides L. 1990. On the universality of human nature and the uniqueness of the individual: the role of genetics and adaptation. *J. Pers.* 58:17–67

Vale JR, Vale CA. 1969. Individual differences and general laws in psychology: a reconciliation. *Am. Psychol.* 24:1093–108

Watson D, Clark LA, eds. 1994. Personality and psychopathology *J. Abnorm. Psychol.* 103 (Special Issue)

Watson D, Clark LA, Harkness AR. 1994. Structures of personality and their relevance to psychopathology. *J. Abnorm. Psychol.* 103:1–14

Watson D, Tellegen A. 1985. Toward a consensual structure of mood. *Psychol. Bull.* 98:219–35

Watts FN. 1993. Neuropsychological perspectives on emotion. *Cognit. Emot.* 7 (Special Issue)

West SG, Graziano WG. 1989. Long-term stability and change in personality. *J. Pers.* 57 (Special Issue)

Westen D. 1990. Psychoanalytic approaches to personality. See Pervin 1990, pp. 21–65

Westen D. 1991. Social cognition and object relations. *Psychol. Bull.* 109:429–55

Widiger TA, Costa PT Jr. 1994. Personality and personality disorders. *J. Abnorm. Psychol.* 103:78–91

Wiggins JS, Pincus AL. 1992. Personality: structure and assessment. *Annu. Rev. Psychol.* 43:473–504

Wilson DS. 1994. Adaptive genetic variation and human evolutionary psychology. *Ethol. Sociobiol.* In press

Wilson DS, Clark AB, Coleman K, Dearstyne T. 1994. Shyness and boldness in humans and other animals. *Trends Ecol. Evol.* In press

Wilson DS, Coleman K, Clark AB, Biederman L. 1993. Shy-bold continuum in pumpkinseed sunfish (*Lepomis gibbosus*): an ecological study of a psychological trait. *J. Comp. Psychol.* 107:250–60

Wilson M, Daly M. 1992. The man who mistook his wife for a chattel. In *The Adapted Mind: Evolutionary Psychology and the Generation of Culture,* ed. JH Barkow, L Cosmides, J Tooby, pp. 289–322. New York: Oxford Univ. Press

Wise RA, Rompre PP. 1989. Brain dopamine and reward. *Annu. Rev. Psychol.* 40:191–225

Yerkes RM, Dodson JD. 1908. The relation of strength of stimuli to rapidity of habit-formation. *J. Comp. Neurol. Psychol.* 18:459–82

York KL, John OP. 1992. The four faces of Eve: a typological analysis of women's personality at midlife. *J. Pers. Soc. Psychol.* 63:494–508

Zinbarg R, Revelle W. 1989. Personality and conditioning—a test of 4 models. *J. Pers. Soc. Psychol.* 57:301–14

Zuckerman M. 1991. *Psychobiology of Personality.* Cambridge: Cambridge Univ. Press

Zuckerman M. 1994. Impulsive unsocialized sensation seeking: the biological foundations of a basic dimension of personality. See Bate & Wachs 1994, pp. 219–55

Annu. Rev. Psychol. 1995. 46:329–53

AGING AND SPEED OF BEHAVIOR: Possible Consequences for Psychological Functioning

James E. Birren and Laurel M. Fisher

Center on Aging, Multicampus Division of Geriatric Medicine and Gerontology, School of Medicine, University of California, Los Angeles, California 90024-1687

KEY WORDS: reaction time, slowness and cognition, information processing speed, speed and intelligence, physiological correlates of speed

CONTENTS

INTRODUCTION

Over one hundred years have passed since Francis Galton studied older persons' speed of reaction to sudden sounds and light. Much of the early research on the speed of response sketched the outlines of issues, some of which are still investigated today. In this review we present a brief overview of some of the important historical contributions to our understanding of speed of response and age-related changes. We limit our review to changes in speed in

0066-4308/95/0201-0329$05.00

normal aging, that is, in relatively disease-free older adults. Because we are interested in how to think about speed of response and how it relates to other cognitive processes, we also limit our review to the biological basis of speed of response, to cognitive correlates of changes in speed, and to some of the consequences of slowed reaction time for intellectual functioning. In the process, we also review some integrative lines of thinking about aging that biologists, psychologists, and sociologists have suggested. In this review, aging is defined as "the regular changes that occur in mature, genetically representative, organisms living under representative environmental conditions" (Birren & Renner 1977, p. 4).

BACKGROUND

In 1884, Galton organized 17 different "anthropometric measurements," including reaction time, for use at the International Health Exhibition in London (Galton 1885). Nearly 9400 subjects aged 5–80 participated, marking the first lifespan reaction-time experiment with enough data points for LISREL modeling analyses. Subsequent analyses of Galton's data by Koga & Morandt (1923) revealed that auditory and visual reaction times were more correlated with each other than auditory reaction time was correlated with auditory acuity or visual reaction time was correlated with visual acuity. Koga & Morandt's analyses provided the first hint that the slowness in behavior shown by older persons lay principally within the central nervous system rather than in the peripheral sensory systems.

In the same manner, Birren & Botwinick (1955) showed that peripheral nerve conduction velocity was not associated with age-related slowing in speed of response. They found that finger, foot, and jaw simple reaction time for young and older adults differed by a constant amount. If peripheral factors had played a role, foot reaction time would have been proportionately slower than finger or jaw reaction time. A neurologist, Magladery (1959), came to much the same conclusion after reviewing the neuropsychological literature: "degenerative changes at the periphery in end organs and nerve pathways, if valid, cannot possibly account for more than a small fraction of the prolongation in motor response times encountered in the old" (p. 183).

In a review of the psychological literature nearly 30 years later, Salthouse (1985) confirmed the small contribution of sensory and motor factors to slowing:

> The great majority of evidence suggests that sensory and motor factors have only slight effects on speed when stimuli are intense, or responses are simple, as those typically found in aging studies of speeded behavior....The controversy now is not whether peripheral or central mechanisms are responsible for the slowing with age, but rather which particularly central mechanism is the

most fundamental....The available evidence is consistent with the hypothesis that the same mechanisms responsible for the slowing phenomenon also contribute to the other cognitive differences observed with increased age (p. 422).

Both early and more recent attempts to account for the slowing with age have regarded response time as a function of a neural network, which points to a global phenomenon of slowness. In one early formulation, Landahl (1959) noted that both young and older adult simple reaction times were faster to high-intensity stimuli. In a model of age differences in reaction time, Landahl introduced terms for stimulus intensities and the number of fibers in a response pathway. At high intensities of signals, age-related differences in response time were proportional to the number of fibers in the pathway. Landahl also examined the age-related tendency for disproportionate increase in reaction time under conditions of increasing difficulty (e.g. degraded stimuli).

Some 30 years later, Cerella (1990) expressed his model of age-related slowing in terms of 1. the number of links that are traversed to reach a response and 2. the time delay within each link. Thus, response time latency equals unit time multiplied by the number of links. Cerella's approach was similar to Landahl's but was couched in terms of the prevailing computer metaphor of cognition.

HIERARCHICAL LEVELS OF EXPLANATION

Another historical trend in scientific exploration of aging issues has been the consideration of the level of explanation afforded by a theory or empirical results. In a review of the aging literature, Miles (1942) held a hierarchical notion of how behavior was organized, stating: "Most significant perhaps in the study of psychological ageing is the discovery of a consistent tendency in reference to the hierarchy of mental functions" (p. 75). The notion of different levels of explanation and a hierarchy of functions continues to plague the psychology of aging in theory building and operalizations of concepts.

It is acceptable to state that an older adult is generally slowed in behavior relative to younger adults. However, the mechanisms whereby the slowing of behavior has an effect on social interactions, decision making, or learning in older adults is an important, but somewhat neglected, question. Intuitively, one suspects that elemental processes, such as inhibition and facilitation, which are closely dependent on neurochemical and neuroanatomical substrata, will in turn influence more complex behaviors such as attention, learning, and reasoning. Without a model of the hierarchical organization of behavior, it is impossible to project the significance of changes at the elemental level to more complex processes, or to project effects from complex processes downward to the more elemental. Empirical results from other traditions have not added to knowledge and systematic explanations of the principal transformations in behavior during adult life. When constructing theories of age-related changes in behavior, we need to be aware of the level of observations made, the level of theoretical statements about behavior, and the need for greater linkages between discrete components and complex behaviors.

The need to create theoretical links across levels of explanation is not unique to studies of aging. Cacioppo & Berntson (1992) called for a "social neuroscience" in order to place data from different levels of analysis into the same theory for explaining behavior. The Gerontological Society of America has recognized the importance of integrating findings across levels of explanation, such that the theme of the 1994 annual meeting was "Aging cells to aging populations" (*Gerontology News,* March 1994). Examination of changes across time and between levels of explanation has placed an increasing emphasis on complexity and the dynamic aspects of older adult behavior, in contrast to single variable correlates of chronological age.

Hoyer & Rybash (1994) suggested an example of theory building integrating across levels. They hypothesized that age-related changes in behavior are "based on the emergence and increased differentiation of domain-ordered knowledge specialization" (p. 10). Knowledge, as presentations of events, is continually updated and differentiated on the basis of ever-increasing experience. The representations include sensory information as well as concepts of meaning. Changing representations result in increasing cognitive complexity with age (Hoyer & Rybash 1994).

Although psychologists observe increasing complexity in the older organisms, physiologists note decreasing biological complexity (Angelucci et al 1991, Lipsitz & Goldberger 1992). These divergent conclusions across disciplines may be the result of different definitions of aging. Investigations should define the level of explanation and the independent variables used in addition to the chronological age of subjects. One of the more general and important integrative questions to be asked of human aging is whether age-related changes are governed by energy (metabolic) change or information change (losses or gains in information) (Salthouse 1993a). Insights into hierarchical organization may be gained by examining clusters of behaviors that show increments, maintenance, or decrements with age, and relating them to imputed causes. The issues discussed above have shaped how the following literature review is organized, moving from the physiological correlates of slowing in speed of behavior, through some basic cognitive changes with age, and, finally, to how slowing affects intellectual abilities across age.

REVIEW OF THE LITERATURE

Physiology of Speed

Clues to the neural basis of changes in speed of processing come from studies of subcortical dementia or white matter dementia (Albert et al 1974; Cummings & Benson 1983; Filley et al 1989a,b; Grafman et al 1990; Junque et al 1990; Rao et al 1989). Cortical dementias, such as Alzheimer's disease, attack neurons in the gray matter of the cortex; subcortical dementias, such as Binswanger's disease and multiple sclerosis, cause demyelination of white matter (Filley et al 1989b). In a study of progressive supranuclear palsy, Albert et al (1974) identified four behavioral features of subcortical damage: impaired memory, inability to manipulate previously acquired knowledge, emotional lability, and slowing of information processing. In addition, investigators have linked white matter dementia impairments with frontal impairments (Filley et al 1989a). Frontal lobe dysfunction has been related to the attention and memory deficits seen in older adults as well (Craik et al 1990, Cummings & Benson 1983). Slowing of information processing has been observed in the major subcortical dementias (e.g. AIDS dementia and progressive supranuclear palsy) (Filley et al 1989a). Thus, damage to white matter structures appears to be a good candidate as a contributor to the slowing with age.

Recent magnetic resonance imaging (MRI) studies have indicated that increased damage to white matter [seen as leuko-ariaosis (LA) on an MRI] is linked with cerebrovascular risk and with decreases in speed of information processing in normal older adults (Junque et al 1990, Rao et al 1989). In an MRI study, Rao et al (1989) assessed young and older subjects on a neuropsychological battery that examined a range from motor functioning to intellectual ability. Ten subjects (out of fifty) showed large amounts of LA and had slower simple reaction times than did subjects with little LA. However, the difference in reaction times was not statistically reliable. Junque et al (1990) also used MRI in an examination of older adults who had cerebrovascular risk factors. They found that LA was not correlated with simple reaction time or finger tapping speed, but it was correlated with slowing of complex cognitive processes, as measured by Stroop interference performance. Taken together, these two studies suggest that MRI evaluation of LA may be helpful in identifying the underlying neurological structures involved in the slowing of response time with normal aging and also in specific disease states, such as risk of cerebrovascular accidents, but more refined and standardized measures of response time are needed across studies.

Electrophysiological measures are also used to demonstrate slowing with age (Ball et al 1989, Bashore et al 1989, Brown et al 1983, Marsh et al 1990, Strayer et al 1987, Surwillo & Iyer 1989). Specific components of EEG waves, event-related potentials (ERPs), have been thought to provide a temporal measurement of various stages of information processing. One of the most frequently examined ERP components in aging is the P300, an ERP component thought to indicate context updating or simple memorial processes (Donchin & Coles 1988). Earlier concerns about the reliability of ERP components in older adults have been allayed somewhat by more recent data indicating good reliability for the P300 in older adults (Pollock & Schneider 1992). However, experiments continue to note differences in ERP waveforms between young and older subjects. The significance of this result is unclear.

Bashore (1990) concluded from his detailed survey of the studies of aging and ERPs that slowing in neuronal processing results in behavioral slowing. Furthermore, Bashore suggested that the temporal nature of ERPs can be used to identify more precisely the focus of the decline of processing speed. Significantly, Bashore stated that the latency of the P300 was "a purer measure of age-related changes in higher order CNS processes" compared to reaction time measures (1990, p. 262). Each ERP component latency points to slowing in specific types of cognitive processing. For example, the N100 and N200 are more indicative of age-related slowing in processes related to the immediate use of information and increased P300 latencies are more indicative of slowing in memorial processes (Bashore 1989, 1990).

Tachibana et al (1992) examined age-related slowing of the latencies of the P300a and P300b subcomponents of the P300 in subjects aged 20–90. P300a presumably represented passive processing of novel stimuli, whereas P300b represented active processing of relevant stimuli. Both components increased in latency with increasing age ($r = .62$ with P300a; $r = .64$ with P300b). Although the subcomponents increased in latency with age, the P300b component showed larger amounts of slowing. Tachibana et al (1992) concluded that both active and passive attentional processing are impaired with age, a conclusion that supports generalized slowing with age.

In Looren de Jong et al's (1989) study, young and older subjects responded to both rare and frequent letters with the left and right hand. Reaction time did not differ across age groups, but older adults were slowed in P300 latencies, and there was no correlation between slowed P300 latencies and reaction time in older adults. These authors concluded that the dissociation of P300 latency and reaction time may have resulted from fewer resources being devoted to the updating of memorial processes with age while the older adults were responding behaviorally.

Iragui et al (1993) investigated slowing of ERP component latencies in young and older adults in an auditory oddball paradigm. They found that latencies of early ERP components (N100 and P200) were increased with age and P300 latencies showed even larger increases with age. However, the P300 latencies were not highly correlated with behavioral reaction time. Iragui et al (1993) concluded that central cognitive processes (e.g. those assessed by

P300) show larger age effects than do peripheral perceptual processes (e.g. those assessed by N100 and P200) and that simple reaction time tasks are not as sensitive to these subtle age changes as are analyses of ERP components. It appears that an analysis of ERPs can provide information about slowing in specific processes that cannot be gained by single examination of reaction time.

At least one study has examined P300 latency and intellectual ability performance in older adults. O'Donnell et al (1992) elicited P300 components both actively and passively using the oddball paradigm with older adults. Passive P300 components were elicited by having subjects listen to a sequence of rare and frequent tones; active P300 components were elicited by requiring subjects to count the target tones within a prescribed sequence. Subjects were also given a battery of intellectual ability measures. Active and passive P300 latency increased with age, as expected. Each P300 component correlated separately and significantly with specific intellectual abilities after age was partialled out. Passively elicited P300 latencies correlated with verbal learning and memory factors. Active P300 latencies correlated with the general intelligence and concentration factors. The authors concluded that measures of neural integrity, in this case, the P300 ERP component, account for some of the individual differences in intellectual ability, beyond the variance associated with age changes (O'Donnell et al 1992).

Measurement of ERP component waveforms provides a window into the temporal nature of neural processing and, thus, provides clues to the slowing in reaction time with age. Differential slowing of separable components apparently can be linked to cognitive processes with which older adults have difficulties. Specifically, slowing directly impacts memorial processes. Slowing also adversely impacts intellectual functioning. Linking slowed ERP components with behavioral measure of reaction time and complex cognitive processing firmly anchors age-related behavioral slowing in biological factors, possibly more affected by disease states in older adults.

Studies of the effects of exercise and cardiovascular fitness on cognitive functioning in older adults provide an additional line of evidence in support of the biological basis for response slowing (Baylor & Spirduso 1988, Clarkson-Smith & Hartley 1989, 1990, Dustman et al 1984, Stones & Kozma 1989). The data suggest that older individuals who exercise regularly and are fit do not demonstrate as much response slowing as do older individuals who do not exercise regularly and are not fit (Bashore 1989).

Reservations to these findings include the amount of exercise and level of cardiovascular fitness necessary for an effect on reaction time. Madden et al (1989) found no effect of exercise on older adults' response time. The authors noted that their subjects did not improve as much in fitness (measured by increase in VO_{2max}) as other studies have reported (e.g. Dustman et al 1984).

Madden et al (1989) suggested that significant improvement in cardiovascular efficiency is a precondition to observing improvement in reaction time in older adults (Blumenthal et al 1989, 1991; Blumenthal & Madden 1988). The fact that regular exercisers show faster reaction time relative to nonexercisers also supports this conclusion (Clarkson-Smith & Hartley 1989).

In another study of exercise in older adults, Hill et al (1993) trained previously sedentary older adults in aerobic exercise and monitored mood and cognitive functioning. The exercised group experienced a 22.5% increase in VO_{2max}, comparable to that found by Dustman et al (1984). This suggests that the level of cardiovascular fitness was near that required for improvement in cognitive functioning. However, the large increase in cardiovascular fitness did not translate into improved cognitive functioning or a decrease in processing time. The reason for the disparate results is not immediately apparent. One possibility is that Hill et al used single measures for each cognitive ability, i.e. there was only one measure of short-term memory, the Wechsler Memory Scale Logical Memory. Also, changes in response time may have been missed because response time was not assessed directly. Another possibility is that subjects had been sedentary for at least two years prior to beginning the study. It may be that continued maintenance of fitness over the lifespan is more beneficial for alleviating the decline in speed with age, whereas once slowing has begun as part of sedentary lifestyle, this slowing may not be easily reversible by beginning an exercise regimen.

A more intriguing possibility exists within the data. Hill et al (1993) report a significant correlation between VO_{2max} and psychomotor speed at pretest ($r = .25$, $p < .01$; p. P15). The posttest correlations between VO_{2max} and psychomotor speed were not reported for either the zero-order correlation or the part correlation partialled for baseline VO_{2max}. However, the presence of a significant correlation indicated that an important relationship between fitness and speed existed at the time of pretest. It is unknown whether the relationship between fitness and speed changed after exercising.

Another intriguing possibility for why several investigators have been unable to find a relationship between increases in cardiovascular fitness and global reaction time or cognitive functioning involves the level of analysis of the problem. Perhaps increases in cardiovascular fitness lead to changes in cardiovascular functions that are indicative of cognitive processes, e.g. heart rate interbeat intervals (IBI), peripheral vascular activity, and blood pressure (Jennings et al 1990a,b; Lacey & Lacey 1974). Jennings et al (1990b) found significant age differences in cardiovascular responses to serial learning memory and simple reaction-time tasks. Young adults typically show increased IBI when anticipating stimuli; older adults do not show much change in IBI when anticipating stimuli. Some of these differences were due to age-related cardiovascular changes, as well as age-related changes in cognitive resource allocation. Perhaps the effects of increased cardiovascular fitness in older adults would show more clearly in psychophysiological measures of cardiac activity and therefore in the cognitive processes underlying the task-related changes in cardiac activity.

The importance of level of analysis and the conceptualization of reaction time measures is illustrated by Bunce et al (1993), who investigated the effect of age and physical fitness on reaction time and mental blocks. Blocks were operationally defined as any reaction time longer than one second on a choice reaction-time task and were thought to indicate inhibitory failures during tasks requiring sustained attention. Fitness was measured with expired volume, vital capacity, body fat, and body mass. Bunce et al (1993) found a significant Age X Fitness interaction effect on the amount of blocks, such that older, less fit subjects experienced more blocks than did older, more fit subjects. Fitness had no effect on blocks in the younger subjects and had no effect on reaction time. The authors concluded that fitness was related to the ability to inhibit extraneous information and not to reaction time, per se. However, Salthouse (1993a) conducted a reanalysis on his own data, and found that attentional blocks were not the direct cause of slowing, thus contradicting Bunce et al.

Bunce et al's (1993) line of reasoning is instructive in that the process behind the slowest reaction times was hypothesized to be inhibitory. From one point of view, fitness had an effect on the slowest reaction times, but not on all reaction times. How one conceptualizes reaction time is crucial to the understanding of the relationship of speed and age. If one asks the question of what causes slowing, one might say a breakdown in inhibitory processes. Thus, Bunce et al's (1993) conclusions can be re-formulated to suggest that fitness and age have an effect on reaction time and that slowed reaction time is the result of impaired inhibition, including slowing of inhibition.

Current data indicate that, given sufficient cardiovascular fitness, exercise is associated with improved cognitive functioning in older adults. Where the focus of improvement is, whether in reaction time, inhibitory processes, arousal, or other processes related to cardiac functions, remains to be investigated. Additional variance in age-related slowing of information processing speed has been associated with health or, as is usually the case, disease states (Dywan et al 1992, Jones et al 1991).

Houx et al (1991) conducted a study in which community dwelling subjects aged 18–63 were assessed for potential risk factors for neurological dysfunction. Risk factors included birth complications, alcohol abuse, and exposure to neurotoxins (Houx et al 1991, p. 250). Half ($n = 40$) of the subjects reported at least one neurological risk event and half did not. Subjects completed a version of the Sternberg memory scanning paradigm. Older subjects were significantly slowed relative to young adults and subjects in the risk group were slowed relative to the no-risk group. The authors concluded that "the existence of risk factors for brain dysfunction aggravate the effects of aging even for subjects younger than 65 years" (p. 255). Aging combined with events associated with neurological problems result in significantly slowed information processing. Nearly 25% of the variance associated with memory scanning speed was associated with the neurological risks experienced by the subjects across the age range (Houx et al 1991). Apparently, response speed can be modulated by age, exercise (or aerobic capacity), and health. It should be noted that older adults tend to experience more events that may lead to neurological dysfunction, e.g. migraine, concussions, general anesthesia, and medication.

Other measures of brain integrity have been associated with speed of processing in older adults. Jones et al (1991) examined 100 men aged 30–80 on an impressive number of variables, from psychosocial functioning and demographic data to cognitive functioning and assessment of brain structure. In a LISREL analysis relating brain and psychosocial functions to cognitive functioning, sulci fluid volume was related significantly to the speed factor, as were education and a measure of general psychiatric symptomology. Relevant to our discussion of the relation of brain integrity to speed of response, the greater the sulci fluid volume, the slower the speed of information processing. As seen in the MRI and ERP componential analyses, brain integrity has a significant relationship to speed of response (Jones et al 1991).

The relationship between the physical health of older adults and cognitive functioning, from processing time to more complex cognitive operations, is not a simple one and is affected by many individual difference variables. Lifestyle variables have long been suspected as contributors to changes in cognition with age. It is presumed that the greater the activities of the person, the less the decline in cognitive processes. In an examination of the relationships between cognitive functioning, self-reported health, and lifestyle factors, Hultsch et al (1993) found significant correlations, albeit modest, between self-reported health and semantic processing time in a sample of normal, healthy adults aged 55–86 years. Furthermore, in older subjects, the correlation between an active lifestyle and processing speed was larger than in the relatively younger subjects. Good self-reported health and the ability to pursue an active lifestyle ameliorated some of the declines in processing speed with age. The beneficial effect of these lifestyle variables was somewhat stronger in the oldest subjects (Hultsch et al 1993).

The separable and independent effects of aging associated with disease were investigated in a multivariate cross-sectional study of older adults aged 65–91 (Anstey et al 1993). Measures of primary aging, defined as maturational processes, included reaction time, muscle strength, vibration sense, and measures of physiological vigor. Measures of secondary aging, defined as disease processes, included self-reported health, number of medications, diagnoses, and education. Subjects were assessed on both fluid and crystallized intelligence tests. The intercorrelation between primary aging and negative secondary aging (health) factors was 0.40.

The results showed that primary aging factors best predicted the fluid intelligence factors, but surprisingly, health factors did not predict fluid intelligence. Reaction time was the best individual predictor of the fluid factor. The authors were puzzled as to the lack of an effect of health on intelligence and speculated that their measures were not good measures of the health construct. However, allowing the health factor to covary with the primary biological aging factor may have confounded health and biological aging measures. Speed is hypothesized to be affected by health and speed, in turn, affects intelligence. Perhaps this hypothesis may help to solve the puzzle in future studies.

Cognitive Implications of Speed of Response

Psychologists have concentrated on defining and manipulating the cognitive processes underlying various tasks, from simple reaction time to typewriting skills; searching for answers to questions about the pervasive nature of slowing of behavior with age and its consequences for other, perhaps more complex processes. Here we review briefly the generalized and specific slowing hypotheses and some of the evidence for declines in working memory and inhibitory processes. Declines in working memory and inhibitory processes are also hypothesized to be a part of the fundamental changes in basic processing that in turn have consequences for more complex cognition.

Generalized or Specific Slowing Theories

Birren (1965, Birren et al 1980) proposed that there is a general factor of speed of the central nervous system (CNS) that is slowed with age. According to Cerella (1985), each component process is slowed and the slowing of performance of a complex task can thus be predicted from the slowing on a simple task. Further, all processes are slowed and are slowed by the same factor, in a linear fashion. The primary methodology used to support generalized slowing has been the Brinley (1965) plot of the mean of the older reaction times across tasks plotted against the mean of the younger reaction times across tasks.

Task-specific slowing hypothesizes that each task component slows at a specific rate, which may or may not be influenced to the rate of slowing of other processes. Thus, there could be slowing of the sensory-motor system that is unrelated to the slowing of more cognitive processes, slowing in the peripheral response system unrelated to central slowing, or slowing of input processes unrelated to output processes. Slowing does not affect task components in the same manner, but in each case, differential amounts of slowing can be observed.

One of the basic questions in this area is how to model generalized or specific slowing. Brinley (1965) plotted older against younger adult mean seconds per cognitive operation across two types of tasks. He found that the resulting regression equation (OLD = (1.68)YOUNG – .27) accounted for 98% (r = .99) of the variance in the means. Brinley concluded that response of speed of the older adult was "simple and accurately described" by the regression on the young response time (p. 131). Old reaction time was a linear function of the young response time, supporting the hypothesis of a generalized slowing across the two tasks.

Cerella's (1985) excellent meta-analysis of young and older adults' reaction times using Brinley plots provided impressive support for the generalized slowing model of reaction time. Cerella (1985) plotted 189 old-young pairs of mean reaction times taken from 18 studies, across 189 task conditions, and found that a general slowing coefficient explained much of the variance in the means. Cerella added one factor to a strong generalized slowing hypothesis. His meta-analysis indicated that there may be a peripheral slowing component and a central slowing component. The size of the slowing coefficient depended on the ratio of peripheral and central processes involved in task performance. How much slowing is observed in the performance of any one task depends on the mix of sensory-motor and central processes, but a general slowing factor affects age-related differences in reaction time performance.

Cerella (1991) stated, "The evidence is near-to-overwhelming that age is experienced, at least to a first approximation, as some sort of generalized slowing throughout the central nervous system, manifested equally in any task that requires the processing of information" (p. 220). Anyone viewing a Brinley plot is sure to be impressed by the regularity of the data points and the amount of variance for which the straight line regression accounts.

Myerson and his colleagues, with minor changes to incorporate a nonlinear factor, also demonstrated the all-pervasive quality of age-related slowing (Hale et al 1987, Lima et al 1991, Myerson et al 1990). They approached modeling age-related changes in response time with the common assumption that mean data from young and older subjects can be plotted without regard to task, underlying distributions of response times, homogeneity of variance, or internal task parameters (such as speed-accuracy tradeoffs), all of which may affect mean response times.

Questions have been raised about the use of Brinley plots to model generalized slowing, usually in the context of an argument in favor of task-specific slowing (Amrhein & Theios 1993, Fisk et al 1992, Laver & Burke 1993, Mayr & Kliegl 1993, Sliwinski et al 1994). Fisk et al (1992) demonstrated that Brinley plots were insensitive for discriminating between a pattern of means that indicated the general slowing model and a pattern of means that indicated the task-specific slowing model. This was especially the case when there was a complete overlap in the mean response times in the younger sample. In addition, because of the dependence of r on the range of data points, the percentage of explained variance is a poor measure of how well a linear model fits the data (see also Cohen & Cohen 1983). Thus, although an r of .98 looks large, it may be spuriously inflated by the selection of data points to include in the model (Fisk et al 1992).

Sliwinski et al (1994) pointed to a related weakness of Brinley plots that has been largely ignored in the aging literature, that is, the dependence of the plot on mean data. Group means are not sufficient for a thorough test of the generalized slowing model. Theoretically, the real question is not, on the average, are older adults slowed, but rather: Is any one older adult slowed across tasks? Furthermore, the size of a mean is completely determined by the number of subjects and the distribution of scores. A mean may not be representative of the distribution from which it was calculated (for an extensive review of this issue, see Wilcox 1987).

In an elegant set of analyses, Sliwinski et al (1994) examined the relationship of young and older subjects' distributions of the time taken to add numbers together. An analysis of distributions showed that the amount of slowing was similar for the extreme ends of the older subjects' distribution, i.e. the fastest and slowest subjects were slowed in the same fashion. Older adults slowed differentially depending on the task subcomponents. Initiating addition caused greater slowing than did incrementing the size of the integer to be added. The results were compatible both with a general slowing factor and with task-specific slowing factors (Sliwinski et al 1994).

Another cited weakness of Brinley plots is that they combine reaction time means without regard to the task or specific experimental manipulation. One could also argue that this is the strength of the plots, that the slowing is task independent. However, an essential assumption of regression analysis is adequate sampling of subjects within the population (Cohen & Cohen 1983). Brinley plot "subjects" are tasks and the tasks chosen may differ in important respects from one another and may not be homogenous or regularly distributed as assumed. Careful attention to incrementally changing task parameters and a demonstration that the tasks are representative of the population from which they come are essential for fulfilling the assumptions of regression analysis.

Mayr & Kliegl (1993) addressed the problem of task selection by increasing the number of task components to be performed by the subjects, thus manipulating the amount of task complexity. The authors were interested in age-related effects on working memory, but it is their analyses of slowing that concern us here. When young mean latencies were plotted against old mean latencies, two regression lines best fit the data, based on the type of task. They found two functions that described the slowing: both general across subjects, yet specific to the tasks. Furthermore, Mayr & Kliegl (1993) concluded that information processing itself is not a static set of steps encountered in a linear fashion, but rather is "a dynamic switching in working memory" of task processes (p. 1317). These results are compatible with a hierarchical notion of the effects of slowing, in that universal slowing of processing is mediated through higher-order components, such as working memory, and may be evidenced in performance differences by task.

Speed and Knowledge as Task Parameters

Salthouse (1982, 1985, 1988, 1991, 1993b) has been at the forefront of theoretical and methodological innovations in the study of age-related changes in speed and the relationship of those changes to cognition. His summaries of the field have been precise and exhaustive, while pointing to new questions. In one of the most interesting contributions to our understanding of generalized and specific slowing issues, Salthouse (1993a) proposed that tasks differ primarily in terms of speed and knowledge requirements of the task. According to Salthouse, "If successful performance is primarily dependent on speed, then the age effects can be expected to be quite large.... If knowledge is an important aspect of the task, as in most of the...verbal tasks..., then the age effects can be expected to be much smaller... (p. P34).

Salthouse (1993a) based his conclusion regarding the relative contributions of knowledge and speed to age-related differences on the results of two studies of young and older adults. Subjects were assessed on a variety of personal characteristics, e.g. education, self-reported health, and amount of time spent reading books and working word puzzles. The subjects completed motor speed, digit symbol, and several word-knowledge tasks (e.g. unscrambling anagrams). Salthouse found that older adults showed small differences from young adults on the tasks dependent on word knowledge and larger differences on tasks more independent of word knowledge.

Placing tasks on a speed-knowledge continuum is an extremely important step forward. The promise of such a continuum is that, given a careful analysis of task components, one would be able to predict the magnitude of age differences in performance. Conversely, one could reason from the pattern of age differences on performance to the relative amounts of knowledge and speed inherent in the task. No longer need attention be paid to formulating the parameters of generalized slowing, but rather to the requirements of the task, to the processes and representations underlying performance.

Speed of Cognitive Processing

Salthouse's conclusions can be supported by data from a number of areas, from the study of intellectual abilities to visual processes. In fact, the distinction between knowledge and speed is reminiscent of the Horn-Cattell fluid-crystallized intelligence distinction in intellectual abilities (discussed below). In this section, we review some studies that appear to support the speed-knowledge continuum. An outgrowth of examining studies that show a reduction in the effect of age-related slowing of response time on task performance is the consideration of other hypotheses for specific declines in performance with age. A review of the age-related changes in working memory, inhibitory processes, and internal noise concludes this section.

Studies of the speed of lexical activation rarely have found age differences between young and older adults, which would be expected if slowing affected all cognitive processes equivalently (e.g. Howard 1988, Howard et al 1986, Madden 1988). In a meta-analysis of lexical decision studies, Lima et al (1991) found that, indeed, older adults were slower to determine whether or not a string of letters was a word. However, the degree of slowing in a lexical task was not as great as would have been predicted on the basis of slowing in nonlexical decision task performance. Generalized versus specific slowing is not the issue according to Lima et al. The authors state that the critical distinction among tasks is the lexical-nonlexical distinction and that research should be directed to understanding what components differ between these types of tasks (see also Laver & Burke 1993).

In an analysis of visual word identification, Madden and his colleagues have conducted a series of studies to indicate that there are age-related speed-knowledge processing differences in specific subcomponents of word-identification task performance (Allen et al 1993; Madden 1992; Madden et al 1992, 1993). For example, Madden (1992) administered a primed lexical decision task to subjects aged 20–78, who had to indicate whether or not the target letter string was a word. Across age, mean reaction time to the targets was slowed; however, the amount of facilitation for related primes was consistent across age. Madden concluded that although slowing of response time was a factor in task performance, there were task components that did not show age-related declines. Specifically, those processes after the initial perceptual processing (e.g. more knowledge-based processes), showed little or no age-related declines in speed (Madden 1992).

Several studies of arithmetic tasks have shown similar dichotomies in age-related performance differences (Allen et al 1992, Geary et al 1993, Geary & Wiley 1991). For example, Geary et al (1993) tested young and older adults on simple and complex subtraction tasks. Older subjects showed a higher level of subtraction strategies relative to those of younger adults and, in complex subtraction, were quicker to execute the borrow function than were young adults. These functions seem to be more dependent on prior knowledge and thus insensitive to age-related changes in speed of processing (Geary et al 1993).

Alternative Explanations

Working memory, inhibitory processes, and internal noise are among the theories used to explain age-related differences in cognitive performance (Allen 1991, McDowd 1994, Salthouse 1991). Within an hierarchical theory of cognition, a notion of generalized slowing and these alternative explanations need not be mutually exclusive. In complex cognitive processing, the contributions of inhibition and working memory may be greater than the contribution of generalized slowing. If, on a particular task, working memory declines and is highly associated with performance differences, it does not negate the contribution of generalized slowing. It indicates that, for that particular task, decline in working memory is the appropriate level at which to make causal inferences. Generalized slowing need not be limited to facilitation, but may influence inhibition and, ultimately, working memory. In solving tasks, a subject needs to keep in mind intentions as well as elements to be combined in a complex response. Attention and working memory are dissipative processes and it seems reasonable that speed of input and output will influence the effectiveness of these functions with age. Understanding how such efforts might be manifest in cognitive performance requires more complex research designs than have previously been used.

In the case of internal noise, slowed neural processing speed may cause incoming stimuli to be represented in a number of different ways. The representation of stimuli will "oscillate" (Allen 1991), causing an increase in internal noise and declines in cognitive processing.

Speed and Intelligence

A hierarchical model of the effects of response speed would predict that individual differences in speed of processing is associated significantly with individual differences in complex cognitive functioning or intellectual ability. The issue is not that processing speed is related to intellectual abilities, but rather is how age-related slowing affects intellectual ability performance. Studies investigating this issue have been primarily correlational and cross-sectional in nature. However, a number of studies have examined longitudinal changes as well. The evidence from these studies supports the evidence from studies of cognitive processing, i.e. age-related slowing in basic processes accounts for much of the variance in a general decline of intellectual abilities.

A few issues need mentioning before reviewing the data. One is that measures of speed of response tend to be different from those in the information processing tradition. This reduces the comparability of perceptual difficulty studies, psychometric studies, and information processing studies. Another is that longitudinal changes in speed have been smaller than cross-sectional studies have suggested. Finally, because of the correlational nature of many of the studies, conclusions about associations and relationships can be made, but more mechanistic conclusions cannot be drawn.

Several psychometric studies have attempted to determine whether there is one general speed factor or several speed factors that change with age (see Cunningham & Tomer 1990, White & Cunningham 1987). Information processing theorists have spent much time examining this issue. Two studies (Hertzog et al 1987, White & Cunningham 1987) report more than one factor that could be called speed factors. This accords well with cognitive literature, i.e. there appear to be task-specific speed-of-response influences. However, in factor analysis, which allows for hierarchical examination of factors, one could examine whether the first-order factor intercorrelates can be subsumed under a second-order factor.

Tomer & Cunningham (1993) investigated the first- and second-order speed factors for performance on five categories of speed tasks (symbolic perceptual speed, figural perceptual speed, choice reaction time, Sternberg reaction times, and card-sorting speed) in 296 subjects (young: 18–33 years of age, old: 58–73 years of age). The first-order factor analysis resulted in a five-factor model fitting the a priori categories of speed tasks. The five speeds were allowed to correlate with one another and the intercorrelations were from .41 to .84. A second-order factor solution accounted for as much variance as the first-order five-factor model, but did not improve the overall fit of the model to the data. The second-order factors were also allowed to intercorrelate and the correlations range from .6 to .8. Tomer & Cunningham (1993) concluded that a one- or even two-factor model of speed did not fit the data, but that at least five factors were needed to describe the data. The authors stated that "higher order analyses of the structure of intellectual speed do not seem very promising..." (p. 21). Tomer & Cunningham do not interpret the high intercorrelations among the second-order factors; the general speed factor may be hidden among the intercorrelations. Thus, Tomer & Cunningham appear to have established a multifactor model of speed; however, an analysis of factor structure only indirectly addresses the question of whether general processes underlie slowing of response speed with age.

One of the defining notions of age-related changes in intellectual abilities today has been the distinction between fluid and crystallized intelligence. Horn (1982) presented data to indicate that fluid intelligence tended to decline with age, was associated with slowing of response speed, and may be more associated with biological factors in aging. Crystallized intelligence, in contrast, tended to increase with age and was less associated with slowing and biological factors. However, Horn (1982) was careful to point out that the data led him to conclude that slowing may be a consequence and not a cause of declines in intellectual ability.

Further psychometric support for the speed-knowledge dichotomy comes from Schaie & Willis (1993), who examined patterns of age differences in intellectual abilities in 1628 subjects. Measures of intellectual ability included inductive reasoning, spatial orientation, numeric and verbal ability, perceptual speed, and verbal memory. Perceptual speed declined across cohorts, with the oldest cohort slowing at about half the rate of the youngest cohorts. Schaie & Willis found that the pattern of age differences varied according to the degree to which the measure depended on speed or knowledge. Those measures dependent on speed tended to decline with age, whereas those dependent on knowledge tended to remain stable across age (Schaie & Willis 1993, Schaie 1989).

According to Hertzog (1989), part of the unexplained variance in age changes in intellectual functioning may be the result of "performance-specific influences of information-processing speed" (p. P645). Hertzog observed significant correlations of speed with Primary Mental Ability (PMA) subtests in a cross-sectional study of adults aged 43–78. Furthermore, a measure of the speed to fill in the PMA answer sheet accounted for some of the differences in intellectual abilities. Hertzog (1989) argued for a "both-and" approach to speed and intellectual abilities. In other words, there is a general negative effect of slowing on intellectual abilities with age and a specific negative effect of slowing.

Support for the hypothesis that there are general and specific effects of speed on intellectual abilities comes from two studies, one cross-sectional and the other longitudinal, of various cognitive tasks across age groups (Hultsch et al 1990, 1992). The cross-sectional study (Hultsch et al 1990) indicated that working memory, in addition to speed of processing, was associated significantly with individual differences in memory performance. Hultsch et al extended the previous studies of speed and complex cognitive functioning by including two measures of working memory. Working memory accounted for differences in complex memory abilities above and beyond speed and no other basic information process or task-specific process accounted for more variance. Perhaps working memory is Schaie's missing component to explain differences in intellectual ability with age.

Hultsch et al's (1992) longitudinal replication supported, for the most part, the cross-sectional findings. However, the longitudinal results revealed a decline in cognitive functioning over the three years of the study that was unrelated to speed and working memory performance. Working memory declined over time even when speed was partialled out of the scores. When the general effects of speed were statistically equated, working memory and other cognitive processes declined, and the decline was unrelated to speed (Hultsch et al 1992).

Lindenberger et al (1993) addressed the question of whether the relationship of speed and intellectual abilities holds within the oldest-old population. Subjects aged 70–103 were assessed on speed, reasoning, memory, knowledge, and word fluency tasks. In a structural equation analysis, the statistical model that associated a general speed factor with intellectual abilities fit the pattern of data well. Allowing speed to affect individual intellectual abilities independently (as in the specific slowing model) did not fit the data. Thus, in the oldest-old, declines in speed of response mediated differences in intellectual abilities. Furthermore, the pervasive nature of the effect of speed was observed in the increased size of intercorrelations among intellectual abilities.

In summary, slowing in speed of response with age underlies much of the decline in intellectual ability with age. The degree to which the effect of speed is observed on performance is the result of the relative amounts of knowledge and speed required for successful task completion. Other studies point to working memory as a significant factor in age-related intellectual ability declines that are not accounted for by speed.

Discussion

This review of the literature on age-related slowing of behavior has examined several thoughts about theory production. One is that the psychology of aging is an interface for many of the psychological conceptions about the organization of behavior. This interface promises gains in understanding as we use our ideas about aging to test our ideas about behavioral organization, and vice versa. Luce (1986) made several relevant observations in his comprehensive survey of response times. He stated that "response time is psychology's ubiquitous dependent variable" (p. 6). The use of response time to investigate behavior assumes that the processing of information is highly structured and different paths through that structure should entail different response times. This represents the traditional experimental design to make inferences from the pattern of response times obtained under different conditions in relation to hypothesized cognitive structures (Luce 1986). Several points relevant for aging research might be added to Luce's thinking on this subject. First, if the structure of the information pathways in the brain is altered because of learning, disease, or aging, then one might also find response-time differences. Changes with age in response time can help to validate our theoretical structures about how cognition is organized. Second, although psychology generally has used response time as a dependent variable, in aging studies, response time can be viewed as an independent variable, as that which is used in explanations.

Third, chronological age is seen increasingly as a "fickle mistress," in that the use of age as a variable should be an initial point of departure to be supplemented and, possibly, to be replaced by other variables. Chronological age is only an index of the passing of time, and correlations with age may be positive or negative; large, small, or zero; and linear or curvilinear. One method for replacing age comes from biological research on aging. In biology, the concept of markers has been used to refer to measures of the status of an organism, other than age alone. Birren & Fisher (1992) discussed criteria that might be used to test the validity of behavioral markers of aging. An example of a behavioral marker is slowing of reaction time. One of the suggested criteria against which to test the significance of slowing is length of life. That is, measures of slowing take on a greater significance if individuals who show the greatest slowing are also the shortest lived. It remains to be demonstrated whether the degree of slowing predicts the remaining years of life. Another criterion is gender differences, as women tend to live longer than men. There may well be identifiable correlates of differences in male and female longevity.

Heikkinen (1994) suggested another useful way to model age-related changes. After reviewing epidemiological and ecological models of aging, Heikkinen proposed the model of an "effective causal complex" (ECC) to represent clusters or groups of factors that may affect patterns of age-related change. Adding ECCs to psychological research allows the examination of functional capacity, length of life, and morbidity in relation to behavioral outcomes. One way to enlarge our scope of ECCs is to examine contemporary models of aging held within the biological, behavioral, and social sciences. While biological scientists study the destructive processes associated with the passage of time, social scientists are interested in the changing course of life in such areas as social roles, achievement, and self-esteem (Marshall 1995).

Yates & Benton (1995) offer the concept of homeodynamics as a useful metaphor to encourage the integration of theory in aging. They distinguish aging from senescence, the latter referring to the degradation of living systems embracing damage, harm, loss, or failure. For psychology, the significance of Yates & Benton lies in the fact that much of the research on aging deals with information and constructive processes that may exist concurrently with the destruction of the multicellular, self-organizing systems. Schroots (1995) discussed the implications for psychology of the notion that entropy is not merely a downward slide toward disorganization; in contrast, order and disorder may emerge over time. Schroots leads again to Heikkinen's causal complexes. Thus, slowness seems to be more closely linked with the biological complex of variables, and crystallized intelligence or knowledge seems to be more closely linked with external factors, such as social structures. These links among causal complexes may replace the imprecision associated with the use of age as our principal index of aging.

SUMMARY AND CONCLUSIONS

Over 100 years of observations have established that slowness of behavior is a characteristic of becoming old, although it is now recognized that health, use of medications, and physical activity may modify the extent of the slowing. Early research indicated that there is a limited contribution to slowing by peripheral sensory-motor factors. Substantial evidence has pointed to the central nervous system as the locus of the slowing.

Recent investigators have expressed divided opinions about whether there is a pervasive general slowing of behavior by the central nervous system or whether there are specific localized mechanisms. This is not unlike early disputed views of the brain as having localized or global behavioral functions: Both principles appear to be simultaneously true. Sufficient research has been conducted to indicate that there are specific factors as well as a general process associated with the slowing of behavior with advancing age. Whether such slowing is a primary or secondary cause of age differences in cognitive processes is a significant scientific issue.

A marked broadening of research on aging has been accompanied by an interest in identifying both the neurophysiological correlates of slowing as well as its role in specific cognitive processes. Yet another aspect of the changing research picture is the trend to move beyond the mere use of chronological age as the sole basis for comparing performance differences. Measurement of more independent variables is suggested as part of clusters or causal complexes that will indicate sources of the changes in speed and other aspects of behavior. These causal complexes include biological indicators such as disease, physiological capacity for work, and length of life, as well as causal complexes of social factors involving such variables as education, occupation, and ethnicity.

There has been considerable discussion of markers of aging. In this approach, factors found to be closely associated with advancing age are used as measures of the effectiveness of attempts to modify the course of aging, e.g. by diet, exercise, new learning, and drugs. Along with other biomarkers of aging, speed of behavior may prove to be a criterion for assessing the impact of interventions on the rate and processes of aging. As a marker of aging, speed needs further exploration that will compare the slowness observed in different subgroups of adults with a wide range of outcomes in their productivity, capacity for adaptation to life's demands, and health.

The present status of information about slowness of behavior with advancing age indicates that it is one of the most reliable features of human life. Its origins remain to be understood in greater detail, as well as its consequences for the well-being of the individual. Research, both longitudinal and experimental, is needed to deepen our understanding of slowing of mediation by the central nervous system and its consequences for complex behaviors.

ACKNOWLEDGMENTS

We would like to thank Gloria Bando for her hard work in the preparation of this manuscript.

Literature Cited

Albert ML, Feldman RG, Willis AL. 1974. The 'subcortical dementia' of progressive supranuclear palsy. *J. Neurol. Neurosurg. Psychiatr.* 37:121–30

Allen P. 1991. On age differences in processing variability and scanning speed. *J. Gerontol.: Psychol. Sci.* 46:P191–201

Allen P, Ashcraft M, Weber T. 1992. On mental multiplication and age. *Psychol. Aging* 7:536–45

Allen P, Madden D, Weber T, Groth K. 1993. Influence of age and processing stage on visual word recognition. *Psychol. Aging* 8: 274–82

Amrhein PC, Theios J. 1993. The time it takes elderly and young individuals to draw pictures and write words. *Psychol. Aging* 8: 197–206

Angelucci L, Alema S, Ferrarisa L, Ghirardia O, Imperato A, et al. 1991. Ordered disorder in the aged brain. In *Plasticity and Regeneration of the Nervous System,* ed. PS Timiras, et al, pp. 277–90. New York: Plenum

Anstey K, Stankov L, Lord S. 1993. Primary aging, secondary aging, and intelligence. *Psychol. Aging* 8:562–70

Ball SS, Marsh JT, Schubarth G, Brown WS, Strandburg R. 1989. Longitudinal P300 latency changes in Alzheimer's Disease. *J. Gerontol.: Med. Sci.* 44:M195–200

Bashore TR. 1989. Age, physical fitness, and mental processing speed. *Annu. Rev. Gerontol. Geriatr.* 9:120–44

Bashore TR. 1990. Age-related changes in mental processing revealed by analyses of event-related brain potentials. In *Event-related Brain Potentials: Basic Issues and Applications,* ed. J Rohrbaugh, R Parasuraman, JR Johnson, pp. 242–75. Oxford: Oxford Univ. Press

Bashore TR, Osman A, Heffley EF. 1989. Mental slowing in elderly persons: a cogni-

tive psychophysiological analysis. *Psychol. Aging* 4:235–44

Baylor AM, Spirduso WW. 1988. Systematic aerobic exercise and components of reaction time in older women. *J. Gerontol.: Psychol. Sci.* 43:P121–126

Birren JE. 1965. Age changes in speed of behavior: its central nature and physiological correlates. In *Behavior, Aging, and the Nervous System,* ed. AT Welford, JE Birren, pp. 191–216. Springfield, IL: Thomas

Birren JE, Botwinick J. 1955. Age differences in finger, jaw, and foot reaction time in auditory stimuli. *J. Gerontol.* 10:429–32

Birren JE, Fisher LM. 1992. Speed of behavior and aging: consequences for cognition and survival. In *1990–91 Nebraska Symposium on Motivation,* pp. 2–37. Lincoln: Univ. Neb. Press

Birren J, Renner V. 1977. Research on the psychology of aging. In *Handbook of the Psychology of Aging,* ed. J Birren, KW Schaie, pp. 30–38. New York: Van Nostrand Reinhold

Birren JE, Woods AM, Williams MV. 1980. Behavioral slowing with age: causes, organization, and consequences. In *Aging in the 1980s: Psychological Issues,* ed. LW Poon, pp. 293–308. Washington, DC: Am. Psychol. Assoc.

Blumenthal J, Emery C, Madden D. George L, et al. 1989. Cardiovascular and behavioral effects of aerobic exercise training in healthy older men and women. *J. Gerontol.* 44:M147–57

Blumenthal JA, Emery CF, Madden DJ, Schniebolk S, Walsh-Riddle M, et al. 1991. Long-term effects of exercise on psychological functioning in older men and women. *J. Gerontol.: Psychol. Sci.* 46: P352–361

Blumenthal JA, Madden DJ. 1988. Effects of aerobic exercise training, age, and physical fitness on memory-search performance. *Psychol. Aging* 3:280–85

Brinley JF. 1965. Cognitive sets, speed and accuracy of performance in the elderly. In *Behavior, Aging, and the Nervous System,* ed. AT Welford, JE Birren, pp. 114–49. Springfield, IL: Thomas

Brown WS, Marsh JT, LaRue A. 1983. Exponential electrophysiological aging: P3 latency. *Electroencephalogr. Clin. Neurophysiol.* 55:277–85

Bunce DJ, Warr PB, Cochrane T. 1993. Blocks in choice responding as a function of age and physical fitness. *Psychol. Aging* 8:26–33

Cacioppo JT, Berntson GG. 1992. Social psychological contributions to the decade of the brain: doctrine of multilevel analysis. *Am. Psychol.* 47:1019–28

Cerella J. 1985. Information processing rates in the elderly. *Psychol. Bull.* 98:67–83

Cerella J. 1990. Aging and information processing rate. In *Handbook of the Psychology of Aging,* ed. JE Birren, KW Schaie, pp. 201–21. San Diego, CA: Academic. 3rd ed.

Cerella J. 1991. Age effects may be global, not local: comment on Fisk and Rogers 1991. *J. Exp. Psychol.: Gen.* 120:215–23

Clarkson-Smith L, Hartley AA. 1989. Relationships between physical exercise and cognitive abilities in older adults. *Psychol. Aging* 4:183–89

Clarkson-Smith L, Hartley AA. 1990. Structural equation models of relationships between exercise and cognitive abilities. *Psychol. Aging* 5:437–46

Cohen J, Cohen P. 1983. *Applied Multiple Regression/Correlation Analysis for the Behavioral Sciences.* Hillsdale, NJ: Erlbaum. 2nd ed.

Craik F, Morris L, Morris R, Loewen E. 1990. Relations between source amnesia and frontal lobe functioning in older adults. *Psychol. Aging* 5:148–51

Cummings JL, Benson DF. 1983. *Dementia: A Clinical Approach.* Boston: Butterworths

Cunningham WR, Tomer A. 1990. Intellectual abilities and age: concepts, theories and analyses. In *Aging and Cognition: Mental Processes, Self Awareness and Interventions,* ed. EA Lovelace, pp. 279–406. Amsterdam: Elsevier

Donchin E, Coles MGH. 1988. Is the P300 component a manifestation of context updating? *Behav. Brain Sci.* 11:357–74

Dustman RE, Ruhling RO, Russell EM, Shearer DE, Bonekat HW, et al. 1984. Aerobic exercise training and improved neuropsychological function of older individuals. *Neurobiol. Aging* 5:35–42

Dywan J, Segalowitz SJ, Unsal A. 1992. Speed of information processing, health, and cognitive performance in older adults. *Dev. Neuropsychol.* 8:473–90

Filley CM, Franklin GM, Heaton RK, Rosenberg NL. 1989a. White matter dementia: clinical disorders and implications. *Neuropsychiatr. Neuropsychol. Behav. Neurol.* 1:239–54

Filley CM, Heaton RK, Nelson LM, Burks JS, Franklin GM. 1989b. A comparison of dementia in Alzheimer's Disease and multiple sclerosis. *Arch. Neurol.* 46:157–61

Fisk AD, Fisher DL, Rogers WA. 1992. General slowing alone cannot explain age-related search effects: reply to Cerella 1991. *J. Exp. Psychol.: Gen.* 121:73–78

Galton F. 1885. On the anthropometric laboratory at the late International Health Exhibition. *J. Anthropol. Inst.* 14:205–21, 275–287

Geary DC, Frensch PA, Wiley JG. 1993. Simple and complex mental subtraction: strategy choice and speed-of-processing differences in younger an older adults. *Psychol. Aging* 8:242–56

Geary DC, Wiley JG. 1991. Cognitive addition: strategy choice and speed-of-processing differences in young and elderly adults. *Psychol. Aging* 6:474–83

Grafman J, Litvan I, Gomez C, Chase TN. 1990. Frontal lobe function in progressive supranuclear palsy. *Arch. Neurol.* 47:553–58

Hale S, Myerson J, Wagstaff D. 1987. General slowing and non-verbal information processing: evidence for a power law. *J. Gerontol.* 42:131–36

Heikkinen E. 1994. Epidemiological-ecological models of aging. *Can. J. Aging.* In press

Hertzog C. 1989. Influences of cognitive slowing on age differences in intelligence. *Dev. Psychol.* 25:636–51

Hertzog C, Raskin C, Cannon C. 1987. Age-related slowing in semantic information processing speed: an individual analysis. *J. Gerontol.* 41:500–2

Hill RD, Storandt M, Malley M. 1993. The impact of long-term exercise training on psychological function in older adults. *J. Gerontol.:Psychol. Sci.* 48:P12–17

Horn JL. 1982. The theory of fluid and crystallized intelligence in relation to concepts of cognitive psychology and aging in adulthood. In *Aging and Cognitive Processes,* ed. FIM Craik, S Trehub, pp. 237–78. New York: Plenum

Houx PJ, Vreeling FW, Jolles J. 1991. Rigorous health screening reduced age effect on memory scanning task. *Brain Cogn.* 15:246–60

Howard DV. 1988. Aging and memory activation: the priming of semantic and episodic memories. In *Language, Memory, and Aging,* ed. LL Light, DM Burke, pp. 77–99. Cambridge: Cambridge Univ. Press

Howard DV, Shaw R, Heisey J. 1986. Aging

and the time course of semantic activation. *J. Gerontol.* 41:195–203

Hoyer WJ, Rybash JM. 1994. Characterizing adult cognitive development. *J. Adult Dev.* 1:7–12

Hultsch DF, Hammer M, Small BJ. 1993. Age differences in cognitive performance in later life: relationships to self-reported health and activity life style. *J. Gerontol.: Psychol. Sci.* 48:P1–11

Hultsch DF, Hertzog C, and Dixon RA. 1990. Ability correlates of memory performance in adulthood and aging. *Psychol. Aging* 5: 356–68

Hultsch DF, Hertzog C, Small BJ, McDonald-Miszczak L, Dixon RA. 1992. Short-term longitudinal change in cognitive performance in later life. *Psychol. Aging* 7:571–84

Iragui VJ, Kutas M, Mitchiner MR, Hillyard SA. 1993. Effects of aging on event-related brain potentials and reaction times in an auditory oddball task. *Psychophysiology* 30:10–22

Jennings JR, Brock K, Nebes R. 1990a. Age and specific processing capacities: a cardiovascular analysis. *J. Psychophysiol.* 4: 51–64

Jennings JR, Nebes RD, Yovetich NA. 1990b. Aging increases the energetic demands of episodic memory: a cardiovascular analysis. *J. Exp. Psychol.: Gen.* 119:77–91

Jones KJ, Albert MS, Duffy FH, Hyde MR, Naeser M, Aldwin C. 1991. Modeling age using cognitive, psychosocial and physiological variables: the Boston normative aging study. *Exp. Aging Res.* 17:227–42

Junque C, Pujol J, Vendrell P, Bruna O, Jodar M, et al. 1990. Leuko-araiosis on magnetic resonance imaging and speed of mental processing. *Arch. Neurol.* 47:151–56

Koga Y, Morandt G. 1923. On the degree of association between reaction times in the case of different senses. *Biometrika* 15: 346–72

Lacey BC, Lacey JI. 1974. Studies of heart rate and other bodily processes in sensorimotor behavior. In *Cardiovascular Psychophysiology,* ed. PA Obrist, J Brener, LV DiCara, pp. 538–64. Chicago: Aldine

Landahl H. 1959. Biological periodicities, mathematical biology, and aging. In *Handbook of Aging and the Individual,* ed. J Birren, pp. 81–115. Chicago: Univ. Chicago Press

Laver GD, Burke DM. 1993. Why do semantic priming effects increase in old age? A meta-analysis. *Psychol. Aging* 8:34–43

Lima SD, Hale S, Myerson J. 1991. How general is general slowing? Evidence from the lexical domain. *Psychol. Aging* 6:416–25

Lindenberger U, Mayr U, Kliegl R. 1993. Speed and intelligence in old age. *Psychol. Aging* 8:207–20

Lipsitz LA, Goldberger AL. 1992. Loss of

'complexity' and aging: potential applications of fractals and chaos theory to senescence. *J. Am. Med. Assoc.* 267:1806–9

Looren De Jong H, Kok A, Van Rooy J. 1989. Stimulus probability and motor response in young and old adults: an ERP study. *Biol. Psychol.* 29:125–48

Luce RD. 1986. *Response Times: Their Role in Inferring Elementary Mental Organization.* New York: Oxford Univ. Press

Madden D. 1988. Adult age differences in the effects of sentence context and stimulus degradation during visual word recognition. *Psychol. Aging* 3:167–72

Madden D. 1992. Four to ten milliseconds per year: age-related slowing of visual word identification. *J. Gerontol.: Psychol. Sci.* 47, P59–68

Madden D, Pierce T, Allen P. 1992. Adult age difference in attention allocation during memory search. *Psychol. Aging* 7:594–601

Madden D, Pierce T, Allen P. 1993. Age-related slowing and the time course of semantic priming in visual word identification. *Psychol. Aging* 8:490–507

Madden DJ, Blumenthal JA, Allen PA, Emery CF. 1989. Improving aerobic capacity in healthy older adults does not necessarily lead to improved cognitive performance. *Psychol. Aging* 4:307–20

Magladery J. 1959. Neurophysiology of aging. In *Handbook of Aging and the Individual,* ed. J Birren, pp. 173–86. Chicago: Univ. Chicago Press

Marsh JT, Schubarth G, Brown WS, Riege W, Strandburg R, et al. 1990. PET and P300 relationships in early Alzheimer's disease. *Neurobiol. Aging* 11:471–76

Marshall V. 1995. Social models of aging. *Can. J. Aging.* In press

Mayr U, Kliegl R. 1993. Sequential and coordinate complexity: age-based processing limitations in figural transformations. *J. Exp. Psychol.: Learn. Mem. Cogn.* 19: 1297–320

McDowd JM. 1994. *Positive thinking about negative priming.* Presented at Cogn. Aging Conf., April, Atlanta, GA

Miles WR. 1942. Psychological aspects of ageing. In *Problems of Ageing,* ed. EV Cowdry, pp. 756–84. Baltimore, MD: Williams & Wilkins

Myerson J, Hale S, Wagstaff D, Poon LW, Smith GA. 1990. The information-loss model: a mathematical theory of age-related cognitive slowing. *Psychol. Rev.* 97: 475–587

O'Donnell BF, Friedman S, Swearer JM, Drachman DA. 1992. Active and passive P3 latency and psychometric performance: influence of age and individual differences. *Int. J. Psychophysiol.* 12:187–95

Pollock VE, Schneider LS. 1992. Reliability of late positive component activity (P3) in healthy elderly adults. *J. Gerontol.: Med. Sci.* 47:M88–92

Rao SM, Mittenberg W, Bernardin L, Haughton V, Leo GJ. 1989. Neuropsychological test findings in subjects with leukoaraiosis. *Arch. Neurol.* 46:40–44

Salthouse TA. 1982. *Adult Cognition: An Experimental Psychology of Human Aging.* New York: Springer-Verlag

Salthouse TA. 1985. Speed of behavior and its implications for cognition. In *Handbook of the Psychology of Aging,* ed. JE Birren, KW Schaie, pp. 400–26. New York: Van Nostrand Reinhold. 2nd ed.

Salthouse TA. 1988. Initiating the formalization of theories of cognitive aging. *Psychol. Aging* 3:3–16

Salthouse TA. 1991. *Theoretical Perspectives on Cognitive Aging.* Hillsdale, NJ: Erlbaum

Salthouse TA. 1993a. Attentional blocks are not responsible for age-related slowing. *J. Gerontol.: Psychol. Sci.* 48:P263–270

Salthouse TA. 1993b. Speed and knowledge as determinants of adult age differences in verbal tasks. *J. Gerontol.: Psychol. Sci.* 48: P29–36

Schaie KW. 1989. Perceptual speed in adulthood: cross-sectional and longitudinal studies. *Psychol. Aging* 4:443–53

Schaie KW, Willis SL. 1993. Age difference patterns of psychometric intelligence in adulthood: generalizability within and across ability domains. *Psychol. Aging* 8: 44–55

Schroots JJF. 1995. Psychology models of aging. *Can. J. Aging.* In press

Sliwinski M, Buschke H, Kuslansky G, Senior G, Scarisbrick D. 1994. Proportional slowing and addition speed in old and young adults. *Psychol. Aging* 9:72–80

Stones MJ, Kozma A. 1989. Age, exercise, and coding performance. *Psychol. Aging* 4: 190–94

Strayer DL Wickens CD, Braune R. 1987. Adult age differences in the speed and capacity of information processing: II. An electrophysiological approach. *Psychol. Aging* 2:99–110

Surwillo WW, Iyer V. 1989. Passively produced P3 components of the averaged event-related potential in aging and in Alzheimer's type dementia: a pilot study. *Neuropsychiatr. Neuropsychol. Behav. Neurol.* 1:177–89

Tachibana H, Toda K, Sugita M. 1992. Age-related changes in attended and unattended P3 latency in normal subjects. *Int. J. Neurosci.* 66:277–84

Tomer A, Cunningham WR. 1993. The structure of cognitive speed measures in old and young adults. *Multivariate Behav. Res.* 28: 1–24

White NA, Cunningham WR. 1987. The age comparative construct validity of speeded cognitive factors. *Multivariate Behav. Res.* 22:249–65

Wilcox R. 1987. *New Statistical Procedures for the Social Sciences: Modern Solutions to Basic Problems.* Hillsdale, NJ: Erlbaum

Yates F, Benton L. 1995. Loss of integration and stability with age: theories and conjectures. *Can. J. Aging.* In press

Annu. Rev. Psychol. 1995. 46:355–374

TEACHING IN SUBJECT MATTER AREAS: Science

Jonathan Sandoval

Division of Education, University of California, Davis, California 95616-8579

KEY WORDS: conceptual change, interest, instruction

CONTENTS

0066-4308/95/0201-0355$05.00

INTRODUCTION

In this survey of research relevant to the teaching of science it is important to first delineate a view of teaching. Psychologists are often focused more on the learner than on the teacher, although it is possible to study teachers' conceptions of what they are doing (Kagan 1992) and how they are behaving in the classroom (Brophy 1988, Druva & Anderson 1983). This review remains in the cognitive psychology tradition by defining teaching in reference to changes that occur in the learner.

The view adopted here is that teaching is the act of facilitating the building of new schemata (or the modification of existing schemata) in the learner through some form of discourse. This definition implies that both human beings and curriculum products (i.e. books or computer software) can engage in teaching. It also implies that many things that teachers do may or may not be teaching. By using the term schemata, moreover, this notion of teaching may exclude the facilitation of some basic forms of learning such as signal learning, stimulus-response learning, chaining, and verbal association (Gagne 1977), although teachers do facilitate these forms of learning.

There is a growing realization that teaching and learning activities are best studied in the subject matter context. In science, learning, and particularly teaching, may have different features than learning and teaching in mathematics, for example. A number of journals have become well established, explicitly devoted to teaching and learning in subject matter areas. All publish work by psychologists, and many of the articles are in the psychological tradition. This review examines teaching in science, although reviews could easily be prepared in reading, mathematics, foreign languages, social studies, writing, or other subject matter topics. Most of this literature is not published in traditional psychological journals, however. In preparing a recent meta-analysis, Guzzetti et al (1993) found only one percent of the studies on science teaching and learning had been published in educational psychology journals.

This review also focuses on studies dealing with children in grades K through 12, although studies with college students make up about 30% of the literature (Guzzetti et al 1993). The teaching of exceptional and remedial populations also is included.

Readers interested in studies related to the efficacy of teacher behaviors are directed to reviews by Druva & Anderson (1983) and Anderson & Burns (1989). This research relates behavioral characteristics of teachers to the learning outcomes of students. Some behaviors may be specific to subject matter or have differential effects in different subject areas (Eggleston 1983).

Teaching is often examined in relationship to particular curricular strategies in science (Shymansky et al 1983). For example, a debate is under way between the proponents of integrating science instruction with other subject matter such as mathematics and literature, and those who are more traditional. This review attempts to examine more general phenomena than specific curricula and examines studies of curricula only as they relate to more general ideas.

In previous decades and continuing in the present, researchers have studied learning and teaching strategies that have applicability across a wide variety of subject matter areas. Mnemonics, for example, have been studied extensively in different learning contexts and have also been studied in science instruction, particularly with special populations (Mastropieri & Scruggs 1992).

CONSTRUCTIVISM

It is heartening to realize that cognitive psychological theories and principles continue to have considerable influence on educators. The dominant conceptual framework in science education over the past two decades is constructivism. Simply stated, constructivism is a cognitive, as opposed to behavioral, view that learners actively construct or formulate their own understandings of phenomena. New knowledge is added in some way to old knowledge with a possible change in the learner's understanding. Learners' cognitive abilities grow through a process of progressively changing conceptual schemes. On the philosophical side, constructivism is related to the epistemological philosophy of science formulations of Kuhn (1962) such as the notion of paradigm shift (Duschl & Gitomer 1991). On the psychological side, three theorists have been influential: Piaget (1950), Ausubel (1968), and Vygotsky (1978). The work of Piaget (1950), a zoologist, had particular appeal to science educators. Piaget traced the development of children's conceptual schemata and described the active process of accommodation and assimilation, emphasizing the role of decolage in learning. Much of his work focused on the child interacting with the physical world through play and exploration.

Ausubel (1968) represents the cognitive learning theorists who trace their ideas to the pioneering work on the construction of memories by Bartlett (1932). Ausubel's work on advance organizers and adjunct questioning was widely investigated in science teaching in the 1970s. His theorizing still influences constructivist thought (cf Mayer 1979), although the emphasis in his theory is on the relationship of new learning to old.

More recently, there has been an interest in the theorizing of Vygotsky (1978), who highlighted the social and cultural nature of learning. Vygotsky emphasized that schema change occurs through interactions of the learner with more capable others in a zone of proximal development.

BUILDING NEW SCHEMATA IN THE PRESENCE OF MISCONCEPTIONS

Rather than focusing on the learning of entirely new information, science educators have most commonly proceeded from the premise that learners come to science with some ideas about the phenomena already in place. An important aspect of instruction in science is the fact that children are often exposed to information in lessons that does not fit their preexisting theories of how the physical world works. Children naturally develop conceptualizations or beliefs about phenomenon that sometimes parallel historical "scientific" conceptualizations of these same phenomenon, e.g. that the earth is flat (Vosniadou & Brewer 1992), or that heavy objects fall faster that light ones (Champagne et al 1985). Science instructors, then, find themselves presenting information that does not fit or that contradicts children's existing preconceptions or naive conceptions of reality. A child's preconceptions may be largely in agreement with existing theory or may conflict with accepted scientific theory. If preconceptions conflict and lead to inaccurate predictions that can be tested, they have been most commonly termed misconceptions, or more neutrally, alternative conceptions. Other nonpejorative labels include "children's science," "preconceptions," "naive conceptions," "intuitive science," and "alternative frameworks" (Guzzetti et al 1993). These misconceptions may come from children's own physical experience with the world, from social interactions with peers or adults, from the general culture through the media, or from formal instruction (Guzzetti et al 1993). Whatever their source, such misconceptions are extremely difficult to alter through traditional instruction and persist after instruction has ended (Brown 1992).

The most influential article discussing the philosophical basis of conceptual change is by Posner et al (1982), who hypothesized that four conditions have to be met before learners change their existing schemata: 1. dissatisfaction (i.e. existing ideas must be found to be unsatisfactory), 2. understanding (i.e. the new idea must be intelligible, coherent, internally consistent, and minimally understood), 3. plausible (i.e. the new idea must be a possible and likely alternative), and 4. fruitful (i.e. the new idea must be preferable to the old viewpoint on the grounds of perceived elegance, parsimony and, particularly, usefulness. Research has tended to focus on the first of these four conditions. Misconceptions have been addressed by presenting students with anomalous data, by giving the students refutational texts, by creating cognitive conflict through dialogue, and by a combination of two or more of these teaching strategies.

The Use of Anomalous Data

Chinn & Brewer (1993), in their review, discuss what happens when children are presented with anomalous data. Children may ignore, hold in abeyance, reject, or exclude the anomalous data, all of which leaves the original preconception intact. Alternatively, they may reinterpret the anomalous data, or make a peripheral change in their theory, both of which leave their preconceptions largely intact. Finally, they may change their core belief and develop a new theory or schema. Chinn & Brewer identify 11 instructional strategies (see Table 1) that they hypothesize will help students become reflective theory changers.

These strategies involve reducing the hold of the previous conceptualization, introducing a clear and plausible alternative theory, providing learners with clear, credible data consistent with the new conceptualization but anomalous to the old conception, and, finally, encouraging the learner to justify or otherwise process the new conceptualization. Such a process is termed "teaching for conceptual change learning" (Roth & Anderson 1988).

Addressing Misconceptions Using Text

Guzzetti et al (1993) conducted a careful meta-analytic study of 23 studies on science education reported in reading education journals. They identified seven strategies that were used to overcome misconceptions: refutational text, nonrefutational text, activation activity, think sheet, discussion strategies,

Table 1 Instructional strategies for promoting reflective theory change (Chinn & Brewer 1993, p. 31) and conditions for schema change (Posner et al 1982).

Strategies	Conditions
Influencing prior knowledge	
1. Reduce the entrenchment of the student's prior theories	dissatisfaction
2. Help students construct appropriate ontological categories	understanding
3. Foster appropriate epistemological commitments	understanding
4. Help students construct needed background knowledge	understanding
Introducing the alternative theory	
5. Introduce a plausible alternative theory	plausible
6. Make sure the alternative theory is of high quality	understanding
7. Make sure the alternative theory is intelligible	understanding
Introducing anomalous data	
8. Make the anomalous data credible	plausible
9. Avoid ambiguous data	understanding
10. Use multiple lines of data when necessary	understanding
Influencing processing strategies	
11. Encourage deep processing	fruitful

other text-based activities, and traditional instruction. The most commonly researched strategies involve the use of refutational text, in which the misconception is explicitly covered and refuted. The next most often studied is some form of nonrefutational text, which presents new information with no direct reference to misconceptions. Activation activities were also examined widely. These strategies involve bringing to mind, or activating, prior knowledge usually supplemented with information that causes the learner to question or correct the misconception because cognitive conflict has been created. Refutational text alone and coupled with activation strategies that causes cognitive conflict or cognitive dissonance are the most effective textbook-based interventions for overcoming misconceptions. Also effective are texts that create dissatisfaction with the student's current understanding and then present new information that helps create a new understanding. Coherent and well-organized texts and texts that contain narrative structures for younger students also help. By themselves, activation strategies that do not stimulate conflict are not effective (Guzzetti et al 1993).

Creating Cognitive Conflict with Discussion

The Discussion Web strategy emerged in Guzzetti et al's (1993) meta-analysis as a powerful intervention for conceptual change. This teaching strategy with high school students consists of a discussion using a graphic aid to explicate and present a group of students' positions on a question. Students must defend their positions using information derived from the text and interact with the teacher and fellow students. The discussion web is similar to a very effective strategy studied by Arnold & Millar (1987), in which discussion and argument about concepts of electricity are encouraged in the classroom, although no graphic aids are used.

Integrated Approaches: The Learning Cycle

Guzzetti and her colleagues observed that science education researchers have tended to design studies in which a number of strategies have been combined and then their focus and impact evaluated. It is difficult to determine from these studies the impact of any one part of the strategy. Of these combined strategies, Guzzetti et al (1993) identify the learning cycle (Lawson 1958) as consistently showing the largest effects in their meta-analysis. The learning cycle consists of a three-stage process: exploration, term introduction, and concept application. In the exploration stage, the students examine and experiment with new materials and ideas with very little direction from the teacher. Students are encouraged to identify questions that are not easily answered and to identify patterns and regular features of the new material. At this stage, students may be asked to predict what will happen if certain interventions are made.

In the term introduction phase, students, with the teacher's help, invent new organizational ideas for the patterns they have discovered previously. The teacher introduces new terms and definitions as needed to help supply labels for newly formed schemata.

In the concept application phase, students extend and apply their new learning. With the teacher's help, they examine the possibilities and limitations of their new conceptualizations and abstract and generalize from concrete examples.

According to Guzzeti et al (1993), "When the Learning Cycle included lecture, teacher-led discussion, nonrefutational text, and audiovisuals, the average effect size was about 1/4 standard deviation over traditional presentations. Even larger effects may be obtained with the inclusion of additional strategies" (p. 146). Additional strategies found to be effective were traditional laboratories and prediction laboratories, where the stress is on the student prediction of experimental outcomes (Guzzetti et al 1993).

Using Analogies to Address Misconceptions

Analogies have been used explicitly to help learners overcome misconceptions (see next section for further discussion of analogies). Both Brown (1992) and Clement (1993) have demonstrated that the use of a "bridge" analogy can be effective, particularly in situations where misconceptions are common. When students consider whether or not a table exerts upward force on a book lying upon it, most high school students believe that it does not. However, they do believe that a spring exerts force when pushed down by their hand. Simply using the spring as an analogy does not usually work to change students' conceptions. Using an intermediate analogy that shares features with both the original case (spring) and analogous case (book), (e.g. a book on a flexible foam pad), was shown by both test data and by qualitative observation of videotaped lessons to be an effective device for bringing high school students' thinking on this and other physics topics in line with physicists' thinking (Clement 1993). Guzzetti et al (1993) noted that, compared to traditional laboratory and discussion, the effect size of a bridging-analogies approach that incorporates students' written predictions, observations, and explanations was about 1.5 standard deviations.

BUILDING NEW SCHEMATA IN THE ABSENCE OF MISCONCEPTIONS

Not all research in science instruction is directed at misconceptions that students bring to learning. Some attention has been given to the use of analogies, examples, models, and discussion.

Analogies

One strategy of teaching is to compare a new phenomenon to be learned to another phenomenon that is familiar. For example, for certain purposes, electrical current can be compared to water flowing through a pipe or a crowd moving through a set of corridors (Gentner & Stevens 1983). Because science instruction often involves explanations based on things that cannot be seen directly, understanding can be facilitated by reference to something observable or that has been experienced in the past. The use of analogy is so popular in science education that the *Journal of Chemical Education* has a regular column, "Applications and Analogies." Some analogies are better than others and some may have features that stimulate new thought. Pointing out that the atom is similar to the solar system may help a learner conceptualize the relationship of the electrons to the nucleus in the atom and it may also stimulate inferences not apparent at first. "For example, in the process of constructing the sun/atom analogy, the individual may conjecture that there might be a gravitational attraction between an electron and the nucleus just as there is between a planet and the sun" (Wong 1993b). However, the student may also develop the misconception that the electrons circle the atom in a single plane. Thus analogies may help or misdirect the learner.

Analogies seem to work by using an easily assimilated problem or explanation structure that is familiar as a source domain and a novel problem or explanation as a target domain. Because the two share structural similarity the learner is able to map the source on the target, encode the two into memory, and subsequently induce a new hybrid schema that contains the abstract similarities of the two domains (Novick & Holyoak 1991). Other explanations for the effectiveness of an analogy are that they act as advance organizers and lead to greater elaboration of schemata in memory (Mayer & Bromage 1980).

Analogies are superior to literal presentations in texts or lessons, particularly when inference, rather than simple comprehension, is called for (Hayes & Tierney 1982) and for learners with minimal background knowledge in the subject being taught (Donnelly & McDaniel 1993). Analogies can be used with new learning or to stimulate conceptual change by comparing situations that learners understand to other situations they misunderstand (Stavy 1991).

Gick & Holyoak (1983) point out from their work on the Duncker radiation problem (using the concept of convergence of power to irradiate a tumor or storm a fortress) that students need to have a well-developed schema in prior knowledge, the ability to recognize the new problem as having similar features to a previous situation, and as being possible instances of the schema in order for them to solve a new, related problem. They call this process mapping an old schema onto a new problem. They write, "...if a current situation can be related to prior knowledge, so that its causally relevant aspects are encoded at an abstract level, then the situation has the potential to be subsequently related to a new analogy from a remote domain" (Gick & Holyoak 1983, p. 33). This notion has stimulated studies using a variety of materials in science.

Thagard (1992) has examined the characteristics of good analogies and bad ones. A good analogy should have great semantic similarity, structural correspondence, and pragmatic relevance. Analogies can get the student thinking about the subject, but the limits of the comparison should be made explicit. Thagard suggests that teachers point out where the analogy breaks down and is not accurate. In addition, "Teachers should take pains to use analogies to matters already familiar to the students and should make clear the semantic and structural correspondences between the analogs that are important for providing the desired explanation" (p. 541).

Because analogies are seldom perfect, some problems are associated with their use. Spiro et al (1989) point out that students may overextend analogies and construct beliefs that are scientifically incorrect. To use an everyday example, many people believe that a thermostat operates like a faucet in heating a home so they turn the dial up to the maximum so the house will heat faster. To counter overgeneralization or misapplication of analogy, these authors propose that multiple analogies be introduced during instruction.

Wong (1993a) points out that much of the research on analogies consists of externally (teacher) supplied analogies and that students need to develop the ability to create their own analogies. In a pilot study with adults, Wong demonstrated the effectiveness of analogies for deepening understanding of air pressure phenomena by stimulating learners to formulate and refine their own analogies. Further research on this approach will be welcome.

Examples

A relatively common teaching practice is the use of examples. Teachers often use multiple examples in the hope that students will induce an abstract schema that contains only the features critical to the concept or principle being taught (Brown 1992). The use and effectiveness of examples has not been studied widely. From a small-group qualitative study, Brown (1992) concluded that good examples must make sense to students and pointed out that several examples in a text on Newton's third law were rated as counter-intuitive to high school students. In his study, examples were less effective in stimulating cognitive change than were analogies.

Conceptual Models

Pictorial models of the phenomenon to be learned are used in science more so than in any other field. According to Mayer (1989), conceptual models are a promising technique to help students learn and understand new material and to help them use these new conceptions in problem solving. Mayer defines conceptual models as "words and/or diagrams that are intended to help learners build mental models of the system being studied; a conceptual model highlights the major objects and actions in a system as well as the causal relations among them" (p. 43). He considers conceptual models as a special kind of advance organizer. Advance organizers (Ausubel 1968) are usually brief textual passages that orient the learner to the subject matter to be learned and relate the new learning to preexisting knowledge.

Mayer argues that good models are complete, concise, coherent, concrete, conceptual, correct, and considerate (i.e. appropriate to the learner). They are most effective for expository material that explains how a system works, and are best used before or during a lesson, not afterward. Because the teacher constructs the pictorial model for the student, such models are usually adjunct to text.

Concept Maps

The concept map is another tool for helping students learn and retain information in science. In concept mapping, the student is taught how and encouraged to draw a map or diagram showing how the concepts in a unit on science are organized relationally and hierarchically. Based on Ausubel's instructional theory, concept maps are intended to mirror the way ideas are organized in cognitive structures. Because these are individual, the instructor does not map concepts for the student. Several kinds of maps have been explored: concept maps or knowledge maps (Dees et al 1992; Evans & Dansereau 1991; Novak 1990a,b; Peel et al 1993), circle diagrams (Wandersee 1990), and vee diagrams. All are two-dimensional diagrams usually consisting of nodes linked to nodes with relational terms attached. They may be used as text supplements, lecture aids, note-taking strategies, and props for cooperative interaction (Wiegmann et al 1992). Figure 1 contains a knowledge map adapted from Evans & Dansereau (1991).

Okebukola (1992) has documented that teachers value cognitive mapping and vee diagramming as instructional tools, particularly in science instruction. Cognitive maps have been used from grade school to university-level instruction. Cognitive map training and the use of cognitive maps have been shown to be effective in a number of studies (see Evans & Dansereau 1991, for a review). Other studies have not found them to be more effective than traditional methods (Lehman et al 1985, Sherris 1984). Map making has also been used as a tool for program evaluation and to explore the conceptual schemata of expert (vs novice) learners. Willerman & Mac Harg (1991) demonstrated that introducing concept maps at the beginning of the lesson as an advance organizer could improve eighth-grade science achievement in the physical sciences.

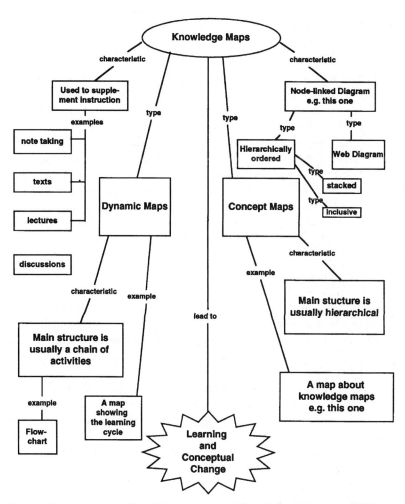

Figure 1   Knowledge map of knowledge maps; adapted from Evans & Dansereau (1991)

Knowledge maps have been most completely explored by Dansereau and his working group at Texas Christian University, who have applied them to a variety of subjects including drug education (Dees et al 1992, Lambiotte & Dansereau 1992, McCagg & Dansereau 1991, Peel et al 1993, Wiegmann et al 1992). One study found that the hierarchical spatial configuration was superior to the web configuration (i.e. where the topic is at the center of the map) and that stacked maps or maps that were cross-referenced were better for students with high–spatial ability, whereas inclusive maps were better for low–spatial ability college students. Having the links between ideas labeled was better for high-ability than for low-ability students (Wiegmann et al 1992).

Discussion and Dialogue

Having students work together in pairs or groups has long characterized science teaching, particularly in laboratory work. There has been increased interest in using student discussion and dialogue between the instructor and the student as a focus for science teaching. Pea (1993) argues that social interaction is critical to the building up of meaning in individuals. Through conversation, "persons collaboratively construct the common ground of beliefs, meanings, and understandings that they share in activity as well as specify their differences" (pp. 268–69). At the same time, through social interactions learners begin to assimilate and accomodate cultural tools and schemata. Pea's research, using an optics simulator and teacher-modeled conversations in small groups in the classroom, has shown the effectiveness of this instructional strategy.

Student-Student Dialogue in Cooperative Learning

Cooperative learning is one device for stimulating student-student interactions and learning. Both Piaget and Vygotsky have emphasized that learning social-arbitrary knowledge, as opposed to physical-observable knowledge, can be learned only in interactions with more knowledgeable others including peers (Slavin 1989).

Lonning (1993), for example, studied two groups of tenth-grade general science students who were taught a four-week unit on the particulate nature of matter with a conceptual change teaching method. The experimental group, who also followed Johnson & Johnson's (1987) cooperative learning method, showed greater achievement gains and engaged in larger numbers of verbal interactions characterized by statements of support (e.g. group members co-constructing and sharing discourse roles), conflict statements (e.g. members challenging and defending each other's arguments), and statements asking for help.

Chang & Lederman (1994), working with seventh-grade physical science students in laboratory groups, found no differences in achievement attributable to cooperative learning, but they did find gains related to the specific teachers involved and to increases in the amount of reading and writing required.

In a structured cooperative situation with two students alternating roles, Dansereau's group has found that when one college student (the recaller) summarizes information from the text, and the second (the listener) corrects errors and omissions, and then the pair work on strategies for both to remember the main ideas, both learn more than do students working alone, although the retention of information acquired in the recaller role is superior. In a series of studies, Dansereau and his colleagues have demonstrated the effectiveness of this scripted cooperation along with the use of structural maps (O'Donnell & Dansereau 1993, Rewey et al 1989).

MOTIVATION AND INTEREST

An important issue for teachers is how to motivate students to learn. Motivation is usually seen as an individual characteristic of students, and current research focuses on student attributions and efforts to reshape them. In subject matter instruction, the problem of motivation has shifted to a consideration of how students' intrinsic motivation can be engaged. One question that might be asked is, Can instructors make a lesson more interesting?

Interest may be conceived as having a personal dimension and a situational dimension (Krapp et al 1992), although the two dimensions obviously interact. Situational interest is interest aroused across individuals by various conditions in the learner's environment. Personal interest is idiosyncratic, develops slowly, and is long-lasting. Personal interest results in increased attention and positive affect in a learning situation. It also results in greater achievement, but this is also a result of the interaction between interest and specific knowledge (Tobias 1994). We tend to be interested in what we already know and gain more knowledge from pursuing our interests. Perhaps of more relevance to the teacher is situational interest, because the conditions or stimuli that make for situational interest are more easily manipulated by the teacher than is personal interest. When interest is activated, learners are thought to process information using more elaboration and to establish more cross references resulting in a qualitatively superior representation of the information and better future recall (Krapp et al 1992).

Interesting Themes

A first question about situational interest would be what features of a text or a lesson are likely to have inherent interest across individuals generally or across members of an age group. Anderson et al (1987) have argued that characters or situations that reflect life themes with which learners can identify, such as sex and change, are more interesting. Hidi and Baird (Hidi & Anderson 1992; Hidi & Baird 1986, 1988) suggest that the character's goal-directed activities and human interest factors are likely to be remembered. Shank has identified topics that he believes to be inherently interesting (e.g. death, danger, chaos, destruction, disease, injury, power, wealth, sex, and romance). These are, of course, the themes of many popular soap operas around the world. He also believes that unexpected events and events that are personally related will be perceived to be interesting (Shank 1979).

In his work on curiosity and interests, Berlyne (1960, 1965) emphasized that the stimulus variables of novelty, surprisingness, incongruity, ambiguity, uncertainty, and complexity can create a state of arousal that facilitates the retention of information (Berlyne 1960, 1965). Iran-Nejad (1987) also suggested that post-surprise incongruity resolution is inherently interesting. Text or lessons may be manipulated to stimulate the reader to resolve an incomplete understanding of the information provided. Because the stimulation of cognitive conflict and the incongruity between misconceptions and other information is at the heart of conceptual change instruction, this form of science instruction should be inherently more interesting to students than instruction that does not point out inconsistencies.

Enhancing Interest in the Classroom

Martinez (1992) distinguishes between three types of interest: cognitive, mastery, and social. Cognitive interest may be simulated by features that stimulate curiosity or that are related to fantasy or mystery. Mastery interest is stimulated by features that appeal to the need to control the environment and consist of challenges from the teacher. For example, to elicit mastery interest, that teachers may use phrases such as "If you can…" or may make the layout of materials more appealing. Social appeal is fostered by structuring the situation to encourage the accomplishment of a common objective. Teachers may pose a question requiring discussion, give a role to each student in an exercise, or use personal references. In his study of junior-high science learning, Martinez found that interest enhancements increased ratings of the appeal of unpopular lessons but not of experiments that were inherently popular. Further, girls were more responsive to interest enhancements than were boys (Martinez 1992).

Enhancing Interest in Text

An important question becomes whether or not these inherently interesting themes can be used to increase comprehension. Hidi and Baird have conducted a series of studies on the relationship of interesting and important material presented in text. After rating the text for interest and importance, the immediate and delayed recalls of subjects were examined. Materials high in interest level, containing high activity levels, character identification, novelty, and life themes produced improved recall.

Garner and her colleagues have found that adding materials to texts to make them more interesting can have negative consequences, in what she calls the "seductive detail" effect. She conducted studies in which vivid details that had situational interest but did not support the main ideas of the passage were added to boring texts. Readers who read short texts without the added interesting but unimportant information recalled much more of the important details than did readers who read the text with the added interesting information

(Garner et al 1989). When interesting details and structurally important ideas are both included in a text, the learners are more likely to remember the interesting details. When the seductive details are separated out and presented in paragraphs separately from the important text, recall is not improved, although versions of text rated "generally interesting" are better at stimulating recall than are those rated "generally uninteresting."

In a similar study by Wade & Adams (1990), college students remembered more unimportant than important information, but all students remembered more interesting than uninteresting information. They recalled, for example, that Lord Nelson had a beautiful mistress and lost an arm, but did not remember that the Battle of Trafalgar won the Napoleonic War for Britain.

In an surprising study by Duffy (Duffy et al 1989), three versions of a history text were prepared: one had the structure of the information and cohesion of the information maximized (by composition teachers), one had a "vivid anecdote" added (by a Time-Life Books editor), and one version (written by linguists) was prepared to improve cohesion. The seductive details added by the editor did not seem to improve recall, but the composition teachers' version was recalled best.

Topical Interest

Within science, there is very little available research on which topics are of interest to different populations or to students in general. An exception is a study by Wandersee (1986), who determined that animals are more interesting to junior high school students than are plants.

REMEDIAL INSTRUCTION AND INSTRUCTION FOR POPULATIONS WITH DISABILITIES

Remediation

Yeany & Miller (1983) searched the literature for studies on a model of remedial instruction in science based on diagnosing pupil problems followed by remedial instruction. They compared diagnosis and diagnostic feedback alone and in combination with remedial efforts, and they concluded that providing diagnostic feedback alone to students was an effective strategy to stimulate achievement. Students aware of what they needed to know were able to manage their own learning without further assistance.

Disabilities

Mastropieri & Scruggs, in their reviews of science for students with disabilities (Mastropieri & Scruggs 1992, Scruggs & Mastropieri 1993), point out that science is one subject that can and should be taught to all children. Often, however, science receives little emphasis by special education teachers, who lack training and resources in this subject and who spend a great deal of time teaching basic skills. Science curriculum, on the other hand, has been developed and evaluated for children with visual impairments, hearing impairments, mental handicaps, learning disabilities, and emotional disturbances. These curricula have been adaptations of the regular educational curriculum. "Interestingly, the types of adaptations and accommodations made for students with varying disabilities were, with few exceptions, very similar across disability areas and relevant to language/literacy, intellectual/cognitive, social/emotional, or sensory/physical domains across categories of exceptionality.... Most investigators modified methods and materials by reducing unnecessary content, providing extra support and guidance, enhancing concrete experiences, and incorporating additional practice and review activities" (Mastropieri & Scruggs 1992, p. 404).

The use of mnemonic devices to learn science terms and labels is by far the most studied intervention for students with disabilities. These studies usually have been directed at children with learning disabilities. In general, mnemonically instructed students gained better science vocabulary than did control students taught with traditional methods (Mastropieri & Scruggs 1992). Learning disabled students also have been assisted by study skills training (Davis 1990) and by carefully designed framed outlines of sequential main ideas and teaching techniques involving vocabulary practice sheets (Lovitt et al 1985, 1986).

Children with mild mental handicaps have been helped to learn material in paleontology by being presented with a high degree of structure with linked concepts (Ferraro et al 1977). This form of support seems appropriate for slow learners.

The teaching and curriculum for exceptional children are often seen as being less challenging than for mainstreamed children. The work on conceptual change and misconceptions has not been extended to exceptional populations. Bay et al (1992) examined more cognitively complex interventions for children with disabilities. These researchers compared the effectiveness of direct instruction versus discovery learning among mildly handicapped upper elementary–grade students. Although direct instruction has been found to benefit low-achieving children in the past (Brophy & Good 1986), discovery learning consists of hands-on activities that demand less sustained attention than do other instructional approaches and may be well-suited to learning- and behavior-disordered children. Although relatively few disabled students completed the study, the authors were able to demonstrate that immediate measures of achievement showed no advantage to one technique, but that learning-disordered students who learned by discovery did better on a delayed test of generalization than did those who had direct instruction (Bay et al 1992).

It will be interesting to see if future research is done using models, concept maps, structured cooperative learning, analogies, and discussion protocols with disabled children. Research in this area is lagging behind the rest of science education.

CONCLUSIONS

The research base on science teaching will benefit from more studies duplicating research across age groups. Research on several topics using a number of creative strategies has been done, but research across a range of ages or populations has not. More research on the effect of single interventions rather than multiple interventions is also needed to determine, for example, on what part of the learning cycle intervention has the greatest impact. The research on conceptual change has a number of parallels with the theory and research on attitude change, such as the use of cognitive dissonance. The fields of cognitive learning and social psychology are too seldom connected, and researchers from both fields might gain inspiration from reading more widely.

Whatever criticisms are made against the research on science teaching, it is important to note that the psychological study of science instruction and learning is a healthy and active enterprise. Because much of what is done is theory driven, a great deal of progress has been made. In general, the researchers combine both developmental and learning approaches so that ultimately we will be able to determine how different strategies are useful at different ages or with different ability groups within ages. Although not highlighted in this review, there may be interesting aptitude by treatment interactions that also will emerge with continued research.

Another feature of studies in science education is the free use of both qualitative and quantitative methodology, often in the same study. Multiple outcomes, both immediate and delayed, and direct and generalized, have been examined. Investigators clearly think complexly and deeply about the phenomena they investigate. Science is a model for the study of the psychology of teaching in subject matter and has blossomed as a field of study over the last decade.

Literature Cited

Anderson LW, Burns RB. 1989. *Research in Classrooms: The Study of Teachers, Teaching and Instruction.* New York: Pergamon

Anderson RC, Shirey LL, Wilson PT, Fielding LG. 1987. Interestingness of children's reading material. In *Aptitude, Learning, and Instruction.* Vol. III: *Conative and Affective Process Analyses,* ed. RE Snow, MJ Farr, pp. 287–99. Hillsdale, NJ: Erlbaum

Arnold M, Millar R. 1987. Being constructive: an alternative approach to the teaching of introductory ideas in electricity. *Int. J. Sci. Educ.* 9:553–63

Ausubel DP. 1968. *Educational Psychology: A Cognitive View.* New York: Holt, Rinehart & Winston

Bartlett FC. 1932. *Remembering.* Cambridge, UK: Cambridge Univ. Press

Bay M, Staver JR, Bryan T, Hale JB. 1992. Science instruction for the mildly handicapped: direct instruction versus discovery teaching. *J. Res. Sci. Teach.* 29:555–70

Berlyne DE. 1960. *Conflict, Arousal, and Curiousity.* New York: McGraw-Hill

Berlyne DE. 1965. *Structure and Direction in Thinking.* New York: Wiley

Brophy J. 1988. Research linking teacher behavior to student achievement: potential implications for instruction of Chapter 1 students. *Educ. Psychol.* 23:235–86

Brophy J, Good TL. 1986. Teacher behavior and achievement. In *Handbook of Research on Teaching,* ed. M Wittrock, pp. 328–75. New York: Macmillan

Brown DF. 1992. Using examples and analogies to remediate misconceptions in physics: factors influencing conceptual change. *J. Res. Sci. Teach.* 29:17–34

Champagne AB, Gunstone RF, Klopfer LE. 1985. Instructional consequences of students' knowledge about physical phenomena. In *Cognitive Structure and Conceptual Change,* ed. LHT West, AL Pines, pp. 61–90. Orlando, FL: Academic

Chang H-P, Lederman NG. 1994. The effect of levels of cooperation with physical science laboratory groups on physical science achievement. *J. Res. Sci. Teach.* 41:167–81

Chinn CA, Brewer WF. 1993. The role of anomalous data in knowledge acquisition: a theoretical framework and implications for science instruction. *Rev. Educ. Res.* 63:1–49

Clement J. 1993. Using bridging analogies and anchoring intuitions to deal with students' preconceptions in physics. *J. Res. Sci. Teach.* 30:1241–57

Davis SJ. 1990. Applying content study skills in co-listed reading classrooms. *J. Read.* 33:277–81

Dees SM, Dansereau DF, Peel JL, Knight K. 1992. Using knowledge maps and scripted cooperation to inform college students about patterns of behavior related to recurring abuse of alcohol. *Addict. Behav.* 17:307–13

Donnelly CM, McDaniel MA. 1993. Use of analogy in learning scientific concepts. *J. Exp. Psychol.: Learn. Mem. Cogn.* 19:975–87

Druva CA, Anderson RD. 1983. Science teacher characteristics by teacher behavior and by student outcome: a meta-analysis of research. *J. Res. Sci. Teach.* 20:467–80

Duffy TM, Higgins L, Mehlenbacher B, Cochran C, Wallace D, et al. 1989. Models for the design of text. *Read. Res. Q.* 24:434–57

Duschl RA, Gitomer DH. 1991. Epistemological perspectives on conceptual change: implications for educational practice. *J. Res. Sci. Teach.* 28:839–58

Eggleston J. 1983. Teacher-pupil interactions in science lessions: explorations and theory. *Br. Educ. Res. J.* 9:113–27

Evans SH, Dansereau DF. 1991. Knowledge maps as tools for thinking and communication. In *Enhancing Learning and Thinking,* ed. RF Mulcahy, RH Short, J Andrews, pp. 97–120. New York: Praeger

Ferraro E, Lee MT, Anderson OR. 1977. The effects of structure in science communications on knowledge acquisition and conceptual organization by students of varying mental maturity. *J. Res. Sci. Teach.* 14:441–47

Gagne RM. 1977. *The Conditions of Learning.* New York: Holt, Rinehart & Winston. 3rd ed.

Garner R, Gillingham MG, White CS. 1989. Effects of "seductive details" on macroprocessing and microprocessing in adults and children. *Cogn. Instruct.* 6:41–57

Gentner D, Stevens AL, eds. 1983. *Mental Models.* Hillsdale, NJ: Erlbaum

Gick ML, Holyoak KJ. 1983. Schema induction and analogical transfer. *Cogn. Psychol.* 15:1–38

Guzzetti BJ, Snyder TE, Glass GV, Gamas WS. 1993. Promoting conceptual change in science: a comparative meta-analysis of instructional interventions from reading education and science education. *Read. Res. Q.* 28(2):116–59

Hayes DA, Tierney RJ. 1982. Developing readers' knowledge through analogy. *Read. Res. Q.* 17:256–80

Hidi S, Anderson V. 1992. Situational interest and its impact on reading and expository writing. In *The Role of Interest in Learning and Development,* ed. KA Renninger, S Hidi, A Krapp, pp. 215–38. Hillsdale, NJ: Erlbaum

Hidi S, Baird W. 1986. Interestingness—a neglected variable in discourse processing. *Cogn. Sci.* 10:179–94

Hidi S, Baird W. 1988. Strategies for increasing text-based interest and students' recall of expository texts. *Read. Res. Q.* 23:465–83

Iran-Nejad A. 1987. Cognitive and affective causes of interest and liking. *J. Educ. Psychol.* 79:120–30

Johnson DW, Johnson RT. 1987. *Learning Together and Alone: Cooperative, Competitive, and Individualistic Learning.* Englewood Cliffs, NJ: Prentice-Hall

Kagan DM. 1992. Implications of research on teacher belief. *Educ. Psychol.* 27:65–90

Krapp A, Hidi S, Renninger KA. 1992. Interest, learning, and development. In *The Role of Interest in Learning and Development,* ed. KA Renninger, S Hidi, A Krapp, pp. 3–25. Hillsdale, NJ: Erlbaum

Kuhn T. 1962. *The Structure of Scientific Revolutions.* Chicago: Chicago Univ. Press

Lambiotte JG, Dansereau DF. 1992. Effects of knowledge maps and prior knowledge on recall of science lecture content. *J. Exp. Educ.* 60:189–201

Lawson CA. 1958. *Language, Thought, and the Human Mind.* East Lansing, MI: Mich. State Univ. Press

Lehman JD, Custer C, Kahle JB. 1985. Concept mapping, vee mapping and achievement: results of a field study on black high school students. *J. Res. Sci. Teach.* 22:663–73

Lonning RA. 1993. Effect of cooperative learning strategies on student verbal interactions and achievement during conceptual change instruction in 10th grade general science. *J. Res. Sci. Teach.* 30:1087–1101

Lovitt T, Rudsit J, Jenkins J, Pious C, Benedetti D. 1985. Two methods of adapting science materials for learning disabled and regular seventh graders. *Learn. Disabil. Q.* 8:275–85

Lovitt T, Rudsit J, Jenkins J, Pious C, Benedetti D. 1986. Adapting science materials for learning disabled and regular seventh graders. *RASE: Remedial and Special Educ.* 7:31–39

Martinez ME. 1992. Interest enhancements to science experiments: interactions with student gender. *J. Res. Sci. Teach.* 29:167–77

Mastropieri MA, Scruggs TE. 1992. Science for students with disabilities. *Rev. Educ. Res.* 62:377–411

Mayer RE. 1979. Twenty years of research on advance organizers: assimilation theory is still the best predictor of results. *Instruct. Sci.* 8:133–67

Mayer RE. 1989. Models for understanding. *Rev. Educ. Res.* 59:43–64

Mayer RE, Bromage BK. 1980. Different recall protocols for technical texts due to advance organizers. *J. Educ. Psychol.* 72:209–55

McCagg EC, Dansereau DF. 1991. A convergent paradigm for examining knowledge mapping as a learning strategy. *J. Educ. Res.* 84:317–24

Novak JD. 1990a. Concept mapping: a useful tool for science education. Special Issue: Perspectives on Concept Mapping. *J. Res. Sci. Teach.* 27:937–49

Novak JD. 1990b. Concept maps and Vee diagrams: two metacognitive tools to facilitate meaningful learning. *Instruct. Sci.* 19:29–52

Novick LR, Holyoak KJ. 1991. Mathematics problem solving by analogy. *J. Exp. Psychol.: Learn. Mem. Cogn.* 17:398–415

O'Donnell A, Dansereau DF. 1993. Learning from lectures: effects of cooperative review. *J. Exp. Educ.* 61:116–25

Okebukola PA. 1992. Attitude of teachers towards concept mapping and vee diagramming as metalearning tools in science and mathematics. *Educ. Res.* 34:201–13

Pea RD. 1993. Learning scientific concepts through material and social activities: conversational analysis meets conceptual change. *Educ. Psychol.* 28:265–77

Peel JL, Dansereau DF, Dees SM. 1993. Identifying the best scenario for using schematic organizers as integration tools for alcohol-related information. *J. Drug Educ.* 23:1–30

Piaget J. 1950. *The Psychology of Intelligence.* Transl. M Piercy, D Berliyne. London: Routledge, Kegan Paul

Posner G, Strike K, Hewson P, Gertzog W. 1982. Accomodations of scientific conception: toward a theory of conceptual change. *Sci. Educ.* 66:211–27

Rewey KL, Dansereau DF, Skaggs LP, Hall RH, Pitre U. 1989. Effects of scripted cooperation and knowledge maps on the processing of technical material. *J. Educ. Psychol.* 81:93–107

Roth K, Anderson C. 1988. Promoting conceptual change learning from science textbooks. In *Improving Learning: New Perspectives,* ed. P Ramsden, pp. 109–41. London: Kogan Page

Scruggs TE, Mastropieri MA. 1993. Current approaches to science education: implications for mainstream instruction of students with disabilities. *RASE: Remedial and Special Educ.* 14:15–24

Shank RC. 1979 Interestingness: controlling inferences. *Artif. Intell.* 12:273–97

Sherris J. 1984. The effects of concept relatedness of instruction and locus of control orientation on the meaningful learning achievements of high school biology students. *J. Res. Sci. Teach.* 21:83–89

Shymansky JA, Kyle WCJ, Alport JM. 1983. The effects of new science curricula on student performance. *J. Res. Sci. Teach.* 20:387–404

Slavin RE. 1989. Cooperative learning and student achievement: six theoretical perspectives. In *Advances in Motivation and Achievement: Motivation Enhancing Environments,* ed. M Maehr, C Ames, pp. 161–78. Greenwich CT: JAI

Spiro RJ, Feltovich PJ, Coulson RL, Anderson DK. 1989. Multiple analogies for complex concepts: antidotes for analogy-induced misconception in advanced knowledge acquisition. In *Similarity and Analogical Reasoning,* ed. S Vosniadou, A Ortony, pp. 498–531. Cambridge: Cambridge Univ. Press

Stavy R. 1991. Using analogy to overcome misconceptions about conservation of matter. *J. Res. Sci. Teach.* 28:305–13

Thagard P. 1992. Analogy, explanation, and education. *J. Res. Sci. Teach.* 29:537–44

Tobias S. 1994. Interest, prior knowledge, and learning. *Rev. Educ. Res.* 64:37–54

Vosniadou S, Brewer WF. 1992. Mental models of the earth: a study of conceptual change in childhood. *Cogn. Psychol.* 24: 535–85

Vygotsky LS. 1978. *Mind in Society.* Cambridge, MA: Harvard Univ. Press

Wade SE, Adams B. 1990. Effects of importance and interest on recall of biographical text. *JRB: J. Literacy* 22:331–53

Wandersee JH. 1986. Concept mapping and the cartography of cognition. Special Issue: Perspectives on Concept Mapping. *J. Res. Sci. Teach.* 27:923–36

Wandersee JH. 1990. Concept mapping and the cartography of cognition. Special issue: perspectives on concept mapping. *J. Res. Sci. Teach.* 27:923–36

Wiegmann DA, Dansereau DF, McCagg EC, Rewey KL, Pitre U. 1992. Effects of knowledge map characteristics on information processing. *Contemp. Educ. Psychol.* 17:136–55

Willerman M, Mac Harg RA. 1991. The concept map as an advance organizer. *J. Res. Sci. Teach.* 28:705–11

Wong ED. 1993a. Self-generated analogies as a tool for constructing and evaluating explanations of scientific phenomena. *J. Res. Sci. Teach.* 30:367–80

Wong ED. 1993b. Understanding the generative capacity of analogies as a tool for explanation. *J. Res. Sci. Teach.* 30:1259–72

Yeany RH, Miller PA. 1983. Effects of diagnostic/remedial instruction on science teaching. *J. Res. Sci. Teach.* 20:19–26

Annu. Rev. Psychol. 1995. 46:375–400

SOCIAL STRUCTURING OF THE SCHOOL: Studying What Is, Illuminating What Could Be

Douglas J. Mac Iver

Center for the Social Organization of Schools, Johns Hopkins University, Baltimore, Maryland 21218

David A. Reuman

Department of Psychology, Trinity College, Hartford, Connecticut 06106

Samuel R. Main

Department of Psychology, Johns Hopkins University, Baltimore, Maryland 21218

KEY WORDS: social organization of schools, motivation in education, opportunities to learn, student evaluation and recognition

CONTENTS

0066-4308/95/0201-0375$05.00

INTRODUCTION

> How can we provide opportunities and rewards for individuals of every degree
> of ability so that individuals at every level will realize their full potentialities,
> perform at their best, and harbor no resentment toward any other level?
>
> J Gardner (1961, p. 115)

For more than 30 years, psychologists and other social scientists interested in
the social psychology of schooling have been studying the effects of school
organization on students' motivation and achievement in school and on their
career success in later life. This area of research is attractive to social scientists
from a variety of disciplines partly because of its social relevance. By studying
potentially alterable aspects of schools—and by understanding the impact of
these aspects on students, teachers, and parents—researchers hope to understand how to create more effective schools. Some of the most important
current research focuses on opportunity structures and on evaluation and reward structures in schools. This research seeks to understand the consequences
of current structures and to learn how schools could restructure (*a*) educational
opportunities to increase the proportion of students who attain high levels of
achievement and (*b*) accountability and recognition practices to increase the
commitment, effort, and performance of students and teachers.

ACCESS TO OPPORTUNITY

A school, at its core, is an organization that exists to provide students with
opportunities to learn. But, opportunities for learning are not equally available
at different schools, and within any one school, learning opportunities are not
equally available to all students (Sorensen 1984). Many researchers have
attempted to measure these differences in students' learning opportunities and
evaluate their impact on students' attainments. In the past, the concept of
opportunity to learn was often operationalized very narrowly in the social
science literature as whether particular tested concepts or skills were taught
beforehand to those who took the test (e.g. Husen 1967, Leinhardt & Seewald
1981). Researchers and policy makers are now broadening the operational
definition of opportunity to learn to include measures of (*a*) students'
access to the core curriculum for their grade level, (*b*) students' access to
college-preparatory, accelerated, and advanced placement courses, (*c*) students' access to the information and anticipatory socialization experiences
needed to successfully negotiate the complexities of the lengthy college preparation and application process, and (*d*) students' access to courses where the
teachers "teach for understanding" and emphasize the development of higher-
order knowledge instead of emphasizing the drill, practice, and recall of facts.

Students' Access to the Core Curriculum for their Grade Level

A recurrent theme of the literature on the social organization of schooling is that much of the systematic variation between and within schools in the amount learned by students can be accounted for by variations in the opportunities given to students to learn the core curriculum for their grade level (e.g. Alexander & Pallas 1984, Cooley & Leinhardt 1980, Husen 1967, McPartland & Schneider 1994). This research provides strong empirical support for the common sense notion that students can't be expected to perform at grade level in a subject if their teacher uses below-grade-level curriculum and materials or even if the teacher uses a grade-level textbook but only covers a small proportion of the text when teaching the course. For example, in their study of 400 first- and third-grade classrooms, Cooley & Leinhardt (1980) found that opportunity was the most important instructional dimension for explaining differences between classrooms in students' attainment of grade-level appropriate reading and mathematics skills. This observation led them to suggest that "the most useful things to do for children with underdeveloped reading and mathematics skills in the primary grades is to provide more direct instruction in these areas. ...It seems clear that what gets taught is a more important consideration than how it is taught" (Cooley & Leinhardt 1980, p. 22).

Unfortunately, a significant proportion of American students do not receive grade-level appropriate learning opportunities (Stevens 1993, Epstein & Mac Iver 1992). For example, when Mac Iver & Epstein (1994) classified the math courses experienced by nonhandicapped eighth graders in public schools in the United States based on teachers' detailed descriptions of course content, they found that 26% of the students experienced a course that predominantly or exclusively emphasized below-grade-level topics (e.g. common fractions, decimal fractions, and percents).

Providing universal access to a full grade-level appropriate curriculum is a distinguishing feature of effective schools; that is, schools that obtain greater student achievement than one would predict based on the socioeconomic and racial compositions of their student populations. In the third phase of the Louisiana School Effectiveness Study, Stringfield & Teddlie (1991) compared the school organizations found in eight matched pairs of elementary schools serving similar student populations but differing markedly in effectiveness. In the effective schools, virtually all the students had grade-level appropriate texts and virtually all classes completed these texts by the end of the school year. In the ineffective schools, classes either moved through grade-level appropriate texts at a much slower pace so that large portions of the texts were never covered or many students were given below-grade-level texts.

When within-classroom ability grouping is used, there often are dramatic differences in students' access to the core curriculum among students who share the same classroom. For example, first-graders assigned to a low reading group receive only half or less of the content covered by their class-mates in average or high-average groups (Dreeben & Barr 1988). Further, for first-graders with low reading readiness, content coverage in reading is influenced by the ability composition of the larger class: Students in classes with a high mean reading readiness receive more content than do students of similar ability in classes with low mean reading readiness (Dreeben & Barr 1988).

Once students are assigned to tracks—often in the middle grades, if not before—within-school differences in students' access to the core curriculum become even more dramatic than under within-class grouping (e.g. Sorensen 1984, Hallinan 1984, Wheelock 1992, Oakes 1990). Low-track classes are much more likely to receive course content focusing on below-grade-level knowledge and skills than are higher-track classes. For example, in low-track English classes, instruction in basic reading skills holds a prominent place and students write simple paragraphs, complete worksheets on English usage, and practice filling out job applications and other "real world" forms. The learning tasks are largely restricted to memorization or low-level comprehension (e.g. Oakes 1986). Similarly, low-track mathematics classes tend to focus on be-low-grade-level computational skills and math facts (e.g. Mac Iver & Epstein 1994).

Learning opportunities in core subjects continue to play a key role in affecting students academic achievements throughout high school. Alexander & Pallas (1984) found that students' access to a common "new basics" core curriculum during high school was a strong predictor of students' senior year academic achievement even after controlling for parents' education, high school grades, and freshman year academic achievement. Researchers comparing Catholic and public high schools have likewise argued that the common core curriculum of demanding content in Catholic schools (contrasted with the differentiated curriculum of many public schools) is an important cause of the more positive educational outcomes reached by poor and minority students in these schools (e.g. Coleman et al 1982, 1987; Greeley 1982). This interpretation of the data is bolstered by recent analyses that directly measure the number and type of academic courses required of students and that show mathematics achievement differences between Catholic and public schools to be accounted for largely by differences in the number of advanced mathematics courses required and, thus, taken (Bryk et al 1993; Lee & Bryk 1988, 1989).

Students' Access to College-Preparatory Coursework

A consistent but disturbing finding in the research on opportunities to learn in high school is that most high schools fail to provide all students who aspire to go to college with the course placements needed to give them a fair chance of gaining admission into a four-year college. For example, Dornbusch (1994) reported that, in the six San Francisco Bay Area high schools he studied, almost half the African-American students and Hispanic students who wanted and expected to graduate from a four-year college and who believed they were taking college preparatory courses were not actually receiving the college preparatory math and science courses they needed in order to have any hope for admission into the University of California or California State University systems. Asians and non-Hispanic Whites who believed they were in the right math and science courses to prepare for them for college and who wanted and expected to graduate from a four-year college were also underserved, although less so. About 20% of these students were not actually taking college preparatory courses in math and science. Even if one looks only at those college aspirants with the strongest prior preparation (e.g. whose eighth-grade math achievement scores are above the fiftieth percentile), the proportion misplaced was substantial (about 30% for African Americans and Hispanics and about 13% for the others).

The downward misplacement problem is not new. Cicourel & Kitsuse observed in 1963 that only 64% of the freshmen in a large, suburban high school who requested a college preparatory curriculum were actually given the full set of college preparatory courses.

One factor that makes large downward misplacement rates possible is a pervasive ignorance of four-year college admission requirements among students and even among teachers. When students at four high schools in Northern California were asked to state the requirements for admission to the University of California system, 55% could not correctly state even one requirement. Similarly, 76% could not state a single California State University requirement. Fewer than 2% of the students knew all the requirements for either system. Although most teachers knew the admission requirements in their own subjects, they could not state the requirements in other subjects. Tragically, the higher the proportions of disadvantaged minorities in a class, the less likely it was for the teacher of that class to be able to correctly state college entrance requirements (Dornbusch 1994).

Schools (and departments within schools) vary greatly in the proportion of students who are misplaced. For example, the proportion of talented students (at the seventy-fifth national percentile in mathematics achievement) who did not receive a college preparatory course in the tenth grade in four California high schools ranged from 7% to 60% in mathematics and from 16% to 66% in science (Garet & Delaney 1988). This variation in the course misplacement rates is largely due to variations in the willingness of schools or departments to create enough college preparatory sections to accommodate all students who aspire to attend college (Delaney 1991, Garet & Delaney 1988, Sorenson 1984). In most schools, many competent college aspirants—especially average students who are enrolled in a singleton course of special interest to them in music, sports, art, or foreign language or who have a job that limits their availability—are frequently assigned to non–college preparatory courses because of scheduling problems. Rather than open new college preparatory sections for students who have a scheduling conflict, many schools assign them to existing non–college preparatory sections that fit the students' schedules but that limit the students' future options. Students don't protest their misplacements partly because, as was documented earlier, they are ignorant of college entrance requirements.

The matching of students, courses, and teaching resources into a master schedule that is completely conflict-free is impossible in most secondary schools (Agnew 1987, Delaney 1991). Thus, some degree of student misplacement is inevitable. This is true even when a school's curriculum, student population, and personnel remain relatively constant, but misplacement rates may soar during years in which there are significant changes in the menu of courses offered (e.g. because of changing graduation requirements or teacher retirements and transfers) and in the types and numbers of students enrolled (Delaney 1991). Delaney presented data on the scheduling process in four California high schools and used these data to argue that many misplacements occur because schools don't have enough technical skill, reliable information on students, information-processing capabilities, and freedom from scheduling restrictions (such as those resulting from negotiated contracts or district or state mandates) to avoid these mismatches. That is, many mismatches result from flaws in schools' scheduling processes rather than from intentional decisions on the part of school personnel or students.

Students' Access to Accelerated Math

Even among those students who gain college admission after receiving access to college preparatory coursework during the middle and high school grades, few are well prepared to successfully complete their college's introductory calculus course, the course that filters students out of quantitatively oriented fields of study. Specifically, more than half of all major fields require college-level calculus as a prerequisite and 35% of those who take calculus in college withdraw from or fail the course (Useem 1992).

School districts can greatly influence the proportion of their college-bound students who successfully pursue quantitative fields in college by adopting course assignment policies that encourage students to pursue an accelerated mathematics curriculum, a sequence of courses that begins with algebra in the eighth grade and ends with calculus in the twelfth grade (Burton 1989, Cipra 1988, Small 1988). Even among districts that are similar in social class, there is astounding variation in the proportion of students, if any, who are given access to eighth-grade algebra (Useem 1992, Epstein & Mac Iver 1992). Some districts require their students to have very high standardized test scores in mathematics (i.e. in the top 2% nationally) to be admitted to eighth-grade algebra whereas other similar districts have far less restrictive criteria or may even require all eighth graders to take eighth-grade algebra. This variation among districts serving similar student populations reflects the considerable division of opinion among educators concerning the importance of learning algebra in middle school (rather than in high school) and of learning calculus in high school (rather than in college).

For the past 12 years, Bob Moses—one of leaders of the civil rights–black voter registration movement in the 1960s—has been advocating that every child be given an algebra course in eighth grade. By offering universal access to algebra in the eighth grade, a school system gives every child five years to complete the full four-year sequence of advanced math required or recommended for admission into the nation's most competitive universities. Further, because less selective colleges require or recommend only three years of advanced math, students actually have two "second chances" built in under this time table. Moses views mathematical literacy rights to be as important as voting rights in opening the doors of opportunity to the poor and disenfranchised. Moses's Algebra Project, which implements universal access to algebra for eighth graders and trains teachers in effective techniques for algebra instruction, was established in Cambridge, Massachusetts, in 1982 and has now spread to many inner cities throughout the nation as well as to the rural south (Jetter 1993, Moses et al 1989).

A basic assumption of the Algebra Project is that the opportunity to push ahead with algebra in middle school will benefit students from all academic tracks regardless of their past success in math. Mac Iver & Epstein (1994) used data from the base year of the National Educational Longitudinal Study of 1988 (NELS:88) to conduct an initial test of this assumption. They found that, even after controlling for various school characteristics and for students' track level, past success in math, socioeconomic status, race, and gender, students who received an algebra course in the eighth grade achieved .3 to .5 standard deviations more on a standardized mathematics test than did other students. The achievement benefits of receiving an algebra course were approximately equal for students in all ability groups. Similar results have been obtained in analyses using 1992 Trial State Mathematics Assessment Data (Mac Iver 1994).

Not only does algebra access in the middle grades have immediate achievement benefits, it also greatly enhances students' chances of eventually taking calculus in high school. Secondary analyses of district-level data reported in Useem (1992, Table 1) indicate that the percentage of eighth graders given a full year of algebra is highly correlated (.84) with the percentage of twelfth graders who enroll in calculus. Although it is also true that a district's average level of parental education is a predictor of both the percentage of eighth graders given a full year of algebra ($r = .33$) and of the percentage of twelfth graders who enroll in calculus ($r = .46$), eighth-grade algebra access in a district still has a highly significant effect on the district's twelfth-grade calculus enrollments even when average parental education is held constant. In fact, when entered as simultaneous predictors of a district's percentage of twelfth graders enrolled in calculus, the percentage of eighth graders given a full year of algebra is a much stronger predictor ($\beta = .77$, $p < .0001$) than is the average level of parental education ($\beta = .21$, $p = .08$).

Students' Access to Teaching for Understanding

Although there is an emerging consensus that teachers should turn their attention from basic skills instruction and focus instead on cultivating their students' conceptual understanding (Becker 1990, Bereiter & Scardamalia 1987, Peterson 1988, Prawat 1989, Newmann 1990, Raudenbush et al 1993), students in the United States have few opportunities to experience teaching for understanding instructional methods, which give students the opportunity to develop knowledge through a process of active construction on performance tasks that require problem solving, critical analysis, and flexible understanding of subject matter. In math, teaching for understanding emphasizes thinking about what a problem means, creative problem-solving, estimation, logic and the logical structure of mathematics, and multiple ways of solving problems rather than just emphasizing drill and practice in math computation (Becker 1993, National Council of Teachers of Mathematics 1991). In science, teaching for understanding involves having students conduct hands-on laboratory research, evaluate arguments based on scientific evidence, and develop scientific writing skills. It also emphasizes scientific methods of discovery rather than just the rote memorization of basic science facts (Collins 1989, Rutherford & Ahlgren 1990). In English, teaching for understanding involves having students engage in the "writing process," which consists of prewriting, planning, writing, editing, and rewriting after peer or teacher review (Daniels & Zemelman 1985) and having students explore ideas in works of literature and engage in literary analysis rather than just giving students drill and practice on vocabulary, punctuation, and grammar (Bereiter & Scardamalia 1987). In history, teaching for understanding involves having students be junior historians (e.g. by writing local histories, collecting oral histories, conducting interviews, and studying archives) in individual or group projects, write compositions that critically evaluate historical accounts or arguments, and use concepts from social science in thoughtful discussions of controversial issues, values, and decisions in history rather than just memorizing important names, dates, and facts of history (Epstein & Salinas 1992, Raudenbush et al 1993).

Hierarchical linear modeling (HLM) analyses of NELS:88 data suggest that when schools provide their eighth graders with frequent opportunities to experience teaching for understanding, mean eighth-grade achievement levels are moderately increased [Effect Size (ES) = .10; Mac Iver & Epstein 1994]. This is true even after controlling for relevant individual-level predictors (e.g. past success in school, socioeconomic status, gender, and minority status) and school-level predictors (e.g. average academic achievement of the school's students upon entry to the school, percentage of minority students in the school, school size, percentage of students whose parents are classified as "professional or managerial personnel").

A school's mean level of student boredom is also partly determined by the instructional approaches typically followed at the school. Specifically, even after statistically holding constant a host of other individual- and school-level predictors of student boredom, schools that emphasize drill, practice, and memorization have higher levels of student boredom (ES = .26) than do other schools (Mac Iver & Epstein 1994).

Although Mac Iver & Epstein (1994) demonstrate that middle grades schools vary reliably in their emphasis on teaching for understanding and that these between-school variations predict differences between schools in students' achievement and affective outcomes, much of the reliable variation in instructional practices in middle schools and high schools is within-teacher variation and between-teacher variation and not between-school variation (Raudenbush et al 1993). A typical teacher does not use teaching for understanding to the same degree with all of his or her classes and there are also important within-school differences between teachers in the emphasis each teacher places on teaching for understanding.

Raudenbush et al (1993) examined emphasis on teaching for higher-order thinking in a sample of 1205 classes taught by 303 academic teachers in 16 high schools. Despite recent calls to deliver teaching for understanding and higher-order thinking to all students (e.g. Peterson 1988, Newmann 1990), Raudenbush et al found that the typical teacher uses teaching for understanding instructional approaches much more frequently in honors- and academic-track classes than in general- or vocational-track classes. These results are consistent with the evidence from many other studies that, to the extent that teaching for understanding is present at all in the middle and high school grades, it occurs far more often in high-track than in low-track classes (e.g. Metz 1978, Oakes 1985, Page 1990).

Although track effects on individual teachers' use of teaching for understanding with specific classes are found in all academic subjects, they are especially large in mathematics and science (Raudenbush et al 1993). In those subjects, the typical teacher uses very different instructional approaches for his or her noncollege and college classes. (The effect sizes for track effects range between 1 and 1.7 standard deviations in math and science and between .4 and .9 standard deviations in social studies and English.) Raudenbush et al (1993) also find that, in social studies and literature, teachers use teaching for understanding more with those courses they feel "very well prepared" to teach than they do with classes outside their areas of specialization ($ES_{social\ studies} = .28$, $ES_{literature} = .38$). Thus, the inclination of a teacher to deliver higher-order instruction may be undermined by mismatches between prior training and specific class assignments.

Extra-Help Opportunities for Students Who Fall Behind

All schools have some students who fall behind or learn more slowly than others. If schools begin to take seriously the challenge to offer all students access to a demanding core curriculum that prepares them for college and that features teaching for understanding, then schools will need to design effective "catch up" programs to provide additional support for students whose current proficiency is considerably below that of their classmates. Virtually every public school currently offers some type of extra-help program for students who fall behind (Mac Iver 1991). Remarkably little data exists concerning the effects of different extra-help opportunities on students' outcomes. Evidence suggests that provision of tutors who work one-on-one or one-on-two with students is reliably effective, especially if these tutors are trained adults who adapt the content and pace of instruction to the needs of individual students and if tutoring is provided in addition to regular classroom instruction and therefore adds to instructional time (Cooledge & Wurster 1985, Devin-Sheehan et al 1976, Mac Iver 1991, Wasik & Slavin 1990, Wilks & Clarke 1988) Despite their effectiveness, many schools cannot afford to hire adult tutors to serve students who need extra help, especially if they have many such students. In fact, schools in which extra-help opportunities are needed most (e.g. in middle schools in which the average achievement of students upon entry to the school is considerably below national norms) are the very schools that are least likely to offer one-to-one tutoring (Mac Iver 1991). Specifically, Mac Iver found that schools with an entering student population whose achievement upon entry is considerably below the national norm are 20% less likely than schools whose student population achievement is considerably above the national norm to offer struggling students one-on-one tutoring in reading or English.

Mac Iver (1991) used data from NELS:88 to investigate the effects of different types of extra-help programs in the middle grades on students' standardized test scores in both reading and math. He found that approaches in which struggling students receive a substantial extra dose of instruction (e.g. offering students the opportunity to take a second period of math or reading during the regular school day instead of other electives or to take Saturday classes or summer classes) were much more effective than less intensive approaches (e.g. small group pull-out programs and before- or after-school coaching classes).

The double period approach to providing extra help, although effective, is rarely used. Only 17% of the nation's middle grades schools use such an approach (Mac Iver 1991). Mac Iver argues that the double period approach has some definite advantages compared to more common remedial programs. Attendance is high because the elective period of academic instruction is part of the regular school day; it is not a pull-out program, so students do not miss regular academic instruction; and it does not stigmatize students because it is viewed as just another elective class to which students disperse. Also, the double period approach can be implemented with little additional cost, if a school is willing to reshuffle priorities and resources. For example, a school can offer roughly 300 students an extra math class without increasing its payroll by hiring two fewer elective subject teachers and two more math teachers. Thus, the double period approach is more cost-effective than are extended day, extended week, or extended year approaches because it does not require schools to keep their buildings open longer, pay their teachers more, or increase their staffing levels.

ACCOUNTABILITY, EVALUATION, AND RECOGNITION PRACTICES

Keeping Students Accountable: Weaknesses in Traditional Evaluation and Recognition Practices

Most of the United States' current official education goals (e.g. "By the year 2000, U.S. students will be first in the world in science and mathematics achievement."; National Education Goals Panel 1991, p. ix) are so unrealistic that many educators have responded to them with derision rather than commitment. But if schools knew how to increase the proportion of their students who regularly "gave their best" in the classroom, it might be possible to obtain world class education outcomes—maybe not by the year 2000—but at least within this generation. American middle and high school students readily admit they are not using 100% effort to learn the subject matter in the courses they take and, as a result, are only working to a fraction of their potential (Mac Iver & Reuman 1993). Although there is no magic bullet to eliminate the student effort shortage, principles of goal-setting theory derived from industrial-organizational psychology (Locke & Latham 1984) and principles of achievement goal theory from educational psychology (Ames 1992) can be used to diagnose major weaknesses in traditional evaluation and recognition practices that render them ineffective in promoting concentrated, persistent student effort.

GOAL-SETTING THEORY   Derivations from goal-setting theory have much to say about why traditional evaluation and recognition practices are ineffective in optimizing student motivation to learn. For example, one principle of goal-setting theory is that goal commitment is highest when the goal is perceived as reachable rather than impossible and when there are clear payoffs such as special recognition associated with attaining the goal (Locke et al 1988, Locke & Latham 1990a). The way we typically evaluate and recognize students' academic accomplishments, however, undermines the commitment of many young adolescents to the goal of academic success because success is defined in such a way as to make the goal unreachable for them; they repeatedly find that their best efforts in the classroom go unnoticed and unrewarded.

Traditional evaluation and recognition practices in schools are based on evaluation systems that compare students' performance to that of other students or to desirable absolute standards of achievement. In both types of systems, students who begin the year far behind grade level in achievement may not be able to obtain a desirable evaluation even if they work very hard. Also, traditional recognition practices often do not adequately recognize the progress that low-achieving students make, because even dramatic progress may still leave them near the bottom of the class in comparative terms and far from the absolute levels of performance that are rewarded and recognized in their school. Once these students begin to realize that there are no clear payoffs associated with their best efforts, they become frustrated with and disengaged from school (Natriello 1982), and their level of effort and rate of progress drop precipitously.

Traditional evaluation and recognition practices do encourage high-performing students to be committed to doing well academically by giving these students reachable goals and clear payoffs for attaining these goals. But, there is strong reason to question whether these practices are effective in encouraging even high-performing students to work up to their potential, especially in heterogeneous classrooms. Because even modest effort on the part of high achievers usually assures them of scores that are near the top of the class in comparative terms or that exceed the "percent-correct" standard needed for a good grade, the evaluation system provides little incentive for these students to stretch themselves by working harder. A basic premise of goal-setting theory is that task performance is heavily influenced by whether individuals are striving for a goal that is easy for them or one that is challenging. Over a hundred studies in the goal-setting literature indicate that goals that are perceived to be challenging but reachable lead to better performance than do easy goals (Locke & Latham 1990b). Unfortunately, current evaluation practices implicitly assign goals to high achievers that may be too easy for them.

Another reason many students do not work up to their potential on assignments, quizzes, and tests is that they approach these tasks with only a vague goal in mind (e.g. "to get this done" or "to do my best"). Research on goal specificity demonstrates that specific goals (e.g. "to beat my current average by 10 points") lead to higher performance than do vague goals or no goals (Chidster & Grigsby 1984, Locke & Latham 1990a). Specific goals lead to increased performance regardless of whether they are assigned (e.g. set unilaterally by the teacher) or participatively set (Dossett et al 1979, Latham & Saari 1979, Latham & Marshall 1982, Latham et al 1982). It is the setting of an appropriate goal that is important rather than the method by which it is set.

ACHIEVEMENT GOAL THEORY   Achievement goal theory is similar to goal-setting theory in that it hypothesizes that the superior performance of some students, classrooms, or schools can be partially attributed to the goals adopted by these students and emphasized in their classrooms and schools. Achievement goal theory differs from goal-setting theory by suggesting the importance of distinguishing two qualitatively different types of goals—task-focused goals and ability-focused goals (Maehr & Midgley 1991, Duda & Nicholls 1992, Nicholls 1984)—that "elicit qualitatively different motivational patterns" (Ames 1992, p. 261). Students are said to have adopted task-focused goals (also known as "learning" or "mastery" goals; Elliott & Dweck 1988, Ames & Archer 1988) when they are concerned primarily with developing new skills, mastering and understanding content, or improving their level of competence (Ames 1992). Students are said to have adopted ability-focused goals (also known as "ego-involved" or "performance" goals) when they are concerned with being judged "smart" (or avoiding being judged "dumb"), and smartness is evidenced by outperforming others or by achieving success with little effort (Maehr & Midgley 1991).

A review of the research on the differential effects of task-focused and ability-focused goal orientations (e.g. Ames 1992) suggests that students who have adopted task-focused goals are more likely than students with ability-focused goals to believe that effort leads to success (Ames & Archer 1988, Nicholls et al 1985), to prefer challenging tasks over easy ones (Ames & Archer 1988, Elliott & Dweck 1988), to report more intrinsic interest in learning activities (Butler 1987, Meece et al 1988, Stipek & Kowalski 1989), to devote more time to learning tasks (Butler 1987), to use more effective learning strategies (Ames & Archer 1988, Meece et al 1988, Nolen 1988, Nolen & Haladyna 1990), and to persist longer in the face of failure (Elliott & Dweck 1988).

Because students' adoption of task-focused rather than ability-focused goals leads to a very positive, productive motivational pattern, it is important to consider how alternative and traditional recognition and evaluation practices may make these different goals salient. The converging literature on this topic suggests that traditional evaluation and recognition practices foster an ability-focused orientation because they (*a*) reward normative success rather than individual improvement, (*b*) bring ability differences among pupils into high resolution by frequently publicizing the relative performance levels of students, (*c*) do not reliably reward strategic effort, and (*d*) do not encourage students to view their initial mistakes and confusions as a normal part of learning new skills (Ames 1992, Marshall & Weinstein 1984, Rosenholtz & Simpson 1984, Mac Iver 1988, Maehr & Midgley 1991).

Effects of Alternative Accountability Techniques on Students' Motivation and Performance

There is a growing literature suggesting practical alternative techniques for evaluation and recognition that overcome some of the major weaknesses of traditional techniques (Covington 1992, de Charms 1972, Frierson 1975, Mac Iver 1993, Mac Iver & Reuman 1993, Vars 1992). Although the specifics of these techniques differ, they all involve "changes in the rules of the learning game" so that (*a*) meaningful rewards are no longer artificially scarce and (*b*) every student is challenged to stretch themselves by pursuing a specific, short-term goal that represents an improvement over their past mastery levels, and thus "the act of learning itself becomes a sought-after goal" (Covington 1992, p. 161).

For example, the Incentives for Improvement (IFI) Program (Mac Iver & Norman 1994) asks students to beat their average previous performance levels, distributes individual performance summaries to students that show their attainment or nonattainment of two types of improvement goals, and provides official recognition to all students who raise their performance levels across time. Students who already have reached a high level of performance also receive official recognition for maintaining that level. Mac Iver (1993) used a matched control group, pretest-posttest design to evaluate the program's effectiveness in raising middle school students' effort, performance, probability of passing, valuing of the subject matter, and self concept of ability by comparing students' pretest adjusted outcomes in 23 middle school classes to 23 matched control group classes. The IFI program had a modest but statistically significant impact on student effort; students in the program reported working harder to master course content, studying harder for quizzes and tests, and working closer to their potential than did students in control classes. This moderate increase in student effort translated into a substantial increase in student performance; students in classes using the IFI program performed almost two thirds of a standard deviation higher on fourth-quarter assessments than did students in control classes.

The IFI program produced marginally significant increases in students' valuing of the subject matter (i.e. their interest and enthusiasm for what they were studying) and their self-concept of ability. Because of its positive impact on student effort and performance, the IFI program significantly increased the probability that at-risk students (i.e. those with failing preintervention performance levels) would pass the course (83% of the at-risk students passed the course in IFI program classes compared with 71% of at-risk students in control classes).

Other researchers have also demonstrated how modest changes in classroom and school practices that encourage students to set manageable self-improvement goals can enhance student motivation (Maehr & Midgley 1991, de Charms 1972, Alschuler 1969). For example, by introducing a simple goal-setting component to a fifth-grade mathematics class (e.g. asking students to indicate in advance what percentage of test problems they would strive to answer on each weekly quiz) and officially recognizing students who met their goals, Alschuler (1969) was able to greatly enhance students' motivation and achievement. Likewise, students' motivation and achievement in spelling may be enhanced by replacing the traditional spelling bee with a self-improvement version (de Charms 1972) in which each student is asked to choose between spelling an easy word (i.e. one the student had spelled correctly on the test several days before), a manageably challenging word (i.e. one he or she had previously misspelled but had studied in the meantime), and a hard word (i.e. one taken from the next spelling assignment, which the student had not yet seen). Students earn three points for spelling hard words, two points for spelling manageably challenging words, and only one point for spelling easy words. These modifications turn the spelling bee into a task that increases students' motivation to learn to spell, especially for those students who would have no chance to experience success in a traditional spelling bee.

The current push for the institution of higher and even world class standards in American schools will be counterproductive if it increases the likelihood that the best efforts of educationally disadvantaged students will go unrecognized and unrewarded just because these students are starting out so far behind. On the other hand, if the establishment of higher standards is accompanied by the adoption of evaluation and recognition structures that (*a*) encourage students to set specific improvement goals and (*b*) provide students with individual performance summaries and rewards for goal attainment that unambiguously indicate whether or not a given goal was attained, then educationally disadvantaged students may have the impetus and support they need to actually reach these higher standards over time.

THE HIDDEN BENEFITS OF (IMPROVEMENT-FOCUSED) REWARDS AND ASSIGNED GOALS   Self-determination theorists counsel caution in the use of extrinsic rewards and assigned goals (e.g. Deci et al 1991) because they fear these "external events designed to motivate" will undermine intrinsic motivation and interfere with the development of autonomous self-regulation. To many critics (e.g. Bandura 1986, Covington 1992, Locke & Henne 1986, Locke & Latham 1990a), the evidence supporting these fears seems weak and inconsistent. Indeed, a recent restatement of self-determination theory indirectly acknowledges these critics by admitting the possibility that rewards, assigned goals, and other motivational techniques can be used in a way that is nondetrimental (i.e. "in a way that does not leave the recipients feeling like pawns;" Deci et al 1991, p. 337). In other words, "assigned goals and incentives will not undermine intrinsic motivation as long as they are not perceived as controlling" (Locke & Latham 1990a, p. 57). When modest rewards (e.g. certificates and pencils, or tokens redeemable for "one free test answer") are given out for meeting assigned improvement goals, the informational value of the reward is emphasized and the bribe-like or controlling nature of the rewards is deemphasized. In fact, there is a growing body of evidence that improvement-oriented goals and modest rewards may have the hidden benefit of increasing students' intrinsic motivation in addition to increasing effort and performance (Mac Iver 1993, Covington 1992).

How do improvement-focused goals and rewards help students develop and maintain interest in what they learn in class? A central axiom of flow theory (Csikszentmihalyi & Nakamura 1989) is that an activity is more likely to be perceived as interesting and enjoyable whenever the challenges of the activity match the individual's ability. The use of improvement-focused goals makes it possible to transform almost any activity into one in which challenges and skills are approximately equal. In progress-oriented evaluation systems, assigned goals become more difficult as students become more competent, thus preventing the activity from becoming boring. Furthermore, increases in students' perceived competence in an activity lead to increases in students' interest in that activity (e.g. Mac Iver et al 1991). Therefore, improvement-focused rewards—especially when they are based on unambiguous performance standards—may lead to increased interest because they clearly signal progress in learning and thus raise perceived competence (Schunk 1991).

Winning the Battle of Requirements Through External Standards and External Graders

The research literature suggests that traditional student accountability and recognition structures suffer from another major weakness: that individual classroom teachers are given the role of standard-setter and dispenser of grades. Waller (1932), in his classic account of the "battle of requirements" may have been the first to point out that teachers, as setters of requirements and graders, have been given duties that hinder their effectiveness as coaches. He vividly described the estrangement that arises between students and teachers whenever teachers strive to establish higher standards for student performance and greater demands for school work than the students perceive to be desirable or feasible.

TREATIES AND BARGAINS   Students who feel that their teachers are asking too much of them begin to respond to their teachers as taskmasters and judges rather than as guides and helpers. They expend great effort in trying to renegotiate the tasks they are assigned and in figuring out an effective method of bribing or threatening the judge into lowering standards and lessening demands. Often, these efforts at renegotiation are successful and they lead to subtle treaties or explicit classroom bargains between students and teachers that lower standards but keep the peace (Sedlak et al 1986, Powell et al 1985). When these efforts to establish bargain-basement standards are unsuccessful, students may become alienated and then drop the course, or begin disrupting and cutting class sections.

Although the battle of requirements occurs in virtually all middle and high school classrooms, it becomes especially severe when a school decides to offer a high-level curriculum to all students in heterogeneous classrooms. Even if improvement-focused grading and recognition is used, each heterogeneous class will have many students who feel overchallenged by the advanced topics and difficult assignments in the class. This will be especially true during the early years of an untracking plan because many former low-track students will have had many years to get used to the dumbed-down curriculum, texts, and standards of the lower track.

THE "LOADING DOWN" OF STANDARDS   When middle and high school teachers try to set higher standards and requirements, not only do they face a losing battle with students; they face a losing battle with the clock as well. The time pressures and student loads faced by these teachers make it extremely difficult for them to use challenging assessments that test students' depth of understanding and critical thinking. It is common for teachers in inner-city schools to teach a total of 175 students (e.g. 5 classes of 35 students each). In districts with unusual resources, a teacher's student load may be closer to 120. Even with this unusually small load, if a teacher were to assign students one higher-order performance task a week (e.g. a one-page paper, a lab report, or an essay exam) and were to spend an average of only five minutes per student in critiquing and grading these tasks—ten hours would be required to evaluate the additional task (Sizer 1985). It's no wonder that teachers rely so heavily on multiple-choice exams and other low-level tasks that can be scored quickly even though these tasks do nothing to promote students' ability to apply course-related knowledge to authentic problems (Newmann 1989) but instead "favor parrot learn-ing...[that is] undesirable not only because it is useless, but also because the parrot-like habit of mind inhibits deeper learning" (Waller 1932, p. 362).

THE TABOO AGAINST BROWNNOSERS   An unfortunate reality is that because the instructor controls the gradebook, student attempts to establish a close personal relationship are viewed by other students with suspicion. Even such seemingly innocent actions as demonstrating alertness or responsiveness in class are often interpreted by other students as strategic behavior designed to bias the instruc-tor's grading. As a result, student norms develop that state that it is "cool" to appear bored in class and to exhibit only grudging cooperation with the teacher's agenda (Mac Iver & Reuman 1993). Students who violate these norms face the "kiss of death:" being labeled by their peers as a teacher's pet, a nerd, or an apple polisher.

Mac Iver & Reuman (1993) conducted a randomized field experiment at Windham High School in Willimantic, Connecticut, to evaluate the Challenge Program, a theory-based multiple component program that offers high-level learning opportunities to students in mixed ability classrooms while attempt-ing to defuse the battle of requirements, prevent the loading down of stand-ards, weaken the taboo against close, cooperative student-teacher relation-ships, and promote proacademic peer norms. The Challenge Program features standards, tests, and graders that are external to the classroom. The standards are set by an examination board composed of all teachers of Challenge classes. The standards are embodied in performance exams that occur three times a quarter. After each exam, improvement awards are given to students and cooperative learning teams that qualify by raising their individual and team performance levels.

Because of the external standards and assessments, both students and teach-ers are freed from the battle of requirements and are allowed to function more like an athletic team. When a team of athletes are faced with frequent challeng-ing games or matches, the athletes realize that it would be counterproductive to pressure their coach to lower standards and lessen demands during training and practice sessions. The athletes might grumble to themselves about how hard they have to work, but they still cooperate with the coach's agenda (if it is clearly designed to help them do well) and encourage their teammates to do likewise.

Similarly, one reason that advanced students work more and complain less in advanced placement (AP) classes than in some of their other demanding courses is because the students know that the AP test is coming. They realize it is counterproductive to complain about being asked to master particularly difficult content, if that content is going to figure prominently on the test. In fact, the teacher is doing them a favor by pushing them, and the students realize this.

Not only is it beneficial to have frequent external assessments (as long as they assess what is essential and important), it is also beneficial to have external graders. In the Challenge Program, a significant portion of the student's grade is derived from evaluations made by external parties (e.g. other teachers who teach different sections of the same course, teachers from the next level of schooling, or other qualified individuals) rather than by the student's own teacher. As a result, students can establish a close, working relationship with the teacher without being accused of brownnosing. Also, because the external graders receive an honorarium (in recognition of the hard work involved in scoring performance assessments), the examination board is not tempted to rely on multiple-choice questions or other "parrot learning" test items.

Teachers are somewhat ambivalent about the presence of external exams, external graders, and improvement-oriented feedback. On the one hand, teachers find that these programs features help them to sustain their own motivation to give their best in the classroom each day because they want to give their students the best possible opportunities to learn the skills and understandings that are going to be evaluated externally. On the other hand, these same program features make it likely that even the best teacher will be embarrassed occasionally by the test results (e.g. when the external grader discovers that students did not understand a particular topic and were thus unable to correctly answer certain questions on the performance exam).

The first full-year course in which the Challenge Program was implemented was a Biology I course. End-of-year data collected and compared against control sections of the course indicate that the Challenge program was effective in reducing anti-academic peer norms by nearly one half of a standard deviation and in increasing peer support for achievement by a similar amount without producing higher levels of test anxiety (Mac Iver & Reuman 1993). On the other hand, the Challenge Program had no effect on students' overall performance on a traditional achievement measure (The National Association of Biology Teachers High School Biology Test). On the whole, Challenge students performed no better (and no worse) than control students on this multiple-choice test. However, there are indications that strong implementation of the program may affect achievement—the Challenge section with the highest measured implementation of program components was significantly higher than the control group on the Genetics and Ecology subscales of the test.

It is an open question whether the results of a longer-term evaluation of the Challenge Program using higher-order achievement measures across multiple years in multiple subject areas will suggest that it is generally effective in combatting anti academic norms among students and in promoting students' higher-order learning and ability to apply knowledge from their coursework to authentic problems. Regardless of what these results eventually indicate, there is an unmistakable need for further work in this area to develop and evaluate the cost and effectiveness of alternative approaches to winning the battle of requirements.

Teacher Evaluation and Recognition Programs

Just as traditional methods of student evaluation and recognition are based partly on the assumption that students will work harder and perform better if they are graded and rewarded competitively on the basis of performance, differential incentive programs for teachers (e.g. merit pay, career ladder, and mentor teacher programs) are based partly on the assumption that teachers will be more likely to give their best efforts if they are paid (or otherwise compensated) competitively on the basis of their teaching effectiveness (Brandt 1990, Cornett & Gaines 1992, Johnson 1984, Firestone & Pennell 1993). Differential incentive programs are popular with the public, which sees them as a fair way to improve compensation for effective teachers without expensive across-the-board salary increases. But, fairness in selection and reward scarcity problems have hampered the effectiveness of differential incentive programs in motivating teachers to improve their instructional practices (Rosenholtz 1987, Smylie & Smart 1990, Natriello & Cohn 1983).

Two different strategies have been followed for judging teacher effectiveness when selecting teachers to receive merit pay or career ladder promotions: (a) directly observing teachers' performance in the classroom and (b) making inferences concerning teachers' effectiveness based on student outcome measures. Teachers frequently perceive direct observations as unreliable because too few class sessions are observed and because vague performance criteria result in different raters giving the same teacher substantially different ratings. Teachers also report that many observers are not well qualified to accurately assess teaching effectiveness in the teacher's specific grade level or subject area or that observers may use the selection process to reward friends and punish enemies (Firestone & Pennell 1993).

Interestingly, teachers respond just like students when their coaches (e.g. principals, department heads, or district-level subject specialists) are given duties incompatible with the coaching role, that is, when evaluative duties require them to select only the top performers for recognition. In such cases, teachers engage in a battle of requirements with administrators in attempts to establish bargain-basement standards or to stack the deck in their favor (e.g. by hiding good ideas from each other, hoarding resources, or negotiating for the honors sections) so that they will look better than their colleagues during observations (Natriello & Cohn 1983, Rosenholtz 1987). In addition, teacher-administrator relations deteriorate as any attempt by a teacher to establish a close, working relationship with their administrators is interpreted and punished by peers as brownnosing (Firestone & Pennell 1993). For example, Malen & Hart (1987) discuss a career ladder program in Utah where teachers who were competitively selected for promotion to the rank of teacher leader were mailed anonymously "a crude drawing depicting a teacher leader kissing the naked buttocks of the school principal" (p. 18).

To overcome these problems, some differential incentive programs use external standards—based on students' performance on standardized achievement tests—to select teachers for merit pay or other incentives (Murnane & Cohen 1986). However, in most if not all schools, these standards will be unfair because of "variations in teacher assignments and student abilities and backgrounds, the inability of teachers to control many of the factors affecting student outcomes, and difficulties in fairly and accurately identifying outstanding or exceptional performance" (Firestone & Pennell 1993, p. 513). If we accept that different sections of students have different short-term potentials because of different starting points, then to measure all teachers against a single standard of performance based on their students' average attainments is not to have a level playing field (Coleman 1993).

As might be expected, teachers react like students when they reach the conclusion that there is not a level playing field and thus their best efforts in the classroom will go unnoticed and unrewarded: They drastically reduce their effort (Murnane & Cohen 1986, Rosenholtz 1987).

One way of leveling the playing field in a differential incentive plan is to provide merit pay and career ladder promotions based on the performance gains achieved by a teacher's students. This type of differential incentive plan has not yet been tried because of a practical difficulty: Any evaluation system that is based on performance gains creates an incentive for teachers' to have one's students perform below their potential on the pretest measure of achievement, thus guaranteeing substantial improvement. Even if a school district were to use independent testers to conduct the pretests and posttests, the district would still need to safeguard against teachers encouraging their students to "play dumb" on the pretest. One such safeguard would be to make each year's posttest scores also serve as the following year's pretest scores. Because of the rewards for performance gains, a students' current teacher would always encourage their students to score high on these end-of-year posttests.

On the other hand, Coleman (1993) has argued for a dual evaluation system for teachers with rewards for both high performance and performance gain because "a system of evaluation with rewards only for gains in achievement lacks the authenticity that one having rewards for level of achievement automatically carries" (p. 22). Whereas dual evaluation systems have been used for student evaluation (e.g. the IFI program), they have not yet been used for teacher evaluation and recognition. Coleman suggests that such a system would resolve fairness in selection and reward scarcity problems while keeping the ultimate goal of high achievement in focus.

CONCLUDING COMMENTS

> Researchers are responsible not only for studying what is, but for illuminating what could be. To the maximum extent possible, education research should be organized to open new pathways toward educational goals. As in medical research, what we need today is not yesterday's leeches, but the cures of tomorrow.
>
> National Academy of Education (1991, p. 35)

Efforts to renew American schools will surely fail unless such efforts are guided by a deep understanding of the effects of school organization on student-teacher relationships, student motivation, and achievement. The research reviewed here suggests that researchers concerned with the social organization of schools are taking seriously their responsibility to illuminate what could be and to seek the cures of tomorrow. Whether or not offering all students a common core of learning opportunities emphasizing higher-order instructional goals and demanding standards is a new pathway to reaching world class student outcomes may depend on whether educational researchers can gain practical insights into effective strategies for teaching heterogeneous classes, means of helping students who are struggling to keep up with high-level coursework, and methods for motivating students and teachers to achieve excellence.

Literature Cited

Agnew EJ. 1987. *Shopping malls and high school schedules.* PhD thesis. Stanford Univ.

Alexander K, Pallas A. 1984. Curriculum reform and school performance: an evaluation of the new basics. *Am. J. Educ.* 92:391–420

Alschuler AS. 1969. The effects of classroom structure on achievement motivation and academic performance. *Educ. Technol.* 9:19–24

Ames C. 1992. Classrooms: goals, structures, and student motivation. *J. Educ. Psychol.* 84(3):261–71

Ames C, Archer J. 1988. Achievement goals in the classroom: students' learning strategies and motivation processes. *J. Educ. Psychol.* 80(3):260–67

Bandura A. 1986. *Social Foundations of Thought and Action: A Social Cognitive View.* Englewood Cliffs, NJ: Prentice-Hall

Becker HJ. 1990. Curriculum and instruction

in middle grade schools. *Phi Delta Kappan* 71:450–57

Becker HJ. 1993. *Mathematics With Meaning.* Baltimore: Johns Hopkins Univ. Cent. Res. Effect. School. Disadv. Stud.

Bereiter C, Scardamalia M. 1987. An attainable version of high literacy: approaches to teaching higher-order thinking skills in reading and writing. *Curric. Inq.* 17:9–30

Brandt RM. 1990. *Incentive Pay and Career Ladders for Today's Teachers: A Study of Current Programs and Practices.* Albany: State Univ. NY Press

Bryk AS, Lee VE, Holland PB. 1993. *Catholic Schools and the Common Good.* Cambridge, MA: Harvard Univ. Press

Burton MB. 1989. The effect of prior calculus experience on "introductory" college calculus. *Am. Math. Mon.* 96:350–54

Butler R. 1987. Task-involving and ego-involving properties of evaluation: effects of different feedback conditions on motivational perceptions, interest, and performance. *J. Educ. Psychol.* 79:474–82

Chidster TR, Grigsby WC. 1984. A meta-analysis of the goal setting performance literature. *Acad. Manage. Proc.*, pp. 202–6. Washington, DC: Acad. Manage.

Cicourel AV, Kitsuse JI. 1963. *The Educational Decision-Makers.* Indianapolis, IN: Bobbs-Merrill

Cipra BA. 1988. Recent innovations in calculus instruction. In *Calculus for a New Century: A Pump, Not a Filter,* ed. LA Steen, pp. 95–103. Washington, DC: Math. Assoc. Am.

Coleman JS. 1993. *The Design of Schools as Output-Driven Organizations.* Chicago: Univ. Chicago Cent. Stud. Econ. State

Coleman JS, Hoffer T, Kilgore S. 1982. *High School Achievement: Public, Catholic, and Private Schools Compared.* New York: Basic

Coleman JS, Hoffer T, Kilgore S. 1987. *Public and Private High Schools: The Impact of Communities.* New York: Basic

Collins A. 1989. Elementary school science curricula that have potential to promote scientific literacy (and how to recognize one when you see one). In *Scientific Literacy,* ed. AB Champagne, BE Lovitts, BJ Calinger, pp. 129–55. Washington, DC: Am. Assoc. Adv. Sci.

Cooledge NJ, Wurster SR. 1985. Intergenerational tutoring and student achievement. *Read. Teach.* 39:343–46

Cooley WW, Leinhardt G. 1980. The instructional dimensions study. *Educ. Eval. Policy Anal.* 2:7–25

Cornett LM, Gaines GF. 1992. *Focusing on Student Outcomes: Roles for Incentive Programs. The 1991 National Survey of Incentive Programs and Teacher Career Ladders.* Atlanta: S. Reg. Educ. Board Career Ladder Clearing House

Covington MV. 1992. *Making the Grade: A Self-Worth Perspective on Motivation and School Reform.* New York: Cambridge Univ. Press

Csikszentmihalyi M, Nakamura J. 1989. The dynamics of intrinsic motivation: a study of adolescents. In *Research on Motivation in Education.* Vol. 3: *Goals and Cognitions,* ed. C Ames, R Ames, pp. 45–72. San Diego, CA: Academic

Daniels H, Zemelman SA. 1985. *Writing Project: Training Teachers of Composition, Kindergarten to College.* Portsmouth, NH: Heinemann

de Charms R. 1972. Personal causation training in the schools. *J. Appl. Soc. Psychol.* 2:95–113

Deci EL, Vallerand RJ, Pelletier LG, Ryan RM. 1991. Motivation and education: the self-determination perspective. *Educ. Psychol.* 26(3/4):325–46

Delaney B. 1991. Allocation, choice, and stratification within high schools: how the sorting machine copes. *Am. J. Educ.* 99(2):181–207

Devin-Sheehan L, Feldman R, Allen V. 1976. Research on children tutoring children: a critical review. *Rev. Educ. Res.* 46:355–85

Dornbusch SM. 1994. *Off the track.* Presidential address to the Soc. Res. Adol., San Diego, February 12

Dossett DL, Latham GP, Mitchell TR. 1979. Effects of assigned vs. participatively set goals, knowledge of results, and individual differences when goal difficulty is held constant. *J. Pers. Soc. Psychol.* 18:105–55

Dreeben R, Barr R. 1988. Classroom composition and the design of instruction. *Sociol. Educ.* 61:129–42

Duda JL, Nicholls JG. 1992. Dimensions of achievement motivation in schoolwork and sport. *J. Educ. Psychol.* 84:290–99

Elliott ES, Dweck CS. 1988. Goals: an approach to motivation and achievement. *J. Pers. Soc. Psychol.* 54:5-12

Epstein JL, Mac Iver DJ. 1992. *Opportunities to Learn: Effects on Eighth Graders of Curriculum Offerings and Instructional Approaches.* Baltimore: Johns Hopkins Univ. Cent. Res. Effect. School. Disadv. Stud.

Epstein JL, Salinas KC. 1992. *Promising Programs in the Middle Grades.* Reston, VA: Natl. Assoc. Second. School Principals

Firestone WA, Pennell JR. 1993. Teacher commitment, working conditions, and differential incentive policies. *Rev. Educ. Res.* 63(4): 489–525

Forgione P. 1990. *Accountability and assessment: the Connecticut approach.* Presented at the Public Educ. Forum, Baltimore, MD, February 15

Frierson EC. 1975. *Grading Without Judgment: A Classroom Guide to Grades and Individual Evaluation.* Nashville, TN: EDCOA

Gardner J. 1961. *Excellence: Can We Be Equal And Excellent Too?* New York: Harper & Row

Garet MS, DeLaney B. 1988. Students, courses, and stratification. *Sociol. Educ.* 61:61–77

Greeley AM. 1982. *Catholic High Schools and Minority Students.* New Brunswick, NJ: Transaction

Hallinan MT. 1984. Ability grouping and student learning. In *The Social Organization of Schools: New Conceptualizations of the Learning Process,* ed. M Hallinan, pp. 41–69. New York: Plenum

Husen T. 1967. *International Study of Achievement in Mathematics: A Comparison of Twelve Countries.* New York: Wiley

Jetter A. 1993. Mississippi learning. *NY Times Mag.* Feb. 21:28–72

Johnson SM. 1984. Merit pay for teachers: a poor prescription for reform. *Harvard Educ. Rev.* 54(2):175–85

Latham GP, Marshall HA. 1982. The effects of self-set, participatively set and assigned goals on the performance of government employees. *Pers. Psychol.* 39:606–17

Latham GP, Saari LM. 1979. Importance of supportive relationships in goal setting. *J. Appl. Psychol.* 64:151–56

Latham GP, Steele TP, Saari LM. 1982. The effects of participation and goal difficulty on performance. *Pers. Psychol.* 35: 677–86

Lee VE, Bryk AS. 1988. Curriculum tracking as mediating the social distribution of high school achievement. *Sociol. Educ.* 61:78–94

Lee VE, Bryk AS. 1989. A multilevel model of the social distribution of high school achievement. *Sociol. Educ.* 62:172–92

Leinhardt G, Seewald A. 1981. Overlap: what's tested, what's taught. *J. Educ. Meas.* 18(2):85–96

Locke EA, Henne D. 1986. Work motivation theories. In *International Review of Industrial and Organizational Psychology,* ed. C Cooper, I Robertson, pp. 101–17. Chichester, England: Wiley

Locke EA, Latham GP. 1984. *Goal-Setting: A Motivational Technique That Works.* Englewood Cliffs, NJ: Prentice-Hall

Locke EA, Latham GP. 1990a. *A Theory of Goal Setting and Task Performance.* Englewood Cliffs, NJ: Prentice-Hall

Locke EA, Latham GP. 1990b. Work motivation and satisfaction: light at the end of the tunnel. *Psychol. Sci.* 1:240–46

Locke EA, Latham GP, Erez M. 1988. The determinants of goal commitment. *Acad. Manage. Rev.* 13:23–39

Mac Iver DJ. 1988. Classroom environments and the stratification of pupils' ability perceptions. *J. Educ. Psychol.* 80:495–505

Mac Iver DJ. 1991 *Helping Students Who Fall Behind: Remedial Activities in the Middle Grades.* Baltimore: Johns Hopkins Univ. Cent. Res. Effect. School. Disadv. Stud.

Mac Iver DJ. 1993. Effects of improvement-focused student recognition on young adolescents' performance and motivation in the classroom. *Adv. Motiv. Achiev.* 8:191–216

Mac Iver DJ. 1994. *Report of major findings: mathematics.* Presented at Inst. Stat. Anal. Educ. Policy, New Orleans, April 10

Mac Iver DJ, Epstein JL. 1994. Impact of Algebra-Focused Course Content and "Active Learning/Teaching for Understanding" Instructional Approaches on Eighth-Graders' Achievement. Baltimore, MD: Johns Hopkins Univ. Cent. Res. Effect. School. Disadv. Stud.

Mac Iver DJ, Norman LA. 1994. *Incentives for Improvement Program Teachers' Manual and Guide to the Electronic Gradebook.* Baltimore, MD: Johns Hopkins Univ. Cent. Res. Effect. School. Disadv. Stud.

Mac Iver DJ, Reuman DA. 1993. Giving their best: grading and recognition practices that motivate students to work hard. *Am. Educ.* 17(4):24–31

Mac Iver DJ, Stipek DJ, Daniels DH. 1991. Explaining within-semester changes in student effort in junior high school and senior high school courses. *J. Educ. Psychol.* 83: 201–11

Maehr ML, Midgley C. 1991. Enhancing student motivation: a schoolwide approach. *Educ. Psychol.* 26(3/4): 399–427

Malen B, Hart AW. 1987. Career ladder reform: a multi-level analysis of initial efforts. *Educ. Eval. Policy Anal.* 9(1):9–23

Marshall HH, Weinstein RS. 1984. Classroom factors affecting students' self-evaluations: an interactional model. *Rev. Educ. Res.* 54: 301–25

McPartland JM, Schneider B. 1994. *Opportunities to Learn and Student Diversity: Prospects and Pitfalls of a Common Core Curriculum.* Baltimore, MD: Johns Hopkins Univ. Cent. Res. Effect. School. Disadv. Stud.

Meece JL, Blumenfeld PC, Hoyle RH. 1988. Students' goal orientations and cognitive engagement in classroom activities. *J. Educ. Psychol.* 80(4):514–23

Metz MH. 1978. *Classrooms and Corridors.* Berkeley: Univ. Calif. Press

Moses RP, Kamii M, Swap SM, Howard J. 1989. The algebra project: organizing in the spirit of Ella. *Harvard Educ. Rev.* 59 (4):27–47

Murnane RJ, Cohen DK. 1986. Merit pay and the evaluation problem: why most merit pay plans fail and a few survive. *Harvard Educ. Rev.* 56(1):1–17

National Academy of Education. 1991. *Research and the Renewal of Education.* Stanford, CA: Natl. Acad. Educ.

National Council of Teachers of Mathematics. 1991. *Professional Standards for Teaching Mathematics.* Reston, VA: Natl. Counc. Teach. Math.

National Education Goals Panel. 1991. *The National Education Goals Report: Building a Nation of Learners.* Washington, DC: US Govt. Print. Off.

Natriello G. 1982. *Organizational Evaluation Systems and Student Disengagement in Secondary Schools. Final report to the National Institute of Education.* St. Louis, MO: Washington Univ.

Natriello G, Cohn M. 1983. *Beyond sanctions: the evolution of a merit pay system.* Presented at Annu. Meet. Am. Educ. Res. Assoc., Montreal, Canada (ERIC Doc. Reprod. Serv. No. ED 238 140)

Newmann FM. 1989. *Student engagement in academic work: a conceptual model.* Presented at Annu. Meet. Am. Educ. Res. Assoc., San Francisco

Newmann FM. 1990. Higher-order thinking in teaching social studies: a rationale for the assessment of classroom thoughtfulness. *J. Curric. Stud.* 22(1):41–56

Nicholls JG. 1984. Achievement motivation: conceptions of ability, subjective experience, task choice, and performance. *Psychol. Rev.* 91:328–46

Nicholls JG, Patashnick M, Nolen SB. 1985. Adolescents' theories of education. *J. Educ. Psychol.* 77:683–92

Nolen SB. 1988. Reasons for studying: motivational orientations and study strategies. *Cogn. Instr.* 5:269–87

Nolen SB, Haladyna TM. 1990. Motivation and studying in high school science. *J. Res. Sci. Teach.* 27:115–26

Oakes J. 1985. *Keeping Track: How Schools Structure Inequality.* New Haven, CT: Yale Univ. Press

Oakes J. 1986. Keeping track. Part 1: The policy and practice of curriculum inequality. *Phi Delta Kappan* 68(1):12–17

Oakes J. 1990. *Excellence and equity: the impact of unequal educational opportunities.* Presented at Annu. Meet. Am. Educ. Res. Assoc., Boston

Page RN. 1990. The lower track curriculum in a college-preparatory high school. *Curric. Inq.* 20:249–82

Peterson PL. 1988. Teaching for higher-order thinking in mathematics: the challenge for the next decade. In *Perspectives on Research on Effective Mathematics Teaching,* ed. DA Grouws, TJ Cooney, 1:2–26. Hillsdale, NJ: Erlbaum

Powell AG, Farrarr E, Cohen DK. 1985. *The Shopping Mall High School: Winners and Losers in the Educational Marketplace.* Boston, MA: Houghton Mifflin

Prawat RS. 1989. Teaching for understanding: three key attributes. *Teach. Teach. Educ.* 5:315–28

Raudenbush SW, Rowan B, Cheong YF. 1993. Higher order instructional goals in secondary schools: class, teacher, and school influences. *Am. Educ. Res. J.* 30(3): 523–53

Rosenholtz SJ. 1987. Education reform strategies: Will they increase teacher commitment? *Am. J. Educ.* 95:534–62

Rosenholtz SJ, Simpson C. 1984. The formation of ability conceptions: developmental trend or social construction? *Rev. Educ. Res.* 54:31–63

Rutherford FJ, Ahlgren A. 1990. *Science for All Americans.* New York: Oxford Univ. Press

Schunk DH. 1991. Self-efficacy and academic motivation. *Educ. Psychol.* 26(3/4):207–31

Sedlak MW, Wheeler, CW, Pullin DC, Cusick PA. 1986. *Selling Students Short: Classroom Bargains and Academic Reform in American High Schools.* New York: Teachers Coll. Press

Sizer TR. 1985. *Horace's Compromise: The Dilemma of the American High School.* Boston: Houghton Mifflin

Small DB. 1988. Transition from high school to college calculus. In *Calculus for a New Century: A Pump, Not a Filter,* ed. LA Steen, pp. 224–29. Washington, DC: Math. Assoc. Am.

Smylie MA, Smart JC. 1990. Teacher support for career enhancement initiatives: program characteristics and effects on work. *Educ. Eval. Policy Anal.* 12(2):139–55

Sorensen AB. 1984. The organizational differentiation of students in schools as an opportunity structure. In *The Social Organization of Schools: New Conceptualizations of the Learning Process,* ed. M Hallinan, pp. 103–29. New York: Plenum

Stevens Fl. 1993. *Opportunity to Learn: Issues of Equity for Poor and Minority Students.* Washington, DC: Natl. Cent. Educ. Stat.

Stipek DJ, Kowalski PS. 1989. Learned helplessness in task-orienting versus performance-orienting testing conditions. *J. Educ. Psychol.* 81(3):384–91

Stringfield S, Teddlie C. 1991. Observers as predictors of schools' multiyear outlier status on achievement tests. *Elem. Sch. J.* 91:357–76

Useem EL. 1992. Getting on the fast track in mathematics: school organizational influences on math track assignment. *Am. J. Educ.* 100(3):325–53

Vars GF. 1992. Humanizing student evaluation and reporting. In *Transforming Middle Level Education: Perspectives & Possibili-*

ties, ed. JL Irvin, pp. 336–65. Boston: Allyn & Bacon

Waller W. 1932. *Sociology of Teaching.* New York: Wiley

Wasik BA, Slavin RE. 1990. *Preventing Early Reading Failure with One-to-One Tutoring: A Best-Evidence Synthesis.* Baltimore: Johns Hopkins Univ. Cent. Res. Effect. School. Disadv. Stud.

Wheelock A. 1992. *Crossing the Tracks: How Untracking Can Save America's Schools.* New York: New Press

Wilks RTJ, Clarke VA. 1988. Training vs. nontraining of mothers as home reading tutors. *Percept. Motor Skills* 67:135–42

Annu. Rev. Psychol. 1995. 46:401–31

PSYCHOLOGICAL CHARACTERISTICS OF MALTREATED CHILDREN: Putative Risk Factors and Consequences

John F. Knutson

Department of Psychology, The University of Iowa, Iowa City, Iowa 52242

KEY WORDS: physical abuse, sexual abuse, neglect, aggression, sexuality, risk factors, consequences of maltreatment

CONTENTS

METHODOLOGICAL AND PUBLIC POLICY ISSUES

Since the publication of *The Battered-Child Syndrome* (Kempe et al 1962) professional interest in child maltreatment has grown dramatically and a related politcal agenda has emerged (cf Best 1990, Nelson 1984). In the United States, this political agenda resulted in the 1974 passage of the Child Abuse

Prevention and Treatment Act (PL 93-247) and has spawned a large amount of research and clinical activity. A recent comprehensive review of the physical abuse and physical neglect literature identified over 1250 articles since 1972 (Knutson & Schartz 1994), and the National Research Council (1993) reviewed over 2000 articles pertaining to maltreatment. Although child maltreatment has attracted a large amount of research attention, the body of work as a whole is fragmented, disorganized, and often methodologically flawed (see Knutson & Schartz 1994, National Research Council 1993).

Research on clinical problems is often compromised by a variety of methodological constraints, but research on the maltreatment of children seems to be plagued by more than the usual number of difficulties. Indeed, review articles in the area routinely call attention to methodological problems in the field and the degree to which conclusions are compromised. One of the major problems in the literature on maltreatment is the use of poorly defined samples or the aggregating of physical abuse, neglect, and sexual abuse into a single category of child maltreatment. Although physical abuse, neglect, and sexual abuse might have characteristics in common (e.g. Cicchetti 1990), there are important differences among these types of maltreatment (e.g. Goldston et al 1989; Widom 1989a,b; Widom & Ames 1994). Furthermore, the operational definition of child abuse and neglect is often left to the agencies or other sources from which research participants have been obtained. Unfortunately, a large body of research indicates that standards for reporting physical abuse, sexual abuse, or neglect differ among professionals (e.g. Dukes & Kean 1989, Giovannoni & Becerra 1979, O'Toole et al 1983, Snyder & Newberger 1986), and that variability is reflected in research in which referral sources have defined maltreatment. In addition, dependency on referral sources to define a sample can result in sampling bias (Widom 1988). In studies of the consequences of maltreatment, Browne & Finkelhor (1986) have argued for the use of natural collectivities (i.e. naturally occuring groups such as high school students or members of a health plan) to minimize sampling biases, but this guideline is rarely followed.

Reliance on single case studies is another methodological problem characterizing research on child maltreatment, as is the presence of studies with no original data. When Knutson & Schartz (1994) reviewed the physical abuse and neglect literature since 1972, they eliminated over 300 articles for these reasons.The National Research Council (1993) also lamented the widespread use of demonstration projects rather than experimental tests of treatment or prevention programs. However, after considering over 1500 intervention articles in the area of abuse, Fantuzzo (1990) identified only two studies that met minimal standards of experimental design. Even outside the treatment literature, only one third of the maltreatment studies provided control groups. When control groups were included they were often not matched on relevant variables (see Beitchman et al 1991, 1992; Plotkin et al 1981). Finally, although the child abuse reporting statutes have been in effect for two decades, and large numbers of maltreated children have been identified, there has been a remarkable paucity of longitudinal research and only a few prospective studies (e.g. Egeland et al 1980, Herrenkohl & Herrenkohl 1979).

When states established mandatory reporting of suspected abuse, they also established central registries of information regarding those abuse reports. Although the registries are often assumed to be valuable resources for epidemiological and outcome data, they have not been beneficial. There is remarkable variability among state registries, as noted in the survey completed by the National Center on Child Abuse and Neglect (1980). For example, most states fail to include extrafamilial maltreatment because such maltreatment would typically be identified through law enforcement agencies, which are usually not required to submit reports to central registries (see Flango et al 1988). In a study by Sullivan & Knutson (1993), when the complete records of a single hospital were merged with child protective registries and law enforcement records within a single state, two thirds of the extrafamilial sexual abuse was only recorded in the law enforcement records (Sullivan & Knutson 1993). Although the central registries have not contributed greatly to research because abuse victims and their families usually come to the attention of researchers through mandatory reporting, it is clear that available data are directly affected by the sampling that is a consequence of mandatory reporting statutes.

Mandatory reporting statutes typically identify those persons who are required to report suspicions of maltreatment, as well as the agency charged with investigating the report. Because the mandatory reporting laws were motivated by the desire to aid children who might be at risk for harm, the statutes specify relatively low standards of evidence necessary to evoke a suspicion; higher standards are required for substantiation. Since they address a broad range of endangering or harmful acts, the statutory definitions of physical abuse and neglect are vague, and there is variability among states (cf Flango 1988). Although the need to have a broad statutory base for defining abuse may be apparent, the possibility of adverse consequences resulting from definitions lacking in specificity has been the focus of considerable debate. Wald (1976, 1982) has argued for statutory definitions of abuse that set stringent standards in terms of the harmful consequences of maltreatment. Such arguments do not seem to have been persuasive in state legislatures. Thus, states continue to embrace a broad approach to defining maltreatment, and research can reflect the statutes operative in the jurisdiction in which the work was conducted.

DEFINING MALTREATMENT FOR RESEARCH PURPOSES

Physical Abuse

Conclusions about the risk factors and consequences of physical abuse are affected by the operational definitions adopted by researchers. Some of those definitions are direct reflections of statutes; others reflect the theoretical positions of investigators (e.g. Besharov 1981, Finkelhor & Korbin 1988, Giovannoni & Becerra 1979, O'Toole et al 1983, Office of Human Development Services 1988). Physical abuse is typically defined as an act of commission by a child caretaker, but the definition may specify an act, an act and a consequence, or merely a consequence of parental action. When the act is the defining characteristic, abuse has been defined as striking a child with some object, blows having some specific topographies, or blows directed at some body loci (see Berger et al 1988, Straus 1980). When the definition of abuse is based on consequences of parental acts, tissue damage ranging from bruises and abrasions to fractures, disfigurement, or life-threatening injury has been the criterion used. Although the consequence approach to defining abuse seems straightforward, setting defining criteria for abuse in terms of degree of tissue damage is only superficially simple (Wald 1982). Because of difficulty in setting a tissue damage standard or because of a concern that a tissue damage criterion would be too stringent, "endangerment" as a consequence has also been adopted as an operational definition of abuse (Office of Human Development Services 1988, Sedlak 1990).

The intentionality of the act has been a major issue in defining physical abuse. The intention of the alleged perpetrator has been important in determining whether physicians, social workers, psychologists, and nurses classified events as abuse (Snyder & Newberger 1986) as well as how courts responded. Intention is typically defined as a desire to harm a victim, but it is often assessed through evaluations of the expressions of socially desirable goals by perpetrators, or assertions that an injury was accidental. Knutson (1978, 1988), however, argued that intentions cannot be assessed unequivocally and, therefore, should not determine whether an act is judged to be abusive. Accordingly, the social desirability of a disciplinary act should not determine its abusive status. Because establishing that an injury was accidental is a challenging enterprise (e.g. Johnson 1990), the alleged accidental nature of an episode should be determined probabilistically, through an assessment of the setting context in which the event occurred, or through base rate information regarding accidents derived from consumer product safety data (cf Wissow & Wilson 1988).

Another approach to operationally defining physical abuse is to include events that have not resulted in significant tissue damage but that are thought to have emotional or psychological sequelae. Although this approach has been criticized for its vagueness (e.g. Nelson 1984, Wald 1982), some investigators have concluded that psychological consequences are at the heart of all maltreatment and such consequences could serve as the defining characteristic of physical abuse (e.g. Garbarino & Stocking 1980, Hart & Brassard 1987). If, however, an investigator is interested in studying consequences of maltreatment, defining maltreatment in terms of consequences becomes an entirely circular exercise.

Contemporary social norms have been used as another strategy for defining maltreatment. Based on a survey of a representative sample of Texans, Sapp & Carter (1978) reported that striking children with some objects (e.g. belts) was not seen as abusive by a majority of respondents, whereas striking children with other objects (e.g. belt buckles) was seen as abusive. According to a majority of those surveyed, any act that resulted in injury to a child was considered abusive. A recent survey of university students in Iowa (Bower 1991) yielded ratings that were comparable to those from Sapp & Carter's study, and a study of subcultural differences in ratings of parental acts as maltreatment did not identify any major group differences (Polansky et al 1983).

Neglect

Although usually defined simply in terms of acts of omission, neglect has also been defined in terms of harmful or endangering consequences of these omissions. Defining neglect in terms of acts of omission intimates that the intention of the parent could be relevant to an operational definition of neglect (see Rohner & Rohner 1980). Of course, determining intention is no easier in neglect than in physical abuse. Unfortunately, with few exceptions, the literature on neglect tends to use operational definitions that do not clearly establish whether neglected children actually experienced harm or were only endangered (cf Zuravin 1989). Taxonomies of deficient and neglectful parenting have also been used (e.g. Giovannoni 1988, Hegar & Yungman 1989). Perhaps the most influential approach to a taxonomy of neglect was provided by the Second National Incidence Study (NIS-2; Office of Human Development Services 1988). The NIS-2 distinguished among physical neglect, educational neglect, and emotional neglect, as well as forms of neglect that could not be placed in the three major categories. Forms of physical neglect included parents refusing to obtain health care for their child or failing to provide adequate supervision. For each type of neglect the distinction was made between the occurrence of harm and endangerment.

Sexual Abuse

Because sexual abuse is specified in the criminal codes of the states, sexual abuse definitions tend to reflect a high degree of specificity with respect to acts and the age of the victim. In some jurisdictions, identification of sexual abuse requires that the child be under 14 years of age, whereas in other jurisdictions older age limits have been adopted. In addition, the age of the perpetrator can be part of the definition. The degree to which force, implicit force, or other elements of coercion are used may also be part of the statutory definition of sexual abuse. Finkelhor & Hotaling (1984) urged that definitions of sexual abuse should include age differentials and elements of coercion as well as the type of act. They recommend an age differential of 5 years or more when the victim is under 12 and a 10-year differential when the child is 13 to 16. In their view, however, the use of force, threat, or exploitation of authority, regardless of age differentials, should always be considered abusive. Russell (1983) takes a different position, noting that sexual abuse of children by peers, siblings, younger children, or by children whose age differential is less than 5 years should not be excluded from databases. The degree to which a youngster can provide informed consent to participate in various sexual acts may also be an important factor in defining sexual abuse (cf Finkelhor 1979b). Such a criterion is particularly important when the victim is handicapped by developmental or communication disorders. Unfortunately, the sexual abuse literature tends to aggregate sexual maltreatment without regard to degree of penetration, injury, force, or even physical contact (see Beitchman et al 1991, 1992), which obviously compromises conclusions about the consequences of sexual abuse.

EPIDEMIOLOGY OF MALTREATMENT

The available epidemiological data on child maltreatment are determined by the definitions adopted by researchers. Since differing criteria are adopted, prevalence estimates of physical abuse and neglect vary widely. In addition, epidemiological estimates depend on the sources used. Finkelhor & Hotaling (1984) have argued there are five different levels of information that are potentially available regarding maltreatment, and prevalence estimates are a function of the degree to which these different levels are assessed. These levels of information range from cases that are known to the state Child Protective Service (CPS) agency (Level One) to abuse in which the incident is known only to the perpetrator and the victim, although the episode is not recognized as abuse by anyone, including the perpetrator and victim (Level Five). It might seem improbable that victims could be involved in truly abusive interactions without recognizing the event as abusive, but evidence indicates that as few as

25% of a sample of abused adolescents or young adults labeled their experiences as physically abusive (Berger et al 1988, Rausch & Knutson 1991).

The National Center on Child Abuse and Neglect has commissioned two national incidence studies. The first (NIS-1) was completed in 1980, and the second (NIS-2) was completed in 1986 (Office of Human Development Services 1988); both studies were designed to obtain data from service providers, so only the first three levels of information noted by Finkelhor & Hotaling (1984) were sampled. Both studies obtained data from counties selected to be nationally representative. The NIS-1 used definitions of maltreatment based on a standard of harm, and the NIS-2 used definitions of maltreatment based on harm or endangerment. With respect to the harm standard, the NIS-2 (Sedlak 1990) estimated the annual incidence of physical abuse at 4.3 per 1000 children, sexual abuse at 1.9, and physical neglect at 2.7. The combined incidence of seriously and moderately injured was 13 per 1000 children. The annual incidence rates based on the endangerment standard were 4.9 per 1000 children for physical abuse, 0.6 for sexual abuse, and 8.1 for physical neglect. These estimates yield a combined estimated total of 437,500 children harmed per year by physical abuse, sexual abuse, or physical neglect and an additional 819,200 endangered by maltreatment.

When the NIS-1 and NIS-2 were contrasted, there seemed to be a large increase in the incidence of maltreatment between 1980 and 1986. However, because the incidence of severely injurious or fatal maltreatment had not changed, and because such maltreatment is not likely to be undetected, the NIS-2 report concluded that the obtained increase reflected greater professional awareness and reporting rather than an actual increase in incidence. Similarly, the American Humane Association (1988) described a 212% increase in reports of maltreatment between 1976 and 1986. Although more cases are being recognized, the evidence provided by the NIS-2 suggests that less than half of the recognized cases are actually reported to CPS agencies. Studies directed at victims also indicate that the incidence of physical abuse has not changed. For example, in a study of 11,660 university undergraduates recruited over a decade, Knutson & Selner (1994) concluded that there has been no systematic change in the report of having experienced physical abuse over the period from 1982 through 1991. Because half of the sample were children before the abuse legislation and half were children after, the Knutson & Selner (1994) data indicate that the abuse agenda has had little impact on prevalence.

The NIS-2 also provided evidence regarding demographic factors related to maltreatment. No statistically significant gender differences were identified in physical abuse nor neglect, although females were at greater risk for injury. This difference was attributable to the much higher rate of sexual abuse of girls and the attendant risk for injury in many sexually abusive acts. Based on

30,901 confirmed reports in the Colorado Central Registry between July 1977 and June 1984, however, Rosenthal (1988) concluded that males were at somewhat greater risk for injury. In the NIS-2, abuse resulting in harm was greater in the 3–5-year-old group relative to the 0–2-year-old group. There was considerable variability in harm as a function of age among children older than five. Thus, the assumption that only very young children are at risk for physical abuse must be seriously questioned. Risk for fatal maltreatment declined markedly after 2 years of age in NIS-2 and in a study by Jason & Andereck (1983). The NIS-2 found an increase in overall neglect associated with increasing age; however, this pattern was attributable to increases in educational neglect. Sexual abuse also showed an increase as a function of age.

Socioeconomic status has been investigated widely in prevalence studies of maltreatment. Although a relatively large literature implicates poverty in child maltreatment, debate continues over the role of economic status in child abuse. The controversy relates in part to how socioeconomic status is measured (e.g. Brown 1984), in part to concerns about sampling biases in research, and in part to public policy issues (e.g. Pelton 1978). Within the NIS-2, when the sample was divided at a family income of $15,000, lower-income children were 4 times as likely to be physically abused, nearly 12 times as likely to be physically neglected, and 4 times as likely to be sexually abused. When indirect indices of economic disadvantage are used, poverty is strongly implicated in abuse and neglect (Dubowitz et al 1987, Zuravin 1989). Although economic disadvantage seems to be a factor in child maltreatment, large segments of economically disadvantaged children are not maltreated (e.g. Farber & Egeland 1987), and there is considerable evidence that maltreatment is represented in all economic strata. The overrepresentation of disadvantaged groups in abuse data is often attributed to their reliance on public agencies that may be more vigilant in reporting maltreatment. For example, Knudsen (1989) reported that 47% of the CPS reports in Indiana reflected reports on children already known to the CPS. However, Bolton & Laner (1986) reported that a majority of the adolescent parents identified as maltreaters over a two-year period were receiving no public assistance. Similarly, Rivara (1985) noted there was no involvement with the social service department prior to the abuse episode for 77% of consecutively referred cases. Although some data indicate that hospitals underreport abuse in higher-income groups (e.g. Hampton & Newberger 1985), there is also evidence supporting Pelton's (1978) position that the sampling bias is overrated. For example, there was a greater rate of nonaccidental injurious child fatalities in lower classes but an equivalence of clearly homicidal death was found across classes (Nixon et al 1981). Since underreporting of fatalities is unlikely, distributions of fatal events may provide a less biased estimate of class-related maltreatment.

When the relationship between ethnicity and maltreatment has been examined, the ethnic groups have often differed on variables other than ethnicity, thus preventing reliable conclusions. Although there are studies that report that African-Americans and Spanish-surnamed groups may be overrepresented in abuse and neglect statistics (e.g. Bolton & Laner 1986, Spearly & Lauderdale 1983), these data may reflect the influence of biased reporting. For example, Buriel et al (1979) noted that, within a random sample of confirmed cases of child abuse in southern California, Mexican-Americans were more often referred to the CPS by professionals as compared to Anglo-American abusers. Hampton & Newberger (1985) provided data strongly indicating that a race bias in reporting could account for ethnic differences in maltreatment rates. The NIS-1 and NIS-2 failed to identify any significant association between incidence rates of maltreatment and victims' ethnicity that was independent of economic disadvantage. Moreover, a reanalysis of the NIS-2 data caused Hampton (1987) to conclude that the overrepresentation of minorities in maltreatment statistics can best be understood as a reflection of economic adversity and discrimination. Consistent with that position, a recent review (Finkelhor & Baron 1986) concluded that sexual abuse is not elevated in African-American populations.

Eckenrode et al (1988) examined 5% of the abuse and neglect reports submitted to the New York Central Registry during a five-month period and found that minority group membership was among the factors that significantly predicted substantiation of physical abuse reports. Eckenrode et al (1988) interpreted this influence of ethnicity as a reflection of process variables rather than a static influence of ethnicity on abuse. The Eckenrode et al (1988) data are certainly consistent with Hampton's (1987) call for studies of maltreating and nonmaltreating families within ethnic groups to empirically determine specific factors that could be contributing to minority overrepresentation in child maltreatment statistics. Interestingly, when studies of maltreatment have been conducted within minority groups (White & Cornely 1981), the data are characterized by considerable within-group variance, which suggests strongly that variables other than ethnicity play a role in determining the occurrence of maltreatment.

Sex of the victim plays an important role in the incidence of sexual abuse: females are victimized at a rate estimated to be approximately four times that of males (e.g. Office of Human Development Services 1988). In a recent summary of epidemiological studies of sexual abuse conducted in 21 countries, Finkelhor (1994) concluded that prevalence estimates were not dramatically different within and outside North America. The early studies were based on cases known to child protective workers and service agencies and did not attempt to determine the occurrence of cases known only to perpetrators and victims, and extrafamilial abuse was underrepresented. Some later studies, however, have attempted to assess victim experiences (e.g. Finkelhor 1979a; Finkelhor et al 1990; Russell 1983, 1984). In a widely cited project, Russell (1983, 1984) completed a probability-based interview survey of adult women in San Francisco. Even after excluding minor events (e.g. being propositioned or being a victim of exhibitionism without contact), 16% of the sample reported intrafamilial sexual abuse prior to age 18, and 12% reported intrafamilial sexual abuse prior to age 14. Extrafamilial sexual abuse involving petting or genital sex prior to age 18 was reported by 31% of the sample, and 20% reported such activities prior to the age of 14. Because of the overlapping experiences, 38% of the sample reported at least one intra- or extrafamilial sexual abuse episode prior to age 18, and 28% reported such episodes prior to age 14. Of the extrafamilial sexual abuse prior to age 18, only 15% was perpetrated by a stranger.

Finkelhor (1979a) conducted a survey of 796 (530 female) students from six New England colleges and universities. The Finkelhor study adopted a less stringent standard of sexual victimization than did the Russell study, but a number of characteristics of the Finkelhor data are congruent with the Russell data. Over 19% of the women and 8.6% of the men reported sexual victimization. Although most episodes were single occurrences, 40% occurred for more enduring periods. The Finkelhor (1979a) data indicate that children are most vulnerable during their prepubescence, that the sexual activity usually includes genital fondling and stimulation, and that it infrequently involves intercourse. Ninety-eight percent of the female and 91% of the male victims reported that the activity was initiated by an older perpetrator, and a majority reported experiencing physical force or threats. In the Russell and Finkelhor studies, women rarely were identified as perpetrators. That 63% of the victimized women and 75% of the victimized men indicated that they had not told anyone about the events underscores the gross underestimation of the prevalence of sexual abuse.

Finkelhor et al (1990) conducted a national survey of 2626 adults of at least 18 years of age. Twenty-seven percent of the women and 16% of the men reported at least one childhood sexual abuse experience, ranging from exposure and "grabbing" to oral sex and intercourse. Abuse by strangers was more prevalent in boys (40%) than girls (21%), and abuse by family members was more likely with girls (29%) than boys (11%). Half of the offenders were characterized by the victims as authority figures. Men were the majority of offenders against both boys (83%) and girls (98%). Most offenders were at least 10 years older than the victims. Sixty percent of the male victims and 49% of the female victims reported actual or attempted intercourse. Boys were more likely (42%) than girls (33%) to have failed to disclose the abuse to anyone.

Epidemiological data do not permit unequivocal determination of the true prevalence of maltreatment, but the data do indicate that the problem is of sufficient magnitude to be a significant health risk for children. Moreover, a large percentage of children receiving services in psychiatric facilities present evidence of maltreatment (e.g. Hillard et al 1988, Leal 1976). Thus, the psychological characteristics of abuse victims is a topic worthy of consideration.

RISK FACTORS IN PHYSICAL ABUSE AND NEGLECT

Within the physical abuse and neglect literature, support is growing for models of maltreatment that reflect the interaction of parent characteristics, child attributes, and environmental factors in the occurrence of abuse or neglect (e.g. Belsky 1993, Cicchetti 1990). The appeal of these models has been facilitated by the general failure of researchers to identify significant psychopathology or other common attributes among maltreating parents (see Knutson & Schartz 1994). These models make possible the identification of child risk factors.

One of the more widely investigated risk factors in abuse and neglect has been prematurity and low birth weight. Early studies (e.g. Faranoff et al 1972; Frodi 1981; Goldberg 1979; Herrenkohl & Herrenkohl 1979, 1981; Klein & Stern 1971) provided evidence suggesting that low birth weight or prematurity placed infants at risk for physical abuse, but other studies (e.g. Egeland & Brunnquell 1979, Egeland & Vaughn 1981, Starr 1988) failed to establish this link. Leventhal (1981) challenged the low birth weight and abuse connection on methodological grounds. Benedict et al (1985) failed to identify any pregnancy history, labor, or delivery factors that were predictive of abuse. Yet, more recently, Leventhal et al (1989) assessed the four-year outcome of infants and demonstrated that the high-risk infants were more likely to be abused or neglected than a matched comparison group.

Although the evidence is inconclusive, some data suggest that low birth weight or prematurity might have an indirect influence on the emergence of abuse or neglect through a disruption of the parent-child attachment process (e.g. Goldberg 1979). Frodi et al (1978, 1981) demonstrated that premature infants emit vocalizations that evoke different responses from abusive and nonabusive parents. Related work has suggested that neonatal characteristics could impair the attachment process and result in the disrupted attachment characterizing some abused infants (e.g. Lyons-Ruth et al 1987).

Egeland & Sroufe (1981) established the presence of an anxious-resistant type of mother-child attachment in neglected children. Schneider-Rosen & Cicchetti (1984) and Crittenden (1988) also documented impaired attachment in abused and neglected children. Although the finding of insecure attachment between abusive mothers and infants has been replicated outside the United States (e.g. Browne & Saqi 1988), considerable controversy exists regarding the specific relation between attachment and abuse (e.g. Schneider-Rosen & Cicchetti 1984, Crittenden 1988). Studies have identified apparently securely attached infants who had experienced abuse, as well as insecurely attached infants who had not been abused (e.g. Browne & Saqi 1988, Schneider-Rosen & Cicchetti 1984, Schneider-Rosen et al 1985). Carlson et al (1989) suggest that the apparent inconsistencies regarding abuse and attachment could be due to the limitations of the three-category attachment classification system proposed by Ainsworth et al (1978). Carlson et al (1989) added a disorganized-disoriented category to the Ainsworth et al (1978) taxonomy and were able to identify the disorganized-disoriented attachment pattern among many maltreated infants.

Early work (e.g. Lynch 1975) yielded speculation that childhood illness could be a stressor that contributes to the emergence of abuse. Sherrod et al (1984) conducted a prospective study to evaluate the contribution of many child characteristics to the emergence of physical abuse, neglect, or failure-to-thrive. During the first three years of life, the abused children were more likely than the control group to have experienced illness and accidental injuries. Starr's (1988) retrospective case-controlled study also presented evidence that abuse may be associated with early childhood illness. The relationship between children's chronic illness and caretaker neglect has also been identified (e.g. Jaudes & Diamond 1986). A wide range of medical problems were found in 44% of 5181 children placed in protective custody in Illinois over a 22-month period (Flaherty & Weiss 1990).

Disabling conditions have also been thought to increase stress and increase risk for abuse or neglect (e.g. Friedrich & Boriskin 1976). Because disabling conditions can result in children who are difficult to manage, who evidence significant cognitive impairments, who are communicatively limited, or who are limited in mobility, disabling conditions can be conceptualized as a chronic stressor for child care providers, as well as disrupters of the attachment process. Unfortunately, most disabling conditions or their behavioral manifestations can be caused by physical abuse or neglect (e.g. Sandgrund et al 1974, Jaudes & Diamond 1985). As a result, it is not surprising that there is controversy regarding disability as a risk factor in abuse. Starr et al (1984), for example, have questioned the role of disabilities as a factor in the occurrence of maltreatment.

Until recently, there were virtually no epidemiological data on disabling conditions among abused groups. Camblin (1982) noted that almost half of the central registries failed to record disabling conditions, and other researchers suggest that many states cannot provide data on the incidence of disabling conditions of children in foster care (Hill et al 1990). Nevertheless, existing foster care data indicate that up to 20% of the children in foster care have some disabling condition (e.g. Hill et al 1990).

A recent study commissioned by the National Center on Child Abuse and Neglect (Westat 1993) followed the same general procedure as that adopted for the NIS-2. Although compromised by the fact that the disabilities were determined by CPS workers, and no law enforcement agencies were sampled, the Westat study indicated that maltreatment was 1.7 times more prevalent in disabled populations. Moreover, the analyses suggested that the disability actually played a role in the maltreatment in 47% of the cases. Another study involving the merging of the complete records of a single hospital over a 10-year period with central registry and law enforcement records identified a strong association between disabilities and maltreatment (Sullivan & Knutson 1993). Unlike the Westat (1993) study, Sullivan & Knutson (1993) used medical evidence to establish disabilities and included law enforcement records to establish extrafamilial abuse. Also, recent research with communicatively-impaired and hearing-impaired children has suggested hearing impairment could be a risk factor in physical and sexual abuse (Sullivan et al 1991).

Several studies indicate that abused and neglected children exhibit significant developmental delays. Elmer (1977) reported a long-term follow-up study in which only 2 of 33 abused children evidenced normal development after 13 years. Similarly, Sandgrund et al (1974) reported that physically abused and neglected children had significantly lower IQ scores than a comparison group matched on age, sex, and socioeconomic status. Similarly, Tarter et al (1984) found that physically abused delinquents had lower verbal IQs than did non-abused delinquents. In a study of 42 closed cases served by a family-based services program, 45% of the families had at least one child with a learning disability, mental retardation, emotional disability, or a physical handicap (Bribitzer & Verdieck 1988). In a sample of consecutively referred physically abused or neglected children seen at a single pediatric clinic, 27% had growth problems and 33% evidenced speech and language or other developmental delays (Taitz & King 1988). Kurtz et al's (1993) study of school-age and adolescent children found pervasive and severe academic problems to be associated with physical abuse and neglect.There was also an increased prevalence of abuse among the mentally retarded children in Sullivan & Knutson's (1993) study.

Although some studies (e.g. Dion 1974, Roscoe et al 1985) have indicated that attractiveness may affect punitive interactions, recent work (e.g. Herrenkohl & Herrenkohl 1981, Starr et al 1984) failed to support the position that physical anomalies contribute significantly to abuse. There are, however, data that implicate unattractive appearance as a disrupter of attachment, which may have an indirect influence on the emergence of physical abuse. For example, craniofacial deformity in infants was associated with consistently less nurturant behavior by mothers when compared with mothers of children without such deformities (Barden et al 1989). Perhaps most importantly, the mothers of the children with craniofacial anomalies were unaware of their less nurturant responses and actually rated their interactions with their children more positively than did the mothers of children without these anomalies.

BEHAVIORAL CHARACTERISTICS OF ABUSED AND NEGLECTED CHILDREN

Like health and developmental status, the behavioral characteristics of abused and neglected children may reflect either antecedents or consequences of abuse. Additionally, reports of children's behavioral characteristics are often based on observations in the presence of a child caretaker. As a result, the behavioral characteristics of the child may actually reflect interactive processes between a maltreating caretaker and a child. Although maltreated children have been described as difficult and demanding, the source of the report is often an abuse perpetrator, so the validity of the report is questionable. For example, Gregg & Elmer (1969) reported that although physicians could not discern any differences between abused and accidentally injured children in a sample of 146 infants, reports from the mothers indicated that they perceived and described the children very differently.

In a study of mothers of physically abused, physically neglected, sexually abused, and control adolescents, Williamson et al (1991) reported that the mothers of the physically abused adolescents reported more conduct-disordered problems than did the mothers of neglected or sexually abused adolescents, who in turn reported more such problems than did the nonmaltreating mothers. Mothers of neglected and physically abused adolescents also reported more socialized aggression than did the mothers of nonmaltreated adolescents. These data are somewhat compromised because the source of the ratings was the mother. Some studies have concluded that abusive parents may view an abused child more negatively and may feel less able to influence that child's behavior compared to nonabused children in the same household (e.g. Herrenkohl & Herrenkohl 1979), but other studies have failed to replicate that finding (e.g. Halperin 1983). In related work, when abusive mothers were compared to mothers who were experiencing parenting difficulties, the perceptions that abusive mothers had of their children were no more negative than the perceptions reported by nonabusive mothers (Rosenberg & Repucci 1983).

Investigators have used ratings by persons outside the family to assess the behavioral attributes of maltreated children. Reidy (1977) found that abused and neglected children were reported to evidence more behavior problems in school than were control children. Teacher ratings in the Reidy (1977) study did not differentiate between abused and neglected children. Salzinger et al (1984) reported that teachers rated the children from abusive families as displaying more negative behavior than did control children. The teachers were able to differentiate the behavior of the target child from an abusive household from that of a nontarget child from the same household. Targeted children were more likely to display conduct-disordered behaviors, to be more hyperactive, to manifest more attentional problems, and to be more anxious than their nontargeted siblings. Moreover, the nontarget children were also rated as displaying more positive behaviors than did the target children. Unfortunately, the Salzinger et al (1984) study aggregated physically abused, sexually abused, emotionally abused, and neglected children in the abused group. The negative ratings of the children could be attributable to the influence of physically abused and neglected children in the sample. Similarly, Goldston et al (1989) observed that the aggressive behavior manifested by some girls in a group of sexually abused girls receiving psychiatric services was probably a function of those girls who had been sexually and physically abused. Such data imply that some behavioral consequences of abuse might be related specifically to the type of abuse sustained. That is, sexual abuse seems to increase the probability of sexualized behavior (see below), and physically abusive parenting tends to be associated with an increase in aggressive behavior. Such a pattern was also noted by Briere & Runtz (1990) in a survey of university women among those who reported childhood histories of physical abuse or sexual abuse.

Some observational analyses of abused children also suggest that children from physically abusive homes are more aggressive than are children from nonabusive but distressed homes. George & Main (1979) reported that abused toddlers were more physically and verbally aggressive with peers and caregivers and more avoidant of other children when compared to matched control toddlers. Burgess & Conger (1977) reported that children in abusive families displayed more aggressive behavior than did children from either neglectful or control families; similar data based on home observations of abusive and nonabusive but deviant families were reported by Reid & Taplin (1976).

Observational studies by Reid et al (1981) contrasted data obtained from nondistressed families recruited from the community, from families referred for child management problems, and from physically abusive families referred for child management problems. The children from the abusive families displayed higher levels of aversive behaviors than did children from either the community control families or the nonabusive families referred for child management difficulties. Because the child management referrals reflected high levels of aggression, antisocial behavior, and conduct-disordered symptoms, the greater level of aggression displayed by the children from the abusive households is indicative of the absolute level of aversive behavior displayed by the children from abusive families. Also based on observations of families, Koverola et al (1985) described either a pattern of reciprocated coercion or a pattern of randomly coercive exchanges in families characterized by abuse. A pattern of reciprocity of aversiveness in the abusive families is consistent with Patterson's (1982) coercion theory of social aggression. Moreover, Reid et al (1982) argued from their observational data that the probability that a parent will abuse, hit, or threaten a child is, in part, influenced by the behavior problems the child presents. Thus, highly aversive children in physically abusive and aggressive households might occasion some maltreatment because of high levels of aversive behavior.

Observations of interactions between physically abusive mothers and their children also suggest that abused children comply less often than do children who are interacting with their nonabusing mothers (George & Main 1979, Schindler & Arkowitz 1986). In a naturalistic study of abused or neglected and nonmaltreated children in a day care setting, Schaeffer & Lewis (1990) noted that the abused children displayed impaired interactions with their mothers, but they did not differ significantly in their interactions with caretakers or nonabused peers. Other data are consistent with the Schaeffer & Lewis (1990) study. For example, Jacobson & Straker (1982) videotaped the interactions of child triads that included abused and control children ranging in age from 5 to 10 years. The observational records did not indicate any greater hostility or aggression by the abused children, but the abused children were less socially interactive than were the nonabused peers. Camras & Rappaport (1993) found similar results among preschoolers engaged in a conflict task. Impaired peer interactions by abused or neglected children have been noted in other studies as well (e.g. Herrenkohl & Herrenkohl 1981, Johnson & Morse 1968).

Based on observational analyses of mother-infant dyads from maltreating and nonmaltreating samples, Crittenden & DiLalla (1988) identified a pattern of child behavior in the maltreated groups that was described as compulsive compliance. This compulsive compliance was viewed as adaptive in the maltreatment setting but as maladaptive in other contexts. The Crittenden & DiLalla (1988) work implicates patterns of mother-child interaction in the ontogeny of inflexible and maladaptive behavior by abused children. These data are consistent with a study by Klimes-Dougan & Kistner (1990), in which the long-term behavioral effects of abuse were assessed by contrasting physically abused and nonabused preschool children in peer interactions. The abused children were more likely to cause distress in their peers and were more likely to respond inappropriately to distress displayed by peers. Similarly, Main & George (1985) found that signs of distress displayed by peers evoked aggressive responses from abused children in a day care setting.

In related research, when abused and neglected children were observed interacting with unfamiliar adults, they were described as evidencing wariness and patterns of avoidance (e.g. Aber & Allen 1987). Such impaired responding to adults could be a factor in the reports that abused children may be less effectively engaged in the school setting (e.g. Hoffman-Plotkin & Twentyman 1984). Interestingly, Fantuzzo et al (1988) demonstrated that peer confederates trained to increase the social behaviors of abused, neglected, or endangered children were more successful than adult caretakers.

Attention deficit hyperactivity disorder (ADHD) was first identified as a risk factor in abuse by Johnson & Morse (1968). More recently, research has suggested that parents are more physically intense and controlling in their interactions with ADHD boys (e.g. Whalen et al 1981), as well as less positive in their interactions with ADHD children (e.g. Campbell 1975, Cunningham & Barkley 1979). Consistent with these studies, Heffron et al (1987) reported that, among attention deficit disordered (ADD) children referred to a psychiatric outpatient facility, documented physical abuse was more prevalent in those patients diagnosed ADD with hyperactivity than in those diagnosed ADD without hyperactivity. In related work, Accardo et al (1990) reported higher rates of abuse and neglect in children referred for an evaluation of hyperactivity and inattention who did not qualify for a diagnosis of ADD than for those who were diagnosed with ADD. Based on models of abuse that include irritable reactivity by parents (e.g. Knutson 1978, Vasta 1982), it is possible that the irritating aspects of hyperactive behavior evoke abusive reactions from some parents. Not all data, however, are consistent with the link between ADHD symptoms and physical abuse.

An adult follow-up study of boys diagnosed with ADHD and their non-ADHD siblings indicated the retrospective recall of punitive disciplinary experiences did not differ between ADHD boys and their non-ADHD siblings (Whitmore et al 1993). When the reports of ADHD boys and their siblings were contrasted with non-ADHD community control subjects, there was a higher level of punitive parenting in the homes of referred ADHD boys, but it was not uniquely targeted at the ADHD child. Consistent with other evidence of elevated aggressiveness associated with abuse, the abused subjects in the Whitmore et al (1993) study were rated as more violent than were the nonabused subjects.

The link between aggressiveness and maltreatment was also demonstrated in a comparison of abused, neglected, and nonabused children receiving psychiatric services (Rogeness et al 1986). In that study, 16% of the female patients and 24% of the male patients could be categorized as physically abused, while an additional 27% of the boys and 17% of the girls could be categorized as neglected (with and without physical abuse). Significantly more of the abused boys and the neglected boys were diagnosed with conduct disorder; the neglected boys evidenced even more undersocialized conduct disorder symptoms than did the other two groups. For girls, significantly more of the abused group were diagnosed with socialized conduct disorder than either the neglected group or the nonabused and nonneglected group. In addition, more of the nonabused and nonneglected girls were diagnosed with dysthymia than were the abused or neglected girls. A link between physical abuse and delinquent and crime activity was also established by Widom (1989a) in a matched cohort design.

Studies of adolescent girls receiving psychiatric services have reported significantly higher rates of physical abuse, neglect, and sexual abuse in groups diagnosed with borderline personality disorder than in comparison groups of adolescent female inpatients (Ludolph et al 1990, Westen et al 1990). Abused and neglected children have also been reported to suffer from depression (Kashani & Carlson 1987, Kazdin et al 1985) and to exhibit an elevated risk for suicide (Deykin 1989, Deykin et al 1985, Kosky 1983). Unfortunately, most of these studies defined abuse or neglect as some type of contact with CPS, which suggests that sexual abuse, emotional abuse, or even risk for abuse may be included in the samples. Based on a survey of 988 adolescents, Bernstein et al (1989) reported that a history of physical abuse was associated with high levels of anxiety. In addition to depression and anxiety, research has noted elevated rates of physical abuse in the histories of self-mutilating patients (e.g. Carroll et al 1980). These data, however, have not been well replicated and it is unreasonable to assert that there is a strong abuse or neglect link to psychological problems other than the constellation of anti-social, aggressive, and conduct disordered behaviors.

TRANSGENERATIONAL PHYSICAL ABUSE

For approximately a decade, the position that abused children become the next generation of abusive parents was supported by an extensive, albeit largely nonempirical, literature (e.g. Baldwin & Oliver 1975, Gelles 1973, Green et al 1974, Justice & Justice 1976, Silver et al 1969, Spinneta & Rigler 1972, Van Stolk 1972). In time, the notion that child abuse leads to abusive parenting became axiomatic among researchers and clinicians. This uncritical accep-tance of the multigenerational hypothesis of abuse, however, was later chal-lenged because of methodological inadequacies (e.g. Berger 1980, de Lisso-voy 1979, Herzberger 1983, Kaufman & Zigler 1987, Rutter 1983, Widom 1989b). Although the methodological challenges to the transgenerational hy-pothesis of abuse have led some to argue that the hypothesis is patently false, recent reviews have suggested that even the methodologically compromised literature supports a more limited transgenerational hypothesis. For example, Widom (1989b) argued that abuse history probably increases risk for abuse, but that the vast majority of abusive parents were not themselves abused. Kaufman & Zigler (1987) estimated a 30% transgenerational persistence of child abuse on the basis of their review and reconsideration of research by others (Hunter & Kilstrom 1979, Herrenkohl et al 1983).

Hunter & Kilstrom (1979) had conducted a prospective study of mothers and newborn infants, but the one-year follow-up period was too short to garner a reliable estimate of a transgenerational pattern. Herrenkohl et al (1983) had conducted follow-up assessments of families cited for abuse or neglect over a 10-year period, as well as of a sample of matched comparison families for whom there was no reason to suspect abuse. Herrenkohl et al then contrasted the current disciplinary activities of the families with the parenting characteristics of the family of origin. By using a relatively large sample and by controlling for social desirability, economic status, and number of children in the home, Herrenkohl et al avoided some of the limitations of other studies in this area. With the prevalence of abuse histories among the abusive parents at 56% and among the nonabusive parents at 38%, Herrenkohl et al (1983) concluded that parental risk of using severely punitive discipline was increased by exposure to abusive parenting as a child. Because 53% of those who had been abused as children did not evidence abusive parenting, it was also noted that the transgenerational transmission of abuse does not reflect a simple relationship.

Evidence of an intergenerational pattern of physical abuse was also obtained by Zaidi et al (1989) from a sample of children who were consecutively admitted to a child psychiatry clinic and who had two parents who could provide data on their own childhood disciplinary experiences. The Zaidi et al (1989) study used an objective questionnaire to assess the childhood disciplinary experiences of the parents, and the abuse status of the child was established from the social history and medical records. The overall rate of physical abuse in the sample of children was 24.3%. Of the referred children who had one parent reporting an abusive childhood, 32% had been abused. A small number of children had two parents who reported a childhood history characterized by physical abuse; of those children, 50% had been physically abused. Other recent studies are consistent with a more limited multigenerational pattern of abuse or neglect (e.g. Cappell & Heiner 1990).

Although Kaufman & Zigler (1987), Pianta et al (1989), and Zaidi et al (1989) suggest that the intergenerational pattern of physical abuse may be far from a one-to-one relationship, a likely 30% transgenerational persistence rate cannot be considered trivial. Although childhood abuse histories may exert a relatively modest influence on the maltreating behaviors of parents (cf Dubowitz et al 1987), even a modest influence may be important. Of course, causal relations have not been established, and other familial or biological variables could contribute to both the abuse and the other characteristics of abused children and the families who are intergenerationally abusive (cf Di-Lalla & Gottesman 1991).

RISK FACTORS IN SEXUAL ABUSE

Beyond the demographic risk factors noted in the epidemiology section above, however, there are relatively few variables that have been established as putting children at risk for sexual abuse. Moreover, those risk factors that have been identified are associated with properties of the environment rather than with properties of the child. For example, the primary risk factors identified by Benedict & Zautra (1993) included the variables of parent absence and conflict. Seven of the eight risk factors identified by Finkelhor (1979a) were also largely familial; the eighth factor was being a socially isolated child. However, with the exception of household poverty, the risk factors identified by Finkelhor (1979a) were not replicated in a recent study (Bergner et al 1994). Although having strong needs for attention has also been identified as putting a child at risk for sexual abuse (Berliner & Conte 1990), the identification of this variable was based on reports of victims rather than on actual epidemiological studies. Data reported by Sullivan & Knutson (1993) suggest that disabilities, especially those associated with residential placements and direct physical management, might increase risk for sexual abuse. As an overall summary, however, the literature identifies sexual abuse risk as an environmental attribute rather than a child attribute.

An irony of the relative absence of child-specific risk factors in sexual abuse is that sexual abuse prevention programs target children rather than identified risk factors related to parenting, supervision, and other environmental variables (see Kolko 1988, Olsen & Widom 1993, Wurtele & Miller-Perrin 1992). However, some data indicate that sexual abuse prevention programs that involve more aggressive targeting of environmental risk factors might not meet with parental approval (Elrod & Rubin 1993). In any event, although there may be behavioral and psychological attributes associated with sexual abuse, the data do not clearly point to those attributes as risk factors.

BEHAVIORAL CORRELATES OF SEXUAL ABUSE

The sexually abusive acts to which children are exposed range from noncontact insults to penetrating violations. Age of abuse, duration of abuse, and the relationship between the victim and the perpetrator also vary. Unfortunately, the literature on the consequences of sexual abuse does not often detail the specifics of the abusive event (see Beitchman et al 1991). Yet it seems reasonable that the sexual abuse of children would have far-reaching emotional and behavioral consequences. To support such a hypothesis, one can easily point to case studies, popularized analyses of sexual abuse, surveys of child psychiatrists (e.g. LaBarbera et al 1980), or books that describe extensive clinical experience (e.g. Kempe & Kempe 1984). Such evidence, however, does not provide the empirical support necessary to make valid conclusions regarding both long-term and short-term consequences of sexual abuse. As in the case of physical abuse, understanding the consequences of sexual abuse is compromised by the lack of prospective studies and a remarkable absence of appropriate control or comparison conditions (see Beitchman et al 1991, 1992).

Survey work with victims (e.g. Finkelhor 1979a; Finkelhor et al 1990; Russell 1983, 1984) has called attention to the widespread nature of sexual abuse, but it also has called attention to one of the major problems in understanding the adverse consequences of abuse. Namely, if a large segment of the general population has experienced some event (i.e. sexual abuse) at a rate far in excess of the base rate of the presumed adverse consequences of the event, it is unreasonable to suggest that the event itself produces the adverse consequences. Importantly, no evidence exists to support the position that the base rate of the presumed adverse consequences of sexual abuse matches the large percentage of women and men reporting some sexually abusive experience. Unfortunately, those who attempt to stimulate public concern and policy changes by reporting the widespread nature of undefined sexual abuse might inadvertently be suggesting that the problem of sexual abuse is not severe in terms of its consequences. As a result, it is important to identify those sexually abusive events that are momentarily problematic for the development of the child and those sexual events that have long-term consequences. Unequivocal evidence is not yet available to make such conclusions, but suggestive evidence has emerged about the contribution of sexual abuse to emotional and behavioral problems.

In the context of assessing consequences of abuse, there is considerable evidence that sexually exploitative events are aversive to victims. For example, Finkelhor (1979a) indicates the aversive qualities of sexually victimizing experiences and suggests that even relatively minor sexually abusive acts are viewed quite negatively by respondents. Although victims do, on occasion, acknowledge some positive aspects of sexual exploitation (i.e. affection, attention, and poorly understood positive physical reactions), it would be a serious misrepresentation of available evidence to suggest that children welcome such overtures.

Most of the evidence regarding adverse effects of sexual victimization is based on clinical experience or research with clinical samples. Characteristics of sexually abused children observed clinically have included withdrawal, altered school performance, change in appearance and weight, precocious sexual behavior, conduct problems, anxiety, and depression. In short, virtually any presenting problem seen at a psychiatric clinic has been linked by some authors to sexual abuse (e.g. Adams-Tucker 1982, Friedrich et al 1986, Gold 1986, Lusk & Waterman 1986). Moreover, when clinicians who provide services to children were surveyed, those who had treated 10 or more sexually abused youngsters rated the consequences of sexual abuse as more severe than those who had treated fewer cases (e.g. LaBarbera et al 1980). Such data indicate that the greater the exposure to sexually abused youngsters, the greater the consequences that are perceived. Clinicians who provide services to children with psychiatric disorders and who serve sexually abused children will necessarily be exposed primarily to sexually abused children who are displaying such disorders. Thus, lacking routine access to appropriate comparison groups, it is not surprising that experienced clinicians report more pernicious consequences of sexual abuse. Researchers, however, often do not provide control or comparison groups.

In a recent review of research on the short-term effects of child sexual abuse, Beitchman et al (1991) noted that 43% of the studies provided no control group and only 7% provided both normal and clinical controls. Thus, most of the literature was characterized by controls or comparisons that would make any conclusions questionable. The literature also was compromised by a failure of researchers to consider covariates of abuse that could influence the outcome measures, such as family dysfunction and the other environmental factors that are associated with sexual abuse and that can influence presenting problems. Consequently, like earlier reviewers (e.g. Browne & Finkelhor 1986), Beitchman et al (1991) could only reach measured conclusions. Those conclusions emphasized that sexual abuse characterized by greater force and penetration are associated with more severe outcomes. Also, more frequent abuse and longer-duration abuse are associated with more adverse outcomes. The most consistent finding reflected in the sexual abuse literature has been that sexual abuse is associated with some degree of sexual maladjustment, often characterized by sexual precocities, promiscuity, or sexual aggression.

A recent review (Friedrich 1993) noted that sexually abused children differed from nonabused children with and without psychiatric diagnoses in their level of sexual behavior, assessed by record review, parent checklists, or self report. The presence of sexual precocities was the primary distinguishing characteristic of sexually abused and nonabused girls seen in a tertiary-care child psychiatry service (Goldston et al 1989). Similarly, Kolko et al (1988) reported that sexually abused psychiatric inpatients evidenced more sexual and internalizing behaviors than did nonabused comparison children and physically abused comparison children in a psychiatric facility. Thus, increased or atypical sexual behavior seems to be the most prevalent short-term outcome of child sexual abuse. The promiscuity or sexual precocity of sexually abused children is thought to reflect an alteration of a child's behavioral norms resulting from premature engagement in sexual activities.

Determining that sexual abuse has occurred can be a challenging diagnostic activity. Diagnosis of the occurrence of sexual abuse is usually made on the basis of two types of information. The first type is the child's description of sexual experiences. Thus, a child who offers a convincing description of sexually abusive or exploitive acts provides the clinician with needed information. Very often, however, the abused or exploited child does not provide complete, detailed, or explicit descriptions of those events, and the second type of information is used. In such cases, clinicians are forced to infer the occurrence of sexual abuse on the basis of indirect evidence consisting of expressive behavior or behavior problems purported to be associated with sexual abuse. Thus, understanding consequences of abuse can be diagnostically important. The most reliable of these markers are the sexually precocious behaviors. Descriptions of a child engaging in sexual precocities, such as adult-like sexual behavior, including lingering kisses, and the fondling of the breasts or genital areas of peers or siblings, can raise questions of sexual abuse. Unfortunately, normative data are only now emerging on sexual play (e.g. Lamb & Coakley 1993) or on the sexual knowledge and activities (e.g. Friedrich et al 1992) of abuse victims or of children in general. Such data will be critically important if consequences of sexual abuse are to be used effectively as markers of sexual exploitation. Although sexual precocities and knowledge of sexual activity well beyond what would be expected for developmental status come close to being markers of sexual abuse, they are not unequivocal (e.g. Friedrich 1993).

An extension of the link between sexual abuse and sexualized outcome is the purported association between sexual abuse and prostitution. For example, based on an assessment of 200 current and former prostitutes from San Francisco, Silbert & Pines (1981) reported that 60% had been sexually abused before age 16. Father figures were the largest proportion of perpetrators, but brothers, extended relatives, and friends of the family were also implicated. Eighty-two percent of the respondents reported experiencing some degree of force in the sexual abuse, and many reported abuse-associated injuries, pregnancies, and venereal disease. The high base-rate of runaway behavior among the juvenile prostitutes suggested that sexual abuse might be a precursor of runaway behavior. Using a matched cohort design, Widom & Ames (1994) also established a link between sexual abuse and runaway behavior, as well as between sexual abuse and arrests for adult prostitution. Importantly, however, there was no direct link between adolescent runaway activity and arrests for prostitution. Also, the association between running away and maltreatment is not confined to sexual abuse; that is, physical abuse and neglect is also associated with running away (cf Janus et al 1987, McCormack et al 1986).

A multigenerational hypothesis of sexual abuse and the development of sexually assaultive behavior following sexual abuse victimization has also received some support. In a study of grandfather-granddaughter incest, Goodwin et al (1983) noted that a majority of cases included evidence that the perpetrator had previously sexually abused his daughter or stepdaughter. Friedrich & Luecke (1988) reported data from sexually abused children, some of whom had become sexually aggressive. The more severe sexual abuse was associated with the development of sexual aggressiveness. In the matched cohort study by Widom & Ames (1994), however, arrests for sexually violent acts of rape or sodomy were associated with physically abusive backgrounds rather than with sexually abusive backgrounds. Such data are consistent with similar matched cohort designs that identify childhood physical abuse as a predictor of violent arrests (Widom 1991). Thus, it is likely that the assaultive coercive aspects of some childhood sexual abuse increase the risk for becoming a sexual abuse perpetrator.

The possible link between posttraumatic stress disorder (PTSD) and sexually abusive experiences has garnered considerable interest and attention. Although several studies have found that a significant percentage of sexually abused children meet some criteria for PTSD (e.g. Deblinger et al 1989, Kiser et al 1988, McLeer et al 1988, Wolfe et al 1994), the data are not unequivocal. For example, Deblinger et al (1989) reported that physically abused and psychiatrically hospitalized children had rates of PTSD symptoms comparable to the rates found in sexually abused children. Other severe clinical consequences associated with prolonged sexual abuse are severe personality disturbances, dissociative symptoms, and even multiple personality disorder symptoms (e.g. Anderson et al 1993, Briere & Zaidi 1989, Coons 1986, Leavitt 1994, Malinosky-Rummell & Hoier 1992, Putnam 1993). However, like PTSD, the dissociative symptoms can also be associated with physically abusive histories (e.g. DiTomasso & Routh 1993).

Alexander & Lupfer (1987) found that sexually abused female undergraduates have lower physical and family self-concepts than do nonabused women. In related work, sexual abuse histories as well as sexual and physical abuse were associated with poorer adult health and reports of greater child and adolescent illness (e.g. Golding 1994, Moeller et al 1993). Thus, a pattern of poor physical health or greater use of health services has also been related to sexual abuse, with greater problems associated with greater levels of maltreatment.

SUMMARY AND CONCLUSION

Although there is considerable evidence that the maltreatment of children is widespread and that it can have significant adverse effects on the victims, specific abuse-outcome patterns are not obvious beyond the link between physical abuse and aggression, and the link between sexual abuse and poor sexual adjustment. Although concepts of invulnerability or child resilience are somewhat controversial (see Rutter 1983), some children from severely maltreating backgrounds do not evidence apparent adverse outcomes (e.g. Farber

& Egeland 1987, Herrenkohl et al 1991). It is unknown whether the more favorable outcomes are the result of child resilience or the influence of environmental buffers. More research clearly is needed to fully understand the behavioral risks and consequences of maltreatment.

Literature Cited

Aber JL, Allen JP. 1987. The effects of maltreatment on young children's socio-emotional development: an attachment theory perspective. *Dev. Psychol.* 23:406–14

Accardo PJ, Blondis TA, Whitman BY. 1990. Disorders of attention and activity level in a referral population. *Pediatrics* 85:426–31

Adams-Tucker C. 1982. Proximate effects of sexual abuse in childhood: a report on 28 children. *Am. J. Psychiatr.* 139:1252–56

Ainsworth MDS, Blehar MC, Waters E, Walls S. 1978. *Patterns of Attachment: A Psychological Study of the Strange Situation.* Hillsdale, NJ: Erlbaum

Alexander PC, Lupfer SL. 1987. Family characteristics and long-term consequences associated with sexual abuse. *Arch. Sex. Behav.* 16:235–45

American Humane Association. 1988. *Highlights of Official Child Neglect and Abuse Reporting 1986.* Denver, CO: Am. Humane Assoc.

Anderson G, Yasenik L, Ross CA. 1993. Dissociative experiences and disorders among women who identify themselves as sexual abuse survivors. *Child Abuse Neglect* 17: 677–86

Baldwin JA, Oliver JE. 1975. Epidemiology and family characteristics of severely-abused children. *Br. J. Prev. Soc. Med.* 29: 205–21

Barden RC, Ford ME, Jensen AG, Rogers-Salyer M, Salyer KE. 1989. Effects of craniofacial deformity in infancy on the quality of mother-infant interactions. *Child Dev.* 60: 819–24

Beitchman JH, Zucker KJ, Hood JE, DaCosta GA, Achman D. 1991. A review of the short-time effects of child sexual abuse. *Child Abuse Neglect* 15:537–56

Beitchman JH, Zucker KJ, Hood JE, DaCosta GA, Achman D, Cassavia E. 1992. A review of the long-term effects of child sexual abuse. *Child Abuse Neglect* 16:101–18

Belsky J. 1993. Etiology of child maltreatment: a developmental-ecological analysis. *Psychol. Bull.* 114(3):413–34

Benedict LLW, Zautra AAJ. 1993. Family environment characteristics as risk factors for child sexual abuse. *J. Consult. Clin. Psychol.* 22:365–74

Benedict MI, White RB, Cornely DA. 1985. Maternal perinatal risk factors and child abuse. *Child Abuse Neglect* 9(2):217–24

Berger AM. 1980. The child abusing family: I. Methodological issues and parent-related characteristics of abusing families. *Am. J. Fam. Ther.* 8:53–66

Berger AM, Knutson JF, Mehm JG, Perkins KA. 1988. The self-report of punitive childhood experiences of young adults and adolescents. *Child Abuse Neglect* 12:251–62

Bergner RM, Delgado LK, Graybill D. 1994. Finkelhor's risk factor checklist: a cross-validation study. *Child Abuse Neglect* 18 (4):331–40

Berliner L, Conte JR. 1990. The process of victimization: the victims' perspective. *Child Abuse Neglect* 14:29–40

Bernstein GA, Garfinkel BD, Hoberman HM. 1989. Self-reported anxiety in adolescents. *Am. J. Psychiatr.* 146(3):384–86

Besharov DJ. 1981. Toward better research on child abuse and neglect: making definitional issues an explicit methodological concern. *Child Abuse Neglect* 5(4): 383–90

Best J. 1990. *Threatened Children. Rhetoric and Concern about Child-Victims.* Chicago: Univ. Chicago Press

Bolton FG, Laner RH. 1986. Children rearing children: a study of reportedly maltreating younger adolescents. *J. Fam. Viol.* 1(2): 181–96

Bower M. 1991. *Classification of disciplinary events and disciplinary choices as a function of childhood history.* Masters thesis. Univ. Iowa, Iowa City, IA

Bribitzer MP, Verdieck MJ. 1988. Home-based, family-centered intervention: evaluation of a foster care prevention program. *Child Welfare* 67(3):255–66

Briere J, Runtz M. 1990. Differential adult symptomatology associated with three types of child abuse histories. *Child Abuse Neglect* 14(3):357–64

Briere J, Zaidi LY. 1989. Sexual abuse histories and sequelae in female psychiatric emergency room patients. *Am. J. Psychiatr.* 146:1602–6

Brown SE. 1984. Social class child maltreatment and delinquent behavior. *Criminology* 22(2):259–78

Browne A, Finkelhor D. 1986. Impact of child sexual abuse: a review of the research. *Psychol. Bull.* 99:66–77

Browne D, Saqi S. 1988. Mother-infant interaction and attachment in physically abusing families. *J. Reprod. Infant Psychol.* 6: 163–82

Burgess R, Conger R. 1977. Family interaction patterns related to child abuse and neglect: some preliminary findings. *Child Abuse Neglect* 1:269–77

Buriel R, Loya P, Gonda T, Klessen K. 1979. Child abuse and neglect referral patterns of Anglo and Mexican Americans. *Hisp. J. Behav. Sci.* 1(3):215–27

Camblin LD. 1982. A survey of state efforts in gathering information on child abuse and neglect in handicapped populations. *Child Abuse Neglect* 6(4):465–72

Campbell SB. 1975. Mother-child interactions: a comparison of hyperactive hearing disabled and normal boys. *Am. J. Orthopsychiatr.* 45:51–57

Camras LA, Rappaport S. 1993. Conflict behaviors of maltreated and nonmaltreated children. *Child Abuse Neglect* 17:455–64

Cappell C, Heiner RB. 1990. The intergenerational transmission of family aggression. *J. Fam. Viol.* 5:135–47

Carlson V, Barnett D, Cicchetti D, Braunwald K. 1989. Disorganized/disoriented attachment relationships in maltreated infants. *Dev. Psychol.* 25(4):525–31

Carroll J, Schaffer C, Spensley J, Abramowitz SI. 1980. Family experiences of self-mutilating patients. *Am. J. Psychiatr.* 137(7): 852–53

Cicchetti D. 1990. The organization and coherence of socioemotional cognitive and representational development: illustrations through a developmental psychopathology perspective on Down Syndrome and child maltreatment. In *Nebraska Symposium of Motivation 1988. Socioemotional Development,* ed. R Dienstbier, RA Thompson, 36:259–366. Lincoln, NE: Univ. Nebr. Press

Coons PM. 1986. Child abuse and multiple personality disorder: review of the litera-

ture and suggestions for treatment. *Child Abuse Neglect* 10:455–62

Crittenden PM. 1988. Distorted patterns of relationship in maltreating families: the role of internal representation models. *J. Reprod. Infant Psychol.* 6:183–99

Crittenden PM, DiLalla DL. 1988. Compulsive compliance: the development of an inhibitory coping strategy in infancy. *J. Abnorm. Child Psychol.* 16(5):585–99

Cunningham CE, Barkley RA. 1979. The interactions of normal and hyperactive children with their mothers in free play and structured tasks. *Child Dev.* 50:217–24

Deblinger E, McLeer SV, Atkins MS, Ralphe D, Foa E. 1989. Post-traumatic stress in sexually abused physically abused and nonabused children. *Child Abuse Neglect* 13:403–8

de Lissovoy V. 1979. Toward the definition of "abuse provoking child." *Child Abuse Neglect* 3:341–50

Deykin EY. 1989. The utility of emergency room data for record linkage in the study of adolescent suicidal behavior. Special Issue: Strategies for studying suicide and suicidal behavior. *Suicide Life Threat. Behav.* 19 (1):90–98

Deykin EY, Alpert JJ, McNamara JJ. 1985. A pilot study of the effect of exposure to child abuse or neglect on adolescent suicidal behavior. *Am. J. Psychiatr.* 142:1299–303

DiLalla LF, Gottesman I. 1991. Biological and genetic contributors to violence—Widom's untold tale. *Psychol. Bull.* 109:125–29

Dion KK. 1974. Children's physical attractiveness and sex as determinants of adult punitiveness. *Dev. Psychol.* 10:722–78

DiTomasso MJ, Routh DK. 1993. Recall of abuse in childhood and three measures of dissociation. *Child Abuse Neglect* 17:477–85

Dubowitz H, Hampton RL, Bithoney WG, Newberger E. 1987. Inflicted and noninflicted injuries: differences in child and familial characteristics. *Am. J. Orthopsychiatr.* 57(4):525–35

Dukes RL, Kean RB. 1989. An experimental study of gender and situation in the perception and reportage of child abuse. *Child Abuse Neglect* 13(3):351–60

Eckenrode J, Powers J, Doris J, Munsch J, Bolger N. 1988. Substantiation of child abuse and neglect reports. *J. Consult. Clin. Psychol.* 56(1):9–16

Egeland B, Breitenbucher M, Rosenberg D. 1980. Prospective study of the significance of life stress in the etiology of child abuse. *J. Consult. Clin. Psychol.* 48:195–205

Egeland B, Brunnquell D. 1979. An at-risk approach to the study of child abuse. *J. Am. Acad. Child Psychiatr.* 18:219–35

Egeland B, Sroufe LA. 1981. Attachment and early maltreatment. *Child Dev.* 52:44–52

Egeland B, Vaughn B. 1981. Failure of "bond formation" as a cause of abuse, neglect and maltreatment. *Am. J. Orthopsychiatr.* 51: 78–84

Elmer E. 1977. *Fragile Families, Troubled Children: The Aftermath of Infant Trauma.* Pittsburgh, PA: Univ. Pittsburgh Press

Elrod JM, Rubin RH. 1993. Parental involvement in sexual abuse prevention education. *Child Abuse Neglect* 17:527–38

Fantuzzo JW. 1990. Behavioral treatment of the victims of child abuse and neglect. Special Issue: Child abuse and neglect. *Behav. Modif.* 14(3):316–39

Fantuzzo JW, Jurecic L, Stovall A, Hightower AD, Goin C, Schachtel D. 1988. Effects of adult and peer social initiations on the social behavior of withdrawn maltreated preschool children. *J. Consult. Clin. Psychol.* 56(1):34–39

Faranoff AA, Kennell JH, Klaus MH. 1972. Follow-up of low birth-weight infants: the predictive value of maternal visiting patterns. *Pediatrics* 49:287–90

Farber EA, Egeland B. 1987. Invulnerability among abused and neglected children. In *The Invulnerable Child,* ed. EJ Anthony, BJ Cohler, pp. 253–88. New York: Guilford

Finkelhor D. 1979a. *Sexually Victimized Children.* New York: Free Press

Finkelhor D. 1979b. What's wrong with sex between adults and children? Ethics and the problem of sexual abuse. *Am. J. Orthopsychiatr.* 49:692–97

Finkelhor D. 1994. The international epidemiology of child sexual abuse. *Child Abuse Neglect* 18(5):409–17

Finkelhor D, Baron L. 1986. High-risk children. In *A Sourcebook on Child Sexual Abuse,* ed. D Finkelhor, S Araji, L Baron, A Browne, SD Peters, GE Wyatt. Beverly Hills, CA: Sage

Finkelhor D, Gelles RJ, Hotaling GT, Straus MA, eds. 1983. *The Dark Side of Families: Current Family Violence Research.* Beverly Hills, CA: Sage

Finkelhor D, Hotaling GT. 1984. Sexual abuse in the National Incidence Study of Child Abuse and Neglect: an appraisal. *Child Abuse Neglect* 8:23–33

Finkelhor D, Hotaling GT, Lewis IA, Smith C. 1990. Sexual abuse in a national survey of adult men and women: prevalence characteristics and risk factors. *Child Abuse Neglect* 14:19–28

Finkelhor D, Korbin J. 1988. Child abuse as an international issue. *Child Abuse Neglect* 12 (1):3–23

Flaherty EG, Weiss H. 1990. Medical evaluation of abused and neglected children. *Am. J. Dis. Child.* 144(3):330–34

Flango CR. 1988. *State Courts' Jurisdiction and Terminology for Child Abuse and Ne-*

glect Cases. Williamsburg, VA: Natl. Cent. State Courts

Flango VE, Casey P, Dibble T, Flango CR, Rubin HT, Bross D. 1988. *Central Registries for Child Abuse and Neglect: A National Review of Records Management, Due Process Safeguards, and Data Utilization.* Williamsburg, VA: Natl. Cent. State Courts

Friedrich WN. 1993. Sexual victimization and sexual behavior in children: a review of recent literature. *Child Abuse Neglect* 17: 59–66

Friedrich WN, Boriskin JA. 1976. The role of the child in abuse: a review of the literature. *Am. J. Orthopsychiatr.* 46:580–90

Friedrich WN, Grambsch P, Damon L, Hewitt SK, Koverola C, et al. 1992 Child sexual behavior inventory: normative and clinical comparisons. *Psychol. Assess.* 4:303–11

Friedrich WN, Luecke WJ. 1988. Young school-age sexually aggressive children. *Prof. Psychol.: Res. Pract.* 19:155–64

Friedrich WN, Urquiza AJ, Beilke RL. 1986. Behavior problems in sexually abused young children. *J. Pediatr. Psychol.* 11:47–57

Frodi AM. 1981. Contributions of infant characteristics to child abuse. *Am. J. Mental Defic.* 85:341–49

Frodi AM, Lamb ME, Leavitt LA, Donovan WL, Neff C, Sherry D. 1978. Fathers' and mothers' responses to the faces and cries of normal and premature infants. *Dev. Psychol.* 14:490–98

Frodi AM, Lamb ME, Wille D. 1981. Mothers' responses to the cries of normal and premature infants as a function of the birth status of their own child. *J. Res. Pers.* 15: 122–33

Garbarino J, Stocking SH. 1980. *Protecting Children from Abuse and Neglect: Developing and Maintaining Effective Support Systems for Families.* San Francisco: Jossey-Bass

Gelles RJ. 1973. Child abuse as psychopathology: a sociological critique and reformulation. *Am. J. Orthopsychiatr.* 43:611–21

George C, Main M. 1979. Social interactions of young abused children: approach avoidance and aggression. *Child Dev.* 50:306–18

Giovannoni J. 1988. *Overview of Issues on Child Neglect. Research Symposium on Child Neglect.* Washington, DC: US Dept. Health Hum. Serv. Off. Hum. Dev. Serv. Admin. Child. Youth Fam., Child. Bur. D4-D9

Giovannoni JM, Becerra RM. 1979. *Defining Child Abuse.* New York: Free Press

Gold ER. 1986. Long-term effects of sexual victimization in childhood: an attributional approach. *J. Consult. Clin. Psychol.* 54: 471–75

Goldberg S. 1979. Premature birth: consequences for the parent-infant relationship. *Am. Sci.* 67:214–20

Golding JM. 1994. Sexual assault history and physical health in randomly selected Los Angeles women. *Health Psychol.* 13(2): 130–38

Goldston DB, Turnquist DC, Knutson JF. 1989. Presenting problems of sexually abused girls receiving psychiatric services. *J. Abnorm. Psychol.* 98:314–17

Goodwin J, Cormier L, Owen J. 1983. Grandfather-granddaughter incest: a tri-generational view. *Child Abuse Neglect* 7:163–70

Green AH, Gaines RW, Sandgrund A. 1974. Child abuse: pathological syndrome of family interaction. *Am. J. Psychiatr.* 131: 882–86

Gregg GS, Elmer E. 1969. Infant injuries: accident or abuse? *Pediatrics* 44:434–39

Halperin SM. 1983. Family perceptions of abused children and their siblings. *Child Abuse Neglect* 7:107–15

Hampton RL. 1987. Race class and child maltreatment. *J. Comp. Fam. Stud.* 18(1):113–26

Hampton RL, Newberger EH. 1985. Child abuse incidence and reporting by hospitals: significance of severity class and race. *Am. J. Public Health* 75:56–60

Hart SN, Brassard MR. 1987. A major threat to children's mental health: psychological maltreatment. *Am. Psychol.* 42(2):160–65

Heffron WM, Martin CA, Welsh RJ, Richard J, Perry P, Moore CK. 1987. Hyperactivity and child abuse. *Can. J. Psychiatr.* 32(5): 384–86

Hegar RL, Yungman JJ. 1989. Toward a causal typology of child neglect. *Child. Youth Serv. Rev.* 11(3):203–20

Herrenkohl EC, Herrenkohl RC. 1979. A comparison of abused children and their nonabused siblings. *J. Am. Acad. Child Psychiatr.* 18:260–69

Herrenkohl EC, Herrenkohl RC. 1981. Some antecedents and developmental consequences of child maltreatment. *New Dir. Child Dev.* 11:57–76

Herrenkohl EC, Herrenkohl RC, Toedter LJ. 1983. Perspectives on the intergenerational transmission of abuse. See Finkelhor et al 1983, pp. 306–16

Herrenkohl RC, Herrenkohl EC, Egolf BP, Wu P. 1991. The developmental consequences of child abuse: the Lehigh Longitudinal Study. In *The Effects of Child Abuse and Neglect,* ed. RH Starr, DA Wolfe, pp. 57–81. New York: Guilford

Herzberger SD. 1983. Social cognition and the transmission of abuse. See Finkelhor et al 1983, pp. 317–29

Hill BK, Hayden MF, Lakin CK, Menke J, Amado ARN. 1990. State-by-state data on children with handicaps in foster care. *Child Welfare* 69:447–62

Hillard JR, Slomowitz M, Deddens J. 1988. Determinants of emergency psychiatric admission for adolescents and adults. *Am. J. Psychiatr.* 145(11):1416–19

Hoffman-Plotkin D, Twentyman CT. 1984. A multimodal assessment of behavioral and cognitive deficits in abused and neglected preschoolers. *Child Dev.* 55:794–802

Hunter RS, Kilstrom N. 1979. Breaking the cycle in abusive families. *Am. J. Psychiatr.* 136(10):1320–22

Jacobson RS, Straker G. 1982. Peer group interaction of physically abused children. *Child Abuse Neglect* 6:321–27

Janus MD, McCormack A, Burgess AW, Hartman C. 1987. *Adolescent Runaways: Causes and Consequences.* Lexington, MA: Lexington

Jason J, Andereck ND. 1983. Fatal child abuse in Georgia: the epidemiology of severe physical child abuse. *Child Abuse Neglect* 7(1):1–9

Jaudes PK, Diamond LJ. 1985. The handicapped child and child abuse. *Child Abuse Neglect* 9:341–47

Jaudes PK, Diamond LJ. 1986. Neglect of chronically ill children. *Am. J. Dis. Child.* 140:655–58

Johnson B, Morse HA. 1968. Injured children and their parents. *Children* 15:147–52

Johnson CF. 1990. Inflicted injury versus accidental injury. *Pediatr. Clin. N. Am.* 37 (4):791–814

Justice B, Justice R. 1976. *The Abusing Family.* New York: Hum. Serv.

Kashani JH, Calson GA. 1987. Seriously depressed preschoolers. *Am. J. Psychiatr.* 144 (3):348–50

Kaufman J, Zigler E. 1987. Do abused children become abusive parents? *Am. J. Orthopsychiatr.* 57(2):186–92

Kazdin AE, Moser J, Colbus D, Bell R. 1985. Depressive symptoms among physically abused and psychiatrically disturbed children. *J. Abnorm. Psychol.* 94(3):298–307

Kempe CH, Silverman FN, Steele BF, Droegemueller W, Silver HK. 1962. The battered child syndrome. *J. Am. Med. Assoc.* 181: 17–24

Kempe RS, Kempe CH. 1984. *The Common Secret: Sexual Abuse of Children and Adolescents.* San Francisco: Freeman

Kiser LJ, Ackerman BJ, Brown E, Edwards NB, McColgan E, et al. 1988. Post-traumatic stress disorder in young children: a reaction to purported sexual abuse. *J. Am. Acad. Child Adol. Psychiatr.* 27:645–49

Klein M, Stern L. 1971. Low birth weight and the battered child syndrome. *Am. J. Dis. Child.* 122:15–18

Klimes-Dougan B, Kistner J. 1990. Physically abused preschoolers' responses to peers' distress. *Dev. Psychol.* 26(4):599–602

Knudsen DD. 1989. Duplicate reports of child

maltreatment: a research note. *Child Abuse Neglect* 13(1):41–43

Knutson JF. 1978. Child abuse research as an area of aggression research. *Pediatr. Psychol.* 3:20–27

Knutson JF. 1988. Physical abuse and sexual abuse of children. In *Handbook of Pediatric Psychology,* ed. DK Routh, pp. 32–70. New York: Guilford

Knutson JF, Schartz HA. 1994. Evidence pertaining to physical abuse and neglect of children as parent-child relational diagnoses. In *DSM-IV, Sourcebook.* Vol. 3, ed. TA Widiger, AJ Frances, HA Pincus, M First, W Davis. Washington, DC: Am. Psychiatr. Assoc. In press

Knutson JF, Selner MB. 1994. Punitive childhood experiences reported by young adults over a 10-year period. *Child Abuse Neglect* 18:155–66

Kolko DJ. 1988. Educational programs to promote awareness and prevention of child sexual victimization: a review and methodological critique. *Clin. Psychol. Rev.* 8: 195–209

Kolko DJ, Moser JT, Weldy SR. 1988. Behavioral/emotional indicators of sexual abuse in child psychiatric inpatients: a controlled comparison with physical abuse. *Child Abuse Neglect* 12(4):529–41

Kosky E. 1983. Childhood suicidal behaviour. *J. Child Psychol. Psychiatr. Allied Disc.* 24 (3):457–68

Koverola C, Manion I, Wolfe D. 1985. A microanalysis of factors associated with child-abusive families: identifying individual treatment priorities. *Behav. Res. Ther.* 23(5):499–506

Kurtz PD, Gaudin JM, Wodarski JS, Howing PT. 1993. Maltreatment and the school-aged child: school performance consequences. *Child Abuse Neglect* 17:581–89

LaBarbera JD, Martin JE, Dozier JE. 1980. Child psychiatrists' view of father-daughter incest. *Child Abuse Neglect* 4:147–51

Lamb S, Coakley M. 1993. "Normal" childhood sexual play and games: differentiating play from abuse. *Child Abuse Neglect* 17:515–26

Leal CA. 1976. Treatment of abused and neglected preschool children in a city hospital. *Psychiatr. Ann.* 6(5):216–26

Leavitt F. 1994. Clinical correlates of alleged satanic abuse and less controversial sexual molestation. *Child Abuse Neglect* 18 (4):387–92

Leventhal JM. 1981. Risk factors for child abuse: methodologic standards in case-control studies. *Pediatrics* 68:684–90

Leventhal JM, Garber RB, Brady CA. 1989. Identification during the postpartum period of infants who are at high risk of child maltreatment. *J. Pediatr.* 114(3):481–87

Ludolph PS, Westen D, Misle B, Jackson A,

Wixom J, Wiss C. 1990. The borderline diagnosis in adolescents: symptoms and developmental history. *Am. J. Psychiatr.* 147 (4):470–76

Lusk R, Waterman J. 1986. Effects of sexual abuse on children. In *Sexual Abuse of Young Children: Evaluation and Treatment,* ed. K MacFarlane, J Waterman, S Conerly, L Damon, M Durfee, S Long, pp. 101–20. New York: Guilford

Lynch MA. 1975. Ill-health and child abuse. *Lancet* 2:317–19

Lyons-Ruth K, Connell DB, Zoll D, Stahl J. 1987. Infants of social risk: relations among infant maltreatment maternal behavior and infant attachment behavior. *Dev. Psychol.* 23:223–32

Main M, George C. 1985. Responses of abused and disadvantaged toddlers to distress in agemates: a study in the day care setting. *Dev. Psychol.* 21:407–12

Malinosky-Rummell RR, Hoier TS. 1992. Validating measures of dissociation in sexually abused and nonabused children. *Behav. Assess.* 13:341–57

McCormack A, Janus MD, Burgess AW. 1986. Runaway youths and sexual victimization: gender differences in an adolescent runaway population. *Child Abuse Neglect* 10: 387–95

McLeer SV, Deblinger E, Atkins MS, Foa EB, Ralphe DL. 1988. Post-traumatic stress disorder in sexually abused children. *J. Am. Acad. Child Adol. Psychiatr.* 27:650–54

Moeller TP, Bachmann GA, Moeller JR. 1993. The combined effects of physical sexual and emotional abuse during childhood: long-term health consequences for women. *Child Abuse Neglect* 17:623–40

National Center on Child Abuse and Neglect. 1980. *Child Abuse and Neglect: State Reporting Laws.* US Dept. Health Hum. Serv. DHHS, Publ. No. OHDS 80–30265. Washington, DC: US Govt. Print. Off.

National Research Council Panel on Research on Child Abuse and Neglect, Commission on Behavioral and Social Sciences and Education. 1993. *Understanding Child Abuse and Neglect.* Washington, DC: Natl. Acad. Press

Nelson BJ. 1984. *Making an Issue of Child Abuse: Political Agenda Setting for Social Problems.* Chicago: Univ. Chicago Press

Nixon J, Pearn J, Wilkey I, Petrie G. 1981. Social class and violent child death: an analysis of fatal non-accidental injury murder and fatal child neglect. *Child Abuse Neglect* 5:111–16

Office of Human Development Services. 1988. *Study Findings: Study of National Incidence and Prevalence of Child Abuse and Neglect: 1988.* Washington, DC: US Dept. Health Hum. Serv.

Olsen JL, Widom CS. 1993. Prevention of

child abuse and neglect. *Appl. Prev. Psychol.* 2:217–29

O'Toole R, Turbett P, Nalepka C. 1983. Theories, professional knowledge and diagnosis of child abuse. See Finkelhor et al 1983, pp. 349–62

Patterson GR. 1982. *Coercive Family Process.* Eugene, OR: Castalia

Pelton LH. 1978. Child abuse and neglect: the myth of classlessness. *Am. J. Orthopsychiatr.* 48(4):608–17

Pianta R, Egeland B, Erickson MF. 1989. The antecedents of maltreatment: results of the Mother-Child Interaction Research Project. In *Child Maltreatment: Theory and Research on the Causes and Consequences of Child Abuse and Neglect,* ed. D Cicchetti, V Carlson, pp. 203–53. Cambridge: Cambridge Univ. Press

Plotkin RC, Azar S, Twentyman CT, Perri MG. 1981. A critical evaluation of the research methodology employed in the investigation of causative factors of child abuse and neglect. *Child Abuse Neglect* 5(4):449–55

Polansky NA, Ammons PW, Weathersby BL. 1983. Is there an American standard of child care? *Social Work* 28(5):341–46

Putnam FW. 1993. Dissociative disorders in children: behavioral profiles and problems. *Child Abuse Neglect* 17:39–45

Rausch K, Knutson JF. 1991. The self-report of personal punitive childhood experiences and those of siblings. *Child Abuse Neglect* 15:29–36

Reid JB, Patterson GR, Loeber R. 1982. The abused child: victim instigator or innocent bystander. In *Response Structure and Organization,* ed. D Berstein, pp. 47–68. Lincoln, NE: Univ. Nebr. Press

Reid JB, Taplin PS. 1976. *A social interactional approach to the treatment of abusive families.* Presented at Annu. Meet. Am. Psychol. Assoc., Washington, DC, September

Reid JB, Taplin PS, Loeber R. 1981. A social interactional approach to the treatment of abusive families. In *Violent Behavior: Social Learning Approaches to Prediction Management and Treatment,* ed. RB Stewart, pp. 88–101. New York: Brunner/Mazel

Reidy TJ. 1977. The aggressive characteristics of abused and neglected children. *J. Clin. Psychol.* 33:1140–45

Rivara FP. 1985. Physical abuse in children under two: a study of therapeutic outcomes. *Child Abuse Neglect* 9(1):81–87

Rogeness GA, Amrung SA, Macedo CA, Harris WR, Fisher C. 1986. Psychopathology in abused or neglected children. *J. Am. Acad. Child Psychiatr.* 25(5):659–65

Rohner RP, Rohner EC. 1980. Antecedents and consequences of parental rejection: a

theory of emotional abuse. *Child Abuse Neglect* 4:189–98

Roscoe B, Callahan JE, Peterson KL. 1985. Physical attractiveness as a potential contributor to child abuse. *Education* 105(4):349–53

Rosenberg MS, Repucci ND. 1983. Abusive mothers: perceptions of their own and their children's behavior. *J. Consult. Clin. Psychol.* 51:674–82

Rosenthal JA. 1988. Patterns of reported child abuse and neglect. *Child Abuse Neglect* 12(2):263–71

Russell DEH. 1983. The incidence and prevalence of intrafamilial and extrafamilial sexual abuse of female children. *Child Abuse Neglect* 7:133–46

Russell DEH. 1984. The prevalence and seriousness of incestuous abuse: step-fathers vs. biological fathers. *Child Abuse Neglect* 8:15–22

Rutter M. 1983. Stress coping and development: some issues and some questions. In *Stress Coping and Development in Children,* ed. N Garmezy, M Rutter, pp. 1–41. New York: McGraw-Hill

Salzinger S, Kaplan S, Pelcovitz D, Samit C, Krieger R. 1984. Parent and teacher assessment of children's behavior in child maltreating families. *J. Am. Acad. Child Psychiatr.* 23:458–64

Sandgrund A, Gaines RW, Green AH. 1974. Child abuse and mental retardation: a problem of cause and effect. *Am. J. Mental Defic.* 79:327–30

Sapp AD, Carter DL. 1978. *Child Abuse in Texas: A Descriptive Study of Texas Residents' Attitudes.* Huntsville, TX: Sam Houston State Univ.

Schaeffer S, Lewis M. 1990. Social behavior of maltreated children: a naturalistic study of day care. *Res. Clin. Cent. Child Dev.* 12:79–117

Schindler F, Arkowitz H. 1986. The assessment of mother-child interactions in physically abusive and nonabusive families. *J. Fam. Viol.* 1:247–57

Schneider-Rosen K, Braunwald KG, Carlson V, Cicchetti D. 1985. Current perspectives in attachment theory: illustrations from the study of maltreated infants. In *Growing Points in Attachment Theory and Research,* ed. I Bretherton, R Waters. *Monogr. Soc. Res. Child Dev.* 209(50):194–210

Schneider-Rosen K, Cicchetti D. 1984. The relationship between affect and cognition in maltreated infants: quality of attachment and the development of visual self-recognition. *Child Dev.* 55:648–58

Sedlak AJ. 1990. *Technical amendment to the study findings—National incidence and prevalence of child abuse and neglect: 1988.* Washington, DC: Natl. Cent. Child Abuse Neglect

Sherrod KB, O'Connor S, Vietze PM, Alte-meier WA III. 1984. Child health and mal-treatment. *Child Dev.* 55:1174–83

Silbert MH, Pines AM. 1981. Sexual abuse as an antecedent to prostitution. *Child Abuse Neglect* 5:407–11

Silver LB, Dublin CC, Lourie RS. 1969. Does violence breed violence? Contributions from the study of the child abuse syn-drome. *Am. J. Psychiatr.* 126:404–7

Snyder JC, Newberger EH. 1986. Consensus and difference among hospital profession-als in evaluating child maltreatment. *Viol. Vict.* 1(2):125–29

Spearly JL, Lauderdale M. 1983. Community characteristics and ethnicity in the predic-tion of child maltreatment rates. *Child Abuse Neglect* 7(1):91–105

Spinetta JJ, Rigler D. 1972. The child-abusing parent: a psychological review. *Psychol. Bull.* 77:296–304

Starr RH. 1988. Pre- and perinatal risk and physical abuse. *J. Reprod. Infant Psychol.* 6:125–38

Starr RH, Dietrich KN, Fischhoff J, Ceresnie S, Zweier D. 1984. The contribution of handicapping condictions to child abuse. *Top. Early Child. Spec. Educ.* 4:55–69

Straus MA. 1980. Stress and physical child abuse. *Child Abuse Neglect* 4:75–88

Sullivan PM, Brookhouser PE, Scanlon JM, Knutson JF, Schulte LE. 1991. Patterns of physical and sexual abuse of comunica-tively handicapped children. *Ann. Otol. Rhinol. Laryngol.* 100(3):188–94

Sullivan PM, Knutson JF. 1993. *The relation-ship between child abuse and neglect and disabilities: implications for research and practice.* Presented at Building Bridges to the Future: 10th Natl. Conf. on Child Abuse and Neglect, Pittsburgh, PA, Nov. 30–Dec. 4

Taitz LS, King JM. 1988. A profile of abuse. *Arch. Dis. Child.* 63(9):1026–31

Tarter RE, Hegedus AM, Winsten NE, Alter-man AI. 1984. Neuropsychological person-ality and familial characteristics of physi-cally abused delinquents. *J. Am. Acad. Child Psychiatr.* 23(6):668–74

Van Stolk M. 1972. *The Battered Child in Canada.* Toronto: McClelland & Stewart

Vasta R. 1982. Physical child abuse: a dual-component analysis. *Dev. Rev.* 2:125–49

Wald MS. 1976. State intervention on behalf of "neglected" children: standards for re-moval of children from their homes. Moni-toring the status of children in foster care and termination of parental rights. *Stanford Law Rev.* 28:623–707

Wald MS. 1982. State intervention on behalf of endangered children: a proposed legal re-sponse. *Child Abuse Neglect* 6:3–45

Westat Inc. 1993. *A Report on the Maltreat-ment of Children with Disabilities.* Wash-ington, DC: Natl. Cent. Child Abuse Ne-glect

Westen D, Ludolph P, Misle B, Ruffins S, Block J. 1990. Physical and sexual abuse in adolescent girls with borderline personality disorder. *Am. J. Orthopsychiatr.* 60(1):55–66

Whalen CK, Henker B, Dotemoto S. 1981. Teacher response to methylphenidate ver-sus placebo status of hyperactive boys in the classroom. *Child Dev.* 52:1005–14

White RB, Cornely DA. 1981. Navajo child abuse and neglect study: a comparison group examination of abuse and neglect of Navajo children. *Child Abuse Neglect* 5(1):9–17

Whitmore EAW, Kramer JR, Knutson JF. 1993. The association between punitive childhood experiences and hyperactivity. *Child Abuse Neglect* 17:359–68

Widom CS. 1988. Sampling biases and impli-cations for child abuse research. *Am. J. Or-thopsychiatr.* 58(2):260–70

Widom CS. 1989a. Child abuse and neglect and adult behavior: research design and findings on criminality, violence and child abuse. *Am. J. Orthopsychiatr.* 59(3):355–67

Widom CS. 1989b. Does violence beget vio-lence? A critical examination of the litera-ture. *Psychol. Bull.* 106(1):3–28

Widom CS. 1991. Childhood victimization: risk factor for delinquency. In *Adolescent Stress: Causes and Consequences,* ed. ME Colten, S Gore, pp. 201–21. New York: Aldine de Gruyter

Widom CS, Ames MA. 1994. Criminal conse-quences of childhood sexual victimization. *Child Abuse Neglect* 18(4):303–18

Williamson J, Borduin C, Howe B. 1991. The ecology of adolescent maltreatment: a mul-tilevel examination of adolescent physical abuse sexual abuse and neglect. *J. Consult. Clin. Psychol.* 59:449–57

Wissow LW, Wilson MH. 1988. The use of consumer injury registry data to evaluate physical abuse. *Child Abuse Neglect* 12(1):25–31

Wolfe DA, Sas L, Wekerle C. 1994. Factors associated with the development of post-traumatic stress disorder among child vic-tims of sexual abuse. *Child Abuse Neglect* 18:37–50

Wurtele SK, Miller-Perrin CL. 1992. *Prevent-ing Child Sexual Abuse.* Lincoln, NE: Univ. Nebr. Press

Zaidi LY, Knutson JF, Mehm JB. 1989. Trans-generational patterns of abusive parenting: analog and clinical tests. *Aggress. Behav.* 15:137–52

Zuravin SJ. 1989. The ecology of child abuse and neglect: review of the literature and presentation of data. *Viol. Vict.* 4(2):101–20

Annu. Rev. Psychol. 1995. 46:433–65

DATA ANALYSIS: Continuing Issues in the Everyday Analysis of Psychological Data

Charles M. Judd, Gary H. McClelland, and Sara E. Culhane

Department of Psychology, University of Colorado, Boulder, Colorado 80309-0345

KEY WORDS: statistical models, anova, multiple regression, hypothesis tests

CONTENTS

INTRODUCTION

The number, variety, and sophistication of data analytic procedures used by psychologists have increased rapidly in the past decade. Yet it is our impression (see also Zuckerman et al 1993) that the basic techniques of regression and analysis of variance are still not fully understood or appropriately used. This review examines issues in these basic procedures that continue to cause problems in the analysis of psychological data.

In particular, psychologists rely almost exclusively on significance tests of null hypotheses and fail to supplement the knowledge gained from such tests

0066-4308/95/0201-0433$05.00

with the knowledge to be gained from estimates of effect size (Rosenthal & Rubin 1985, Tukey 1991). Issues of statistical power are often ignored (Sedlmeier & Gigerenzer 1989). Omnibus tests of hypotheses are used when focused tests would be more appropriate and informative (Rosenthal & Rosnow 1985). There seems to be continuing difficulty with the interpretation of interactions (Dawes 1990, Rosnow & Rosenthal 1991). Finally, there is a marked tendency to ignore violations of those assumptions upon which parametric statistics are based (i.e. normality, homogeneity of variance, and independence of observations; Kenny & Judd 1986, Tomarken & Serlin 1986). The purpose of this review is to increase understanding of these five issues and to make recommendations regarding the proper application of basic data analysis techniques.

Our treatment of these issues is guided by what we call a "model comparison" approach to data analysis (Judd & McClelland 1989, Lunneborg 1994, Maxwell & Delaney 1990). This is a unified approach that emphasizes the estimation of theoretically motivated models of data rather than exclusive reliance on traditional significance testing.

THE MODEL COMPARISON APPROACH TO DATA ANALYSIS

Statisticians have long realized (Cohen 1968, Tatsuoka 1993a) that most parametric inferential tests are closely related. They all derive from the general linear model and usually rely on least-squares estimation. Psychologists, however, have traditionally learned a set of seemingly discrete statistical tests, each test appropriate for only a specific question and/or a specific data structure. As a result, when faced with the task of analyzing a data set, psychologists first attempt to locate the appropriate test in a statistics textbook and then to find the procedure for that test in the computer manual for a statistical package. This approach constitutes what we call the cookbook approach to data analysis. Although most introductory and many classic statistics textbooks are commendable on other grounds, they share this cookbook approach. The problem with this approach is that psychologists do not learn that all these statistical tests are special cases of a general model for data analysis. As a result, when faced with a question or a data structure that cannot be located in the textbook or the computer manual, they do not know how to proceed.

A "model comparison" approach (Estes 1991, Judd & McClelland 1989, Lunneborg 1994, Maxwell & Delaney 1990), on the other hand, de-emphasizes specific statistical tests in favor of developing a reasonable and theoretically guided model of the data. The purpose of data analysis "is to organize an important argument from quantitative evidence, using a form of principled rhetoric" (Abelson 1995). The model or the argument is not the same thing as the data. Rather it is a construction that the researcher derives from theoretical considerations and imposes on the data, recognizing that the goal of efficient communication requires that the model be a simplification of the data. Thus,

DATA = MODEL + ERROR[1]   1.

The contrast between the traditional approach and the model comparison approach to data analysis can be illustrated by considering a hypothetical data set described by Estes (1991). The data set, presented in Figure 1, consists of memory search times for different set sizes. The traditional approach to these data would first use analysis of variance to test whether there exist significant differences among the means for the different set sizes, and, if so, use pairwise comparison procedures to test for differences among specific pairs of set sizes. The model comparison approach, on the other hand, would propose and compare alternative models to describe the data. Possible models for these set-size data include (*a*) a simple model, specifying no effect of set size, (*b*) a linear model in which search time increases linearly with set size, and (*c*) a full model in which a separate mean is estimated for each set size. As can be seen in Figure 1, the linear model provides a much better description of the data than does the simple model, but the full model does not offer much improvement over the linear model.

As this example illustrates, the model comparison approach emphasizes building reasonable models to describe the data rather than using specific inferential tests. One starts with a series of theoretically motivated and increasingly complex models that might explain the data, and then asks whether the increase in complexity from model to model is warranted by substantially better descriptions of the data. More complex models will always do a better job of describing the data. The question is whether the reduction in the errors that separate the model and the data is worth the additional complexity.

Generally the question is answered by calculating the sum of squared errors for a simpler model (variously called the "base" or "restricted" or "compact" model) and a more complex model (known as the "full" or "augmented" model). A comparison of these two sums of squared errors yields an *F* statistic that indicates whether the additional complexity of the augmented model is worth the reduction in error. Such comparisons can be iterated as often as there are models to be compared.

It should be obvious that standard regression and analysis of variance procedures can be subsumed under the model comparison approach. Indeed, nearly all of the parametric statistical tests used by psychologists can be framed as model comparisons. But the difference between the cookbook appli-

---

[1]

   Tukey (1991) has suggested the following equivalent expression: DATA = FIT + RESIDUAL.

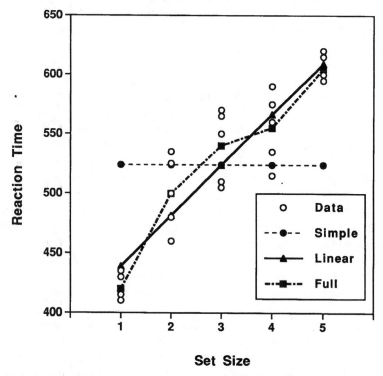

Figure 1   Model comparisons for memory search times (after Estes 1991)

cation of these tests and the model comparison approach lies in the effort extended to build theoretically reasonable models of the data. The cookbook approach imposes a set of standard or traditional models on the data with little consideration of whether the questions being asked are the most theoretically important questions that might be asked. The model comparison approach, on the other hand, examines the models that are most interesting regardless of whether they conform to those that receive standard definitions in the statistics cookbooks. Also, because the model comparison approach is a single unified approach, it frequently offers insights that the cookbook approach does not.

Because the model comparison approach emphasizes the construction of theoretically reasonable models of data, rather than set inferential tests, the emphasis is necessarily upon the models that are developed and their capacity to describe the data meaningfully and efficiently. This means that the researcher is much more likely to pay attention to the interpretation of model parameters and other indices of effect size instead of relying exclusively on the results of inferential tests. This is a distinct advantage of the approach.

Just as the emphasis in this approach is on the model as a compact description of the data, so too does the approach focus attention on the ways in which the model fails to describe the data. That is, one is led to consider the errors as well as the model. Accordingly, the detection of outliers, particularly unusual cases that are poorly described by the model, becomes more routine.

The following sections address four issues that have been the focus of much recent literature: significance tests and effect estimates; the importance of asking focused questions of data; statistical power; and the testing and interpretation of interactions. Insight into these issues is gained, we believe, through the model comparison approach.

Significance Tests and Effect Estimates

The nearly exclusive reliance of psychologists on significance testing has been justifiably criticized both in the past (Bakan 1966, Grant 1962, Morrison & Henkel 1970) and more recently (Cohen 1990, Folger 1989, Loftus 1991, Rosenthal & Rubin 1985, Rosnow & Rosenthal 1989b, Tukey 1991). This literature argues against significance testing on three grounds. First, the goal of significance testing is different from the goal of scientific inference. What we really want to ask, consistent with a Bayesian perspective on inference, is "Given the data, what is the probability of the research hypothesis?" But significance tests instead ask "Given that the null hypothesis is true, what is the probability of the data?" These two questions are obviously not the same, yet psychologists act as if they were. Moreover, even if the second question is of interest, the null hypothesis is typically not the most informative hypothesis we might test. Its rejection may not tell us much about the research hypothesis, because numerous competitors to the research hypothesis may also result in the rejection of the null hypothesis.

Second, the null hypothesis is in fact virtually never correct and so its rejection tells us little. Tukey (1991) argues that it is foolish to ask if, for example, the effects of A and B are different, because we know that they must be different, at least in some decimal place. Because null hypotheses, regardless of whether they are formulated as the absence of mean differences (i.e. the effects of A and B are identical) or as statements that two variables are unrelated, are only very implausibly correct, a significance tells us more about the power of a study than about the validity of a research hypothesis.

Third, by adopting a fixed alpha level for the rejection of the null hypothesis, one turns a continuum of uncertainty into a dichotomous reject/do-not-reject decision. This strategy has two unfortunate consequences. First, it often means that a do-not-reject decision is interpreted as an accept decision. In their review of 440 studies published in the *Journal of Abnormal Psychology,* Sedlmeier & Gigerenzer (1989) note that a substantial number of authors interpret the failure to reject the null hypothesis as a confirmation of its truth.

Cook & Campbell (1979, pp. 44–50) provide a set of compelling reasons why such interpretations are nearly always erroneous. Second, the dichotomous decision rule means that we may conclude that two studies differ in their conclusions (with one rejecting the null hypothesis and one failing to do so) when the two studies differ only in the precision with which they estimate the identical effect. To quote an apt phrase from Rosnow & Rosenthal (1989b, p. 1277), "surely, God loves the .06 nearly as much as the .05."

Although a significance test does not tell us much about the always implausible null hypothesis, it does provide us with a confidence estimate about whether the direction of the difference between the effects of A and B is positive, negative, or uncertain (Tukey 1991). Being uncertain emphatically does not mean we accept the null hypothesis. And, once we have determined the direction of an effect (as consistent or inconsistent with the research hypothesis), then we should ask the next question about the magnitude of the effect. Unlike significance tests, estimates of the magnitude of effects are generally not dependent on the power of studies; they also discourage the reliance on dichotomous decision making and inappropriate acceptance of a null hypothesis (see Zuckerman et al 1993).

Important results do not necessarily require large effect sizes. Prentice & Miller (1992) and Rosenthal (1990) demonstrate that small effect sizes can be of both theoretical and practical importance. One needs to calibrate the magnitude of an effect by the benefit possibly accrued from that effect (Tukey 1991).

Due in part to the popularity of meta-analysis and its reliance on effect size estimates, there now exists a large number of ways to estimate the magnitude of an effect (for review, see Cohen 1988, Maxwell & Delaney 1990, Tatsuoka 1993b). We offer only a general classification of effect size estimates and discuss the relative merits of each class.

The most basic estimate of effect size is the unstandardized or raw regression coefficient or slope, indicating the expected difference on the dependent variable given a unit change on the independent variable. Its interpretation depends on the meaningfulness of the measurement metrics of the independent and dependent variables. Thus, in comparing the effects of A and B, its interpretation assumes we know the number of units that actually separate treatments A and B.

If the metric of the independent variable is not known, an arbitrary one can be used to represent the A − B distinction to compute the slope. In essence, this defines a standard metric for the independent variable. For instance, if we use a contrast coding convention (or, equivalently, analysis of variance), the slope estimates the A − B difference acting as if these two treatments are two units apart (since they are coded as −1 and +1). The dummy coding convention acts as if they are only one unit apart.

Other estimates of effect size standardize on the basis of the dependent variable. For example, Cohen's d (Cohen 1988) and Hedges' g (Hedges 1992) both divide the slope by slight variations on the pooled within-group standard deviation or the root mean squared error. The advantage of this standardization is that it permits comparison of effect sizes across different dependent variables having different metrics. The disadvantage is that if the dependent variable has a common and well-known metric (e.g. pounds or years or time units), it seems peculiar to talk in terms of standard deviation units rather than in terms of the original metric. Note that these estimates require either knowledge of the metric of the independent variable or an arbitrary one. Cohen's d and Hedges' g both assume a metric for the independent variable equivalent to the dummy coding convention.

Finally, a number of estimates of effect size standardize on the basis of both the independent and dependent variables. Examples include standardized regression coefficients, correlations, proportional reduction in error measures (e.g. Judd & McClelland 1989, Maxwell & Delaney 1990), and the binomial effect size display (Rosenthal & Rubin 1982). The advantage of this dual standardization is that it permits one to compare effect size estimates for both independent and dependent variables that have different metrics. For example, we can compare the correlation between stress and coping in two different studies that use entirely different measures of both variables. The disadvantage of standardized effect estimates, however, is that they confound differences in variance between studies with differences in effect sizes. Accordingly, the tendency to compare correlation coefficients obtained in two different studies (or groups) is problematic. Differences in the variability of the independent variable in the two studies may result in different correlations even when the two raw slopes are equivalent. Given a common metric for both the independent and dependent variables, raw slopes ought to be compared.

One of the distinct advantages of the model comparison approach to data analysis is that both unstandardized and standardized effect estimates are provided automatically. First, in estimating a model, raw regression slopes for every effect of interest are always generated. One cannot simply rely on inferential statistics; one necessarily focuses on the parameter estimates that constitute the model. Second, statistical inference in this approach involves the comparison of two models, differing in whether one or more additional parameters are estimated. This comparison focuses on the reduction in error achieved by the additional parameters. Expressed as a proportion of the error in the compact or restricted model, this measure is a standardized effect size estimate.

As an example of interplay of models, significance tests, and effect sizes in the model comparison approach, consider the following models that correspond to the models of Figure 1, where *Lin, Quad,* etc. refer to orthogonal contrast codes for linear, quadratic, etc effects:

Simple: $\hat{Y} = 524;$ $SSE = 108,200$
Linear: $\hat{Y} = 524 + 42.5Lin;$ $SSE = 17,887.5$
Full: $\hat{Y} = 524 + 42.5Lin - 6.1Quad + 7.5Cub + 0.64Quart;$ $SSE = 12,350$

The linear model is an important improvement over the simple model, with a proportional reduction in error of PRE = (108,200 − 17,887.5)/108,200 = 83%. For a traditional significance test, PRE can be compared to critical values (Judd & McClelland 1989) or converted to an F statistic [in this case, $F(1,23)$ = 116.25]. The parameters of the model provide an efficient description of the data: The average reaction time is 524 ms and reaction times increase (decrease), on average, by 42.5 ms for each increase (decrease) in set size. The full model, which allows for deviations from linearity, improves over the linear model by PRE = 31%, or about 10% for each additional parameter. Although this improvement is not quite significant according to the traditional comparison [$F(3,20)$ = 2.99], the effect size of .31 reminds us not to dismiss the hypothesis of nonlinearity. Thus, the model comparison approach turns the focus on models of data and the effect sizes of those models, while still allowing traditional significance tests.

Focused Comparisons

The model comparison approach to data analysis encourages asking the questions that are of primary theoretical interest to the researcher rather than the relatively unfocused questions that are typical of the traditional approach. The model comparison approach is thus consistent with a growing trend to recommend the use of specific focused comparisons or contrasts among cell means in an experimental design rather than reliance on omnibus, multiple-degrees-of-freedom-in-the-numerator (MDFN) tests (Judd & McClelland 1989, Maxwell & Delaney 1990, Rosenthal & Rosnow 1985).[2]

This recommendation stems from three problems with MDFN tests. First, the rejection of an omnibus null hypothesis indicates that there are at least some differences among treatment means but does not locate those differences. The omnibus test must always be followed by more focused comparisons in order to identify significant treatment differences. Second, if the researcher has a hypothesis about particular treatment differences, exclusive

---

2

This discussion is phrased in analysis of variance terms, involving comparisons of cell means. The same problems exist in multiple regression where an omnibus test of the overall reliability of R^2 is typically uninformative about particular research hypotheses.

reliance on an MDFN test can lead to both biased conclusions and the loss of statistical power. Bias occurs when there are reliable differences among treatments that do not follow the researcher's predictions. A conclusion about the reliability of those predictions based on the results of the omnibus test is then unwarranted. On the other hand, if the researcher's hypothesis is exclusively correct, then reliance on an MDFN test results in a substantial loss of statistical power because the sum of squares associated with the predicted treatment difference is diluted by dividing it by multiple irrelevant degrees of freedom. Finally, substantial bias can occur in repeated-measures or mixed-model analysis of variance designs when an omnibus test is conducted using the traditional univariate analytic approach. The omnibus test makes a strong assumption about the homogeneity of variances and covariances of the repeated observations, i.e. the homogeneity of treatment-difference variances assumption (Maxwell & Delaney 1990) or, equivalently, the sphericity assumption (Huynh & Feldt 1970). Omnibus tests of within-subject differences are far from robust to violations of this assumption (McCall & Appelbaum 1973). Focused single-degree-of-freedom comparisons involving within-subject treatment differences do not require this assumption if the correct contrast-specific error term (rather than the omnibus or pooled-error term) is used (Judd & McClelland 1989, Lewis 1993, Maxwell & Delaney 1990).

The application of single-degree-of-freedom contrasts within a particular experimental design is not always straightforward. Consider a simple experimental design with four treatment groups, A, B, C, and D. Many sets of three orthogonal contrasts can be used to decompose the total between-group variation. Three possibilities are:

	A	B	C	D
Set 1	3	-1	-1	-1
	0	2	-1	-1
	0	0	1	-1
Set 2	-3	-1	1	3
	-1	1	1	-1
	1	-3	3	-1
Set 3	1	1	-1	-1
	1	-1	1	-1
	1	-1	-1	1

Each of these sets partitions the total between-group sum of squares in a different way. The first set of codes, known as Helmert codes, compares each group with all subsequent groups, thereby assuming that they are ordered. The codes in the second set are known as orthogonal polynomials. Their interpretation as such assumes that the four groups vary along a single dimension in the specified order and at equal intervals. The third set of codes is equivalent to the traditional decomposition of a 2×2 factorial design with the groups arranged as follows:

	Column Factor	
Row Factor	A	B
	C	D

The first, second, and third codes in this last set estimate the row main effect, the column main effect, and the row by column interaction, respectively. Thus, factorial analysis of variance can be seen as the application of a particular set of contrast codes to a one-way layout of groups (Judd & McClelland 1989, Rosenthal & Rosnow 1985).

The choice of any particular set of contrast codes depends on theoretical assumptions about the underlying constructs or processes that differentiate the groups. If these assumptions are incorrect, then one can be seriously misled by an inappropriate choice of contrast codes. For example, consider the following treatment group means:

A	B	C	D
2	0	0	-2

Assume that these means are generated by the additive effects of two crossed factors (i.e. codes 1 and 2 of set 3). The mean square associated with each of these two codes equals $4n$, where n is the group size. If one mistakenly tested the codes of set 1, the mean square for the first code of that set equals $5.33n$. Depending on the size of the mean square error, one could easily find this last contrast to be reliable while neither of the earlier two that actually capture the generating process are statistically significant. It is easy to turn this example around, so that some of the codes in set 3 have larger mean squares than those of set 1, even though the underlying generating process might best be described by set 1.

The lesson to be learned from these examples is that the choice of contrast codes depends on theoretical considerations or hypotheses about underlying processes responsible for group differences. No one set of codes is necessarily superior to any other set of codes except as a result of theoretical considerations. The data can only lend credence to a particular hypothesis concerning processes responsible for group differences. Confirmation of those processes is impossible except through extended replication.

The sets of contrast codes given above all involve orthogonal contrasts within sets, assuming equal treatment group sizes. Even if group sizes are unequal, they still ask orthogonal questions about differences among group means. Occasionally, one might be interested in simultaneously testing contrasts that are not orthogonal. Maxwell & Delaney (1990) and Rosenthal & Rosnow (1985) suggest that the mean squares associated with such nonorthogonal contrasts be computed in the usual way. Then the interpretation of the results should include an acknowledgment that the questions being asked about the differences among group means are partially redundant.[3]

When observations between groups are not independent of each other (e.g. they come from the same subject or are grouped in other ways), then contrasts must be computed within subjects. For each contrast, one computes a contrast score for each subject, weighting the subject's score in each condition by the appropriate contrast weight and summing these across conditions. One then computes the mean contrast score across subjects and uses a single sample t test to examine whether its mean differs from zero. The mean square error in this test equals the mean square due to the interaction between the within-subject contrast and subjects.

In a design with p conditions and subjects measured in each condition, a total of $p - 1$ orthogonal within-subject contrast scores can be computed. Each is tested by dividing its mean square by its unique error mean square. This approach is consistent with the multivariate approach to analyzing within-subject designs (Lewis 1993, O'Brien & Kaiser 1985).[4] The use of unique error terms for each within-subject contrast avoids the problematic assumption that the variance of all within-subject differences are homogeneous. This assumption arises when one uses a pooled error term, as is standard in the univariate repeated measures analysis of variance. Accordingly, adjustments to the resulting Fs to allow for heterogeneity of treatment differences (Box 1954, Geisser & Greenhouse 1958, Huynh & Feldt 1976) are unnecessary.

Decisions about within-subject contrast codes involve the same theoretical considerations as decisions about between-subject contrast codes. If the within-subject observations can be ordered along a single underlying continuum such as time, then orthogonal polynomial codes may be appropriate. The resulting contrast scores then amount to within-subject slopes that estimate changes in observations over time. If there is a sufficient number of observations for each subject, these slopes can be computed even if there are missing

---

[3]
 Alternatively, one might compute mean squares and F statistics for each nonorthogonal contrast, partialing out the others. In a model comparison format, this is easily done by including the entire set of nonorthogonal codes in an augmented model and testing each in turn by deleting it to form a compact model. One should recognize, however, that the comparison among cell means coded by a particular contrast changes when additional nonorthogonal contrasts are controlled. Hence, when testing a contrast that controls for other partially redundant contrasts, one may not be making the comparison one wishes to make.

[4]
 The multivariate approach uses multivariate procedures to examine the omnibus question of whether any of the mean contrast scores are different from zero. This approach tests the set of $p - 1$ orthogonal within-subject contrasts simultaneously.

observations and differences among subjects in the patterns of missing observations. One can then test the reliability of these within-subject slopes by asking whether their means differ from zero. One can also ask whether the slopes depend on various between-subject variables of interest. These analyses of within-subject slopes are equivalent to recent recommendations concerning the analysis of growth or change (Bryk & Raudenbush 1987, Francis et al 1991, Goldstein 1987, Rogosa et al 1982), where separate growth functions are estimated within each subject (essentially regressing the dependent variable on time and other variables within each subject) and then differences in growth functions are examined between subjects.

The simultaneous testing of numerous contrasts, whether within or between subjects, necessitates consideration of inflated α levels. We selectively review the extensive literature on the topic of controlling experiment-wise error rates when multiple comparisons are tested (Hochberg & Tamhane 1987, Toothaker 1991, Wilcox 1985). With an a priori set of κ contrasts, the Bonferroni adjustment to control experiment-wise error rates at level α requires that one uses α/κ as the nominal level in the test of any individual contrast. Rosenthal & Rubin (1984) and Tukey (1991) suggest that the experiment-wise error rate need not be divided up equally among the κ planned contrasts. Contrasts that are more important may be given a greater share of the experiment-wise error rate in order to decrease the chance of Type II errors for such tests. Ryan (1985) correctly notes that these weighted Bonferroni adjustments also imply unequal tolerance of Type I errors across different contrasts.

Recent work has suggested that the Bonferroni adjustment may be overly conservative. This is clearly the case when nonorthogonal contrasts are used (Maxwell & Delaney 1990). Additionally, Holland & Copenhaver (1988) and Klockars & Hancock (1992) review modifications to the standard Bonferroni adjustment that result in greater power. Although such modifications may often be appropriate, the increase in power over the traditional Bonferroni adjustment is usually not large. These modifications also have the disadvantage of not allowing the estimation of confidence intervals. The standard Bonferroni procedure is also overly conservative when the planned contrasts are the set of $p(p - 1)/2$ pairwise comparisons among the means of all p groups, since these are necessarily nonorthogonal. Tukey's WSD procedure is preferred in this case (Maxwell & Delaney 1990).

Where contrasts are unplanned and follow upon the inspection of the group means, the Scheffé procedure (1953) is appropriate but conservative. The Scheffé procedure and the one-way omnibus test of no group differences are inextricably linked: Unless the overall hypothesis of no group differences is rejected, none of the possible contrasts will be significant using the Scheffé procedure. We feel that the very conservative Scheffé procedure ought to be used only rarely.

Among other widely used procedures for multiple comparisons, Fisher's LSD (1935) and Newman-Keuls's (Keuls 1952, Newman 1939) are the two most popular (Jaccard et al 1984). Unfortunately, these procedures fail to control the experiment-wise error rate at the specified level (Keselman et al 1991, Maxwell & Delaney 1990) unless the omnibus null hypothesis of no group differences is true. Keselman et al (1991) have suggested appropriate modifications.

Statistical Power

Due largely to Cohen's recommendations (1969, 1988, 1992), there has been a dramatic increase over the past 20 years in the attention paid to issues of statistical power. Discussions of power calculations and factors affecting power are now a routine part of statistics and data analysis textbooks. Numerous articles have appeared comparing the power benefits of alternative design and analysis strategies (e.g. Maxwell et al 1991). A number of computer programs exist for conducting power analyses (reviewed in Goldstein 1989). And a necessary component of research proposals, if they are to compete successfully for funding, is a section claiming to demonstrate adequate power for the proposed work. This increased attention to issues of power does not seem to be reflected, however, in the actual conduct of research. Sedlmeier & Gigerenzer (1989) report that studies recently published in the *Journal of Abnormal Psychology* typically have no greater power than those reviewed in a similar survey conducted 25 years ago (Cohen 1962). In fact, due to an increase in attention paid to the issue of adjusting alpha levels to compensate for use of multiple comparisons or contrasts, the power of many of the statistical tests in recent studies is lower than that of tests in the earlier studies. Thus, the adjustment strategies for multiple contrasts have power implications that are often unrecognized.

In any study, four factors are intimately related: the power of the study, the effect size, the sample size, and the α level. Any three of these determine the fourth. The common assumption in the literature seems to be that in order to increase statistical power, one must increase a study's sample size. Increases can also be produced by changing the other two factors, effect size and α level. These other strategies deserve greater attention, particularly because subjects should be seen as a scarce and valuable resource (Engeman & Shumake 1993).

Changing the α level to achieve greater power may seem like a radical recommendation. However, as we have said earlier, there is nothing sacred about an alpha level arbitrarily set at .05. When the sample size is small and constrained, an increase in power at somewhat greater risk of Type I error may be worthwhile. This is often true in applied research. If one is evaluating a large intervention that is already in place, Type II errors may be particularly costly (Cook & Campbell 1979, Judd & Kenny 1981).

Increases in power can also be produced by changing a study's design so that a larger effect size is anticipated. One way to do this is to reduce the error variance of the dependent variable. The two kinds of error, systematic and random, require different strategies (Maxwell et al 1991). In the case of random errors, or unreliability, power can be increased by standard methods of improving the reliability of the dependent variable, such as the use of better measures and of multiple measures. In the case of systematic error, power can be increased by controlling the error through design modifications or the inclusion of covariates. Thus power increases can be achieved by more complete models of data.

One design modification that increases power involves the use of a blocking factor and random assignment of subjects to levels of the experimental factor within levels of the blocking factor. The blocking factor is then included in the analysis of variance in order to reduce the error variance. If the blocking factor is a pretest measurement of the dependent variable or some other variable known to be linearly related to the dependent variable, an analysis of covariance that allocates only a single degree of freedom to the blocking factor has more power. A number of papers have explored the relative advantages of these two analytic strategies (e.g. Feldt 1958, Maxwell et al 1984). A generally unwise procedure in this sort of pretest-posttest design is the use of a repeated measures analysis of variance that treats time as a within-subject factor. Such an analysis will generally have less power than the analysis of covariance and may have even less power than the analysis of variance of the posttest scores that ignores the pretest scores (Huck & McLean 1975, Jennings 1988, Judd & McClelland 1989).

An inappropriate approach to power analysis is common in many research proposals. At the suggestion of R Dawes (personal communication), we call this a "backward power analysis." A researcher adopting this approach starts with a desired level of power, a set α level, and a sample size constrained by financial and/or practical limits. The researcher then derives the effect size that will yield the necessary power, calls this the predicted effect size, and confidently assures the reader that the proposed study has adequate power. Such an approach is misleading at best.

Interactions

As research in a domain becomes increasingly sophisticated, researchers generate hypotheses that the effect of one independent variable on the dependent variable depends on the level of another independent variable, that one independent variable moderates the effect of another, or, equivalently, that two independent variables interact to affect the dependent variable. Data analysis techniques must be able to test these sophisticated hypotheses. Unfortunately, a review of the recent literature in psychology reveals an embarrassing confusion about the definition, testing, power, and interpretation of interaction hypotheses not only for continuous variables but even for the simplest 2×2 experimental designs.

DEFINITION AND TESTING   When the sum of the separate effects of two independent variables does not equal their joint effect, the two variables are said to interact. For both categorical and continuous variables X and Z, the appropriate test of an interaction is the test of whether $\beta_3 = 0$ for the product XZ in the following model:

$$Y_i = \beta_0 + \beta_1 X_i + \beta_2 Z_i + \beta_3 X_i Z_i + \varepsilon_i. \qquad 2.$$

In the model comparison approach, this model is compared to a model without the product term (i.e. an additive model). For two-level categorical variables, X and Z represent codings (dummy, effects, or contrast). The model shown here demonstrates that the interaction is the residual after removing the separate effects of X and Z (Cohen 1978).

At least three misguided alternatives for defining and testing interactions have been proposed. First, on the basis of an unwarranted concern about the collinearity between XZ and its components, some researchers (e.g. Morris et al 1986) have proposed that the interaction be assessed by testing the product without controlling for its components. However, the presence of the collinearity that motivates this suggestion means that testing XZ rather than its residual confounds the separate effects with the interaction (Cronbach 1987, Dunlap & Kemery 1987). Also, this test is not invariant under alternative codings or linear transformations, and is thus dependent on a researcher's arbitrary scaling choices.

Second, Bobko (1986) has proposed testing alternatives to cross-over interactions. For example, a $[-1, -1, -1, +3]$ contrast coding might be used for the four cells of a 2×2 design. Although there may be valid reasons for expecting and testing such a pattern of means, it is not appropriate to refer to it as an interaction because it confounds traditional main effects and interactions (Dawes 1990; Rosnow & Rosenthal 1989a, 1991).

Third, researchers sometimes claim interactions when a test reveals an effect of X on Y for one group (or at one level of Z) but a separate test finds no such effect for another group (or at another level of Z). This is a problematic claim because of the implicit acceptance of the null hypothesis in the second test. The difference supporting the claim of an interaction might be trivial if, for example, the first test statistic barely exceeds its critical value and the second barely falls short of its critical value. Comparing correlation coefficients between groups as a test of interaction is also inappropriate because there may be different standardizations of the variables within each group. For example, if the variance of X is different within each group, the rs for the groups can be different even though the proper test of the XZ term reveals no interaction. Alternatively, the rs for the groups can be the same even though the proper test of the XZ term reveals an interaction. In short, there is no valid alternative to defining and testing the interaction as the residual product XZ after removing the separate effects of X and Z.

Aiken & West (1991) and Jaccard et al (1990) provide excellent advice on testing and interpreting interactions for continuous variables. Care must be taken not to introduce spurious interactions or to preclude finding interactions by using median splits (Maxwell & Delaney 1993) or by failing to test the nonlinearity of X and Z by including their quadratic terms X^2 and Z^2 (Lubinski & Humphreys 1990). Standardized regression weights (called "beta weights" in some computer programs) require special care in calculation and interpretation (Aiken & West 1991, Friedrich 1982) because the product of two standardized components does not equal the standardized value of the product of the raw components.

POWER   Several issues of statistical power plague the testing of interactions. In a 2×2 design the test of the interaction involves a comparison of the average of two cell means (one diagonal) against the average of the other two cell means (the other diagonal) just as tests of the row and column main effects involve comparisons of averages of two cell means. In multiple regressions including product variables, the test of the interaction coefficient is just like the test of any other coefficient. So, in principle, the test of the interaction potentially has equivalent statistical power to tests of the component effects. However, in practice, the statistical power of the interaction is greatly reduced when the moderating effect of Z is not large enough to reverse the sign of the slope of the X-Y relationship within the range of X and Z in the data collected. Not having a sign reversal for the slope in the range of the data constrains the magnitude of the interaction and thereby reduces the power of the test of the interaction (McClelland & Judd 1993). When sign reversals make no sense theoretically, it is useful to compare the obtained interaction coefficient to the theoretical maximum interaction given the estimated coefficients for the components of the interaction.

ANOVA designs in which one or more variables have multiple levels exacerbate the power problems considered earlier when there are multiple degrees of freedom in the numerator (MDFN). If X has p levels and Z has q levels, then the omnibus test of the interaction has $(p-1)(q-1)$ degrees of freedom for the numerator. If the interaction is concentrated in a few possible patterns (say, the linear × linear interaction), then it might be lost statistically in the MDFN omnibus test. The omnibus test implicitly includes tests of, for example, the quartic × quintic interaction, an interaction that is unlikely to be hypothesized. This problem can be solved by testing specific one-degree-of-freedom contrasts (orthogonal to the main effects) when particular interactions are expected.

Interactions involving continuous variables (including tests of the homogeneity of regression in ANCOVA) have an additional power problem (McClelland & Judd 1993). A key determinant of the power for detecting an interaction is the residual variance of the product XZ after controlling for the separate components. The residual variance of the product, and hence the statistical power for the interaction, is greatly reduced for variables whose distributions are center-peaked and asymmetric compared to variables whose values are concentrated at the extremes (as they are in 2×2 experimental designs, for example). Also, nonlinear scales and measurement error have especially deleterious effects on the identification of interactions involving continuous variables (Aiken & West 1991, Busemeyer & Jones 1983).

INTERPRETATIONS IN INTERACTION MODELS   Once detected, interactions and moderating effects are difficult to interpret. Rosnow & Rosenthal (1989a, 1991) and Meyer (1991) have debated whether ANOVA interactions can be interpreted and described by examining graphs of cell means. Cell means necessarily include not only the interaction but also the main effects so that what is seen in the graph is not equivalent to what is tested statistically. For categorical independent variables, Judd & McClelland (1989), Tukey et al (1991), and

Table of Means

		Z1	Z2	Z3
Means	X1	32	26	17
	X2	17	19	9

Classical ANOVA Decomposition
(Sweeping out Common and Main effects)

			Z1	Z2	Z3	
X x Z Interaction	X Main	X1	2.5	-1.5	-1	5
	Effects	X2	-2.5	1.5	1	-5
Z Main Effects	Common		4.5	2.5	-7	20

Simple Effects of Z at Levels of X
(Recombining Common, Z, and X x Z)

			Z1	Z2	Z3	
Z@X	X Main	X1	27	21	12	5
(Z Effects by Rows)	Effects	X2	22	24	14	-5

Figure 2   Tabular decomposition of ANOVA table (after Tukey 1991).

Tukey (1991) suggest tabular decompositions of cell means such as those shown in Figure 2. Rosnow & Rosenthal (1989a) prefer the classical decomposition (the middle tables in Figure 2) because it depicts the interaction with the main effects removed. Tukey (1991) is not averse to recombining a main effect and an interaction (the bottom tables in Figure 2) in order to examine the conditional effect of one variable at fixed levels of the other variable. Graphing these conditional effects facilitates understanding of how the effect of one variable depends on the levels of the other (see Figure 3). If there were no interaction, the lines in Figure 3 would be superimposed. Cleveland (1993) illustrates other techniques for producing conditioning plots or co-plots. Schmid (1991) provides another useful graphical technique for displaying and comparing the magnitudes of main effects, interactions, and the residual errors (see Figure 4). Because interactions are sufficiently difficult to interpret, it is useful to examine them with many different tabular and graphical techniques.

Interpreting interactive models with continuous variables or with 0–1 dummy codes for categorical variables is even more difficult. Expressing the model as the relationship between the dependent variable and one of the independent variables, as in the following equation, leads naturally to the correct interpretation (Cohen & Cohen 1983, Judd & McClelland 1989):

$$Y_i = (\beta_0 + \beta_2 Z_i) + (\beta_1 + \beta_3 Z_i) X_i + \varepsilon_i. \qquad\qquad 3.$$

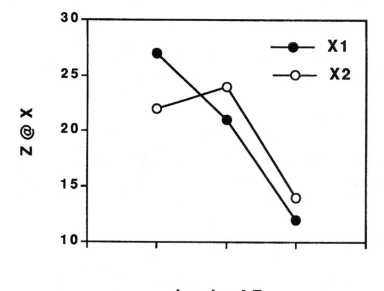

Figure 3 Graph of Z@X to examine interaction (lines would be superimposed if no interaction).

The term in the second set of parentheses represents the relationship or slope between X and Y at particular levels of Z. The fact that this slope depends on Z indicates the interaction or the moderating effect of Z on the X-Y relationship. (Equivalently, one could express the interaction in terms of the relationship between Z and Y as moderated by X.) The coefficient β_3 represents the interaction: For a unit change in Z, the slope of the X-Y relationship is moderated (changed) by amount β_3.

When a variable W is partially redundant with X and Z, it is well known that adding it to a regression model changes the interpretation of the effects tested by the partial regression coefficients for X and Z. There are additional interpretation complications when $W = XZ$. Most linear model tests are invariant under linear transformations of the variables; however, in the interaction model, the test of X is not invariant under linear transformations of Z. As a consequence, it is not appropriate, as has been done in a number of published studies, to interpret tests of X and Z as tests of main effects analogous to those in classical ANOVA designs. The previous equation shows that the coefficient β_1 does not represent the main or direct effect of X; instead, it is the slope of the X-Y relationship when and only when $Z = 0$. Depending on the scaling of Z, a value

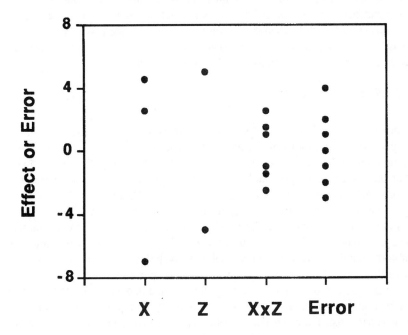

Figure 4 The effects (the classical decomposition from Figure 2) and the errors (after Schmid 1991).

of zero may not even be meaningful. By subtracting the mean so that the average value of Z is zero, the test of β_1 becomes a test of the effect of X on Y when Z is at its average value. This is not the same as the average effect of X, nor is it the same as a main effect in ANOVA. The main or average effect of X is estimated by β_1^* in the following model, which does not include the interaction:

$$Y_i = \beta_0 + \beta_1^* X_i + \beta_2^* Z_i. \qquad\qquad 4.$$

β_1 is assured to equal β_1^* only for balanced designs with equal numbers of observations in each cell and when Z has a mean of zero. The error term from the interaction model can be used to test the average effect represented by β_1^*.

ASSUMPTIONS: VIOLATIONS AND SOLUTIONS

Parametric statistical analyses assume that errors or residuals are independently and randomly sampled from a single normally distributed population. This assumption is often expressed as three separate assumptions about the distribution of errors: 1. normality, 2. homogeneity of variance, and 3. independence. Recent studies have investigated the magnitude and direction of the bias that can result when these assumptions are violated. We first consider distributional problems (i.e. nonnormality and heterogeneity of variance) and their remedies and then turn to independence problems.

Distributional Problems

NORMALITY   Traditional wisdom asserts that parametric tests are robust with respect to departures from normality. For example, numerous analytic and simulation studies (e.g. Boneau 1960, Glass et al 1972, Ito 1980) have shown that the t statistic is reasonably robust if group sample sizes are large and approximately equal, and two-tailed tests are used. Bradley (1977, 1982) has questioned these conclusions, arguing that violations of normality are more common and more severe in distributions of real data than in the distributions analyzed in the robustness literature. Micceri (1989) examined the distributions of 440 large data sets from educational and psychological research. Consistent with Bradley's claims, he found that almost none showed the normal shape and that many departed from the normality in ways that had not been considered in the robustness literature. Sawilowsky & Blair (1992) report simulation results based on the distribution shapes that Micceri found to be common in educational and psychological research. Their conclusions are consistent with traditional wisdom even for these more realistic distributions. That is, they found t tests to be relatively robust to Type I errors for large and approximately equal sample sizes. They also found *t* to be relatively robust with respect to Type II errors, although they agree with other authors (Blair & Higgins 1980, 1985) that nonparametric procedures may be more powerful than parametric tests for nonnormal distributions. However, this difference may be entirely attributable to the presence of a few outliers (Zimmerman & Zumbo 1993).

HOMOGENEITY OF VARIANCE   Traditionally, violation of the homogeneity of variance assumption in ANOVA has been viewed as relatively unproblematic if there are an equal number of observations in the cells of an experimental design (Glass et al 1972). Recent research has shown, however, that the Type I error rate may be somewhat affected if heterogeneity is marked, even if cell sizes are equal (Harwell et al 1992). This seems to be particularly true as the number of cells in the design increases (Rogan & Keselman 1977, Tomarken & Serlin 1986, Wilcox et al 1986). If cell sizes are unequal, ANOVA is not robust to violation of the homogeneity assumption. The direction of the bias in the Type I error rate depends on the match between cell size and variance size. When the larger cells have the larger variance, traditional tests are overly conservative. When the larger cells have the smaller variance, traditional tests are overly liberal.

Bryk & Raudenbush (1988) argue persuasively that heterogeneity of variance should not only be viewed as a statistical problem to be eliminated, but additionally might be considered substantively interesting. If treatment effects depend on characteristics of the sampled population, then different treatments may induce different variances. Detecting treatment by subject interactions, via an analysis of the differences in variances, may be an important part of data analysis.

OUTLIERS AND INFLUENTIAL OBSERVATIONS   Sometimes violations of the normality and homogeneity assumptions are not general distributional problems but occur as a result of a few very discrepant observations (outliers). These observations may be recording errors or they may be genuinely different observations. The least-squares minimization procedures that underlie many statistical techniques are not robust to the presence of as few as one or two extreme outliers. Rousseeuw & Leroy (1987) note that analyses of data reflecting modest relationships (such as those typically found in psychological research) are the most vulnerable to outliers. Thus, it is crucial to identify these observations before proceeding with the data analysis. Despite the availability of many excellent guides to detecting outliers (e.g. Atkinson 1985, Barnett & Lewis 1984, Belsley et al 1980, Chatterjee & Hadi 1988, Cook & Weisberg 1982, Hossain & Naik 1989, Judd & McClelland 1989, Stevens 1984), and procedures in statistical packages, mentions of outlier analysis in published research articles remain rare. Many psychologists are suspicious of analyses in which outliers are deleted. However, just as with statistical testing, one must also consider the other kind of error—reporting a least-squares model that because of a few outliers does not describe *any* of the data adequately. Data should always be examined for outliers and the impact of those outliers on the analysis and conclusions should be considered, whether or not one decides to remove them. To ignore them entirely is just as much "cheating" as is removing them from the data.

There are three relatively independent questions to be addressed in outlier analysis. First, is the predictor (or set of predictors) for an observation unusual? Unusual predictor values artificially inflate the predictor's variance, which in turn inflates effect sizes and test statistics, and can lead to Type I errors in which the rejection of the null hypothesis depends entirely on only one or two observations. Levers (entries on the diagonal of the "hat" matrix used in regression computations) and Mahalanobis distances can detect unusual predictors. Unusual predictors are never a problem for balanced ANOVA designs with equal cell sizes, but may be a substantial problem for regression analyses and unbalanced ANOVA designs when not analyzed by unweighted means procedures. Second, is the value of the dependent variable for an observation unusual relative to the observed (or modeled) values of the dependent variable for the other observations? A single highly discrepant observation may account for a substantial proportion of the mean squared error and hence increase the likelihood of Type II errors. That is, a single outlier can produce so much error as to make the detection of other effects impossible. The Studentized deleted residual (the scaled residual for an observation relative to a model determined by only the other observations) can identify an unusual value of the dependent variable and indicate whether it would be useful to add a predictor (dummy code) for just that observation. Unusual dependent variables can be problematic in any analyses, including balanced ANOVA designs. Third, is the observation unusually influential in determining the model? That is, do the estimated cell means or regression coefficients depend on whether or not that observation is included? An observation's influence is essentially an interaction between the answers to the previous two questions. An observation with an unusual set of values for the predictor variables but a value of the dependent variable close to that predicted by a model of the other observations will not have unusual influence. However, an observation can have values for the predictor variables and the dependent variable that would not be detected as unusual individually but that have an inordinate joint influence on the final model. A few highly influential observations can produce either Type I or II errors by yielding a model that describes only those few observations, even though that model appears to be based on the complete set of observations. These highly influential observations can be identified by Cook's D (Cook 1977) or DFFTS (Belsley et al 1980). Pendleton

(1985) and Hossain (1991) suggest that slightly different influence measures (e.g. Welsch-Kuh distance) may be more informative for ANOVA and MANOVA models. Visual detection of all three types of unusual observations is facilitated by special plots such as partial regression leverage plots (Belsley et al 1980), partial residual plots (Ezekiel & Fox 1959), and influence-enhanced scatter plots (Thissen et al 1981). The detection of multiple outliers poses special problems (Davies & Gather 1993).

Remedies for Distributional Problems

Transformations—reexpressions of Y, X, or both—and differential weighting of observations (according to procedures to be described later) can often solve distributional problems of nonnormality and heterogeneity of variance. Transformations and differential weighting often lead to simpler models. Some statisticians (Emerson 1991, Tukey et al 1991) suggest that producing simpler models is an even more important function of these remedies than are their normalizing and variance-stabilizing effects. Although certain variance-stabilizing transformations (e.g. the arcsin and the logit for probabilities and proportions, Fisher's Z for correlations, and to a lesser extent the log for reaction times) have been well received by psychologists, transformations and differential weighting in general remain controversial (e.g. see the lively exchange between Games 1983, 1984; Levine et al 1992; Levine & Dunlap 1982, 1983). Statisticians are much more sympathetic to transformations and differential weighting than are psychologists. Some statisticians also believe that psychologists are overly concerned with Stevens' scale types (e.g. ordinal, interval, ratio) and their implications for data analysis (Velleman & Wilkinson 1993). As psychologists begin to emphasize building good models of data over the testing of null hypotheses, transformations should become less controversial because there will be less concern with the possibility that a transformation might change the result of a significance test.

The recent surge in transformation-related research among statisticians is partly the result of improvements in computer technology that make new graphical and computer-intensive procedures feasible. We briefly review some of these procedures, and consider their benefits, costs, and potential problems.

TRANSFORMATIONS OF Y A large class of transformation techniques seeks a monotonic function $g()$ to reexpress Y so that the errors ε_i in the model

$$g(Y_i) = f(X_i, \beta) + \varepsilon_i \qquad\qquad 5.$$

are approximately normal and homogeneous. The function $f()$ represents a particular combination of the predictor variables X and the parameter vector β. For example, a typical function would be the familiar linear model

$$f(X_i,\beta) = \beta_0 + \beta_1 X_{i1} + \beta_2 X_{i2} + \ldots. \qquad 6.$$

The log and power transformations popularized by Box & Cox (1964, 1982) and Tukey's (1977) ladder of powers provide a large class of candidate functions. Box & Cox (1964) recommended maximum-likelihood estimation procedures for finding the best transformation to make the errors symmetric. Lin & Vonesh (1989) use a nonlinear data-fitting approach to make the errors normal. Berry (1987) formally minimizes skewness and kurtosis; but Emerson's (1991) simple graphical techniques to find a transformation yielding a simpler model are usually sufficient and much less complicated. One disadvantage of these transformations is that it is sometimes difficult to interpret the dependent variable in the new metric. In these cases, predicted values can be retransformed to the original metric, but it must be done carefully to avoid bias (Miller 1984, Taylor 1986). Carroll & Ruppert (1984, 1988), Ruppert & Aldershof (1989), and Snee (1986) considered transformation of both sides of a model:

$$g(Y_i) = g[f(X_i,\beta)] + \varepsilon_i. \qquad 7.$$

This dual transformation allows theoretical models to be preserved in terms of $f()$.

Nonparametric statistical techniques are often used to avoid the distributional assumptions of parametric techniques. However, many nonparametric techniques depend on stronger assumptions than most users realize. For example, the Mann-Whitney (or Wilcoxon) and Kruskal-Wallis tests avoid the normality assumption but require that the distribution of observations, whatever it is, must be the same within each cell (Maxwell & Delaney 1990). Conover & Iman (1981) illustrate that many familiar nonparametric statistical techniques can be represented as modeling the ranks of the dependent variable; that is,

$$\text{Rank}(Y_i) = f(X_i,\beta) + \varepsilon_i. \qquad 8.$$

The resulting least-squares test statistics are often equivalent or monotonically related to the corresponding nonparametric test statistics. Unfortunately, attempts to generalize the rank transformation from simple regression and one-way ANOVA to multiple regression and factorial ANOVA have not been successful (Sawilowsky et al 1989).

GENERALIZED LINEAR MODELS   Sometimes a single transformation cannot solve all distributional problems. Generalized linear models (Aitkin et al 1989, Hastie & Pregibon 1992, Healy 1988, McCullagh & Nelder 1983), not to be confused with the General Linear Model, allow more flexibility by using separate functions to address (*a*) nonlinearity in the relationship between *Y* and the predictors and (*b*) heterogeneity of variance. Hastie & Pregibon (1992) note that "generalized linear models are closer to a reparametrization of the model than to a reexpression of the response." Generalized linear modeling requires specification of (*a*) a link function $g()$ relating the expected value of Y to the predictors, that is,

$$E(Y_i) = \mu_i = g[f(X_i, \beta)],$$ 9.

where $f()$ is the usual linear function, and (*b*) a variance function $V()$ relating the variance of Y to the expected value of Y, that is,

$$\sigma_i^2 = \sigma^2 V[E(Y_i)] = \sigma^2 V(\mu_i).$$ 10.

Sometimes an error distribution is specified (e.g. Poisson, binomial, normal, gamma) that implies the variance function to be used. With appropriate selection of link and variance functions, many modeling techniques, including log-linear models for contingency tables and logistic regression, are particular types of generalized linear models. For example, logistic regression is the generalized linear model for which the link function is the logit

$$\log \frac{\mu_i}{(1 - \mu_i)},$$ 11.

and the variance function is

$$V(\mu_i) = \frac{\mu_i (1 - \mu_i)}{n}.$$ 12.

The increasing availability of software (e.g. in S+ and PROC MODELS in SAS) should lead to greater use of generalized linear models, which have the advantage of being "summarized by statistics, tables, and plots that are natural generalizations of their linear model counterparts" (Hastie & Pregibon 1992, p. 196).

EMPIRICAL WEIGHTING   Procedures for empirically weighting observations use the data to estimate how much weight an observation should be given in the analysis. One disadvantage of the generalized linear model approach is that the data analyst must specify the appropriate link and variance functions on the basis of theoretical considerations about the type of data. Although these functions allow for a greater variety of distributions, the fit of real data to these assumed distributions may not be exact. Carroll & Ruppert (1988) consider techniques for empirically estimating either the weights for each observation (inversely proportional to its variance) or the variance function itself.

In the special case of ANOVA, there is a large literature on empirical weighting procedures to redress heterogeneity of variance (see review in Maxwell & Delaney 1990, pp. 697–713). In most situations, it appears that Welch's (1951) procedure effectively controls the Type I error rate while maximizing power (Tomarken & Serlin 1986). However, alternative procedures continue to be proposed (Rice & Gaines 1993, Wilcox 1989). Additionally, Welch's procedure is not a panacea because it has an inflated Type I error rate in the presence of nonnormality (Harwell et al 1992). As noted previously, our strong preference is that researchers use single-degree-of-freedom contrasts rather than omnibus, multiple-degree-of-freedom tests. However, considerable bias can result from unequal variances when a pooled variance estimate is used to test individual comparisons among subsets of the cell means, even with relatively equal cell sizes. In this case, Maxwell & Delaney (1990) recommend a variation on the Welch (1951) procedure that relies on separate variance estimates from the cells that are involved in the contrast.

TRANSFORMATIONS OF X Reexpressing the predictors solves distributional problems less often than does reexpressing Y, but transformations of X often lead to simpler models. The goal is to find functions $h()$ of the predictors so that an additive combination of the transformed X variables predicts Y; that is,

$$Y_i = \beta_0 + h_1(X_{i1}) + h_2(X_{i2}) + \ldots + \varepsilon_i. \qquad\qquad 13.$$

Lubinski & Humphreys (1990) demonstrate that including polynomial terms, probably the most common way to reexpress X, can produce simpler models without interaction terms. It has long been known that transforming X can remove ordinal interactions (Busemeyer & Jones 1983, Scheffé 1959). Tukey (1977) recommends graphic techniques to find simplifying transformations of X. Generalized additive models (Hastie & Tibshirani 1990, Hastie 1992) use nonparametric scatterplot smoothing techniques such as splines and locally weighted regression (Cleveland 1993, Cleveland & Devlin 1988, Cleveland et al 1992) to estimate arbitrary functions $h()$ relating the predictors to the dependent variable. Often it is difficult to calculate the equivalent number of parameters estimated in fitting the arbitrary functions of X although various ad hoc (Hastie 1992) and special case (Cleveland et al 1992) procedures exist. As a result, standard errors and confidence intervals are commonly estimated using computer-intensive bootstrap methods (Efron & Tibshirani 1991, 1993).

ROBUST ESTIMATORS   Rousseeuw & Leroy (1987) argue that none of the outlier detection methods is entirely satisfactory. They suggest using robust estimation procedures, such as the least-median-of-squares method, to avoid the undesirable effects of distributional problems on model estimates. Robust alternatives to least-squares methods were suggested as early as the late nineteenth century (Edgeworth 1887; see Emerson & Hoaglin 1985, Hampel et al 1986, Rousseeuw & Leroy 1987, for historical reviews), but they did not become feasible until the advent of high-speed computing. Rousseeuw & Leroy's approach uses deviations from a model estimated using least-median-squares to weight observations in a subsequent weighted least-squares regression; hence, these robust estimators might reasonably be grouped with the empirical weighting procedures.

Nonindependence of Observations

Parametric statistical tests are not robust to violations of the independence assumption. Violations of the assumption can lead to serious underestimation or overestimation of the probability of Type I errors. Kenny & Judd (1986) discuss situations in which the independence assumption is likely to be violated and the consequences if dependence is ignored. The most frequent violation in psychological data arises from nestings or groupings of observations that are ignored in the analysis. Although psychologists generally recognize dependence resulting from the grouping of observations within subjects (and handle this dependence appropriately by using within-subject analysis of variance), they often ignore other groupings in their data (e.g. students grouped in classrooms, siblings grouped in families, subjects who interact with each other in laboratory studies, matched or yoked subjects). In general, to avoid nonindependence problems, any grouping factor in the data must be incorporated into the analysis, either as a fixed or a random effect. If groups are ignored and if observations within groups are more similar (positive dependence) or less similar (negative dependence) than observations between groups, then substantial bias in testing the effects of the independent variable of interest is likely to occur. The direction of the bias depends jointly on the sign of the dependence and on whether groups are crossed with or nested under levels of the independent variable of interest. With a nested design, dependence leads to inflated F values, and negative dependence leads to F values that are too small. For a crossed design, the direction of bias is reversed (Kenny & Judd 1986).

The appropriate analysis strategy that avoids these biases depends on whether group is considered to be a fixed or random effect. Typically it ought to be considered random, thus permitting generalization of the effect of the independent variable across groups. The appropriate analysis in this case treats group, rather than the individual observation, as the unit of analysis. With a nested design, the independent variable is thus a between-group factor. With a crossed design, the independent variable is a within-group factor and appropriate analyses involve tests of within-group contrasts or slopes. If group is considered fixed, then one simply partials the group differences out of the individual observations and proceeds to treat those observations as the unit of analysis.

A more complicated situation arises when the independent variable varies both within and between groups. Consider, for example, a situation where students are grouped in classrooms and one wants to examine the effects of teachers' expectations at the start of the term on performance at the end. Expectations vary both within and between classrooms. In this situation, one needs to conduct a multilevel analysis (Bryk & Raudenbush 1992; DA Kenny, DA Nashy, NC Bolger, unpublished manuscript) in which the relationship between the independent and dependent variables is examined both between and within groups (or classrooms). For the between-groups part of the analysis, one treats the group as the unit and examines the relationship between group averages on the independent and dependent variables, perhaps weighted by group size or some other factor. For the within-groups part, one calculates the relationship between the independent and dependent variables in each group (i.e. a within-group contrast or slope) and tests the reliability of these slopes across groups, perhaps again weighted by group size or some other factor. These two parts of the analysis need not produce consistent conclusions. In the above example, it might be that teachers with higher average expectations have students who achieve more poorly on average, yet within classrooms, expectations and achievement are positively related.

Computer algorithms are available to perform these multilevel analyses simultaneously at the within- and between-group levels, using maximum likelihood and other estimation procedures (Bryk & Raudenbush 1987, 1992; DeLeeuw & Kreft 1986; Goldstein 1987; Raudenbush 1988).

CONCLUSIONS

In this review, we have made numerous recommendations, some explicit, others implicit, for the proper application of basic data analytic techniques. These recommendations were prompted by our impression that the basic techniques of analysis of variance and regression are often misunderstood and misused by psychologists.

We recommend that psychologists use the model comparison approach to data analysis. Within the framework provided by the model comparison approach, we make other, more specific recommendations. We urge psychologists to emphasize model content and to ask focused questions of their data—questions of theoretical interest that can be phrased as single degree-of-freedom tests. We also urge psychologists to compute estimates of effect size and to use these estimates to supplement the information gained from significance tests. In the tradition of Cohen (1988) and others, we urge psychologists to perform power analyses when designing experimental and field research. Increases in power can be accomplished not only by increasing sample sizes but also by adjusting alpha levels and reducing error variance.

We make similar recommendations with respect to interactions: Focus on the interaction questions of interest. Understand that interactions are the residual products of two or more independent variables after removing the separate effects of these variables. Test interactions as single degree-of-freedom contrasts. Compute effect estimates for interactions. And finally, conduct power analyses for tests of interactions, but recognize that constraints on the magnitude of the interaction reduce power as do independent variables with center-peaked distributions. If implemented, these recommendations should alleviate many of the problems that plague the definition and interpretation of interactions.

We end with three recommendations for dealing with violations of the assumptions upon which parametric statistics are based: assumptions of normality, homogeneity of variance, and independence of observations. First, we recommend that psychologists pay attention to these assumptions and identify violations as they occur. Second, we encourage psychologists to seek transformations and other solutions that correct for violations of these assumptions. Third, we caution psychologists that failure to adjust for nonindependence or outliers in their data can produce seriously misleading models and statistical tests.

ACKNOWLEDGMENTS

Preparation of this chapter was partially supported by NIMH grant R01 MH-45049. We acknowledge with gratitude the superb editorial suggestions of Carol Nickerson. Additionally, we thank Robert Abelson, Jacob Cohen, Robyn Dawes, David Kenny, and Steve West for their very helpful comments on an earlier draft.

Literature Cited

Abelson RP. 1995. *Statistics as Principled Argument.* Hillsdale, NJ: Erlbaum

Aiken LS, West SG. 1991. *Multiple Regression: Testing and Interpreting Interactions.* Newbury Park, CA: Sage

Aitkin MA, Anderson DA, Francis BJ, Hinde JP. 1989. *Statistical Modeling in GLIM.* Oxford: Oxford Univ. Press

Atkinson AC. 1985. *Plots, Transformations, and Regression: An Introduction to Diagnostic Regression Analysis.* Oxford: Clarendon

Bakan D. 1966. The effect of significance testing in psychological research. *Psychol. Bull.* 66:423–37

Barnett V, Lewis T. 1984. *Outliers in Statistical Data.* New York: Wiley. 2nd ed.

Belsley DA, Kuh E, Welsch RE. 1980. *Regression Diagnostics: Identifying Influential Data and Sources of Collinearity.* New York: Wiley

Berry DA. 1987. Logarithmic transformations in ANOVA. *Biometrics* 43:439–56

Blair RC, Higgins JJ. 1980. A comparison of the power of the Wilcoxon's rank-sum statistic to that of the student's *t* statistic under various non-normal distributions. *J. Educ. Stat.* 5:309–35

Blair RC, Higgins JJ. 1985. Comparison of the power of the paired samples *t* test to that of

Wilcoxon's signed-ranks test under various population shapes. *Psychol. Bull.* 97:119–28

Bobko P. 1986. A solution to some dilemmas when testing hypotheses about ordinal interactions. *J. Appl. Psychol.* 71:323–26

Boneau CA. 1960. The effects of violations of assumptions underlying the *t* test. *Psychol. Bull.* 57:49–64

Box GEP. 1954. Some theorems on quadratic forms applied in the study of analysis of variance problems: II. Effects of inequality of variance and of correlation between errors in the two-way classification. *Ann. Math. Stat.* 25:484–98

Box GEP, Cox DR. 1964. An analysis of transformations. *J. R. Stat. Soc. Ser. B* 26:221–52

Box GEP, Cox DR. 1982. An analysis of transformations revisited (rebutted). *J. Am. Stat. Assoc.* 77:209–10

Bradley JV. 1977. A common situation conducive to bizarre distribution shape. *Am. Stat.* 31:147–50

Bradley JV. 1982. The insidious L-shaped distribution. *Bull. Psychomet. Soc.* 20:85–88

Bryk AS, Raudenbush SW. 1987. Application of hierarchical linear models to assessing change. *Psychol. Bull.* 101:147–58

Bryk AS, Raudenbush SW. 1988. Heterogeneity of variance in experimental studies: a challenge to conventional interpretations. *Psychol. Bull.* 104:396–404

Bryk AS, Raudenbush SW. 1992. *Hierarchical Linear Models: Applications and Data Analysis Methods.* Newbury Park, CA: Sage

Busemeyer JR, Jones LE. 1983. Analysis of multiplicative combination rules when the causal variables are measured with error. *Psychol. Bull.* 93:549–62

Carroll RJ, Ruppert D. 1984. Power transformation when fitting theoretical models to data. *J. Am. Stat. Assoc.* 79:321–28

Carroll RJ, Ruppert D. 1988. *Transformation and Weighting in Regression.* New York: Chapman & Hall

Chambers JM, Hastie TJ, eds. 1992. *Statistical Models in S.* Pacific Grove, CA: Wadsworth

Chatterjee S, Hadi AS. 1988. *Sensitivity Analysis in Linear Regression.* New York: Wiley

Cleveland WS. 1993. *Visualizing Data.* Summit, NJ: Hobart

Cleveland WS, Devlin SJ. 1988. Locally weighted regression: an approach to regression analysis by local fitting. *J. Am. Stat. Assoc.* 83:596–610

Cleveland WS, Grosse E, Shyu WM. 1992. Local regression models. See Chamber & Hastie 1992, pp. 309–76

Cohen J. 1962. The statistical power of abnormal-social psychological research: a review. *J. Abnorm. Soc. Psychol.* 65:145–53

Cohen J. 1968. Multiple regression as a general data-analytic system. *Psychol. Bull.* 70:426–43

Cohen J. 1969. *Statistical Power Analysis for the Behavioral Sciences.* San Diego, CA: Academic

Cohen J. 1978. Partialed products are interactions; partialed powers are curve components. *Psychol. Bull.* 85:858–66

Cohen J. 1988. *Statistical Power Analysis for the Behavioral Sciences.* Hillsdale, NJ: Erlbaum. 2nd ed.

Cohen J. 1990. Things I have learned (so far). *Am. Psychol.* 45:1304–12

Cohen J. 1992. A power primer. *Psychol. Bull.* 112:155–59

Cohen J, Cohen P. 1983. *Applied Multiple Regression/Correlation Analysis for the Behavioral Sciences.* Hillsdale, NJ: Erlbaum. 2nd ed.

Conover WJ, Iman RL. 1981. Rank transformations as a bridge between parametric and nonparametric statistics. *Am. Stat.* 35:124–29

Cook RD. 1977. Detection of influential observations in linear regression. *Technometrics* 23:15–18

Cook RD, Weisberg S. 1982. *Residuals and Influence in Regression.* New York/London: Chapman & Hall

Cook TD, Campbell DT. 1979. *Quasi-Experimentation: Design and Analysis Issues for Field Settings.* Boston: Houghton Mifflin

Cronbach LJ. 1987. Statistical tests for moderator variables: flaws in analyses recently proposed. *Psychol. Bull.* 102:414–17

Davies L, Gather U. 1993. The identification of multiple outliers (with discussion). *J. Am. Stat. Assoc.* 88:782–801

Dawes RM. 1990. Monotone interactions: It's even simpler than that. *Behav. Brain Sci.* 13:128–29

DeLeeuw J, Kreft I. 1986. Random coefficient models for multilevel analysis. *J. Educ. Stat.* 11:57–85

Dunlap WP, Kemery ER. 1987. Failure to detect moderating effects: Is multi-collinearity the problem? *Psychol. Bull.* 102:418–20

Edgeworth FY. 1887. On observations relating to several quantities. *Mermathena* 6:279–85

Efron B, Tibshirani RJ. 1991. Statistical data analysis in the computer age. *Science* 253:390–95

Efron B, Tibshirani RJ. 1993. *An Introduction to the Bootstrap.* New York: Chapman & Hall

Emerson JD. 1991. Introduction to transformation. See Hoaglin et al 1991, pp. 365–400

Emerson JD, Hoaglin DC. 1985. Resistant multiple regression, one variable at a time.

In *Exploring Data Tables, Trends, and Shapes,* ed. D Hoaglin, F Mosteller, JW Tukey, pp. 241–80. New York: Wiley

Engeman RM, Shumake SA. 1993. Animal welfare and the statistical consultant. *Am. Stat.* 47:229–33

Estes WK. 1991. *Statistical Models in Behavioral Research.* Hillsdale, NJ: Erlbaum

Ezekiel M, Fox KA. 1959. *Methods of Correlation and Regression Analysis.* New York: Wiley. 3rd ed.

Feldt LS. 1958. A comparison of the precision of three experimental designs employing a concomitant variable. *Psychometrika* 23:335–53

Fisher RA. 1935. *The Design of Experiments.* Edinburgh, UK: Oliver & Boyd

Folger R. 1989. Significance tests and the duplicity of binary decisions. *Psychol. Bull.* 106:155–60

Francis DJ, Fletcher JM, Stuebing KK, Davidson KC, Thompson NM. 1991. Analysis of change: modeling individual growth. *J. Consult. Clin. Psychol.* 59:27–37

Friedrich RJ. 1982. In defense of multiplicative terms in multiple regression equations. *Am. J. Polit. Sci.* 26:797–833

Games PA. 1983. Curvilinear transformations of the dependent variable. *Psychol. Bull.* 93:382–87

Games PA. 1984. Data transformations, power, and skew: a rebuttal to Levine and Dunlap. *Psychol. Bull.* 95:345–47

Geisser S, Greenhouse SW. 1958. An extension of Box's results on the use of the F distribution in multivariate analysis. *Ann. Math. Stat.* 29:885–91

Glass GV, Peckham PD, Sanders JR. 1972. Consequences of failure to meet assumptions underlying the fixed effects analysis of variance and covariance. *Rev. Educ. Resch.* 42:237–88

Goldstein H. 1987. *Multilevel Models in Educational and Social Research.* London: Oxford Univ. Press

Goldstein R. 1989. Power and sample size via MS/PC-DOS computers. *Am. Stat.* 43:253–60

Grant DA. 1962. Testing the null hypothesis and the strategy and tactics of investigating theoretical models. *Psychol. Rev.* 69:54–61

Hampel FR, Ronchetti EM, Rousseeuw PJ, Stahel WA. 1986. *Robust Statistics: The Approach Based on Influence Functions.* New York: Wiley

Harwell MR, Rubinstein EN, Hayes WS, Olds CC. 1992. Summarizing Monte Carlo results in methodological research: the one- and two-factor fixed effects ANOVA cases. *J. Educ. Stat.* 17:315–39

Hastie TJ. 1992. Generalized additive models. See Chambers & Hastie 1992, pp. 249–308

Hastie TJ, Pregibon D. 1992. Generalized linear models. See Chambers & Hastie 1992, pp. 195–247

Hastie TJ, Tibshirani R. 1990. *Generalized Additive Models.* London: Chapman & Hall

Healy MJR. 1988. *GLIM: An Introduction.* Oxford: Clarendon

Hedges LV. 1992. Meta-analysis. *J. Educ. Stat.* 17:279–96

Hoaglin DC, Mosteller F, Tukey JW, eds. 1991. *Fundamentals of Exploratory Analysis of Variance.* New York: Wiley

Hochberg Y, Tamhane AC. 1987. *Multiple Comparison Procedures.* New York: Wiley

Holland BS, Copenhaver MD. 1988. Improved Bonferroni-type multiple testing procedures. *Psychol. Bull.* 104:145–49

Hossain A. 1991. Influential observations in ANOVA and MANOVA models. *J. Stat. Comp. Simul.* 39:9–19

Hossain A, Naik DN. 1989. Detection of influential observations in multivariate regression. *J. Appl. Stat.* 16:25–37

Huck SW, McLean RA. 1975. Using a repeated measures ANOVA to analyze data from a pretest-postest design: a potentially confusing task. *Psychol. Bull.* 82:511–18

Huynh H, Feldt LS. 1970. Conditions under which mean square ratios in repeated measurements designs have exact F-distributions. *J. Am. Stat. Assoc.* 65:1582–89

Huynh H, Feldt LS. 1976. Estimation of the Box correction for degrees of freedom from sample data in randomized block and split-plot deisgns. *J. Educ. Stat.* 1:69–82

Ito PK. 1980. Robustness of ANOVA and MANOVA test procedures. In *Handbook of Statistics,* ed. PR Krishnaiah, pp. 199–236. Amsterdam: North-Holland

Jaccard J, Becker MA, Wood G. 1984. Pairwise multiple comparison procedures: a review. *Psychol. Bull.* 96:589–96

Jaccard J, Turrisi R, Wan CK. 1990. *Interaction Effects in Multiple Regression.* Newbury Park, CA: Sage

Jennings E. 1988. Models for pretest-postest data: repeated measures ANOVA revisited. *J. Educ. Stat.* 13:273–80

Judd CM, Kenny DA. 1981. *Estimating the Effects of Social Interventions.* New York: Cambridge Univ. Press

Judd CM, McClelland GH. 1989. *Data Analysis: A Model Comparison Approach.* San Diego, CA: Harcourt, Brace, Jovanovich

Kenny DA, Judd CM. 1986. Consequences of violating the independence assumption in analysis of variance. *Psychol. Bull.* 99:422–31

Keren G, Lewis C, eds. 1993a. *A Handbook for Data Analysis in the Behavioral Sciences: Statistical Issues.* Hillsdale, NJ: Erlbaum

Keren G, Lewis C, eds. 1993b. *A Handbook for Data Analysis in the Behavioral Sci-*

ences: Methodological Issues. Hillsdale, NJ: Erlbaum

Keselman HJ, Keselman JC, Games PA. 1991. Maximum familywise Type I error rate: the Least Significant Difference, Newman-Keuls, and other multiple comparison procedures. Psychol. Bull. 110:155–61

Keuls M. 1952. The use of the "Studentized range" in conjunction with analysis of variance. Euphytica 1:112–22

Klockars AJ, Hancock GR. 1992. Power of recent multiple comparison procedures as applied to a complete set of planned orthogonal contrasts. Psychol. Bull. 111:505–10

Levine A, Liukkonen J, Levine DW. 1992. Predicting power changes under transformations in ANOVA tests. Commun. Stat.: Theory Methods 21:679–92

Levine DW, Dunlap WP. 1982. Power of the F Test with Skewed Data: Should one transform or not? Psychol. Bull. 92:272–80

Levine DW, Dunlap WP. 1983. Data transformation, power, and skew: a rejoinder to Games. Psychol. Bull. 93:596–99

Lewis C. 1993. Analyzing means from repeated measures data. See Keren & Lewis 1993a, pp. 73–94

Lin LI, Vonesh EF. 1989. An empirical nonlinear data-fitting approach for transforming data to normality. Am. Stat. 43:237–43

Loftus GR. 1991. On the tyranny of hypothesis testing in the social sciences. Contemp. Psychol. 36:102–5

Lubinski D, Humphreys LG. 1990. Assessing spurious "moderator effects": illustrated substantively with the hypothesized ("synergistic") relation between spatial and mathematical ability. Psychol. Bull. 107:385–93

Lunneborg CE. 1994. Modeling Experimental and Observational Data. Belmont, CA: Duxbury

Maxwell SE, Cole DA, Arvey RD, Salas E. 1991. A comparison of methods for increasing power in randomized between-subjects designs. Psychol. Bull. 110:328–37

Maxwell SE, Delaney HD. 1990. Designing Experiments and Analyzing Data: A Model Comparison Perspective. Belmont, CA: Wadsworth

Maxwell SE, Delaney HD. 1993. Bivariate median splits and spurious statistical significance. Psychol. Bull. 113:181–90

Maxwell SE, Delaney HD, Dill CA. 1984. Another look at ANCOVA versus blocking. Psychol. Bull. 95:136–47

McCall RB, Appelbaum MI. 1973. Bias in the analysis of repeated-measures designs: some alternative approaches. Child Dev. 44:401–15

McClelland GH, Judd CM. 1993. Statistical difficulties of detecting interactions and moderator effects. Psychol. Bull. 114:376–90

McCullagh P, Nelder JA. 1983. Generalized Linear Models. London: Chapman & Hall

Meyer DL. 1991. Misinterpretation of interaction effects: a reply to Rosnow and Rosenthal. Psychol. Bull. 110:571–73

Micceri T. 1989. The unicorn, the normal curve, and other improbable creatures. Psychol. Bull. 105:156–66

Miller DM. 1984. Reducing transformation bias in curve fitting. Am. Stat. 38:124–26

Morris JH, Sherman J, Mansfield ER. 1986. Failures to detect moderating effects with ordinary least squares moderated multiple regression: some reasons and a remedy. Psychol. Bull. 99:282–88

Morrison DE, Henkel RE, eds. 1970. The Significance Test Controversy. Chicago: Aldine

Newman D. 1939. The distribution of the range in samples from a normal population expressed in terms of an independent estimate of standard deviation. Biometrika 31:20–30

O'Brien RG, Kaiser MK. 1985. MANOVA method for analyzing repeated measures designs: an extensive primer. Psychol. Bull. 97:316–33

Pendleton OJ. 1985. Influential observations in the analysis of variance. Commun. Stat.: Theory Methods 14:551–65

Prentice DA, Miller DT. 1992. When small effects are impressive. Psychol. Bull. 112:160–64

Raudenbush SW. 1988. Educational applications of hierarchical linear models: a review. J. Educ. Stat. 13:85–116

Rice WR, Gaines SD. 1993. Calculating P values for ANOVA with unequal variances. J. Stat. Comp. Simul. 46:19–22

Rogan J, Keselman H. 1977. Is the ANOVA F-test robust to variance heterogeneity when sample sizes are equal? An investigation via a coefficient of variation. Am. Educ. Res. J. 14:493–98

Rogosa D, Brandt D, Zimowski M. 1982. A growth curve approach to the measurement of change. Psychol. Bull. 92:726–48

Rosenthal R. 1990. How are we doing in soft psychology. Am. Psychol. 45:775–76

Rosenthal R, Rosnow RL. 1985. Contrast Analysis: Focused Comparisons in the Analysis of Variance. Cambridge: Cambridge Univ. Press

Rosenthal R, Rubin DB. 1982. A simple, general purpose display of magnitude of experimental effect. J. Educ. Psychol. 74:166–69

Rosenthal R, Rubin DB. 1984. Multiple contrasts and ordered Bonferroni procedures. J. Educ. Psychol. 76:1028–34

Rosenthal R, Rubin DB. 1985. Statistical analysis: summarizing evidence versus establishing facts. Psychol. Bull. 97:527–29

Rosnow RL, Rosenthal R. 1989a. Definition and interpretation of interaction effects. *Psychol. Bull.* 105:143–46

Rosnow RL, Rosenthal R. 1989b. Statistical procedures and the justification of knowledge in psychological science. *Am. Psychol.* 44:1276–84

Rosnow RL, Rosenthal R. 1991. If you're looking at the cell means, you're not looking at only the interaction (unless all main effects are zero). *Psychol. Bull.* 110:574–76

Rousseeuw PJ, Leroy AM. 1987. *Robust Regression and Outlier Detection.* New York: Wiley

Ruppert D, Aldershof B. 1989. Transformation to symmetry and homoscedasticity. *J. Am. Stat. Assoc.* 84:437–46

Ryan TA. 1985. "Ensemble-adjusted p values": How are they to be weighted? *Psychol. Bull.* 97:521–26

Sawilowsky SS, Blair RC. 1992. A more realistic look at the robustness and type II error properties of the *t* test to departures from population normality. *Psychol. Bull.* 111:352–60

Sawilowsky SS, Blair RC, Higgins JJ. 1989. An investigation of the Type I error and power properties of the rank transform procedure in factorial ANOVA. *J. Educ. Stat.* 14:255–67

Scheffé H. 1953. A method for judging all contrasts in the analysis of variance. *Biometrika* 40:87–104

Scheffé H. 1959. *The Analysis of Variance.* New York: Wiley

Schmid CH. 1991. Value splitting: taking the data apart. See Hoaglin et al 1991, pp. 72–113

Sedlmeier P, Gigerenzer G. 1989. Do studies of statistical power have an effect on the power of studies? *Psychol. Bull.* 105:309–16

Snee RD. 1986. An alternative approach to fitting models when reexpression of the response is useful. *J. Qual. Tech.* 18:211–25

Stevens JP. 1984. Outliers and influential data points in regression analysis. *Psychol. Bull.* 95:334–44

Tatsuoka M. 1993a. Elements of the general linear model. See Keren & Lewis 1993a, pp. 3–41

Tatsuoka M. 1993b. Effect size. See Keren & Lewis 1993b, pp. 461–80

Taylor JMG. 1986. The retransformed mean after a fitted power transformation. *J. Am. Stat. Assoc.* 81:114–18

Thissen D, Baker L, Wainer H. 1981. Influence-enhanced scatterplots. *Psychol. Bull.* 90:179–84

Tomarken A, Serlin R. 1986. Comparison of ANOVA alternatives under variance heterogeneity and specific noncentrality structures. *Psychol. Bull.* 99:90–99

Toothaker LE. 1991. *Multiple Comparisons for Researchers.* Newbury Park, CA: Sage

Tukey JW. 1977. *Exploratory Data Analysis.* Reading, MA: Addison-Wesley

Tukey JW. 1991. The philosophy of multiple comparisons. *Stat. Sci.* 6:100–16

Tukey JW, Mosteller F, Hoaglin DC. 1991. Concepts and examples in analysis of variance. See Hoaglin et al 1991, pp. 1–23

Velleman PF, Wilkinson L. 1993. Nominal, ordinal, interval, and ratio typologies are misleading. *Am. Stat.* 47:65–72

Welch B. 1951. On the comparison of several mean values: an alternative approach. *Biometrika* 38:330–336

Wilcox RR. 1985. New designs in analysis of variance. *Annu. Rev. Psychol.* 38:29–60

Wilcox RR. 1989. Adjusting for unequal variances when comparing means in one-way and two-way fixed effects ANOVA models. *J. Educ. Stat.* 14:269–78

Wilcox RR, Charlin V, Thompson K. 1986. New Monte Carlo results on the robustness of the ANOVA F, W, and F* statistics. *Commun. Stat.: Simul. Comp.* 15:933–44

Zimmerman DW, Zumbo BD. 1993. The relative power of parametric and nonparametric statistical methods. See Keren & Lewis 1993b, pp. 481–518

Zuckerman M, Hodgins HS, Zuckerman A, Rosenthal R. 1993. Contemporary issues in the analysis of data: a survey of 551 psychologists. *Psychol. Sci.* 4:49–53

Annu. Rev. Psychol. 1995. 46:467–92

SPEECH PERCEPTION:
From Signal to Word

Joanne L. Miller

Department of Psychology, Northeastern University, Boston, Massachusetts 02115

Peter D. Eimas

Department of Cognitive and Linguistic Sciences, Brown University, Providence, Rhode Island 02912

KEY WORDS: spoken language processing, speech perception, lexical access, modularity, interaction, context effects, development, language-specificity

CONTENTS

INTRODUCTION

Over the past several decades enormous progress has been made in the study of psycholinguistics, a now very large and sophisticated area of inquiry that involves researchers from a variety of diverse disciplines (for recent reviews, see Gernsbacher 1994, Miller & Eimas 1994; see also Foss 1988). Our review focuses on one of the core issues in psycholinguistics, the comprehension of spoken language. More specifically, we concentrate on the earliest stages of comprehension, during which listeners analyze the continuous signal of speech and map initial representations onto the lexical items of their language. We focus first on how listeners map the continuous signal of speech onto discrete prelexical linguistic representations, for example, how they convert the acoustic signal to the sequences of consonants and vowels that comprise spoken utterances. We then examine how listeners map the acoustic signal onto lexical representations themselves. These two foci have often been considered in terms of two rather distinct literatures, one on speech perception and the other on word recognition. However, these areas of inquiry are very closely intertwined, and, as we shall see, many of the same issues arise in both domains.

MAPPING FROM ACOUSTIC SIGNAL TO INITIAL REPRESENTATIONAL UNITS

Over four decades of research have provided a vast amount of information on the nature of the mapping between the acoustic signal of speech and the initial prelexical linguistic units that comprise a given utterance. The central finding of this research is that the relation between acoustic signal and linguistic structure is highly complex: Elements of the acoustic signal do not stand in a simple one-to-one relation with linguistic units. As a consequence of this discovery, a major challenge in speech perception has been to provide an account of how listeners are able to map the continuously varying speech signal onto the discrete linguistic categories of their language. A closely related problem has been how best to characterize the representational units themselves, for example, as phonetic features, phonetic segments, diphones, or syllables.

We first briefly characterize the nature of the complex mapping between acoustic signal and linguistic structure and, in the course of doing so, provide an overview of major theoretical positions in the field. Next, we highlight progress on four specific issues that are currently the focus of considerable interest and debate. Our discussion is necessarily selective; for example, we do not consider such critical topics as the perceptual organization of speech (Remez et al 1994) or the contribution of visual information to phonetic perception (Summerfield 1987). More comprehensive reviews are provided by Jusczyk (1986) and Nygaard & Pisoni (1994) (see also Pisoni & Luce 1987, Klatt 1989).

The Basic Problem

When speakers talk, they do not produce each phonetic segment (consonant or vowel) sequentially, one at a time (see Liberman et al 1967). Rather, they produce segments in a coarticulated fashion, such that at any given point in time the state of the vocal tract (and hence the acoustic signal) reflects not only the current segment being produced, but also previous and subsequent segments. Although such coarticulation allows for the rapid transmission of linguistic information, it vastly complicates the mapping between signal and segment, in that the form of the acoustic information specifying a given segment is highly dependent on the preceding and following segments. Not only does this produce a lack of invariance between acoustic property and phonetic category (whether defined in terms of segment or feature), but it also makes it impossible to divide the speech signal into discrete acoustic segments that correspond, in a one-to-one fashion, to given phonetic segments. Thus the information for a given segment is not only context-dependent, but it also overlaps in time with the information for other segments.

Coarticulation is only one of many factors introducing variation into the mapping between acoustic signal and linguistic unit. For example, speakers vary in the size and shape of their vocal tracts (especially across age and gender), and they alter their rates of speech when they talk. These factors also introduce variation in the acoustic properties specifying phonetic identity (Miller 1981, Nearey 1989). To further complicate matters, any given phonetic segment (or feature) is typically specified not by a single property of the acoustic signal, but rather by multiple properties (e.g. Lisker 1986) that enter into perceptual trading relations and that vary with phonetic context (Repp 1982; see also Gordon et al 1993).

Much of the research in speech perception has focused on how listeners cope with such variability when deriving the phonetic form of the utterance. This view on variability has not gone unquestioned, however. Longstanding attempts have been made to find invariant properties that specify phonetic structure (e.g. Kewley-Port 1983, Stevens & Blumstein 1981, Sussman et al 1991). The basic argument is that the presumed lack of invariance is more apparent than real and that under the proper acoustic (auditory) description, often involving higher-order, relational properties, an invariant mapping between acoustic signal and phonetic feature (or segment) might be found. The search for higher-order invariants continues to provide important information about the nature of acoustic information underlying phonetic perception. However, finding invariant properties, per se, has proved difficult, and there is evidence that even when invariant properties are available in the signal, listeners also rely on context-dependent properties (e.g. Lahiri et al 1984). Thus the problem of how context-dependent acoustic information is mapped onto an invariant phonetic percept remains a central issue.

The extensive literature on speech perception makes it clear that listeners are exquisitely sensitive to the systematic variation introduced by changes in phonetic context, speaker, speaking rate, and the like, and that they take this variation into account when mapping particular values of acoustic properties onto phonetic categories (see e.g. Repp & Liberman 1987). What remains elusive, despite decades of study, is the nature of the underlying mechanisms responsible for mapping the acoustic signal to the representational units during the earliest stages of language processing. Current views offer fundamentally different proposals.

For example, according to the motor theory of speech perception developed by Liberman and his colleagues (Liberman & Mattingly 1985), listeners recover phonetic structure from the highly encoded speech signal through the operation of a specialized, species-specific, innately given processing system that computes the intended phonetic gestures of the speaker. Thus, speech perception is accomplished by reference to speech production. The direct-realist view of speech perception (Fowler 1986) also takes the objects of speech perception to be articulatory in nature. However, in this view no specialized mechanism is involved in perceiving the articulatory gestures that constitute phonetic form. Instead, the acoustic signal, which is structured by the gestures, is assumed to contain sufficient information to directly specify them; thus no specialized processing is required. In contrast to these theories is a set of views that, although different in various ways from one another, share the assumption that phonetic perception involves neither the recovery of articulatory events nor the operation of a specialized speech processing mechanism; instead, general principles of auditory processing, learning, and categorization underlie the listener's ability to map the acoustic signal onto phonetic categories (e.g. Diehl & Kluender 1989; Kuhl 1986, 1992; Massaro 1987a; Pastore 1981, 1987). A final example is TRACE, an interactive-activation model of speech perception. One version of the model (Elman & McClelland 1986) uses real speech as input and focuses on the mapping from acoustic signal to features and phonemes. Another version (McClelland & Elman 1986), which will be discussed in the second part of this review, uses simulated (speech-like) input and focuses on phoneme- and word-level recognition.

Although much of the experimental work in speech perception has been aimed at distinguishing the major theoretical alternatives, there is no consensus on the relative viability of each approach. Nonetheless, although progress on an overarching theory of phonetic processing has been slow, there continues to be considerable progress on an array of specific issues and phenomena, if not on the specific mechanisms that underlie them. In the next section we highlight four particularly active areas of research; taken together, they underscore the diversity of topics being addressed in the field today.

Internal Structure of Phonetic Categories

As discussed above, a major challenge for a theory of speech perception is to specify how a listener maps the continuous acoustic signal onto discrete categorical representations. Over the past few years there has been a striking change in how the categorization process and the resulting representations are viewed.

Much of the early work on speech categorization was concerned with the phenomenon of categorical perception (Harnad 1987, Liberman et al 1957, Repp 1984). The early view was that when listeners process the speech signal to recover the phonetic segments of their language, they largely strip away irrelevant, within-category acoustic differences, primarily retaining only the linguistic, categorical information about segmental identity. Evidence supporting this view came from experiments that compared the identification and discrimination of stimuli along an acoustic continuum that ranged from one perceived phonetic segment to another. The main phenomenon, known as categorical perception, was that discrimination of two stimuli was considerably better when the stimuli straddled the phonetic boundary than when they did not, even when acoustic differences were kept constant.

Although the early literature focused on the relative (often considerable) difficulty in perceiving within-category distinctions, there is now evidence that listeners can discriminate such distinctions with a high degree of accuracy under certain circumstances (e.g. Carney et al 1977, Samuel 1977; see also van Hessen & Schouten 1992). Of particular importance is increasing evidence that not only can listeners perceive within-category distinctions, but that some category members are perceived as better exemplars, or more prototypical, than others (Kuhl 1991, Massaro 1987b, Miller & Volaitis 1989, Samuel 1982). That is, phonetic categories have a graded structure (cf Medin & Barsalou 1987, Rosch 1978). Evidence for such structure comes from experiments showing that listeners are able to make very fine-grained, overt judgments of category goodness when presented with randomized stimuli from within a given category (Kuhl 1991, Miller & Volaitis 1989). Furthermore, as stimuli vary in judged category goodness, so too do they vary in their perceptual effectiveness in tasks such as dichotic listening (Miller 1977, Repp 1977) and selective adaptation (Miller et al 1983, Samuel 1982). In addition, stimuli in the centers of categories (i.e. the category prototypes) may assimilate nearby stimuli, thus effectively shrinking the perceptual space around the prototypes (Kuhl 1991; cf Samuel 1982).

We noted earlier that among the major factors contributing to the complexity in mapping between acoustic signal and phonetic category are context effects and the multiple specification of category identity. Traditionally, the effects of context and multiple properties have been measured as shifts in the location of the boundaries between categories (Repp & Liberman 1987). Evidence now indicates that these effects are not limited to the boundary region where, by definition, there is ambiguity in category membership. Rather, they extend to the centers of categories, resulting in a systematic shift in the location of the category's best exemplars (see Miller 1994; cf Oden & Massaro 1978). This indicates that the centers of categories are not represented as singular, abstract prototypes, per se, but rather as structures that retain fine-grained detail about the acoustic-phonetic form of the language. Whether these detailed representations are based on some type of context-dependent summary description (Rosch 1978) or on stored category exemplars, presumably weighted for frequency (Nosofsky 1988), remains to be resolved (Li & Pastore 1992, Medin & Barsalou 1987). Also unknown is the level at which the detailed representations are best described, for example, whether in terms of featural, segmental, or syllabic categories. Finally, the shift in emphasis from abstract representations that code only phonetic category identity to representations that also code fine-grained detail about the acoustic-phonetic form of the language is consistent with the increasingly accepted view that variation in the speech signal is not "noise" to be discarded, but rather provides a rich source of information that plays a prominent role in speech processing (Elman & McClelland 1986, Nygaard & Pisoni 1994).

Infant Speech Perception

The literature on infant speech perception provides strong evidence that the abilities of adults to map the inherently variable speech signal onto categorical representations finds its origins in the earliest, probably innately given perceptual abilities of infants (for reviews, see Eimas et al 1987, Jusczyk 1994). For example, infants in the first days, weeks, and months of life are sensitive to and attracted by human speech (e.g. Bertoncini et al 1989, DeCasper & Fifer 1980, Fernald 1984, Mehler et al 1978). They are also seemingly able to distinguish all (or nearly all) of the phonetic distinctions found in human languages and do so by processes that yield organized categorical representations (e.g. Eimas et al 1971, Eimas & Miller 1992). Furthermore, for infants, as for adults, the mapping between acoustic signal and categorical representation is not invariant. The boundary between infant categories can be altered by varying contextual factors (Eimas & Miller 1991, Levitt et al 1988, Miller & Eimas 1983), and similarly, the categorical representations of infants are specified by multiple properties of the acoustic signal that enter into perceptual trading relations (Eimas 1985, Miller & Eimas 1983). In addition, by six months of age infants can form equivalence classes, despite acoustic variation from differences in speakers, intonation, and phonetic context (e.g. Kuhl 1979, 1983). These phenomena show that infants, like adults, listen through the natural variation in speech, a necessary ability if infants are to experience perceptual constancy and develop a repertoire of the basic constituents of language.

Experiments indicating categorical perception or the existence of equivalence classes in infants do not reveal whether the infants' representations are linguistic in nature. Nor do they inform us whether the initial categories represent features, segments, or syllables [but see Bijeljac-Babic et al (1993) for evidence of syllabic representations in neonates]. Nevertheless, by 12 months of age the processes of perception provide representations that are appropriate for the discovery and construction of words and syntactic constituents (e.g. Christophe et al 1994, Gerken et al 1994, Hirsh-Pasek et al 1987, Hohne & Jusczyk 1994, Jusczyk et al 1992, Morgan 1994).

Experiments have also explored the role of experience with the parental language on the infant's perception of speech (Best 1994, Best et al 1988, Polka & Werker 1994, Werker 1993, Werker & Lalonde 1988, Werker & Tees 1984a). Evidence for a very early effect of the parental language on speech perception is found in the preference of neonates for their native language (Bahrick & Pickens 1988, Mehler et al 1988). Additionally, although infants appear to perceive phonetic distinctions without constraint by the parental language during the first few months of age (Best 1994, Werker 1993), experience with the native language modifies phonetic perception during the first year of life. The perception of vowels begins to be constrained by the native language by six months of age (Kuhl et al 1992, Polka & Werker 1994), and Werker & Tees (1984a) have shown that the perception of consonantal contrasts undergoes reorganization near the end of the first year of life. Infants born into Canadian-English speaking families, for example, were by 10 to 12 months of age no longer able to discriminate nonnative consonantal contrasts found in Hindi and Salish, a North American Indian language. Interestingly, however, Best et al (1988) found that infants at ages up to 14 months (as well as adults) could discriminate a nonnative consonantal Zulu click contrast. Best and her colleagues (e.g. Best 1994) suggest that the degree to which nonnative contrasts can be discriminated by older infants (and adults) depends on the relation of the contrast to the developing phonological categories of the native language (see the section below on cross-language speech perception). Finally, there is evidence that sensitivity to native language prosodic structure (Jusczyk et al 1993a) and phonotactic structure (Jusczyk et al 1993b) also emerges within the first year of life. In summary, although the infant's speech processing system is initially highly developed, it shows an equally early sensitivity to the specific sound patterns of the native language.

Cross-Language Speech Perception

As noted in the previous section, over the course of development the highly sophisticated abilities of infants to perceive speech in terms of categorical representations are shaped by the native language. As a consequence, phonetic perception in adults is highly language-specific (for early evidence of such specificity, see Lisker & Abramson 1970). In particular, although infants appear to be able to distinguish all (or nearly all) of the phonetic contrasts used in the world's languages, adults often find it difficult to distinguish nonnative contrasts (Aslin & Pisoni 1980). However, they do not find all nonnative contrasts equally difficult to distinguish, and there is considerable interest in determining why this is so.

Burnham (1986) has proposed that the phonetic contrasts used in the world's languages form a continuum from fragile to robust, and that the position of a contrast on the continuum, which is largely based on psychoacoustic salience, determines the relative difficulty of nonnative contrasts. However, independent measures of psychoacoustic salience have remained elusive, and there is now considerable evidence that linguistic as well as psychoacoustic factors play an important role. For example, Werker and her colleagues (Tees & Werker 1984, Werker et al 1981) have suggested that the ability to perceive a nonnative contrast depends in part on whether the phonetic properties of the nonnative contrast appear allophonically in the native language (i.e. the contrast occurs in the language, although it is not used to distinguish among phonemes). Evidence supporting the role of allophonic experience came in part from studies showing that English-speaking adults could more readily perceive a nonnative Hindi contrast that occurrs allophonically in English than one that does not. However, more recent data suggest that exposure to allophonic variation, per se, is not the critical factor. For example, Zulu click sounds do not occur in English, even allophonically, and yet, as noted earlier, English-speaking adults can readily discriminate them (Best et al 1988).

In an attempt to accommodate these findings, Best (1994, Best et al 1988) has proposed that native language phonology plays a critical role, but in a somewhat different way. She suggests that adults assimilate incoming speech sounds (both native and nonnative) to the phonological categories of their native language (cf Flege 1992). The ability to perceive a nonnative contrast is assumed to depend on the nature of the assimilation; for example, whether the two nonnative sounds are not assimilated to any native category, whether they are assimilated to the same or different native categories, and, if they are assimilated to the same category, whether to a comparable extent. This approach appears promising in that it can account for many of the differences in discriminability that have been found across a variety of contrasts, and it incorporates aspects of acoustic salience and allophonic variation (Best 1994; cf Polka 1992). What remains to be developed is a set of criteria for determining, a priori, what type of assimilation any given nonnative contrast should undergo.

A closely related question is whether it is possible for adults to relearn to distinguish nonnative contrasts that they find difficult (see Pisoni et al 1994). For some time, the answer was generally taken to be no (Strange & Jenkins 1978). This conclusion fit well with the view, prominent at the time, that the lack of exposure to a particular phonetic contrast results in a loss of sensitivity to the linguistically-relevant acoustic information, perhaps through the atrophy or retuning of sensory mechanisms such as feature detectors (Eimas 1978).

More recently, researchers have argued that the inability to perceive certain nonnative phonetic contrasts is not due to a sensory-based loss, but instead derives from a reorganization of perceptual abilities in terms of the phonological categories of the native language (e.g. Best et al 1988, Werker & Tees 1984b), perhaps through the operation of attentional mechanisms that produce changes in the relative salience of linguistically relevant acoustic properties of speech (Jusczyk 1993). Evidence supporting this view comes from studies showing that even difficult nonnative contrasts can often be discriminated, given more sensitive testing procedures (Werker & Logan 1985), and that certain training procedures, especially those emphasizing stimulus variability and identification procedures with feedback, yield improved performance even on difficult nonnative contrasts (e.g. Jamieson & Morosan 1986, Logan et al 1991). It should be noted, however, that the effects of laboratory training are often rather modest (cf MacKain et al 1981) and it is not known whether these effects will transfer to more naturalistic listening conditions involving connected discourse.

Effects of Higher-Level Linguistic Context

One of the most pervasive themes in perceptual research concerns the way in which higher-level contextual information is integrated with stimulus information during speech processing (Fodor 1983, Neisser 1967). Within the domain of phonetic perception, the issue is how higher-level linguistic information (e.g. from the word or sentence) combines with information from the acoustic signal to determine category identity. A major finding is that, as in other domains of perception, higher-level contextual information affects the outcome of categorization; that is, categorization is not based solely on the acoustic properties of the speech signal (e.g. Ganong 1980; see also Miller et al 1951). What remains unresolved is where in the categorization process higher-level context has its effect.

Research on context effects has focused primarily on contextual information provided by the lexicon, underscoring the view that speech perception and lexical access are closely related. Two major alternative views of how lexical information influences phonetic categorization have provided the general framework for much of this research. The first alternative, within the tradition of autonomous models (also called feed-forward or modular models) of processing (Fodor 1983), is that during an initial stage the acoustic signal is analyzed in terms of potential category identity, with context operating on the output of this process to influence the final categorization response. The second alternative, within the tradition of interactive models of processing (e.g.

McClelland & Elman 1986), is that the higher-level contextual information feeds down to affect the initial perceptual analysis.

The literature does not present a clear-cut choice between these alternatives. For example, Samuel (1981) found that increasing the availability of lexical information produced changes in sensitivity in a signal detection task that assessed the perceptual restoration of phonemes in degraded speech. He concluded that the lexicon can produce true top-down effects (interestingly, sentence-level context did not produce such changes in sensitivity, suggesting an important distinction between types of higher-level contextual effects). Using a paradigm that measures the influence of lexical status on the speed of phonetic categorization (cf Ganong 1980), Connine & Clifton (1987) also found evidence consistent with an interactive effect of lexical information, and the same paradigm produced evidence for a noninteractive effect of sentence-level context (Connine 1987). Further support for an interactive influence of lexical information comes from Elman & McClelland's (1988) study, which showed evidence of perceptual compensation for coarticulatory effects, mediated through the lexicon. However, other findings favor a noninteractive effect of lexical information. For example, Massaro (1989) reported an independent (i.e. noninteractive) influence of phonological context (assumed to be mediated via the lexicon) on phonetic categorization, and McQueen (1991) provided evidence more consistent with at least certain types of autonomous models (e.g. Cutler et al 1987) than with interactive models such as TRACE (McClelland & Elman 1986). Thus the empirical findings are inconclusive.

The problem runs deeper than this, however. Versions of interactive models seem to be able to accommodate empirical findings generally taken to support noninteractive views, and conversely, some types of noninteractive models can accommodate findings thought to provide evidence for true interaction between lexical and phonetic levels of processing. For example, Massaro (1989) modeled his empirical evidence for independent effects of phonological (lexical) context and acoustic-phonetic information with the noninteractive fuzzy logical model of perception. However, McClelland (1991; but see Massaro & Cohen 1991) has argued that these empirical effects can also be accommodated by a version of an interactive-activation model. Working in the opposite direction, Norris (1993) has shown that the Elman & McClelland (1988) findings that demonstrate lexically mediated perceptual compensation for coarticulation, originally taken to provide strong support for an interactive-activation model, can also be modeled by a version of a feed-forward model. Thus, although there is no doubt that higher-level context can influence phonetic categorization, and even some evidence that lexical-level and sentence-level effects may be qualitatively different, the precise nature of the underlying processes giving rise to these effects remains highly controversial and elusive.

MAPPING FROM ACOUSTIC SIGNAL TO LEXICON

We now examine how the acoustic signal is mapped onto the lexical items of the language. In some views (e.g. McClelland & Elman 1986), this is a well-specified multi-level process: The acoustic signal is first mapped onto prelexical linguistic representations (such as features and phonetic segments), and then these prelexical representations are used to access lexical items. In other views (e.g. Klatt 1979), an auditory representation of the acoustic signal is mapped directly onto lexical forms. Yet other views (Marslen-Wilson & Tyler 1980) are noncommittal about the existence or nature of possible prelexical linguistic representations that mediate between acoustic signal and lexical form. In other words, there is no tidy division between the traditional issues of speech perception and issues of lexical processing. As we have pointed out, it is increasingly clear that these two domains of research are closely interrelated. Perhaps not surprisingly, then, some of the issues we have already touched upon (e.g. the nature of the representational units and the role of native-language experience) surface here as well, albeit with somewhat different emphases.

The mapping of the speech signal onto the lexicon can be construed in terms of the processes of lexical access, selection, and integration with the developing discourse model (see Forster 1979; Frauenfelder & Tyler 1987; Marslen-Wilson 1984, 1987, 1989b, 1993; McClelland & Elman 1986; Norris 1986). We use this approach to structure our discussion. We begin with a brief overview of two major theoretical positions, cohort theory (Marslen-Wilson & Welsh 1978; Marslen-Wilson 1987, 1989b) and TRACE (McClelland & Elman 1986). We then examine, in light of these views, the segmentation and representation of spoken words, which are presumed to be necessary for lexical access to occur. Next, we turn to the process of lexical access itself. Finally, we consider lexical selection from the often large number of accessed items (Cole & Jakimik 1980; Marslen-Wilson 1987, 1989b, 1993; Marslen-Wilson & Tyler 1980; Marslen-Wilson & Welsh 1978; Morton 1969; but see Forster 1979), a process that in some theoretical positions rests in part on the extent to which an accessed item can be integrated with the existing discourse model (Marslen-Wilson 1987, 1989b; see also Norris 1986).

Theoretical Positions

COHORT THEORY   Cohort theory is a qualitative description of word recognition (Marslen-Wilson 1987, 1989b; Marslen-Wilson & Tyler 1980; Marslen-Wilson & Welsh 1978). It rests on the assumption that "...each memory element in the lexicon will be a computationally active processing entity" (Marlsen-Wilson & Welsh 1978, p. 56).

In early versions of the model, these memory entities process both bottom-up acoustic-phonetic and top-down syntactic-semantic information, provided by the developing discourse model (cf Morton 1969). The role of higher knowledge sources is restricted, however. Lexical access is only triggered by acoustic-phonetic input and thus no preselection of words based on context can occur. The initial, roughly 150 to 200 ms stretch of speech, however represented, activates in an all-or-none manner a cohort of items that match this initial representation. Activation makes available the phonological, syntactic, and semantic information associated with each lexical entry. As the acoustic-phonetic evidence accumulates over time, members of the cohort are affirmed and retained or disconfirmed and removed. Recognition occurs when the cohort is reduced to a single candidate. This may occur prior to the end of the word, at the uniqueness point—the point at which a target word is differentiated from all other members of its cohort. Given the presence of a developing discourse model, it is also possible for recognition to occur before the uniqueness point; inappropriate syntactic and semantic information can eliminate members of the cohort. Recognition is assumed to be optimally efficient in part because the processes of access and selection can make use of contextual information—a view directly opposed to modular theories of word recognition.

In later versions of cohort theory (Marslen-Wilson 1987, 1989b), there were three major revisions. First, access was no longer considered an all-or-none phenomenon. Words were activated in a graded manner, determined in part by the similarity between the input signal and the stored lexical representation. This change was prompted by the need to accommodate the obvious variability in speech arising from variation in articulation and noisy environments and our obvious ability to understand speech despite this variability. The special importance of word onsets was also relaxed. It was recognized that as long as the sequential nature of the incoming speech was registered, a word could be activated, even if the initial segment or segments were misperceived. Finally, the influence of contextual information was relegated to postperceptual processes of integration. Context could no longer eliminate members of the cohort. Selection must now be made on the basis of the prelexical goodness-of-fit between signal and activated word and the postlexical goodness-of-fit between cohort members and the discourse model, and without the possibility that contextual information might override the match between acoustic-phonetic information and stored representations.

THE TRACE MODEL   TRACE is a quantitative model, designed originally to recognize speech at the segmental level and later extended to simulate the recognition of words, but now from preprocessed input rather than from the acoustic signal (Elman & McClelland 1986, McClelland & Elman 1986).

TRACE is an interactive-activation model of processing in which information flows in both directions, from the bottom up and from the top down. There are three levels of representation—phonetic features, phonemes, and words—and although the model is connectionist in nature, the representations are local and prewired and not distributed and learned. These representations are actually processing elements (or units) that are activated in proportion to the strength of the hypothesis that a unit represents. To accommodate the sequential, time-dependent nature of speech, each set of representations is repeated over arbitrary units of time. The activation of a representation, a hypothesis about information currently being received, is the TRACE and, in accord with a concept of a mental trace, may be altered with further processing within the time window, permitting both preceding and following contextual information to affect the trace.

At the level of features, the units representing phonetic features are defined in terms of the acoustic information that both precedes and follows the feature of concern—an attempt to accommodate consequences of coarticulation and the temporal overlap of cues. Activated features feed upward to activate phonemic units, which in turn activate word units, and both phonemic and word units activate supporting units at the adjacent lower level of representation. Within a level of representation and within a restricted time-frame, individual units are connected by inhibitory mechanisms, whereas across levels, the flow of activation in either direction is excitatory. There is no presegmentation; segmentation is a consequence of recognition. The strength of all activated word units depends on past and current input (i.e. on excitatory inputs from lower levels and on inhibitory inputs from the same level of representation). Recognition of the more strongly activated word representation may occur when a criterial time has elapsed or when some criterion of relative strength is achieved. As is apparent, TRACE has many features in common with cohort theory and was developed to accommodate in a quantitative manner the qualitative expectations of cohort theory.

Segmentation and Representation

As noted above, a characteristic of spontaneous spoken language is its continuous nature. There are no invariant acoustic indicants to mark the beginnings and endings of individual words (but for some possible cues, see Nakatani & Dukes 1977, Nakatani & Shaffer 1978), let alone the beginnings and endings of phonetic segments or syllables. Nevertheless, there have been a number of attempts to find a solution to the segmentation problem, at lexical and sublexical levels, not all of which are necessarily mutually exclusive. As Norris & Cutler (1985) have noted, the segmentation problem involves two components: The first is the physical segmentation of the speech stream into lexical and sublexical units, and the second is what they call the classification problem—the classification of these segmented units into representational structures of a linguistic nature that provide the basis for accessing the lexicon. As noted earlier, prelexical linguistic structures need not be available; in some views, access is achieved directly by means of auditory representations (Klatt 1979). Representations of a linguistic nature have been hypothesized to take a number of forms, from phonetic features (e.g. Marslen-Wilson 1987) and underspecified phonological features (Lahiri & Marslen-Wilson 1991, Marslen-Wilson 1993) to phonetic segments (e.g. Foss & Gernsbacher 1983, Pisoni & Luce 1987), morae (subsyllabic units such as the vocalic nucleus) (Otake et al 1993), and syllables (e.g. Cutler et al 1986, Mehler et al 1981, Mehler et al 1990, Segui et al 1990). The segmentation-representational strategy used appears to be determined in part by the listener's native language.

One segmentation procedure that is a consequence of a postlexical strategy (Frauenfelder 1985) is an integral part of the early version of cohort theory (e.g. Marslen-Wilson & Welsh 1978; see also Cole & Jakimik 1980). Given knowledge of the beginning of an utterance (e.g. a long pause), listeners can begin to access the initial word (and the members of its cohort) after the first 150 to 200 ms of speech. On the further assumption that the initially activated cohort of possible words could be reduced to a single word on perception of the last phonetic segment or even before, given an early uniqueness point, then listeners' knowledge of the phonological representation associated with the perceived word determines its ending and importantly the beginning of the next word. This word-by-word view of lexical segmentation rests heavily on the assumption that word endings can be determined without reference to subsequent information and, when this is not possible, that the number of ambiguities would be few (e.g. those arising from words such as *can, cant,* and *canter*). However, Luce (1986a) has shown that approximately 60% of the words in continuous speech do not possess uniqueness points, and thus the beginning of the next word cannot be predicted as easily as early cohort theory would have us believe. Suffixes create a similar problem, as do words that may or may not be a single word (*lettuce* vs *let us*). The postlexical strategy would thus seem inadequate as a general principle of segmentation. In contrast, TRACE (McClelland & Elman 1986) and recent versions of the cohort theory (Marslen-Wilson 1987) do not require an explicit segmentation process—segmentation is simply a consequence of the ongoing processes of recognition (see also Frauenfelder & Peeters 1990).

A prerecognition view of segmentation is found in the work of Cutler and her associates (Cutler 1990, Cutler & Butterfield 1992, Cutler & Carter 1987, Cutler & Mehler 1993, Cutler & Norris 1988, Norris & Cutler 1985), who have posited a metrical segmentation strategy for English, which is a stress-timed language, as opposed to French, for example, which is syllable timed. In essence, they have assumed that segmentation is initiated by strong syllables (i.e. syllables with a full vowel). This full vowel, together with a syllable onset and coda, and all following weak syllables up to the next strong syllable, would trigger a lexical search (Cutler & Norris 1988, Cutler & Butterfield 1992). [See Cutler (1990) for a summary of the characteristics of English word structure that favor a metrical segmentation strategy; see also Grosjean & Gee (1987), who suggest that lexical access may be driven by stressed syllables alone].

In French, as noted, rhythm is based on the syllable and native speakers appear to base their segmentation of speech on syllabic structures that, once delineated, may reasonably be assumed to be the basis for lexical access. Mehler et al (1981) found that French listeners responded more quickly to consonant-vowel or consonant-vowel-consonant syllabic targets when they matched word-initial syllables than when there was a mismatch, despite the fact that the initial three phonetic segments were the same in both cases. English listeners showed no evidence for a syllable-based segmentation strategy. For them, access presumably was based on sequences of phonetic segments. Furthermore, French listeners responded to English as they did to French and English listeners responded to French as they did to English (Cutler et al 1986, Cutler et al 1992) (for evidence that attention can be allocated to syllables by French and Spanish listeners, see Pallier et al 1993).

At issue is what specific factors in the phonology of a language and its realization in speech drive these different strategies. Sebastian-Gallés et al (1992) have outlined a number of possibilities, including the presence or absence of variable stress, contrastive stress, ambisyllabicity, and vowel reduction as well as the number of vowels. However, it has not been possible to determine which factor or set of factors underlies the use of a syllabic versus nonsyllabic segmentation strategy. For example, Sebastian-Gallés et al (1992) found evidence of a syllabic segmentation unit in Catalan, but only for unstressed initial syllables. Syllabic segmentation was not found in Spanish, regardless of stress, unless reaction times were relatively slow (but see Bradley et al 1993) and thus possibly a consequence of postlexical processing (see Bard 1990). Based on the presence of a syllabic segmentation strategy in Dutch listeners (Zwitserlood et al 1993), regardless of whether target words were ambisyllabic, ambisyllabicity would thus seem not to be critically related to a syllabic segmentation strategy as was first believed. It is important to note that the syllable is not the only prelexical linguistic unit (above the phonetic segment) used for segmentation. Otake et al (1993) have shown that Japanese listeners use the subsyllabic unit, the mora. Zwitserlood et al (1993) have suggested that syllables (and by extension, subsyllabic units) may not be stored representations, but rather may be computed during processing from a listener's knowledge of phonology and its acoustic realization (cf Frazier 1987). It remains to be determined how computational procedures or models of word recognition generate the observed differences across languages. Indeed, it even remains to be shown whether language-specific strategies are involved in the on-line processing of continuous discourse. Studies (Eimas & Nygaard 1992, Foss 1982) have indicated that speech perception differs markedly when listeners hear individual lexical items as opposed to connected discourse.

Lexical Access

The information in speech is temporally organized, a fact recognized in both versions of cohort theory (Marslen-Wilson & Welsh 1978, Marslen-Wilson 1987) and in TRACE (McClelland & Elman 1986; see also Norris 1990, 1993). In the original version of cohort theory, Marslen-Wilson & Welsh (1978) presumed that the onsets of words were of special importance in activating a cohort of possible candidates (cf Tyler 1984). Thus, the initial segments /s/ and /p/ in the word *spell* would activate all words beginning with these sounds (e.g. *spell, split, spill,* and *spite*). Moreover, the activated cohort could not be altered to include a mispronounced word (e.g. *tribe* rather than *bribe*) except by some form of late backtracking. TRACE and later versions of cohort theory permit lexical access (actually the activation of running cohorts) on the basis of any information in the incoming signal, regardless of its position, although its sequential position must be preserved. Nevertheless, TRACE gives priority to word-initial information in that activated words inhibit all other words, and the strength of inhibition between words increases with the growing activation strength of words that were first accessed.

Experimental results have shown that word-initial information takes precedence, but not absolutely, as might be expected on intuitive grounds. For example, the detection of mispronunciations is more easily accomplished in word-initial than noninitial position (Cole 1973, Marslen-Wilson & Welsh 1978). These results support the hypothesis that words are efficiently recognized—not all the acoustic information need be perceived given an early uniqueness point; thus, phonetic segments occurring after the uniqueness point may receive very little attention, making late mispronunciations difficult to detect. Using a cross-modal semantic priming task (Swinney 1979), Marslen-Wilson & Zwitserlood (1989) showed that priming was reliable for the original word but not for real-word or nonword rhymes. Nonetheless, real-word and nonword rhyme primes did have some subtle effects [see also Marslen-Wilson (1993) and Bard (1990) for a discussion of these effects]. Furthermore, Connine et al (1993) found reliable cross-modal semantic priming with nonword rhyming primes but only when they differed by no more than two phonetic features from the original word [but see Salasoo & Pisoni 1985; see Norris (1990) for a connectionist model of recognition given input variability].

Minimal alterations in the initial segmental information do not seem to preclude a word from entering a cohort of possibly intended words. This is

also true for words with perceptually ambiguous onsets [Connine et al 1994; but see Marslen-Wilson (1993) for constraints on priming by perceptually ambiguous information]. Nevertheless, the entry of mispronounced words would seem not to be without cost to activation levels and their perception may not be the same as that for correctly pronounced words (Marslen-Wilson 1993, Marslen-Wilson & Zwitserlood 1989). In sum, marked, but not subtle, alterations in the initial segment may preclude a word's entry into a cohort, and mismatches late in a word (Zwitserlood 1989) may have immediate and strong inhibitory effects on the activation of the target word.

Marslen-Wilson (1987, 1993) has argued that these data have implications for the representation of speech and for the view that the activation of lexical items is a graded phenomenon. With regard to the former, the claim is that representations must be tolerant of the natural variation in speech; we need, for example, to be able to recognize allophonic variations and even the word *cigarette* if *shigarette* is pronounced. More specifically, a featural description of segments, especially underspecified phonological features, can accommodate these and other forms of variation in the acoustic signal that arise from processes of production, including variation from mispronunciations that does not specify marked phonological features (Lahiri & Marslen-Wilson 1991, Marslen-Wilson 1993). It should be noted, however, that a sparse phonological representation runs directly counter to recent findings, noted earlier, that the representation of speech is incredibly detailed (for a review, see Nygaard & Pisoni 1994).

As for the activation of lexical items, a representation of the input signal in terms of underspecified (i.e. unmarked) phonological features or phonetic features permits a cohort of lexical items with the activation of each member increasing as the similarity between signal and stored lexical representations increases (Marslen-Wilson 1987). Warren & Marslen-Wilson (1987, 1988) and Marslen-Wilson (1989b) argue that their findings indicating the continuous uptake of acoustic information during word recognition necessitates pre-lexical representations of a featural nature or units no larger than a phonetic segment. There is also evidence favoring the graded activation of cohort members in that word frequency is related both to the speed of recognition and the relative strength of cross-modal priming effects (e.g. Marslen-Wilson 1990, Shillcock 1990, Zwitserlood 1989; see also Morton 1969). However, the frequency effect may be quite short-lived, occurring only during the earliest stages of activation (Marslen-Wilson 1990, Zwitserlood 1989), when levels of activation are free to vary.

Finally, Luce (1986b; Luce et al 1990) has presented evidence supporting the idea that cohort density (i.e. the number of items activated by the acoustic signal) also influences lexical access, presumably by making differentiation of the intended item more difficult and recognition slower in dense as opposed to sparse lexical environments. More recently, however, contradictory evidence has been obtained (e.g. Shillcock 1990; cf Marslen-Wilson 1993). Moreover, Bard & Shillcock (1993) have shown on the basis of statistical properties of English that neighborhood effects may have been a consequence of word frequency, in particular the presence of a single high-frequency competitor that is more likely with high- than low-density cohorts.

Lexical Selection and Integration

A major assumption of cohort theory, and one that is readily accommodated by TRACE, is that there is early selection of words (i.e. the word recognition process is optimally efficient). Evidence favoring this position is found in experiments in which listeners closely shadow (repeat) connected speech or make detection responses to preassigned targets that are identical to the input or a rhyme of the target, for example. In these experiments (e.g. Marslen-Wilson 1973, Marslen-Wilson & Welsh 1978, Marslen-Wilson & Tyler 1980), correct selection may occur as soon as 200 to 300 ms of the target has been heard, which often provides less information than is necessary to determine the uniqueness point, let alone the entire word. The preceding context must have been used by listeners in making their decisions. A similar conclusion comes from gating studies (e.g. Grosjean 1980; see also Marslen-Wilson 1987). Although the evidence cited above is robust and clearly supports a process of early selection aided by contextual information, it is not the entire story about selection.

It is simply not possible to recognize all words early. Luce (1986a) showed that most words in continuous speech do not have uniqueness points. There are additional problems with potentially embedded words and words that cross potential word boundaries as well as problems with properly segmenting, accessing, and selecting the unstressed, highly-reduced function words (see Cutler & Carter 1987, Shillcock 1990). These phenomena indicate that selection must often be delayed in order to resolve the ubiquitous ambiguity present in language by means of later-occurring contextual information (for evidence and additional arguments favoring frequent late selection, see Bard et al 1988, Connine et al 1991, Grosjean 1985, Grosjean & Gee 1987, Shillcock 1990, Taft & Hambly 1986).

Swinney (1979, 1981; Onifer & Swinney 1981) and Tanenhaus et al (1979) have published seminal papers on the effects of context on lexical selection. Using a cross-modal lexical decision task, they found that biasing sentential contexts failed to constrain the activation of the multiple meanings of words. For example, the semantically ambiguous word *bug* immediately primed both *ant* and *spy,* dominant and subordinate meanings of *bug*—evidence in accord with a modular view of lexical access (Fodor 1983). However, as expected, if the target word was delayed by about 200 ms the ambiguity was resolved in line with the biasing sentence, indicating that nonlexical knowledge sources influence lexical processing, but they do so postlexically (see Norris 1986, Onifer & Swinney 1981, Tanenhaus et al 1979). Similarly, the noun and verb meanings of a word (e.g. *watch*) were likewise found to be unaffected by contexts that bias one or the other meaning, but again for only brief intervals between the priming and target words (Seidenberg et al 1984, Tyler & Wessels 1983; for reviews, see Tanenhaus et al 1987, Tanenhaus & Lucas 1987).

In contrast, Seidenberg et al (1982) have found that sentential contexts that biased alternate noun interpretations by both pragmatic and semantic factors did constrain the immediate activation of meaning (for additional evidence, see Zwitserlood 1989; for an alternative interpretation of Zwitserlood, see Marslen-Wilson 1987, 1989b). However, no such constraints were found for noun-verb meanings (for a possible explanation of the difference between noun-noun and noun-verb meanings, see Tanenhaus et al 1987, Tanenhaus & Lucas 1987). Forster (1979), among others, has noted that the presence of contextual constraints may arise from intralexical associations (see Collins & Loftus 1975) and thereby be in accordance with a modular architecture. On the other hand, biasing sentential contexts can be arranged to be based on extra-lexical conceptual features (but see Koriat 1981, Glucksberg et al 1986; cf Burgess et al 1989, Seidenberg et al 1984). The view that modularity may not be an all-or-none phenomenon (cf Tanenhaus et al 1987, Tanenhaus & Lucas 1987) has guided the research of Tabossi and her colleagues (Tabossi 1988a,b; Tabossi et al 1987; Tabossi & Zardon 1993). Their findings support the idea that our understanding of contextual constraints requires more than simple yes or no answers to questions of their presence and the locus of their effects; a description of the causal conditions, as well as where and when these effects occur, is now essential.

This position finds further support in connectionist models that are attempting to capture the conditions under which contextual constraints are operative and the conditions when they are not in evidence (Kawamoto 1993, Norris 1993, Tanenhaus et al 1987, Tanenhaus & Lucas 1990; see also Seidenberg 1994). Some of these models (e.g. Kawamoto 1993, Norris 1993), although interactive in the sense that contextual information is operative during percep-tual processing, do not accommodate contextual effects by means of classical interactive architectures that involve the top-down flow of information, but rather by distributed lexical representations that are enriched in a bottom-up fashion by the contextual information itself. As we noted above, a similar blurring of the distinction between interactive and modular architectures is also taking place at lower levels of the system, where the issue is the influence of lexical information on phonetic processing.

Given these developments in theory, and the empirical findings we have discussed confirming the seemingly natural relation between the earliest stages of speech perception and the processes of word recognition, a major task of future research will be to describe the architecture that underlies the commonalities of the early components of spoken language comprehension. This will involve at minimum an explication of the representations that are involved in these early stages of processing and a specification of the processing mechanisms themselves.

ACKNOWLEDGMENTS

Preparation of this chapter was supported in part by NIH Grants DC 00130 (JL Miller) and HD 05331 (PD Eimas).

Literature Cited

Altmann GTM, ed. 1990. *Cognitive Models of Speech Processing: Psycholinguistic and Computational Perspectives.* Cambridge, MA: MIT Press

Altmann GTM, Shillcock R, eds. 1993. *Cognitive Models of Speech Processing.* East Sussex, UK: Erlbaum

Aslin RN, Pisoni DB. 1980. Some developmental processes in speech perception. In *Child Phonology,* ed. GH Yeni-Komshian, JF Kavanagh, CA Ferguson, pp. 67–96. New York: Academic

Bahrick LE, Pickens JN. 1988. Classification of bimodal English and Spanish language passages by infants. *Infant Behav. Dev.* 11: 277–96

Bard EG. 1990. Competition, lateral inhibition, and frequency: comments on the chapters of Frauenfelder and Peeters, Marslen-Wilson, and others. See Altmann 1990, pp. 185–210

Bard EG, Shillcock R. 1993. Competitor effects during lexical access: chasing Zipf's Tail. See Altmann & Shillcock 1993, pp. 235–76

Bard EG, Shillcock RC, Altmann GTM. 1988. The recognition of words after their acoustic offsets in spontaneous speech: effects of subsequent context. *Percept. Psychophys.* 44:395–408

Bertoncini J, Morais J, Bijeljac-Babic R, McAdams S, Peretz I, Mehler J. 1989. Dichotic perception and laterality in neonates. *Brain Lang.* 37:591–605

Best CT. 1994. The emergence of native-language phonological influences in infants: a perceptual assimilation model. See Goodman & Nusbaum 1994, pp. 167–224

Best CT, McRoberts GW, Sithole NM. 1988. Examination of perceptual reorganization for nonnative speech contrasts: Zulu click discrimination by English-speaking adults and infants. *J. Exp. Psychol: Hum. Percept. Perform.* 14:345–60

Bijeljac-Babic R, Bertoncini J, Mehler J. 1993. How do 4-day-old infants categorize multisyllabic utterances? *Dev. Psychol.* 29:711–21

Bradley DC, Sánchez-Casas RM, García-Albea JE. 1993. The status of the syllable in the perception of Spanish and English. *Lang. Cogn. Proc.* 8:197–233

Burgess C, Tanenhaus MK, Seidenberg MS. 1989. Context and lexical access: implications of nonword interference for lexical ambiguity resolution. *J. Exp. Psychol.: Learn. Mem. Cogn.* 15: 620–32

Burnham DK. 1986. Developmental loss of speech perception: exposure to and experience with a first language. *Appl. Psycholinguist.* 7:207–40

Carney AE, Widin GP, Viemeister NF. 1977. Noncategorical perception of stop consonants differing in VOT. *J. Acoust. Soc. Am.* 62:961–69

Christophe A, Dupoux E, Bertoncini J, Mehler J. 1994. Do infants perceive word boundaries? An empirical study of the bootstrapping of lexical acquisition. *J. Acoust. Soc. Am.* 95:1570–80

Cole RA. 1973. Listening for mispronunciations: a measure of what we hear during speech. *Percept. Psychophys.* 13:153–56

Cole RA, Jakimik J. 1980. A model of speech perception. In *Perception and Production of Fluent Speech,* ed. RA Cole, pp. 133–63. Hillsdale, NJ: Erlbaum

Collins AM, Loftus EF. 1975. A spreading-activation theory of semantic processing. *Psychol. Rev.* 82:407–28

Connine CM. 1987. Constraints on interactive processes in auditory word recognition: the role of sentence context. *J. Mem. Lang.* 26: 527–38

Connine CM, Blasko DG, Hall M. 1991. Effects of subsequent sentence context in auditory word recognition: temporal and linguistic constraints. *J. Mem. Lang.* 30: 234–50

Connine CM, Blasko DG, Titone D. 1993. Do the beginnings of spoken words have a special status in auditory word recognition? *J. Mem. Lang.* 32:193–210

Connine CM, Blasko DG, Wang J. 1994. Vertical similarity in spoken word recognition: multiple lexical activation, individual differences and the role of sentence context. *Percept. Psychophys.* In press

Connine CM, Clifton C Jr. 1987. Interactive use of lexical information in speech perception. *J. Exp. Psychol.: Hum. Percept. Perform.* 13:291–99

Cutler A. 1990. Exploiting prosodic probabilities in speech segmentation. See Altmann 1990, pp. 105–121

Cutler A, Butterfield S. 1992. Rhythmic cues to speech segmentation: evidence from juncture misperception. *J. Mem. Lang.* 31: 218–36

Cutler A, Carter DM. 1987. The predominance of strong initial syllables in the English vocabulary. *Computer Speech Lang.* 2:133–42

Cutler A, Mehler J. 1993. The periodicity bias. *J. Phonet.* 21:103–8

Cutler A, Mehler J, Norris D, Segui J. 1986. The syllable's differing role in the segmentation of French and English. *J. Mem. Lang.* 25:385–400

Cutler A, Mehler J, Norris D, Segui J. 1987. Phoneme identification and the lexicon. *Cogn. Psychol.* 19:141–77

Cutler A, Mehler J, Norris D, Segui J. 1992. The monolingual nature of speech segmentation by bilinguals. *Cogn. Psychol.* 24: 381–410

Cutler A, Norris D. 1988. The role of strong syllables in segmentation for lexical access. *J. Exp. Psychol.: Hum. Percept. Perform.* 14:113–21

DeCasper AJ, Fifer WP. 1980. Of human bonding: newborns prefer their mothers' voices. *Science* 208:1174–76

Diehl RL, Kluender KR. 1989. On the objects of speech perception. *Ecol. Psychol.* 1: 121–44

Eimas PD. 1978. Developmental aspects of speech perception. In *Handbook of Sensory Physiology,* ed. R Held, H Leibowitz, HL

Teuber, pp. 357–74. New York: Springer-Verlag

Eimas PD. 1985. The equivalence of cues in the perception of speech by infants. *Infant Behav. Dev.* 8:125–38

Eimas PD, Miller JL, eds. 1981. *Perspectives on the Study of Speech.* Hillsdale, NJ: Erlbaum

Eimas PD, Miller JL. 1991. A constraint on the discrimination of speech by young infants. *Lang. Speech* 34:251–63

Eimas PD, Miller JL. 1992. Organization in the perception of speech by young infants. *Psychol. Sci.* 3:340–45

Eimas PD, Miller JL, Jusczyk PW. 1987. On infant speech perception and the acquisition of language. See Harnad 1987, pp. 161–95

Eimas PD, Nygaard LC. 1992. Contextual coherence and attention in phoneme monitoring. *J. Mem. Lang.* 31:375–95

Eimas PD, Siqueland ER, Jusczyk P, Vigorito J. 1971. Speech perception in infants. *Science* 171:303–6

Elman JL, McClelland JL. 1986. Exploiting lawful variability in the speech wave. In *Invariance and Variability in Speech Processes,* ed. JS Perkell, DH Klatt, pp. 360–85. Hillsdale, NJ: Erlbaum

Elman JL, McClelland JL. 1988. Cognitive penetration of the mechanisms of perception: compensation for coarticulation of lexically restored phonemes. *J. Mem. Lang.* 27:143–65

Fernald A. 1984. The perceptual and affective salience of mothers' speech to infants. In *The Origins and Growth of Communication,* ed. L Feagans, C Garvey, R Golinkoff, pp. 5–29. Norwood, NJ: Ablex

Flege JE. 1992. Speech learning in a second language. In *Phonological Development: Models, Research, and Implications,* ed. CA Ferguson, L Menn, C Stoel-Gammon, pp. 565–604. Parkton, MD: York

Fodor JA. 1983. *The Modularity of Mind.* Cambridge, MA: MIT Press

Forster KI. 1979. Levels of processing and the structure of the language processor. In *Sentence Processing: Psycholinguistic Studies Presented to Merrill Garrett,* ed. WE Cooper, ECT Walker, pp. 27–85. Hillsdale, NJ: Erlbaum

Foss DJ. 1982. A discourse on semantic priming. *Cogn. Psychol.* 14:590–607

Foss DJ. 1988. Experimental psycholinguistics. *Annu. Rev. Psychol.* 39:301–48

Foss DJ, Gernsbacher MA. 1983. Cracking the dual code: toward a unitary model of phoneme identification. *J. Verb. Learn. Verb. Behav.* 22:609–32

Fowler CA. 1986. An event approach to the study of speech perception from a direct-realist perspective. *J. Phonet.* 14:3–28

Frauenfelder UH. 1985. Cross-linguistic approaches to lexical segmentation. *Linguistics* 23:669–87

Frauenfelder UH, Peeters G. 1990. Lexical segmentation in TRACE: an exercise in simulation. See Altmann 1990, pp. 50–86

Frauenfelder UH, Tyler LK. 1987. The process of spoken word recognition: an introduction. *Cognition* 25:1–20

Frazier L. 1987. Structure in auditory word recognition. *Cognition* 25:157–87

Ganong WF III. 1980. Phonetic categorization in auditory word perception. *J. Exp. Psychol.: Hum. Percept. Perform.* 6:110–25

Gerken L, Jusczyk PW, Mandel DR. 1994. When prosody fails to cue syntactic structure: 9-month-olds' sensitivity to phonological versus syntactic phrases. *Cognition* 51:237–65

Gernsbacher MA, ed. 1994. *Handbook of Psycholinguistics.* San Diego, CA: Academic

Glucksberg S, Kreuz RJ, Rho SH. 1986. Context can constrain lexical access: implications for models of language comprehension. *J. Exp. Psychol.: Learn. Mem. Cogn.* 12:323–35

Goodman JC, Nusbaum HC, eds. 1994. *The Development of Speech Perception: The Transition from Speech Sounds to Spoken Words.* Cambridge, MA: MIT Press

Gordon PC, Eberhardt JL, Rueckl JG. 1993. Attentional modulation of the phonetic significance of acoustic cues. *Cogn. Psychol.* 25:1–42

Grosjean F. 1980. Spoken word recognition processes and the gating paradigm. *Percept. Psychophys.* 28:267–83

Grosjean F. 1985. The recognition of words after their acoustic offset: evidence and implications. *Percept. Psychophys.* 38:299–310

Grosjean F, Gee JP. 1987. Prosodic structure and spoken word recognition. *Cognition* 25:135–55

Harnad S, ed. 1987. *Categorical Perception.* New York: Cambridge Univ. Press

Hirsh-Pasek K, Kemler Nelson DG, Jusczyk PW, Cassidy KW, Druss B, Kennedy L. 1987. Clauses are perceptual units for young infants. *Cognition* 26:269–86

Hohne EA, Jusczyk PW. 1994. Two month-old infants' sensitivity to allophonic differences. *Percept. Psychophys.* In press

Jamieson DG, Morosan DE. 1986. Training non-native speech contrasts in adults: acquisition of the English /D/-/T/ contrast by francophones. *Percept. Psychophys.* 40: 205–15

Jusczyk PW. 1986. Speech Perception. In *Handbook of Perception and Human Performance.* Vol. 11: *Cognitive Processes and Performance,* ed. KR Boff, L Kaufman, JP Thomas, pp. 2-49. New York: Wiley

Jusczyk PW. 1993. From general to language-specific capacities: the WRAPSA model of how speech perception develops. *J. Phonet.* 21:3–28

Jusczyk PW. 1994. Language acquisition: speech sounds and the beginnings of phonology. See Miller & Eimas 1994. In press

Jusczyk PW, Cutler A, Redanz N. 1993a. Preference for predominant stress patterns of English words. *Child Dev.* 64: 675–87

Jusczyk PW, Friederici AD, Wessels JMI, Svenkerud VY, Jusczyk AM. 1993b. Infants' sensitivity to the sound patterns of native language words. *J. Mem. Lang.* 32: 402–20

Jusczyk PW, Hirsh–Pasek K, Kemler Nelson DG, Kennedy LJ, Woodward A, Piwoz J. 1992. Perception of acoustic correlates of major phrasal units by young infants. *Cogn. Psychol.* 24:252–93

Kawamoto AH. 1993. Nonlinear dynamics in the resolution of lexical ambiguity: a parallel distributed processing account. *J. Mem. Lang.* 32:474–517

Kewley-Port D. 1983. Time-varying features as correlates of place of articulation in stop consonants. *J. Acoust. Soc. Am.* 73:322–35

Klatt DH. 1979. Speech perception: a model of acoustic-phonetic analysis and lexical access. *J. Phonet.* 7:279–312

Klatt DH. 1989. Review of selected models of speech perception. See Marslen-Wilson 1989a, pp. 169–226

Koriat A. 1981. Semantic facilitation in lexical decision as a function of prime-target association. *Mem. Cogn.* 9:587–98

Kuhl PK. 1979. Speech perception in early infancy: perceptual constancy for spectrally dissimilar vowel categories. *J. Acoust. Soc. Am.* 66:1668–79

Kuhl PK. 1983. Perception of auditory equivalence classes for speech in early infancy. *Infant Behav. Dev.* 6:263–85

Kuhl PK. 1986. Theoretical contributions of tests on animals to the special-mechanisms debate in speech. *Exp. Biol.* 45:233–65

Kuhl PK. 1991. Human adults and human infants show a "perceptual magnet effect" for the prototypes of speech categories, monkeys do not. *Percept. Psychophys.* 50:93–107

Kuhl PK. 1992. Psychoacoustics and speech perception: internal standards, perceptual anchors, and prototypes. In *Developmental Psychoacoustics,* ed. LA Werner, EW Rubel, pp. 293–332. Washington, DC: Am. Psychol. Assoc.

Kuhl PK, Williams KA, Lacerda F, Stevens KN, Lindblom B. 1992. Linguistic experience alters phonetic perception in infants by 6 months of age. *Science* 255: 606–8

Lahiri A, Gewirth L, Blumstein SE. 1984. A reconsideration of acoustic invariance for place of articulation in diffuse stop consonants: evidence from a cross-language study. *J. Acoust. Soc. Am.* 76:391–404

Lahiri A, Marslen-Wilson W. 1991. The mental representation of lexical form: a phonological approach to the recognition lexicon. *Cognition* 38:245–94

Levitt A, Jusczyk PW, Murray J, Carden G. 1988. Context effects in two-month-old infants' perception of labiodental/interdental fricative contrasts. *J. Exp. Psychol.: Hum. Percept. Perform.* 14:361–68

Li X, Pastore RE. 1992. Evaluation of prototypes and exemplars in perceptual space for place contrast. In *The Auditory Processing of Speech: From Sounds to Words*, ed. MEH Schouten, pp. 303–8. Berlin: de Gruyter

Liberman AM, Cooper FS, Shankweiler DP, Studdert-Kennedy M. 1967. Perception of the speech code. *Psychol. Rev.* 74:431–61

Liberman AM, Harris KS, Hoffman HS, Griffith BC. 1957. The discrimination of speech sounds within and across phoneme boundaries. *J. Exp. Psychol.* 54:358–68

Liberman AM, Mattingly IG. 1985. The motor theory of speech perception revised. *Cognition* 21:1–36

Lisker L. 1986. "Voicing" in English: a catalogue of acoustic features signaling /b/ versus /p/ in trochees. *Lang. Speech* 29:3–11

Lisker L, Abramson AS. 1970. The voicing dimension: some experiments in comparative phonetics. *Proc. Int. Congr. Phonet. Sci., 6th, Prague, 1967*, pp. 563–67. Prague: Academia

Logan JS, Lively SE, Pisoni DB. 1991. Training Japanese listeners to identify English /r/ and /l/: a first report. *J. Acoust. Soc. Am.* 89:874–86

Luce PA. 1986a. A computational analysis of uniqueness points in auditory word recognition. *Percept. Psychophys.* 39:155–58

Luce PA. 1986b. *Neighborhoods of words in the mental lexicon.* PhD thesis. Indiana Univ., Bloomington, Indiana

Luce PA, Pisoni DB, Goldinger SD. 1990. Similarity neighborhoods of spoken words. See Altmann 1990, pp. 122–47

MacKain KS, Best CT, Strange W. 1981. Categorical perception of English /r/ and /l/ by Japanese bilinguals. *Appl. Psycholinguist.* 2:369–90

Marslen-Wilson W. 1973. Linguistic structure and speech shadowing at very short latencies. *Nature* 244:522–23

Marslen-Wilson W. 1984. Function and process in spoken word recognition. In *Attention and Performance X: Control of Language Processes*, ed. H Bouma, DG Bouwhuis, pp. 125–50. Hillsdale, NJ: Erlbaum

Marslen-Wilson W. 1987. Functional parallelism in spoken word-recognition. *Cognition* 25:71–102

Marslen-Wilson W, ed. 1989a. *Lexical Representation and Process.* Cambridge, MA: MIT Press

Marslen-Wilson W. 1989b. Access and integration: projecting sound onto meaning. See Marslen-Wilson 1989a, pp. 3–24

Marslen-Wilson W. 1990. Activation, competition, and frequency in lexical access. See Altmann 1990, pp. 148–72

Marslen-Wilson W. 1993. Issues of process and representation in lexical access. See Altmann & Shillcock 1993, pp. 187–210

Marslen-Wilson W, Tyler LK. 1980. The temporal structure of spoken language understanding. *Cognition* 8:1–71

Marslen-Wilson W, Welsh A. 1978. Processing interactions and lexical access during word recognition in continuous speech. *Cogn. Psychol.* 10:29–63

Marslen-Wilson W, Zwitserlood P. 1989. Accessing spoken words: the importance of word onsets. *J. Exp. Psychol.: Hum. Percept. Perform.* 15:576–85

Massaro DW. 1987a. *Speech Perception By Ear and Eye: A Paradigm for Psychological Inquiry.* Hillsdale, NJ: Erlbaum

Massaro DW. 1987b. Categorical partition: a fuzzy-logical model of categorization behavior. See Harnad 1987, pp. 254–83

Massaro DW. 1989. Testing between the TRACE model and the Fuzzy Logical Model of Speech Perception. *Cogn. Psychol.* 21:398–421

Massaro DW, Cohen MM. 1991. Integration versus interactive activation: the joint influence of stimulus and context in perception. *Cogn. Psychol.* 23:558–614

McClelland JL. 1991. Stochastic interactive processes and the effect of context on perception. *Cogn. Psychol.* 23:1–44

McClelland JL, Elman JL. 1986. The TRACE model of speech perception. *Cogn. Psychol.* 18:1–86

McQueen JM. 1991. The influence of the lexicon on phonetic categorization: stimulus quality in word-final ambiguity. *J. Exp. Psychol.: Hum. Percept. Perform.* 17:433–43

Medin DL, Barsalou LW. 1987. Categorization processes and categorical perception. See Harnad 1987, pp. 455–90

Mehler J, Bertoncini J, Barriere M, Jassik-Gerschenfeld D. 1978. Infant recognition of mother's voice. *Perception* 7:491–97

Mehler J, Dommergues JY, Frauenfelder U, Segui J. 1981. The syllable's role in speech segmentation. *J. Verb. Learn. Verb. Behav.* 20:298–305

Mehler J, Dupoux E, Segui J. 1990. Constraining models of lexical access: the onset of word recognition. See Altmann 1990, pp. 236–62

Mehler J, Jusczyk P, Lambertz G, Halsted N, Bertoncini J, Amiel-Tison C. 1988. A precursor of language acquisition in young infants. *Cognition* 29:143–78

Miller GA, Heise GA, Lichten W. 1951. The intelligibility of speech as a function of the context of the test materials. *J. Exp. Psychol.* 41:329–35

Miller JL. 1977. Properties of feature detectors for VOT: the voiceless channel of analysis. *J. Acoust. Soc. Am.* 62:641–48

Miller JL. 1981. Effects of speaking rate on segmental distinctions. See Eimas & Miller 1981, pp. 39–74

Miller JL. 1994. On the internal structure of phonetic categories: a progress report. *Cognition* 50:271–85

Miller JL, Connine CM, Schermer TM, Kluender KR. 1983. A possible auditory basis for internal structure of phonetic categories. *J. Acoust. Soc. Am.* 73:2124–33

Miller JL, Eimas PD. 1983. Studies on the categorization of speech by infants. *Cognition* 13:135–65

Miller JL, Eimas PD, eds. 1994. *The Handbook of Perception and Cognition.* Vol. 11: *Speech, Language, and Communication.* San Diego, CA: Academic. In press

Miller JL, Volaitis LE. 1989. Effect of speaking rate on the perceptual structure of a phonetic category. *Percept. Psychophys.* 46:505–12

Morgan JL. 1994. Converging measures of speech segmentation in prelingual infants. *Infant Behav. Dev.* In press

Morton J. 1969. Interaction of information in word recognition. *Psychol. Rev.* 76:165–78

Nakatani LH, Dukes KD. 1977. Locus of segmental cues for word juncture. *J. Acoust. Soc. Am.* 62:714–19

Nakatani LH, Shaffer JA. 1978. Hearing "words" without words: prosodic cues for word perception. *J. Acoust. Soc. Am.* 63: 234–45

Nearey TM. 1989. Static, dynamic, and relational properties in vowel perception. *J. Acoust. Soc. Am.* 85:2088–2113

Neisser U. 1967. *Cognitive Psychology.* Englewood Cliffs, NJ: Prentice-Hall

Norris D. 1986. Word recognition: context effects without priming. *Cognition* 22:93–136

Norris D. 1990. A dynamic-net model of human speech recognition. See Altmann 1990, pp. 87–104

Norris D. 1993. Bottom-up connectionist models of 'interaction'. See Altmann & Shillcock 1993, pp. 211–34

Norris D, Cutler A. 1985. Juncture detection. *Linguistics* 23:689–705

Nosofsky RM. 1988. Similarity, frequency and category representations. *J. Exp. Psychol.: Learn. Mem. Cogn.* 14:54–65

Nygaard LC, Pisoni DB. 1994. Speech perception: new directions in research and theory. See Miller & Eimas 1994. In press

Oden GC, Massaro DW. 1978. Integration of featural information in speech perception. *Psychol. Rev.* 85:172–91

Onifer W, Swinney DA. 1981. Accessing lexical ambiguities during sentence comprehension: effects of frequency of meaning and contextual bias. *Mem. Cogn.* 9: 225–36

Otake T, Hatano G, Cutler A, Mehler J. 1993. Mora or syllable? Speech segmentation in Japanese. *J. Mem. Lang.* 32:258–78

Pallier C, Sebastian-Gallés N, Felguera T, Christophe A, Mehler J. 1993. Attentional allocation within the syllable structure of spoken words. *J. Mem. Lang.* 32:373–89

Pastore RE. 1981. Possible psychoacoustic factors in speech perception. See Eimas & Miller 1981, pp. 165–205

Pastore RE. 1987. Categorical perception: some psychophysical models. See Harnad 1987, pp. 29–52

Pisoni DB, Lively SE, Logan JS. 1994. Perceptual learning of nonnative speech contrasts: implications for theories of speech perception. See Goodman & Nusbaum 1994, pp. 121–66

Pisoni DB, Luce PA. 1987. Acoustic-phonetic representations in word recognition. *Cognition* 25:21–52

Polka L. 1992. Characterizing the influence of native language experience on adult speech perception. *Percept. Psychophys.* 52:37–52

Polka L, Werker JF. 1994. Developmental changes in perception of nonnative vowel contrasts. *J. Exp. Psychol.: Hum. Percept. Perform.* 20:421–35

Remez RE, Rubin PE, Berns SM, Pardo JS, Lang JM. 1994. On the perceptual organization of speech. *Psychol. Rev.* 101:129–56

Repp BH. 1977. Dichotic competition of speech sounds: the role of acoustic stimulus structure. *J. Exp. Psychol.: Hum. Percept. Perform.* 3:37–50

Repp BH. 1982. Phonetic trading relations and context effects: new experimental evidence for a speech mode of perception. *Psychol. Bull.* 92:81–110

Repp BH. 1984. Categorical perception: issues, methods, findings. In *Speech and Language: Advances in Basic Research and Practice,* ed. NJ Lass, pp. 243–335. New York: Academic

Repp BH, Liberman AM. 1987. Phonetic category boundaries are flexible. See Harnad 1987, pp. 89–112

Rosch E. 1978. Principles of categorization. In *Cognition and Categorization,* ed. E Rosch, BB Lloyd, pp. 28–48. Hillsdale, NJ: Erlbaum

Salasoo A, Pisoni DB. 1985. Interaction of knowledge sources in spoken word identification. *J. Mem. Lang.* 24:210–31

Samuel AG. 1977. The effect of discrimination training on speech perception: noncategorical perception. *Percept. Psychophys.* 22: 321–30

Samuel AG. 1981. Phonemic restoration: insights from a new methodology. *J. Exp. Psychol.: Gen.* 110:474–94

Samuel AG. 1982. Phonetic prototypes. *Percept. Psychophys.* 31:307–14

Sebastian-Gallés N, Dupoux E, Segui J, Mehler J. 1992. Contrasting syllabic effects in Catalan and Spanish. *J. Mem. Lang.* 31:18–32

Segui J, Dupoux E, Mehler J. 1990. The role of the syllable in speech segmentation, phoneme identification, and lexical access. See Altmann 1990, pp. 263–80

Seidenberg MS. 1994. Visual word recognition: an overview. See Miller & Eimas 1994. In press

Seidenberg MS, Tanenhaus MK, Leiman JM, Bienkowski M. 1982. Automatic access of the meanings of ambiguous words in context: some limitations of knowledge-based processing. *Cogn. Psychol.* 14:489–537

Seidenberg MS, Waters GS, Sanders M, Langer P. 1984. Pre- and postlexical loci of contextual effects on word recognition. *Mem. Cogn.* 12:315–28

Shillcock R. 1990. Lexical hypotheses in continuous speech. See Altmann 1990, pp. 24–49

Stevens KN, Blumstein SE. 1981. The search for invariant acoustic correlates of phonetic features. See Eimas & Miller 1981, pp. 1–38

Strange W, Jenkins JJ. 1978. Role of linguistic experience in the perception of speech. In *Perception and Experience,* ed. HL Pick Jr, RD Walk, pp. 125–69. New York: Plenum

Summerfield Q. 1987. Some preliminaries to a comprehensive account of audio-visual speech perception. In *Hearing By Eye: The Psychology of Lip Reading,* ed. B Dodd, R Campbell, pp. 3–51. Hillsdale, NJ: Erlbaum

Sussman HA, McCaffrey HA, Matthews SA. 1991. An investigation of locus equations as a source of relational invariance for stop place categorization. *J. Acoust. Soc. Am.* 90:1309–25

Swinney DA. 1979. Lexical access during sentence comprehension: (re)consideration of context effects. *J. Verb. Learn. Verb. Behav.* 18:645–59

Swinney DA. 1981. Lexical processing during sentence comprehension: effects of higher order constraints and implications for representation. In *The Cognitive Representation of Speech,* ed. T Myers, J Laver, J Anderson, pp. 201–9. Amsterdam: North Holland

Tabossi P. 1988a. Accessing lexical ambiguity in different types of sentential context. *J. Mem. Lang.* 27:324–40

Tabossi P. 1988b. Effects of context on the immediate interpretation of unambiguous nouns. *J. Exp. Psychol.: Learn. Mem. Cogn.* 14:153–62

Tabossi P, Colombo L, Job R. 1987. Accessing lexical ambiguity: effects of context and dominance. *Psychol. Res.* 49:161–67

Tabossi P, Zardon F. 1993. Processing ambiguous words in context. *J. Mem. Lang.* 32:359–72

Taft M, Hambly G. 1986. Exploring the cohort model of spoken word recognition. *Cognition* 22:259–82

Tanenhaus MK, Dell GS, Carlson G. 1987. Context effects in lexical processing: a connectionist approach to modularity. In *Modularity in Knowledge Representation and Natural-Language Understanding,* ed. JL Garfield, pp. 83–108. Cambridge, MA: MIT Press

Tanenhaus MK, Leiman JM, Seidenberg MS. 1979. Evidence for multiple stages in the processing of ambiguous words in syntactic contexts. *J. Verb. Learn. Verb. Behav.* 18:427–40

Tanenhaus MK, Lucas MM. 1987. Context effects in lexical processing. *Cognition* 25:213–34

Tees RC, Werker JF. 1984. Perceptual flexibility: maintenance or recovery of the ability to discriminate non-native speech sounds. *Can. J. Psychol.* 38:579–90

Tyler LK. 1984. The structure of the initial cohort: evidence from gating. *Percept. Psychophys.* 36:417–27

Tyler LK, Wessels J. 1983. Quantifying contextual contributions to word-recognition processes. *Percept. Psychophys.* 34:409–20

van Hessen AJ, Schouten MEH. 1992. Modeling phoneme perception. II: a model of stop consonant discrimination. *J. Acoust. Soc. Am.* 92:1856–68

Warren P, Marslen-Wilson W. 1987. Continuous uptake of acoustic cues in spoken word recognition. *Percept. Psychophys.* 41:262–75

Warren P, Marslen-Wilson W. 1988. Cues to lexical choice: discriminating place and voice. *Percept. Psychophys.* 43:21–30

Werker JF. 1993. Developmental changes in cross-language speech perception: implications for cognitive models of speech processing. See Altmann & Shillcock 1993, pp. 57–78

Werker JF, Gilbert JHV, Humphrey K, Tees RC. 1981. Developmental aspects of cross-language speech perception. *Child Dev.* 52:349–55

Werker JF, Lalonde CE. 1988. Cross-language speech perception: initial capabilities and developmental change. *Dev. Psychol.* 24:672–83

Werker JF, Logan JS. 1985. Cross-language

evidence for three factors in speech perception. *Percept. Psychophys.* 37:35–44

Werker JF, Tees RC. 1984a. Cross-language speech perception: evidence for perceptual reorganization during the first year of life. *Infant Behav. Dev.* 7:49–63

Werker JF, Tees RC. 1984b. Phonemic and phonetic factors in adult cross-language speech perception. *J. Acoust. Soc. Am.* 75:1866–78

Zwitserlood P. 1989. The locus of the effects of sentential-semantic context in spoken-word processing. *Cognition* 32:25–64

Zwitserlood P, Schriefers H, Lahiri A, van Donselaar W. 1993. The role of syllables in the perception of spoken Dutch. *J. Exp. Psychol.: Learn. Mem. Cogn.* 19:260–71

Annu. Rev. Psychol. 1995. 46:493–523

CLINICAL ASSESSMENT OF MEMORY DISORDERS IN AMNESIA AND DEMENTIA

Nelson Butters and Dean C. Delis

Pscyhology Service, San Diego Department of Veterans Affairs Medical Center, San Diego, California 92161 and Department of Psychiatry, University of California, San Diego, School of Medicine, La Jolla, California 92093

John A. Lucas

Department of Psychiatry and Psychology, Mayo Clinic Jacksonville, Jacksonville, Florida 32224 and Department of Psychiatry, University of California, San Diego, School of Medicine, La Jolla, California 92093

KEY WORDS: learning, neuropsychology, cognitive psychology, Alzheimer's disease

CONTENTS

0066-4308/95/0201-0493$05.00

INTRODUCTION

Amnesia and dementia are the two major classes of memory disorders seen in clinical populations. Amnesia refers to a specific, acquired difficulty in learning new information and/or remembering information from the past. The memory disturbance may be strikingly circumscribed and may occur in the absence of significant impairment of other cognitive or social skills. Dementia is a more broadly defined cognitive disorder, of which amnesia is the primary feature. The fourth edition of the *Diagnostic and Statistical Manual of Mental Disorders* (*DSM IV*; APA 1994) describes dementia as "the development of multiple cognitive deficits that include memory impairment and at least one of the following cognitive disturbances: aphasia, apraxia, agnosia, or a disturbance in executive functions" (p. 134).

By definition, the cognitive disturbance seen in dementia must reflect a decline from a higher premorbid level of functioning and be severe enough to interfere with social or occupational responsibilities. Prevalence estimates for dementia increase significantly with age, and approximately 6% of individuals over age 65 and 20% over age 80 suffer from a medically or socially disabling degree of dementia (Plum 1987). Statistics such as these, coupled with increases in life expectancy and the resulting changes in population demographics, have led to an upsurge of scientific interest in the dementias over the last several decades.

Dementia and amnesia are not homogeneous entities, but instead are associated with a wide range of etiologies and neuropathological correlates. Consequently, a single pattern of preserved and impaired cognitive abilities does not apply to all dementing illnesses or amnesic syndromes. Moreover, although impaired memory is the cardinal feature of both dementia and amnesia, the specific aspects of memory that are preserved and impaired vary considerably among these disorders.

The past 25 years have witnessed substantial changes in our understanding of the neurological and cognitive processes that comprise memory. This review summarizes important theoretical divisions of memory that have arisen from the cognitive psychological literature, presents a critical overview of traditional and experimental neuropsychological techniques used in the clinical assessment of memory functioning, and discusses the characteristic memory deficits associated with selected dementing illnesses and amnesic syndromes.

CONCEPTUAL DIVISIONS OF MEMORY

Perhaps the most important contribution of cognitive psychology to the study of the neuropsychology of memory is the recognition that memory is a heterogeneous entity comprised of several distinct yet interacting systems and subsystems (Heindel et al 1993). The validity of these distinctions and their interrelationships is a topic of ongoing debate, and the lack of universally accepted terminology can lead different investigators to use the same terms to reflect different constructs, or different terms to reflect the same construct (Cermak 1984, Delis 1989, Warrington & Weiskrantz 1973). Therefore, we begin with an overview of some of the more widely accepted conceptual divisions of memory.

Short-Term vs Long-Term Memory

In 1890, William James proposed a distinction between two different types of memory, one that endured for a very brief time and one that lasted after the experience had been "dropped from consciousness" (James 1890, p. 648). The former is commonly referred to as short-term memory (STM) and the latter as long-term memory (LTM). STM is demonstrated by the recall of material immediately after it is presented or during uninterrupted rehearsal. It is of limited capacity, holding an average of seven "bits" of information at any one time. This information can be held for up to several minutes but will be lost or replaced by new information unless it is sustained by rehearsal (Lezak 1983). In contrast, LTM is demonstrated by the ability to recall information after an interval during which attention is focused away from the target information (Miller 1956). Capacity for LTM is believed to be extraordinarily large, with the potential of holding information indefinitely without the need for continued rehearsal.

The clinical significance of the distinction between STM and LTM is best exemplified in cases of amnesia (see Butters & Cermak 1980, Milner et al 1968, Scoville & Milner 1957, Squire & Moore 1979, Teuber et al 1968). In perhaps the most famous case study in the neuropsychological literature, the patient H.M. underwent bilateral resection of the medial temporal lobes for treatment of intractable epilepsy. Following the surgery, H.M. showed no disruption in STM, but a profound deficit in LTM was observed.

Despite rather eloquent demonstrations of how STM and LTM can be dissociated, this dichotomy remains controversial. There is disagreement over the temporal definitions of STM and LTM, and over the very concept of staging memory processes (Klatzky 1980). Some investigators argue that the phenomena that comprise STM and LTM can be divided into three or more separate stages, while others believe that levels of learning and memory exist on a continuum (see Crowder 1982, Wickelgren 1973). Squire (1987), however, argues that the abrupt decline in memory performance demonstrated by amnesic patients as soon as they are distracted from the target material provides strong clinical justification for the distinction between a short-term and long-term memory store. Moreover, there is a lack of compelling evidence in the neuropsychological and experimental psychological literatures warranting the subdivision of the STM-LTM dichotomy into additional stages.

Encoding vs Retrieval

Encoding is the process by which information is transformed into a stored, mental representation. Retrieval is the process of bringing the stored memory back into consciousness. Patients with cerebral disorders vary in terms of whether their memory problems are at the level of encoding or retrieval. One common way to illustrate this distinction is to present new information, such as a story or word list, to the patient and compare his or her memory for that information using both free recall and recognition paradigms. If information has been encoded successfully but cannot be retrieved, performance will be poor on free recall, which places maximal demands on retrieval processes, and disproportionately better on recognition testing, which places minimal demands on retrieval. Patients with encoding-level deficits will perform equally poorly on both free recall and recognition testing, because the information was not stored successfully in the first place.

Retroactive vs Proactive Interference

Events or information encountered before or after presentation of material that is to be remembered can interfere with later recall of the target material. The mechanisms responsible for memory failure in such instances are retroactive and proactive interference. Retroactive interference refers to the disrupting effect of later learning on the ability to recall previously learned information (see Slamecka 1960).

Proactive interference refers to the opposite situation; that is, the disruptive effect that earlier learning has on the ability to learn new information at a later time. Studies show that the degree of proactive or retroactive interference is a function of the degree of similarity between the target and interfering information. The more similar the interference items are to the target items, the poorer the recall of the target items (Klatzky 1980, Reitman 1971). Likewise, in a phenomenon known as release from proactive interference, recall can be facilitated by making target items dissimilar to the interference information (see Randolph et al 1992).

Anterograde vs Retrograde Memory Functioning

Anterograde memory refers to the ability to recall or recognize information or events that are newly encountered. An anterograde memory deficit typically affects a wide variety of new learning. Retrograde memory refers to the ability to recall or recognize information or events that were encountered in the past (see Milner 1966, Milner et al 1968, Scoville & Milner 1957).

Patients with retrograde amnesia are unable to remember events that occurred prior to the onset of their memory disorder. The ability to recall factual information not related to specific contexts or experiences, however, remains relatively intact. For example, patients with true retrograde amnesia will typically retain previously acquired factual knowledge such as the name of the first President of the United States, as well as salient personal facts (McCarthy & Warrington 1990). Patients who suffer complete loss of personal history and identity are rare and typically reflect psychological, rather than neurological, etiologies (Kopelman 1987).

Recent vs Remote Memory

The distinction between recent and remote memory is typically applied to the temporal dimension of retrograde amnesia. Recent memory most often refers to the information acquired just prior to the onset of a memory disorder. Remote memory refers to information regarding events or experiences acquired years or decades before the disorder began. Patients with retrograde amnesia may demonstrate a temporal gradient in which memory for more recent events is disrupted to a greater extent than memory for remote events. This gradient is seen, for example, in the case study of the patient P.Z., a distinguished scientist who became amnesic secondary to Alcoholic Korsakoff syndrome when he was in his sixties (Butters & Cermak 1986). The patient demonstrated substantially poorer memory for recent events and experiences than for events from his early life.

Declarative vs Nondeclarative Memory

One of the most important insights to emerge from modern neuropsychological research is the distinction between declarative and nondeclarative memory, also known as explicit and implicit memory, respectively. Declarative memory refers to the acquisition of facts, experiences, and information about events and is directly accessible to conscious awareness. In contrast, nondeclarative memory refers to unconscious changes in task performance attributed to prior exposure to information. These include skill and habit learning, classical conditioning, the phenomenon of priming, and other situations in which memory is expressed through performance rather than recollection (Heindel et al 1993, Squire et al 1993).

According to Squire et al (1993), declarative memory is relatively fast and flexible. Fact-based information, for example, can usually be expressed relatively quickly via a number of different response systems. Declarative memory, however, is not always reliable, as is evident in everyday problems with retrieval of information and forgetting. In contrast, nondeclarative memory is considered quite reliable but is often slow and inflexible. The information present in a learned skill, for example, can often be expressed most readily only by the response systems that were involved in the original learning of that skill.

EPISODIC VS SEMANTIC MEMORY   Declarative knowledge can be divided into episodic and semantic memory (Tulving 1983). Episodic memory refers to information learned at a particular place and time in one's life. Asking individuals to recall what they had for breakfast that morning or what they were doing when they first heard of the Space Shuttle *Challenger* disaster taps into episodic memory. To recall the target information correctly, the individual must be able to access information regarding the time and place of the original event. Semantic memory, on the other hand, refers to general knowledge of the world and is not linked to a particular temporal or spatial context. For example, asking an individual to define the word "breakfast" or to state what a space shuttle is does not require recall of where or when the information was originally learned. Both episodic and semantic memory are declarative, however, in that retrieval of information is carried out explicitly, on a conscious level.

TYPES OF NONDECLARATIVE MEMORY   The study of nondeclarative memory is a relatively recent pursuit, and a complete classification scheme has yet to be developed. Nondeclarative memory includes several different forms of learning and memory abilities, including procedural memory, some forms of classical conditioning, and priming (Squire et al 1993).

Procedural memory   Procedures are motor, perceptual, or cognitive skills that are learned and used by an individual to operate effectively in the world (e.g. tying a shoe or driving a car). Procedural memory refers to the process of retrieving information that underlies these skilled performances. Although some aspects of skills can be declared, the skill itself is most often automatically performed without conscious retrieval of information regarding the procedure. Recent evidence suggests that the brain structures required for acquisition and performance of learned skills and procedures (i.e. the corticostriatal system) are distinct from those that are important to declarative memory (i.e. the medial temporal lobe and diencephalic systems; see Squire et al 1993). Consequently, amnesic patients and patients with dementias that do not involve the neostriatum typically demonstrate intact skill learning and memory regardless of whether or not they have conscious recall of learning the task (Cermak et al 1973, Eslinger & Damasio 1986, Heindel et al 1989, Martone et al 1984).

Conditioning   In the typical classical conditioning paradigm, a stimulus that naturally produces a desired response [i.e. an unconditioned stimulus (UCS) that produces an unconditioned response (UCR)] is identified and paired with a neutral stimulus. After repeated pairings, the neutral stimulus [conditioned stimulus (CS)] alone will elicit some version of the same response [conditioned response (CR)].

Some have argued that conditioning in humans requires conscious awareness of the CS-UCS contingency (Marinkovic et al 1989); however, studies of patients with amnesic disorders strongly suggest that associations can be conditioned without declarative knowledge (e.g. Daum et al 1989). In one such study, Weiskrantz & Warrington (1979) paired the presentation of a puff of air to the eye with a sound and flash of light. The puff of air (UCS) reflexively elicits an eye-blink (UCR). Amnesic patients were able to acquire a conditioned eye-blink response to the sound and light flash despite their inability to recall 24 hr later any relevant details about the training session. Conditioning in amnesic patients has not, however, been compared to that of normal control subjects. Therefore, although conscious awareness may not always be necessary for conditioning to occur, it has not been established that amnesics acquire the conditioned response at a normal rate. If differences in acquisition exist between amnesic subjects and normal controls, some aspects of conditioning may indeed rely on declarative knowledge.

Priming   Priming is a phenomenon in which prior experience with perceptual stimuli temporarily and unconsciously facilitates the ability to later detect or identify those stimuli. Priming is said to have occurred when task performance for previously presented stimuli is superior to that for new stimuli.

For example, in a study of semantic priming, Salmon et al (1988) showed normal subjects 10 words (e.g. *motel, abstain*) one at a time. Subjects were later given 20 three-letter word stems (e.g. *mot-, abs-*) and asked to complete each stem with the first word that came to mind. Half of the word stems could be completed by using words presented previously, while the other half could not. Subjects displayed a significantly greater tendency to complete the word stems with words that were presented previously, thus demonstrating a priming effect.

Priming has been shown to be independent of the ability to consciously recall or recognize stimuli. Warrington & Weiskrantz (1970), for example, presented amnesic subjects and normal controls with printed lists of words and later tested them by one of three techniques: free recall, recognition, or the above-mentioned stem-completion task. As expected, amnesics performed significantly worse than normal controls on recall and recognition measures; however, patients and controls demonstrated equivalent priming effects on the stem-completion task.

CLINICAL ASSESSMENT OF MEMORY

Although revolutionary advances have been made in cognitive approaches to memory functioning, the publishers of major clinical assessment measures often take a conservative stance with regard to so-called breakthroughs in cognitive science. Thus, the development of instruments for the clinical assessment of memory has tended to lag about 10 years behind the cognitive literature (Butters 1992). In recent years, several improved memory measures have emerged that incorporate the most important and reliable findings from the cognitive literature of the 1970s and early 1980s, including measures of recognition, sensitivity to proactive interference, encoding strategies, and rates of forgetting. Techniques for the clinical assessment of retrograde memory functioning have also been developed. For the most part, these new and improved memory tests demonstrate superior sensitivity and specificity in detecting not only the presence of memory disorder but also the severity and type of dysfunction present. What follows is a description of some of the more commonly used clinical memory tests.

Memory Scales

The clinical assessment of memory should cover a number of different abilities, including immediate retention of information, rate and pattern of learning and forgetting, retrieval efficiency, and susceptibility to interference (Spreen & Strauss 1991). Although several batteries of tests have been developed in an attempt to provide a thorough assessment of memory, their success in meeting the above goals has been limited.

WECHSLER MEMORY SCALE-REVISED (WMS-R)   Perhaps more than any other clinical test of memory, the revised version of the WMS (WMS-R; Wechsler 1987) reflects the strength of the impact of cognitive neuropsychological research on clinical practice. The original WMS (Wechsler 1945) consisted of seven subtests assessing such memory functions as orientation, span of attention, immediate recall of stories and novel geometric figures, and the ability to learn words paired in couplets. The raw scores for these subtests were summed and added to an age-correction factor, which was then converted to a summary score called the memory quotient (MQ).

The WMS was criticized extensively for a number of weaknesses involving its validity, standardization, and psychometric properties (see Erickson & Scott 1977, Loring & Papanicolaou 1987, Prigatano 1978). Moreover, the entire concept of the MQ was assailed for confounding several cognitive and memory constructs.

The WMS-R represents a significant improvement over the original. It includes 13 subtests, including updated versions of the original seven plus six additional measures. Delayed recall procedures are included, as are more tests of visuospatial memory. The scoring rules have been clearly delineated, more extensive normative studies have been conducted, and the singular MQ index has been eliminated. Based on factor analytic results from a sample of 316 normal subjects and 346 clinical patients, five composite standardized scores were derived for the WMS-R: general memory, attention-concentration, verbal memory, visual memory, and delayed recall. In addition, percentile scores have been computed for several of the more widely used subtests.

Despite these improvements, the WMS-R met with almost immediate criticism upon publication (see Loring 1989). Some of the criticisms leveled against the instrument represent limitations inherent to any short battery that attempts to measure a broad spectrum of memory functions. For example, memory for specific sensory information (e.g. tactile or olfactory), autobiographical events, and learned procedures and skills are not assessed (Zielinski 1993). Other criticisms, however, highlight significant design flaws. Although delayed recall measures have been included in the revised battery, the WMS-R still does not provide cued recall or recognition measures that could help distinguish encoding from retrieval deficits. In addition, subtests purporting to measure nonverbal memory are subject to varying degrees of verbal encoding and are confounded by perceptual and visuomotor factors.

The WMS-R normative sample represents a marked improvement over the WMS. The sample was based on 1980 US census data plus more recent special-purpose census reports to achieve desired demographic representations (i.e. age, sex, race, geographic region, and education). Norms are stratified across nine age levels from 16 years, 0 months to 74 years, 11 months; however, the WMS-R has been criticized for using estimation procedures, rather than actual subject data, to obtain some of its age norms (i.e. 18–19, 25–34, 45–54). Moreover, the lack of normative data for subjects age 75 and over is a serious limitation, especially given the need for memory assessment in elderly populations. Finally, although the WMS-R standardization sample included representative proportions of the population with regard to other demographic variables such as sex, race, and level of education, norms are not stratified by these variables.

An effort is underway to address these limitations and further improve the WMS. Despite its shortcomings, however, recent investigations indicate that the WMS-R has considerable utility in characterizing the memory disorders of patients with diverse disorders, including Alzheimer's disease, Huntington's disease, multiple sclerosis, Alcoholic Korsakoff syndrome, long-term alcoholism, psychiatric illness, closed head injury, and exposure to neurotoxins (Butters et al 1988, Chelune & Bornstein 1988, Fischer 1988, Ryan & Lewis 1988).

MEMORY ASSESSMENT SCALES (MAS)   The MAS (Williams 1991) was introduced four years after the publication of the WMS-R in an effort to address some of the criticisms leveled against that instrument. The MAS consists of several subtests measuring attention, verbal memory, and nonverbal memory, many of which are analogous to subtests of the WMS-R. The MAS provides four summary scores, including verbal memory, visual memory, global memory, and short-term memory. These are comparable to the verbal memory, visual memory, general memory, and attention-concentration indices of the WMS-R.

The MAS represents several improvements compared to the WMS-R . It provides cued recall and recognition trials for some measures, and a list-learning task allows measurement of memory variables not assessed by the WMS-R, including learning strategy and error types. There is also a test of memory for the names of people shown in photographs, which may be more ecologically valid with regard to everyday memory functioning. Norms are based on census data for 1995 using middle series projections of the US population for age and sex (Zielinski 1993). This is believed to be the best current and near-future representation of population demographics (Williams 1991). Normative data are available for subjects up to age 90 and are stratified at three different education levels (i.e. less than or equal to 11 years, 12 years, and greater than or equal to 13 years).

Although the MAS is more psychometrically sophisticated and better normed than the WMS-R, it also has weaknesses. For example, the visual memory tasks of the MAS are confounded by visuoperceptual and visuomotor abilities. In addition, despite the inclusion of delayed recall measures, the MAS does not provide a separate summary score reflecting delayed recall. This information is available to the clinician, however, via comparison of immediate and delayed recall measures on individual subtests. Because it is a relatively new instrument, data are not yet available to fully examine the strengths and weaknesses of the MAS with regard to various patient populations. Overall, however, the MAS appears to be a promising memory instrument.

RANDT MEMORY TEST (RMT)   The RMT (Randt & Brown 1983) is comprised of seven subtests, including tests of general information, immediate span of auditory-verbal attention, verbal learning and recall, picture recognition, and an incidental learning test of the names of the previous tasks. On some of the subtests, a Brown-Peterson distraction task is used in which the examinee must count backward by threes between presentation and recall. Twenty-four-hour delayed recall is also solicited. As the authors state, the test attempts to provide a global survey of patients' memory complaints; it is not intended to help localize brain lesions or functions, nor is it intended to tap every type of memory.

An advantage of the RMT is that five alternative forms are available, thus allowing for multiple testing over short intervals of time. There are, however, several disadvantages. First, test instructions are at times complex and difficult to understand, especially if the examinee suffers from a significant memory disturbance. Second, the manual instructs the examiner to change the nature of the distraction task (i.e. count backward by twos or ones) if the patient is too impaired to count backward by threes. Such unsystematic variation in administration may lessen the test's psychometric rigor. Third, examinees are told before tasks of new learning that they will have to remember the material "again tomorrow." This instruction may be a confound, because highly motivated examinees have the opportunity to write down and study target items after leaving the examination. Finally, visuospatial memory is not assessed adequately by this battery, because the stimuli presented for picture recognition are common objects (e.g. telephone) and can be encoded verbally with little or no difficulty.

LURIA-NEBRASKA NEUROPSYCHOLOGICAL BATTERY (LNNB) MEMORY SCALE The LNNB (Golden et al 1983) contains 14 scales, one of which is a memory scale. This scale has drawn extensive criticism, primarily because of low content validity, heterogeneity of items (e.g. confounding memory with nonmemory questions and verbal with visuospatial items), and failure to assess delayed recall (Adams 1980, Spiers 1981, Russell 1986). Although the LNNB has been useful in identifying cerebral dysfunction, the psychometric weaknesses of the memory scale makes it impossible to use this measure to determine the integrity of specific memory functioning.

Verbal Tests

IMMEDIATE RECALL SPAN   The repetition of information immediately after its initial presentation requires attentional abilities and short-term memory capacity. Patients with classic amnesic syndromes often perform within, or close to, the normal range on such tests whereas individuals with impaired attentional skills, such as patients with severe depression, often perform poorly (Breslow et al 1980, Stromgren 1977).

Digit span   The most commonly used attention span tests are those found on Wechsler's scales (Wechsler 1981, 1987). The examiner presents increasingly long sequences of digits, and the examinee is asked to repeat each sequence in the same order presented. Once a maximum digit span is achieved in the forward direction, a second series of digits is presented, which the examinee is asked to repeat backward.

One of the major criticisms of using this particular method to determine immediate recall span is that digits forward and backward have traditionally been collapsed into one score despite wide recognition that each taps different cognitive processes. Repeating digits backward, for example, places more demand on mental control and symbol transformation than does repeating them in the same order presented. Consequently, a single score can obscure findings in which only one or the other process is impaired. Amnesic patients, for example, typically show a normal forward digit span and an impaired backward span.

Some have argued that repetition of digits in sequence, whether forward or backward, may not be the best measure of an examinee's immediate verbal recall span. Most tests of verbal memory do not require that the target items be recalled in the exact order in which they were presented; consequently, the length of a digit sequence accurately repeated, regardless of the order of the digits, may be the better measure of immediate recall span. A method for evaluating this ability has been incorporated into a new scoring system for Wechsler's digit span subtest (Kaplan et al 1991).

Word and sentence span   Tests have been developed that require the examinee to repeat increasingly long sequences of words or sentences (Miller 1973, Benton & Hamsher 1976, Goodglass & Kaplan 1983). Lezak (1983), however, points out that a number of variables can confound interpretation of such tests, including the number of syllables per word and the frequency, abstractness, imageability, and meaningfulness of words, phrases, or sentences used.

MEMORY FOR WORD LISTS

Verbal paired associates   In this subtest of the WMS-R, which uses a technique known as paired-associate learning, the examinee is read eight word pairs: In four of the word pairs, the second word has an obvious association with the first; in the other four pairs, there is little or no association. The examiner then presents the first word of each pair and asks the examinee to provide the word with which it is paired. Errors are corrected and the procedure is repeated for up to six learning trials. Examiners then have the option of assessing recall for the word pairs after an intervening delay period.

Some clinicians include an additional recall trial after the first three learning trials are completed. In this procedure, the examiner reads the second word of each pair and the examinee must report the first word. Patients who encode word pairs on a more superficial, phonetic level, rather than a deeper semantic level, often perform worse on this trial compared to the third learning trial because the phonemic sequence of the word pairs is altered.

Selective reminding   In this procedure, a word list is read to the subject, who is then asked to recall as many words as possible. On the next trial, the subject is presented only those words he or she failed to recall on the preceding trial, after which recall for the entire list is again elicited. This procedure is repeated until the examinee recalls all the target words on two consecutive trials, or until a predetermined number of trials has been administered (Buschke 1973, Buschke & Fuld 1974, Hannay & Levin 1985). Delayed recall, cued recall, and recognition procedures have also been developed for this test (see Hannay & Levin 1985).

The selective reminding procedure represents one of the first attempts to bridge the gap between clinical assessment and cognitive science. Several memory constructs are operationally defined and quantified by the procedure. For example, once a word is recalled on two consecutive trials, it is believed to be encoded in long-term storage (LTS). Recall of words that have entered LTS is believed to reflect long-term retrieval (LTR), while recall of words that have not entered LTS represents short-term retrieval (STR). Although the parceling of verbal memory into component processes is desirable, the validity of some of the constructs defined in selective reminding has been called into question. Loring & Papanicolaou (1987), for example, argue that the distinction between LTS and LTR is arbitrary. As noted above, Buschke proposes that LTS is achieved when a word is recalled on two consecutive trials. It is by this definition only, however, that failure to recall a word after meeting the two-consecutive-trial criterion is due to failure of retrieval. It seems equally likely that recall failure could be caused by weak or degraded storage. In such cases, the LTR score would be low, but the errors would be due to poor encoding rather than retrieval difficulties.

It has also been suggested that the operational definition of LTS may be altogether invalid for certain patient populations. Ober et al (1985) found that patients with moderate to severe dementia of the Alzheimer's type (DAT) showed better LTS on a selective reminding test than did patients with mild DAT. This finding is opposite that expected and may be explained by the more severe DAT patient's tendency to perseverate one or two words across the majority of trials. Such perseveration arbitrarily inflates LTS scores and provides an incorrect characterization of this pathological performance.

Rey Auditory Verbal Learning Test   On Rey's test, a list of 15 unrelated words is presented in its entirety over each of five learning trials, with immediate recall assessed following each presentation. Following the fifth learning trial, a second list of unrelated words is presented one time as an interference task. Recall for the original 15 words is then assessed, followed by recognition testing. Many examiners also test for recall of the target list again after a delay interval. Normative data are readily available for each of these indices (Lezak 1983, Spreen & Strauss 1991). In addition, the examiner can make qualitative interpretations about various learning parameters, such as primacy-recency effects, learning rate across trials, and vulnerability to proactive and retroactive interference.

The California Verbal Learning Test (CVLT)   The general format of the CVLT (Delis et al 1987) was modeled after Rey's test. One major difference between the two tests is that the 16 list words of the CVLT are comprised of four words from each of four different semantic categories (e.g. fruits or tools). Words from the same category are never presented consecutively, which affords an assessment of the degree to which an examinee uses an active semantic clustering strategy in recalling the words. The CVLT scoring system quantifies and provides normative data for numerous learning and memory variables in addition to total levels of recall and recognition.

The advantage of the CVLT for clinical practice is that its scoring system quantifies the strategies, processes, and errors an examinee displays in learning verbal material. Normative data from 273 normal subjects and 145 carefully diagnosed neurological patients are provided for 26 memory variables. An alternate form is available, and there is now a children's version of the CVLT.

CERAD word-list learning   The Consortium to Establish a Registry for Alzheimer's Disease (CERAD) was organized to develop brief standardized assessment measures of the clinical and neuropsychological manifestations of Alzheimer's Disease (Welsh et al 1991). The CERAD word-list learning test consists of immediate and delayed recall trials, as well as recognition testing. Subjects are presented 10 words, each printed separately on index cards. When all words have been presented, recall is assessed and the words are presented again. After the third learning trial, an intervening task is administered for five to eight minutes, after which free recall is again assessed. A word-list recognition procedure is administered next, during which subjects are shown 20 words (10 target words and 10 distractors), one at a time, and asked to indicate whether each word was or was not from the list.

The CERAD word-list learning test is an efficient and effective tool in the diagnosis of dementia (Welsh et al 1991). Using a cutoff score of two standard deviations below the mean, Welsh et al (1991) found that the measure of delayed recall could correctly classify 96% of control subjects, 86% of patients with mild DAT, and 96% of patients with moderate to severe DAT. A discriminant function analysis of CERAD measures identified the delayed recall score as the single best discriminator between patients with mild DAT and normal elderly controls. When combined with the number of correct "no" responses on recognition testing, the discriminant function formula classified 91% of mildly demented and normal subjects correctly. All memory measures from the CERAD word-list learning test discriminate between normal elderly control subjects and patients with moderate or severe DAT; however, use of measures other than delayed recall and correct "no" responses on recognition testing is not useful for discriminating between controls and mildly demented patients. In fact, emphasis on these other measures may lead to false-negative errors in diagnosis (Welsh et al 1991).

MEMORY FOR STORIES   Although several clinical tests of story memory have been developed (see Heaton et al 1991, Lezak 1983, Randt & Brown 1983, Williams 1991), the Logical Memory subtest of the WMS-R is the most popular (Wechsler 1987). In its standardized format, two brief paragraphs are read to the examinee. Recall is assessed after immediate presentation of each story and again following a 30-minute delay. The total number of ideas recalled across the two stories are summed to achieve recall scores. These scores can then be converted to percentile ranks using the WMS-R normative sample.

Despite improvements in scoring criteria and normative information, this test has several shortcomings. For example, learning is not assessed beyond one trial of immediate recall, and there is no formal measure of retroactive or proactive interference despite the presentation of two sets of similar information in succession. There is no formal measure of recognition, making it difficult to distinguish between encoding and retrieval difficulties. Heaton et al (1991) avoid some of these problems by presenting one story for up to five trials or until a learning criterion score is reached, whichever comes first. Others have added their own versions of multiple-choice or recognition testing and rely on their own normative data or clinical acumen to help detect the presence of encoding or retrieval difficulties.

The prose memory subtest of the MAS (Williams 1991) differs from the above-mentioned story memory tests in that it does not assess recall of story segments. Instead, patients are read a story aloud and are scored on their ability to answer nine specific questions related to that story. Thus, rather than measuring retrieval processes, as is the case with Logical Memory and other story memory tests, the prose memory test measures encoding and consolidation of information.

Nonverbal Tests

Nonverbal memory is often more difficult to assess than verbal memory. Finding stimuli that cannot be encoded verbally and procedures that do not confound deficits in visual memory with impaired visuoperception, visuospatial analysis, and visuomotor construction is challenging. Some confounds can be sorted out by assessing component processes and employing recognition techniques; however, the problem of verbal encoding is typically more difficult to control.

IMMEDIATE RECALL SPAN   Procedures for testing immediate recall span for visuospatial stimuli parallel those of auditory-verbal stimuli described earlier. Most of these procedures represent a variation of the Corsi Block test (see Lezak 1983). In this test, nine one-inch cubes are fastened in a random but standardized pattern on a board. The examiner touches increasingly long sequences of blocks, and the examinee is asked to recreate each sequence in the same order. Once the length of forward span has been established, the procedure is repeated with the examinee touching each sequence in the reverse order presented by the examiner. This test represents a spatial analog of the digit span subtest (described earlier), and the same cautions apply. A similar, 10-block test is included as a supplemental neuropsychological subtest of the Wechsler Adult Intelligence Scale-Revised (Kaplan et al 1991), while a two-dimensional, pictorial version of this task is included in the WMS-R (Wechsler 1987).

MEMORY FOR VISUALLY-PRESENTED STIMULI   The majority of clinical tests of memory for visual information require subjects to view figures presented by the examiner and later reproduce these figures in free-hand drawing. The number and complexity of figures presented varies from one measure to another as well as within tests themselves.

Benton Visual Retention Test (BVRT)   The BVRT (Benton 1974) is a test of memory for geometric designs. The examinee is presented 10 stimulus cards, one at a time. The first two stimuli consist of one geometric shape each, and the remaining eight contain three figures each: two large main figures and one small peripheral figure, which may be to the left or right of the main figures, in the upper or lower hemispace. The examiner can choose between three alternate forms and four different administration conditions (e.g. immediate vs delayed recall). The BVRT was one of the first clinical instruments to use a scoring system that quantifies and provides normative data for multiple variables, including accuracy and error types. It has been used extensively in neuropsychological investigations (e.g. Benton 1974, Marsh & Hirsch 1982, Sterne 1969) and has been found to be sensitive to hemispatial processing deficits in unilateral brain-damaged patients (Heilbrun 1956). Several procedures developed by Benton and his colleagues can be used to rule out possible confounding constructional or perceptual difficulties (Benton 1974, Spreen & Strauss 1991). For example, the examinee may be asked to copy the same designs he or she previously drew from memory or to match each target design to its exact duplicate displayed among several similar designs. The figures used, however, are relatively common geometric shapes and can easily be encoded verbally.

Visual reproduction   On this subtest of the WMS-R (Wechsler 1987), subjects are asked to reproduce geometric figures immediately following a 10-second exposure to each stimulus and later following a 30-minute delay. Four stimulus cards are used. Three of these contain one design each; the fourth displays two designs side by side. Like the BVRT, however, the figures are relatively simple, can easily be verbalized, and can be confounded by perceptual and/or constructional deficits. Although these latter confounds can be addressed clinically in ways similar to those described above, standard procedures, recognition stimuli, and normative information are not provided by the publisher of the test.

Figure Memory Test (FMT)   Prior to its revision in 1987, the visual reproduction subtest consisted of only three stimulus cards (two single-figure cards and one with two figures) and assessed immediate recall only. Heaton et al (1991) used these original stimuli to assess learning and recall of visual information. In Heaton's FMT, the cards are displayed one at a time for 10 seconds each; however, the examinee is not allowed to draw until after all three cards (i.e. four designs) have been presented. This procedure is repeated for up to five trials or until the examinee reaches a criterion score; thus allowing the assessment of learning beyond immediate recall. Memory for the drawings is assessed based on the amount of information lost over a four-hour delay. Normative data for over 150 normal subjects are available for this procedure (Heaton et al 1991).

California Global-Local Learning Test (CGLT)   Unilateral brain pathology tends to disrupt analysis of wholes and parts selectively (Kaplan 1983), and the CGLT (see Delis et al 1988) was developed specifically to quantify this phenomenon more rigorously. The test involves the presentation of visual hierarchical stimuli consisting of a larger letter or shape constructed from numerous smaller letters or shapes. These stimuli provide precise demarcation between features perceived as larger wholes (i.e. the global letter or shape) and smaller details (i.e. the local letter or shape). To control for the ease of verbalizing the stimuli, three types of stimuli are used: linguistic forms (i.e. letters), high-frequency nonlinguistic forms (i.e. shapes with established names, such as a square or trapezoid), and low-frequency nonlinguistic forms (i.e. shapes without established names). Stimuli are presented in pairs, with one stimulus in each hemispace. Each of three pairs of visual hierarchical stimuli are presented for five seconds, followed by recall drawing of each pair immediately after its presentation. The pairs are presented for three trials to assess learning of visuospatial material; free recall, recognition, and copy are assessed following a 20-minute delay.

The CGLT provides indices and normative data for learning rate and retention of forms that are global or local, linguistic or nonlinguistic, and presented in left or right hemispace. Studies have found that left-hemisphere-damaged patients are selectively impaired in learning local forms, especially when they are presented in right hemispace, whereas right-hemisphere-damaged patients are selectively impaired in learning global forms, especially when they are presented in left hemispace (Delis et al 1986, 1988).

Recognition Memory Test for Faces (RMFT)   Unlike the previous measures described, the RMTF (Warrington 1984) does not have a visuoconstructional component. Instead, this test assesses recognition memory for 50 photographs of unfamiliar faces. Examinees are presented each photograph one at a time and are asked to rate each one as pleasant or unpleasant in order to ensure attention to each stimulus. After all the stimuli have been viewed, pairs of photographs are presented side by side. One photograph is new, the other has been presented previously. Subjects are asked to identify which of the two faces they have seen before. Normative data for this and a verbal analog (recognition of 50 printed words following the same procedure described above) are provided for over 300 subjects. This test affords a rigorous assessment of modality-specific recognition memory and is sensitive to unilateral brain damage (Warrington 1984).

MEMORY FOR TACTILE INFORMATION   Although primarily a measure of psychomotor problem solving, the Tactual Performance Test (Reitan & Wolfson 1985) can be used to measure memory for tactually presented information. The examinee sits blindfolded in front of a formboard and is asked to place cutout shapes of geometric figures into their appropriate spaces as quickly as possible. This procedure is performed first with the preferred hand, then with the non-preferred hand, and finally, with both hands. Once the test is completed, the equipment is removed, the blindfold is taken off, and the examinee is asked to draw the shapes of the figures with attention to their appropriate spatial relationships to one another on the board. Normative data for close to 500 normal subjects have been gathered for the total number of figures recalled correctly and the number of figures recalled in their correct location (Heaton et al 1991).

Retrograde Memory Tests

The assessment of memory for events that occurred prior to the onset of brain dysfunction can often be done informally by eliciting autobiographical recall. When using this technique, however, it is important to obtain verification of memories from relatives or ask the same questions a second time after a delay interval, because patients with retrograde amnesia are occasionally prone to fabricating answers (Schacter et al 1982). If the responses are valid, a time-line can be constructed reflecting the presence, nature, and extent of a patient's retrograde amnesia (Squire & Slater 1983).

BOSTON RETROGRADE AMNESIA BATTERY (BRAB)   The original BRAB (Albert et al 1979) assessed familiarity with historical events and individuals who were in the public spotlight from the 1940s through the 1970s; however, a new experimental version of this test has been updated through 1993. Subjects are asked to provide the names of famous individuals presented in photographs and answer questions regarding major events that have occurred over the past six decades. Cued recall and multiple-choice recognition testing are also included. If a retrograde memory deficit is present, the number of correct responses to items from each decade can be plotted to reveal whether the deficit is equally severe (i.e. flat) or temporally graded across decades.

TELEVISION TEST   A methodological problem inherent in testing retrograde memory is the difference in item difficulty across decades. For example, patients may show better memory for celebrities from the remote past than from the recent past because celebrities from the remote past have had a longer period of exposure and fame, thereby making them easier to recall. To circumvent this problem, Squire & Slater (1975) developed a test to maximize the potential for equivalent public exposure across years. They used as test items television programs that were broadcast for only one season and employed both recall and recognition techniques. This test has been useful in documenting the nature of retrograde amnesia in depressed patients who have undergone electroconvulsive therapy (Squire et al 1975) and in amnesic patients (Cohen & Squire 1980), and it has been validated by repeated administrations of updated versions to subjects over a seven-year period (Squire & Fox 1980).

MEMORY PROFILES ASSOCIATED WITH DEMENTIA

Analysis of the characteristics of memory loss associated with dementia can often provide insight into the differential diagnosis of the specific dementing illness. In the past, standardized memory tests have been useful in detecting the presence of a memory deficit but inadequate in characterizing the underlying nature of the memory disorder. The newer generation of standardized tests, however, incorporates theoretical rationales from the cognitive neuropsychological literature and are much more useful in this regard.

Dementia of the Alzheimer Type

Anterograde amnesia for semantic and episodic types of declarative knowledge is often the first neuropsychological finding of dementia of the Alzheimer type (DAT; Zec 1993). Memory difficulties typically begin insidiously and progress gradually, becoming the most prominent and disproportionately impaired cognitive symptom. By the middle stages of the disorder, memory is severely impaired while other cognitive functions, including language, visuospatial abilities, and executive functions are at least moderately impaired. In later stages, the patient becomes progressively disoriented to time, place, and finally, person.

The memory disorder associated with DAT is typically characterized by poor learning and retention of information over time. DAT patients fail to show learning over repeated trials (Moss et al 1986, Ober et al 1985, Wilson et al 1983) and tend to recall items from the recency region of word lists, reflecting a highly passive learning style (Delis et al 1987, Wilson et al 1983). They also make numerous intrusion errors (Kramer et al 1988). Information is lost rapidly over relatively brief delays (e.g. within 10 min) and is evidenced by poor performance on both recall and recognition testing (Ober et al 1985, Moss et al 1986, Tröster et al 1993, Wilson et al 1983). The consistent finding of rapid loss of information even on tasks that have minimal retrieval demands suggests that the memory disorder in DAT is one of information storage, rather than retrieval (Zec 1993).

In addition to the anterograde memory deficits described above, patients with DAT also demonstrate impaired retrograde memory. Patients with moderate to severe DAT demonstrate marked retrograde memory deficits equally across all past decades of their lives (i.e. flat retrograde amnesia; Albert et al 1981b, Wilson et al 1983). In earlier stages, however, there is evidence of a temporal gradient, in which remote events are remembered better than more recent events (Beatty et al 1987).

There is mounting evidence of significant variability in the cerebral regions most affected by the neuropathological process of DAT. Positron emission tomography indicates that DAT patients show significantly more lateral asymmetry of brain glucose metabolism than age-matched normal subjects (Friedland et al 1985, Haxby et al 1985). Especially in the early stages of the disease, patients with greater metabolic dysfunction in one or the other cerebral hemisphere tend to demonstrate asymmetry of memory deficits consistent with the hemisphere most affected.

A recent study by Massman et al (1993) demonstrated asymmetric visuospatial memory profiles in subgroups of DAT patients. Patients were divided into groups based on their performance on clinical tests of verbal and visuospatial ability. One subgroup consisted of patients who performed significantly better on verbal measures than on visuospatial measures (high-verbal); the second subgroup was comprised of patients who performed significantly better on visuospatial than verbal measures (high-spatial). Patients who obtained similar normative scores on tests of both verbal and visuospatial functioning comprised the third subgroup (equal). All patients were administered a modified version of the California Global-Local Learning Test (described earlier). The investigators found pronounced dissociations among the DAT subgroups on this test. Patients in the high-spatial subgroup had particular difficulty processing details (i.e. local forms), whereas patients in the high-verbal subgroup exhibited marked deficits in processing the configural aspects (i.e. global forms). No significant dissociation in global or local processing was seen in the equal subgroup.

Several studies have shown a dissociation of subtypes of nondeclarative memory abilities in DAT. Lexical and semantic priming deficits have been reported in patients with DAT (e.g. Salmon et al 1988, Shimamura et al 1987), as have deficits in the classical conditioning of an eye-blink response (Solomon et al 1991). Procedural learning, however, as demonstrated by a subject's ability to become proficient at visuomotor tasks such as using a mirror to trace line drawings (i.e. mirror-tracing) and maintaining contact between a hand-held stylus and a rotating metallic disk (i.e. pursuit-rotor) remains intact in DAT (Heindel et al 1988, Eslinger & Damasio 1986).

Frontal Lobe Dementia

The frontal lobes account for approximately half of the cerebrum and consist of the primary motor area (i.e. motor strip), premotor areas (i.e. Broca's area, supplementary motor area, and frontal eye fields), and the prefrontal cortex. Given its size, the chances that the frontal lobes will be involved in any diffuse pathological process are high; however, some dementing disorders preferentially affect the frontal lobes. These include Pick's disease and Jakob-Creutzfeldt disease, both of which are relatively rare conditions. Recent evidence, however, suggests that a more common degenerative dementia specific to the frontal lobes may exist that is histopathologically distinct from these and other known dementing illnesses (see Gustafson et al 1990, Knopman et al 1990, Neary & Snowden 1991).

Although it may be too early to establish frontal lobe dementia as a distinct diagnostic entity, several features appear to be indicative of dementia associated with frontal lobe dysfunction. The patient with frontal lobe features typically presents with reports of a change in personality or adaptive behaviors that precede the onset of cognitive symptoms. When cognitive deficits appear, they typically involve disorders of planning, organization, mental flexibility, and memory (Sungaila & Crockett 1993). The memory deficits associated with frontal lobe dementia typically reflect poor organization, use of inefficient learning strategies, and increased susceptibility to interference (Mayes 1988). Ability to sustain attention is disturbed; however, there is no evidence of rapid forgetting of information, such as is seen in DAT (Shimamura et al 1991). Errors in recall are quite common, and include perseverations, intrusions, and source memory problems (e.g. recalling words from an interference list when asked to recall the original target list). Release from proactive interference may also be disturbed in frontal lobe dementia; however, this is not a consistent finding (see Shimamura et al 1991).

Subcortical Dementia

The concept of subcortical dementia has generated much discussion (Mahurin et al 1993). Although the pattern of cognitive impairment originally described was in specific reference to progressive supranuclear palsy (PSP), this pattern has since been associated with a multitude of disorders affecting subcortical structures and pathways, including Parkinson's disease, Huntington's disease, multiple sclerosis, Wilson's disease, and brainstem-cerebellar degenerative disorders such as olivopontocerebellar atrophy. The predominant feature in all of these disorders is motor dysfunction (e.g. tremor, choreoform movements, and/or bradykinesia); however, significant cognitive disturbances are often present as well (see Cummings & Benson 1992).

Most neuropsychological studies of memory disturbance in subcortical dementia have focused on Parkinson's disease (PD) and Huntington's disease (HD). When compared to DAT patients with equivalent overall severity of cognitive dysfunction, patients with PD and HD display equally impaired free recall of information immediately following presentation; however, patients with subcortical disorders demonstrate superior retention of information over delay intervals than do patients with DAT (Butters et al 1985, Helkala et al 1988). PD and HD patients also tend to benefit more from rehearsal and the provision of cues than do DAT patients (Helkala et al 1988). When presented with multiple trials of different verbal stimuli, HD patients demonstrate normal sensitivity to proactive interference and make significantly fewer intrusion and perseveration errors than do DAT patients (Butters et al 1976, Kramer et al 1988, Massman et al 1990).

Recognition performance, though impaired, tends to be disproportionately better in HD and PD patients than in DAT patients (Butters et al 1985, Kramer et al 1988, Snodgrass & Corwin 1988). This has led some to propose that the mechanism of memory failure in subcortical dementias may be deficient retrieval search (Butters et al 1986, Massman et al 1990). A recent study, however, reported that HD patients in the most advanced stages of illness are as impaired as DAT patients in recognition discriminability (Kramer et al 1988). This suggests that although retrieval failure may account for memory deficits throughout much of HD, encoding abilities may become more affected as the illness progresses.

HD patients have impaired retrograde memory, showing a flat retrograde amnesia with equally deficient recall of events from all decades (Beatty et al 1987, Albert et al 1981a). The performance of recently diagnosed HD patients improves on recognition testing of remote events, which further implicates a retrieval search deficit in this group of patients (Beatty et al 1987). PD patients show a similar, temporally graded retrograde memory deficit (Sagar et al 1988).

Much like patients with DAT, patients with PD and HD evidence selective impairments on a subset of related measures of nondeclarative memory. The pattern of preserved and impaired abilities observed in PD and HD, however, is distinct from that seen in DAT. Specifically, PD and HD patients demonstrate marked impairment in their ability to acquire and retain rule-based motor and cognitive skills (i.e. procedural memory; Bondi & Kaszniak 1991, Eslinger & Damasio 1986, Saint-Cyr et al 1988); such abilities are relatively preserved in DAT. In contrast, HD patients demonstrate normal lexical priming and better than normal pictorial priming (Heindel et al 1989, 1990); DAT patients demonstrate significant impairment on these measures. Results of priming studies in PD are less straightforward. Normal lexical priming has been observed in nondemented PD patients (Bondi & Kaszniak 1991); however, demented PD patients display impaired lexical priming (Heindel et al 1989). These studies suggest that the memory deficits seen in demented PD patients may reflect a combination of features associated with DAT and HD.

Alcoholic Dementia

It is well known that long-term, chronic alcoholism often leads to impaired cognitive abilities. Detoxified chronic alcoholics often display mild to moderate deficits on more challenging tests of new learning and memory (Brandt et al 1983, Miglioli et al 1979, Ryan & Butters 1980, Ryan & Lewis 1988). Memory for visuospatial stimuli is often worse than for verbal material (Miglioli et al 1979), which parallels findings that these patients tend to show greater dysfunction in visuospatial skills relative to verbal abilities (Glosser et al 1977, Kapur & Butters 1977, Wilson et al 1987). Relatively young alcoholics (in their thirties) may show little neuropsychological impairment due to alcohol (Grant et al 1984), and older alcoholics may show improvement in cognitive functioning after at least five years of sobriety (Brandt et al 1983).

Some chronic alcoholics, however, develop a global dementia that persists despite abstinence from alcohol. This alcoholic dementia is typically characterized by severe impairment of memory, conceptualization, problem-solving, and visuospatial abilities (Salmon et al 1993). The memory disturbance is characterized by rapid forgetting of information over time, rather than retrieval or encoding difficulties. In addition, patients with alcoholic dementia are more sensitive to and do not demonstrate normal release from proactive interference. They do, however, demonstrate preserved priming abilities on word-stem completion tasks (Salmon et al 1988, Shimamura et al 1987; see also Shimamura 1986).

MEMORY PROFILES ASSOCIATED WITH AMNESIA

Damage to the medial temporal lobe or medial diencephalon typically results in a severe disturbance of declarative memory. If the damage does not extend beyond these regions, the patient will demonstrate an amnesic syndrome in which other cognitive functions remain relatively intact despite the presence of markedly impaired memory abilities. The more common etiologies associated with such amnesic disturbances include surgical interventions (i.e. temporal lobectomy), infectious diseases (e.g. herpes encephalitis), cerebrovascular accidents involving the posterior cerebral artery, anoxic episodes, and Alcoholic Korsakoff syndrome.

Temporal Lobe Amnesia

The importance of the medial temporal lobe region in memory functioning was firmly established in the 1950s, when bilateral resections of medial temporal lobe structures were performed to treat patients with intractable epilepsy (Scoville & Milner 1957). Bilateral damage to medial temporal lobe structures results in marked anterograde memory deficits for both verbal and nonverbal material, as well as profound, temporally graded retrograde memory deficits. In contrast, nondeclarative memory functioning, including procedural learning and priming, remains relatively intact (but see Jernigan & Ostergaard 1993, for evidence of medial temporal lobe involvement in priming).

Based on the study of patients with unilateral temporal lobe resections, it was established that the left and right temporal lobes were responsible for material-specific memory functioning, with the left temporal lobe (LTL) responsible for verbal memory and the right temporal lobe (RTL) responsible for nonverbal memory (Gerner et al 1972, Milner 1971). Subsequent findings, however, have indicated that patients with RTL damage also suffer subtle deficits in verbal memory functioning and that LTL patients are impaired in remembering certain types of visual stimuli.

On tests of story memory, for example, RTL patients may remember an equivalent number of idea units as normal controls; however, they are more prone to lose the gist of the story (Wapner et al 1981). They tend to recall exact wordings rather than paraphrasing the words of stories that do not fit into their everyday vocabulary. These patients also tend to introject personal information into their recall, which can further obscure the original gist of the story (Wapner et al 1981). On tests of list learning and recall such as the CVLT, RTL patients do not adopt an active semantic clustering strategy and recall fewer words than do normal controls (Villardita 1987).

Kaplan (1983) observed that LTL patients displayed more impairment in remembering the internal details of complex visual stimuli. RTL patients, on the other hand, tend to recall the details but cannot reproduce the overall configuration of the figure. Delis et al (1988) found that LTL patients were selectively deficient in remembering local forms of visual hierarchical stimuli, especially when they were presented in right hemispace. In contrast, RTL patients were selectively impaired in remembering global forms, especially when the stimuli were presented in left hemispace. These findings occurred whether or not the patients displayed visual field cuts, hemi-inattention, or aphasic deficits (Delis et al 1986, 1988).

Patients with amnesia secondary to medial temporal lobe or medial di-encephalic damage are not, however, as totally memory disabled as was once believed. When assessed using measures of nondeclarative memory, it is readily shown that the performance of patients with amnesia can be influenced by previous experiences. For example, facilitation of the processing of words to which the individual has had recent exposure (i.e. recognition priming) is frequently normal in amnesic patients despite severe deficits in explicit recognition memory for those same words (Graf et al 1984, Jernigan & Ostergaard 1993). In addition, no differences are found between normal control subjects and amnesic patients on measures of lexical priming (i.e. Salmon et al 1988, Shimamura et al 1987). Amnesic patients have also been shown to have normal procedural learning on mirror-tracing and pursuit-rotor tasks (Cermak et al 1973). Moreover, the ability to learn and retain cognitive skills such as mirror reading is also preserved in these patients (Cohen & Squire 1980).

Alcoholic Korsakoff Syndrome

Alcoholic Korsakoff (AK) syndrome results from damage to the medial di-encephalon, including the dorsomedial nucleus of the thalamus and the mammillary bodies. For these patients, intelligence and immediate recall span range from average to low average, but the ability to encode new information into more permanent storage is severely impaired (Butters & Cermak 1980, see also Cermak et al 1985). This severe anterograde amnesia is restricted to declarative knowledge; nondeclarative memory abilities, including procedural learning and semantic priming, are preserved (Shimamura et al 1987, Cohen & Squire 1980). Declarative anterograde amnesia in AK syndrome encompasses all stimulus categories (e.g. verbal and visuospatial material) and stimulus features (e.g. global and local forms). Patients with AK syndrome demonstrate a flat learning curve across repeated trials. On delayed recall tasks, they frequently have no recollection of having been exposed to the target items. Minimal, if any, improvement is seen on recognition testing, where patients typically adopt a liberal response bias, saying that they recognize all stimuli, including both target items and distractors (Butters et al 1988). High rates of intrusion errors and increased sensitivity to proactive interference are also common.

When recall of past autobiographical events and public information is assessed, AK patients typically demonstrate a severe retrograde amnesia characterized by a temporal gradient. Generally speaking, memory for events from the 20- to 30-year period immediately preceding onset of the disorder is much worse than memory for remote events from childhood and early adulthood (Butters & Stuss 1989). Some have suggested that the temporal gradient of retrograde amnesia in AK patients is an artifact of a primary progressive deficit in anterograde memory over the period of their alcohol abuse (Albert et al 1979, Squire & Cohen 1982). That is, chronic alcoholics with AK syndrome may recall less information from more recent times because they were able to acquire fewer and fewer new memories over that period of time. Perhaps the most convincing evidence against this hypothesis comes from the case study of P.Z. (Butters & Cermak 1986). P.Z. demonstrated a temporally graded retrograde amnesia secondary to AK syndrome, including an inability to recall any personal episodes or facts from the immediately preceding 20-year period. By all accounts and documentation, however, he possessed complete autobiographical knowledge just three years prior to his development of the disorder. Thus, the temporal gradient of P.Z.'s retrograde amnesia cannot be attributed to his not having acquired the information in the first place.

Cermak (1984) has proposed that the temporal gradient seen in AK syndrome may reflect a dichotomy of remote memories. According to this proposal, more recent autobiographical knowledge and acquired information may be episodic in nature, and thus may be more reliant on temporal and spatial contexts. With time, however, these memories may become less dependent on temporal and spatial contexts and become part of semantic memory. The temporally graded retrograde amnesia seen in AK syndrome may therefore represent a specific vulnerability of episodic memory to the type of damage incurred in the disorder (i.e. medial diencephalic damage).

CONCLUSION

As the investigation of cognitive processes associated with memory functioning continues to move forward, so will our ability to measure and characterize memory disorders at both the structural and functional level. Recognition of the existence of two dissociable memory systems has led to an explosion of interest in the neurology of memory and the search for brain structures that mediate nondeclarative memory systems (see Heindel et al 1993, Jernigan & Ostergaard 1993, Squire et al 1993). Determinations concerning the structure-function relationships of procedural memory and priming will become more evident as neuropsychological studies involving cognitive psychological procedures and advanced neuroimaging techniques accumulate in the literature.

Unfortunately, the revolution incited by the discovery of nondeclarative types of memory has thus far had little, if any, impact on how memory is assessed in clinical settings. A review of the major catalogs of neuropsychological assessment measures reveals the virtual absence of tests of nondeclarative memory. If the lag between breakthroughs in cognitive neuropsychological science and the development of new clinical tests of memory remains true to form, the next few years should witness not only a refinement and development of new techniques for assessing nondeclarative memory in the laboratory, but the introduction of standardized measures of implicit memory into clinical practice as well. Such a development would provide a means of better defining the extent and nature of memory impairment in patient populations and will aid in differential diagnosis. The ability to measure nondeclarative memory for clinical purposes may also have important implications for cognitive rehabilitation of individuals with memory deficits. Whether patients can be trained to use intact nondeclarative memory systems to ameliorate or circumvent deficits in explicit memory is yet to be determined.

Certainly, the improvements in declarative measures of memory reviewed in this chapter (e.g. the inclusion of indices of delayed recall, recognition, sensitivity to interference, learning strategies, error analysis, retrograde memory deficits, and rates of forgetting) have produced a generation of tests that are far superior to their predecessors with regard to sensitivity and selectivity. Consequently, today's clinical neuropsychologist is better able to detect the presence of early dementia, differentiate between dementias of various etiologies, and distinguish dementing illnesses from amnesic syndromes.

Any *Annual Review* chapter, as well as any article cited in an *Annual Review* chapter, may be purchased from the Annual Reviews Preprints and Reprints service. 1-800-347-8007; 415-259-5017; email: arpr@class.org

---

Literature Cited

Adams KM. 1980. In search of Luria's battery: a false start. *J. Consult. Clin. Psychol.* 48: 511–16

Albert MS, Butters N, Brandt J. 1981a. Development of remote memory loss in patients with Huntington's disease. *J. Clin. Neuropsychol.* 3:1–12

Albert MS, Butters N, Brandt J. 1981b. Patterns of remote memory in amnesic and demented patients. *Arch. Neurol.* 38:495–500

Albert MS, Butters N, Levin J. 1979. Temporal gradients in the retrograde amnesia of patients with alcoholic Korsakoff disease. *Arch. Neurol.* 36:211–16

American Psychiatric Association. 1994. *Diagnostic and Statistical Manual of Mental Disorders*, pp. 133–55. Washington, DC: Am. Psychiatr. Assoc. 4th ed.

Beatty WW, Salmon DP, Butters N, Heindel WC, Granholm EP. 1987. Retrograde amnesia in patients with Alzheimer's disease or Huntington's disease. *Neurobiol. Aging* 9:181–86

Benton AL. 1974. *The Revised Visual Retention Test*. New York: Psychol. Corp. 4th ed.

Benton AL, Hamsher KdeS. 1976. *Multilingual Aphasia Examination*. Iowa City: Univ. Iowa Press

Bondi MW, Kaszniak AW. 1991. Implicit and explicit memory in Alzheimer's disease and Parkinson's disease. *J. Clin. Exp. Neuropsychol.* 13:339–58

Brandt J, Butters N, Ryan C, Bayog R. 1983. Cognitive loss and recovery in long-term alcohol abusers. *Arch. Gen. Psychiatr.* 40: 435–42

Breslow R, Kocsis J, Belkin B. 1980. Memory deficits in depression: evidence utilizing the Wechsler Memory Scale. *Percept. Motor Skills* 51:541–42

Buschke H. 1973. Selective reminding for analysis of memory and behavior. *J. Verb. Learn. Verb. Behav.* 12:543–50

Buschke H, Fuld PA. 1974. Evaluating storage, retention, and retrieval in disordered memory and learning. *Neurology* 24:1019–25

Butters N. 1992. Memory remembered: 1970–1991. *Arch. Clin. Neuropsychol.* 7:285–95

Butters N, Cermak LS. 1980. *Alcoholic Korsakoff's Syndrome.* New York: Academic

Butters N, Cermak LS. 1986. A case study of the forgetting of autobiographical knowledge: implications for the study of retrograde amnesia. In *Autobiographical Memory*, ed. D Rubin, pp. 253–72. New York: Cambridge Univ. Press

Butters N, Salmon DP, Cullum CM, Cairns P, Tröster AI, et al. 1988. Differentiation of amnesic and demented patients with the Wechsler Memory Scale-Revised. *Clin. Neuropsychologist* 2:133–48

Butters N, Stuss DT. 1989. Diencephalic amnesia. In *Handbook of Neuropsychology*, ed. F Boller, J Grafman, 3:107–48. Amsterdam: Elsevier

Butters N, Tarlow S, Cermak LS, Sax D. 1976. A comparison of the information processing deficits in patients with Huntington's chorea and Korsakoff's syndrome. *Cortex* 12:134–44

Butters N, Wolfe J, Granholm E, Martone M. 1986. An assessment of verbal recall, recognition and fluency abilities in patients with Huntington's disease. *Cortex* 22:11–32

Butters N, Wolfe J, Martone M, Granholm E, Cermak LS. 1985. Memory disorders associated with Huntington's disease: verbal recall, verbal recognition, and procedural memory. *Neuropsychologia* 23:729–43

Cermak LS. 1984. The episodic-semantic distinction in amnesia. In *Neuropsychology of Memory*, ed. LR Squire, N Butters, pp. 55–62. New York: Guilford

Cermak LS, Lewis R, Butters N, Goodglass H. 1973. Role of verbal mediation in performance of motor tasks by Korsakoff patients. *Percept. Motor Skills* 37:259–62

Cermak LS, Talbot N, Chandler K, Wolbarst LR. 1985. The perceptual priming phenomenon in amnesia. *Neuropsychologia* 23:615–22

Chelune GJ, Bornstein RA. 1988. Wechsler Memory Scale-Revised patterns among patients with unilateral brain lesions. *Clin. Neuropsychol.* 2:121–32

Cohen N, Squire LR. 1980. Preserved learning and retention of pattern analyzing skill in amnesia: dissociation of knowing how and knowing that. *Science* 210:207–9

Crowder RG. 1982. The demise of short-term memory. *Acta Psychol.* 50:291–323

Cummings JL, Benson DF. 1992. *Dementia: A Clinical Approach.* Boston: Butterworth-Heinemann. 2nd ed.

Daum I, Channon S, Canavar A. 1989. Classical conditioning in patients with severe memory problems. *J. Neurol. Neurosurg. Psychiatr.* 52:47–51

Delis DC. 1989. Neuropsychological assessment of learning and memory. In *Handbook of Neuropsychology*, ed. F Boller, J Grafman, 3:3–33. Amsterdam: Elsevier

Delis DC, Kiefner M, Fridlund AJ. 1988. Visuospatial dysfunction following unilateral brain damage: dissociations in hierarchical and hemispatial analysis. *J. Clin. Exp. Neuropsychol.* 10:421–31

Delis DC, Kramer JH, Kaplan E, Ober BA. 1987. *The California Verbal Learning Test.* New York: Psychol. Corp.

Delis DC, Robertson LC, Efron R. 1986. Hemispheric specialization of memory for visual hierarchical stimuli. *Neuropsychologia* 24:205–14

Erickson RC, Scott ML. 1977. Clinical memory testing: a review. *Psychol. Bull.* 84: 1130–49

Eslinger PJ, Damasio AR. 1986. Preserved motor learning in Alzheimer's disease: implications for anatomy and behavior. *J. Neurosci.* 6:3006–9

Fischer JF. 1988. Using the Wechsler Memory Scale-Revised to detect and characterize memory deficits in multiple sclerosis. *Clin. Neuropsychol.* 2:149–72

Friedland RP, Budinger TF, Koss E, Ober BA. 1985. Alzheimer's disease: anterior-posterior and lateral hemispheric alterations in cortical glucose utilization. *Neurosci. Lett.* 53:235–40

Gerner P, Ommaya A, Fedio P. 1972. A study of visual memory: verbal and nonverbal mechanisms in patients with unilateral lobectomy. *Int. J. Neurosci.* 4:231–38

Glosser G, Butters N, Kaplan E. 1977. Visuoperceptual processes in brain damaged patients on the Digit Symbol Substitution test. *Int. J. Neurosci.* 7:59–66

Golden CJ, Hammeke TA, Purisch AD. 1983. *The Luria Nebraska Neuropsychological Battery.* Los Angeles: Western Psychol. Serv.

Goodglass H, Kaplan E. 1983. *The Assessment of Aphasia and Related Disorders.* Philadelphia: Lea & Febinger. 2nd ed.

Graf P, Squire LR, Mandler G. 1984. The information that amnesic patients do not forget. *J. Exp. Psychol. Learn. Mem. Cogn.* 10:164–78

Grant I, Adams K, Reed R. 1984. Aging, abstinence, and medical risk factors in the prediction of neuropsychologic deficit among long-term alcoholics. *Arch. Gen. Psychiatr.* 41:710–18

Gustafson L, Brun A, Risberg J. 1990. Frontal lobe dementia of the non-Alzheimer type. In *Advances in Neurology.* Vol. 51: *Alzheimer's Disease,* ed. RJ Wurtman. New York: Raven

Hannay HJ, Levin HS. 1985. Selective reminding test: an examination of the equivalence of four forms. *J. Clin. Exp. Neuropsychol.* 7:251–63

Haxby JV, Duara R, Grady CL, Cutler NR, Rapoport SI. 1985. Relations between neuropsychological and cerebral metabolic asymmetries in early Alzheimer's disease. *J. Cerebr. Blood Flow Metab.* 5:193–200

Heaton RK, Grant I, Matthews CG. 1991. *Comprehensive Norms for an Expanded Halstead-Reitan Battery.* Odessa, FL: Psychol. Assess. Resourc.

Heilbrun AB. 1956. Psychological test performance as a function of lateral localization of cerebral lesion. *J. Comp. Physiol. Psychol.* 49:10–14

Heindel WC, Butters N, Salmon DP. 1988. Impaired learning of a motor skill in patients with Huntington's disease. *Behav. Neurosci.* 102:141–47

Heindel WC, Salmon DP, Butters N. 1990 . Pictorial priming and cued recall in Alzheimer's and Huntington's disease. *Brain Cogn.* 13:282–95

Heindel WC, Salmon DP, Butters N. 1993. Cognitive approaches to memory disorders of demented patients. In *Comprehensive Handbook of Psychopathology,* ed. PB Sutker, HE Adams, pp. 735–61. New York: Plenum. 2nd ed.

Heindel WC, Salmon DP, Shults CW, Walicke PA, Butters N. 1989. Neuropsychological evidence for multiple implicit memory systems: a comparison of Alzheimer's, Parkinson's and Huntington's disease patients. *J. Neurosci.* 9:582–87

Helkala EL, Laulumaa V, Soinninen H, Riekkinen PJ. 1988. Recall and recognition memory in patients with Alzheimer's and Parkinson's diseases. *Ann. Neurol.* 24:214–17

James W. 1890. *Principles of Psychology.* New York: Holt

Jernigan TL, Ostergaard AL. 1993. Word priming and recognition memory are both affected by medial temporal lobe damage. *Neuropsychology* 7:14–26

Kaplan E. 1983. Process and achievement revisited. In *Toward a Holistic Developmental Psychology,* ed. S Wapner, B Kaplan. Hillsdale, NJ: Erlbaum

Kaplan E, Fein D, Morris R, Delis DC. 1991. *WAIS-R as a Neuropsychological Instrument.* New York: Psychol. Corp.

Kapur N, Butters N. 1977. An analysis of visuoperceptive deficits in alcoholic Korsakoffs and long term alcoholics. *J. Stud. Alcohol* 38:2025–35

Klatzky RL. 1980. *Human Memory: Structures and Processes.* San Francisco: Freeman. 2nd ed.

Knopman DS, Mastri AR, Frey WH, Sung JH, Rustan T. 1990. Dementia lacking distinctive histologic features: a common non-Alzheimer degenerative dementia. *Neurology* 40:251–56

Kopelman MD. 1987. Amnesia: organic and psychogenic. *Br. J. Psychiatr.* 150:428–42

Kramer JH, Delis DC, Blusewicz MJ, Brandt J, Ober BA, Strauss M. 1988. Verbal memory errors in Alzheimer's and Huntington's dementias. *Dev. Neuropsychol.* 4:1–5

Lezak MD. 1983. *Neuropsychological Assessment.* Oxford: Oxford Univ. Press. 2nd ed.

Loring DW. 1989. The Wechsler Memory Scale-Revised or the Wechsler Memory Scale-Revisited. *Clin. Neuropsychologist* 3:59–69

Loring DW, Papanicolaou AC. 1987. Memory assessment in neuropsychology: theoretical considerations and practical utility. *J. Clin. Exp. Neuropsychol.* 9:340–58

Mahurin RK, Feher EP, Nance ML, Levy JK, Pirozzolo FJ. 1993. Cognition in Parkinson's disease and related disorders. See Parks et al 1993, pp. 308–49

Marinkovic K, Schell AM, Dawson ME. 1989. Awareness of the CS-UCS contingency and classical conditioning of skin conductance responses with olfactory CSs. *Biol. Psychol.* 29:39–60

Marsh GG, Hirsch SH. 1982. Effectiveness of two tests of visual retention. *J. Clin. Psychol.* 38:115–18

Martone M, Butters N, Payne M, Becker J, Sax DS. 1984. Dissociations between skill learning and verbal recognition in amnesia and dementia. *Arch. Neurol.* 41:965–70

Massman PJ, Delis DC, Butters N, Levin BE, Salmon DP. 1990. Are all subcortical dementias alike? Verbal learning and memory in Parkinson's and Huntington's disease patients. *J. Clin. Exp. Neuropsychol.* 12:729–44

Massman PJ, Delis DC, Filoteo JV, Butters N, Salmon DP, Demadura TL. 1993. Mechanisms of spatial impairment in Alzheimer's disease subgroups: differential breakdown of directed attention to global-local stimuli. *Neuropsychology* 7:172–81

Mayes AR. 1988. The memory problems caused by frontal lobe lesions. In *Human Organic Memory Disorders,* ed. AR Mayes, pp. 102–23. Cambridge: Cambridge Univ. Press

McCarthy RA, Warrington EK. 1990. *Cognitive Neuropsychology: A Clinical Introduction.* San Diego: Academic

Miglioli M, Buchte, HA, Campanin T, DeRisio C. 1979. Cerebral hemispheric lateralization of cognitive deficits due to alcoholism. *J. Nerv. Ment. Dis.* 167:212–17

Miller E. 1973. Short- and long-term memory in patients with presenile dementia. *Psychol. Med.* 3:221–24

Miller GA. 1956. The magical number seven: plus or minus two. Some limits on our capacity for processing information. *Psychol. Rev.* 9:81–97

Milner B. 1966. Amnesia following operation on the temporal lobes. In *Amnesia,* ed. CWM Whitty, OL Zangwill, p. 113. London: Butterworth

Milner B. 1971. Interhemispheric differences in the localization of psychological processes in man. *Br. Med. Bull.* 27:272–77

Milner B, Corkin S, Teuber HL. 1968. Further analysis of the hippocampal amnesic syndrome: a 14-year follow-up study of H.M. *Neuropsychologia* 6:215–34

Moss MB, Albert MS, Butters N, Payne M. 1986. Differential patterns of memory loss among patients with Alzheimer's disease, Huntington's disease, and alcoholic Korsakoff's syndrome. *Arch. Neurol.* 43:239–46

Neary D, Snowden JS. 1991. Dementia of the frontal lobe type. *J. Neurol. Neurosurg. Psychiatr.* 51:353–61

Ober BA, Koss E, Friedland RP, Delis DC. 1985. Processes of verbal memory failure in Alzheimer-type dementia. *Brain Cogn.* 4:90–103

Parks RW, Zec RF, Wilson RS, eds. 1993. *Neuropsychology of Alzheimer's Disease and Other Dementias.* Oxford: Oxford Univ. Press

Plum F. 1987. Dementia. In *Encyclopedia of Neuroscience,* ed. G Adelman, 1:309–12. Boston: Birkhäuser

Prigatano GP. 1978. Wechsler Memory Scale: a selective review of the literature. *J. Clin. Psychol.* 34:816–32

Randolph C, Gold JM, Carpenter CJ, Goldberg TE, Weinberger DR. 1992. Release from proactive interference: determinants of performance and neuropsychological correlates. *J. Clin. Exp. Neuropsychol.* 14:785–800

Randt CT, Brown ER. 1983. *Randt Memory Test.* Bayport, NY: Life Sci.

Reitan RM, Wolfson D. 1985. *The Halstead-Reitan Neuropsychological Test Battery.* Tucson, AZ: Neuropsychology

Reitman JS. 1971. Mechanisms of forgetting in short-term memory. *Cogn. Psychol.* 2:185–95

Russell EW. 1986. The psychometric foundation of clinical neuropsychology. In *Handbook of Neuropsychology,* ed. SB Filskov, TJ Boll, 2:45–80. New York: Wiley

Ryan C, Butters N. 1980. Learning and memory impairments in young and old alcoholics: evidence for the premature aging hypothesis. *Alcoholism* 4:288–93

Ryan JJ, Lewis CU. 1988. Comparison of normal controls and recently detoxified alcoholics on the Wechsler Memory Scale-Revised. *Clin. Neuropsychol.* 2:173–80

Sagar HJ, Cohen NJ, Sullivan EV, Corkin S, Growdon JH. 1988. Remote memory function in Alzheimer's disease and Parkinson's disease. *Brain* 111:185–206

Saint-Cyr JA, Taylor AE, Lang AE. 1988. Procedural learning and neostriatal dysfunction in man. *Brain* 111:941–59

Salmon DP, Butters N, Heindel WC. 1993. Alcoholic dementia and related disorders. See Parks et al 1993, pp. 186–209

Salmon DP, Shimamura AP, Butters N, Smith S. 1988. Lexical and semantic priming deficits in patients with Alzheimer's disease. *J. Clin. Exp. Neuropsychol.* 10:477–94

Schacter D, Wang PL, Tulving E, Freedman PC. 1982. Functional retrograde amnesia: a quantitative case study. *Neuropsychologia* 20:523–32

Scoville WB, Milner B. 1957. Loss of recent memory after bilateral hippocampal lesions. *J. Neurol. Neurosurg. Psychiatr.* 20:11–21

Shimamura AP. 1986. Priming effects in amnesia: evidence for a dissociable memory function. *Q. J. Exp. Psychol.* 38a:619–44

Shimamura AP, Janowski JS, Squire LR. 1991. What is the role of frontal damage in memory disorders? In *Frontal Lobe Function and Dysfunction,* ed. HS Levin, HM Eisenberg, AL Benton, pp. 173–95. Oxford: Oxford Univ. Press

Shimamura AP, Salmon DP, Squire LR, Butters N. 1987. Memory dysfunction and word priming in dementia and amnesia. *Behav. Neurosci.* 101:347–51

Slamecka NJ. 1960. Retroactive inhibition of connected discourse as a function of practice level. *J. Exp. Psychol.* 59:104–8

Snodgrass JG, Corwin J. 1988. Pragmatics of measuring recognition memory: applications to dementia and amnesia. *J. Exp. Psychol.* 117:34–50

Solomon PR, Levine E, Bein T, Pendlebury WW. 1991. Disruption of classical conditioning in patients with Alzheimer's disease. *Neurobiol. Aging* 12:283–87

Spiers P. 1981. Have they come to praise Luria or to bury him? The Luria-Nebraska Battery controversy. *J. Consult. Clin. Psychol.* 49:331–41

Spreen O, Strauss E. 1991. *A Compendium of Neuropsychological Tests: Administration,*

Norms, and Commentary. Oxford: Oxford Univ. Press

Squire LR. 1987. *Memory and Brain.* Oxford: Oxford Univ. Press

Squire LR, Cohen NJ. 1982. Remote memory, retrograde amnesia, and the neuropsychology of memory. In *Human Memory and Amnesia,* ed. LS Cermak, pp. 275–303. Hillsdale, NJ: Erlbaum

Squire LR, Fox MM. 1980. Assessment of remote memory: validation of the television test by repeated testing during a seven-year period. *Behav. Res. Methods Instrum. Comput.* 12:583–86

Squire LR, Knowlton B, Musen G. 1993. The structure and organization of memory. *Annu. Rev. Psychol.* 44:453–95

Squire LR, Moore RY. 1979. Dorsal thalamic lesions in a noted case of chronic memory dysfunction. *Ann. Neurol.* 6:503–6

Squire LR, Slater PC. 1975. Forgetting in very long-term memory as assessed by an improved questionnaire technique. *J. Exp. Psychol. Hum. Learn. Mem.* 104:50–54

Squire LR, Slater PC. 1983. Electroconvulsive therapy and complaints of memory dysfunction: a prospective three-year follow-up study. *Br. J. Psychiatr.* 142:1–8

Squire LR, Slater PC, Chase PM. 1975. Retrograde amnesia: temporal gradient in very long term memory following electroconvulsive therapy. *Science* 187:77–79

Sterne DM. 1969. The Benton, Porteus, and WAIS Digit Span tests with normal and brain injured subjects. *J. Clin. Psychol.* 25:173–75

Stromgren LS. 1977. The influence of depression on memory. *Acta Psychiatr. Scand.* 56:109–28

Sungaila P, Crockett DJ. 1993. Dementia and the frontal lobes. See Parks 1993, pp. 235–64

Teuber HL, Milner B, Baughan HG. 1968. Persistent anterograde amnesia after stab wound of the basal brain. *Neuropsychologia* 6:267–82

Tröster AI, Butters N, Salmon DP, Cullum CM, Jacobs D, et al. 1993. The diagnostic utility of savings scores: differentiating Alzheimer's and Huntington's diseases with the Logical Memory and Visual Reproduction tests. *J. Clin. Exp. Neuropsychol.* 15:773–88

Tulving E. 1983. *Elements of Episodic Mem-*

ory. Oxford: Clarendon

Villardita C. 1987. Verbal memory and semantic clustering in right hemisphere damaged patients. *Neuropsychologia* 25:277–80

Wapner W, Hamby S, Gardner H. 1981. The role of the right hemisphere in the apprehension of complex linguistic material. *Brain Lang.* 14:15–32

Warrington EK. 1984. *Recognition Memory Test.* Windsor: Nfer-Nelson

Warrington EK, Weiskrantz L. 1970. Amnesic syndrome: consolidation or retrieval? *Nature* 228:628–30

Warrington EK, Weiskrantz L. 1973. An analysis of short-term and long-term memory defects in man. In *The Physiological Basis of Memory,* ed. JA Deutsch, pp. 365–95. New York: Academic

Wechsler D. 1945. A standardized memory scale for clinical use. *J. Psychol.* 19:87–95

Wechsler D. 1981. *Manual for the Wechsler Adult Intelligence Scale-Revised.* New York: Psychol. Corp.

Wechsler D. 1987. *Wechsler Memory Scale-Revised.* New York: Psychol. Corp.

Weiskrantz L, Warrington EK. 1979. Conditioning in amnesic patients. *Neuropsychologia* 17:187–94

Welsh K, Butters N, Hughes J, Mohs R, Heyman A. 1991. Detection of abnormal memory decline in mild cases of Alzheimer's disease using CERAD neuropsychological measures. *Arch. Neurol.* 48:278–81

Wickelgren WA. 1973. The long and short of memory. *Psychol. Bull.* 80:425–38

Williams JM. 1991. *Memory Assessment Scales Professional Manual.* New York: Psychol. Corp.

Wilson B, Kolb B, Odland L, Whishaw IQ. 1987. Alcohol, sex, age, and the hippocampus. *Psychobiology* 15:300–7

Wilson RS, Bacan LD, Fox JH, Kaszniak AW. 1983. Primary memory and secondary memory in dementia of the Alzheimer type. *J. Clin. Neuropsychol.* 5:337–44

Zec RF. 1993. Neuropsychological functioning in Alzheimer's disease. See Parks et al 1993, pp. 3–80

Zielinski JJ. 1993. A comparison of the Wechsler Memory Scale-Revised and the Memory Assessment Scales: administrative, clinical, and interpretive issues. *Prof. Psychol.: Res. Pract.* 3:353–59

Annu. Rev. Psychol. 1995. 46:525–59

DEDUCTIVE INFERENCE

Rachel Joffe Falmagne and Joanna Gonsalves

Department of Psychology, Clark University, Worcester, Massachusetts 01610-1477

KEY WORDS: deduction, reasoning, semantics, thinking, language

CONTENTS

INTRODUCTION

The research area of deduction is shaped by its historical origins in rationalist philosophy. Though many rationalist assumptions have been relaxed, transformed, and woven with others in cognitive theories of deduction, some of the major theories are descendents of this tradition, directly or indirectly. More recently, the extensive developments in linguistic semantics have also brought to the fore the complex relations between language and logic and informed

0066-4308/95/0201-0525$05.00

theories of deduction. Further, as one recent tradition envisions thought and language as an evolutionary, biologically based process, nativist and evolutionary proposals for deduction have appeared. Finally, psychology's increasing attention to the societal context of human functioning, and the resulting emphasis on the pragmatic context of thought and language comprehension has yielded some situated approaches to deduction, a shift consonant with the pragmatic turn in philosophy and linguistics. Not surprisingly, deduction as a central cognitive activity is the meeting ground of those broad concerns.

Deductive inference is an activity coordinated with other linguistic and nonlinguistic activities and carried out in context, so the proper object of study is not a disembodied process but a person, though the focus is on one particular segment of that person's cognitive activity. For this reason, we selectively discuss topics that interface or intersect with deduction, drawing on philosophical, linguistic, and cognitive work, and research and theory on deduction is considered within that perspective. Though we do not discuss development here, issues of acquisition are addressed selectively.

With few exceptions, psychological theory and research generally has described the deductive process as disembodied and encapsulated, despite important theoretical differences in other respects. The existing collective description of deductive processes treats those as largely self-contained, but several recent theories have recognized the significant links between deductive and linguistic processes or have attempted to describe deduction as pragmatically driven.

An important theme in the literature is an ostensible conflict between abstract and contextual elements of thought. This problematic spans the study of language, lexical semantics, and cognitive approaches to deduction. Until recently, most discussions of deductive inference have been oppositional in that regard, although some integrative proposals have begun to emerge. Both aspects of thought are needed for a comprehensive understanding of deductive processes; they are in duality, not in conflict (Falmagne 1994). We adopt this perspective when focusing on the interplay between formal and contentful factors in semantics and in deduction.

Throughout the chapter our critical assessment of the literature is oriented toward moving theoretical discussions beyond oppositional forms, and acknowledging the complexity and interconnectedness of cognitive processes, which any mature account of deduction must reflect.

Logic, Language, Mind and Reality

Deductive inference is but one component of cognitive activity, therefore its relation to linguistic and nonlinguistic processes is critical. The status of logic in relation to language in philosophy and linguistics informs this question because logical processes are likely ingredients of deductive inference.

The broad philosophical issue of whether logic formalizes linguistic relations or nonlinguistic relations between events spins a web of interconnected questions (see e.g. Haack 1978). The question especially germane here is whether the objects capable of truth and falsity, and therefore capable of standing in logical relations with one another, are sentences (i.e. grammatical strings of a natural language; e.g. Quine 1970), statements (i.e. the content of utterances in context; Strawson 1971), or abstract propositions (e.g. Frege 1956). That question has been reformulated in accordance with new developments in linguistic semantics and new views on propositions. Theories reviewed adopt different options on the issue of truth-bearers. Much of linguistic semantics views logical relations as purely linguistic, whereas Barwise (1989) grounds these relations in situation schemas that include both nonlinguistic and linguistic aspects, and Stalnaker (1984) bases deduction in nonlinguistic propositions. Psychological theories reflect similar choices.

Even if logic formalizes linguistic relations, it also applies to the world, in which language is semantically grounded (Tarski 1952). However, the foundation adopted has substantive consequences for both logic and cognition (Falmagne 1988). Adequacy criteria for logic hinge on whether it is dedicated to formalizing key aspects of natural language such as connectives or presupposition (e.g. Strawson 1971) or, alternatively, to capturing nonlinguistic epistemological concepts (e.g. modal notions of necessity and possibility; Lewis 1918, von Wright 1951).

Likewise, cognitive theories are predicated on either a linguistic, a nonlinguistic, or a joint construal of logic and deduction. Cognitively, the question is whether logical knowledge is primarily about linguistic structures or about the structure of events; that is, how logical knowledge and deductive principles functionally articulate with other knowledge domains in the organization of mind.

The linguistic and philosophical approaches reviewed below, and the associated psychological research, span a range of perspectives on the relation between deduction, linguistic processes, and world knowledge, and together provide a broad conceptual framework of interpretation of deductive phenomena.

THE LOGIC-LANGUAGE INTERFACE IN LINGUISTIC SEMANTICS AND COGNITION

Psychological theory and research on deduction has focused on inference from natural language and hence draws on the links between linguistic and deductive processes. The interface between language and logic described in linguistic semantics is a complex interweaving of processes residing at three levels: (a) the process whereby the logical form of sentences is identified or constructed, (b) the interpretation of lexical items that encode logical concepts, and (c) the supra-sentential discourse processes contributing to comprehension and inference. Cognitively, all three levels yield processes relevant to deduction.

Sentential Logical Form

At the sentential level, current discussions focus on two issues. One is the nature of semantic relations. The other concerns the relations between syntax and logical form. The concept of logical form has been central to semantic theory since its earliest developments. Kempson (1990a) and McCawley (1993) provide a clear survey of state-of-the-art issues regarding the nature of semantic relations, and Kempson (1990b) includes substantive proposals from several theoretical perspectives. Regardless of how, specifically, logical form is construed in each theory, it is taken to be the core logical structure of the sentence, relevant for semantic interpretation. Further, across specific theoretical variations, it is linguistic entities, or propositions construed linguistically, that are truth-bearers.

There are significant relations between logic and syntax. Both are formal systems underlying natural language, and both interface with semantics (e.g. Lycan 1984). Debates center on the degree to which logical structures and syntactic structures coincide and on the manner in which each contributes to semantic structure. The putative parallelism between syntax and semantics (Chomsky 1965) has been called into question (e.g. McCawley 1968, Chomsky 1981). Currently, the status of logical form as a distinct level of representation (e.g. May 1985, Hornstein 1984) is no longer unquestioned. For Kempson (1988), it is the interface between grammar and cognition.

Logical form within any perspective is a semantic construct, but the ingredients of semantic interpretation are debated. Model-theoretic semantics formalizes semantic interpretation in terms of truth conditions. One version, possible-worlds semantics, originally developed as a semantics for modal logic (Kripke 1963), has become pivotal in semantics for natural languages (Partee 1986). The meaning of a sentence (i.e. the proposition it expresses) is characterized by the set of possible worlds in which it is true. Meanings intractable in extensional semantics, such as necessity and possibility, are represented by suitable sets of possible worlds. Although some psychologists have questioned the value of the possible-worlds construct for cognition, arguing that our capacity to construct alternative construals of reality is computationally limited (Johnson-Laird 1978, 1983), this is not a valid problem. Any linguistic theory must be modulated by psychological assumptions when incorporated into a cognitive account. Recent developments utilizing possible-worlds semantics within a pragmatic framework have provided psychologically plausible theories of a range of phenomena (Kratzer 1980, Stalnaker

1968, 1984). The contribution of possible-worlds semantics to the study of deduction is to provide a framework for modal reasoning as well as a theoretically motivated notion of supposition that can be incorporated in the semantics of connectives.

Situation semantics (Barwise & Perry 1983, 1985), another model-theoretic semantics, grounds meaning in situations and in the cognitive agent's relations to those and applies to linguistic as well as nonlinguistic meaning. Objects, relations (including abstract relations), facts, and situation types arise from uniformities across situations. Meaning lies in systematic relations between types of situations. Likewise, linguistic meaning is contextual: It is not disembodied sentences that have meaning, but rather statements, embedded in their circumstances. Fenstad et al (1987) analyze the relation between linguistic form and situation schemata. The cognitive appeal of situation theory is to formalize linguistic and nonlinguistic relations within the same theoretical language, thus yielding a unified theory of linguistic and nonlinguistic inference (see below).

The considerable attention, both theoretical and critical, that situation theory has elicited perhaps attests to its importance. The ontological and cognitive relations between situations and possible worlds have been discussed (Stalnaker 1986; Partee 1985, 1986), especially regarding the treatment of context, for which situations are evidently better suited. Alternative accounts of specific linguistic phenomena have been developed reactively (Neale 1988). The theory has been criticized for not being representational (Fodor 1987, Jackendoff 1985). But, although it originally stemmed from an ecological perspective, its substantive assumptions about meaning structures can be assimilated within a representational framework (Falmagne 1990a), and its later development is cognitive in nature (Barwise 1989).

The imperfect correspondence between logical connectives and natural language connectives, and other complexities of language, are sometimes taken to imply that logic is irrelevant to deduction. The work reviewed above on logical form in linguistic semantics reveals that this conclusion is misguided and rests on a facile construal of linguistic structure as surface structure only. Two ramifications of that work are of special relevance to cognitive concerns.

First, linguistic theory underscores the importance of syntactic aspects of logical form. This suggests that syntactic processing must be at work when the logical form of an expression is uncovered and used in the course of deductive inference. This point, and the substantial interface between syntactic and logical structures, lends plausibility to theories assuming that human reasoning relies on a set of formal principles represented mentally and capturing what statements can be derived from which other statements on the basis of their form (e.g. Braine et al 1984; Braine & O'Brien 1991; Falmagne 1988, 1990b; Rips 1990, 1994).

Second, logical form remains the backbone of meaning for any semantic theory, whether language-of-thought or model-theoretic. Even situation semantics with its contextual foundation defines abstract logical relations. An important lesson from work in linguistic semantics is that inference inherently operates on the form of sentences in that sense. This point is often hidden from view in theories of deduction that argue that reasoning hinges on the semantic representation but not the form of an argument (e.g. Johnson-Laird & Byrne 1991, Johnson-Laird et al 1992).

Logico-Lexical Semantics

Lexical elements whose meaning encodes deductive relations contribute to logical structure and are central to deduction. This point extends beyond logical connectives. Recent theories in cognitive semantics isolate a number of logical constituents of lexical meaning, including necessity, factivity, and causality (Jackendoff 1983, Pinker 1984, Reuland & Abraham 1993). Descriptions of interlexical relations in semantic networks have also revealed logical categories. Thus, Miller & Fellbaum (1991) describe entailment or synonymy as central semantic relations. Those lexical items enable the smooth inferencing that drives language comprehension.

CONDITIONALS   The semantics of conditional markers such as *if* is key to any theory of reasoning because they drive inferences about real and hypothetical contingent relations. The traditional truth-functional characterization, imported into semantics and psychology from standard logic, is now recognized to present serious problems, both philosophically and psychologically (e.g. Edgington 1984). It inherits the general limitations of extensional semantics in failing to capture non-truth-functional elements of meaning such as logical consequence. And, people rarely interpret *if-then* as material implication. In particular, pragmatic aspects of conditionals are key to their meaning and modulate their inferential use (e.g. Van der Auwera 1986, Fillenbaum 1986).

Stalnaker (1968, 1984) uses possible-worlds semantics to represent the property that the consequent of a conditional is necessarily and not fortuitously implied by the antecedent, a property not conveyed by truth-functional implication. This enrichment has been claimed insufficient to capture the constraint that the antecedent be relevant to the consequent (Anderson & Belnap 1975), but this criticism is arguable in light of the pragmatic assumptions of the theory.

An alternative characterization, also overcoming the problems of truth-functional semantics, is to posit that the meaning of *if* and other connectives is defined by the inferences they yield. Braine & O'Brien (1991) detail a psychological theory, well supported empirically, in which the lexical entry of *if* includes two deductive schemas, Modus Ponens (if p then q; p; therefore q) and a schema of conditional proof deriving a conditional statement from a supposition. Linguistic pragmatic principles inform the interpretation of the connective, and suppositions must be consistent with prior assumptions and arguments.

The move to possible worlds reflects the importance of supposition in an adequate semantic description of the conditional, whose reference to hypothetical states of affairs is critical. Supposition is key in theories of counterfactual meaning (e.g. Lewis 1973) and in conditional reasoning. It appears to be present in the meaning of *if* along with hypotheticality and entailment at least as early as six years of age (Jorgensen & Falmagne 1992).

Although there is little variation in the logic and syntax of conditional markers across languages, the hypotheticality they convey varies considerably (Comrie 1986). Some languages, such as English, distinguish counterfactuals, hypotheticals, and constructions presupposing the referent events, while others appear not to mark explicitly distinctions in degree of hypotheticality. In Mandarin, hypotheticality is conveyed contextually instead, thus enabling counterfactual reasoning (Liu 1985), despite prior proposals to the contrary (Bloom 1981). Interestingly, Bowerman (1986) suggests that English-speaking two-year-olds signal hypotheticality in pseudoconditional constructions prior to the use of *if*.

A well-documented finding is that both adults and children often treat *if-then* as if it were bi-conditional. However, few theorists have concluded that this is the core meaning of *if* for adults because nonlogical, pragmatic factors are probably responsible for biconditional interpretations (Braine & O'Brien 1991, Politzer 1986, Grice 1989, Comrie 1986). Alternatively, George (1992) argues that the interpretation is governed by informational rather than pragmatic aspects of content. Those discussions raise the theoretical question of whether *if* is best characterized by one or two lexical entries. The choice hinges on the theoretical articulation of form and content.

MODALS   The modal system is another semantic domain important to deduction. In English, modal verbs such as *must* and *can* express concepts of necessity and possibility central to modal logics (Hughes & Cresswell 1968). However, modal verbs not only convey logical concepts but also signal epistemic information about the speaker's relative certainty about the truth of propositions. Further, they can also receive deontic interpretations as actions that can, cannot, or must be taken, and recent proposals that deductive processes are pragmatically driven are closely related to deontic modal reasoning (e.g. Over & Manktelow 1993).

This apparent plurality of meaning raises issues as to whether modal verbs are ambiguous terms (requiring a separate lexical entry for logical, epistemic, and deontic meanings) or whether there is a core meaning (presumably logical) at the heart of each term. Linguists often have favored the latter option and have used relations between possible worlds to handle the variations, seen as context sensitive (Kratzer 1980, Palmer 1986, Partee 1986). This tension between logical and pragmatic meaning finds its echo in current theories of deduction that contrast natural logics (e.g. Braine et al 1984) with pragmatic schemas (e.g. Cheng & Holyoak 1985).

Deontic and epistemic meanings appear earlier in development and are later superseded by logical modal concepts (Pieraut-Le Bonniec 1980, Coates 1988; Shatz & Wilcox 1991; Bassano et al 1992, Hickman et al 1993; Gonsalves 1991). As is the case for *if* and other connectives, children's early productions of modals are pragmatically restricted, governed by parents' and children's concerns of social regulations and routines (McCabe et al 1983, Peterson 1986, Stephany 1986, Peterson & McCabe 1988), apparently reflecting a generalization about logico-lexical acquisition.

Logical aspects of meaning, once acquired, are at first fragile and stabilize only gradually, suggesting that logico-lexical knowledge is coordinated increasingly strongly by executive processes in the course of acquisition. Although young children display a lexical understanding of possibility and necessity, inadequate executive control prevents them from explicitly manipulating sets of possibilities in tasks requiring a logical evaluation of necessity or indeterminacy (Gonsalves 1991).

FACTIVE VERBS   Factive verbs (e.g. *know, is aware*) presuppose the truth of their sentential complement. For instance, a speaker who asserts "Mary knows that the door is open" also takes "The door is open" to be true. Factivity has been defined as a logical relation since the presupposition ("The door is open") holds even when *know* is negated, as in "Mary does not know that the door is open" (Kiparsky & Kiparsky 1974).

Although the relative role of logic and pragmatics in factivity is debated (e.g. Chierchia & McConnell-Ginet 1992, Burton-Roberts 1989), the semantic rather than pragmatic interpretation is preferred, as factive verbs robustly presuppose the truth of their complements. Falmagne et al (1994), using complementary tasks and scaling procedures, found that the factive properties of verbs are distinct from their epistemic senses for adults. For instance, both *know* and *is sure* carry high epistemic strength, but *know* is factive for adults and older children whereas *is sure* is not. In contrast, young children's judgments of the certainty of events are governed by the epistemic confidence conveyed by verbs and not by their factive status (see also Moore & Furrow 1991, Moore & Davige 1989). Thus, later in acquisition, factivity becomes a logical component of meaning, with a status superseding that of other facets of meaning.

Discourse Processes

Deductive processes are deployed routinely in comprehending text and spoken language and in constructing coherent discourse, drawing on logical structures in discourse. A number of recent linguistic analyses take up meaning at the discourse level, and in particular specify discourse-level logical relations. Asher (1993) and Zucchi (1993) extend Barwise & Perry's theory to discourse-level meaning. Though the implications for deduction are not yet fully developed, this work paves the way for a discourse-level treatment of deductive relations, applying to both propositions and events. Seuren (1985) introduces the notion of a discourse domain and characterizes the meaning of a proposition in terms of the structural changes it yields when added to previous assertions made by the same speaker in the same discourse domain.

Discourse representation theory (Kamp 1984, 1988; see also Spencer-Smith 1987) stresses the cumulative aspects of meaning in connected discourse. The theory relies on model-theoretic techniques to yield the truth conditions holding across multiple sentence contexts. Mental discourse representations are built by integrating multiple sentences and contextual elements; these representations are mapped onto partial models. The theory, originally developed to account for anaphora and for quantified and conditional sentences, has been extended to include an explicit treatment of logical relations (Kamp 1993) and of the content of belief states (Asher 1986).

Sperber & Wilson (1986) describe inference as one tier of verbal comprehension, drawing on semantic entailments, syntactic logical implications, and discourse-level contextual assumptions. Contextual implication is obtained through interaction between new information and contextual assumptions. New assumptions are defined as relevant if they have some contextual effect in this sense and require no or little cognitive effort. Despite the semi-circularity of this notion of relevance, it is more analytical than previous psychological discussions and richer than some formal proposals (Anderson & Belnap 1975).

One line of research examines the role of deductive inference in recovering meaning in discourse. Following Grice (1975, 1989), pragmatic inferences are standardly assumed to shape language interpretation. Likewise, in reasoning contexts, people often rely on pragmatic language conventions rather than logic conventions, and these may conflict with logic (Politzer 1986, Moore 1986). The primary goal of linguistic activities is to recover meaning, not to assess validity or to evaluate the truth of a speaker's assertion. Manktelow & Over (1990) comprehensively survey the contribution of linguistic inference, general knowledge, pragmatic principles, and logic to comprehension. Sperber & Wilson (1986) and Wilson & Sperber (1986) argue that deduction plays a central role in recovering speakers' meaning (see also Allwood 1986, Sales-Wuillemin 1993). Thus, deduction is involved in integrating contextual assumptions, an enterprise at the heart of pragmatic interpretation.

A second line of empirical research centers on deduction as deployed in text comprehension and examines how it interfaces with other cognitive components. Subjects routinely make basic deductive inferences during text comprehension (Lea et al 1990, Fisch 1991) involving negation, conjunction, and the conditional, and appear to have difficulty distinguishing information logically inferred from information stated (Lea et al 1990). This finding echoes those on script-based inferences (Graesser & Bower 1990) and suggests that deductive inferences are normally and automatically made in the service of text integration. However, we must keep track of key propositions for deduction to be successful (Hudson & Slackman 1990), which suggests that logical inference involves more explicit representations. Related to this conjecture, Kintsch (1993) views logical inferences as controlled rather than automatic processes, unlike other text-based inferences. The control, however, is flexible. Deductive inference is only one of many cognitive goals in text processing, but it can be activated by suitable primes and helped by readily formalizable premises (Carlson et al 1992).

Causal inferences, though not strictly logical, are pertinent to deduction because the causal antecedent entails the consequent within the inference context. The interplay between form and content is complex, but recent developments of pragmatic schema theory for deduction suggest that causality is an important contentful structure in deduction (Cheng & Nisbett 1993, Cummins 1994). Causal inferences are normally made in the course of comprehension (van den Broek 1990), as are transitive inferences between causal relations (Trabasso et al 1989). Inferences may be generated either immediately or with delay, depending on content-driven factors (Magliano et al 1993), but their deployment is undisputed.

The format of discourse-level representations is debated but most theories assume multi-level representations. Some proposals stress that a situation model is constructed, integrating explicit and inferred information, either aside from the propositional text base (Fincher-Kiefer 1993, Perrig & Kintsch 1985) or instead of it (Johnson-Laird 1983). In the latter case, discourse coherence is defined through the ease of constructing a single model of the information. For instance, Byrne (1989a) reports that more inferences are made from transitive conditional sequences than from pairs of simple arguments, presumably because they yield one integrated model.

PERSPECTIVES ON INFERENCE AND COGNITIVE ACTIVITY

Inference as a Global Process

In Sperber & Wilson's (1986) theory, deductive inferencing is a global process in two ways. First, it is assumed to draw on all conceptual information in memory and on background assumptions. Concepts have encyclopedic, lexical, and logical entries, with the logical entry consisting of deductive rules applying to the logical forms of which the concept is a constituent, and the encyclopedic entry consisting, roughly, of the world knowledge related to that concept. This view is useful for conceptualizing the interplay of form and content in deduction. Second, importantly, context undergoes retroactive reshaping as a function of new information, so as to maximize relevance. These features are conceptually useful to a broad perspective on deduction, although their implications for psychological research have not been fully pursued.

Situated Inference

Developed on philosophical grounds as an extension of situation semantics, Barwise's (1989) approach sees speech, thought, and inference as situated activities carried by embodied, limited agents and occurring within restricted portions of the environment. Though the theory was motivated by philosophical concerns, it has important cognitive ramifications. First, in jointly describing linguistic and nonlinguistic relations, it supplies a useful conceptual bridge for cognitive theories that encompass both the linguistic and nonlinguistic underpinnings of deduction and logical development. Falmagne (1990a,b) argues that, cognitively, logical relations hold both within linguistic meaning and between nonlinguistic states of affairs. Thus, logical knowledge can be gained from both linguistic and nonlinguistic sources. Therefore, the two acquisitions must merge into a coherent logical system and require a common representational format; situation semantics, as a theoretical language for representing both linguistic and nonlinguistic meaning, can serve this function. Second, situated inference is strongly contextual in the sense that context is fully incorporated in the primitive of the theory (the situation), rather than being treated as an extraneous factor affecting or modulating semantic interpretation, as it is in other approaches.

Barwise's (1989) treatment of logic and of situated inference mechanisms are in the early stages of elaboration, but these mechanisms exploit environmental constants, draw circumstantial rules of inference, and make explicit those parameters typically implicit in a situation. Situated inference mechanisms are not assumed to capture all deductive thought, and indeed the theory allows for some formal relations, but it prioritizes the importance of the embedding circumstances on thought and on inference. Because statements rather than sentences or propositions are the linguistic objects capable of having meaning, the primitive objects of logic, capable of being true or false, are statements as well.

Deduction in the Context of Inquiry

Whereas Barwise's theory of inference spans linguistic and nonlinguistic contexts, Stalnaker (1984) explicitly provides a nonlinguistic underpinning for deduction. Deduction operates on propositions that, in contrast to other views, are nonlinguistic objects of thought. Propositions are defined in terms of possible worlds in which they are true, and thus have no structural resemblance to the sentences that express them.

Stalnaker (1984) describes inference within a pragmatic theory of mental representation and as one component of the process of inquiry leading to rational action, broadly construed. Two critical aspects of the theory are its ontological stance on the constituents of mental representation, which are described by the functions they play in characterizing action, and its pragmatic approach to propositional attitudes and deductive inference. The commitment to a possible-worlds view on propositions allows Stalnaker to view belief states as an agent's acceptance of certain possible worlds and potential actions. It also places deduction within the context of broader inquiry involving the acceptance, supposition, and presupposition of propositions (i.e. the adjustment of attitudes toward the truth of subsets of possible worlds) at the service of rational action. The theory is congruous with current psychological theorizing about pragmatic reasoning.

Reasoning as Belief Revision

Starting from the view that the object of investigation of reasoning is the determinant of belief revision, Harman (1986) foregrounds the role of current interrelated beliefs and of knowledge of the world in that process, while recognizing that logical principles may be part of people's knowledge base. The goal of reasoning is to achieve coherence among beliefs.

Whereas Stalnaker's theory is placed within the context of specific mental activities such as hypothesis formation, investigation, and explanation, Harman holds the broader goal of describing reasoning as reasoned change in view and suggests that such a holistic account of rational action is an idealization from ordinary practice. Belief revision is governed by principles such as avoidance of inconsistency and clutter avoidance, whereby the acquisition history of current beliefs is erased.

Thus the reasoning process integrates the various elements of a person's knowledge base rather than giving precedence to abstract, formal knowledge. Logic enters the process in the form of immediate implications and inconsistencies, not in the form of formal principles. The process furthermore requires no semantics, since it operates on beliefs, not on truth-conditional statements. For cognitive psychology, the theory is suggestive in situating reasoning within the natural course of belief updating.

THE INTERPLAY OF FORM AND CONTENT IN DEDUCTION

The psychological study of deduction is dominated by four proposals about the fundamental processes involved. Deduction is taken to be driven by (*a*) deductive schemas hinging on the logical form of premises (formal schemas), (*b*) context-specific, pragmatically based inferential rules (pragmatic schemas and their variants), (*c*) processes relying on mental representations of meaning (mental models), or (*d*) world knowledge and beliefs as opposed to any deductive principle (for review see Evans et al 1993, Evans 1989, Johnson-Laird & Byrne 1991, Rips 1994).

Until recently, most discussions have advocated the exclusivity of either one or the other process in deduction, a "right or wrong" rhetoric so characteristic of the current discourse of cognitive science. Typically, analyses are radicalized into extreme, opponent accounts, each claiming to explain the phenomenon in its entirety with a single theoretical language and a few constructs, and focusing the bulk of analytical and rhetorical effort on establishing the supremacy of one extreme account over the other.

Less militant arguments consider processes other than the core processes in the theory but treat those as peripheral additions to the historical core. Though the recent literature has gradually moved in a more integrated direction, the prevalence of the oppositional rhetoric is strong enough to warrant putting forth explicitly some metatheoretical principles before reviewing the current status of the issues.

First, for complex cognitive processes, oppositional debate between radical proposals is a questionable strategy. Any radical theory has built-in limitations in explanatory range (Falmagne 1992, 1993), and theories are often complementary, as illustrated by the recent bridging of symbolic theories of cognition and connectionist models (Holyoak & Spellman 1993). The criterion of parsimony often invoked is grounded in one particular view of scientific inquiry. A more compelling goal is to capture the deductive process theoretically in a way that is commensurate with its complexity and flexibility, thus integrating descriptions of formal, meaningful, and pragmatic aspects of deductive thought.

Second, those universalizing theories that offer a uniform account of deduction (or of any cognitive process) without points of entry for motivated variations raise fundamental issues regarding both implicit theoretical commitments and method, as pointed out by respondents to Cohen's (1981) influential article on the putative irrefutability of logic as a cognitive theory. Cohen's argument is incapable of handling inherent variations according to age, schooling, and culture, variations that are constitutive of, not peripheral to, the cognitive process. Similar theoretical dilemmas are posed for universalizing theories by individual differences, especially when qualitative and systematic (Roberts 1993).

Third, the fact that assessment of logical knowledge is mediated by access, retrieval, and response processes (Falmagne 1975b) implies that this assessment is inherently task dependent. Yet, for the most part, arguments for mental logic, mental models, and pragmatic schemas rely on three nonoverlapping empirical domains: propositional inference, quantified inference, and the Wason selection task, in which subjects are asked to test a rule. This fact, generally unaddressed in the associated theoretical debates, poses serious limitations for the comparability of theoretical claims.

A Preliminary Framework

Any theory of deductive inference must be informed by two requirements, whose conjunction stands in dialectical tension. Clearly, people's reasoning draws on content and knowledge of the world, an assumption well supported empirically. Equally compellingly, a natural logic must be part of people's knowledge base, in order to account for the smooth automatic inferencing that underlies deduction across content domains. Falmagne (1990b) points out that it is indisputable on both intuitive and empirical grounds that an adult untutored in logic, upon being told that "If Sarah fibbles, then she thabbles" and that "Sarah fibbles," would deduce that Sarah thabbles. Thus, a theory must afford abstract relations that apply across contents, and in that sense are formal, whatever notational variant is used to characterize them.

A central focus for theory is to describe the functional interplay between formal and concrete modes of representation in the deductive process. One proposal motivated by this aim (Falmagne 1989a, 1994) is used here as an organizing framework. Deduction draws on two distinct levels of mental representation: permanent knowledge, including a set of deductive schemas based on logical form amidst other knowledge domains such as syntax, event knowledge, concepts, and semantic relations; and the functional representation of the problem in working memory, where the actual deductive work is done for a specific inference token.

Construction of the functional representation is a complex process. Recognizing the logical form of the problem entails a formalization process that exploits the syntax of the sentences, surface cues, and semantic and contextual cues. A representation highlighting the logical form of the statement among other aspects of meaning is then constructed and serves as explicit input to the pertinent deductive schema.

However, the formalization may be overridden if cues pointing to logical structure lack salience or if other aspects of meaning are more compelling. The functional representation may then be ordinary event schemas or domain-specific schemas (Cheng & Holyoak 1985); it may be imagistic when the content is imageable (Clement & Falmagne 1986); or it may rely on prototypical exemplars of the referent relations (Johnson-Laird & Byrne 1991). Or, if cognitive limitations render a formal representation ineffective, a more concrete representation may be constructed as has been found in children with quantified problems (Falmagne 1975a, Falmagne et al 1989). The distinction between logical knowledge and the ongoing functional representations provides a theoretical structure for considering empirically how form, content, and world knowledge articulate in deduction.

In addition, aside from its representational function, logical knowledge has an executive function: It controls the construction of the functional representation, whether formal or not, and it orchestrates the program of subsequent deductive steps. Thus, the entire process is monitored by the logical executive. Although event knowledge or mental models may yield responses fortuitously converging with logic, these cannot be valid unless directed by the logical executive. This tenet is motivated both conceptually and empirically. For instance, although imagery is functional for some inferences, it is only supportive; without logical executive control of imagistic processes, imagery cannot help and indeed does not (RJ Falmagne, J Singer, & C Clement, unpublished information). Similar findings are obtained for representational and executive factors in recognition of indeterminacy in children (Falmagne et al 1989). Thus, formal and nonformal processes are conceptualized not as disjoint or mutually exclusive but as two interdependent poles of the same cognitive process.

Formal Schemas and Their Acquisition

Some recent proposals submit that reasoning relies on deductive schemas specifying inferences that can be made from propositions with particular forms (Braine 1978; Braine et al 1984; Braine & O'Brien 1991; Falmagne 1988, 1990b; Johnson-Laird 1975; Osherson 1975; Rips 1983, 1994; O'Brien 1993; Sperber & Wilson 1986). There are some consequential differences between theories regarding the functional articulation of formal and other processes, but the differences among the inference schemas proposed are minimal. For example, all theories assume Modus Ponens and *and*-elimination. Braine & O'Brien (1991) and Rips (1994) assume the schema of conditional proof, that is, these models theorize that people have the ability to make suppositions and examine their entailments; Rips (1983) but not Braine et al (1984) proposes a schema for disjunction-introduction. Sperber & Wilson's (1986) deductive rules include entailment and formal rules for connective elimination. In some models, in addition to the inference schemas, a reasoning program specifies how schemas are selected and used, either stepwise (Braine & O'Brien 1991) or via a control structure with forward and backward rules governing the deployment of deductive steps, a heuristic process formulating goals and sub-goals, and a bipartite memory (Rips 1994). O'Brien (1993) rightly stresses that the reasoning program, through which schemas are implemented, is in need of empirical investigation as it is a major source of reasoning errors.

Theories differ in how they treat linguistic and contextual processes. Sperber & Wilson (1986) provide the most fully developed description of pragmatic and contextual factors operating in conjunction with deductive schemas, within a general account of linguistic communication. Deduction proceeds from explicit premises and context jointly via inference schemas and contextual assumptions whose strength is modulated by new information, although this assumption needs to be enriched, as premises may be left unstated by the speaker (Hagert & Waern 1986).

Elaborating on Braine (1978) and on Braine et al's (1984) revised theory, Braine & O'Brien (1991) describe comprehension processes through which natural language sentences are mapped onto their logical form, thus incorporating the translation process into the theory. Pragmatic information affects interpretation of *if* statements; e.g. Gricean principles are assumed to yield invited inferences leading to biconditional interpretations (see also Politzer 1986, O'Brien 1993). By building two formal schemas into the lexical entry for *if* (Modus Ponens and conditional proof), the theory nicely exploits the rich logic-language interface at the lexical level.

Rips's (1994) theory extends Rips (1983) to reasoning with variables, with other elaborations. Rips discusses this theory of mental proof in relation to broader issues such as belief revision and the role of deduction in thought, but the model itself is computational. Assertions are represented as sentences, and deductive schemas rely on English connectives in surface structure. Hence, truth-bearers are sentences rather than statements or propositions. Philosophically and linguistically, this is a problem. Translation from natural language to formal schemas is implicitly assumed to be automatic because schemas operate on surface structure and no comprehension processes are postulated. The theory explicitly distinguishes the role of long-term and working memory in deduction, but working memory for Rips simply has a highlighting function and keeps track of current assertions in a uniformly sentential representational format, thus providing no potential interface with processes other than sentential.

Support for inference schema theories comes from studies that predict error rates (Rips 1983, Braine et al 1984), subjective judgments of difficulty (Braine et al 1984), and response times based on the number of inference schemas required to solve a problem (Braine et al 1984). Verbal protocols of subjects' solving of a logical problem are also consistent with inference schema models (Rips 1983). Rips' (1994) theory predicts well the difficulty of many arguments in tasks involving evaluating conclusions and comprehending and remembering proofs. Braine and colleagues predict the order in which a series of intermediate inferences would be made as indicated by verbal protocols (MDS Braine, DP O'Brien, IA Noveck, MC Samuels, SM Fisch, RB Lea & Y Yang, unpublished information.

Smith et al's (1992) useful methodological discussion outlines content, performance, and training criteria for establishing the psychological reality of rules, whether formal or pragmatic. Though most empirical tests in the literature do not have that form, the evidence cited above meets two of Smith et al's criteria for the existence of rules (that performance be a function of the number of rules and that the rules be verbalized). Regarding content, Smith et al assume (probably too strongly overall) that concreteness or content familiarity should not affect difficulty. This seems to be the case for Modus Ponens in all studies.

In relation to Smith et al's training criteria for the cognitive reality of schemas, Falmagne (1990b) found that exposure to thematic inferences and feedback were sufficient for children to abstract the common logical form (Modus Tollens, i.e. if p then q; not q; therefore not p) spanning thematic and syntactic variations. The concept abstracted was based on logical form, rather than on surface syntactic cues, as demonstrated by transfer to problems with nonsense content and with different surface structure. Training on one of the two indeterminate conditional inferences (Denying the Antecedent) transferred to its companion inference (Affirming the Consequent), showing that the deep logical structure of conditional relations was abstracted (Bennett-Lau 1983). Because training materials were meaningful, these conclusions accord generally with Cheng et al's (1986) findings on the effectiveness of pragmatic training, but they stress instead that formal schemas were learned as a result.

If formal schemas underlie deduction, one immediate issue concerns their origins, particularly in relation to language, and the contribution of learning processes and innate constraints to their acquisition. The complex interface of logic and language is discussed by Falmagne (1988, 1990b) and Braine (1993), who believe that language acquisition research can inform questions about mental logic and its acquisition but who take the issue in two different directions.

Falmagne (1988; 1990a,b) assumes that once children acquire language, formal deductive principles are derived from linguistic sources, not unlike the process of syntax acquisition. The links between logic and syntax, and their common interface with semantics, are taken as an a priori argument for this hypothesis. The interplay of innate constraints, input, and learning processes documented for the acquisition of complex syntactic rules (e.g. MacWhinney

1987) is assumed for deductive structures as well. Logical structures, initially embedded in the child's early contextual (e.g. causal or pragmatic) representations become formal through a process of abstraction from context-bound inferences in which the child is engaged and that have similar logical form. The account relies on semantic bootstrapping as does early syntax acquisition (e.g. Pinker 1984). Studies summarized above, where children acquired new logical properties from linguistic input, support the cognitive feasibility of this process, and Scholnick & Wing's (1991, 1992) findings that conversations between parents and young children contain many examples of thematic conditional inferences show that the needed input is present. Abstractions from nonlinguistic states of affairs and the structure of their representation contribute to logical acquisitions as well. The merging of both acquisitions is ensured by the fact that language is semantically grounded.

Braine (1993) assumes that Modus Ponens and other simple inference schemas must be innate and speculates that schemas are universal across languages and cultures. To date, the only evidence to support this claim is the observation that elementary connectives appear early in children across a few languages. However, such evidence is not pertinent to the claim that the formal schema is innate, since young children's early meanings for logical terms are pragmatically based and context-bound, as noted earlier. What is at issue for the innateness claim is whether schemas are represented formally and can be deployed without reliance on pragmatics or content. What might be the case, however, is that simple logical properties are embedded in the core lexical entry for those early pragmatic meanings, though not dissociated yet from the pragmatic components of representation (J Gonsalves, unpublished information).

Braine (1993) also speculates that the mental logic must constitute the syntax of the language of thought in which knowledge is putatively recorded from the earliest ages. This argument and Macnamara's (1986) claim that logical notions must be innate because they underlie language learning are appealing conceptually but call for caution. In particular, discussions that conceptualize acquisition as an instantaneous phenomenon are driven to nativist solutions to the acquisition puzzle by that idealization. The recursive and temporally extended nature of acquisition cannot be ignored, nor can transformations in the representational capacities of the cognitive system engaged in acquisition (Falmagne 1989b, 1992).

Macnamara (1986) argues that logical notions such as *true* must be innate, because their learning putatively relies on the truth-functional connective *if and only if* and, hence, would be circular, and that the meaning of elementary connectives must be innate too. However, this impasse is linked to Macnamara's specific task analysis and to his reliance on a constant representational register to describe acquisition. Those truth-functional meanings may derive developmentally either from pragmatic, content-bound meanings or from a logic of action.

Whereas Braine's speculations bear on primitive representations and their putative logical-syntactic structure and Falmagne's address the underlying structure of inferential processes, one of Macnamara's (1994) claims is that logic does not describe mental states but is an essential constituent of the theory of cognition in the same way that calculus and mechanics constrain each other (see also Macnamara & Reyes 1994). Thus, those acquisition proposals are tuned to three different levels: Macnamara (1994) largely focuses on the infrastructure of cognition.

Despite those differences, there is general consensus that acquisition is both potentiated and constrained by innate capacities. However, these are not sufficient. Cognitive constraints only set boundaries on the outcome of learning processes; they do not constitute an acquisition theory. Innate constraints on the forms of grammar the child can acquire are highly abstract, leaving much of the burden of acquisition to processes that exploit linguistic and nonlinguistic data; the substance of an acquisition account lies in describing those, as well as developmental transformations (Falmagne 1992). Braine (1994) likewise argues that nativism must be supplemented by an account of learning and developmental processes in language acquisition.

Pragmatic Schemas versus Formal Schemas

Cheng & Holyoak's (1985) proposal that reasoning relies on domain-specific rules specialized for classes of goal-driven relationships, such as permission and obligation, has instigated a vast literature aimed at isolating the relevant content factors and the specific cognitive basis for those effects. More importantly, both the original proposal and its counterproposals have introduced into discussions of inference fresh attention to the pragmatic, deontic, and situated context in which it is embedded.

However, despite their intended reach, these theories have relied exclusively on one paradigm, the Wason selection task. This narrow empirical basis is unfortunate given the scope of the claims made in that literature. But more critically, the nature of the task itself makes it an indirect assessment of deductive processes. The Wason selection task tests whether people will search for appropriate evidence that might disconfirm a conditional rule. It thus crucially involves hypothesis-testing strategies and the heuristics of verification and falsification in addition to conditional deductive processes (George 1990, Xiao 1994). Theories based on this task reflect its idiosyncratic nature, and their generalizability for deduction can be questioned. Evans et al (1993) and Holyoak & Spellman (1993) provide good reviews of the literature on the Wason selection task.

Permission and obligation schemas are sets of production rules specifying necessary relations between preconditions and actions, and isomorphic to formal schemas but restricted to deontic domains. In support of the theory, deontic content as well as abstract deontic rules improve selection performance both in adults (e.g. Politzer & Nguyen-Xuan 1992) and in children (e.g. Light et al 1990). And training with abstract deontic tasks yields transfer to both concrete and arbitrary materials (Cheng et al 1986, Light et al 1989). The theory has been expanded to include a causal schema for explanation and prediction, relying on probabilistic contingencies (Cheng & Nisbett 1993; Cheng & Novick 1991), an extension essential for the general claim that reasoning relies on domain-sensitive knowledge.

There is an obvious, but underexplored connection between pragmatic situations and deontic language. Platt & Griggs (1993) report effects of modal language in pragmatic-schema tasks and Higgins (1994) finds that subjects use modal language spontaneously when drawing conclusions from permission and obligation scenarios. Exploration of the interface between modal semantics and pragmatic situations has only just begun (Cummins 1994, Over & Manktelow 1993).

Cosmides (1989) posits instead specialized algorithms for dealing with social exchange, specifically with the breaking of contracts with a cost-benefit structure. Predictions are supported in the original study and others (Platt & Griggs 1993) but only when subjects are cued into the perspective of someone who can be cheated (Gigerenzer & Hug 1992). However, these schemas cover a narrow content domain, and permission contexts not involving social exchange improve performance as well (e.g. Girotto 1991, Pollard 1990). Cosmides' broader claim that those schemas result from natural selection clearly is separable from the substantive proposal (see below).

Manktelow & Over (1991, 1992), while drawing on previous proposals, stress that deontic rules are normative, seek to guide behavior, and involve a non–truth-functional semantics and pragmatic as well as social elements. A conditional obligation or permission issued by an agent guides the behavior of an actor on grounds other than its truth or falsity. Thus, procedures for determining whether a rule is violated differ between the agent and the actor. It is argued that in deontic thought, mental models are enriched with pragmatic information about subjective utilities of outcomes, though this enrichment seems unnecessary to Johnson-Laird & Byrne (1992).

Although it seems indisputable that deontic and other domain-specific contents improve selection in the Wason task, a broader empirical base is needed to ground theories of content. Studies not using the selection task are few, but suggest that some effects do not extend to syllogistic tasks with similar materials (Markovits & Savary 1992). Higgins (1994), using syllogisms embedded in a story context, found that permission and obligation contents function differentially for certain inference forms, and draws on Barwise (1989) to provide a broader interpretation of those effects in terms of classes of situations. Content effects are also not restricted to the pragmatic or social domain. They exist in causal reasoning (Cummins 1994). Clement & Falmagne (1986) found improved syllogistic reasoning when conditional clauses were both strongly related via a general event schema and imageable. Findings are interpretable in terms of general event knowledge and thus call into question the idea that pragmatic or social schemas are the primary determinants of content effects.

The origins of pragmatic schemas and their variants have been debated. Cheng & Holyoak (1985) take these to be induced from ordinary life experience. Cosmides (1989) draws from theory in evolutionary biology to argue that social exchange must be regulated by Darwinian algorithms, resulting in modular information-processing procedures necessary for species survival (an argument extended to cognitive function in general by Cosmides & Tooby 1994). Acceptance of Cosmides' hypothesis is contingent on endorsing sociobiological theory of cognition. As Cheng & Holyoak (1989) point out, the pragmatic usefulness of social schemas is not in question, but there are many ways that they could be acquired, and nonsocial schemas are equally useful.

Another strand of argumentation has contrasted pragmatic schemas and their variants with formal schemas. After years of oppositional debate taking evidence for one process to demonstrate the fundamental inadequacy of the other, that discussion has evolved in a more integrative direction. As mentioned previously, those theories at present rely on largely nonoverlapping empirical domains (propositional reasoning and the Wason task); thus, integration is especially welcome. Two directions of progress can be noted.

First, the issue has shifted from one of exclusivity to one of relative primacy. Accounts invoking pragmatic schemas no longer suggest that these supplant any formal processes but rather postulate that they have primacy in driving deduction, with formal schemas as defaults (Cheng & Nisbett 1993). Mental logic accounts have been enriched by auxiliary processes that exploit the richness of the linguistic input and nonlinguistic context from which logical form is read. Braine & O'Brien (1991) suggest that in addition to Modus Ponens and conditional proof, the lexical entry of *if* includes pragmatic knowledge, possibly in the form of pragmatic schemas. Rips (1990, 1994) recommends that formal schema theories explore rules from modal logics for deontic reasoning. The increasing concern about context by rule theorists reflects a welcome move in the field toward integration and away from the rhetoric of opposition; yet, context and pragmatics often are still viewed as extraneous factors modulating deduction. Alternatively, situation semantics (Barwise 1989) incorporates both form and context into the primitives of the theory.

Second, questions concerning the functional relations between the two modes of reasoning have begun to emerge. Politzer (1986) holds that there is evidence for two competing systems of linguistic knowledge (pragmatic and logical) and that the tension between them accounts for most phenomena observed in reasoning studies. Noveck et al (1991) propose that pragmatic and logical inferences perform complementary functions in discourse processing and other natural cognitive activities. Falmagne's (1989, 1994) two-level theory makes it possible for domain-specific construals to be constructed in working memory when engaged by problem content, while formal schemas in the permanent knowledge system remain available. Sperber & Wilson (1986) propose that context (pragmatic assumptions or world knowledge) enriches a problem's representation by adding additional premises that then are processed by a deductive component; thus, the deductive device itself is formal, but operates on rich arrays of contextual assumptions shaped by pragmatic factors. D Cummins (unpublished information) argues that prior beliefs and pragmatic schemas are constitutive of the very logical form of representations.

Mental Models versus Formal Schemas

Mental model theory (Johnson-Laird 1983, Johnson-Laird & Byrne 1991) proposes that deduction is based on streamlined representations, of the state of affairs described in the premises, that rely on linguistic meaning and on knowledge of the world. The contrast with formal schema theory has been conceptualized as hinging on whether inference is semantically or syntactically based, though the issue is more complex than it appears (see below).

An additional claim is that deduction relies exclusively on semantic processes and structures and that no logical rules are needed (Johnson-Laird & Byrne 1991, Johnson-Laird 1986). Clearly, this exclusivity claim and the claim for the involvement of models are distinct and must be evaluated as such. Good evidence exists for the cognitive reality of models in some reasoning domains, but the exclusivity claim is questionable. First, it overlooks the contribution of syntax and logic to the construction of mental models. Second, models are best thought of as functional representations in working memory; therefore, empirical support for models does not address the nature of permanent logical knowledge. Thus, only one part of the issue is empirical. Conceptually, critical attention must be given to the status of mental models as semantic representations and to the resulting subtleties of interpretation of findings. Because the specific workings of mental models vary from one domain to another, as does their nature as representational devices, we evaluate research separately for quantified and for propositional reasoning.

Quantified inference relies on prototypical exemplars of the premises. Models of the referent states of affairs are built and combined so as to preserve semantic information and yield new information. If tentative conclusions are obtained, their necessity is tested by building alternative models (Johnson-Laird & Byrne 1991). Errors result from working-memory limitations and from failures to search exhaustively for counter-examples or to adequately represent information initially. The key prediction that error rates depend on the number of models required to reach a valid conclusion has been well supported (Johnson-Laird & Bara 1984, Johnson-Laird et al 1989; see also Evans et al 1993), although it has been argued that the theory does not specify how we combine models or search for alternatives (e.g. Rips 1994, Bach 1993, Chater 1993, Polk 1993). Differential predictions based on the putative complexity of the initial model have also been supported for *all* and *only* (Johnson-Laird & Byrne 1989).

Thus, the use of models in quantified inference seems plausible. Although this finding cannot be used to claim an exclusively semantic foundation for reasoning, it appears that, within the cognitive architecture, semantic processes may play a functionally distinct role. Their specific cognitive status must be defined carefully, however. Theoretically, mental models are functional, intermediate representations in working memory, constructed through the logical executive function (Falmagne 1994). In particular, for quantified problems, the construction of composite models must be guided by an understanding of supra-sentential constraints in predicate logic, defining the scope and compositional properties of quantifiers.

Quantified reasoning is a highly specialized domain of reasoning, rarely represented in natural inferential contexts, whether textual, conversational, or spontaneous. The prominence of quantified reasoning in research on deduction is most certainly due to the historical roots of that topic in Aristotelian logic, which continues to shape cognitive research. Most linguistic inferences are not quantified and rely instead on either propositional or lexical processes.

Applied to propositional reasoning, mental model theory holds that deduction only requires knowledge of the meaning of connectives and that the meaning of a connective lies in its truth conditions (Johnson-Laird & Byrne 1991, Johnson-Laird et al 1992). The meaning of a proposition consists of symbols representing the states of affairs the connective permits. The initial model may leave the full set of truth conditions implicit, to be fleshed out later in deduction; if so, this property is marked symbolically in the initial model. If the initial model exhaustively captures all possibilities, it includes a "propositional tag" (Falmagne 1975a) indicating that no alternative state of affairs is possible.

Johnson-Laird et al (1992) predict the relative difficulty of different conditional inferences and of other connectives from the number of explicit models required, and the greater difficulty of particular inference forms for conditional than for biconditional *if* (but see Evans 1993, Wetherick 1993). However, most findings can be accounted for by rule theories, as Johnson-Laird et al recognize for their own data and those of Braine et al (1984). Rips (1994) accounts for the greater ease of Modus Ponens from a biconditional than from a conditional sentence. Braine et al (1984) predict Modus Tollens to be more difficult than Modus Ponens because the absence of a basic schema requires indirect reasoning routines, so Legrenzi et al's (1993) predictions to that effect are not discriminative. That inclusive disjunctions are more difficult than exclusive disjunctions, putatively due to the number of models, supports the involvement of models at some stage in the process. So do Bauer & Johnson-Laird's (1993) findings that diagrams improve reasoning in their task, but with barren people-in-places problems with multiple premises, it is not surprising that working memory benefits from diagrams.

Byrne's (1989b) finding on the ostensible suppression of Modus Ponens by a second premise, putatively refuting formal schemas, has generated a mini-debate predicated on questionable assumptions. Both the original interpretation (Byrne 1989b, 1991; Evans et al 1993) and the replies that the second conditional simply weakens the believability of the first (e.g. Politzer & Braine 1991, Over 1993) assume that logical form is restricted to isolated sentences. If, however, deduction is seen as a global process with suprasentential logical forms exploiting discourse-level relations, there is no problem in positing that a compound logical form with joint conditions is constructed.

Johnson-Laird & Byrne's (1991) assertion that rule theories are incapable of handling content effects finds a match in Holyoak & Spellman's (1993) point that mental model theory cannot explain how world knowledge affects model building without auxiliary assumptions, because the procedures that manipulate models are formal (see also Rips 1994). Rule theories can address content effects by adding contextual assumptions (Sperber & Wilson 1986). When rules are supplemented with pragmatic schemas (Braine & O'Brien 1991), content involving permission or causality can be accounted for as well. D Cummins (unpublished information) reaches a similar conclusion, and George (1992) shows that formal cues from content are used to deduce the initial interpretation of conditional connectives on either theory.

Conceptually, support for the use of models does not discount either the syntactic or the logical underpinnings of deduction. As semantic representations, the construction of models must exploit the syntactic and logical properties of the sentence, which are, after all, the backbones of meaning (Falmagne 1993), as work in linguistic semantics makes clear. Johnson-Laird & Byrne acknowledge, of course, that syntactic processing operates, but they do not use this fact substantively nor do they attend to its implication that semantics embodies syntax and therefore logic. Stenning (1992) lucidly discusses the corresponding point about the model-theoretic and proof-theoretic implementations of logic. Relatedly, Rips (1994) points out that models, especially those for propositional reasoning, contain variables and thus are functionally equivalent to propositional statements. Thus, regardless of notational style, the models themselves symbolize propositions.

Put differently, the logical executive must guide the construction of mental models for these to be adequate and reflect the logic of the problem (Falmagne 1989a, 1994). A vivid illustration of this point involves the symbols signaling that a state of affairs is exhausted: For the conditional *if p then q,* the initial model contains a *p,* signaled to be exhaustive with a *q,* so that another *p* without a *q* cannot occur should the initial model be fleshed out. Clearly, the entire logic of conditionals is embodied in the model itself, dictating which models are exhaustive, which are fit to be implicit, and how they are unfolded explicitly as directed by the logical executive function. The search for alternative models likewise must be designed to preclude illegitimate possibilities (see also Pollard 1993). Politzer & Braine (1991) and Braine (1993) likewise argue that a mental logic underlies models, and Holyoak & Spellman (1993) similarly point out that the construction and fleshing out of models must be guided by retrieval of relevant knowledge from long-term memory.

Another serious problem with the theory of propositional reasoning is that despite their initial motivation as complex semantic representations, models for propositions exclusively represent extensional properties of sentences, because the deductive process only considers the presence or absence of a state of affairs. Johnson-Laird et al (1992) see models as less bulky than truth tables since they only represent admissible states of affairs. This may be so, but the fundamental problem faced by truth-functional semantics remains, calling into question the adequacy of the theory for the propositional domain. Using a different approach, relying on the meaning of connectives as cornerstones of propositional reasoning but avoiding this problem, Braine & O'Brien (1991) characterize the meaning of *if* and other connectives as inference schemas.

These problems notwithstanding, the exclusivity claim is unwarranted. First, it would be entirely natural for the human mind to abstract a rule such as Modus Ponens from repeated contentful applications, and empirical evidence noted previously supports that conjecture. Second, the research reviewed in the previous section suggests that rules (formal schemas, pragmatic schemas, or both) are applied at some point in the deductive process. Thus, evidence for the cognitive reality of models must be integrated with those findings.

The manner in which formal schemas and models of states of affairs can be articulated in a unified theory is illustrated in an early analysis of deductive processes in children for simple quantified inferences. Falmagne (1975a) and Falmagne et al (1989) describe alternative representations of the premise as propositional, schematic, and concrete, and argue that the initial representation is propositional, encoding indeterminate information as default values. This representation is sufficient for the simpler inferences, but a fully specified representation of the concrete potential objects is unfolded in the process of answering the more difficult indeterminate inferences, with a propositional tag of tentativeness attached to the representation of the concrete alternatives, and a quasi-combinatorial analysis operating on them. A basic understanding of indeterminacy is needed to maintain the tentative tags throughout this process and to orchestrate the combinatorial analysis. This work predates the upsurge of mental model theory, but it introduces several of its concepts, within an integrative analysis.

Beliefs

Beliefs play a significant role in cognition, and belief updating is a key process in knowledge representation. For Harman (1986) and Stalnaker (1984), and more generally within philosophy of mind, belief is one of a handful of attitudes one may hold toward a proposition. Stalnaker defines acceptance as a generic propositional attitude subsuming presupposition, assumption, and belief. To accept a proposition is to treat it as true in one way or another; thus, belief and assumption of premises are treated within a unified theory. Harman sees beliefs as constitutive of a rational activity aimed at coherence in worldview. In contrast, in the psychological literature, belief has been viewed mostly as inducing distortions from rationality and affecting heuristic, nonlogical processes.

Empirically, beliefs have been shown to affect deduction by shaping the representation of premises (Revlin & Leirer 1978, Revlin et al 1980), by controlling the intuitive acceptability of conclusions, and by modulating the deductive process itself. The first process is insufficient to account for findings, and most recent research has focused on the second and third.

Three recent hypotheses, generated to account for different clusters of findings, each provide fragmentary insights on the interplay of beliefs and logic (see Evans et al 1993, Oakhill & Garnham 1993, Newstead & Evans 1993). Evans' (1989) selective scrutiny model predicts that conclusions that are believable are more readily accepted (Evans et al 1983, Evans & Pollard 1990). The model assumes preanalytic representational heuristics selecting aspects of the problem deemed relevant, such as the believability of conclusions, and a second, analytic stage.

This hypothesis cannot explain that belief bias is found for indeterminate invalid syllogisms only: Conclusions that are indeterminate are recognized as such more readily when they are also unbelievable, but believability does not affect determinate false conclusions. Two competing accounts address those findings. Barston (1986) assumes that people misunderstand logical necessity and that, when a conclusion is neither falsified nor determined by premises, they rely on its believability rather than judging it indeterminate. Alternatively, Oakhill et al (1989) suggest that when conclusions are unbelievable, alternative models are elicited more readily, a key process in their general account of inference. Both processes hold jointly, according to Newstead et al's (1992) results from five experiments manipulating logic, believability, and number of models. To explain additional findings, Oakhill et al speculate that beliefs also filter conclusions, a process akin to the first stage of selective scrutiny, as Oakhill & Garnham (1993) recognize, but crucially occurring at the end of the deductive process.

Thus, in the selective scrutiny model, belief takes precedence over logic in processing: Logical analysis occurs for unbelievable conclusions only. In the misinterpreted necessity model, belief operates as a default when no definite conclusion is reached, thus blocking recognition of indeterminacy. In mental model accounts, belief affects the deductive process itself by modulating the generation of alternatives and secondarily filters conclusions. Those notions are interestingly distinct and have complementary aspects, but it is important to note that the research has used quantified syllogisms, a highly specific reasoning domain.

Beliefs and prior knowledge play a constitutive role in reasoning (Harman 1986, Stalnaker 1984). They may yield additional premises in problems, or be used as grounds for deciding whether to accept the conventions of the deductive task at all. Formal arguments and syllogistic tasks are a culture-specific "genre" (Scribner 1977); thus, agreeing to suspend ordinary knowledge and rely on arbitrarily asserted premises is less a matter of rationality than compliance. Logic aims at insuring true conclusions if the premises are true; its intended epistemic function is thus to reason from true premises.

Recent theorizing stresses consistency of beliefs more generally. Stalnaker (1984) and Harman (1986) ground their theories of reasoning in this notion, although for Harman cognitive agents do not keep a track record of belief updating, thus making it possible to have inconsistent beliefs unwittingly. Braine & O'Brien's (1991) theory of *if* uses a limited notion of consistency. One constraint on the schema for conditional proof is that premises must be consistent with prior assumptions, although this constraint is flexible so as to allow for counterfactual reasoning, in which certain beliefs can be suspended when reasoning explicitly.

CONCLUDING COMMENTS

Although the involvement of formal processes in deduction is well substantiated, it is equally clear that they are interwoven with contentful and contextual elements of thought. In our view the dialectic between form, content, and context is the central question for theory on deductive inference at the present time, and we have evaluated research from that angle.

The distinction between content and context is theory-dependent and contingent on what the purely deductive segment consists of, and pragmatic perspectives on meaning render the distinction complex. Content itself is defined in two different ways. The construal predominant in the deduction literature is propositional content, i.e. what the proposition is about. In particular, theories stressing background knowledge or believability rely on this construal, as belief is a propositional attitude. Alternatively, content has been construed pragmatically, as consisting in the functional rather than the referential properties of a statement, in line with pragmatic theories of meaning.

Virtually every recent theory posits some type of content-sensitive reasoning process. Two basic options have been adopted in that regard. One theoretical device is to assume that propositional content affects reasoning by being constitutive of semantic representations. Mental model theory (e.g. Johnson-Laird & Byrne 1991) uses that option, although for propositional and quantified reasoning, representations are in fact impoverished to solely include abstract tokens standing for the objects of propositions, so that the impact of content on the reasoning process is narrow. In the second device, the content of a statement triggers a knowledge structure with domain-sensitive rules (Cheng & Holyoak 1985, Cosmides 1989). One issue for research is the level of abstraction of these knowledge structures. Another issue, currently underexamined, is the relative contribution of linguistic and situational cues to the activation of these structures.

Pragmatic content raises an important question regarding the relation between logical knowledge and pragmatic knowledge. For example, permission and obligation schemas, putatively drawing on pragmatic content, share similarities with deontic logic, which is a formal, logical system (e.g. Platt & Griggs 1993, Rips 1994). So the boundaries between what is considered content and form become complex, as are the boundaries between what is considered pragmatic and logical.

The increasing recognition that supra-sentential and nonlinguistic context inform deduction calls for an articulated cognitive theory of context. Some of the theories reviewed above pave the way in that direction, taking different theoretical options and with different explanatory scope. Context has been characterized as integral to deductive forms (Barwise 1989) or, alternatively, as extraneous and modulating other processes. Context modulates by enriching representations (Sperber & Wilson 1986), by informing the interpretive process (Braine & O'Brien 1991), or by restricting the domain of application of deductive processes, as do pragmatic schemas (Cheng & Holyoak 1985, Cheng & Nisbett 1993).

The ostensible tension between formal knowledge on the one hand and pragmatic contextual knowledge on the other is a continuous thread spanning both deductive processes and lexical semantics. In reviewing logico-lexical semantics, we encountered this tension for *if* and other lexical items: The lexical semantics of those terms must include pragmatic aspects of meaning along with formal properties. The theoretical issue of whether the core lexical entry contains both formal and pragmatic components or whether pragmatic information is extraneous in affecting contextual interpretation (Braine & O'Brien 1991) echoes that just discussed for deductive schemas. The associated issue of whether one or several lexical entries are needed for capturing pragmatically driven meaning variations has its parallel for deductive schemas as well. Both issues are key to an integrative theory of deductive inference.

Broader pragmatic aspects of deduction are made evident by recent analyses. Stalnaker's (1984) pragmatic view, based on mental acts and attitudes, posits that mental states, and not linguistic expressions, are primarily representational, and that what they are about (their intentionality) is defined by the conditions that caused them as much as it is by their objects. Stalnaker's theoretical account of deduction is grounded in the naturalistic and pragmatic view of cognitive activity: Deduction is embedded within the activities of rational action.

An important question is how abstract and concrete forms of knowledge interact. Harman's (1986) theory of reasoning, in stressing coherence of beliefs, gives epistemological precedence to concrete modes of knowledge drawing broadly from a person's knowledge base over abstract, formal knowledge. On entirely different grounds, Ilyenkov (1977) stresses the inherently contextual nature of knowledge and prioritizes the concrete over the abstract epistemologically, in contrast to traditional conceptions. Logic is a network of concrete universal laws and concepts, not an abstract system and, in that sense, is akin to scientific theory. Falmagne (1994) discusses Ilyenkov's ideas and their contrasts and resonances with issues in cognitive science. Scribner's (1977) observation that Kpelle people appear to hold an epistemic view that takes empiric knowledge to be needed for formal argument, is an interesting illustration of this worldview.

The formal schema and the mental models approaches reviewed here have tended to rely on a linguistic construal of deduction, while emphasis on pragmatic factors and biases has been partly motivated by nonlinguistic considerations. Linguistic and nonlinguistic elements of deduction intersect, of course. A case in point is the relation between pragmatic schemas and deontic logic, a relation that is evident on theoretical and empirical grounds but is in need of a fuller treatment capturing the semantics of deontic terms. Because deontic information is conveyed by modal terms via their semantics, and because this type of information is also an excellent candidate for nonlinguistic, situationally defined meaning, this domain instantiates the merging of linguistic and nonlinguistic elements of reasoning in a particularly felicitous way.

The centrality of deduction in thought renders these questions particularly consequential. Though fundamental theoretical choices always are necessary, we have argued that a mature understanding of deduction entails recognizing its complexity and focusing attention in integrative directions. Recent research and theory have been remarkably productive in the past two decades and provide rich data for such an integration if used with this aim in mind.

ACKNOWLEDGMENTS

We thank Joyce Lee for her help throughout the preparation of the manuscript and Karlina Lyons for help with references. We thank colleagues who kindly sent us recent materials and regret that space limitations and the resulting constraints in the scope of discussion forced us to omit valuable contributions and topics.

Literature Cited

Allwood J. 1986. Logic and spoken interaction. See Myers et al 1986, pp. 67–91

Anderson AR, Belnap ND. 1975. *Entailment.* Princeton NJ: Princeton Univ. Press

Asher N. 1986. Belief in discourse representation theory. *J. Philos. Logic* 15:127–89

Asher N. 1993. *Reference to Abstract Objects in Discourse.* Hingham, MA: Kluwer

Bach K. 1993. Getting down to cases. *Brain Behav. Sci.* 16(2):334–36

Barston JL. 1986. *An investigation into belief biases in reasoning.* PhD thesis. Univ. Plymouth, UK

Barwise J. 1989. *The Situation in Logic.* Stanford, CA: Cent. Stud. Lang. Info.

Barwise J, Perry J. 1983. *Situations and Attitudes.* Cambridge, MA: Bradford

Barwise J, Perry J. 1985. Semantic innocence and uncompromising situations. In *The Philosophy of Language,* ed. AP Martinich, pp. 401–13. New York: Oxford Univ. Press

Bassano D, Hickmann M, Champaud C. 1992. Epistemic modality in French children's discourse: to be sure or not to be sure? *J. Child Lang.* 19:389–413

Bauer MI, Johnson-Laird PN. 1993. How diagrams can improve reasoning. *Psychol. Sci.* 4(6):372–78

Bennett-Lau S. 1983. *The learning of indeterminate arguments by children in the context of a syllogistic task.* PhD thesis. Clark Univ., Worcester, MA

Bloom AH. 1981. *The Linguistic Shaping of Thought: A Study in the Impact of Language on Thinking in China and the West.* Hillsdale, NH: Erlbaum

Bowerman M. 1986. First steps in acquiring conditionals. See Traugott et al 1986, pp. 285–308

Braine MDS. 1978. On the relation between the natural logic of reasoning and standard logic. *Psychol. Rev.* 85:1–21

Braine MDS. 1990. The "natural logic" approach to reasoning. In *Reasoning, Necessity, and Logic: Developmental Perspectives,* ed. WF Overton, pp. 263–340. Hillsdale, NJ: Erlbaum

Braine MDS. 1993. Mental logic and how to discover it. In *The Logical Foundations of Cognition,* ed. J Macnamara, G Reyes, pp. 241–63. Oxford: Oxford Univ. Press

Braine MDS. 1994. Is nativism sufficient? *J. Child Lang.* 21:9–31

Braine MDS, O'Brien DP. 1991. A theory of If: a lexical entry, reasoning program, and pragmatic principles. *Psychol. Rev.* 98(2):182–203

Braine MDS, Reiser BJ, Rumain B. 1984. Some empirical justifications for a theory of natural propositional logic. In *The Psychology of Learning and Motivation,* ed. GH Bower, 18:313–71. New York: Academic

Burton-Roberts G. 1989. *The Limits to Debate: A Revised Theory of Semantic Presupposition.* New York: Cambridge Univ. Press

Byrne RMJ. 1989a. Everyday reasoning with conditional sequences. *Q. J. Exp. Psychol.* 41A:141–66

Byrne RMJ. 1989b. Suppressing valid inferences with conditionals. *Cognition* 31:61–83

Byrne RMJ. 1991. Can valid inferences be suppressed? *Cognition* 30:71–78

Carlson R, Lundy D, Yaure R. 1992. Syllogistic reasoning in meaningful text. *Am. J. Psychol.* 105(1):75–99

Chater N. 1993. Mental models and nonmonotonic reasoning. *Brain Behav. Sci.* 16(2): 340–41

Cheng PW, Holyoak KJ. 1985. Pragmatic reasoning schemas. *Cogn. Psychol.* 17:391–416

Cheng PW, Holyoak KJ. 1989. On the natural selection of reasoning theories. *Cognition* 33:285–313

Cheng PW, Holyoak KJ, Nisbett RE, Oliver LM. 1986. Pragmatic versus syntactic approaches to training deductive reasoning. *Cogn. Psychol.* 18:293–328

Cheng PW, Nisbett RE. 1993. A pragmatic constraint on causal deduction. In *Rules for Reasoning: Implications for Cognitive Science and Education,* ed. RE Nisbett, pp. 207–27. Hillsdale, NJ: Erlbaum

Cheng PW, Novick LR. 1991. Causes versus enabling conditions. *Cognition* 40(1–2): 83–120

Chierchia G, McConnell-Ginet S. 1992. *An Introduction to Semantics.* Cambridge, MA: MIT Press

Chomsky N. 1965. *Aspects of a Theory of Syntax.* Cambridge, MA: MIT Press

Chomsky N. 1981. *Lectures on Government and Binding.* Dordrecht: Foris

Clement C, Falmagne RJ. 1986. World knowledge, mental imagery and logical reasoning: interconnections in cognitive processes. *Mem. Cogn.* 14(4):299–307

Coates J. 1988. The acquisition of meanings in modality in children aged eight to twelve. *J. Child Lang.* 15:425–34

Cohen LJ. 1981. Can human irrationality be experimentally demonstrated? *Behav. Brain Sci.* 4(3):317–70

Comrie B. 1986. Conditionals: a typology. See Traugott et al 1986, pp. 77–99

Cosmides L. 1989. The logic of social exchange: Has natural selection shaped how humans reason? Studies with the Wason Selection Task. *Cognition* 31:187–276

Cosmides L, Tooby J. 1994. Beyond intuition and instinct blindness: toward an evolutionarily rigorous cognitive science. *Cognition* 50:117–82

Cummins DD. 1994. Naive theories and causal deduction. *Mem. Cogn.* In press

Edgington D. 1984. Do conditionals have truth conditions? In *Conditionals,* ed. F Jackson, pp. 176–201. New York: Oxford Univ. Press

Evans JStBT. 1989. *Bias in Human Reasoning: Causes and Consequences.* Hove, UK: Erlbaum

Evans JStBT. 1993. The mental model theory of conditional reasoning. *Cognition* 48:1–20

Evans JStBT, Barston JL, Pollard R. 1983. On the conflict between logic and belief in syllogistic reasoning. *Mem. Cogn.* 11:295–306

Evans JStBT, Newstead SE, Byrne RM. 1993. *Human Reasoning: The Psychology of Deduction.* Hillsdale, NJ: Erlbaum

Evans JStBT, Pollard P. 1990. Belief bias and problem complexity in deductive reasoning. In *Cognitive Biases,* ed. JP Caverini, JM Fabre, M Gonzalez, pp. 131–54. Amsterdam: North-Holland

Falmagne RJ. 1975a. Deductive processes in children. See Falmagne 1975c, pp. 175–200

Falmagne RJ. 1975b. Reasoning, representation and process: an overview. See Falmagne 1975c, pp. 247–64

Falmagne RJ, ed. 1975c. *Reasoning, Representation, and Process.* Hillsdale, NJ: Erlbaum

Falmagne RJ. 1988. *Language as a constitutive factor in logical knowledge: cognitive, philosophical, and linguistic considerations. Cogn. Sci. Lab., Tech. Rep. 28.* Princeton, NJ: Princeton Univ.

Falmagne RJ. 1989a. *Formal and nonformal aspects of deduction.* Presented at Annu. Meet. Soc. Philos. Psychol., Tucson, Ariz.

Falmagne RJ. 1989b. The place of logical primitives in cognition. [Review of John Macnamara, A border dispute]. *Contemp. Psychol.* 34(4):327–28

Falmagne RJ. 1990a. *Situations, statements and logical relations.* Presented at 20th Anniv. Symp. Jean Piaget Soc. (Soc. Stud. Knowl. Dev.), Philadelphia, PA

Falmagne RJ. 1990b. Language and the acquisition of logical knowledge. In *Reasoning, Necessity, and Logic: Developmental Perspectives,* ed. WF Overton, pp. 111–31. Hillsdale, NJ: Erlbaum

Falmagne RJ. 1992. Reflections on acquisition processes. In *Analytic Approaches to Human Cognition,* ed. J Alegria, D Holender, J Junça de Morais, M Radeau, pp. 395–413. New York: Elsevier

Falmagne RJ. 1993. On modes of explanation. *Behav. Brain Sci.* 16(2):346–47

Falmagne RJ. 1994. The abstract and the concrete. In *Cross-cultural Psychology and Activity Theory: Essays in Honor of Sylvia Scribner,* ed. K Nelson, L Martin, E Tobach. New York: Cambridge Univ. Press. In press

Falmagne RJ, Gonsalves J, Bennett-Lau S. 1994. Children's linguistic intuitions about factive presuppositions. *Cogn. Dev.* 9:1–22

Falmagne RJ, Mawby RA, Pea RD. 1989. Linguistic and logical factors in recognition of indeterminacy. *Cogn. Dev.* 4:141–76

Fenstad JE, Halvorsen P, Langholm T, van Be-
them J. 1987. *Situations, Language and
Logic.* Dordrecht: Reidel

Fillenbaum S. 1986. The use of conditionals in
inducements and deterrents. See Traugott
et al 1986, pp. 367

Fincher-Kiefer R. 1993. The role of predictive
inferences in situation model construction.
Disc. Process. 16:99–124

Fisch S. 1991. *Mental logic in children's reasoning and text comprehension.* PhD thesis. New York Univ.

Fodor JA. 1987. A situated grandmother?
Some remarks on proposals by Barwise
and Perry. *Mind Lang.* 2:64–81

Frege G. 1956. The thought: a logical inquiry.
Reprinted in *Mind* 65:289–311

George C. 1990. Dissotiation des difficultes
dans la tache de selection de Wason. *Anee
Psychol.* 90:169–93

George C. 1992. Rules of inference in the interpretation of the conditional connective.
Eur. Bull. Cogn. Psychol. 12(2):115–39

Gigerenzer G, Hug K. 1992. Domain specific
reasoning: social contracts, cheating, and
perspective change. *Cognition* 43(2):127–
71

Girotto V. 1991. Deontic reasoning: the pragmatic reasoning schemas approach. *Intellectica* 11:15–52 (Special issue)

Gonsalves J. 1991. *Logico-semantic development: the development of modality in children three to six.* MA thesis. Clark Univ.,
Worcester, Mass.

Graesser AG, Bower GH, eds. 1990. *The Psychology of Learning and Motivation: Inferences and Text Comprehension.* New
York: Academic

Grice HP. 1975. Logic and conversation. In
Syntax and Semantics, ed. P Cole, JL Morgan, 3:41–58. New York: Academic

Grice HP. 1989. *Studies in the Way of Words.*
Cambridge, MA: Harvard Univ. Press

Haack S. 1978. *Philosophy of Logics.* New
York: Cambridge Univ. Press

Hagert G, Waern Y. 1986. On implicity assumptions in reasoning. See Myers et al
1986, pp. 93–115

Harmann G. 1986. *Change in View: Principles of Reasoning.* Cambridge, MA: Bradford

Hickmann M, Champaud C, Bassano D. 1993.
Pragmatics and metapragmatics in the development of epistemic modality: evidence
from French children's reports of think-
statements. *First Lang.* 13:359–89

Higgins T. 1994. *The situation in human reasoning.* MA thesis. Clark Univ., Worcester,
MA

Holyoak KJ, Spellman BA. 1993. Thinking.
Annu. Rev. Psychol. 44:265–315

Hornstein N. 1984. *Logic as Grammar.* Cambridge, MA: MIT Press

Hudson J, Slackman E. 1990. Children's use of

scripts in inferential text processing. *Disc.
Process.* 13(4):375–85

Hughes GE, Cresswell MJ. 1968. *An Introduction to Modal Logic.* London: Methuen

Ilyenkov EV. 1977. *Dialectical Logic.* Moscow: Progress

Jackendoff R. 1983. *Semantics and Cognition.*
Cambridge, MA: MIT Press

Jackendoff R. 1985. Information is in the mind
of the beholder. *Linguist. Philos.* 8:23–33

Jackson F, ed. 1991. *Conditionals.* Oxford:
Oxford Univ. Press

Johnson-Laird PN. 1975. Models of deduction.
See Falmagne 1975c, pp. 7–54

Johnson-Laird PN. 1978. The meaning of modality. *Cogn. Sci.* 2:17–26

Johnson-Laird PN. 1983. *Mental Models.* New
York: Cambridge Univ. Press

Johnson-Laird PN. 1986. Reasoning without
logic. See Myers et al 1986, pp. 13–50

Johnson-Laird PN, Bara BG. 1984. Syllogistic
inference. *Cognition* 16:1–61

Johnson-Laird PN, Byrne RMJ. 1989. Only
reasoning. *J. Mem. Lang.* 28(3):313–30

Johnson-Laird PN, Byrne RMJ. 1991. *Deduction.* Hove, UK: Erlbaum

Johnson-Laird PN, Byrne RMJ. 1992. Modal
reasoning, models, and Manktelow and
Over. *Cognition* 43(2):173–82

Johnson-Laird PN, Byrne RMJ, Schaeken W.
1992. Propositional reasoning by model.
Psychol. Rev. 99(3):418–39

Johnson-Laird PN, Byrne RMJ, Tabossi P.
1989. Reasoning by model: the case of
multiple quantification. *Psychol. Rev.* 96
(4):658–73

Jorgensen J, Falmagne RJ. 1992. Aspects of
the meaning of "if...then" for older preschoolers: hypotheticality, entailment, and
suppositional processes. *Cogn. Dev.* 7:
189–212

Kamp H. 1984. A theory of truth and semantic
representation. In *Truth, Interpretation and
Information,* ed. J Groenendijk, TMV
Janssen, M Stokhof, pp. 1–41. Dordrecht:
Foris

Kamp H. 1988. Conditionals in DR theory. In
*Representation and Reasoning: Proceed-
ings of the Stuttgart Conference Workshop
on Discourse Representation, Dialogue
Tableaux and Logic Programming,* ed. J
Hoepelman, pp. 67–124. Tubingen: Nie-
meyer Verlag

Kamp H. 1993. *From Discourse to Logic:
Introduction to Model Theoretic Se-
mantics, Formal Logic and Discourse
Representation Theory.* Hingham, MA:
Kluwer

Kempson RM. 1988. Logical form: the gram-
mar-cognition interface. *J. Linguist.* 24:
393–431

Kempson RM. 1990a. The relation between
mind, language and reality. See Kempson
1990b, pp. 3–25

Kempson RM. 1990b. *Mental Representations: The Interface Between Language and Reality.* New York: Cambridge Univ. Press

Kintsch W. 1993. Information accretion and reduction in text processing: inferences. *Disc. Process.* 16:193–202

Kiparsky P, Kiparsky C. 1974. Fact. In *Semantics,* ed. DD Steinberg, LA Jakobovits, pp. 370–93. London: Cambridge Univ. Press

Kratzer A. 1980. Possible worlds semantics and psychological reality. *Linguist. Berichte* 66:1–14

Kripke S. 1963. Semantic considerations on modal logic. *Philos. Fennica* 16:83–94

Lea R, O'Brien D, Fisch S, Noveck I, Braine MD. 1990. Predicting propositional logic inferences in text comprehension. *J. Mem. Lang.* 29(1):361–87

Legrenzi P, Girotto V, Johnson-Laird PN. 1993. Focussing in reasoning and decision making. *Cognition* 49:37–66

Lewis CI. 1918. *A Survey of Symbolic Logic.* Berkeley: Univ. Calif. Press

Lewis DK. 1973. *Counterfactuals.* Cambridge: Cambridge Univ. Press

Light P, Blaye A, Gilly M, Girotto V. 1989. Pragmatic schemas and logical reasoning in 6- to 8-year-old children. *Cogn. Dev.* 4: 49–64

Light PH, Girotto V, Legenzi P. 1990. Children's reasoning on conditional premises and permissions. *Cogn. Dev.* 5:369–83

Liu LG. 1985. Reasoning counterfactually in Chinese: Are there any obstacles? *Cognition* 21:239–70

Lycan W. 1984. *Logical Form in Natural Language.* Cambridge, MA: MIT Press

Macnamara J. 1986. *A Border Dispute: The Place of Logic in Psychology.* Cambridge, MA: MIT Press

Macnamara J. 1994. Logic and cognition. In *The Logical Foundation of Cognition,* ed. J Macnamara, GE Reyes, pp. 9–32. New York: Oxford Univ. Press

Macnamara J, Reyes GE. 1994. Introduction. In *The Logical Foundations of Cognition,* ed. J Macnamara, GE Reyes, pp. 1–8. New York: Oxford Univ. Press

MacWhinney B, ed. 1987. *Mechanisms of Language Acquisition.* Hillsdale, NJ: Erlbaum

Magliano JP, Baggett WB, Johnson BK, Graesser AG. 1993. The time course of generating causal antecedent and causal consequence inferences. *Disc. Process.* 16: 35–53

Manktelow KL, Over DE. 1990. *Inference and Understanding.* London: Routledge

Manktelow KL, Over DE. 1991. Social roles and utilities in reasoning with deontic conditionals. *Cognition* 39(2):85–105

Manktelow KL, Over DE. 1992. Utility and deontic reasoning: some comments on

Johnson-Laird and Byrne. *Cognition* 43 (2):183–88

Manktelow KL, Over DE, eds. 1993. *Rationality: Psychological and Philosophical Perspectives.* London: Routledge

Markovits H, Savary F. 1992. Pragmatic schemas and the selection task. To reason or not to reason. *Q. J. Exp. Psychol.* 45A: 133–48

May R. 1985. *Logical Form: Its Structure and Derivation.* Cambridge, MA: MIT Press

McCabe AE, Evely S, Abramovitch R, Corter CM, Pepler CJ. 1983. Conditional statements in young children's spontaneous speech. *J. Child Lang.* 10:253–58

McCawley JD. 1968. The role of semantics in a grammar. In *Universals in Linguistic Theory,* ed. E Bach, RT Harms, pp. 125–69. New York: Hold, Rinehart & Winston

McCawley JD. 1993. *Everything That Linguists Have Always Wanted To Know About Logic...But Were Ashamed To Ask.* Chicago: Univ. Chicago Press. 2nd ed.

Miller GA, Fellbaum C. 1991. Semantic networks of English. *Cognition* 41:197–230

Moore C, Davige J. 1989. The development of mental terms: pragmatics or semantics? *J. Child Lang.* 16:633–41

Moore C, Furrow D. 1991. The development of the language of belief: the expression of relative certainty. In *Children's Theories of Mind: Mental States and Social Understanding,* ed. D Frye, C Moore, pp. 173–93. Hillsdale, NJ: Erlbaum

Moore T. 1986. Reasoning and inference in logic and in language. See Myers et al 1986, pp. 51–66

Myers T, Brown K, McGonigle B, eds. 1986. *Reasoning and Discourse Processes.* New York: Academic

Neale S. 1988. Events and logical form. *Linguist. Philos.* 11:303–21

Newstead SE, Evans JStBT. 1993. Mental models as an explanation of belief bias effects in syllogistic reasoning. *Cognition* 46(1):93–97

Newstead SE, Pollard P, Evans JStBT, Allen J. 1992. The source of belief bias in syllogistic reasoning. *Cognition* 45(3):257–84

Noveck IA, Lea RB, Davidson GM, O'Brien DP. 1991. Human reasoning is both logical and pragmatic. *Intellectica* 11:81–109

Oakhill J, Garnham A. 1993. On theories of belief bias in syllogistic reasoning. *Cognition* 46(1):87–92

Oakhill J, Johnson-Laird PN, Garnham A. 1989. Believability and syllogistic reasoning. *Cognition* 31:117–40

O'Brien DP. 1993. Mental logic and human irrationality: We can put a man on the moon, so why can't we solve those logical reasoning problems? See Manktelow & Over 1993, pp. 110–35

Osherson D. 1975. Logic and models of logical thinking. See Falmagne 1975, pp. 81–91

Over D. 1993. Deduction and degrees of belief. *Behav. Brain Sci.* 16:361–62

Over D, Manktelow KL. 1993. Rationality, utility and deontic reasoning. See Manktelow & Over 1993, pp. 231–59

Palmer FR. 1986. *Mood and Modality.* London: Cambridge Univ. Press

Partee BH. 1985. Situations, worlds and contexts. *Linguist. Philos.* 8:53–58

Partee BH. 1986. *Possible worlds in model-theoretic semantics: a linguistic perspective.* Nobel Symp. Possible Worlds Arts Sci.

Perrig W, Kintsch W. 1985. Propositional and situational representations of text. *J. Mem. Lang.* 24:503–18

Peterson C. 1986. Semantic and pragmatic usages of "but." *J. Child Lang.* 13:583–90

Peterson C, McCabe A. 1988. The connective "and" as discourse glue. *First Lang.* 8:19–28

Pieraut-Le Bonniec G. 1980. *The Development of Modal Reasoning.* New York: Academic

Pinker S. 1984. *Language Learnability and Language Development.* Cambridge, MA: Harvard Univ. Press

Platt RD, Griggs RA. 1993. Darwinian algorithms and the Wason selection task: a factorial analysis of social contract selection task problems. *Cognition* 48:163–92

Politzer G. 1986. Laws of language use and formal logic. *J. Psycholinguist. Res.* 15(1): 47–92

Politzer G, Braine MD. 1991. Responses to inconsistent premises cannot count as suppression of valid inferences. *Cognition* 38: 103–8

Politzer G, Nguyen-Xuan A. 1992. Reasoning about conditional premises and warnings: Darwinian algorithms, mental models, relevance judgements or pragmatic schemas. *Q. J. Exp. Psychol.* 44A(3):401–21

Polk TA. 1993. Mental models more or less. *Brain Behav. Sci.* 16(2):362–63

Pollard P. 1990. Natural selection for the selection task: limits to the social exchange theory. *Cognition* 36:195–204

Pollard P. 1993. There is no need for (even fully fleshed out) mental models to map onto formal logic. *Behav. Brain Sci.* 16: 363–64

Pollock JL. 1987. Defeasible reasoning. *Cogn. Sci.* 11:481–518

Quine WV. 1970. *Philosophy of Logic.* Englewood Cliffs, NJ: Prentice-Hall

Reuland E, Abraham W. 1993. *Knowledge and Language: Lexical and Conceptual Structures,* Vol. 2. Hingham, MA: Kluwer

Revlin R, Leirer VO. 1978. The effects of personal biases on syllogistic reasoning: rational decisions from personalized representations. In *Human Reasoning,* ed. R

Revlin, RE Mayer, pp. 51–80. New York: Wiley

Revlin R, Leirer VO, Yopp H, Yopp R. 1980. The belief bias effect in formal reasoning: the influence of knowledge on logic. *Mem. Cogn.* 8:584–92

Rips LJ. 1983. Cognitive processes in propositional reasoning. *Psychol. Rev.* 90:38–71

Rips LJ. 1990. Paralogical reasoning: Evans, Johnson-Laird and Byrne on liar and truthteller puzzles. *Cognition* 36:291–314

Rips LJ. 1994. *The Psychology of Proof: Deductive Reasoning in Human Thinking.* Cambridge, MA: Bradford

Roberts MJ. 1993. Human reasoning: deduction rules or mental models, or both? *Q. J. Exp. Psychol.* 46:569–89

Sales-Wuillemin E. 1993. De l'apprehension des significations implicites: les syllogismes tronques. *Anee Psychol.* 93:345–78

Scholnick EK, Wing CS. 1991. Speaking deductively: preschools' use of IF in conversation and in conditional inference. *Dev. Psychol.* 27(2):249–58

Scholnick EK, Wing CS. 1992. Speaking deductively: using conversation to trace the origins of conditional thought in children. *Merrill-Palmer Q.* 38(1):1–20

Scribner S. 1977. Modes of thinking and ways of speaking: culture and logic reconsidered. In *Thinking: Reading in Cognitive Science,* ed. PN Johnson-Laird, PC Wason, pp. 483–500. Cambridge: Cambridge Univ. Press

Seuren PAM. 1985. *Discourse Semantics.* Oxford: Blackwell

Shatz M, Wilcox SA. 1991. Constraints on the acquisition of the English modal. In *Perspectives on Language and Thought,* ed. SA Gelman, JP Byrnes, pp. 319–53. New York: Cambridge Univ. Press

Smith EE, Langston C, Nisbett RE. 1992. The case for rules in reasoning. *Cogn. Sci.* 16: 99–102

Spencer-Smith R. 1987. Semantics and discourse representation. *Mind Lang.* 2:1–26

Sperber D, Wilson D. 1986. *Relevance: Communication and Cognition.* Cambridge, MA: Harvard Univ. Press

Stalnaker RC. 1968. A theory of conditionals. In *Studies in Logical Theory,* ed. N Rescher, pp. 98–112. Oxford: Blackwell

Stalnaker RC. 1984. *Inquiry.* Cambridge, MA: MIT Press

Stalnaker RC. 1986. Possible worlds and situations. *J. Philos. Logic* 15:109–23

Stenning K. 1992. Distinguishing conceptual and empirical issues about mental models. In *Models in the Mind: Theory, Perspective, and Application,* ed. Y Rogers, A Rutherford, PA Bibby, pp. 29–48. New York: Academic

Stephany V. 1986. Modality. In *Language Ac-*

quisition, ed. P Fletcher, M Garman, pp. 375–400. New York: Cambridge Univ. Press

Strawson PF. 1971. *Logico-linguistic Papers.* London: Methuen

Tarski A. 1952. The semantic conception of truth. In *Semantics and the Philosophy of Language,* ed. L Linsky, pp. 13–47. Chicago: Chicago Univ. Press

Trabasso T, van den Broek P, Suh S. 1989. Logical necessity and transitivity of causal relations in the representation of stories. *Disc. Process.* 12:1–25

Traugott EC, ter Meulen A, Reilly JS, Ferguson CA, eds. 1986. *On Conditionals.* New York: Cambridge Univ. Press

van den Broek P. 1990. Causal inferences in the comprehension of narrative text. See Graesser & Bower 1990, pp. 175–96

Van der Auwera J. 1986. Conditionals and speech acts. See Traugott et al 1986, pp. 197–214

von Wright GH. 1951. *An Essay in Modal Logic.* Amsterdam: North-Holland

Wetherick NE. 1993. More models just means more difficulty. *Behav. Brain Sci.* 16(2): 367–68

Wilson D, Sperber D. 1986. Inference and implicature in utterance interpretation. See Myers et al 1986, pp. 241–64

Xiao MA. 1994. *Logical and heuristic aspects of the Wason selection task.* MA thesis. Clark Univ., Worcester, MA

Zucchi A. 1993. *The Language of Propositions and Events.* Hingham, MA: Kluwer

Annu. Rev. Psychol. 1995. 46:561–84

MULTIPLE HYPOTHESIS TESTING

Juliet Popper Shaffer

Department of Statistics, University of California, Berkeley, California 94720

KEY WORDS: multiple comparisons, simultaneous testing, p-values, closed test procedures, pairwise comparisons

CONTENTS

INTRODUCTION

Multiple testing refers to the testing of more than one hypothesis at a time. It is a subfield of the broader field of multiple inference, or simultaneous inference, which includes multiple estimation as well as testing. This review concentrates on testing and deals with the special problems arising from the multiple aspect. The term "multiple comparisons" has come to be used synonymously with

0066-4308/95/0201-0561$05.00

561

"simultaneous inference," even when the inferences do not deal with comparisons. It is used in this broader sense throughout this review.

In general, in testing any single hypothesis, conclusions based on statistical evidence are uncertain. We typically specify an acceptable maximum probability of rejecting the null hypothesis when it is true, thus committing a Type I error, and base the conclusion on the value of a statistic meeting this specification, preferably one with high power. When many hypotheses are tested, and each test has a specified Type I error probability, the probability that at least some Type I errors are committed increases, often sharply, with the number of hypotheses. This may have serious consequences if the set of conclusions must be evaluated as a whole. Numerous methods have been proposed for dealing with this problem, but no one solution will be acceptable for all situations. Three examples are given below to illustrate different types of multiple testing problems.

SUBPOPULATIONS: A HISTORICAL EXAMPLE   Cournot (1843) described vividly the multiple testing problem resulting from the exploration of effects within different subpopulations of an overall population. In his words, as translated from the French, "…it is clear that nothing limits…the number of features according to which one can distribute [natural events or social facts] into several groups or distinct categories." As an example he mentions investigating the chance of a male birth: "One could distinguish first of all legitimate births from those occurring out of wedlock,…one can also classify births according to birth order, according to the age, profession, wealth, or religion of the parents…usually these attempts through which the experimenter passed don't leave any traces; the public will only know the result that has been found worth pointing out; and as a consequence, someone unfamiliar with the attempts which have led to this result completely lacks a clear rule for deciding whether the result can or can not be attributed to chance." (See Stigler 1986, for further discussion of the historical context; see also Shafer & Olkin 1983, Nowak 1994.)

LARGE SURVEYS AND OBSERVATIONAL STUDIES   In large social science surveys, thousands of variables are investigated, and participants are grouped in myriad ways. The results of these surveys are often widely publicized and have potentially large effects on legislation, monetary disbursements, public behavior, etc. Thus, it is important to analyze results in a way that minimizes misleading conclusions. Some type of multiple error control is needed, but it is clearly impractical, if not impossible, to control errors at a small level over the entire set of potential comparisons.

FACTORIAL DESIGNS   The standard textbook presentation of multiple comparison issues is in the context of a one-factor investigation, where there is evidence from an overall test that the means of the dependent variable for the different levels of a factor are not all equal, and more specific inferences are desired to delineate which means are different from which others. Here, in contrast to many of the examples above, the family of inferences for which error control is desired is usually clearly specified and is often relatively small. On the other hand, in multifactorial studies, the situation is less clear. The typical approach is to treat the main effects of each factor as a separate family for purposes of error control, although both Tukey (1953) and Hartley (1955) gave examples of $2 \times 2 \times 2$ factorial designs in which they treated all seven main effect and interaction tests as a single family. The probability of finding some significances may be very large if each of many main effect and interaction tests is carried out at a conventional level in a multifactor design. Furthermore, it is important in many studies to assess the effects of a particular factor separately at each level of other factors, thus bringing in another layer of multiplicity (see Shaffer 1991).

As noted above, Cournot clearly recognized the problems involved in multiple inference, but he considered them insoluble. Although there were a few isolated earlier relevant publications, sustained statistical attacks on the problems did not begin until the late 1940s. Mosteller (1948) and Nair (1948) dealt with extreme value problems; Tukey (1949) presented a more comprehensive approach. Duncan (1951) treated multiple range tests. Related work on ranking and selection was published by Paulson (1949) and Bechhofer (1952). Scheffé (1953) introduced his well-known procedures, and work by Roy & Bose (1953) developed another simultaneous confidence interval approach. Also in 1953, a book-length unpublished manuscript by Tukey presented a general framework covering a number of aspects of multiple inference. This manuscript remained unpublished until recently, when it was reprinted in full (Braun 1994). Later, Lehmann (1957a,b) developed a decision-theoretic approach, and Duncan (1961) developed a Bayesian decision-theoretic approach shortly afterward. For additional historical material, see Tukey (1953), Harter (1980), Miller (1981), Hochberg & Tamhane (1987), and Shaffer (1988).

The first published book on multiple inference was Miller (1966), which was reissued in 1981, with the addition of a review article (Miller 1977). Except in the ranking and selection area, there were no other book-length treatments until 1986, when a series of book-length publications began to appear: 1. *Multiple Comparisons* (Klockars & Sax 1986); 2. *Multiple Comparison Procedures* (Hochberg & Tamhane 1987; for reviews, see Littell 1989, Peritz 1989); 3. *Multiple Hypothesenprüfung (Multiple Hypotheses Testing)* (Bauer et el 1988; for reviews, see Läuter 1990, Holm 1990); 4. *Multiple Comparisons for Researchers* (Toothaker 1991; for reviews, see Gaffan 1992, Tatsuoka 1992) and *Multiple Comparison Procedures* (Toothaker 1993); 5. *Multiple Comparisons, Selection, and Applications in Biometry* (Hoppe 1993b; for a review, see Ziegel 1994); 6. *Resampling-based Multiple Testing*

(Westfall & Young 1993; for reviews, see Chaubey 1993, Booth 1994); 7. *The Collected Works of John W. Tukey, Volume VII: Multiple Comparisons: 1948–1983* (Braun 1994); and 8. *Multiple Comparisons: Theory and Methods* (Hsu 1996).

This review emphasizes conceptual issues and general approaches. In particular, two types of methods are discussed in detail: (*a*) methods based on ordered p-values and (*b*) comparisons among normally distributed means. The literature cited offers many examples of the application of techniques discussed here.

ORGANIZING CONCEPTS

Primary Hypotheses, Closure, Hierarchical Sets, and Minimal Hypotheses

Assume some set of null hypotheses of primary interest to be tested. Sometimes the number of hypotheses in the set is infinite (e.g. hypothesized values of all linear contrasts among a set of population means), although in most practical applications it is finite (e.g. values of all pairwise contrasts among a set of population means). It is assumed that there is a set of observations with joint distribution depending on some parameters and that the hypotheses specify limits on the values of those parameters. The following examples use a primary set based on differences $\mu_1, \mu_2, \ldots, \mu_m$ among the means of m populations, although the concepts apply in general. Let δ_{ij} be the difference $\mu_i - \mu_j$; let δ_{ijk} be the set of differences among the means μ_i, μ_j, and μ_k, etc. The hypotheses are of the form $H_{ijk\ldots}:\delta_{ijk\ldots} = 0$, indicating that all subscripted means are equal; e.g. H_{1234} is the hypothesis $\mu_1 = \mu_2 = \mu_3 = \mu_4$. The primary set need not consist of the individual pairwise hypotheses H_{ij}. If $m = 4$, it may, for example, be the set H_{12}, H_{123}, H_{1234}, etc, which would signify a lack of interest in including inference concerning some of the pairwise differences (e.g. H_{23}) and therefore no need to control errors with respect to those differences.

The *closure* of the set is the collection of the original set together with all distinct hypotheses formed by intersections of hypotheses in the set; such a collection is called a *closed set*. For example, an intersection of the hypotheses H_{ij} and H_{ik} is the hypothesis $H_{ijk}: \mu_i = \mu_j = \mu_k$. The hypotheses included in an intersection are called components of the intersection hypothesis. Technically, a hypothesis is a component of itself; any other component is called a proper component. In the example above, the proper components of H_{ijk} are H_{ij}, H_{ik}, and, if it is included in the set of primary interest, H_{jk} because its intersection with either H_{ij} or H_{ik} also gives H_{ijk}. Note that the truth of a hypothesis implies the truth of all its proper components.

Any set of hypotheses in which some are proper components of others will be called a *hierarchical set*. (That term is sometimes used in a more limited way, but this definition is adopted here.) A closed set (with more than one hypothesis) is therefore a hierarchical set. In a closed set, the top of the hierarchy is the intersection of all hypotheses: in the examples above, it is the hypothesis $H_{12...m}$, or $\mu_1 = \mu_2 = ... = \mu_m$. The set of hypotheses that have no proper components represent the lowest level of the hierarchy; these are called the *minimal hypotheses* (Gabriel 1969). Equivalently, a minimal hypothesis is one that does not imply the truth of any other hypothesis in the set. For example, if all the hypotheses state that there are no differences among sets of means, and the set of primary interest includes all hypotheses H_{ij} for all $i \neq j = 1,...m$, these pairwise equality hypotheses are the minimal hypotheses.

Families

The first and perhaps most crucial decision is what set of hypotheses to treat as a family, that is, as the set for which significance statements will be considered and errors controlled jointly. In some of the early multiple comparisons litera- ture (e.g. Ryan 1959, 1960), the term "experiment" rather than "family" was used in referring to error control. Implicitly, attention was directed to relatively small and limited experiments. As a dramatic contrast, consider the example of large surveys and observational studies described above. Here, because of the inverse relationship between control of Type I errors and power, it is unreason- able if not impossible to consider methods controlling the error rate at a conventional level, or indeed any level, over all potential inferences from such surveys. An intermediate case is a multifactorial study (see above example), in which it frequently seems unwise from the point of view of power to control error over all inferences. The term "family" was introduced by Tukey (1952, 1953). Miller (1981), Diaconis (1985), Hochberg & Tamhane (1987), and others discuss the issues involved in deciding on a family. Westfall & Young (1993) give explicit advice on methods for approaching complex experimental studies.

Because a study can be used for different purposes, the results may have to be considered under several different family configurations. This issue came up in reporting state and other geographical comparisons in the National Assessment of Educational Progress (see Ahmed 1991). In a recent national report, each of the 780 pairwise differences among the 40 jurisdictions in- volved (states, territories, and the District of Columbia) was tested for signifi- cance at level .05/780 in order to control Type I errors for that family. How- ever, from the point of view of a single jurisdiction, the family of interest is the 39 comparisons of itself with each of the others, so it would be reasonable to test those differences each at level .05/39, in which case some differences would be declared significant that were not so designated in the national report. See Ahmed (1991) for a discussion of this example and other issues in the context of large surveys.

Type I Error Control

In testing a single hypothesis, the probability of a Type I error, i.e. of rejecting the null hypothesis when it is true, is usually controlled at some designated level α. The choice of α should be governed by considerations of the costs of rejecting a true hypothesis as compared with those of accepting a false hypothesis. Because of the difficulty of quantifying these costs and the subjectivity involved, α is usually set at some conventional level, often .05. A variety of generalizations to the multiple testing situation are possible.

Some multiple comparison methods control the Type I error rate only when all null hypotheses in the family are true. Others control this error rate for any combination of true and false hypotheses. Hochberg & Tamhane (1987) refer to these as weak control and strong control, respectively. Examples of methods with only weak error control are the Fisher protected least significant difference (LSD) procedure, the Newman-Keuls procedure, and some nonparametric procedures (see Fligner 1984, Keselman et al 1991a). The multiple comparison literature has been confusing because the distinction between weak and strong control is often ignored. In fact, weak error rate control without other safeguards is unsatisfactory. This review concentrates on procedures with strong control of the error rate. Several different error rates have been considered in the multiple testing literature. The major ones are the *error rate per hypothesis, the error rate per family,* and *the error rate familywise* or *familywise error rate.*

The *error rate per hypothesis* (usually called PCE, for per-comparison error rate, although the hypotheses need not be restricted to comparisons) is defined for each hypothesis as the probability of Type I error or, when the number of hypotheses is finite, the average PCE can be defined as the expected value of (number of false rejections/number of hypotheses), where a false rejection means the rejection of a true hypothesis. The *error rate per family* (PFE) is defined as the expected number of false rejections in the family. This error rate does not apply if the family size is infinite. The *familywise error rate* (FWE) is defined as the probability of at least one error in the family.

A fourth type of error rate, the *false discovery rate,* is described below. To make the three definitions above clearer, consider what they imply in a simple example in which each of n hypotheses $H_1, \ldots, H_n$ is tested individually at a level α_i, and the decision on each is based solely on that test. (Procedures of this type are called *single-stage*; other procedures have a more complicated structure.) If all the hypotheses are true, the average PCE equals the average of the α_i, the PFE equals the sum of the α_i, and the FWE is a function not of the

α_i alone, but involves the joint distribution of the test statistics; it is smaller than or equal to the PFE, and larger than or equal to the largest α_i.

A common misconception of the meaning of an overall error rate α applied to a family of tests is that on the average, only a proportion α of the rejected hypotheses are true ones, i.e. are falsely rejected. To see why this is not so, consider the case in which all the hypotheses are true; then 100% of rejected hypotheses are true, i.e. are rejected in error, in those situations in which any rejections occur. This misconception, however, suggests considering the proportion of rejected hypotheses that are falsely rejected and trying to control this proportion in some way. Letting V equal the number of false rejections (i.e. rejections of true hypotheses) and R equal the total number of rejections, the proportion of false rejections is $Q = V/R$. Some interesting early work related to this ratio is described by Seeger (1968), who credits the initial investigation to unpublished papers of Eklund. Sorić (1989) describes a different approach to this ratio. These papers (Seeger, Eklund, and Sorić) advocated informal consideration of the ratio; the following new approach is more formal. The *false discovery rate* (FDR) is the expected value of $Q =$ (number of false significances/number of significances) (Benjamini & Hochberg 1994).

Power

As shown above, the error rate can be generalized in different ways when moving from single to multiple hypothesis testing. The same is true of power. Three definitions of power have been common: the probability of rejecting at least one false hypothesis, the average probability of rejecting the false hypotheses, and the probability of rejecting all false hypotheses. When the family consists of pairwise mean comparisons, these have been called, respectively, any-pair power (Ramsey 1978), per-pair power (Einot & Gabriel 1975), and all-pairs power (Ramsey 1978). Ramsey (1978) showed that the difference in power between single-stage and multistage methods is much greater for all-pairs than for any-pair or per-pair power (see also Gabriel 1978, Hochberg & Tamhane 1987).

P-Values and Adjusted P-Values

In testing a single hypothesis, investigators have moved away from simply accepting or rejecting the hypothesis, giving instead the p-value connected with the test, i.e. the probability of observing a test statistic as extreme or more extreme in the direction of rejection as the observed value. This can be conceptualized as the level at which the hypothesis would just be rejected, and therefore both allows individuals to apply their own criteria and gives more information than merely acceptance or rejection. Extension of this concept in its full meaning to the multiple testing context is not necessarily straightforward. A concept that allows generalization from the test of a single hypothesis to the multiple context is the *adjusted p-value* (Rosenthal & Rubin 1983). Given any test procedure, the adjusted p-value corresponding to the test of a single hypothesis H_i can be defined as the level of the entire test procedure at which H_i would just be rejected, given the values of all test statistics involved. Application of this definition in complex multiple comparison procedures is discussed by Wright (1992) and by Westfall & Young (1993), who base their methodology on the use of such values. These values are interpretable on the same scale as those for tests of individual hypotheses, making comparison with single hypothesis testing easier.

Closed Test Procedures

Most of the multiple comparison methods in use are designed to control the FWE. The most powerful of these methods are in the class of closed test procedures, described in Marcus et al (1976). To define this general class, assume a set of hypotheses of primary interest, add hypotheses as necessary to form the closure of this set, and recall that the closed set consists of a hierarchy of hypotheses. The *closure principle* is as follows: A hypothesis is rejected at level α if and only if it and every hypothesis directly above it in the hierarchy (i.e. every hypothesis that includes it in an intersection and thus implies it) is rejected at level α. For example, given four means, with the six hypotheses H_{ij}, $i \neq j = 1,\ldots, 4$ as the minimal hypotheses, the highest hypothesis in the hierarchy is H_{1234}, and no hypothesis below H_{1234} can be rejected unless it is rejected at level α. Assuming it is rejected, the hypothesis H_{12} cannot be rejected unless the three other hypotheses above it in the hierarchy, H_{123}, H_{124}, and the intersection hypothesis H_{12} and H_{34} (i.e. the single hypothesis $\mu_1 = \mu_2$ and $\mu_3 = \mu_4$), are rejected at level α, and then H_{12} is rejected if its associated test statistic is significant at that level. Any tests can be used at each of these levels, provided the choice of tests does not depend on the observed configuration of the means. The proof that closed test procedures control the FWE involves a simple logical argument. Consider every possible true situation, each of which can be represented as an intersection of null and alternative hypotheses. Only one of these situations can be the true one, and under a closed testing procedure the probability of rejecting that one true configuration is $\leq \alpha$. All true null hypotheses in the primary set are contained in the intersection corresponding to the true configuration, and none of them can be rejected unless that configuration is rejected. Therefore, the probability of one or more of these true primary hypotheses being rejected is $\leq \alpha$.

METHODS BASED ON ORDERED P-VALUES

The methods discussed in this section are defined in terms of a finite family of hypotheses H_i, $i = 1,\ldots, n$, consisting of minimal hypotheses only. It is assumed that for each hypothesis H_i there is a corresponding test statistic T_i with a distribution that depends only on the truth or falsity of H_i. It is further assumed that H_i is to be rejected for large values of T_i. (The T_i are absolute values for two-sided tests.) Then the (unadjusted) p-value p_i of H_i is defined as the probability that T_i is larger than or equal to t_i, where T refers to the random variable and t to its observed value. For simplicity of notation, assume the hypotheses are numbered in the order of their p-values so that $p_1 \le p_2 \le \ldots \le p_n$, with arbitrary ordering in case of ties. With the exception of the subsection on Methods Controlling the FDR, all methods in this section are intended to provide strong control of the FWE.

Methods Based on the First-Order Bonferroni Inequality

The first-order Bonferroni inequality states that, given any set of events A_1, $A_2,\ldots, A_n$, the probability of their union (i.e. of the event A_1 or A_2 or…or A_n) is smaller than or equal to the sum of their probabilities. Letting A_i stand for the rejection of H_i, $i = 1,\ldots, n$, this inequality is the basis of the Bonferroni methods discussed in this section.

THE SIMPLE BONFERRONI METHOD   This method takes the form: Reject H_i if $p_i \le \alpha_i$, where the α_i are chosen so that their sum equals α. Usually, the α_i are chosen to be equal (all equal to α/n), and the method is then called the unweighted Bonferroni method. This procedure controls the PFE to be $\le \alpha$ and to be exactly α if all hypotheses are true. The FWE is usually $< \alpha$.

This simple Bonferroni method is an example of a single-stage testing procedure. In single-stage procedures, control of the FWE has the consequence that the larger the number of hypotheses in the family, the smaller the average power for testing the individual hypotheses. Multistage testing procedures can partially overcome this disadvantage. Some multistage modifications of the Bonferroni method are discussed below.

HOLM'S SEQUENTIALLY-REJECTIVE BONFERRONI METHOD   The unweighted method is described here; for the weighted method, see Holm (1979). This method is applied in stages as follows: At the first stage, H_1 is rejected if $p_1 \le \alpha/n$. If H_1 is accepted, all hypotheses are accepted without further test; otherwise, H_2 is rejected if $p_2 \le \alpha/(n - 1)$. Continuing in this fashion, at any stage j, H_j is rejected if and only if all H_i have been rejected, $i < j$, and $p_j \le \alpha/(n - j + 1)$.

To prove that this method controls the FWE, let k be the number of hypotheses that are true, where k is some number between 0 and n. If $k = n$, the test at the first stage will result in a Type I error with probability $\le \alpha$. If $k = n - 1$, an error might occur at the first stage but will certainly occur if there is a rejection at the second stage, so again the probability of a Type I error is $\le \alpha$

[because there are $n - 1$ true hypotheses and none can be rejected unless at least one has an associated p-value $\leq \alpha/(n - 1)$]. Similarly, whatever the value of k, a Type I error may occur at an early stage but will certainly occur if there is a rejection at stage $n - k + 1$, in which case the probability of a Type I error is $\leq \alpha$. Thus, the FWE is $\leq \alpha$ for every possible configuration of true and false hypotheses.

A MODIFICATION FOR INDEPENDENT AND SOME DEPENDENT STATISTICS   If test statistics are independent, the Bonferroni procedure and the Holm modification described above can be improved slightly by replacing α/k for any $k = 1,\ldots, n$ by $1 - (1 - \alpha)^{(1/k)}$, always $> \alpha/k$, although the difference is small for small values of α. These somewhat higher levels can also be used when the test statistics are *positive orthant dependent,* a class that includes the two-sided t statistics for pairwise comparisons of normally distributed means in a one-way layout. Holland & Copenhaver (1988) note this fact and give examples of other positive orthant dependent statistics.

Methods Based on the Simes Equality

Simes (1986) proved that if a set of hypotheses $H_1, H_2,\ldots, H_n$ are all true, and the associated test statistics are independent, then with probability $1 - \alpha$, $p_i > i\alpha/n$ for $i = 1,\ldots, n$, where the p_i are the ordered p-values, and α is any number between 0 and 1. Furthermore, although Simes noted that the probability of this joint event could be smaller than $1 - \alpha$ for dependent test statistics, this appeared to be true only in rather pathological cases. Simes and others (Hommel 1988, Holland 1991, Klockars & Hancock 1992) have provided simulation results suggesting that the probability of the joint event is larger than $1 - \alpha$ for many types of dependence found in typical testing situations, including the usual two-sided t test statistics for all pairwise comparisons among normally distributed treatment means.

Simes suggested that this result could be used in multiple testing but did not provide a formal procedure. As Hochberg (1988) and Hommel (1988) pointed out, on the assumption that the inequality applies in a testing situation, more powerful procedures than the sequentially rejective Bonferroni can be obtained by invoking the Simes result in combination with the closure principle. Because carrying out a full Simes-based closure procedure testing all possible hypotheses would be tedious with a large closed set, Hochberg (1988) and Hommel (1988) each give simplified, conservative methods of utilizing the Simes result.

HOCHBERG'S MULTIPLE TEST PROCEDURE   Hochberg's (1988) procedure can be described as a "step-up" modification of Holm's procedure. Consider the set of primary hypotheses $H_1,\ldots, H_n$. If $p_j \leq \alpha/(n - j + 1)$ for any $j = 1,\ldots, n$, reject all hypotheses H_i for $i \leq j$. In other words, if $p_n \leq \alpha$, reject all H_i; otherwise, if $p_{n-1} \leq \alpha/2$, reject $H_1, \ldots, H_{n-1}$, etc.

HOMMEL'S MULTIPLE TEST PROCEDURE   Hommel's (1988) procedure is more powerful than Hochberg's but is more difficult to understand and apply. Let j be the largest integer for which $p_{n-j+k} > k\alpha/j$ for all $k = 1, \ldots, j$. If no such j exists, reject all hypotheses; otherwise, reject all H_i with $p_i \leq \alpha/j$.

ROM'S MODIFICATION OF HOCHBERG'S PROCEDURE   Rom (1990) gave slightly higher critical p-value levels that can be used with Hochberg's procedure, making it somewhat more powerful. The values must be calculated; see Rom (1990) for details and a table of values for small n.

Modifications for Logically Related Hypotheses

Shaffer (1986) pointed out that Holm's sequentially-rejective multiple test procedure can be improved when hypotheses are logically related; the same considerations apply to multistage methods based on Simes' equality. In many testing situations, it is not possible to get all combinations of true and false hypotheses. For example, if the hypotheses refer to pairwise differences among treatment means, it is impossible to have $\mu_1 = \mu_2$ and $\mu_2 = \mu_3$ but $\mu_1 \neq \mu_3$. Using this reasoning, with four means and six possible pairwise equality null hypotheses, if all six are not true, then at most three are true. Therefore, it is not necessary to protect against error in the event that five hypotheses are true and one is false, because this combination is impossible. Let t_j be the maximum number of hypotheses that are true given that at least $j - 1$ hypotheses are false. Shaffer (1986) gives recursive methods for finding the values t_j for several types of testing situations (see also Holland & Copenhaver 1987, Westfall & Young 1993). The methods discussed above can be modified to increase power when the hypotheses are logically related; all methods in this section are intended to control the FWE at a level $\leq \alpha$.

MODIFIED METHODS   As is clear from the proof that it maintains FWE control, the Holm procedure can be modified as follows: At stage j, instead of rejecting H_j only if $p_j \leq \alpha/(n - j + 1)$, H_j can be rejected if $p_j \leq \alpha/t_j$. Thus, when the hypotheses of primary interest are logically related, as in the example above, the modified sequentially-rejective Bonferroni method is more powerful than the unmodified method. For some simple applications, see Levin et al (1994).

   Hochberg & Rom (1994) and Hommel (1988) describe modifications of their Simes-based procedures for logically related hypotheses. The simpler of the two modifications the former describes is to proceed from $i = n$, $n - 1$, $n - 2$, etc until for the first time $p_i \leq \alpha/(n - i + 1)$. Then reject all H_i for which $p_i \leq \alpha/t_{i+1}$. [The Rom (1990) modification of the Hochberg procedure can be improved in a similar way.] In the Hommel modification, let j be the largest integer in the set $n, t_2,\ldots, t_n$, and proceed as in the unmodified Hommel procedure.

Still further modifications at the expense of greater complexity can be achieved, since it can also be shown (Shaffer 1986) that for FWE control it is necessary to consider only the number of hypotheses that can be true given that the specific hypotheses that have been rejected are false. Hommel (1986), Conforti & Hochberg (1987), Rasmussen (1993), Rom & Holland (1994), and Hochberg & Rom (1994) consider more general procedures.

COMPARISON OF PROCEDURES   Among the unmodified procedures, Hommel's and Rom's are more powerful than Hochberg's, which is more powerful than Holm's; the latter two, however, are the easiest to apply (Hommel 1988, 1989; Hochberg 1988; Hochberg & Rom 1994). Simulation results using the unmodified methods suggest that the differences are usually small (Holland 1991). Comparisons among the modified procedures are more complex (see Hochberg & Rom 1994).

A CAUTION   All methods based on Simes's results rest on the assumption that the equality he proved for independent tests results in a conservative multiple comparison procedure for dependent tests. Thus, the use of these methods in atypical multiple test situations should be backed up by simulation or further theoretical results (see Hochberg & Rom 1994).

Methods Controlling the False Discovery Rate

The ordered p-value methods described above provide strong control of the FWE. When the test statistics are independent, the following less conservative step-up procedure controls the FDR (Benjamini & Hochberg 1994): If $p_j \leq \alpha/n$, reject all H_i for $i \leq j$. A recent simulation study (Y Benjamini, Y Hochberg, & Y Kling, manuscript in preparation) suggests that the FDR is also controlled at this level for the dependent tests involved in pairwise comparisons. VSL Williams, LV Jones, & JW Tukey (manuscript in preparation) show in a number of real data examples that the Benjamini-Hochberg FDR-controlling procedure may result in substantially more rejections than other multiple comparison methods. However, to obtain an expected proportion of false rejections, Benjamini & Hochberg have to define a value when the denominator, i.e. the number of rejections, equals zero; they define the ratio then as zero. As a result, the expected proportion, given that some rejections actually occur, is greater than α in some situations (it necessarily equals one when all hypotheses are true), so more investigation of the error properties of this procedure is needed.

COMPARING NORMALLY DISTRIBUTED MEANS

The methods in this section differ from those of the last in three respects: They deal specifically with comparisons of means, they are derived assuming normally distributed observations, and they are based on the joint distribution of all observations. In contrast, the methods considered in the previous section are completely general, both with respect to the types of hypotheses and the distributions of test statistics, and except for some results related to independence of statistics, they utilize only the individual marginal distributions of those statistics.

Contrasts among treatment means are linear functions of the form $\Sigma c_i \mu_i$, where $\Sigma c_i = 0$. The pairwise differences among means are called simple contrasts; a general contrast can be thought of as a weighted average of some subset of means minus a weighted average of another subset. The reader is presumably familiar with the most commonly used methods for testing the hypotheses that sets of linear contrasts equal zero with FWE control in a one-way analysis of variance layout under standard assumptions. They are described briefly below.

Assume m treatments with N observations per treatment and a total of T observations over all treatments, let $\bar{y}_i$ be the sample mean for treatment i, and let MSW be the within-treatment mean square.

If the primary hypotheses consist of all linear contrasts among treatment means, the Scheffé method (1953) controls the FWE. Using the Scheffé method, a contrast hypothesis $\Sigma c_i \mu_i = 0$ is rejected if $| \Sigma c_i \bar{y}_i | \geq \sqrt{\Sigma c_i^2 (MSW/N)(m-1)} \, F_{m-1,T-m;\alpha}$, where $F_{m-1,\ T-m}$; α is the α-level critical value of the F distribution with $m-1$ and $T-m$ degrees of freedom.

If the primary hypotheses consist of the pairwise differences, i.e. the simple contrasts, the Tukey method (1953) controls the FWE over this set. Using this method, any simple contrast hypothesis $\delta_{ij} = 0$ is rejected if $| \bar{y}_i - \bar{y}_j | \geq \sqrt{MSW/N} \, q_{m,T-m;\alpha}$, where $q_{m,T-m;\alpha}$ is the α-critical value of the studentized range statistic for m means and $T-m$ error degrees of freedom.

If the primary hypotheses consist of comparisons of each of the first $m-1$ means with the mth mean (e.g. of $m-1$ treatments with a control), the Dunnett method (1955) controls the FWE over this set. Using this method, any hypothesis $\delta_{im} = 0$ is rejected if $| \bar{y}_i - \bar{y}_m | \geq \sqrt{2MSW/N} \, d_{m-1,T-m;\alpha}$, where $d_{m-1,\ T-m}$; α is the α-level critical value of the appropriate distribution for this test.

Both the Tukey and Dunnett methods can be generalized to test the hypotheses that all linear contrasts among the means equal zero, so that the three procedures can be compared in power on this whole set of tests (for discussion of these extended methods and specific comparisons, see Shaffer 1977). Richmond (1982) provides a more general treatment of the extension of confidence intervals for a finite set to intervals for all linear functions of the set.

All three methods can be modified to multistage methods that give more power for hypothesis testing. In the Scheffé method, if the F test is significant, the FWE is preserved if $m - 1$ is replaced by $m - 2$ everywhere in the expression for Scheffé significance tests (Scheffé 1970). The Tukey method can be improved by a multiple range test using significance levels described by Tukey (1953) and sometimes referred to as Tukey-Welsch-Ryan levels (see also Einot & Gabriel 1975, Lehmann & Shaffer 1979). Begun & Gabriel (1981) describe an improved but more complex multiple range procedure based on a suggestion by E Peritz [unpublished manuscript (1970)] using closure principles, and denoted the Peritz-Begun-Gabriel method by Grechanovsky (1993). Welsch (1977) and Dunnett & Tamhane (1992) proposed step-up methods (looking first at adjacent differences) as opposed to the step-down methods in the multiple range procedures just described. The step-up methods have some desirable properties (see Ramsey 1981, Dunnett & Tamhane 1992, Keselman & Lix 1994) but require heavy computation or special tables for application. The Dunnett test can be treated in a sequentially-rejective fashion, where at stage j the smaller value $d_{m-j,\ T-m;\ \alpha}$ can be substituted for $d_{m-1,\ T-m;\ \alpha}$.

Because the hypotheses in a closed set may each be tested at level α by a variety of procedures, there are many other possible multistage procedures. For example, results of Ramsey (1978), Shaffer (1981), and Kunert (1990) suggest that for most configurations of means, a multiple F-test multistage procedure is more powerful than the multiple range procedures described above for testing pairwise differences, although the opposite is true with single-stage procedures. Other approaches to comparing means based on ranges have been investigated by Braun & Tukey (1983), Finner (1988), and Royen (1989, 1990).

The Scheffé method and its multistage version are easy to apply when sample sizes are unequal; simply substitute N_i for N in the Scheffé formula given above, where N_i is the number of observations for treatment i. Exact solutions for the Tukey and Dunnett procedures are possible in principle but involve evaluation of multidimensional integrals. More practical approximate methods are based on replacing MSW/N, which is half the estimated variance of $\bar{y}_i - \bar{y}_j$ in the equal-sample-size case, with $(1/2)$ MSW $(1/N_i + 1/N_j)$, which is half its estimated variance in the unequal-sample-size case. The common value MSW/N is thus replaced by a different value for each pair of subscripts i and j. The Tukey-Kramer method (Tukey 1953, Kramer 1956) uses the single-stage Tukey studentized range procedure with these half-variance estimates substituted for MSW/N. Kramer (1956) proposed a similar multistage method; a preferred, somewhat less conservative method proposed by Duncan (1957) modifies the Tukey multiple range method to allow for the fact that a small difference may be more significant than a large difference if it is based on larger sample sizes. Hochberg & Tamhane (1987) discuss the implementation of the Duncan modification and show that it is conservative in the unbalanced one-way layout. For modifications of the Dunnett procedure for unequal sample sizes, see Hochberg & Tamhane (1987).

The methods must be modified when it cannot be assumed that within-treatment variances are equal. If variance heterogeneity is suspected, it is important to use a separate variance estimate for each sample mean difference or other contrast. The multiple comparison procedure should be based on the set of values of each mean difference or contrast divided by the square root of its estimated variance. The distribution of each can be approximated by a t distribution with estimated degrees of freedom (Welch 1938, Satterthwaite 1946). Tamhane (1979) and Dunnett (1980) compared a number of single-stage procedures based on these approximate t statistics; several of the procedures provided satisfactory error control.

In one-way repeated measures designs (one factor within-subjects or subjects-by-treatments designs), the standard mixed model assumes sphericity of the treatment covariance matrix, equivalent to the assumption of equality of the variance of each difference between sample treatment means. Standard models for between-subjects-within-subjects designs have the added assumption of equality of the covariance matrices among the levels of the between-subjects factor(s). Keselman et al (1991b) give a detailed account of the calculation of appropriate test statistics when both these assumptions are violated and show in a simulation study that simple multiple comparison procedures based on these statistics have satisfactory properties (see also Keselman & Lix 1994).

OTHER ISSUES

Tests vs Confidence Intervals

The simple Bonferroni and the basic Scheffé, Tukey, and Dunnett methods described above are single-stage methods, and all have associated simultaneous confidence interval interpretations. When a confidence interval for a difference does not include zero, the hypothesis that the difference is zero is rejected, but the confidence interval gives more information by indicating the direction and something about the magnitude of the difference or, if the hypothesis is not rejected, the power of the procedure can be gauged by the width of the interval. In contrast, the multistage or stepwise procedures have no such straightforward confidence-interval interpretations, but more complicated intervals can sometimes be constructed. The first confidence-interval interpretation of a multistage procedure was given by Kim et al (1988), and Hayter & Hsu (1994) have described a general method for obtaining these intervals. The intervals are complicated in structure, and more assumptions are required for them to be valid than for conventional confidence intervals. Furthermore, although as a testing method a multistage procedure might be uniformly more powerful than a single-stage procedure, the confidence intervals corresponding to the former are sometimes less informative than those corresponding to the latter. Nonetheless, these are interesting results, and more along this line are to be expected.

Directional vs Nondirectional Inference

In the examples discussed above, most attention has been focused on simple contrasts, testing hypotheses $H_0:\delta_{ij} = 0$ vs $H_A:\delta_{ij} \neq 0$. However, in most cases, if H_0 is rejected, it is crucial to conclude either $\mu_i > \mu_j$ or $\mu_i < \mu_j$. Different types of testing problems arise when direction of difference is considered: 1. Sometimes the interest is in testing one-sided hypotheses of the form $\mu_i \leq \mu_j$ vs $\mu_i > \mu_j$, e.g. if a new treatment is being tested to see whether it is better than a standard treatment, and there is no interest in pursuing the matter further if it is inferior. 2. In a two-sided hypothesis test, as formulated above, rejection of the hypothesis is equivalent to the decision $\mu_i \neq \mu_j$. Is it appropriate to further conclude $\mu_i > \mu_j$ if $\overline{y}_i > \overline{y}_j$ and the opposite otherwise? 3. Sometimes there is an a priori ordering assumption $\mu_1 \leq \mu_2 \leq \ldots \leq \mu_m$, or some subset of these means are considered ordered, and the interest is in deciding whether some of these inequalities are strict.

Each of these situations is different, and different considerations arise. An important issue in connection with the second and third problems mentioned above is whether it makes sense to even consider the possibility that the means under two different experimental conditions are equal. Some writers contend that a priori no difference is ever zero (for a recent defense of this position, see Tukey 1991, 1993). Others, including this author, believe that it is not necessary to assume that every variation in conditions must have an effect. In any case, even if one believes that a mean difference of zero is impossible, an intervention can have an effect so minute that it is essentially undetectable and unimportant, in which case the null hypothesis is reasonable as a practical way of framing the question. Whatever the views on this issue, the hypotheses in the second case described above are not correctly specified if directional decisions are desired. One must consider, in addition to Type I and Type II errors, the probably more severe error of concluding a difference exists but making the wrong choice of direction. This has sometimes been called a Type III error and may be the most important or even the only concern in the second testing situation.

For methods with corresponding simultaneous confidence intervals, inspection of the intervals yields a directional answer immediately. For many multistage methods, the situation is less clear. Shaffer (1980) showed that an additional decision on direction in the second testing situation does not control the FWE of Type III for all test statistic distributions. Hochberg & Tamhane (1987) describe these results and others found by S Holm [unpublished manuscript (1979)] (for newer results, see Finner 1990). Other less powerful methods with guaranteed Type I and/or Type III FWE control have been developed by Spjøtvoll (1972), Holm [1979; improved and extended by Bauer et al (1986)], Bohrer (1979), Bofinger (1985), and Hochberg (1987).

Some writers have considered methods for testing one-sided hypotheses of the third type discussed above (e.g. Marcus et al 1976, Spjøtvoll 1977, Berenson 1982). Budde & Bauer (1989) compare a number of such procedures both theoretically and via simulation.

In another type of one-sided situation, Hsu (1981,1984) introduced a method that can be used to test the set of primary hypotheses of the form $H_i : \mu_i$ is the largest mean. The tests are closely related to a one-sided version of the Dunnett method described above. They also relate the multiple testing literature to the ranking and selection literature.

Robustness

This is a necessarily brief look at robustness of methods based on the homogeneity of variance and normality assumptions of standard analysis of variance. Chapter 10 of Scheffé (1959) is a good source for basic theoretical results concerning these violations.

As Tukey (1993) has pointed out, an amount of variance heterogeneity that affects an overall F test only slightly becomes a more serious concern when multiple comparison methods are used, because the variance of a particular comparison may be badly biased by use of a common estimated value. Hochberg & Tamhane (1987) discuss the effects of variance heterogeneity on the error properties of tests based on the assumption of homogeneity.

With respect to nonnormality, asymptotic theory ensures that with sufficiently large samples, results on Type I error and power in comparisons of means based on normally distributed observations are approximately valid under a wide variety of nonnormal distributions. (Results assuming normally distributed observations often are not even approximately valid under nonnormality, however, for inference on variances, covariances, and correlations.) This leaves the question of How large is large? In addition, alternative methods are more powerful than normal theory-based methods under many nonnormal distributions. Hochberg & Tamhane (1987, Chap. 9) discuss distribution-free and robust procedures and give references to many studies of the robustness of normal theory-based methods and of possible alternative methods for multiple comparisons. In addition, Westfall & Young (1993) give detailed guidance for using robust resampling methods to obtain appropriate error control.

Others

FREQUENTIST METHODS, BAYESIAN METHODS, AND META-ANALYSIS   Frequentist methods control error without any assumptions about possible alternative values of parameters except for those that may be implied logically. Meta-analysis in its simplest form assumes that all hypotheses refer to the same parameter and it combines results into a single statement. Bayes and Empirical Bayes procedures are intermediate in that they assume some connection among parameters and base error control on that assumption. A major contributor to the Bayesian methods is Duncan (see e.g. Duncan 1961, 1965; Duncan & Dixon 1983). Hochberg & Tamhane (1987) describe Bayesian approaches (see also Berry 1988). Westfall & Young (1993) discuss the relations among these three approaches.

DECISION-THEORETIC OPTIMALITY   Lehmann (1957a,b), Bohrer (1979), and Spjøtvoll (1972) defined optimal multiple comparison methods based on frequentist decision-theoretic principles, and Duncan (1961, 1965) and coworkers developed optimal procedures from the Bayesian decision-theoretic point of view. Hochberg & Tamhane (1987) discuss these and other results.

RANKING AND SELECTION   The methods of Dunnett (1955) and Hsu (1981, 1984), discussed above, form a bridge between the selection and multiple testing literature, and are discussed in relation to that literature in Hochberg & Tamhane (1987). Bechhofer et al (1989) describe another method that incorporates aspects of both approaches.

GRAPHS AND DIAGRAMS   As with all statistical results, the results of multiple comparison procedures are often most clearly and comprehensively conveyed through graphs and diagrams, especially when a large number of tests is involved. Hochberg & Tamhane (1987) discuss a number of procedures. Duncan (1955) includes several illuminating geometric diagrams of acceptance regions, as do Tukey (1953) and Bohrer & Schervish (1980). Tukey (1953, 1991) gives a number of graphical methods for describing differences among means (see also Hochberg et al 1982, Gabriel & Gheva 1982, Hsu & Peruggia 1994). Tukey (1993) suggests graphical methods for displaying interactions. Schweder & Spjøtvoll (1982) illustrate a graphical method for plotting large numbers of ordered p-values that can be used to help decide on the number of true hypotheses; this approach is used by Y Benjamini & Y Hochberg (manuscript submitted for publication) to develop a more powerful FDR-controlling method. See Hochberg & Tamhane (1987) for further references.

HIGHER-ORDER BONFERRONI AND OTHER INEQUALITIES   One way to use partial knowledge of joint distributions is to consider higher-order Bonferroni inequalities in testing some of the intersection hypotheses, thus potentially increasing the power of FWE-controlling multiple comparison methods. The Bonferroni inequalities are derived from a general expression for the probability of the union of a number of events. The simple Bonferroni methods using individual p-values are based on the upper bound given by the first-order inequality. Second-order approximations use joint distributions of pairs of test statistics, third-order approximations use joint distributions of triples of test statistics, etc, thus forming a bridge between methods requiring only univariate distributions and those requiring the full multivariate distribution (see Hochberg & Tamhane 1987 for further references to methods based on second-order approximations; see also Bauer & Hackl 1985). Hoover (1990) gives results using third-order or higher approximations, and Glaz (1993) includes an extensive discussion of these inequalities (see also Naiman & Wynn 1992, Hoppe 1993a, Seneta 1993). Some approaches are based on the distribution of combinations of p-values (see Cameron & Eagleson 1985, Buckley & Eagleson 1986, Maurer & Mellein 1988, Rom & Connell 1994). Other types of inequalities are also useful in obtaining improved approximate methods (see Hochberg & Tamhane 1987, Appendix 2).

WEIGHTS   In the description of the simple Bonferroni method it was noted that each hypothesis H_i can be tested at any level α_i with the FWE controlled at $\alpha = \Sigma \alpha_i$. In most applications, the α_i are equal, but there may be reasons to prefer unequal allocation of error protection. For methods controlling FWE, see Holm (1979), Rosenthal & Rubin (1983), DeCani (1984), and Hochberg & Liberman (1994). Y Benjamini & Y Hochberg (manuscript submitted for publication) extend the FDR method to allow for unequal weights and discuss various purposes for differential weighting and alternative methods of achieving it.

OTHER AREAS OF APPLICATION   Hypotheses specifying values of linear combinations of independent normal means other than contrasts can be tested jointly using the distribution of either the maximum modulus or the augmented range (for details, see Scheffé 1959). Hochberg & Tamhane (1987) discuss methods in analysis of covariance, methods for categorical data, methods for comparing variances, and experimental design issues in various areas. Cameron & Eagleson (1985) and Buckley & Eagleson (1986) consider multiple tests for significance of correlations. Gabriel (1968) and Morrison (1990) deal with methods for multivariate multiple comparisons. Westfall & Young (1993, Chap. 4) discuss resampling methods in a variety of situations. The large literature on model selection in regression includes many papers focusing on the multiple testing aspects of this area.

CONCLUSION

The field of multiple hypothesis testing is too broad to be covered entirely in a review of this length; apologies are due to many researchers whose contributions have not been acknowledged. The problem of multiplicity is gaining increasing recognition, and research in the area is proliferating. The major challenge is to devise methods that incorporate some kind of overall control of Type I error while retaining reasonable power for tests of the individual hypotheses. This review, while sketching a number of issues and approaches, has emphasized recent research on relatively simple and general multistage testing methods that are providing progress in this direction.

ACKNOWLEDGMENTS

Research supported in part through the National Institute of Statistical Sciences by NSF Grant RED-9350005. Thanks to Yosef Hochberg, Lyle V. Jones, Erich L. Lehmann, Barbara A. Mellers, Seth D. Roberts, and Valerie S. L. Williams for helpful comments and suggestions.

Literature Cited

Ahmed SW. 1991. Issues arising in the application of Bonferroni procedures in federal surveys. *1991 ASA Proc. Surv. Res. Methods Sect.,* pp. 344–49

Bauer P, Hackl P. 1985. The application of Hunter's inequality to simultaneous testing. *Biometr. J.* 27:25–38

Bauer P, Hackl P, Hommel G, Sonnemann E. 1986. Multiple testing of pairs of one-sided hypotheses. *Metrika* 33:121–27

Bauer P, Hommel G, Sonnemann E, eds. 1988. *Multiple Hypothesenprüfung. (Multiple Hypotheses Testing.)* Berlin: Springer-Verlag (In German and English)

Bechhofer RE. 1952. The probability of a correct ranking. *Ann. Math. Stat.* 23:139–40

Bechhofer RE, Dunnett CW, Tamhane AC. 1989. Two-stage procedures for comparing treatments with a control: elimination at the first stage and estimation at the second stage. *Biometr. J.* 31:545–61

Begun J, Gabriel KR. 1981. Closure of the Newman-Keuls multiple comparison procedure. *J. Am. Stat. Assoc.* 76:241–45

Benjamini Y, Hochberg Y. 1994. Controlling the false discovery rate: a practical and powerful approach to multiple testing. *J. R. Stat. Soc. Ser. B.* In press

Berenson ML. 1982. A comparison of several k sample tests for ordered alternatives in completely randomized designs. *Psychometrika* 47:265–80 (Corr. 535–39)

Berry DA. 1988. Multiple comparisons, multiple tests, and data dredging: a Bayesian perspective (with discussion). In *Bayesian Statistics,* ed. JM Bernardo, MH DeGroot, DV Lindley, AFM Smith, 3:79–94. London: Oxford Univ. Press

Bofinger E. 1985. Multiple comparisons and Type III errors. *J. Am. Stat. Assoc.* 80:433–37

Bohrer R. 1979. Multiple three-decision rules for parametric signs. *J. Am. Stat. Assoc.* 74:432–37

Bohrer R, Schervish MJ. 1980. An optimal multiple decision rule for signs of parameters. *Proc. Natl. Acad. Sci. USA* 77:52–56

Booth JG. 1994. Review of "Resampling Based Multiple Testing." *J. Am. Stat. Assoc.* 89:354–55

Braun HI, ed. 1994. *The Collected Works of John W. Tukey.* Vol. VIII: *Multiple Comparisons:1948–1983.* New York: Chapman & Hall

Braun HI, Tukey JW. 1983. Multiple comparisons through orderly partitions: the maximum subrange procedure. In *Principals of Modern Psychological Measurement: A Festschrift for Frederic M. Lord,* ed. H Wainer, S Messick, pp. 55–65. Hillsdale, NJ: Erlbaum

Buckley MJ, Eagleson GK. 1986. Assessing large sets of rank correlations. *Biometrika* 73:151–57

Budde M, Bauer P. 1989. Multiple test procedures in clinical dose finding studies. *J. Am. Stat. Assoc.* 84:792–96

Cameron MA, Eagleson GK. 1985. A new procedure for assessing large sets of correlations. *Aust. J. Stat.* 27:84–95

Chaubey YP. 1993. Review of "Resampling Based Multiple Testing." *Technometrics* 35:450–51

Conforti M, Hochberg Y. 1987. Sequentially rejective pairwise testing procedures. *J. Stat. Plan. Infer.* 17:193–208

Cournot AA. 1843. *Exposition de la Théorie des Chances et des Probabilités.* Paris: Hachette. Reprinted 1984 as Vol. 1 of Cournot's *Oeuvres Complètes,* ed. B Bru. Paris: Vrin

DeCani JS. 1984. Balancing Type I risk and loss of power in ordered Bonferroni procedures. *J. Educ. Psychol.* 76:1035–37

Diaconis P. 1985. Theories of data analysis: from magical thinking through classical statistics. In *Exploring Data Tables, Trends, and Shapes,* ed. DC Hoaglin, F Mosteller, JW Tukey, pp.1–36. New York: Wiley

Duncan DB. 1951. A significance test for differences between ranked treatments in an analysis of variance. *Va. J. Sci.* 2:172–89

Duncan DB. 1955. Multiple range and multiple F tests. *Biometrics* 11:1–42

Duncan DB. 1957. Multiple range tests for correlated and heteroscedastic means. *Biometrics* 13:164–76

Duncan DB. 1961. Bayes rules for a common multiple comparisons problem and related Student-t problems. *Ann. Math. Stat.* 32:1013–33

Duncan DB. 1965. A Bayesian approach to multiple comparisons. *Technometrics* 7:171–222

Duncan DB, Dixon DO. 1983. k-ratio t tests, t intervals, and point estimates for multiple comparisons. In *Encyclopedia of Statistical Sciences,* ed. S Kotz, NL Johnson, 4: 403–10. New York: Wiley

Dunnett CW. 1955. A multiple comparison procedure for comparing several treatments with a control. *J. Am. Stat. Assoc.* 50:1096–1121

Dunnett CW. 1980. Pairwise multiple comparisons in the unequal variance case. *J. Am. Stat. Assoc.* 75:796–800

Dunnett CW, Tamhane AC. 1992. A step-up multiple test procedure. *J. Am. Stat. Assoc.* 87:162–70

Einot I, Gabriel KR. 1975. A study of the powers of several methods in multiple comparisons. *J. Am. Stat. Assoc.* 70:574–83

Finner H. 1988. Abgeschlossene Spannweitentests (Closed multiple range tests). See Bauer et al 1988, pp. 10–32 (In German)

Finner H. 1990. On the modified S-method and directional errors. *Commun. Stat. Part A: Theory Methods* 19:41–53

Fligner MA. 1984. A note on two-sided distribution-free treatment versus control multiple comparisons. *J. Am. Stat. Assoc.* 79:208–11

Gabriel KR. 1968. Simultaneous test procedures in multivariate analysis of variance. *Biometrika* 55:489–504

Gabriel KR. 1969. Simultaneous test procedures—some theory of multiple comparisons. *Ann. Math. Stat.* 40:224–50

Gabriel KR. 1978. Comment on the paper by Ramsey. *J. Am. Stat. Assoc.* 73:485–87

Gabriel KR, Gheva D. 1982. Some new simultaneous confidence intervals in MANOVA and their geometric representation and graphical display. In *Experimental Design, Statistical Models, and Genetic Statistics,* ed. K Hinkelmann, pp. 239–75. New York: Dekker

Gaffan EA. 1992. Review of "Multiple Comparisons for Researchers." *Br. J. Math. Stat. Psychol.* 45:334–35

Glaz J. 1993. Approximate simultaneous confidence intervals. See Hoppe 1993b, pp. 149–66

Grechanovsky E. 1993. *Comparing stepdown multiple comparison procedures.* Presented at Annu. Jt. Stat. Meet., 153rd, San Francisco

Harter HL. 1980. Early history of multiple comparison tests. In *Handbook of Statis-*

582 SHAFFER

tics, ed. PR Krishnaiah, 1:617–22. Amsterdam: North-Holland

Hartley HO. 1955. Some recent developments in analysis of variance. *Commun. Pure Appl. Math.* 8:47–72

Hayter AJ, Hsu JC. 1994. On the relationship between stepwise decision procedures and confidence sets. *J. Am. Stat. Assoc.* 89: 128–36

Hochberg Y. 1987. Multiple classification rules for signs of parameters. *J. Stat. Plan. Infer.* 15:177–88

Hochberg Y. 1988. A sharper Bonferroni procedure for multiple tests of significance. *Biometrika* 75:800–3

Hochberg Y, Liberman U. 1994. An extended Simes test. *Stat. Prob. Lett.* In press

Hochberg Y, Rom D. 1994. Extensions of multiple testing procedures based on Simes' test. *J. Stat. Plan. Infer.* In press

Hochberg Y, Tamhane AC. 1987. *Multiple Comparison Procedures.* New York: Wiley

Hochberg Y, Weiss G, Hart S. 1982. On graphical procedures for multiple comparisons. *J. Am. Stat. Assoc.* 77:767–72

Holland B. 1991. On the application of three modified Bonferroni procedures to pairwise multiple comparisons in balanced repeated measures designs. *Comput. Stat. Q.* 6:219–31. (Corr. 7:223)

Holland BS, Copenhaver MD. 1987. An improved sequentially rejective Bonferroni test procedure. *Biometrics* 43:417–23. (Corr:43:737)

Holland BS, Copenhaver MD. 1988. Improved Bonferroni-type multiple testing procedures. *Psychol. Bull.* 104:145–49

Holm S. 1979. A simple sequentially rejective multiple test procedure. *Scand. J. Stat.* 6: 65–70

Holm S. 1990. Review of "Multiple Hypothesis Testing." *Metrika* 37:206

Hommel G. 1986. Multiple test procedures for arbitrary dependence structures. *Metrika* 33:321–36

Hommel G. 1988. A stagewise rejective multiple test procedure based on a modified Bonferroni test. *Biometrika* 75:383–86

Hommel G. 1989. A comparison of two modified Bonferroni procedures. *Biometrika* 76: 624–25

Hoover DR. 1990. Subset complement addition upper bounds—an improved inclusion-exclusion method. *J. Stat. Plan. Infer.* 24:195–202

Hoppe FM. 1993a. Beyond inclusion-and-exclusion: natural identities for P[exactly t events] and P[at least t events] and resulting inequalities. *Int. Stat. Rev.* 61:435–46

Hoppe FM, ed. 1993b. *Multiple Comparisons, Selection, and Applications in Biometry.* New York: Dekker

Hsu JC. 1981. Simultaneous confidence intervals for all distances from the 'best'. *Ann. Stat.* 9:1026–34

Hsu JC. 1984. Constrained simultaneous confidence intervals for multiple comparisons with the best. *Ann. Stat.* 12:1136–44

Hsu JC. 1996. *Multiple Comparisons: Theory and Methods.* New York: Chapman & Hall. In press

Hsu JC, Peruggia M. 1994. Graphical representations of Tukey's multiple comparison method. *J. Comput. Graph. Stat.* 3:143–61

Keselman HJ, Keselman JC, Games PA. 1991a. Maximum familywise Type I error rate: the least significant difference, Newman-Keuls, and other multiple comparison procedures. *Psychol. Bull.* 110:155–61

Keselman HJ, Keselman JC, Shaffer JP. 1991b. Multiple pairwise comparisons of repeated measures means under violation of multisample sphericity. *Psychol. Bull.* 110:162–70

Keselman HJ, Lix LM. 1994. Improved repeated-measures stepwise multiple comparison procedures. *J. Educ. Stat.* In press

Kim WC, Stefansson G, Hsu JC. 1988. On confidence sets in multiple comparisons. In *Statistical Decision Theory and Related Topics IV,* ed. SS Gupta, JO Berger, 2:89–104. New York: Academic

Klockars AJ, Hancock GR. 1992. Power of recent multiple comparison procedures as applied to a complete set of planned orthogonal contrasts. *Psychol. Bull.* 111:505–10

Klockars AJ, Sax G. 1986. *Multiple Comparisons.* Newbury Park, CA: Sage

Kramer CY. 1956. Extension of multiple range tests to group means with unequal numbers of replications. *Biometrics* 12:307–10

Kunert J. 1990. On the power of tests for multiple comparison of three normal means. *J. Am. Stat. Assoc.* 85:808–12

Läuter J. 1990. Review of "Multiple Hypotheses Testing." *Comput. Stat. Q.* 5:333

Lehmann EL. 1957a. A theory of some multiple decision problems. I. *Ann. Math. Stat.* 28:1–25

Lehmann EL. 1957b. A theory of some multiple decision problems. II. *Ann. Math. Stat.* 28:547–72

Lehmann EL, Shaffer JP. 1979. Optimum significance levels for multistage comparison procedures. *Ann. Stat.* 7:27–45

Levin JR, Serlin RC, Seaman MA. 1994. A controlled, powerful multiple-comparison strategy for several situations. *Psychol. Bull.* 115:153–59

Littell RC. 1989. Review of "Multiple Comparison Procedures." *Technometrics* 31: 261–62

Marcus R, Peritz E, Gabriel KR. 1976. On closed testing procedures with special reference to ordered analysis of variance. *Biometrika* 63:655–60

Maurer W, Mellein B. 1988. On new multiple

tests based on independent p-values and the assessment of their power. See Bauer et al 1988, pp. 48–66

Miller RG. 1966. *Simultaneous Statistical Inference.* New York: Wiley

Miller RG. 1977. Developments in multiple comparisons 1966–1976. *J. Am. Stat. Assoc.* 72:779–88

Miller RG. 1981. *Simultaneous Statistical Inference.* New York: Wiley. 2nd ed.

Morrison DF. 1990. *Multivariate Statistical Methods.* New York: McGraw-Hill. 3rd ed.

Mosteller F. 1948. A k-sample slippage test for an extreme population. *Ann. Math. Stat.* 19:58–65

Naiman DQ, Wynn HP. 1992. Inclusion-exclusion-Bonferroni identities and inequalities for discrete tube-like problems via Euler characteristics. *Ann. Stat.* 20:43–76

Nair KR. 1948. Distribution of the extreme deviate from the sample mean. *Biometrika* 35:118–44

Nowak R. 1994. Problems in clinical trials go far beyond misconduct. *Science* 264:1538–41

Paulson E. 1949. A multiple decision procedure for certain problems in the analysis of variance. *Ann. Math. Stat.* 20:95–98

Peritz E. 1989. Review of "Multiple Comparison Procedures." *J. Educ. Stat.* 14:103–6

Ramsey PH. 1978. Power differences between pairwise multiple comparisons. *J. Am. Stat. Assoc.* 73:479–85

Ramsey PH. 1981. Power of univariate pairwise multiple comparison procedures. *Psychol. Bull.* 90:352–66

Rasmussen JL. 1993. Algorithm for Shaffer's multiple comparison tests. *Educ. Psychol. Meas.* 53:329–35

Richmond J. 1982. A general method for constructing simultaneous confidence intervals. *J. Am. Stat. Assoc.* 77:455–60

Rom DM. 1990. A sequentially rejective test procedure based on a modified Bonferroni inequality. *Biometrika* 77:663–65

Rom DM, Connell L. 1994. A generalized family of multiple test procedures. *Commun. Stat. Part A: Theory Methods, 23.* In press

Rom DM, Holland B. 1994. A new closed multiple testing procedure for hierarchical families of hypotheses. *J. Stat. Plan. Infer.* In press

Rosenthal R, Rubin DB. 1983. Ensemble-adjusted p values. *Psychol. Bull.* 94:540–41

Roy SN, Bose RC. 1953. Simultaneous confidence interval estimation. *Ann. Math. Stat.* 24:513–36

Royen T. 1989. Generalized maximum range tests for pairwise comparisons of several populations. *Biometr. J.* 31:905–29

Royen T. 1990. A probability inequality for ranges and its application to maximum range test procedures. *Metrika* 37:145–54

Ryan TA. 1959. Multiple comparisons in psychological research. *Psychol. Bull.* 56:26–47

Ryan TA. 1960. Significance tests for multiple comparison of proportions, variances, and other statistics. *Psychol. Bull.* 57:318–28

Satterthwaite FE. 1946. An approximate distribution of estimates of variance components. *Biometrics* 2:110–14

Scheffé H. 1953. A method for judging all contrasts in the analysis of variance. *Biometrika* 40:87–104

Scheffé H. 1959. *The Analysis of Variance.* New York: Wiley

Scheffé H. 1970. Multiple testing versus multiple estimation. Improper confidence sets. Estimation of directions and ratios. *Ann. Math. Stat.* 41:1–19

Schweder T, Spjøtvoll E. 1982. Plots of P-values to evaluate many tests simultaneously. *Biometrika* 69:493–502

Seeger P. 1968. A note on a method for the analysis of significances en masse. *Technometrics* 10:586–93

Seneta E. 1993. Probability inequalities and Dunnett's test. See Hoppe 1993b, pp. 29–45

Shafer G, Olkin I. 1983. Adjusting p values to account for selection over dichotomies. *J. Am. Stat. Assoc.* 78:674–78

Shaffer JP. 1977. Multiple comparisons emphasizing selected contrasts: an extension and generalization of Dunnett's procedure. *Biometrics* 33:293–303

Shaffer JP. 1980. Control of directional errors with stagewise multiple test procedures. *Ann. Stat.* 8:1342–48

Shaffer JP. 1981. Complexity: an interpretability criterion for multiple comparisons. *J. Am. Stat. Assoc.* 76:395–401

Shaffer JP. 1986. Modified sequentially rejective multiple test procedures. *J. Am. Stat. Assoc.* 81:826–31

Shaffer JP. 1988. Simultaneous testing. In *Encyclopedia of Statistical Sciences,* ed. S Kotz, NL Johnson, 8:484–90. New York: Wiley

Shaffer JP. 1991. Probability of directional errors with disordinal (qualitative) interaction. *Psychometrika* 56:29–38

Simes RJ. 1986. An improved Bonferroni procedure for multiple tests of significance. *Biometrika* 73:751–54

Sorić B. 1989. Statistical "discoveries" and effect-size estimation. *J. Am. Stat. Assoc.* 84:608–10

Spjøtvoll E. 1972. On the optimality of some multiple comparison procedures. *Ann. Math. Stat.* 43:398–411

Spjøtvoll E. 1977. Ordering ordered parameters. *Biometrika* 64:327–34

Stigler SM. 1986. *The History of Statistics.* Cambridge: Harvard Univ. Press

Tamhane AC. 1979. A comparison of procedures for multiple comparisons of means with unequal variances. *J. Am. Stat. Assoc.* 74:471–80

Tatsuoka MM. 1992. Review of "Multiple Comparisons for Researchers." *Contemp. Psychol.* 37:775–76

Toothaker LE. 1991. *Multiple Comparisons for Researchers.* Newbury Park, CA: Sage

Toothaker LE. 1993. *Multiple Comparison Procedures.* Newbury Park, CA: Sage

Tukey JW. 1949. Comparing individual means in the analysis of variance. *Biometrics* 5: 99–114

Tukey JW. 1952. Reminder sheets for "Multiple Comparisons." See Braun 1994, pp. 341–45

Tukey JW. 1953. The problem of multiple comparisons. See Braun 1994, pp. 1–300

Tukey JW. 1991. The philsophy of multiple comparisons. *Stat. Sci.* 6:100–16

Tukey JW. 1993. Where should multiple comparisons go next? See Hoppe 1993b, pp. 187–207

Welch BL. 1938. The significance of the difference between two means when the population variances are unequal. *Biometrika* 25:350–62

Welsch RE. 1977. Stepwise multiple comparison procedures. *J. Am. Stat. Assoc.* 72: 566–75

Westfall PH, Young SS. 1993. *Resampling-based Multiple Testing.* New York: Wiley

Wright SP. 1992. Adjusted p-values for simultaneous inference. *Biometrics* 48:1005–13

Ziegel ER. 1994. Review of "Multiple Comparisons, Selection, and Applications in Biometry." *Technometrics* 36:230–31

Annu. Rev. Psychol. 1995. 46:585–624
Copyright © 1995 by Annual Reviews Inc. All rights reserved

WHAT WE CAN LEARN FROM INVERTEBRATE LEARNING

Franklin B. Krasne

Department of Psychology and Brain Research Institute, University of California, Los Angeles, California 90024

David L. Glanzman

Department of Physiological Science and Brain Research Institute, University of California, Los Angeles, California 90024

KEY WORDS: synaptic plasticity, conditioning, long-term potentiation, cellular mechanisms, physiological mechanisms

CONTENTS

INTRODUCTION

Interest in the learning abilities of lower animals dates back to Romanes (1895), who argued that ability to learn provides an operational definition of mind. However, about 30 years ago a special interest in invertebrate learning was kindled in a search for learning phenomena that might yield to physiological analysis. Progress was rapid and striking, and instances of habituation, sensitization, and classical conditioning began to be analyzed in terms of cellular mechanism. However, soon after the first important invertebrate studies appeared, synapses of the mammalian hippocampus that were subject to one kind of long-term potentiation (LTP; recent reviews in Hawkins et al 1993, Bliss & Collingridge 1993) were found to have the features that Hebb (1949) had speculated might underlie associative learning. Attempts to circumscribe parts of the mammalian brain involved in learning were also increasingly successful, and some of the regions identified were found to contain synapses subject to LTP (see Carlson 1994). An explosion of interest in mammalian LTP has resulted.

Nevertheless, the exact relationship between findings at the cellular level and the behavioral phenomenon of learning remain complex and obscure in mammals. With invertebrate preparations, however, relationships between cellular and behavioral phenomena are much more readily clarified. Also, as rapid as progress has been in understanding mammalian LTP, the cellular understanding of certain forms of invertebrate plasticity is significantly more advanced.

WHAT INVERTEBRATES LEARN

Simple decreases of the innate response to a stimulus with repetition (habituation) or increases as a result of repetition or strong stimulation (types of sensitization) occur in all invertebrates, even the protozoa (e.g. Jennings 1906), and associative learning, at least in particular contexts and situations, is well developed in cephalopod molluscs and in many arthropods (see Corning et al 1973). Such learning can be robust, play significant roles in the lives of the animals, and last a very long time. Thus, a bee's recollection of the color or location of a flower from which it received nectar can last a lifetime (Menzel 1990); and from a single inspection flight lasting only a few minutes, a digger wasp can memorize the locations and amounts of food needed to provision some 15 burrows containing developing young (Baerends 1941 as cited in Gould 1982).

Though the nervous systems of invertebrates that can learn have many fewer neurons than do typical vertebrate species in which learning is studied, their nervous systems are far from simple and, like ours, are ill understood.

The physiologist requires specific behavior patterns that are produced by neural circuitry simple enough to understand, but that are also subject to modification by experience. The relative ease of elucidating neural circuits of behavior in invertebrates follows perhaps less from their simplicity than from their nonredundant use of neurons. Processing tasks that in vertebrates appear to involve massive numbers of neurons of rather similar function operating in parallel are carried out in invertebrates by circuitry in which each individual neuron has a relatively unique role. Once these unique neurons are found and characterized, the same identified neuron can be studied from one animal to another, greatly facilitating the task of functional analysis. It is unknown whether this difference between vertebrate and invertebrate nervous systems leads to different processing strategies.

Physiologically Analyzed Learning Paradigms

MODIFICATION OF *APLYSIA* DEFENSIVE WITHDRAWAL REFLEXES If a sea hare (*Aplysia*) is stimulated at appropriate bodily locations, it protectively withdraws its gill, respiratory siphon, and/or tail. A siphon-gill withdrawal reflex of the abdominal ganglion mediates withdrawal of the siphon and gill in response to stimulation of mechanoreceptors on the siphon and part of the mantle shelf (see Kandel 1976), and a tail-siphon reflex of the pleural-pedal and abdominal ganglia mediates withdrawal of the tail and siphon in response to stimulation of tail mechanoreceptors (see Walters et al 1983). These two reflexes appear to have sufficiently similar properties that here we do not usually distinguish them.

Defensive withdrawal to gentle stimulation habituates (i.e. gets weaker and less prolonged) when stimuli are repeated (e.g. 5–10 stimuli at 1 per 3 min) and becomes sensitized following one or a few strong stimulations of various body parts including the head and tail (Pinsker et al 1970). Habituation and sensitization produced by limited training lasts under an hour, but with sufficiently spaced training they persist for weeks (Carew et al 1972, Carew & Kandel 1973, Pinsker et al 1973).

Although strong stimulation sensitizes reflex reactions somewhat to all stimuli, much more profound sensitization occurs for stimuli that are applied just before (ideally 1/2 s) each sensitization-producing stimulus (Carew et al 1981, Carew et al 1983, Hawkins et al 1983, Walters & Byrne 1983). Thus, the reflex can be classically conditioned to particular stimuli. Conditioning also shows some response specificity. The form of reflexive siphon withdrawals is adapted to help direct a defensive ink secretion toward the source of disturbance, and when a rostral conditioned stimulus (CS) is paired with a caudal unconditioned stimulus (UCS), the conditioned response adopts a caudal form (Walters & Erickson 1986, Walters 1989, Hawkins et al 1989). Classical conditioning can last for more than three days (Carew et al 1972), but its duration has not been evaluated fully.

MODIFICATIONS OF LATERAL GIANT ESCAPE IN CRAYFISH   When threatened, crayfish produce all-or-none flexions of their abdomens that thrust them through the water away from the source of disturbance (see Krasne & Wine 1987 for a review). Most studied has been a lateral giant (LG) neuron–mediated response caused by mechanical stimulation of the abdomen. The probability of LG escape diminishes with repeated stimulation. This habituation recovers partially over a period of several hours but accumulates over days with repeated experience (Wine et al 1975, Krasne & Teshiba 1994). Traumatic stimulation also increases the probability of LG escape to its normal stimuli for up to a few hours (sensitization; Krasne & Glanzman 1986), but associative conditioning of the response has not been reported.

CONDITIONED SUPPRESSION OF *HERMISSENDA* PHOTOTAXIS   The marine gastropod *Hermissenda crassicornis* is normally positively phototactic but innately adheres to available surfaces under turbulent conditions. Following repeated simultaneous pairing of vestibular stimulation (produced by rotation but intended to simulate turbulence) and light (e.g. 50 pairings/day for 3 days), but not after asynchronous light and rotation, phototaxis is suppressed for as long as 18 days (Alkon 1974, Harrigan & Alkon 1985). Training reduces responses to contrast differences, slows onset of movement and rate of locomotion, and causes shortening of the foot, which also occurs as part of the unconditioned response to vestibular stimulation (Lederhendler et al 1986, Lederhendler & Alkon 1987); these changes are presumed to be responsible for reduced phototaxis.

CLASSICALLY CONDITIONED RESPONSES TO ODOR IN INSECTS AND SLUGS Classical conditioning persisting for days is reliably produced in bees, fruit flies (*Drosophila*), and the slug, *Limax maximus,* by one or a few pairings of an odorant (the CS) with either positive or negative stimuli. In bees, the odorant is presented just before sugar water, which elicits innate proboscis extension; after conditioning the odorant elicits a similar response (Takeda 1961, Bitterman et al 1983; see Menzel 1990). In *Drosophila* (Tully & Quinn 1985) and *Limax* (Sahley et al 1981a) subjects are exposed simultaneously to the odorant and either shock (*Drosophila*) or a bitter substance (*Limax*). When subsequently given a choice between the CS and a different odor, subjects avoid the CS.

Choice of Paradigms

Most physiological studies have used simple classical conditioning paradigms because it was suspected that the associative bond presumed to form during such conditioning might be due to the strengthening of synaptic connections between neurons whose activity represents the events associated. However, over the past 20 years the discovery of phenomena such as blocking (Kamin 1969) and attenuation of learning by unpredicted UCSs (Rescorla 1967) has made it clear that vertebrate classical conditioning is governed by statistical features of the flow of events more sophisticated than the mere co-occurrence of CSs and UCSs.

Rescorla & Wagner (1972) have argued that most observations can be understood if it is assumed that co-occurrence of a CS and UCS leads to the formation of an association between them only if other CSs present at the same time are not already strongly associated to the UCS. However, Gallistel (1990) has argued forcefully that the full range of phenomena of classical conditioning, as now understood, shows that what an animal learns is not a connection between representations of events but rather the times, locations, and descriptions of significant events, which are then utilized to guide performance at the time of testing. Learning, he argues, is a matter of storing values of variables, not forming connections. Therefore, he reasons, physiologists should utilize learning situations, such as those involving navigation, in which it is apparent that values of variables are being learned.

To what degree do invertebrates in fact show the features of classical conditioning that raise these questions? *Limax* trained to avoid a mixture of carrot and potato odors subsequently avoid potato; but such learning is attenuated if the animals were previously trained to avoid carrot, a clear blocking result (Sahley et al 1981b). Similarly, classical conditioning of *Aplysia* defense responses is attenuated if animals are trained in a context where they were previously shocked (Colwill et al 1988). But conditioning of proboscis extension responses in bees does not seem to be subject to blocking (Menzel 1990, Couvillon et al 1983).

Unpaired UCS presentations appear to attenuate conditioning of defensive withdrawal in *Aplysia* (Hawkins et al 1986), phototactic suppression in *Hermissenda* (Farley et al 1987a,b), and, to a slight extent, proboscis extension in bees (Menzel 1990). However, these effects may have been at least partly due to habituation to additional UCS presentations. Furthermore, the unpaired UCS presentations in *Hermissenda* were only effective in attenuating conditioning if they came immediately after the offset of light and rotation. This specificity, which can be explained by vestibular inhibition of the long-lasting depolarization (a depolarization that follows pairing and is suspected of inducing neural changes; see below) suggests that contingency degradation in *Hermissenda* is not comparable to that in vertebrates.

Thus, although blocking and contingency degradation effects can occur in invertebrates, they are not general and are unlikely to be a consequence of fundamental cellular mechanisms. Hawkins & Kandel (1984) have suggested plausible circuit-based explanations for some invertebrate blocking and contingency degradation results, and several authors have suggested that even in mammals, blocking may depend on specialized circuitry (Fanselow 1986, Thompson 1990).

We know of nothing in the invertebrate literature that would force abandonment, as Gallistel proposes, of the view that conditioning is the result of strengthening of synapses in circuits mediating conditioned responses. Furthermore, it is widely believed that nervous systems code the values of variables by activating populations of neurons from within multidimensional topographic maps having the variable values as axes. Given this, the formation of connections between neurons representing a qualitative event and the neurons representing a value such as the time or location of the event seems a plausible information storage strategy, even for the kinds of learning that Gallistel considers basic.

Phenomena such as associative conditioning of *Aplysia* defensive withdrawal or *Hermissenda* phototactic suppression may work because investigators have capitalized fortuitously on neural attributes that are not necessarily used for learning in the life of the animals and that therefore may not tell us how animals really learn. For example, Walters and colleagues have suggested that apparent classical conditioning in *Aplysia* may be the product of a mechanism that evolved to increase the local sensitivity of skin regions that have been traumatically stimulated (Walters 1987, Woolf & Walters 1991). Thus, it may be only an accident of the way those mechanisms work that allows pairing of a traumatic stimulus in one bodily location with a neutral stimulus in another to increase responses to the neutral stimulus and so meet the formal requirements for classical conditioning. Such arguments are not easy to answer. However, they do not seem to apply to the kinds of learning studied in insects and in *Limax*, which is one reason for pursuing with more vigor physiological analyses in those animals.

LOCI OF FUNCTIONAL CHANGES RESPONSIBLE FOR LEARNING

In invertebrates, where one is commonly dealing with relatively well-defined neural circuits, one seeks specific circuit elements whose functions are altered rather than anatomically defined locations. One can envisage a variety of aspects of neuron function that might change. However, characteristics such as critical firing levels and resting potentials that would be expected to simultaneously affect a neuron's responses to input over many of its many input lines would not allow nearly as large a storage capacity as changes at individual synapses. Therefore, synapses are commonly expected to be the site of functional changes responsible for learning.

Aplysia

As first characterized by Kupfermann & Kandel (1969; see also Kandel 1976) the circuit for defensive withdrawal is monosynaptic; sensory neurons innervating various parts of the body make direct synapses with the motor neurons that produce the response (Figure 1). Early studies of short-term habituation found pronounced depression of transmission at the sensory-motor synapses and detected no significant contribution of either sensory adaptation or neuromuscular fatigue to the decline of the behavioral response (Castellucci et al 1970, Kupfermann et al 1970, Byrne et al 1978). These transmission changes were due to reductions of excitatory postsynaptic potential (EPSP) amplitude, and analysis of the statistical properties of variations in EPSP amplitude due to probabilistic release of transmitter from single synaptic vesicles (quantal analysis) indicated that decreased release from sensory neuron terminals was responsible (Castellucci & Kandel 1974). EPSP depression occurred normally when firing of interneurons was prevented by the use of high divalent cation bathing media to reduce excitability; thus, depression was apparently intrinsic to the sensory neurons rather than being the result of presynaptic inhibitory modulation from outside the basic circuit (Kandel 1976). This conclusion is supported by the observation that short-term depres-

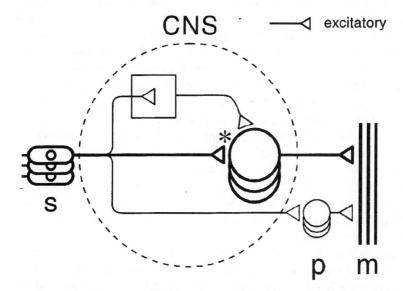

Figure 1 Circuit for *Aplysia* defensive withdrawal. Most fully studied circuitry is in bold; * indicates the most studied site of plasticity. The relevant central nervous system (CNS) circuitry is primarily within abdominal and pedal-pleural ganglia; s = sensory neurons; m = muscles; p = peripheral motor neurons; box = interneuron circuitry.

sion of EPSPs occurs when sensory neurons that have formed synapses on motor neurons in cultures of isolated sensory and motor neurons are stimulated at frequencies similar to those used in behavioral experiments (Montarolo et al 1988, Rayport & Schacher 1986).

Long-term habituation was also found to be associated with decreased monosynaptic transmission (Castellucci et al 1978), but it apparently cannot be established by repetitive activity at cultured sensory-motor synapses and might involve presynaptic inhibition at least during its induction (Montarolo et al 1988; see Initiation of Change section below). Both short- (Kupfermann et al 1970, Castellucci & Kandel 1976) and long-term (Frost et al 1985) sensitization were similarly shown to be due to facilitated transmission at sensory-motor neuron synapses. Quantal analysis showed short-term facilitation to be due to increased transmitter release (Castellucci & Kandel 1976), and broadening of the sensory neuron action potential (see below) provided further evidence of presynaptic change.

Sensitization appears to be induced by facilitatory neurons that release transmitters to the presynaptic terminals of sensory neurons (see below). One of several transmitters used is 5-HT; exogenous 5-HT produces effects similar to those caused by sensitizing stimuli (Brunelli et al 1976) and has been used in many experiments to produce neural changes thought to underlie sensitization. Application of 5-HT to cultured sensory-motor synapses causes facilitation lasting for minutes when applied briefly and lasting at least 24 hr when applied repeatedly or for a longer period, showing that the facilitation of transmission is intrinsic to the sensory-motor synapses (Montarolo et al 1986, Rayport & Schacher 1986). Quantal analysis at cultured synapses has also established that long-term facilitation is due to increased transmitter release, without changes in postsynaptic sensitivity to transmitter (Dale et al 1988).

Classical conditioning procedures produce EPSP and sensory neuron changes similar to those produced during simple facilitation (see below), but they are exaggerated in extent in those sensory neurons that were active just before traumatic stimulation or serotonin application (Hawkins et al 1983, Walters & Byrne 1983, Abrams 1985). Hence, classical conditioning is said to be due to an activity-dependent amplification of facilitation (or activity-dependent facilitation) and is believed to result from the same kinds of changes that occur during sensitization.

Thus, habituation, sensitization, and classical conditioning of *Aplysia* defensive withdrawal are all associated with alterations of transmitter release at the monosynaptic connection between sensory and motor neurons, and the biophysical and molecular biological bases of these alterations, which are discussed below, have been studied intensively. However, these changes appear to be merely the tip of the iceberg.

Sensitizing events also can cause threshold decreases to mechanical stimulation (Walters 1987, Billy & Walters 1989a,b), other sensory neuron changes (Klein et al 1986), motor neuron input impedance increases (Pieroni & Byrne 1992), and persisting increases of spontaneous firing rates, with resulting development of neuromuscular facilitation (Frost et al 1988). More importantly, evidence is accumulating that defensive withdrawal responses are by no means primarily monosynaptic. Eberly & Pinsker (1984) have shown that interneurons that normally produce spontaneous "respiratory pumping" movements of gill and siphon (Byrne 1983) are also responsible for a large fraction of motor output in reflexive responses of freely behaving animals though not of acute preparations. And in acute preparations, suppression of almost all interneuron firing by elevating divalent cation concentration reduces the area under motor neuron EPSPs by more than 75% (Trudeau & Castellucci 1992). Thus, understanding learned changes in defensive withdrawal will require analyzing changes in the polysynaptic as well as monosynaptic pathways (see Figure 1).

Excitation of interneurons that contribute to defensive withdrawal is normally truncated by an immediately following inhibition (Trudeau & Castellucci 1993a, Fischer & Carew 1993), and reduction of this inhibition is substantially responsible for response increases due to sensitizing stimulation (Trudeau & Castellucci 1993a,b). Augmentations of the inhibition during repetitive stimulation may also contribute to habituation (Fischer & Carew 1993), and it has been reported that habituation of the tail-siphon reflex is entirely due to the polysynaptic pathway (Stopfer & Carew 1994).

Some complexities are also introduced by the existence outside the CNS of a neural plexus containing additional motor neurons that under some circumstances contribute to defensive withdrawal (see Pearlman 1979, Lukowiak 1979). In addition, Colwill et al (1988) found that, in freely behaving *Aplysia,* defensive reactions to constant test stimuli are heightened in animals placed in a situation where they were previously shocked. This means that the circuitry that mediates defensive withdrawal is subject to learning-induced external modulation, and it opens the possibility that in freely behaving animals, learning-altered defensive behavior with training is due to altered modulation originating in circuitry outside the defensive reflex pathway itself.

Crayfish

The lateral giant (LG) escape response of the crayfish is named for the bilateral pair of LG command neurons of the circuit that mediates the behavior (Figure 2; see Krasne & Wine 1987). The LGs fire, usually only once, when they receive sufficient summed input from primary afferents and sensory interneurons (monosynaptic input alone is usually subthreshold); the single firing produces a vigorous tail flip. Presumably as an adaptation favoring rapid-

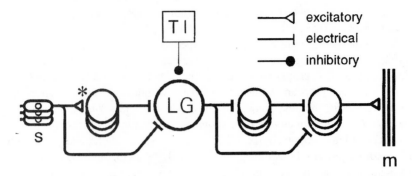

Figure 2 Circuit for crayfish LG escape. Most fully studied circuitry is in bold; * indicates the most studied site of plasticity; s = sensory neurons; m = muscles; TI = tonic inhibitory system.

ity, most of the synapses of the circuit are electrical; only those between sensory neurons and first-order interneurons are purely chemical (cholinergic) (Zucker 1972a, Edwards et al 1991, Miller et al 1992).

Most evidence has pointed to these chemical synapses as the locus of change responsible for habituation because they are depressed, at least partly due to lowered release, by repetitive activation, whereas transmission of other circuit synapses is fairly stable (Krasne 1969, Zucker 1972b, Krasne 1976). However, recent findings (Krasne & Teshiba 1994), though confirming that intrinsic depression makes some contribution to behavioral habituation, appear to have established that in the freely behaving crayfish, cessation of response is mostly due to the onset of activity in a descending tonic inhibitory pathway (Figure 2; Vu et al 1993) that directly innervates the LGs.

Sensitization also has been associated with altered transmission at the chemical sensory neuron synapses (Krasne & Glanzman 1986). Octopamine in crayfish, like serotonin in *Aplysia,* facilitates transmission at these synapses (Glanzman & Krasne 1983), though the relation of this effect to sensitization by traumatic stimulation is speculative. Individual primary afferents appear to make multiple synapses, some strong and some with little effect, on their interneuronal targets; octopamine augments transmission mainly at those synapses that initially were not effective (Bustamante & Krasne 1991). Thus, plasticity could reside in a subset of synaptic contacts specialized for the purpose.

As with the excitatory interneurons for defensive withdrawal in *Aplysia,* the excitation of the LGs is normally truncated by activity of an inhibitory pathway that parallels the excitatory one (Vu et al 1987). However, in crayfish there is no evidence that excitability of escape is altered by changes in this inhibition.

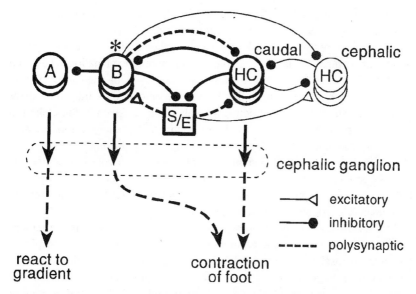

Figure 3 Circuit for *Hermissenda* phototaxis. Most fully studied circuitry is in bold; * indicates the most studied site of plasticity; A = type A and B = type B photoreceptors; HC = vestibular hair cells; S/E = S/E optic ganglion cells (see text).

Hermissenda

Whereas the circuits for *Aplysia* defensive withdrawal and crayfish LG escape span the entire reflex arcs, only the afferent end of the circuit involved in *Hermissenda*'s conditioned suppression response is worked out in detail (Figure 3). The eye possesses two types of photoreceptors, denoted A and B (Alkon 1973). Statocysts, which provide information about bodily displacements and are the sensors of the rotational UCS used in conditioned suppression experiments, also contain two cell types, cephalic and caudal, which are differentiated on the basis of their responses in a centrifugal force field (Farley & Alkon 1980). As explained below, the B photoreceptors and the caudal hair cells (but not the A photoreceptors or cephalic hair cells), along with a class of optic ganglion neurons called the S/E cells, are part of a network of mutually interacting neurons that appear to play a role in detecting the coincidence of visual CSs and vestibular UCSs and thus in determining whether a conditioned response will develop (see below).

Although the charting of the circuitry that stands between the photoreceptors and motor apparatus is incomplete, this preparation has been able to provide a great deal of interesting information, because training produces changes in the B photoreceptors themselves, which show an augmented response to light after CS-UCS pairing but not after various appropriate control procedures (Crow & Alkon 1980, West et al 1982). It seems paradoxical that an increased response to light should decrease phototaxis. A definitive resolution of this conundrum is not available, but a proposed explanation is based on the fact that A photoreceptors, which are suspected of mediating turning toward the light, are inhibited by B photoreceptors; thus they may drive turning less strongly in conditioned animals (Goh & Alkon 1984, Goh et al 1985, Lederhendler & Alkon 1987). In contrast, B photoreceptors are suspected of promoting antagonistic responses that disrupt locomotion (e.g. clinging to the substrate); these responses would increase in conditioned animals (Akaike & Alkon 1980, Lederhendler et al 1986). The inhibitory synapses of type B onto type A photoreceptors may also become strengthened by training (Schuman & Clark 1994, Frysztak & Crow 1994).

Increased responses of photoreceptors of trained animals to light after surgical removal of the synaptic portion of the receptors indicates that the photoreceptors themselves are altered (West et al 1982), but since testing was done soon after removal, it is not certain to what degree these clearly intrinsic changes are self sustaining. Pairing of light and intracellular depolarization of a single type B photoreceptor, which is meant to mimic the effects of paired light and rotation on the cell (see below), causes behavioral phototactic suppression 24 hr later (Farley et al 1983). This observation indicates that the changes in the B photoreceptor contribute significantly to altered behavior, although this treatment may also have caused central nervous system activity leading to changes elsewhere in the system.

Insects

Some of the brain structures thought to be important for olfactory learning in bees are shown in Figure 4. With a few exceptions, analysis in terms of identified neurons has not yet been possible. Olfactory information projects to antennal lobes and thence to the calyces of the so-called mushroom bodies (MBs) (see Menzel 1990, Hammer 1993, Mauelshagen 1993, Mobbs 1984). A neuron that appears to mediate reinforcement by the UCS (Hammer 1993; see below) also distributes profusely to the antennal lobes, lateral protocerebrum, and calyces of the MBs, making all three sites points of CS-UCS convergence. Studies of the effects on learning of local cooling (Erber et al 1980, Menzel 1990), selective destruction of MB neuroblasts (de Belle & Heisenberg 1994), and MB structural mutations (Heisenberg et al 1985) as well as localization of abnormal gene products in learning mutants (Han et al 1992, Nighorn 1991) and findings of anatomical changes produced by various forms of experience (see Belle & Heisenberg 1994) all point to the MBs as having a special role in learning.

Intrinsic Change or Extrinsic Modulation?

In most of the work reviewed above the focus has been on changes intrinsic to the neurons of the circuits that actually mediate the learned behaviors. It may seem somewhat surprising that animals with some degree of encephalization should abdicate to what is rather low-level circuitry, analogous to our spinal reflexes, control over the excitability of behavior patterns that may be crucial

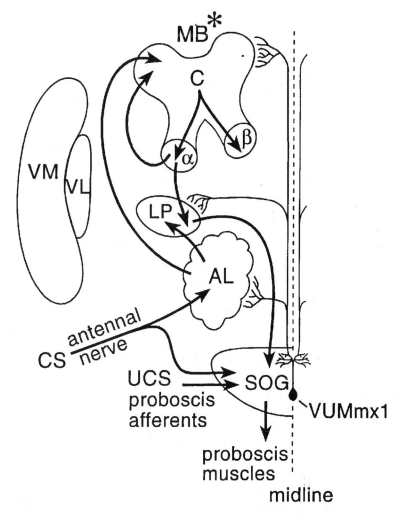

Figure 4   Neural structures involved in insect olfactory conditioning. * indicates the most studied site of plasticity; MB = mushroom body; AL = antennal lob; SOG = sub-esophageal ganglion; VUMmx1 = VUMmx1 neuron; VM = visual medulla; VL = visual lobula.

for survival. That training produces changes paralleling behavioral learning in such circuitry seems clear. But the role of higher-level control circuitry may be underestimated because it is liable to be dysfunctional in more or less dissected and restrained animals. There is now evidence both from crayfish and *Aplysia* that the role of extrinsic modulation by higher-level circuitry in freely behaving animals cannot be ignored. The detailed analysis of changes in the low-level circuitry has progressed remarkably, but this analysis may tell only a small part of the story.

Parallel Distributed Processing?

Parallel distributed processing theories of learning propose that learning may be the result of a multiplicity of changes in neural circuits each of which is too small to affect behavior significantly on its own but that in the aggregate can produce large effects on behavior when the circuits are used in certain ways. Thus, the changes responsible for learning (engrams) are said to be "distributed." Lockery & Sejnowski (1993) have used a back-propagation algorithm to generate distributed engrams that would produce the sorts of behavioral changes seen during leech habituation and sensitization. In the circuits produced by the algorithm, changes at individual synapses were all near or below practical limits of detectability, and the behavioral consequences of changes at any one synapse would have been negligible.

Sensitization and habituation of defensive behavior in *Aplysia* and crayfish clearly are due to changes in synaptic efficacy (resulting from intrinsic change or extrinsic modulation) distributed over a number of sites within the circuits that mediate the behaviors. However, in contrast to the leech modeling results, changes at individual synapses are detectable and are thought to have significant behavioral consequences. Indeed, Falk et al (1993), using voltage-sensitive dyes, have visualized altered responses of hundreds of abdominal ganglion neurons that are engaged by test stimuli during habituation training in *Aplysia,* and Frost et al (1988) have speculatively proposed specific, qualitatively different functions such as determination of response specificity or response duration for various changes they found during sensitization.

Nevertheless, some of the fundamental properties of parallel distributed processing might be operative in these invertebrate circuits. This would be the case if it could be shown, for example, that enhanced transmitter output of sensory neurons in sensitized *Aplysia* contributed substantially to augmented defensive responses when combined with changes at interneuronal synapses but not when responses not involving interneurons were tested. The same principle might be demonstrable in the crayfish LG circuit if first-synapse depression operating in conjunction with tonic inhibition of the LGs were an essential ingredient in LG habituation but had relatively little influence on slow flexion reflexes innervated by the same afferent pathways.

THE FUNCTIONAL EXPRESSION OF ENGRAMS

Altered Ion Channels

Ion channel alterations appear to be an important cause of learned changes of behavior. In *Aplysia*, strong stimulation or 5-HT application causes statistically increased closures of a serotonin sensitive K^+ channel (here called K_S; Klein & Kandel 1978, 1980; Klein et al 1982; Siegelbaum et al 1982) and also decreases the delayed voltage-dependent K^+ current that promotes repolarization following action potentials (Baxter & Byrne 1989). Both effects increase the duration of sensory neuron spikes, thus extending the period during which Ca^{++} enters terminals and hence the amount of transmitter released to excite defense reflex motor neurons (Klein & Kandel 1978, 1980; but see Klein 1994). These effects also cause a slight depolarization of the sensory neuron and contribute to a decreased tendency toward accommodation. Long-term sensitization has also been associated with reductions of an outward current thought to be mediated by closure of the K_S channels (Scholz & Byrne 1987).

Activity-dependent increases in transmission are associated with exaggerated broadening of presynaptic spikes, and decreases of a presumptive K_S current, suggesting that activity merely amplifies the effects produced during ordinary sensitization (Hawkins et al 1983, Abrams 1985, Hawkins & Abrams 1984). Conversely, the synaptic depression responsible for habituation is associated with a slight shortening of presynaptic spikes and has been attributed to inactivation of Ca^{++} channels (Klein & Kandel 1980, Eliot et al 1994b). Much of this picture emerges from voltage-clamp and patch-clamp studies, which must be done on sensory neuron somata rather than on the presynaptic terminals themselves. Although the soma and terminal cannot be counted on to have the same channel types, findings from terminals using Ca^{++}-sensitive dyes (Eliot et al 1993) and growth cones (Belardetti et al 1986) are consistent with those from somata.

Closure of K^+ channels is also thought to be responsible for the increased responsiveness of type B photoreceptors associated with suppression of phototaxis in *Hermissenda*. Input resistance of the photoreceptors increases, resulting in stronger (less shunted) responses to light both acutely (Crow & Alkon 1980) and a day or more following more protracted training (West et al 1982). Voltage-clamp studies indicate that the resistance increases result from decreases in a rapidly activating and inactivating depolarization-dependent K^+ current (I_A) and a Ca^{++}-dependent K^+ current (I_{K-Ca}) (Alkon et al 1982, 1985). Using patch-clamp recording, a 64 pS K^+ channel, possibly the mediator of I_A, has been found in which the probability of opening is greatly reduced at 24 hr after classical conditioning (Etcheberrigaray et al 1991, 1992).

Undefined Physiological Changes

The discovery of ion channel changes as the cause of altered function in learning is appealing because of the well-defined nature of the change, which can then be studied in still more detail (see below). However, modeling studies first suggested that the quantitative details of neither the synaptic facilitation thought to be responsible for sensitization nor the depression responsible for habituation in *Aplysia* can be accounted for by the K^+ and Ca^{++} channel changes initially thought responsible for them, and physiologically undefined processes labeled "transmitter mobilization" and "depletion" were postulated to account for the discrepancies (Gingrich & Byrne 1985). Experimental evidence obtained subsequently showed that 5-HT enhances transmission via mechanisms independent of the presynaptic spike broadening produced by altered K^+ currents (Hochner et al 1986a,b; Pieroni & Byrne 1992; Klein 1994). It has been suggested that alterations in Ca^{++} handling (Boyle et al 1984) or a modulation of the release process itself (Pieroni & Byrne 1992) might be responsible. Increases in spontaneous miniature EPSPs appear to be a correlate of this spike broadening–independent process (Dale & Kandel 1990).

Anatomical Change

In *Aplysia*, both repeated traumatic stimulations leading to long-term sensitization in vivo (Bailey & Chen 1988a,b) and 5-HT application causing synaptic facilitation that lasts more than a day in sensory and motor neuron co-cultures (Glanzman et al 1990) cause increases in presynaptic varicosities, synaptic active zones, length of active zones, and numbers of synaptic vesicles immediately adjacent to these zones. Conversely, repeated stimulation leading to behavioral habituation that lasts weeks, as well as applications of FMRFamide, which causes long-term decreases of synaptic efficacy in culture (see below), result in effects largely opposite to those produced by sensitizing procedures (Bailey & Chen 1988a, Schacher & Montarolo 1991). In the case of 5-HT–produced facilitation, some changes have been detected within 30 min of the start of 5-HT application (Bailey et al 1993). Elevated numbers of varicosities and active zones in behaviorally trained animals persist about as long as does augmented transmission (>3 weeks), but increases in active zone length and numbers of adjacent vesicles outlast training by only a few days (Bailey & Chen 1989).

Pairing of light and rotation that causes suppression of phototaxis in *Hermissenda* decreases the range of the neuronal arbor of B photoreceptors (Alkon et al 1990). It has been suggested that this could reflect a selection process in which a few "useful" branches increase while others decrease.

THE INDUCTION OF NEURONAL CHANGES RESPONSIBLE FOR LEARNING

Phosphorylation is the predominant means used to regulate the activity of proteins such as enzymes and receptors in animal cells. Thus, it is not surprising that this mechanism is intimately involved in the changes responsible for learning (see Byrne et al 1993). Indeed, understanding the induction of changes largely reduces to understanding what activates the second messenger cascades responsible for triggering phosphorylation (i.e. how change is *initiated*) and understanding what the cascades do (i.e. how changes are *implemented*).

Initiation of Change

SENSITIZATION   Induction of sensitized defensive reactions must be triggered by evidence of danger. Because significant danger generally causes defensive reactions, vigorous activity of the motor circuitry that produces these reactions might provide a signal that could trigger the responsible changes. But in *Aplysia* much of this motor circuitry is also engaged during spontaneous respiratory pumping (see above) and therefore cannot provide a reliable signal of danger; thus, independent circuitry is used to recognize danger. Such circuitry is ill-charted but some of the output neurons involved have been identified. These output neurons, which are believed to be relatively few in number, fire in response to strong stimuli and distribute widely, innervating the presynaptic terminals of defense reflex sensory neurons at their contacts with both motor and interneurons (Mackey et al 1989, Hawkins et al 1981, Hawkins & Schacher 1989). The release of transmitters to their presynaptic targets induces the facilitated state. Facilitators differ with respect to receptive field and output properties, as would be expected from differences in response topography for traumatic stimulation of various bodily regions (see above; Walters & Erickson 1986, Erickson & Walters 1988). Facilitators also differ with respect to transmitter released, duration of firing to a transient stimulus, and post-activity persistence of the facilitation they produce (both on the order of seconds to tens of minutes) (Mackey et al 1989).

The transmitters released by facilitators have not been fully characterized. Serotonin, as well as two endogenous peptides, the small cardioactive peptides (SCPs), mimic most of the effects of trauma (Brunelli et al 1976, Abrams et al 1984), although 5-HT appears to be the more faithful mimic. Serotonergic processes are found near terminals of defense reflex primary afferents (Kistler et al 1985, Longley & Longley 1986), and SCPs are present in abdominal ganglion neuropile (Lloyd et al 1985). The properties of the facilitation produced by activity of some facilitators are somewhat different from those of any of the known mimetic agents (Hawkins & Schacher 1989). But some facilitators have been identified as serotonergic (Mackey et al 1989), and pharmacological disruption of serotonergic transmission has been shown to reduce behavioral sensitization and its neural correlates (Brunelli et al 1976, Glanzman et al 1989b, Mercer et al 1991). Thus, 5-HT is accepted as one known mediator of sensitization. Its effects, both on intact *Aplysia* ganglia and sensory-motor synapses grown in culture, have been studied extensively. Brief applications cause presynaptic facilitation lasting several minutes (Rayport & Schacher 1986, Eliot et al 1994a), whereas multiple spaced or a single longer application produce sensitization lasting days (Montarolo et al 1986).

Both 5-HT and strong stimulation, acting via a membrane G-protein (Castellucci et al 1983, Schwartz et al 1983), stimulate adenylyl cyclase to catalyze production of cAMP (Bernier et al 1982). As in other cells, cAMP exerts its physiological effects by activating a cAMP-dependent protein kinase (PKA). Thus, direct elevation of cAMP produces enhanced sensory-motor transmission, sensory neuron spike broadening, and K_S channel closure (Brunelli et al 1976, Klein & Kandel 1978, Siegelbaum et al 1982). Conversely, drugs that prevent PKA from phosphorylating its target proteins prevent these effects (Castellucci et al 1982). PKA is formed by the association of two catalytic subunits with two regulatory subunits that inhibit catalytic activity, and cAMP activates the enzyme by binding to sites on the regulatory subunits, which causes them to dissociate from the catalytic units, freeing them to act. Direct injection of the catalytic subunit produces the same effects as exposure to cAMP (Castellucci et al 1980). There may also be a modest contribution of the Ca^{++}- and phospholipid-dependent protein kinase (PKC) system to spike broadening and enhanced transmission (Sugita et al 1992).

As discussed below, procedures causing changes that persist on the order of days involve new protein synthesis. Daily repetition of treatments in which individual measured effects do not last as long as the intertreatment intervals can trigger long-term change. Where and how the requisite integration is being made is unknown, but during extended periods of 5-HT treatment, the pattern of protein phophorylation undergoes sequential changes (Homayouni et al 1991) that could be involved in the requisite processing (see further below).

In crayfish, sensitization-like effects on the lateral giant escape circuit are produced by the naturally occurring neuromodulator, octopamine (Glanzman & Krasne 1983), which also facilitates insect evasion responses (Casagrand & Ritzman 1992, Sombati & Hoyle 1984). Octopamine appears to be a general arthropod analog of adrenalin (e.g. Evans 1985, Orchard 1982, Battelle & Kravitz 1978), but its actual role in sensitization is speculative.

HABITUATION   Habituation of the protective responses studied in physiological work becomes appropriate when evidence accumulates that a specific disturbance can be safely ignored. To be adaptive, habituation must be somewhat stimulus specific. In principle its induction could be triggered either by activity per se or by receipt of a special safety signal analogous to the danger signal provided by the facilitators that trigger sensitization. Insofar as habituation is the result of tonic inhibitory modulation, as in crayfish LG escape, its analysis must await charting of the circuitry that generates the inhibition. However, remarkably little is known even about mechanisms of intrinsic depression.

Depression has been ascribed to processes such as inactivation of Ca^{++} currents, depletion of transmitter available for release, and reduced invasion of spikes in terminal arbors (see above and Zucker 1989). At least in the short-run such changes might be expected to be the result of intrinsically slow rates of recovery of the relevant processes (e.g. transmitter mobilization, recovery from Ca^{++} channel inactivation; see Zucker 1989 for a discussion of proposed mechanisms); however, active down-regulation mediated via phophorylation or dephosphorylation cannot be discounted, although it has been little discussed.

One possible scenario involves presynaptic transmitter autoreceptors. Many presynaptic terminals have autoreceptors whose stimulation down-regulates release (e.g. Trimmer & Weeks 1989, Chesselet 1984), and in guinea pig ileum, synaptic depression that develops at low stimulation frequencies is prevented by blocking presynaptic muscarinic autoreceptors pharmacologically (Morita et al 1982). The depression-prone first-order synapses of the crayfish LG reflex are also known to have muscarinic autoreceptors whose transient activation by cholinergic agents appears to produce a depression of release lasting about 90 min (Miller et al 1992); however, there is presently no evidence that these autoreceptors play a role in habituation.

Although short-term depression occurs normally at cultured *Aplysia* sensory-motor synapses, repetitive activation does not lead to long-term depression of transmission, suggesting the need for a factor that is not present in these simple co-cultures (Montarolo et al 1988). In fact, several spaced 5-min applications of FMRFamide, a peptide that causes presynaptic inhibition of release from *Aplysia* sensory neurons via an arachadonic acid second messenger cascade, causes cultured synapses to undergo a long-term, protein-synthesis–dependent reduction of transmission accompanied by the same kinds of morphological changes seen following long-term habituation training (Piomelli et al 1987, Schacher & Montarolo 1991, Schacher et al 1993, Bailey et al 1992). Thus, the intrinsic changes responsible for long-term habituation in *Aplysia* may require receipt of a special FMRFamide-like safety signal. To achieve the stimulus specificity required of habituation, this signal would have to be directed selectively to those sensory neurons activated by the repeating stimulus, or the long-term effects of the FMRFamide-like agent would have to be activity-dependent, which FMRFamide's short-term inhibitory effects in fact are (Small et al 1989).

Dishabituation   Habituation resulting from intrinsic depression, whatever the means of its induction, can only be adaptive if it can be prevented from developing and reversed under conditions of danger, and there is considerable evidence that traumatic stimulation breaks up both short-term and long-term habituation (Krasne & Glanzman 1986, Pinsker et al 1970, Carew et al 1971, Carew et al 1979, Fitzgerald et al 1990). The same mechanisms used for sensitization might mediate dishabituation. But in *Aplysia*, dishabituation (i.e. trauma-produced recovery of habituated reflexes) appears before sensitization (i.e. enhancement of unhabituated reflexes) during development (reviewed in Carew 1989; but see Glanzman et al 1989b), and recovery from synaptic depression is heavily dependent on transmitter mobilization not involving presynaptic spike broadening and K_S channel closure (Hochner et al 1986 a,b). This mobilization, which like sensitization is well mimicked by 5-HT (Hochner et al 1986b, Pieroni & Byrne 1992), appears to be dependent on PKC-catalyzed phosphorylation, although PKA-mediated processes amplify it somewhat (Braha et al 1990, but see Ghiradi et al 1992). A separate mechanism for dishabituation could provide a means of restoring excitability to prehabituation levels in a way that does not result in heightened sensitivity to novel stimuli, but this would require an unknown external means of recruiting the PKC- and not the PKA-mediated process.

ASSOCIATIVE LEARNING   Conditioned responses become appropriate when the environment provides evidence that one stimulus predicts another in a biologically significant context.

Activity-dependent facilitation in Aplysia   The condition for development of activity-dependent facilitation in *Aplysia* is pairing of noxious stimulation with the activity of defense reflex sensory neurons. Thus, the facilitation is believed to be simply an exaggerated form of simple facilitation (see above). Consistent with this theory, pairing of 5-HT exposure with sensory neuron activity (or depolarization by K^+) causes a more than additive increase in (*a*) cAMP production (Abrams 1985, Ocorr et al 1985), (*b*) degree of presynaptic spike broadening (Eliot et al 1994a, Abrams 1985), and (*c*) transmitter release per spike (assessed by the evoked EPSP; Eliot et al 1994a) in intact ganglia and/or co-cultured sensory and motor neurons.

Sensitivity to the conjunction of presynaptic activity and trauma or 5-HT input depends on the presence of extracellular Ca^{++} (Abrams 1985), suggesting that Ca^{++} entering presynaptic terminals during activity potentiates the cAMP-producing effects of 5-HT. Ca^{++}, acting via calmodulin, does in fact enhance the effectiveness of the enzyme, adenylyl cyclase, that catalyzes the formation of cAMP (Abrams et al 1991). In addition, PKA and Ca^{++}/cal-modulin-dependent protein kinase (CaM kinase) both can phosphorylate protein [cAMP-responsive-element (CRE)–binding protein; see below] that triggers induction of long-term facilitation when its phophorylated form binds to a specific DNA recognition sequence. Moreover, PKA plus CaM kinase causes more transcription than does either kinase alone in a cell-free test system (Dash et al 1991). Therefore, transcription-triggering protein could provide another site sensitive to the conjunction of trauma and sensory neuron activity.

Classical conditioning in intact *Aplysia*, and activity-dependent facilitation of EPSP amplitude in isolated ganglia, depend on close forward pairing (0.5 s ISI) of sensory neuron activity and traumatic stimulation (Hawkins et al 1986, Clark 1984). It is not obvious how the biochemical conjunction–detecting mechanisms just described would produce this order sensitivity. Biochemical experiments have provided some evidence that rate of 5-HT–stimulated adenylyl cyclase catalysis of cAMP production is enhanced by Ca^{++}/calmodulin pulses that precede onset of 5-HT exposure (Yovell & Abrams 1992, Abrams et al 1991), but the time scale of these experiments is in minutes rather than seconds. It remains to be determined whether the precise temporal requirement for classical conditioning is an intrinsic property of the sensory neuron. In sensory-motor neuron co-cultures, activity and 5-HT exposure produce more facilitation when they overlap than when they are separated by a full minute (Eliot et al 1994a), but measurements of precise timing and order dependence have not been done. It has been suggested that perhaps prevention of backward conditioning is due to network properties; e.g. presynaptic inhibition that follows traumatic stimulation might prevent such conditioning by preventing amplification of facilitation by presynaptic activity (Mackey et al 1987).

Classical conditioning in insects   Analysis of classical conditioning of the proboscis extension reflex of bees and of odor avoidance in *Drosophila* (see above) has provided evidence for the generality of the mechanisms seen in *Aplysia* as well as promising preparations for more detailed analysis.

A variety of *Drosophila* mutants (*amnesiac, turnip, rutabaga, dunce,* and others) with learning disorders but few other behavioral abnormalities have been established (Dudai et al 1976, Quinn et al 1974, Tully & Quinn 1985). Continuing analysis of the primary biochemical deficits of these mutants (see Tully 1988, Dudai 1989) indicates that *dunce* has low cAMP phosphodiesterase (see Qiu et al 1991), that *rutabaga* adenylyl cyclase is not activated by Ca^{++}/calmodulin (see Levin et al 1992), and that *turnip* has somewhat less active than normal adenylyl cyclase as well as drastic reductions in PKC activity (Smith et al 1986). These findings are striking, given the importance attributed to the PKA system in *Aplysia* and the postulated role of adenylyl cyclase Ca^{++}/calmodulin sensitivity in associative phenomena, as well as evidence for major involvement of the PKC system in a variety of other learning phenomena (see above and below).

Induction of classically conditioned responses to odor in insects may also depend on the activity of special neurons analogous to the facilitators of *Aplysia* defensive reflexes. In bee brain a neuron has been identified that fires in response to sugar water UCSs and that when driven by direct intracellular depolarization produces no behavior but serves quite effectively in lieu of sugar water as a reinforcement in conditioning experiments (Hammer 1993). This neuron, the VUMmx1 cell (Figure 4), which is thought to be one of a small population of similar cells, has dendrites in the subesophageal ganglion and projects a profoundly branching axonal arbor into several structures including the calyces of the mushroom bodies, which, as reviewed above, are candidate loci for engrams. It might be expected from the *Aplysia* analogy that the cAMP pathway products of *dunce* and *rutabaga* genes would be localized preferentially in the calyces where the bee VUMmx1 cells terminate. This is true for the *dunce* phosphodiesterase, but *rutabaga* Ca^{++}/calmodulin-sensitive adenylyl cyclase seems to be concentrated more along axons or at terminals of the mushroom body neurons.

Long-term potentiation in Aplysia   Activity-dependent facilitation provides a means of selectively enhancing transmission at synapses whose presynaptic activity coincides with a widely broadcast facilitatory message. It does not, however, allow such enhancement to be limited to synapses between particular co-active pre- and postsynaptic neurons. Enhancement of transmission at co-active synapses was postulated by Hebb and subsequently established as the mechanism for one type of long-term potentiation (associative LTP) in mammalian brain (see Hawkins et al 1993, Bliss & Collingridge 1993). Initial tests for a role of postsynaptic activity in the activity-dependent facilitation of *Aplysia* found that depolarizing the postsynaptic neuron during presynaptic activity did not cause facilitation, and hyperpolarizing the neuron during pairing of traumatic stimulation and presynaptic activity did not reduce facilitation (Hawkins et al 1983, Carew et al 1984).

However, in these experiments the somatically injected current may not have adequately affected dendrites, and recent experiments on co-cultured sensory and motor neurons of *Aplysia* show that a phenomenon extremely similar to mammalian associative LTP occurs at *Aplysia* sensory-motor synapses (Lin & Glanzman 1994a,b). Repeated, brief sensory neuron tetani cause a persistent enhancement of transmission that is prevented by postsynaptic hyperpolarization. Pairing a weak presynaptic tetanus with direct depolarization of the motor neuron also causes enhancements, and these are blocked by the NMDA antagonist, APV, or postsynaptic injection of the Ca^{++} chelator, BAPTA. This *Aplysia* LTP-like mechanism (apLTP) is obviously quite independent of activity-dependent facilitation, since no facilitators are present in the culture. Similarly, leech protective responses, which are also sensitized by a 5-HT–dependent mechanism, can still be classically conditioned, but not sensitized, after 5,7-DHT poisoning of their serotonergic systems (Sahley 1993).

If operative in vivo (Cui & Walters 1994), apLTP could be the basis for response-selective associative conditioning such as that reported by Walters (1989) and Hawkins et al (1989), which were attributed to other mechanisms. However, because gill and siphon motor neurons are activated during spontaneous respiratory pumping, fortuitous sensory activity during pumping could result in adventitious conditioned responses due to apLTP. Suitable three-way interaction effects between sensory, facilitator, and motor neuron activity (i.e. interactions between activity-dependent facilitation and apLTP) could resolve this problem. Indeed, this system could provide a useful model for physiological investigations of interactions between contiguity and reinforcement.

Classically conditioned phototactic suppression in Hermissenda   Light applied to *Hermissenda*'s type B photoreceptors, whose increased responses and synaptic outputs are believed to be responsible for learned suppression of phototaxis, causes a strong depolarization, which at light-offset does not entirely abate for several minutes (Alkon & Grossman 1978). This persistent after-depolarization, which occurs even when the distal synapse–containing portion of a photoreceptor is cut away, is referred to as the LLD (long-lasting depolarization). Recordings during training show that pairing regimens that lead to successful conditioning are associated with enhanced LLDs, which tend to summate from one light-vestibular stimulation pairing to the next to produce a cumulative depolarization that may last for hours (Alkon 1979, Tabata & Alkon 1982, Farley & Alkon 1987, Alkon 1980). These augmented post-stimulation depolarizations might be secondary to decreased shunting associated with developing K^+ current reductions, but the possibility that they play a causative role in establishing longer term changes has received considerable attention.

How pairing might enhance the LLD, so that it could in turn cause long-term change, has been explained with reference to the network connecting B photoreceptors and hair cells (Figure 3; Tabata & Alkon 1982, Farley & Alkon 1987, Alkon 1979). Type B photoreceptors (here called B cells) and caudal (but not rostral) hair cells provide convergent hyperpolarizing inhibitory input to a group of S/E optic ganglion cells that in turn send excitatory input back to the B cells and inhibitory input to the hair cells. The S/E cells are prone to post-inhibitory rebound. Thus, when they are inhibited particularly strongly because of pairing of light and caudal hair cell stimulation, they produce substantial rebound excitation of the B cells at offset of light and vestibular stimulation. This excitation is further enhanced because the otherwise tonically firing caudal hair cells are uninhibited and thereby prevented from inhibiting the B cells. The result is a barrage of EPSPs to the B cells that sum with the intrinsic light–produced LLD. If this explanation of the LLD enhancement following pairing is correct, and if it really does cause learning, then rotations designed to selectively stimulate the rostral hair cells, or light-vestibular stimulation pairings that do not co-terminate, should not cause conditioning. Both predictions have been confirmed (Farley & Alkon 1980, Grover & Farley 1987).

Voltage-clamp and use of the Ca^{++}-sensitive dye, Arsenazo III, show that the nonsynaptic portion of the LLD is due to a light- and depolarization-dependent Ca^{++} current (Alkon 1979) that, presumably because of its voltage dependence, is somewhat self-sustaining. Arsenazo measurements also show that light flashes paired with injections of depolarizing current, which start with the flash and extend for about a minute beyond it, simulating the effects of the S/E cell input that occurs during pairing, cause augmented Ca^{++} responses (Connor & Alkon 1984). A similar regimen of B-cell stimulation results in behavioral learning measured a day later (Farley et al 1983). Thus, B photoreceptor Ca^{++} elevations, acting via Ca^{++}-dependent protein kinases such as PKC or CaM kinase, have been suggested as the event that triggers learning-induced changes.

Both CaM kinase and PKC, under conditions intended to elevate intracellular Ca^{++}, as well as phorbol ester, which directly activates PKC, cause reductions of I_A and I_{K-Ca} (Sakakibara et al 1986a,b; Alkon et al 1986, 1988; Farley & Auerbach 1986); however, the PKC-mediated effect is thought to mimic that of training more closely. Conversely, PKC inhibitors prevent induction of both early (Matzel et al 1990) and more persistent (>24 hr) learning-produced changes (Farley & Schuman 1991). As would be expected, changes do not develop in B photoreceptors injected with the Ca^{++} chelator, EGTA (Matzel et al 1992).

In the picture that thus emerges, sensitivity to pairing is partly a consequence of the convergence of photoreceptors and hair cells on the S/E cells, resulting in post-inhibitory depolarizing input to the photoreceptors, and partly to the joint dependence of a photoreceptor Ca^{++} current on light and depolarization. The assumptions of this schema have been incorporated in an equivalent circuit model that rather faithfully reproduces many experimental results (Werness et al 1992, 1993), but this is difficult to evaluate because the values of the many parameters used in the simulation have not been given.

In the above scenario, an LLD-associated Ca^{++} elevation is supposed to foster B photoreceptor change. But Matzel et al (1992) have reported that abolishing the LLD by clamping the photoreceptor membrane potential to its resting level right after paired light and vestibular input does not prevent development of conditioned changes.

Several other findings also complicate the picture. For example, exposure to exogenous 5-HT has been found to produce changes apparently similar, though not identical, to those produced by behavioral conditioning procedures (Crow & Bridge 1985, Schuman & Clark 1994, Farley & Wu 1989, Acosta-Urquidi & Crow 1993), and pairing 5-HT with light amplifies this 5-HT effect (Crow & Forrester 1986, 1991; Frysztak & Crow 1994). Kinase inhibition using the partially selective PKC inhibitors H7 and sphingosine prevents induction of this effect in the short term, but long-term changes still develop (Crow & Forrester 1993a,b). Serotonergic neurons that respond to both visual and vestibular stimulation and innervate the B photoreceptors have been found (Cheyette & Farley 1989), but a role for them in learning has not been established. Finally, procedures that interfere with 5-HT release or action reduce short-term conditioning effects of paired light and caudal hair cell stimulation (Grover et al 1989). Thus, as with the original scheme, sensitivity to CS and UCS pairing may be dependent on both convergence on a common target (the serotonergic cells) and on an intrinsic B cell interaction between synaptic input and light.

A quite different possibility is suggested by the recent discovery that when GABA, which may be the transmitter the caudal hair cells release to the B photoreceptors during paired light and vestibular stimulation, is applied to depolarized B cells, an increase in input resistance occurs similar to that produced by training (Matzel & Alkon 1991). This effect requires external Ca^{++} and is H7-sensitive. Pairing of GABA and depolarization also seems to transform the hyperpolarizing inhibition produced by hair cell synapses on B photoreceptors into a depolarizing response that is apparently caused by release of Ca^{++} from internal stores (Alkon et al 1992). This hair cell–engendered Ca^{++} response could also contribute to the induction of further B cell changes.

THE LOCUS OF DECISIONS TO CHANGE—GENERALITIES The initiation of change depends on an evaluation that can be made by the potentially changing cell itself (i.e. proximally) or by other neurons (i.e. distally). Of the cases we have examined, *Aplysia* sensitization, which simply depends on whether facilitators fire, falls into the latter category whereas *Aplysia* short-term habituation seems to fall into the former. Sensitivity to pairing in classical conditioning of *Aplysia* appears to be dependent on a proximal integration at the level of adenylyl cyclase and perhaps also at the CRE-binding protein, whereas in *Hermissenda* it depends, at least in one theory, on both the distal network illustrated in Figure 3 and a synergistic interaction between synaptically induced depolarization and light stimulation of the B photoreceptor.

Two general points need to be made about these differing scenarios. First, distal strategies have the advantage that change can be made contingent on potentially sophisticated computations made anywhere in the nervous system. Thus, it seems likely that at least in higher animals the distal approach will be the one commonly taken. Second, the information processing capabilities of single cells should not be underrated. The "and" gate formed by adenylyl cyclase's joint Ca^{++} and 5-HT dependence is an example of a kind of biochemical information processing that could be elaborated to an extraordinary degree as the various second messenger and protein kinase systems of a cell interact. Sophisticated logical analysis based on various types of input to a cell as well as timing and counting operations are all at least in principle single-cell capabilities (Bray 1990).

Implementation of Change

Although there is significant information regarding the cytoplasmic signals activated by various training regimens in invertebrate learning paradigms, considerably less is known about the cellular changes that result from activation of these signals. One important common theme is that development and expression of short-term learning may involve covalent modifications of preexisting proteins, whereas induction of long-term change usually requires protein synthesis (Goelet et al 1986).

Thus, although short-term sensitization in *Aplysia,* and generator potential enhancements produced by pairing light and 5-HT exposure in *Hermissenda* photoreceptors, develop in the presence of protein synthesis inhibitors, inhibition of protein synthesis during periods of training, or during exposure to facilitatory or inhibitory neuromodulators, prevents the development of the corresponding long-term changes (Castellucci et al 1989, Crow & Forrester 1990, Montarolo et al 1986). It also prevents the structural changes described above (Bailey et al 1992), long-lasting changes in protein phosphorylation (see below; Sweatt & Kandel 1989), and decreases in PKA regulatory subunits (see below) (Bergold et al 1990). However, inhibition of protein synthesis does not prevent long-term learning in bees (Wittstock et al 1993), and its effects have not been tested on long-term habituation in *Aplysia* or crayfish.

PATTERNS AND ROLES OF PHOSPHORYLATION   During short-term sensitization, and at 24 hr after induction of long-term sensitization in *Aplysia,* a common set of 17 sensory neuron proteins show increased phosphorylation (Sweatt & Kandel 1989). The commonality of these patterns suggests a role for phosphorylation in expression rather than in induction of the sensitized state. However, because structural changes are probably developing at 24 hr after induction of long-term sensitization, it is surprising that the biochemical acitivity involved is not associated with some alterations in phosphorylation. Four *Hermissenda* eye proteins also show increased phophorylation 24 hr after induction of phototactic suppression (Nelson et al 1990).

One of the phosphorylated *Aplysia* proteins could be the K_S channel itself or a closely associated membrane protein, because application of the catalytic subunit of PKA directly to inside-out patches of sensory neuron membrane causes closure of its channels (Shuster et al 1985). Also, one of the proteins that becomes phosphorylated by *Hermissenda* training reduces the two conditioning sensitive K^+ currents when injected into B photoreceptors (Nelson et al 1990).

In *Aplysia* the presynaptic inhibitory neuromodulator FMRFamide suppresses resting phosphorylation levels of 10 proteins, all of them within the group of 17 whose phosphorylation increases during sensitization. When applied in conjunction with 5-HT or cAMP, FMRFamide prevents all 17 increases of phophorylation (Sweatt & Kandel 1988) as well as preventing any functional sensitization (Sweatt et al 1989, Belardetti et al 1987), possibly by activating phosphatases that break down phosphate-protein bonds (Ichinose & Byrne 1991).

Although short- and long-term sensitization are said to ultimately produce similar patterns of phosphorylation, these patterns change dynamically during extended periods of serotonin treatment (Homayouni et al 1991). This could reflect protein kinase system involvement in the evaluation of whether the history of facilitator input warrants initiation of long-term change (see Generalities section above). And some later developing phosphorylation could be involved in the recruitment of protein synthesis.

Cyclic AMP can induce transcription of a variety of so-called immediate early genes. This induction is thought to occur when cAMP-activated PKA phosphorylates certain proteins, the cAMP-responsive-element binding proteins, that in turn bind to a particular DNA nucleotide sequence called the cAMP responsive element (CRE) (Brindle & Montimony 1992). There is now considerable evidence that this sequence of events is involved in 5-HT–induced long-term facilitation in *Aplysia*: 1. Serotonin exposures that cause long-term sensitization, but not more limited exposures, cause fluorescently labeled catalytic subunits of PKA to break away from cAMP-bound regulatory units and enter the nucleus (Bacskai et al 1993). 2. *Aplysia* sensory neuron DNA contains the CRE (Schacher et al 1990a). 3. Foreign CREs fused to *Escherichia coli lacZ* genes injected into sensory neurons express LacZ gene product when the neuron is stimulated by a 5-HT protocol that produces long-term facilitation (Kaang et al 1993). 4. Injection of short nucleotide chains containing the CRE sequence in abundance, which should tend to capture limited amounts of natural phosphorylated CRE-binding proteins and thereby prevent transcription, prevented expression of the *lacZ* gene in the above experiment and also prevented induction of long-term but not short-term facilitation (Dash et al 1990). Alberini et al (1994) have identified a protein (ApC/EBp) that is produced by a cAMP-inducable gene and appears to be essential for induction of long-term sensitization.

These data suggest intriguing possible roles for phosphorylation in producing long-term change. However, the lack of effect of kinase inhibitors on long-term *Hermissenda* photoreceptor conditioning produced by pairing 5-HT with light (see above) should not be forgotten.

PATTERNS AND ROLES OF PROTEIN SYNTHESIS   Repeated 5-HT applications induce a complex, temporally orchestrated, pattern of increased and decreased synthesis of specific proteins in *Aplysia* sensory neurons (Barzilai et al 1989). Some of this synthesis must be associated with regulatory gene actions that establish altered patterns of continuing synthesis (see Castellucci et al 1988). Also, of 15 proteins whose rate of transcription alters within 15–30 min of the start of 5-HT exposure and continues for 1–3 hr (so-called early proteins), 5 appear to be related to structural changes. Four of these proteins, whose synthesis decreases, are *Aplysia* homologues of the vertebrate neural cell adhesion molecules (Schacher et al 1990a, Mayford et al 1992). These presumed *Aplysia* cell adhesion molecules (apCAMs) appear to play a role in neurite outgrowth and synapse formation. Thus, monoclonal antibodies to apCAM cause sensory neuron processes in culture to defasciculate (Mayford et al 1992), a process associated with the formation of synapses in sensory-motor neuron co-cultures (Glanzman et al 1989a, 1990). The application of 5-HT to sensory neurons, in addition to down-regulating apCAM synthesis, also causes protein synthesis–dependent endocytosis of existing cell surface apCAM molecules (Mayford et al 1992, Bailey et al 1992). One of the early proteins whose synthesis is increased is in fact critical for apCAM endocytosis and has been identified as the light chain of *Aplysia* clathrin, a protein homologous to one known to regulate receptor-mediated endocytosis in vertebrate cells (Hu et al 1993). Synthesis of several other known proteins such as actin, intermediate filament protein, and several endoplasmic reticulum proteins is also altered (Noel et al 1993, Kennedy et al 1992, Kuhl et al 1992).

Another consequence of altered protein synthesis is suggested by the discovery that 5-HT treatments that induce long-term facilitation cause a long-lasting reduction in concentration of regulatory (but not catalytic) subunits of PKA (Greenberg et al 1987, Bergold et al 1990). Thus, the phosphorylations normally mediated by cAMP can occur at lower concentrations of cAMP and possibly become endogenous, potentially explaining the persistence of the short-term pattern of K_S channel closure and protein phophorylation after induction of long-term sensitization. Extended 5-HT treatment reduces regulatory subunits at 24 hr even in isolated synaptic terminals (Greenberg et al 1987), but integrity of protein synthesis during induction is necessary for regulatory subunits to remain low in intact cells, presumably because replacement subunits eventually get synthesized unless their synthesis is down-regulated or synthesis of a protease is up-regulated as a protein synthesis–dependent result of the induction process.

In *Hermissenda*, long-term (>24 hr) phototactic suppression is associated with altered synthesis rates of a number of mRNA species (Nelson & Alkon 1990). However, the functions of the associated proteins are unknown.

MEMORY

Sensitization of *Aplysia* defensive withdrawal has provided a useful model for investigating the mechanism of retention over time. Since sensitization is mediated by protein phosphorylation, it might be expected that sensitization would be relatively long lasting because phosphates link to proteins via inherently stable covalent bonds. However, cells are rich in protein phosphatases that limit the longevity of these bonds; in *Aplysia* the activity of phophatases is indicated by prolongation of spike broadening effects in the presence of phosphatase inhibitors (Ichinose & Byrne 1991). Indeed, injection of a protein kinase inhibitor into a sensory neuron abolishes spike broadening previously established by exposure to 5-HT within a few minutes, indicating that the phosphorylation responsible for broadening is not inherently stable (Castellucci et al 1982a). In fact, the short-term effects of 5-HT last only about 5 min (Bernier et al 1982, Eliot et al 1994a, Schacher et al 1990b, or perhaps less (Yovell et al 1987), after 5-HT exposure ends. Thus, the duration of short-term sensitization may be mostly dependent on sustained exposure to a facilitatory transmitter. This could result from persistent activity of facilitators (Mackey et al 1989), the mechanism for which is still unknown. It is also unknown how the effects of multiple 5-HT exposures separated by 15 min can sum to induce protein synthesis. Perhaps even very low levels of cAMP, when prolonged, can trigger protein synthesis or there may be some slowly degraded phosphoproteins that span the interstimulus interval.

Long-term sensitization involves growth, which is associated with altered levels of several proteins, and decreased levels of PKA regulatory subunit, presumably resulting from lowered synthesis or from increased production of a protease. Altered behavior due to structural changes or presence (or absence) of particular proteins would be expected to be more stable than that due to protein phosphorylation, but because cytoplasmic and cell membrane molecules turn over, persistence on the order of weeks and longer must still be explained. Induction of sensitization may establish a new self-maintaining pattern of gene expression analogous to the transcriptional and perhaps post-transcriptional controls that are put in place as cells differentiate during development. Long-term sensitization would then be the result of continuing export of particular proteins at regulated concentrations to sensory terminals. Emptage & Carew (1993) have shown that at 24 hr after a 1.5 hr exposure of a sensory neuron soma to 5-HT, the terminals are sensitized even though they were not exposed to the facilitator and never displayed short-term sensitization (see also Clark & Kandel 1993).

Such a mechanism might well mediate *Aplysia* sensitization, in which all the terminals of a given sensory neuron may change in the same way. But it is believed that associative learning in vertebrates demands a capability for independent regulation of each of thousands of synapses of a given neuron, and it is implausible to suppose that the status of each of those synapses could be coded by self-sustaining patterns of gene expression. Thus, this sort of cell memory is not a suitable storage medium for large-scale associative learning. Rather, it must be supposed that changes established locally at each synapse, perhaps involving cooperative pre- and postsynaptic changes (Schuman & Madison 1994), are individually self renewing, (see Lisman 1985, Crick 1984, Hanson & Schulman 1992), albeit with presumed logistical support from the cell nucleus. It will be interesting to exploit *Aplysia* neuron co-cultures of the kind used to study LTP (Lin & Glanzman 1994a,b) or sensory neurons that have spatially well-separated output synapses (Emptage & Carew 1993, Clark & Kandel 1984, 1993) to study the development and maintenance of long-term changes that are specific to particular synapses.

CONCLUSIONS

The findings reviewed here provide an extent and depth of insight into mechanisms of simple learning that go far beyond anything that could have been envisaged a few decades ago. We find particularly impressive the analysis of sensitization in *Aplysia*, where one can trace an almost unbroken causal chain from experiential events responsible for the learning to anatomical and physiological changes responsible for the altered behavior. The relative simplicity of the neural circuits that mediate the learned responses demonstrates clearly the relationship between the cellular responses studied and the resulting behavior; this is the tremendous strength of the approach. We can feel quite confident that what is being studied are really mechanisms of learning and not laboratory curiosities or phenomena unrelated to learning. However, we can also see that the surface has only been scratched; there is extensive evidence that the changes studied so far are only a small part of the totality. Thus, behavioral learning has not yet really been explained, even in invertebrates. But the way seems clear to continuing the analysis with the same approaches that have brought us this far.

Literature Cited

Abrams TW. 1985. Activity-dependent presynaptic facilitation: an associative mechanism in *Aplysia*. *Cell. Mol. Neurobiol.* 5:123–45

Abrams TW, Castellucci VF, Camardo JS, Kandel ER, Lloyd PE. 1984. Two endogenous neuropeptides modulate the gill and siphon withdrawal reflex in *Aplysia* by presynaptic facilitation involving cAMP-dependent closure of a serotonin-sensitive potassium channel. *Proc. Natl. Acad. Sci. USA* 81:7956–60

Abrams TW, Karl KA, Kandel ER. 1991. Biochemical studies of stimulus convergence during classical conditioning in *Aplysia*: dual regulation of adenylate cyclase by Ca²⁺/calmodulin and transmitter. *J. Neurosci.* 11:2655–65

Acosta-Urquidi J, Crow T. 1993. Differential modulation of voltage-dependent currents in *Hermissenda* type B photoreceptors by serotonin. *J. Neurophysiol.* 70:541–48

Akaike T, Alkon DL. 1980. Sensory convergence on central visual neurons in *Hermissenda*. *J. Neurophysiol.* 44:501–13

Alberini CM, Ghirardi M, Metz R, Kandel ER. 1994. C/EBP is an immediate-early gene required for the consolidation of long-term facilitation in *Aplysia*. *Cell* 76:1099–1114

Alkon DL. 1973. Neural organization of a molluscan visual system. *J. Gen. Physiol.* 61:444–61

Alkon DL. 1974. Associative training of *Hermissenda*. *J. Gen. Physiol.* 64:70–84

Alkon DL. 1979. Voltage-dependent calcium and potassium ion conductances: a contingency mechanism for an asociative learning model. *Science* 205:810–16

Alkon DL. 1980. Membrane depolarization accumulates during acquisition of an associative behavioral change. *Science* 210:1375–76

Alkon DL, Grossman Y. 1978. Long-lasting depolarization and hyperpolarization in eye of *Hermissenda*. *J. Neurophysiol.* 41:1328–42

Alkon DL, Ikeno H, Dworkin J, McPhie DL, Olds JL, et al. 1990. Contraction of neuronal branching volume: an anatomic correlate of Pavlovian conditioning. *Proc. Natl. Acad. Sci. USA* 87:1611–14

Alkon DL, Kubota M, Neary JT, Naito S, Coulter D, Rasmussen H. 1986. C-Kinase

activation prolongs Ca²⁺-dependent inactivation of K⁺ currents. *Biochem. Biophys. Res. Commun.* 134:1245–53

Alkon DL, Lederhendler I, Shoukimas JJ. 1982. Primary changes of membrane currents during retention of associative learning. *Science* 215:693–95

Alkon DL, Naito S, Kubota M, Chen C, Bank B, et al. 1988. Regulation of *Hermissenda* K⁺ channels by cytoplasmic and membrane-associated C-Kinase. *J. Neurochem.* 51:903–17

Alkon DL, Sakakibara M, Forman R, Harrigan J, Lederhendler I, Farley J. 1985. Reduction of two voltage-dependent K⁺ currents mediates retention of a learned association. *Behav. Neural Biol.* 44:278–300

Alkon DL, Sanchez-Andres J-V, Ito E, Oka K, Yoshioka T, Collin C. 1992. Long-term transformation of an inhibitory into an excitatory GABAergic synaptic response. *Proc. Natl. Acad. Sci. USA* 89:11862–66

Bacskai BJ, Hochner B, Mahaut-Smith M, Adams SR, Kaang BK, et al. 1993. Spatially resolved dynamics of cAMP and protein kinase A subunits in *Aplysia* sensory neurons. *Science* 260:222–26

Baerends GP. 1941. Fortpflanzungsverhalten und orientierung der grabwespe. *Tijd. Entomol.* 84:68–275

Bailey CH, Chen M. 1988a. Long-term memory in *Aplysia* modulates the total number of varicosities of single identified sensory neurons. *Proc. Natl. Acad. Sci. USA* 85:2372–77

Bailey CH, Chen M. 1988b. Long-term sensitization in *Aplysia* increases the number of presynaptic contacts onto the identified gill motor neuron L7. *Proc. Natl. Acad. Sci. USA* 85:9356–59

Bailey CH, Chen M. 1989. Time course of structural changes at identified sensory neuron synapses during long-term sensitization in *Aplysia*. *J. Neurosci.* 9:1774–80

Bailey CH, Chen M, Kandel ER, Schacher S. 1993. Early structural changes associated with long-term presynaptic facilitation in *Aplysia* sensory neurons. *Soc. Neurosci. Abstr.* 19:16

Bailey CH, Montarolo PG, Chen M, Kandel ER, Schacher S. 1992. Inhibitors of protein and RNA synthesis block structural changes that accompany long-term heterosynaptic plasticity in *Aplysia. Neuron* 9: 749–58

Barzilai A, Kennedy TE, Sweatt JD, Kandel ER. 1989. 5-HT modulates protein synthesis and the expression of specific proteins during long-term facilitation in *Aplysia* sensory neurons. *Neuron* 2:1577–86

Battelle BA, Kravitz EA. 1978. Targets of octopamine action in the lobster: cyclic nucleotide changes and physiological effects in hemolymph, heart and exoskeletal muscle. *J. Pharmacol. Exp. Ther.* 205:438–48

Baxter DA, Byrne JH. 1989. Serotonergic modulation of two potassium currents in the pleural sensory neurons of *Aplysia. J. Neurophysiol.* 62:665–79

Belardetti F, Kandel ER, Siegelbaum SA. 1987. Neuronal inhibition by the peptide FMRFamide involves opening of S K^+ channels. *Nature* 325:153–56

Belardetti F, Schacher S, Kandel E, Siegelbaum SA. 1986. The growth cones of *Aplysia* sensory neurons: modulation by serotonin of action potential duration and single potassium channel currents. *Proc. Natl. Acad. Sci. USA* 83:7094–98

Bergold PJ, Sweatt JD, Winicov I, Weiss KR, Kandel ER, Schwartz JH. 1990. Protein synthesis during acquisition of long-term facilitation is needed for the persistant loss of regulatory subunits of the *Aplysia* cAMP-dependent protein kinase. *Proc. Natl. Acad. Sci. USA* 87:3788–91

Bernier L, Castellucci VF, Kandel ER, Schwartz JH. 1982. Facilitatory transmitter causes a selective and prolonged increase in adenosine 3′:5′-monophosphate in sensory neurons mediating the gill and siphon withdrawal reflex in *Aplysia. J. Neurosci.* 2:1682–91

Billy AJ, Walters ET. 1989a. Long-term expansion and sensitization of mechanosensory receptive fields in *Aplysia* support an activity-dependent model of whole-cell sensory plasticity. *J. Neurosci.* 9:1254–62

Billy AJ, Walters ET. 1989b. Modulation of mechanosensory threshold in *Aplysia* by serotonin, small cardioactive peptide$_B$ (SCP$_B$), FMRFamide, acetylcholine, and dopamine. *Neurosci. Lett.* 105:200–4

Bitterman ME, Menzel R, Fietz A, Schafer S. 1983. Classical conditioning of proboscis extension in honeybees (*Apis mellifera*). *J. Comp. Psychol.* 97:107–19

Bliss TVP, Collingridge GL. 1993. A synaptic model of memory: long-term potentiation in the hippocampus. *Nature* 361:31–39

Boyle MB, Klein M, Smith SJ, Kandel ER. 1984. Serotonin increases intracellular Ca^{2+} transients in voltage-clamped sensory neurons of *Aplysia californica. Proc. Natl. Acad. Sci. USA* 81:7642–46

Braha O, Dale N, Hochner B, Klein M, Abrams TW, Kandel ER. 1990. Second messengers involved in two processes of presynaptic facilitation that contribute to sensitization and dishabituation in *Aplysia* sensory neurons. *Proc. Natl. Acad. Sci. USA* 87:2040–44

Bray D. 1990. Intracellular signalling as a parallel distributed process. *J. Theor. Biol.* 143:215–31

Brindle PK, Montimony MR. 1992. The CREB family of transcription activators. *Curr. Opin. Genet. Dev.* 2:199–204

Brunelli M, Castellucci VF, Kandel ER. 1976. Synaptic facilitation and behavioral sensitization in *Aplysia*: possible role of serotonin and cyclic AMP. *Science* 194:1178–81

Bustamante J, Krasne FB. 1991. Effects of octopamine on transmission at the first synapse of the crayfish lateral giant escape pathway. *J. Comp. Physiol. A* 169:369–77

Byrne JH. 1983. Identification and initial characterization of a cluster of command and pattern-generating neurons underlying respiratory pumping in *Aplysia californica. J. Neurophysiol.* 49:491–508

Byrne JH, Castellucci VF, Carew TJ, Kandel ER. 1978. Stimulus-response relations and stability of mechanoreceptors and motor neurons mediating defensive gill-withdrawal reflex in *Aplysia. J. Neurophysiol.* 41:402–17

Byrne JH, Zwartjes R, Homayouni R, Critz SD, Eskin A. 1993. Roles of second messenger pathways in neuronal plasticity and in learning and memory. In *Advances in Second Messenger and Phosphoprotein Research*, ed. S Shenolikar, AC Nairn, 27: 47–108. New York: Raven

Carew TJ. 1989. Developmental assembly of learning in *Aplysia. Trends Neurosci.* 12: 389–94

Carew TJ, Castellucci VF, Kandel ER. 1971. An analysis of dishabituation and sensitization of the gill-withdrawal reflex in *Aplysia. Int. J. Neurosci.* 2:79–98

Carew TJ, Castellucci VF, Kandel ER. 1979. Sensitization in *Aplysia*: restoration of transmission in synapses inactivated by long-term habituation. *Science* 205: 417–19

Carew TJ, Hawkins RD, Abrams TW, Kandel ER. 1984. A test of Hebb's postulate at identified synapses which mediate classical conditioning in *Aplysia. J. Neurosci.* 4: 1217–24

Carew TJ, Hawkins RD, Kandel ER. 1983. Differential classical conditioning of a defensive withdrawal reflex in *Aplysia californica. Science* 219:397–400

Carew TJ, Kandel ER. 1973. Acquisition and retention of long-term habituation in *Aplysia*: correlation of behavioral and cellular processes. *Science* 182:1158–60

Carew TJ, Pinsker HM, Kandel ER. 1972. Long-term habituation of a defensive withdrawal reflex in *Aplysia. Science* 175:451–54

Carew TJ, Walters ET, Kandel ER. 1981. Classical conditioning in a simple withdrawal reflex in *Aplysia californica. J. Neurosci.* 1:1426–37

Carlson NR. 1994. *Physiology of Behavior,* Vol. 5. Boston: Univ. Mass. Press. 704 pp.

Casagrand JL, Ritzman RE. 1992. Biogenic amines modulate synaptic transmission between identified giant interneurons and thoracic interneurons in the escape system of the cockroach. *J. Neurobiol.* 23:644–55

Castellucci VF, Bernier L, Schwartz JH, Kandel ER. 1983. Persistant activation of adenylate cyclase underlies the time course of short-term sensitization in *Aplysia. Soc. Neurosci. Abstr.* 9:169

Castellucci VF, Blumenfeld H, Goelet P, Kandel ER. 1989. Inhibitor of protein synthesis blocks long-term behavioral sensitization in the isolated gill-withdrawal reflex in *Aplysia. J. Neurobiol.* 20:1–9

Castellucci VF, Carew TJ, Kandel ER. 1978. Cellular analysis of long-term habituation of the gill-withdrawal reflex of *Aplysia californica. Science* 202:1306–8

Castellucci VF, Kandel ER. 1974. A quantal analysis of the synaptic depression underlying habituation of the gill-withdrawal reflex in *Aplysia. Proc. Natl. Acad. Sci. USA* 71:5004–8

Castellucci VF, Kandel ER. 1976. Presynaptic facilitation as a mechanism for behavioral sensitization in *Aplysia. Science* 194:1176–78

Castellucci VF, Kandel ER, Schwartz JH, Wilson FD, Nairn AC, Greengard P. 1980. Intracellular injection of the catalytic subunit of cyclic AMP-dependent protein kinase simulates facilitation of transmitter release underlying behavioral sensitization in *Aplysia. Proc. Natl. Acad. Sci. USA* 77:7492–96

Castellucci VF, Kennedy TE, Kandel ER, Goelet P. 1988. A quantitative analysis of 2-D gels identifies proteins in which labeling is increased following long-term sensitization in *Aplysia. Neuron* 1:321–28

Castellucci VF, Nairn A, Greengard P, Schwartz JH, Kandel ER. 1982. Inhibitor of adenosine 3':5'-monophosphate-dependent protein kinase blocks presynaptic facilitation in *Aplysia. J. Neurosci.* 2:1673–81

Castellucci VF, Pinsker HM, Kupfermann I, Kandel ER. 1970. Neuronal mechanisms of habituation and dishabituation of the gill-withdrawal reflex in *Aplysia. Science* 167:1745–48

Chesselet MF. 1984. Presynaptic regulation of neurotransmitter release in the brain: facts and hypothesis. *Neuroscience* 12:347–75

Cheyette BN, Farley J. 1989. Localization of 5-HT containing meurons which modulate *Hermissenda* type B cell excitability. *Soc. Neurosci. Abstr.* 15:1284

Clark GA. 1984. A cellular mechanism for the temporal specificity of classical conditioning of the siphon-withdrawal response in *Aplysia. Soc. Neurosci. Abstr.* 10:268

Clark GA, Kandel ER. 1984. Branch specific heterosynaptic facilitation in *Aplysia* siphon sensory cells. *Proc. Natl. Acad. Sci. USA* 81:2577–81

Clark GH, Kandel ER. 1993. Induction of long-term facilitation in *Aplysia* sensory neurons by local application of serotonin to remote synapses. *Proc. Natl. Acad. Sci. USA* 90:11411–15

Colwill RM, Absher RA, Roberts ML. 1988. Context-US learning in *Aplysia californica. J. Neurosci.* 8:4434–39

Connor J, Alkon DL. 1984. Light- and voltage-dependent increases of calcium ion concentration in molluscan photoreceptors. *J. Neurophysiol.* 51:745–52

Corning WC, Dyal JA, Willows AOD, eds. 1973. *Invertebrate Learning,* Vols. 1–3. New York: Plenum

Couvillon PA, Klosterhalfen S, Bitterman ME. 1983. Analysis of overshadowing in honeybees. *J. Comp. Psychol.* 97:154–66

Crick F. 1984. Memory and molecular turnover news. *Nature* 312:101

Crow TJ, Alkon DL. 1980. Associative behavioral modification in *Hermissenda*: cellular correlates. *Science* 209:412–14

Crow TJ, Bridge MS. 1985. Serotoin modulates photoresponses in *Hermissenda* type-B photoreceptors. *Neurosci. Lett.* 60:83–88

Crow TJ, Forrester J. 1986. Light paired with serotonin mimics the effect of conditioning on phototactic behavior in *Hermissenda. Proc. Natl. Acad. Sci. USA* 83:7975–78

Crow TJ, Forrester J. 1990. Inhibition of protein synthesis blocks long-term enhancement of generator potentials produced by one-trial in vivo conditioning in *Hermissenda. Proc. Natl. Acad. Sci. USA* 87:4490–94

Crow TJ, Forrester J. 1991. Light paired with serotonin in vivo produces both short- and long-term enhancement of generator potentials of identified B-photoreceptors in *Hermissenda. J. Neurosci.* 11:608–17

Crow TJ, Forrester J. 1993a. Down-regulation of protein kinase C and kinase inhibitors dissociate short- and long-term enhancement produced by one-trial conditioning of *Hermissenda. J. Neurophysiol.* 69:636–41

Crow TJ, Forrester J. 1993b. Protein kinase inhibitors do not block the expression of established enhancement in identified *Hermissenda* B-photoreceptors. *Br. Res. Bull.* 613:61–66

Cui M, Walters ET. Homosynaptic LTP and

PTP of sensorimotor synapses mediating the tail withdrawal reflex in *Aplysia* are reduced by postsynaptic hyperpolarization. *Soc. Neurosci. Abstr.* 20:1072

Dale N, Kandel ER. 1990. Facilitatory and inhibitory transmitters modulate spontaneous transmitter release at cultured *Aplysia* sensorimotor synapses. *J. Physiol.* 421:203–22

Dale N, Schacher S, Kandel ER. 1988. Long-term facilitation in *Aplysia* involves increase in transmitter release. *Science* 239:282–85

Dash PK, Hochner B, Kandel ER. 1990. Injection of the cAMP-response element into the nucleus of *Aplysia* sensory neurons blocks long-term facilitation. *Nature* 345:718–21

Dash PK, Karl KA, Colicos MA, Prywes R, Kandel ER. 1991. cAMP response element-binding protein is activated by Ca^{2+}/calmodulin- as well as cAMP-dependent protein kinase. *Proc. Natl. Acad. Sci. USA* 88:5061–65

de Belle JS, Heisenberg M. 1994. Associative odor learning in *Drosophilia* abolished by chemical ablation of mushroom bodies. *Science* 263:692–95

Dudai Y. 1989. *The Neurobiology of Memory: Concepts, Findings, Trends.* Oxford: Oxford Univ. Press. 340 pp.

Dudai Y, Jan Y-N, Byers D, Quinn WG, Benzer S. 1976. *Dunce*, a mutant of *Drosophilia* deficient in learning. *Proc. Natl. Acad. Sci. USA* 73:1684–88

Eberly LB, Pinsker HM. 1984. Neuroethological studies of reflex plasticity in intact *Aplysia. Behav. Neurosci.* 98:609–30

Edwards DH, Heitler WJ, Leise EM, Fricke RA. 1991. Postsynaptic modulation of rectifying electrical synaptic inputs to the LG escape command neuron in crayfish. *J. Neurosci.* 11:2117–29

Eliot LS, Hawkins RD, Kandel ER, Schacher S. 1994a. Pairing-specific, activity-dependent presynaptic facilitation at *Aplysia* sensory-motor neuron synapses in isolated cell culture. *J. Neurosci.* 14:368–83

Eliot LS, Kandel ER, Hawkins RD. 1994b. Modulation of spontaneous transmitter release during depression and posttetanic potentiation of *Aplysia* sensory-motor neuron synapses isolated in culture. *J. Neurosci.* 14:3280–92

Eliot LS, Kandel ER, Siegelbaum SA, Blumenfeld H. 1993. Imaging terminals of *Aplysia* sensory neurons demonstrates role of enhanced Ca^{2+} influx in presynaptic facilitation. *Nature* 361:634–37

Emptage NJ, Carew TJ. 1993. Long-term synaptic facilitation in the absence of short-term facilitation in *Aplysia* neurons. *Science* 262:253–56

Erber T, Masuhr T, Menzel R. 1980. Localization of short term memory in the brain of the bee, *Apis mellifera. Physiol. Entomol.* 5:343–58

Erickson MT, Walters ET. 1988. Differential expression of pseudoconditioning and sensitization by siphon responses in *Aplysia*: novel response selection after training. *J. Neurosci.* 8:3000–10

Etcheberrigaray R, Huddie PL, Alkon DL. 1991. Gigaohm single-channel recording from isolated *Hermissenda crassicornis* type B photoreceptors. *J. Exp. Biol.* 156:619–23

Etcheberrigaray R, Matzel LD, Lederhendler II, Alkon DL. 1992. Classical conditioning and protein kinase C activation regulate the same single potassium channel in *Hermissenda crassicornis* photoreceptors. *Proc. Natl. Acad. Sci. USA* 89:7184–88

Evans PD. 1985. Octopamine. In *Comprehensive Insect Physiology, Biochemistry, and Pharmacology*, ed. GA Kerkut, LI Gilbert, 11:499–530. New York: Permagon

Falk CX, Wu J, Cohen LB, Tang AC. 1993. Nonuniform expression of habituation in the activity of distinct classes of neurons in the *Aplysia* abdominal ganglion. *J. Neurosci.* 13:4072–81

Fanselow MS. 1986. Conditioned fear-induced opiate analgesia: a competing motivational state theory of stress analgesia. *Ann. NY Acad. Sci.* 467:40–54

Farley J. 1987a. Contingency learning and causal detection in *Hermissenda*: I. Behavior. *Behav. Neurosci.* 101:13–27

Farley J. 1987b. Contingency learning and causal detection in *Hermissenda*: II. Cellular mechanisms. *Behav. Neurosci.* 101:28–56

Farley J, Alkon DL. 1980. Neural organization predicts stimulus specificity for a retained associative behavioral change. *Science* 210:1373–75

Farley J, Alkon DL. 1987. In vitro associative conditioning of *Hermissenda*: cumulative depolarization of type B photoreceptors and short-term associative behavioral changes. *J. Neurophysiol.* 57:1639–68

Farley J, Auerbach S. 1986. Protein kinase C activation induces conductance changes in *Hermissenda* photoreceptors like those seen in associative learning. *Nature* 319:220–23

Farley J, Richards WG, Ling LJ, Liman E, Alkon DL. 1983. Membrane changes in a single photoreceptor cause associative learning in *Hermissenda. Science* 221:1201–3

Farley J, Schuman E. 1991. Protein kinase C inhibitors prevent induction and continued expression of cell memory in *Hermissenda* type B photoreceptors. *Proc. Natl. Acad. Sci. USA* 88:2016–20

Farley J, Wu R. 1989. Serotonin modulation of *Hermissenda* type B photoreceptor light responses and ionic currents: implications for mechanisms underlying asociative learning. *Brain Res. Bull.* 22:335–51

Fischer TM, Carew TJ. 1993. Activity-dependent potentiation of recurrent inhibition: a mechanism for dynamic gain control in the siphon withdrawal reflex in *Aplysia. J. Neurosci.* 13:1302–14

Fitzgerald K, Wright WG, Marcus EA, Carew TJ. 1990. Multiple forms of non-associative plasticity in *Aplysia*: a behavioural, cellular and pharmalogical analysis. *Philos. Trans. R. Soc. London Ser. B* 329:171–78

Frost WN, Castellucci VF, Hawkins RD, Kandel ER. 1985. Monosynaptic connections made by the sensory neurons of the gill- and siphon-withdrawal reflex in *Aplysia* participate in the storage of long-term memory for sensitization. *Proc. Natl. Acad. Sci. USA* 82:8266–69

Frost WN, Clark GA, Kandel ER. 1988. Parallel processing of short-term memory for sensitization in *Aplysia. J. Neurobiol.* 19:297–334

Frysztak RJ, Crow TJ. 1994. Enhancement of type B and A photoreceptor inhibitory synaptic connections in conditioned *Hermissenda. J. Neurosci.* 14:1245–50

Gallistel CR. 1990. *The Organization of Learning.* Cambridge: MIT Press

Ghirardi M, Braha O, Hochner B, Montarolo PG, Kandel ER, Dale N. 1992. Roles of PKA and PKC in facilitation of evoked and spontaneous transmitter release at depressed and nondepressed synapses in *Aplysia* sensory neurons. *Neuron* 9:479–89

Gingrich KJ, Byrne JH. 1985. Simulation of synaptic depression, posttetanic potentiation, and presynaptic facilitation of synaptic potentials from sensory neurons mediating gill-withdrawal reflex in *Aplysia. J. Neurophysiol.* 53:652–69

Glanzman DL, Kandel ER, Schacher S. 1990. Target-dependent structural changes accompanying long-term synaptic facilitation in *Aplysia* neurons. *Science* 249:799–802

Glanzman DL, Kandel ER, Schacher S. 1989a. Identified target motor neuron regulates neurite outgrowth and synapse formation of *Aplysia* sensory neurons in vitro. *Neuron* 3:441–50

Glanzman DL, Krasne FB. 1983. Serotonin and octopamine have opposite modulatory effects on crayfish's lateral giant escape reaction. *J. Neurosci.* 3:2263–69

Glanzman DL, Mackey SL, Hawkins RD, Dyke AM, Lloyd PE, Kandel ER. 1989b. Depletion of serotonin in the nervous system of *Aplysia* reduces the behavioral enhancement of gill withdrawal as well as the heterosynaptic facilitation produced by tail shock. *J. Neurosci.* 9:4200–13

Goelet P, Castellucci VF, Schacher S, Kandel E. 1986. The long and the short of long-term memory—a molecular framework. *Nature* 322:419–22

Goh Y, Alkon DL. 1984. Sensory, interneuronal, and motor interactions within *Hermissenda* visual pathway. *J. Neurophysiol.* 52:156–69

Goh Y, Lederhendler I, Alkon DL. 1985. Input and output changes of an identified neural pathway are correlated with associative learning in *Hermissenda. J. Neurosci.* 5:536–43

Gould JL. 1982. *Ethology: The Mechanisms and Evolution of Behavior.* New York/London: Norton. 544 pp.

Greenberg SM, Castellucci VF, Bayley H, Schwartz JH. 1987. A molecular mechanism for long-term sensitization in *Aplysia. Nature* 329:62–65

Grover LM, Farley J. 1987. Temporal order sensitivity of associative neural and behavioral changes in *Hermissenda. Behav. Neurosci.* 101:658–75

Grover LM, Farley J, Auerbach SB. 1989. Serotonin involvement during in vitro conditioning of *Hermissenda. Br. Res. Bull.* 22:363–72

Hammer M. 1993. An identified neuron mediates the unconditioned stimulus in associative olfactory learning in honeybees. *Nature* 366:59–63

Han P-L, Levin LR, Reed RR, Davis RL. 1992. Preferential expression of the *Drosophilia rutabaga* gene in mushroom bodies, neural centers for learning in insects. *Neuron* 9:619–27

Hanson PI, Schulman H. 1992. Neuronal Ca^{2+}/calmodulin-dependent protein kinases. *Annu. Rev. Biochem.* 61:559–601

Harrigan JF, Alkon DL. 1985. Individual variation in associative learning of the nudibranch mollusc *Hermissenda Crassicornis. Biol. Bull.* 168:222–38

Hawkins RD, Abrams TW. 1984. Evidence that activity-dependent facilitation underlying classical conditioning in *Aplysia* involves modulation of the same ionic current as normal presynaptic facilitation. *Soc. Neurosci. Abstr.* 10:268

Hawkins RD, Abrams TW, Carew TJ, Kandel ER. 1983. A cellular mechanism of classical conditioning in *Aplysia*: activity-dependent amplification of presynaptic facilitation. *Science* 219:400–5

Hawkins RD, Carew TJ, Kandel ER. 1986. Effects of interstimulus interval and contingency on classical conditioning of the *Aplysia* siphon withdrawal reflex. *J. Neurosci.* 6:1695–1701

Hawkins RD, Castellucci VF, Kandel ER. 1981. Interneurons involved in mediation and modulation of gill-withdrawal reflex in *Aplysia* II. Identified neurons produce heterosynaptic facilitation contributing to behavioral sensitization. *J. Neurophysiol.* 45: 315–26

Hawkins RD, Kandel ER. 1984. Is there a cellbiological alphabet for simple forms of learning? *Psychol. Rev.* 91:375-91

Hawkins RD, Kandel ER, Siegelbaum SA. 1993. Learning to modulate transmitter release: themes and variations in synaptic plasticity. *Annu. Rev. Neurosci.* 16:625–65

Hawkins RD, Lalevic N, Clark GA, Kandel ER. 1989. Classical conditioning of the *Aplysia* siphon withdrawal reflex exhibits response specificity. *Proc. Natl. Acad. Sci. USA* 86:7620–24

Hawkins RD, Schacher S. 1989. Identified facilitator neurons L29 and L28 are excited by cutaneous stimuli used in dishabituation, sensitization, and classical conditioning of *Aplysia. J. Neurosci.* 9:4236–45

Hebb DO. 1949. *The Organization of Behavior.* New York: Wiley

Heisenberg M, Borst A, Wagner S, Byers D. 1985. Drosophilia mushroom body mutants are deficient in olfactory learning. *J. Neurogenet.* 2:1–30

Hochner B, Klein M, Schacher S, Kandel ER. 1986a. Action-potential duration and the modulation of transmitter release from the sensory neurons of *Aplysia* in presynaptic facilitation and behavioral sensitization. *Proc. Natl. Acad. Sci. USA* 83:8410–14

Hochner B, Klein M, Schacher S, Kandel ER. 1986b. Additional component in the cellular mechanism of presynaptic facilitation contributes to behavioral dishabituation in *Aplysia. Proc. Natl. Acad. Sci. USA* 83: 8794–98

Homayouni R, Zwarties R, Byrne JH, Eskin A. 1991. Changes in protein phosphorylation in pleural sensory neurons of *Aplysia* vary depending on the duration of serotonin treatments. *Soc. Neurosci. Abstr.* 17: 1589

Hu Y, Barzilai A, Chen M, Bailey CH, Kandel ER. 1993. 5-HT and cAMP induce the formation of coated pits and vesicles and increase the expression of clathrin light chain in sensory neurons of *Aplysia. Neuron* 10: 921–29

Ichinose M, Byrne JH. 1991. Role of protein phosphates in the modulation of neuronal membrane currents. *Br. Res. Bull.* 549: 146–50

Jennings HS. 1906. *Behavior of the Lower Organisms.* New York: Columbia Univ. Press. 366 pp.

Kaang BK, Kandel ER, Grant SGN. 1993. Activation of cAMP-responsive genes by stimuli that produce long-term facilitation in *Aplysia* sensory neurons. *Neuron* 10: 427–35

Kamin LJ. 1969. Predictability, surprise, attention, and conditioning. In *Punishment and Aversive Behavior,* ed. BA Campbell, RM

Church, pp. 276–96. New York: Appleton-Century-Crofts

Kandel ER. 1976. *Cellular Basis of Behavior: An Introduction to Behavioral Neurobiology.* San Francisco: Freeman

Kandel ER, Schwartz JH. 1982. Molecular biology of learning: modulation of transmitter release. *Science* 218:433–42

Kennedy TE, Kuhl D, Barzilai A, Sweatt JD, Kandel ER. 1992. Long-term sensitization training in *Aplysia* leads to an increase in Calreticulin, a major presynaptic calciumbinding protein. *Neuron* 9:1013–24

Kistler HB Jr, Hawkins RD, Koester J, Steinbusch HWM, Kandel ER, Schwartz J. 1985. Distribution of serotonin-immunoreactive cell bodies and processes in the abdominal ganglion of mature *Aplysia. J. Neurosci.* 5:72–80

Klein M. 1994. Synaptic augmentation by 5-HT at rested *Aplysia* sensorimotor synapses: independence of action potential prolongation. *Neuron* 13:159–66

Klein M, Camardo JS, Kandel ER. 1982. Serotonin modulates a specific potassium current in the sensory neurons that show presynaptic facilitation in *Aplysia. Proc. Natl. Acad. Sci. USA* 79:5713–17

Klein M, Hochner B, Kandel ER. 1986. Facilitatory transmitters and cAMP can modulate accommodation as well as transmitter release in *Aplysia* sensory neurons: evidence for parallel processing in a single cell. *Proc. Natl. Acad. Sci. USA* 83:7994–98

Klein M, Kandel ER. 1978. Presynaptic modulation of voltage-dependent Ca^{2+} current: mechanism for behavioral sensitization in *Aplysia californica. Proc. Natl. Acad. Sci. USA* 75:3512–16

Klein M, Kandel ER. 1980. Mechanism of calcium current modulation underlying presynaptic facilitation and behavioral sensitization in *Aplysia. Proc. Natl. Acad. Sci. USA* 77:6912–16

Krasne FB. 1969. Excitation and habituation of the crayfish escape reflex: the depolarizing response in lateral giant fibres of the isolated abdomen. *J. Exp. Biol.* 50:29–46

Krasne FB. 1976. Invertebrate systems as a means of gaining insight into the nature of learning and memory. In *Neural Mechanisms of Learning and Memory,* ed. MR Rosenzweig, EL Bennett, pp. 401–29. Cambridge, MA: MIT Press. 637 pp.

Krasne FB, Glanzman DL. 1986. Sensitization of the crayfish lateral giant escape reaction. *J. Neurosci.* 6:1013–20

Krasne FB, Teshiba TM. 1994. Habituation of an invertebrate escape reflex due to modulation by higher centers rather than local events. *Proc. Natl. Acad. Sci. USA.* In press

Krasne FB, Wine JJ. 1987. Evasion response of the crayfish. In *Aims and Methods in Neuroethology,* ed. DM Guthrie, 1:10-45.

Wolfeboro, NH: Manchester Univ. Press. 310 pp.

Kuhl D, Kennedy TE, Barzilai A, Kandel ER. 1992. Long-term sensitization training in *Aplysia* leads to an increase in the expression of BiP, the major protein chaperone of the ER. *J. Cell Biol.* 119:1069–76

Kupfermann I, Castellucci VF, Pinsker HM, Kandel ER. 1970. Neuronal correlates of habituation and dishabituation of the gill-withdrawal reflex in *Aplysia*. *Science* 167:1743–45

Kupfermann I, Kandel ER. 1969. Neuronal controls of a behavioral response mediated by the abdominal ganglion of the *Aplysia*. *Science* 164:847–50

Lederhendler II, Alkon DL. 1987. Associatively reduced withdrawal from shadows in *Hermissenda:* a direct behavioral analog of photoreceptor responses to brief light steps. *Behav. Neural Biol.* 47:227–49

Lederhendler II, Gart S, Alkon DL. 1986. Classical conditioning of *Hermissenda:* origin of a new response. *J. Neurosci.* 6:1325–31

Levin LR, Han P-L, Hwang PM, Feinstein PG, Davis RL, Reed RR. 1992. The *Drosophilia* learning and memory gene *rutabaga* encodes a Ca^{2+}/calmodulin-responsive adenylyl cyclase. *Cell* 68:479–89

Lin XY, Glanzman DL. 1994a. Hebbian induction of long-term potentiation of *Aplysia* sensorimotor synapses: partial requirement for activation of an NMDA-related receptor. *Proc. R. Soc. London Ser. B* 255:113–18

Lin XY, Glanzman DL. 1994b. Long-term potentiation of *Aplysia* sensorimotor synapses in cell culture: regulation by postsynaptic voltage. *Proc. R. Soc. London Ser. B* 255:215–21

Lisman JE. 1985. A mechanism for memory storage insensitive to molecular turnover: a bistable autophosphorylating kinase. *Proc. Natl. Acad. Sci. USA* 82:3055–57

Lloyd PE, Mahon AC, Kupfermann I, Cohen JL, Scheller RH, Weiss KR. 1985. Biochemical and immunocytological localization of molluscan small cardioactive peptides in the nervous system of *Aplysia californica*. *J. Neurosci.* 5:1851–61

Lockery SR, Sejnowski TJ. 1993. A lower bound on the detectability of nonassociative learning in the local bending reflex of the medicinal leech. *Behav. Neural Biol.* 59:208–24

Longley RD, Longley AJ. 1986. Serotonin immunoreactivity of neurons in the gastropod *Aplysia californica*. *J. Neurobiol.* 17:339–58

Lukowiak K. 1979. L9 modulation of gill withdrawal reflex habituation in *Aplysia*. *J. Neurobiol.* 10:255–71

Mackey SL, Glanzman DL, Small SA, Dyke AM, Kandel ER, Hawkins RD. 1987. Tail shock produces inhibition as well as sensitization of the siphon-withdrawal reflex of *Aplysia:* possible behavioral role for presynaptic inhibition mediated by the peptide Phe-Met-Arg-Phe-NH_2. *Proc. Natl. Acad. Sci. USA* 84:8730–34

Mackey SL, Kandel ER, Hawkins RD. 1989. Identified serotonergic neurons LCB1 and RCB1 in the cerebral ganglia of *Aplysia* produce presynaptic facilitation of siphon sensory neurons. *J. Neurosci.* 9:4227–35

Matzel LD, Alkon DL. 1991. GABA-induced potentiation of neuronal excitability occurs during contiguous pairings with intracellular calcium elevation. *Br. Res. Bull.* 554:77–84

Matzel LD, Lederhendler II, Alkon DL. 1990. Regulation of short-term associative memory by calcium-dependent protein kinase. *J. Neurosci.* 10:2300-7

Matzel LD, Rogers RF, Fass DM. 1992. Calcium transients, not accumulation, induce biophysical correlates of learning in *Hermissenda*. *Soc. Neurosci. Abstr.* 18:15

Mauelshagen J. 1993. Neural correlates of olfactory learning paradigms in an identified neuron in the honeybee brain. *J. Neurophysiol.* 69:609–25

Mayford M, Barzilai A, Keller F, Schacher S, Kandel ER. 1992. Modulation of an NCAM-related adhesion molecule with long-term synaptic plasticity in *Aplysia*. *Science* 256:638–44

Menzel R. 1990. Learning, memory, and "cognition" in honey bees. In *Neurobiology of Comparative Cognition,* ed. RP Kesner, DS Olton, pp. 237–91. London: Erlbaum

Mercer AR, Emptage NJ, Carew TJ. 1991. Pharmacological dissociation of modulatory effects of serotonin in *Aplysia* sensory neurons. *Science* 254:1811–13

Miller MW, Vu ET, Krasne FB. 1992. Cholinergic transmission at the first synapse of the circuit mediating the crayfish lateral giant escape reaction. *J. Neurophysiol.* 68:2174–84

Mobbs PG. 1984. Neural networks in the mushroom body of the honey bee. *J. Insect Physiol.* 30:43–58

Montarolo PG, Goelet P, Castellucci VF, Morgan J, Kandel ER, Schacher S. 1986. A critical period for macromolecular synthesis in long-term heterosynaptic facilitation in *Aplysia*. *Science* 234:1249–54

Montarolo PG, Kandel ER, Schacher S. 1988. Long-term heterosynaptic inhibition in *Aplysia*. *Nature* 333:171–74

Morita D, North RA, Tokimasa T. 1982. Muscarinic presynaptic inhibition of synaptic transmission in myenteric plexus of guinea-pig ileum. *J. Physiol.* 333:141–49

Nelson TJ, Akon DL. 1990. Specific high molecular weight mRNAs induced by associative learning in *Hermissenda. Proc. Natl. Acad. Sci. USA* 87:269–73

Nelson TJ, Collin C, Alkon DL. 1990. Isolation of a G protein that is modified by learning and reduces potassium currents in *Hermissenda. Science* 247:1479–83

Nighorn A, Healy MJ, Davis RL. 1991. The cyclic AMP phosphodiesterase encoded by the *Drosophilia dunce* gene is concentrated in the mushroom body neuropil. *Neuron* 6: 455–67

Noel F, Nunez-Regueiro M, Cook R, Byrne JH, Eskin A. 1993. Long-term changes in synthesis of intermediate filament protein, actin and other proteins in pleural sensory neurons of *Aplysia* produced by an in vitro analogue of sensitization training. *Mol. Brain Res.* 19:203–10

Ocorr KA, Walters ET, Byrne JH. 1985. Associative conditioning analog selectively increases cAMP levels of tail sensory neurons in *Aplysia. Proc. Natl. Acad. Sci. USA* 82:2548–52

Orchard I. 1982. Octopamine in insects: neurotransmitter, neurohormone and neuromodulator. *Can. J. Zool.* 60:659–69

Pearlman AJ. 1979. Central and peripheral control of siphon-withdrawal reflex in *Aplysia californica. J. Neurophysiol.* 42: 510–29

Pieroni JP, Byrne JH. 1992. Differential effects of serotonin, FMRFamide, and small cardioactive peptide on multiple, distributed processes modulating sensorimotor synaptic transmission in *Aplysia. J. Neurosci.* 12:2633–47

Pinsker HM, Hening WA, Carew TJ, Kandel ER. 1973. Long-term sensitization of a defensive withdrawal reflex in *Aplysia. Science* 182:1039–42

Pinsker HM, Kupfermann I, Castellucci VF, Kandel ER. 1970. Habituation and Dishabituation of the gill-withdrawal reflex in *Aplysia. Science* 167:1740–42

Piomelli D, Volterra A, Dale N, Siegelbaum SA, Kandel ER, et al. 1987. Lipoxygenase metabolites of arachidonic acid as second messengers for presynaptic inhibition of *Aplysia* sensory cells. *Nature* 328:38–43

Qiu Y, Chen C-N, Malone T, Richter L, Beckendorf SK, Davis RL. 1991. Characterization of the memory gene *dunce* of *Drosophilia melanogaster. J. Mol. Biol.* 222:553–65

Quinn WG, Harris WA, Benzer S. 1974. Conditioned behavior in *Drosophilia melanogaster. Proc. Natl. Acad. Sci. USA* 71:708–12

Rayport SG, Schacher S. 1986. Synaptic plasticity in vitro: cell culture of identified *Aplysia* neurons mediating short-term habituation and sensitization. *J. Neurosci.* 6: 759–63

Rescorla RA. 1967. Pavlovian conditioning and its proper control procedures. *Psychol. Rev.* 74:71–80

Rescorla RA, Wagner AR. 1972. A theory of Pavlovian conditioning: variations in the effectiveness of reinforcement and nonreinforcement. In *Classical Conditioning II,* ed. AH Black, WF Prokasy. New York: Appleton-Century-Crofts

Romanes GJ. 1895. *Mental Evolution in Animals.* New York: Appleton. 411 pp.

Sahley C. 1993. 5HT depletion eliminates sensitization but only partially disrupts classical conditioning. *Soc. Neurosci. Abstr.* 19: 579

Sahley C, Gelperin A, Rudy JW. 1981a. One-trial associative learning modifies food odor preferences of a terrestrial mollusc. *Proc. Natl. Acad. Sci. USA* 78:640–42

Sahley C, Rudy JW, Gelperin A. 1981b. An analysis of associative learning in a terrestrial mollusc. *J. Comp. Physiol. A* 144:1–8

Sakakibara M, Alkon DL, DeLorenzo R, Goldenring JR, Neary JT, Heldman E. 1986a. Modulation of calcium-mediated inactivation of ionic currents by Ca^{2+}/calmodulin-dependent protein kinase II. *Biophys. J.* 50: 319–27

Sakakibara M, Alkon DL, Neary JT, Heldman E, Gould R. 1986b. Inositol trisphosphate regulation of photoreceptor membrane currents. *Biophys. J.* 50:797–803

Schacher S, Glanzman D, Barzilai A, Dash P, Grant SGN, et al. 1990a. Long-term facilitation in *Aplysia:* persistant phosphorylation and structural changes. *Cold Spring Harbor Symp. Quant. Biol.* 55:187–202

Schacher S, Kandel ER, Montarolo PG. 1993. cAMP and arachidonic acid simulate long-term structural and functional changes produced by neurotransmitters in *Aplysia* sensory neurons. *Neuron* 10:1079–88

Schacher S, Montarolo PG. 1991. Target-dependent structural changes in sensory neurons of *Aplysia* accompany long-term heterosynaptic inhibition. *Neuron* 6:679–90

Schacher S, Montarolo PG, Kandel ER. 1990b. Selective short- and long-term effects of serotonin, small cardioactive peptide, and tetanic stimulation on sensorimotor synapses of *Aplysia* in culture. *J. Neurosci.* 10:3286–94

Scholz KP, Byrne JH. 1987. Long-term sensitization in *Aplysia:* biophysical correlates in tail sensory neurons. *Science* 235:685–87

Schuman EM, Clark GA. 1994. Synaptic facilitation at connections of *Hermissenda* type B photoreceptors. *J. Neurosci.* 14: 1613–22

Schuman EM, Madison DV. 1994. Locally distributed synaptic potentiation in the hippocampus. *Science* 263:532–36

Schwartz JH, Bernier L, Castellucci VF, Palazzolo M, Saitoh T, et al. 1983. What molecular steps determine the time course of the memory for short-term sensitization in *Aplysia? Cold Spring Harbor Symp. Quant. Biol.* 58:811–19

Shuster MJ, Camardo JS, Siegelbaum SA, Kandel ER. 1985. Cyclic AMP-dependent protein kinase closes the serotonin-sensitive K$^+$ channels of *Aplysia* sensory neurons in cell-free membrane patches. *Nature* 313:392–95

Siegelbaum SA, Camardo JS, Kandel ER. 1982. Serotonin and cyclic AMP close single K$^+$ channels in *Aplysia* sensory neurones. *Nature* 299:413–17

Small SA, Kandel ER, Hawkins RD. 1989. Activity-dependent enhancement of presynaptic inhibition in *Aplysia* sensory neurons. *Science* 243:1603–6

Smith RF, Choi K-W, Tully T, Quinn WG. 1986. Deficient protein kinase C activity in *turnip*, a *Drosophilia* learning mutant. *Soc. Neurosci. Abstr.* 12:399

Sombati S, Hoyle G. 1984. Central nervous sensitization and dishabituation of the reflex action in an insect by the neuromodulator octopamine. *J. Neurobiol.* 15:455–80

Stopfer M, Carew TJ. 1994. Homosynaptic depression in tail sensory neurons is not the mechanism of habituation of tail-induced tail or siphon withdrawal in *Aplysia. Soc. Neurosci. Abstr.* 20:1073

Sugita S, Goldsmith JR, Baxter DA, Byrne JH. 1992. Involvement of protein kinase C in serotonin-induced spike broadening and synaptic facilitation in sensorimotor connections of *Aplysia. J. Neurophysiol.* 68: 643–51

Sweatt D, Volterra A, Siegelbaum SA, Kandel ER. 1988. Molecular convergence of presynaptic inhibition and presynaptic facilitation on common substrate proteins of individual sensory neurons of *Aplysia. Cold Spring Harbor Symp. Quant. Biol.* 53:395–405

Sweatt JD, Kandel ER. 1989. Persistant and transcriptionally-dependent increase in protein phosphorylation in long-term facilitation of *Aplysia* sensory neurons. *Nature* 339:51–54

Tabata M, Alkon DL. 1982. Positive synaptic feedback in visual system of nudibranch mollusk *Hermissenda crassicornis. J. Neurophysiol.* 48:174–91

Takeda K. 1961. Classical conditioning responses in the honey bee. *J. Insect Physiol.* 6:168–79

Thompson RF. 1990. Neural mechanisms of classical conditioning in mammals. *Philos. Trans. R. Soc. London Ser. B* 329:161–70

Trimmer BA, Weeks JC. 1989. Effects of nicotinic and muscarinic agents on an identified motoneurone and its direct afferent inputs in larval *Manduca Sexta. J. Exp. Biol.* 144: 303–37

Trudeau LE, Castellucci VF. 1992. Contribution of polysynaptic pathways in the mediation and plasticity of *Aplysia* gill and siphon withdrawal reflex: evidence for differential modulation. *J. Neurosci.* 12: 3838–48

Trudeau LE, Castellucci VF. 1993a. Functional uncoupling of inhibitory interneurons plays an important role in short-term sensitization of *Aplysia* gill and siphon withdrawal reflex. *J. Neurosci.* 13:2126–35

Trudeau LE, Castellucci VF. 1993b. Sensitization of the gill and siphon withdrawal reflex of *Aplysia*: multiple sites of change in the neuronal network. *J. Neurophysiol.* 70: 1210–20

Tully T. 1988. On the road to a better understanding of learning and memory in *Drosophilia melanogaster*. In *Modulation of Synaptic Transmission and Plasticity in Nervous Systems,* ed. G Hertting, H-C Spatz, H19:401-17. Berlin/Heidelberg: Springer-Verlag

Tully T, Quinn WG. 1985. Classical conditioning and retention in normal and mutant *Drosophilia melanogaster. J. Comp. Physiol. A* 157:263–77

Vu ET, Lee SC, Krasne FB. 1987. Anatomical and physiological evidence for a novel inhibitory circuit in the crayfish lateral giant escape reflex. *Soc. Neurosci. Abstr.* 13:143

Vu ET, Lee SC, Krasne FB. 1993. The mechanism of tonic inhibition of crayfish escape behavior: distal inhibition and its functional significance. *J. Neurosci.* 13:4379–93

Walters ET. 1987. Multiple sensory neuronal correlates of site-specific sensitization in *Aplysia. J. Neurosci.* 7:408–17

Walters ET. 1989. Transformation of siphon responses during conditioning of *Aplysia* suggests a model of primitive stimulus-response association. *Proc. Natl. Acad. Sci. USA* 86:7616–19

Walters ET, Byrne JH. 1983. Associative conditioning of single sensory neurons suggest a cellular mechanism for learning. *Science* 219:405–8

Walters ET, Byrne JH, Carew TJ, Kandel ER. 1983. Mechanoafferent neurons innervating tail of *Aplysia*. I. Response properties and synaptic connections. *J. Neurophysiol.* 50:1522–42

Walters ET, Erickson MT. 1986. Directional control and the functional organization of defensive responses in *Aplysia. J. Comp. Physiol. A* 159:339–51

Werness SA, Fay SD, Blackwell KT, Vogl TP, Alkon DL. 1992. Associative learning in a network model of *Hermissenda crassicornis. Biol. Cybern.* 68:125–33

Werness SA, Fay SD, Blackwell KT, Vogl TP, Alkon DL. 1993. Associative learning in a network model of *Hermissenda crassicornis*. II. Experiments. *Biol. Cybern.* 69: 19–28

West A, Barnes E, Alkon DL. 1982. Primary changes of voltage responses during retention of associative learning. *J. Neurophysiol.* 48:1243–55

Wine JJ, Krasne FB, Chen L. 1975. Habituation and inhibition of the crayfish lateral giant fibre escape response. *J. Exp. Biol.* 62:771–82

Wittstock S, Kaatz HH, Menzel R. 1993. Inhibition of brain protein synthesis by cycloheximide does not affect formation of long-term memory in honeybees after olfactory conditioning. *J. Neurosci.* 13:1379–86

Woolf CJ, Walters ET. 1991. Common patterns of plasticity contributing to nociceptive sensitization in mammals and *Aplysia*. *Trends Neurosci.* 14:74–78

Yovell Y, Abrams TW. 1994. Temporal asymmetry in activation of Aplysia adenylyl cyclase by calcium and transmitter may explain temporal requirements of conditioning. *Proc. Natl. Acad. Sci. USA* 89:6526–30

Yovell Y, Kandel ER, Dudai Y, Abrams TW. 1987. Biochemical correlates of short-term sensitization in *Aplysia*: temporal analysis of adenylate cyclase stimulation in a perfused-membrane preparation. *Proc. Natl. Acad. Sci. USA* 84:9285–89

Zucker RS. 1972a. Crayfish escape behavior and central synapse. I. Neural circuit exciting lateral giant fiber. *J. Neurophysiol.* 35:599–620

Zucker RS. 1972b. Crayfish escape behavior and central synapses. II. Physiological mechanisms underlying behavioral habituation. *J. Neurophysiol.* 35:621–37

Zucker RS. 1989. Short-term synaptic plasticity. *Annu. Rev. Neurosci.* 12:13–31

Annu. Rev. Psychol. 1995. 46:625–54

GENES AND HUMAN BEHAVIOR

Richard J. Rose

Department of Psychology, Indiana University, Bloomington, Indiana 47405-1301

KEY WORDS: behavior genetics, cognitive abilities, personality, health habits, psychopathology

CONTENTS

INTRODUCTION

This volume of the *Annual Review of Psychology* marks anniversaries of both old and new approaches to human behavioral genetics. This review of genes and human behavior appears 35 years after the field of behavior genetics was christened with a monograph bearing that name (Fuller & Thompson 1960), and 25 years after the Behavior Genetics Association was founded and its journal, *Behavior Genetics,* launched. This volume appears 15 years after recognition of the utility of using DNA markers for gene-mapping, which initiated the use of restriction fragment length polymorphisms (RFLPs) for genetic linkage studies. And 1995 is the fifth year of the United States Human Genome Project, a project to map the human DNA sequence, one so successful that three years into it, a new, more ambitious five-year plan was launched (Collins & Galas 1993). There are exciting developments in both old (quantitative) and new (molecular) approaches to human behavioral genetics; this review attempts to highlight the excitement, promise, and controversy surrounding contemporary human behavior genetics.

Cover-story reports of behavior genetics (*Science* 1994) testify to the field's vitality and visibility, but controversy follows. The most influential popular periodical in US science headlined "The dubious link between genes and behavior," subtitling its "lack-of-progress report" in behavior genetics as "Eugenics Revisited" (Horgan 1993). Others charge that the "allure of genetic explanations" (Alper & Natowicz 1992) for complex social behavior leads to poor science and pernicious social policy, and that problems endemic to the old genetic analyses will reoccur in the new (Billings et al 1992). Amid such controversy, an initiative to enhance NIH funding for violence research was put on hold, and an NIH-funded conference on "Genetic Factors in Crime" was canceled. A gene for a form of familial aggression was announced by Dutch scientists (Brunner et al 1993), who subsequently were denounced (Simm 1994) for studying violent behavior as a phenotype. And while the media debates whether genes affect behavioral outcomes, some behavioral geneticists declare the nature-nurture war to be over (Scarr 1987) and, presuming they have won, now throw down a gauntlet to "socialization theorists," arguing that children's behavioral individuality is a product of children's unique genes. The notion that parental behaviors, and the home environments parents create, cause differences in children's outcomes is rejected: "Being reared in one family, rather than another...makes few differences in children's personality and intellectual development" (Scarr 1992, p. 3; for replies, see Baumrind 1993, Jackson 1993). A new monograph, provocatively entitled *The Limits of Family Influence,* broadly extends that theme (Rowe 1994). Such claims about the nature of nurture challenge basic social and scientific assumptions; hopefully, the challenge will elicit empirical replies and redirect inquiry into the interplay of genes and behavior.

Except among monozygotic (MZ) co-twins, an exception of central importance to behavior genetics, each of us has a unique genotype. Our genetic individuality is at the core of our personal lives, rendering us differentially susceptible to life events and leading us to seek environmental niches within which to behaviorally express our genetic dispositions. Evidence from behavior genetic research on fruit flies and rodents (Barinaga 1994), success in gene targeting mouse embryos (Capecchi 1994), and progress in identifying genetic etiologies of neurological disease (Martin 1993) raise profound questions relating genes to behavior (Wiesel 1994). The questions are not whether genes matter, but, rather, how they matter and how genetic effects are modulated across lifespans of environmental interactions. This review explores the treatment of such questions in recent research.

COGNITIVE ABILITY AND DISABILITY

Cognitive Abilities: General and Specific

Recent research has been directed to models that disentangle genetic and environmental influences on change and continuity in cognitive abilities over time (Boomsma 1993, Molenaar et al 1991). Data for such models have come from biological and adopted siblings studied within the Colorado Adoption Project (CAP), begun in 1975 and now yielding informative analyses across the first decade of childhood (DeFries et al 1994). Developmental models ask whether age-to-age correlations are the result of early genetic and environmental effects that persist across time, or whether new effects are exerted at specific ages. Typical models used in the CAP combine a single general factor present at all ages with a simplex model of specific effects that arise at each age but persist to later ages, a model first formulated by Eaves et al (1986).

CONTINUITY AND CHANGE IN COGNITIVE ABILITIES IN CHILDHOOD   In CAP data, observed and latent sources of individual differences in general cognitive ability have been analyzed in adopted and nonadopted siblings at ages one to nine years, sometimes adding data from twins assessed from one to three years. These analyses have found that observed continuity in cognitive ability arises from both age-specific effects that persist over time and from developmental influences that are static and unchanging (Cardon et al 1992a; Cherny & Cardon 1994). Genes account for age-specific, persistent effects, while siblings' shared environmental effects are constant from ages one to nine. Thus, genetic influences are a major source of both continuity and change, while shared environmental effects contribute to continuity; environmental experience unique to individuals contributes to developmental change. (Cardon et al 1992a, Fulker & Cardon 1993). CAP analyses suggest that the complexity of developmental processes resides in the genotype, and both continuity and change contribute to rank ordering of behaviors at ages one to three. There is no new genetic variation at age four, but at seven years of age, new variation again arises, attributed by Fulker et al (1993) to novel environmental demands of a year of schooling. One message from the CAP data is that stability of mental development is, in part, caused by unchanging familial environmental influences (e.g. social class) shared by siblings throughout childhood development. Across ages one to nine, the proportion of phenotypic variance explained by genetic factors (heritability or h^2) is fairly constant at approximately .55. What of shared environmental effects? Adoptive siblings directly assess their importance, for such effects are the only cause of their resemblance. Correlations of adoptive siblings in the CAP provide only modest evidence of shared environmental effects, but that fact must be interpreted cautiously because most adoptive siblings in the CAP are brother-sister pairs, and all CAP adopted siblings, necessarily, differ in age (on average, by three years). So CAP analyses cannot detect environmental effects uniquely shared by like-sex siblings and must underestimate effects of trait-relevant experience shared by age-matched co-twins (Cherny & Cardon 1994). With that caveat, the important developmental changes in sources of individual variation in IQ appear to be an increase in heritability from infancy to childhood and a decrease in effects of common familial environments during adolescence (Boomsma 1993).

SUBSEQUENT AGE-DEPENDENT CHANGES   What happens later? Do genetic and environmental influences on IQ vary across adolescence and adulthood? One answer is found in analyses (McGue et al 1993a) of the approximately 13,500 twin pairs whose IQ data are reported in world literature. Analyzed by age, from four to six years to late adulthood, MZ twin correlations continuously increase throughout life, while those for dizygotic (DZ) co-twins drop off after late adolescence. The correlations suggest that the proportion of IQ variance associated with additive genes increases throughout development, especially after age 20. Conversely, the proportion of individual variation associated with shared environmental factors is relatively constant (~ 30%) until early adulthood, but then declines to zero. It is of no surprise that shared environmental effects are greatest while twins are cohabiting. But do these effects not endure beyond cohabitation? Perhaps the meta-analysis misleads, for it compares data collected over decades in different cultures with different methods. But McGue et al (1993a) report the same result from their own standardized research with twins, aged 11–88. Again, MZ twins' similarity for tested IQ increases with age, that for DZ twin pairs does not; estimated heritability of IQ increases from about 50% in preadolescence to about 80% in adulthood, while shared environmental effects decrease from about 20% in preadolescence to near zero in adulthood. Thus, age-modulation of sources of individual variation in tested IQ is a robust finding, and the data suggest that (*a*) effects of common environment, evident in childhood and adolescence, do not persist beyond cohabitation and (*b*) heritability increases throughout development, especially after age 20, as resemblance of MZ twins increases. Important questions remain, however. There are few adult twin studies, and none are long-term longitudinal in design.

DIFFERENTIAL HERITABILITY AT DIFFERENT LEVELS OF ABILITY? If heritability, h^2, varies with age, does it also vary with level of cognitive ability? Three research groups explored this question, and each group reported a different answer. Detterman et al (1990) found higher h^2 at lower levels of ability, prompting a review (Bailey & Ravelle 1991) of previous twin studies that found the opposite effect (i.e. higher heritability at higher levels of cognitive ability). And with twins assessed at ages one, two, and three years, Cherny et al (1992) found little evidence that h^2 varies as a function of ability level. The issue, of practical and theoretical interest, will not be resolved without much larger twin samples.

BEHAVIOR GENETICS OF SPECIFIC COGNITIVE ABILITIES   A recent development is a hierarchical longitudinal path model for analysis of twin and sibling data to assess shared and independent etiologies for groups of measures on multiple occasions (Cardon & Fulker 1994). The model provides information on consistency and change in relationships among variables over time. Applied to CAP data, obtained at ages 3, 4, 7, and 9, results indicate that the genetic continuity observed for general intelligence in childhood is due to stability of the specific components of which general intelligence is composed, not to genetic influences on general intelligence itself (Cardon 1994, Cardon & Fulker 1993). At ages 3 and 4, both genetic and environmental influences on specific abilities are evident; the genetic effect is largely a general one, the environmental effects largely those unique to individuals. There is little evidence, in early childhood, of genetic variance specific to specific cognitive ability. But data obtained at age seven for verbal, spatial, and memory abilities did suggest ability-specific genetic influences (Cardon et al 1992b). At age 9, on data from smaller samples, only verbal ability showed such specific genetic influence, while shared environmental effects contributed to spatial and perceptual speed abilities (Cardon 1994). The shifts at ages 7 and 9 are intriguing: Does genetic differentiation of specific cognitive ability emerge in childhood? Do shared environmental effects on specific abilities emerge late in childhood? Or are these apparent effects confounds of measurement variance, arising from different assessments at different ages and smaller samples at older ages?

Developmentally removed from CAP analyses of infants' cognitive ability is research on individual differences in memory among elderly twins. Data from Minnesota twin pairs aged 60–88 (Finkel & McGue 1993) indicate that 55% of variance in memory performance was attributable to additive genetic effects. Genetic variance in memory performance of elderly Swedish twins (Pedersen et al 1992b) appears comparable (Finkel et al 1994). Bivariate analyses of the Minnesota data examined cross-correlations of memory performance in one twin with cognitive variables or intellectual activities in the co-twin; the cross-correlations suggest that relationships between memory and its components are genetic, while those between memory and lifestyle variables (e.g. time spent in leisure reading) arise from effects of common environments.

GENETIC ANALYSES OF NEUROPHYSIOLOGICAL CORRELATES OF IQ   IQ test scores correlate with nerve conduction velocity (NCV): Faster NCV is associated with higher IQ (Vernon 1991). Faster NCV also is associated with shorter reaction time (RT) (Vernon & Mori 1992), and a multivariate analysis of twins' IQs and RTs found a genetic correlation between these variables (Baker et al 1991). A twin study of NCV, RT, and IQ should be informative. Data have been reported for NCV, RT, and a measure of cognitive ability for more than 200 Dutch twins tested at age 16 (Rijsdijk et al 1994a,b). Significant h^2 was found for both NCV and RT, but gene expression was sex-limited for RT, with h^2 higher for males. Faster NCV was associated with shorter RTs, but correlations were modest (−0.11). Performance on each of the RT tasks correlated significantly with test scores on the Raven Matrices (average $r = -0.21$): Shorter RTs were associated with higher Raven's scores. But NCV did not correlate with Raven's scores. Perhaps NCV-IQ correlations are measure-specific: A follow-up study of the Dutch twins with the Wechsler Adult Intelligence Scale, now in progress, may find an answer to this question.

SEARCH FOR QUANTITATIVE TRAIT LOCI IN COGNITIVE ABILITIES   Recent behavior genetic research on cognitive ability includes the first allelic association study (Plomin et al 1994a). Frequency differences were sought in 60 DNA markers, in or near genes thought relevant to neural functioning, in children at extremes of tested ability. Forty-two (twin) children formed two subsamples with average IQs of 82 and 130. Forty-four singleton school children formed replication samples with mean IQs of 59 and 142. The search was unsuccessful: Replicated differences in allelic frequencies were not found. Given the limited statistical power of the small samples and uncertain utility of the DNA markers employed, this result is not surprising. With larger samples and more functional DNA polymorphisms, the power of this approach will be enhanced. But it remains uncertain whether, and, if so, how quickly, at what cost, and to what end, a search for allelic associations in IQ test scores will pay off. Despite skeptics (see Aldhous 1992), however, quantitative trait loci (QTL) research on IQ and other continuously varying dimensions of human behavior is well under way, and some (e.g. Plomin et al 1994b) optimistically forecast its success.

Reading Disability

Evidence from the Colorado Family Reading Study (CFRS; DeFries & Gillis 1993) documents familial aggregation of reading disability, establishes that heritable variation underlies the aggregation, and encourages a search for major genes. The CFRS compares reading-disabled children with controls matched on age, gender, school, and home neighborhood. Siblings and parents of probands exhibit significant reading deficits, relative to performance of parents and siblings of matched controls—compelling evidence that reading disability is familial. A recent analysis (Pennington et al 1991) added independent samples to families in the CFRS and used segregation analysis to test for a major gene. Results suggested that major gene transmission occurs in some families with reading-disabled children. Earlier efforts found suggestive evidence of linkage to chromosome 15, a finding weakened by follow-up and inclusion of additional families, a pattern that is, alas, common in linkage studies of behavioral disorder. More recent efforts (Smith et al 1991) analyzed sibling pairs, rather than cross-generational family data, with results suggesting possible linkages to both chromosomes 6 and 15. In a reanalysis of these sibling-pair data, Fulker et al (1991) used discriminate scores on reading disability for each pair, together with information on their genetic identity-by-descent (ibd) at markers for which QTLs may be linked. Information on marker loci on the siblings and their parents was used to estimate the proportion of alleles each sibling pair shares ibd at various marker loci; that proportion assumes values 0, 0.5, or 1 for siblings who share zero, one, or two alleles ibd at each locus. Siblings with a value of zero are no more alike than unrelated strangers at that locus; at value 0.5, they are as alike as ordinary siblings, and at value one, they are, at that locus, as alike as MZ co-twins. Each sibling's discriminant reading ability score then became the dependent variable in regressions, in which each sibling's reading score and the pair's ibd estimate, π, for RFLP markers on chromosome 15, were entered as independent variables. This promising approach provides additional evidence that major genes on chromosome 15 influence reading ability. Fulker & Cardon (1994) have extended analytic techniques for sibling-pair analyses and have begun further research with informative sibling-pairs; early results (Fulker 1994) offer less evidence of chromosome 15 markers, but suggest that the HLA histocompatibility complex on chromosome 6 may be relevant.

Fragile-X Syndrome and Triplet Repeats

Fragile-X Syndrome is the most common form of inherited mental retardation, with a population frequency of about 1 in 1250 males. A characteristic of the syndrome is that risk increases across generations, a phenomenon known as anticipation: The disease tends to be more severe and occurs with earlier onset in later generations of a pedigree. The molecular basis of Fragile-X is now known to be a triplet repeat, and the lessons learned may elucidate other psychiatric conditions. Instability of the repeat, transmitted through affected pedigrees, explains anticipation and the unusual segregation pattern of the phenotype. The mutation makes genes markedly increase in size by adding extra copies of a 3 base-pair repeated sequence of DNA. Fragile-X results from amplification of the CGG repeat found in the untranslated region of the *FMR-1* gene on the X chromosome (Verkerk et al 1991). The normal *FMR-1* gene carries, at most, 50 copies of the CGG trinucleotide. When the gene begins to mutate, the expansion increases to as many as 200 copies, although these gene carriers are not retarded. But children who inherit the gene from carriers, and who develop mental retardation and the other stigmata of the Fragile-X Syndrome, exhibit hundreds to thousands of CGG repeats. Thus, the Fragile-X genotype is characterized by an unstable region of DNA—a trinucleotide repeat of variable copy number (Oberlé et al 1991, Yu et al 1991, Yu et al 1992). Because the Fragile-X genotype is defined by the extent of amplification of the trinucleotide repeat, the length of the unstable sequence correlates with the variable phenotype. McConkie-Rosell et al (1993) studied six brothers who showed a continuum of phenotypic expression of the syndrome, ranging from mental retardation to specific learning disability with normal intelligence, and a range from severe to mild physical characteristics. Phenotypic variability correlated with size of the CGG repeat. With triplet instability, phenotypic variability occurs because the mutation is not uniform—those with longer repeats exhibit severe symptoms. Fragile-X can be subdivided into pre- and full mutations: those with a premutation, an increase in the size of the repeat ≤ 200, are clinically normal. The premutations are unstable and may expand to full mutations (> 200 repeats), but only when transmitted by a female. Daughters of male carriers have only a premutation and are normal, but their children carry a risk of mental retardation.

Discovery of a polymorphic trinucleotide repeat in Fragile X was unexpected, but it is now apparent that triplet repeats characterize several, perhaps many, heritable human diseases (Caskey 1993, Martin 1993, Morell 1993). A CCC triplet repeat that results in mental retardation was discovered during screening of families for Fragile X (Knight et al 1993). This repeat differs from Fragile X in that it can contract or expand and is equally unstable whether passed by male or female carriers. Huntington's Disease, which exhibits anticipation across generations, is attributable to a triplet repeat. And anticipation has been reported in bipolar affective disorder, generating the hypothesis that a triple repeat may play a role in its etiology (McInnis et al 1993). Clearly, inheritance of unstable regions of DNA, which become progressively more unstable in succeeding generations, is an important finding; its implication for psychiatric genetics may be great.

PERSONALITY, LIFESTYLES, AND HEALTH HABITS

Personality

There are noteworthy trends in behavior genetic research on personality: Assessments based on direct observation by neutral observers are supplementing or replacing parental ratings of children and adolescents, longitudinal research is replacing single-occasion studies, population-based twin registries are replacing volunteer twin samples, and research with juvenile twins increasingly includes their parents and non-twin siblings in the sampling structure. Each development adds a burden of cost and time, but each significantly enhances the data-yield. Observational assessments address a consistent, disconcerting finding from parental ratings of twin children: substantial resemblance of MZ co-twins, but negligible, often negative resemblance of DZ co-twins and non-twin siblings. Greater sibling similarity may be expected for observable behaviors (e.g. Hoffman 1991), because they are directly available to reinforcement effects of child-rearing; if so, the newer assessment efforts should find greater sibling similarity. They do. Longitudinal behavior genetic research on personality, like that on ability, uniquely addresses causes of continuity and change over the lifespan. Such research is optimal with population-based twin registries recently developed in the United States (e.g. Lykken et al 1990, Kendler et al 1992b, Hewitt et al 1993), the Netherlands (Boomsma et al 1994), and Nordic countries, where population registries permit exhaustive identification of living twins. A new Danish registry (Kyvik et al 1994) includes more than 20,000 twin pairs born 1953–1982; in Sweden, 16,000 twin pairs born 1968–1990 have been ascertained (NL Pedersen, personal communication); and in Finland, approximately 22,000 twin pairs born 1959–1985 form the younger Finnish twin cohort (Kaprio et al 1990a), permitting studies of consecutive birth cohorts of twin adolescents, with compliance rates approximately 90% (Rose et al 1993). Dutch and Finnish research includes parents of twins in the sampling structure, to yield analyses of assortative mating and estimation of cultural transmission from parent to (twin) child (e.g. Viken et al 1994a).

ARE DZ CO-TWINS AND NON-TWIN SIBLINGS BEHAVIORALLY SIMILAR?   Surprisingly, behavior genetic data, limited to parental ratings, frequently fail to show that DZ co-twins and non-twin siblings are behaviorally similar. In new data, from direct observations and assessments by raters other than parents, resemblance of siblings and DZ co-twins is not only statistically significant, it approximates half that observed for MZ co-twins, as expected by simple genetic models. One of the new US twin panels is the MacArthur Longitudinal Twin Study (MALTS), which recruited twins from statewide birth reports. Similarities of 200 pairs of MALTS twins were assessed at 14 months of age (Emde et al 1992) at home and in the laboratory with observational measures of behavioral inhibition and shyness and standardized observer ratings. The results are strik-ing: Although parents reported no resemblance of DZ co-twins, significant DZ resemblance was found for parallel, observational measures; substantial contrast effects must bias parental reports of infant twins of known zygosity. Correlations for MZ twins pairs were significantly higher for most measures, documenting, again, genetic influences on individual differences for domains of early tem-perament. But the more noteworthy finding is the dramatic difference between observational and parental report measures of DZ twins for the same behavioral domains. Follow-up studies, six (Plomin et al 1993) and ten (Robinson et al 1992) months later, replicate that finding: DZ co-twins were significantly similar for observational measures of temperament, although no resemblance was attributed to them in parental ratings. At 24 months, correlations for DZ twin brothers (.33) and sisters (.30) were at least half those observed for age-matched MZ twin pairs. Such evidence is not limited to twins: Braungart et al (1992) obtained significant similarities in behavior ratings at one and two years of age for biological siblings in the CAP, and Schmitz (1994) reported similar results for temperament dimensions in CAP siblings at age seven. Compelling evidence that siblings significantly resemble one another in social behavior is found in multimethod comparisons of siblings and unrelated pairs formed from the siblings' classmates and matched on sex and grade (Lewin et al 1993). No sibling pairs were in the same classroom, but independent teacher and peer ratings, and direct observations of classroom and playground behav-iors, found sibling similarities for social behaviors on the playground, in peer popularity ratings, and in teachers' behavior elicited by and directed toward target siblings. No correlation for classmate-matched pairs was significant. And sibling correlations were high: .50 for peer social preference, .42 for direct observation of positive playground behavior, .64 for teacher disapproval in the classroom, and .63 for teacher-rated school adjustment.

GENETIC CONTRIBUTIONS TO INDIVIDUAL DIFFERENCES IN PERSONALITY
Loehlin (1992) offers an engaging survey of the Big Five dimensions of personality: extraversion, emotional stability (neuroticism), agreeableness, con-scientiousness, and culture (or openness). In Loehlin's analysis of extraversion, genetic effects account for 35–40% of observed individual variation, but be-cause self-reported resemblance of MZ twins routinely exceeds twice that found for DZ twin pairs, either nonadditive genetic variance (Lykken et al 1992) or unequal resemblance of MZ and DZ twins' environments must be assumed. Similarly, for each of the other four personality dimensions, additive genetic variance accounts for most of the observed variance, but either epistatic genetic variance or, alternatively, special MZ twin environments, accounts for the next-largest portion. Loehlin finds "appreciable effects" of additive genes (~ 20–45%) across all five personality factors, but, unless nonadditive genes are

invoked, effects of special MZ environments must be. Whichever it turns out to be, it accounts for 10–20% of the variance on the first four factors, less on the last (culture/openness). Similar inferences are drawn (Bouchard 1994) in analyses that highlight Minnesota studies of separated twins. Genetic factors contribute at least 40% of phenotypic variance in major personality traits, but an alternative model, of more modest additive variance with special MZ environmental effects, cannot be excluded with existing data. Nonadditive genetic variance is an intriguing hypothesis to account for the frequent finding, across behavioral and psychophysiological measures, of MZ-DZ correlation ratios that exceed 2.0 (Lykken et al 1992), but scaling effects (Miller 1993) offer an alternative explanation. If, instead, environmental effects uniquely shared by MZ twins explain the MZ-DZ correlation ratios, the environmental effects appear to be complex and phenotype specific: Sibling contact is sometimes cause and sometimes consequence (Kaprio et al 1990b, Rose et al 1990) of sibling similarity. Another caveat is that analyses of personality dimensions other than extraversion and neuroticism are based on limited data from a "miscellaneous collection of scales" (Loehlin 1992); more data are needed, especially with alternatives to assessment based on self-report. In an important illustration, Heath et al (1992) compared self-reported extraversion and neuroticism from adult twins with ratings obtained from their co-twins. Significant rater bias was found for extraversion, and the analyses suggest that reciprocal rating data usefully supplement conventional self-report measures of personality; the combined data can be modeled to explicitly assess some biases in self-perception and in perception of others.

LONGITUDINAL ANALYSES: CONTINUITY AND CHANGE IN PERSONALITY   Recent behavior genetic studies of personality use longitudinal designs to identify causes of consistency and change over the lifespan. The analyses partition genetic and environmental components into those unique to each test occasion and those persisting across occasions. Analyses of personality employ longitudinal models similar to those for research on cognitive ability; typically, a genetic simplex model with causal pathways between effects on adjacent occasions is used to assess the contribution of genetic and environmental factors to both stability and change. The simplex model has been extended to include simultaneous analysis of phenotypic means and covariance structures (Dolan et al 1991, 1992) to address trends in average development, as well as stability of individual differences. Recent longitudinal analyses document genetic contributions to age-to-age continuity and change across development, from early infancy (Plomin et al 1993) to late adolescence and early adulthood (McGue et al 1993b), through mid-adulthood (Viken et al 1994b), and in late life (Pedersen 1993). Viken et al (1994b) tested approximately 15,000 Finnish twins, aged 18–53 at baseline, on two occasions six years apart. Heritability of both extraversion and neuroticism decreased after late adolescence, and there was little or no new genetic influence on individual differences after age 30, but significant new environmental effects emerged at every age. In elderly Swedish twins, tested on two occasions three years apart, no new genetic effects appeared at follow-up for neuroticism, while for extraversion, genetic effects unique to the second occasion accounted for modest variance on that occasion (Pedersen et al 1992a). Most nonshared environmental variance (accounting for half of the total observed variance) was unique to each occasion. Longitudinal analysis of personality dimensions other than extraversion and neuroticism should be a priority for future research.

Sexual Orientation

A behavioral phenotype subject to recent genetic study, and generating extensive publicity as a consequence, is sexual orientation—a phenotype self-identified by fantasy, attraction, and behavior. The phenotype is not new to behavior genetic research (e.g. Heston & Shields 1968). What is new are larger samples, offering better evidence that sexual orientation is familial and heritable, and modern molecular analyses, offering initial evidence linking sexual orientation to a chromosomal locus.

FAMILIALITY AND HERITABILITY OF SEXUAL ORIENTATION   Moderate familial aggregation has been found for both male and female homosexuality (Bailey & Bell 1993, Bailey & Benishay 1993), and twin data suggest that heritable variation underlies the familial aggregation. Bailey & Pillard (1991) studied twin and adoptive brothers of homosexual male probands, reporting that > 50% of the probands' MZ twin brothers, > 20% of their DZ twin brothers, and 11% of their adoptive brothers were homosexual, yielding h^2 estimates from .3–.7, dependent on assumptions of population prevalence. Similar analyses on twin and adoptive sisters of lesbian probands (Bailey et al 1993) offer similar results. A small twin study from the United Kingdom (King & McDonald 1992) and another from the United States (Whitam et al 1993) add evidence that sexual orientation is a (moderately) heritable behavioral phenotype. For critics, that evidence is as uncertain as the (un)representativeness of the proband samples and the (in)adequacy of measures of sexual orientation (Baron 1993, Byne & Parsons 1993, Byne 1994). Can unbiased samples of homosexual adults who are twins and whose co-twins agree to be studied be found by advertising for them in lesbian and gay publications? How can a phenotype of sexual orientation be defined? And how can the adequacy of its measurement be insured in self-report and in reports by relatives?

LINKAGE   More controversial is a report (Hamer et al 1993) linking male homosexual orientation to the X chromosome. The linkage effort was predicated on pedigree analyses that preceded it: Pedigrees of homosexual male probands revealed a marked excess of gay male relatives restricted to maternal uncles and maternal cousins. The pedigree results were interpreted as implicating X-chromosome transmission, for which the androgen receptor might be a candidate gene; accordingly, DNA samples were collected from pairs of gay brothers in families selected because the families gave no evidence of male transmission. One stretch of X chromosome, containing five markers and near the end of the long arm, was shared by 33 of the 40 brother-brother pairs. Chance expectation is 20/40, because brothers on average share one half the DNA on each chromosome. The linkage yielded a highly significant LOD score, and subsequently (Hamer 1993), five more families were added to the analysis, and the LOD score increased to 4.4. Clearly, the putative gene cannot account for all male homosexuality, because seven pairs of brothers in the sample were concordantly gay but failed to share the stretch of X chromosome. Beyond that fact, little is certain. No one knows what the gene might do: Sequence variation of the androgen receptor gene appears irrelevant to development of male sexual orientation (Macke et al 1993). These gay brothers were selected deliberately, in a biased way to exclude paternal transmission and minimize heterogeneity, but at the cost of uncertain generalizability. No one knows what proportion of gay men carry an X-linked allele influencing their sexual orientation, nor how frequent the allele may be among heterosexual males (King 1993). X-linkage has not been replicated in gay men, nor attempted in lesbians. Scientific criticism of the work centers on uncertain assumptions made about population prevalence of homosexuality and on criticisms of the sib-pair method. The more searching questions are social, rather than scientific: Do we want to know whether there is a gene for homosexuality? What use will be made of that knowledge? If a gene is found, a screening test to identify those who carry it will likely follow; who will use the screen and for what purpose? The questions are far more obvious than are answers.

Health Habits: Smoking and Drinking

Analyses of alcohol use in nonselected twin samples are distinguished from analyses of twin pairs, in which one or both co-twins meet diagnosable criteria. The distinction is empirical: Genetic influences on initiation and persistence of social drinking differ from one another and from others that influence alcoholism. Genetic pathways in transitions from social use of alcohol to its sustained, serious abuse are multiple (e.g. Heath 1993, Hodgkinson et al 1991, McGue 1993). This section begins with behavior genetic studies of smoking because (*a*) research on drinking habits in nonselected twin samples invariably includes smoking, as well as drinking, and the behaviors covary and (*b*) a common genetic pathway may explain the covariance.

BEHAVIOR GENETICS OF SMOKING   For smoking, as for drinking, data from adolescent twins document significant influences of shared environmental experience. For example, Boomsma et al (1994) assessed smoking in more than 1300 families of adolescent Dutch twins, aged 13–22, and found but modest genetic effects; almost 60% of the variation in adolescent smoking habits was attributed to effects of shared environmental influences, and, among twin sisters, genetic effects became evident only after age 19. Shared environmental effects were imperfectly correlated in co-twins of brother-sister twin pairs, suggesting that different environmental factors influence smoking in adolescent boys and girls. There was no evidence of parental social modeling: Parent-offspring resemblance was wholly accounted for by genetic transmission. Evidence of genetic effects on initiation of smoking was found in juvenile Australian twins (Hopper et al 1992), where MZ twins were approximately 16 times more likely to smoke, if their co-twins were smokers, against a 7-fold increase found for DZ pairs. But odds ratios conditioned on smoking by a twin's peers were about as great as those conditioned on reciprocal smoking by DZ co-twins, suggesting significant effects of shared experience, as well.

With adult twin samples, research on smoking has moved from the question of whether genes influence smoking to more interesting issues: Are genetic influences on initiation of smoking independent of those influencing its persistence? Are the genetic and familial environmental effects on smoking the same as those affecting drinking? Genetic factors are significant for initiation of smoking and for age at which smoking begins. Among WWII veteran twins, surveyed when 40–50 years old and again 16 years later (Carmelli et al 1992), all three components of smoking—initiation, persistence, and quitting—were influenced by genetic factors. It is fascinating that a genetic component contributed to smoking initiation in veteran twins, all heavily exposed to smoking promotion and offered free cigarettes during their military service. Among adult Australian twins, genetic effects on initiation were independent of those on persistence (Heath & Martin 1993). A twin's smoking status (e.g. non-smoker, ex-smoker, current smoker) was cross-classified by that of the co-twin, to compare smoking among co-twins of persistent smokers with co-twins of ex-smokers. If initiation and persistence are independent liability dimensions, no difference is expected; but if a single liability underlies initiation and persistence, odds of smoking in co-twins of persistent smokers will exceed that of co-twins of ex-smokers. For Australian twins at least 30 years of age, results supported the independent liability model.

BEHAVIOR GENETICS OF DRINKING   Among adolescent twins, Australian data (Hopper et al 1992) suggest genetic influences on early drinking among boys, but not girls. In Holland (Koopmans & Boomsma 1993), the opposite was found (i.e. no genetic effect in boys and a substantial one in girls). It is not clear whether this discrepancy arises from sample differences in age composition or from cultural modulation of trait-relevant experiences in boys and girls. Drinking habits of a population-based sample of Finnish twins, all tested at age 16 (Rose et al 1993), suggest substantial, and equivalent, genetic variance in both males and females, but in the context of sex-specific effects. Again, questions arise about such a result: Is it due to sex-limitation of gene expression, gender differences in relevant experiences, or some other factor? Longitudinal studies of young twins and their peers may resolve these important issues.

Prescott et al (1994) report data on alcohol use from a volunteer sample of elderly twins, 75% female, with mean age 67. The data indicated that determinants of whether one drinks in older age are not the determinants of how much or how often one drinks. Consistent with earlier data, alcohol consumption was greater among males, abstinence more common in older twins, and twins in more frequent social contact were more similar for lifetime and current alcohol use. Both additive genes and shared experiences significantly contributed to initiation of alcohol use in both men and women. For lifetime abstinence, twin resemblance was substantial, regardless of gender or zygosity, reflecting significant influences from shared experience. But among current drinkers, shared genes, not shared experiences, contributed most to twin resemblance for alcohol use. These data suggest that different genetic and environmental factors influence consumption across patterns of alcohol use. Nonmetrical multidimensional scaling of twin-pair data (Heath et al 1991a,b) confirms that finding. Abstinence is influenced significantly by familial environmental factors, but consumption patterns among users exhibit substantial genetic effects.

So, genes influence tobacco use and genes influence alcohol use, but are they the same genes? Swan et al (1994) reported multivariate analyses of smoking, drinking, and coffee consumption from male twin pairs 52–66 years of age. Tobacco use, alcohol consumption, and caffeine intake were intercorrelated, provoking a more interesting question: What are the genetic and environmental sources of their covariation? A model with independent genetic and environmental causal paths to each of the three phenotypes was compared to one incorporating a single latent pathway (labeled "polysubstance use"). The common pathway model provided an adequate, parsimonious fit: Smoking, alcohol, and caffeine use each exhibited genetic variance (h^2 from .36 to .56), and the common factor accounted for a significant proportion of genetic effect on each phenotype, especially smoking, for which most heritable variance was shared with the polysubstance-use phenotype. In a similar analysis of adolescent Dutch twins (Koopmans & Boomsma 1993), shared environmental effects on drinking and smoking correlated ($r = .64$) in brothers, while the association of smoking and drinking in sisters was influenced by both correlated genetic ($r = .69$) and familial environmental ($r = .30$) effects.

LONGITUDINAL STUDY OF DRINKING HABITS   Alcohol consumption patterns in adults are stable, and genetic contributions are largely responsible. In a six-year follow-up of adult Finnish twins, aged 18–43 at baseline, genes contributed to both consistency and change in patterns of alcohol use, and the greater stability observed in older twins was shown to be a consequence of greater influence of both genetic and environmental effects (Kaprio et al 1992). A 16-year follow-up of adult male twins found that genes accounted for more than 80% of the stable variation in alcohol consumption, but shared environmental effects influenced choice of specific beverage consumed (Carmelli et al 1993).

PSYCHOPATHOLOGY AND NEUROLOGICAL DISORDERS

Huntington's Disease

After 12 years of effort, the Huntington's Disease (HD) gene was isolated (MacDonald et al 1993), and the molecular basis for HD was identified as a triplet repeat, a CAG mutation with a mechanism similar to that earlier described for Fragile-X Syndrome (i.e. the larger the expansion, the more severe the disease and the earlier its onset). The CAG repeat has a normal range ≤ 34, but the repeat increases to > 100 in HD; cases with early onset average 61 repeats, those with onset after 65 years of age average 41 repeats (Craufurd & Dodge 1993). Early onset is associated with inheritance of the disease allele from the father—an illustration of genomic imprinting, in which a gene's expression is modulated by its parental origin. Genomic imprinting may have important implications for genetics of behavioral phenotypes, including alcoholism (Durcan & Goldman 1993).

Traditional Twin Methods in Psychiatric Genetics

Dramatic success of the new (molecular) genetics has not made the old (quantitative) genetics obsolete. Traditional methods remain central to the resolution of many problems, including those of diagnosis. Categorical definitions of psychiatric phenotypes constrain research (e.g. Pauls 1993), and twin data can help investigators explore new diagnostic distinctions (McGuffin et al 1993) as forerunners of molecular studies. Twin data are critical in evaluating continuous measures of latent liability. Typical models assume that a latent quantitative liability, normally distributed, underlies categorical diagnostic states, and that illness occurs when a threshold in a distribution of liability is reached. Such models fit an array of diagnostic outcomes, from alcoholism to phobias (Kendler et al 1992b) and panic disorder (Kendler et al 1993a,b,c). Twin data address a related issue, the relationship of normal variation in personality to psychopathology. For example, Carey & DiLalla (1994) use direction-of-causation models to explore correlations between a disorder and a personality trait. Continuity of clinical phenotypes with normal variation can be evaluated with latent class analyses of twin data (e.g. Eaves et al 1993, Meyer et al 1992, Slutske et al 1994). Such research suggests that both dimensional and categorical models may be useful for some forms of psychopathology, because in the context of single genes with large effects, dimensional ordering of severity of symptomatology may be evident in the behavioral phenotype.

New developments include advances in model fitting (Neale & Cardon 1992); applications of bivariate analyses to assess comorbidity [e.g. of major depression with alcoholism (Kendler et al 1993a,b) and with phobias (Kendler et al 1993bc)]; bivariate analyses of direction-of-causation in cross-sectional data (Heath et al 1993); extended twin-family designs, adding adolescent twins' parents or adult twins' children to the sampling structure (Rose 1991); and development of methods (e.g. Nance 1994) that incorporate measured genotypes into twin comparisons. Such developments ensure that traditional twin methods will remain basic tools in human behavior genetics (Kendler 1993).

Alcoholism

QUANTITATIVE METHODS   Pickens et al (1991) used treatment records in Minnesota to identify alcoholic probands who were twins, finding that risk for alcohol abuse, characterized by impaired social-occupational function, was mostly attributable to shared environmental factors, while alcohol dependence, characterized by tolerance and/or withdrawal, was largely due to genetic effects. Genetic contributions to liability were consistently greater in males; genes made no apparent contribution to liability for alcohol abuse in females. McGue et al (1992) found similar results in a follow-up questionnaire study of more than 350 twin pairs, in each of which the proband twin met criteria for alcohol abuse-dependence. Genetic effects appeared substantial only in early-onset male alcoholism. No evidence of genetic effects on alcohol abuse-dependency was found in female twins, and significant cross-sex transmission was observed in male-female DZ pairs: Male co-twins of female DZ probands had more alcohol problems than did male co-twins of male DZ probands. For men, early-onset alcohol problems had much higher h^2; for women, h^2 did not differ with proband's age of onset. Caldwell & Gottesman (1991) reported gender differences in genetic effects on alcoholism in twins similarly selected.

In contrast, twins from population-based samples show no gender modulation of gene expression. Data on adult twin sisters, identified from state records in Virginia, yielded h^2 estimates for liability to alcoholism $\geq .5$ (Kendler et al 1992a). Studies of population-based twin samples from Australia offer similar findings. In 6000 adult Australian twins, correlations, estimated under a threshold model, suggest no gender differences in magnitude of genetic contributions to risk for alcohol dependence (Heath et al 1994b). The h^2 of alcoholism in women (67%) is comparable to that for men (71%), and multivariate analyses found a substantial genetic correlation ($r_G = .66$) between alcoholism and conduct disorder in women, challenging conventional wisdom that prediction of alcohol risk from early antisocial behavior is sex limited (Heath et al 1994a).

The likely explanation of discrepant results from these twin studies are the differences in how the twin samples were selected. If relatively few women with alcohol problems seek treatment, those that do may be atypical of the general population of women with alcohol problems. And if treatment-seeking is a function of social-environmental influences, community-based samples of female twins will show higher h^2 than will clinically selected female twin samples (Kendler et al 1992a).

MOLECULAR METHODS   Recent molecular genetic research on alcoholism has centered on the *A1* allele of the D2 dopamine receptor gene, first associated with alcoholism in autopsy analyses of brain samples from 35 alcoholics and matched controls (Blum et al 1990). The dopamine D2 receptor is a candidate gene for allelic association, because it is mapped (onto chromosome 11), and because it is involved, or implicated, in alcohol metabolism and alcohol-seeking behavior. The alcoholics studied by Blum et al (1990) represented severe cases: A majority had experienced repeated treatment failures, and their deaths were attributable to alcohol-induced pathologies. DNA samples from the 70 brains included 31 possessing the *A1* allele of the D2 gene; 24 of the 31 were from alcoholics. Of the 39 DNA samples lacking an *A1* allele, 28 of the 39 were from controls. The report, the first using RFLP analysis to associate a candidate gene with a major behavioral disorder, immediately stimulated efforts to replicate or disprove it. A meta-analysis of those efforts (Pato et al 1993) found the box score even: 4 replications, 4 failures. An updated box-score, as of this writing, is 6 replicates, 9 failures. Problems inescapable in association studies (e.g. variable frequency of the target allele across populations; ethnic heterogeneity among probands and controls; disagreement on whether, and how, to screen controls; differences in severity of alcoholism in probands) all contribute to the variable results and their discrepant interpretation. Association of the *A1* allele with alcoholism is convincing to some (Nobel 1993) and discredited by others (Holden 1994). Cook et al (1993) report a successful linkage analysis that might resolve the matter.Their sibling-pair analysis of the *A1* allele addresses criticism that population stratification caused spurious associations between the *A1* allele and alcoholism in the original study and its replications. In an informative identity-by-descent analysis (genotyping both siblings and their parents) of 29 sibling pairs, Cook et al (1993) found significant evidence that the dopamine D2 receptor locus contributes both to liability to develop heavy drinking and to diagnosed alcoholism. Recent reports associate the allele, in discordant DZ co-twins (Christian et al 1994) and sons of alcoholics (Noble et al 1994), with electrocortical variables relevant to alcoholism risk. But if the D_2 locus does have a causal role in alcoholism, it is not specific to alcoholism: The *A1* allele is elevated not only in alcoholics, but in polysubstance abusers (e.g. Noble et al 1993) as well.

Alzheimer's Disease

As recently as 1991, relatively little was known of the causes of Alzheimer's Disease (AD). Since then, replicate twin studies have found genetic influences on late-onset AD, and techniques of molecular genetics have identified or linked relevant genes. The unfolding story of genetic research on Alzheimer's has several chapters, one in quantitative twin data and the other in molecular genetics.

TWIN STUDIES   The twin data from Norway and Finland reveal genetic etiologies for late-onset AD. This is surprising because one expects early onset to be the more heritable form of behavior disorder. Both Nordic studies linked population twin registries to nationwide hospital discharge data to identify twin probands with possible AD. In Norway (Bergem 1993), proband twins met the established criteria, at mean onset age of 73 years, in 64 twin pairs. The MZ-DZ concordance rates were high and approximated a 2 to 1 ratio, suggesting that late-onset AD is both familial and heritable. The Finnish data (Räihä et al 1994) linked approximately 14,000 twin pairs with hospital discharge records: 83 pairs (45 MZ and 38 DZ) of twins met *DSM III-R* criteria; all were more than 65 years of age. Compared to Norwegian results, concordance rates were lower in Finnish twins, but MZ-DZ ratios were higher.

ASSOCIATION STUDIES   Genetic variability for different forms of familial AD has been identified on three chromosome loci: mutations in the beta-amyloid precursor protein gene (Murell et al 1991) on chromosome 21, a locus on chromosome 14 (Schellenberg et al 1992), and in the apolipoprotein E (ApoE) gene on chromosome 19. The *E4* allele of ApoE dramatically modulates risk for late-onset AD (Corder et al 1993); heterozygotes were three times more likely to develop the disease than were those carrying alleles for other isoforms of ApoE, and homozygotes for *E4* were eight times more likely to develop AD than were those homozygous for the more usual ApoE allele. That startling finding has been replicated (Liddell et al 1993) in data that indicate a tenfold risk of late-onset AD among Apo *E4* homozygotes. Clearly, this is the most dramatic and most important allelic association with behavior yet discovered, one creating new dilemmas in presymptomatic genetic testing: The *E4* allele can be identified with a test widely used for screening a cholesterol-transport disorder, but should its carriers be told? Clearly, too, it is a mystery: ApoE is an amyloid-binding protein we all carry. How does its *E4* allele raise the risk for AD?

Schizophrenias and Affective Disorders

Genetic studies of major psychiatric disorders are assuming new directions amid explosive developments in molecular technology (Ciaranello & Ciaranello 1991, McGuffin & Murray 1991, Papolos & Lachman 1994). But here, as elsewhere, traditional techniques, with some new twists (Gottesman & Bertelsen 1991), remain useful. For example, Torrey et al (1994) report on six years of research focused on MZ twins discordant for schizophrenic outcome. Such research tells us little about genes but may provide much information about nongenetic factors in the developmental history of schizophrenia. Major findings of this study are that perinatal factors were important in at least 30% of the ill co-twins; widespread early CNS dysfunctions were found; changes in brain structure were common among affected twins and were interpreted as an integral part of the schizophrenia disease process; and, in contrast to earlier analyses of unselected series, there were no clinical differences in onset or expression of schizophrenia in the ill twins from concordant and discordant pairs. Gottesman (1991) offers a concise overview of what is known of the genesis of schizophrenia, and, with clarity and compassion, interweaves poignant personal accounts with themes of empirical research.

Evidence of triplet repeats in neurological disorders encourages a search for them in the psychopathologies. Because triplet repeats cause clinical anticipation, a search can begin by asking whether anticipation characterizes a particular psychiatric disorder. McInnis et al (1993) report finding it in bipolar affective disorder (BPAD): Across generations of families ascertained for linkage research, BPAD cases in the second generation experienced onset 9–14 years earlier and with 1.8–3.4 times the severity.

Aggression

A large Dutch kindred included 14 male probands behaviorally characterized by impulsive violence (Brunner et al 1993). The behavior phenotype, found in different sibships living in different parts of the country at different times, included episodes of aggression, sometimes violent, triggered by anger, out of proportion to provocation. Aggressive behavior was episodic, typically confined to 24–72 hours, during which time affected males would sleep little and experience frequent night terror. The pedigree allowed linkage analyses, focused on the X-chromosome, which identified a stretch containing genes for two monoamine oxidase (MAO) enzymes, and 24-hour urine analyses of affected males proved them deficient in one of the two enzymes. As a result, the locus for the disorder was assigned to the monoamine oxidase Type A (MAOA) locus of X (Brunner et al 1993). These dramatic, but interim, results leave important questions unanswered: The frequency of the defective gene in the male population is unknown and the magnitude of variation of MAOA activity and its association with aggression in the normal population are uncertain. In addition, data from the Dutch kindred do not address a major question: How does too much of a monoamine messenger stimulate violence?

NEW IDEAS AND ENDURING ISSUES

Twin Comparisons: New Twists

An important variation on conventional twin studies contrasts MZ co-twins who differ in exposure to an environmental experience; the contrast offers an incisive test of effects of specific experience. For example, Goldberg et al (1990) evaluated posttraumatic stress disorder (PTSD) among 715 MZ veteran twin pairs; both twin brothers in each pair were military veterans during 1965–1975, but only one twin in each pair had been in active military service in Southeast Asia. That service was strongly associated with PTSD, especially among those with high levels of combat exposure; e.g. twins who had high combat exposure in the Vietnam War were 12 times as likely as their identical twin brothers to reexperience traumatic events of military service in nightmares and painful memories 15 years later.

Two other novel twin comparisons have been made. Neither tests for a genetic effect; instead, the comparisons illustrate ways in which twin data address behavioral sequelae of *in utero* experience. One approach compares monozygotic twin pairs who differ in timing of embryological splitting and, therefore, in their placentation; the other evaluates female members of male-female DZ twin pairs for possible behavioral effects of *in utero* androgenization.

PLACENTATION   Differentiated by placental type, MZ twin pairs can assess an aspect of prenatal environment on subsequent behavioral development. Placentation differences result from differential timing in separation of the cell mass. Dichorionic (DC) MZ twins result from early separation of blastomeres; monochorionic (MC) MZ twins duplicate later and develop within a single chorionic membrane, sharing a placenta with possible vascular anastomosis. For some traits, at some developmental ages, there is suggestive evidence (Rose 1991) that MC MZ co-twins are more alike than are DC MZ pairs. Three new studies add to that evidence (see Beekmans et al 1993, Carlier et al 1994, Sokol et al 1994). The replicability, mechanisms, and magnitude of placental effects are uncertain, but placental information is available in several new twin registries, so answers can be sought.

ANDROGENIZATION IN SISTERS OF TWIN BROTHERS   Prenatal androgenization is documented in litter-bearing animals. Recent research has tested whether similar effects occur in female members of opposite-sex (OS) DZ twin pairs, following prenatal exposure to their brother's androgens. Positive evidence was inferred for the personality dimension of sensation-seeking (Resnick et al 1993), and, in data less vulnerable to alternative psychosocial explanations, in rate of otoacoustic emissions (McFadden 1993). But extensive data from the population-based Finnish Twin Cohort are negative, both for a measure of feminine interests at age 16 and in life-events analyses of fertility among more than 12,000 adult women from like-sex and OS twin pairs (Rose et al 1994). Several population-based twin registries include representative numbers of OS DZ twin pairs, and more incisive analyses of this issue, on diverse behavioral and attitudinal variables, should soon be available.

Enduring Issues

DOES SHARED ENVIRONMENT MATTER?   The profound issues raised by developments in molecular genetics (e.g. gene testing and gene therapy) cause understandable controversy among lay people and medical ethicists. But for psychologists, the more controversial issue in behavior genetics may be the claim that family environment is irrelevant to children's behavioral outcomes. Can the claim be correct? The belief that family environment has little impact on behavioral development had its origins in adoption data showing no reduced risk for a child of a schizophrenic mother when the child was removed from mother at birth and reared by non-relatives; the belief was reinforced by other adoption data that found little resemblance in behavior or personality of adoptive siblings and little difference in similarity of MZ co-twins, whether the twins were reared together or apart. And, finally, the impact of familial environmental effects was challenged by reports that focused on differential behaviors of siblings who shared family environments. These several sets of data have been interpreted widely to imply that sibling similarity, and the similarity of parents and their children, is solely attributable to shared genes; that although environmental experiences are influential in development of individual differences in behavior, only experiences unique to individuals, not those shared within families, are relevant.

Perhaps "the obituary for the shared environmental effect has been written too soon" (Goodman 1991). Goodman argues that the assumptions and methods of behavior genetics inflate the importance of nonshared environmental experience and minimize that of common, familial environment; similar arguments have been advanced by others (e.g. Hoffman 1991). Such arguments are bolstered by convincing evidence of family environmental effects. Sibling similarity too great to be wholly attributed to siblings' shared genes is found in observational assessments by neutral observers (Lewin et al 1993), and shared family influences account for substantial variation in delinquent behaviors reported by siblings (e.g. Rowe et al 1992), behaviors subject to significant reciprocal influences between twins and non-twin siblings (Carey 1992). And for some dimensions of experience, studies of separated twins yield direct evidence of the importance of family rearing: In analyses of elderly Swedish twins reared together and apart, Gatz et al (1992) report "early experiences shared by family members shape individual differences in depressive symptoms later in life," accounting for one third of the variance in self-reported depression. Finally, effects of family rearing have been reported in a US adoption study (McGue et al 1994). Adoptive adolescent siblings reared together but genetically unrelated were significantly alike ($r = .46$ for 43 pairs of brothers, .41 for 62 pairs of sisters) in their alcohol and smoking patterns, a finding consistent with substantial effects of common environment found in adolescent twin research on health habits.

Perhaps we are misled by a research focus that reflects funding priorities but ignores the prosocial behaviors valued by parents and society—helpfulness, kindness, and generosity. We limit too much of our data to twins, rely too much on their self-reports, and focus too narrowly on well-studied dimensions of personality. We pay too little attention to measurement issues, and model effects of family environment from residual variance, rather than measuring the effects directly. Too rarely are parents and peers of twins included in sampling strategies.

GENE-BEHAVIOR ASSOCIATIONS   Interpretation of behavior genetic research by the general press consistently presents each gene-behavior association, whether associating a gene with disease or divorce, obesity or occupation, alcoholism or aggression, as an association attributable to a specific gene for that association. The implication of a gene for each behavioral phenotype is drawn not by behavioral geneticists, who remain unwilling, on present evidence, to infer specific genes for *any* specific behaviors (e.g. Sokolowski, quoted in Barinaga 1994); it is a too-ready inference of the popular press, described as "wilful public misunderstanding of genetics" (Maddox 1993). But if public misunderstanding is wilful, it is fostered by application of genetic models to behavioral phenotypes for which gene-behavior pathways can only be highly indirect—e.g. voting (Martin & Heath 1993), volunteering for military combat (Lyons et al 1993), and watching TV (Plomin et al 1990). That genetic dispositions make some indirect contribution to individual differences in voting behavior, combat exposure, and TV viewing habits may be true; perhaps no dimension of human behavioral variation is immune to effects, however indirect, of genetic variation. But genetic analyses of such phenotypes are of uncertain meaning (Prescott et al 1991). For example, no gene for TV watching, a behavioral phenotype nonexistent three generations ago, could plausibly exist. Important caveats are acknowledged and indeed, emphasized, in original reports of these findings (e.g. see Lyons et al 1993), but the public and the press too readily assume discrete gene-behavior associations and too easily presume that genetic differences consign us to different behavioral outcomes. My earlier admonitions (Rose 1992) bear repeating.

LIMITS OF GENETIC EFFECTS ON BEHAVIOR   We do not uniformly react to environmental situations, nor do the situations we encounter "just happen." We actively seek opportunities to develop and display our dispositional characteristics, so adult personality differences reflect, not fixed consequences of hereditary variance, but interactive processes of lifestyle selection. With rare exceptions (e.g. Huntington's Disease), genes do not mandate life outcomes. Less than half the variance observed in typical behavioral phenotypes is attributable to heritable effects, and those effects are largely indirect, from gene-environment interactions and correlations. Consider obesity. Genetic contributions to variation in adult weight are well documented. But popular interpretations (*Time* 1990) are wrong. Pairs of MZ twins show very different weight changes in response to uniform diet (Bouchard et al 1990b) or standardized exercise (Bouchard et al 1990a). But such compelling evidence of gene-environment interaction does not consign anyone to a lifetime of uncontrollable obesity. In real life, people do not choose uniform diets, nor do they engage in uniform exercise patterns. The behavioral choices adults make in dietary habits and exercise patterns contribute to their weight problems. Genes do not make people obese.

DISPOSITIONS NOT DESTINIES   We inherit dispositions, not destinies. Life outcomes are consequences of lifetimes of behavior choices. The choices are guided by our dispositional tendencies, and the tendencies find expression within environmental opportunities that we actively create. Lives are not simple consequences of genetic consignments. Genetic determinism is improbable for simple acts of the fruit fly, implausible for complex human behavior.

CONCLUSIONS

In the four years since the *Annual Review of Psychology* last reviewed human behavior genetics, genetic mechanisms for Huntington's Disease and Fragile-X Syndrome have been identified; linkages for Alzheimer's Disease, developmental dyslexia, and a form of familial aggression have been reported; extensive new twin registries have been created, and powerful tools for both quantitative and molecular analyses of their data yields have been developed. Few areas of psychology are changing as rapidly as human behavior genetics. Few are as filled with excitement and promise. Few are as surrounded by controversy. Future reviews of the field are likely to read very differently than this one. And they should be interesting to read.

Literature Cited

Aldhous P. 1992. The promise and pitfalls of molecular genetics. *Science* 257:164

Alper JS, Natowicz MR. 1992. The allure of genetic explanations. *Br. Med. J.* 305:666

Bailey JM, Bell AP. 1993. Familiality of female and male homosexuality. *Behav. Genet.* 23:313–22

Bailey JM, Benishay DS. 1993. Familial aggregation of female sexual orientation. *Am. J. Psychiatr.* 150:272–77

Bailey JM, Pillard RC. 1991. A genetic study of male sexual orientation. *Arch. Gen. Psychiatr.* 48: 1089–96

Bailey JM, Pillard RC, Neale MC, Agyei Y. 1993. Heritable factors influence sexual orientation in women. *Arch. Gen. Psychiatr.* 50:217–23

Bailey JM, Revelle W. 1991. Increased heritability for lower I.Q. levels? *Behav. Genet.* 21:397–404

Baker LA, Vernon PA, Ho HZ. 1991. The genetic correlation between intelligence and speed of information processing. *Behav. Genet.* 21:351–67

Barinaga M. 1994. From fruit flies, rats, mice: evidence of genetic influence. *Science* 264: 1690–93

Baron M. 1993. Genetics and human sexual orientation. *Biol. Psychol.* 33:759–61

Baumrind D. 1993. The average expectable environment is not good enough: a response to Scarr. *Child Dev.* 64:1299–1317

Beekmans K, Thiery E, Derom C, Vernon PA, Vlietinck R, Derom R. 1993. Relating type of placentation to later intellectual development in monozygotic (MZ) twins. *Behav. Genet.* 23:547–48 (Abstr.)

Bergem A. 1993. Estimation of concordance rate in demented twin pairs as a function of age of onset and age of sample. *Psychiatr. Genet.* 3:139 (Abstr.)

Billings PR, Beckwith J, Alper JS. 1992. The genetic analysis of human behavior: a new era? *Soc. Sci. Med.* 35:227–38

Blum K, Noble EP, Sheridan PJ, Montgomery A, Ritchie T, et al. 1990. Allelic association of human dopamine D2 receptor gene

in alcoholism. *J. Am. Med. Assoc.* 263: 2055–60

Boomsma DI. 1993. Current status and future prospects in twin studies of the development of cognitive abilities: infancy to old age. See Bouchard & Propping 1993, pp. 67–82

Boomsma DI, Koopmans JR, Van Doornen LJP, Orlebeke JM. 1994. Genetic and social influences on starting to smoke: a study of Dutch adolescent twins and their parents. *Addiction* 89:219–26

Bouchard TJ Jr. 1994. Genes, environment, and personality. *Science* 264:1700–1

Bouchard TJ Jr, Propping P, eds. 1993. *Twins as a Tool of Behavioral Genetics,* West Sussex, England: Wiley. 310 pp.

Bouchard C, Perusse L, Leblanc C. 1990a. Using MZ twins in experimental research to test for the presence of a genotype-environment interaction effect. *Acta Genet. Med. Gemellol.* 39:85–89

Bouchard C, Tremblay A, Després JP, Nadeau A, Lupien PJ, et al. 1990b. The response to long-term overfeeding in identical twins. *New Engl. J. Med.* 322:1477–82

Braungart JM, Plomin R, DeFries JC, Fulker DW. 1992. Genetic influence on tester-rated infant temperament as assessed by Bayley's Infant Behavior Record: nonadoptive and adoptive siblings and twins. *Dev. Psychol.* 28:40–47

Brunner HG, Nelen M, Breakefield XO, Ropers HH, Van Oost BA. 1993. Abnormal behavior associated with a point mutation in the structural gene for monoamine oxidase A. *Science* 262:578–80

Byne W. 1994. The biological evidence challenged. *Sci. Am.* 270:50–55

Byne W, Parsons B. 1993. Human sexual orientation. The biologic theories reappraised. *Arch. Gen. Psychiatr.* 50:228–41

Caldwell CB, Gottesman II. 1991. Sex differences in the risk for alcoholism: a twin study. *Behav. Genet.* 21:563 (Abstr.)

Capecchi MR. 1994. Targeted gene replacement. *Sci. Am.* 270:52–59

Cardon LR. 1994. Specific cognitive ability. See DeFries et al 1994, pp. 57–76

Cardon LR, Fulker DW. 1993. Genetics of specific cognitive abilities. See Plomin & McClearn 1993, pp. 99–120

Cardon LR, Fulker DW. 1994. A model of developmental change in hierarchical phenotypes with application to specific cognitive abilities. *Behav. Genet.* 24:1–16

Cardon LR, Fulker DW, DeFries JC, Plomin R. 1992a. Continuity and change in general cognitive ability from 1 to 7 years of age. *Dev. Psychol.* 28:64–73

Cardon LR, Fulker DW, DeFries JC, Plomin R. 1992b. Multivariate genetic analysis of specific cognitive abilities in the Colorado adoption project at age 7. *Intelligence* 16: 383–400

Carey G. 1992. Twin imitation for antisocial behavior: implications for genetic and family environment research. *J. Abnorm. Psychol.* 101:18–25

Carey G, DiLalla DL. 1994. Personality and psychopathology: genetic perspectives. *J. Abnorm. Psychol.* 103:32–43

Carlier M, Spitz E, Reed T, Lavenu MCV, Busnel MC. 1994. *Effect of chorion type on MZ twins on a sample of French children: preliminary results.* Presented at Int. Symp. Genetic Epidemiology of Twins and Twinning. Amsterdam, April

Carmelli D, Heath AC, Robinette D. 1993. Genetic analysis of drinking behavior in World War II veteran twins. *Genet. Epidemiol.* 10: 201–13

Carmelli D, Swan GE, Robinette D, Fabsitz R. 1992. Genetic influence on smoking—a study of male twins. *New Engl. J. Med.* 327:829–33

Caskey CT. 1993. *Trinucleotide repeats as a cause of heritable human disease.* Presented at 17 Int. Congr. Genet., Birmingham, England, August

Cherny SS, Cardon LR. 1994. General cognitive ability. See DeFries et al 1994, pp. 46–56

Cherny SS, Cardon LR, Fulker DW, DeFries JC. 1992. Differential heritability across levels of cognitive ability. *Behav. Genet.* 22:153–62

Christian JC, Edenburg H, O'Connor SJ, Conneally M, Wheeler P, Li TK. 1994. Associations of dopamine D_2 polymorphisms with brain electrophysiology. *Alcohol.: Clin. Exp. Res.* 18:449

Ciaranello RD, Ciaranello AL. 1991. Genetics of major psychiatric disorders. *Annu. Rev. Med.* 42:151–58

Collins F, Galas D. 1993. A new five-year plan for the U.S. Human Genome Project. *Science* 262:43–46

Cook CCH, Holmes D, Brett P, Curtis D, Gurling HMD. 1993. Linkage analysis confirms a genetic effect at the D_2 dopamine receptor locus in heavy drinking and alcoholism. *Psychiatr. Genet.* 3:130 (Abstr.)

Corder EH, Saunders AM, Strittmatter WJ, Schmechel DE, Gaskell PC, et al. 1993. Gene dose of apolipoprotein E type 4 allele and the risk of Alzheimer's disease in late onset families. *Science* 261:921–23

Craufurd D, Dodge A. 1993. Mutation size and age at onset in Huntington's disease. *Psychiatr. Genet.* 3:139 (Abstr.)

DeFries JC, Gillis JJ. 1993. Genetics of reading disability. See Plomin & McClearn 1993, pp. 121–145

DeFries JC, Plomin R, Fulker DW. 1994. *Nature, Nurture During Middle Childhood.* Cambridge, MA: Blackwell. 368 pp.

Detterman DK, Thompson LA, Plomin R. 1990. Differences in heritability across groups differing in ability. *Behav. Genet.* 20:369–84

Dolan CV, Molenaar PC, Boomsma DI. 1991. Simultaneous genetic analysis of longitudinal means and covariance structure in the simplex model using twin data. *Behav. Genet.* 21:49–65

Dolan CV, Molenaar PC, Boomsma DI. 1992. Decomposition of multivariate phenotypic means in multigroup genetic covariance structure analysis. *Behav. Genet.* 22:319–35

Durcan MJ, Goldman D. 1993. Genomic imprinting: implications for behavioral genetics. *Behav. Genet.* 23:137–43

Eaves LJ, Long J, Heath A. 1986. A theory of developmental change in quantitative phenotypes applied to cognitive development. *Behav. Genet.* 16:143–62

Eaves LJ, Silberg JL, Hewitt JK, Rutter M, Meyer JM, et al. 1993. Analyzing twin resemblance in multi-symptom data: genetic applications of a latent class model for symptoms of conduct disorders in juvenile boys. *Behav. Genet.* 23:5–20

Emde RM, Plomin R, Robinson J, Corley R, DeFries J, et al. 1992. Temperament, emotion, and cognition at fourteen months: the MacArthur Longitudinal Twin Study. *Child Dev.* 63:1437–55

Finkel D, McGue M. 1993. The origins of individual differences in memory among the elderly: a behavior genetic analysis. *Psychol. Aging* 8:527–37

Finkel D, Pedersen N, McGue M. 1994. *Genetic influences on memory performance in the second half of the lifespan: comparison of Minnesota and Swedish twin data.* Presented at Annu. Meet. Behav. Genet. Assoc., 24th, Barcelona, July

Fulker D. 1994. *A behavior-genetic perspective on development.* Presented at Int. Soc. Study Behav. Dev., 13th, Amsterdam, July

Fulker DW, Cardon LR. 1993. What can twin studies tell us about the structure and correlates of cognitive abilities? See Bouchard & Propping 1993, pp. 33–52

Fulker DW, Cardon LR. 1994. A sib-pair approach to interval mapping of quantitative trait loci. *Am. J. Hum. Genet.* 54:1092–1103

Fulker DW, Cardon LR, DeFries JC, Kimberling WJ, Pennington BF, Smith SD. 1991. Multiple regression analysis of sib-pair data on reading to detect quantitative trait loci. *Read. Writ. Interdisc. J.* 3:299–313

Fulker DW, Cherny SS, Cardon LR. 1993. Continuity and change in cognitive development. See Plomin & McClearn 1993, pp. 77–97

Fuller JL, Thompson WR. 1960. *Behavior Genetics.* New York: Wiley

Gatz M, Pedersen NL, Plomin R, Nesselroade JR, McClearn GE. 1992. Importance of shared genes and shared environments for symptoms of depression in older adults. *J. Abnorm. Psychol.* 101:701–8

Goldberg J, True WR, Eisen SA, Henderson WG. 1990. A twin study of the effects of the Vietnam War on posttraumatic stress disorder. *J. Am. Med. Assoc.* 263:1227–32

Goodman R. 1991. Growing together and growing apart: the non-genetic forces on children in the same family. See McGuffin & Murray 1991, pp. 212–24

Gottesman II. 1991. *Schizophrenia Genesis: The Origins of Madness.* New York: Freeman. 296 pp.

Gottesman II, Bertelsen A. 1991. Schizophrenia: classical approaches with new twists and provocative results. See McGuffin & Murray 1991, pp. 85–97

Hamer DH. 1993. Genetics of sexual orientation. *Psychiatr. Genet.* 3:115 (Abstr.)

Hamer DH, Hu S, Magnuson VL, Hu N, Pattatucci AML. 1993. A linkage between DNA markers on the X chromosome and male sexual orientation. *Science* 261:321–27

Heath AC. 1993. What can we learn about the determinants of psychopathology and substance abuse from studies of normal twins? See Bouchard & Propping 1993, pp. 273–85

Heath AC, Bucholz KK, Dinwiddie SH, Madden PAF, Slutske WS, et al. 1994a. *Pathways from genotype to alcoholism risk in women.* Presented at Annu. Meet. Behav.Genet.Assoc., 24th, Barcelona, July

Heath AC, Kessler RC, Neale MC, Hewitt JK, Eaves LJ, Kendler KS. 1993. Testing hypotheses about direction of causation using cross-sectional family data. *Behav. Genet.* 23:29–50

Heath AC, Madden PAF, Bucholz KK, Dinwiddie SH, Slutske WS, et al. 1994b. Genetic contribution to alcoholism risk in women. *Alcohol.: Clin. Exp. Res.* 18:448 (Abstr.)

Heath AC, Martin NG. 1993. Genetic models for the natural history of smoking: evidence for a genetic influence on smoking persistence. *Addict. Behav.* 18:19–34

Heath AC, Meyer J, Eaves LJ, Martin NG. 1991a. The inheritance of alcohol consumption patterns in a general population twin sample: I. multidimensional scaling of quantity/frequency data. *J. Stud. Alcohol* 52:345–52

Heath AC, Meyer J, Jardine R, Martin NG. 1991b. The inheritance of alcohol consumption patterns in a general population twin sample: II. determinants of consumption frequency and quantity consumed. *J. Stud. Alcohol* 52:425–33

Heath AC, Neale MC, Kessler RC, Eaves LJ, Kendler KS. 1992. Evidence for genetic influences on personality from self-reports and informant ratings. *J. Pers. Soc. Psychol.* 63:85–96

Heston LL, Shields J. 1968. Homosexuality in twins. A family study and a registry study. *Arch. Gen. Psychiatr.* 18:149–60

Hewitt JK, Eaves LJ, Silberg JL, Rutter M, Simonoff E, et al. 1993. The Virginia Twin Study of Adolescent Behavioral Development. *Psychiatr. Genet.* 3:175 (Abstr.)

Hodgkinson S, Mullan M, Murray RM. 1991. The genetics of vulnerability to alcoholism. See McGuffin & Murray 1991, pp. 182–97

Hoffman LW. 1991. The influence of the family environment on personality: accounting for sibling differences. *Psychol. Bull.* 110: 187–203

Holden C. 1994. A cautionary genetic tale: the sobering story of D2. *Science* 264:1696–97

Hopper JL, White VM, Macaskill GT, Hill DJ, Clifford CA. 1992. Alcohol use, smoking habits and the Junior Eysenck Personality Questionnaire in adolescent Australian twins. *Acta Genet. Med. Gemellol.* 41: 311–24

Horgan J. 1993. Trends in behavioral genetics: eugenics revisited. *Sci. Am.* 268:122 –31

Jackson JF. 1993. Human behavioral genetics, Scarr's theory, and her views on interventions: a critical review and commentary on their implications for African American children. *Child Dev.* 64:1318–32

Kaprio J, Koskenvuo M, Rose RJ. 1990a. Population-based twin registries: illustrative applications in genetic epidemiology and behavioral genetics from the Finnish Twin Cohort Study. *Acta Genet. Med. Gemellol.* 39:427–39

Kaprio J, Koskenvuo M, Rose RJ. 1990b. Change in cohabitation and intrapair similarity of monozygotic (MZ) cotwins for alcohol use, extraversion, and neuroticism. *Behav. Genet.* 20:265–76

Kaprio J, Viken R, Koskenvuo M, Romanov K, Rose RJ. 1992. Consistency and change in patterns of social drinking: a 6-year follow-up of the Finnish twin cohort. *Alcohol.: Clin. Exp. Res.* 16:234–40

Kendler KS. 1993. Twin studies of psychiatric illness: current status and future directions. *Arch. Gen. Psychiatr.* 50:905–16

Kendler KS, Heath AC, Neale MC, Kessler RC, Eaves LJ. 1992a. A population-based twin study of alcoholism in women. *J. Am. Med. Assoc.* 268:1877–82

Kendler KS, Heath AC, Neale MC, Kessler RC, Eaves LJ. 1993a. Alcoholism and major depression in women. *Arch. Gen. Psychiatr.* 50:690–91

Kendler KS, Neale MC, Kessler RC, Heath AC, Eaves LJ. 1992b. The genetic epidemiology of phobias in women. *Arch. Gen. Psychiatr.* 49:273–81

Kendler KS, Neale MC, Kessler RC, Heath AC, Eaves LJ. 1993b. Major depression and phobias: the genetic and environmental sources of comorbidity. *Psychol. Med.* 23:361–71

Kendler KS, Neale MC, Kessler RC, Heath AC, Eaves LJ. 1993c. Panic disorder in women: a population-based twin study. *Psychol. Med.* 23:397–406

King M, McDonald E. 1992. Homosexuals who are twins. *Br. J. Psychiatr.* 160:407–9

King M-C. 1993. Sexual orientation and the X. *Nature* 364:288–89

Knight SJL, Flannery AV, Hirst MC, Campbell L, Christodoulou Z, et al. 1993. Trinucleotide repeat amplification and hypermethylation of a CpG island in *FRAXE* mental retardation. *Cell* 74:127–34

Koopmans JR, Boomsma DI. 1993. Bivariate genetic analysis of the relation between alcohol and tobacco use in adolescent twins. *Psychiatr. Genet.* 3:172

Koopmans JR, Boomsma DI, Van Doornen LJP, Orlebeke JF. 1993. Alcohol use, smoking, and personality in adolescent twins. *Behav. Genet.* 23:556 (Abstr.)

Kyvik KO, Green A, Beck-Nielsen H. 1994. *The new Danish twin registry.* Presented at Int. Symp. Genetic Epidemiology of Twins and Twinning, Amsterdam, April

Lewin LM, Hops H, Davis B, Dishion TJ. 1993. Multimethod comparison of similarity in school adjustment of siblings and unrelated children. *Dev. Psychol.* 29:963–69

Liddell M, Williams J, Bayer A, Keiser F, Owen M. 1993. Association between the e4 allele of apolipoprotein E and Alzheimer's disease. *Psychiatr. Genet.* 3:138 (Abstr.)

Loehlin JC. 1992. *Genes and Environment in Personality Development.* Newbury Park, CA: Sage. 145 pp.

Lykken DT, Bouchard TJ Jr, McGue M, Tellegen A. 1990. The Minnesota Twin Family Registry: some initial findings. *Acta Genet. Med. Gemellol.* 39:35–70

Lykken DT, McGue M, Tellegen A, Bouchard TJ Jr. 1992. Emergenesis. Genetic traits that may not run in families. *Am. Psychol.* 12:1565–77

Lyons MJ, Goldberg J, Eisen SA, True W, Tsuang MT, et al. 1993. Do genes influence exposure to trauma? A twin study of combat. *Am. J. Med. Genet. (Neuropsychiatr. Genet.)* 48:22–27

MacDonald ME, Ambrose CM, Duyao MP, Myers RH, Lin C, et al. 1993. A novel gene containing a trinucleotide repeat that is expanded and unstable on Huntington's disease chromosomes. *Cell* 72:971–83

Macke JP, Hu N, Hu S, Bailey M, King VL, et al. 1993. Sequence variation in the androgen receptor gene is not a common determinant of male sexual orientation. *Am. J. Hum. Genet.* 53:844–52

Maddox J. 1993. Wilful public misunderstanding of genetics. *Nature* 364:281

Martin JB. 1993. Molecular genetics of neurological diseases. *Science* 262:674–76

Martin NG, Heath AC. 1993. The genetics of voting: an Australian twin-family study. *Behav. Genet.* 23:558 (Abstr.)

McConkie-Rosell A, Lachiewicz AM, Spiridigliozzi A, Tarleton J, Schoenwald S, et al. 1993. Evidence that methylation of the FMR-1 locus is responsible for variable phenotypic expression of the Fragile X Syndrome. *Am. J. Hum. Genet.* 53:800–9

McFadden D. 1993. A masculinizing effect on the auditory systems of human females having male co-twins. *Proc. Natl. Acad. Sci.* 90:11900–4

McGue M. 1993. From proteins to cognitions: the behavioral genetics of alcoholism. See Plomin & McClearn 1993, pp. 245–68

McGue M, Bouchard TJ Jr, Iacono WG, Lykken DT. 1993a. Behavioral genetics of cognitive ability: a life-span perspective. See Plomin & McClearn 1993, pp. 59–76

McGue M, Pickens RW, Svikis DS. 1992. Sex and age effects on the inheritance of alcohol problems: a twin study. *J. Abnorm. Psychol.* 101:3–17

McGue M, Sharma AR, Benson PL. 1994. *Shared environmental influences on adolescent adjustment in a U.S. adoption cohort.* Presented at Annu. Meet. Behav. Genet. Assoc., 24th, Barcelona, July

McGue M, Bacon S, Lykken DT. 1993b. Personality stability and change in early adulthood. A behavioral genetic analysis. *Dev. Psychol.* 29:96–109

McGuffin P, Murray R, eds. 1991. *The New Genetics of Mental Illness.* Oxford, England: Butterworth-Heinemann. 304 pp.

McInnis MG, McMahon FJ, Chase GA, Simpson SG, Ross CA, DePaulo JR Jr. 1993. Anticipation in bipolar affective disorder. *Am. J. Hum. Genet.* 53:385–90

Meyer JM, Heath AC, Eaves LJ. 1992. Using multidimensional scaling on data from pairs of relatives to explore the dimensionality of categorical multifactorial traits. *Genet. Epidemiol.* 9:87–107

Miller MB. 1993. Comment on Lykken et al. *Am. Psychol.* 48:1295–97

Molenaar PCM, Boomsma DI, Dolan CV. 1991. Genetic and environmental factors in a developmental perspective. In *Problems and Methods in Longitudinal Research: Stability and Change,* ed. D Magnusson, LR Bergman, G Rudinger, B Törestad, pp. 250–73. Cambridge: Cambridge Univ. Press

Morell V. 1993. The puzzle of the triple repeats. *Science* 260:1422–23

Murrell J, Farlow M, Ghetti B, Benson MD. 1991. A mutation in the amyloid precursor protein associated with hereditary Alzheimer's disease. *Science* 254:97–99

Nance WE. 1994. *The future of twin research.* Presented at Int. Symp. Genetic Epidemiology of Twins and Twinning, Amsterdam, April

Neale MC, Cardon LR. 1992. *Methodology for Genetic Studies of Twins and Families.* Dordrecht, Netherlands: Kluwer

Noble EP. 1993. The D_2 dopamine receptor gene: a review of association studies in alcoholism. *Behav. Genet.* 23:119–29

Noble EP, Berman SM, Ozkaragoz TZ, Ritchie T. 1994. Prolonged P300 latency in children with D_2 dopamine receptor A1 allele. *Am. J. Hum. Genet.* 54:658–68

Noble EP, Blum K, Khalsa ME, Ritchie T, Montgomery A, et al. 1993. Allelic association of the D_2 dopamine receptor gene with cocaine dependence. *Drug Alcohol. Depend.* 33:271–85

Oberlé I, Rousseau F, Heitz D, Kretz C, Devys D, et al. 1991. Instability of a 550-base pair DNA segment and abnormal methylation in Fragile X Syndrome. *Science* 252:1097–102

Papolos DF, Lachman HM. 1994. *Genetic Studies in Affective Disorders: Overview of Basic Methods, Current Directions, and Critical Research Issues.* New York: Wiley

Pato CN, Macciardi F, Pato MT, Verga M, Kennedy JL. 1993. Review of the putative association of dopamine D_2 receptor and alcoholism: a meta-analysis. *Am. J. Med. Genet. (Neuropsychiatr. Genet.)* 48:78–82

Pauls DL. 1993. Twin studies as an approach to differential manifestations of childhood behavioral disorders across age. See Bouchard & Propping 1993, pp. 195–204

Pedersen NL. 1993. Genetic and environmental continuity and change in personality. See Bouchard & Propping 1993, pp. 147–62

Pedersen NL, McClearn GE, Plomin R, Nesselroade JR. 1992a. Effects of early rearing environment on twin similarity in the last half of the life span. *Br. J. Dev. Psychol.* 10:255–67

Pedersen NL, Plomin R, Nesselroade JR, McClearn GE. 1992b. A quantitative genetic analysis of cognitive abilities during the second half of the lifespan. *Psychol. Sci.* 3:346–53

Pennington BF, Gilger JW, Pauls D, Smith SA, Smith SD, DeFries JC. 1991. Evidence for major gene transmission of developmental dyslexia. *J. Am. Med. Assoc.* 266:1527–34

Pickens RW, Svikis DS, McGue M, Lykken DT, Heston LL, Clayton PJ. 1991. Heterogeneity in the inheritance of alcoholism. *Arch. Gen. Psychiatr.* 48:19–28

Plomin R, Corley R, DeFries JC, Fulker DW. 1990. Individual differences in television viewing in early childhood: nature as well as nurture. *Psychol. Sci.* 1:371–77

Plomin R, Emde RN, Braungart JM, Campos J, Corley R, et al. 1993. Genetic change and continuity from 14 to 20 months: the MacArthur Longitudinal Twin Study. *Child Dev.* 64:1354–76

Plomin R, McClearn GE, eds. 1993. *Nature, Nurture, & Psychology.* Washington, DC: Am. Psychol. Assoc. 498 pp.

Plomin R, McClearn GE, Smith DL, Vignetti S, Chorney MJ, et al. 1994a. DNA markers associated with high versus low IQ: The IQ Quantitative Trait Loci (QTL) Project. *Behav. Genet.* 24:107–18

Plomin R, Owen MJ, McGuffin P. 1994b. The genetic basis of complex human behaviors. *Science* 264:1733–39

Prescott CA, Hewitt JK, Heath AC, Truett KR, Neale MC, Eaves LJ. 1994. Environmental and genetic influences on alcohol use in a volunteer sample of older twins. *J. Stud. Alcohol* 55:18–33

Prescott CA, Johnson RC, McArdle JJ. 1991. Genetic contributions to television viewing. *Psychol. Sci.* 2:430–31

Räihä I, Koskenvuo M, Kaprio J, Rajala T, Sourande L. 1994. *Occurrence of dementia in the Nationwide Finnish Twin Cohort.* Presented at Int. Symp. Genetic Epidemiology of Twins and Twinning, Amsterdam, April

Resnick SM, Gottesman II, McGue M. 1993. Sensation seeking in opposite-sex twins: an effect of prenatal hormones? *Behav. Genet.* 23:323–29

Rijsdijk FV, Boomsma DI, Vernon PA. 1994a. Genetic analyses of peripheral nerve conduction velocity in men and its relation with I.Q. *Behav. Genet.* In press

Rijsdijk FV, Boomsma DI, Vernon PA. 1994b. Nerve conduction velocity and reaction time development in twins. In *Abstracts of the Thirteenth Biennial Meetings of the International Society for the Study of Behavioural Development,* ed. W Koops,

B Hopkins, P Engelen, p. 537. Leiden: Logan

Robinson JL, Reznick JS, Kagan J, Corley R. 1992. The heritability of inhibited and uninhibited behavior: a twin study. *Dev. Psychol.* 28:1030–37

Rose RJ. 1991. Twin studies and psychosocial epidemiology. In *Genetic Issues in Psychosocial Epidemiology,* ed. MT Tsuang, KS Kendler, MJ Lyons, pp. 12–32. New Brunswick, NJ: Rutgers Univ. Press

Rose RJ. 1992. Genes, stress and cardiovascular reactivity. In *Individual Differences in Cardiovascular Response to Stress,* ed. JR Turner, A Sherwood, KC Light, pp. 87–102. New York: Plenum

Rose RJ, Kaprio J, Williams CJ, Viken R, Obremski K. 1990. Social contact and sibling similarity: facts, issues, and red herrings. *Behav. Genet.* 20:763–78

Rose RJ, Kaprio J, Viken RJ, Winter T, Romanov K, Koskenvuo M. 1993. Use and abuse of alcohol in adolescence: a population study of Finnish twins at age 16. *Psychiatr. Genet.* 3:142 (Abstr.)

Rose RJ, Kaprio J, Winter T, Koskenvuo M. 1994. Femininity and fertility in sisters of twin brothers: neither prenatal androgenization nor cross-sex socialization. In *Abstracts of the Thirteenth Biennial Meetings of the International Society for the Study of Behavioural Development,* ed. W Koops, B Hopkins, P Engelen, p. 535. Leiden: Logan

Rowe DC. 1994. *The Limits of Family Influence.* New York: Guilford. 232 pp.

Rowe DC, Rodgers JL, Meseck-Bushey S. 1992. Sibling delinquency and the family environment: shared and unshared influences. *Child Dev.* 63:59–67

Scarr S. 1987. Three cheers for behavior genetics: winning the war and losing our identity. *Behav. Genet.* 17:219–28

Scarr S. 1992. Developmental theories for the 1990s: development and individual differences. *Child Dev.* 63:1–19

Schellenberg GD, Bird TD, Wijsman EM, Orr HT, Anderson L, et al. 1992. Genetic linkage evidence for a familial Alzheimer's disease locus on chromosome 14. *Science* 258:668–71

Schmitz S. 1994. Personality and temperament. See DeFries et al 1994, pp. 120–40

Science. 1994. Genes & Behavior. (Special Issue) 264:1686–739

Simm M. 1994. Violence study hits a nerve in Germany. *Science* 264:653

Slutske WS, Heath AC, Eaves LJ, Madden PA, Bucholz KK, et al. 1994. An examination of the classification of alcoholism using latent class analysis. *Alcohol.: Clin. Exp. Res.* 18:492 (Abstr.)

Smith SD, Kimberling WJ, Pennington BF. 1991. Screening for multiple genes influencing dyslexia. *Read. Writ. Interdisc. J.* 3:285–98

Sokol DK, Moore CA, Rose RJ, Williams CJ, Reed T, Christian JC. 1994. Intra-pair differences in personality and cognitive ability among young monozygotic twins distinguished by chorion type. In press

Swan GE, Cardon LR, Carmelli D. 1994. The consumption of tobacco, alcohol, and caffeine in male twins: a multivariate genetic analysis. Presented at Annu. Meet. Soc. Behav. Med., Boston, April

Time. 1980. Chubby? Blame those genes. June 4:80

Torrey EF, Bowler AE, Taylor EH, Gottesman II. 1994. *Schizophrenia and Manic-Depressive Disorder: The Biological Roots of Mental Illness as Revealed by the Landmark Study of Identical Twins.* New York: Basic

Verkerk AJMH, Pieretti M, Sutcliffe JS, Fu Y, Kuhl DPA, et al. 1991. Identification of a gene *(FMR-1)* containing a CGG repeat coincident with a breakpoint cluster region exhibiting length variation in Fragile X Syndrome. *Cell* 65:905–14

Vernon PA. 1991. Studying intelligence the hard way. *Intelligence* 15:389–95

Vernon PA, Mori M. 1992. Intelligence, reaction times, and peripheral nerve conduction velocity. *Intelligence* 16:273–88

Viken RJ, Rose RJ, Kaprio J, Koskenvuo M. 1994b. A developmental-genetic analysis of adult personality: extraversion and neuroticism from 18 to 59. *J. Pers. Soc. Psychol.* 66:722–30

Viken RJ, Rose RJ, Kaprio J, Koskenvuo M. 1994a. *Genetic and cultural transmission of personality: adolescent twins and their parents.* Presented at Int. Soc. Stud. Behav. Dev., 13th, Amsterdam, July

Whitam FL, Diamond M, Martin J. 1993. Homosexual orientation in twins: a report on 61 pairs and three triplet sets. *Arch. Sex. Behav.* 22:187–206

Wiesel TN. 1994. Genetics and behavior. (Editorial). *Science* 264:1647

Yu S, Mulley J, Loesch D, Turner G, Donnelly A, et al. 1992. Fragile-X Syndrome: unique genetics of the heritable unstable element. *Am. J. Hum. Genet.* 50:968–80

Yu S, Pritchard M, Kremer E, Lynch M, Nancarrow J, et al. 1991. Fragile X genotype characterized by an unstable region of DNA. *Science* 252:1179–81

Annu. Rev. Psychol. 1995. 46:655–87

PERSONALITY DEVELOPMENT IN SOCIAL CONTEXT

Willard W. Hartup

Institute of Child Development, University of Minnesota, Minneapolis, Minnesota 55455

Cornelis F. M. van Lieshout

Department of Psychology, University of Nijmegen, 6500 HE Nijmegen, The Netherlands

KEY WORDS: temperament, parent-child relationships, peer relationships

CONTENTS

INTRODUCTION

The behavior of children and adolescents reflects the social conditions in which they live. Aggressive and disruptive children commonly live in aggressive and violent circumstances; similarly, supportive and empathic environments figure prominently in the developmental histories of responsible children and adolescents. These concordances, however, are relatively modest. Many individuals who grow up in violent circumstances are not aggressive or antisocial, and numerous individuals growing up under empathic circumstances are egoistic and antisocial. Developmental pathways from childhood to adulthood are thus both "straight and devious" (Robins & Rutter 1990).

Recent studies are slowly tracing these paths. First, the dimensions of individuality are now described in more detail. Second, individual-to-individual variations that can be traced to genetic factors are better specified. Third, variations in child and adolescent development traceable to both social structural variables (e.g. community or neighborhood) and social relationships are better established. Fourth, the sequences linking social events to one another and to individual variations are being more clearly documented and alternative developmental pathways have been identified.

Progress has also been made in the areas of design and analysis. Most ontogenetic studies use correlational designs, but regression and structural equation models are being used with greater frequency to specify developmental sequences. Multiple measurement of key constructs is increasingly common; different levels of analysis occur within studies rather than always across them. New longitudinal data sets are available on-line, thereby expanding the database with which developmental models can be tested. Older data sets are used, too, but with improved conceptual models and more refined quantitative methods. These efforts are achieving excellent results.

This review differs from the most recent ones appearing in the *Annual Review of Psychology* under the title "Social and personality development" (Parke & Asher 1983, Collins & Gunnar 1990). Greater emphasis is given to central orientations existing in child and adolescent behavior (i.e. dimensions characterizing the individual from an early age that pervade many different areas of functioning; see Bronson 1966) as well as to the continuities and discontinuities that characterize them.

We first discuss theoretical and measurement issues in describing personality and temperament in children and adolescents. Descriptive and dimensional studies are considered, emphasizing the close connection between work with children and adolescents, on the one hand, and work with adults, on the other. Developmental continuities are considered next. Variable-centered approaches (e.g. aggression and social withdrawal) and person-centered approaches (e.g. individualities in the organization of behavior) are distinguished. Finally, developmental pathways are examined within three central orientations: antisocial behavior, social inhibition and withdrawal, and social responsibility. Developmental sequences are emphasized, and because relationships are the nexuses through which these sequences move, we organize our remarks concerning antisocial behavior, social inhibition, and social responsibility using a relationships scheme. Gene-environment transactions are mentioned only briefly because other recent reviews have dealt with them (cf Plomin & Rende 1991).

PERSONALITY AND TEMPERAMENT

Dimensional Issues

PERSONALITY   Personality has many different meanings. Attributes encompassed by the construct range from emotional reactivity to attitudes, expectations, values, and instrumental behaviors. Because consensus does not exist concerning the specific attributes that constitute personality, few measuring instruments cover every dimension assumed to be relevant.

Personality is commonly studied at many different levels ranging from the concrete (e.g. behavioral responses) to the abstract (e.g. central orientations or behavioral styles that typify individuals across different situations). Digman (1990) describes this enterprise in terms of a four-tiered hierarchy that includes (*a*) specific acts or interactions that occur in specific situations, (*b*) typical or modal responses occurring in prototypical situations (e.g. generalized habits or dispositions), (*c*) trait facets or characteristics, and (*d*) superordinate constructs or traits (e.g. extraversion). Hierarchical representations of this kind usually assume that lower-order characteristics are uniquely related to higher-order constructs. And yet, empirical studies based in natural language show that only about 50% of personality-related descriptors (e.g. adjectives) are related to single traits; almost as many are related to two factors, and a small number to more than two. Circumplexes, created by pitting constructs or traits against one another (e.g. agreeableness vs extraversion), are thus attractive alternative models (Hofstee et al 1992). Using several hundred descriptive adjectives, these authors were able to propose a taxonomy that they thought "comparable in function to the periodic table of chemical elements" (p. 146).

Factor analyses based on self- and other-descriptions of adults generally yield five orientations or dimensions, known as the Big Five or the Five Factor Model: extraversion, agreeableness, conscientiousness, emotional (in)stability, and openness (Digman 1990, Goldberg 1993). The Five Factor Model is robust across many different subjects, item pools, instruments, and methods of factor analysis as well as across different languages and cultures. Some writers (e.g. Goldberg 1993) suggest that the framework can subsume most earlier taxonomies and theoretically derived schemas including Cattell's (1956) Sixteen Personality Factors and Eysenck's (1970) Superfactors (psychoticism, extraversion, and neuroticism). Such assertions have elicited heated arguments (Eysenck 1993), although wide replicability of the Five Factor Model is sparking many new studies, including several with children and adolescents (Halverson et al 1994).

Main questions are whether the five factors assessed in adult personality also apply to the description of children's personality and how infant temperament develops into adult personality (Halverson et al 1994). Although a consensus does not exist, certain studies with children now confirm earlier results of studies with adults. For example, among both children and adolescents in the Netherlands and the United States, strong resemblance has been reported between the first five factors in the California Child Q-set (Block & Block 1980) and the Five Factor Model (van Lieshout & Haselager 1994, John et al 1994). Ego-resiliency and ego-control are also linked to the Five Factor Model. Other studies from four countries (the Netherlands, the United States, Belgium, and Surinam) reveal that 70–80% of the characteristics mentioned by parents in describing their children can be classified within the Five Factor Model. Moreover, the proportions of these characteristics assigned to each factor are remarkably similar across countries and languages and across reports obtained from both mothers and fathers for both boys and girls (Kohnstamm et al 1994).

TEMPERAMENT   Temperament is usually defined as a substrate for personality development, consisting of simple, basic styles that emerge early and that are tied closely to distinctive modes of emotional expression. Temperament ordinarily encompasses attributes including activity level, irritability or emotionality, soothability or self-regulation, fearfulness, and sociability (Goldsmith et al 1987). These attributes, in turn, can be divided into two broad groups (Rothbart 1989): reactivity (i.e. arousability of affect and motor activity) and self-regulation (e.g. attention, approach-withdrawal, inhibition, and self-soothing).

Factor-analytic studies reveal considerable isomorphism between the structure of early temperament and the structure of child and adolescent personality. Studies with infants in the United States, Europe, Australia, and China, using two well-known temperament questionnaires, reveal five to seven factors very similar in meaning to four of the Big Five: Activity level and inhibition are positive and negative poles (respectively) of a factor resembling extraversion; flexibility and control of negative affect reveal aspects of agreeableness; negative emotionality, activity level, irritability, and inhibition define a temperamental factor similar to neuroticism; and task persistence resembles conscientiousness (Martin et al 1994). Openness does not emerge in these analyses because relevant items are not contained in the infant temperament scales; intellectual ability, however, may be the basis for this factor. Rhythmicity (i.e. regularity of biological functions such as eating, defecating, and sleeping) emerges as a separate factor in these studies but is not usually regarded as relevant to personality development (Goldsmith et al 1987).

The manner in which temperament serves as a substrate for personality development is not well understood. Temperament is thought to be constitutionally based (i.e. influenced by heredity, maturation, and experience), although it is not more genetically determined or biologically rooted than is personality. In fact, the extent to which temperament is more genetically based than is personality remains an empirical question (Goldsmith et al 1987, Loehlin 1992). Temperament is believed to interact with experience in four main ways (Rothbart et al 1994): (a) by determining the child's effective experience, thus accounting for the different effects that similar experiences have on different children; (b) by affecting the child's sensitivity to rewards and punishments; (c) by moderating or controlling the effects of other temperamental characteristics (e.g. effortful control may moderate aggression); and (d) by influencing the learnability of social behaviors (e.g. social responsibility or conscience). Personality development is affected pervasively by these interactions between temperament and experience. First, certain temperamental factors are elaborated or modulated by these means into personality structure (e.g. low irritability and difficultness into agreeableness). Second, temperament interacts with parental characteristics and caretaking behaviors, affecting both the construction of relationships between parent and child and the child's socialization. Much remains to be learned, however, about these elaborations.

SUMMARY   The dimensions of temperament and the dimensions of personality are sometimes difficult to distinguish from one another. Early temperament is structured in some ways that are similar to the manner in which child and adolescent personality is structured. Continuities exist from childhood into adolescence and adulthood in both temperament and personality organization although the elaborations of temperament into personality are not well understood. Turning to these elaborations, we first examine stability and change in personality development. We then examine the complex transactions occurring between temperament, personality, and interpersonal relationships.

Developmental Issues

Personality development involves multidimensional and multidirectional elements in a constant state of organization and reorganization. Two main strategies are used to examine these processes—variable- and person-centered approaches (cf Block 1971, Magnusson & Törestad 1993). Variable-centered approaches stress correlations between the same variables or dimensions measured across time. Stability, then, is the extent to which individuals maintain their relative scores or rank orderings in these time-repeated measurements. This stability may occur together with normative change, that is, change that occurs across time in mean scores. Considerable stability may also co-occur with instability because some individuals maintain their rank orderings on the measures in question while others do not.

Person-centered approaches are based on ipsative stability, that is, the relative rank ordering among different behavioral characteristics occurring within a person across repeated measurements. Consistency then refers to the extent to which the personality profile remains constant over time (Caspi et al 1994).

Examples of a person-centered approach include cross-time relations between patterns of child behavior and patterns of contextual characteristics (e.g. in the mother's behavior), comparisons between clinical and nonclinical samples with respect to constellations of adjustment problems at different points in the life course, and comparisons across age in behavior and personality patterns between males and females.

Although variable- and person-centered views sometimes seem to be in opposition, mixing them can be advantageous (Ozer & Gjerde 1989). Such mixtures, however, carry strict methodological requirements with them. Demonstrating either interindividual stability or intraindividual consistency assumes continuity in the temperament or personality dimensions being measured. Continuities exist when the categories representing these dimensions are conceptually equivalent across time. Even heterotypic continuity (Kagan 1980), in which behavioral indicators of a construct are assumed to change with maturation, requires age-equivalence across indicators (Asendorpf 1992). Otherwise, discontinuity would indicate change in the measurement structure or meaning of the behavioral constellation. In short, interindividual stability and change can be investigated in relation to intraindividual consistency only as long as continuity in the dimensions of temperament and personality can be assumed.

VARIABLE-CENTERED STUDIES   Pedlow et al (1993) convincingly demonstrated that continuity of a construct over time is needed in the assessment of variable-centered stabilities (cf Wohlwill 1973). Using age-appropriate temperament questionnaires, the investigators first showed measurement equivalence between infancy and age eight in approach (inhibition), irritability, cooperation-manageability, inflexibility, rhythmicity, and task persistence. (Irritability and cooperation-manageability during the first two years combined subsequently to create an inflexibility construct during middle childhood.) Interindividual stabilities were substantially greater (modal values ranging between .57 and .78) than those reported in earlier studies. Similarly, when strong continuities in shyness were established between early childhood and adulthood, stability coefficients ranged between .51 and .75 from ages four through eight (Asendorpf 1992).

These temperamental stabilities resemble the stability coefficients (approximately .70) reported in the personality domain among Big Five factor scores obtained in several studies across six- to seven-year intervals between early adulthood and old age (Costa & McCrae 1994). Current results thus suggest that interindividual stabilities in childhood temperament are similar to interindividual stabilities in adult personality. One must remember, however, that these stabilities occur simultaneously with normative change: Neuroticism and extraversion decrease from early to late adulthood, for example, while agreeableness and conscientiousness increase (Costa & McCrae 1994, McGue et al 1993).

PERSON-CENTERED STUDIES   Lifelong development involves temperament and personality in continuous transactions that encompass physiological processes, social expectations, and interpersonal relationships. Many writers argue that stability and change can be meaningfully construed only in terms of organization across these domains. Consequently, assessment must involve diverse functions including neurophysiological and endocrine processes as well as personological assessments made by independent observers, significant others, and the self. Personological assessments from three sources are needed because no one source is a proxy for another: Independent observers provide assessments that are relatively unbiased by the subject's attributions; significant others establish the subject in relational context with reference to the goals, cognitions, coregulated rules, and affective expectations that mark interpersonal relationships; self-evaluations are constituent elements of the self-concept and thus reflect the subject's self-perceived roles and identities. Assessment must occur simultaneously across these domains because quality of adaptation cannot be completely measured otherwise. Overall, the person-oriented argument is well taken: Personality development should not be viewed in terms of a set of static traits, but rather in terms of more or less stable organizational features that qualify a person's dyadic and group relationships and that may change over the life course (Berscheid 1994).

Developmental differences in temperament begin to covary with changing qualities of relationships in early infancy. Based on analyses of infant and mother behaviors between one and six months postpartum, irritable and nonirritable babies are known to differ in positive and negative emotionality as well as in interest in the environment. Developmental trajectories also differ. Concordantly, maternal behavior is more positive with nonirritable as compared with irritable babies, and the mothers' behaviors also change differentially over time. Growth curves in the activities of the mothers of nonirritable babies, for example, differ from the growth curves for mothers of irritable babies in visual contact, effective stimulation, physical contact, soothing, noninvolvement, and responsiveness to the baby's signals (van den Boom & Hoeksma 1994). Further, intervention with the mothers of irritable babies (between six and nine months postpartum) results in the experimental mothers becoming more responsive, stimulating, and controlling than are the mothers of irritable babies in comparison groups. Their babies also become more sociable, self-soothing, and exploratory; and they cry less. Finally, at 12 months postpartum, the experimental babies and their mothers are more often securely attached to one another than are the control babies and their mothers (van den Boom 1994).

Early childhood temperament also has been linked to subsequent behavior across longer periods. For example, restless three-year-olds turn out to be relatively impulsive, danger-seeking, aggressive, and socially alienated as eighteen-year-olds; inhibited youngsters, in contrast, score significantly lower on these measures. Confident children tend to be impulsive as young adults, whereas reserved children become relatively unforceful and indecisive (Caspi & Silva 1994). Early control difficulties are also more strongly associated with externalizing (e.g. aggression, inattention, impulsivity, hyperactivity) than internalizing (e.g. anxiety, somatic complaints, social withdrawal) problems later on. Reservedness is associated with internalizing problems later among boys; sluggishness is related to anxiety and inattention, especially among girls (Caspi et al 1994).

Other studies extend differential patterns occurring in childhood even further into adulthood. In one investigation (Pulkkinen & Ronka 1994), behavioral factors (e.g. school success and problem behavior) and social context (e.g. socioeconomic status) in childhood and adolescence were both correlated among 26-year-olds with positive orientations (e.g. personal control over development, positive evaluation of the future, and identity formation) and motivated questioning (e.g. identity exploration, future orientation, and dissatisfaction with present achievements).

In a second instance (Block & Robins 1993), consistency and change in self-esteem were studied from early adolescence into adulthood. Although continuity in self-esteem scores (i.e. perceived self–ideal self differences) was similar in males and females, change was correlated with different personality characteristics in the two sexes. Females whose Q-scores showed them to be protective, sympathetic, generous, and humorous at age 14 tended to increase in self-esteem through age 23, whereas those who were negative and irritable tended to decrease in self-esteem. Males rated as calm, relaxed, and unanxious in adolescence tended to increase in self-esteem, while others who were anxious and fantasized frequently decreased in self-esteem. But these results do not tell the whole story. The correlates of self-esteem varied with both gender and developmental status: Girls with high self-esteem tended to be poised, assertive, and socially influential during both early and late adolescence, remaining so through early adulthood. Clear-cut correlates did not emerge for males until early adulthood, at which time they were not very different from the correlates of self-esteem among females. These analyses reveal change and continuity occurring together in the context of gender socialization. Overall, these changes and continuities are consistent with the notion that socialization connects self-esteem to social responsibility among females but to the control of anxiety among males. More intensive investigation is needed to better understand how these continuities and changes are maintained. Without a person-centered orientation, however, the dialectics involving these continuities and changes in self-esteem would be difficult to detect.

NATURE AND NURTURE   Differences among individuals in temperament and personality appear to be generated by a combination of environmental and genetic factors. For the Big Five, additive genetic effects (i.e. added effects of several genes) account for between 22% and 46% of individual variation in the samples studied; nonadditive effects (i.e. effects of specific configurations of genes) account for between 11% and 19% (except for openness, which shows between 2% and 5%), and shared family environment accounts for between 0% and 11%. The remaining variation, 44% to 55%, represents some combination of environmental effects unique to the individual, genotype-environment interaction, and/or measurement error (Loehlin 1992).

Heritability estimates differ according to age: Significant heritabilities are rare for temperament assessments obtained at birth or during the first year but gradually increase during and beyond the second year toward magnitudes characterizing adolescents and adults. Current studies suggest that stability and change in early temperament are to some extent heritable in some populations (Plomin et al 1993, Saudino et al 1994a).

SUMMARY   Temperament and personality development are being studied in a relatively integrated fashion. Variable-oriented and person-oriented approaches to personality development are in vogue, and closer attention to basic assumptions (e.g. continuity in the measurement structure) is improving the results. Short- and long-term stability and change are being documented with emphasis on the manner in which temperament is elaborated into personality. Relatively little is known about the manner in which temperament, socialization pressures, and interpersonal relationships are intertwined in personality development. Beginnings are being made, however, as evidenced by advances in three areas: antisocial behavior, inhibition and withdrawal, and responsibility.

THREE BEHAVIORAL ORIENTATIONS

Antisocial Behavior

STABILITIES   The stability of antisocial behavior from childhood through adolescence is substantial, approximating the consistencies across time reported for measured intelligence (Olweus 1979, Vuchinich et al 1992). Among aggressive individuals, biological factors (e.g. low autonomic activity and reactivity) and temperamental styles in early childhood (e.g. resisting control and hyperactivity) are associated with externalizing symptoms and aggressiveness in childhood, adolescence, and young adulthood (Caspi et al 1994, Magnusson 1994,

Sampson & Laub 1994). Extraversion, agreeableness, and conscientiousness are also associated with externalizing symptoms (inversely for the latter two) in adolescence (John et al 1994).

Differences among individuals in the stability of antisocial behavior, however, are substantial. Antisocial behavior is stable for very aggressive persons (Stattin & Magnusson 1991) but decidedly unstable for many others (Caspi & Moffitt 1994). Some children are aggressive at an early age and remain so, whereas others only become aggressive during the transition to adolescence (Moffitt 1993, Patterson et al 1991). Among "early starters," different subtypes can be traced: Some individuals engage in aggression and antisocial behavior continuously through childhood and adolescence (i.e. persistors), whereas others discontinue their aggression before serious delinquency begins (i.e. desistors). Consensus has not been reached concerning the risk dynamics represented by these discontinuities. Some investigators (Moffitt 1993) believe that adolescence-limited aggression is largely due to the accelerating peer pressure that favors antisocial behavior during pre- and early adolescence. Others believe that late-starting aggression is rooted in the same disordered relationships that characterize early starters (see below) but that it involves children who are more socially skilled (Patterson et al 1992). Although late starters cannot be distinguished from early starters in many ways during adolescence, early starters are more seriously at risk in social development than are late starters (Dishion et al 1994b).

What conditions support these stabilities among early-starters? Behavior-genetic studies have not shown convincingly that aggressiveness and antisocial behavior in childhood and adolescence are heritable. Substantial heritabilites have been reported for criminality among older individuals in some populations, but the evidence for aggressiveness in children and adolescents is thin (Dilalla & Gottesman 1989). At the same time, consistencies across time exist in the social and demographic circumstances under which most individuals live: Poverty, exposure to community violence, and exposure to stress and coercion within family and peer relationships are more likely than not to persist across childhood and adolescence. New evidence, however, indicates that genetic factors contribute to measures of the family environment. That is, more than a quarter of the variance in a diverse array of environmental measures is accounted for by genetic differences among the children in one investigation (Plomin et al 1994). Additionally, the stability of antisocial behavior is known to reflect child effects on the family environment, environmental effects on the child's antisocial behavior, and reciprocal effects simultaneously (Vuchinich et al 1992). The dialectics between heredity and environment in this area are indeed complex.

SOCIETAL CONTEXT   Epidemiological studies (Offord et al 1991, Loeber & Wikstrom 1993, Dodge et al 1994) show that aggression and/or conduct disorder are maximized in certain populations: males, blacks, residents in inner city or lower income neighborhoods, families suffering economic privation, and large families headed by single parents. Gender is related to aggression independent of the other conditions. Family size and single parent status also account independently for significant variance in aggression and conduct disorder in some data sets (Offord et al 1991, Dodge et al 1994, Sampson & Laub 1994), but race does not seem to account for aggressiveness beyond the effects of social class (Dodge et al 1994).

Social class and economic stress are risk factors for early- but not late-starting aggression. Among early-starters, economic stress heightens aggression even with family structure and functioning taken into account; the child's progress toward both overt and covert delinquency is accelerated (Loeber & Wikstrom 1993). These social dynamics are becoming more clear. Dodge et al (1994) found that socioeconomic status in kindergarten was strongly and inversely related to peer-rated aggression—both at the time and over the next three years. Social class was also inversely correlated with harsh parental discipline, lack of maternal warmth, exposure to aggressive models, positive maternal attitudes toward aggression, family stress, lack of social support, and restricted cognitive stimulation. Because both teacher-rated externalizing problems and peer-rated aggression were correlated with these family characteristics, regression analyses were needed to demonstrate that the connection between social class and aggression is actually mediated by socialization within the family. Results showed that economic effects on aggression were only partially mediated by family socialization, indicating that the search for additional mediators (e.g. neighborhood) must continue. Among adolescents, the effects of socioeconomic status on aggression are mediated through family socialization, especially ineffective discipline and poor supervision (Lempers et al 1989, Sampson & Laub 1994).

Other data sets clarify the social processes that mediate the correlation between economic conditions and family relationships. Conger and his colleagues (Conger et al 1992, 1993) show that economic hardship forecasts, first, depression and demoralization in both mothers and fathers which, in turn, forecast marital conflict as well as hostility and inconsistency in parents' dealings with their children. These conditions, in turn, correlate with antisocial behavior during adolescence. This model applies generally to both boys and girls in cross-sectional data, and it has been replicated in two laboratories (Conger et al 1994b). Longitudinal data across the transition to adolescence also support the model (Conger et al 1994a): Economic stress, parent mood, and marital conflict were measured in seventh grade, conflicts over money and parent hostility were measured a year later, and adolescent adjustment was assessed after yet another year. Extensions to other samples are needed (these studies were conducted with rural families), but the results suggest interesting hypotheses concerning the affective and social mediators that link the societal context to adolescent aggression.

PARENT-CHILD RELATIONSHIPS   Standard attachment classifications with infants predict aggression during the preschool years in some studies (e.g. Renken et al 1989) but not others (Fagot & Kavanagh 1990). Some writers claim that attachment insecurity better predicts conflict with others than aggression (Perry et al 1992). With relationship assessments made later (e.g. at age six or in adulthood), correlations between attachment insecurity and aggressiveness are more consistent (Speltz et al 1990).

Conflict and resistance characterize insecure attachments and are correlated with temperamental difficultness (Bates et al 1991), maternal depression (Radke-Yarrow et al 1985), asynchronicity, nonsensitivity, and rejection in maternal reactions to the infant (Isabella & Belsky 1991). It is unknown whether the child's difficultness and the mother's insensitivity arise from common sources (e.g. gene-environment transactions). Behavior-genetic studies, however, show (*a*) that parents and their biological children are more similar in conflict and negativity than are parents and their adopted children, (*b*) monozygotic twins are more similar than dizygotic twins, and (*c*) twins and biological siblings are more similar than step-siblings and unrelated siblings living in blended families (Reiss et al 1993). Whatever their origins, the concordances involving insensitive mothering, conflict-resistance by the child, and insecure attachment represent conditions that are strikingly similar to the disordered contingencies known to be training grounds for antisocial behavior among preschoolers (Hinde et al 1993a) and older children (Patterson et al 1992). Only one data set, however, has been obtained that links poor parent-child attachment in early childhood to delinquency in adolescence (Sampson & Laub 1994).

Conflict and fighting within the family system are strongly correlated with childhood aggression (Holden & Ritchie 1991). Marital conflict and its concomitants are among the best predictors of childhood aggression, much better than marital dissatisfaction. Conflicts between husbands and wives about childrearing have especially deleterious effects (Jouriles et al 1991). One concomitant of marital conflict is diminished efficacy in parenting: Children are more likely to be rejected under these circumstances, and control efforts are more likely to be ineffective. These mediators account for more variance in externalizing difficulties among children and adolescents than does marital conflict alone (Fauber et al 1990). But "background anger" cannot be discounted because marital conflict distresses children directly, elicits angry reactions, and increases aggression toward others through modeling (Cummings et al 1989).

Gradually emerging from troubled parent-child relationships are training conditions that increase aggression and antisocial behavior. Based on extensive work with families of aggressive, "out-of-control" boys, Patterson and his associates (Patterson et al 1992, Patterson et al 1989, DeBaryshe et al 1993) have shown that family interaction provides most children with ample opportunities to learn aversive, aggressive, and antisocial acts. "Problem" families differ from "control" families in two ways that affect the performance of these antisocial acts: (a) coercion (i.e. exchanges in which mothers and children attempt to force one another to stop behaving aversively but actually maintain these actions through negative reinforcement) and (b) poor monitoring (i.e. indifferent or inadequate tracking of the children's whereabouts, the kinds of companions they keep, and the types of activities in which they engage). These conditions also establish mistrust of others and attributions favoring hostile interpretations of ambiguous events among both mothers and their children (MacKinnon-Lewis et al 1992). Patterson et al (1992) remain cautious about the causal status of the constructs in this model because the empirical evidence is mainly correlational. Success in changing these conditions (Kazdin 1987, Yoshikawa 1994) as well as recent structural equation models suggest strongly, however, that antisocial behavior (at least among early-starters) emerges in the sequence described above.

SIBLING RELATIONSHIPS   Conflict and aggression are common in sibling interaction although frequencies vary greatly across dyads. Certain child characteristics are correlated with sibling aggression (e.g. sex and temperament). Brothers evince more aggressiveness than do sisters, but opposite-sex siblings are more aggressive with one another than are same-sex siblings (Vandell & Bailey 1992). Emotional intensity and activity level are related to negativity and conflict between siblings (Stocker et al 1989). Negative interactions, however, occur most frequently when older siblings are more active than younger ones (Dunn & Munn 1986a). Causal direction is difficult to establish in this case, although fussy and difficult nine-month-olds have been reported to engage in more conflicts with siblings at five years than do children who were temperamentally calmer as infants (Volling 1990).

Significant sibling concordances in delinquency have been reported by numerous investigators, with some results suggesting that shared rather than unshared environmental influences are responsible (Rowe et al 1992). Marital conflict and contentious parent-child relationships are both correlated with sibling aggression from an early age (MacKinnon 1989, Volling & Belsky 1992). Differential treatment also exacerbates sibling aggression among both children and adolescents (Stocker et al 1989, Brody et al 1992). Support thus exists for the hypothesis that the developmental pathway from family coercion to antisocial behavior may be mediated to some extent by sibling conflict. Other evidence suggests, however, that coercive interaction between siblings contributes to the development of coercive behavioral styles independently of the contribution made by parent behavior (Patterson et al 1992).

Positive interactions vastly exceed negative ones in most sibling relationships. These interactions are correlated with affection and support (Volling & Belsky 1992) and may have sanguine developmental outcomes. When siblings are exposed to simulated conflicts between their mothers and other adults, for example, affectionate exchanges increase among girls and prosocial exchanges increase among boys (Cummings & Smith 1993). Quality of the sibling relationship is also important: Child symptoms associated with marital conflict are not as frequent when the sibling relationship is close as when it is not (Jenkins 1992).

PEER RELATIONSHIPS   Early-starters continue their antisocial behaviors at school (Ramsey et al 1990). Other children dislike them, as much for their deviant and disruptive behavior as for fighting (Juvonen 1991). Family coercion and poor monitoring actually affect the child's sociometric status indirectly rather than directly, because these effects are mediated through the children's antisocial acts and academic failures (Dishion 1990, DeBaryshe et al 1993). Developmental dynamics vary from child to child. Many aggressive children are not rejected, and many rejected children are not aggressive (Cillessen et al 1992). Children who are both aggressive and rejected, however, are more likely to continue toward delinquency and externalizing behavior than are children who are one or the other (Coie & Lenox 1994).

Because being aggressive and being disliked are correlated with one another, developmental dynamics are not entirely clear. Longitudinal studies, however, reveal that aggression and peer rejection in childhood contribute separately to externalizing behavior in preadolescence (Hymel et al 1990). For example, among third graders who are both aggressive and rejected, 62% experience serious difficulties in the sixth grade as compared with 18% who are neither aggressive or rejected. Problem occurrence is 40% among nonrejected aggressive children and 34% among rejected nonagressive children. Taken together, these results suggest that being aggressive and being disliked are additive conditions in antisocial development (Coie et al 1992).

Peer rejection is ordinarily assessed with sociometric tests, and thus reflects collective "dislike" by classmates rather than the frequencies with which children suffer ostracism or exclusion. Surprisingly, disliked children are more likely to be disregarded and to suffer loneliness when they are nonaggressive than when they are aggressive (Parkhurst & Asher 1992). Although some aggressive children do not belong to classroom cliques and others are peripheral members, many belong to social networks (Cairns et al 1988), and others have neighborhood friends (Dishion 1990). Antisocial children come from the same neighborhoods as their friends and resemble them in antisocial behavior and sociometric status. Marked by considerable bossiness and coercion, however, these relationships are relatively unstable, are regarded by the children as marginally satisfactory, and tend to end acrimoniously (Dishion et al 1994a). Antisocial boys, then, associate with other deviant children and, in so doing, probably socialize themselves in coercion. Opportunities for effective socialization are simultaneously constricted.

Deviant friends have long been known to support delinquent behavior among adolescents. What, then, is the connection between family experience and these affiliations, especially since negativity in family relationships seems not to be directly correlated with negativity in friendship interaction (Andrews & Dishion 1994)? Longitudinal analysis shows that poor parental discipline and monitoring predict peer rejection and academic failure among school children; these conditions, in turn, predict increasing involvement with antisocial friends (Dishion et al 1991). The effects of deviant peers may not be evident until mid-adolescence (Patterson et al 1991), but these relationships now seem to be the most immediate connection to serious conduct difficulties among early-starting adolescents. Among late-starters, the scenario is less certain although some investigators contend that early starters set the stage for them in adolescence by eliciting antisocial behavior in various ways (e.g. by modeling).

Behavioral Inhibition and Social Withdrawal

STABILITIES   Several investigators have studied the perseverance of "behavioral inhibition to the unfamiliar" in early childhood. Representative results show inhibition to be weakly stable between 16 and 40 months (Broberg et al 1990), using composited measures that combine behavioral inhibition with indications of negative affect (e.g. fussing and crying). Other studies show that, with negative affect not included, inhibition is moderately stable through the first three years, although more so in extreme cases than in representative samples (Kagan et al 1988). It has been contended that extreme cases are qualitatively different from "modal children" in terms of emotional regulation, but such comparisons inflate the results (Asendorpf 1993). Structural equation modeling also reveals considerable continuity in temperamental approach between the ages of four months and eight years (Pedlow et al 1993).

Among older children (ages four through ten years), stability in behavioral inhibition is evident when assessed during confrontations with strangers (Asendorpf 1990). But behavioral inhibition toward strangers differs from shyness displayed in familiar settings. Shyness toward strangers, for example, is stable between four and six years, but shyness toward familiar classmates is not. Under unfamiliar circumstances (e.g. school entrance or family moves), stranger inhibition and classmate inhibition are correlated with one another, but these concordances decrease with age, suggesting the existence of two shynesses among older individuals (Asendorpf 1990).

Neurophysiological and endocrine processes in inhibition have been suggested (Gray 1982), and significant heritabilities for behavioral inhibition and shyness in early childhood have been demonstrated in twin studies (Matheny 1989). Model-fitting exercises show further that genetic factors support change in these traits between 14 and 20 months, and they also support continuity. Either genes contribute directly to change or, more likely, the genes affecting inhibition at 14 months differ from those affecting the trait at 20 months (Plomin et al 1993). Person characteristics, including IQ, are also associated with decreasing inhibition and shyness in middle childhood (Asendorpf 1994), suggesting that more intelligent children can better overcome inhibition than can less intelligent children.

Long-term continuities in shyness have been detected but may be heterotypic rather than homotypic. Early childhood shyness is associated with low self-esteem in middle childhood (Asendorpf & van Aken 1994). Childhood shyness is only weakly related to internalizing problems in early and late adolescence (Caspi et al 1994) but is more strongly related (negatively) to impulsivity, danger-seeking, aggression, and social efficacy (Caspi & Silva 1994). In another instance, shyness in middle childhood was weakly correlated with shyness, withdrawal, and negative affect in adulthood, but was more strongly related to delayed marriage and vocational decisions—among men only. Shyness, then, may be more consequential in the long term for men than for women in age-specific adaptations (Caspi et al 1988).

SOCIETAL CONTEXT   Behavioral inhibition and social withdrawal have not been studied epidemiologically because the risk status of these attributes is only beginning to be established. Epidemiological studies have been suggested (Weissman 1989), but compelling reasons are lacking for conducting such studies because no one yet knows whether shyness and inhibition are latent traits for psychopathology. Sociodemographic correlates of the affective disorders have been examined, but results are inconclusive because these disorders are relatively rare in childhood. One long-term investigation shows that socioeconomic status predicts separation anxiety from childhood to adolescence but not the other affective disorders (Velez et al 1989). Most studies show that parental depression, family dysfunction, and family stress predict affective disturbance more consistently than do socioeconomic conditions (Fleming & Offord 1990). Person-by-situation interaction effects may also exist: For example, economic exigency is correlated with depression among women when a history of child-hood neurosis also exists (Rodgers 1990).

Although socioeconomic status may not bear a consistent relation to the affective disorders, economic pressures may be correlated with internalizing symptoms. Conger et al (1994a) report that the connection between economic pressure and internalizing behavior among adolescents is mediated by family interaction in a manner similar to the mediation of antisocial behavior. That is, economic pressure elicits parental depression and marital conflict, which, in turn, increase parents' hostility and conflict with their children as well as adolescent internalizing behavior. Similarities in the developmental models that account for internalizing and externalizing undoubtedly reflect the correlation between these orientations (Cicchetti & Toth 1991).

PARENT-CHILD RELATIONSHIPS   Most investigators assume that inhibition and social withdrawal cycle through family interaction in determining developmental outcomes. Controversy has raged, however, concerning whether behavioral inhibition is a stable, constitutionally determined orientation that circumscribes the child's social interactions and relationships or whether the reverse is more accurate (i.e. the child's inhibition and withdrawal are derivatives of insensitive-insecure interactions and relationships). Recent studies do not answer the origins question conclusively, but the child's inhibition and mother-child relationships seem more clearly than ever to be co-constructed. Developmental outcomes, then, may be related to the goodness-of-fit between individual characteristics and relationships rather than to the child's inhibition alone (Thomas & Chess 1977).

Meta-analysis shows proneness to distress or fearfulness in the young child (indexed by long latencies in approaching unfamiliar situations and fussiness or crying) to be related to attachment insecurity but with relatively small effect sizes (Goldsmith & Alansky 1987). Current results also suggest that avoidant, secure, and resistant attachments, respectively, reflect low, moderate, and high degrees of the child's inhibition (Calkins & Fox 1992). Assessments in these and other studies, however, were drawn from the same laboratory sessions and/or respondent reports, so concordance between inhibition and attachment classification might reflect the mother's involvement more than the child's temperament. Indeed, when behavioral inhibition is assessed in the absence of maternal involvement (and fussiness is not used as a criterion), a direct relation between inhibition and attachment security is either not apparent (Mangelsdorf 1990, Nachmais et al 1994) or involves different groupings of attachment subcategories (Belsky & Rovine 1987).

Consistent with the view that the attachment between mother and child is a dyadic entity rather than an attribute of either the child or the mother, maternal personality (e.g. rigidity and constraint) relates to attachment insecurity among distress-prone but not among nondistress-prone infants (Mangelsdorf et al 1990). In addition, maternal encouragements to the child (which mothers generally use more frequently with inhibited than noninhibited toddlers) are associated with stress reactivity (measured by elevations in salivary cortisol)—but only among inhibited children with insecure attachments. Inhibited–insecurely attached toddlers also do not seek information from their mothers about novel events as frequently as do securely attached toddlers. Among some children, then, behavioral inhibition seems to be a means of coping with the threat deriving from unfamiliar events; secure relationships with the mother support this coping, whereas insecure ones do not (Nachmais et al 1994).

Developmental scenarios beyond early childhood reveal that gender differentiates behavioral inhibition among preschool-aged children, although greater prevalence among girls than boys is not noted in every sample (Reznick et al 1989, Broberg 1993). Family correlates, however, show greater parental support and fewer efforts to change shyness in girls than in boys. Girls experience fewer negative consequences in social relationships generally (Stevenson-Hinde & Hinde 1986).

Concurrent correlational studies show that relatively extreme withdrawal in nursery school (e.g. frequently being alone and unoccupied) is associated among both boys and girls with frequent social overtures (dependency) between mother and child at home as well as negative behavior directed by the mother to the child (Hinde et al 1993b). Laboratory observations show mothers of withdrawn children to engage in less contingent interaction with the child as well as more negative reciprocity and superfluous efforts to control the child than do mothers of nonwithdrawn children (LaFreniere & Dumas 1992). Observations thus confirm self-reports showing that mothers are more directive, angry, and coercive in dealing with withdrawn children than are mothers of average children (Rubin & Mills 1990). Predictive studies reveal further that the combination of maternal depression and insecure mother-infant attachments is associated with social inhibition among five-year-olds (Rubin et al 1991). Concordantly, among boys in middle childhood, passive withdrawn individuals are overrepresented when early relationships with their mothers were insecure or avoidant and when mothers were not agentic, enthusiastic, or sensitive but instead were neglectful (Renken et al 1989).

Parenting differences are not well documented in middle childhood and adolescence. Socially withdrawn girls and their parents perceive their relationships with one another as less supportive than do average children and their parents; boys' parents regard their relationships with withdrawn children similarly. Most notably, socially withdrawn children and their parents disagree about the supportiveness of their relationships more than do other children and their parents (East 1991).

SIBLING RELATIONSHIPS   Evidence is scarce concerning sibling relationships and behavioral inhibition. Among young children, the birth of a sibling increases social withdrawal (Teti 1992). In this instance, social withdrawal is traceable to changes in attention received from the mother and changes in her behavior toward the child. One small-scale investigation also suggests that individual differences in approach to strangers, which otherwise are modestly stable during the second and third years, are destabilized by the birth of a sibling (Arcus & McCartney 1989). Although these sibling effects may be acute, their long-term significance is unclear.

Close ties to a sibling generally offset insecurity, anxiety, and internalizing problems in middle childhood, suggesting that the quality of sibling relationships may affect social withdrawal (East & Rook 1992). These results, however, could reflect general relationship disturbances rather than the contributions of sibling relationships to the child's adaptation. Behavior-genetic studies suggest that the environmental experiences responsible for sibling differences are mostly nonshared rather than shared; hence, differences rather than similarities in family and sibling interaction may be related to social withdrawal. Indeed, the extent to which mothers are more controlling and less affectionate toward the older of two siblings accounts for 34% of the variance in the internalizing behavior of the older ones (Dunn et al 1990).

PEER RELATIONSHIPS   Solitary children are thought to lack opportunity to learn the social skills needed to work out effective adaptations both in childhood and later life. Recent studies demonstrate, however, that one must distinguish between inhibited (reticent) children, who fear unfamiliar situations; shy children, who fear negative evaluation by others; and unsociable children, who are disinterested or lack motivation to interact with others (Rubin & Asendorpf 1993a). Substantial correlations between mother-rated shyness and solitary-passive behavior with peers are not evident among four-year-olds but appear gradually over the next four years (Asendorpf 1991), suggesting that behavioral inhibition is elaborated into social withdrawal only with time and only for some children.

Ratings and observations are used to establish correlations between behavioral inhibition and peer interaction. Kagan and his associates (Reznick et al 1986, Kagan et al 1988, Gersten 1989) have shown that inhibition in the child's reactions to unfamiliar events, measured during the second and third years, is negatively correlated with social involvement with unfamiliar children—encountered either singly or in small groups. Modest concurrent correlations between inhibition and peer involvement are evident through early childhood and across time, especially when extremely inhibited and uninhibited children are compared with each other.

Cross-time comparisons, however, must be based on differentiated temperament and social measures. Mothers' ratings of their toddlers' shyness, for example, are correlated with both the amount and quality (i.e. maturity) of the young child's exchanges with other children—including the frequency with which reciprocity and complementarities occur (Broberg et al 1990). When social inhibition is differentiated from nonsocial inhibition, outcomes are similarly differentiated, that is, social inhibition predicts the frequency of shy or inhibited behavior with other children, whereas nonsocial inhibition negatively predicts associative and cooperative interaction (Kochanska & Radke-Yarrow 1992).

Among school-aged children, behavioral inhibition is most often equated with social withdrawal. Sometimes measured with mother or teacher ratings, sometimes with peer ratings, and sometimes with observations, this variable increasingly correlates negatively with popularity during the elementary school years but not consistently with social behavior (Hymel et al 1990). Reticence must be differentiated from sociability in these studies and considered in relation to situational demands. Reticent second graders, for example, converse less frequently than do nonreticent children in unfamiliar but not in familiar situations; unsociable children, on the other hand, spend the least time and converse the least frequently in moderately unfamiliar situations (Asendorpf & Meier 1993). Reticence and sociability thus seem to involve different coping mechanisms employed differently by different children for dealing with unfamiliar situations.

One behavioral constellation including shyness, unsociability, and social withdrawal nevertheless characterizes certain children in middle childhood. Co-occurring with social withdrawal are low sociometric status, lack of self-esteem, loneliness, and unhappiness (Hymel et al 1990, Hymel et al 1993, Renshaw & Brown 1993). Although loneliness and sadness appear as correlates of social withdrawl in these data sets, correlations with childhood depression are not clear. Sometimes aggression accompanies social withdrawal, in which case, developmental risk is great (Hymel et al 1993). Shyness and withdrawal may also be consequences of long-term treatment by other children as indicated by their recovery when interventions are aimed at controlling the behavior of bullies (Olweus 1991).

Continuities between early and late childhood in social withdrawal, peer acceptance, self-attitudes, and internalizing symptoms are not clear. Only one major investigation dealing with shyness and social withdrawal covers this age range, and the numerous reports based on this work are not in complete agreement (cf Rubin & Mills 1988, Hymel et al 1990, Rubin 1993). Generally, observational measures of sociability are not good predictors from second to fifth grade or for adolescence in this data set. Teacher ratings of anxiety and internalizing only predict similar traits across time. On the other hand, peer ratings are good predictors of subsequent social behaviors that include isolation, lack of popularity, anxiety and shyness, negative self-evaluations, and feelings of loneliness.

SUMMARY   Current results provide an increasingly comprehensive, but still fragmented view of inhibition and its developmental significance. Both the quantity and the quality of the data in this area are less sophisticated than the data bearing on aggression and antisocial behavior. Quantitative methods used in this area are correspondingly weak. Mothers and children almost certainly construct their earliest relationships to accomodate—for better or worse—the inhibition or shyness of the children. Results suggest alternative pathways by which early inhibition may be implicated in social relationships during middle childhood and adolescence. One cannot assert, however, that early behavioral inhibition is a direct source of internalizing symptoms or depression. Developmental pathways need to be better understood and the causal status of variables bearing on inhibition and its sequelae needs to be better established.

Social Responsibility: Prosocial Behavior and Conscience Development

STABILITIES   Social responsibility consists of both "doing good" and "not doing bad" (as well as ameliorating the negative consequences of one's misbehavior). Empathy, altruism, guilt, and resistance to temptation are relevant constructs. Personality concomitants of responsibility are thought to include agreeableness and conscientiousness (Graziano & Eisenberg 1994); temperamental substrates are believed to include negative affectivity (especially the internalizing dimensions of sadness and anxiety) and effortful control (Rothbart et al 1994, Kochanska 1993). "Doing good" and "not doing bad," however, may have different temperamental bases because mothers' ratings of their school-aged children show effortful control to be substantially correlated with both empathy and guilt, but negativity (fear and sadness) is associated with guilt alone (Rothbart et al 1994). Mothers stress "safety first" in their earliest compliance demands, usually in the form of prohibitive interventions (Gralinski & Kopp 1993).

Compliance to these demands (one manifestation of responsibility) is modestly stable beginning in the second year and predicts guilt, reparation, and discomfort with wrongdoing from ages two to eight (Kochanska 1991). Prosocial behavior also emerges during the second year. Empathic concern shows weak stabilities and prosocial behavior shows slightly stronger ones, based on children's reactions to simulated distress at 14 and 20 months (Zahn-Waxler et al 1992a). The most stable empathic reactions occur when the child causes the distress. Giving assistance, in contrast, is more stable when distress is witnessed than when it is caused by the child (Zahn-Waxler et al 1992b). Sharing, comforting, and helping are also somewhat stable during this time (Dunn & Munn 1986b), and modest stability coefficients have been reported for donating behavior and empathy in children between eight and ten years of age (Eisenberg et al 1987).

Considerable interest has been expressed in the heritability of empathy because many writers regard it as the bedrock of responsible behavior. Among toddlers, significant heritabilities have been reported at 14 months but not at 20 months (Zahn-Waxler et al 1992a). Change in empathy scores does not show significant genetic variance but continuity does (Plomin et al 1993). Because sociability and empathy are correlated in many data sets, and because sociability possesses significant heritabilities (Saudino et al 1994b), this temperamental variable may be partially responsible for the observed stability—as well as for certain changes. Accordingly, positive sociability assessed at 14 months turns out to be associated both with maintenance of high empathy scores through 20 months and with increases in these scores among children who were not empathic initially. Sociability thus seems to support an "other-orientation" over time among some children as well as increases in this orientation among others (Robinson et al 1994).

Continuities are also evident in the family context. Mothers who endorse authoritative childrearing philosophies (i.e. expressing warmth and making moderate demands) when their children are toddlers, use positive incentives and avoid prohibitive interventions with their children two to three years later. Conversely, those endorsing authoritarian rearing (i.e. making high demands and exerting punitive controls) use prohibitive rather than positive controls later on (Kochanska 1990). Stability in social reponsibility thus seems to reside in both the social context and the child.

SOCIETAL CONTEXT   Cultural variations are associated with prosocial behavior in children, especially cooperation and nurturance. Children in complex societies (i.e. those marked by occupational and religious specialization, settlement differentiation, and social stratification) are not as nurturant and helpful toward one another as are children in simpler societies (Whiting & Whiting 1975). Similarly, societies in which children socialize with children of many different ages (including sibling caretaking) are marked by greater cooperation and prosocial behavior than more age-graded ones. Cultural variations in conscience development are not well documented although much attention has been given to guilt and shame in cross-cultural studies.

Sociodemographic correlates of altruism within industrialized societies are unclear. Socioeconomic status, for example, is not related to either prosocial or prohibitive responsibility among children in the United States and Western

Europe except for the social and emotional regulation relating to conduct disorder and antisocial behavior (see above).

PARENT-CHILD RELATIONSHIPS   Parent-child relationships are thought to be the well springs of social responsibility. Beginning with maternal demands and the child's compliance to them, responsibility requires internalization (i.e. a gradual shift from exogenous to endogenous behavior regulation). Compliance to maternal demands may be an early manifestation of internalization, especially when the child is committed to or eager in complying with the mother's agenda. Situational compliance, in contrast, does not seem to be related to self-regulation (Kochanska & Aksan 1994).

The shift from other-regulation to self-regulation has been explained in two main ways (Hoffman 1970): (a) internalization is believed to rest on social exchanges in which consistent demands on the child are made with inductive reasoning and moderate power assertion (i.e. conditions that foster encoding and storage of social rules without undue anxiety) and (b) self-regulation arises mainly from warmth and responsiveness in mother-child relationships (i.e. conditions that motivate the child to comply and self-regulate). These contrasting beliefs remain with us, augmented by arguments that child characteristics (including temperament) moderate the effects on the child of both power assertion and warmth. Other moderators may include the specific demands to which the child is exposed and the child's understanding and acceptance of them (Grusec & Goodnow 1994). Longitudinal studies based on these augmented hypotheses are rare, but even so, alternative pathways leading to responsible individuality are being identified.

Not surprisingly, toddlers whose attachments are secure exhibit more empathy as children than do those whose attachments are not secure (Kestenbaum et al 1989). Empathic socialization (e.g. modeling) occurs within secure attachments, and children may also acquire generalized expectations or working models for "doing good" in these relationships. Concordantly, maternal empathy and emotional expressiveness in distress situations are correlated with empathic behavior among young children (Fabes et al 1994); maternal responsiveness, mediated by the induction of positive mood, supports compliance (Lay et al 1989); and mutual positive affect in the mother-child relationship is correlated with committed compliance and internalization (Kochanska & Aksan 1994). Among older children, maternal empathy, perspective-taking, responsiveness, and involvement with the child continue to be correlated with the child's empathic concerns (Fabes et al 1990). Maternal involvement remains a relatively strong predictor of empathic concern from childhood into adulthood, along with toleration of the child's dependency (Koestner et al 1990). Correlations between the child's empathy, on the one hand, and maternal empathy, responsiveness, and reasoning, on the other, are more consistent for girls than for boys; committed compliance also occurs more frequently among girls (Kochanska 1994). These sex differences may reflect the greater importance of same-sex parent-child relationships than of opposite-sex relationships in the socialization of altruism (Eisenberg et al 1991). Father-child relationships have not been studied sufficiently, however, to verify this hypothesis.

Reasoning, especially about the distress of others in relation to the child's own experience, is a well-known correlate of empathic behavior beginning in the second year. Recent evidence also shows induction to be related to empathy among preschool-aged children (Eisenberg et al 1992) as well as to advances in moral reasoning among older children (Walker & Taylor 1991). Power assertion is usually associated negatively with empathy and internalization, although the construct needs differentiation, and the evidence is not altogether consistent (Grusec & Goodnow 1994).

Maternal responsiveness, inductive discipline, and gentle control thus seem to foster social responsibility. Effect sizes are modest, however, and results are not entirely uniform when these childrearing dimensions are studied separately. Constellations of these childrearing behaviors have been examined (e.g. authoritativeness), and longitudinal results indicate, according to some accounts, that "...Authoritative childrearing was the only pattern that consistently produced optimally competent children [that is, children high in social competence and social responsibility] and failed to produce incompetent children in the preschool years and in middle childhood, and this was true for both girls and boys" (Baumrind 1989, p. 364).

Parent-child relationships, however, may have different consequences for different children. Even authoritative childrearing may not always produce a responsible child. Indeed, Kochanska (1991) found that authoritative treatment of toddlers (i.e. rational rather than coercive guidance, encouragement of independence, and mutual expression of affect) was associated with internalized conscience six years later, but only for children who were initially prone to fearful arousal. Other data indicate that the specific dimensions constituting authoritative discipline (e.g. responsiveness or warmth, and moderate control) have different consequences depending on the child's temperament: (a) Among fearful or anxious toddlers, both committed compliance and internalization are greater when mothers employ gentle controls and de-emphasize power assertion; at the same time, attachment security is unrelated to internalization. (b) Among nonfearful or nonanxious children, the situation is reversed; compliance is correlated with attachment security but not gentle control (Kochanska 1994). Alternative pathways to social responsibility are thus indicated: Among fearful children, gentle control may induce responsibility because it produces moderate (optimal) arousal; among fearless children, empathic mother-child relationships may be necessary to supply the motivation necessary for internalization.

SIBLING RELATIONSHIPS   Older siblings show empathic concern and exhibit simple acts of helping when their younger siblings are infants, suggesting that empathy emerges in the sibling context at about the same time as elsewhere in family relationships (i.e. the second year). Social exchanges between older siblings also contain many kindnesses, including sharing and cooperation as well as talk about positive feelings and behavior. Although maternal encouragement of empathy supports children's empathy individually (see above), sibling interaction contains more references to feelings when the mother is absent than when she is present (Howe 1991). Older children also consider their siblings to be relatively important sources of affection, companionship, and intimacy (Buhrmester 1992). Sibling interaction thus contains most of the elements needed to foster responsibility.

Accordingly, longitudinal studies show significant cross-lagged correlations between cooperation by older siblings and cooperation by their younger siblings measured six months later. Similarly, when younger children share and cooperate, older siblings are more likely to behave prosocially later on (Dunn & Munn 1986b). Causality is difficult to infer from these results, however, because maternal encouragement also may be involved. Sibling interaction thus could be a special arena for the development of empathic responding, although the evidence does not demonstrate conclusively that these relationships contribute to responsibility more than do other family relationships.

PEER RELATIONSHIPS   Children are attracted to other children for their friendliness, cooperativeness, and social competence as well as for their kindness and helpfulness. Peer and teacher ratings of altruism are correlated with sociometric status (Dekovic & Janssens 1992), as are parent-child relationships (e.g. authoritativeness). What pathways, then, best describe these connections, given that the data consist entirely of concurrent correlations?

Covariance analyses show that, among preschool-aged children, prosocial behavior remains correlated with popularity even when parent authoritativeness is taken into account (Hart et al 1992). Regression analyses with school-aged children, on the other hand, suggest that altruism (rated by both teachers and other children) only partially mediates the connection between authoritative childrearing and sociometric status; direct effects also exist (Dekovic & Janssens 1992). These direct effects could also be mediated through child behaviors that were not measured in the investigation (e.g. aggression; see above). Parent emphasis on achievement and joint decision-making are also correlated with popularity through the child's own achievement and self-reliance (Brown et al 1993)—yet another indication that parent-child and peer relationships are mediated by the child's behavior. Longitudinal studies are lacking, however, so causal status is difficult to establish in this area. Similarly, the relative effects of social responsibility and sociometric status on subsequent adjustment have not been specified.

Children's friendships are generally marked by sociability, cooperativeness, and mutuality, so friendship experience may promote responsibility. Scattered evidence supports this generalization. Among preschool-aged children, those who have friends (both popular and rejected individuals) are more responsive and reciprocal in their dealings with others than are children who do not have friends (Howes 1988). Among older children, those who have friends are more likely to be altruistic and more mature perspective-takers. Children express more sympathy in response to a friend's distress than to an acquaintance's and are more motivated to relieve the distress of their friends (Costin & Jones 1992). Because children select one another on the basis of similarities between them, these correlations may not, however, reflect socialization effects. Correlations are modest, too, perhaps because friendships between antisocial children are not marked by the same reciprocity and stability that characterize the friendships of other children (see above).

SUMMARY   New evidence suggests that child temperament, parent characteristics, and parent-child relationships combine to create alternate pathways to social responsibility in childhood and adolescence. Parent-child relationships are correlated, via the child's responsibility, with peer relationships, which themselves are differentiated according to social responsibility. Only circumstantial evidence suggests, though, that peer relationships themselves contribute additional variance to the likelihood of a child's "doing good" and "not doing bad."

CONCLUSION

Research dealing with personality development has entered a new era. Psychologists have argued the merits of person-centered and contextually oriented approaches to personality development for many years but, with a few exceptions (Block & Block 1980, Magnusson 1992, Pulkkinen & Ronka 1994), have not acquired databases that would confirm or disconfirm many of their ideas. Resources (e.g. hardware and software) have sometimes been lacking or attention has been directed elsewhere (e.g. to situational effects on child behavior). But the sampling of current work cited in this review attests to greatly changed strategies for studying individuality in developmental perspective.

This review reveals, too, that psychologists stand only on the threshold of this new era: Greater conceptual clarity is needed in many areas, especially in defining the boundaries between temperament and personality. Certain developmental gaps loom large, for example, the years between infancy and middle childhood and the transition into adolescence. But current investigators are remarkably willing to commit themselves to long-term multivariate studies. One expects these gaps to be filled sooner rather than later.

Dominating current thinking is the dictum "continuity occurs amidst change and change amidst continuity." These words are consistent with existing results but, as Block & Robins (1993) state, are bland and simplistic. Personality development has been described this way for centuries. What remains is the formidable task of disentangling causal status among the variables in the developmental sequence, including the transactions that turn genetic chemistry into behavioral individuality and the ways in which social context and social relationships are implicated in both stability and change.

Research must move in several directions at once. Developmental transitions need intensive scrutiny, including both normative ones (e.g. the child's entrance to school) and nonnormative ones (e.g. chronic illness). Nonnormative transitions, such as marital transitions and economic exigency, have taught us a great deal about personality development, but we have not exploited many other opportunities to examine these turning points. Not enough is known about secular changes and developmental individuality. Intervention studies must be used more extensively (as ethically feasible) to test causal hypotheses as well as to alleviate social suffering. Finally, the laboratory experiment must not be discarded. Longitudinal data sets and correlational methods will remain *sine qua non* for understanding personality development. Other methods and substantial time will be needed, however, before the processes of personality development are understood as well as is its substance.

ACKNOWLEDGEMNTS

The authors gratefully acknowledge the assistance of Art Sesma in preparing this manuscript as well as their debt to W. Andrew Collins and Marcel A. G. van Aken for criticisms and suggestions.

Literature Cited

Andrews DW, Dishion TJ. 1994. The microsocial structure underpinnings of adolescent problem behavior. In *Adolescent Problem Behavior*, ed. M Lamb, R Ketterlinus, pp. 187–207. Hillsdale, NJ: Erlbaum

Arcus D, McCartney K. 1989. When baby makes four: family influences in the stability of behavioral inhibition. See Reznick 1989, pp. 197–218

Asendorpf JB. 1990. Development of inhibition during childhood: evidence for situational specificity and a two-factor model. *Dev. Psychol.* 26:721–30

Asendorpf JB. 1991. Development of inhibited

children's coping with unfamiliarity. *Child Dev.* 62:1460–74

Asendorpf JB. 1992. A Brunswikean approach to trait continuity: application to shyness. *J. Pers.* 60:53–77

Asendorpf JB. 1993. *Inhibition toward strangers: discrete type or continuous trait?* Presented at Bienn. Meet. Soc. Res. Child Dev., New Orleans, March 25–28

Asendorpf JB. 1994. The malleability of behavioral inhibition: a study of individual developmental functions. *Dev. Psychol.* In press

Asendorpf JB, Meier GH. 1993. Personality effects on children's speech in everyday life: sociability-mediated exposure and shyness-mediated reactivity to social situations. *J. Pers. Soc. Psychol.* 64:1072–83

Asendorpf JB, van Aken MAG. 1994. Traits and relationship status: stranger versus peer group inhibition and test intelligence versus peer group competence as early predictors of later self-esteem. *Child Dev.* In press

Bates JE, Bayles K, Bennett DS, Ridge B, Brown MM. 1991. Origins of externalizing behavior problems at eight years of age. See Pepler & Rubin 1991, pp. 93–120

Baumrind D. 1989. Rearing competent children. In *Child Development Today and Tomorrow,* ed. W Damon, pp. 349–78. San Francisco: Jossey-Bass

Belsky J, Rovine M. 1987. Temperament and attachment security in the Strange Situation: an empirical rapprochement. *Child Dev.* 58:787–95

Berscheid E. 1994. Interpersonal relationships. *Annu. Rev. Psychol.* 45:75–129

Block J. 1971. *Lives Through Time.* Berkeley, CA: Bancroft

Block J, Robins RW. 1993. A longitudinal study of consistency and change in self-esteem from early adolescence to early adulthood. *Child Dev.* 64:909–23

Block JH, Block J. 1980. The role of ego-control and ego-resiliency in the organization of behavior. In *Development of Cognition, Affect, and Social Relations. Minn. Symp. Child Psychol.,* ed. WA Collins, 13:39–101. Hillsdale, NJ: Erlbaum

Broberg AG. 1993. Inhibition and children's experience of out-of-home care. See Rubin & Asendorpf 1993, pp. 151–76

Broberg AG, Lamb ME, Hwang P. 1990. Inhibition: its stability and correlates in sixteen-to forty-month-old children. *Child Dev.* 61:1153–63

Brody GH, Stoneman Z, McCoy JK, Forehand R. 1992. Contemporaneous and longitudinal associations of sibling conflict with family relationship assessments and family discussions about sibling problems. *Child Dev.* 63:391–400

Bronson WC. 1966. Central orientations: a study of behavior organization from childhood to adolescence. *Child Dev.* 37:125–55

Brown BB, Mounts N, Lamborn SD, Steinberg L. 1993. Parenting practices and peer group affiliation in adolescence. *Child Dev.* 64:467–82

Buhrmester D. 1992. The developmental courses of sibling and peer relationships. In *Children's Sibling Relationships: Developmental and Clinical Issues,* ed. F Boer, J Dunn, pp. 19–40. Hillsdale, NJ: Erlbaum

Cairns RB, Cairns BD, Neckerman HJ, Gest S, Gariepy JL. 1988. Peer networks and aggressive behavior: peer support or peer rejection? *Dev. Psychol.* 24:815–23

Calkins SD, Fox NA. 1992. The relations among infant temperament, security of attachment, and behavioral inhibition at twenty-four months. *Child Dev.* 63:1456–72

Caspi A, Elder GH, Bem DJ. 1988. Moving away from the world: life-course patterns of shy children. *Dev. Psychol.* 24:824–31

Caspi A, Henri B, McGee RO, Moffitt TE, Silva PA. 1994. Temperamental origins of child and adolescent behavior problems: from age 3 to age 15. *Child Dev.* In press

Caspi A, Moffitt TE. 1994. The continuity of maladaptive behavior: from description to understanding in the study of antisocial behavior. In *Manual of Developmental Psychopathology,* Vol. 1, ed. D Cicchetti, D Cohen. New York: Wiley. In press

Caspi A, Silva PA. 1994. Temperamental qualities at age 3 predict personality traits in young adulthood: longitudinal evidence from a birth cohort. *Child Dev.* In press

Cattell RB. 1956. Second-order personality factors. *J. Consult. Psychol.* 20:411–18

Cicchetti D, Toth SL, eds. 1991. *Internalizing and Externalizing Expressions of Dysfunction: Rochester Symposium on Developmental Psychopathology.* Hillsdale, NJ: Erlbaum

Cillessen AHN, van Ijzendoorn HW, van Lieshout CFM, Hartup WW. 1992. Heterogeneity among peer-rejected boys: subtypes and stabilities. *Child Dev.* 63:893–905

Coie JD, Lenox KF. 1994. The development of antisocial individuals. In *Progress in Experimental Personality and Psychopathology Research,* ed. D Fowles, P Sutker, S Goodman, pp. 45–72. New York: Springer

Coie JD, Lochman JE, Terry R, Hyman C. 1992. Predicting early adolescent disorder from childhood aggression and peer rejection. *J. Consult. Clin. Psychol.* 60:783–92

Collins WA, Gunnar MR. 1990. Social and personality development. *Annu. Rev. Psychol.* 41:387–416

Conger RD, Conger KJ, Elder GH, Lorenz FO, Simons RL, et al. 1992. A family process

model of economic hardship and adjustment of early adolescent boys. *Child Dev.*
63:526–41

Conger RD, Conger KJ, Elder GH, Lorenz FO,
Simons RL, et al. 1993. Family economic
stress and adjustment of early adolescent
girls. *Dev. Psychol.* 29:206–19

Conger RD, Ge X, Elder GH, Lorenz FO, Simons RL. 1994a. Economic stress, coercive family process, and developmental
problems of adolescents. *Child Dev.* 65:
541–61

Conger RD, Patterson GR, Ge X. 1994b. It
takes two to replicate: a mediational model
for the impact of parents' stress on adolescent adjustment. *Child Dev.* In press

Costa PT, McCrae RR. 1994. Stability and
change in personality from adolescence
through adulthood. See Halverson et al
1994. In press

Costin SE, Jones DC. 1992. Friendship as a
facilitator of emotional responsiveness and
prosocial interventions among young children. *Dev. Psychol.* 28:941–47

Cummings EM, Smith D. 1993. The impact of
anger between adults on siblings' emotions
and social behavior. *J. Child Psychol. Psychiatr.* 34:1425–33

Cummings JS, Pellegrini DS, Notarius CI,
Cummings EM. 1989. Children's responses to angry adult behavior as a function of marital distress and history of inter-
parent hostility. *Child Dev.* 60:1035–45

DeBaryshe BD, Patterson GR, Capaldi DM.
1993. A performance model for academic
achievement in early adolescent boys. *Dev.
Psychol.* 29:795–804

Dekovic M, Janssens JMAM. 1992. Parents'
child-rearing style and child's sociometric
status. *Dev. Psychol.* 28:925–32

Digman JM. 1990. Personality structure: emergence of the five-factor model. *Annu. Rev.
Psychol.* 41:417–40

Dilalla LF, Gottesman II. 1989. Heterogeneity
of causes for delinquency and criminality:
lifespan perspectives. *Dev. Psychopathol.*
1:339–49

Dishion TJ. 1990. The family ecology of boys'
peer relations in middle childhood. *Child
Dev.* 61:874–92

Dishion TJ, Andrews DW, Crosby L. 1994a.
Antisocial boys and their friends in early
adolescence: relationship characteristics,
quality, and interactional process. *Child
Dev.* In press

Dishion TJ, Patterson GR, Griesler PC. 1994b.
Peer adaptations in the development of an-
tisocial behavior: a confluence model. In
*Current Perspectives on Aggressive Behav-
ior,* ed. LR Huesmann. pp. 61–95. New
York: Plenum

Dishion TJ, Patterson GR, Stoolmiller M,
Skinner M. 1991. Family, school, and behavioral antecedents to early adolescent in-

volvement with antisocial peers. *Dev. Psychol.* 27:172–80

Dodge KA, Pettit GS, Bates JE. 1994. Socialization mediators of the relation between
socioeconomic status and child conduct
problems. *Child Dev.* 65:649–65

Dunn J, Munn P. 1986a. Sibling quarrels and
maternal intervention: individual differences in understanding and aggression. *J.
Child Psychol. Psychiatr.* 27:583–95

Dunn J, Munn P. 1986b. Siblings and the development of prosocial behaviour. *Int. J.
Behav. Dev.* 9:265–84

Dunn J, Stocker C, Plomin R. 1990. Nonshared
experiences within the family: correlates of
behavioral problems in middle childhood.
Dev. Psychopathol. 2:113–26

East PL. 1991. The parent-child relationships
of withdrawn, aggressive, and sociable
children: child and parent perspectives.
Merrill-Palmer Q. 37:425–44

East PL, Rook KS. 1992. Compensatory patterns of support among children's peer relationships: a test using school friends,
nonschool friends, and siblings. *Dev. Psychol.* 28:163–72

Eisenberg N, Fabes RA, Carlo G, Troyer D,
Speer AL, et al. 1992. The relations of maternal practices and characteristics to children's vicarious emotional responsiveness.
Child Dev. 63:583–602

Eisenberg N, Fabes RA, Schaller M, Carlo G,
Miller PA. 1991. The relations of parental
characteristics and practices to children's
vicarious emotional responding. *Child Dev.*
62:1393–408

Eisenberg N, Shell R, Pasternack J, Lennon R,
Beller R, et al. 1987. Prosocial development in middle childhood: a longitudinal
study. *Dev. Psychol.* 23:712–18

Eysenck HJ. 1970. *The Structure of Human
Personality.* London: Methuen. 3rd ed.

Eysenck HJ. 1993. Comment on Goldberg.
Am. Psychol. 48:1299–1300

Fabes RA, Eisenberg N, Karbon M, Bernzweig
J, Speer AL, et al. 1994. Socialization of
children's vicarious emotional responding
and prosocial behavior: relations with
mothers' perceptions of children's emotional reactivity. *Dev. Psychol.* 30:44–55

Fabes RA, Eisenberg N, Miller PA. 1990. Maternal correlates of children's vicarious
emotional responses. *Dev. Psychol.* 26:
639–48

Fagot BI, Kavanagh K. 1990. The prediction of
antisocial behavior from avoidant attachment classification. *Child Dev.* 61:864–73

Fauber R, Forehand R, Thomas AM, Wierson
M. 1990. A mediational model of the impact of marital conflict on adolescent adjustment in intact and divorced families:
the role of disrupted parenting. *Child Dev.*
61:1112–23

Fleming JE, Offord DR. 1990. Epidemiology

of childhood depressive disorders: a critical review. *J. Am. Acad. Child Adol. Psychiatr.* 29:571–80

Gersten M. 1989. Behavioral inhibition in the classroom. See Reznick 1989, pp. 71–92

Goldberg LR. 1993. The structure of phenotypic personality traits. *Am. Psychol.* 48: 26–34

Goldsmith HH, Alansky JA. 1987. Maternal and infant temperamental predictors of attachment: a meta-analytic review. *J. Consult. Clin. Psychol.* 55:805–16

Goldsmith HH, Buss AH, Plomin R, Rothbart MK, Thomas A, et al. 1987. Roundtable: What is temperament? Four approaches. *Child Dev.* 58:505–29

Gralinski JH, Kopp CB. 1993. Everyday rules for behavior: mothers' requests to young children. *Dev. Psychol.* 29:573–84

Gray JA. 1982. *The Neuropsychology of Anxiety: An Enquiry into the Functions of the Sept-hippocampal System.* Oxford: Oxford Univ. Press

Graziano WG, Eisenberg NH. 1994. Agreeableness: a dimension of personality. In *Handbook of Personality Psychology,* ed. R Hogan, J Johnson, S Briggs. San Diego: Academic. In press

Grusec JJ, Goodnow JJ. 1994. The impact of parental discipline methods on the child's internalization of values: a reconceptualization of current points of view. *Dev. Psychol.* 30:4–19

Halverson CF, Kohnstamm GA, Martin RP, eds. 1994. *The Developing Structure of Temperament and Personality from Infancy to Adulthood.* Hillsdale, NJ: Erlbaum. In press

Hart CH, DeWolf DM, Wozniak P, Burts DC. 1992. Maternal and paternal disciplinary styles: relations with preschoolers' playground behavioral orientations and peer status. *Child Dev.* 63:879–92

Hinde RA, Tamplin A, Barrett J. 1993a. Home correlates of aggression in preschool. *Aggress. Behav.* 19:85–105

Hinde RA, Tamplin A, Barrett J. 1993b. Social isolation in 4-year-olds. *Br. J. Dev. Psychol.* 11:211–36

Hoffman M. 1970. Moral development. In *Carmichael's Manual of Child Psychology,* ed. PH Mussen, pp. 261–359. New York: Wiley

Hofstee WKB, de Raad B, Goldberg LR. 1992. Integration of the big five and circumplex approaches to trait structure. *J. Pers. Soc. Psychol.* 63:146–63

Holden GW, Ritchie KL. 1991. Linking extreme marital discord, child rearing, and child behavior problems: evidence from battered women. *Child Dev.* 62:311–27

Howe N. 1991. Sibling-directed internal state language, perspective taking, and affective behavior. *Child Dev.* 62:1503–12

Howes C. 1988. Peer interaction of young children. *Mongr. Soc. Res. Child Dev.* 53(Ser. No. 217):1–78

Hymel S, Bowker A, Woody E. 1993. Aggressive versus withdrawn unpopular children: variations in peer and self-perceptions in multiple domains. *Child Dev.* 61:2004–21

Hymel S, Rubin KH, Rowden L, LeMare L. 1990. Children's peer relationships: longitudinal prediction of internalizing and externalizing problems from middle to late childhood. *Child Dev.* 61:2004–21

Isabella RA, Belsky J. 1991. Interactional synchrony and the origins of infant-mother attachment. *Child Dev.* 62:373–84

Jenkins J. 1992. Sibling relationships in disharmonious homes: potential difficulties and protective effects. In *Children's Sibling Relationships,* ed. F Boer, J Dunn, pp. 125–38. Hillsdale, NJ: Erlbaum

John OP, Caspi A, Robins RW, Moffitt TE, Stouthamer-Loeber M. 1994. The "little five": exploring the nomological network of the five-factor model of personality in adolescent boys. *Child Dev.* 65:160–78

Jouriles EN, Murphy CM, Farris AM, Smith DA, Richters JE, et al. 1991. Marital adjustment, parental disagreements about child-rearing, and behavior problems in boys: increasing the specificity of the marital assessment. *Child Dev.* 62:1424–33

Juvonen J. 1991. Deviance, perceived responsibility, and negative peer interactions. *Dev. Psychol.* 27:672–81

Kagan J. 1980. Perspectives on continuity. In *Constancy and Change in Human Development,* ed. OG Brim, J Kagan, pp. 26–74. Cambridge, MA: Harvard Univ. Press

Kagan J, Reznick JS, Snidman N, Gibbons J, Johnson MO. 1988. Childhood derivatives of inhibition and lack of inhibition to the unfamiliar. *Child Dev.* 59:1580–89

Kazdin AE. 1987. Treatment of antisocial behavior in children: current status and future directions. *Psychol. Bull.* 102:187–203

Kestenbaum R, Farber EA, Sroufe LA. 1989. Individual differences in empathy among preschoolers: relation to attachment history. In *New Directions in Child Development,* ed. N Eisenberg, 44:51–64. San Francisco: Jossey-Bass

Kochanska G. 1990. Maternal beliefs as long-term predictors of mother-child interaction and report. *Child Dev.* 61:1934–43

Kochanska G. 1991. Socialization and temperament in the development of guilt and conscience. *Child Dev.* 62:1379–92

Kochanska G. 1993. Toward a synthesis of parental socialization and child temperament in early development of conscience. *Child Dev.* 64:325–47

Kochanska G. 1994. Children's temperament, mothers' discipline, and security of attachment: multiple pathways to emerging internalization. *Child Dev.* In press

Kochanska G, Aksan N. 1994. Mother-child mutually positive affect, the quality of child compliance to requests and prohibitions, and maternal control as correlates of early internalization. *Child Dev.* In press

Kochanska G, Radke-Yarrow M. 1992. Inhibition in toddlerhood and the dynamics of the child's interaction with an unfamiliar peer at age five. *Child Dev.* 63:325–35

Koestner R, Franz C, Weinberger J. 1990. The family origins of empathic concern: a 26-year longitudinal study. *J. Pers. Soc. Psychol.* 58:709–17

Kohnstamm GA, Bates JE, Rothbart MK, eds. 1989. *Temperament in Childhood.* Chichester, UK: Wiley

Kohnstamm GA, Halverson CF, Havill VL, Mervielde I. 1994. Parents' free descriptions of child characteristics: a cross-cultural search for the roots of the big five. In *Parents' Cultural Belief Systems: Cultural Origins and Developmental Consequences,* ed. S Harkness, CM Super. New York: Guildford. In press

LaFreniere P, Dumas JE. 1992. A transactional analysis of early childhood anxiety and social withdrawal. *Dev. Psychopathol.* 4: 385–402

Lay KL, Waters E, Parke KA. 1989. Maternal responsiveness and child compliance: the role of mood as a mediator. *Child Dev.* 60: 1405–11

Lempers JD, Clark-Lempers D, Simons RD. 1989. Economic hardship, parenting, and distress in adolescence. *Child Dev.* 60:25–39

Loeber R, Wikstrom PH. 1993. Individual pathways to crime in different types of neighborhood. In *Integrating Individual and Ecological Aspects of Crime,* ed. DP Farrington, RJ Sampson, PH Wikstrom. *Swedish National Council for Crime Prevention Report* 1:169–204

Loehlin JC. 1992. *Genes and Environment in Personality Development. Individual Differences and Development Series.* Newbury Park, NY: Sage

MacKinnon C. 1989. An observational investigation of sibling interactions in married and divorced families. *Dev. Psychol.* 25: 36–44

MacKinnon-Lewis C, Lamb ME, Arbuckle B, Baradaran LP, Volling BL. 1992. The relationship between biased maternal and filial attributions and the aggressiveness of their interactions. *Dev. Psychopathol.* 4:403–15

Magnusson D. 1992. Individual development: a longitudinal perspective. *Eur. J. Pers.* 6: 119–38

Magnusson D. 1994. The patterning of antisocial behavior and the autonomic reactivity. In *The Neurobiology of Clinical Aggression,* ed. DM Stoff, RB Cairns. Hillsdale, NJ: Erlbaum. In press

Magnusson D, Törestad B. 1993. A holistic view of personality: a model revisited. *Annu. Rev. Psychol.* 44:427–52

Mangelsdorf S, Gunnar M, Kestenbaum R, Lang S, Andreas S. 1990. Infant proneness-to-distress temperament, maternal personality and mother-infant attachment: associations and goodness of fit. *Child Dev.* 61: 820–31

Martin RP, Wisenbaker J, Huttunen M. 1994. Review of factor analytic studies of temperament measures based on the Thomas-Chess structural model: implications for the big five. See Halverson et al 1994. In press

Matheny AP. 1989. Children's behavioral inhibition over age and across situations: genetic similarity for a trait during change. *J. Pers.* 57:215–35

McGue M, Bacon S, Lykken DT. 1993. Personality stability and change in early adulthood: a behavioral genetic analysis. *Dev. Psychol.* 29:96–109

Moffitt TE. 1993. Adolescence-limited and life-course-persistent antisocial behavior: a developmental taxonomy. *Psychol. Rev.* 100:674–701

Nachmias M, Gunnar M, Mangelsdorf S. 1994. Behavioral inhibition and stress reactivity: the moderating role of attachment security. *Child Dev.* In press

Offord DR, Boyle MH, Racine YA. 1991. The epidemiology of antisocial behavior. See Pepler & Rubin 1991, pp. 31–54

Olweus D. 1979. Stability of aggressive reaction patterns in males: a review. *Psychol. Bull.* 86:852–75

Olweus D. 1991. Bully/victim problems among school children: basic facts and effects of a school-based intervention program. See Pepler & Rubin 1991, pp. 411–48

Ozer DJ, Gjerde PF. 1989. Patterns of personality consistency and change from childhood through adolescence. *J. Pers.* 57: 483–507

Parke RD, Asher SR. 1983. Social and personality development. *Annu. Rev. Psychol.* 34: 465–509

Parkhurst JT, Asher SR. 1992. Peer rejection in middle school: subgroup differences in behavior, loneliness, and interpersonal concerns. *Dev. Psychol.* 28:231–41

Patterson GR, Capaldi DM, Bank L. 1991. An early starter model for predicting delinquency. See Pepler & Rubin 1991, pp. 139–68

Patterson GR, DeBaryshe BD, Ramsey E. 1989. A developmental perspective on antisocial behavior. *Am. Psychol.* 44:329–35

Patterson GR, Reid JB, Dishion TJ. 1992. *Antisocial Boys.* Eugene, OR: Castalia

Pedlow R, Sanson A, Prior M, Oberklaid F. 1993. Stability of maternally reported temperament from infancy to 8 years. *Dev. Psychol.* 29:998–1007

Pepler DJ, Rubin KH, eds. 1991. *The Development and Treatment of Childhood Aggression.* Hillsdale, NJ: Erlbaum

Perry DG, Perry LC, Kennedy E. 1992. Conflict and the development of antisocial behavior. See Shantz & Hartup 1992, pp. 301–29

Plomin R, Emde RN, Braungart JM, Campos J, Corley R, et al. 1993. Genetic change and continuity from fourteen to twenty months: the MacArthur Longitudinal Twin Study. *Child Dev.* 64:1354–76

Plomin R, Reiss D, Hetherington EM, Howe GW. 1994. Nature and nurture: genetic contributions to measures of the family environment. *Dev. Psychol.* 30:32–43

Plomin R, Rende R. 1991. Human behavioral genetics. *Annu. Rev. Psychol.* 42:161–90

Pulkkinen L, Ronka A. 1994. Personal control over development, identity formation, and future orientation as components of life orientation: a developmental approach. *Dev. Psychol.* 30:260–71

Radke-Yarrow M, Cummings EM, Kuczynski L, Chapman M. 1985. Patterns of attachment in two- and three-year olds in normal families and families with parental depression. *Child Dev.* 56:884–93

Ramsey E, Patterson GR, Walker HM. 1990. Generalization of the antisocial trait from home to school settings. *J. Appl. Dev. Psychol.* 11:209–23

Reiss D, Plomin R, Hetherington EM, Howe GW, Rovine M, et al. 1993. The separate worlds of teenage siblings: an introduction to the study of the nonshared environment and adolescent development. In *Separate Social Worlds of Siblings: The Impact of Nonshared Environment on Development,* ed. EM Hetherington, D Reiss, R Plomin, pp. 63–109. Hillsdale, NJ: Erlbaum

Renken B, Egeland B, Marvinney D, Mangelsdorf S, Sroufe LA. 1989. Early childhood antecedents of aggression and passive-withdrawal in early elementary school. *J. Pers.* 57:257–81

Renshaw PD, Brown PJ. 1993. Loneliness in middle childhood: concurrent and longitudinal predictors. *Child Dev.* 64:1271–84

Reznick JS, ed. 1989. *Perspectives on Behavioral Inhibition.* Chicago: Univ. Chicago Press

Reznick JS, Gibbons J, Johnson M, McDonough P. 1989. Behavioral inhibition in a normative sample. See Reznick 1989, pp. 25–49

Reznick JS, Kagan J, Snidman N, Gersten M, Baak K, et al. 1986. Inhibited and uninhibited children: a follow-up study. *Child Dev.* 57:660–80

Robins LN, Rutter M, eds. 1990. *Straight and Devious Pathways from Childhood to Adulthood.* Cambridge: Cambridge Univ. Press

Robinson JL, Zahn-Waxler C, Emde RN. 1994. Patterns of development in early empathic behavior: environmental and child constitutional influences. *Soc. Dev.* 3:125–45

Rodgers B. 1990. Influences of early-life and recent factors on affective disorder in women: an exploration of vulnerability models. See Robins & Rutter 1990, pp. 314–27

Rothbart MK. 1989. Temperament and development. See Kohnstamm et al 1989, pp. 187–247

Rothbart MK, Ahadi SA, Hershey KL. 1994. Temperament and social behavior in children. *Merrill-Palmer Q.* 40:21–39

Rowe DC, Rodgers JL, Meseck-Bushey S. 1992. Sibling delinquency and the family environment: shared and unshared influences. *Child Dev.* 63:59–67

Rubin KH. 1993. The Waterloo longitudinal project: correlates and consequences of social withdrawal from childhood to adolescence. See Rubin & Asendorpf 1993b, pp. 291–314

Rubin KH, Asendorpf JB. 1993a. Social withdrawal, inhibition, and shyness in childhood: conceptual and definitional issues. See Rubin & Asendorpf 1993b, pp. 3–17

Rubin KH, Asendorpf JB, eds. 1993b. *Social Withdrawal, Inhibition, and Shyness in Childhood.* Hillsdale, NJ: Erlbaum

Rubin KH, Both L, Zahn-Waxler C, Cummings EM, Wilkinson M. 1991. Dyadic play behaviors of children of well and depressed mothers. *Dev. Psychopathol.* 3:243–51

Rubin KH, Mills RSL. 1988. The many faces of social isolation in childhood. *J. Consult. Clin. Psychol.* 56:916–24

Rubin KH, Mills RSL. 1990. Maternal beliefs about adaptive and maladaptive social behaviors in normal, aggressive, and withdrawn preschoolers. *J. Abnorm. Child Psychol.* 18:419–35

Sampson RJ, Laub JH. 1994. Urban poverty and the family context of delinquency: a new look at structure and process in a classic study. *Child Dev.* 65:523–40

Saudino KJ, DeFries JC, Campos J, Plomin R. 1994a. Tester-rated temperament at 14, 20, and 24 months: environmental change and genetic continuity. *Dev. Psychol.* In press

Saudino KJ, McGuire S, Reiss D, Hetherington EM, Plomin R. 1994b. Clarifying the confusion: parent ratings of EAS temperaments in twins, full siblings, half siblings, and step siblings. *J. Pers. Soc. Psychol.* In press

Shantz CU, Hartup WW, eds. 1992. *Conflict in*

Child and Adolescent Development. Cambridge: Cambridge Univ. Press

Speltz ML, Greenberg MT, Deklyen M. 1990. Attachment in preschoolers with disruptive behavior: a comparison of clinic-referred and nonproblem children. *Dev. Psychopathol.* 2:31–46

Stattin H, Magnusson D. 1991. Stability and change in criminal behaviour up to age 30. *Br. J. Criminol.* 31:327–46

Stevenson-Hinde J, Hinde RA. 1986. Changes in associations between characteristics and interaction. In *The Study of Temperament: Changes, Continuities and Challenges,* eds. R Plomin, J Dunn, pp. 115–29. Hillsdale, NJ: Erlbaum

Stocker C, Dunn J, Plomin R. 1989. Sibling relationships: links with child temperament, maternal behavior, and family structure. *Child Dev.* 60:715–27

Teti DM. 1992. Sibling interaction. In *Handbook of Social Development,* ed. VB van Hasselt, M Hersen, pp. 201–26. New York: Plenum

Thomas A, Chess S. 1977. *Temperament and Development.* New York: Bruner Mazel

Vandell DL, Bailey MD. 1992. Conflict between siblings. See Shantz & Hartup 1992, pp. 242–69

van den Boom DC. 1994. The influence of temperament and mothering on attachment and exploration: an experimental manipulation of sensitive responsiveness among lower class mothers with irritable infants. *Child Dev.* 65:1449–69

van den Boom DC, Hoeksma JB. 1994. The effect of infant irritability on mother-infant interaction: a growth-curve analysis. *Dev. Psychol.* 30:581–90

van Lieshout CFM, Haselager GJT. 1994. The big-five personality factors in Q-sort descriptions of children and adolescents. See Halverson et al 1994. In press

Velez CN, Johnson J, Cohen P. 1989. A longitudinal analysis of selected risk factors for childhood psychopathology. *J. Am. Acad. Child Adol. Psychiatr.* 28:861–64

Volling BL. 1990. *Mother-child and father-child relationships as contemporaneous correlates and developmental antecedents of sibling conflict and cooperation.* PhD thesis. Penn. State Univ.

Volling BL, Belsky J. 1992. The contribution of mother-child and father-child relationships to the quality of sibling interaction: a longitudinal study. *Child Dev.* 63:1209–22

Vuchinich S, Bank L, Patterson GR. 1992. Parenting, peers, and the stability of antisocial behavior in preadolescent boys. *Dev. Psychol.* 28:510–21

Walker LJ, Taylor JH. 1991. Family interactions and the development of moral reasoning. *Child Dev.* 62:264–83

Weissman MM. 1989. Anxiety disorders in parents and children: a genetic-epidemiological perspective. See Reznick 1989, pp. 241–54

Whiting BB, Whiting JWM. 1975. *Children of Six Cultures.* Cambridge, MA: Harvard Univ. Press

Wohlwill JF. 1973. *The Study of Behavioral Development.* New York: Academic

Yoshikawa H. 1994. Prevention as cumulative protection: effects of early family support and education on chronic delinquency and its risks. *Psychol. Bull.* 115:28–54

Zahn-Waxler C, Radke-Yarrow M, Wagner E, Chapman M. 1992a. Development of concern for others. *Dev. Psychol.* 28:126–36

Zahn-Waxler C, Robinson JL, Emde RN. 1992b. The development of empathy in twins. *Dev. Psychol.* 28:1038–47

AUTHOR INDEX

A

Abbot BB, 220
Abelson RP, 434
Aber JL, 416
Abney SP, 97
Abraham W, 530
Abrahamson E, 240
Abramovitch R, 532
Abramowitz SI, 418
Abrams DB, 39
Abrams TW, 587, 592, 599, 601, 604–6, 613
Abramson AS, 473
Absher RA, 589, 593
Accardo PJ, 417
Achenbach TM, 266, 271, 279
Achman D, 403, 406, 420, 421
Achtenhagen F, 171
Acioly NM, 157
Ackerman BJ, 424
Ackerman PL, 305, 306
Acosta-Urquidi J, 609
Adams B, 369
Adams KM, 503, 515
Adams MJ, 167
Adams SR, 611
Adams-Tucker C, 421
Addis ME, 32, 42, 43
Adey PS, 165
Adinoff B, 131
Adler NJ, 252
Adler PS, 70, 74, 249
Adrian C, 283
Affleck G, 301
af Klinteberg B, 315
Aggleton JP, 222
Agnew EJ, 380
Agras WS, 40
Agyei Y, 308, 636
Ahadi SA, 314, 659, 675
Ahlgren A, 382
Ahmed SW, 565, 566
Ahwesh E, 166
Aiken LS, 448, 449
Ainsworth MDS, 412
Aitkin MA, 456
Aizley HG, 140
Ajjanagadde V, 102, 113
Akaike T, 596
Akon DL, 610, 613
Aksan N, 677
Alansky JA, 671
Alberini CM, 611
Albers W, 185, 187, 190
Albers Mohrman S, 73

Albert ML, 104, 333
Albert MS, 337, 338, 511, 512, 514, 518
Albrecht JE, 111
Alden LS, 41
Aldershof B, 456
Aldhous P, 630
Aldwin C, 337, 338
Alema S, 332
Alexander JF, 28, 31, 32, 34, 39, 40, 42, 43, 46, 49, 159
Alexander K, 377, 378
Alexander PA, 168
Alexander PC, 424
Alexander RD, 191
Alger SA, 145
Alheid G, 226
Alkon DL, 588, 595, 596, 599, 600, 607–11
Allain AN Jr, 129
Allbritton DW, 110
Allen GM, 246
Allen JP, 416, 550
Allen P, 343, 344
Allen PA, 335, 336
Allen R, 166
Allen S, 159, 172
Allen V, 384
Allgood SM, 49
Alliger RJ, 133
Allison ST, 196–98
Allport G, 299
Allport GW, 296
Allwood J, 534
Al-Mufti R, 127, 136
Alper JS, 626
Alpert JJ, 418
Alport JM, 357
Alsaker FD, 273
Alschuler AS, 389
al-Shabbout M, 280
Altemeier WA III, 412
Alterman AI, 134, 413
Althauser RP, 251
Altieri P, 104
Altmann G, 98
Altmann GTM, 484
Alvarez EB, 251
Amado ARN, 412
Amaral DG, 224, 226
Ambrose CM, 640
Ambrosini PJ, 280, 283
Amburgey TL, 81
Amelang M, 313
Ames C, 385, 387, 388
Ames MA, 402, 423, 424
Amiel-Tison C, 473
Amigues R, 162

Ammons PW, 405
Amrhein PC, 340
Amrung SA, 417
Amsel E, 163
Anagnopoulos C, 104
Anastopoulos AD, 40
Andereck ND, 408
Andersen AE, 127, 136
Anderson AR, 530, 533
Anderson CM, 29, 39, 359
Anderson DA, 456
Anderson DK, 363
Anderson G, 130, 145, 424
Anderson KJ, 306, 312, 314, 316, 318
Anderson LW, 356, 643
Anderson NH, 9, 21
Anderson OR, 370
Anderson RC, 367
Anderson RD, 356
Anderson SW, 49
Anderson V, 367
Andersson B, 159
Andersson T, 315
Andreas S, 672
Andreasen NC, 133, 144
Andreski P, 128, 145
Andrews DW, 669
Andrews G, 128, 129
Andrews JA, 128, 281
Andrusiak P, 110
Angelucci L, 332
Angleitner A, 314
Angold A, 269, 279, 281
Angst J, 136, 137
Anstey K, 338
Anthony EJ, 273
Anton R, 131
Anton SF, 129, 130
Apostolakis G, 78
Appelbaum MI, 441
Apple R, 129, 130
Apter MJ, 320
Aquino K, 192, 194
Arbisi P, 312
Arbuckle B, 667
Archer J, 387
Arcus DM, 313, 315, 673
Arias I, 50
Arkowitz H, 416
Arndt S, 133
Arneric S, 213
Arnold GS, 276
Arnold MB, 223, 360
Arnow BA, 40
Arria A, 146
Arts W, 135
Arvey RD, 252, 445

SUBJECT INDEX

A

Accountability
  students and, 385–90
Achievement goal theory
  motivation to learn and, 387–88
Action theory
  organization and, 67–70
Activation activity
  overcoming misconceptions and, 359–60
Acute stress disorder, 140
AD
  See Alzheimer's disease
Adaptive functioning
  adolescent development and, 271
Adaptive processing
  neural networks and, 19
Additive conjoint measurement, 7
Adjustment disorder
  comorbidity, 128
Adolescence
  acting out
    family-based intervention models, 28
    needs for autonomy and control and,
      276
    research on problems, 274–84
  theory and research
    emergent themes, 267–71
Adolescent development, 265–88
  emergent themes, 285–87
  models, 266
  pathways and trajectories, 271–73
  processes of risk and resilience, 273–74
Advanced manufacturing technology (AMT),
  74–75
  human resource management and, 244
Affective disorders
  genetic studies, 644
Affective psychosis, 133
Affective reaction
  positive
    neural basis, 222
Age
  behavioral couple therapy and, 42
Agency theory
  human resource management and, 242–43
Aggression
  abused/neglected children and, 415–16
  adolescence and, 272, 274–79
  developmental pathways, 277–78
  familial
    gene, 626
  genetic studies, 644–45
  psychoticism and, 313
  societal context, 665–66
Aggressiveness
  child maltreatment and, 417–18
  sexual
    child sexual abuse and, 424

Aging
  sentence comprehension and, 104
  speed of behavior and, 329–50
Agnosia, 494
Agoraphobia
  comorbidity, 129
  couple and family therapy, 40
Agreeableness, 657, 660–61, 675
  genetic contributions, 634–35
AIDS dementia, 333
Alcohol abuse
  delinquent behavior and, 278
  neurological dysfunction and, 337–38
Alcohol abuse/dependence
  comorbidity, 128
  subtypes, 134–35
Alcoholic dementia, 515
Alcoholic Korsakoff syndrome
  amnesia and, 497
  memory and, 501, 517–18
Alcoholism, 641–43
  comorbidity, 129–30
  couple and family therapy, 39
  depression and, 131
  genomic imprinting and, 640
  memory and, 501–2
  molecular research, 642–43
  quantitative research, 641–42
Alcohol use
  behavior genetics, 638–39
  longitudinal study, 640
Algebra Project, 381
Algebra word problem
  language processing deficit and, 157
Altruism
  sociodemographic correlates, 676–77
Alzheimer's disease (AD), 333, 643–44
  association studies, 643–44
  memory and, 501
  twin studies, 643
Ambiguity
  retention of information and, 367–68
Ambiguity processing, 102
American Association for Marriage and Family Therapy, 28
American Family Therapy Academy, 28, 45
American Humane Association, 407
American Medical Association
  Adolescent Medicine branch, 266
American Psychiatric Association (APA), 122
American Psychological Association Family
  Psychology Division, 28
American Sign Language (ASL), 105
Amnesia, 493–519
  anterograde, 511
  infantile, 229
  memory profiles associated, 516–18
  retrograde, 497
  short-term/long-term memory and, 495

CUMULATIVE INDEXES

CONTRIBUTING AUTHORS, VOLUMES 36–46

CHAPTER TITLES, VOLUMES 36–46

VISION

See SENSORY PROCESSES